# THE
# COLLECTED LETTERS
## OF
# W. B. YEATS

GENERAL EDITOR: JOHN KELLY

# THE
# COLLECTED LETTERS
## OF
# W. B. YEATS

*General Editor* · JOHN KELLY

---

VOLUME FOUR

# 1905–1907

EDITED BY

## JOHN KELLY

AND

## RONALD SCHUCHARD

OXFORD
UNIVERSITY PRESS

# OXFORD

UNIVERSITY PRESS

Great Clarendon Street, Oxford OX2 6DP

Oxford University Press is a department of the University of Oxford.
It furthers the University's objective of excellence in research, scholarship,
and education by publishing worldwide in

Oxford New York

Auckland Cape Town Dar es Salaam Hong Kong Karachi
Kuala Lumpur Madrid Melbourne Mexico City Nairobi
New Delhi Shanghai Taipei Toronto

With offices in

Argentina Austria Brazil Chile Czech Republic France Greece
Guatemala Hungary Italy Japan Poland Portugal Singapore
South Korea Switzerland Thailand Turkey Ukraine Vietnam

Oxford is a registered trade mark of Oxford University Press
in the UK and in certain other countries

Published in the United States
by Oxford University Press Inc., New York

© in the compilation, introduction, and editorial matter John Kelly 2005
© 2005 by Michael Yeats

The moral rights of the author have been asserted

Database right Oxford University Press (maker)

First published 2005

British Library Cataloguing in Publication Data

Data available

Library of Congress Cataloging in Publication Data

Data available

Typeset by Kolam Information Services Pvt. Ltd, Pondicherry, India
Printed in Great Britain
on acid-free paper by
Antony Rowe Ltd,
Chippenham, Wiltshire

ISBN 0-19-812684-0   978-0-19-812684-3

1 3 5 7 9 10 8 6 4 2

# ACKNOWLEDGEMENTS

Our thanks are due first to the late Anne Yeats, and to Michael and Gráinne Yeats, without whose help and hospitality this edition would not have been possible. We also gratefully acknowledge the generosity of those who have allowed us to make copies of Yeats material in their possession: Joann M. Andrews, W. Barrington Baker, Stuart Bennett, Lord Bridges, the late Alan Clodd, Jim Edwards, Stephen Fay, the late James Gilvarry, David Gould, Mrs Basil Gray, Richard Lancelyn Green, Terry Halladay, William F. Halloran, the late Richard M. Kain, Declan Kiely, Francis King, Mary McGee, the late Michael Maclagan, Douglas Sealy, Ann Weygandt, Anna MacBride White, and the Hon. Gerald Yorke.

This volume has been greatly assisted by grants and other financial help from the British Academy, the AHRB, the Leverhulme Trust, the President and Fellows of St John's College, Oxford, the Oxford English Faculty, and Emory University.

Our particular thanks go to Catherine Morris for her assiduous research assistance, and to Deirdre Toomey and Warwick Gould, who placed their unrivalled knowledge and expertise at our disposal in reading through and commenting upon the final drafts of this volume.

We are also indebted for help and advice to Mark Abley, Montreal; Geoffrey Alderman, Middlesex University; Jonathan Allison, University of Kentucky; Robin Alston, University College London; Philip Attwood, British Museum; Pamela Baker, University of London Library; Irena Balgalvis, Boston Public Library; Christopher Barth, Kenyon College; Peter Beal, Sotheby's; Robert Bearman, Shakespeare Birthplace Trust; Robert S. Becker; Karl Beckson, New York; Charles Benson, Trinity College Library, Dublin; Morris L. Bierbrier, British Museum; Jennifer Booth, Tate Gallery Archive; Michael Bott, Reading University Library; David C. Braasch, Morris Library, Southern Illinois University; George Brennan, London School of Economics; the Hon. Robert O. Bridges; Sir Henry Brooke; the Rt. Hon. Peter Brooke; Iain G. Brown, National Library of Scotland; Mark N. Brown, Brown University Library; Sally Brown, British Library; Margaret Campbell, London; Kathleen Cann, Cambridge University Library; Peter Caracciolo, Royal Holloway College, London; Wayne K. Chapman, Clemson University; Diana Chardin, Trinity College Library, Cambridge; the late Alan Denson; Laurie M. Deredita, Connecticut College; Denis Donoghue, New York University; the Earl of Cromartie;

the late Richard Ellmann; Stephen Enniss, Emory University; Catherine Fahy, National Library of Ireland; Rosita Fanto, Monte Carlo; Catherine Farragher, Galway County Libraries; Rosalind Field, Royal Holloway College, London; Mirjam Foot, British Library; Roy Foster, Hertford College, Oxford; Adrian Frazier, NUI, Galway; Jason Freeman; R. A. Gekoski, London; R. A. Gilbert, Bristol; Sophie Goldsworthy; David Gould, London; Mary K. Greer, Wet Hill, Nevada; T. Affleck Greeves, Bedford Park Society, London; Terry Halladay, New Haven; William F. Halloran, University of Wisconsin-Milwaukee; Bobbie Harper, Florida; George Harper, Florida State University; the late Sir Rupert Hart-Davis; John Harwood, The Flinders University of South Australia; Kate Hedworth, Christie's; Narayan Hegde, SUNY at Stony Brook; Elizabeth Heine, New Jersey; Cathy Henderson, Ransom Center, University of Texas at Austin; the Historical Society of Pennsylvania; Sara S. Hodson, Huntington Library; John Hunter, England; Elizabeth Ingli-James, Victoria and Albert Museum; Elizabeth James, British Library; the late A. Norman Jeffares, Fife Ness; Klaus Peter Jochum, University of Bamberg; Declan Kiely, Berg Collection, New York Public Library; Kristen Knyitray, SUNY, Sony Brook, G. Krishnamurti, London; Peter Kuch, University of New South Wales; Mark Samuels Lasner, Washington; Roger Lhombreaud, France; A. Walton Litz, Princeton University; Andrew Lockett; Rena Lohan, University College, Dublin; Elizabeth Loizeaux, University of Maryland; Patricia Lysaght, University College, Dublin; Colin McDowell, Caulfield North, Australia; Jim McGarry, Colloony, Co. Sligo; Peggy L. McMullen; Brenda Maddox, London; Edward Maggs, Maggs Bros., London; Rosemary Magnus, England; Nicholas Mann, Warburg Institute, London; Sean Manning, Inverin, Co. Galway; Edward Marx, Kyoto University; Michel Mansuy, France; Phillip L. Marcus, Florida International University; Stephen Massil, University of London Library; Linda Matthews, Woodruff Library, Emory University; James Mays, University College, Dublin; Bernard Meehan, Trinity College Library, Dublin; Nisha Mithani, India Office Collections, British Library; Bruce Morris, Palo Alto; Maureen Murphy, Hofstra University; William M. Murphy, Union College, Schenectady; Eric R. Nitschke, Emory University; Kristen J. Nyitray, SUNY, Stony Brook; Stephen O'Brien, Cork City Library; Beairthe O'Conaire, An Spideal, Co. na Gaillimhe; Fr Liam O'Connell SJ, Conglowes Wood College, Co. Kildare; William H. O'Donnell, University of Memphis; Bernard O'Donoghue, Wadham College, Oxford; Leonard Orr, Washington State University; Stuart O'Seanoir, Trinity College Library, Dublin; Roger Nyle Parisious, Ohio; Stephen Parrish, Cornell University; James Pethica, Williams College, Schenectady; Andrew Phillips, British Library; Amanda Piesse, Trinity College, Dublin; John Pitcher, St John's College,

Oxford; Omar Pound, Princeton; J. V. Price; Susan C. Pyzynski, Brandeis University; Fiona Robertson, Dingwall Library, Ross-shire; Will Ryan, Warburg Institute, London; Ann Saddlemyer, University of Toronto; Christa Sammons, Beinecke Library, Yale; Helen Q. Schroyer, Purdue University Library; the late Kim Scott Walwyn; Michael Sidnell, University of Toronto; S. M. Simpson, National Library of Scotland; William Simpson, Trinity College, Dublin; Christine Smith, Ashford Borough Council; Colin Smythe, Gerrard's Cross; Thomas F. Staley, Ransom Center, University of Texas at Austin; Jon Stallworthy, Wolfson College, Oxford; John D. Stinson, New York Public Library; the late Lola Szladits, Berg Collection, New York Public Library; Norah Toomey; J. B. Trapp, London; Sarah Tyacke, Keeper of Public Records; Mr and Mrs J. Victor, London; Katie Wales, Royal Holloway College, London; Janet Wallwork, John Rylands Library, Manchester; David Ward, Royal Holloway College, London; George Watson, University of Aberdeen; Robert Welch, University of Ulster, Coleraine; Tara Wenger, University of Texas; Trevor West, Trinity College, Dublin; Ann Weygandt, Philadelphia; Frances Whistler, Boston University; Anna MacBride White, Dublin; Compton Whitfield; Patricia C. Willis, Beinecke Library, Yale University; Melanie Yolles, New York Public Library; Sibylle Zemitis, California State Library; Hans-Joachim Zimmermann, Heidelberg University.

# CONTENTS

# CHRONOLOGY

**1865**  **13 June**  William Butler Yeats (WBY), eldest child of John Butler Yeats (JBY) and Susan Mary Yeats (née Pollexfen), born at 3 (later 5) Sandymount Avenue, Dublin.

**1866**  **Jan**  JBY called to the Irish Bar. **25 Aug**  Susan Mary (Lily) Yeats (SMY) born at Enniscrone, Co. Sligo.

**1867**  **Late Feb/early Mar**  JBY gives up the law, and moves to London to enrol at Heatherley's Art School. **Late July**  Susan Yeats, WBY, SMY, and Isabella Pollexfen (aunt) join JBY at 23 Fitzroy Road, Regent's Park.

**1868**  **11 Mar**  Elizabeth Corbet (Lollie) Yeats (ECY) born in Fitzroy Road. **Summer**  Family holiday in Sligo.

**1869**  **Summer**  Family holiday in Sligo; children remain there until Dec.

**1870**  **27 Mar**  Robert Corbet (Bobbie) Yeats born in Fitzroy Road. **Apr**  WBY ill with scarlatina. **Summer**  Family holiday in Sligo.

**1871**  **29 Aug**  John Butler (Jack) Yeats born in Fitzroy Road. **Sept**  Short family holiday in Sligo.

**1872**  **23 July**  Yeatses leave London for Sligo, where Susan Yeats and the children remain for more than two years, living at Merville.

**1873**  **3 Mar**  Bobbie Yeats dies suddenly in Sligo. **Oct–Dec**  JBY painting portraits at Muckross Abbey.

**1874**  **Winter–spring**  JBY painting portraits at Stradbally Hall; rejoins his family in Sligo in the summer. **Late Oct**  Yeatses move back to London, settling at 14 Edith Villas, North End (West Kensington).

**1875**  **29 Aug**  Jane Grace Yeats born at Edith Villas.

**1876**  **6 June**  Jane Grace Yeats dies of bronchial pneumonia; the same month, JBY's mother dies of cancer in Dublin. **Summer**  Yeatses holiday in Sligo. JBY returns alone to London, and, having decided to abandon portrait painting for landscapes, spends extended periods at Burnham Beeches. **Autumn**  WBY joins his father at Burnham Beeches, lodging with the Earles in Farnham Royal.

1877   **Jan**   Susan Yeats and the other children return to Edith Villas.
**26 Jan**   WBY enrolled at the Godolphin School, Iffley Road,
Hammersmith.

1879   **Spring**   Yeatses move to 8 Woodstock Road, Bedford Park. **Summer**   Family holiday at Branscombe, Devon.

1881   **Easter**   WBY leaves the Godolphin School. **Summer**   JBY's
chronic financial difficulties worsen; in the autumn he rents a
Dublin studio. **Late autumn**   JBY brings his family (except
Jack, who is living permanently in Sligo with grandparents) to
Dublin, and they settle at Balscaddan Cottage in Howth. WBY
enrolled at the Erasmus Smith High School, Harcourt Street.

1882   **Spring**   Yeatses move from Balscaddan Cottage to Island View,
Harbour Road, Howth. **Autumn**   WBY meets his distant cousin
Laura Armstrong, and is attracted to her.

1883   **20 Nov**   Attends lecture by Oscar Wilde in Dublin. **Dec**   Leaves
the Erasmus Smith High School.

1884   **8 Jan**   Begins play, *Vivien and Time*, for Laura Armstrong. **Early
spring**   Yeats family forced by financial considerations to leave
Howth for 10 Ashfield Terrace, in the south Dublin suburb of
Terenure. **May**   WBY enrols as a student at the Metropolitan
School of Art, Dublin. **Sept**   Laura Armstrong marries Henry
Byrne.

1885   **19 Jan**   John O'Leary returns from exile in Paris; WBY meets him
later in the year. **Mar**   WBY's first publications, 'Song of the
Faeries' and 'Voices', in the *Dublin University Review* (*DUR*).
**Apr–July**   *The Island of Statues* published in *DUR*. **16 June**
First meeting of Dublin Hermetic Society, WBY presiding. **Late
June**   C. H. Oldham introduces WBY to Katharine Tynan at her
house in Clondalkin. **Aug**   JBY's finances deteriorate after death of
Matthew Yeats, his uncle and agent. **21 Nov**   Contemporary Club
founded by Oldham. **18 Dec**   Attends meeting of Young Ireland
Society.

1886   Poems, plays, and literary articles appearing regularly in *DUR*, *Irish
Monthly*, and *Irish Fireside*. **Apr**   Leaves the Metropolitan School
of Art. **10, 11 Apr**   Hears William Morris lecture in Dublin, and
meets him at the Contemporary Club. **Oct**   *Mosada*, WBY's first
publication in book form, privately printed in Dublin. Begins first
part of 'The Wanderings of Oisin'. **11 Dec**   Discussion of historical drama with Hyde at the Contemporary Club.

1887   **10 Jan**   Accompanies Katharine Tynan to a meeting of the Protestant Home Rule Association. **3 Mar**   JBY goes to London to
arrange for family's return there. **Early Apr**   The family join JBY
in England; WBY lodges at 6 Berkeley Road, Regent's Park,
London, until the family house is ready. **Early May**   WBY joins
the family at 58 Eardley Crescent, South Kensington. **May**   Meets
Ernest Rhys. WBY out of sorts; works on reviews, articles, and
poems at the Art Library, South Kensington Museum. First visit to
Mme Blavatsky, lately arrived in London. **19 June**   Attends lec-
ture at William Morris's house in Hammersmith; meets May
Morris. Thereafter WBY regularly attends the Morris 'Sunday
Nights'. **11 Aug**   Arrives in Sligo to stay with his uncle George
Pollexfen, at Rosses Point; working on 'Oisin'. **Late summer**   -
Susan Yeats has her first stroke. **Oct**   WBY moves into Sligo town
to stay with his grandparents. **18 Nov**   Finishes 'Oisin'. **22
Nov**   To Dublin, where he stays with Katharine Tynan; O'Leary
begins to organize subscriptions for WBY's book of poems. **Dec**   -
Susan Yeats suffers another stroke, and falls down a back stair.

1888   **Jan**   WBY experiences severe nervous disturbance at a Dublin
seance. **26 Jan**   Returns to London. **Feb**   Commissioned by
Rhys to edit a book of Irish folklore. **12 Feb**   Meets George
Bernard Shaw at William Morris's house. **12 Mar**   Deposits MS
of *The Wanderings of Oisin and Other Poems* with Kegan Paul.
**21 Mar**   First visit to the Southwark Irish Literary Club. **24 Mar**
Yeats family moves to 3 Blenheim Road, Bedford Park. Susan Yeats
and SMY go there from Yorkshire on 13 Apr. **Apr**   WBY
attending French lessons at the Morrises'. **Early May**   Publication of *Poems and Ballads of Young Ireland*. **13 June**   WBY lectures
to the Southwark Irish Literary Club on 'Sligo Fairies'. **28 July**
Meets Lady Wilde, and becomes a frequent guest at her Saturday
afternoon 'at homes'. **11 Aug**   In Oxford copying out Caxton's
edition of Aesop's *Fables* at the Bodleian. **Late Sept**   *Fairy and
Folk Tales of the Irish Peasantry* published. **Nov**   Attacked by
'lunar influences'. Joins Esoteric Section of the Theosophical
Society. **1 Dec**   SMY begins work as embroidress at May
Morris's. **Mid-Dec**   Composes 'The Lake Isle of Innisfree'.
**25 Dec**   Spends Christmas Day with the Oscar Wildes.

1889   *c.* 10 Jan   *Oisin* published. **Late Jan**   Yeats family financial problems particularly acute. **30 Jan**   WBY meets Maud Gonne (MG)
for the first time when she visits Blenheim Road. **31 Jan**   WBY
dines with MG in London. **Feb**   Begins *The Countess Cathleen*.

3 Mar   Spends night at the Ellises', probably to discuss a proposed edition of *The Works of William Blake*. 1 May   In Oxford copying Blake's *The Book of Thel*. 6 May   Reads *The Countess Cathleen* to Florence Farr (FF). 29 May   Lectures on Mangan to the Southwark Irish Literary Society. 6 Aug   In Oxford copying an Elizabethan book for Nutt. 23 Aug   *Stories from Carleton*. 15 Oct Ellen O'Leary dies in Cork. 20–3 Oct   WBY sees O'Leary in London. 20 Dec   Meets with Annie Besant and other members of the Esoteric Section of the Theosophical Society to renew their pledges to Mme Blavatsky. Late Dec   Ellis and WBY discover Linnell's MS of Blake's *Vala*.

1890   Early Jan   Ill with Russian influenza. 11 Jan   With Rhys, founds the Rhymers' Club. 7 Mar   WBY initiated into the Hermetic Order of the Golden Dawn (GD) in Moina Bergson's studio, 17 Fitzroy Street. 16 Mar   Dispatches MS of *Representative Irish Tales*. 5 May   Attends performance of Todhunter's *A Sicilian Idyll* at the Club House in Bedford Park. Aug   Ellis signs contract with Quaritch for publication of *The Works of William Blake*. 11 Oct   First number of the short-lived *Weekly Review*, to which WBY and other Rhymers contribute. Mid-Oct   Asked to resign from the Esoteric Section of the Theosophical Society. Autumn   In state of semi-collapse; a slight heart ailment is diagnosed. 18 Nov   Verdict in the O'Shea divorce case precipitates a political crisis in the Irish Party. 1–6 Dec   Irish Party debate on the leadership crisis ends in a split between Parnellite and anti-Parnellite factions.

1891   Mar   *Representative Irish Tales*. 8 May   Mme Blavatsky dies in London. *c.* 17 July   WBY arrives in Dublin. 22 July   Meets MG in Dublin; his love for her revives. 23 July   Stays with Charles Johnston near Downpatrick. Early Aug   Returns to Dublin, to stay at various addresses while writing 'Rosy Cross Lyrics'. 31 Aug   MG's illegitimate son dies in Paris. 17 Sept   Inaugural Meeting of the Young Ireland League, organized by WBY and O'Leary to unite various Irish literary societies. 7 Oct   Charles Stewart Parnell dies in Brighton. Funeral in Dublin on 11 Oct. *c.* 21 Oct   WBY returns to London. Early Nov   *John Sherman and Dhoya*. 13 Nov   WBY at a meeting of the Rhymers' Club. 16 Nov   Calls on Elkin Mathews with G. A. Greene and Lionel Johnson to discuss the publication of *The Book of the Rhymers' Club*. 28 Dec   Meeting at Blenheim Road to plan an Irish Literary Society.

1892   Jan   WBY planning a new Library of Ireland. 13 Jan   Present at meeting which formally decides to establish an Irish Literary Society in London. **17 Jan** Lectures on 'Nationality and Literature' to the Clapham Branch of the Irish National League. **Feb** *The Book of the Rhymers' Club.* **8 Feb** Fisher Unwin takes over unsold stock of *Oisin* from Kegan Paul. **May** *Irish Fairy Tales.* **6 May** Copyright performance of *The Countess Cathleen* at the Athenaeum Theatre, Shepherd's Bush. **Mid-May** WBY arrives in Dublin to found a central Irish Literary Society. **9 June** Speaks at Public Steering Committee meeting of the National Literary Society held at the Rotunda. **14 June** WBY and MG appointed to the Libraries Sub-committee of the National Literary Society. **8 Aug** Public meeting at the Mansion House, Dublin, to discuss plans for the revival of Irish literature and the foundation of a publishing company. **16 Aug** Inaugural Meeting of the National Literary Society with Gavan Duffy in the chair; address by Sigerson; WBY also speaks. **Late Aug** *The Countess Kathleen and Various Legends and Lyrics.* **Early Sept** Newspaper controversy over proposed New Irish Library. **22 Sept** WBY appointed secretary of the Library Committee of the National Literary Society. **Oct** In Sligo, where his grandmother, Elizabeth Pollexfen, dies on 2 Oct. **29 Oct** Rolleston and Gavan Duffy begin negotiations with Fisher Unwin for publication of the New Irish Library, thus angering WBY and O'Leary. **12 Nov** William Pollexfen dies in Sligo. **20 Nov** WBY returns to Dublin from Sligo. **25 Nov** Hyde inaugurates the first lecture session of the National Literary Society. **Mid-Dec** WBY goes to London to confer with the Committee of the Irish Literary Society, London, and Fisher Unwin about the rival schemes for the New Irish Library. **Late Dec** Preparing for the Portal examination of the GD.

**1893** **20 Jan** Performs the Portal ritual for entry to the Second Order of the GD; also takes the 1st Point part of the $5° = 6°$ grade, the lowest grade of the Second Order. **21 Jan** Takes 2nd and 3rd Points of $5° = 6°$ grade. **22 Jan** Arrives in Dublin. **23 Jan** Travels to Cork with Hyde to promote the National Literary Society at a public meeting. **Late Jan** Small-paper version of *The Works of William Blake* ready; large-paper version appears in mid-Feb. **Mid-Feb** Brief visit to Sligo, where he stays with George Pollexfen. **4 Mar** Delivers the address at the National Club, Dublin, on Robert Emmet. **21 Mar** Formal agreement for setting up the New Irish Library signed by Fisher Unwin and Gavan Duffy. **4 May** Katharine Tynan marries Henry Albert Hinkson. **19 May** WBY lectures on 'Nationality and Literature' to the National Literary Society. **Late May** Returns to London. **30 May** Attends a

Council of Adepts at the Second Order of the GD, Clipstone Street, where he continues to pay regular visits throughout the summer. **31 July**   Gaelic League founded in Dublin. **29 Aug**   Begins small white notebook, in which many of the poems to be published in *The Wind Among the Reeds* are drafted. **Mid-Sept**   Returns to Dublin with Lionel Johnson, to plan an Irish literary magazine. **4 Oct**   Present at Annual General Meeting of the National Literary Society. **21 Nov**   Lectures to the Belfast Naturalists' Field Club. **Late Nov**   *The Poems of William Blake.* **Dec**   *The Celtic Twilight.* **Late Dec**   Returns to London.

1894   **7 Feb**   Stays with the Matherses in Paris. Sees MG and Verlaine, but fails to meet Mallarmé. **26 Feb**   Accompanies MG to a performance of Villiers de l'Isle Adam's *Axël* at the Théâtre de la Gaîté. *c.* **27 Feb**   Returns to London. **Mar**   Begins to rewrite *The Shadowy Waters.* **29 Mar**   *The Land of Heart's Desire* produced at the Avenue Theatre, London, until 14 Apr. **16 Apr**   Meets Olivia Shakespear (OS). **Apr**   *The Land of Heart's Desire* published, and on 21 Apr revived at the Avenue Theatre with Shaw's *Arms and the Man* until 12 May. **June**   *The Second Book of the Rhymers' Club* published; meets Augusta, Lady Gregory (AG), for the first time. **6 Aug**   MG's daughter Iseult born. **23 Aug**   Present at marriage of Jack Yeats to Mary Cottenham White. **10 Oct**   Arrives in Dublin. **25 Oct**   Goes to stay with George Pollexfen in Sligo. Spends much time writing *The Shadowy Waters* and revising poems and plays for a collected edition. **Mid-Nov**   Stays at Lissadell, and contemplates asking Eva Gore-Booth to marry him. Collects folklore and lectures on fairy tales.

1895   **Mid-Jan**   Joins in a controversy with Edward Dowden over Irish literature. **27 Feb**   Begins a controversy in the Dublin *Daily Express* over 'The Best 30 Irish Books'. **Late Feb**   WBY and George Pollexfen ill with influenza. **Early Mar**   *A Book of Irish Verse.* **27 Mar**   Finishes revision of his poems for collected edition. **13 Apr** Leaves Sligo to visit Hyde at Frenchpark, Co. Roscommon. **16 Apr**   Visits Castle Rock in Lough Key. Returns to Sligo on 1 May. **4 May**   Leaves Sligo for London via Dublin. **19 May**   Calls on Oscar Wilde to offer sympathy and support during his trial. **July–Oct**   Four articles on Irish literature in the *Bookman.* **16 July**   Visits Kent with OS. **13 Sept**   Aunt Agnes Pollexfen Gorman arrives at Blenheim Road, having escaped from a mental home. **Early Oct**   WBY leaves the family house, and takes rooms with Arthur Symons in Fountain Court, the Temple. **Oct**   Delivers the address at a Parnell Commemorative Meeting in London.

1896   **Late Feb**   WBY moves from the Temple to rooms at 18 Woburn Buildings. Begins an affair with OS; starts work on *The Speckled Bird*. **Summer**   Visits Aran Islands. **Dec**   To Paris, where on 21 Dec he meets Synge.

1897   **Mid-Jan**   Returns to London. **Mar**   Visits Robert Bridges. **Apr**   *The Secret Rose*. **May**   In Sligo. **June**   *The Adoration of the Magi*. Visits Edward Martyn at Tillyra Castle. **Late July**   To Coole to stay with AG for two months; WBY collects folklore and they discuss the possibility of a 'Celtic Theatre'. **Nov–Dec**   Returns to Dublin and thence back to London.

1898   Working at 'Celtic mysticism' with MG and members of GD. **Jan**   Synge calls on him in London. **Early Mar**   Short visit to Dublin. **1 Apr**   Meets Wilfrid Blunt. **Late Apr–May**   Visits Paris to discuss Celtic mysticism with Mathers and MG. Successfully lobbies MPs to change theatrical licensing laws in Dublin. **May**   Sits to Rothenstein for portrait. **8 June**   To Dublin, and thence to Coole on 20th. **Mid-Aug**   In London and Dublin for '98 banquets and celebrations. Controversy with AE and John Eglinton over 'Literary Ideals in Ireland' in Dublin *Daily Express*. **Sept–Nov**   Staying with George Pollexfen in Sligo. **Late Nov**   To Dublin, where MG tells him she has long been in love with him but cannot marry him.

1899   **Late Jan**   Returns to London. **Feb**   Short visit to Paris, where he again proposes to MG. Returns to London to arrange rehearsals of Irish Literary Theatre plays with FF, George Moore, and Martyn. **Late Mar**   Martyn worried by supposed heresy of *The Countess Cathleen*, but is reassured. **Apr**   *The Wind Among the Reeds*. F. H. O'Donnell attacks *The Countess Cathleen* with support of Cardinal Logue. **8 May**   *The Countess Cathleen* performed at the Antient Concert Rooms as first production of Irish Literary Theatre (ILT). **May**   Revised edition of *Poems*. At Coole until Nov except for short trips to Dublin and Belfast. **Late Oct**   Begins collaboration with Moore on *Diarmuid and Grania*: **17 Nov**   Returns to London.

1900   **3 Jan**   Susan Yeats dies. **19–24 Feb**   Second season of the ILT. **Mar–Apr**   Protests against Queen Victoria's visit to Dublin. **17–25 Apr**   Mathers sends Aleister Crowley to seize the GD headquarters but WBY evicts him and guards the rooms against him. **June**   Takes on A. P. Watt as his literary agent. **23 June**   To Dublin and thence to

Coole. **14 Oct** Returns to London. Disputes with Moore over writing of *Diarmuid and Grania*; play finished on **12 Dec.**

**1901** **Jan** Contributes to *Ideals in Ireland*. **Feb** Trouble in GD. WBY resigns from Committee of the ILS because Moore has been black-balled. **30 Mar** Impressed by stage scenery in Gordon Craig's production of Purcell's *Dido and Aeneas*. **Late Apr** Visits Stratford. **9 May** To Dublin, and on to Sligo, 20 May until late June. **July** At Coole, writing a series of poems on the Irish heroic age. **Late Aug** Attends Pan Celtic Conference in Dublin. Sees the Fays act. **29 Aug** Attends Galway Feis. **21–2 Oct** *Diarmuid and Grania* produced at the Gaiety Theatre. **21 Oct–3 Nov** JBY's Dublin exhibition. **Mid-Nov** WBY returns to London; begins experiments with the psaltery.

**1902** **26 Jan** Allows Fays to rehearse *Cathleen ni Houlihan*, and they produce it, with AE's *Deirdre*, on 2 Apr. **5 Apr** Meeting with Fays and others to discuss an Irish National Theatre. **8 Apr** Returns to London. **Spring and Summer** Public lectures on the psaltery. **21 June** To Ireland, where he helps prevent the destruction of Tara. **8 Aug** Fays' company move into the Camden Street Hall, and begins rehearsals. **Late Aug** WBY meets John Quinn. **Sept– Oct** Quarrel with Moore over *Where There Is Nothing*. **4 Oct** Lionel Johnson dies. **29 Oct–1 Nov** Irish National Theatre Society (INTS) productions, including *The Pot of Broth*. **Early Nov** Meets James Joyce. **Late Nov** Dun Emer Press set up. **2 Dec** Meets Joyce in London, and tries to find him reviewing work. **Mid-Dec** Discovers Nietzsche.

**1903** **21 Feb** MG marries Major John MacBride in Paris. WBY lecturing on the psaltery with FF. **12 Mar** To Dublin for plays by the INTS. **17 Mar** Announces the setting up of the Masquers Theatrical Society in London. **2 May** INTS's first visit to London a resounding success. **May** *Ideas of Good and Evil* published. **8–13 June** Stays with Hyde at Frenchpark. **14–21 June** Visits George Pollexfen at Rosses Point, Sligo. *c.* **21 June** Goes from Rosses Point to Coole. **Aug** *In the Seven Woods* published. **Late Sept** MG, Hyde, Digges, and Maire Quinn withdraw from the INTS in protest against *In the Shadow of the Glen*. **8 Oct** INTS produce *The King's Threshold* and *In the Shadow of the Glen* at the Molesworth Hall. **4 Nov** WBY leaves from Liverpool for extended lecturing tour of USA. **11 Nov** Arrives in New York, and lectures there and in north-eastern states. **28 Dec** Lunches with President Roosevelt at the White House.

1904    3 Jan   Lectures on 'The Intellectual Revival in Ireland' at Carnegie Hall, and meets a deputation from the Clan-na-Gael. **4 Jan**
Leaves New York for St Louis at the beginning of a tour of the
Midwest and California, returning to New York on 14 Feb by way
of Canada. **9 Mar**   Quinn gives farewell dinner for WBY, who
afterwards sails on the *Oceanic*. **16 Mar**   Arrives in Liverpool.
**26 Mar**   INTS performs at the Royalty Theatre, London; WBY
given a curtain call. **Mid-Apr**   In Dublin to discuss purchase
of Mechanics' Institute and its conversion into the Abbey Theatre.
**26–9 June**   Stage Society production of *Where There Is Nothing* in
London. **29 June**   Meets Queen Alexandra at Stafford House.
**Aug**   Abbey Theatre granted a patent. **31 Aug**   WBY, AG, and
Quinn attend first rehearsal at the Abbey Theatre. **27 Dec**   First
productions at the Abbey Theatre.

1905    1 Jan   Meets Louis Esson at AE's house. **Early Jan**   Returns to
London; sees Laurence Housman's *Prunella* and Carr's production
of *The Knight of the Burning Pestle*. **9 Jan**   Learns that MG is
seeking a divorce. **11 Jan**   Shocked by Mrs Clay's account of
MG's marital problems; in evening discusses the divorce with
Barry O'Brien. **15 Jan**   Lunches with D. S. MacColl to enlist his
support for Lane's purchase of pictures. **16 Jan**   Travels to Dublin
from London to oversee scenery for Synge's *The Well of the Saints*.
**Late Jan**   Press controversy over Synge's *In the Shadow of the
Glen*; WBY rewriting *On Baile's Strand* and *The King's Threshold*.
**1 Feb**   Attends meeting of the INTS Reading Committee.
**12 Feb**   Colum reads part of his new play, *The Land*, to WBY.
**18 Feb**   MG sues MacBride for divorce. **23 Feb**   WBY reads Fay
a new version of *On Baile's Strand*. **24 Feb**   Quarrels with AE over
drama and MG's divorce; later discusses the divorce with Henry
Dixon. **28 Feb**   *The Pot of Broth* begins a series of matinées in
London. **1 Mar**   'Red Hanrahan's Vision' (story) published in
*McClure's Magazine*. **Early Mar**   Crosses to London; disgusted
with production of *The Pot of Broth*; visits the Whistler Exhibition;
sees Bullen. **13 Mar**   Attends Stage Society production of Brieux's
*The Three Daughters of M. Dupont*; in the evening Maclagan at
WBY's 'Monday Evening'. *c.* **20 Mar**   Crosses to Dublin from
London. **24 Mar**   Attends dress rehearsal of *Kincora*. **25 Mar**
First production of AG's *Kincora* at the Abbey Theatre. **Late
Mar** Rewriting *The King's Threshold*. **30 Mar**   *The Hour-Glass*
produced in Chicago by Anna Morgan. **1 Apr**   'America and the
Arts' published in the *Metropolitan Magazine*. Attends last perform-

ance of *Kincora*, and AG's party afterwards. **7 Apr**    Gogarty calls
on WBY and AEFH at the Nassau Hotel. **8 Apr**    WBY replies
to Cruise O'Brien's paper at the Literary and Historical Society.
*c.* **10 Apr**    Travels with Colum to Coole. Resumes work on *Deirdre*. **15 Apr**    Special performance of the INTS on behalf of the
proposed Gallery of Modern Art. *c.* **20 Apr**    Returns to Dublin
from Coole. **24 Apr**    Attends revival of *Kincora* at the Abbey with
AG and Synge. **26 Apr**    At performance of *Kincora* and party
afterwards. **28 Apr**    Attends another performance of *Kincora* and
to tea with AG afterwards. **5 May**    He and AG hunt for folklore in
Dundrum. *c.* **10 Apr**    Crosses to London from Dublin. **11 Apr**
Sees Irving in Tennyson's *Becket*. *c.* **12 Apr**    Attends Carr's production of Jonson's *The Silent Woman*. **13 Apr**    Attends first
production in England of Wilde's *Salome*. Inscribes *Stories of Red
Hanrahan* (1905) to AEFH. **Mid-Apr**    Advises Roberts and Hone
on establishing the Maunsel Press. *c.* **18 Apr**    Sends Hone to seek
Bullen's advice on the Maunsel Press. **21 Apr**    Attends first performance of Shaw's *Man and Superman*. **23 Apr**    Goes to Stratford
to see Bullen; discusses forthcoming publications and the *Collected
Edition*; buys 40-vol. edition of Balzac. *c.* **28 Apr**    Sees Carr's
production of W. S. Gilbert's *The Palace of Truth*. **3 June**    Symons
calls on WBY. **8 June**    Sees French production of Molière's *Les
Précieuses ridicules* at the Shaftesbury Theatre. **9 June**    Catches
day boat to Dublin with AG; they see Colum's *The Land* in evening.
**10 June**    WBY sits up to small hours discussing theatrical
matters with Fay. **13 June**    Friends give WBY a copy of the
Kelmscott *Chaucer* for his 40th birthday. **18 June**    Attends General Meeting of the INTS. **19 June**    Catches morning boat to
England and dines with FF in evening. **20 June**    Dines with FF
after rehearsal of *The Shadowy Waters*. **Late June**    WBY attends
rehearsals of *The Shadowy Waters*. **24 June**    Dines with Masefield
at Woburn Buildings and afterwards speaks at the Lyceum Club.
**29 June**    Accompanies FF to Pinero's *The Cabinet Minister*.
**30 June**    Calls to see Ricketts in the evening, and talks discour-
agingly about Ireland and disparagingly about Gorki. **1 July**    Takes
Frank Fay to a rehearsal of *The Shadowy Waters*. **8 July**    *The
Shadowy Waters* produced at the Annual Congress of the Theosophical Society. **10 July**    FF recites to the psaltery at WBY's
'Monday Evening'. *c.* **11 July**    Leaves London for Coole.
**Mid-July–Aug**    Radical rewriting of *The Shadowy Waters*. **19
July**    Dines with Martyn at Tillyra. **Aug**    Corresponds with AE
on reorganization of the INTS. **9 Aug**    MG granted a legal separ-

ation. **Mid-Aug**   The Countess of Cromartie and Lady Margaret Sackville visit Coole. **19 Aug**   AG takes WBY to Recess in Connemara for a few days. **27 Aug**   WBY and AG attend General Meeting of the INTS in Dublin. **Sept**   'Queen Edaine' (poem) published in *McClure's Magazine*. **15 Sept**   Jack and Cottie Yeats leave Coole after a fortnight's visit. **16 Sept**   WBY, AG, and Synge hold policy meeting at Coole to plan the reorganization of the INTS. *c.* **17 Sept**   AEFH arrives in Coole. **20 Sept**   WBY, Synge, and AEFH travel to Dublin from Coole. **21 Sept**   Sees AEFH and AE about theatrical reorganization; visits Jack Yeats's exhibition. **22 Sept**   Attends General Meeting of the Irish National Theatre Society which turns it into a limited liability company. **23 Sept**   Attends meeting of the Contemporary Club and discusses Oscar Wilde with Robert Sherard, Wilde's biographer. AE, Synge, and John O'Leary also present. **24 Sept**   In morning Sherard calls on WBY in Dublin. **25 Sept**   Hammers out details of organization of the new National Theatre Society with AE, Synge, and Ryan. **29 Sept**   Discusses organization of Theatre Society with AE. In evening attends rehearsal of *The Building Fund* and *The Land* at the Abbey Theatre, accompanied by AEFH and Synge. **30 Sept**   Catches bad cold at the Abbey and is indisposed for several days. **Oct**   'Do Not Love Too Long' published in the *Acorn*. **Early Oct**   AG typing a prose scenario of *Deirdre* for WBY, as well as changes in *The King's Threshold* and his notes for *Samhain*. **9 Oct**   Attends General Meeting of the National Theatre Society. **13 Oct**   In morning WBY gives evidence to Inquiry into work at the Dublin art schools; later attends rehearsal at the Abbey. **24 Oct**   Dismisses George Roberts from role of Conchubar; National Theatre Society formally registered as a limited company. **28 Oct**   Attends with AG and Edward Martyn performances of Dinneen's plays in Irish given by the Keating Branch of the Gaelic League at the Abbey Theatre. **29 Oct**   Reads new version of *The Shadowy Waters* to members of the Abbey Company at the Nassau Hotel. **31 Oct**   Attends Cumann na nGaedheal plays at the Molesworth Hall with AG. They see Hyde's *Teach na mBocht* and first performance of Martyn's *The Tale of a Town*. Major John MacBride also in the audience. **Nov**   Edits and contributes to *Samhain*. **1 Nov**   Leaves Dublin for London by morning boat. **2 Nov**   Consults Mathews about future publication of *The Wind Among the Reeds*. Sees Bourchier's production of *The Merchant of Venice* in the evening. **3 Nov**   Calls on Ricketts and Shannon and is much impressed with Ricketts's paintings. **5 Nov**   Reads new version of *The Shadowy Waters* to FF and later to Symons. **7 Nov** Calls on Shaw and persuades him to publish an early story in the *Shanachie*. **8 Nov** Hyde sails from Cork on his USA tour. WBY calls on AEFH and finds her ill. **9 Nov** Goes to Cambridge with O'Donovan; lunches with Professor of Arabic, and makes speech at Newnham College. **10 Nov** Goes to John Murray's about republication of AG's books; calls on AEFH; in evening meets Hughes, the musician, at FF's apartment. *c.* **14 Nov** Sees Rhys's *Guinevere* at the Coronet Theatre. **22 Nov** Travels to Oxford with Synge; gives lecture. **23 Nov** Attends Abbey performances at Oxford. **24 Nov** With Abbey Company at Cambridge. **26 Nov** Addresses the Dramatic Debaters at Frascati's on 'The Drama as it is and What it Might Be', with J. T. Grein in the chair. **27–8 Nov** With the Abbey Company at St George's Hall, London. **1 Dec** Dines with Synge at Ricketts's and Shannon's house, and Hind calls in later. Synge's *The Well of the Saints* with WBY's introduction appears early this month. **2 Dec** 'Never Give All the Heart' (poem) published in *McClure's Magazine*. WBY denounces the printed book at an 'Original Night' at the ILS. **3 Dec** Calls on Gosse and discusses Ibsen. *c.* **4 Dec** Goes from London to Dublin. **9 Dec** Attends first performance of AG's *The White Cockade*. **12 Dec** At another performance of *The White Cockade* and introduces the audience to Arthur Darley who plays the violin between the acts. **14 Dec** Lectures on 'What is National Literature?' at Cork. **16 Dec** Sees AE who tells him Colum is complaining about the position of his plays in the London programme. Serious dissension in the new National Theatre Society. **20 Dec** Goes to Dundrum to persuade Maire Walker to sign acting contract; discusses problem with Fay and Synge in evening. **21 Dec** Goes through Abbey accounts with Ryan to apportion shares for costumes; sees Maire Walker later. **22 Dec** Two long interviews with Maire Walker; dines with Tom Kettle in the evening. **23 Dec** Maire Walker signs contract. *c.* **27 Dec** Returns to London from Dublin. **30 Dec** Learns that Maire Walker is backing out of her contract and threatens her with legal action.

**1906** **1 Jan** Dines with Vera Esposito in London and offers her an acting job at the Abbey; Masefield reads him his 'magnificent play' *The Campden Wonder*. **3 Jan** Controversy over prosecution of Maire Walker continues; working on lyrical parts of *On Baile's Strand*. **4 Jan** Decides to drop threat to prosecute Maire Walker.

**6 Jan** Hears that a rival theatre group (later the Theatre of Ireland) are rehearsing Colum's *The Land*. **7 Jan** Goes to Edinburgh as guest of Alexander Carmichael. **10 Jan** Lectures on 'Irish Heroic Poetry' to the Celtic Union in the Hall of the Philosophic Institution, Edinburgh. **11 Jan** Travels to Dundee where he lectures on 'Literature and the Living Voice'. **12 Jan** Lectures to Aberdeen University Literature Society on 'Literature and the Living Voice'. Afterwards entertained to supper in the University Union. **13 Jan** Leaves Aberdeen by morning train to be the guest of the Countess of Cromartie and her husband at Leod Castle, Strathpeffer; where he remains until 19 Jan, working at *On Baile's Strand*. **20 Jan** Arrives back in Dublin and undertakes a number of informal lectures. **23 Jan** Discusses the inadequate heating at the Abbey Theatre with the architect, Joseph Holloway. **25 Jan** Lectures on 'The Ideal in Art' at Royal Hibernian Academy. **1 Feb** Speaks in a discussion after AE's lecture 'Art and Literature' at the Royal Hibernian Academy. **5 Feb** Speaks at the NLS to a paper by George Sigerson, 'The Irish Theatre and the Peasant'. **6 Feb** Travels to Coole 'to spend a couple of weeks of most unwilling industry' on *The Player Queen*. Begins 'eastern meditations' in attempt to 'lay hands upon some dynamic and substantialising force'. *c.* **17 Feb** Returns to Dublin from Coole. **18 Feb** Sees Synge who tells him about the rival drama company, the Theatre of Ireland; visits his father's studio. *c.* **19 Feb** Returns to London where he dines out 'a great deal'. **26 Feb** Abbey Company visit Wexford; remain there until 27 Feb. **3 Mar** Stays with Lord Howard de Walden until 5 March. **8 Mar** Robert Gregory calls and reads the additions to *On Baile's Strand*. **10 Mar** Stays with Mrs Ladenburg at Melton Mowbray until 12 March. **14 Mar** Lectures on 'Poetry and the Living Voice' at the Leeds Arts Club. **15 Mar** Lectures in Liverpool. **16 Mar** Returns to London from Liverpool. **17 Mar** Abbey Company playing in Dundalk. **18 Mar** Accompanies AG and Robert Gregory to Charles Shannon's studio to view Shannon's portrait of Robert. **Late March** Working hard, rewriting his introduction to Spenser and his play; dines with T. P. O'Connor and meets Prince Christian. **28 Mar** Goes to see Pinero's new play, *His House in Order*, and does not like it. **29 Mar** Tea with Mrs Albert Montgomery. Sees *Hippolytus*. **30 Mar** Finishes dictating a new version of his Spenser introduction; goes to the theatre in the afternoon and also sees Stephen Phillips's *Nero* in the evening. **1 Apr** Goes to see Sydney Cockerell at Richmond, and afterwards to T. Sturge Moore's play *Aphrodite against Artemis*, which he pronounces a failure.

**2 Apr** Sturge Moore at WBY's 'Monday Evening'. **3 Apr** In evening accompanies AEFH to Anstey's play *The Man from Blankley's*. **4 Apr** In afternoon collects two theatre wigs from Clarkson's, and in the evening crosses to Dublin. **6 Apr** Attends rehearsal of *On Baile's Strand* at the Abbey Theatre. **7 Apr** Reading Shaw's plays for possible performance at the Abbey. **11 Apr** Attends dress rehearsals of *On Baile's Strand* and AG's version of Molière's *Doctor in Spite of Himself* at the Abbey. **13 Apr** Attends final dress rehearsal of the two plays. **14 Apr** Present at first night of AG's version of *The Doctor in Spite of Himself* and the revised *On Baile's Strand*. **17 Apr** Discusses Molière and revised *On Baile's Strand* with Joseph Holloway at the Abbey Theatre. **23 Apr** Attends Abbey Company's performances at the Midland Hall, Manchester; remains there until 24 April. **27–28 Apr** Abbey Company in Leeds. **29 Apr** Goes to Coole, where he remains until *c.* 20 May, working on his play *Deirdre*. **May** 'Against Witchcraft' and 'The Praise of Deirdre' (poems) published in the *Shanachie*. **9 May** Meeting of seceders from INTS plans the Theatre of Ireland. **15 May** Abbey Company playing in Dundalk **18 May** First meeting to inaugurate the Theatre of Ireland. **24 May** Attends AGM of the National Theatre Society at the Abbey Theatre. **26 May** Abbey Company, managed by Alfred Wareing, begins an extended tour to Cardiff, Glasgow, Aberdeen, Newcastle, Edinburgh, and Hull, which lasts until 9 July. **27 May** With the Abbey Company at Theatre Royal, Cardiff. **30 May** Addresses a luncheon at the Royal Hotel, Cardiff, on the Celtic Revival and the desirability of National Theatres. **June** Writing a series of short essays later published as 'Discoveries'. **1 June** WBY and Rothenstein visit Ricketts and Shannon in the evening and discuss the theatre. **7 June** In Edinburgh with the Abbey Company, where he remains until *c.* 12 June, giving two lectures and spending much time looking at Phoebe Traquair's paintings. **8 June** Dispatched to Glasgow by AEFH to sort out a dispute between William Fay and Bell over theatre make-up. **11 June** Abbey Company in Aberdeen, until 16 June. **15 June** Calls on Ricketts in the evening, Hind also there. **18 June** Abbey Company in Newcastle until 23 June. **25 June** Visits Bullen in Stratford-upon-Avon to discuss publication of 'Discoveries'; Abbey Company in Edinburgh until 30 June. **30 June** The *Athenaeum* quotes Algernon Swinburne's attack on WBY. **30 June** Spends a 'delightful' weekend at Margaret Horner's Elizabethan manor house at Mells in Somerset, with

Sydney Cockerell, Lady Cromartie, Lady Margaret Sackville, and Raymond Asquith. **1 July**   Reads Agnes Tobin's translations of Petrarch to Miss Horner's house party. In evening talks of ghosts and reincarnation. **2 July**   Abbey Company in Hull until 7 July. **3 July**   WBY calls on Agnes Tobin in London. **8 July**   Consults Alfred Wareing about hiring a manager for the Abbey Theatre. **10 July**   WBY crosses to Dublin in the morning; in the afternoon has a long talk with Frank Fay about the company's unruly behaviour on the recent tour. **11 July**   Sees William Fay and John Synge about the bad behaviour on the recent Abbey tour. **12 July**   Accompanies the Abbey Company on its visit to Longford; remains until 13 July. **14 July**   WBY at Coole for a series of Abbey Directors' meetings to discuss the reorganization of the Company; William Fay also present. **17 July**   John Synge joins AG, WBY, and William Fay at Coole, and together they put the Abbey Company on a new footing. **Late July**   WBY corrects the proofs of the New York edition of his poems, condenses his selection from Spenser's poetry, and flirts with Dorothy Carleton, Wilfrid Scawen Blunt's mistress, who is visiting Coole. **27 July**   Karel Mušek, the Czech theatre director, visits Coole and stays until 31 July. **29 July**   After spending day going through a second Dun Emer selection of AE's poems, WBY sends an imperious letter to ECY demanding the book be postponed. **1 Aug**   Letitia Darragh's arrival at Coole to see if she would make a suitable Deirdre leads to a dispute with the Fays over whether Darragh or Allgood should play the heroines in *The Shadowy Waters* and *Deirdre*. **Mid-Aug**   Quarrels with ECY over books for the Dun Emer Press, and resigns as literary adviser; working on *Deirdre* and 'Discoveries'. **6 Sept**   W. G. Fay visits Coole. **18 Sept**   Abbey Company plays at Galway until 19 September. **15 Sept**   'My Thoughts and my Second Thoughts' (essays) published in the *Gentleman's Magazine*. **Mid-Sept**   Reading Jonson, Donne, and Jacobean dramatists. **Late Sept**   WBY's edition of *The Poems of Spenser* published; he is 'absorbed' in *Deirdre*. **1 Oct**   'Literature and the Living Voice' (essay) published in the *Contemporary Review*. *Poems, 1899–1905* published. WBY sets out his terms for continuing to act as editor and adviser to the Cuala Press; these are finally accepted by ECY in late Nov. W. A. Henderson takes up duties as secretary to Abbey Theatre. **8 Oct**   WBY in Dublin for the opening of Jack Yeats's exhibition 'Sketches of Life in the West of Ireland'. **9 Oct**   In Dublin with AG watching rehearsals at the Abbey. **13 Oct**   Travels from Coole for Abbey Theatre 'At Home' in Dublin and makes speech on the achievements and plans of the Irish Dramatic Movement. **14 Oct** Before returning to Coole, leaves copy for the periodical the *Arrow* with William Fay. **15 Oct** 'My Thoughts and my Second Thoughts' (Part II) published in the *Gentleman's Magazine*. **19 Oct** Attends dress rehearsal of *The Mineral Workers* and *The Gaol Gate* at the Abbey. **20 Oct** Attends productions of William Boyle's *The Mineral Workers* and AG's *Gaol Gate* at the Abbey. One thousand copies of the occasional theatrical periodical the *Arrow*, edited and largely written by WBY, are posted to subscribers to the Abbey. **23 Oct** At rehearsals at the Abbey, and has a long talk on theatre business with Synge. **29 Oct** William Fay and Brigit O'Dempsey married in Glasgow. **2 Nov** Meets Synge in afternoon at the Abbey Theatre, and dines with him and AG in evening. **3 Nov** At the Abbey Theatre for packed revival of *Doctor in Spite of Himself*, *Hyacinth Halvey*, and *Riders to the Sea*. **13 Nov** Synge reads *The Playboy of the Western World* to WBY and AG. **15 Nov** 'My Thoughts and my Second Thoughts' (Part III) published in the *Gentleman's Magazine*. **16 Nov** WBY and AG in Dublin at a rehearsal of his *Deirdre*. **23 Nov** WBY at a rehearsal of *Deirdre* and speaks to Joseph Holloway about the play. **24 Nov** Attends first night of *Deirdre*, with Miss Darragh in leading role. **29 Nov** WBY and AG at a sparsely attended Abbey Theatre. **1 Dec** ECY accedes to WBY's right of veto over Cuala books and their decorations. First ever matinée performance at the Abbey Theatre inaugurates a regular practice. **2 Dec** Writes memo calling for changes in the National Theatre Society; advocates more capital, a larger company, more foreign plays, guest actresses, and a managing director to take non-artistic work off W. G. Fay's shoulders. **3 Dec** Begins selection of KT's poems for the Cuala Press. **7 Dec** Attends Theatre of Ireland's first productions at the Molesworth Hall. **8 Dec** Attends Abbey productions of the revised version of his *The Shadowy Waters* and AG's *The Canavans*, with Miss Darragh playing Dectora. **9 Dec** Gives interview to the *Freeman's Journal* on the proposed reform of the Royal Hibernian Academy. **10 Dec** Speaks after lecture by Padraic Colum to the NLS on the need for Irish actors for Irish plays. **15 Dec** Meeting with Synge and AG at Abbey to discuss reorganization of the Company. **16 Dec** Travels to London from Dublin. **17 Dec** Dines in London with AEFH. **20 Dec** Lunches with Sidgwick, and hears that 800 copies of *Poems, 1899–1905* have been sold, the quickest sale he has ever had. **21 Dec** Sees FF in evening. **22 Dec** Making revisions and correcting proofs for vol. II of the American edition of *The Poetical Works*. **Late Dec** Epistolary discussions between WBY, AG, AEFH, and Synge about the management and reorganization of the Abbey Company; difficulties centre on the position and personality of William Fay.

**1907** **1 Jan** Reads *Deirdre* to FF. **3 Jan** Writes to AG telling her of AEFH's objections to Fay, and insisting that Fay must not be left in charge of the Abbey Company. **7 Jan** Consults Vedrenne about a hiring a stage manager for the Abbey. **8 Jan** Attends first night of Masefield's play *The Campden Wonder*. **10 Jan** WBY sees Holroyd about Lane's Municipal Gallery. *c.* **12 Jan** Sees Mrs William Sharp, lately widowed, who confirms that William Sharp was 'Fiona Macleod', giving him full details of that relationship. **14 Jan** Sees Vedrenne again about a new manager for the Abbey Theatre; in evening sees Masefield and discusses the shocked reception of *The Campden Wonder* with him. **15 Jan** Lunches with Ella Hepworth Dixon at the Lyceum. **16 Jan** Invites Ben Iden Payne to be manager of the Abbey. **18 Jan** FF leaves for a lecturing tour in USA; in the evening WBY goes to see Ricketts and discusses Miss Darragh's acting with him. **21 Jan** Despite 'a frightful cold', goes to see Sidgwick at Bullen's about the price of his proposed *Collected Edition*. **22 Jan** Sees AEFH, who is just back from Algeria. **23 Jan** Sees AEFH; in the late evening goes to a party at Miss Stone's. **25 Jan** Lectures in Aberdeen on 'The Heroic Poetry of Ireland' under the auspices of the Franco-Scottish Society. **26 Jan** Remains in Aberdeen until 27 Jan as the guest of H. P. R. Grierson. In Dublin the first performance of *The Playboy of the Western World* breaks up in a riot at the word 'shift'. Disturbances continue over the following week. **29 Jan** WBY, back in Dublin, makes a speech in front of the Abbey curtain inviting the protesters to a discussion about *The Playboy* on 4 Feb. Police present in the theatre, and students from Trinity College shout for the play. **30 Jan** In morning WBY attends trials of Patrick Columb and Piaras Beaslai for causing a riot at the Abbey Theatre; in the evening attends the Abbey for production of *The Playboy*. **1 Feb** WBY at trial of Patrick Hughes and John Duane for causing riot at the Abbey Theatre; in evening attends performance of *The Playboy* where there are more arrests. **2 Feb** Calls at the *Leader* office to get a copy of the Christmas issue which attacked William Boyle. At matinée and evening performances of *The Playboy*. **4 Feb** Speaks at public debate on 'The Freedom of the

Theatre', to discuss dispute over *The Playboy*. **6 Feb**  WBY goes
to Wexford, where Ben Iden Payne is on tour, to discuss his new
duties at the Abbey; remains until 7 Feb. **9 Feb**  Goes to visit
Synge at his mother's house, but Synge is too ill to see him; in the
evening given a curtain call at the Abbey after a performance of
*Cathleen ni Houlihan*. **16 Feb**  Calls to see Synge at his mother's
house in Glenageary, but Synge still too ill to see him. **23 Feb**  Edits
and contributes to the *Arrow*. **25 Feb**  Present at George
Sigerson's lecture 'The Peasants of the West' at the NLS. *c.* **28
Feb**  Goes from Dublin to London. **1 Mar**  Sees Shaw who
refuses permission for Abbey to produce *John Bull's Other Island*;
visits AEFH in afternoon; in evening sees Agnes Tobin to discuss
the possibility of Frohman arranging an American tour for the
Abbey Company. **2 Mar**  Sees Cecil French in afternoon and
hears news of Althea Gyles. **6 Mar**  Goes to A. P. Watt to arrange
for transfer of his books to Bullen prior to the *Collected Edition*; sees
Frohman about possible American tour for the Abbey; takes the
revised *Deirdre* to be copied for the American edition; in the evening
Norreys Connell reads his play *The Piper* to WBY at AEFH's flat.
**8 Mar**  Sees AEFH; receives MS of Lionel Johnson's *Essays*.
**12 Mar**  AG arrives in London and WBY reads *The Piper* to her.
**13 Mar**  WBY and AG see Bullen at the Euston Hotel and exult
over the downfall of the publisher Oldmeadow. **14 Mar**  WBY
travels from London to Dublin, lending Bullen his rooms while he
is away. **16 Mar**  Death of John O'Leary. **19 Mar**  WBY chooses
not to attend O'Leary's funeral. That evening he makes a speech at
the Bohemians Club, giving his reminiscences of Oscar Wilde, and
revealing that the Abbey would produce four new plays next season.
**21 Mar**  Attends performances of the Theatre of Ireland at the
Rotunda, accompanied by AG and a number of the Abbey company. *c.* **22 Mar**  WBY goes to London for a few days to see
Aeschylus' *The Persians*, designed by Charles Ricketts, at Terry's
Theatre. Stays at the Euston Hotel because he has lent his rooms to
Bullen. **30 Mar**  Back in Dublin, attends performance of *The
Pagans* and *The Turn of the Road* given by the Ulster Literary
Theatre at the Abbey. **31 Mar**  Visits Synge who is recuperating
at Glendalough House. **1 Apr**  Attends Abbey performances of his
revised *Deirdre* and Winifred Letts's *The Eyes of the Blind*. Froh-
man, the American theatre impresario, also there, accompanied by
J. M. Barrie. **2 Apr**  Consults with AG and Ben Iden Payne at the
Abbey. Meets the Company to steel their nerve for the production
of *The Playboy* in England. **3 Apr**  At the Abbey with AG to see

performances of *The Poorhouse*, *Gaol Gate*, *Deirdre*, and *The Jack-daw*. **5 Apr**   Sees Synge and AG at the Nassau Hotel. **6 Apr**   At the Abbey with AG to see Maeterlinck's *Interior* (which replaced his own *Deirdre* because of the illness of Mona Limerick), *The Poor-house*, *The Rising of the Moon*, and *The Jackdaw*. *c.* **7 Apr**   Returns to London from Dublin. **10 Apr**   Leaves London to join AG and Robert Gregory in Florence; they remain in Italy until *c.* 21 May. **5 May**   WBY and the Gregorys visit San Marino. **11 May**   Ab-bey Company begins tour to Glasgow, Cambridge, Birmingham, Oxford, and London. **Mid-May**   Visits Venice with the Gregorys, driving in carriages through the Apennines, and by Urbino to Ravenna, to approach the city for the first time by sea. **22 May** Arrives back from Italy, summoned by a telegram telling him that the Lord Chamberlain might refuse to license *The Playboy* for performance in Britain. **27 May**   Holbrook Jackson and Orage at WBY's Monday evening to discuss performances of *The Playboy* on the Abbey's British tour. *c.* **28 May**   WBY in Birmingham with the Abbey Company; remains there until 1 June. **31 May**   WBY sees William Fay about the Abbey Company's lack of discipline on their British tour. **1 June**   Edits and contributes to the *Arrow*. **3 June**   WBY in Oxford with Abbey Company, staying with George Mair at Christ Church; remains there until 5 June. **7 June**   Temporarily resigns as Director of the Abbey following a dispute with AEFH. **9 June**   With Ben Iden Payne attends matinée of the Stage Society's production of Charles McEvoy's *David Ballard*. **10 June**   Attends opening production of Abbey Company at the Great Queen Street Theatre, London, and after-wards dines with Synge, Lord Dunraven, and Annette Meakin. **11 June**   Attends rehearsal of *The Shadowy Waters* at the Great Queen Street Theatre with AG and Synge. In evening attends the performances of *Riders to the Sea*, *The Jackdaw*, *Spreading the News*, and *The Shadowy Waters* with AG. **12 June**   Attends rehearsals at the Great Queen Street Theatre with AG and Synge. In evening attends performance of *The Hour-Glass* and *The Playboy of the Western World*, and talks to George Bernard Shaw. **14 June**   Pre-sent during a minor disturbance during performance of *The Playboy of the Western World* at the Great Queen Street Theatre. **15 June**   Last performance of the Abbey's London tour: WBY receives a special curtain call. **16 June**   Visits AEFH with Payne and they discuss the possibility of her setting up another theatrical initiative, using Dublin 'as a pied-à-terre'. **17 June**   Sees AEFH, who tells him that she is abandoning Dublin, and invites him to join her new theatrical venture in Manchester; she also announces that she is withdrawing as patron of the Abbey Theatre, but will continue her subsidy until the end of 1910. **19 June**  Has conference with AG and W. G. Fay about AEFH's decision to withdraw her support for the Abbey; in evening discusses Abbey finances with AEFH. **22 June**  Ben Iden Payne formally resigns from managership of the Abbey Theatre. **25 June**  Meets Fay and Payne in the morning: they decide to fire W. A. Henderson and put Vaughan into his job as secretary; they also plan a tour to Glasgow, Edinburgh, and Manchester during Advent. **26 June**  Dines with Mrs Myers to meet the Revd Reginald John Campbell. **1 July**  Travels from London to Coole, where he begins to prepare copy text for the *Collected Works*, to write *The Golden Helmet*, and to turn *Where There Is Nothing* into *The Unicorn from the Stars*. Feeling unwell and close to a nervous breakdown. **8 July**  Vol. 11 of the US edition of *The Poetical Works* published in New York. **10 July**  Sends Bullen a rewritten version of 'Maid Quiet'. **28 July**  Sends Bullen a corrected version of 'The Hollow Wood', with an improved rhyme scheme. **9 Aug**  At Coole, continuing work on the *Collected Works*. **4 Aug**  Finishes *The Golden Helmet*. *c.* **18 Aug**  *Deirdre* published. **Late Aug**  Declines romantic liaison with American poet Agnes Tobin. Enraged at appointment of George Plunkett as director of the Irish National Museum instead of Hugh Lane. *c.* **30 Aug**  Sees W. G. Fay while in Dublin on his way to London from Coole. **1 Sept**  In London visits his dentist, and sees Agnes Tobin and Granville-Barker. **4 Sept**  With FF attends performance of Binyon's play *Attila* at His Majesty's Theatre. **6 Sept**  Returns to Ireland from London. **7 Sept**  Travels down to Coole, where he returns to revisions for the *Collected Works*, reads North's *Plutarch*, and is sketched by Augustus John. **13 Sept**  Synge in the Elphis nursing home for an operation on his neck glands; remains there until 26 Sept. **23 Sept**  Augustus John leaves Coole after sketching WBY. First performance of AEFH's 'Playgoers' Theatre' in Manchester. **1 Oct**  'Discoveries' (essays) published in the *Shanachie*. **3 Oct**  WBY travels from Coole to Dublin to attend first production of George Fitzmaurice's *The Country Dressmaker* at the Abbey Theatre. **4 Oct**  Meets the Italian painter Antonio Mancini and is delighted with him; in the evening he sees Forbes-Robertson's production of Shaw's *Caesar and Cleopatra*. **5 Oct**  Visits Synge who is recuperating after the operation on his neck. In evening sees another performance of *The Country Dressmaker*. **6 Oct**  Mancini paints a portrait of him in pastels. **10 Oct**  Attends a Directors'

Meeting at the Abbey Theatre with AG and Synge. **11 Oct** Present at a special Abbey matinée for the Beerbohm Tree and Forbes-Robertson companies who are performing in Dublin. **17 Oct** Stays with Lord Dunraven at Adare Manor, Adare; remains until 19 Sept, when he returns to Dublin. **19 Oct** Attends Abbey with AG to see revival of Colum's *The Land*. **24 Oct** Attends a dinner at the United Arts Club in honour of Mrs Pat Campbell, and pays tribute to her genius as an actress. **25 Oct** At a special Abbey matinée in honour of Mrs Pat Campbell's company. Mrs Campbell touches him by offering to take the title role in his *Deirdre* at the Abbey in November 1908. **26 Oct** Attends performance of *Magda* by Mrs Pat Campbell at the Gaiety Theatre; she makes a speech from the stage calling WBY 'my dear friend and your great poet'. **29 Oct** Signs public protest against stage censorship. **31 Oct** Attends first production of AG's *Dervorgilla* at the Abbey Theatre. **2 Nov** At the Abbey Theatre, and has a meeting with AG and Synge there afterwards. *c.* **7 Nov** Visits the Irish International Exhibition. **10 Nov** Sees Ella Young to discuss astrology, and dines later with the actor-manager John Martin Harvey. **13 Nov** Dines with Lawrence Binyon at the Arts Club, Dublin, and afterwards attends a discussion there on Modernism, introduced by William Gibson. **14 Nov** Attends lecture by Martin Harvey at the Theatre Royal, Dublin, to inaugurate the Dublin Branch of the British Empire Shakespearean Society. In the evening speaks on behalf of an Irish Catholic University at a dinner arranged by the Corinthian Club at the Gresham Hotel in honour (although WBY did not know this in advance) of Lady Aberdeen, wife of the Lord-Lieutenant. **15 Nov** Present at a special Abbey matinée for the Martin Harvey and Frank Benson companies who are performing in Dublin. **19 Nov** Dines with William Poel, the actor and producer, Synge, and AG. Speaks at the inaugural meeting of the Dublin University Gaelic Society. **20 Nov** At AEFH's behest he sees the manager of the Theatre Royal, Dublin, to make sure that no Abbey actors were involved in the demonstration against Forbes-Robertson's production of Rosamund Langbridge's *The Spell*. In the evening sees Shaw's *John Bull's Other Island* with AG at the Royalty Theatre. **21 Nov** In afternoon present at a lecture by William Poel at the Abbey Theatre on the Elizabethan Playhouse, and in evening attends first production of *The Unicorn from the Stars*. Writes to the *Leader* to defend his presence at the Corinthian Club dinner of 14 Nov. **24 Nov** Talks with Edward Evans; Abbey Company begin advent tour to Manchester, Glasgow, and Edinburgh. The tour lasts until 15 Dec and intensifies the antagonism between the Company and William Fay. **30 Nov**  Present at the Contemporary Club, Dublin, for a discussion on Shaw's *John Bull's Other Island*. **2 Dec**  Sees AG and Synge; casts Synge's horoscope, and hears of his proposal to write *Deirdre of the Sorrows*. JBY painting WBY's portrait on a commission from John Quinn. **4 Dec**  WBY, AG, and Synge hold a long meeting in Dublin to discuss W. G. Fay's troublesome behaviour on the Abbey tour; in evening WBY and Synge attend a debate at the Arts Club. **5 Dec**  Sits to JBY. **6 Dec**  Sits to JBY. **7 Dec**  Travels from Dublin to London where he sees a very bad-tempered AEFH in the evening. **8 Dec**  Sees FF. **9 Dec**  Sees a much subdued AEFH, and FF also calls. Orage calls in later and discusses clairvoyance with WBY. **13 Dec**  Attends lecture at the New Gallery and hears Rothenstein praise Mancini's portrait of Hugh Lane; in evening dines with the astrologer Ralph Shirley. **14 Dec**  Works in the British Museum Library. **15 Dec**  *Discoveries* published by the Dun Emer Press; WBY goes to Ralph Shirley for lesson in astrology. Flurry of correspondence between the Abbey directors about W. G. Fay's position in the Abbey Company continues until the end of the month. **16 Dec**  Receives two etched portraits of himself from Augustus John and shows them to AEFH, who dislikes them. **18 Dec**  Synge sees W. G. Fay and Kerrigan in Dublin about disputes during the recent British tour. **19 Dec** WBY dines with Norreys Connell to discuss the proposed production of his play *The Piper*. **20 Dec**  Calls on Ricketts and Shannon to arrange for Shannon's portrait of him. **21 Dec**  JBY and SMY sail for a short trip to New York aboard the *Carmania*, but JBY is destined to remain there for the rest of his life.

**1908**  **13 Jan**  Fays resign from the Abbey Company. **Spring**  WBY starts a love affair with Mabel Dickinson. **Late June**  Visits MG in Paris. **Sept–Dec**  *Collected Works* published in 8 vols. **Nov**  Mrs Patrick Campbell plays *Deirdre* in Dublin and London. **Dec**  WBY goes to Paris to work on *The Player Queen*.

**1909**  **Feb**  AG's illness causes concern. **24 Mar**  Synge dies. **Aug** Quarrel with John Quinn. Dispute with Dublin Castle over production of Shaw's *Blanco Posnet*. **Late autumn**  Plans for buying out AEFH's interest in the Abbey.

**1910**  **May**  Stays with MG in Normandy. **7 May**  Abbey remains open following death of Edward VII, causing violent row with AEFH. **June**  Jack Yeats moves from Devon to Ireland. **9 Aug**  WBY

granted a Civil List pension of £150 per annum. **Sept** George
Pollexfen dies. **Autumn** Talk of WBY taking up Edward Dow-
den's TCD professorship. **Dec** *The Green Helmet and Other
Poems.*

1911 **Late Jan** C. P. Scott offers to arbitrate in the dispute between
AEFH and the Abbey Directors. **Mar** WBY meets Winston
Churchill. **Apr** Visits Paris, where Ezra Pound calls on
him. **May** Scott finds in favour of the Abbey Directors.
**26 July** *Synge and the Ireland of his Time.* **13 Sept** Accompanies
the Abbey Players to USA. **23 Oct** Returns to London. **Nov–
Dec** Helps Nugent Monck with the Abbey School in Dublin.

1912 **Jan** Abbey Players arrested in Philadelphia. **May** Third Home
Rule Bill introduced. **June** Meets Tagore. **Aug** Stays with
MG in Normandy. **Sept** Solemn League and Covenant in North-
ern Ireland. **Oct** WBY staying with the Tuckers in Devon.
**Nov** Severe nervous indigestion. **13 Nov** *The Cutting of an
Agate.* **Dec** AG in USA with Abbey Players.

1913 **Jan** Home Rule Bill thrown out by House of Lords. **Spring**
Visiting Mabel Beardsley in hospital. Active in getting support for
Lane's Dublin Art Gallery. **4 Apr** Dowden's death renews WBY's
interest in Chair of English at TCD. **May** AG and Abbey Players
return from USA. Ulster and National Volunteers organized. **Sum-
mer** Experiments in automatic writing with Elizabeth Radcliffe.
**Oct** *Poems Written in Discouragement.* Rents Stone Cottage in
Sussex, with Pound as his secretary from Nov.

1914 **31 Jan** Leaves for American tour. **Mar** Resumes broken friendship with John Quinn. **Apr** Returns to London. **May** Investi-
gates miracle at Mirabeau with MG and Everard Feilding.
**25 May** *Responsibilities.* **July** Home Rule Bill passed, but suspended because of European situation. **4 Aug** First World War
begins. **Autumn** Begins his memoirs.

1915 **Jan–Feb** At Stone Cottage with Ezra and Dorothy Pound. Read-
ing Wordsworth. **May** Hugh Lane drowned on the *Lusitania.*
**Summer** WBY helps to obtain a grant for Joyce from the Royal
Literary Fund. **Dec** Refuses a knighthood.

1916 **Jan–Mar** At Stone Cottage with the Pounds. **20 Mar** *Reveries
over Childhood and Youth.* **Late Mar** Macmillan becomes his
publisher. **4 Apr** *At the Hawk's Well*, first of WBY's Noh plays,
produced at Lady Islington's. **24 Apr** Easter Rising in Dublin.
**July–Aug** Stays with MG in Normandy, and on 1 July asks her to

marry him. Reads the modern French poets with Iseult Gonne, and discusses marriage with her. **Oct–Dec** AG and WBY begin campaign to have the Lane pictures brought to Dublin.

**1917** **Jan** Quarrel with D. S. MacColl over Lane biography. **Late Jan** Elected to the Savile Club. **Late Mar** Buys the Tower (Thoor Ballylee) from the Congested Districts Board. **7 Aug** Arrives in Normandy to stay with MG; proposes to Iseult, but is refused. **Late Aug** Lectures in Paris. *c.* **24 Sept** Proposes to George Hyde-Lees and is accepted. **Early Oct** Visits Coole. **20 Oct** Marries George Hyde-Lees at Harrow Road Registry Office. Honeymoon in Ashdown Forest, WBY depressed. **27 Oct** George Yeats (GY) begins the automatic writing that is eventually to form the basis of *A Vision*. **8 Nov** Moves to Stone Cottage with GY. **17 Nov** *The Wild Swans at Coole*. **20 Dec** After a short stay in London, Yeatses move to Ashdown Cottage to escape Zeppelin raids.

**1918** **Jan–early Mar** Move to Oxford. **18 Jan** *Per Amica Silentia Lunae*. **23 Jan** Robert Gregory killed in action. **Mar–early Apr** To Ireland, to stay at Glendalough and Glenmalure. **6 Apr** Visit to Coole. **May–Sept** At Ballinamantane House, near Coole, to supervise restoration of Thoor Ballylee. **Late Sept** Move into Ballylee. In Dublin, WBY rents 73 Stephen's Green. **Nov** GY seriously ill with pneumonia. **11 Nov** First World War ends. **Late Nov** Quarrel with MG. **14 Dec** General Election, in which Sinn Fein scores resounding success.

**1919** **Jan** *Two Plays for Dancers*. **26 Feb** Anne Yeats born. **9 May** WBY returns to England. **25 May** Stage Society produces *The Player Queen*. **25 June** Gives up 18 Woburn Buildings. **Summer** At Ballylee. **July** Invitation to Japan. **Oct** Yeatses move to 4 Broad Street, Oxford. Guerrilla warfare in Ireland.

**1920** **13 Jan** With GY, sails for USA on the *Carmania*; lectures in America until 29 May. **Aug** Invited to Ireland by MG to help resolve Iseult's marital problems. GY has miscarriage. **Oct** Gogarty removes WBY's tonsils. **Autumn** Guerrilla war in Ireland intensifies.

**1921** **Feb** *Michael Robartes and the Dancer*. **17 Feb** WBY denounces British policy in Ireland at the Oxford Union. **Apr–June** Oxford house let; move to Minchin's Cottage, Shillingford. **May** Lectures for the Abbey Fund. **28 June** Move to Cuttlebrook House, Thame. **11 July** Truce in Anglo-Irish War. **22 Aug** Michael Yeats born in Thame; has operation in Dublin in Sept. **7 Oct** The

Yeatses return to Oxford. **28 Oct**   *Four Plays for Dancers*. **Late Oct**   Michael Yeats operated on in London. **Nov**   WBY lectures in Scotland. **Dec**   *Four Years*. Anglo-Irish Treaty debated by the Dáil.

**1922**   **7 Jan**   Dáil ratifies the Treaty, leading to civil war in Ireland. **Mid-Jan**   WBY and GY attend Irish Race Conference in Paris. **3 Feb**   JBY dies in New York. **20 Mar**   The Yeatses move from Oxford to 82 Merrion Square, Dublin. **Mar–Sept**   At Ballylee; Civil War raging. **19 Aug**   Ballylee bridge blown up by Republicans. **20 Sept**   Return to Dublin. **Oct**   *The Trembling of the Veil*. **3 Dec**   Dines with T. S. Eliot in London. **11 Dec**   Becomes a senator. **20 Dec**   Honorary degree from TCD. **24 Dec**   Bullets fired into the Yeatses' house.

**1923**   **Jan–Feb**   In London campaigning for Dublin's right to the Lane pictures. **12 Apr**   First production of O'Casey's *Shadow of a Gunman* at Abbey. **July**   To London to arrange a nursing home for SMY, who is seriously ill. **Nov**   Awarded the Nobel Prize. **27 Nov**   *Plays and Controversies*. **Dec**   In Stockholm for Nobel Prize ceremony.

**1924**   **6 May**   *Essays*. **June–July**   Helps with the short-lived publication *Tomorrow*. **11 July**   Honorary degree at Aberdeen. **29 July**   John Quinn dies in New York. **Aug**   WBY attends the celebrations connected with the Tailteann Games. **Autumn**   Suffering from high blood pressure.

**1925**   **Jan–Feb**   Visit to Sicily and Rome. **11 June**   Speech on divorce in Senate causes controversy.

**1926**   **15 Jan**   *A Vision*. **Feb**   *The Plough and the Stars* causes controversy at the Abbey. **Early Apr**   WBY has slight rupture and measles. **19 May**   Appointed chairman of the committee on coinage design. **July**   Reads Spengler's *Decline of the West*. **5 Nov**   *Autobiographies*. **Nov**   In London seeing leading politicians and public figures about Lane pictures.

**1927**   **Jan–Feb**   Violent attack of arthritis followed by influenza. **10 July**   Assassination of Kevin O'Higgins. **Nov**   Yeatses at Algeciras, Seville, and Cannes; WBY seriously ill with congestion of the lungs.

**1928**   **Jan**   At Cannes. **14 Feb**   *The Tower*. **17 Feb**   To Rapallo to look for an apartment. **Early Apr**   Return to Dublin. **Early June**   Controversy over rejection by the Abbey of O'Casey's *The Silver Tassie*. **31 July**   Sells 82 Merrion Square and moves to a flat at 42 Fitzwilliam Square. **Sept** Resigns from the Senate. **Nov** To Rapallo flat for the winter.

**1929** **Early Jan** Visit to Rome. **Mar** Meets Gerhart Hauptmann and George Antheil. **Early May** Return to Dublin by way of London, where he meets Wyndham Lewis. **Nov** Haemorrhage of lungs delays departure for Rapallo. **Dec** Dangerously ill in Rapallo with Malta fever; makes an emergency will witnessed by Pound and Basil Bunting.

**1930** **Jan–Mar** Slow convalescence at Rapallo. Reads Swift. **3 July** Leaves Italy by sea to arrive in Dublin, via London, on 17 July. **23 July–6 Aug** Portrait painted at Renvyle by Augustus John. **Sept–Oct** At Coole. **Early Nov** Visits Oxford, where on 5 Nov Masefield organizes a recitation of his poems. Visits May Morris at Kelmscott, and meets Walter de la Mare and Virginia Woolf at Garsington. **Nov–Feb 1931** Winter in Dublin.

**1931** **Feb–May** Stays at South Hill, Killiney. **May** Cuala Industries in financial difficulties, and bailed out by WBY. **26 May** Honorary D.Litt. at Oxford. **1 June** Delivers bulk of MS for proposed 'Edition de Luxe' to Macmillan. **July–Aug** Works on Berkeley with Mario Rossi. AG in decline, and WBY spends most of the autumn and winter at Coole. **Sept** Broadcasts for BBC Belfast.

**1932** **Winter and spring** At Coole. **Feb** Reads the autobiography of Shri Purohit Swami in MS. **16 Feb** General Election, after which de Valera and Fianna Fáil form government. **Early Apr** In London, WBY discusses setting up of an Irish Academy of Letters with Shaw. Acts as unofficial go-between in Anglo-Irish controversy over the oath of allegiance. **10 Apr** Broadcasts for BBC London. **22 May** AG dies at Coole. **July** Moves to his last Irish home, Riversdale, Rathfarnham, Dublin. **Sept** Foundation of Irish Academy of Letters. **21 Oct** Sails from Southampton on last tour of USA. **26 Oct–7 Nov** Lectures in New York and north-east. **Nov** Midwest and Canada. **14 Nov** *Words for Music Perhaps.* **Dec** Lectures in New York to raise funds for Irish Academy of Letters.

**1933** **22 Jan** Sails from New York. **Mar** Meets de Valera. **June** In London, Oxford, and Cambridge. **July–Aug** Becomes involved in the Blueshirt movement; their march in Dublin on 12 Aug banned. **19 Sept** *The Winding Stair and Other Poems.* **Nov** *Collected Poems.*

**1934** **Jan–Mar** In Dublin. **5 Apr** To London for Steinach operation. **June** With GY to Rapallo to dispose of their flat. **Oct** Speaks on

'The Dramatic Theatre' at 4th Congress of the Alessandro Volta Foundation in Rome. Begins friendship with Margot Collis. **Late Oct** In London for discussions about the Group Theatre. **13 Nov** *Wheels and Butterflies*. **30 Nov** *Collected Plays*. **7 Dec** To London to arrange for committee meetings of Group Theatre; preparing poems for *A Full Moon in March*. **Late Dec** Begins friendship with Ethel Mannin.

**1935** **11 Jan** Returns to Dublin. **Mid-Jan–early Mar** Renewed congestion of lungs causes collapse and confinement to bed. **Late Mar** In London on Group Theatre business, suffers a further attack of congestion. **Late Apr** GY goes to London to look after him. **3–4 June** Stays with Dorothy Wellesley in Sussex for the first time. **13 June** Celebrations in Dublin for his 70th birthday, including a PEN dinner on 27 June. **17 July** AE dies in Bournemouth; WBY attends his funeral in Dublin on 20 July. **14–23 Aug** Visits Dorothy Wellesley with Anne Yeats. **Early Sept** Clerical attacks on the Abbey. **16 Oct** Operation to remove a lump on his tongue. **27 Oct** In London for special 'birthday' production of *The Player Queen* at the Little Theatre. **22 Nov** *A Full Moon in March*. **28 Nov** WBY sails from Liverpool for Majorca, where he and Shri Purohit Swami are to collaborate on a translation of the Upanishads. **9 Dec** *Dramatis Personae*. **From 12 Dec** In Majorca working on the Upanishads and *The Herne's Egg*.

**1936** **Late Jan** Severe collapse, with heart and kidney ailments; GY, summoned by the doctor, flies to Majorca on 2 Feb. **Feb–Apr** Slow recovery from illness. *c.* **14 May** Margot Collis arrives unexpectedly, suffering from a temporary fit of insanity. Yeatses go to Barcelona to help. On return to Majorca WBY sees Shri Purohit Swami off for India. **25 May** Leaves by steamer for London. **June** In London and Sussex. **Late Sept–early Nov** In London for BBC broadcast and to arrange distribution of *Broadsides*. **19 Nov** *Oxford Book of Modern Verse* causes controversy.

**1937** **Feb** Broadcast of WBY's poems from Abbey stage by Radio Eireann not a technical success. **16 Feb** Elected a member of the Athenaeum. **Early Mar–24 Apr** In London. **Apr** BBC broadcast 'In the Poet's Pub'. Begins friendship with Edith Shackleton Heald. **18 Apr** *The Ten Principal Upanishads*. **22 Apr** BBC broadcast 'In the Poet's Parlour'. **26 May** Announces his retirement from public life. **8 June–21 July** BBC broadcast 'My Own Poetry'. **17 Aug** Irish Academy of Letters dinner for Patrick

MacCartan and WBY's Irish-American benefactors. **9 Sept–
1 Nov**   In London, at Steyning and Penns in the Rocks.
**7 Oct**   Revised edition of *A Vision*. **29 Oct**   BBC broadcast 'My
Own Poetry Again'. **Nov–Dec**   Planning *On the Boiler* and helping
to reorganize the Cuala Press. **14 Dec**   *Essays 1931 to 1936*.

**1938**   **8 Jan**   Leaves Dublin for south of France, where GY joins him in
Menton on **4** Feb. **23 Mar**   Arrives in London; remains in England, visiting Steyning and Penns in the Rocks, until 13 May.
**18 May**   *New Poems*. **June**   In Dublin to arrange affairs at the
Cuala Press and the Abbey. **Early July–8 Aug**   In England.
**10 Aug**   First production of *Purgatory* at the Abbey causes theological controversy. **3 Oct**   OS dies. **Late Oct**   WBY leaves
Dublin for England. **26 Nov**   With GY, leaves London for south
of France.

**1939**   **28 Jan**   Dies. Buried at Roquebrune. **10 July**   *Last Poems and
Two Plays*. **Sept**   *On the Boiler*.

# A NOTE ON
# EDITORIAL PRINCIPLES

The ambition in this volume, as in the edition as a whole, is to give as accurate and yet readable a text as possible. In the case of Yeats this modest aim presents more difficulties than one might wish. As he wrote to Katharine Tynan in March 1888 when seeking employment, 'Todhunter says my bad writing and worse spelling will be much against me ...' (1. 56). These faults, together with lack of punctuation and a failure to date his letters, continued into later life and are also much against editors who wish to be at once true to what Yeats wrote and tactful to the reader. The poet himself was eager that his letters should be emended when they appeared in print. He instructed Katharine Tynan to show him any of his letters that she intended to publish in her memoirs so that he could correct them, and as late as 1938 asked his wife, when passing on a letter to his daughter, to 'put spelling right & make it legible'. But to correct and regularize as he would have wished would be to lose much of the immediacy and personality of his correspondence. Besides, we could even argue that in our editorial practices we are following his own lead, for in a letter to Edwin Ellis of February 1893, discussing the publication of Blake's poems, Yeats writes: 'I incline myself, to the irregular text on the ground that the "tincture" to quote the Lavatar Notes "has entered into the errors & made them physiognomic"' (1. 353).

We have, therefore, attempted to reproduce the physiognomy of his letters, orthographic warts and all, but endeavouring always to hold back from an officious pedantry that would involve the reader in unnecessary confusion. To have marked with '*sic*' every misspelling or solecism would have been wilfully tiresome, and so errors in spelling and punctuation are silently reproduced. Any editorial emendations appear within square brackets—as, for instance, where we have supplied letters or sometimes whole words omitted through carelessness, when such omission would be otherwise confusing or unprofitably irksome. Where Yeats has used a word obviously in error for another we have given, again in square brackets, the most likely intended reading—for example (p. 10), 'serious [*for* series]'. The poet's hand can be extremely difficult, and uncertain readings are preceded by a query in square brackets. Where proper names have been so grievously mangled as to be unrecognizable or misleading, we have supplied the correct form in square brackets. Careless repetitions and false starts are silently excised, as are directions (such as 'P.T.O.' or 'Second Page') no longer applicable to the form of the letter as printed. Significant cancelled passages, where they can be deciphered, are printed within angle brackets (< >). Words underlined once in the original are printed in italics, twice in small capitals, three times in full capitals. Yeats's use of superscript letters—'M$^r$', 'D$^r$', 'R$^d$'—has been adhered to throughout. Punctuation follows the original, except that full stops have been supplied where clearly intended, and where their omission would cause confusion. Opening or closing brackets and opening or closing inverted commas have also been supplied where Yeats has forgotten them; and single and double inverted commas have been regularized where they are mismatched in the original.

The format of the letters has been slightly standardized, in that addresses and dates, where present, are always placed at the top right regardless of where they occur in the MS, with vertical rules to indicate the original line-divisions. Printed and blind-stamped addresses are given in small capitals. Yeats's abbreviated complimentary closes—for example, 'Sincly', 'Yrs trly'—have not been expanded, and no points are used in signatures. Postscripts are placed uniformly at the end of the letter (thus following the temporal sequence of composition), with a note in square brackets indicating their position in the original. Letters to newspapers and periodicals follow the original published form exactly except for the signature, which has been regularized.

Each letter is headed by a line giving the addressee, if known, and the date. Since Yeats rarely dated his letters in full, many of these dates, the most accurate we have been able to fix upon, are conjectural and appear within square brackets, often with a preceding query or '*c.*' A line following each letter identifies the copy-text and describes it (ALS, TS, etc.; see List of Abbreviations and Short Forms), recording where possible the postmark and the address (in Yeats's spelling) to which the letter was sent; gives its present location; and lists the first and/or most significant instances of previous publication.

Synge wrote that all art is collaboration, and we might add that this is also true of some of Yeats's letters. On occasion he and Lady Gregory would write what amount to joint letters (see, for example, p. 208), and we have included all such letters, even when not actually signed by Yeats. We have also included those letters written under instruction from Yeats, even if not directly dictated by him, as for instance the letters by Lady Gregory and John Synge on behalf of all the Abbey Directors (see pp. 319–20). We have also tried to reconstruct, or at least cite, lost or untraced letters from other sources such as references in replies, memoirs, diaries, and so on (see, for example, p. 177). Necessarily, many of these recoveries must be conjectural as to both content and date, and by the nature of things we would not claim that our list is exhaustive. We consider such items, no matter how slight, worth including for the light they throw upon Yeats's biography, work, and range of interests.

This volume sees Yeats's relationships with publishers increasingly complex and his immersion in the business of the Abbey almost total, and these interests generated a number of business documents, memoranda, draft proposals, and the like. We have printed all the material of this kind that we have been able to trace. We also reproduce printed dedications to books when cast in an epistolary form. In this period, as ever, Yeats was ready to plunge into public controversy, and he contributed letters and articles to the press with some frequency. On occasion his letters were subedited into the form of articles, and we have included any item for which there is internal or external evidence that this has occurred.

Yeats is an allusive correspondent, and so the footnotes attempt not only to identify individuals and to provide information on particular points or references but also to supply wider contextual material. References in the footnotes are made where possible to accessible printed sources, and full citations are given. In those cases where our reading of an original document differs from the printed version we have given the location of the original, followed by the printed source preceded by 'cf.' (see p. 306, n. 1). Certain important correspondents and other individuals, institutions, and themes which figure largely in this volume are given fuller treatment in the Appendix at p. 837, unless they have already appeared in earlier volumes, in which case the relevant back-reference is provided. References to Yeats's works (see List of Abbreviations) are to the original editions or, where a collected edition is in question, to the best text available at the time of this volume's preparation; *Variorum Poems* and *Variorum Plays*, together with the two-volume *Uncollected Prose*, are cited where possible.

# LIST OF MANUSCRIPT SOURCES

## INSTITUTIONS

| | |
|---|---|
| Belfast | City of Belfast Public Libraries |
| Berg | The Henry W. and Albert A. Berg Collection, New York Public Library |
| BL | British Library |
| Bodleian | Department of Western MSS, Bodleian Library, Oxford |
| Boston College | John J. Burns Library, Boston College, Chestnut Hill, Mass. |
| Brandeis | University Library, Brandeis University, Waltham, Mass. |
| Butler College | The Library, Butler University, Indianapolis, Indiana |
| Buffalo | Lockwood Memorial Library, State University of New York at Buffalo |
| Cambridge | University Library, University of Cambridge |
| Connecticut College | The Library, Connecticut College, New London, Conn. |
| Emory | Robert W. Woodruff Library, Emory University, Atlanta, Ga. |
| Fredonia | Daniel Read Library, State University of New York at Fredonia |
| Gainesville | University of Florida Libraries, Gainesville, Fla. |
| Getty | The Getty Research Institute, Los Angeles, Calif. |
| Harvard | Houghton Library, Harvard University, Cambridge, Mass. |
| Holy Cross | Dinand Library, College of the Holy Cross, Worcester, Mass. |
| Huntington | Henry E. Huntington Library, San Marino, Calif. |
| Illinois | University Library, University of Illinois at Urbana-Champaign |
| Indiana | Lilly Library, Indiana University, Bloomington |
| India Office | India Office Papers, British Library |
| Kansas | Kenneth Spencer Research Library, University of Kansas Libraries, Lawrence |

| | |
|---|---|
| Kentucky | University of Kentucky Library, Lexington |
| Kingston | Douglas Library, Queen's University, Kingston, Ont. |
| Leeds | Brotherton Library, University of Leeds |
| NCAD | National College of Art and Design, Dublin |
| NLA | National Library of Australia |
| NLI | National Library of Ireland |
| NLS | National Library of Scotland |
| Northwestern | Northwestern University, Evanston, Ill. |
| Pierpont Morgan | Pierpont Morgan Library, New York |
| Plunkett Foundation | Plunkett Foundation, Long Hanborough, Oxford |
| Princeton | Princeton University Library, Princeton, NJ |
| Providence College | Phillips Memorial Library, Providence College, Rhode Island |
| Reading | University of Reading Library, Whiteknights, Reading |
| St John's Seminary | E. L. Doheny Memorial Library, St John's Seminary, Camarillo, Calif. |
| Southern Illinois | Morris Library, Southern Illinois University at Carbondale |
| Sydney | The Mitchell Library, State Library of New South Wales, Sydney |
| TCD | Trinity College Library, University of Dublin |
| Texas | Harry Ransom Humanities Research Center, University of Texas at Austin |
| UCD | Archives Department, University College, Dublin |
| UCLA | William Andrews Clark Memorial Library, University of California at Los Angeles |
| Wake Forest | The Smith Reynolds Library, Wake Forest University, Winston-Salem, NC |
| Warburg | The Warburg Institute, London |
| Watt | A. P. Watt Ltd., London |
| Wellesley | Wellesley College Library, Wellesley, Mass. |
| West Sussex | West Sussex Record Office, Chichester |

## PRIVATE OWNERS

| | |
|---|---|
| Anne Yeats | The late Anne Yeats, Dublin |
| MBY | Mr Michael B. Yeats, Dublin |

Other MSS designed 'Private' are in the hands of the following individuals:

Irene Dwen Andrews Collection, Yucatan, Mexico

Mr Stuart Bennett, Bath
Mr Docker Drysdale, Abingdon
Mr Jim Edwards, Potomac, Maryland
Mr Stephen Fay, London
Mr David Gould, London
Mrs Basil Gray, Abingdon
Mr Richard Lancelyn Green, London
Mr Terry Halladay, New Haven, Conn.
Mr William F. Halloran, Milwaukee, Wis.
Mr John Hunter, England
Dr David Walker, University of New South Wales
Miss Ann Weygandt, Landenberg, Pa.
Mrs Anna MacBride White, Dublin

# LIST OF ABBREVIATIONS
## AND SHORT FORMS

AE = George Russell
AEFH = Annie Horniman
AG = Lady Augusta Gregory
ECY = Elizabeth Corbet Yeats (Lolly)
FF = Florence Farr Emery
GD = Order of the Golden Dawn
GY = Mrs George Yeats
IAOS = Irish Agricultural Organization Society
ILS = Irish Literary Society, London
ILT = Irish Literary Theatre
INTS = Irish National Theatre Society
JBY = John Butler Yeats
KT = Katharine Tynan Hinkson
MG = Maud Gonne
NTS = National Theatre Society
OS = Olivia Shakespear
SMY = Susan Mary Yeats (Lily)
WBY = W. B. Yeats

The following abbreviations are used in the description given with the provenance at the foot of each letter:

AD          autograph draft
AL          unsigned autograph letter
ALCS        autograph lettercard signed
ALS         autograph letter signed
ANI         autograph note initialled
APS         autograph postcard signed
Dict        dictated
Frag        fragment
MS copy     handwritten copy in another hand
Printed Doc Printed document
TL          unsigned typed letter
TLS         typed letter signed
TS copy     typewritten copy
TS Doc      typed document
TS memo     typed memorandum

## Principal Sources Cited or Quoted
### PUBLISHED

BY W. B. YEATS

| | |
|---|---|
| *Aut* | *Autobiographies* (1955) |
| *AVA* | *A Vision* (1925) |
| *AVB* | *A Vision* (1937) |
| Bax | *Florence Farr, Bernard Shaw, W. B. Yeats Letters*, ed. Clifford Bax (1946) |
| Bridge | *W. B. Yeats and T. Sturge Moore: Their Correspondence 1901–1937*, ed. Ursula Bridge (1953) |
| *The Countess Kathleen* | *The Countess Kathleen and Various Legends and Lyrics* (1892) |
| *CP* | *Collected Poems* (1933) |
| *CW* | *Collected Works*, 8 vols. (1908) |
| *Druid Craft* | *Druid Craft: The Writing of The Shadowy Waters*, ed. Michael J. Sidnell, George P. Mayhew, and David R. Clark (1971) |
| *E & I* | *Essays and Introductions* (1961) |
| *Expl* | *Explorations*, sel. Mrs W. B. Yeats (1962) |
| *I & R* | *W. B. Yeats Interviews and Recollections*, ed. E. H. Mikhail, 2 vols. (1977) |
| *IGE* | *Ideas of Good and Evil* (1903) |
| *LNI* | *Letters to the New Island*, ed. George Bornstein and Hugh Witemeyer (New York, 1989) |
| *Mem* | *Memoirs*, ed. Denis Donoghue (1972) |
| *Myth* | *Mythologies* (1959) |
| *OBMV* | *The Oxford Book of Modern Verse*, ed. W. B. Yeats (1936) |
| *Oisin* | *The Wanderings of Oisin, and Other Poems* (1889) |
| *P & I* | *Prefaces and Introductions*, ed. William H. O'Donnell (1988) |
| Saddlemyer | *Theatre Business*, ed. Ann Saddlemyer (1982) |
| *SB* | *The Speckled Bird*, ed. William H. O'Donnell (Toronto, 1976) |
| *UP I* | *Uncollected Prose*, ed. John P. Frayne, vol. I (1970) |
| *UP II* | *Uncollected Prose*, ed. John P. Frayne and Colton Johnson, vol. II (1975) |

| | |
|---|---|
| *VP* | *The Variorum Edition of the Poems of W. B. Yeats*, ed. Peter Allt and Russell K. Alspach (1957, rev. 1966) |
| *VPl* | *The Variorum Edition of the Plays of W. B. Yeats*, ed. Russell K. Alspach (1966) |
| *VSR* | *The Secret Rose, Stories by W. B. Yeats: A Variorum Edition*, ed. Warwick Gould, Phillip L. Marcus, and Michael J. Sidnell (1981, rev. 1992) |
| Wade | *The Letters of W. B. Yeats*, ed. Allan Wade (1954) |
| *YA* | *Yeats Annual* nos. 1–11 (1982–94) |
| *YL* | Edward O'Shea, *A Descriptive Catalog of W. B. Yeats's Library* (New York, 1985) |

## OTHER WORKS

| | |
|---|---|
| *Abbey Theatre* | *Joseph Holloway's Abbey Theatre*, ed. Robert Hogan and Michael J. O'Neill (Carbondale, Ill., 1967) |
| *ASSL* | *Arthur Symons: Selected Letters, 1880–1935*, ed. Karl Beckson and John M. Munro (1989) |
| *Bibl* | *A Bibliography of the Writings of W. B. Yeats*, ed. Allan Wade, rev. Russell K. Alspach, 3rd edn. (1968) |
| Blunt | Wilfrid Scawen Blunt, *My Diaries*, 2 vols. (1919, 1920) |
| *BSCL* | *Bernard Shaw Collected Letters*, ed. Dan H. Lawrence, 5 vols. (1972–90) |
| Cave | George Moore, *Hail and Farewell*, ed. Richard Cave (Gerrards Cross, 1976, rev. 1985) |
| Denson | *Letters from AE*, ed. Alan Denson (1961) |
| *Fays of the Abbey* | W. G. Fay and Catherine Carswell, *The Fays of the Abbey Theatre* (1935) |
| Fingall | Elizabeth, Countess of Fingall, *Seventy Years Young: Memories as Told to Pamela Hinkson* (1937) |
| *Friends of a Lifetime* | *Friends of a Lifetime: Letters to Sydney Carlyle Cockerell*, ed. Viola Meynell (1940) |
| Gilcher | Edwin Gilcher, *A Bibliography of George Moore* (DeKalb, Ill., 1970) |
| Gwynn | Denis Gwynn, *Edward Martyn and the Irish Revival* (1930) |

| | |
|---|---|
| *G–YL* | *The Gonne–Yeats Letters 1893–1938*, ed. Anna MacBride White and A. Norman Jeffares (1992) |
| Harper | George Mills Harper, *Yeats's Golden Dawn* (1974) |
| Himber | *The Letters of John Quinn to William Butler Yeats*, ed. Alan Himber (Ann Arbor, 1983) |
| Hogan and Kilroy | *The Modern Irish Drama*, ed. Robert Hogan and James Kilroy, vols. I–V (Dublin, 1975–84) |
| Hone | J. M. Hone, *W. B. Yeats 1865–1939*, rev. edn. (1962) |
| Howe | Ellic Howe, *Magicians of the Golden Dawn* (1972) |
| Hugh Lane | Lady Gregory, *Sir Hugh Lane: His Life and Legacy* (Gerrards Cross, 1973) |
| *JBYL* | J. B. Yeats, *Letters to his Son W. B. Yeats and Others*, ed. Joseph Hone (1944) |
| *JMSCL* | *The Collected Letters of John Millington Synge*, ed. Ann Saddlemyer, 2 vols. (Oxford, 1983, 1984) |
| *JMSCW* | *J. M. Synge Collected Works*, 4 vols. (1962–8) |
| *Journals* | *Lady Gregory's Journals*, ed. Daniel J. Murphy, 2 vols. (Gerrards Cross, 1978, 1987) |
| *LBP* | *Letters from Bedford Park*, ed. William M. Murphy (Dublin, 1972) |
| *LWBY* | *Letters to W. B. Yeats*, ed. Richard J. Finneran, George Mills Harper, William M. Murphy, with Alan B. Himber, 2 vols. (1977) |
| *Many Lines* | Oliver St John Gogarty, *Many Lines to Thee: Letters to G. K. A. Bell, 1904–1907*, ed. James F. Carens (Dublin, 1971) |
| *Men and Memories* | Sir William Rothenstein, *Men and Memories: Recollections of William Rothenstein 1872–1900* (1931) |
| Murphy | William M. Murphy, *Prodigal Father: The Life of John Butler Yeats 1839–1922* (1978) |
| Nic Shiubhlaigh | *The Splendid Years, Recollections of Maire Nic Shiubhlaigh; as told to Edward Kenny* (Dublin, 1955) |
| *OIT* | Lady Gregory, *Our Irish Theatre: A Chapter of Autobiography* (Gerrards Cross, 1972) |
| Pethica | *Lady Gregory's Diaries 1892–1902*, ed. James Pethica (Gerrards Cross, 1996) |

| | |
|---|---|
| *70 Years* | *Seventy Years: Being the Autobiography of Lady Gregory*, ed. Colin Smythe (Gerrards Cross, 1974) |
| Sharp | Elizabeth A. Sharp, *William Sharp (Fiona Macleod), a Memoir* (1910) |
| *Some Memories* | John Masefield, *Some Memories of W. B. Yeats* (Dublin, 1940) |
| *SP* | Charles Ricketts, *Self-Portrait*, ed. T. Sturge Moore and Cecil Lewis (1939) |
| *SQ* | Maud Gonne MacBride, *A Servant of the Queen*, rev. edn. (Gerrards Cross, 1994) |
| *Ulysses* | *'Ulysses': A Critical and Synoptic Edition*, prepared by Hans Walter Gabler, 3 vols. (1984) |
| *Visions and Beliefs* | *Visions and Beliefs in the West of Ireland*, collected and arranged by Lady Gregory (Gerrards Cross, 1970) |
| *Works and Days* | Michael Field, *Works and Days*, ed. T. and D. C. Sturge Moore (1933) |
| *Works of William Blake* | The Works of William Blake Poetic, Symbolic, and Critical, ed. Edwin John Ellis and William Butler Yeats, 3 vols. (1893) |
| *Y & H* | *W. B. Yeats and W. T. Horton: The Record of an Occult Friendship*, ed. George Mills Harper (1980) |
| *Y & T* | *Yeats and the Theatre*, ed. Robert O'Driscoll and Lorna Reynolds (1975) |

All other published sources are cited in full at the first mention. The place of publication is London unless otherwise indicated.

## UNPUBLISHED

| | |
|---|---|
| Belfast | City of Belfast Public Libraries |
| Berg | The Henry W. and Albert A. Berg Collection, New York Public Library |
| Columbia | Nicholas Murray Butler Library, Columbia University, New York |
| Cornell | Olin Library, Cornell University, Ithaca, NY |
| Emory | Robert W. Woodruff Library, Emory University, Atlanta, Ga. |
| Galway | The Library, University College, Galway |
| Huntington | Henry E. Huntington Library, San Marino, Calif. |
| India Office | India Office Papers, British Library |

| | |
|---|---|
| Iowa | The University of Iowa Library, Iowa City, Ia. |
| LC | Library of Congress, Washington, DC |
| London | University of London Library, Senate House |
| MBY | Michael B. Yeats, Dublin |
| NLI | National Library of Ireland |
| NLS | National Library of Scotland |
| NYPL | New York Public Library |
| OUP | Oxford University Press, Oxford |
| Princeton | Princeton University Library, Princeton, NJ |
| PRO | Public Record Office, Kew, London |
| Queen's | The Queen's University, Kingston, Canada |
| Rylands | John Rylands Library, Manchester |
| Southern Illinois | Morris Library, Southern Illinois University at Carbondale |
| Stratford | The A. H. Bullen Archive, The Shakespeare Birthplace Trust, Shakespeare Centre, Stratford-upon-Avon |
| TCD | Trinity College Library, University of Dublin |
| Texas | Harry Ransom Humanities Research Center, University of Texas at Austin |
| Tulsa | McFarlin Library, University of Tulsa, Okla. |
| UCD | Archives Department, University College, Dublin |
| Warburg | The Warburg Institute, University of London |
| Widener | Widener Library, Harvard University, Cambridge, Mass. |

Other MS material in private hands is designated 'Private' when cited or quoted in the notes.

# INTRODUCTION TO VOLUME IV

## I

In 1905 Yeats entered those years of 'Theatre business, management of men'. Because that business involved shifting coalitions of overlapping but often antagonistic constituencies, and since his skills in man-management left much to be desired, these were also and inevitably years of controversy and conflict, in both his public and private lives. A friend later assured him that such experiences had 'made a man' of him, but looking back in 1931 he disagreed: 'I doubt the value of the embittered controversy that was to fill my life for years, but certainly they rang down the curtain so far as I was concerned on what was called "The Celtic Movement". An "Irish Movement" took its place.'

As the letters of this period show, the uncompromising positions he adopted during these conflicts exacerbated their intensity. This was due not to social ineptitude nor sheer bloody-mindedness—for Yeats could be flexible and guileful enough when necessary—but to a conscious attitude. His experience of earlier battles—the outcry over the first production of *The Countess Cathleen* and the quarrel in the Golden Dawn, as well as his recent reading of Nietzsche and the confidence-boosting success of his late American tour—had given him an assurance he previously lacked, and brought him to the conclusion, as he told Lady Gregory early in 1905, 'that strength shapes the world about itself, & that weakness is shaped about the world—& that the compromise is weekness'. This stance was partly a compensation—even overcompensation—for unquelled self-doubts, his ruffling 'in a manly pride | For all his timid heart', as he was later to put it. But it was also more than mere bravura, and grew out of a conviction he articulated in a letter of 1906, that 'one has at times to act on something which is the reverse of scient[if]ic reasoning or scholourly reasoning'. Instead of 'merely deducing ones actions from existing circumstances', one had, he insisted, 'to act so as to create new circumstances by which one is to be judged. It is all faith.'

If action grew out of faith rather than thought, Yeats's faith was predicated on two firm tenets. One was the strong antipathy of good to bad, the insistence that in the Arts originality, personality, energy, and sincerity were not to be sacrificed to political expediency, cronyism, or fear of censure. His other credo was that all great movements in art took their indelible stamp from the outset, while the plastic was still pliable. 'A moment comes in every country', he was shortly to argue, 'when its character expresses itself through some group of writers, painters, or musicians, and it is this moment . . . which fixes the finer elements of national character for generations.' It was crucial, therefore, to get things right from the start; to betray the given moment by compromise or timidity was to distort irredeemably whatever came afterwards. From the beginning Yeats had inclined to an apocalyptic rather than evolutionary interpretation of history, and his adamant refusal to traffic his ideas or truckle to opposition is grounded in this outlook. Unhappily, the strong finger he felt necessary to shape the cultural future of Ireland seemed to his less sympathetic compatriots too often raised in an offensively haughty gesture to all they held dear.

Yet in January 1905 it was not obvious that controversies were inevitable, let alone that they would prove to be so bitter or prolonged, and the letters in this volume begin on an optimistic note, with Yeats, as he told Constance Masefield, 'in a whirl of varying occupations'. The opening of the Abbey Theatre, the first subsidized repertory theatre in the English-speaking world, had been a palpable success and the future of the Irish dramatic movement seemed assured. 'The country is in its first plastic state', Yeats assured Gilbert Murray, 'and takes the mark of every strong finger. We have a beautiful little theatre and . . . I believe we are going to make a great dramatic school here.' Yeats's views on the primary plastic nature of Irish thought were as suspect now as they had been fifteen years earlier, when the 'mind of Ireland' seemed to him 'like soft wax'. He was soon to learn that molten plastic is capable of burning even strong fingers, but for the moment he could ground his optimism in a variety of cultural initiatives that seemed to be coming to fruition. Dublin was not only to enjoy a National Theatre dedicated to the best in modern Irish drama, but also a Municipal Gallery dedicated to the best in modern art, and on 5 January 1905 he joined eight other Irish writers in a public letter seeking, with every anticipation of success, funds to secure for the city and nation a core collection of distinguished pictures assembled by Lady Gregory's nephew, Hugh Lane. In London Yeats sought out the influential art critic D. S. MacColl, to enlist his help with the campaign, and wrote letters to potential supporters and donors. The arrival of a new ten-volume anthology of Irish writing was further cause for rejoicing. Yeats told Quinn that he thought 'it could have hardly have been done better' and that only a decade before 'it could not have been done at all. It is the evidence of the scholarship and criticism of a generation.' Here was tangible proof that his tireless and frequently unpopular efforts—the application of 'the strong finger'—

to establish a more rigorous taste in Ireland were justifying themselves. Meanwhile another project, long dear to his heart, also seemed suddenly to be possible. This was a commercial publishing house, based in Dublin and dedicated to the work of aspirant as well as seasoned Irish writers. In the summer of 1904 James Starkey had revived the modest house of Whaley & Co. and now he and George Roberts, with the active help of Yeats, were trying to turn it into a more ambitious and financially secure company. As a token of their intentions they issued an Irish edition of Synge's *The Well of the Saints* in February, and later that spring Yeats took an instrumental role in the founding of the new firm of Maunsel and Co. by encouraging the young Joseph Hone to fund the project and by getting A. H. Bullen to initiate both Hone and Roberts into the mysteries of the publishing trade. But he regarded his most important contribution to the project as circumventing AE's attempts to become the firm's literary adviser as one of an unwieldy board of seven directors. Such a scheme 'would mean seven cooks spoiling the broth & as small as possible monetary liability apiece', he warned Roberts, and wagged his strong finger in admonition: 'There is no use mincing words in this matter. Russell will never make a successful publishing firm, if he have any influence over the choice of books; & I foresee that his spoon would be somewhere among those 7 cooks.' In the end he succeeded in keeping AE out of the business, and the new company survived, though not without vicissitudes, until the 1920s, publishing five of Yeats's plays in 1905, as well as issuing subsequent editions of *The Secret Rose*, *Ideas of Good and Evil*, and *The Celtic Twilight*.

## II

With so many cultural possibilities to be realized, the first souring of the promise of these days turned out to be private rather than public. Shortly after returning to London, and while still basking in the successful launch of the Abbey Theatre, Yeats had a visit from Maud Gonne's sister May Clay. She had 'very miserable news' to impart. Maud Gonne's marriage to John MacBride was over and she was seeking a divorce on grounds of his alleged drunkenness, violence, and, finally, child-abuse. Yeats had been aware for two years that the marriage was not a success, but nothing could prepare him for the catastrophe that was about to unfold. A 'frightful scandal' seemed inevitable, but he rallied at once to Maud's aid, accepting without question her version of the events and denouncing a compromise proposal as too propitiative. His support was of immense emotional and psychological importance to her, but its practical value was more questionable. His attempts to put her case to MacBride's adviser Barry O'Brien had little effect, while the counsel's opinion, procured with Lady Gregory's help, proved to be of only marginal value. He set John Quinn to investigate MacBride's alleged bad behaviour in New York, but this had only limited success, and the mission of Annie Horniman (by a very long way the least suitable of all his acquaintances for such an office) to spy on the MacBride family in their native Westport drew a predictable blank. More directly, he himself rallied Maud Gonne's friends and tried to confound her enemies in Dublin but, even here, his schemes backfired: his too insistent recital of the causes of the marriage's failure seems to have left MacBride with no alternative but to face down the more lurid accounts of his conduct by challenging them in open court.

Yeats had, from the beginning, an unrealistic estimation of the strength of Maud Gonne's position, and, spurred by his new conviction that compromise was weakness, initially encouraged her to press too hard and so reject proposals put forward by AE, Ella Young, and Henry Dixon that might have led to a less clear-cut but also less acrimonious outcome. In this sense, the affair's public dimension affected him as deeply as its private anguish by opening his eyes to the hypocrisy of Irish social and political life. He was shocked that Barry O'Brien, in defence of whose integrity he had resigned from the committee of the Irish Literary Society in 1899, tried to coerce Maud Gonne into an unsatisfactory settlement for 'the sake of the country' and to ensure that 'the Mac Bride legend must keep its lustre'. Old friends, including the morally fastidious John O'Leary, unhesitatingly took MacBride's part, while another acquaintance, the Fenian Henry Dixon, seemed to think 'M$^{rs}$ Mac Brides objection to drunkenness a morbid peculiarity'. 'The trouble with these men', Yeats complained, 'is that in their eyes a woman has no rights.'

There was also personal agony, although he was surprised to discover that while 'the whole thing has made me very wretched', it 'awakened nothing of the old feeling.. no feeling but pity & anger'. These, however, were potent enough emotions, and as darker details of MacBride's behaviour were divulged he began to feel as if he 'had been through a circle of Hell'. He appealed to Lady Gregory to play Virgil to his anguished Dante, but she chose to remain at Coole, limiting her assistance to seeking out legal advice and offering long-distant support by letter. For a time it looked as if the private aspect of the crisis would spill into the public. Maud Gonne's case was weakened by her own colourful past, particularly her long affair with the French politician and journalist Lucien Millevoye. MacBride's lawyers made full use of this as a supposed example of her general moral laxity, and MacBride even tried to blackmail her by threatening to name Yeats (together with W. T. Stead and Amilcare Cipriani) as a co-respondent. He was deterred from doing so not, evidently, by her protestations, but by Barry O'Brien, who ingenuously assured him that 'that kind of thing never seemed to interest Yeats'. Yeats was nevertheless tickled to learn that MacBride intended to shoot him: 'This is the only cheerful peice of news I have had for days—it gives one a sense of hightened life.' Yeats's master plan was that Maud Gonne should prepare a detailed account of her charges against her husband, in the expectation that the appalling facts would 'make it obvious that Mac Bride must dissappear'. This hugely overestimated the credence and respect the Irish people placed in Maud Gonne, and in similar measure underestimated the affection and esteem which they had for MacBride. The Fenians supported the husband to a man, and the case dragged on for another three years, ending in, at best, a damaging draw.

## III

One of MacBride's chief allies in Ireland was the founder of the Sinn Fein movement, Arthur Griffith, with whom Yeats crossed swords later in January 1905. The cause was not Maud Gonne but John Synge. The recent revival and publication of *In the Shadow of the Glen*—in which a husband feigns death to catch his wife in an adulterous relationship—had rekindled a 1903 controversy over the play's morality and authenticity, and Griffith's paper, the *United Irishman*, revived the charge that the play was Greek in origin and anti-Irish in theme and sentiment. Yeats defended the piece robustly but also astutely, pressing Griffith for the questionable sources of his allegations, forcing him to publish a letter by Synge he had tried to suppress, and adroitly associating Synge's theme with the seventeenth-century divine Jeremy Taylor. But, despite all Yeats's refutations and counter-examples, Griffith remained implacable in his view that the main justification of art lay in its propagandist value: 'No Irishman', he wrote, 'may set up his spade or his lyre and say "This first." The spade finds its true work in delving for Ireland—the lyre its true voice in singing for Ireland.'

It was not simply a question of nationalism. *In the Shadow of the Glen* touched upon sexual taboos ostensibly long forbidden to the Irish mind and imagination. It offended the myth of the pure Irishwoman and chaste 'manly' Irishman—an idealization Griffith was pushing with particular vigour at this time to point a contrast with the licentiousness of Britain in general and the British army in particular. The historical and social roots of this taboo were complex, and its self-righteous energy drew on a local manifestation of a more general Victorian prudery, intensified by the distorting lenses of a colonial position. For Yeats there was a grim irony in the fact that Griffith was denouncing Synge's portrayal of a dysfunctional Irish marriage at the same time as he was defending MacBride's alleged marital and sexual excesses, but, although he may have felt that he had got the better of Griffith intellectually in this dispute, Irish suspicion of Synge, and, by extension, of the moral and political direction of the Abbey Theatre as a whole, was to fester malignantly before erupting in the riots at the first production of *The Playboy of the Western World*.

## IV

For the moment these deeper social and ideological questions were less pressing than the day-to-day problems thrown up by the attempt to transform an amateur dramatic society into a professional national theatre. Not that at the beginning of 1905 'professional' was an appropriate description, since none of the players was actually being paid. Yeats confided to Quinn that William Fay was putting part of the scanty profits on their productions 'into the fund which is to be used to pay enough of the players to go on tour with', but predicted that it would 'take us a little time amassing enough of money'. Refunding the players for their loss of regular earnings during extended tours was clearly essential, but even at home in Dublin the problem of the actors' welfare was becoming so urgent that the 'little time' needed to establish the required float seemed likely to be insufficient. The fragile health of Maire Walker, one of the leading actresses, was giving cause for concern, since she was working full-time by day at the Dun Emer Press and spending most of her evenings in rehearsal or performance. As early as April 1905 her doctor warned AE that she was close to a breakdown and that she could either continue with her daytime job or in the theatre, but not both. Fay's fund was still far short of the sum required to make regular payment possible, but in late June, primed by Yeats, Miss Horniman agreed to pump a further £400 a year unto the Theatre's budget to guarantee a weekly wage for the leading actors.

The decision to pay the actors had unforeseen but far-reaching consequences for the Irish National Theatre Society. To put the proposal into effect it was necessary to alter the existing rules and when first discussed by William Fay and AE in early August 1905 this seemed a reasonably straightforward matter. However, as AE worked on the revisions, it became obvious that the constitution promulgated in 1903 under the Friendly Societies' Act would no longer serve. A permanent and professional theatre could not tolerate the friction and muddle generated by the elaborate committees and subcommittees of the existing constitution, and the loose-knit co-operative practices of the early years would have to give way to the more rigorous discipline of a regular company. Initially, Yeats left the redrafting to AE and Fred Ryan, both of whom had worked on the original co-operative constitution and both of whom enjoyed, as he did not, the goodwill of the Company as a whole. He contented himself with a watching brief from Coole, and during these early redraftings, when the aim was still to rejig the existing rules, his main concerns centred on the desirability of having intelligent members of the Society appointed to the crucial committees. But as revision continued, the legal status of the Society gradually changed from a friendly society to a limited liability company. Although this greatly suited Yeats, he also believed—and genuinely—that the new arrangements would benefit those players who were prepared to commit themselves wholeheartedly to the Theatre. It would, he maintained, put them 'into the way of earning their living at work they are supreme in instead of drifting through life ingloriously at work they do not care for, or sacrificing their health by trying to do both', but this, he warned, could only be done by getting 'the theatre on a business foundation'. Since things were shaping up so well he was more than content to leave the matter in AE's hands, even ending one letter on an infuriatingly casual note: 'It is a very complicated business and requires a great deal of tact, that is why we are leaving it to you. I am just going out fishing.'

But not all his time at Coole was spent with rod and line. While AE was busy revising the rules for the Irish National Theatre Society in Dublin, Yeats was busy revising his plays for the Irish National Theatre Society in Galway. The Abbey had provided him with an unrivalled testing-ground for his plays and dramatic theories, and he was eager to exploit its resources. He began to revise *On Baile's Strand* almost as the final curtain fell on its first production in January 1905, and rewriting was to continue for the rest of the year and beyond, resulting not only in the sharpening of the conflict between Conchubar and Cuchulain, but also in a whole new oath-taking scene. In December, after a further performance of the play, he actually held up the publication of the already half-printed *Poems, 1899–1905* while he worked on it again. 'It had already been re-written twice since its publication', he told Quinn, 'I think I am getting it right this time.' The production of a revised version of *The King's Threshold*, in late April 1905, convinced him that it needed even more radical attention, and he began by shortening and breaking up King Guaire's 83-line opening speech. He had always been an enthusiastic reviser and access to a permanent theatre sharpened his appetite for such work, since he could test the effectiveness of his alterations almost immediately on the stage. Indeed, so habitual did the practice become that regular theatregoers like Joseph Holloway and W. J. Lawrence grumbled that cherished and familiar felicities had been ruthlessly excised from new versions to, as far as they could see, no good effect.

Perhaps the most significant of his dramatic revisions in 1905 was provoked not by an Abbey performance, but by Florence Farr's staging of *The Shadowy Waters* for a convention of the Theosophical Society in London. This production forced the mature Yeats to confront his earlier self, and the encounter filled him with horror. He managed to displace some of his consternation onto Robert Farquharson, the actor who played his hero, Forgael, and whom he considered 'the most despicable object I ever set eyes on—effeminate, constantly emphatic, never getting an emphasis in the right place, vulgar in voice and ridiculous with a kind of feeble feminine beauty . . . a sort of wild excited earth-worm of a man, turning and twisting out of sheer weakness of character'. While the camp Farquharson was clearly far from ideal as the brooding Forgael, the very vehemence of Yeats's invective betrays an acute discontent with his own play and with a style which he had now outgrown. He immediately retired to Coole to begin a thorough rewriting, and after a few weeks was able to inform Florence Farr that he was 'making Forgaels part perfectly clear and straightforward' and that the play now hinged 'upon one single idea'. In some ways finding the play so bad was, as he confessed to Arthur Symons, 'a comfort, for it shows me how much I have learned by watching rehearsals in Dublin and by altering my plays and other people's for the stage'.

This almost total immersion in the theatre meant that he wrote little new lyric verse, and in May 1906 he apologized to Witter Bynner, at that time assistant editor of *McClure's Magazine*, for having 'no lyric to send because I have been buried in plays this last year. I think of nothing else, for the existence of my little company gives me an opportunity that no dramatic poet has had for generations of mastering the technique of dramatic verse. I shall have time for lyrics later on.' In fact, this dedicated reworking of his dramatic verse had a profound effect on his lyric poetry, and accelerated the transition from transcendent symbolism to rooted experience and embodiment that he had been working towards since the turn of the century. He congratulated himself on introducing references to 'liquorice roots' and squeaking shoes into the previously symbolic *Shadowy Waters*, and allows a sailor in the same play to announce that he is so randy he would even bed 'Red Biddy with the squint'. All this is far from the exquisitely wrought phrases of his early style: Red Biddy is out of Synge's Red Dan's Sally's ditch rather than the Mausoleum of Villiers de l'Isle Adam's Axël, Count of Auersperg. As Yeats explained to Arthur Symons, he had 'learned a great deal about poetry generally' in the process of revision, 'and one thing I am now quite sure of is that all the finest poetry comes logically out of the fundamental action, and that the error of late periods like this is to believe that some things are inherently poetical, and to try and pull them on to the scene at every moment'.

Not that the change in style was entirely due to his increasing mastery of dramatic poetry: emotional and temperamental as well as artistic developments were at work. The earlier versions of *The Shadowy Waters* had been inspired by his love for the unattainable Maud Gonne, and, indeed, she had accompanied him to the production of Villiers de l'Isle Adam's *Axël* in Paris which spurred him to take up the play again in 1894. By contrast, the theosophist production of 1905 was directed by Florence Farr, with whom he was having a physical relationship, and whom he regaled with erotic dreams in which she featured. He travelled England with her, lecturing on the psaltery, and, writing from Dublin, suggested a bicycle trip to Canterbury with her when he returned to England: 'I do not see why we should not go with some harmless person to keep up appearances.' The desire for what was a clearly to be a profane modern pilgrimage to Canterbury was inspired by his reading of the *Canterbury Tales* in his fortieth birthday present, the fine Kelmscott edition of Chaucer. Yeats read the book avidly during the summer of 1905 and contrasted the abundant variety of the medievals with the monotony of the moderns, noting that Chaucer 'follows his noble *Knight's Tale* with an unspeakable tale told by a drunken miller. If Morris had done the like – everyone would have read his *Earthly Paradise* for ever.' He also applauded Chaucer's description of Alison in *The Miller's Tale* as 'white and small as a weasel': 'Does it not bring the physical type clearly to the minds-eye? I think one wants that sort of vivid irresistible phrase in all verse to be spoken aloud—it rests the imagination as upon the green ground.' The Kelmscott Chaucer was not merely a handsome present marking Yeats's passage into middle age, but also an index of the difference between the early Pre-Raphaelite Yeats and his more earthy maturity. The fact that the book was published by his youthful mentor William Morris made this contrast the more pointed and ironic.

## V

In late September 1905 Yeats decided that the time had come to leave Coole to join more actively in the discussions over the restructuring of the Irish National Theatre Society, and the autumn and winter of 1905 were almost entirely occupied with theatre business. By 21 September he could report to Lady Gregory that AE had himself proposed a limited liability company, with her, Yeats, and Synge as Directors. At a meeting on the following day the Society formally agreed to change its legal status, but the devil was in the detail and Yeats spent the following weeks hammering out the Articles of Association with Synge, Ryan, and AE. The crucial point for him was the division of shares and therefore of voting power. Some in the Company were troubled to find that the new scheme gave the Directors, on Yeats's own admission, 'an over mastering influence', and the socialist accountant Fred Ryan urged that each member should have only one vote no matter how many shares they owned. Yeats was 'quite resolute about making no concessions' on this point and concocted a letter with Annie Horniman in which she insisted that voting rights in the new Company should be directly commensurate with the number of shares held. Although Ryan tried to resist this policy to the end, it was finally adopted at a General Meeting on 9 October, and Yeats assured Lady Gregory that under the new arrangements 'the directors reserve the right to refuse transfer of shares and nobody but the directors can allot shares'. This, as he pointed out, made the Directors 'absolutely supreme in everything': 'They will appoint all Committees and all Officers and decide on the programme of plays etc.' Although he described this scheme as a 'compromise', it was in fact a financial and constitutional coup which delivered the Theatre entirely into hands of the directoral triumvirate.

Without the support of AE, this triumph would hardly have been conceivable, especially since Yeats's own interventions in the delicate negotiations nearly proved disastrous. 'He would wreck anything he is concerned with', an exasperated AE complained to Lady Gregory, 'by his utter incompetence to understand the feelings or character of anybody he is dealing with.' This inability, or unwillingness, to empathize with members of the company soon shattered the fragile concordat that AE had tactfully pieced together, and even those he had initially hoped to include in his team, such as Thomas Keohler and James Starkey, ended up opposing him. But he had calculated the odds shrewdly and by mid-October could even contemplate losing Maire Walker, since he estimated that the Directors would still be 'entirely certain of a perfectly sufficient group of actors going with us whatever happens'. Nor was it a mere matter of numbers; he foresaw (correctly as it turned out) that the Directors would take 'all the really competent people with us certainly'. He began to exercise his new powers immediately, overriding the objections of both the Fays by summarily putting George Roberts out of the part of Conchubar, and peremptorily demanding alterations to William Boyle's play *The Eloquent Dempsy*: 'Now that we are going to have a position of so much more authority we needn't be so diplomatic.'

'Hitherto the democratic arrangements have made it impossible to look ahead and settle dates and all that kind of thing,' Yeats had pointed out in welcoming the new constitution, and a further consequence of the more efficient management structure and payment of actors was that more ambitious tours could be planned. In late November the Company set off

for Oxford, Cambridge, and London. Yeats had already joined Miss Horniman on an advance publicity tour to Cambridge, and devoted himself to
arranging music and finding suitable theatres. The actors were delighted by
their success in the two university towns, where the educated audiences
were quick to pick up allusions and appreciate the dramatic and literary
subtleties of the plays. The Company was dined in a college hall, entertained by professors and their wives, and put up in private houses. London
was not quite so dazzling; as Yeats explained to Quinn, their 'own audience
which is a particularly fashionable one is only there during the meeting of
Parliament, and we fell on the rather flat general public; but they came in
very considerable numbers, which is the great point.' But back at home
discontent continued to simmer: Dublin alleged it had been abandoned
while the Directors whored after metropolitan success, and that in its
pursuit they had even fixed the London programme so as to push their
own plays into the most prominent slots while condemning work by Colum
and Boyle to less popular times.

## VI

Against this background of grumbling discontent Yeats set about wooing
the members of the old Society into the new Company with enticing offers
of shares and acting roles. The most important of the waiverers, and
probably the only one he really cared about, was Maire Walker, but she
was also the most difficult to pin down. Not only were her lover James
Starkey and her brother Frank opposed to the new arrangements, but she
was also bitterly jealous of Sara Allgood, and insisted on being paid a higher
wage than her. Yeats thought he had managed this difficulty with consum-
mate diplomacy by appointing her wardrobe mistress at five shillings a
week in addition to her acting duties. Under pressure, if not quite duress,
she consented to this arrangement and signed the contract, but almost
immediately thought better of it. Yeats, by now back in London and in
consultation with Miss Horniman (who once again promised him any
necessary extra financial backing), decided to make an example of her
and, through her, of the 'combination' behind her. While his exasperation
is understandable, his proposed response—to drag a popular young
working-class woman of extremely straitened means and known to be in
fragile health through a police court over a contract she had only signed
after he became on his own admission 'rather angry' and 'emphatic'—was
unlikely to teach Dublin to improve any of its business habits. He could not
see this; nor could he see as anything but 'futility' that the terms of
his brusque letter appointing her wardrobe mistress were wounding to

precarious sensitivities about class and status. He held up to derision her mother's social pretensions, uttered in 'that dirty room of hers', not apparently comprehending that this was the very point of the daughter's susceptibilities. When the whole sorry affair was over he confessed to Lady Gregory that he had 'no doubt I was wrong ... I was very tired out—this theatre row has been a good deal of a strain.' During the controversy he had not so much stifled these doubts as hidden them under a mask of joyful action. 'I am really rather enjoying the game,' he informed Lady Gregory with less than total candour and, on withdrawing his threat, telegraphed Synge (to whom, significantly, he never admitted his self-doubts) 'painted devil back in his box'. The mask is evidently not yet Nietzschean, rather the melodramatic property of grand guignol.

The fitting and adjusting of the mask of public man, defiantly taking on the conformist, trafficking world, is a recurrent feature of these years. The falling-out with Maire Walker and the other seceders from the Irish National Theatre Society was but one of many quarrels he was involved in at this time. It had been preceded by a public controversy in Cork, where he was charged with slighting local drama groups, and he was engaged simultaneously in an exchange with an incandescent Sarah Purser, whom he had accused of sacrificing the artistic integrity of her stained-glass business to commercial success. Each of these disputes involved questions of artistic distinction and independence and in such matters Yeats was not only correct but courageous. What he often failed to gauge was the difference between being right and being forthright to the point when insensitivity became counter-pro-ductive. 'Yes of course I have no tact, and bully people,' he perhaps too cheerfully assured AE, 'That is why I am leaving the whole matter to you.' He clearly came close to bullying Maire Walker in late December 1905 and his treatment of his sister Elizabeth, provoking although she could be, was often so disdainful and abrupt that his father found it necessary to warn him that 'men whom Nietche's [sic] theory fits are only great men of a sort, a sort of Yahoo greatness. The struggle is how to get rid of them, they belong to the clumsy & brutal side of things.' AE deplored Yeats's dismissal of Dublin writers as 'singing canaries' and 'poultry gardans' [sic], and complained that there was 'probably not one of the younger people of whom you have not said some stinging and contemptuous remark'. Yeats remained defiant both in his letters—'I desire the love of very few people, my equals or my superiors. The love of the rest would be a bond & an intrusion'—and in his verse, where the poem 'To a Poet, who would have me Praise certain Bad Poets, Imitators of His and Mine' (*VP*, 262) offers an epigrammatic riposte to AE's objections.

The problems in the theatre were compounded by divisions within both the Company and the Directorship. The Company itself was an amalgam-ation of disparate elements—a central core of the Fay's original amateur troop, the Ormonde Society, had been augmented by the Daughters of Erin, who were more committed to the national question than to perfection of their dramatic arts, and by the Dublin theosophists, for whom drama had never been more than a hobby. The two latter groups saw less need to put the theatre onto a professional footing since that involved far more time and effort than they thought dramatic representation warranted. In addition, the centralization of power into the hands of a small directorate, and the generally more systematic structures required by a professional society, offended against their ideas of democracy and co-operation. This, ironically, was particularly true of AE and the socialist Fred Ryan, the two men who did most to make the reorganization of the society a success. Even those who saw themselves as professional players, and remained in the new Company, increasingly resented the dictatorial manner and unpredictably violent temper of W. G. Fay, and nursed resentments that were to boil over in December 1907.

Yeats's quarrel with Maire Walker deepened the fissure between the two wings of the dramatic movement and the seceders hived off to form a rival society. This new organization, later to be named 'The Theatre of Ireland', did not at first worry Yeats since he correctly predicted that their lax discipline and poor taste would contrast unfavourably with the Abbey's more accomplished work: 'Everything they do would only reveal the superiority of our work. . . . They will either collapse after a performance or two or they will become more and more crudely propagandist playing up to that element in the country.' Moreover the Abbey had the ongoing advantage of Miss Horniman's subsidy: 'We have now £400 a year to spend on salaries & a fine theatre—all we have to do is to hold firm.' Thus, when Padraic Colum appealed to him to bring the Society back together, he permitted himself the cavalier reply that 'a re-united society would be "five-wild cats struggling in a bag"' and added airily that he was 'off lecturing & would have no certain address for some time & that he had better see Synge'.

But while he could be confident about the long-term artistic outcome of the split, more immediate legal consequences prevented confidence turning into smugness. In mid-January 1906 he was brought up short when he was reminded that the Patent under which the Abbey operated had been granted not to the Theatre itself, nor to Miss Horniman, but to the Irish National Theatre Society, and that if that Society were dissolved (which was in effect what was happening), the Patent was void and no plays could be performed at the Abbey. He immediately changed tack. 'Not being able to fight them as I should like', he now proposed 'a scheme so generous that it will as I think help us with the public as well as in the long run bring back everybody we want.' At this time it was unclear that the seceders understood the full implications of the Patent, but a sharp exchange between them and Lady Gregory (acting for the Directors [pp. 329–33]) and a tendentious article in the *United Irishman* on 10 March 1906, stating that the Limited Company was in fact the seceding faction, caused the Directors deep consternation. In the end negotiations behind the scenes carried the day. The Directors promised to induce Miss Horniman to allow the new Company the use of the Abbey Theatre and agreed to hand over £50 remaining in the kitty to them. Armed with this sum, the new Society held a provisional meeting on 18 May, and many of its members formally resigned from the Irish National Theatre Society at that time, so that the Annual General Meeting on 26 May turned out to be far less contentious and close-run than Yeats had feared. He was re-elected President, and the committees were packed with his supporters. In the following days, the seceders formally constituted themselves the Theatre of Ireland, thus abandoning their potentially dangerous claim to the title of Irish National Theatre and so obviating the threat to the Patent.

## VII

During these upheavals the Abbey Company had not been idle. It had mounted regular productions and, although it prudently kept mainly to familiar pieces during this time of reorganization, on 16 April 1906 staged for the first time Lady Gregory's version of Molière's *The Doctor in Spite of Himself*, together with a much-revised version of Yeats's *On Baile's Strand*. It also mounted tours to Wexford and Dundalk, as well as to Manchester, Leeds, and Liverpool. As hitherto, these visits were of short duration, and even that to three of the major English cities lasted only a week. But now, with full-time actors and Miss Horniman's subsidy, a far more ambitious British tour became possible.

Although the Abbey's British tour in the summer of 1906 was not its most important overseas venture, the long-term effects were highly significant. For a new and still developing company it was wildly ambitious, extending over six tiring weeks and taking in six major cities, none of which had been visited before. The management was divided, with Alfred Wareing, an English professional actor-manager, who had little previous acquaintance with the Irish theatre, taking the main responsibility and William Fay looking after the night-by-night performances. Under these conditions, the defects in the Company's acting and technique were cruelly exposed, and raw sensibilities were further grated when John J. Bell, a Scottish commercial manager, called Fay's stage management into question. All this came as an unwelcome eye-opener to Miss Horniman. If one of her reasons for purchasing the Abbey Theatre had been to provide Yeats with a venue for his dramatic aspirations, another was to promote herself as a benefactor of the arts. She had hoped, as Yeats saw, that the English tours would supply her 'with what she called a career'. She now began to fear that the Company, far from enhancing her name and prestige, were turning her into a laughing-stock. This was especially irksome in Edinburgh, where she had a number of friends and where, as she complained to Yeats, the Company's acting had been 'shocking': 'Dead amateurs not caring for anything. Every word clear throughout the theatre but articulated by dolls.' She insisted, such was her nature, on offering her advice, and a turning point in the history of the Abbey hinged on a bad-tempered encounter with the no doubt over-harassed William Fay on the stage of the King's Theatre in Glasgow.

Fay had already irritated Miss Horniman with his lax business habits, especially over money, in which matters she took an over-scrupulous and almost self-defining pride, but the flare-up in Glasgow turned mild vexation to an obsessive detestation. Yeats did not realize how signal and serious the incident had been, and later reproached himself for not getting Fay to apologize at once. Egged on by the Wareings, Miss Horniman now made a detailed inventory of the Company's shortcomings and misdemeanours: the young women had been seen in public with their hair down and sitting on the men's knees, they leant out of carriage windows, shouting to people on the platform, the actor Arthur Sinclair was drunk at Cardiff station and wanted to travel through the night in Brigit O'Dempsey's railway compartment, her flirtatious sister Eileen wore 'outrageous low dresses' and made an 'assignation with a stranger, overheard by Miss Horniman', as well as tootling on a toy trumpet during the frequent train journeys and at night in Liverpool and Leeds (where Miss Horniman was mortified to be scolded by the proprietress of the Trevelyan Hotel). Yeats knew that behind this excess of high spirits 'the company is very harmless and innocent', but he was worried by the dangerously adverse attention their public behaviour might attract in Ireland, and he saw it as part of a wider problem, 'the carelessness in all details, the absence of precise habits', which had also involved sloppy stage management, a woeful lack of rehearsals, and the neglect of production values.

Both he and Miss Horniman laid the final blame for this situation with William Fay (although Synge's relationship with Maire O'Neill was also causing both them and Lady Gregory alarm). Miss Horniman's generosity did not cease, but henceforth she declined 'to have anything more to do with the company until they have all learned to be worth my troubling about them' (a resolution she predictably found impossible to keep). With the Directors' approval, she resolved that they should appoint a business manager, who would take the financial business out of Fay's hands, including the paying of actors. This arrangement made the actors directly dependent on the Directors, and so gave them 'an opportunity of insisting on the work being done properly and on orderly behaviour'. After canvassing opinion, W. A. Henderson, the secretary of the National Literary Society and an enthusiastic student of the theatre, was appointed to the post, and with his help the Abbey prospered. He devised a new scheme for marketing tickets and, at the same time, Miss Horniman was induced to halve the price of the cheapest seats in the Theatre. This led to increased audiences during the autumn season and on 19 October Yeats was able to report that people had to be turned away because the theatre was full; by 11 November he was even more upbeat: 'The theatre is now a success, if it goes on as it is now we are through all our troubles. . . . People standing up both in gallery and pit. The audience have been steadily going up and this is the best yet.'

Although delighted with this commercial success he was more worried by his own artistic position in the theatre. As early as May 1906, he had voiced his concern that the Abbey was too exclusively associated with comedy and feared that without 'work more burdened with thought', audiences would 'expect comedy and resent anything else. Comedy must make the ship sail, but the ship must have other things in the cargo.' That autumn he pointed out that Synge, Boyle and Lady Gregory were now enjoying far superior productions than they could have hoped for from any English company and that, while this was also true of his own prose plays, he was 'essentially a verse writer' and 'could get a much better performance taken as a whole in England of a play like Deirdre'. One of the main problems facing him was the Company's lack of a passionate female lead, a lacuna he hoped to full with Letitia Darragh, 'an Irish star on the English stage', as he described her, who also had the added advantage of being one of Miss Horniman's friends. Although she took the lead in the Abbey productions of Yeats's Deirdre and The Shadowy Waters, she was never accepted by the Company, who found her technique alien to their manner, nor by Lady Gregory, who thought the passion detected in her by Yeats was no more than an over-intense sensuality.

The Company's resentment of Miss Darragh, orchestrated by the two Fays, did nothing to compose Yeats's mind. Nor was all peace and harmony within the Directorship more generally. Synge, never comfortable with Yeats's high-handed treatment of the Company, was intermittently suspicious that his plays were being neglected in order to advance those of the other two Directors, and that the Society, with Lady Gregory's connivance, was being shaped to suit Yeats's work. Indeed, Lady Gregory told him directly that the Abbey's main mission was to further Yeats's dramatic aspirations. Relationships with Annie Horniman were even more fraught; Synge became an object of scorn to her and Lady Gregory was worried, not without justification, about her power over Yeats and by the hints of 'secret treaties' between the two of them. Miss Horniman, increasingly frustrated by the failure of her pursuit of Yeats and by the Irish rather than European orientation of the Abbey Theatre, became ever more captious and unpredictable. As a loose cannon she was perilously well armed, since she held the economic power and through that the legal power, as the Patent was dependent upon her continuing benefactions. Over the period 1905 to 1907 she was to fall out with practically every member of the Company except Yeats, but in truth from the beginning only he really had her ear. It was for him that she had purchased the theatre and it was the success of his plays alone that interested her. Yeats in turn used this privileged position to add extra weight to his views—whether it was scotching the production of plays of which he disapproved ('I am not at all sure of the effect of a play of this kind on Miss Horniman who has spent four thousand pounds on us already'), or of insisting that votes in the restructured society should be proportional to the shares by concocting a letter with her insisting upon this. But she was no mere Spenlow to his Jorkins, for she had very obstinate views of her own and her letters to him, a perplexing and infuriating mixture of ingenuous flirtation, pedantic nagging, snide insinuation, all intercut with acts of breathtaking generosity, were to cause him sentiments of guilt, irritation, amusement, gratitude, and anger.

These warring emotions were intensified over the winter of 1906-7. Both he and she were convinced that not only was William Fay overworked but that he had no gift for tragedy or for poetic drama, and that few of the other actors, with the exception of Frank Fay, were capable of performing Yeats's work satisfactorily. Things came to a head with a flurry of manifestos in December 1906, and in close consultation with Miss Horniman, Yeats proposed the appointment of a new Managing Director, at the then very handsome salary of £500 a year, to take charge of the production of verse plays and foreign masterpieces, as well as the casting of actors and actresses from outside the Company to perform in his and foreign work. His fellow Directors were less convinced. Lady Gregory thought that it would give Miss Horniman too much power and that they should not over-diversify their repertoire at this early point in their development. Synge was also opposed to giving Miss Horniman any extra power or to swamping the creative Irish element in the Abbey with a heterogeneous mass of foreign plays as she advocated. Four-way negotiations took place during December and January between the three Directors and Miss Horniman, who was on holiday in North Africa, but all seemed lost when Fay, naturally suspicious that the new arrangements would lessen his influence, turned the final proposal down. Both Lady Gregory and Synge took Fay's part, but Yeats persisted, claiming that 'the existence of the movement is at stake—& that I am bound by my obligation to the movement, to Miss Horniman & above all to the company as a whole—our young people have no future but with us— to press them'. His will finally prevailed, but not until Miss Horniman had permanently alienated Lady Gregory by describing the Abbey Theatre as an 'Irish toy' of extrinsic interest to her, and roused her and Synge's fears that there was a secret understanding between her and Yeats as to future claims on his work. Nevertheless, Ben Iden Payne, a gifted English actor and stage director, was recruited as the new manager from early February 1907.

## VIII

Ironically the ructions over the first production of Synge's *The Playboy of the Western World* helped to shore the Theatre against the forces of disintegration. In the face of nationwide hostility, it was no time to be airing internal disagreements. Yeats was not present on the play's fateful first evening, but lecturing in Scotland, where he was handed a telegram sent by Lady Gregory after the end of the second act, announcing 'Play great success'. In the early hours of the following morning another wire arrived with the news that the 'Audience broke up in disorder at the word shift'. It was not until Tuesday that he could get back to Dublin. The previous evening no word of the play had been heard, but he was determined to fight. Henderson recalled that he rushed into the theatre excitedly exclaiming that they must take columns in the press and hire thirty or forty sandwich-board men to advertise the play. Payne also remembered Yeats's resolve and exaltation at this time, rejecting out of hand Synge's suggestion that they might withdraw the play: 'His manner was high-spirited, even elated. The fire of combat lighted up his eyes as he said they must at all hazards give the play its full allotted time. If they gave way to clamor, he said, they would ever afterward be at the mercy of the whims and prejudices of their audiences.'

This was the most important event in the early history of the Abbey Theatre, and Yeats at once recognized it as such. The play went on, but not without cost. Yeats defended its right to be heard from the stage on the Tuesday night, and, when his argument was disregarded, he and Lady Gregory authorized the deployment of police to keep order—a reasonably common procedure in the Dublin commercial theatres, but which was thought inappropriate in an institution claiming to be a 'National' theatre. The police were also in present in force on the following night, when the faction opposed to the play was confronted by a group of students from Trinity College, who supported it no less vociferously. Yeats pressed the

prosecution of the rioters, prompting one of them to deride the sight of
'Mr. W. B. Yeats, once a patriot and still a poet, prosecuting men in the
Police Courts for hooting a bad play at his theatre', and among those fined
£2 and bound over in surety of £10 was Padraic Colum's father.

Yeats's determination not to surrender to the rioters paid off. By Thursday night the disturbances were much subdued and on the following two
evenings there were very few interruptions, although the services of the
police were retained. The longer-term consequences were less clear-cut.
William Boyle, angered as much by Miss Horniman's triumphalism as
Synge's supposed indecency, withdrew his very popular plays from the
Abbey repertoire. District councils throughout rural Ireland passed resolutions denouncing the Abbey, and the Gort Board of Guardians forbade
the workhouse children under its jurisdiction attending Lady Gregory's
picnics at Coole Park. A number of regular patrons ceased to frequent the
Abbey, and the overflowing auditoria of the previous autumn dwindled to
sometimes painfully thin audiences. But the audience, if smaller, was more
sophisticated and sympathetic, and at the productions following *The Playboy* (which cannily included his most popular nationalist play, *Cathleen ni
Houlihan*) Yeats was delighted to get 'an extraordinary reception from the
audience, which was certainly meant to imply approval of our action'. On 5
February he spoke at a heated debate on the production of *The Playboy*,
refusing to be shouted down by his opponents. Although the majority at the
meeting had been noisily opposed to him, he accounted the whole experience a signal victory: 'It has been the first real defeat to the mob here, and
may be the start of a party of intellect in the Arts, at any rate.' He was
convinced that the opposition had been orchestrated by the political clubs,
and, as such, represented a falling away of the ideals of Irish nationalism in
the present generation. It also, like the reaction to Maud Gonne's divorce
proceedings, pointed to the hypocrisy in contemporary Irish life: 'At the
second performance of Synges play', he told Quinn, 'a doctor said to Synge
"I wish medical etiquette permitted me to go down & stand in front of that
pit & point out among the protesters in the name of Irish virtue the patients
I am treating for venereal disease". What drama.'

## IX

The work of restoring the Theatre's fortunes continued through the spring
and given Synge's prolonged ill health much of the administration fell on
Yeats. On 15 February a formal agreement appointed William Fay as
producer of plays in dialect while Payne looked after verse work and foreign
plays, and so, for a time at least, that problem seemed to have been solved to

everyone's satisfaction. But, as Yeats confided to Quinn, it would 'take some time to measure the consequences' of *The Playboy* dispute. One of the imponderable consequences was the likely reception of the play in America, a question which was given urgency by the prospect of its publication there, and by the visit to the Abbey by the influential impresario Charles Frohman. It was supposed that if Frohman liked what he saw he might arrange an Abbey tour in the USA, and one of the actors confidently informed Joseph Holloway that they 'probably would go to America in September'. But, despite inside advice from Agnes Tobin, a friend of Frohman's, and a carefully selected bill (a selection which infuriated Synge as another example that his work was being neglected in favour of plays by the other two Directors), nothing came of the visit. Although Frohman attended a performance on 1 April 1907 and later said complimentary things about the Theatre, he did not meet Yeats on that occasion ('Is Yeats the long black fellow who was passing continually between the audience and the footlights?', he later inquired) and discussions about a transatlantic trip came to nothing.

## X

Meanwhile one of Yeats's long-cherished schemes was, with the crucial financial assistance of Miss Horniman, finally put in train. This was a lavish eight-volume edition of his *Collected Works*. The partners of the publisher A. H. Bullen had been sceptical about the economic viability of this undertaking (a scepticism that proved to be justified) and Yeats had reconciled himself to a far more modest publication. In March 1907, however, Miss Horniman once again put her purse at his service and early that month he saw Watt about the transference of all his books to Bullen to facilitate the project. On 14 March Miss Horniman formally stated her terms to Bullen, agreeing to a guarantee of £1,500, and insisting that the volumes should be 'done as well as possible, with new portraits'. Her motivation in all this is suggested in a concluding paragraph: 'I will do all in my power to protect Mr Yeats' *time* from the theatre; in future I hope that he will get more opportunity for direct literary work.'

## XI

It had been a punishing year for Yeats and Lady Gregory, who was still encountering local hostility in Gort over her involvement with *The Playboy*, and in March they planned to get away from it all with an extended visit to Italy accompanied by Robert Gregory. Theatre controversies dogged them almost to the point of departure and were to be responsible for dragging them prematurely back to England. Another extended British tour to Glasgow, Cambridge, Birmingham, Oxford, and London was being planned for May and June, largely organized by Payne and Miss Horniman, but the prospect of *The Playboy* being staged in England provoked William Boyle to an intemperate article in the London *Catholic Herald*. As well as general vituperation, he hinted at a political agenda in reviving the play, pointing out that it 'appears when Home Rule is again prominently before the English public', and in an accompanying editorial the paper practically incited the London Irish to physical violence, supposing that they would 'feel an insatiable itching to get their fingers on Mr. Synge and express their feelings with blows and knocks neither apostolic nor restrained'. Boyle's article was reprinted in the *Freeman's Journal* and caused consternation in the Company; Yeats was obliged to call them together two days before he left for Italy to and 'win them over by speach (explaining our motives, reasons, & so forth)'. His pep-talk worked and he 'left them very resolute', a state of mind which survived until their departure on 11 March, when Holloway, who saw them off, recorded that they 'were all in great spirits, & laughed & joked about what was to happen to them in London when *The Playboy* was put on'.

By then Yeats had been in Italy for a month. It was the first time he had been east of Paris and Lady Gregory planned the trip with great care, using Florence as a base for the first part and from there making expeditions to other Renaissance cities. 'We had chosen Florence and Siena', she later recalled, 'and then to please that student of Castiglione's *Courtier* we drove across the Apennines to Urbino, and descended to Pesaro and Ravenna.' In Florence Yeats went every day to the Baptistery or to the Duomo, telling Florence Farr that he thought the perpetual hum in the latter 'was mass at first but found it was only people reading out the guide book—the old age of faith'. Theatre business pursued him even in Italy and he corresponded with Miss Horniman about the details of the Abbey's British tour as well as sending Payne copy for a new number of the *Arrow*. Meanwhile, after a further trip to San Marino, the party journeyed on to Venice by way of Ferrara. Lady Gregory had been at some pains to make sure that Yeats's first sight of Venice should be from the most impressive direction: 'taking steam-boat at Chioggia we came before the sun had set to our haven, not to the jangle and the uproar of the railway station, but to set foot first upon the very threshold of the city's beauty, the steps leading to the Grand Piazza, to the Duomo, of St. Mark.' There she left Yeats, entranced by the rich colouring and the beauty of the Venetian night.

It was as well that he drank in the beauties of Venice at the first opportunity as there were to be few others. On 17 May Miss Horniman interrupted a business letter to Lady Gregory to tell her that the English censor, George Redford, terrified by the prospect of a row in London over the production of *The Playboy of the Western World*, was 'consulting the Home Office & Lord Chamberlain'. This was followed by a telegram urging her and Yeats to return at once, and they arrived in Cambridge on 22 May. In the circumstances they decided to withdraw *The Playboy* from Birmingham, a decision that provoked the threat of resignation from Synge, but to retain it in Oxford and London. Yeats had resolved to go to prison rather than submit to censorship, but this proved unnecessary; Redford granted a licence for the play on 23 May, subject to the omission of Pegeen's reference in Act I to 'loosèd khaki cut-throats' and 'any other allusion derogatory to the army'.

## XII

The successful English productions of *The Playboy* did not end the difficulties in the Theatre. Miss Horniman had been spoiling for trouble during most of the year. In March there had been a dispute over whether *The King's Threshold* was a poetic play (and therefore Payne's concern) or a dialect play and part of Fay's remit. Yeats's prolonged trip to Italy and his consequent cancellation of speaking engagements she had made for him without his knowledge had also annoyed her. Smarting under a sense of being rebuffed, she began to seek out even more desperate occasions for offence. An error in the printing of a new batch of Abbey stationery, still showing Fay as manager, led her to accuse the Directors of chicanery. A few weeks later she wrote an arch letter purporting to believe that the arrangement with Payne as manager had broken down and that this had been kept from her either though incompetence or deceit. An incensed Yeats responded with a letter resigning his Directorship and it seemed that the Abbey Theatre experiment was at an end.

But a week is as long a time in theatrical as in party politics, and a few days after his outraged resignation of 7 June he called on Miss Horniman with Payne to suggest that she should set up an entirely new theatrical scheme, assigning his plays to the new company and treating the Abbey as a Dublin 'pied à terre'. After a day's reflection she concluded that she had had enough of Lady Gregory, Synge, William Fay, and Dublin, and of 'the obloquy of connection with the Abbey there', and discussion turned to other possible bases, including Manchester. Although this was a scheme which she insisted Yeats 'had suggested yourself', he could not finally reconcile himself to it, and withdrew himself and his plays from the project. She strongly suspected that he had abandoned the idea at Fay's insistence, since, increasingly hostile to Irish nationalism, she did not understand that, ambivalent as it might be, his commitment to Ireland was his primary impulse. 'I understand my own race & in all my work, lyric or dramatic I have thought of it,' he wrote in a letter of explanation, adding that if the Abbey failed he might or might not go on writing plays 'but I shall write for my own people—whether in love or hate of them matters little—probably I shall not know which it is'.

The withdrawal of Miss Horniman and Payne concentrated the minds of the Directors. Yeats had hoped for a further £25,000 from her, but she now earmarked this for setting up the Gaiety Theatre in Manchester, and it became clear that while she would go on paying the subsidy she had promised to the Abbey, she would give nothing extra, and stop that after the period of the Patent ended in 1910. In this situation, yet another reorganization of the Abbey became an urgent necessity. William Fay returned to the position he had held before the engagement of Payne and the hapless Henderson was fired, ostensibly for economic reasons, but largely because he had offended Miss Horniman, who exerted relentless pressure on Yeats to get rid of him. The Theatre's income and funds were audited with the help of professional accountants and Ernest Vaughan, whom the Directors had been looking forward to dismissing for over a year, was instead appointed business manager in Henderson's place. It was a far from satisfactory arrangement, as Yeats immediately confessed, and it was not destined to last long.

## XIII

'Theatre business, management of men' was taking its toll. Yeats fell ill in the summer of 1907, revealing to Maud Gonne that he was close to a nervous breakdown. In June he confessed to Lady Gregory that he felt he had 'lost' himself: 'my centre as it were, has shifted from its natural interests, and . . . it will take me a long time finding myself again.' Miss Horniman, he divulged, wanted him to resign from the theatre entirely, but he was 'afraid to do that, as I think my presence in it is a protection to it against her capriciousness'. At the beginning of July, however, he retired to Coole for three months to devote himself to preparing the copy for *The Collected Works*. This was not to be the leisurely occupation he hoped for. As so often in his dealings with Bullen, the contractual arrangements were vague; he had understood that each volume would take between six and eight weeks to print, so giving him over a year to complete his revisions. Now, to his chagrin, he discovered that Bullen intended to print at the rate of three weeks per volume, leaving him less than six months to produce a final and definitive text, and he feared that so short a time to revise 'so much that is immature or inexperienced as there is in my already published books would do me a very great injury'. He saw as his main task the rewriting of his rushed play of 1902, *Where There Is Nothing*, but Lady Gregory came to his aid and together they refashioned it as *The Unicorn from the Stars*. The dispute over the copyright status of *The Wind Among the Reeds* also dragged on, largely owing to the sharp business practices of the publisher John Lane backed with quiet connivance by Elkin Mathews, but finally the Macmillan Company of New York called Lane's bluff and the disputed poems appeared in the first volume of *The Collected Works*.

Bullen agreed to give Yeats more time and even at this late stage the whole project was rethought so that the exact contents of individual volumes remained fluid until comparatively late in the project. So did the choice of portraits, which both Yeats and Miss Horniman considered essential to the work. Finally the edition included portraits by John Singer Sargent, Charles Shannon, Antonio Mancini, and a drawing by John Butler Yeats. The Sargent portrait was a replacement for one commissioned from Augustus John (originally, in its turn, a substitute for one by Charles Shannon). John, who was shortly to be Robert Gregory's best man, happened to be visiting Coole in September 1907 and was commissioned by Lady Gregory to do an etching of Yeats. It was an experience he found as interesting as Yeats, informing one of his mistresses that, despite Yeats's sentimental prejudice in favour of his soulful early self, he thought him 'far more interesting as he is, as maturity is more interesting than immaturity. But my unprejudiced vision must seem brutal and unsympathetic to those in whom direct vision is supplanted by a vague and sentimental memory.' He was right; the portrait gave Yeats a horrified shock of recognition, and he recalled in 1930 that when he saw it for the first time he 'shuddered' in discovering in it an 'Anglo-Irish solitude, a solitude I have made for myself, an outlawed solitude'. The rest of his friends, as well as Bullen, experienced the shock without the recognition, and, in spite of his wishes, the etching was not included in the book.

The portrait by Antonio Mancini was included, even though Miss Horniman disliked it. Hugh Lane had invited Mancini over from Italy to paint Lady Gregory and his sister Ruth Shine, and so the extra portrait of Yeats was, like the John, something of an accident. Yeats recorded in Quinn's copy of *The Collected Works* that if only he had resembled the portrait he would 'have defeated all my enemies here in Dublin', and revealed that Mancini 'did it in an hour or so working at the last with great vehemence and constant cries, "Cristo, O", and so on'. Given the general hostility to John's portrait a replacement was commissioned from Sargent, and the original plan of commissioning a picture from Charles Shannon was resuscitated.

## XIV

On 3 October the Abbey reopened for its doors for the autumn season, and Yeats went up to Dublin to oversee the performances and rehearse the first production of *The Unicorn from the Stars*. The Theatre had adopted a radically new programming policy. Previously performances had been given for six days in one week per month, with extra shows on Saturday; now they ran for three days in three weeks of the month. The first production of the new season, *The Country Dressmaker*, by the young Kerry playwright George Fitzmaurice, was such a hit that its run was extended, although Yeats, who thought the play a poor imitation of Synge, resented its success and temporarily underrated it. With Miss Horniman's support now more precarious than hitherto, the Directors could not afford to trail their coats too ostentatiously in Dublin, even while defending the right of free speech they had won at such a cost. As Yeats wrote to Norreys Connell, a new and potentially controversial Abbey dramatist, they were 'fighting a very difficult battle in Dublin, and though resolved to fight on, producing every good work we can, I confess that one grows a little weary of the fight, and we do not want more fighting than we can help'. Given the highly charged atmosphere of Dublin this was a difficult line to draw, and as the autumn progressed it became clear that the Directors and William Fay were drawing it in significantly different places. He was anxious to put on as little dangerous work as possible, and to press for performances of the cruder and more successful plays over the less popular work of the Directors.

An innovation which helped the Directors' campaign was the inauguration of 'Professional Matinées', to which visiting companies playing at the large Dublin commercial theatres were invited. These events became a shop-window for the Abbey's work and raised its prestige in the theatre world. The compliments of the visiting stars also did much to stem the facile disparagement of the Theatre in post-*Playboy* Dublin. A bonus of this scheme that Yeats could not have foreseen was the unstinted acclaim of Mrs Patrick Campbell, whose company had been invited to a matinée in late October. She not only praised the plays and acting enthusiastically, but promised publicly to come and act with the Company for a week the following year, and improved even this shining hour by describing Yeats in a farewell speech from the stage of the Gaiety Theatre as 'my dear friend and your great poet'. Yeats, noting bitterly that every one of the Irish newspapers omitted the epithet 'great', explained that this gesture was more than a merely personal tribute: her endorsement would 'do more than anything else to break down the feeling on the Unionist side here that our plays cannot be good because they are "Irish", and the feeling among a considerable number of Nationalists that they cannot be good because they are cultivated and intellectual'. Mrs Campbell's generous promise strengthened the Directors' resolve 'of keeping the Theatre precisely as it has always been'.


## XV


William Fay's predilection for 'safe' work was not the only problem he posed. Without Payne as a counterweight, the balance of power in the Company had passed back into his far from certain hands. Yeats was 'very doubtful of his being able to hold the company together, considering his queer temper, but I dont see what else we can do'. His first response was to 'give Fay every opportunity to acquire experience and amend his faults', observing gloomily that the Theatre was 'now a desperate enterprise and we must take desperate measures'.

The desperate measures did not work. Fay's abrasive personality had been one of the reasons for the number of secessions from the Company in late 1905—including that of Maire Walker. The actor Ambrose Power had complained of his victimization at Fay's hands during a London tour, and there had been a fist fight in the theatre between the Fay brothers on the important night when Frohman had been unofficially auditioning the Company for an American tour. But relations between Fay and the Company reached a new low during the 1907 Advent tour to Manchester, Glasgow, and Edinburgh. Here he compounded his chronic inconsistency (on one day he would condone their bad timekeeping, and on the next bawl them out in violent language) with new displays of arrogance. Besides including *The Hour-Glass* on the bill against Yeats's express wishes, he allowed his wife to appear instead of the indisposed Sara Allgood without announcing the change from the stage or in the programmes. This had attracted adverse publicity in the press, and resulted in two of the leading actors, Sara Allgood and Arthur Sinclair, fishing for jobs at Miss Horniman's Gaiety Theatre.

For his part, Fay was depressed and discouraged. He felt that the Directors were pushing their own unpopular plays—he had a particular aversion to Lady Gregory's *The Canavans*—at the expense of more feasible work. The growing insubordination and resentment of the Company, which he looked upon as his own creation, also exasperated him. He complained to Joseph Holloway that 'he had trained several companies & had arrived at the age of 35—& had made nothing', and claimed that he 'was for chucking the whole thing'. Instead of 'chucking the whole thing', he submitted a list of impossible demands to the Directors, among them being that he should dismiss the whole Company and personally re-engage those he wanted to retain. Once reappointed, such actors would lose all rights of appeal to the Directors, thus putting them and their careers entirely in the arbitrary power of his uncertain temper. These terms the Directors turned down, although they tried to defuse the situation by declaring the need for better discipline and suggested a committee of actors to help advise on this.

The situation simmered dangerously but could not be brought to a crisis. Despite his remarks to Holloway, it was clear that Fay had no intention of resigning, and the Directors, already unpopular and abused in Dublin, had no wish to be seen as acting in a high-handed way. Any initiative to remove Fay must come from the Company itself, but the Company seemed loath to act. Yeats suggested that they should present a formal account of their complaints in writing, but both he and Lady Gregory doubted 'their spirit'. In fact this highly unsatisfactory situation dragged on until early February 1908, when William Fay and his wife finally resigned from the Company and were joined by Frank Fay. The split, when it came, was initially passed off as a friendly parting of the ways, but within a few weeks things turned acrimonious, and the Abbey had generated yet another quarrel.

## XVI

And so the period of 'Theatre business, management of men' continued and was destined to continue for many more years. And as it did so, the 'Celtic Movement' turned inexorably into the 'Irish Movement'. Yeats, like Augustus John, was acutely conscious of the alteration that time and experience was making to his writing and personality, and, like John, open to the idea that he was becoming 'far more interesting as he is, as maturity is more interesting than immaturity'. After a series of speaking engagements in February 1906 he told Florence Farr that he found he could 'move people by power not merely—as the phrase is—by "charm" or "speaking beautifully"—a thing I always resented. I feel this change in all my work and that it has brought a change into the personal relations of life—even things seemingly beyond control answer strangely to what is within. I once cared only for images about whose necks I could cast various "chains of office" as it were. They were so many aldermen of the ideal, whom I wished to master the city of the soul. Now I do not want images at all, or chains of office being contented with the unruly soul.' This was an important and defining insight; no less significant for his future work would be the discovery that those with unruly souls rarely remain contented for long.

# THE LETTERS
# 1905–1907

# 1905

*To Lady Gregory,*[1] *[early January 1905]*

18 Woburn Buildings | Euston Road.

My dear Lady Gregory: Has a copy of that American anthology reached Coole for me. One was sent. If it has arrived please bring it to Dublin if you are coming.[2] Nothing new here—I saw "the Knight of the Burning Pestle" last—A delight, joyful, extravigant thing & finely played.[3] 'Prunnella' at

[1] Lady Augusta Gregory (1852–1932; see III. 703–7), Irish folklorist and playwright, was WBY's closest friend, patron, and correspondent from 1897, when he began to spend his summers at her house, Coole Park, in Co. Galway.

[2] *Irish Literature*, a ten-volume anthology edited by the Irish politician and man of letters Justin McCarthy (1830–1912); see III. 484, 493–4, 649–50. The project had been seen through the press by George James Bryan (1852–1915), and Charles Welsh, managing editor of J. D. Morris & Co., Philadelphia. Although WBY did not join the editorial and advisory board (which included Douglas Hyde and AG), he was listed as one of the authors of 'Biographies and Literary Appreciations', which are identified in the index. AE had made a selection of WBY's poems, prefaced with a biographical and critical introduction. The volumes had arrived safely, and AG brought them to Dublin at the end of this month.

[3] Philip Comyns Carr's production of Francis Beaumont's comedy *The Knight of the Burning Pestle* (1613) ran at the Royalty Theatre from 26 Dec 1904 to 4 Jan 1905. Annie Horniman (AEFH, 1860–1937; see III. 709–13), the patron of the Abbey Theatre, had evidently accompanied WBY on this occasion, for in a letter of 15 Feb 1908 (NLI) she recalled 'how you enjoyed "The Knight of the Burning Pestle" long ago', and told him that she intended to revive it at the Gaiety Theatre, Manchester: 'Your wriggles of laughter made me think that it would do well. Of course I'll mount it with more taste than Phillip Carr did.' The plot, in which a Jacobean London citizen, his family, and his apprentice insist on putting on their own play during a performance of a romantic tragedy at a public theatre, may have had some influence on WBY's experiments in breaking the dramatic illusion, as at the beginning of *The Death of Cuchulain*. In *The Cutting of an Agate* (*E & I*, 280) WBY recalled as an example of the superiority of imagination and personality over logic and detached observation that 'I saw with delight *The Knight of the Burning Pestle* when Mr. Carr revived it, and found it none the worse because the apprentice acted a whole play upon the spur of the moment and without committing a line to heart'. WBY had first met Carr (1874–1957) at one of AG's dinner parties on 15 Dec 1897, shortly after he had come down from Oxford (Pethica, 161).

the Court—Barkers & Housemans play—has on the other hand no merit.[4]
I am dictating letters to Miss Horniman.[5]

Y ev
W B Yeats

ALS Berg.

## *To the Editor of the* Irish Times, [*5 January 1905*]

Sir,—We, the undersigned Irish writers, ask our friends and readers to help us in a most urgent matter. We are most anxious to keep in Ireland the extraordinarily important collection of pictures by modern—chiefly modern French—artists now being exhibited at the Royal Hibernian Academy, chosen by experts from the Staats-Forbes and Durand-Ruel collections, and admitted to be the finest representation of modern French art outside Paris.[1]

Among the pictures there are 12 paintings by Corot, 14 by Constable, 16 drawings by Millet, and many works by Daubigny, Diaz, Troyon, Courbet, Fantin Latour, Whistler, Bastien Lepage, Israels, Mauve, and Maris.[2]

---

[4] Harley Granville-Barker's and Laurence Housman's *Prunella; or, Love in a Dutch Garden*, a 'play in three acts for grown-up children', was the Christmas attraction at the Court Theatre from 23 Dec 1904. The dramatists hoped to make their fortunes with this fantasy in which a simple country girl wins, loses, and regains the love of a Pierrot, but the first production of Barrie's smash hit *Peter Pan* overshadowed it and it folded on 14 Jan, although it was revived for a series of matinée performances in late April and early May 1905, and again, at the Duke of York's Theatre, in April 1910.

[5] AEFH often acted as WBY's amanuensis to save his always precarious eyesight (see II. 103).

[1] This letter appeared in a number of Dublin newspapers, including the *Irish Times*, and was published in the London *Times* on 6 Jan (8); it was also distributed in a slightly revised form as a printed circular entitled 'A Modern Art Gallery for Dublin'. It was the latest round in what was proving to be a prolonged fight to purchase pictures from the late James Staats-Forbes's collection and from the Parisian connoisseur and dealer Paul Durand-Ruel as the nucleus for Hugh Lane's proposed Gallery of Modern Art (see III. 608, 680–2). Hugh Percy Lane (1875–1915), AG's nephew, a member of the Board of Governors of the Irish National Gallery, and a successful art-dealer and collector, had mounted an exhibition, largely of modern French paintings, in the Royal Irish Academy in the autumn of 1904, and was hoping that funds could be raised to purchase them for the nation. Responding to this letter in an editorial of 6 Jan 1905, the *Irish Times* acknowledged that the pictures were worth £30,000 (some correspondents had disputed this), but pointed out that £30,000 was a large sum to raise in a poor country like Ireland, and announced that Hugh Lane and Sir William Armstrong (1850–1918), art critic, Director of the National Gallery of Ireland from 1892 to 1914, and a supporter of Lane, were to select a smaller number of pictures from the collections, up to a value of £20,000.

[2] Jean-Baptiste Camille Corot (1796–1875), one of the major French landscape painters of the 19th century; John Constable (1776–1837), English landscape painter who strove to achieve 'a pure apprehension of natural effect'; Jean François Millet (1814–75), French artist of rustic life, whose drawings are more prized than his paintings; Charles-François Daubigny (1817–79), Narcisse-Virgile Diaz (1811–89), and Constant Troyon (1810–65), French landscape painters associated with the Barbizon School, which opposed classical convention and sought direct representation of nature for its own sake; Gustave Courbet (1819–77), realist French painter of everyday life; Ignace Henri-Jean Théodore Fantin-Latour (1836–1904), French painter admired for his figures and groups and also for his still lifes, a friend of the American artist James Abbott McNeill Whistler (1834–1903), who had trained in Paris and lived most of his life in London, and whose work was a harbinger of Impressionism; Jules Bastien-Lepage (1848–84), French realist painter, much disliked by WBY (see *Aut*, 125, 168–70); Josef

There are also the two great pictures by Manet, "The Strolling Musician" and "the portrait of Eva Gonzales";[3] the "Beheading of John the Baptist," by Puvis de Chavannes, considered by him as his masterpiece,[4] and three fine examples of Claude Monet.[5]

Should it be impossible to raise the £30,000 or £40,000 necessary to buy all the pictures, we may at least keep some of the best of them. Some thousands of pounds have been already collected in Ireland; but some of the pictures, including those by Claude Monet and by Manet, so essential to a study of modern art, are to be removed from Ireland unless from £10,000 to £15,000 can be raised before January 7.[6]

It is hoped, however, to get the time extended during which Ireland has the option of purchasing the other pictures.

Donations for the Purchase Fund will be gratefully received by any of us, or by the Hon. Treasurer, Modern Art Gallery, care of the Hibernian Bank, Dublin.

| | |
|---|---|
| JANE BARLOW. | E. O. E. SOMERVILLE. |
| S. H. BUTCHER. | EMILY LAWLESS. |
| AUGUSTA GREGORY. | GEORGE RUSSELL (A.E.). |
| DOUGLAS HYDE. | W. B. YEATS. |
| MARTIN ROSS.[7] | |

Printed letter, the *Irish Times*, 5 January 1905 (6).

Israels (1824–1911), Antoine Mauve (1838–88), and Jacob Maris (1837–99), members of the Hague School, the Dutch counterpart of the Barbizon group, dedicated to the representation of realist landscapes and peasant life.

[3] The French artist Édouard Manet (1832–83) was associated with the Impressionists, and developed the technique of *peinture claire*, which achieved rich qualities by working darker tones into passages of light pigment while they were still wet. This technique is seen to effect in *The Strolling Musician*, usually known as *Le Concert aux Tuileries* (1860), which depicts the leading artists, writers, and musicians of the Second Empire — including Baudelaire, Gautier, Offenbach, and Manet himself — listening to music in the Tuileries gardens, and in *Mademoiselle Éva Gonzalès* (1870), a full-length portrait of Manet's young pupil seated painting at an easel in a flowing white dress. In his essay 'The Tragic Theatre' (*E & I*, 242), WBY recalls that he could not understand 'the new French painting . . . until Sir Hugh Lane brought the *Eva Gonzales* to Dublin'. According to Thomas Bodkin (*Hugh Lane*, [1934], plate XLII), Lane acquired his Manets from Durand-Ruel in 1906 in exchange for pictures by Lancret and Gainsborough.

[4] Pierre Puvis de Chavannes (1824–98), a French symbolist and mural painter, was one of WBY's favourite artists in the 1890s. In his *The Martyrdom of St John the Baptist* (*c.* 1870), which was acquired by Lane in 1906, St John kneels in the centre of the composition, stripped to the waist, while on the left the Executioner has raised his sword, ready to behead him. On the right is a group comprising a seated weeping girl, Salome standing and holding a platter, and a steward.

[5] Claude Oscar Monet (1840–1926) was by 1905 already acknowledged as the most important of the French Impressionists. Among the three fine examples of his work owned by Lane was *Vétheuil, Sunshine and Snow* (1881), which depicts a row of small cottages facing a line of bare trees beside a river where two small boats are moored.

[6] For obvious reasons, the words after the semicolon were omitted in the printed circular.

[7] Jane Barlow (1857–1917), a popular novelist and short-story writer, was best known for her *Bog-Land Studies* (1891) and *Irish Idylls* (1892), which went into numerous editions; Samuel Henry Butcher (1850–1910), the classical scholar and former Professor of Greek at Edinburgh University, had published his influential *Aristotle's Theory of Poetry and Fine Art* (1895) and collaborated with Andrew Lang on a prose translation of *The Odyssey*; Douglas Hyde (1860–1949; see I. 493–5) wrote in Irish and

## *To Maud Gonne,* [*9 January 1905*]

Mention in next letter and in a letter from MG, 'Tuesday' [10 January 1905]. Commiserating with her over her marital difficulties,[1] telling her that he and May Clay[2] think the terms she has offered MacBride are too generous, offering to come to Paris to help her,[3] and telling her that the opening of the Abbey Theatre has been a success.[4]

*G–YL*, 184–5.

was co-founder and president of the Gaelic League; 'Martin Ross' (Violet Martin, 1862–1915) and Edith Oenone Somerville (1858–1949), who wrote popular novels and short stories under the joint pseudonym 'Somerville and Ross', had achieved success with *The Real Charlotte* (1894) and celebrity with *Some Experiences of an Irish RM* (1898); the Hon. Emily Lawless (1845–1913), novelist and poet, was best known for *Hurrish* (1886), *Grania* (1892), *Malecho* (1895), and her volume of poems *With the Wild Geese* (1902). George Russell, who wrote under the pseudonym AE (1867–1935; see I. 509–11), attended the Metropolitan School of Art with WBY and became one of his closest friends. He had joined the Irish Agricultural Organization Society in 1897, and was to be appointed editor of the *Irish Homestead* later this year.

[1] WBY's long-standing devotion to Maud Gonne (MG, 1865–1953; see I. 488–92) had received a devastating shock when in February 1903 she married Major John MacBride (1865–1916), but by later that spring he already knew that the marriage was unhappy (see III. 314–17, 356–7, 359). The relationship, however, had deteriorated rapidly after the birth of their son Séan on 26 Jan 1904, and on 25 Nov 1904, while MG was away from their home in Paris, MacBride returned to Ireland, leaving an offensive letter telling her that their marriage was over. Despite this, they continued to correspond, and even arranged to meet in Dublin on 18 Dec, but MG went to London instead, where she and her solicitor informed MacBride's brother Anthony that they were preparing a document which would require MacBride to admit his marital transgressions and agree to live in America for the rest of his life. MacBride, summoned by his brother, arrived in London on 21 Dec and arranged to meet his wife at the house of Barry O'Brien, an Irish lawyer and journalist, the following day. Advised by O'Brien, he refused to sign the deed of separation and negotiations over this continued for several weeks. In the meantime MG returned to Paris on 2 Jan, and on 7 Jan her solicitor, Philip Witham, wrote to tell her (*G–YL*, 184) that the 'whole position is a very unpleasant and very serious one and I should have been very glad if you could have got some friend whom you trust to go over the whole thing again for you and finally decide on your course of action. If you decide to have a judicial separation you had better make up your mind as soon as you can because evidently your husband grasps at every concession and uses them to try and get new terms.' MG immediately asked her cousin May Clay to see WBY and explain the situation to him. The negotiations over her divorce dragged on throughout the year and were ultimately unsuccessful, although MG was eventually granted a legal separation. Among the numerous poems written in dejection in the months and years following the marriage is a bitter quatrain in WBY's 1909 diary (*Mem*, 145): 'My dear is angry that of late | I cry all base blood down | As though she had not taught me hate | By <kindness> kisses to a clown.'

[2] Mrs Mary Kemble (May) Clay, née Gonne (1863–1929), MG's cousin, had married N. S. Bertie-Clay, an English civil servant, in May 1902. She trained as a nurse and frequently cared for MG when she was ill, became guardian of MG's illegitimate daughter Iseult when MG married John MacBride, and later shared MG's house near Calvados in Normandy.

[3] WBY's letter is now lost, but MG was grateful for it, replying on 10 Jan (*G–YL*, 184): 'It is generous & it is like you & I am very glad to get it.' She dissuaded him from coming to Paris because of her husband's jealous insinuations.

[4] The Abbey Theatre (see III. 694–6) had opened for the first time on 27 Dec 1904 with productions of WBY's *On Baile's Strand* and *Cathleen ni Houlihan* (alternating with Synge's *The Shadow of the Glen*), and AG's *Spreading the News*. Both the Theatre and this programme, which ran until 3 Jan 1905, were enthusiastically welcomed by the audiences and by the Irish and English press (see III. 690). In her reply MG said she was 'so glad the theatre was so successful. I longed to be in Dublin for the opening.'

## To Lady Gregory, [9 January 1905]

18 Woburn Buildings | Euston Road.
Monday

*Private*

My dear Lady Gregory: very miserable news has waited me here. I went to M^rs^ Clays[1]—her sister a Miss Gonne took the children out of the room[2]—& M^rs^ Clay began to tell me about M^rs^ MacBrides affairs—which they are trying to keep quiet. MacBride has been a half insane brute from the very first. On one occassion he kicked his wife in a drunken fury.[3] He has carried on with the servants & now at last "there has been a very serious offence and the children cannot be trusted with him" & M^rs^ MacBride came to London three weeks ago to start divorce proceedings. I cannot imagine what the final offence has been—but it has evidently been very serious.[4] M^rs^ MacBride suffered all the rest in silence, defending him always. She went to

[1] Mrs Clay lived at 39 Alexandra Court, 171 Queensgate, London, SW. The 'Miss Gonne' was her sister and MG's cousin Katherine (Chotie) Gonne (1861–1931). AG had long known that MG's marriage was unhappy; as early as 5 May 1903 WBY had told her of MG's confession that she had married 'in a sudden impulse of anger', and that she was already repenting it (III. 356–7).

[2] MG's surviving children were Iseult Gonne (1894–1954), whose father was Lucien Millevoye and to whom WBY was to propose marriage in 1916 and 1917, and MacBride's son Séan MacBride (1904–88), barrister, statesman, and leader of organizations for peace and human rights. He served as Irish Minister for External Affairs from 1948 to 1951, and received the Nobel Peace Prize in 1974. Another son, Georges, had died as an infant in 1891.

[3] This was alleged to have taken place on 25 Dec 1903, shortly before the birth of her son, when, according to MG's legal petition (NLI), 'Mr. MacBride entered the conjugal domicile in a state of absolute shameful drunkenness, accompanied by one of his friends [Vance Thompson] in a similar condition; they dined, drank champagne, and at the end of the repast Mr. MacBride was so drunk that he could not stand upright. He picked a quarrel with his friend and was looking in his pocket for a revolver when the petitioner intervened and succeeded, after having received several kicks from her husband, in dragging him into the bedroom where he went to bed dressed.'

[4] These allegations were spelt out in the petition MG presented to the Civil Tribunal in Paris on 9 Aug this year (NLI):

> 6. Mr. MacBride made obscene propositions to the cook and his attitude towards her was most improper; one day, viz: at the end of the first fortnight in October, in the absence of his wife, his attitude was downright coarse, he went as far as to brutalise the cook Mrs. B. and tried to outrage her.
> 7. Mr. MacBride continued to persecute the cook [Joséphine Pillon] with his compromising attentions and two or three days after he made her come up to his bedroom at 9 o'clock at night with a letter which he had recommended her to bring as it was very hurried. Mr. MacBride was in bed and quite naked. He threw himself on Mrs. B., seized her by the throat and tried again to outrage her.
> 8. He made to Miss M.B.D. [Mary Barry Delaney], governess, the same obscene propositions and on several occasions tried to get into the bedroom which she occupied in the neighbourhood of the Trocadero.

MG also alleged a sexual relationship between MacBride and MG's illegitimate 17-year-old half-sister Eileen Wilson, who subsequently married MacBride's elder brother Joseph. Her petition to the Civil Tribunal maintained that MacBride 'was so audacious and cynical that he even went so far as to compromise a young girl, Miss E . . . W . . . to whom his petitioner had shown hospitality, and in the

the family lawyer[5]—beleiving divorce necessary for the childrens sake. Then Barry O Brien came. For the sake of the country there must be no divorce & so on—the Mac Bride legend must keep its lustre.[6] He dominated everybody including M[rs] Mac Bride—whose will seems to be gone—& got a deed of seperation drawn up in which M[rs] MacBride undertakes to keep the child in Ireland nine months of every year that MacBride may see it once a month.[7] Mean while Mac Bride on whom his wife settled a capital sum enough to give him a hundred a year, at the marr[i]age, is living on her capital drinking hard & generally going to the devil. <The family>M[rs] Clay

absence of his wife at Colleville, namely, during the summer of 1903 he had adulterous relations with her.' The 'very serious' final offence was that MacBride had allegedly indecently exposed himself to MG's 10-year-old illegitimate daughter Iseult.

[5] The family lawyer was Philip Witham (1843–1921), a partner in the firm of Roskell, Witham, Munster, & Weld, Solicitors, at 1 Gray's Inn Square, who looked after the Gonne Trust.

[6] R. Barry O'Brien (1847–1918), Irish barrister, historian, journalist, and writer. Born in Co. Clare, he was called to the Irish Bar in 1874 and the English Bar in 1875, and practised for a short time as a barrister in England before moving into politics and literature. He was on the editorial staff of the *Speaker*, a Liberal weekly paper published in London to which WBY had occasionally contributed, and he wrote a number of works on Irish history, including *The Autobiography of Wolfe Tone* (1893). O'Brien remained faithful to Parnell after 1890, acting for a period as his unofficial private secretary, and in 1898 he published an influential two-volume biography of him, *The Life of Charles Stewart Parnell 1846–1891*. WBY knew and admired O'Brien through the ILS and various political societies, and they had met frequently in the 1890s. O'Brien took an enthusiastic interest in the Irish drama and helped to arrange the visits of the INTS to London in 1903 and 1905. MacBride went to see O'Brien almost immediately after his arrival in London on 22 Dec and O'Brien told him 'that at all hazards public scandal ought, if possible, to be avoided'. When MacBride started to refute MG's charges, 'Mr O'Brien refused to listen to any details. He said "I am not in a position to judge on this matter, all that I see is that there has been a grave quarrel between you and your wife, that you must separate and that this separation must be brought about without a public scandal. My interest is Ireland." ' When MG saw O'Brien on the following day she again refused to listen to any of the allegations against MacBride, but insisted that there should be a separation not a divorce, and that 'the first thing to be done must be to avoid public scandal, both you and your husband must think of Ireland'. O'Brien then went to see Philip Witham (who happened to be a great personal friend of his), and persuaded him that a separation without scandal was the best course. Over the following week both lawyers and their clients deliberated over the deed of separation, the chief issue being the upbringing of Séan MacBride. O'Brien put his views on the separation in a letter to MG of 1 Jan (NLI): 'Take care that you do not allow yourself to be dominated by English political and family influences in a matter where the interests of our country are concerned. This is no ordinary case of differences between husband and wife. Were it so the charges and countercharges made by you and your husband against each other would call for no interference from me. But this is a case in which Irish National considerations must be taken into account. Therefore I cannot regard with indifference the prospect of seeing you and your husband made the subjects of ridicule and contempt by the press of this country.' He went on to insist that they were 'bound to think of the Irish cause with which you have been for so many years associated. Those who undertake public duties have public obligations. Your husband recognized this fact. You will recognize it too—if you are true to Ireland.'

[7] Philip Witham had sent O'Brien MG's deed of separation on 3 Jan 1905. The document did not go into the reasons for the separation and was almost entirely concerned with the custody, upbringing, and education of Séan MacBride. In a covering note, Witham said that if MacBride 'refuses there is an end of it and they must fight it out', but on 6 Jan MacBride insisted on countering with demands of his own. MG's conditions stated that Séan MacBride was to be under her entire control until he reached the age of 10, that he was to be raised as a Catholic and a nationalist at her expense, that he was to live for at least nine months every year in Ireland, that MacBride should have access to him once a month when in

beleives that the settlement is a great mistake, & is even afraid that it may lead
to a personal attack on M^{rs} Mac Bride or some other disgraceful scene. She
even I imagine fears for her life. She thinks the only solution is a divorce or
Mac Bride going to America for good. Mac Bride has replied to the divorce
proposal by threatening to publish the Milvoye episode.[8] M^{rs} Clay (& I
conclude the family generaly) think that this should be risked. I have written
supporting her advice. A frightful scandal, seems inevitable sooner or later
but the brave course seems generaly the best. M^{rs} MacBride being a catholic
complicates things as they object to divorce.[9] It will [be] a frightful business
but anything seems better than a drunken & violent father. MacBride has
been furiously je[a]lous to add to the general mess.

    The whole thing has made me very wretched but has awakened nothing
of the old fealing—a little to my surprize—no fealing but pity & anger.
M^{rs} Clay tells me that M^{rs} MacBride is quite friendless in Paris—she has
not seen Milvoye since her marriage.[10] She thinks that if she could have
gone to Dublin & seen Russell & myself all might have been well but Mac
Bride was there. She went to Paris a week ago. I feal, as I always feal about
these things—that strength shapes the world about itself, & that weakness
is shaped about the world—& that the compromise is weekness.

    Do not speak of these things to any one.

    I have got scenery from Pixie Smith. I saw her last night.[11]

Yrs alway<br>W B Yeats

ALS Berg, with envelope addressed to Coole, postmark 'LONDON JA 9 05'.

Ireland, and that MacBride should renounce all rights to MG's property. MacBride acceded to most of
these demands but wanted MG's sole custody to extend only to the age of 8, and insisted that he should
have access to his son once a fortnight, not once a month. MacBride sent his draft to Barry O'Brien on 6
Jan with the gloss that ten years was too long to leave the child under the control of his mother, and that
he had given way on a number of points 'in order to prevent the possibility of any scandal arising from
public recriminations between my wife and myself'. And he ended his letter with the 'hope that I have
now seen the last of this dramatic lady'.

  [8] Lucien Millevoye (1850–1918), French Boulangist deputy, political journalist, and editor of *La
Patrie*, had become MG's lover in 1888 and she bore him two children, Georges and Iseult (see p. 7,
n. 2). The affair had come to an end in 1898, when he took up with an actress, whom, to MG's indignation,
he introduced to Iseult. Despite its length, MG's relationship with Millevoye was not generally known in
Ireland or England, although MacBride was to make much of it in his counter-petition.

  [9] Much to WBY's alarm, and against his urging, MG had become a Catholic on 17 Feb 1903, shortly
before her marriage to MacBride; see III. 314.

  [10] In fact, MG still had a number of loyal friends in Paris, including the journalist and feminist Mme
Ghénia Avril (1856–1939) and the Irish journalist Mary Barry Delaney (d. 1947). In his counter-
petition MacBride alleged (NLI) that MG had seen Millevoye on a number of occasions after their
marriage, and had even suggested inviting him to their house.

  [11] Corinne Pamela Colman ('Pixie') Smith (1878–1951), artist, stage designer, book illustrator, and
folklorist, was born in London of American parents, but grew up in Jamaica. As a young girl she had
toured with the Irving company, and she remained close to the Terry–Craig circle, Ellen Terry giving

## *To Lady Gregory, [11 January 1905]*

18 Woburn Buildings

My dear Friend: I have just come from M^rs Clay, who at M^rs Mac Brides request has told me all. I feal as if I had been through a circle of Hell with no peaceful <Dante> Virgil by my side.[1] I may not tell you now, what that most serious offence was—I can but say that the blackest thing you can imagine will probably be the truth.[2] M^rs Mac Bride, who was, I now beleive, genuinely in love with Mac Bride is utterly crushed & humiliated.[3] I am urging her to anul all steps she has taken up to this & leave the affair in the hands of some person chosen by M^rs Clay & myself. I am utterly certain that she must get divorce or legal seperation, with entire control of her child—divorce if possible. I shall urge this on her ceaselessly. <The worst of> Some person other than M^rs Mac Bride should see lawyers <& have all in their hands> etc. The worst of it is that my hands are rather tied, as Mac Bride has made a serious [*for* series] of lying counter charges—in which as you can well imagine I am involved.[4] <Mac Bride seems> I have seen a

---

her the nickname 'Pixie' (see II. 429–30). She studied art at the Pratt Institute, New York, in the mid-1890s, executed stage designs for *The Countess Cathleen* in the summer of 1899, and was currently designing the scenery for Synge's *The Well of the Saints*. She collaborated with Jack Yeats on *A Broad Sheet*, and edited *The Green Sheaf* (1903–4). Her interest in WBY's methods of chanting poetry led her to join FF's 'psaltery people'; she helped illustrate one of his lectures at Cliffords Inn in May 1903, and, as a member of the 'Chelsea Mummers', played the Faery Child in a production of *Land of Heart's Desire* on 22 Mar and 4 June 1904, reciting the part 'after the manner of an Irish lilt'. She later impressed small New York audiences by chanting WBY's poetry in the Farr manner. In later life she moved to Cornwall, where she remained until her death.

[1] In her letter of 10 Jan (see p. 6, n. 3) MG had told WBY that she was instructing Mrs Clay to 'tell you the whole story, you will be able to judge then better of the situation & understand why for the children's sake as well as from an Irish point of view I wish this thing if possible kept out of court'. WBY's perception of Dante's journey through hell, guided by Virgil, was largely mediated by the drawings of William Blake, 'the one perfectly fit illustrator for the *Inferno*' (see *E & I*, 144).

[2] i.e. MacBride's alleged indecent exposure to Iseult; in her letter of 10 Jan MG asked WBY to 'be careful not to tell others. It is so serious I think you will be.'

[3] In an interview with MG on 30 Dec (NLI) O'Brien had attacked her for going straight to an English lawyer instead of first giving MacBride an opportunity of answering the allegations against him, and had pointed out that if the case came to court in England the details of her liaison with Millevoye, as well as the allegations of her affairs with other lovers, would become notorious: 'you will be cross-examined on every incident of your life, and let me tell you, Mrs MacBride, that you will come out of this case thoroughly besmirched.' The following day, against the advice of both lawyers, she saw MacBride at O'Brien's house, broke down, and compromised her position, explaining later to O'Brien that her nerves had 'been terribly overstrained lately'.

[4] In his depositions, MacBride maintained that 'most of her [MG's] complaints were absolutely false. The origin of all difference between us was my wife's efforts to force her ex-lovers on me. She had no conception of delicacy and no idea of truth.' He alleged (NLI) that he had never wanted to marry MG, and only did so at her tearful supplication that it would be good for Ireland and for her, that from the day of their marriage she wanted to keep up a correspondence with her ex-lovers and bring them to the house, that she had confessed to being the mistress of three different men, by one of whom she had had

letter of Mac Brides which seems to contain the essence of all the cads of all ages.[5] The worst of it is that part of M$^{rs}$ MacBrides case is a charge of such an unspeakable nature, that it seems hardly possible to bring it into court— certainly not unless it can be heard in camera (& this a genuine secresy) for others are involved. I feal I am rather incoherent but I have really had a shock over this business. The state of matters at this moment is that Mac Bride (who is full [*for* fool] enough to hesitate) has been given until Saturday to sign that too generous settlement. I want M$^{rs}$ Mac Bride to withdraw the option.

Yr ev

W B Yeats

ALS Berg, with envelope addressed to Coole, postmark 'LONDON JA 11 05'.

## To Lady Gregory, [*12 January 1905*]

18 Woburn Buildings | Euston Road.

My dear Lady Gregory: I saw O Brien last night. MacBride has not signed, & he beleives will not sign "the settlement" so that is out of the way & M$^{rs}$ Mac Bride will take steps to get a legal seperation at any rate.[1] Mac Bride charged, in speaking to O Brien, three people with having been her lovers, besides Milvoye. The three are an unnamed man (probably Stead) Chi-

two illegitimate children and two miscarriages, that she had visited a brothel in Marseilles with Millevoye, and that she had met WBY surreptitiously in London a few months after her marriage. In her letter of 10 Jan MG told WBY that MacBride was 'insinuating that every man who has ever been a friend of mine, is a lover'.

[5] This was probably the letter that MacBride left to await MG's return to Paris in late November, telling her that their marriage was over. Even in his own deposition (NLI), he admitted that the letter was a mistake: 'It was a foolish letter to write and annoyed her considerably. In a nutshell it amounted to this—That our life was not a happy one owing to her being unable to rise above a certain level. That it was very painful to me to see that she was only the weak [im]itation of a weak man. I also advised her in case I was hanged or died in prison to get married again, [as] she was a woman that could not live without some man or other behind her; that it was better for her if she was really interested in the cause of Ireland to be married, even if she were a little unhappy, than to live an impure life.' MacBride added that it 'was a letter I should not have written: but she had made life simply intolerable by her complete lack of all womanly delicacy, by constantly lying, and by trying to force her ex-lovers on me. In her first letter to Westport she complained of the above mentioned letter and said she would have it out with me when we met.'

[1] On 6 Jan O'Brien had called on Witham with MacBride's latest terms, but Witham warned him (NLI) that he was sure MG would not agree to them as she was 'now in Paris and she has been finding out other things and is less favourable to agreement'. On 9 Jan he wrote to tell O'Brien that, as he had anticipated, 'Mrs MacBride will agree to no alteration at all in the terms. I will treat them as open for acceptance until Saturday. After that please consider them as withdrawn.' O'Brien replied that he could 'do no more in the matter', and so the negotiations ended.

priani & myself.[2] O Brien told him it was baseless in my case (as "that kind of thing never seemed to interest Yeats")[3] & thinks he put it out of his head—which I doubt. My plan is for M[rs] Mac Bride to press on her case, get her evidence ready & then for someone—D[r] Mark Ryan[4] perhaps—to be shown it, or told enough of it to make it obvious that Mac Bride must dissappear. M[rs] MacBride *seems* prepared to admit the Milvoye affair if necessary, denying the lying stories—she can be cross examined on all her past life with a view to credit. But one must do everything to keep Mac Bride from opposing at all, if possible. He should go to America. I shall want to talk over it all with you very soon. The worst of it is that MacBride is evidently a very reckless character. I have another plan which I do not

---

[2] William Thomas Stead (1849–1912), journalist, editor of the *Pall Mall Gazette* (1883–90), and founder of the *Review of Reviews* (1890), met MG in Russia in 1887. In *SQ* she recalled him (80) as 'a man with puritanical beliefs constantly warring with a sensual temperament, which induced in him a sex obsession'. In an article in the *Review of Reviews* of 25 Jan 1892 (4) he described her as 'one of the most beautiful women in the world. She is an Irish heroine, born a Protestant, who became a Buddhist, with theories of pre-existence, who in all her pilgrimings from shrine to shrine, never ceased to cherish a passionate devotion to the cause of Irish independence. . . . Everywhere her beauty and her enthusiasm naturally make a great impression.' They met intermittently in following years, but the relationship foundered. Stead shared WBY's interest in spiritualism and the occult. He perished on the *Titanic*.

Amilcare Cipriani (1844–1918), Italian revolutionary, had joined Garibaldi's forces, after which he emigrated to Greece and then to Egypt, engaging in revolutionary activity in both countries. In 1870 he went to Paris to fight in the Franco-Prussian War, distinguishing himself at the Battle of Montretout, after which he was offered (and refused) 'La Croix'. He then joined the Communards, and was imprisoned and deported to New Caledonia. Freed in 1881, he returned to Italy where he was condemned to twenty-five years in jail but was released in 1888 after a public protest. He moved to Paris, but in 1897 fought on the Greek side in a brief uprising against the Turks. He had become a close friend of MG's in Paris in the early 1890s (*SQ*, 171–2) and accepted her invitation to help with the 1798 centenary commemorations. WBY recalled him (*Aut*, 410) as a 'magnificent-looking old man . . . Maud Gonne had brought him to Ireland to work out a scheme for insurrection, then to some London Irish to make his report.' He thought Cipriani 'the handsomest man [he had] ever seen' and was impressed with his remark, 'As for me, I believe in nothing but cannon' (*Aut*, 370).

[3] O'Brien was wrong; in *Mem* (71– 2) WBY recalled that during the years of his unsuccessful wooing of MG: 'I was tortured by sexual desire. . . . I knew that my friends had all mistresses of one kind or another and that most, at need, went home with harlots. . . . At Hammersmith I saw a woman of the town walking up and down in the empty railway station. I thought of offering myself to her, but the old thought came back, "No, I love the most beautiful woman in the world".' Although O'Brien did not believe that WBY had had adulterous relations with MG, it did not deter him from using the allegation of her liaisons to cow her into submission during their interview on 30 Dec (see p. 10, n. 3): 'whether they occurred or not, a suspicion will hang over you regarding them. Now mark the dragging in of the name of B [i.e. WBY] would be a very serious thing for him; he is a young man and it will be a misfortune to have his career destroyed serving Ireland as he does; you will be asked about him; your husband will swear to this statement, he probably will be called; just think of the scandal and the ruin that all means.'

[4] Dr Mark Ryan (1844–1940), a Fenian agent and London physician, was a close friend of John O'Leary, through whom WBY had met him in the late 1880s. A founder-member of the ILS and the Gaelic League, he was active in numerous Irish societies in London, and a member of the Supreme Council of the Irish Republican Brotherhood. His autobiography, *Fenian Memories*, appeared in 1945. He was a long-time friend of both MG and MacBride, whose brother, Dr Anthony MacBride, was his trusted partner and locum in several London medical practices. As a high-ranking Fenian and a friend of both parties, Ryan's intervention would have been a powerful factor, but he, like John O'Leary, sided with John MacBride and refused to adjudicate.

care to write—it may be impossible, but if possible I will need your help in it.[5]

I am sorry you are still so ill you seemed better in Dublin.[6]

Yours affectionately

W B Yeats

ALS Berg, with envelope addressed to Coole, postmark 'LONDON JA 12 05'.

## *To Constance Masefield,*[1] *12 January 1905*

18 Woburn Buildings, | Euston Road.

Jan. 12th, | 05.

*dictated*

My dear M[rs] Masefield,

I am afraid that I have left your letter a long time unanswered, but I have been in a whirl of varying occupations. I am here in London but only for a few days & short as the time is, so much work which requires the seeing of many people, has come upon me, that I cannot hope to get down to Greenwich for the present.[2]

---

[5] Presumably WBY's 'wild project' for getting MacBride out of the country (see p. 19); although he may have been hoping that AG might allow MG and her children to take refuge at Coole: he was to make a similar suggestion in 1920, when he proposed that Iseult Gonne might go to Coole during a rift in her marriage to Francis Stuart.

[6] A severe bout of illness—fever, headaches, neuralgia, and coughs—had prevented AG attending the opening of the Abbey in late December 1904, and had persisted well into the new year. Nevertheless, she had gamely come up to Dublin in the first week of January, and informed Quinn on 9 Jan (NYPL) that she was 'home again, very well pleased with what I saw of the plays—the last 3 nights—for they were beautifully acted & very well received . . . I gave the players a party on the last night, at the picture gallery.'

[1] Constance Masefield, née Crommelin (1867–1960), came from a Co. Antrim family, and had been a Senior Optime in the Cambridge Mathematical Tripos. She had married John Masefield in July 1903, but WBY found her views opinionated and her manner overbearing, and thought her argumentative influence had impaired Masefield's creativity, writing to Jack Yeats in 1912 (Anne Yeats): 'I find him surrounded with such a crew of female political economists & emotional journalists—forced on him by his wife I suppose. His friends are no longer the people who know & have taste—& I think few men who live with their inferiors keep their critical capacity.' This antipathy is probably partly responsible for his refusal of her invitation, although his preoccupation with MG's marital problems would have made any visit extremely difficult at this time. John Masefield (1878–1967), the poet, novelist, and dramatist, had met WBY in the autumn of 1900 (see II. 595–6).

[2] In October 1904 the Masefields took a semi-detached Regency house at 1 Diamond Terrace, Greenwich. Masefield, working as a journalist in Manchester and making occasional visits to Greenwich, had written to WBY (*LWBY* I. 144) that they were going to live in 'a little lonely house not very far from the river, and I hope that sometimes, when there are some fine ships to see, you will come with me to see them'.

I shall be at home on Monday evening[3] & if either you or your husband or both of you happen to be in town, I hope that you will come in. I would ask you to dinner but an Astrologer bursting with some message from the stars has written that he must see me & he will need the room to himself till the message is delivered.[4]

Yrs sinrly
W B Yeats

Dict AEFH, signed WBY; Texas.

## To Maud Gonne, [c. *12 January 1905*]

Mention in letter from MG, 'Friday' [13 January 1905].
Telling her that Mrs Clay has told him all the facts about MacBride's behaviour,[1] that he is rallying support for her,[2] that he has seen Barry O'Brien

---

[3] WBY had started his weekly 'Monday Evenings', during which he kept informal open house, shortly after he moved into Woburn Buildings in February 1896 (see II. 8); they became a permanent feature of his London life, and he continued to hold them when he moved to Oxford and Dublin.

[4] The astrologer was probably William Thomas Horton (1864–1919, see II. 683–6), mystic and artist. WBY had been introduced to him in late 1895 by Aubrey Beardsley, and the two remained friends until Horton's death. WBY wrote an introduction to his volume of drawings *A Book of Images* (1898), and recalls him in 'All Soul's Night' (*VP*, 471) as one who 'loved strange thought'. He regularly brought WBY horoscopes, and often attended WBY's Monday Evenings.

[1] As well as giving WBY an oral report on 11 Jan (see p. 10), May Clay had also, on the same day, sent him a letter (Emory) repeating the main charges against MacBride, explaining that MG had asked her 'to write more fully about her troubles, so that you may understand them, without her having to make you the very painful explanations': 'On one of her returns to Paris, Maud was told that MacBride owing I suppose to drink had given way to most indecent conduct, & had been very careless in the arrangement of his clothes (with intention) & spoken to Miss Delany while in this state, on indecent subjects, & had tried to go to her room at night. But what is worse, he had allowed Iseult to come into his rooms, when his clothes were disarranged, & asked her to come up & play with him in a most disgusting way. The poor little girl's modesty was terribly upset, & he added to her horror, when she tried to escape by terrifying her with threats. This is a criminal charge, & in France means at least 2 years imprisonment. But this would mean exposing the fact whose child Iseult is, & also a bad scandal for the child herself, which is what frightens & hampers Maud. Since all this came out, other terrible stories have been told against him. The servants werent safe, & the cook was attacked in the same indecent fashion as de Lainey [*sic*] & Iseult. & another very bad story he tempted Eileen Wilson, successfully, when she was engaged to his brother, & who she has now married. It was very bad of Eileen for she has to thank Maud for all the advantages she has had in making such a good start in life. She was the natural daughter of Maud's father, & though at his death my Father & Uncle were willing to help her, they would only have brought her up to service, but Maud intervened, & had her brought up by an old servant at whose death, Maud took Eileen into her own house. Then lots of nasty details, & tales of his being drunk, & Maud helping him to bed, & dreadful things like that, but I think I have told you the most important.'
She added that MG intended to take action for a judicial separation if MacBride had not signed the Deed of Separation by Saturday, but that she thought 'Maud makes a mistake in not getting a complete divorce, as all the scandals will be let loose by him, in any case'.
In her reply to the present letter, MG told WBY: 'I am glad you know all. Thank you for your letter & thank you for all the trouble you are taking for me.'

[2] Besides enlisting AG's help, WBY was to encourage John Quinn and AEFH to gather evidence on MG's behalf, as well as championing her cause among mutual acquaintances in London and Dublin.

on her behalf, who revealed that MacBride has not accepted the terms she is offering, and telling her that he is sending a copy of *Samhain* to her.[3]

*G–YL*, 136–7.

## *A. P. Watt to the Editor of the* Metropolitan Magazine, *12 January 1905*

January 12, 1905.

(Copy)
R. H. Russell Esq.,
    "The Metropolitan Magazine",[1]
        3, West 29th Street,
            NEW YORK, U.S.A.

Dear Mr. Russell,

I take pleasure in sending you herewith, per book post registered, typewritten 'copy' of a new article by Mr. W. B. Yeats entitled "AMERICA AND THE ARTS".[2]

As at present arranged this article will be published in this country in 'The Fortnightly Review' on a date hereafter to be fixed and of which I would of course give you due notice.[3] I shall be glad to hear that you are willing to purchase the American serial rights for use, on or shortly after the date upon which it will be published in 'The Fortnightly Review' in 'The Metropolitan Magazine' and on terms likely to be satisfactory to the author.[4]

[3] The 1904 edition of the annual theatrical periodical *Samhain*, published in December, marked the opening of the Abbey Theatre and, constituting a manifesto of WBY's thinking on the theatre, was the fullest of the whole series. It contained WBY's notes on 'The Dramatic Movement', his essays on 'First Principles' and 'The Play, the Player, and the Scene', the texts of Synge's *In the Shadow of the Glen* and AG's *The Rising of the Moon*, as well as AEFH's letter offering the Abbey Theatre to the INTS. In her reply, MG acknowledged receipt of the magazine, although she had 'not read it yet—but it looks very interesting—I shall read it tonight'.

[1] Robert Howard Russell (*c.*1846–1916) was the publisher of the *Metropolitan Magazine*, a popular monthly which had been founded in 1895. At first dedicated to social gossip, topical feature articles, and numerous pictures of glamorous young women, it grew more serious from 1898.

[2] WBY had been eager to place his article 'America and the Arts' (*UP* II. 338–42) on both sides of the Atlantic since the previous July. Giving an account of his impressions of America during his lecturing tour there from November 1903 to March 1904, he considered it 'a good article', and had first suggested that Watt might send it to *McClure's Magazine* (see III. 669).

[3] In fact, although the *Fortnightly Review* had offered 6 guineas for the article on 31 Oct. 1904, it never appeared there, nor in any other British or Irish journal.

[4] The *Metropolitan Magazine* paid WBY $40 for the article. Quinn, who read an advance copy of the April number, told WBY on 21 Mar 1905 (Himber, 70) that he thought it 'a very good and all too-short article. You saw the best side of this country—the other side is seamy enough but it is one of the privileges of the artist and the poet to overlook or ignore the seamy sides.'

Please note that this offer is made subject to your taking all such steps as may be necessary properly to secure Mr. Yeats' American copyright in his own name and to copies of 'The Fortnightly Review' containing the article being exported from this country to the United States and elsewhere as usual.

Awaiting your early decision and trusting that it may be a favourable one,

I am,

Yours sincerely,
(Sgd) A. P. WATT

'Copy' per book
post registered.

TS copy Watt.

## *To A. H. Bullen,*[1] [c. *14 January 1905*]

Mention in following letter and in a letter from Bullen to George Roberts, 30 January 1905.

Asking Bullen for the MS of Synge's *The Well of the Saints*, and impressing on him that the play is not to be published before it has been copyrighted in America, since sales in the theatre would constitute publication.[2]

---

[1] Arthur Henry Bullen (1857–1920), Elizabethan scholar and publisher, had published WBY's *The Celtic Twilight* (1893) and *The Secret Rose* (1897). On 9 Nov 1904 he had written to WBY (TCD) agreeing to publish *The Well of the Saints* by the Irish dramatist John Millington Synge (1871–1909; see III. 731–3), as part of the Plays for an Irish Theatre series, paying a royalty of 15% on the published price. On 14 Jan, Synge had returned the corrected proofs of the first half of the play to him (*JMSCL* I. 104), apologizing for the number of corrections to the stage directions in the first act, and explaining that this was because the copy had been used by the prompter and that 'Mr Yeats promised to send me back this MS. to revise stage-directions etc. before it went to press, but he seems to have forgotten all about it at the last minute'.

[2] It was important that the play should not be published in England or Ireland before it was copyrighted in the USA, as otherwise the American rights would be lost. The text of the play was, in fact, first published by George Roberts in February 1905 from Bullen's sheets in a limited edition for sale in the Abbey Theatre during the first production. Bullen's edition, with an introduction by WBY, did not appear until December this year, partly because the binders mislaid the sheets. In his letter of 30 Jan Bullen warned Roberts (NLI) that even limited publication would compromise the American copyright.

## *To John Quinn,*[1] [*14 January 1905*]

18 Woburn Buildings | Euston Road.
Saturday.

My dear Quinn: I have asked Bullen [for] the MS of Synges play. I want you to get it copyrighted, and send me the bill. There is no time to be lost as we want to publish on Feb 4 or as near to it as we can—that is the date of acting. I hope there will be time. I am afraid it will give you a great deal of trouble.[2]

I am in the midst of the most painful affair of my life. M[rs] MacBride after enduring a horrible life with her husband has suffered the most intolerable wrong & is seeking divorce or seperation. She is stunned, & heartbroken & I am doing what I can about lawyers & so on.[3] Mac Bride seems to have eroto-mania from drink—it is the only thing one can say in his defence. The case will I expect have to be tried in Camera. It is by the by an unimportant incident that he threatened to shoot me some while back.[4] Be discreet about what I tell you. For her childs sake M[rs] MacBride will have to screne [*for* screen] her husbands worst offences & I dont yet know quite what part of the story will have to be made public. The true & full story is unspeakably horrible. I am just writing to Lady Gregory to come to London to advise about lawyers & so on.

Yrs alway
W B Yeats

ALS NYPL, with envelope addressed to 1 West 87 St, New York, postmark 'LONDON. W.C. JA 14 05'.

[1] John Quinn (1870–1924; see III. 728–31), the Irish-American company lawyer and patron of the arts, had first corresponded with WBY in late 1901, and the two met when he visited Dublin in August 1902. Quinn suggested and organized WBY's successful first American lecturing tour in 1903–4, and gave financial assistance to the nascent INTS. He took it upon himself to look after WBY's and the Abbey Theatre's interests in the USA, and had copyrighted a number of plays there, beginning with WBY's *Where There Is Nothing* (see III. 238). At this time he was a junior partner in the firm of Alexander & Colby.

[2] Quinn had fifty paper-covered copies of *The Well of the Saints* privately printed from linotype to secure the American copyright. This edition was registered on 7 Feb 1905.

[3] Quinn also rallied to MG's side and tried to get witnesses to testify to MacBride's drunkenness in New York. He collected depositions from Maire Quinn that she had seen MacBride at the Vanderbilt Hotel 'many times during the month of July 1904, and on nearly every occasion . . . he was more or less intoxicated. On some occasions the said MacBride was so intoxicated that he was maudlin and incoherent in his speech.' But in answer to this, and a deposition from Frank McLaughlin, a cab-driver, who claimed to have seen MacBride drunk or with drink taken on at least twenty occasions in May 1904, MacBride's American lawyers collected twenty-four affidavits, including statements from the manager of the Vanderbilt Hotel and John J. Delany, a retired captain of the New York Police Department, that MacBride was abstemious.

[4] In her letter of 13 Jan (see p. 14), MG had revealed that MacBride was 'insanely jealous & utterly unscrupulous, he has accused, at some time or other, every man who he has ever heard of being my friend or whose photo he has ever seen at my house of having been my lover. On one occasion he told me

## *To Lady Gregory,* [*14 January 1905*]

18 Woburn Buildings

Dear Friend: I am going to put you to a great deal of trouble. I want you to come to London. I will meet you in Dublin on Wednesday unless I wire to the contrary. I will see about Synges scenery & come back here on Thursday. I cannot bear the burden of this terrible case alone—I know nothing about lawyers & so on.[1] I see that I shall have to do a great deal—I have had a letter to day from M$^{rs}$ Mac Bride, which shows that she is utterly broken down. At one moment she asks me about lawyers, at another she begs me 'to keep out of this horrible affair' she 'brought this trouble on herself' she should 'fight it alone' & so on.[2] Her cousin, who is a very charming woman, does not seem to know what to do. You alone can help us all, I think. It will

he had intended to kill you—Even Russell he declared was my lover & that Mrs Russell was mad with jealousy!!' MacBride's unreasonable jealousy was a major charge in MG's case against him; her affidavit to the Civil Tribune of the Seine prepared later this year (NLI) cited 'the jealous, suspicious and violent temper of her husband' and charged that 'his intemperate habits, his unbridled licentiousness, et [*sic*] his unscrupulous immorality constitute a dangerous environment for the petitioner and rendered life with him unsupportable'. Although MacBride's depositions complained that MG had kept up her friendship with Millevoye after her marriage, and displayed pictures of him and WBY in the house, he denied in a document entitled 'Stray Ideas' (Emory) that he was jealous of WBY: 'Why the lady should say I was jealous of Mr Yeats is more than I know for I never bothered my head about the man except to laugh at some of his foolishly mystic writings.' MG, he went on to reveal, had told him that 'before marriage she & Mr Yeats used to indulge in crystal gazing & that they had some wonderful visions. One night in Ireland they visited a cave together and conversed with the fairies.' He was, however, angry that WBY was, as he thought, slandering him: 'Since this case started I have been informed that Mr Yeats is the originator of a number of false & disgusting stories about me in Dublin in connection with the present action. I know for a fact that he tried to poison Mr Barry O'Brien's mind against me.'

[1] In her letter of 13 Jan (see p. 14) MG had implored WBY to help her find a good Irish barrister, since MacBride 'was trying so hard to get political & religious sympathy to cover his vices & is making a great point against me that I have been to an English solicitor, it would be well to get an Irish barrister.... Would you make enquiries & advise me on this matter.... To have a really good counsel <barrister> is necessary, & if you will help me in this you will do me a great service, but apart from this Willie, for your sake for Ireland's sake & for your own work as well as for mine try & keep quite clear of this affair, don't even think of it too much. I know the generosity of your nature makes you want to help me & to defend me but it would only add to my trouble to know your life was touched in any way by this miserable tragedy—That I have your friendship what ever happens is a great comfort to me.' AG did not apparently travel to London, but wrote for advice to her friend, the lawyer Sir William Nevill Montgomerie Geary, whose reply she sent to WBY to transmit to MG. AG also consulted Geary's *The Law of Marriage and Family Relations* (1892), a presentation copy of which he had sent her in June 1893, and marked passages that shed light on the Gonne–MacBride case in chapter VII, 'Dissolution of Marriage', chapter VIII, 'Judicial Separation Protection Order', and chapter XIV, 'Infancy', regarding 'Forfeiture of Parental Rights by Misconduct of Waiver'. On 6 May AG was to complain to Quinn (NYPL) that the 'MacBride affair' had 'killed' WBY's 'own work through a great part of this winter—constant letters asking him to find out this or that, things that wd. have been more fitting for an attorney or a detective'.

[2] In her letter of 13 Jan MG complained that her nerves were 'so shattered by all I have gone through, not only since I knew this horrible thing, but ever since my marriage, where insane scenes of jealousy, & an atmosphere of base intrigue have rendered life almost unbearable—that I find it hard to think out the

probably be legal seperation but that is for the lawyer to say— M^rs Clay is anxious that it should be divorce as she thinks Mac Bride will be on the watch, for any imprudence of M^rs Mac Brides to trump up a case against her—she thinks she will never have any security, especially <as she is incapable of produci>, I dare say, because of her habitual imprudence.[3] M^rs Mac Bride seems indifferent as to whether it is seperation or divorce.[4] There is another reason why it may be necessary to *prepare* a case for divorce—Mac Bride may be got to leave the country & let a seperation suit go by default if threatened with the whole scandal. I think M^rs Mac Bride should *proffess* a readiness to go into the whole case—this <would involve> the whole case would involve him ultimately in a criminal prosecution. I have, what is perhaps a wild project, for the getting of Mac Bride out of the country & about this I rather want to see you *in Dublin.*[5] When you know the story you will feal that if she were the uttermost stranger, if ones bitterest enemy, one would have none the less, even to the putting aside of all else, to help her. You will be a protection to me, though I need hardly say I am not thinking of that. If I am too active it will make him drag my name in of a certainty, as well as perhaps damage her. Mac Bride threatened a while back I hear to shoot me. This is the only cheerful peice of news I have had for days—it gives one a sense of hightened life.

I cannot do the new 'Baile Strand' without your help over the opening conversations.[6] I wish I could attend to those highly intelligent Academicians but I cant know [ *for* now].[7]

Yr alway

W B Yeats

ALS Berg, with envelope addressed to Coole, postmark 'LONDON. W. JA 14 05'.

situation fully.' She went on to thank him for his 'kind letters' and 'generous sympathy', but told him, 'I don't want you to get mixed up in this horrible affair. By my marriage *I brought all this trouble on myself*, and as far as I can I want to fight it alone. This is why I have spoken to none of my friends. Why should they who are engaged on noble work be mixed up with a sordid horror of this sort.'

[3] Even at their first meetings WBY had noticed 'something declamatory, Latin in a bad sense' in MG's behaviour (*Mem*, 41), and in his poem 'A Bronze Head' meditates on the enigma of her character: 'I saw the wildness in her and I thought | A vision of terror that it must live through | Had shattered her soul' (*VP*, 619).

[4] In her letter MG said that events were 'shaping them selves', and that 'the only thing left is to apply for judicial separation or divorce, it seems to me indifferent which. Which ever is easiest to obtain, as I believe both give me complete security for the control of the children.'

[5] WBY never divulged his 'wild scheme', which he quietly abandoned.

[6] In fact, WBY was to subject the whole play to such a radical revision over the coming months that the text printed in *Poems, 1899–1905* has very little in common with that published in *In the Seven Woods* (1903) and the edition of 1904.

[7] The call to establish a Gallery of Modern Art in Dublin (see pp. 4–5) had provoked a vigorous discussion in the Dublin press, as well as opposition from the Royal Hibernian Academy, led by its president Sir Thomas Drew (1838–1910). On 9 Jan the Council of the Academy met to draw up a long

## *To Maud Gonne,* [c. *14 January 1905*]

Mention in letter from MG, 'Monday' [16 January 1905].
Giving an account of his activities on her behalf, sending her a letter from
AG's lawyer about divorce proceedings,[1] telling her that a publishing house
is being started in Ireland,[2] and describing Synge's new play.

*G–YL*, 137.

and pompous 'Statement', giving its views on the subject, and this was published on 11 Jan in the *Irish Times* (9) and the Dublin *Daily Express* (5) at the request of Stephen Catterson Smith (1849–1912), portrait painter and secretary to the Academy. The 'Statement' pointed out that while the Academy was well disposed towards the proposed gallery, Lane's exhibition was not mounted under its auspices, and its members had played no part in selecting the pictures. It went on to classify the pictures under three headings: (1) pictures of great quality and highly desirable in a modern gallery; (2) pictures which, although by great artists, did not represent the full measure of those artists' genius; (3) pictures of negligible quality, which would occupy undue space, and 'which it would not be judicious to accept even if generously offered as gifts'. The statement concluded with an 'appeal to those of the Irish public who have evinced a generous impulse to do a great service to art in Ireland and make it a practicable one, that their contributions should be conditional on a more deliberative procedure than has been advocated by some writers in the Press', and urged that the pictures selected for the gallery 'should be those of pre-eminent and individual fame, selected under associated expert and independent advice, with unhurried judgement, and from wider fields than the sources of this Exhibition'. It also advocated that such deliberative selection should take some 'works of artists of Irish origin'. The frequent references to Lane's 'enthusiasm' created the impression that he was a headstrong and injudicious arbiter of value, and the statement could not fail to dampen the interest in the pictures that he had aroused. AG had evidently asked WBY to join in the controversy.

[1] Many of the letters that AG wrote to WBY at this time are missing, and were probably destroyed by AG or WBY as revealing too much of the MacBride scandal. But it is evident that AG asked Sir William Geary for advice (see p. 18, n. 1), and sent on a letter in which he advocated suing for divorce not separation, and doing so in France, not England or Ireland. The advice was probably close to that he gave in chapter VII of his *The Law of Marriage and Family Relations* (which AG had marked in her copy): 'If the husband has only been guilty of adultery alone, and his wife obtains a judicial separation in consequence, she runs the risk of never being able to turn her remedy into a dissolution; for *ex necessitate rei* after a judicial separation a husband cannot be guilty of cruelty or desertion, and subsequent simple adultery, not incestuous or bigamous, will give her no further rights. In fact, in such a case, unless the husband commits the somewhat unusual matrimonial offences of incestuous adultery, bigamy, and adultery or sodomy, she will never be able to obtain solution. But it is a wise and prudent course for a wife to obtain a judicial separation for cruelty or desertion, as after this, in the event of her husband committing subsequent adultery, she will have the option of petitioning for a dissolution.' AG has queried in the margin (246), 'Open trial?'

In her reply, MG thanked WBY for 'all the trouble you have taken for me—I saw the French lawyer this morning & showed him the letter to Lady Gregory, he was very pleased, as it exactly confirmed what he had said, that the divorce should take place in France because of it being my husband's domicile. It has taken a great weight off my mind not having to appeal to English justice....Will you thank Lady Gregory very much for me for having written to Mr Grey [*for* Geary]. His opinion is most valuable. It is very kind of her troubling.'

[2] James Starkey had revived the Irish publishing house of Whaley in the summer of 1904 to issue his own slim volume of poems *The Twilight People*, AE's *The Mask of Apollo*, and Standish James O'Grady's *The Flight of the Eagle*. Subsequently—probably in December 1904—Starkey had been introduced to George Roberts by James Cousins, and the two, with the advice of Stephen Gwynn, were trying to establish a new and more financially secure company, to be launched later this year as Maunsel & Co.

# To D. S. MacColl,[1] *15 January 1905*

18 Woburn Buildings, | Euston Road, | London.
Jan. 15th, | 05.

Dear M[r] Mc'Coll,

My father has asked me to explain to you about the picture situation in Dublin.[2] I am a member of Lane's Committee & know about matters from the beginning. The worst of it is, that I may probably have to go to Dublin to-morrow night & not return until the end of the week. Meanwhile matters in Dublin are pressing. Will you be in town to-morrow & if so can you lunch with me at the Austrian Restaurant. I name the Austrian Restaurant as I believe that you go to the British Museum & may be able to combine the Museum & our talk. If however any other restaurant would suit you better please write & tell me. The Austrian is the big corner house immediately opposite Mudies'.[3] When I left Dublin things were going well there & if only we can overcome the opposition which has

---

MG was 'glad you are starting a publishing house in Ireland & hope it will be a great success. It should be.' She also wished that she could be in Dublin for the production of Synge's *The Well of the Saints*, 'but alas for the present I must stay here'.

[1] Dugald Sutherland MacColl (1859–1948), editor, and art critic successively for the *Spectator*, the *Saturday Review*, and the *Week-end Review*, had recently published *Nineteenth Century Art* (1902). He was, with George Moore, one of the most influential champions of contemporary French art. He helped found the National Art Collections Fund and served as keeper of the Tate Gallery (1906–11) and of the Wallace Collection (1911–24). He was also a close friend of Hugh Lane, and AG appointed him Lane's official biographer in 1915, but quickly engineered his resignation when she discovered that he disagreed with her over the interpretation of Lane's will and intentions concerning the location of his collection of modern paintings.

[2] See p. 4, n. 1. WBY's father John Butler Yeats (1839–1922; see I. 518–20) had denounced the Royal Hibernian Academy's 'Statement' on the proposed art gallery in the *Irish Times* on 11 Jan (see p. 19, n. 7), and wished to enlist MacColl's help and authority in the campaign. He had written to WBY on 'Saturday' (14 Jan 1905; NLI), enclosing MacColl's address, and urging him to see him: 'I am certain he would help us. I have already written to him sending him the manifesto and also my reply.... Probably if you wrote to him he would arrange for you to go there in the evening (probably dine) and you might talk matters over.'

[3] This was the Vienna Café which occupied the first floor above the Anglo-Austrian Confectionery Co., about a hundred yards from the British Museum on the corner of New Oxford Street and Museum Street, opposite Mudie's Library. It was a regular meeting place for those working at the Museum and is vividly described in Sir Henry Newbolt's *My World as in My Time* (1932), 209–10. MacColl evidently kept the appointment with WBY, for he attacked the 'Statement' in the *Saturday Review* of 21 Jan (74–5) and commended JBY's letter of refutation. Much to JBY's satisfaction the Irish morning papers 'reproduced his remarks. So that I hope from this on the Academy is out of the Saga' (*JBYL*, 81). Lane cited MacColl's article in an interview in the *Irish Times* on 15 Mar 1905 (6), and in his *Catalogue of Pictures*, dated 15 May 1905, reported (10) that 'Mr. D. S. MacColl, the famous Art Critic, has again and again strenuously helped us...'. MacColl was also to praise the pictures as 'excellent and enviable' in a letter to the *Irish Times* on 14 June 1905 (8).

now got a voice in the Academy, we may be able to buy a fair number of pictures.[4]

> Yrs sinely
> W B Yeats

Dict AEFH, signed WBY; Glasgow.

## *To Lady Gregory,* [*15 January 1905*]

Dear Friend: I am very anxious to see you, I turn to you in every trouble— perhaps it is not kind to ask you to share in every trouble.[1]

> Yr ev
> W B Yeats

ALS Berg, with envelope addressed to Coole, postmark 'LONDON W JAN 16 1905'.

## *To Gilbert Murray,*[1] *24 January* [*1905*]

> Nassau Hotel | Dublin
> Jan 24

My dear Murray,
  Will you translate Edipus Rex for us?[2] We can offer you nothing for it but a place in heaven, but if you do, it will be a great event. Our company are excited at the idea. The Fays have read it, and believe we can give a fine

[4] The executors of the Staats-Forbes estate had agreed to divide the collection, and permitted Lane's committee to make a smaller selection of 160 paintings (out of the original 4,000) for £20,000 rather than £220,000. A subscriber's circular issued at this time listed the revised selections and prices, and announced that the pictures would be on view in the Round Gallery of the Science and Art Museum, Kildare Street, until 25 March.

[1] WBY had similarly turned to AG during a previous crisis with MG; see II. 320

[1] Gilbert Murray (1866–1957), classical scholar and translator, had been on the committee of J. T. Grein's Independent Theatre. In 1899 he resigned his Chair of Greek at Glasgow and moved to Surrey, where he wrote poetic drama, joined the committee of the Stage Society, and renewed his efforts to help William Archer found an English National Theatre. His verse translations of Euripides began to appear in 1902 and led to a revival of Attic drama at the Court Theatre in 1904. He was appointed Regius Professor of Greek at Oxford in 1908. He had met WBY briefly at Edmund Gosse's house in 1896, and the acquaintanceship had been renewed in 1903 (see III. 308–9).

[2] The discovery, during his American tour, that Sophocles' *Oedipus Rex* had been staged at the University of Notre Dame inspired WBY to attempt a production in Dublin, especially since it was banned in England because of the incest theme. Murray, his first choice as translator, immediately declined on the grounds that it had 'nothing Irish about it: no religion, not one beautiful action, hardly a stroke of poetry' (*LWBY* I. 145). Having failed with Murray, WBY turned to Oliver Gogarty for a translation, and then to John Eglinton. When Gogarty failed to deliver and Eglinton's version proved unsatisfactory, WBY decided to attempt his own version, working at first from Jebb's translation, and

performance.³ There is no censor here to forbid it as it has been forbidden in England. It is much better worth writing for us than for Granville Barker.⁴ Nothing has any effect in England, but here one never knows when one may affect the mind of a whole generation. The country is in its first plastic state, and takes the mark of every strong finger.⁵ We have a beautiful little theatre and can stage it well. Do not ask us to play Euripides instead, for Euripides is rapidly becoming a popular English dramatist, and it is upon Sophocles that we have set our imaginations.⁶ Besides, I am always trying to persuade Ireland, which does not understand the game, that she is very liberal, abhors censors delights in the freedom of the arts, is prepared for anything. When we have performed Edipus the King, and everybody is proud of having done something which is forbidden in England, even the newspapers will give [up] pretending to be timid. As it is the people here who are ready to make an outcry because Lady Gregory has dramatized a virtuous policeman,⁷ havn't found anything wrong in

later from that by Paul Masqueray. Although he began his translation in 1910, WBY's *Sophocles' King Oedipus* was not produced at the Abbey until 7 Dec 1926, because, as he explained in the *New York Times* of 15 Jan 1933 (section 9, p. 1), 'when I had finished the dialogue in the rough and was still shrinking at the greater labor of the choruses the English censor withdrew his ban and I lost interest'. While far more interested in Euripides, Aeschylus, and Aristophanes, Murray did finally publish a translation of *Oedipus at Colonus* in 1948.

³ William G. Fay (1873–1947) and Frank J. Fay (1870–1931), founder-members and leaders of the INTS (see III. 699–703). Stage-struck from youth, they had set up the amateur Ormond Dramatic Society in the 1880s, and W. G. Fay worked for a series of fit-up companies touring Ireland and Britain. In August 1901 WBY was delighted with the Fays' productions in Dublin, and he subsequently gave them permission to stage his *Cathleen ni Houlihan* in April 1902, performances which led to the founding of the Irish National Theatre Society, and the Abbey Theatre in 1904. Over the next six years Frank Fay took leading parts in most of the major INTS productions, scoring his greatest successes in WBY's poetic tragedies, most notably with his interpretation of Seanchan in *The King's Threshold* and Cuchulain in *On Baile's Strand*. When AEFH bought the Mechanics' Institute to convert into the Abbey Theatre in 1904, W. G. Fay gave up his job as an electrician to become full-time manager of the Company, a post that he was to hold until 1908. From the summer of 1906 his relationship with AEFH, WBY, and, finally, the Company deteriorated; things came to a head early in 1908 when both brothers resigned from the Abbey.

⁴ The actor and playwright Harley Granville-Barker (1877–1946) was director of the Stage Society, and his adventurous management of the Court Theatre with J. E. Vedrenne (1868–1930) was a focus of the dramatic revival in London 1904–7. Barker had produced Murray's translation of Euripides' *Hippolytus* at the Court Theatre in October 1904 and was to stage his versions of *The Trojan Women* in April 1905, *Electra* in January and March 1906, and a revival of *Hippolytus* in March 1906.

⁵ WBY had long entertained the idea of Ireland's impressionability at this period in history. In *Aut* (199) he recalled that in the early 1890s he had had 'the sudden certainty that Ireland was to be like soft wax for years to come', and wondered whether this 'was a moment of supernatural insight'.

⁶ Although the Greek dramatist Euripides (*c*. 485–*c*. 406 BC) was only slighter younger than Sophocles (*c*. 496–406 BC), his attitude to Greek religion and myth was more sceptical, and his style less elevated, neither of which attributes would have endeared him to WBY. Recent developments in classical studies had brought him into prominence, a popularity that Murray had done much to foster through his translations and critical writings.

⁷ The policeman in AG's one-act play *The Rising of the Moon* allows a Fenian suspect to escape, despite a £100 reward, when reminded of his own nationalist past. This had upset 'a few extreme

language which the English censor protested against in licensing my last
play. " 'amorous women and lascivious goddesses' " he said "are phrases
that would give pleasure to no one and pain too many".[8]

We can give you plenty of time over Sophocles, for we have so many
plays coming on that we can hardly produce the Edipus before our autumn
session. I believe we are going to make a great dramatic school here. We
produce on February 4th a three act play by Synge which is I believe a great
play,[9] and we have other long plays to follow. I wish you could come over
and see our work. The first production of a play by us is a good chance of
meeting most of the people of interest here.

Yrs sinly
W B Yeats

ALS Bodleian.


## *To George Roberts,*[1] *[late January 1905]*

Nassau Hotel

My dear Roberts,
    Why not suggest to Bullen that you get cover for cheap edition made in
Dublin & *put programe design* upon it. There should be time to do this if it is
done in Dublin.

Yrs ev
W B Yeats

ALS Harvard.

---

nationalists', who, as the *Northern Whig* reported on 14 Jan 1905 (10), could not accept the play 'because
it shows a policeman in a favourable light, and "the Dublin crowds should be kept of so high a heart that
they will fight the police at any moment"'. As WBY recalled in *Aut* (566), this political hostility
prevented the play's production for two years: 'One well-known leader of the mob wrote to me, "How
can the Dublin mob be expected to fight the police if it looks upon them as capable of patriotism?"
When performed at last the play was received with enthusiasm, but only to get us into new trouble. The
chief Unionist Dublin newspaper denounced us for slandering His Majesty's forces, and Dublin Castle
denied to us a privilege . . . of buying, for stage purposes, the cast-off clothes of the police.' The play was
not produced until 9 Mar 1907.

[8] These quotations are from *On Baile's Strand*: 'She was an amorous woman—a proud, pale,
amorous woman' (*VPl*, 521), and 'how lecherous these goddesses are' (*VPl*, 458). The English censor
was George Alexander Redford (1840–1916), a former bank manager, who had been appointed
Examiner of Plays in 1875. A TS version of the play is among the Lord Chamberlain's files at the BL.
[9] i.e. *The Well of the Saints*, first produced on 4 Feb 1905.

[1] George Roberts (1873–1953), a native of Belfast, had joined the INTS in 1903, and played the part
of Dan Burke in the first production of *In the Shadow of the Glen*. He was now secretary of the Society, a
post he combined with his regular employment as a commercial traveller, but was hoping to set up a

## *To the Editor of the* United Irishman,[1] *[28 January 1905]*

Mr. Yeats writes to us—we owe him an apology for the delay in the insertion of the letter—a delay occasioned through the borough elections:

DEAR SIR—You say of Mr. Synge's "Shadow of the Glen" in one of your paragraphs on the performances at the Abbey Theatre, "The story is two thousand years old—it was invented by the decadent Greeks—the reputation of womankind has suffered in every century from it. Mr. Synge heard the story, he called the Greek dame Nora Burke; her husband, Dan Burke; and the robber with whom in the original, she goes away, while the Greek husband and the Greek lover remain, 'a Tramp.' He calls Ephesus, a Wicklow Glen, and lo! the thing is staged and dubbed an Irish play." If the names have been changed from Greek to Irish, they have not been changed by him, but by the unknown Irish peasant who first told the story in Ireland. You will find the Irish form of the story in Mr. Synge's forthcoming book on the Aran Islands.[2] You, yourself, once suggested that it was imported by the hedge schoolmasters.[3] I do not, myself, see any evidence to prove what country it first arose in, or whether it may not have had an independent origin in half-a-dozen countries. The version of the Widow of Ephesus that I know differs from Mr. Synge's plot, and also from the Irish folk-story on which he has founded his play. I would be very much obliged if you would give me the reference to the story referred to by you in the paragraph I have quoted. I do not remember it in the "Decameron," which

publishing firm in Dublin. He was just about to issue *The Well of the Saints*, with sheets imported from Bullen, as the first volume in the Abbey Theatre series (see p. 16), and WBY presumably thought that the use of the Abbey device on the paper covers would give the book a more authentically Irish tone, as well as advertising the theatre. Roberts adopted the suggestion at once and had wrappers for the cheap (1s.) paper-bound edition of the play printed in Dublin by Hely's, with the same design on the front cover as that on Abbey programmes and posters, a line block of Queen Maeve and an Irish wolfhound by Elinor Monsell (1878–1954), reduced to 4″ × 4¼″. This design appeared on the front covers of all the subsequent books in the series until 1911, when it was replaced by a line block of a boy holding a theatrical mask.

[1] Arthur Griffith (1872–1922; see III. 707–9) was founder and editor of the *United Irishman*, a nationalist weekly which put politics before art. Although initially well disposed towards WBY and the Irish dramatic movement, Griffith had attacked the first production of Synge's *In the Shadow of the Glen* in November 1903, and from that time became increasingly hostile to WBY's views on the relationship between literature and nationality.

[2] The recent revival and publication of *In the Shadow of the Glen*—in which a husband feigns death to catch his wife, Norah Burke, in an adulterous relationship—had stirred up the 1903 controversy over its morality and authenticity (see III. 439–49, 451–3), and on 7 Jan 1905 the *United Irishman* (5) had revived the charge of its Greek origins in the words WBY (slightly inaccurately) quotes here. Synge's direct source for the tale was Pat Dirane, the Aran story-teller, whose version he first published in *The Aran Islands* (1907); it appears in *JMSCW* II. 70–2.

[3] After the opening performance of *In the Shadow of the Glen*, Griffith had written in the *United Irishman* of 17 Oct 1903 (1): 'It is a staging of a corrupt version of that old-world libel on womankind— the "Widow of Ephesus", which was made current in Ireland by the hedge-schoolmaster.'

I have lately read.[4] This story may, however, be exactly the same as some Greek or Italian story, and we be no nearer its origin.

Among the audience at the last performance of "On Baile's Strand" there was a famous German scholar who had just edited the old German version of the world-wide story of the king who fights with his own son. Yet, no man can say whether that story came from Ireland to Germany or from Germany to Ireland, or whether to both countries from some common source.[5]

There is certainly nothing in the accounts that travellers give of mediaeval Ireland or in Old Irish or Middle Irish literature to show that Ireland had a different sexual morality from the rest of Europe.[6] And I can remember several Irish poems and stories in which the husband feigns death for precisely the reason that the husband does in Mr. Synge's play; one of them a very beautiful ballad found in the Aran Islands by Mr. Fournier.[7]

But after all, if Mr. Synge had found the story in some Greek writer and had changed the names into Irish names, or even if he had found it in the "Decameron" itself, as you suggest, he would have precedents to encourage him. Shakespeare laid the scene of Cymbeline in his own country, but he found the story in the "Decameron".[8]

I do not reply to the matters of opinion in dispute between us, for to do so would be to repeat what I have already written in my introduction to "A Book of Irish Verse," in the Irish part of "Ideas of Good and Evil," and in the last

---

[4] While Giovanni Boccaccio's 14th-century collection of stories, the *Decameron* (of which WBY owned a two-volume edition, translated by J. M. Rigg and published by Bullen in 1903 [*YL*, 231]) has numerous tales of sexual infidelity, none is close to the plot of Synge's play, and WBY had misread Griffith in supposing that he had claimed this. What Griffith wrote was that if *In the Shadow of the Glen* 'had been allowed to go unchallenged, there was no reason why its author should not have constructed fifty "Irish" plays out of the Decameron'. In his reply, printed immediately after this letter, Griffith said he could 'not understand how Mr. Yeats came to think that we suggested a story which is 2,000 years old had been taken from the Decameron'. The version of the Widow of Ephesus that WBY knew was that in another Italian collection of stories, Gian Francesco Poggio Bracciolini's version of Aesop's *Fables* (see III. 452).

[5] WBY is thinking of a German's rather than a German version, for the Hamburg-born scholar Kuno Meyer (1858–1919) had recently published his translation of 'The Death of Connla', the tale of how Cuchulain slew his son, in the first number of *Ériu* (Dublin, 1904), 113–21. WBY had already used the theme in his poem 'Cuchulain's Fight with the Sea' (*VP*, 105–11) and his play *On Baile's Strand* (*VPl*, 456–525).

[6] Griffith returned to this point the following week, complaining that 'Mr. Yeats fails to tell us who the "mediaeval travellers" were . . . who led him to believe that Irishwomen were of the same class with the Ephesian dame, and where in Old or in Middle Irish literature he found confirmation for the impression these "mediaeval travellers" made upon him.'

[7] This ballad, 'An Gruagach Uasal' ('The Noble Enchanter'), found apparently on Tory Island rather than the Aran Islands by E. E. Fournier d'Albe, had appeared in the *Irish Homestead* in December 1901. WBY used it as the source for the song 'Going the Road One Day' in *The Hour-Glass*, and frequently described it as a ballad from Aran. Fournier had lectured to the National Literary Society on 'A Fortnight in Tory Island' on 4 Dec 1899. Edmund Edward Fournier d'Albe (1868–1933), born in London of Franco-Irish parents, had thrown himself enthusiastically into the Celtic movement. He was editor of *Celtia*, a proponent of Celtic national costume, and, as secretary of the Celtic Association, organized Pan Celtic Congresses in Dublin (1901), Caernarvon (1904), and Edinburgh (1907). He was also a physicist and inventor, and was to become secretary of the Dublin Society for Psychical Research.

[8] Shakespeare drew on a number of sources for *Cymbeline*; the story of Iachimo's wager and the bedroom scene owe much to the ninth story of the second day in the *Decameron*, in which Ambrogiuolo

number of "Samhain."[9] It is no bad thing that our two so different points of view should find full and logical expression, for as William Blake says: "All progress is by contraries";[10] but differences that arise out of mistakes of fact are useless.

[*Unsigned*]

Printed letter, *United Irishman*, 28 January 1905 (1). *UP* II. 331–3.

## To John Quinn, 29 January [*1905*]

Nassau Hotel
Jan 29

My dear Quinn,

I am dictating to Lady Gregory as usual. We have both come to Dublin, I from London and she from Coole, to attend the rehearsals and performance of Synge's play. We have been making decorative scenery—William Fay doing the painting, Pixie Smith and Lady Gregory the designs, and I the criticism. I dont know how it will turn out, for we have no time for experiments, and it is quite a new thing. It is our first attempt to do decorative open air scenes. We feel though I cant exactly explain our idea, that the remoteness, the abstractedness of the scenic arrangements, will make the play safer.[1]

---

deceives Bernabò into believing that he has slept with his wife. Shakespeare knew little Italian, and his direct source may have been *Frederyke of Jennen*, an English version of Boccaccio's tale. In his reply, Griffith asserted that *Cymbeline* was 'an English national play—a work of English genius. Imogen is a glory, not a slander on her countrywomen. Mr. Synge's Norah Burke is not an Irish Norah Burke—his play is not a work of genius—Irish or otherwise—it is a foul echo from degenerate Greece.'

[9] After an early attempt, under John O'Leary's influence, to write verse in the popular political tradition of Thomas Davis and the Young Irelanders, WBY wearied of the obviousness of its themes and the carelessness of its technique. Since 1895 he had been attempting to establish a rival tradition founded upon writers like Ferguson and Allingham, and his introduction to *A Book of Irish Verse*, many of the essays in *IGE*, and his article 'First Principles' in *Samhain* (1904) were written to this end. Griffith, firmly in the Young Ireland tradition, deplored WBY's insistence that imaginative and aesthetic qualities should take precedence over political correctness in literature, and on 7 Jan had proclaimed that neither 'Irishman nor Irishwoman has the right to think of himself or of herself before thinking of Ireland. In the acceptance and realisation of this truth lies the national redemption.... No Irishman may set up his spade or his lyre and say "This first." The spade finds its true work in delving for Ireland—the lyre its true voice in singing for Ireland.' These disagreements were shortly to lead to a breach in their earlier friendship.

[10] Blake, 'The Marriage of Heaven and Hell', plate 3: 'Without Contraries is no progression. Attraction and Repulsion, Reason and Energy, Love and Hate, are necessary to Human existence.' This proverb had a particular significance for WBY and underlies his later notion of antinomy; see *Works of William Blake* II. 62–3.

[1] On 4 Feb, the day of the first production, AG wrote to Quinn (NYPL) that Synge 'has been frightfully nervous this last week—& WBY has been in a fidget about scenery & Mr Fay has had bad neuralgia—I feel we shall have more peace next week.... We are a little anxious—for it is hard to know how it will be taken—I am giving a party in the theatre afterwards, to help to bring people.' The scenic arrangements received a mixed press, as did the play.

I have written a preface for it, and we are awaiting your wire about copyright that we may publish.[2] I am afraid we are giving you a great deal of trouble, and there is more trouble to come, unless you suggest to us some ordinary routine of business, which will enable us to copyright plays. Kincora is to be played and published some time in March. Lady Gregory is very sorry but she is afraid she will have to send it to you, but she begs you to simply give it to a publisher to print as cheaply as possible, and let him deal with her direct. She hopes to get it off this week.[3] Plays are beginning to come in to us here, we will have a whole dramatic literature before long. Colum was round the other night with the scenario of a [play] he talked over with you. He has got it simple at last, and what is more unexpected, has written some very good dialogue. Dialogue full of country idiom and character.[4] Synge has a long new play drawing to an end, but there will be no hurry about that, for we cannot play it till the autumn.[5] What is getting us into difficulties over the copyright is that we are starting an Abbey Theatre series of plays, two or three shillings for the ordinary edition, and a shilling edition for sale at the theatre. Synge is to be Vol l. Lady Gregory's Kincora Vol II. We will then be guided by the sales as to how far we can venture with plays at present. <It is quite possible that a real Irish publishing house may be started here in connection with the theatre. Bullen who is an Irishman going into it. I am expecting to hear every post, but the series comes off in any case. We feel that it is necessary to help us towards a true critical public.> Bullen has been nibbling at the idea of an

---

[2] WBY's introduction to *The Well of the Saint*, 'Mr. Synge and his Plays', is dated 'Abbey Theatre, January 27th, 1905', but it was not published until Bullen brought out the English edition of the play as vol. IV of 'Plays for an Irish Theatre' in December 1905 (see p. 16, n. 2). Quinn copyrighted the play in America on 7 Feb (see p. 17, n. 2).

[3] AG's three-act historical play *Kincora*, first produced at the Abbey Theatre on 25 Mar 1905, with Frank Fay playing King Brian Boru, dramatizes the intrigues of Queen Gormleith to thwart Brian's attempts to bring peace to Ireland, which culminate in the Battle of Clontarf of 1014. AG sent Quinn the MS of the play on 4 Feb (NYPL), asking him to 'send it to be copyrighted in whatever way is easiest & cheapest—It will probably be published & played here 11th March—I believe it is not necessary to print the whole thing to get copyright, that abt half the pages can be left out—If this is so, it would save expense.... But perhaps you have already managed some automatic method for us.' In fact, Quinn had fifty copies of *Kincora* privately printed on 25 Mar to secure the American copyright, and AG's typescript of the play became a part of his growing collection of literary MSS. She inscribed a copy of the 1905 Dublin edition to him in March 1905. AG had great difficulty with the play's construction and subsequently radically revised it.

[4] Padraic Colum (1881–1972; see III. 696–7), poet, playwright, novelist, and man of letters, was an original member of the INTS, which had staged his *Broken Soil* on 3 Dec 1903. His new play was *The Land*, although WBY was to find the dialogue lacking in vividness when it was produced in June. Colum had been at pains to find an appropriate idiom, and had spent time in the spring of 1904 down in the country, writing to Maire Garvey (NLI) that the people there were witty and poetical without knowing it, and that he had 'got characters for a tragic-comedy'. He had evidently discussed the play with Quinn during the latter's visit to Ireland the previous autumn.

[5] Synge's long new play was *The Playboy of the Western World*, not produced until 26 Jan 1907, and at this time entitled 'The Murderer (A Farce)'. Synge had begun it in September 1904, and it was to go through numerous drafts over the next two years.

Irish publishing house. A week or two ago it seem[ed] likely to come to something at once, and now it has faded again for a while.[6]

The ten volume anthology has just come to me, and I shall write them a letter of commendation. It is a very admirable book, and none of us need regret any time or trouble spent upon it. My standard for Irish scholarship is not high, for I remember the Cabinet of Irish Literature and other books of a like kind, but I dont think I am judging this anthology by any lax Irish standard.[7] Considering the size of the book and the material dealt with it could hardly have been done better. Ten years ago it could not have been done at all. It is the evidence of the scholarship and criticism of a generation. Almost every part of the book I turn to shows me a careful selection of material. I have been reading some bits out of old plays, and out of old novels. There are one or two curious slips, but that is inevitable. Maturin for instance is left out. I have always supposed him to have been an Irishman and a remarkable one. He certainly lived in Ireland and was a relation of Oscar Wilde's who used to talk to me about him.[8] I wish I thought the anthology would have any sale here, but the country is too poor. What astonishes me about this anthology is that when I turn to any writer I find little but his best or nothing but his best, whereas the one volume anthologies published in this country always give vast quantities of the writer's worst. How ten volumes have managed to be so much more exclusive than one, I cannot imagine. One thing is, you in America are free from our local influences. I think that I have noticed a slightly less exclusive temper when it comes to American-Irish writers. Lady Gregory is saddened by some verses inserted by the Craoibin in her translation of

---

[6] Since 1901 the INTS had been publishing the texts of new plays in *Samhain*, but had now decided to issue selected titles regularly in book form as 'The Abbey Theatre Series'. The First Series, comprising fifteen volumes, appeared between February 1905 and June 1911; a Second Series of nine plays was issued between October 1911 and January 1922. The first three volumes—*The Well of the Saints*, AG's *Kincora*, and Colum's *The Land*—were published by the Abbey Theatre itself, but in the autumn of 1905 the series was transferred to the newly established publishing firm of Maunsel & Co. The series had the active support of A. H. Bullen, who provided the sheets of his English edition of *The Well of the Saints*, and a specially printed title page, for the separate Dublin edition, which went on sale in February 1905 as vol. 1 of the 'Abbey Theatre Series'. Although he did not establish an Irish publishing firm, Bullen continued to supply the sheets and new title pages when the Series was transferred to Maunsel & Co.

[7] See p. 3; Charles Anderson Read's *The Cabinet of Irish Literature*, a far less satisfactory selection from 'the works of the chief poets, orators and prose writers of Ireland', originally appeared in four volumes (1879–80). In 1902 Katharine Tynan Hinkson brought[ out a revised and enlarged edition.

[8] Charles Robert Maturin (1780–1824), Dublin-born novelist and dramatist, is best known for his Gothic novel *Melmoth the Wanderer* (1820). His reputation went into a steep decline in Ireland and Britain after his death, although he retained a readership in France. He was a great-uncle of Oscar Wilde, who had adopted the pseudonym 'Sebastian Melmoth' after his release from Reading Gaol.

'the Boers curse...' verses he wrote after she had made her translation. The line 'whelm a warship' fills her with dismay.[9]

I never thanked you for the two bottles of rye whiskey. I asked Bullen to dine on the strength of it, and he got through a great part of a bottle and went home sober. He was evidently very happy at not having the eyes of his two nieces fixed upon him. They do not allow him anything until ten o'clock.[10] If I had been in London with the other a few days ago, the new Irish publishing house would I have little doubt be already started.

I am re-writing Baile's Strand; and then I have to go on with the re-writing of the King's Threshold, and after that to return to Deirdre— Granville Barker is putting the Pot of Broth on at the Court.[11]

I shall hand the proceeds over to the company in some form.

I hope you have had your poster by this.[12] Lady Gregory wrote that she was sending it; I said I would send it; and then because I didn't know in the least how one sends through the post a long flipperty-flopperty thing like that, I gave it to Roberts and asked him to send it, thinking that he would know how, as he is a publisher among other things. When I came over from London a few days ago I found he had been considering the same problem

---

[9] AG's 1901 translation of 'The Curse of the Boers on England' appeared in vol. x of *Irish Literature*, 3929–33. The penultimate stanza of the poem, as altered by Hyde, an associate editor, reads: 'Every single tear | Shall have power in that day, | To whelm a warship | In the great deep.' In fact, AG had other complaints about the edition, and the following day was to protest to Quinn (NYPL) that she had received neither payment not acknowledgement, although she had done 'the work asked for—besides a good deal of reading & looking through books by myself, I had Dr Hyde at Coole for a week, during which we both worked hard at the anthology for several hours every day—My name has been largely used in advertisements of it.'

[10] Bullen, who was a heavy drinker, was looked after by two sisters, Edith Georgina and Alys Oswald Lister (1863–1938), although 'nieces' may be a euphemism since the latter appears to have been his mistress. Edith Lister (1859–1938), known as 'Mickey' or sometimes 'Michael' to her friends, assisted Bullen in his publishing business and was to help see WBY's *CW* though the press 1907–8. She also contributed an article, 'The Writings of Mr. W. B. Yeats', to the *Fortnightly Review* in February 1909 (signed E.M.D.), as well as writing verse as 'E. M. Martin' and under other pseudonyms. In *Experiences of a Literary Man* (1926) Stephen Gwynn remarks (151) that Bullen inherited 'the taste for whisky, of which he consumed a bottle daily' from his father, but that he did not inherit the father's 'constitution which enabled him to survive this regimen to the age of eighty—and which no doubt inspired him in his last years to marry again and disinherit the son with whom he had quarrelled. A. H. Bullen was nervous, thin and excitable as compared with that stout old warrior, and had not the talent for prospering commercially.'

[11] *The Pot of Broth* was performed at the Court Theatre for nine matinées from 28 Feb to 17 Mar 1905 in a triple bill with Arthur Schnitzler's *In the Hospital* and Shaw's *How He Lied to Her Husband*.

[12] The poster for the newly opened Abbey Theatre, displaying the woodcut of Queen Maeve and an Irish wolfhound designed by Elinor Monsell, the artist and illustrator (see pp. 24–5, n. 1, and III. 650, 678–9). Quinn confirmed the arrival of his copies on 24 Feb: 'I received the posters for the new theatre last week and am very much obliged to you for sending them to me as well as for the copy of *Samhain* and the other papers' (Himber, 66).

at intervals ever since. He had however got so far as to buy some large sheets of pasteboard to roll it up in so I suppose its off by this.[13]

Yours ever

W B Yeats

TLS NYPL, with envelope addressed to 1 West 87 Street, New York, postmark 'DUBLIN FE 1 05'.

## *To the Editor of the* United Irishman, *4 February 1905*

Two or three weeks ago you wrote of Mr. Synge's "Shadow of the Glen," "The story is two thousand years old—it was invented by the decadent Greeks—the reputation of womankind has suffered in every century from it. Mr. Synge heard the story, he called the Greek dame Nora Burke; her husband, Dan Burke, and the robber with whom in the original she goes away, while the Greek husband and the Greek lover remain, 'a tramp.' He calls Ephesus a Wicklow Glen, and, lo! the thing is staged and dubbed an Irish play." I wrote to you that I would be very much obliged if you would give me the reference to the story referred to by you in the paragraph I have quoted.[1] You replied, "Mr. Yeats is mistaken in supposing the story of the Ephesian widow a folk-story. It is a story invented by the wits of decadent Greece, and introduced, with amendments, into Latin literature by the most infamous of Roman writers, Petronius Arbiter, the pander of Nero. But Mr. Synge could not have ventured to produce Petronius's version on the stage of any civilised country."

You have wasted some of my time. There is no such story in Petronius, and I must again ask you for your reference. He does, indeed, tell the well-known story of the Ephesian widow.[2] You will find a rather full paraphrase

---

[13] For George Roberts see p. 24. In the early spring of 1904, while continuing as a commercial traveller, Roberts succeeded Fred Ryan as secretary of the INTS, and from Dec 1904 received a salary of £1 a week. Among his duties were the preparation and production of posters and programmes, and arranging publicity. He was to help set up the publishing house of Maunsel & Co. later this year (see p. 20) and early in 1906 seceded from the Abbey Theatre.

[1] See p. 25.

[2] Petronius (d. *c.* AD 66), Roman satirist, credited with writing *The Satyricon*. A connoisseur of taste, he took his sobriquet from Tacitus, who styled him in *Annales* as *arbiter elegantiae* of Nero's court. The story of the Ephesian widow is told by the poet Eumolpus in sections 3 ff. of *The Satyricon*, described later this year by WBY (*Expl*, 195) as a novel 'which satirises, or perhaps one should say celebrates, Roman decadence'. In 'Upon a Dying Lady' WBY describes (*VP*, 362) visitors at Mabel Beardsley's hospital bed 'matching our broken-hearted wit against her wit, | Thinking of saints and of Petronius Arbiter'. In his reply, Griffith doubted whether WBY had ever read Petronius and advised him 'not to trust too implicitly in Mr. Whibley's scholarship and his definitions. . . . Petronius brought the story out of Greece, where it had been invented by the decadents, and altered it.' In his satirical skit 'National Drama', Synge lists among the books of a narrow-minded nationalist critic 'The Pedigree of

of his version in chapter 5 of Jeremy Taylor's "Holy Living." It is an admirable fable. It has been described by a good scholar and masterly writer as "the very model of its kind, and withal the perfection of ironic humour," but it is not Mr. Synge's story nor the story of your paragraph.[3]

Here it is: "A widow mourning on the tomb of her husband surrenders to the love of a soldier who has been sent to watch over the hanged body of a robber. In the night the robber's friends steal his body away, and the widow hangs her husband's body in its place to save the life of the soldier who had otherwise been executed for neglect of duty." This is a bare summary, and does no justice to a fable that has gone through the whole world. It was not invented by the decadent Greeks, for you will find, if you look in Dunlop's "History of Fiction," that it is one of the oldest of Eastern tales. It is in that most ancient book of fables, "The Seven Wise Masters," and is extant in a very vivid form in old Chinese writings.[4] Ireland may, I think, claim all the glory of Mr. Synge's not less admirable tale. The only parallels I can remember at this moment to the husband who pretends to be dead that he may catch his wife and his wife's lover, are Irish parallels. One is in a ballad at the end of "The Love Songs of Connacht," and the other in a ballad taken down in Tory Island by Mr. Fournier.[5]

In everything but the end of the play Mr. Synge has followed very closely the Aran story, which he has, I believe, sent to you; but it is precisely the end of the play that puts him at once among men of genius. For this there is no parallel in any story that I know of. The sitting down together of the husband and the lover is certainly "the perfection of ironic humour."[6]

the Widow of Ephesus. The complete works of Petronius and Boccaccio, unabridged' ( *JMSCW* III. 221).

   [3] The story occurs not in *Holy Living* (1650) but in section 8, chapter 5 of *The Rule and Exercise of Holy Dying* (1651), also by the 17th-century Anglican clergyman Jeremy Taylor (1613–67). WBY had picked up the reference to Taylor and the quotation about ironic humour from pp. 46–7 of *Studies in Frankness* (1898) by the 'good scholar and masterly writer' Charles Whibley (1859–1930), journalist and man of letters, whom WBY had met at W. E. Henley's in the late 1880s and early 1890s.

   [4] *The History of Fiction* (1814) by John Dunlop (1785–1842), 'a critical account of the most celebrated prose works of fiction from the Earliest Greek Romances to the Novels of the Present age', went into five editions during the 19th century. Dunlop describes *The Seven Wise Masters* as an ancient Indian work that influenced Italian writers, and identifies one of the stories, 'The Widow who was Comforted', as 'the Ephesian matron of Petronius Arbiter'. In his reply Griffith poured scorn on Dunlop's accuracy.

   [5] 'The Roman Earl', the last poem in Hyde's *Love Songs of Connacht*, which had been republished in July 1904 by Dun Emer Press, recounts how a wealthy Roman feigns death to see if his wife will give him the lavish funeral she has promised. In fact she shrouds him in sackcloth that does not even reach his hips, but when she upbraids her she argues that, attired thus, he will run fastest on Judgement Day and come first to God's bliss. For Fournier's Tory Island ballad see p. 26.

   [6] At the end of Synge's play the wife leaves with the tramp while her husband and lover sit down to drink together.

It is not my business to dispute with you about the character of Petronius. I know little about him, but I do know that his identification with Arbiter Elegantarium is considered very uncertain by good scholars, and that little that is certain is known of either Petronius or Arbiter. Mr. Charles Whibley, a sound critic and, as I have always understood, a sound scholar, has said of Petronius, "One thing only is certain, he was a gentleman, and incomparably aristocratic."[7]

The Aran story and the Ephesian story are alike stories of wrong-doing; but so, too, is Bluebeard, and we are none of us a penny the worse.[8]

[*Unsigned*]

Printed letter, *United Irishman*, 4 February 1905 (1). *UP* II. 334–6.

## To Maud Gonne, [c. 10 February 1905]

Mention in letter from MG, 'Tuesday evening' [14 February 1905]. Telegram telling her that Henry Dixon's proposals for a compromise between MG and MacBride have been withdrawn.[1]

*G–YL*, 189.

[7] See n. 3 above. Whibley makes this comment in the concluding paragraph of his essay 'Petronius' in *Studies in Frankness* (47): 'Who was he? What was he? Whence came he? These questions must remain for ever without an answer. One thing only is certain, he was a gentleman, and incomparably aristocratic.'

[8] In 'La Barbe Bleue', a story which gained a European circulation following its inclusion in Charles Perrault's collection of fairy tales *Contes de ma mère l'oye* (1697), 'Bluebeard' (perhaps based on Gilles de Retz [d. 1440]) instructs his new wife never to enter a certain room in the house, but during his absence she does so, and discovers the bodies of his former wives, whose throats he has cut. He is about to mete out the same treatment to her, because of her disobedience, when her brothers arrive and save her.

[1] Henry Dixon (1858–1928), a solicitor's clerk, was from an advanced nationalist background and had become politically active in the early 1880s. At the time he met WBY in 1892 he was being described by the Dublin police as 'a fanatic', but together they initiated a plan to establish libraries throughout Ireland (*Mem*, 58). By 1897 he had become a member of the Fenian group the INA, and he appears anonymously in George Moore's *Ave* as 'a revolutionary of some kind (after business hours), a follower of Miss Gonne.... [a] mild-eyed clerk.... A dried-up, dusty fellow' (Cave, 117, 119). He later became a friend of John MacBride, and with Arthur Griffith had called to see him in Dublin on 24 Jan 1905 to ask him about the rumours of his differences with MG. MacBride recalled (NLI) that he 'gave both of them a fair idea of the charges made against me without mentioning Es name & contented myself with denying them. In response to a question from Mr. Dixon I said that I was prepared to do anything reasonable without loss of honour to avoid public recriminations between my wife & myself. Dixon said: "That was what he expected of me." I read for their benefit one of the letters to Barry O'Brien, Mr Witham's ... draft & my draft. Dixon & Griffith like all who have heard of the nasty business deplored it deeply.' Since negotiations between MG and MacBride had broken down (see p. 11, n. 1), Dixon tried to draw up a compromise settlement to the dispute, but in her reply MG told WBY that she was glad it had been withdrawn 'as I felt it would not do'. On 27 Nov of this year Dixon was to appear with John O'Leary as a witness for MacBride during the *enquête* in Paris into the divorce suit.

## *To the Editor of the* United Irishman, *11 February 1905*

I don't see how we can go on with the controversy about the origin of the "Shadow of the Glen" until you have printed Mr. Synge's letter to you, with its enclosure giving the Irish original,[1] and given me a more definite reference than "The Palais Royal."[2] I must, however, contradict a statement you have made about myself. You say, "In America he told his audiences the Castle lived in fear of his Theatre, and sent forty baton-bearing myrmidons down to its each performance." This is as true as the statement made to me by an American journalist that you were paid by the British Government to abuse the Irish Party. I described in many of my American lectures the attack made upon the "Countess Cathleen" by Mr. F. H. O'Donnell and the *Nation* newspaper. I have my exact words among my papers in London. This seems to be the origin of your extravagant charge, doubtless sent to you by some imaginative correspondent, or copied from some inaccurate newspaper. I mentioned neither Dublin Castle nor politics of any kind.[3]

*[Unsigned]*

Printed letter, *United Irishman*, 11 February 1905 (1). *UP* 11. 336–8.

Dixon was closely associated with Griffith and the Sinn Fein movement, of which he was elected a vice-president in 1906. In the same year he became a member of the editorial board when Griffith transformed the *United Irishman* into *Sinn Fein*, and he was imprisoned after the 1916 Rising. As a founder and secretary of Cumann na Leabharlann (the Irish Libraries Association), he helped promote public libraries and reading rooms.

[1] Griffith, alleging lamely that this was 'the first intimation we had that Mr. Synge intended his letter for publication, and not for our personal enlightenment', grudgingly printed it below WBY's letter: 'SIR—I beg to enclose the story of an unfaithful wife which was told to me by an old man on the Middle Island of Aran in 1898, and which I have since used in modified form in "The Shadow of the Glen". It differs essentially from any version of the story of the "Widow of Ephesus" with which I am acquainted. As you will see, it was told to me in the first person, as not infrequently happens in folk-tales of this class — Yours, J. M. Synge.' Griffith, however, refused to publish the story, claiming that it was 'we regret to say, of insufficient merit to entitle it to a place in our columns'. Griffith chose to interpret WBY's opening sentence as indicating that he had decided 'not to continue the controversy he begun', and commented that in this 'we think Mr. Yeats is acting wisely'.

[2] On 28 Jan (1) the *United Irishman* had claimed that Synge's story was 'a stock one in the Quartier Latin, and which he could have purchased in the Palais Royal', and the following week (1) it repeated the charge: 'If Mr. Yeats refers again to our reply to his question, Where he may procure the prurient Greek story Mr. Synge has dubbed "In a Wicklow Glen" [*sic*], he will find the answer, In the Palais Royal.'

[3] Frank Hugh O'Donnell (1846–1916; see 11. 707–12), author and politician, had been expelled from the Irish Parliamentary Party by Parnell, and fallen out with WBY over his activities in the '98 Centennial Committee, when he had attacked Michael Davitt and Maud Gonne (see 11. 265–6, 272). Reprimanded by WBY and John O'Leary, he had taken his revenge by attacking WBY and *The Countess Cathleen* in his pamphlet *Souls for Gold! Pseudo-Celtic Drama in Dublin*, which he circulated widely in Dublin in late April 1899 (see 11. 674–80), and which prompted Cardinal Logue's condemnation of the play. The Dublin Catholic weekly the *Nation* had supported his attacks. In 'The Intellectual Revival in

## *To Maud Gonne,* [c. *11 February 1905*]

Mention in letter from MG, 'Tuesday evening' [14 February 1905]. Letter giving an account of his activities on her behalf,[1] telling her that MacBride has talked over several people in Dublin, and has been alleging that her mind is unbalanced,[2] assuring her that the verdict of the court in her favour will be the surest way of putting an end to the lies MacBride has been telling about her,[3] and discussing the success of the theatre, the thinness of the audiences,[4] the dispute over *The Shadow of the Glen*, and Synge's talent.[5]

*G–YL,* 189–90.

Ireland', one of the lectures he gave in America, WBY had recalled the disturbances at the first production of *The Countess Cathleen*: 'I saw thirty policemen in the theatre to keep order. Then I said, "Now we have a passionate audience". Shakespeare wrote for passionate audiences. The modern theatregoer goes to the theatre to digest his dinner. When I saw the thirty police in that theatre I said, "We have a great national theatre. Now let us create the literature." ' This passage was widely reported in the American press, but the only 'imaginative' report of it seems to have appeared in the London *Daily News*, where WBY was quoted as saying that the INTS dramatists 'now study what the people want, and then we give it to them in such form that thirty or forty police must often be stationed inside the theatre to prevent riots'. Even this report did not cite any mention by WBY of Dublin Castle or politics, but Griffith got round this by tartly observing: 'That Mr. Yeats never mentioned Dublin Castle nor politics of any kind in America is all the more wonderful in view of the fact that he delivered a public address to a Nationalist audience on Robert Emmet there. An address on Robert Emmet with all reference to the Castle and politics left out eclipses the record of the stage manager who successfully produced "Hamlet" with the part of the Prince of Denmark omitted.' In his speech 'Emmet the Apostle of Irish Liberty', delivered in New York on 28 Feb 1904 (see III. 535, 538), WBY had mentioned Dublin Castle and politics in passing but the main emphasis of the lecture was the superiority of idealism over practical politics and was mainly devoted to the progress of the Irish cultural revival.

[1] WBY had followed up his recent telegram (see p. 33) with a letter, and she thanked him 'for all the trouble you are taking for me'.

[2] MG replied that she was 'not the least surprised that John MacBride has talked over several people in Dublin, he is quite unscrupulous & very plausible, when sober. Also I have not told any of the facts of the case; in Dublin I have only written to Mr Russell, to Ella Young and to Miss Machen & to these I have merely stated that I am separating from my husband for very serious reasons.'

[3] MG thought WBY was 'quite right in saying that the verdict of the court in my favor will be the surest way of putting an end to the lies my husband has been telling or may yet tell & my lawyers are quite certain I will get the verdict'. She went on to say that although French divorces were heard in camera, the judgments were public. She was unperturbed by MacBride's comments on her mental health, because she did not believe that anyone in Paris 'would believe in his talk about my mind being unhinged, besides the case will rest on the evidence of others, not on mine'.

[4] MG was glad that the plays were 'succeeding so well', but suggested that the audiences would improve if the cheapest seat were priced at sixpence rather than a shilling.

[5] WBY had evidently told MG of his dispute with Griffith over *The Shadow of the Glen*, which she had just read for the first time in the current number of *Samhain*. Although she had resigned her vice-presidency of the INTS in September 1903 over its production (see III. 435, n. 2), she now agreed with WBY about Synge's 'really remarkable force & talent as a dramatic writer, though still I think this play is not for the many in Ireland & not helpful to the movement as we were trying to carry it out at that time'.

## *To Charles Welsh,*[1] *12 February* [*1905*]

The Abbey Theatre | Dublin
Feb. 12

Dear Sir:

I thank you very much for the "Irish Literature," the most admirable Irish anthology I have seen. I would have thanked you more promptly, but I have been reading a great deal in it, turning the leaves here and there, now to some writer whose books I have not opened for years; now to some writer whose works I have never read, and again to see what you have chosen from some writer I know well. I have been constantly delighted by the results of careful selection and research. Nobody ever agrees wholly with any anthology, for no two people select in the same way, but I cannot imagine that our generation will see any rival to this book of yours. A generation ago this book could not have been made—for there were not then enough minds at once cultivated and learned among Irish students. One thing, however, puzzles me very much. When I turn to the productions of any writer I know in this many-volumed anthology, I find his best, and little else. When I turn to the Irish anthologies of some years ago, which were nearly all small books, I find great quantities of every writer's worst. Why is it that a big book is so much more exclusive than a small one?

Yrs sincerely
W B Yeats

TLS Private

---

[1] This letter was written to Charles Welsh (1850–1914; see III. 524), managing editor of the ten-volume compendium of *Irish Literature* (see pp. 3, 29), and an edited typed version of it is among his papers at Providence College. An energetic man of letters, Welsh had written a biography of Goldsmith's friend John Newbery, and then devoted himself to producing multi-volume series and children's books. He was general editor of Heath's Home and School Classics, the twenty-volume Young Folks' Library, and the four-volume Famous Battles of the Nineteenth Century. He had worked on *Irish Literature* for over five years, aided by a team of copy- and sub-editors, as well as by a selection committee which included AG, Hyde, AE, Stephen Gwynn, Standish O'Grady, D. J. O'Donoghue, and F. N. Robinson of Harvard (1871–1966). The Irish collaborators' joy in the project was tarnished somewhat by Welsh and Bryan's reluctance to pay them, and Quinn had to go over their heads to the publisher, J. D. Morris, to get the fees promised to WBY, AG, and AE.

## *To John Quinn, 15 February 1905*

Nassau Hotel, | South Frederick Street, | Dublin
15th. Feby '05.

My dear Quinn,

I send you a copy of Synges play. Moore has written to the Irish Times saying that it is a great play, more remarkable than any original play produced in England during his time. I rather wonder why he has been converted for he abused the play when he saw an Act of it in rehearsal some months ago. He has also praised the acting in the most strenuous way. I imagine that his dislike of our work was artificial and that he has gradually come to feel that he would make himself absurd. He is now unbounded in his enthusiasm both in public and private which makes Miss Horniman perfectly furious. She threatens us with all kinds of pains and penalty should we accept of any help from him. That quarrel is just now the only little annoyance in a very promising state of things.[1] We had rather thin audiences for Synge's play, but they were always sufficient to play to and make expenses and a little more. Our first production this year "Baile's strand" etc, left us £90 after we had paid expenses. Synge's play left us £30. In the case of the first production however, our expenses were heavier as we gave the actresses something, so the disparity between the two plays was greater than appears in the figures. Fay did not feel entitled to give anything to the actresses this time as he is most anxious to put as much as possible into the fund which is to be used to pay enough of the players to go on tour with. It will take us a little time amassing enough of money but with reasonable luck we should be able to do it.

I count "The well of the Saints" in spite of the thin audiences as a success. It was, I think, the finest piece of acting as a whole the company has done. Nobody was really bad. It ranked with a good professional perform-ance. And of course ranked above any possible professional performance as

---

[1] Synge's *The Well of the Saints* played until 11 Feb. The praise of George Moore (1852–1933), the novelist and dramatist, was a surprise since he had attacked W.G. Fay as a director in *Dana* in September 1904 (see III. 630, 639–40), where he had alleged that Fay did 'not know his A.B. and C. of stage management'. Ironically, Moore's enthusiastic letter, describing the production as an event of 'exceeding rarity', was not published until 13 Feb, after the run had finished. He maintained that he had 'never seen in London any play written originally in English that I can look upon as dramatic literature . . . whereas Mr. Synge's little play seems to me to be of a new growth', and went on to praise William Fay as 'wholly admirable as the blind beggar', Frank Fay as 'very good as the saint', and the blind beggarwoman 'so well played by Miss Vernon [Vera Esposito] that I am afraid . . . I shall not find words wherewith to praise it enough'. AEFH, who disliked Moore, had written to WBY on 9 Feb (NLI) complaining that Moore was taking credit for the Abbey Theatre, and threatening to contribute nothing more to the project unless WBY put a stop to this.

a presentation of Irish peasant character. You will have judged of the play for yourself. The audiences always seemed friendly but the general atmosphere has for all that been one of intense hostility.[2] Irish National Literature, though it has produced many fine ballads and many novels written in the objective spirit of a ballad has never produced an artistic personality in the modern sense of the word. Tom Moore was merely an incarnate social ambition, and Clarence Mangan differed merely from the impersonal ballad writers about him in being miserable. He was not a personality as Edgar Poe was. He had not thought out or felt-out a way of looking at the world peculiar to himself.[3] We will have a hard fight in Ireland before we get the right for everyman to see the world in his own way admitted. Synge is

[2] The paucity of the audience was noted by several reviewers, and the play itself came in for severe criticism. The *Irish Times* of 6 Feb (7) suggested that the 'by no means crowded' house indicated the wrong choice of plays, and found the subject 'commonplace . . . and its action barren of anything really noteworthy. The play, in fact, is chiefly given over to wearisome dialogues. . . . These usually take the form of mutual recrimination, and there is not much point in the rustic repartee. The author, too, beats out certain peculiarities of Irish speech threadbare.' The Dublin *Evening Mail* of 6 Feb (2) thought it 'hardly worth while analyzing Mr. Synge's intentions for the simple reason that out of such intangible and fantastic material it will never be possible to build up a national Irish drama'. The *United Irishman* characteristically insisted on 11 Feb (1) that Synge's play was a 'failure': 'His peasants are not Irish, and the language they use in strife is pure Whitechapel. The dialogue is most uneven, varying from passages of lyric beauty to violent eruptions of no real strength; the duologues are lengthy, iterative, and apt to become wearisome. The imperfections of the play are numerous, and it is dragged out to three times its natural length. . . . What there is "Irish," "national," or "dramatic" about it even Oedipus might fail to solve. How is it that the Irish National Theatre, which started so well, can now only alternate a decadent wail with a Calvinistic groan.' Nevertheless, there was grudging praise for the actors. The *Freeman's Journal* reported that the 'players did excellently in the measure of their opportunity. Mr. W. G. Fay is a comedian of rare powers, and in the subtler touches of his part was excellent. His explosions were not convincing, but that, perhaps, was not his fault. Miss Emma Vernon [Vera Esposito] as the blind woman was also admirable. Her brogue is perfect, and the peasant manner is given without strain or stiffness.' The *Irish Times* noted resignedly that, despite its strictures, 'the audience appeared to appreciate the play, and the author was called before the curtain for an ovation at the close of the last act', and that William Fay as Martin Doul 'certainly made the most of the part, frequently evoking laughter'. The knock-on effect of this poor reception was felt in the reduced audiences for AG's *Kincora* in March, and she explained to Quinn on 29 Mar (NYPL) that there was 'a strong undercurrent of feeling against Synge—The company believe we lost a part of our audience during Well of Saints, & that it will be hard to coax it back again—It is a fine play, but only appeals to the few, & has the orthodox against it.'

[3] The Irish poet Thomas Moore (1779–1852) achieved enormous popularity in his time for the songs and lyrics in his ten-volume *Irish Melodies* (1808–34), although later Irish writers, including WBY, were more critical of him. The son of a Dublin grocer and without private means, he nevertheless rose in society through both his talent and the assiduous cultivation of the great. He became the friend and biographer of Byron, who observed that he 'dearly loved a lord', and in *BIV* (1895) WBY commented (p. xiii) that the 'Irish Melodies are to most cultivated ears but excellent drawing-room songs, pretty with a prettiness which is contraband of Parnassus', and remarked that in England Moore's reputation was over 'but in Ireland numbers think him the first of lyric poets, and no persuasion can make them believe that poetry has cast him out because he has not distinction of style'. James Joyce concurred with this view, and Stephen Dedalus pointed to Moore's social climbing in describing him as 'a Firbolg in the borrowed cloak of a Milesian' (see I. 32, n. 7).

James Clarence Mangan (1803–1849), the Dublin poet, had led a wretched life, working at first as a law scrivener and later as a cataloguer in the TCD Library. Worn out by poverty, alcohol, and probably

invaluable to us because he has that kind of intense narrow personality, which necessarily raises the whole issue. It will be very curious to notice the effect of his new play. He will start next time with many enemies but with very many admirers. It will be a fight like that over the first realistic plays of Ibsen.[4] I have done a preface for the more expensive addition [*for* edition] of his play but it not out yet.[5]

I daresay you've seen my squabble with Arthur Griffith. I could not very well avoid it as the story that he had taken a plot from Petronius' and pretended that it was Irish was calculated to do a deal of mischief.

Lady Gregory has greatly improved "Kincora" since that version went out to you. She has added a new scene at the beginning and heightened and ennobled the second and third acts a good deal.[6] The scenery is now being made. It will be a fine spectacle I think, with its rich harmonious colour, which reminds me that our decorative scenery for Synge's play has been generally liked. It was scrambled thro' in a great hurry and cost, I think, about £5, and yet was, I am certain, tho' often mistaken in execution, obviously right in principle, we were in despair over it for a while.[7]

opium, he succumbed to the cholera epidemic of 1849. His life and works are often compared to his American contemporary Edgar Allan Poe (1809–49), and he had been one of the 'neglected' Irish writers whom WBY wanted to revive in the 1890s. WBY published eight of his poems in *A Book of Irish Verse*, but he subsequently narrowed his admiration to only two, writing in *Aut* (396) of 'the Clarence Mangan of the *Dark Rosaleen* and *O'Hussey's Ode to The Maguire*, our one poet raised to the first rank by intensity, and only that in these or perhaps in the second of these poems'.

[4] The effect of his new play was to be as tumultuous as WBY here prophesies; *The Playboy of the Western World* caused a riot at the Abbey when it was first produced in January 1907. The London productions of the realist plays of the Norwegian dramatist Henrik Ibsen (1828–1906) had provoked fierce controversy in the 1880s and early 1890s, particularly that of *Ghosts* at the Royalty Theatre in 1891. In *Aut* (279) WBY recalls the hostility of audience and critics to a production of *A Doll's House* which he saw in 1889.

[5] WBY's introduction is dated 'Abbey Theatre, January 27th, 1905'; see p. 28.

[6] The construction of AG's three-act historical drama *Kincora* had given her considerable trouble (see p. 28, n. 3). She had just added a short 'Prologue' before Act I in which two armed men find Brian sleeping in a wood, and agree that he alone is capable of driving the Danes out of Ireland. After they leave, the Celtic spirit Aoibhell of the Grey Rock visits Brian to persuade him to give up the thankless task of serving Ireland, and to live with her in peace, happiness and immortality. But he refuses: 'I will not give up Ireland. For it is a habit of my race to fight and to die, but it never was their habit to see shame or oppression put on their country by any man on earth.' The play was produced on 25 Mar of this year, but radically revised thereafter. On 24 Feb Quinn told AG (NYPL) that she had 'improved "Kincora" very much' and predicted that it would be 'a great popular success'. And in his reply to this letter (Himber, 67), he said that if AG did not intend to publish *Kincora* by 11 Mar, he 'would prefer to print the revised form of it'.

[7] The scenery for *The Well of the Saints* received mixed notices. The *Irish Times* of 6 Feb complained (7) that the play was 'particularly crude in its scenic equipment' and that 'more scenic effects must be utilised', but the *Belfast Evening Telegraph* of the same day thought (5) that 'really wonderful effects have been produced by the simplest means. Flat cloths and faint tints suggested surprising semblances of rugged lands and sombre skies.'

Miss Horniman has undertaken to make the arrangements for our London expedition this year.[8] We expect to bring there "Baile's Strand" (re-written since performance) "Spreading the News" "Kathleen Ni houlihan" and "The well of the Saints". Synge is pretty sure of a big success in London. We are to follow "Kincora" with a revival of "The King's Threshold" (partly re-written) and a new play by Boyle.[9] We shall probably follow these a month later with Colum's three-act play. He read me an act last Sunday really very good, simple and coherent, and with a curious dialect. Unlike Synge and Lady Gregory, his is the dialect of a non-Irish speaking district. In addition to a certain number of phrases containing Gaelic construction, there are quantities of phrases out of the School reading Books and out of newspapers; it gives a very curious sense of reality tho' rather a horrid one. There is a certain amount too of the pompous English of the hedge school-master days. It is unbeautiful Ireland and he will contrast finely with our western dialect makers. He writes of his own Longford of course. I think he is really going to come off as a writer, but it will be as a harsh realist, rather of the German kind.[10]

Yrs sinly<br>W B Yeats

TLS NYPL, with envelope addressed to 120 Broadway, New York, postmark 'DUBLIN FE 15 05'. Wade, 446–8.

## *To Henry G. O'Brien, 15 February 1905*

NASSAU HOTEL, | Sth. Frederick St., | Dublin<br>15/2/'05.

Dear Mr. O'Brien,

I hardly know how to address you. Are you Father O'Brien or Brother O'Brien now?[1] I thought I had answered your letter telling me that you

---

[8] The Company was to visit London in November of this year.

[9] William Boyle's three-act comedy *The Building Fund* was produced at the Abbey Theatre on 25 Apr with a revised version of WBY's *The King's Threshold*. *The Building Fund*, in which a son and niece compete to threaten and cajole their way into a miserly old woman's will, only to discover when the will is read that she has left her money to a building fund for a new church, was an immediate success, and was revived frequently at the Abbey.

[10] Padraic Colum's three-act play *The Land* (see p. 28) was produced at the Abbey Theatre on 9 June, the last production of the INTS, which was thereafter absorbed into the National Theatre Society, Ltd. Colum (see p. 28, n. 4) had been born in Longford, and WBY had advised him to read Ibsen and Sudermann in December 1902 (see III. 287–8, 293–4). Hedge schoolmasters, who presided over unofficial schools until the establishment of a national system of education in 1831, were noted for their extravagant rhetoric, described by Hyde as a 'sesquipedalian style, teeming with classical names and allusions'.

[1] Henry G. O'Brien (1883–1971) was born in Mitchelstown, Co. Cork, and attended Clongowes College 1894–6. He subsequently joined the Royal Navy, and served as a midshipman on HMS *Argonaut*

were going to become a priest.[2] Certainly I had no intention to leave it
unanswered, but I'm very careless about letters, and sometimes think I have
answered one when I have not. My bad eyesight, which forces me to wait
till I can get a typewriter[3] or the like, often a difficult thing when I am in the
country, makes me a very bad correspondent. Do you ever come up to
London? I would find it so much easier to explain to you personally when
[*for* what] I am doing than to write to you about it. If you let me know
before hand I would make an appointment. I am to and fro between Dublin
and London constantly, and unless I knew beforehand, you would never be
certain of finding me. When I am in Dublin I'm always here, but 18,
WOBURN BUILDINGS, Euston Rd. will always find me sooner or later.

Our work is going on very well I think, and perhaps some day you may be
able to help it, or what is more likely find some aspect of this great
intellectual stir and awakening now coming up on Ireland which would
be your work and no one elses

Yrs sny
W B Yeats

TLS Pierpont Morgan.

## *To Maud Gonne, [18 February 1905]*

Mention in following letter and in letters from MG, 'Sunday' [19 February
1905], and 25 February [1905].
Telegram, enquiring 'Is all well?'[1]

*G–YL*, 191, 192.

---

on the China Station. While based at Weihaiwei in the summer of 1902 he came across (and temporarily
purloined) *John Sherman and Dhoya* in the officers' club, and wrote to tell WBY (*LWBY* 1. 109–11) that
he had failed his sub-lieutenant examination and was, with some cause, regarded as one of the slackest
officers on the ship. He explained that he lacked nautical zeal because he was constantly daydreaming
about Ireland, and that he wished to be an Irish farmer and write books like WBY's (see pp. 997–8). He
was dismissed from the navy and returned to England in the summer of 1903, but became a priest, not a
farmer. At this time he was still training for the priesthood; he was ordained Father O'Brien in 1909, and
subsequently served for many years as the parish priest of Kingsbridge, Devon.

[2] Both O'Brien's letters are untraced; the first evidently disclosed that he was studying to be a priest,
and the second enquired about WBY's latest writings. O'Brien recalled (Pierpont Morgan) that he was
'then a church student and was passing thro London for a holiday with school friends near Madrid &
must have written a few lines; alas, we were not destined to meet.'

[3] i.e. a typist.

[1] WBY was eager to know how the reconciliation tribunal, held earlier this day, had gone.

## To Lady Gregory, [20 February 1905]

Nassau Hotel

My dear Lady Gregory: I wired to M^rs Mac Bride on Saturday night. I asked 'Is all well' & this morning came the answer 'All well, writing'. I conclude the case is going on. If it had been postponed she would have wired 'postponed' & of course would have wired if it was over.[1]

I did not go to the doctor as I am much better.[2] I went round to the theatre to day & found Fay pouring paper pulp into a shield mold. He [had] a very gloomy & care worn look. The look he had when he was trying to colour the lamp with hat die—yet all seemed going well.

I am all but finished with 'Baile Strand', but must make a clean copy & some six lines more.

Moore proffessed great interest in 'Kincora' & even gently commended 'Spreading of the News'.

Yr ev
W B Yeats

PS.

I expect Gogorty to discuss his being turned out. He is just due.[3]
[*On back of envelope*]
I shall be here some days yet.
WBY.

ALS Berg, with envelope addressed to Coole, postmark 'DUBLIN FE 20 05'.

[1] MG had petitioned the Civil Tribunal of the Seine for a divorce on 3 Feb, and, in accordance with French law, the Tribunal authorized her to call MacBride before the court on 18 Feb to see if a reconciliation could be effected, meanwhile forbidding him access to the conjugal home. The attempted reconciliation failed, and on 24 Feb the court granted her custody of her son pending a final adjudication. Her petition for a final decree was heard on 26 July, and on 9 Aug the judge ordered MacBride to pay MG 1,500 francs, granted her custody of the child, but also ordered a new 'enquête' (an inquiry based on oral evidence given to a judge by witnesses) into both MG's allegations and the counter-charges by MacBride. The *enquête* did not take place until 20 and 27 Nov 1905.

[2] WBY was replying to a letter from AG of 'Monday' (Berg) in which she asked: 'Have you been to a doctor? What does he say? Have you any news from Paris? Have you got on with Baile's Strand?' WBY had been suffering from 'bad neuralgia', as AG told Quinn on 4 Feb (NYPL).

[3] Oliver St John Gogarty (1878–1957), surgeon, poet, writer of memoirs, athlete, and wit, was born in Dublin and educated at Stonyhurst and Trinity College, Dublin. He had cultivated WBY's friendship since meeting him early in 1902 (see III. 170), and they were to remain friends for the rest of WBY's life. Gogarty served in the Irish Senate from 1922 to 1936. Among his volumes of verse are *Poems and Plays* (1920), *An Offering of Swans* (1924), *Others to Adorn* (1938), and *Elbow Room* (1939), and his books of memoirs include *As I Was Going Down Sackville Street* (1937), *Tumbling in the Hay* (1939), and *It Isn't This Time of Year at All!* (1954). He had shared the Martello Tower at Sandymount with James Joyce in the summer of 1904, and became the model for 'Buck Mulligan' in *Ulysses*. He was only periodically in residence there after the autumn of 1904, having gone to Oxford to take his medical exams, which he failed, and having spent some time in a Trappist monastery at the insistence of his

## *To Lady Gregory, [21-24 February 1905]*

Nassau Hotel
Tuesday

My dear Lady Gregory: I got a letter from M$^{rs}$ Mac Bride last night. It was however dated Sunday & there was nothing new. Mac Bride had 'sat & cried' all through 'the confrontation' on Saturday. 'He did himself as much harm as possible in the eyes of the judge.' He goes about 'crying & making insinuations against' her & so on.[1] I may get more news to-night. I am waiting on here till the case is decided, or practically so; & until I have given a complete script of 'Baile's Strand' to Fay. I have worked well & am now copying out what I have written. I have nothing new except a few connecting lines to write. I am very pleased with my work. Frank Fay was delighted with some lines I showed him. When I give Fay the final text we will settle dates.[2]

Friday.

No more news from Paris. I am a little anxious. Russell who regularly exausts two hours or an hour & a half of my time every day when he heard there was no news said in a voice, that suggested he was pleased 'no news is bad news'. Fay says he argues wholly on Mac Brides side. I dont let him now. I have told him that if I wish to discuss academic moral propositions I shall go to history, not to the intimate affairs of my friends, for subject matter. He told me for the first time on Tuesday that he & Miss Young had something to do with launching the arbitration proposal—they were wholly responsible I thought

mother. He now lived mainly at the Gogarty family home, 5 Rutland Square, and was evidently being turned out of the Tower. After Gilbert Murray rejected his request for a translation of Sophocles (see p. 22), WBY turned to Gogarty, who wrote to G. K. A. Bell in February 1905: 'I am preparing a trans. (verse) of "Oedipus Rex" for Yeats!' (*Many Lines*, 73). The translation was never published or produced.

[1] MG had written from Paris on 'Sunday' (19 Feb 1905; *G–YL*, 191), the day after the abortive attempt at a legal reconciliation, explaining that by 'a stupid forgetfulness the telegram I wrote in answer to yours was not sent—I am so sorry.' She went on to tell him that things were 'going on fairly well. I have the best lawyer in Paris Mr Crouppi to defend me. He hopes things will go quickly. The confrontation was very painful, my husband sat & cried all the time & talked about wanting no scandal & wanting arbitration & at the same time trying to make insinuations against me—I think he did himself as much harm as possible in the eyes of the judge.' MacBride's account of the proceedings (NLI) records that he 'attended with his wife alone before the Judge', and, when asked whether there was any chance of a reconciliation, he replied 'that he was willing to do anything in that direction subject to safeguarding his honour'. The judge then asked MG if she would be party to a reconciliation 'and she shook her head and said "No", firmly. The judge then said to her "you want to be free?" and she said she did.' In her reply of 'Saturday' (Berg), AG hoped that all had 'gone well in Paris & that your mind will soon be at rest'.

[2] WBY had been rewriting *On Baile's Strand* over the previous six weeks (see p. 30), and in her reply AG said that she was 'delighted to hear of Baile's Strand, & long to see the new bits'.

at first but next day he was vaguer.[3] Griffith is the last cat who shows for a Griffen in his eyes.

I read my new Bailes Strand to Fay last night. He was delighted but suggested one or two very slight changes which I shall make. He thinks that Kinkora would suffer if he got it up for the special show.[4] I have suggested 'The Hour Glass' & I think this will be done but he wants to play it with plain sacking instead of the green. He says the dies [*for* dyes] would cost about £4-10 & this is too much for one performance. I have half consented though unwillingly to the plain. What do you think. Nothing is settled.[5]

I am afraid some cuts are wanted in Act 2 of Kinkora. There are bits that stop the action. Fay is urgent & I feal with him. I am to go through it to day & I will send you a suggested text. Fay is very much against working from so slight a design as Roberts one for the backcloth & will wait till I go to London. He says Robert should give us a detailed design to scale, which we need not depart from at all, or leave it to us wholly. He says there was a lack of unity in Singes scenery through the need of altering Pamela Smiths inadequate sketches. He would sooner wait till the last moment for a sufficient design than start on a mere sketch. I hope to go to London next week. I do not like leaving this while things in Paris are uncertain or while there is a chance of doing something here.

Yr sny<br>W B Yeats

[3] Ella Young (1865–1956), poet and writer of children's stories, was the sister of the actress Elizabeth Young. She had been born in Co. Antrim but moved to Dublin, where she took a BA in Law and Political Science. She joined the Dublin Theosophical Society, and AE encouraged her to collect fairy folklore, as well as including her in his anthology *New Songs*. She cast horoscopes with WBY, but came to epitomize for him the complaisant and spiritualized sentimentality that he despised in the AE circle. A friend of MG's, she espoused the nationalist cause and supported the Republicans in the Civil War. In 1925 she emigrated to America and lectured on Celtic mythology at the University of California. She and AE had evidently helped Dixon to formulate his arbitration proposal (see p. 33), and had tried to arrange a meeting between MG and Dixon and Griffith 'in London with a view to arriving at a settlement without scandal, they told Ella that John was very reasonable & wanted settlement. I wrote back that I had given him every opportunity of settling things quietly, that he had refused, that now my friends in Dublin could do no good by trying to arrange a settlement as I had already applied for divorce in the French courts' (*G–YL*, 189). In her reply (see n. 1) AG commented that 'Russell is a queer creature'.

[4] Lady MacDonnell was organizing a special INTS benefit performance of *The Hour-Glass*, *A Pot of Broth*, and *Spreading the News* for 15 Apr, all proceeds going to the new Municipal Gallery of Modern Art. See pp. 4, 21.

[5] In her reply (see n. 1) AG thought it would be 'a pity if the Hour Glass can't be green', and suggested that perhaps 'my wood scene sacking [from the prologue to *Kincora*] may be dyed green first & would do. However I am writing to Robert about it. The plain sacking would not look bad.'

3.30

I wired to M^rs Clay on Tuesday night asking "is all well". I have just received a wire saying "All well, Gonne". So my mind is at ease.[6] I notice that she drops the word "Mac Bride" for the first time.

Russell has just been in. I told him apropose of something or other that 'he was a bad critic of drama'. He got very angry & said, a little irrelevantly that I had told Madame <Marcrevittsch> Marcovitch that he "would not do for Lanes Curator as he would do jobs all the time". I never thought or said such a thing I need hardly say.[7]

ALS Berg, with envelope addressed to Coole, postmark 'DUBLIN FE 25 05'.

## To May Clay, [21 February 1905]

Mention in previous letter and in a letter from May Clay of 23 February. A telegram asking 'Is all well' and a letter informing her that MacBride might be arrested if he returned to Ireland.[1]

---

[6] On 25 Feb MG explained to WBY (*G–YL*, 192) that his 'telegram was badly transcribed here & May did not understand it wanted an answer so it was only on receiving your letter that I found it did, the telegram read "All well here!"'

[7] AE was still an organizer for the Irish Co-operative Society (IAOS), but an increasingly disgruntled one, and on 23 Jan he had told Thomas Mosher (NLI) that he hoped he would soon be able to retire. In these circumstances, and as a painter himself and a member of Lane's Picture Committee, the post of curator of the new gallery would have been tempting to him. Constance Gore-Booth (1868–1927), now the Countess Markiewicz, artist, suffragette, nationalist, and politician, was the daughter of Sir Henry Gore-Booth of Lissadell, Sligo. After studying art at the Slade School in the early 1890s, she went in 1897 to Julian's Academy in Paris to study under Jean-Paul Laurens. There she met a Polish artist, Casimir Dunin, Count de Markiewicz, whom she married as his second wife in September 1900. They settled in Dublin in 1903, and were now playing a vigorous part in artistic and theatrical circles. She was a friend and neighbour of AE, and the two collaborated in mounting annual summer exhibitions of their paintings. After her husband's return to Europe in December 1913 she became increasingly involved in Sinn Fein politics, was sentenced to death for her part in the Easter Rising of 1916, but reprieved—events recorded in WBY's poem 'On a Political Prisoner' (*VP*, 397)—and was later a member of the first Dáil Eireann and a cabinet minister. WBY's elegy for her and her sister Eva Gore-Booth, 'In Memory of Eva Gore-Booth and Con Markiewicz' (*VP*, 475–6), was written shortly after her death.

[1] In her reply of 23 Feb (Emory) May Clay told WBY that his letter and telegram had arrived the previous day, '& they have rather troubled me, for I think MacBride's arrest might interfere fatally with the divorce & that is an essential thing for Maud's future. If he is arrested, would it not stop all legal proceedings, I am certain it would have an affect on her mind. If there is really any fear of his being arrested on his return to Ireland do you think it would be possible for some of his friends to warn him. Anything that I said here, to his journalist friends, would give rise to the suspicion, that I was using Government help & that would be bad for Maud.' She added that the 'legal part is as good as possible, & it all depends on how much obstruction MacBride raises for how long it will last'.

## To Maud Gonne, [c. 24 February 1905]

Mention in letter from MG, 25 February [1905].
Asking for news,[1] telling her that Edward Martyn is on her side,[2] and assuring her that the Irish cause is above being injured by the unworthiness of one of its servants.[3]

*G–YL*, 192.

## To Lady Gregory, [27 February 1905]

Nassau Hotel

My dear Lady Gregory: I am very glad you think of coming.[1] The sooner you come the better as it may be necessary for me to go to London before Robert gets those designs right.[2] In any case unless of course you could stay on until the play I had better go to London between your visit & the play. The Second Act wants considerable cutting—some of Brians most cherished speaches should go out & Fay thinks <Rory &> Derrick & one other servent should be cut out of Act III & I think he is right. These cuts will improve

---

[1] In her reply MG reported that there was little news: 'things are going wearily on here. I believe the assignation has been sent, & John will then have to name a French lawyer who will state his line of defence but I think he has still 10 days' delay to do this. Then the tribunal fixes a day & our Lawyers fight it out between them & the judges decide whether or no the Court can pronounce at once or must order an enquiry. If John is at all wise he will let the divorce be pronounced then but he is not at all wise.'

[2] Edward Martyn (1859–1923; see II. 686–95), Galway landlord, playwright, Irish nationalist, and first president of Sinn Fein. He had first met WBY in London in 1896, and helped him and AG found the Irish Literary Theatre in 1897. He underwrote the first performances of the ILT and his plays *The Heather Field* and *Maeve* were produced under its auspices. As a member of the Sinn Fein movement, Martyn also knew MG well and the two had been leaders of rambunctious protests against the visit of Edward VII to Ireland in May 1903 (see III. 377–8). Despite this, it was far from certain that he would take MG's part on religious grounds: as a devout Catholic he was opposed to divorce, and later in the year his scruples on this point were indeed to lead him to reconsider his support for her (see p. 172). In her reply, MG said that she was 'glad Mr Martyn is a friend of mine, for I like & respect him very much. As for the others when the verdict is given against John I suppose they will be convinced anyhow it is not for me to bother about convincing them.'

[3] MG replied that WBY was 'quite right in saying the Irish Cause is above being injured by the unworthiness of one of its servants. Though because of his love of that cause I would rather have spared him, if he would have made it possible—'

[1] AG had remained in Coole to recover her health, but had suggested in a letter of the previous day (Berg) that she should perhaps go up to Dublin to decide about the scenery for *Kincora*, and 'to see a rehearsal or two'. 'What are you doing?' she asked WBY. 'I could go up in about a week for a day or two. Let me know your plans.'

[2] Robert Gregory was designing the scenery for AG's *Kincora*, but communication was difficult and in her letter AG had complained that she was 'in the dark as it [is] very hard to get an answer out of either you or Robert or W. Fay'.

the play & they are made necessary in \<adit> \<adition> edition by the play being Fay says considerably too long. If they are to be done they should be made at once by Fay & myself or you should come up & make them. They may involve three or four new sentences & the sooner they are right the better. With these cuts the play will go very swiftly & movingly.[3] Could you not come up before the end of the week—there is a Shakespear actor called Tearle who is much admired by Fay. He plays Julius Ceasar on Friday & Hamlet on Saturday. He is one of Fays old fashioned actors 'who know how to speak'. He does 'Macbeth' on Wednesday—Fay thinks finely—but I suppose you could not be in time for that. Do come.[4]

I am not anxious about Paris. It goes on slowly & may still I am told take weeks. I can see from his friends desire to get Mac Bride in prison that they know his case is hopeless. Or rather I am only anxious for fear she may be bullied into some weakness. I had Henry Dixon[5] here on Friday & I think sadened him. The trouble with these men is that in their eyes a woman has no rights. I could see that he thinks M^rs Mac Brides objection to drunkenness a morbid peculiarity. I feal at every turn that by turning catholic she put herself in their hands—she accepted their code & that is for woman a code of ignoble submission.

I think you will learn a good deal by some rehearsals & by seeing why Fay wants these changes. Do come I am 'desolate else, left by mankind'.[6]

---

[3] Act II of the 1905 version of *Kincora* takes place after the successful Battle of Glenmama, at which Brian has defeated and captured King Maelmora of Leinster, his nephew Sitric, the Danish commander, and Gormleith, the treacherous wife of his ally, the High King Malachi. King Malachi condemns the prisoners to death, but Brian intervenes to save them, so causing a breach with Malachi. However, Malachi finds himself unable to raise an army to challenge Brian and surrenders both the high kingship and his wife Gormleith to him. Derrick is one of Brian Boru's servants, who also sees himself as a poet. Despite Fay's advice, AG retained him in the first and third scenes of Act III of this version, although she cut him entirely when revising the play in 1909.

[4] WBY may have confused Osmond with Edmund Tearle. Edmund Tearle (1856–1913), an English actor-manager, produced *Othello*, *Macbeth*, *Julius Caesar*, and *Hamlet* in Dublin from 27 Feb to 4 Mar, supported by Kate Clinton and a specially selected company. On 22 Feb 1902 Frank Fay had written in the *United Irishman* (5) that 'although he is not an *artist*, he is a good rough-and-ready actor, and I confess I have a great admiration for him. Here is an actor who, without any lavish mounting or newspaper puffing, has gone on . . . playing Shakespeare to people who don't want Shakespeare at all.' But Fay admired Osmond Tearle far more, telling WBY on 23 July 1901 (Private) that he was 'the only English tragedian worth a rap in my opinion', and on 18 Dec 1902 (Private) claiming that he was superior to Forbes-Robertson. He held to this opinion, and on 14 Oct of this year was to tell Joseph Holloway (NLI) that he preferred Osmond Tearle's portrayal of Shylock to that of Henry Irving.

[5] See p. 33.

[6] See the second quatrain of Lionel Johnson's sonnet 'The Church of a Dream': 'Still in their golden venture the old saints prevail; | Alone with Christ, desolate else, left by mankind.' It appeared in *Poems* (1895), and it became one of WBY's favourites among Johnson's poems; he included it in the revised edition of *A Book of Irish Verse* (1900) and in *OBMV*. He also quoted the whole poem in a fund-raising speech, 'Friends of my Youth', in March 1910, and again in his 1936 broadcast 'Modern Poetry'. It was probably in his mind at this time because he had just reread it in the Dun Emer anthology of Johnson, *Twenty-One Poems*, published on 21 Feb 1905. The line lingered in WBY's memory for a lifetime, and

I am making my lyric[7] for Pamela Smith.

Yrs ev<br>W B Yeats

ALS Berg, with envelope addressed to Coole, postmark 'DUBLIN FE [?]27 05'.

## *To Maud Gonne, [early March 1905]*

Mention in an undated letter from MG, [early March 1905]. Apparently asking the name of the correspondent of the *Morning Leader*,[1] discussing the announcement of divorce proceedings in the Irish papers, offering to stay on in Dublin to look after her affairs,[2] and telling her of the forthcoming production of AG's *Kincora*.[3]

*G–YL*, 193–4.

was reworked in his poem of 1938 'An Acre of Grass': 'Forgotten else by mankind, | An old man's eagle mind' (*VP*, 576).

[7] Presumably 'O Do Not Love Too Long' (*VP*, 211–12), apparently written before 23 Feb 1905, and probably promised to the *Green Sheaf*, which Pamela Colman Smith planned to turn into a quarterly, but which was discontinued before the poem could appear there. It was eventually published in the *Acorn* in October 1905.

[1] News of the Gonne–MacBride proceedings became public on 27 Feb, when the London *Morning Leader*'s 'own correspondent' reported from Paris that 'Miss Gonne-McBride famous lady agitator' was suing for divorce: 'Mrs McBride alleges infidelity and intemperance, which the husband absolutely and emphatically denies. The major is well-known and popular in Irish and Irish-American circles in Paris.' This report was copied by the Irish papers and appeared in the Dublin press on 27 and 28 Feb, as well as in the London *Daily Mail* and *Daily Mirror*. In her reply (*G–YL*, 193), MG told WBY that the correspondent of the *Morning Leader*, Cozens Hardy, was in love with the daughter of MacBride's best friend in Paris, Victor Collins: 'It is his note that the Irish papers have reproduced . . . so John has again his own friends to thank for the glaring announcement in the Irish papers as he had for the announcement in the American press.' She added that the report had caused great sorrow to MacBride's 'poor old mother in Westport for whom I feel very sorry, of course she says she believes nothing against her son but is terribly upset & miserable'. MG also correctly foresaw that the now inescapable publicity would harden MacBride's position: 'the effect of this announcement will be to make John defend himself to the utmost, as now it is more difficult for him to accept what my lawyers were willing to offer that the divorce should be pronounced without dishonoring considerations & on the minimum offence.'

[2] WBY had evidently offered to remain in Dublin to rally support for MG and her cause, but she would not hear of this: 'Thank you so much for offering to stay in Dublin, but PLEASE don't alter your plans at all on my account. You have been so helpful & so kind all through this trouble, but I don't want you to do any more. It is such a horrid thing to keep one's mind on.' In fact, WBY left for London shortly after receiving this letter.

[3] In her reply MG wished she 'was in Dublin. I should love to see the plays. I am sure *Kincora* will be a great success with the people.'

## *To Maud Gonne,* [c. *9 March 1905*]

Mention in letter from MG, 'Friday' [10 March 1905].
Sending her a copy of Lionel Johnson's poems.[1]

*G–YL,* 192–3.


## *To John Quinn, 11 March* [*1905*]

18 Woburn Buildings | Euston Road
March 11.

My dear Quinn: I write to you on another business. On something I want
you to do or get done in your professional capacity. You know that M^{rs}
MacBride is divorcing her husband. It is a very bad case. She went through
great misery with him. She kept silent about it pretending that all was going
well, even to her own sister. Then something unspeakable happened & she
came to London to ask legal advice.[1] Barry O'Brien came in to the affair as
representing the fenians who did not want a scandal. He drew up a
settlement which M^{rs} Mac Brides lawyer & friends thought very unwise
from her point of view. She agreed to it for the sake of the cause but Mac
Bride to everybody's surprize refused it. She then took divorce proceedings. The charge against him is infidelity cruelty & drunkenness (an offence
under the French marriage law).[2] There are certain very serious features in
the case, other people involved & so on & this makes it very desirable that
M^{rs} Mac Bride should get her case on the minor offences. I tell you in strict
confidence that the offence that made M^{rs} Mac Bride seperate from him
was an assault of a criminal nature upon a child, nearly related to M^{rs} Mac
Bride. For the childs sake, & other reasons, that has to be kept out of the
trial if possible. She has therefore to make as much as she can out of such
comparative small beer as an assault upon the cook, drunkenness, & an
intreague or two. His moral sense has been destroyed by drink. A week ago
I got a letter from M^{rs} Clay—her cousin & friend & helper in this business.
I enclose the letter. I know you will not mind my having crossed out the
name in the phrase 'the news of——'s marriage'. It is the name of a poor

---

[1] WBY had sent MG a copy of the Dun Emer anthology of Johnson, *Twenty-One Poems*, published
on 21 Feb 1905 (see III. 619–20, 645). MG would have met the poet and scholar Johnson (1867–1902;
see I. 496–7) at WBY's rooms and at the ILS in the early 1890s, and he proposed the toast at a '98
Banquet on 9 Aug 1898 at which she also spoke (see II. 259).

[1] The 'unspeakable thing' was MacBride's alleged indecent exposure to Iseult (see pp. 7–8, 10–11).

[2] See 'Easter 1916' (*VP,* 393): 'This other man I had dreamed | A drunken, vainglorious lout. | He
had done most bitter wrong | To some who are near my heart.'

girl who may have to be brought into the case.[3] It is one of the painful & scandalous parts I spoke of. I do not think much of ordinary morals but this man has been a drunken cad from the first. I replied to this letter by saying that you were my one New York friend & suggesting that you be invited to act in your proffesional capacity, & asking that her lawyer write to you & give you authority. To day I got the enclosed. I know you will do what you can. If too busy, you will know who could be put to do it. Please tell me what it would cost or if you like write direct to M$^{rs}$ Clay in Paris.

You can understand that this all has been a deep trouble to me. M$^{rs}$ Clay asked my help at the outset, & I have written many letters & received many about it & perhaps been of a little use. Mac Bride at the outset made & is still making I beleive, wild counter charges—including a charge against me. He has had mad fits of jelousey from the very outset of this marriage & in one of these has threatened to shoot me. I am afraid neither of his counter charges— which are lies—nor of his revolver which is probably empty, but I am deeply troubled & worried about M$^{rs}$ Mac Bride for whom I have an affection of the most lasting kind. I do not say that it is any kind of passion but it is the feeling one has for some near & dear relation. I have had a very low-spirited letter from her this morning. She feals that her work is over & is spending her time painting in a study that she may not think.[4] She [is] acting as she is merely because she looks upon it as a duty to get absolute control of her child, the father being unworthy.[5] She refused to think that the cause can suffer because of any mans unworthiness & so though ready to go far was not ready to go to all lengths to prevent scandal. The accounts in the papers are all coming from her husbands friends & acquaintances for she is keeping silent.

Very many thanks for that money & for all the trouble you have taken[6]— 'The Pot of Broth' was performed at a London theatre last week but the

[3] Both of May Clay's letters are untraced. The first apparently asked for the name of an American lawyer, rehearsed the charges against MacBride, and gave the latest news of the divorce proceedings. The deleted name is that of MG's half-sister Eileen Wilson, who had married Joseph MacBride (1860–1938), John MacBride's eldest brother, in August 1904. MG alleged that John MacBride had had sexual relations with the 17-year-old Eileen in the summer of 1903 at her house at Colleville while she was away (see p. 7, n. 4), and that the marriage was a way of hushing this up. In spite of her misgivings, the incident was brought forward as grounds for divorce, and denied by MacBride.

[4] MG was painting in the studio of Joseph Grainié (1866–1955) at 17 rue de l'Annonciation: 'He lets me come down and draw with him', she wrote on 10 Mar (*G–YL*, 193), 'I don't draw much. . . . In the mornings I work at Julian's Academy. As usual with me I am trying to fill my life so as not to think . . . it may be the Gods have no more use for me & want a younger voice & energy to carry on the work.'

[5] The custody and upbringing of Séan MacBride had been the major concern of both parties in the negotiations over the break-up of the marriage (see p. 8), and on 25 Feb MG had told WBY (*G–YL*, 192): 'All I care about is to safeguard my child . . . between John whose usefulness is I should think over & little Seagan whose work has not yet begun there can be no hesitation.'

[6] The money was for performing rights and came from Phillip Bayard Veiller, who was currently managing his wife Margaret Wycherly in an American tour of WBY's plays *Cathleen ni Houlihan*, *The Hour-Glass*, and *The Land of Heart's Desire* (see III. 614, 663–4). She had first performed the latter

acting—I had been in Dublin during rehersal—was bad & vulgar beyond words. Caubeen—tailed coat & all the rest of it—a most injurious business from every point of view. I get £5 which I give to the company—that is all the gain to set against the loss.[7]

Yr ev

W B Yeats

PS. I have reopened this to say that I missed the mail yesterday through thinking that it went at night instead of noon. I want you, if you can does [*for* do] this work—perhaps I should have addressed you as Alexander & Colby—to wire to M^rs Clay, at my expense 'It will cost about such & such a sum'. She can then get her lawyer to write. Do not forget to send me the bill for the wire—the delay is my fault.[8]

ALS NYPL, with envelope addressed to 120 Broadway, New York, postmark 'LONDON. N.W. MR 13 05'. New York postmark 'MAR 24 1905' and 'DUE 10 CENTS'.

## To Maud Gonne, [c. 11 March 1905]

Mention in letter from MG, 'Sunday' [? 12 March 1905].
Informing her that Dr. Joseph Quinn is on her side,[1] asking if there is any truth in the announcement in the *Irish Independent* that she has come to an

---

two pieces in San Francisco on 29 Apr 1904, and added *Cathleen ni Houlihan* to the repertoire when she toured New England that autumn. Veiller withheld the royalties due from performances in Boston in November, but, when they moved to the Hudson Theatre in New York on 22 Feb 1905, Quinn insisted that he pay what was owing from Boston as well as the New York rights and on 3 Mar was able to send WBY $60 in sterling, in addition to the $200 he had remitted on 24 Feb. Phillip Bayard Veiller (1869–1943), playwright, journalist, and theatre manager, had married Margaret Wycherly in 1901 and became her manager before he began his own career as a prolific playwright, best known for *Within the Law* (1912), *The Thirteenth Chair* (1916), and *The Trial of Mary Dugan* (1927).

[7] Robert Pateman (1840–1924), a well-known English actor, played the Tramp in the Stage Society production of *The Pot of Broth*. Amy Lamborn, ingénue and character actress, took the part of Sibby Coneely, and George F. Tully (1876–1930), an Irish actor making his first appearance on the London stage, that of John Coneely. WBY's disgust with the acting was not universally shared: *MAP* on 11 Mar (223) asserted that it 'would be worth going to see the little piece for Mr. Robert Pateman's acting alone. His study of the artful tramp . . . is one of the completest things this strangely versatile actor has ever done.' The *Stage* of 2 Mar also enjoyed the performance (16), noting that 'Mr. Robert Pateman, besides singing acceptably some snatches of song, gave a very clever and humorous performance of the Tramp who lives on his wits', and the *Morning Post* of 1 Mar similarly found (5) that 'Mr. Robert Pateman as the tramp was extremely clever'.

[8] On 31 Mar, shortly after receiving this letter, Quinn cabled Mrs Clay (Emory): 'Will forward best papers can as soon as possible without any charge.'

[1] Joseph Patrick Quinn (1854–1916), son of a labourer from Claremorris, the 'young Mayo doctor' (*Mem*, 71) whose Dublin lodgings at 56 North Circular Road WBY shared in 1893 and 1894. Quinn had

arrangement with MacBride and stopped divorce proceedings,[2] and telling her that he proposes to have songs and poems between the plays at the Abbey Theatre.[3]

*G–YL*, 194–5.


## To May Clay, [early and mid-March 1905]

Mention in letter from MG, 'Tuesday' [March 1905].
A series of sympathetic letters about MG's marital problems.

*G–YL*, 195.


## To Lady Gregory, [12 March 1905]

18 Woburn Buildings | Euston Road.
Sunday

My dear Lady Gregory: I have just found the MSS after a long search.[1] I have not done any writing yet—the first day I was tired out & after that I had to see Bullen & the Whistler Show[2] & the Pot of Broth. The poor Pot of Broth was played & *gagged* with unspeakable vulgarity. Pateman played

served as assistant secretary of the Land League in 1881, and in this connection was imprisoned in Kilmainham Jail from October 1881 to June 1882. An admirer of Michael Davitt, he continued to work for the land movement and the Irish National League throughout the 1880s; and he was also a member of the Irish Republican Brotherhood, the extreme nationalist organization founded in 1858 by James Stephens. He later took up medicine, and in 1892 helped WBY found the National Literary Society. He had known MG through his political work and as a member of the ILS. In her reply to this letter MG told WBY that it was 'good getting your letters. You always know the right things to say. I am glad some of my old friends like Dr Quinn are capable of standing firm. As for the others they are like water & can be pushed aside but they will return again as surely.'

[2] MG ridiculed these reports: 'Of course there is no truth in the announcement in the Independent that an arrangement has been come to & divorce proceedings will be stayed. After the lies John MacBride has been telling & publishing about me nothing but the divorce judgment given in my favor can reply.'

[3] In fact, the Abbey settled for music between plays rather than recitations, although MG thought 'your idea of having song & poems between the plays very good, couldn't you get the author sometimes to come & recite their own poems, as they did at the *Chat Noir* in Paris. It used to be very interesting.'

[1] This was the MS of *The King's Threshold*, which WBY was rewriting for a new production. In a letter of 9 Mar (Berg) AG hoped 'Senchan goes well—& has been found', and on 29 Mar she wrote to Quinn (NYPL): 'WBY is at this moment writing his new version of "King's Threshold" which is to be given next month—He hasn't got back to Deirdre yet, & won't I expect until I have got him back to Coole.'

[2] The James Abbott McNeill Whistler Memorial Exhibition opened at the New Gallery, Regent Street, on 22 Feb and continued to 15 Apr under the auspices of the International Society of Sculptors, Painters, and Gravers, of which Whistler (1834–1903) had been first president.

in a stage Irish man-hat & coat & *rolled* his eyes & showed his teath—he was the stage Irishman of tradition & vulgar at that. The others were merely incompetent & had got themselves up like an English coachman & his wife. The cottage was a coachmans cottage too. The whole thing was careless & disgraceful beyond words & has I am afraid done some mischief.[3]

Bullen says he is too unwell for business now but wants me to go to Stratford-on Avon & stay with him in April & then to settle about collected edition.[4]

Yours always
W B Yeats

ALS Berg, with envelope addressed to Coole, postmark 'LONDON. N. W. MAR 13 05'.

# *To A. C. Benson,*[1] *12 March 1905*

18 Woburn Buildings, | Euston Road,
March 12th, | 05.

*Dictated.*
Dear Sir,
I have answered your letter as you will see.[2] "The Wind among the Reeds" contains what most people believe to be my best lyrical work.[3]

Yrs sry
W B Yeats

Dict AEFH, signed WBY; Cambridge.

---

[3] See p. 51, n. 7.

[4] WBY had long intended a collected edition (or, as he sometimes called it, a 'collective' edition; see III. 554–6), but this is the first definite mention of the *Collected Works* (*CW*) of 1908, published by Bullen in eight volumes at the Shakespeare Head Press, Stratford-upon-Avon.

[1] Arthur Christopher Benson (1862–1925), poet, essayist, and biographer, was a son of Edward White Benson (d. 1896), Archbishop of Canterbury 1883–96. He had been a schoolmaster at Eton College 1885–1903, and had sent WBY his collection of supernatural tales *The Hill of Trouble* in October 1903 (see III. 453). In 1904 he was elected to a fellowship at Magdalene College, Cambridge, and he became master of the College from 1915 to his death. In writing to congratulate WBY on the award of the Nobel Prize on 15 Nov 1923, Benson extolled him (MBY) for keeping his 'mind & spirit so resolutely turned away from all the worst as well as all the subtlest temptations of the writer & the artist—away from all narrow effect & cheap credit & secondrate applause', and added that he had 'read most if not all of your books . . . & I am sure that you differ from all the writers of the time in having the best sort of detachment—the detachment from the urgent *present* which ends by bringing an artist, if he is a great enough artist, into line with the Great Spirits of the past & the future.'

[2] Benson's letter is untraced, but was apparently asking for WBY's comments on the current state of his work.

[3] *The Wind Among the Reeds* was published in London on 15 Apr 1899, and filed for copyright at the Library of Congress on 13 Apr. Its initial print run was probably 1,500 copies, 500 each for the English

## To Archibald Henderson,[1] 12 March 1905

18 Woburn Buildings, | Euston Road, | London.
March 12th | 05.

Dear Sir,

I am afraid the special occasion you wanted my photograph for will have passed by this.[2]

I have been very busy this Winter & your letter was forgotten with many others. I send you the photograph however, but will not send you any criticism on Bernard Shaw. I have written nothing about him & would not like to do so, unless at considerable length & after weighing my words; he is a very brilliant man & my friend.[3] I send you an annual of mine full of dramatic criticism which may be of interest to you.[4]

Yrs sny
W B Yeats

Dict AEFH, signed WBY; N. Carolina.

first edition, an English second edition printed (and issued in error by Mathews simultaneously), and an American edition for Lane. By 1900 a third English edition was needed, and in 1902 a further 493 copies were printed for Lane. There were other English editions in 1903, 1907, and 1911, and more American editions in 1905 and 1911. The book was widely reviewed, and received favourable notices from, among others, Dora Shorter in the *Illustrated London News* of 22 July 1899 (104), Arthur Symons in the *Saturday Review* of 6 May 1899 (553), Annie Macdonnell in the *Bookman* of May 1899 (45–6), and Dora M. Jones in the *London Quarterly Review* of July 1900 (61–70). Other critics found the book too unworldly, and many complained of the large number of notes (see II. 305, n. 2, 306, n. 4).

[1] Archibald Henderson (1877–1963), an Assistant Professor of Mathematics at the University of North Carolina, Chapel Hill, and a prolific writer on science, history, literature, and philosophy, had become a disciple of G. Bernard Shaw after seeing a performance of *You Never Can Tell* in Chicago in February 1903. When in June 1904 he wrote to Shaw, asking for information for the biography he intended to write, Shaw assured him that 'the best authority on Shaw is Shaw', and then proceeded to prove this by sending him fifty-four pages of notes about his early life (*BSCL* II. 427, 479–506). Partly owing to Shaw's active interest in the project, and his delays in transmitting material to Henderson, the biography, *George Bernard Shaw: His Life and Works*, did not appear until 1911, when it repeated, as the 'cleverest and truest remark about *John Bull*', WBY's observation that it was 'the first play of Bernard Shaw's that has a genuine geography' (378).

[2] Henderson had probably requested WBY's photograph and comments on Shaw for his article, 'Two Irish Dramatists: William B. Yeats and George B. Shaw', published in the Charlotte (NC) *Daily Observer* on 17 Apr 1904.

[3] This categorization simplifies a more complex relationship. In *Aut* (133–4) WBY recalls that 'when Wilde said, "Mr. Bernard Shaw has no enemies but is intensely disliked by all his friends", I knew it to be a phrase I should never forget, and felt revenged upon a notorious hater of romance, whose generosity and courage I could not fathom'. In the late 1880s WBY and his circle 'all hated him with the left side of our heads, while admiring him immensely with the right side' (*Aut*, 147), and this contradiction, despite joint enterprises such as their collaboration over the Irish Academy of Letters in the 1930s, was never resolved. Significantly, Shaw also refused to write on WBY, when invited by Stephen Gwynn in 1939: 'Somehow I cannot write about Yeats' (see below, p. 79, n. 1).

[4] *Samhain* of December 1904, which contained 'First Principles' and 'The Play, the Player, and the Scene'.

## *To Hugh Lane, 12 March 1905*

18 Woburn Buildings, | Euston Road. | London.
March 12<sup>th</sup>,|05.

*Dictated.*
Dear Lane,

Miss Eva Hamilton[1] has sent me the name of a friend of hers, a titled person[2] to whom I am to send circulars of the pictures.[3] Would you mind sending me a set of them. I shall be here until the week ends.

Yours sinly
W B Yeats

Miss Horniman is excited about *Joli Coeur*[4]

Dict AEFH, signed WBY; NLI.

[1] Eva Henrietta Hamilton (1876–1960), portrait and landscape artist, was born in Meath and studied at the Metropolitan School of Art, Dublin, where she came under the influence of William Orpen. She specialized in portraiture, particularly of children, until financial necessity obliged her to move to Castleknock, where she turned to landscape painting. She exhibited at the Royal Hibernian Academy from 1904 to 1945, and at the Irish International Exhibition in 1907.

[2] This was Edward John Moreton Drax Plunkett, 18th Baron Dunsany (1878–1957), poet and playwright, educated at Eton and the military academy at Sandhurst. He had succeeded his father in 1899, and served with the Coldstream Guards in the Boer War. Nearly 6′ 6″ tall and energetically athletic, he wrote fantasies and fairy stories, and was to publish his first book, a novel called *The Gods of Pagana*, in October of this year. He went on to become a prolific author and in 1909, at WBY's suggestion, wrote *The Glittering Gate* for the Abbey Theatre, and followed this with a number of other plays, including *King Argimenes and the Unknown Warrior* (1911), *A Night at an Inn* (1916), *The Tents of the Arabs* (1920), and *The Gods of the Mountain* (1929). For a few years after 1909 he and WBY were close friends, but later became estranged, and in *Poets in the Flesh* (1961) R. F. Rattray recalls (9) Dunsany bridling at the mention of WBY: ' "Yeats!" exclaimed Dunsany: "Did you ever hear of Yeats doing anybody a good turn? No. Why not? Because pigs don't fly." ' In July 1938 WBY, inscribing *Selections from the Writings of Lord Dunsany* (Dublin, 1912) for James A. Healy (Stanford), described Dunsany as 'a fine writer but a nuisance of a man'.

[3] The Women's Picture League, of which AG was a committee member, had prepared a circular to enlist further support for the proposed Municipal Art Gallery in Dublin.

[4] AEFH had purchased Dante Gabriel Rossetti's oil painting *Joli Cœur* (1867), a characteristic portrait of a young woman, at auction in 1888, and had frequently loaned it for public display, most recently to the Bradford Exhibition of Fine Arts of the previous year. She may have planned to lend it to Lane for exhibition, or possibly to allow its purchase by subscription. She finally bequeathed it to the Manchester City Art Gallery, where it now hangs.

## To Lady Gregory, [*14 March 1905*]

18 Woburn Buildings | Euston Road.
Tuesday

My dear Lady Gregory: I have the MSS very safely but have done nothing at it yet.[1] I have had a multitude of things to do—I have dictated scores of letters, & have had Masefields plays read to me,[2] have written a long letter to Quinn for M[rs] Clay & so on.[3] To morrow night I hope to meet Hughes the Irish musician Synge is always speaking of.[4] Do you go to Dublin next Saturday? I shall I hope go there Saturday night.[5]

I saw a "stage society" play yesterday—a dramatized opinion through out—clever & I think false—I was greatly bored.[6]

Symons has written a review of Gwynns Tom Moore for I think the 'Fortnightly' & in this he reproves me for saying in my 'Book of Irish Verse' & [*for* that] Moore had written two good poems. He adds that doubtless I would not say this now. He thinks Moore never wrote anything good. I wish some Irish paper would quote this reproof.[7]

---

[1] i.e. the MS of *The King's Threshold*; see p. 52.

[2] The MSS of at least two plays written by Masefield after his move to Greenwich, *The Buccaneer* and *The Wrecker's Corpse*, have not survived. Two others, *The Sweeps of '98* and *The Locked Chest*, were not published until 1916.

[3] i.e. the letter of 11 March; see pp. 49–51.

[4] Herbert Hughes, 'Padraic MacAodh O'Neill' (1882–1937), folk musician and composer, was founder and co-editor of the *Journal of the Irish Folk Song Society*. In 1904 he had arranged the airs in *Songs of Uladh* with words by Joseph Campbell and transcribed the *caoin* in the first production of Synge's *Riders to the Sea*. He also set WBY's 'Down by the Salley Gardens'. He later became music critic for the *New Age* and the *Daily Telegraph*. In 1931 he invited WBY to contribute to *The Joyce Book*, containing 'Pomes Penyeach' set to music by various composers, recalling (MBY) that he 'used to meet you now and again with Florence Farr . . . many years ago. I had attic rooms immediately over Mrs. Emery's in Holland Road and I was greatly honoured one evening when you came upstairs with Synge and Robert Gregory to look at the ceiling decorations I had improvised with candle smoke!'

[5] WBY probably did travel to Dublin on Saturday, 18 Mar. He was to have lectured to the ILS on that evening, but a lecture on 'The Irish House of Commons' by John Boland, the Nationalist MP for Kerry South, was substituted for his talk at the last minute.

[6] *The Three Daughters of M. Dupont* (1897), by the French social realist playwright Eugène Brieux (1858–1932), translated by St John Hankin, was produced at the National Sporting Club 12–14 Mar. The play has as its theme the iniquity of arranged marriages and *petit bourgeois* materialism. Charlotte and George Bernard Shaw both admired Brieux and the Stage Society staged four of his plays between 1904 and 1907.

[7] Stephen Gwynn's book on Thomas Moore in the *English Men of Letters* series was reviewed by Symons in the *Fortnightly Review* on 1 Apr 1905 (686): ' "All he had of high poetry", says Mr Yeats in his *Book of Irish Verse*, "is probably in 'The light of other days,' and in the exquisite lines beginning, 'At the mid hour of night' ". It is true that Mr Yeats wrote that ten years ago; I am not sure that he would write it now. To be "exquisite," or to attain "high poetry," requires qualities which Moore never possessed, and in neither of those two lyrics . . . can I find an exception to those qualities of strictly second-rate skill in verse writing which he did possess.' Writing to James Starkey on 19 Feb of this year (TCD) Symons had commented that WBY 'thinks Moore worth two poems. I am not disposed to go so far!'

Maclaggan who came in last night is well contented with his South Kensington post—he is in charge of the Ecclesiastical Embroidery.[8]

Bullen wants fine covers designed for my collected edition. I wonder, who is to do them.[9]

Yours ever

W B Yeats

ALS Berg, with envelope addressed to Coole, postmark 'LONDON. N. W. MAR 14 '05'.

## *To Miss G. E. Moore,*[1] *14 March 1905*

18 Woburn Buildings, | Euston Road. | London.

March 14<sup>th</sup>,|05.

Dear Madam,

Many thanks for your plays. I have sent them in to the Reading Committee of the Irish National Theatre Society Abbey Theatre, Dublin. I imagine that that was your purpose in sending them to me. I think however that they are outside the scope of our work, we are restricted by our patent to plays on Irish subjects or by Irish writers & have always hitherto looked upon both these requirements as essential.

I have kept your plays beside me hoping that I should find time to read them myself, but I hope that you will permit a great deal of work & very little eye-sight to be my excuse for not having done so.

I send this care of your publisher as I have mislaid your letter.[2]

Yrs snly

W B Yeats

Dict AEFH, signed WBY; Private.

[8] WBY had met Eric R. D. Maclagan (1879–1951), then an Oxford undergraduate, in May 1902 (see III. 185, 186). He subsequently became an expert in ecclesiastical embroidery, and assisted WBY and SMY with advice and designs for the banners Dun Emer Industries made for Loughrea Cathedral (see III. 406–7, 410–11, 460). He had recently joined the Victoria and Albert Museum as an assistant in the Department of Textiles, and was eventually to become director.

[9] The eight volumes of *CW* were handsomely covered in quarter vellum binding with grey linen sides, lettered in gold on the front cover and spine.

[1] Although AEFH read the second initial as 'E', this is probably the American author Grace B. Moore, who described herself as 'an active member of the Self-Culture Society', and who wrote a number of books promoting its aim of fostering self-improvement: *Practical Self-Help* (Chicago, 1901), *What the World Wants* (Chicago, 1901), and *Nature's Way in Love, Courtship and Marriage* (Chicago, 1905). As WBY foresaw, the Reading Committee did reject her plays, and they do not appear to have been published. They were presumably intended to dramatize and popularize the teachings of the Society.

[2] Grace Moore's previous books had been published by the Self-Culture Society at 56 High Holborn, London, and 4714 Evans Avenue, Chicago.

## *To Lord Dunsany, [mid-March 1905]*

Mention in letter to Eva Hamilton, 5 April 1905.
Sending Dunsany a circular about the new Municipal Gallery and asking him for a subscription.


## *To Maud Gonne, [mid-March 1905]*

Mention in letter from MG, 'Tuesday' [? 21 March 1905].
Sending her encouragement and sympathy,[1] discussing the position of Inghinidhe na hEireann in the nationalist controversy over the divorce,[2] and saying that he thinks making things is more amusing than drawing pictures.[3]

*G–YL*, 195–6.

[1] In her reply MG thanked WBY for his letter to her and for those to her cousin May 'which were also written to help me. When one is in trouble one finds out who are one's real friends.'

[2] MG had founded the women's nationalist organization Inghinidhe na hEireann (Daughters of Ireland) in 1900, and took the chair at its inaugural meeting on 5 Oct 1900. The Society mounted a number of demonstrations, plays, and *tableaux vivants* with political themes, and several of its members had played an active part in the early days of the INTS. The Society was now disturbed by MG's marital problems, which seemed to set revolutionary and sexual politics at odds. In her reply, MG told WBY that she had received 'letters from many Inghinide & Mary Quinn from America sent me letters from others who had not liked to write to me but who were warm in their sympathy'. She confessed, however, that she was 'distressed about Inghinide. This is not the sort of fight I want them to be in & yet what can I do? If I sent my resignation as president just now it would I think make their position more difficult, as many of them wouldn't accept it, & even if they did it would weaken them & be used against them. I have written to some of them telling them not to fight at all on this matter & to refuse altogether to discuss it or to try & defend me, the verdict in the court will do that, but I know it is very hard for them.'

[3] MG replied that she agreed with him 'that it is more amusing *making things* than *pictures*, but for every thing *drawing* is necessary & it interests me very much'.

## *To A. J. Baker,*[1] *18 March 1905*

18 Woburn Buildings, | Euston Road. | London.
March 18th, | 05.

Dear Sir,
You are entirely right about the authorship of "Father Tom". I made that book a long time ago when I was very young & knew no better. I had hoped that it was in its grave.[2]

Yr sny
W B Yeats

Dict AEFH, signed WBY; McGill.

## *To John Quinn, 29 March 1905*

NASSAU HOTEL. | Sth. Frederick Street,
29th. March, 1905.

My dear Quinn:—
You have done great things for me. I never prospered until you took up my affairs.[1] I wonder how Miss Wycherly will get on with the "Countess Kathleen".[2] I hardly know what sort of a play it is. It was produced in such

---

[1] Possibly Alfred Baker (1848–1942), Professor of Mathematics at Toronto University, who had literary interests, and who had met WBY on his visit to Toronto in February 1904.
[2] In *Representative Irish Tales* (1891) WBY had erroneously attributed Sir Samuel Ferguson's short story 'Father Tom and the Pope' (1838) to William Maginn (1794–1842); see I. 256. The tale had commonly been attributed to both Maginn and John Fisher Murray (1811–65) prior to the confirmation by Ferguson himself of the authorship in the 'Ante-Preface' to the American pirated edition of 1868: 'It was written by me in the summer of 1838. . . . No one else had any hand in it. . . . I am flattered by its having been ascribed to Maginn, for whose genius I entertain a high admiration. I have never made any secret of the authorship; but as I have constantly endeavoured in any literary work I have been able to do for many years back to elevate the Irish subject out of the burlesque, I have an indisposition to place my name on the title page of so very rollicking a piece as "Father Tom".'
Baker was telling WBY nothing that he did not already know, for as early as July 1891 the *Irish Monthly* had pointed out his mistake, and he corrected it in a letter to the Dublin *Daily Express* on 27 Feb 1895 (see I. 441–2). In *Sir Samuel Ferguson in the Ireland of his Day* (1894), Lady Ferguson claims (I. 105) that the tale was 'a humorous skit, suggested by a controversial encounter between Father Tom Maguire, a well-known priest of that day, and Mr. Pope, a clergyman of the Church of Ireland, champions respectively of their opposing faiths'.
[1] Quinn had continued his relentless pursuit of Bayard Veiller and Margaret Wycherly for WBY's unpaid royalties (see p. 50, n. 6). On 17 Mar he had written that Veiller owed him $30 for the performances at the Hudson Theatre and, despite being sent two reminders, was prevaricating, although he now promised 'to pay all the back royalties'.
[2] Having produced *Cathleen ni Houlihan*, *The Hour-Glass*, and *The Land of Heart's Desire* for two well-received matinees at the Hudson in late February, Miss Wycherly announced matinée

an artificial atmosphere, absurd controversies darkening the air: and it was so ill-staged that I hardly know what to think of it. I had no stage experience when I wrote it and I am afraid it rambles all over the place. I have always intended, as soon as I thought the time had come to play it here—to put more logic into the construction. There is nothing however that I can do at short notice except perhaps cut the spirits out of Act Three, and Fay rather urges me not to do that. He says that they will go all right if Miss Wycherly does not make them pantomime spirits. We cut one batch of them when we played it here.[3] We also and this involved a few lines writing, reduced the Angels at the end to one. We did this last because we were only playing in a Hall and had no proper stage machinery. I think it was a mistake. The stage should get darker and darker until it is pitch dark. In the darkness the Cottage Scene should be lifted up showing another Scene set behind it. In this other Scene the light should show armed angels. If one does not get this effect—if one does not get the gradual darkening of the stage, a wakening expectation of some event—the play seems to go on too long after the death of the Countess.[4] I daresay Miss Wycherly's

performances of *The Countess Cathleen* at the Madison Square Theatre on 28 and 31 Mar. Margaret Wycherly, stage name of Margaret De Wolf (1884–1956), was born in London but moved to Nova Scotia as a child. She took her stage name from the English dramatist William Wycherly, from whom she claimed to be descended through her mother, and began her acting career with Richard Mansfield and later Ben Greet. She moved to San Francisco, where she married Phillip Veiller and under his managership toured WBY's plays 1904–5 (see p. 50, n.6). In a letter of 31 Mar, which crossed with this, Quinn informed WBY (Himber, 71–2) that Veiller had undertaken to pay $30 for each performance of *The Countess Cathleen* in advance, but, despite good audiences, had not yet paid anything, and that he intended 'to sue him for back royalties and the papers are prepared and will be served tomorrow. I can get judgment for the royalties due under his contract and the next performance he gives of *The Countess Cathleen* I will attach the receipts at the Box Office.'

[3] WBY had not seen *The Countess Cathleen* since its Dublin production in May 1899 had provoked attacks by Frank Hugh O'Donnell, Cardinal Logue, and the students of the Catholic University (see II. 410–12, 669–80). In an unpublished typed fragment (NLI) he recalled that 'it was at that time a very bad play and left to itself would I think have failed. But the quarrel made the audience alive, the play was of no importance.' The most heavily revised of all WBY's plays, it was first published in 1892 but did not get its final form until *Poems* (1913). In the original versions of the play the demon merchants call up an 'elemental populace' of damned souls, sheogues, sowlths and thivishes, described as '*less than the size of men and women, and … dressed in green jackets, with red caps, trimmed with shells*' (*VPl*, 86), to steal the Countess's gold so that she cannot use it to alleviate the hunger of the poor. As early as October 1898 George Moore had warned WBY that these creatures did 'not add to the reality of the play—they take away' (see II. 273–4), and for the 1899 performance WBY excised references to sheogues and cut back the roles of the thivishes and sowlths, subsequently amalgamating them into 'spirits' in editions of the play published between 1901 and 1912.

[4] All versions of the play involve the Countess Cathleen selling her own soul to redeem her starving peasants who have sold their souls to demon merchants in a time of famine. Overcome by this sacrifice, she dies, but in the earlier versions this happens offstage and angelic spirits, bathed in a bright light, report how they have fought off the demons and conducted her soul to heaven. In subsequent versions, the fight between good and evil is represented on the stage with thunder and lightning; the transition from darkness to 'visionary light' is far more dramatic and the angelic spirits more warlike: '*Half in the light, half in the shadow, stand armed angels. Their armour is old and worn, and their drawn*

Manager[5] may have to cut a line here and there throughout the play. If there is time and Miss Wycherly wants it and cares to send me a telegram I will cut those spirits altogether out of Act III. and make the demons steal that treasure with their own hands. The play however is so broken up that one does not know where to begin on it. Perhaps I over-rate its defects, for, I have been thinking of very little but construction for a couple of years now. It is not constructed worse than some Elizabethan plays but then an Elizabethan play is sometimes the very devil.

I wish my "Dierdre" were ready for it would much better suit Miss Wycherly's purposes.[6] I shall not be a little nervous till I hear how "Countess Kathleen" goes. I think Lady Gregory is a little depressed about "Kincora". I don't think she need be. We have had a magnificent success so far as the people in the theatre are concerned and the Newspapers. It is bound to draw great audiences before long. A theatre like ours makes no sudden leaps as I have told the Company from the beginning. We have now about a thousand people who come to everything we do. If we are very lucky they will be twelve or fourteen hundred before the session ends and so on.[7]

I have finished the new version of "The King's Threshold". I wonder how it would go in Miss Wycherly's hands? The poet is so symbolical a personage that it might be no worse for her to play him than for Miss

---

*swords dim and dinted. They stand as if upon the air in formation of battle and look downward with stern faces'* (*VPl*, 167).

[5] i.e. Bayard Veiller, Margaret Wycherly's husband as well as her manager. WBY was to be introduced to Margaret Wycherly by Signe Toksvig in Dublin in July 1933 (Signe Toksvig's *Irish Diaries* [Dublin, 1994], 250).

[6] WBY had evidently already offered her the rights to *Deirdre*. An undated clipping from the New York *World* of late autumn 1904 announced that she had 'received a cable dispatch from Mr Yeats ...informing her that the American rights to all of the plays to be presented this year by the Irish National Theatre have been given her'. Miss Wycherly told the *World* that besides the plays she already had in repertoire she would stage 'a new version' of *The King's Threshold* and would also 'give the first production on any stage to Mr Yeats new poetic tragedy, "Deirdre", on which the poet is now at work'. The *World* concluded that this meant 'the practical establishment in this country of the Irish drama, and the presentation here of a number of plays hitherto entirely unknown to the American public'.

[7] *Kincora* was first produced on 25 Mar to general approbation, and in response to repeated urgings and applause AG took a curtain call. The *Evening Herald* of 27 Mar (2) thought it 'in several respects the best play produced under the auspices of the National Theatre Society'; the *Leader* of 1 Apr (90–1) deemed it 'an unquestioned success'; and the *Freeman's Journal* reported on 27 Mar (5) that it had 'roused the audience to great enthusiasm' and that no play 'to which the new dramatic movement has given birth is so likely to achieve popularity'. The *Irish Times* of the same day (7) also stressed its popular appeal, and praised AG for making her historical characters 'live again in the modern imagination' in a play 'replete with lofty and beautiful dialogue, full of heroic energy'. Significantly, the reviewer detected the emergence of what would become known as the Abbey style of acting: 'The playing throughout was different in its ideal from that of any other company. The players appear to have trained themselves to perform Irish types of character and to catch the sentiment of Irish legend. They move but little, subordinating gesture to fine speaking, recognising that in any play which gets part of its effect out of

Maddison [*for* Matthison] to play the hero in "Every Man".[8] It would be ten times better of course if she could get some good speaker of verse who is a man to play it and be the sweetheart herself, but I doubt of there being much chance of getting any speaker of verse from the ordinary theatre good enough an orator to carry thro' a part where the drama is so much in the ideas.

I wish you could see the scenery of "Kincora". It is severely decorative, the most rigorous following of my formula, and yet there are moments when I think it the most beautiful in effect that I have ever seen. The extraordinary thing is that it is beautiful and yet never makes one look away from the actors. It has conquered everybody. I have not heard of anybody here who does not accept the decorative idea now.[9]

---

literature speech is of paramount importance.' Despite uniformly excellent reviews, the audience, which had been large on the first night (despite adverse weather), dwindled away, and by 29 Mar Holloway was complaining (*Abbey Theatre*, 54) of 'the thinness of the audience at the Abbey Theatre'. As Protestants, WBY and AG had failed to appreciate the effect Lent would have in reducing the numbers of their Catholic patrons. Writing to Quinn on this day, AG told him: 'Kincora came off on Saturday—a good house—great applause—everyone apparently delighted—the papers splendid . . . there was not one unkind word in any paper—We were elated, but alas on Monday, the audience had fallen very low—It slightly increased last night—& all who came seem delighted with play, acting, & scenery—but it is a little disappointing not getting better support.' She also suggested that, besides Lent, Synge's unpopularity had reduced audiences (see p. 38, n. 2).

[8] Edith Wynne Matthison (1875–1955), a member of Ben Greet's company, had created a sensation with her performance in the medieval morality play *Everyman* in London and New York in 1902, and was advertised as about to take the title role in a revival at the Shaftesbury Theatre 17–22 Apr 1905. In fact, Margaret Wycherly had alternated with her in the role during the New York run.

[9] The staging of *Kincora* (see pp. 39, 46, n. 2) drew particular comment and was described at length in a preview in the *Freeman's Journal* of 25 Mar (4): 'The scenic treatment is practically a new departure here. It is merely decorative and suggestive—not realistic or spectacular at all. The object is to admit nothing on the stage calculated to distract the attention of the audience from the words and action. . . . Then as to costumes, a certain scheme of colour has been adhered to with the view of making dress and character accord with one another as much as possible. The background for the Prologue consists of hangings on which tree forms appear, thus suggesting without picturing a wood.' The costumes of the leading male characters were, it reported, 'similar—red with a grey cloak and sword, and a minn or ancient Irish coronet on the head. No glaring embroidery or glittering jewellery. Chief among the female personages is Queen Gormleith; and she wears a very bright orange dress ornamented with black and gold. The costume of the Danish warriors . . . is to be black with yellow facings. Attendants of the palace are clad in green and brown on grey green . . . all the costumes and the scenic backgrounds have been designed by Mr. Robert Gregory, and made and painted in the theatre . . . ' After the first night the same paper commented (27 Mar 1905, p. 5) that the last scene 'reminded one of those old Italian triptyche, with their simple backgrounds and rare colour schemes . . . It was a unique contribution of talent.' The *Irish Times* (see n. 1) also noted that Robert Gregory's design was 'rich in tone, and forms a fitting framework for the play. No attempt is made to paint any scene realistically, the artist's aim evidently being suggestion rather than imitation. The colours in the background contrast and harmonize effectively with the dresses of the company.' In her letter to Quinn of 29 Mar (see above), AG described the scenery as 'quite beautiful, wonderful colour effects, & all from painted or dyed sacking & sheeting—Robert has worked like a day-labourer, painting as well as designing & modelling, & Orpen who was there last night shared in the general admiration of it.' In a further letter of 2 Apr (NYPL) she recalled that 'Robert's scenery was an enormous help, the severe grey hall, & the mysterious wood, & the splendid colour of the tent scene seemed to give force to the idea all though'.

I hope I have not left out of this letter any necessary thing, but I am writing in a great hurry. I got the money you sent of course and for it many thanks.[10]

Yrs snly ever

W B Yeats

TLS NYPL, with envelope addressed to 120 Broadway, New York, postmark 'DUBLIN MR 29 05; New York postmark 'APR 5 1905, DUE 10 CENTS'.

## To Maud Gonne, [c. 29 March 1905]

Mention in letter from MG, 'Thursday evening' [? 30 March 1905]. Sending her an account of the success of AG's *Kincora*.[1]

*G–YL*, 196–7.

## To J. P. Quinn, [30 March 1905]

Nassau Hotel | South Fredrick St. | Dublin.
Thursday.

My dear Quinn:[1] Have you been to see Kinkora? If you have not, come Saturday & stay behind afterwards. Lady Gregory always has a party for the players on the last day of a play & she has asked me to invite you to this one.[2]

Yr alway

W B Yeats

<hr>

[10] See p. 59. Quinn's insistence that Veiller should pay back royalties on the productions of WBY's plays was succeeding, and on 3 Mar he was able to send WBY (Himber, 68) a 'London draft for twelve pounds, five shillings and eleven pense; the proceeds of the $60 paid me by Veiller yesterday, for the two matinees on Tuesday and today (Friday) of this week. He squirmed but I demanded and got my check yesterday. He agreed, when I jumped on him and he paid the $200, which I sent you last week, to pay $30 a performance till the back royalties were paid.'

[1] MG was 'so glad to read of the success of Kincora how I wish May & I could have seen it—we will one day I hope—All my congratulations to Lady Gregory. The book of the play arrived today & I have only had time to read a few pages. I am looking forward to reading it this evening.'

[1] Quinn had remained loyal to MG (see p. 51), and WBY wanted to see him again to strengthen his support, and to use his influence to bring Michael Davitt in behind MG in her legal struggle with MacBride.

[2] The performance and party were also attended by Martin Ross, who reported (*Selected Letters of Somerville and Ross*, ed. Gifford Lewis [1989], 272–3) that after the final curtain AG had 'swept me and the Morris's [*sic*] and Killanin and others to tea afterwards, *on the stage*. A stranger thing I have seldom

I rather want to know if Davitt is in Ireland, perhaps you will be able to tell me.[3]

ALS NLI.


## *To George Brett,*[1] *31 March* [*1905*]

Nassau Hotel | Dublin
March 31 —

Dear M[r] Brett—
I have just received your letter sent on to me from London. I am afraid I shall not return there for some weeks though I am not quite sure — This,

done — and Oh the discomfort of the sloping stage floor. . . . I was introduced to the tragedy queen — who had swallowed a poker, in token of sovereignty — but had retained her brogue through all — and I was also introduced by Augusta (who swept me about as if I were blind and drunk) to Lord Monteagle, who was wholly uninterested in me and is a great rebel (Emily tells me) — I then talked very enjoyably to the leading comedian — Fay — a first rate little actor — and as common as a little Dublin cab man — but most agreeable to talk to. The Dermod O'Briens were also there . . . then W B Yeats — and *very* highclass conversation — inspired by sips of black tea and a cheese cake.'

[3]  Michael Davitt (1846–1906), agrarian agitator and labour leader, was born in Mayo, but emigrated with his family as a child to Lancashire. In 1870 he was sentenced to fifteen years' penal servitude for IRB gun-running; released on ticket-of-leave in 1877, he founded the Land League which organized tenant farmers against exploitation by landlords, and was subsequently reimprisoned. Although a revolutionary socialist, he had been a close associate of Parnell, but opposed him after the O'Shea divorce in 1890. In 1899 he resigned his seat in Parliament in protest against the Boer War (see II. 464–6) and visited Africa, Russia, and America as a journalist and as a fund-raiser for the Irish Party. Although of a very different political persuasion, WBY had great respect for Davitt, and when he met him with several others on 28 Dec 1897 at a '98 Centennial Meeting could 'remember nothing of what passed but the manner and image of Michael Davitt. He seemed hardly less unfitted for such negotiation, perhaps even for any possible present politics, than I myself, and I watched him with sympathy. . . . [He] suggested to me a writer, a painter, an artist of some kind, rather than a man of action' (*Aut*, 356). WBY and MG tried to defend him against the calumnies of his erratic political enemy Frank Hugh O'Donnell in 1899, and WBY wanted to see him now to enlist his help in MG's battle to prevent MacBride being granted access to her son. As she explained in her letter of 30 Mar (see above), MacBride was 'going to propose that my child should spend part of each year' with his grandmother who kept a public house in Westport. Since the matter was 'of the utmost importance' to MG, she wanted WBY to 'get evidence as to the drunkenness which goes on there', and suggested he might obtain it from Davitt, who had stated in a pamphlet 'that Mrs MacBride kept "*a low shebeen house*"'. She explained that self-interest would prevent both the Westport priests and police from speaking out against the MacBrides but that William O'Brien and the United Irish League were 'bitter enemies of the MacBride family. United Irish Leaguers of the neighborhood would be sure to know everything against them that was why I thought Davitt likely to be well informed but United Irish Leaguers also hate me so I can't ask them directly. Dr Quinn could easily find out as he is friends with the United Irish Leaguers as I think Mr Russell might be able to find out.'

[1]  George Platt Brett (1859–1936), a London-born publisher who was now president of the Macmillan Company of New York, had established a business relationship with WBY when his firm issued *Where There Is Nothing* in May 1903. On 1 Jan 1904 WBY opened negotiations whereby the firm was to

however, need not delay our arrangements. A. P. Watt has made all my English arrangements for me for a long time now,[2] and I am sending him your letter, agreement, etc.[3] He can settle the matter in the spirit of our correspondence—It would have been necessary to bring him in in any case, as there are one or two slight complications involving previous arrangements.[4] I would have written to you about the matter but I have only just finished the revision of the plays. With the exception of the making of a clean copy of some parts the text of your proposed edition is now ready. The complications I spoke of are as follows—You may not remember but I told you about two of them when I saw you in London—

1st　John Lane got the American right of 'Wind Among the Reeds' in '97—The arrangement was made with him by Elkin Matthews—A. P. Watt has a letter written by Matthews & giving his recollection of the terms. The arrangement gives the book back into my hands this year. Unfortunately however John Lane has never sent an agreement, never furnished an account, never paid a penny, never answered a letter. (A. P. Watt was not looking after my affairs when John Lane got into them)—[5]

become his sole American publishers (see III. 503–5), and later that year the Macmillan Company published editions of *In the Seven Woods* and *The Hour-Glass and Other Plays*. WBY met Brett for the first time in London on 18 Mar 1904, when they discussed the terms on which WBY might become a Macmillan author, and decided that the firm should publish that autumn 'a collected edition of all my verse—plays & lyrics' (see III. 557–8). In the event, both these decisions took longer to implement than anticipated. WBY was cautious about committing his works entirely to one American publisher, and the copy for the 'collected edition' was delayed, partly by the difficulty of retrieving the American rights to *The Wind Among the Reeds* from the unscrupulous John Lane, and partly because WBY was constantly revising the text and contents of the second volume, which printed his plays.

[2] Alexander Pollock Watt (1837–1914) was born in Edinburgh; after a period in his brother-in-law's publishing firm, he began to act for the Scottish novelist George MacDonald, and quickly became the foremost British literary agent. He introduced the flat fee of 10% of royalties that became the standard agents' charge, and was skilled at placing books and articles for both authors and publishers. He became WBY's exclusive agent in May 1901.

[3] The agreement was for WBY's two-volume *The Poetical Works of William B. Yeats*, vol. I of which ('Lyrical Poems') appeared in November 1906, and vol. II ('Dramatic Poems') in July 1907. The agreement was not finally drawn up until 26 June of this year (see below, pp. 121–3).

[4] WBY had written to Brett on 21 June 1904 (III. 607–8) questioning the draft agreement for *The Poetical Works* and future relations between them: 'for one thing I don't think that the proposal that you surrender past books at a price settled by mutual agreement would amount to much. It would be too easy for us to fall out over the price. Nor do I think it advisable for me to absolutely pledge all my future work as it would be pledged by Clause 11 of the Draft Agreement.'

[5] After dissolving their joint firm in September 1894 (see II. 115, 156–8), Mathews took over the English rights to *The Wind Among the Reeds* (see p. 53) and Lane the American ones. Both men proved difficult, and WBY finally decided not to include poems from the book in his next collection, *Poems, 1899–1905* (1906). Mathews brought out further editions in 1907 and (in breach of an agreement) in 1911, but could not stop its inclusion in *The Poetical Works* and vol. I of Bullen's *CW* in 1908. Lane was even less accommodating; he tried to hang on to rights he no longer possessed but, although he managed to delay the publication of vol. I of *The Poetical Works*, he could not finally prevent the poems being published there.

2<sup>nd</sup>    Dodd, Mead & Co have a poem of mine 'The Shadowy Waters'—but I imagine would surrender. They have not many copies left.[6]

3<sup>rd</sup>    Bullen has proposed to me the bringing out of an expensive collected edition of my writings in 6 or 7 volumes—10/- a volume. I want you to see M<sup>r</sup> Bullen if possible about this—& to speak of it to M<sup>r</sup> A. P. Watt— Could you not make some arrangement by which this edition could be taken up by you in America? It could not interfere with the sale of a cheap collected edition in one or two volumes—It would be an edition de luxe—[7]

M<sup>r</sup> Quinn is of opinion that your edition of my poetry should be in two volumes, one of plays, one of poems.

*[Vertically on first page]*
Yours sincely
W B Yeats

Dict AG, signed WBY; NYPL. Marked in another hand 'Ans Apl 6'.

## To John Quinn, 1 April 1905

Nassau Hotel, | Dublin.
April 1<sup>st</sup>,/05.

*Dictated.*

My dear Quinn,

Very many thanks for your letter about Miss Wycherley. M<sup>rs</sup> Ford wrote a letter to my sisters the other day, evidently intended for my eyes. She said in the letter that Miss Wycherley had done badly in Boston, that her friends had stood to her & that as she was doing better each time, she ought to make a success in the end. She said also that Miss Wycherley & Billier [*for* Veiller] had put all they possessed into the venture & lost their all in Boston. I am too far from the seat of battle to give an opinion & am perfectly confident, I need hardly say, in your judgement.[1] I am not really very anxious for a performance of the Countess Kathleen as I am not at all confident of the play in its present shape. If it proved convenient to you in any way, you could say this & use it as a means of getting out of the bargain. At the same time I have no very strong convictions and you may do as you

---

[6] Dodd, Mead & Co. had published an American edition of *The Shadowy Waters* in April 1901, and were, as WBY anticipates, now happy to surrender their rights in it.

[7] Despite urging from John Quinn and Bullen, as well as WBY, the Macmillan Company did not issue *CW* (see p. 53) in America, owing ostensibly to copyright difficulties.

[1] Quinn had written to WBY on 21 Mar, enclosing a copy of a letter about Wycherly and Veiller that he had sent to Mrs Simeon Ford, née Julia Ellsworth Shaw (1859–1950), the wife of the wealthy New York hotelier and property developer Simeon Ford (1855–1933). She had evidently written to remonstrate with Quinn over his treatment of the Veillers, and repeated their hard-luck story, but he was implacable, explaining to WBY that 'Mrs. Veiller, alias Miss Wycherly, is, in my opinion, working poor Mrs. Ford.

please in the matter. I shall of course be greatly interested in the result of the performance. If it comes off, I know that I shall be very sorry, not being over there to see it. One learns something from every performance of a play of one's own. "Kincora" has drawn steadily increasing audiences, we have found out that Lent is the thing that is against us, & we are putting the play on again at Easter, alternating it with Boyle's comedy & "The King's Threshold".[2] I met Sir Anthony MacDonnell in the street yesterday & he said "the more I think of that play of "Kincora", the more does it loom in my imagination. It is a great business."[3] A drunken man was also seen balancing himself against the door-post after Wednesday's performance and saying "I am never moved like this in a Music Hall". Another man cried at Gormleigh's farewell to Brian in the last act, but explained himself by saying "it isn't so much the acting, but I know the little girl".[4]

Yrs ev

W B Yeats

Dict AEFH, signed WBY; NYPL, with envelope addressed to 120 Broadway, New York, postmark 'DUBLIN AP 1 05'.

I *know* she is only trying to make a name for herself. I hope you approve of the position I have taken. . . . I know Mrs. Ford well enough to feel sure that she won't misunderstand me or be hurt by anything I say. I know you will tell me frankly what you think about it.' WBY also knew Mrs Ford: she had studied his work at a New York literary class (see *JBYL*, 285) and met him at Yale on 16 Nov 1903. Her article 'The Neo-Celtic Poet — William Butler Yeats', written in collaboration with Kate V. Thompson, had appeared in the Winter 1903 *Poet-Lore*, and she had arranged for WBY to lecture on 'Poetry' at the New York Arts Club on 20 Dec 1903, during his American tour (see III. 516). In 'Julia Ellsworth Ford: An Appreciation', published in the *Yale University Library Gazette* of April 1952, Francis Bangs records (154) that on that occasion WBY 'because of a crisis in cravats, wore a pair of Mrs. Ford's black silk stockings in lieu of the customary adornment'. On a visit to Ireland in October of this year she called, at Quinn's insistence, on WBY's sisters at Dun Emer, but bought nothing, and SMY confided to Quinn on 10 Oct 1905 (NYPL) that they 'did wish she would listen more and talk less'. She made some amends by acting as ECY's hostess during her trip to America in the autumn of 1906. She founded the Friday Night Literary Dinner Club, attended on occasion by JBY after he moved to New York, and became a playwright, novelist, and children's film producer. JBY stayed in her Grand Union Hotel for the first eighteen months of his residence in New York.

[2] i.e. *The Building Fund* which was produced with the revised version of *The King's Threshold* on 25 Apr. The two plays alternated through that week with *Kincora*, which was revived in a slightly altered form on 24 Apr.

[3] Sir Antony Patrick MacDonnell (1844–1925), an Irish-born Liberal statesman and Catholic. Educated at Queen's College, Galway, he had enjoyed a distinguished career in the Indian administration before being appointed Under-Secretary for Ireland in 1902 by the Conservative Chief Secretary George Wyndham, 'rather as a colleague than as a mere Under-Secretary to register my will'. He gave Wyndham valuable service in preparing the Land Act of 1903, and, unusually and controversially, retained office under the new Conservative Irish Secretary Walter Long, as well as, on the return of the Liberals, under James Bryce and Augustine Birrell, resigning in 1908, when he was created 1st Baron MacDonnell of Swinford. In 1904 he had advised WBY and AEFH about securing a patent for the Abbey Theatre (see III. 580).

[4] In Act III scene iii of the first version of *Kincora*, Queen Gormleith delivers a valediction over her slain husband Brian Boru: 'From this time out I must go from country to country, driven by rough

## *To T. Fisher Unwin,* [c. *4 April 1905*]

Mention in letter to G. K. A. Bell, 7 April.
Asking permission for Bell to include some of his poems in an anthology.[1]

## *To Lady Gregory,* [*5 April 1905*]

Nassau Hotel | Dublin.
Wed

My dear Lady Gregory: I am going to dictate a letter for you to Miss Horniman. I am well of my cold but it has left my eyes very bad & know you will not mind my dictating under the circumstance as I have to tell some detailed matters.

Yr ever
W B Yeats

ALS Berg.

## *To Lady Gregory, 5 April 1905*

Nassau Hotel, | Dublin.
April 5th, | 05.

*Dictated.*
Dear Lady Gregory,
    I had intended to go down to Coole this morning with Colum,[1] but a matter connected with Paris detained me here.[2] Then I meant to go down to-morrow morning, but Colum came in a couple of hours ago, to say

---

winds over rough seas, driven from place to place, with beaten men. (*They draw her away, she turns as she goes out.*) My thousand farewells to you, Brian of the victories!' (*Collected Plays* II. 353). In this production she was played by Maire Walker.

    [1] See below, p. 71.

    [1] Colum was writing *The Land* (see p. 28), dealing with emigration and the recent settling of the Land Question.

    [2] Davitt being away, MG was still enlisting WBY's help in finding a witness who would provide her lawyers with evidence that MacBride's mother lived in a low drinking den in Westport, and that its proprietor, her son Patrick, was a drunkard, so that this was no place to bring up a young child (see p. 64, n. 3). WBY approached MG's friend, the artist Sarah Purser, but she refused, and he was now seeking the aid of AEFH. She accepted the mission, and was to spend some time in Mayo trying to gather evidence of the MacBrides' intemperance — but to no avail.

that he was afraid that he could not get away for some time; some man he had to see about something, and he was afraid that he could not get a hold of him until next Thursday. He was evidently greatly disappointed. He went off to make a last attempt to get a hold of this man. If he can arrange to come in the next two or three days, I will take him down & probably not return for the special performance, at least if that will suit your plans.[3] I don't like to disappoint him. And besides it may be really important to him, that we get him & his play to ourselves. In case he can't come I won't go until after Saturday evening. There is a lecture at the Historical Society of the Royal University upon our dramatic movement. They wrote to me a very complimentary letter calling me an "illustrious leader" or something of the kind. I wrote that I should not be in Dublin. But unless I hear from Colum to-night that he can start at once, I will go & speak. Frank Fay was very anxious that I should go & I think it really of some little importance.[4] I am desperately tired however of city life & have a great longing for country quiet. I suppose that there will be no objection to my missing the Special Performance & coming up on the Thursday say, before Easter Monday. This would give me time to work up the press. I could do something in any case by letter from Coole. My cold has been rather exhausting, I am sorry to say that owing to a combination of my cold & some letters I got on Monday morning, I did not see Orpen. I of course sent your letter.[5]

I have forgotten the most interesting piece of information until the end. They made up the Kincora accounts last night; the takings were

---

[3] Lady Henrietta MacDonnell, née MacDonnell, wife of the Under-Secretary for Ireland, had organized a special INTS performance of *The Hour-Glass*, *A Pot of Broth*, and *Spreading the News* for 15 Apr, all proceeds going to the new Gallery of Modern Art (see p. 44, n. 4). The show was a success, and on 19 Apr AG wrote to Quinn (NYPL) 'to say how well the special performance went': 'Hugh Lane writes that the players surpassed themselves and that he never saw a more attentative and enthusiastic audience. Orpen said he had never been held by a play as he was with the Hour Glass. All plays went well, there was a double call after each, even Frank Fay the gloomy, writes cheerfully. He evidently gave a very fine performance of the Wise Man. We haven't heard yet how much money was cleared for the pictures, but the audience was a very good one, and prices had been advanced.' On 24 Mar the Dublin Corporation had passed a resolution approving £500 a year for the maintenance of such a gallery.
[4] WBY did speak; see below p. 77.
[5] William Orpen (1878–1931), a friend of Lane (who had commissioned him to do portraits of a number of distinguished Irishmen), was among those who promised a work of art for the new gallery. Educated at the Metropolitan School of Art, Dublin, he taught there for six years before the First World War, when be became an official war artist in France. He was a member of the New English Art Club and became president of the International Society of Sculptors, Painters, and Gravers in 1921. His *Stories of Old Ireland and Myself* (1924) gives a lengthy account of Lane's struggle to establish the Municipal Gallery and recalls (80) WBY in pre-war Dublin 'walking along with his head in the air, his thoughts blinding him to the sight of you'. AG's letter may have been an invitation to Coole; in an undated reply to her (Emory) he regrets that he cannot accept her invitation as he is going to London.

about 20 per cent better than in the case of Synge. There was a profit of £50.

Yrs sny<br>
W B Yeats

Dict AEFH, signed WBY; Berg, with envelope addressed to Coole, postmark 'AP 6 05'.

## *To Eva Hamilton, 5 April 1905*

Nassau Hotel, | Dublin.<br>
April 5<sup>th</sup>, | 05.

*Dictated.*

Dear Miss Hamilton,

I am dictating this as my eyes have been made sensitive by a cold. I wrote to Lord Dunsany but without result.[1] I hear that Lane got three hundred letters written to persons of wealth and got in answer—twenty shillings.

Nothing is definitely settled about the date of our London performances, but they are not likely to come before June. Our performance for the pictures is on the 15<sup>th</sup> of this month & on Easter Monday we begin a week's performances. At the end of May, or early June, we shall open again. After that I have no doubt that it will be London.[2]

Yrs sny<br>
W B Yeats

Dict AEFH, signed WBY; NLI.

---

[1] See p. 55. WBY had evidently written c/o Dunsany Castle, but Lord Dunsany was in London. The situation was not so precarious as WBY supposed, for the appeal was just getting under way and eventually over 130 wealthy patrons, including the Prince and Princess of Wales, became subscribers, either contributing pictures or helping to purchase over forty items from the Staats-Forbes and Durand-Ruel exhibition. When the Municipal Gallery of Modern Art opened in January 1908, the catalogue listed 300 pictures.

[2] The London productions did not take place until 27–8 Nov.

# To G. K. A. Bell,[1] 7 April 1905

Nassau Hotel, | Dublin
April 7th,| 05.

*Dictated.*

Dear M' Bell,

I heard from Gogherty the other day[2] that you wanted to include a couple of short poems from the book of my verse published by Fisher Unwin. I wrote to Unwin and got the enclosed in reply. You may have the poems and without any payment. The charge is meant to keep off publishers, compilers of school-books, musicians, makers of books for reciters & so on.

It was never meant to keep poets from selecting what they have a mind to.

Yrs sny
W B Yeats

Dict AEFH, signed WBY; Routledge.

[1] George Kennedy Allen Bell (1883–1958), Oliver Gogarty's friend and sometime lodger at the Martello Tower, read Classics at Oxford, and won the Newdigate Poetry Prize in 1904. He was editor of the eight-volume Golden Anthologies (1905–7), the first of which, *Poems of Love* (1905), included WBY's 'The Pity of Love' and 'The Sorrow of Love'. He subsequently published 'A Dream of a Blessed Spirit' in *Poems of Life and Death* (1906), and 'A Faery Song' in *Poems of Marriage* (1907). Bell took holy orders in 1907, wrote extensively on the Church of England and Christian values, and became Bishop of Chichester in 1929.

[2] Gogarty also wrote to Bell on 7 Apr (*Many Lines*, 87), hoping that he had received Unwin's permission to publish WBY's poems, and describing a visit to WBY at the Nassau Hotel, where he was received by AEFH: 'In the parlour were: "letters to Mr Watt", "Yeats Plays".... Many letters in a portfolio which he showed me saying: "Miss Horniman writes all my letters now—I leave them for a week and then we answer them all in an afternoon." Miss Horniman said "Do you know, Mr Gogarty, that sometimes we have to go out to ask how to spell a word." I made some little jocular vacuity about Yeats' writing saving his spelling, but that with her handwriting she had to be correct.'

## To Maud Gonne, [c. 8 April 1905]

Mention in letter from MG, 'Monday' [? 10 April 1905].
Telling her that AEFH will go to Westport to spy on the MacBrides,[1] that
Sarah Purser has refused to help,[2] that he is taking Colum with him on a
visit to Coole,[3] and that he has a cold.

G–YL, 198.

## To Hugh Lane, 14 April 1905

COOLE PARK, | GORT, | CO. GALWAY.
April 14. 1905

My dear Lane: I enclose Lord Dunsanys letter. Please send him a receipt—
I only got his note & checque to day—sent on from London.[1]

Yr sny
W B Yeats

ALS NLI.

[1] See p. 68, n. 2. In her reply MG said that she had written and telegraphed AEFH 'accepting her offer because my lawyer thought it of great importance. I don't know how to express my gratitude to her for her more than kindness. Kindness I would hardly have expected or ventured to ask from even a great friend—'

[2] Sarah Henrietta Purser (1848–1943), the portrait painter and well-known Dublin wit had been a friend of MG's since the late 1880s, when she painted a portrait of her with a monkey, now in the Dublin Municipal Gallery. They visited each other frequently in Dublin and Paris, and MG had stayed at the Pursers while recovering from a carriage accident in June 1898 (see II. 236). But Purser had little time for MG's political activities and told WBY (*Mem*, 61) that she talked 'politics in Paris, and literature to you, and at the Horse Show she would talk of a clinking brood mare'. She also held her distance from any emotional engagement, and upset the youthful WBY by meeting him 'with the sentence, "So Maud Gonne is dying in the South of France, and her portrait is on sale," and went on to tell how she had lunched with Maud Gonne in Paris and there was a very tall Frenchman there—and I thought she dwelt upon his presence for my sake—and a doctor, and the doctor had said to her, "They will be both dead in six months."' In her reply MG said that she was 'not surprise[d] Sarah refused. I knew she would, but it was too late to telegraph you not to trouble yourself to ask her.'

[3] See p. 68. MG replied that she was 'glad you have taken Colm down to Coole, it will do him good. He is such a charming boy & his work is so interesting.'

[1] See pp. 55, 70. Dunsany's letter is untraced, but he appears on the list of subscribers and, with others, he presented one of Millet's studies for *The Gleaners* (the final version of which hangs in the Louvre) to the new gallery.

## *To A. H. Bullen, 14 April* [*1905*]

COOLE PARK, | GORT, | CO. GALWAY.
April 14

My dear Bullen: I enclose a letter just received from Brett— sent on from London—had you not better see Watt or Brett. The last paragraph means I suppose that Brett objects to sale of your big collected edition in America. It should be possible for you to arrange with him so as to make it worth his while. If the big collected edition will be much more expensive than his small one & if he have a share in the handling of it he should not object. It would be better perhaps for you to see Watt or Brett before Brett has gone back.

I shall be over at end of month.

I am anxious to leave Watt as free as possible in settling the complex bother of my American affairs.

They have just played my "Countess Cathleen" out there—not I think very succesfully. I would not have consented to it—for it wants re-construction as a play—but John Quinn had taken so much trouble I did not care to interfear.

Yrs ev
W B Yeats


[*With enclosure*]
Dear M^r Yeats                                                  April 6 5

I saw M^r Watt today & he agreed to endeavor to arrange with Dodd & Lane for the two small volumes.[1] Even if it should be impossible to get them we might still go ahead explaining their absence in the preface.

I asked M^r Watt to send me the agreement when I will at once forward the duplicate & I sincerely trust for all our sakes that we shall get the edition out by early autumn as we are all I think by postponement losing a really good opportunity of sale.

I quite agree with Quinn's excellent suggestion that the book should be in two volumes ie one of plays & one of poems.

---

[1] i.e. Dodd, Mead & Co. American publishers of *The Shadowy Waters*, and John Lane, American publisher of *The Wind Among the Reeds* (see p. 65).

I explained my view fully to M^r Watt on the Bullen edition which cannot I think legally be imported into the United States *for sale*.²

Yours faithfully,<br>
George P. Brett

W. B. Yeats Esq.

ALS Harvard and NYPL.

## To John Quinn, 15 April [1905]

Coole Park, | Gort,<br>
April 15

My dear Quinn,

A great many thanks for all the trouble you have taken about Miss Wycherly.¹ If you saw the play yourself I would be very glad if you wrote and told me quite frankly what part went well and what badly. My feeling about it is that in its present form it is not likely to have a real stage success. I wrote it before I had any real experience of the theatre, constructed indeed the whole story before I had ever seen a theatre from behind the footlights, or much of one from in front. Sooner or later I shall have to make an adaption for our own people here, and find it very hard to see the play without a fresh eye. I would also like to know what cuts she made if any, if you happened to notice them. I dont much mind what the ordinary dramatic critics say, I am anxious for your own impression. At the same time I think the New York papers have been extremely fair. I have no doubt the play affected the audience as they say it did.² I have had a letter from

---

² Although there was an apparent marketing clash between the Macmillan *Poetical Works of William B. Yeats* and Bullen's proposed *Collected Works*, the difference in scale and cost meant that they were in fact appealing to different constituencies. Brett's objection, to which he adhered despite intense lobbying from Bullen and Quinn, was that the importation of Bullen's sheets and plates, on the scale envisaged, would breach the American copyright laws and render his firm vulnerable to piracy.

¹ See pp. 50, 59–63. Quinn was still locked in battle with Veiller and Miss Wycherly, who had misused his name in publicity letters and failed to pay the performing fees they had promised. The quarrel was no longer merely business but had become personal and he told WBY on 31 Mar that he intended to sue Veiller for back royalties and attach the receipts for *The Countess Cathleen*: 'This Canadian Jew may think that he can beat me. He may. But I don't think he will.'

² Quinn had included newspaper reviews of Margaret Wycherly's production of *The Countess Cathleen* with his letter of 31 Mar, commenting that he had been 'assured by a reporter that everything "fed up to the press" was favorable to her acting and that Veiller didn't care a Damn how you came out in the matter'. Quinn's informant seems to have been right: the New York press of 29 Mar was almost

Brett and things are now being definitely arranged about the edition of my poems in America. He agreed to your suggestion of two volumes, one of plays, one of poems. I shall do a preface, that is all that remains.[3]

I keep constantly hearing the praises of Kincora, and I believe it has scattered whatever suspicion of us there may have been. Colum is here, and has read us a good part of his new play. It is much more nearly finished than when I wrote to you last about it, and we are all agreed that it is a really fine work. He is working very hard I think.[4] We hope to have it performed this season and possibly in London. This is the night of the special performance

unanimous in its praise of Miss Wycherly's performance at the expense of the play and WBY's dramatic powers. The New York *Evening Sun* complained that WBY had provided 'New York with a most dismal afternoon. The only persons to be congratulated were those Thousands of Patriotic Irishman who love their poet but studiously stayed away from his play's performance—Miss Wycherly, although charming strove vainly to arouse interest in "The Countess Cathleen".... That William Butler Yeats is a poet there is no doubt... but that he is not a playwright nor has the slightest idea of stage construction or dramatic values was proved yesterday afternoon.... There were about fifty people in the house, so there was plenty of gloom for everybody.' The reviewer thought Miss Wycherly 'charming to look upon as the Countess, and her bewitching voice intoned and recited the long speeches beautifully', but he warned that 'if as her friends declare, Miss Wycherly is giving these matinées to bring her work before the managers, then she may as well be told frankly at once that "The Countess Cathleen" is not the sort of vehicle for her to appear in if she really wants to show what she can do as an actress not as a reciter.' The New York *Mail and Express* of the same day, noting the play's 'remoteness of interest', gave a similar account: 'Even the delight Miss Wycherly gives... cannot quite compensate for the infliction of tediousness put upon the spectator by Mr Yeats. It is his pleasure to take a strong theme and to see how quickly he can make it vanish into thin air.' *The World*, while also praising Miss Wycherly's acting, considered that Yeats's drama was 'not suited to practical histrionic purposes. Though its imagination travels along the path of the sublime, the course is laid dangerously near the verge of the ridiculous.' The *Globe* also found the source tale appealing but 'curiously impotent except for isolated passages on the stage.... It pleases Yeats in theory and practice to disclaim, not merely threadbare tricks of the theatre, but the essential means by which character, incident, speech and atmosphere, pass from the stage to the audience. Much that he writes for the theatre seems bald, artificial, thin, even dull, because he cannot or he will not give it theatrical body.' Two of the few exceptions in this litany of complaint were the *New York Herald* and the *New-York Times*. The *Herald* claimed that not only was Miss Wycherly's performance 'delightful', but the play was a *succès d'estime* and well received: 'such meaning as the drama conveys was addressed more to brain than to heart.... There was applause at every curtain, but the applause was more a personal tribute to the actors than to the play itself.' The *New-York Times* was almost alone in preferring the play to Miss Wycherly: on 29 Mar (9) it pronounced the production lacking in impressiveness and, while acknowledging her pains-taking efforts, found that her company did 'not meet requirements which would tax any but the most sympathetic and gifted players', and thought that she herself had 'no such variety of expression as is needed to convey the melodious color of Mr. Yeats's richly imaginative verse'. Quinn was so incensed with Veiller that he probably could not bring himself to attend the performances.

[3] WBY's preface to vol. I of *The Poetical Works* (1906) is dated July 1906.

[4] Colum wrote to Maire Garvey from Coole on 20 Apr: 'Here's from the Seven Woods. I'm working very hard here trying to finish the play this week. Lady Gregory is holding me up as an example to Yeats. Yeats and I have been fishing. We have had talks about the Society and I have put our point of view very strongly. He is quite aware of WG's [i.e. Fay's] prejudices, and I do not think is much influenced by them' (Hogan and Kilroy III. 30). In her letter to Quinn of 19 April (see p. 69, n. 3), AG disclosed that WBY was 'taking infinite trouble with Colum... who is getting his play into good shape. It is a great thing getting him on to right lines, there is no critical standard in Dublin, and lads fritter away their talent in careless work.'

for the Art Gallery, The Hour Glass, Pot of Broth and Spreading the News. Next Monday week we re-open with Kincora, alternated with Senchan and Boyle's play. We shall go to Dublin for that.

There is nothing new about Mrs MacBride's affair. The first hearing will be I think at the end of May. Mrs Clay mentioned in a recent letter that Mary Quinn knew something about MacBride's habits in New York. In fact I rather think it was she who wrote to them about it, but I am not sure.[5]

Arnold Dolmetsch has written to me from Chicago. He had seen a performance of the Hour Glass of which I enclose the programme. He wanted to do music for a miracle play for me. I suppose all these nice young ladies who have I suppose infringed Miss Wycherley's rights were among the people I saw there and made speeches to and heard speeches by. They have got out a very good programme.[6]

I am working at a rather elaborate article on the necessity of having verse sung or spoken. It is for the International Review.[7] But whether I have finished it or not, Lady Gregory has announced that I am to return to Deirdre next Monday. I have not touched it since I left here in October.[8]

---

[5] Quinn was finding it difficult to obtain affidavits testifying to MacBride's drunkenness and antisocial behaviour (see pp. 49–50), and was to write to WBY on 6 May (Himber, 73): 'I have been met by opposition and silence at every turn. MacBride has had his friends here notified and they apparently take his side of the case and those who do not say that the scandal is hurtful to the cause generally and that the sooner it is hushed up the better.' The former INTS actress Maire T. Quinn (d. 1947), who often Anglicized her forename in America, knew both MG and MacBride well. She had been a member of the Inghinidhe na hEireann and assisted MG in the 'Battle of Coulson Avenue' (see III. 417). John Quinn did not manage to see her until mid-June, but she then, as he reported to WBY on 17 June (Himber, 75), 'made a strong affidavit, fully corroborating the affidavits that had been sent from here to Paris', and testified that MacBride had been drunk most of his time in New York in the summer of 1904. At the preliminary hearing of the divorce petition on 26 July, MacBride's counsel dismissed the evidence collected by John Quinn as 'that of a cab-driver and of the coachman of an actress . . . picked up in the street, and . . . of comparatively no importance' (*Irish Independent*, 27 July 1905, p. 5).

[6] The French-born Arnold Dolmetsch (1858–1940) had studied at the Brussels Conservatoire before moving to the Royal College of Music. In London he led the revival of early English music, played for the Rhymers' Club, was championed by Shaw, and provided the music for William Poel's Elizabethan Stage Society. He became interested in WBY's and FF's chanting experiments after they attended one of his concerts in February 1901, and designed and made a psaltery to assist them (see III. 68, 91, 194–5). He had set out on his second American tour in November 1904, and had now decided to remain there, signing a contract with Chickerings of Boston to open a new department of keyboard instruments, lutes, and viols. While in Chicago to arrange the music for Ben Greet's 'Shakespeare Festival', he sent WBY a programme of Anna Morgan's eight performances of *The Hour-Glass* (30 Mar–21 Apr), saying that he would like 'to make some music for such a morality play, Angelic music, introduced as you would. It would be beautiful' (*LWBY* 1. 148). In the 1903 *Samhain* (*Expl*, 109) WBY had wished for the Angel to 'sound like the voice of an Immortal . . . spoken upon pure notes which are carefully recorded and learned as if they were the notes of a song'. Dolmetsch never wrote the music. Against Quinn's advice, WBY had attended a performance of *The Land of Heart's Desire* given by the Chicago University drama group on 14 Jan 1904 (see III. 518–19).

[7] 'Literature and the Living Voice' was published not in the *International Review* but in the *Contemporary Review* of October 1906 (see below, pp. 383, 400).

[8] Quinn was pleased at this news. Writing on 24 Feb (see p. 30, n. 12) he had urged WBY to 'go on and finish *Deirdre* for there I think you have one of the greatest themes in the world and that you will

The Historical Society of the Catholic College in Stephens Green invited me to speak there a week ago. I had a fine reception and a good part of the audience applauded my praise of Synge, so I think times are changing. A man who spoke after me read out an extract from Huyssman supposing it to be by Maeterlinck, as an example of absurd unintelligible symbolism. He wound up by asking me if I could explain what it meant. I got up looking as bothered in my head as I could. I asked the chairman's leave to ask the young man a question. I said I had missed the name of the author and asked was it S John of the Cross. I knew it must be one of the Catholic medieval writers but wasn't sure which. The audience saw what I was at at once and applauded me very loudly. The young man was on a heresy hunt.[9]

Yrs sincerely<br>W B Yeats

TLS NYPL, addressed (in AG's hand) to 120 Broadway, New York, postmark 'ORAN-MORE AP 15 05', enclosing theatre programme.

make a great play of it', and on 29 Apr he advised AG (NYPL): 'Now that Yeats is started at "Deirdre" again you can do nothing better than keep him at it until he has finished. I know that . . . he is likely to be distracted by other things but he has great opportunity here to write the greatest play—the greatest poem—that he ever has written.'

[9] See p. 69. The Literary and Historical Society of University College met on 8 Apr, with AE presiding. Francis Cruise O'Brien (1885–1927), later a friend of WBY, read a paper on 'The New School of Literature and Drama in Ireland', focusing on the symbolism of AE, WBY, AG, Synge, and Edward Martyn. The *Freeman's Journal* of 11 Apr 1905 (6) printed WBY's reply and his remark that if 'Mr Synge lived another twenty years he would have a European reputation. He had the most intense artistic individuality of any man in Ireland.' The *Leader* of 15 Apr (125–7) reported that WBY 'delivered a clever and witty speech, quite devoid of mystery. The audience keenly enjoyed his tussle with Mr. J. Kennedy over the question, whether *Huysman* [*sic*] is meaningless or meaningful.' Joseph Holloway took a rather more jaundiced view of the proceedings, recording in his diary (NLI) that 'Mr O'Brien is a silly-looking individual with long hair plastered down at either side of his face over his ears from the division at the centre. He wears a big Etonesque collar & speaks in a slow-somewhat-affected voice & altogether reminded one of Bunthorne in *Patience*. His *paper* was like a series of blind alleys leading nowhere. He was ever raising points only to drop them unsolved & one gained very little information of a definite kind when he sat down. . . . The great W B Yeats followed & explained his views & aims in his usual enthusi-astic manner accompanied by his strange gesticulation which seldom carry out Shakespeare's advice to suit the word to the action & the action to the word. Words flow in rapid blocks of speech, as it were, from him, with slight intervals between each burst of eloquence. For much if not all, of his speech is eloquent. He praised Synge beyond measure, & said the fight for the theatre would certainly be round him. One time he exclaimed that he could not believe that "the Irish peasant was such a *monster of virtue* as many would have us suppose!" amid applause & laughter. If he wasn't very convincing he was very entertaining. Mr J. E. Kennedy who followed . . . struck an attitude, by leaning against the reading desk . . . & spoke with an air of cock suredness in slightly satirical voice, that was sad to behold. Conceit oozed out of him, therefore, no one was sorry that he got well sat upon in the end. Incompetent affectation met well with its just reward in his case!' Quinn relished this anecdote and on 29 Apr (see n. 8) asked AG to tell WBY 'that I enjoyed reading his letter very much and particularly his misunderstanding of Huysman's [*sic*] name. . . . Indeed Yeats was not so far wrong, for Huysman [*sic*] will compress into three pages what St. John would gush out in thirty-three.' The French novelist Joris-Karl Huysmans (1848–1907) moved from an early admiration for Zola's naturalism to aestheticism and mysticism, and had exercised a significant influence on Wilde and George Moore. WBY's initial admiration for the work of the Belgian symbolist Maurice

## *To Maud Gonne,* [c. *21 April 1905*]

Mention in letter from MG, 'Sunday' [? 23 April 1905].
Complaining of rheumatism, telling her that AEFH has failed to enlist any witnesses to drunkenness in the MacBride family in Westport,[1] and asking whether MacBride visits his son every day.[2]

*G–YL*, 199.

## *To Maud Gonne,* [c. *24 April 1905*]

Mention in letter from MG, 'Wednesday' [? 26 April 1905].
Sending her a book of stories,[1] saying that it will be impossible to find the actor Dudley Digges a job at the Abbey Theatre,[2] and giving W. G. Fay's

Maeterlinck (1862–1949) had waned after the turn of the century, and he was to tell Masefield that 'Maeterlinck must be a godsend to the parodist' (*Some Memories*, 10).

[1] See pp. 64, n. 3, 68, n. 2. AEFH had arrived in Westport by 10 Apr and, entering enthusiastically into the cloak-and-dagger spirit of the adventure, decided to report back to AG (Berg) 'because I don't think that your name & address would be as interesting to anybody as that of Mr. Yeats'. She realized that she needed 'an exact statement that Patrick Mc'Bride drinks': 'He does not look a nice sort of person, or rather not a pleasant character; but that without drinking would not be considered important.' By 11 Apr she had interviewed two local solicitors and taken depositions from them, but they both vouched for the rectitude of the MacBride family. One, R. C. Garvey, 'a wholesome looking young man', had 'a brother in the army by the bye, yet he spoke most highly of Patrick Mc'Bride... & he is certain that he is a perfectly sober person & of solid financial status'. Garvey also enquired whether MG 'took herself seriously as no one else did'.

AEFH immediately announced the unwelcome news of Patrick MacBride's temperance in two telegrams, cunningly written in German, a language she evidently supposed to be wholly unknown to the natives of the west of Ireland: 'Man sagt dass er sauft nicht' and 'Der andere aucht sagt dass er sauft nicht'. Happily, her trip was not an entire disaster: 'The weather has been absolutely lovely & I have really enjoyed myself here.'

MG replied that she had also heard from AEFH about her lack of success, but that she knew 'how timid & suspicious people are in the country towns in Ireland, & it was only to be expected they would not speak out to a stranger. Also the fact of the bishop having shown favor to the MacBride family lately means that everyone will hesitate how they speak about them. Also I am sorry to say Drunkenness is so usual in the country towns that a man must be in the last stages before any one speaks of it. I think I must do without this evidence.'

[2] MG indignantly refuted the Dublin rumour that MacBride had daily visiting rights to his son: '*Of course* it is a lie that MacBride visits Seagan every day. Once a week is all that is permitted by the Court.' She added that MacBride was now in Dublin.

[1] Probably an advance copy of *Stories of Red Hanrahan*. The book was officially published by the Dun Emer Press on 16 May 1905, but WBY had inscribed a copy for AG on 18 Apr 1905 (Private).

[2] John Dudley Digges (1880–1947) had acted with the Fays' original Ormond Company, and was a founding member of the INTS. He and Maire Quinn (see p. 76, n. 5) resigned from the Society in November 1903 over the production of *In the Shadow of the Glen*, and in 1904 they emigrated to the USA to act in Irish plays at the St Louis Exhibition. Dismissed for protesting about the 'stage-Irish' aspects of these productions (see III. 609–10), Digges had moved to New York with Maire Quinn (whom he married in 1907), and was at present a poorly paid clerk in a wholesale clothiers, while she was a research assistant

estimation of the Digges family,³ telling her that things are going well with him.⁴

*G–YL*, 201–2.

## *To George Bernard Shaw,*¹ [*1 May 1905*]

Nassau Hotel | South Fredrick Sᵗ | Dublin.

My dear Shaw: all right give that green elephant to Calvert.² We all admire it but dont feal that we could do the English men at all. We might be able to play it but it is all uncertain & the great thing is to get it done here. Calvert will do it far better than we could.

Yrs ever
W B Yeats

ALCS Texas, addressed to 10 Adelphi Terrace, London, postmark 'DUBLIN MY 1 05'.

in the New York Public Library. She had lately been in correspondence with MG about affidavits as to MacBride's drunkenness (see p. 76), and in one of her letters, which MG sent on to WBY on 20 Apr (*G–YL*, 200–1), reported that, owing to Digges's prolonged and serious illness, they were almost destitute, and that the doctor had warned that his lungs would not stand another New York winter. In her covering letter MG asked WBY whether it would be possible to find Digges a job in the Abbey, so that the couple could return to Ireland, and offered to subsidize his salary there. In his reply WBY had evidently told MG that this was impossible: neither he nor the Fays would have relished the return of Digges or Maire Quinn, known for their touchiness on political and religious matters, to the theatre, and it would have been difficult in any case to reabsorb two powerful and outspoken ex-members into the INTS. In her reply MG said that she quite understood the difficulty, and emphasized that the suggestion had been entirely hers, and that neither Digges nor Maire Quinn knew anything of it.

³ Fay's estimation of the Digges family has not been traced. In a letter Maire Quinn had told MG that 'Digges has a starving father, mother & sister & brothers at home, to whom he sends help every week'.

⁴ In her reply MG said she was 'delighted to hear things are going on so well with you'.

¹ George Bernard Shaw (1856–1950) had known WBY since February 1888 (see 1. 50), and, although at this time both men were suspicious of each other's attitudes, they had a friendly relationship (see p. 54). WBY disliked what he regarded as Shaw's mechanistic view of life (in a memorable nightmare he imagined him as 'a sewing-machine, that clicked and shone, but...smiled, smiled perpetually') and his debunking of romantic sentiments, but appreciated Shaw's formidable polemical powers, recognizing that, while they had not the same friends, they had the same enemies, and Shaw 'could hit my enemies...as I could never hit' (*Aut*, 283). Shortly after WBY's death, Shaw told Stephen Gwynn (Bucknell) that he 'was always on very good terms with him personally; but I was not on literary terms with him; did not read enough of him to pontificate about his work; and did not get into his movement at all. At first he amused me because of Gilbert's entirely unsuccessful attempt to put Wilde on the stage as Bunthorne in Patience. Bunthorne was not a bit like Wilde; but he presently came to life in the person of W.B.Y., who out Bunthorned him enough to make him seem commonplace.' It was not until Shaw spent some time with WBY at Coole in 1910 that he discovered 'what a penetrating critic and good talker he was; for he played none of his Bunthorne games, and saw no green elephants, at Coole'.

² i.e. *John Bull's Other Island*, Shaw's four-act Irish play, which WBY thought elephantine in being 'immensely too long' (III. 661), and perhaps, since he was given to seeing green elephants following people of whom he disapproved (*I & R*, 401–2), also uncongenial. The play examines the paradoxical

# *To Wilfrid Scawen Blunt,*[1] *7 May* [*1905*]

Abbey Theatre | Dublin
May 7.

Dear Mr Blunt,

I am dictating this letter because my eyesight makes letter writing nearly impossible, and my handwriting nearly unreadable. I have long been intending to write to you about your play, but waited to have some definite decision from the company.[2] The play, with the second act left out, and some shortening of speeches here and there is passionate and beautiful, and should be a strong play upon the stage. William Fay is particularly content because of what he called its masculine vigour and were it not for a difficulty with the verse we could come to a definite decision about its performance and give you a date. Frank Fay, our best speaker of verse and our teacher of elocution has not only come round to read passages to me and to hear me read them, and this several times, but he has tried it in private a great deal.

---

attitudes towards Ireland of the supposedly hard-headed English civil engineer, Thomas Broadbent, who sentimentalizes over Irish stereotypes on a trip to develop the village of Rosscullen into a holiday resort, and his Irish partner Larry Doyle, who looks on with shrewd and despairing realism. Although commissioned for the INTS, the play was not produced at the Abbey (see III. 268, 390, 660–3), since WBY later claimed (*Expl*, 103) that 'we felt ourselves unable to cast it without wronging Mr. Shaw. We had no "Broadbent" or money to get one.' Louis Calvert (1859–1923), one of the leading actors at the Court Theatre during the Vedrenne–Barker management, played the role of Broadbent when the play first opened there in November 1904, and, although he was not Shaw's first choice, made a great success in the part. He now wanted the touring rights, including Ireland, where the Abbey still had first refusal. It was produced in Dublin for the first time at the Royalty Theatre on 20 Nov 1907, under the auspices of J. E. Vedrenne and Harley Granville-Barker and with WBY and AG in the audience, although on that occasion Broadbent was played by Nigel Playfair.

[1] Wilfrid Scawen Blunt (1840–1922), poet, horseman, and traveller, was born in Sussex and entered the British diplomatic service at the age of 18, serving in legations at Athens, Frankfurt, Madrid, Paris, Lisbon, Buenos Aires, and Berne. In 1869 he left the service and married Lady Anne Noel, a descendant of Lord Byron, with whom he travelled in the Middle East and India. He became a flamboyant anti-Imperialist and a champion of nationalism in Ireland, Egypt, and India. From December 1882 to July 1883 he had been AG's lover, and her sequence of poems 'A Woman's Sonnets' was inspired by this affair and published under his name in 1892. In 1888 he served two months in Galway Gaol for resisting the police during the suppression of a Land League meeting at Woodford, Co. Galway, an exploit which WBY celebrated in an article in *United Ireland* on 28 Jan 1888 (*UP* 1. 122–30). AG had introduced WBY to him on 1 Apr 1898, and the two met occasionally in London.

[2] Blunt had been awaiting this letter since 19 Feb 1905, when he recorded in his diary (II. 119): 'Lady Gregory writes that Yeats has read my play "Fand" to his company and that they are anxious to act it, and perhaps it will be put on the stage in April. Yeats, she says, has declared that if I had begun to write plays when I was thirty, I should now have a European reputation.' Blunt's three-act play *Fand*, based on the same legend as WBY's *Only Jealousy of Emer*, had first been mooted in June 1902 (see III. 202–3), and a privately published edition of the play, entitled *Fand of the Fair Cheek*, had appeared in December 1904. Its production was delayed until 20 Apr 1907, when Frank Fay played Cuchulain and Sara Allgood, Maire O'Neill, and Maire Garvey the parts of the three women Emer, Fand, and Eithne in a shortened, two-act version.

He is very much alarmed at the difficulty of anything so new to our people as the Alexandrine. If Cuchulain had an overmastering part in the play, Frank Fay's own speaking would hold the play together, but the overmastering part lies for a great part of the play between three women. At the present moment we have only two women who can be relied upon in the speaking of blank verse, and one of them has never been tested in any important part. If it were blank verse we could train somebody, or rather the general work of our theatre must train somebody during the summer, but the Alexandrines will throw a great deal of work upon everybody who has to speak it for their experience in blank verse will not help them very greatly. Now if you care to leave the play with us, I think I will be able to get a performance of a competent kind, but unfortunately I cannot say when. Probably not until we have had some more verse plays. A number of new people joined us last Christmas, and they have all to be drilled in verse. We believe that the company very shortly will have to become a regular paid company, and this will give us much more time for rehearsal. The difficulty of the moment is Frank Fay who has argued the whole thing out with me, and declared it impossible to give an adequate performance under present circumstances. I had originally hoped to have it performed this season. We had discussed the possibility of doing it in May, and I was about to propose putting it early in the autumn, when these difficulties with the verse cropped up. I feel that this delay is in some ways very unfair to you, and if you have any other way of getting it performed we have no desire to stand in the way. It would not interfere with our performance. The play is so admirable in construction that I would think that somebody would be got to try it in London. I do not mean of course that there would be any chance of its acceptance by the ordinary theatre, but there are various groups of experimentalists there now. Possibly however it needs an audience like ours already interested in the subject matter and without any prejudice against eloquent speech. I wish you had written the play in blank verse, but I imagine that you felt the necessity of breaking from the English tradition of dramatic speech.[3] This is our last month of performance, for the season. We are trying to get the Royalty or some other theatre in London for a couple of days in June, but nothing is settled yet. I shall be in London next week. Some day I shall probably have to discuss with you the placing of

---

[3] Blunt wrote in reply on 7 May (*LWBY* I. 148–9): 'As to the metre I equally cd. not have written it in blank verse. I have been preaching against blank verse any time for the last five & twenty years as the one thing which has always stood in the way of any progress in the direction of good verse drama on the English stage . . . I was brought up, as far as play going went, mostly in Paris & used to attribute the success of the French poetic drama largely to their having so infinitely better a medium than ours in the Alexandrine.' WBY may well have been influenced by *Fand* in using the alexandrine for the metre of his own play *The Green Helmet.*

some of your caesuras, but it is too soon for that. A small number of lines I notice give F. Fay trouble.

Yrs sincely
W B Yeats

TLS Texas.

## To Maud Gonne, [c. 9 May 1905]

Mention in an undated letter from MG, [May 1905].
Telling her that MacBride has announced his intention of transferring the divorce case from France to England.[1]

*G–YL*, 202–4.

## To Lady Gregory, [12 May 1905]

18 Woburn Buildings | Euston Road | London
Friday.

My dear Lady Gregory: I send you a letter, which I have just received. Please send it on to Russell. MacBride makes what is I suspect the first move towards a 'surrender'. After you have read the letter please send it to Russell but ask him to send it to me. I saw 'Beckett' last night. The 'Beckett' scenes are good, though not as good as I thought but the rest is sentimental melodrama, with nothing to act, & therefore no acting. The worst & most sentimental melodramatic scene roused the audience to enthusiasm it seems. It was the bit where Beckett appears from behind a tree in time to keep Queen Elinor from stabbing Rosimond. There was a child, & a garrish [*for* garish] wood & much sentiment & I heard the people behind me saying from time to time 'How beautiful'. Irving played finely but I think more out of manner & habit than in old days, & all the rest—well they were a good deal below our level. With good parts they might have done well. The construction of the play is childlike & the character drawing of the stage.[1]

Yrs ev
W B Yeats

---

[1] This did not happen.

[1] Shortly before his death in October 1892, Alfred Lord Tennyson had cut and adapted his play *Becket* (1880) for stage production by Henry Irving. Irving, who took the title role in February 1893, was now in his 'Farewell Season' at the Theatre Royal, Drury Lane, where he alternated *Becket* with Shakespeare's *The Merchant of Venice* and the adaptation *A Story of Waterloo* from 29 Apr to 10 June. On 13 Oct of this year, while on tour in Bradford, Irving collapsed on stage and, professional to the last, died

[*With enclosure*]²
My dear Willie
   The day I got your letter telling me of my husband's announced intention of asking for the transfer of the divorce case from France to England, I also got a letter from my lawyer saying he had had a visit from MacBride's solicitor Mr Kelly.³ On my husband's behalf he offered to let the divorce suit go undefended if I would take back the citation containing the charges & arrange some other charges not so dishonoring. He admits being drunk on *two occasions*!⁴ Also that I would sign a paper, which it was explained would not be even legally binding, to agree to the submitting the question for the custody of the child to arbitrators named by MacBride & by myself in seven years' time.⁵ Failing my agreement to these terms Mr Kelly said

on cue shortly after declaiming the closing line of *Becket*, 'Into thy hands, O Lord'. A fault of the play is that the plot concerning the power struggle between Henry II and his former friend Becket, now Archbishop of Canterbury, hardly engages with a romantic secondary plot, centring on the murderous hatred of Henry's queen, Eleanor of Aquitaine, for his mistress Rosamund de Clifford. The melodramatic scene, which WBY describes accurately, is Act III scene iii, and takes place near Rosamund's secret country refuge, when Becket appears from nowhere to prevent Eleanor stabbing Rosamund and her (and King Henry's) child Geoffrey. The lavishly designed set by Hawes Craven (1837–1910) depicted an extensive and thick-set wood. The play is a series of short episodes, which hardly give the characters opportunity to develop, and although Irving found playing Becket a moving experience, Ellen Terry, the original Rosamund, complained that 'She is not there, she does not exist' (R. Manvell, *Ellen Terry* [1968], p. 210). According to T. R. Henn WBY had met Irving in his early teens, and Irving told JBY (*The Lonely Tower* [1950], 248) 'if your son ever thinks of becoming an actor, send him to me'. Although WBY did not take up the offer, Irving's performance of Hamlet exercised a lasting influence on him as 'an image of heroic self-possession . . . a combatant of the battle within myself' (*Aut*, 47). He later recalled (*Aut*, 125) that 'Irving, the last of the sort on the English stage . . . never moved me but in the expression of intellectual pride', an association that recurs in 'A Nativity' (*VP*, 625): 'What brushes fly and moth aside?' | Irving and his plume of pride.'

   ² In her reply of 'Sunday' (Berg) AG thanked WBY for 'sending Mrs. MacB's. I hope she, & every woman with a drunken husband, may succeed in getting free. Where I don't quite agree with you is the probability of her being able to do any more work in Ireland. I think that is over for her. But I may be wrong.' AG did send MG's letter on to AE, who returned it to her on 15 May, commenting (Berg) that he feared it would 'end in a bad scandal and everything will be public. I would have preferred an arrangement of mutual consent. But as that was vetoed there is nothing Mrs MacBride's friends can do but wait.'
   ³ Edmond Kelly was MacBride's lawyer in Paris, with offices at 82 boulevard Haussmann.
   ⁴ In the long 'Statement of Facts on behalf of Major MacBride' (NLI) MacBride denied MG's many citations of his inebriety, and could 'only recollect two occasions during my married life when I was sick from overdrinking. On one of these occasions my wife was at home (the day after Xmas) and on the other she was away, on neither was I sick in the room. On the occasion on which she was at home, viz: the day after Christmas, I was sick in the water closet, no one saw this but myself and I made no filth there. My wife was then at home. On the second occasion, when my wife was away I was sick in the toilet room in the slop basin.' His lawyer deleted the whole of this passage with the comment 'Entirely unnecessary'.
   ⁵ See p. 87, n. 10. MG's position was that the arbitrators over the custody and bringing up of Séan MacBride should be the Archbishop of Dublin and two nationalist friends, one to be named by MacBride and one by her. MacBride rather more elaborately insisted that an Irish nationalist named by him and MG 'should have a voice in directing the education of the child, and in the event of the father and mother and the chosen Nationalist not agreeing about the selection of such nationalist then the matter shall be referred to the President of the Gaelic League for the time being. And if the mother and chosen Nationalist do not agree in the matter of the education of the child the question be referred to the Archbishop of Dublin' (NLI).

they would push the defence in such a way that my reputation & political work would be ruined completely.[6]

I replied I would concede nothing whatever in regard to the complete custody of the child & as I knew it was always possible for MacBride to reopen this question in the English Courts (where French divorce is recognised but where the question of the custody of the child can be contested), I could not allow the charges against my husband to be made too light, though the one of adultery with E. I would gladly withdraw though I have complete proof;[7] if the other charges could be made to satisfy English as well as French law & that my husband allowed the divorce to be pronounced at once and undefended.

My lawyer said he didn't think Kelly would allow MacBride to give in without scandal. I replied that telling lies against me in open court unsupported by evidence & with a crushing verdict against him would do far less harm to me, to my work than the whispered lies he & his friends are circulating against me in Ireland & which would be strengthened by any sign of weakness or compromise on my part. My lawyer fully agreed with me. He is certain I will win my case, but says there is no means of preventing MacBride & his council telling what lies they like against me, or from getting these lies copied in the *foreign* press. The French press never publishes divorce affairs & in France a wife cannot attack her husband or her husband's lawyer for defamation—The verdict given however will be the answer to these lies. MacBride has no grounds for getting the case removed to England, he knows well he can't do it. I think it is only to prepare opinion for a verdict against him, or for possibly letting the case go by default that he is beginning to express want of confidence in French justice.

May has a cable from Mr Quinn saying he has sent by this mail two affidavits.[8]

Mr Kelly is the legal adviser of the American as well as the English Embassys[9] from his name he is Irish & MacBride & Collins[10] have got a

---

[6] In his handwritten 'Observations on the evidence of Petitioner's Witnesses' (NLI) MacBride also insisted that MG was 'politically dead in Ireland. If she were a paid emissary of the British government she could not have done England['s] work more effectively than she is doing to-day by trying to bring disgrace on me and the cause with which I have been associated.'

[7] i.e. Eileen Wilson; see pp. 7, 50.

[8] Quinn had managed to get affidavits as to MacBride's drunkenness in New York only from Maire Quinn and the cab-driver Frank McLaughlin (see p. 17, n. 3).

[9] Kelly's dealings with the British and American Embassies are unclear, but since both delegations had their own legal departments, it is unlikely that he was deeply implicated with either of them, and MG's allegations of collusion probably owe more to her predilection for conspiracy theories than to fact. Kelly's surviving correspondence with MacBride is scrupulous and shows no evidence of undue pressure.

[10] Victor Collins was French correspondent of the New York *Sun*. He had acted as MG's sponsor on her admission into the Catholic Church in 1903, but was totally committed to MacBride's cause in the

legend that he was a fenian & his father defended fenian prisoners on some occasions or some story of that sort—He was describing MacBride's heroism to M. Cruppi my lawyer[11] who stopped him at once, saying oh yes of course a hero if you like but a drunkard & an exhibitionist, except for that a hero: The fenian lawyer Mr Kelly replied 'Well as for drunkenness what could she expect if she married an Irishman!' Maître Cruppi said 'It will be for your council to bring forward that excuse for your client in Court.'

I *know* that Kelly refused to have anything to do with John MacBride's case at first, I heard (but this last is only *hear* say & I am not sure of the source) that it was only at the suggestion of the English Embassy who wanted the scandal as big as possible that he took it up. I am afraid that I cannot comfort myself with the thought that by my stand against a black-guard & drunken husband I am doing more than protecting Seagan & Iseult & that I am helping other women in Ireland in similar circumstances. Several horrible cases of this sort have come to my knowledge in Ireland & I have never dared to tell the unhappy women to act as I am doing, for too often the drunken brute was the breadwinner & in each case the women had big families & no means of supporting them & no means of getting judicial assistance. One of these women wrote me the other day asking why I had given her different advice to that on which I myself am acting—I replied that in her case as in mine our lives are on the decline, & therefore of less importance than the lives of the children who still contain in them possi-bilities of great fulfilment, therefore the safety of the children must be our 1st consideration in such matters. In her case she would have to have left a helpless family to the tender mercies of a Drunkard as having to get a situation she couldn't have taken them with her—I on the contrary had the power of turning the drunkard out, & so saving the children the scandal of his presence, so I did it for the same reasons that she had to stay, *the protection of the children.* She wrote me she understood & wished me all success.

I think the horror with which drunkenness is regarded in France would do good if realised in Ireland. Here it is no excuse for a man who commits a crime to say 'I was drunk'.

present case. Apart from his friendship for MacBride, he also apparently blamed MG for the death of his 9-year-old son Dan, who had been drowned while staying with her at Colleville in the summer of 1903 (NLI). He later returned to Ireland and taught at the Mount St Benedict school in Co. Wexford.

[11] MG's lawyer was Maître Jean-Charles-Marie Cruppi (1855–1933), an advocate in the Cour d'Appel de Paris, who later served as président of the Conseil General and Senator for la Haute-Garonne. He was already becoming more interested in politics than the law and served as French Minister of Education in 1907, Commerce and Industry in 1908, Foreign Affairs in 1911, and Justice 1911–12. Maurice Ravel dedicated the fugue in the piano version of his suite *Le Tombeau de Couperin* to his son (also Jean), who was killed in the First World War.

What a dull letter I am writing my mind tends to be occupied with dull things just now. I have had to take a week off from my painting to devote to the full consideration of my affairs. I manage to get so absorbed in painting that I don't worry over things much, but at times I have to come out of that peace to see that things go on as they should.

I remain
> my dear friend

> > Always yours very sincerely
> > Maud Gonne

ALS Berg, with envelope addressed to Coole, redirected to 22 Dominick Street, Galway,[12] postmark 'LONDON W. MY 12 05'.

## To A. H. Bullen, 15 May 1905

> 18 Woburn Buildings, | Euston Road. | London.
> May 15th,/05.

*Dictated.*

My dear Bullen,

I am back from Ireland, but doubt if I can get to you for a few days. However, here is a business matter which you may as well know about at once. When I wrote to you at Xmas urging the setting up of Roberts as your agent in Dublin & the starting of some sort of publishing branch there, even though it were but nominal, I had an instinct that if you didn't some other man would get his toes into your boots. He has.[1] Shortly before I left Dublin Roberts came round to consult me, Russell had found a young man called

---

[12] AG was staying with her sister Arabella (1850–1924), who had married the landowner Robert William Waithman (1828–1914) as his second wife in 1891. In her reply to this letter (see n. 2), AG said that she was in Galway because Coole was in the hands of the workmen: 'There is fine weather here, & Galway looks very bright & many-coloured, at least it did yesterday when the market was going on.... Old Waithman is away for a few days, rent-collecting—a great mercy! & he has taken the carriage so I can't be taken out visiting, another mercy!'

[1] WBY's letter to Bullen is untraced, but it had evidently alerted him to the fact that Starkey had revived the Irish publishing house of Whaley & Co. (see p. 20, n. 2) and had now joined with George Roberts to establish a more ambitious Irish publishing firm. In early January 1905 Stephen Gwynn, who, as literary adviser to Macmillan of London, had probably persuaded them to co-publish AE's *The Mask of Apollo* with Whaley, and who had liaised with Roberts on planning the INTS visits to London, drafted a six-point agreement for Roberts (Harvard) as a blueprint for a Dublin publishing company. Since neither Roberts nor Starkey (who soon withdrew from the venture) had the necessary capital, they were looking for a wealthy partner, and WBY hoped that Bullen, whose father was Irish and who sometimes spoke of setting up a Dublin branch, would join them. In the autumn of 1904 Bullen, as Starkey recalled in *The Rose and Bottle* (27–8), had in fact agreed to co-publish his *The Twilight People* with Whaley & Co.: 'that fine scholar and genial soul, A. H. Bullen, consented to come to our rescue,

Hone with about £1,000 to adventure & he had drawn up a scheme by which Hone, Roberts & Starkie were to start publishing;[2] Starkie nominal literary adviser, Russell real one. I knew that this arrangement was impossible; Russell, who has great influence over Starkie, would get all the bad poets in Dublin printed. And what they already call in Ireland "The Twilight School" would sap up everybody's vitality.[3] Hone's money would be lost & enterprise discouraged. I tried to find out if Hone would throw in his lot with you. Roberts' impression was that he would not.[4] I succeeded however in getting Stephen Gwynn to take the matter up with Hone & arrange a practicable scheme. Gwynn has of course plenty of publishing experience.[5]

and lend us his name. He was probably induced to do so by reason of the fact (of which we were careful to inform him) that the final selection of the poems in my projected volume was made by W. B. Yeats, and so, in the spring of 1905 I had the thrilling experience of seeing my first book ... with its pleasant blue and silver wrapper, launched on the world.'

[2] Joseph Maunsel Hone (1882–1959), editor, publisher, biographer, historian, and translator, was the first biographer of WBY. From a well-to-do Dublin Protestant family, he had been educated in England and at this time was studying law at Jesus College, Cambridge. Although he had no experience or knowledge of the business, he wrote to Starkey on 14 Apr 1905 (TCD) to say that his father was 'more or less favourable to the idea of my taking up publishing', but that he needed to get a few points clear. He thought he could raise £500 to float the company, but wanted to know whether they would both devote all their time to the enterprise: 'I have been reading for the bar but, no doubt, I would give that up should I have no time & should the matter be started seriously.' He also wanted to know what part Bullen might play in the scheme: 'Mr Russell spoke of Bullen's contention to start a branch of his firm in Dublin, would not that clash greatly with & be very harmful to any other enterprising publishing?' He was eager to sound out Bullen on these points and also to get his advice on the project, and on 10 May had written to Roberts (Harvard): 'I didn't find Yeats in & so could not see him re Bullen but if you think it would be a good idea for me to see latter, write to me at Cambridge.' As a result of these conversations, he did join the publishing house, which took its title from his second name, but seems to have withdrawn from active participation in 1909, although he retained a financial interest in the firm until 1920. In their first year Maunsel published editions of five of WBY's plays 'for sale in Ireland only' at a reduced price and, in conjunction with Bullen, issued *Poems, 1899–1905* (1906) and *Deirdre* (1907). Hone also edited the firm's literary quarterly, the *Shanachie* (1906–7), as well as publishing a number of books with them: *Persia in Revolution with notes of travel in the Caucasus* (1910), co-authored with Page Dickinson, and translations of Ernest Seillière's *The German Doctrine of Conquest* (1914) and Émile Montégut's *John Mitchel* (1915). The first of his works on WBY, *William Butler Yeats: The Poet in Contemporary Ireland*, appeared as one of Maunsel's Irishmen of Today series in late 1915. His later books included *Bishop Berkeley* (1931), introduced by WBY, *The Life of George Moore* (1936), *W. B. Yeats 1865–1939* (1942), and an edition of JBY's letters (1944).

[3] Starkey was a great admirer of AE and had revived Whaley & Co. partly to publish his collection of stories *The Mask of Apollo*, but WBY, who had praised his early poetry, now thought AE a bad influence on his younger imitators. In April 1904 he had criticized the contents of AE's anthology *New Songs*, with its 'sweet insinuating feminine voice of the dwellers in the country of shadows & hollow images' (see III. 576–9). Their aesthetic and personal differences were to lead to a rupture in their friendship early in 1906.

[4] Bullen did in fact meet Hone on 19 May and reported to WBY two days later (*LWBY* I. 149–50) that he 'appears to have a thorough dislike of his manager Roberts.... I did not commit myself to anything definitely.... Hone has a great admiration for you, & would like to work with you & me if Roberts could be got out of the way; but he says that A.E. won't allow Roberts to be ousted.'

[5] Stephen Lucius Gwynn (1864–1950), journalist, novelist, critic, poet, and nationalist politician, was born in Co. Dublin; his father was Professor of Divinity at Trinity College, Dublin, and his mother

He is the literary adviser & Hone will I believe act on his advice. I believe that the new firm can easily be got to work in with you & that the ultimate foundation of a Printing Press in Ireland, such as you described, is not made more difficult. I think Hone will at any rate in the first case insist on keeping his seperate identity, or, perhaps I should say, his freedom of action. I say this because Gwynn thinks that he should. I enclose Gwynn's letter, I think you should write to Hone & make an appointment. I could then see you either at Stratford or here & talk the matter out, so that you could be posted in everything before you met him. At the stage when I got news of this adventure, it was impossible to do more than I have done in the matter. I couldn't get it out of the way. Roberts would have refused to go into it if I had advised that, but Starkie would have been in possession then. All I could do was to see that this new ship was properly manned. You must do the rest.

If any arrangement could be made whereby the ultimate popular edition of my own writings should have an Irish printers' name & the name of some Irish publishing house side by side with your own on the title-page, I am confident that the Irish sales would be greatly increased. The one reproach against me in Ireland is—that I write for the English market.[6] It shall be as you wish, but I think that you will be wise, with a view to Irish books generally, to come into some friendly or business relation with the Dublin House. Wisely managed, this new venture might ultimately be absorbed in an Irish Publishing House with you in the saddle, as I imagine that you must be a somewhat better rider than Hone; or if it prove the other way, you may as well have a seat on the crupper. I hope that the big Shakespeare is going well & that the German Emperor will get all his subjects to subscribe.[7] I will really look out that

---

a daughter of the Young Irelander and patriot William Smith O'Brien. After a brief career teaching classics, Gwynn gave up schoolmastering in 1896 to become a freelance journalist in London. He was one of WBY's earliest admirers, subscribing for four copies of *The Wanderings of Oisin* in 1888, and in 1900, after his appointment as literary adviser to Macmillan, tried unsuccessfully to persuade the firm to become WBY's publishers (see II. 519–21, 528). As secretary to the Irish Literary Society he arranged the Irish National Theatre Society's London visits in May 1903 and March 1904, and he published influential articles on Irish literature and culture in the British and Irish press. He returned to Ireland in 1904, and had now joined Roberts and Hone on the board of Maunsel & Co., but gave up this post when he was elected Nationalist MP for Galway City in 1906. His letter is untraced, but he had been in correspondence with Roberts about the new firm over the previous winter (Harvard).

[6] Although Bullen never published a 'popular' edition of WBY's works, in 1908 he prepared approximately fifty sets of the more expensive *CW* with Maunsel's name on the title page.

[7] Bullen, who had embarked on his ten-volume *Stratford Town Shakespeare*, was constantly looking for financial support for the project. His partner, Frank Sidgwick, wrote in his diary for 14 Mar 1905: 'We are sending out written applications to all the crowned heads of Europe, enclosing prospectuses, French and German' (*Frank Sidgwick's Diary* [1975], 54).

preface & let you have it this week. A thousand things have put it out of my head.[8]

Yours sny
W B Yeats

Dict AEFH, signed WBY; Kansas.

## To Lady Gregory, [18 May 1905]

18 Woburn Buildings | Euston Road. | London.
Thursday

My dear Friend: I am very sorry this must indeed be very painful to you—but do not allow yourself to act weakly for the sake of peace. Life in its last analysis is a war of forces & it is right that it should be, for it makes us strong & I think that is the root of happiness—certainly not to fear is. This is a peice of ignorant tactics, I mean the kind of idea that occurs to the narrow supicious brain of the half educated. As likely as not it has been put into their heads by some obscure politician who dislikes you because you are friendly with the people & on their side. Or it may be mere peasant cunning; but at any rate a day comes in everything almost when one has to fight, & wisdom is not in avoiding it but in keeping no bitterness when the day is over. Of course one should do all one can for peace & see that one is just, but after this—firmness & an easy mind. I think Robert has too much philosophy & knowledge of life to forget old friendliness because of the roughness of peasant bargaining.[1]

---

[8] 'Mr. Synge and his Plays', the preface to Synge's *The Well of the Saints*, not published by Bullen until December 1905; see p. 28.

[1] AG, like many landowners in Co. Galway and elsewhere, was in conflict with the grass farmers on her estate over the tenant purchase provisions of the recent Wyndham's Land Act. The agitation was orchestrated by the United Irish League, which protested that the landlords were charging too much rent, not selling enough grazing land, and in some cases, when forced to sell, even buying it back surreptitiously. AG had some cause to be concerned because on 2 Mar her younger brother Henry H. Persse (1855–1928) had exchanged shots with a group who had attacked his house at Woodville, Co. Galway, an incident which, as the *Irish Times* of 4 Mar reported (7), 'left a very uneasy feeling amongst persons who have become obnoxious to the United Irish League in the district'. A meeting between AG's nephew John Shawe-Taylor (1866–1911), the Bishop of Galway, and representatives of the United Irish League, held at Loughrea on 12 Mar, did little to defuse the situation, and on 1 May a large conference of League delegates, including representatives from AG's district of Gort, as well as the neighbouring parishes of Kinvarra, Craughwell, and Loughrea, applauded when told by Michael Reddy MP that Parliament had passed an Act to abolish landlordism, and the men of Connaught must see 'that law carried out in the spirit and intention. . . . The heather now was on fire from the Shannon to the sea to get possession of the grazing ranches for the people', and he urged his audience to 'act like men and assert their rights as citizens and Irishmen and show their English rulers that the land of Ireland must

I wish you could have seen 'The Silent Woman' at Carrs theatre, that and 'the Knight of the Burning Pestle' are just such extravagant joyous comedy as we are trying to make.[2] I think we can get Carr's theatre for middle of June—but company seem tired judging by a letter from Frank Fay.[3] I have heard from Roberts about publication scheme—seven directors means Starkie & Russell but I think that can be got rid of.[4] I have got my ticket for 'Man & Superman'.[5] I have written a new passage of some length for 'Bailes Strand' & am just setting out on the changing of the long opening speach in 'The Kings Threshold'.[6] I have taken 'Shadowy Waters' from M^rs Emery. She would not agree to our scheme of colour but wanted one of her own & as I thought her colours in 'Salome' very bad there was nothing else to be done.[7] It is a releif. I enclose a letter I have had from

belong to the Irish people' (*Irish Times*, 2 May 1905, pp. 5–6). On 17 May AG had written to WBY (Berg) that she was 'in great trouble', as her brother Frank Persse (1854–1928), who acted as the Coole agent, had wired on 15 May 'Tenants demand 6/- in the pound reduction—no rents paid': 'This was a shock & gave me a sleepless night, & in the morning I had a letter from him saying the tenants are trying to blackmail us—& that he is making preparations to seize their cattle end of this week or beginning of next, which he will he thinks bring them to reason, especially as the bulk of them are really anxious to pay—I wrote to Father Fahy to do what he could, but this morning I decided to go home this afternoon—though Frank had told me not to come, as the cattle will be impounded in Coole, & I would be nervous—But I must do what I can to keep peace—I dont know what outside pressure has been brought to bear on them, for they had paid full rents up to this, & this is not a bad year. My terror is that if their cattle are seized they may retaliate by maiming ours, & that would give Robert a turn against them for ever—It is a great shock & sorrow.'

[2] Philip Carr's Mermaid Repertory Theatre performed Ben Jonson's *Epicoene; or, The Silent Woman* (1609) at the Great Queen Street Theatre from 8 to 13 May. The complicated plot centres on machinations through which a disinherited nephew is reinstated when he tricks his cantankerous uncle into marrying a silent woman, who turns out to be a shrew and is then revealed as a boy in disguise. In *Samhain* for 1905 WBY wrote (*Expl*, 181) that Carr's 'revivals of Elizabethan plays and old comedies have been the finest things one could see in a London theatre'. He had seen Carr's production of *The Knight of the Burning Pestle* earlier in the year (see p. 3).

[3] Fay's letter has not been traced, but the still-amateur Company had put on six different plays during April, while holding down their regular jobs, and were evidently feeling the strain.

[4] Roberts's letter is now lost, but AG had been in correspondence with AE about the new publishing house (Berg), and on 23 May was to tell Roberts (Harvard) that she did not like the idea of seven directors.

[5] Shaw's *Man and Superman* ran for a series of matinées at the Court Theatre from 21 May to 16 June.

[6] Revisions to *On Baile's Strand* (see pp. 30, 43) were to continue for the rest of the year and beyond. The recent production of the revised *King's Threshold* (see pp. 30, 40, 52, n. 1) convinced WBY that it needed even more radical rewriting, and he began by shortening and breaking up King Guaire's eighty-three-line opening speech (*VPl*, 257–62).

[7] Mrs Emery was the married name of WBY's long-time friend, the actress and occultist Florence Farr (FF; see below, p. 112), and despite these misgivings she finally persuaded him to allow her to produce *The Shadowy Waters* for a Theosophical Congress in July this year. From the first WBY had been very particular about the staging of this play and had forced Sturge Moore to alter his original design in March 1903 (see III. 336–9), instructing him that the play was 'dreamy & dim & the colour should be the same—(say) a blue green sail, against [*sic*] an indigo blue backcloth, & the mast & bulwark indigo blue. The persons in blue & green with some copper ornaments. By making one colour predominate only slightly in backcloth & one only slightly in persons the whole will be kept dim &

Quinn—I dont know what to do about it. I feal that M^rs^ Mac Bride should know about the expense he has been put to.[8]

Yours always<br>W B Yeats

I am not working badly.
I find I have mislaid Quinn's letter but will send it later on.

ALS Berg, with envelope addressed to Coole, postmark 'LONDON N.W. MY 18 05'.

## To George Roberts, 18 May 1905

18 Woburn Buildings, | Euston Road, | London.<br>May 18^th^,/05.

*Dictated.*
Dear Roberts,
    I had hardly read your letter before Hone himself turned up. I have sent him straight down to Stratford-on-Avon to see Bullen. I don't think that you will have any difficulty in re-adjusting your relations with him. He is willing, I understand, to give you a guarantee of your present income for three years & a share of profits from the second year. The only point at issue between you is the ultimate partnership. I think he would give you any reasonable guarantee, but I think he will rather hesitate about the partnership as it might complicate things with the other person you spoke of.[1] He may give way on the point. Of course something, I have no doubt, would depend on the amount of money you could put into the firm after three

mysterious & like the waters themselves.' FF had directed the first English production of Oscar Wilde's *Salome* (1893), presented in two private performances by the New Stage Club at the Bijou Theatre, Archer Street, Bayswater, on 10 and 13 May 1905.

[8] See pp. 49–50, 76. Quinn had written on 6 May enclosing a letter to Mrs Clay about affidavits, and confiding that he had paid £12 to private detectives to secure evidence of MacBride's drunken behaviour.

[1] See pp. 86–8. Hone looked down upon Roberts as a social inferior, as Bullen was to point out to WBY in his letter of 21 May (see p. 100), but finally accepted him as a co-director with Stephen Gwynn. In an undated letter, written shortly after his return from England (NLI), Hone told Roberts that, on his father's advice, he had offered Gwynn a partnership and that Gwynn was thinking it over. He proposed to meet Roberts the following day to discuss some points with regard to 'a partnership for you'. Although a talented book designer, Roberts was never a good businessman, and while the firm published books by WBY, AG, and handsome editions of Synge, it was to be dogged by financial difficulties, as well as by disputes with its authors (including WBY and AG), unhappy at what they considered Roberts's sharp practice. An arrangement with the London firm of George Allen & Unwin in 1915 worked to the firm's disadvantage, but in 1916 the offices in Abbey Street were burnt down during the Easter Rising, and generous compensation from the government kept it from bankruptcy. From 1917 to 1920 it traded under the name 'George Roberts' and thereafter as 'Maunsel and Roberts, Ltd.' After a period of expensive overproduction, the business fell into decline and in 1923 all the directors except Roberts resigned. The company went into liquidation in 1925, and was subsequently taken over by the Talbot Press.

years. I think that if I were in your position I would be satisfied with the
three years guarantee & a share of the profits from the second year.

A share of the profits given in this way is substantially a partnership but
without risk in case of bankruptcy. If you became a partner in this business
you would practically risk all you have. At the end of the three years, you
will if the firm is going well, be necessary to it; you will have a great deal of
practical power. You will be the efficient businessman of the concern in all
probability. If on the other hand it is going ill, you will have undergone no
monetary risk. You have to weigh this new position against your prospects,
whatever they are, in the business you are already at.[2] I think if it were my
own case I would steer clear of partnership, until I knew how things were
going; at least if I had any money. I don't see any possibility of the Limited
Liability Company succeeding enough to cover the cost of floatation. Seven
directors in *this* country means seven people who want to make money; in
Dublin it would mean seven cooks spoiling the broth & as small as possible
monetary liability apiece. There is no use mincing words in this matter.
Russell will never make a successful publishing firm, if he have any
influence over the choice of books; & I foresee that his spoon would be
somewhere among those 7 cooks. Stephen Gwynn has the necessary experience of the business & what you want in this case, is not merely literary
knowledge, but knowledge of publishing. You & he have experience &
don't add any more inexperienced people than you can help. Hone should
be quite enough. I know that practically none of our writers would have to
do with the firm if they were not satisfied with the business-like nature of
the control. Every bad Irish book published injures the whole trade in Irish
books. Gwynn has for instance impressed it upon Hone, that he must
publish no books "on commission" & that he (Gwynn) must advise upon
every book published.

Hone will be in Dublin in a few days, so please do nothing until you see
him. Try & see the matter from Hone's point of view as well as your own;
your risks are about equal. You may not like him in the end & he may not
get on with you. He puts in his money & his time; you put in your time &
your prospects; but it is he that stands to lose money. It is generally a

---

[2] Roberts had been a commercial traveller in women's underwear, an occupation that had prompted
Bullen to dub him 'this ex-Knight of the Garter' and Joyce and Gogarty to play practical jokes on him.
In the summer of 1904 they had discovered his travelling bag in the deserted rooms of the Hermetic
Society and, as Stanislaus Joyce narrates (*My Brother's Keeper* [1958], 249): 'Gogarty found a pair of
open drawers in the bag, stretched them out by tying the strings to two chairs, and by means of another
chair fixed the handle of the Hermetic broom between the legs of the drawers, while on the hoisted head
of it he hung a placard bearing the legend "I never did it" and signed "John Eglinton".' A Dublin
rumour alleged that the two then helped themselves to the remaining wares for distribution among their
delighted lady friends (see Gogarty's *Mourning Became Mrs Spendlove* [1948], 53–5).

mistake in dealing with a man to try & tie him down too closely for it makes him suspicious; all life is a gamble, we bet on "black or white".

I hope that this letter is not too dogmatic, but I find that dictation in some curious way changes my style & makes me more emphatic than I want to be.

Yrs sny
W B Yeats

Dict AEFH, signed WBY; NLI.

## To Lady Gregory, [21 May 1905]

18 Woburn Buildings | Euston Road
Sunday

My dear Lady Gregory: I certainly do not think you have been weak. I think you have done entirely right. I should have known that your alert will would find some positive thing to do—that you would never be merely inactive. I am always so afraid of the sensitiveness, created by imaginative culture, making one over yielding that I perhaps push things the other way. I have always been anxious over this purchase question—afraid that it would bring you trouble. It is a releif to know that all is well for the moment.[1] I have had a good deal of negociation to do about that publishing

---

[1] AG had sent a postcard to WBY on the evening of 18 May (Berg), enclosing a copy of a long letter she had written to her son Robert earlier in the day, giving a detailed account of the compromise she had reached with the Coole tenants over rents (see p. 89, n. 1). 'I think I have done right', she told WBY, 'it is hard to know', and she added that she was 'very tired—I stay here for the present'. In the enclosed letter to Robert (*Journals* II. 367–8), she explained that on her return to Coole late on 17 May she found her brother Frank determined to seize cattle in lieu of rent as he 'said there was no possibility of a settlement, that it was the effect of the Leagues about the country that made the people so stiff, that they were determined not to pay without the 6/- reduction which of course it would be impossible to give without giving up everything. He had offered them 2/- which they scorned.' There was also a dispute over the tenants' buying-out period under the Land Act; they had offered a period of twenty-one years, but Frank Persse maintained that 'we could not take the 21 years offer unless second term tenants gave 23 or 24, and there is a reasonable price offered for the grass lands'. He had planned to begin impounding cattle on Friday, 19 May (although the tenants knew nothing of this), but AG arranged a meeting of interested parties at the priest's house in Gort on the afternoon of 18 May. In the meantime she persuaded Frank Persse to accept a rent reduction of 3s. rather than 2s. in the pound by offering to pay the extra shilling ('over £50') out of her own pocket, and she also enlisted the help of the parish priest, Fr. Jerome Fahey (1843–1919), in talking round the tenants. After some hard negotiating they reluctantly agreed to the 3s. reduction, and 'went off, rather dissatisfied I hear, thinking Father F. could have got another shilling if he tried. I found F[rank] who had waited at the Office in a fairly good humour, though he says he feels quite a reaction, having his blood up for tomorrow.' She added that she felt 'a fool not to go away and spend my £50 otherwise', but defended herself by explaining that she and her servants were convinced that the seizure of cattle if an agreement had not been reached would have

house—letters from Roberts, and Gwynn, & a visit from Hone, who has gone down to Stratford to see Bullen. I think Russell is definitely out of it but Roberts, urged by Russell is holding out for a partnership at the end of three years on the condition of his putting money in. Hone offers a share of profits from second year but not partnership as he has a certain presumably moneyed partner in his eye. I think Roberts is asking too much as from Hone's point of view he is a young man with little experience about whose business capacity he knows nothing.[2] He offers Roberts as well as a share of profits a guarrantee of his present income for 3 years. I notice that in Russells letter which I return there is a scratched out sentence which seems to be something about the books he would choose being what were wanted.[3] That is the real trouble. I have I beleive succeeded in preventing Phillip Carr, who knows nothing about a play unless an old one, from producing 'Dierdre' (urged by Miss Young).[4] It is an absurd situation— but Russell has to be faught & once that influence is confined to what he really understands we will have a quiet time again. I send you Quinns letter—do please advise me—He forbids me to tell M^{rs} MacBride about the expense he has been under & yet I am not sure that she out [*for* ought] not to know—I sent you her letter & got you [to] send it to Russell because of her husbands offering to let the case go undefended. I thought it only right that you & above all Russell should know that he practically admits the case against him. I had hoped that she would be able to accept an offer such as he has made but do not know enough about the legal aspects to judge the matter. I have had a little struggle with M^{rs} Emery this week. She

had disastrous consequences, and that even Frank Persse had belatedly confessed to her that 'he would have required police after this'. AG's diary entry for May 1905 (*70 Years*, 428) recorded: 'Estate business has settled down, but I have had a very bad fortnight and could not have left home for a day, I just prevented war with the grass farmers, and I am very much in want of sleep.' She also received a reassuring letter from Fr. Fahey: 'All well with the tenants ... through your great kindness we have the old kindly relations preserved. I can assure you of the gratitude of the tenantry and of mine.' She had, in fact, behaved with great prudence: on 2 Dec of this year her nephew Frank Shawe-Taylor and his wife narrowly escaped death when they were ambushed by four of their disgruntled tenants.

    [2] Hone's potential moneyed partner is unidentified and did not join the firm; in 1910 Hone tried, again unsuccessfully, to bring another wealthy young man, Dominick Spring Rice (1889–1940), into it. At 32, Roberts was nearly ten years older than Hone.

    [3] i.e. AE's letter to AG of 'Monday' (see below).

    [4] i.e. AE's two-act play *Deirdre*, which both AG and WBY thought insipid (see III. 148–9, 581), but which was now being touted in Dublin as a more wholesome treatment of Irish legend and life than the plays of WBY and Synge. Elizabeth Young, the sister of MG's friend Ella Young, acted under the name of Violet Mervyn and had played the title role in the first production of the play in April 1902, with, according to WBY, 'a general lack of intensity' (see III. 172). She had also performed in the play as a member of the Irish company at the World Fair in St Louis from late April to early June 1904, and was now seeking theatrical engagements in London and Dublin. She had mounted 'A Dramatic Recital and Concert' at the Abbey Theatre on 28 Jan this year, but had since moved to London, where she remained until 1910, when she returned permanently to Ireland.

demanded to be given a free hand to 'stage Shadowy' Waters in her own way. I withdrew the play. She has now agreed to accept any <competent> good artist I like—but rather wants Harry Paget as he knows about ancient boats & so forth.—I have said I must approve any design.[5] She thinks that our scheme would be difficult on the Court stage, as we will be more or less limited to a great blue cloth, not of our shade, which they have. The designing of the boat is the problem. I proposed Robert & she would have worked with him very gladly but then it occured to me that he will be in Ireland on July 7 (when play is performed) & she always goes wrong unless there is somebody on the spot to bully her. But if we could get things made now that might be different. If you think he would care to do it please wire me his address. Dont say anything to him as I may have to arrange with Paget. If so I will try & get Paget to make our scheme of colour workable. The thing is not very important as it is a performance for Theosophists & there will be but few probably of the general public there.[6] I am contemplating a change in the play to make the spell from the harp seem real. Stage to darken & harp to glow with internal fire (electric) till all the light comes from it. Ricketts suggested this. Paget tempts me a little because his mechanical genius would delight in this harp which we could buy for Dublin afterwards at half price. I am afraid on the other hand of Paget being too realistic. I suppose I shall have to come over for performance—that I may judge of this effect—an experiment that may work out well or ill. If it is good I will embody it in text for the American edition. One must try all kind of things. An effect of this kind may kill the words or it may heighten them. Something is wanted to make the spell beleivable—to give a real situation to a place where the 'scene is always dropped' a little.[7] I have practically finished my breaking up of the long opening speach of the King in 'The Kings Threshold'. I have lost

[5] The artist and book illustrator Henry Mariott Paget (1856–1936) was FF's brother-in-law. He had been a neighbour of the Yeatses during their time in Bedford Park, and had painted WBY's portrait in April 1889 (see I. 159). The set for *The Shadowy Waters* was constructed after a model designed by Paget, whose painting often took second place to his fascination with gadgetry for, as WBY describes (*Aut*, 118–19), 'he had half filled his studio with mechanical toys of his own invention, and perpetually increased their number'. WBY was particularly concerned to get the harp right, as it had caused adverse comment in the reviews of the Dublin production.

[6] *The Shadowy Waters* was produced with FF's and OS's *The Shrine of the Golden Hawk* on 7 and 8 July for the Annual Congress of the Federation of the European Sections of the Theosophical Society. The reporter from *Black and White* (15 July, p. 86) described the audience, which included Maeterlinck, as 'one of the most cosmopolitan . . . that ever assembled to witness a dramatic entertainment. For myself, I was surrounded by a great company of vari-coloured and strange-tongued persons, sicklied o'er in a very special degree with the pale cast of thought. I was a tiny oasis of normal Englishman, as it were, in a desert of foreign faces and esoteric emotions.'

[7] A radically revised acting version of *The Shadowy Waters* was included in vol. II of *The Poetical Works* in 1907, where the glowing harp is part of the final stage directions.

nothing & gained much. The Company does not come to London until November. Carr offered his theatre[8] for middle or end of June but Fay said they had not time to rehearse & were too tired. M$^{iss}$ Horniman is indignant—says they kept her six weeks in London looking for a theatre. Column is to be played in second week in June. Will you come to London after that— or stay on in Dublin a bit. I feal rather lost without you. This July the 7$^{th}$ show rather upsets my plans—<I was inclined to ?finish 'Naisi' myself> I wonder when you will go to Coole—whether I shall go there first for a bit or not. All the papers here are abusing Ben Johnson's 'Silent Woman' which I thought the most joyful laughable, wonderful cup of youth—my uncle was not less delighted than I—it was all so simple & radical. I wish you could have seen it—it was even nearer to folk than Moliére.[9]

Yrs ev
W B Yeats


[*With enclosures*]

May 6, 1905


My dear Yeats: Enclosed I send you copy of a letter to Mrs. Clay about the affidavits. I have been met by opposition and silence at every turn. MacBride has had his friends here notified and they apparently take his side of the case and those who do not say that the scandal is hurtful to the cause generally and that the sooner it is hushed up the better. I have tried to convince them that the best way is to meet it head on and have a separation or divorce and that she was anxious to have a divorce without any more scandal than was necessary

---

[8] i.e. The Great Queen Street Theatre. The Abbey were to lease it for their London tour of June 1907.
    [9] See p. 90, n. 2. In *Discoveries* (1907) WBY recalled with disgust the unperceptive critical reception of the production (*E & I*, 280): 'When *The Silent Woman* rammed a century of laughter into the two hours' traffic, I found with amazement that almost every journalist had put logic on the seat where our Lady Imagination should pronounce that unjust and favouring sentence her woman's heart is ever plotting, and had felt bound to cherish none but reasonable sympathies and to resent the baiting of that grotesque old man.' As WBY says, the play had been generally disliked. Max Beerbohm, writing in the *Saturday Review* of 13 May (623), maintained that it depended on a tedious practical joke: 'I (as a duty to my readers) sit the play out; but smile I really cannot; and indeed, as the joke happens to be a barbarous one . . . I should be rather ashamed of smiling at it. . . . Ben Jonson's humour was ever purely intellectual. Ben Jonson had no high spirits. I shall make haste to forget "The Silent Woman". And so, I trust, will our very admirable Mermaid Society.' The *Athenaeum* of the same day (603) thought the revival could 'have none but purely archaeological interest', and William Archer in the *World* of 16 May commented (835–6) that the play was an example of 'mediaeval droll, which, both in invention and expectation, stands on a far lower place of intellectual effort than even a second-rate drama or comedy of to-day'. He went on to insist that 'in this play' Jonson 'did an essentially trivial thing, though he did it with characteristic vigour and gusto'. WBY's uncle was George Pollexfen (1839–1910), with whom he often stayed in Sligo. A leading freemason, and dedicated astrologer, he made regular trips to London. As a melancholic and inveterate hypochondriac, his delight was an even more remarkable testimony to the play than WBY's.

and that putting it on the ground of drunkenness was the simplest way. The impression here is that he will fight and that if he does the counter charges will be made. I hope that this will not be true. I hope to have another affidavit next Tuesday and will forward that direct to Messrs. Turner.[10]

I have paid out so far about £12 to detectives in connection with this, but I don't want you ever to mention that to Mrs. MacBride or say anything about it to anybody else. I am very sorry that I have not been more successful and I would not think of having her pay a penny of the expenses on this side, or permit anybody friendly to her doing so.

This is only a hasty line to catch today's steamer and I will write about the plays and other things fully in my next letter. Yours very truly,

[John Quinn]

[*In WBY's hand at the top of following letter*: 'Note reconstructed sentence crossed out bit—the real point.']

Monday

Dear Lady Gregory,

I return Mrs MacBrides letter. I am afraid it will end in a bad scandal and every thing will be public. I would have preferred an arrangement by mutual consent, but as that was vetoed there is nothing Mrs MacBrides friends can do but wait.

Arran should be like one of the Isles of the Blessed in this weather. But it would be the weather not the place itself which would make it liveable. There are a hundred beautiful nooks in Ireland I know of I would prefer to Arran. But I suppose it is the Gaelic which is the attraction.[11] Violet I am glad to say is much better these last few days & has been out a little only hobbling but it is a great improvement on lying down.[12] I dont approve of the suggested

---

[10] E. F. Turner & Sons, solicitors of 101 Leadenhall Street, to whom Witham had evidently entrusted the collection of affidavits on behalf of MG.

[11] On 14 May AG (Berg) had written to WBY from her sister's house in Galway that she was thinking of going to the Aran Islands (which she had visited in 1893 and 1898), although the trouble with the Coole grass farmers probably prevented this trip. WBY had made his only visit to the Aran Islands, the Irish-speaking archipelago off the Galway coast, in August 1896 (see II. 47). AE's favourite part of Ireland was Donegal.

[12] AE had married Violet Rose North (1869–1932), an English theosophist who had moved to Dublin in 1895, in June 1898. She contributed to the *Irish Theosophist* (later the *Internationalist*) under the pseudonym 'Laon', and was later to publish *Heroes of the Dawn* (Dublin, 1913), a collection of Irish myths retold for children. George Moore thought she was the ideal wife for a sage, but was warned by John Eglinton 'to be very careful what I said about AE's home life' (Cave, 585), and, according to Monk Gibbon, SMY described the marriage as 'a failure' (*Early Years*, 25). Mrs Russell enjoyed chronic ill-health, and although AG had evidently asked for news of her, the two women disliked each other. On her first and only visit to Coole in 1900 AG found her 'very untidy & dirty in attire & hard in manner' (Pethica, 274); for her part, Violet Russell thought AG had patronized her and resolved never to visit Coole again (*SQ*, 321).

arrangement with Hone. Starkey was to be pushed out. Roberts to be employed at a salary but no partnership on any terms. I advised Roberts to refuse & to hold out for a partnership say one fifth share at least. There is no reason why he should work up a business which Hone does not understand at present & be in the position of an employee who could be discharged later on. Hone has another person in his mind to join him later on if the project showed signs of success & Roberts might be left out. Roberts I believe has written Hone holding out for partnership. I should for many reasons have preferred my own suggestion of Starkey Roberts & Hone joining, and if Hone & Roberts dont agree I think I will be able to arrange publishing otherwise with Starkey Roberts & some others in partnership. <I should trust my own judgement about the kind of books ? which would sell in Ireland more than to Gwynne [indecipherable]>.[13] Brian is flourishing. He is getting a real little boy but shows no signs of grace abounding anywhere.[14]

I hope you will enjoy Arran.

Yours ever
George Russell

ALS Berg, with envelope addressed to Coole, postmark 'LONDON MY 22 05'. Enclosures NYPL and Berg.

## To Lady Gregory, [22 May 1905]

18 Woburn Buildings | Euston Road

My dear Lady Gregory: Here is the result of Russells last move. I wrote to Roberts, before I knew anything of Hones fealing on the matter saying that he should not press for a partnership. He had already at Russells urging written making his getting one a condition. It will be the devil of a business if he is put out as through Bullen having my books I shall be mixed into the new firm & this will make matters difficult in the company—so far as Roberts & Miss Garvey & their friends are concerned. On the other hand Hone is obviously free to do as he likes. He has the money & can employ

---

[13]  This was the sentence to which WBY drew AG's attention in his note at the head of this letter, and he wrote out the cancelled words to help her. The other 'person' Hone had in mind was evidently Stephen Gwynn.

[14]  Brian Hartley Russell, the elder of the Russells' two surviving children, had been born in 1903, and given the same name as an elder brother, who had died in infancy. AG had a poor opinion of child-rearing skills in the Russell household: when the elder Bryan was brought to Coole in July 1900 she recorded that Violet Russell 'slaps & shakes the child, says she hates it near her, & wd rather have a bundle of old manuscripts. . . . The maids furious, as she sits reading a novel, or having her tea, while it is catching & eating flies at the window—The end is, that I am chief nurse & am at this moment with it while asleep, Mr. and Mrs. R[ussell] being on the lake' (Pethica, 274–5).

who he likes.[1] Miss Horniman is writing to Roberts—not on my suggestion—saying that she gave him the right to use the name 'Abbey Series' for
the plays & will not withdraw it.[2] At the same time she thinks Hone should
not make Roberts a partner, or anything more than than manager <and not
that if he does not want it>. Bullen, who thinks Roberts very un-business
like may exagerate Hones fealing. I beleive I shall go to see Bullen, at
Stratford to morrow & stay till thursday or Friday. You might write to me
C/o A H Bullen, Shakespear Head Press, Stratford-on-Avon. I shall have
to think things out—I must either drop out of the matter, I think, or urge
Roberts on them as manager (not as Partner)—manager for a certain
period. Hone has offered a guarrantee of 3 years & a share of profits &
that seems to me generous. The Argument in favour of Roberts from Hones
point of view is the Abbey Series, & getting rid of a possible opposition
firm. I wish these arguments were more weighty. I saw 'Man & Super man'
last night & liked the last act a good deal & the first two with half my mind. I
thought the construction bad—there was no cumulating effect except in
last act.[3]

Yr ev

W B Yeats

[1] On reading Bullen's letter, AG wrote to Roberts on 23 May (see p. 90, n. 4) urging him to accept the
new post on Hone's terms, warning him that she did not think Hone would take him into partnership,
and telling him that she did not like the idea of appointing seven Directors. Roberts was engaged to the
actress Maire Garvey (d. 1946), whom he later married.

[2] The Abbey Theatre series of Irish plays was inaugurated in February 1905 when Synge's *The Well
of the Saints* was published by the Abbey Theatre (see p. 29, n, 6). In the autumn of 1905 the series was
transferred to Maunsel, as was *Samhain*. Fifteen volumes were published in the First Series (1905–11)
and nine in the Second Series (1911–22). In a letter to Roberts of 22 May (Harvard) AEFH told him: 'I
am writing to you to formally make it clear that I have given you the permission to call that series of
plays "The Abbey Theatre Series". I gave it with the intention that it should include only those plays
produced by the Irish National Theatre Society. If in the future you wish to include a play or plays
produced by any other actors in that theatre, I reserve the right to being consulted on the subject. The
right to sell your books in the theatre rests with you, subservient of course to the wish of whoever may be
my tenants; either the Irish National Theatre Company or any other tenant.' And, to strengthen his
hand in the present negotiations, she added: 'I want you to understand that I have no intention of giving
anyone else the right to use that title unless you should ask me to do so.' AG's *Kincora* had appeared in
the series in April.

[3] Now Act IV; the present Act III, 'Juan in Hell', was not performed in London until June 1907. In a
Shavian reversal of the Don Juan theme, John Tanner, the Faustian metaphysician hero of *Man and
Superman*, does not pursue but is pursued by Doña Elvira in the character of Ann Whitefield, who,
impelled by the Life Force, tracks him from London to the Sierra Nevada, where they are captured by
bandits. Shaw had been working on the play since 1901, and it had been published in 1903. WBY is
expressing a received idea about Shaw's dramaturgy: A. B. Walkley complained in the *TLS* on 26 May
(170) that because of the plot's 'weakness, its haphazardness, its unnaturalness . . . one finds the play as a
play unsatisfying', and William Archer argued in the *World* on 30 May (914) that Shaw was 'not really a
good dramatist. He has brilliant moments, but no staying-power'. On the other hand, Max Beerbohm,
previously sceptical of Shaw's plots, 'found that as a piece of theatrical construction it was perfect'
(Michael Holroyd, *Bernard Shaw* II. [1989], 71).

What do you think about this whole business. I am afraid of letting my fear of a temporary trouble in the company & of my wish not to hurt Roberts, making me unjust to Hone. I told Hone that I thought Roberts about as good a manager as he was likely to get in Dublin—but serious pressure is another thing. Hone did not show me his real fealing about Roberts.

[*At top of first page*]
I enclose a note of Masefields also.[4]

[*With enclosure*]

THE SHAKESPEARE HEAD PRESS, | STRATFORD-ON-AVON.
21/v/1905

*Private*
My dear Yeats,
   Young Hone came on Friday. He appears to have a thorough dislike of his manager Roberts; in fact cannot speak about him with patience. Evidently he would be glad to back out of the arrangement if he could find a decent excuse; but he stands in some fear of 'A.E.' I found Hone pleasant enough & felt some sympathy for him; for Russell wants eventually to thrust Roberts on him as a partner, & Hone's alarm at the prospect is tempered with disgust—as Roberts is of course his social inferior. He asked whether I would co-operate with him if he were to throw over Roberts (this ex-Knight of the Garter); but I did not commit myself to anything definitely. We can talk over the matter when you come down: let me hear when you are coming. Hone has a great admiration for you, & would like to work with you & me if Roberts could be got out of the way; but he says that A.E. won't allow Roberts to be ousted.

Yours sincerely
A. H. Bullen

ALS Berg, with envelope addressed to Coole, postmark 'LONDON. N. W. MAY 22 '05'. Enclosure MBY.

   [4] John Masefield and his wife had stayed at Coole as a guest of AG in September 1904. The note was probably his undated letter (Berg) in praise of the revised and recently published Dun Emer edition of *Stories of Red Hanrahan* (see p. 78), which Masefield had 'just finished': 'I have always been fond of the Hanrahan tales, as you know; but I would like to tell you how very deeply they have moved me in their new form. They are by far the most beautiful stories I have ever read. I have never read any stories that gave me such a sense of the beauty of life or so deep a pleasure in the reading.' Later this summer Masfield was to help AG secure the lectern and Kelmscott edition of Chaucer as a fortieth birthday present for WBY.

## *To John Quinn,* [29] *May 1905*

18, Woburn Buildings, | Euston Road,
May 30th, 1905.

My dear Quin,

A great many thanks for all the trouble you have taken about Mrs. McBride's affair. I know she is very grateful to you.[1] I am glad that you have not written too sternly to Miss Anna Morgan, the paper which reached me in due course showed that she and her pupils had really played my work, with sympathetic intelligence.[2] I was afraid that they were

---

[1] See pp. 76, 94, 96–7. Quinn was continuing to take an active interest in the case and in his letter of 19 May informed WBY that he had sent three affidavits to Paris, but 'got a cable on Monday saying that the dates in the affidavits were wrong and that Mac Bride had been here May, June and July. I at once cabled to Paris to have them withhold the affidavits and that I would send new affidavits with corrected dates. I have thus far succeeded in getting one of the men down. It is the devil's job to do anything with these men, for the Irish Societies have done all they could to shield MacBride. I wish I had known the exact dates of MacBride's being in New York because I could then have got the affidavits right in the first instance, but that was a detail that Mrs. Clay assumed, I suppose, that I was familiar with, although as a matter of fact I was not and could not get any exact information on the point from MacBride's friends here.'

[2] Anna Morgan (1851–1936), drama teacher and founder of the Anna Morgan School of Expression in Chicago, presented American premières of plays by Ibsen, Shaw, and Maeterlinck, as well as mounting the recent performances of WBY's *The Hour-Glass* (see p. 76, n. 6). As early as 1894 she had discarded elaborate realistic settings for simple draperies, and she produced WBY's play with the sort of symbolic set he had advocated in *Samhain* and elsewhere. Quinn had pointed out to her that her performances of *The Hour-Glass* infringed copyright and, as he informed WBY on 19 May (Himber, 74), 'got back a very penitential letter from her pleading that she knew nothing about the copyright, etc., and I wrote her a polite note saying in effect that I attributed no bad faith to her but thought it was well to put the matter right'. The paper which reached WBY was the Chicago *Sunday Record Herald* of 2 Apr 1905, which contained James O'Donnell Bennett's enthusiastic review of the production under the headline 'Practical Test of Mr. Yeats' Idea'. Praising 'the lovely effects which a little band of amateur players was able to produce against a severely simple background of draperies', Bennett found that WBY's ideas on staging his plays turned out to be 'profoundly practical truths'. He noted that Miss Morgan's studio 'was quite barren of most of the mechanical contrivances which are considered essential . . . for a dramatic performance. A little stage filled one end of the room, and it was softly lighted by concealed lamps. There was a restful abundance of shadow, even of gloom, but it was easy to distinguish the shades of expression in the faces of the players. The shadows met and blended with dark green draperies, which, though they were hung not more than a dozen feet from the front of the stage, somehow produced an impression of ample space on the stage proper and of something behind and beyond it.' Bennett went on to observe that WBY's stage directions 'were followed in the main by Miss Morgan, any variation from them being in the direction of increased meagerness. And yet the result was not suggestive of a lack of resources or of make-shifts, but of added dignity and of voluntary reticence in display . . . the draperies and the shadows, the desk of the scholar, which was so simple as to be quite unnoticed, and the hourglass in a dim recess, served all the purposes of a perfect investiture. Nothing seemed lacking, and yet nothing obtruded. . . . Most important, however, was the fact that play and players were given the chance that comes of commanding undivided attention. The characters in the little drama stood like silhouettes against the simple scene, every one of them distinct and significant, yet everyone blending softly into the subdued tone of the picture. There was no suggestion of clutter or fussiness, no distraction, no garishness, none of the inevitable disillusion that becomes the more explicit the more elaborate and painstaking is the make-believe. The experiment was an unqualified success, not only from a pictorial point of view, but from the histrionic as well.'

infringing Miss Wycherley's right and so sent you that programme. You have got much more money out of Miss Wycherley than I had ever hoped.[3] I suppose Kelly is adrift now.[4] Fay and his people are not coming to London until November. A theatre here offered to take them on sharing terms in June, but they were too tired out after their Dublin season to do the extra rehearsing. It will be as much as they can do before the holidays to perform Colum's play. It comes on about the 10th, and "The Hour Glass" is to be revived with it. It will be a week as usual, I shall go over for it, returning here for a couple of weeks as Mrs. Emery is to give a performance of "The Shadowy Waters" for some Theosophists. I don't expect much success for the play which is hardly suitable for more than about 50 people who know my work well. I gave her leave as I want to try some experiments. I have written in several new passages and hope to use a harp made of dim glass and lighted from inside by electricity, so that the harp will seem to burn with supernatural fire. It is an effect Charles Rickett's suggested to me. I have also made some one or two other slight changes of an

---

[3] In his letter of 19 May, Quinn had informed WBY that Margaret Wycherly owed all her actors 'from one to two hundred dollars apiece' and that she owed WBY 'nearly five hundred dollars'. He also reported that he had officially drawn the attention of Veiller ('a liar and a sneak') 'to the section of the United States Revised Statutes providing for criminal prosecution upon "wilful violation of the copyright laws," so that if I hear of him giving any more unauthorized performances I will call the matter to the attention of the United States District Attorneys for criminal prosecution.... You never would have gotten a cent out of the matter if it had not been that I had caught him here on the hip and made him pay up to the extent that he did.' In fact, Quinn's ingrained anti-Semitism and legalistic aggression had almost certainly done an injustice to Veiller and Miss Wycherly, one of whose intentions had been to promote WBY's plays as part of a more demanding and fulfilling contemporary theatre and who had lost a good deal of money in the attempt. Summing up her disastrous season in the *New York Commercial* of 1 Sept 1905 under the headline 'WHY YEATS FAILED', Margaret Wycherly laid the blame on the taste of the typical theatregoer: 'I have devoted the better part of a year and several thousand dollars to the effort, to make this form of drama popular, and I have failed absolutely; the public does not care for this style of play.' In future, she went on, she would 'endeavor to present plays with a wider appeal, a more human note, and of more modern construction': 'One must go with the tide unless one has a position much more firmly established than mine and a reputation a thousand times greater than the little bit of notice that has come to me. I have made my effort, have failed and I am quite willing to admit that I am beaten. Let someone else do the rest.' She concluded by warning theatre managers that they 'would be extremely foolish to throw away their money in such ventures for the limited few who are anxious to see plays of this type'.

[4] The Irish actor P. J. Kelly (b. 1883) had taken the part of Shaun Bruin in Margaret Wycherly's production of *The Land of Heart's Desire*. Kelly, who had acted with the Fays' amateur companies from 1900, was a founder-member of the INTS, but, much to WBY's sorrow, had been expelled on 6 Apr 1904 after he had joined the Digges–Quinn company to play at the St Louis World Fair (see III. 568). Reviewing his performance in WBY's play on 22 Feb 1905, the *New-York Times* (7) described him as 'a young actor with a fine voice, who reads poetry well'. After leaving the Wycherly tour Kelly remained in the USA, joining the Edward Sothern Company, and subsequently playing with a number of other American companies, including Deborah Beirne's Irish Players and the Walter Hampden Company. In his recollections, 'The Early Days of the Irish National Theatre', published in the *New-York Times* on 1 June 1919, Kelly described WBY as probably 'the most interesting figure in the Irish literary renaissance...a man of lofty idealism.... It was sometimes extremely difficult, however, to follow his thought' (Mikhail, 51).

experimental nature. I want to get the three recent verse plays "The King's Threshold", "Baile's Strand" and "Shadowy Waters" as perfect as revision after performance can make them. I have already re-written every word of "Baile's Strand" up to the entrance of the young man from Aoife's Country, and made it, I think, a strong play. I have also made "The King's Threshold" much more animated throughout breaking up the long opening speech and so on. If A. P. Watt can make the necessary arrangements about "The Shadowy Waters" and "Wind among the Reeds" Brett will bring out in America in early autumn that two volume edition of all my verse, one volume of plays one of poems and at the same time Bullen here will bring out a volume containing all my poetical works since 1895, when the Unwin volume was published. I shall call this English volume "Poems, a new Series, 1895–1905". I saw Bullen at Stratford-on-Avon last week and we arranged this, deciding to postpone the expensive collected edition until next year as this will give me an opportunity of completing my revision of "Where there is Nothing" and some other parts of the prose. When I have a lot of unrevised work I feel as I do when somebody calls (some lady) and finds me unshaven and in my dressing gown. Just as I think that she is thinking of nothing except my untidy appearance so I feel that my readers are thinking of nothing but the untidy writing. A great many thanks for the little Oscar Wilde book. It is an interesting historical record of what is I should say a very early phase of his development. It was written, I should think, at College.[5] I saw the performance of his "Salome" here and did not like it. His wonderful sense of the stage evidently deserted him when he got away from comedy. His comedies were written according to a technique perfected by the modern theatre and he was able to learn from his contemporaries but when he got to tragedy—well, he wrote exactly as any other writer of unactable literary drama. The play has every sort of fault, the speeches don't work to any climax, and there are moments when the principal people have nothing to do but look like fools, and as if they would like to twiddle their thumbs. There has been a great outcry here against its repulsiveness, but I felt nothing of that I would indeed have been glad for any sort of a thrill, however disagreeable.[6] The audience was

[5] Quinn sent WBY a pirated edition of Wilde's *The Rise of Historical Criticism* (Hartford, Conn.: Privately Printed by Sherwood Press, 1905), commenting that he had 'only hastily glanced through the book and I must admit that I was disappointed with it but I thought you might be curious to look at it. . . . The book-making and book-selling hyenas are now burrowing around poor old Wilde's remains trying to make a little profit on his name.' Wilde wrote the essay at Oxford in 1879 as an unsuccessful entry for the Chancellor's English Essay Prize.

[6] See p. 90, n. 7. The *Athenaeum* of 13 May (603) thought the play 'verbose and tedious' and its sole attraction 'a pronounced form of eroticism', while Max Beerbohm in the *Saturday Review* of the same day (623) described it as 'too horrible for definite and corporeal presentment . . . we suffer something

curiously reverential and as I came away I said to somebody "Nothing kept us quiet but the pious memory of the sainted author". I took Mrs. Worthington to see it and I think it pleased her to be so evidently at the heart of some kind of shrine.[7] Lady Drogheda has arranged for Fay and his Company to give performances in her neighbourhood in July. She is paying all expenses, hiring a whole hotel to hold them and the town hall for the play-house.[8] This will be a fine beginning for our touring of the country.

I should have said at the beginning of this letter that McBride's lawyer has offered in McBride's name to let the case go by default if Mrs. McBride will agree to withdraw the more dishonouring charges and to submit the question of the custody of the child to arbitration after seven years. She has refused to make any concession whatever about the child, and thought when writing that she could not withdraw any of the charges, as she has to make the case strong enough to hold good in the English Courts, should he bring a case in them in connection with the custody of the child. You will understand these legal questions better than I do, but so far as I could see by her last letter, McBride's expressed intention (as she would not give way on these points) was to go on with the case.[9] He threatened to say everything he could against her. She however keeps to the one point that she has no right to surrender to him any influence over the child's future. Her knowledge of the extreme badness of the Irish Catholic Schools would I should say be sufficient to make her hold out at every cost[10] even if Mac Bride were less of a rogue, when in his cups—rogue is a mild word, but I find that dictation takes from the precision of one's style.

beyond the rightful tragic thrill: we suffer qualms of physical disgust'. Despite his criticism of the play, WBY was to use the motif of dancer and severed head in his plays *A Full Moon in March* (1935) and *The King of the Great Clock Tower* (1935).

[7] Mrs Julia H. Worthington (1856–1913), a socialite with an interest in the arts, was a friend of Quinn, and WBY had stayed at her house on the Hudson during his American tour. On 8 Apr she had written to tell Quinn (NYPL) that she was sailing for England, and to ask him for WBY's address as she would 'be in London for May and I hope to see Mr Yeats. I expect to be home again the middle of June. Perhaps you will call then and hear about him.' JBY wrote from New York in 1910 (*JBYL*, 127) that she was 'a sort of Duchess over here. Socially clever and a friend to all the distinguished people.'

[8] Anne, Countess of Drogheda (d. 1924), had evidently asked Fay to perform in the town hall of Monasterevan, Co. Kildare, near her residence, Moore Abbey, as part of the festivities to mark the coming of age of her only son, Viscount Henry Charles Ponsonby Moore (1884–1957). When the event had to be postponed, because Lord Moore was on the Continent, the Company withdrew and the townspeople and distinguished guests were entertained on 29 Aug by Sealy Jeffares singing comic songs and Pamela Colman Smith (see p. 9) performing folk songs from the West Indies.

[9] i.e. that of 10 May, which WBY had sent on to AG and, via her, to AE (see pp. 83–6).

[10] MG opposed the system of National Schools in Ireland and in the 1912 Christmas number of the *Irish Worker* attacked them as 'a system invented by England and carried out by ourselves ... the children are taught ... to forget the high deeds of their ancestors, the language they spoke and the songs of their poets, and they are taught also to forget the beauty and the sacredness of the land. ... They come out of those terrible schools ... unable to help themselves or their nation.'

The price suggested for that poem is quite enough. I should have said this in my last letter but it went out of my mind. I hope this has not inconvenienced you. I suppose they will use it within a reasonable time, as I can send Brett the MS. for his collected edition the very moment A. P. Watt has got through the preliminaries, and I would like to put the poem beginning "Never give all the heart" into the "Seven Woods" section.[11] The Reverend Mother of the Girls College at Notre Dame invited me to their annual celebration, and I got a St. Patrick's Day invitation from San Francisco. I was pleased at the compliment.[12] Yesterday I met an American woman who knew you. I wish I could remember her name, but she was a librarian at San Francisco a few years ago, and prosecuted a clergyman for libel. The libel being that he publicly prayed that she might have a change of heart. She won her action. She struck me as a very spirited person, vital and merry, but as ugly as the Devil.[13]

Yours always
W B Yeats

TLS NYPL, with envelope addressed to 120, Broadway, New York, postmark 'LONDON. W.C. MY 29 05'.

---

[11] Witter Bynner (1881–1968), poetry editor of *McClure's Magazine*, had offered $40 for 'Queen Edaine' and 'Never Give All the Heart', in a letter that Quinn had forwarded on 17 Mar, asking WBY to let 'me know what you think about it and I will take it up with him promptly' (Himber, 69). This WBY failed to do, and on 19 May Quinn reminded him that he had 'not answered Bynner's letter . . . about the publication of the chorus from *Deirdre*' (Himber, 74). The two poems were published in *McClure's Magazine* in September and December of this year, and WBY's fair copy of them is among Bynner's papers at Harvard. They were included both in vol. 1 of *The Poetical Works* and in *Poems, 1899–1905*.

[12] Mother Mary Pauline O'Neill (1854–1935), of the Sisters of the Holy Cross, became the first president of St Mary's College, Notre Dame, in March 1903. WBY had lectured there on 15 Jan 1904 during his American tour (see III. 519–21). The San Francisco invitation probably came from James Duval Phelan (1861–1930), former mayor of San Francisco (1897–1902), who had helped arrange WBY's lectures and acted as his host during his visit to California in late January 1904 (see III. 538–43).

[13] This may have been the feisty Ina D. Coolbrith, née Smith (1841–1928), who was librarian of the Bohemian Club in San Francisco, where WBY had dined on 1 Feb 1904 with Quinn's friend James Phelan and local literary people (see II. 543 n.). After travelling to California by wagon train at the age of 10 and a disastrous early marriage that ended in divorce, she became librarian of the Oakland Public Library in 1874, but was dismissed for obscure reasons in 1893 and, after a brief period at the Mercantile Library in San Francisco, moved to the Bohemian Club in late 1899. No details of her libel case have come to light, but it may have been concerned with her dismissal from the Oakland Library, which involved in part religious prejudice. Ina Coolbrith was herself a poet and a member of the San Francisco group which included Joaquin Miller, Bret Harte, Mark Twain, and Ambrose Bierce.

## To Maud Gonne, [c. 29 May 1905]

Mention in letter from MG, 1 June [1905].
Enclosing a letter from Quinn to WBY giving details of his outside expenses in seeking evidence in New York on her behalf,[1] giving her details of the new Maunsel Press, and complaining of the heat.

*G–YL*, 204–5.

## To Lady Gregory, 30 May [1905]

18, Woburn Buildings, | Euston Road,
May 30th, 1903.

My dear Lady Gregory.

When do you go to Dublin? Will you wait till the very end or go up a few days before the opening. I shall go there I suppose Tuesday or Wednesday of next week. It will take me, I should think, three or four days solid struggle to get that new stool for the Hour-Glass out of William Fay.[1] I have just completed the revision of "Shadowy Waters" but have a few lines more to do on "The King's Threshold". Did I tell you that I have arranged with Bullen for him to bring out in the early autumn a volume containing all my poems since the Unwin book. I will call it "Poems, a New Series, 1895–1905".[2] The three verse-plays will be in it in their revised form. We are to put off the expensive collected edition until next year. I think this new book should sell very well for it will be the first big mass of verse that I have published for years, and will get a constant advertisement from the plays at the Abbey Theatre. Bullen is to publish enough copies to last him until 1907 when the Unwin copyright returns to me.[3] He can then issue a

---

[1] See pp. 96–7. In her reply (G–YL, 204–5) MG said that she 'had already written to Mr Quinn to thank him. I am writing again to tell him my gratitude & am sending £12 which I am begging him to allow me to pay for the outside expenses. I said I knew through you he had taken all this trouble out of friendship, but that I had written you begging you to find out for me at least what the outside expenses were.'

[1] The stage directions for *The Hour-Glass*, which was produced with Colum's *The Land* from 9 to 16 June, called for a 'creepy stool' to be placed close to the hourglass, and the Fool sits on this at a significant moment in the play.

[2] In fact the book was called *Poems, 1899–1905*; it did not finally appear until October 1906, and did not contain the poems published in *The Wind Among the Reeds*. It did, however, print the new versions of the poetic plays *The Shadowy Waters*, *On Baile's Strand*, and *The King's Threshold*.

[3] Thomas Fisher Unwin (1848–1935), who founded his firm in 1882, had been WBY's main publisher since 1891, when he issued *John Sherman and Dhoya*. He had the rights to WBY's *Poems*, first published in 1895, and, despite WBY's expectation that this copyright would expire in 1907, retained them until his company was taken over by Ernest Benn in October 1926.

complete edition of the Poems. I have heard nothing more about Hone, Bullen liked him very much and would have liked him still better if he could have got that thousand pounds for his own business. I found Bullen a very charming person to stay with. He is really a great scholar probably the greatest Elizabethan scholar now. He seems to have lost all desire to write. He was very cross with Sydney Lee an old friend of his, because he had not mentioned the Stratford Shakespeare in some speech, and would have attacked him for some theory about Shakespeare's sonnets, through desire of vengeance if I had not dissuaded him.[4] It was very beautiful at Stratford, and Marie Corelli pressed her gondola upon me but I did not want to be paragraphed as going about in her gondola, or rather Bullen's womenkind, who look upon me as one of the assets of the firm did not want me to. She asked after you.[5] The heat here is beyond words, indeed but for the heat I should be writing this and not dictating it. I came out to dictate letters in desperation of keeping sufficiently upright in a chair to hold a pen, with the forty volumes of Balzac which I have bought from Bullen calling me to the armchair.[6] I did some lines, not very many, of the new King's Threshold and then came out. Philip Carr wants to bring out a play simultaneously with our production of it in Dublin. It might be well to let him have Deirdre or perhaps one of yours. I daresay they would think all the better of us in Dublin for having a theatre here producing us so promptly. Carr has not been doing very well and will stop until the autumn when he makes another attempt. I saw The Palace of Truth at his Theatre, and thought it rather a bad play though written round an idea full of dramatic possibilities. There was no detailed life, no sense of character, and of course no speech, nothing but the central idea, the difference after the Elizabethan comedy

---

[4] Sidney Lee (1859–1924), Shakespearian scholar and editor of the *Dictionary of National Biography*, had been at school with Bullen, but the two fell out when Bullen derided his critical interpretations in the Shakespeare Head Press edition of *Shakespeare's Sonnets* (1905). Lee retaliated by ignoring Bullen's ongoing edition of Shakespeare in a speech at the Annual Shakespeare Commemoration Banquet on 28 Apr of this year (*The Times*, 29 Apr 1905, p. 10). The rift was widened when Lee (who was having a clandestine affair with her) sought financial compensation for Bullen's estranged wife.

[5] Marie Corelli, pseudonym of Mary Mackay (1855–1924), became one of the most popular novelists in Britain after the publication of *The Sorrows of Satan* (1895). She moved to Stratford-upon-Avon in 1898, where she was often in conflict with the local authorities as she sought to save the town from modernization. Her ostentatious use of a 'gondola' (which boasted a boatman but more nearly resembled a punt) was part of her campaign to have steam-launches and other modern craft banished from the Avon.

[6] WBY had purchased the 1901 New York edition of George Saintsbury's forty-volume edition of the *Comédie humaine* (*YL*, 76–111), which he was to read and reread throughout his life, seeing himself as belonging 'to a generation that returns to Balzac alone' (*E & I*, 445). He had been introduced to Balzac's novels in his teens by his father, who would use 'incident or character as an illustration for some profound criticism of life' (*Aut*, 48). WBY was to value Balzac for counteracting Shelley's influence on him, keeping him (*E & I*, 425) 'from the pursuit of a beauty that, seeming at once absolute and external, requires, to strike a balance, hatred as absolute', and he placed among his six sacred authors 'Balzac, who saved me from Jacobin and Jacobite' (*E & I*, 447).

was startling. In the Elizabethan comedy, the Silent Woman for instance, the details were full of invention and vitality, and the language was like a torrent.[7]

Yours always<br>W B Yeats

TLS Berg. Wade, 449–50.

## To John Millington Synge, 1 June 1905

18 Woburn Buildings, | Euston Road, | London.<br>June 1st/05

*Dictated.*

Dear Synge,

Delighted to hear about the Manchester Guardian.[1]

The great thing about translation rights is not to give a man permission until you know that he has got a publisher & not then I should say for an indefinite period. I will find out about the business terms in detail.[2] Symonds is coming here on Saturday evening and I will ask him. If there is any hurry, I would write if I were you, to your translator & say—"I will give you the translators rights as soon as I hear you have a publisher".

Yours sny<br>W B Yeats

Dict AEFH, signed WBY; TCD, with envelope addressed to 31 Crossthwaite Park, Kingston, Co. Dublin, postmark 'LONDON JU 1 05'. Saddlemyer, 68.

[7] The Mermaid Repertory Theatre production of W. S. Gilbert's *The Palace of Truth*, a 'Fairy Tale in Three Acts', opened at the Great Queen Street Theatre on 23 May. In the play, which was first produced and published in 1870, a year before he began his collaboration with Sir Arthur Sullivan, the characters cannot stop themselves telling the truth on entering the palace. Strictly speaking *The Silent Woman*, written in 1609, is a Jacobean play.

[1] The *Manchester Guardian* had commissioned Synge to write a series of articles, illustrated by Jack Yeats, on the poorest areas of Connemara. The two were in west Galway and Mayo from 3 June to 3 July, and the twelve illustrated articles appeared periodically as 'In the Congested Districts' between 10 June and 26 July. Jack Yeats's note 'With Synge in Connemara' appeared in WBY's *Synge and the Ireland of his Time* (1911).

[2] Dr Max Meyerfeld (1875–1952), German theatre critic and translator of Robert Burns, John Galsworthy, George Moore, and Oscar Wilde, had written to Synge on 22 May (TCD) asking for permission to translate *The Well of the Saints* into German, and Synge had sent him a copy of the play on 26 May. In thanking him for this, Meyerfeld pointed out that the language of the play was very strange and difficult to translate, and asked whether Synge could send him 'an English transcript of the play'. Synge took WBY's advice and on 14 June (*JMSCL* I. 113) told Meyerfeld that he did 'not want to give away the rights of translation unless you are sure of finding a publisher for the work'. The poet and man

## To Lady Gregory [2 June 1905]

My dear Friend

Man in City says 'between 2 & 4'. I need not go till near 4.[1]

Yrs ev<br>W B Yeats

ALS Berg, with envelope addressed to Queen Annes Mansions, postmark 'LONDON. N.W. JUN 2 '05'. Both letter and envelope are written in pencil.

## To George Brett, 5 June 1905

18 Woburn Buildings, | Euston Road, | London.<br>June 5<sup>th</sup>,/05.

Dear M' Brett,

I have not yet had the agreement. I understand however from A. P. Watt that you have arranged matters satisfactorily with him.[1]

I am merely waiting on some decision about the "Shadowy Waters" & "The Wind amongst the Reeds".

You may announce a book of my poems for the Autumn, the two volumes if you like, but it may perhaps be better not to go into details until I know whether I can get "The Wind among the Reeds" and the "Shadowy Waters".[2]

Yours sny<br>W B Yeats

Dict AEFH, signed WBY; NYPL.

of letters Arthur Symons had numerous literary contacts on the Continent and was well versed in questions of translation.

[1] AG's arrival in London had taken WBY by surprise because she was there for the still secret presentation of his fortieth birthday present, a copy of the Kelmscott Chaucer. The man in the city is unidentified, but may have been the broker through whom WBY had invested the money from his American tour of 1903–4.

[1] Brett was negotiating the agreement for the two-volume American edition of WBY's works (see pp. 64–6), and on 17 May 1905 Watt had sent him details of WBY's amendments to the contract. Brett had accepted these and Watt must have sent the new agreement to WBY later in this month, for on 1 July he returned it, signed by WBY, to Brett.

[2] On 1 July (NYPL) Watt informed Brett that in a recent letter WBY 'tells me that he can let you have the "copy" at once whenever matters are settled with Messrs. Dodd, Mead and with Mr. Lane. I am in communication with Messrs. Dodd, Mead & Co. and I believe Mr. Yeats has asked the Author's Society of which he is a member to deal with Mr. Lane.' Dodd, Mead & Co. readily assented to resign their American rights in *The Shadowy Waters*, but negotiations with Lane over *The Wind Among the Reeds* were to drag on into the next year.

## To Eric Maclagan, [8 June 1905]

18 Woburn Buildings
Thursday

My dear Maclagan: I thank you a great many times for that most beautiful book.[1] It will be a great delight to read practically for the first time Sir Thomas Browne[2] & Chaucer, under such conditions of pleasure.[3] I am a slow reader & though I read very thoroughly have never even dipped here & there in books most know well. Sir Thomas Browne I hardly know at all, & I was most anxious to have this book just because I intend to know it from end to end. It has been very generous of you.

I shall not be back for about ten days but hope to be here again next Monday week, to start the rehersals of 'Shadowy Waters'.

I notice that Ricketts uses borders which are 'greyer' in colour, less black & white than Morris. That is I should think because his type is more like modern type, while Morris gives the impression of black letter.[4] I shall keep this in mind when the time comes for my sisters to use ornament—I am hoping to get Gregory to make some experiments, & shall bring both books

[1] Since WBY was to be in Dublin for his fortieth birthday, Maclagan (see p. 57) had given him as an advance birthday present a copy of the Vale Press edition of Sir Thomas Browne's *Religio Medici, Urn Burial, Christian Morals and Other Essays* (1902), decorated by Ricketts, and inscribed on the flyleaf 'To W B Yeats | 13.6.1905 | from | E. Maclagan' (*YL*, 291).

[2] Sir Thomas Browne (1605–82), the English physician and antiquarian, was educated at Oxford and on the Continent, and lived for most of his life in Norwich. The first authorized edition of his most famous work, *Religio Medici*, an extended meditation upon religious, philosophical, and scientific questions, distinguished for the quality of its distinctive prose style, appeared in 1643. *Hydriotaphia, Urne-Buriall* (1658) is an account of ancient burial rites and a reflection on the transitoriness of life. *Christian Morals* appeared posthumously in 1716. WBY had some knowledge of Browne as early as 1896, when his narrator describes *Rosa Alchemica* as 'somewhat in the manner of Sir Thomas Browne' (*VSR*, 126), and in an interview in the *Daily News and Leader* on 3 Jan 1913 (7–8), he stated that he preferred Browne to Swift.

[3] As well as the edition of Browne, WBY was given a copy of the Kelmscott edition of *The Works of Geoffrey Chaucer* (1896), generally recognized as the Press's finest achievement, for his fortieth birthday on 13 June.

[4] The Kelmscott Press, founded by William Morris 1890, had three main founts: the Golden type, based on the work of 15th-century Venetian printers, notably Nicolas Jenson; the Troy type, a Gothic face in Great Primer, modelled in particular on Peter Schoeffer's Mainz Bible of 1462; and the Chaucer type, a smaller, pica version of the Troy fount, designed in 1892 especially for *The Works of Geoffrey Chaucer* after Morris had discovered that Troy type would prove too large. Morris had great difficulty in finding an ink sufficiently black (and red for headings) to give the striking contrasts that WBY mentions here, but finally discovered the firm of Jaenecke of Hamburg, which used a traditional mixture of linseed oil and lamp-black. By these means he hoped to produce reader-friendly black-letter books 'which would have a definite claim to beauty, while at the same time they should be easy to read and should not dazzle the eye, or trouble the intellect of the reader by eccentricity of form in the letters', and thus 'to redeem the Gothic character from the charge of unreadableness which is commonly brought against it' (*A Note by William Morris on his Aims in Founding the Kelmscott Press* [1898], 1, 3).

Charles Ricketts was deeply influenced by Morris's example when he founded the Vale Press in 1896, although, as he explained in his pamphlet *A Defence of the Revival of Printing* (1899), he preferred the Golden fount and based his type on the 'the sunny pages of the Venetian printers' (19), rather than Gothic models. Even here he amended Venetian practice, finding that while in 'spirit and intention the Italian founts are admirable indeed' they were not always so in execution. While putting Jenson in the

to Ireland with that object in part.[5] There is also some body else there I want to start.[6]

Yours always
W B Yeats

ALS Private.

## *To Lady Gregory, [8 June 1905]*

18 Woburn Buildings | Euston Road.
Thursday.

My dear Friend: I am so sorry you have been ill. I will be at station at about twenty before 11.[1] The Molèire play to day was wonderful—one can get no idea from the unacted words.[2]

Yours ever
W B Yeats

ALS Berg, with envelope addressed to 1 Old Albermarle St,[3] near Regents St, postmark 'LONDON. N.W. JUN 8 '05'.

first place as a designer, he devised a mixture of Jenson's and Vindelinus de Spira's types for the Vale Press, as well as altering the angle of their serifs and making his type slightly more open and larger, insisting that 'imitation pure and simple of some Venetian fount would . . . mount up in the long run to an affectation of archaism' (27). This gives his books a more 'modern' appearance than those of Morris, as does his use of decoration, which he approved in the Kelmscott editions but which he thought had become debased in the hands of less able imitators, resulting in 'a new cumbersome trade article' (12). He advocated that decoration should only be employed 'when it can be urged as an added element of beauty to the book, let it accompany the text, and not gobble it up' (36), and in his edition of Browne only the first page has a decorated border. He also argued that type should be inked up gradually, noting that fine old books were 'often slightly under-pressed' (35), and in contrast with Morris's emphatic inking this gives Vale Press publications the 'greyer' look that WBY notes. Charles Ricketts (1866–1931), one of the most eminent of art nouveau book illustrators, had been the close companion of Charles Haslewood Shannon (1863–1937) from 1882, when they were both apprenticed to a wood-engraver. WBY had evidently been introduced to them by Lionel Johnson in the later 1890s (see *Aut*, 169), and frequently attended their Friday evening at-homes. Although the Vale Press ceased in 1904, Ricketts was to design the cover for WBY's *Later Poems* (1922), as well as costumes for *On Baile's Strand* and *The King's Threshold* in 1915. WBY described him as one of his 'chief instructors' in artistic matters (*Aut*, 169), and as 'one of the greatest connoisseurs of any age, an artist whose woodcuts prolonged the inspiration of Rossetti' (*E & I*, 495). Both Ricketts and Shannon had subscribed to WBY's Kelmscott Chaucer.

[5] Apart from press-marks and colophon, the Dun Emer and Cuala books were unadorned, but in their type, inking, and design they owe more to Morris and his adviser Emery Walker than to Ricketts. Robert Gregory did not design any of the books.

[6] Presumably George Roberts of the Maunsel Press.

[1] WBY was arranging to meet AG at Euston Station on 9 June to catch the morning boat-train for Ireland.

[2] Constant-Benoît Coquelin and company, on a 'flying visit' from the Théâtre de la Gaîté, Paris, performed Rostand's *Les Romanesques* and Molière's *Les Précieuses ridicules* on the afternoon of 8 June at the Shaftesbury Theatre.

[3] For this short visit AG had evidently rented a service flat at 1 Albermarle Street (there was no 'Old' Albermarle Street), near her publisher, John Murray, at 50 Albermarle Street.

## To Florence Farr,[1] [*11 June 1905*]

Nassau Hotel | South Fredrick St | Dublin.
Sunday.

My Friend: Colums play has played finely—wonderfully simple & natural & wonderfully played. I will send you a copy of the book in the morning.[2] We have done 12 plays since Xmas—six of them being new & all I think good & all staged in a more or less new way. We hope to start the company, or rather some of them who will be paid, touring the small towns this summer. Fay came in last night & sat up to the small hours talking. He would be delighted if you played Emer in Blunts play & thinks you would be a draw.[3] I should think that his support makes the matter certain—I wish my 'Deirdre' could come at the same time—you could then play in that too & look after the chorus. There is a general meeting next Saturday—the day after the last day of play & I shall return to London at once—perhaps that night. It will be hard to settle the exact hour of starting until news of the meeting—I have to arrange about paying the company & so forth & the meeting may last too long for me to get the boat. Beautiful

---

[1] WBY's long friendship with the actress Florence Farr (1860–1917; see 1. 485–6) had now developed into a physical relationship. WBY met her in May 1890 when her performance in an amateur production of Todhunter's *A Sicilian Idyll* greatly impressed him. Her marriage to the actor Edward Emery came to an end in the late 1880s and she divorced him in 1894. In the early 1890s she had had an affair with Shaw, under whose guidance she took a number of roles in his and Ibsen's plays, although her lack of motivation as an actress was to annoy both him and WBY. In 1894 she acted in the first public production of a play by WBY, *The Land of Heart's Desire*, at the Avenue Theatre, London, and she was also associated with WBY in the Golden Dawn, which she joined in 1890, although her inefficiency and heterodoxy as Praemonstratrix of the London Temple brought her into conflict with him and AEFH. WBY appointed her general manager for the first season of the ILT in 1899, and she played Aleel in the first production of *The Countess Cathleen*. During the first decade of the new century she frequently accompanied WBY in his experiments of speaking verse to the psaltery, a twenty-six-string lyre-like instrument (see III. 725–8). She was currently appearing in plays at the Court Theatre, and was about to produce and act in the Theosophical Society's production of *The Shadowy Waters*.

[2] See p. 40. *The Land* opened on 9 June, and was published as vol. III in the Abbey Theatre series. The *Irish Times* of 10 June, describing Colum (8) as 'a young author, who seems to possess the dramatic instinct, and can apply it with effect in portraying some phases of rural life', reported that he had thanked WBY and the Fays in a curtain speech 'for having made it possible to start an Irish dramatic movement with every prospect of success'. The play was generally greeted with enthusiasm, the *Freeman's Journal* of 10 June in particular describing the dialogue (8) as 'admirable . . . strong, coloured, subtle' and commending the play's 'curious formal excellence': 'No play yet produced in the Abbey Theatre has so gripped and held captive an audience. There have been fuller houses, but never more enthusiastic. What we have been waiting for was a play that should be at once good and popular. Mr Yeats has proved a little too abstruse, and Mr. Synge a little too bizarre to get fully down to the hearts of the people. . . . Mr. Colum has caught up his play out of the mid-current of actual, Irish life.' Even the reviewers who were not as exuberant as this noted the play's originality, and most commented upon the excellence of the acting.

[3] i.e. *Fand*; see pp. 80–2. When the play was produced on 20 Apr 1907, Sara Allgood took the part of Emer.

weather again—I wish we could have a day in the country when I get back—but such plans have a way of coming to nothing when rehersals are in question. There is a very wise book here—at least as wise as that book of pious reveries—it is very rare—I may be able to get a sight of it.[4] People are taking [*for* talking] round me & it is hard not to be very scrappy—I wish you would send me your horoscope—do please send it at once. I want to tell you about some of the aspects I saw in my hasty glance in London & to look up some aspects between it & mine.[5]

Yrs always
W B Yeats

PS. At Colums play I saw the Irish Times reporter writing his notice in the hall while the play was going on. Column came up & he asked him for some information about the plot. Column said "Had not you better go in & see the play". "Oh, no" said the reporter "plays depress my spirits".[6] 'The Irish Times' is the most influential paper here—so God help us—or rather he does for we find the papers have no influence on our public.

ALS Texas.

## *To Maud Gonne,* [c. *13 June 1905*]

Mention in letter from MG, 'Thursday night' [? 15 June 1905].
Sending her a copy of Colum's play *The Land* and describing its production,[1] and enquiring how her case is proceeding.[2]

*G–YL*, 192–3.

---

[4] The 'wise' book is unidentified, but the book of pious reveries was probably Mahatma Sri Agamya Guru Paramahamsa's recently published *Sri Brahma Dhārā (Shower from the Highest)*, a series of dialogues on spiritual matters between variously named students and a variously named master. FF transcribed a letter of 23 Nov 1904 from Paramahamsa to Helen Rand into her occult notebooks (Private), which suggested that 'the whole world exists as a blissful wave in the Brahmic consciousness' and mentioned that his book was in the press.

[5] As an occultist FF was deeply interested in astrology and did give WBY a copy of her horoscope, although not apparently until September 1907.

[6] Despite this—or perhaps because of it—the opening performance of *The Land* was reviewed both favourably and at length in the *Irish Times* of 10 June (8).

[1] MG would have been particularly interested in the production of Colum's play since, as she informed WBY on 1 June (*G–YL*, 205), 'Colum told me a lot about his play on the land & the tyranny of the old & I think it will be very interesting. It is cruel not to be able to see it.'

[2] MG replied that the trial was definitely fixed for 26 July, although she supposed that MacBride and his lawyers would insist on an *enquête*, 'which means that things will drag on till the Autumn but I should think after the first trial John MacBride's power for harm will be considerable diminished'.

## *To Florence Farr,* [c. *16 June 1905*]

Nassau Hotel | South Frederick St | Dublin

This damned beautiful weather is keeping our audiences very thin[1]—
however we have enough money now to pay half a dozen of our people
who are to go on tour. I sent you the play-book. I could not send it as soon
as I said for somebody stole out of the Green Room the copy I had bought
for the purpose.[2] General meeting has been put off till Sunday. I shall
therefore start home on Monday morning in time for my usual 'Monday'.
You might come and dine that day if you have nothing else to do and keep
Tuesday evening free for me. You can dine with me after the rehearsal.
I may have nobody on Monday but most likely somebody will turn up. I was
very glad to get your letter—a dip into the river of life changes even an old
handwriting and gives it a new and meaning face.[3]

I have not a moment [to] write in. I am expecting an unknown caller who
was described to me by the hotel messenger boy as 'a gentleman with a
shaking mouth called by a name something like Holmes'. Examination of
the boy reduced 'a shaking mouth' to a stutter.[4] I met Roberts a while
ago—he has been to an Irish printer to arrange for the new publishing
house's first book. He said 'How much for a novel of 80,000 words?' The
printer said 'Are they long words or short?'[5] The path of a patriot is—well
it is described by a popular phrase that has become common since my play,
'The Thorny path of Kathleen-ni-Houlihan'.[6] *The Hour-Glass* is beautiful

---

[1] The *Irish Daily Independent* of 15 June 1905 reported 'Light or moderate S. E. breezes; fair or fine;
warm'. The weather had been fair and mild for several days. The production also coincided with the
Whitsun holidays, and Holloway recorded a very small audience on Whit Monday, 12 June, but on
Friday, 16 June, reported that 'the poor houses of the opening nights were forgotten in the cheery ones
of to-night and last night, but large or small there was no lack of enthusiasm for *The Land*' (Hogan and
Kilroy III. 33).

[2] i.e. Colum's *The Land*, which WBY had promised to send on 11 June (see p. 112).

[3] The tone and frequency of his letters at this time bear witness to WBY's and FF's new relationship
(see p. 112. n. 1). She had evidently altered her attitude towards him, for on 30 Jan 1903 she had
confided to Nevinson (Bodleian) that 'Yeats is not personally attractive to her, not as a lover, nor she
thinks to other women'. The affair did not last long, as Mrs Yeats later recalled (Bax, 43–4): 'WBY once
said to me "She was the only person to whom I could tell *everything*." He thought her career as an
actress had given her a solitary, perhaps unhappy, personal life and quoted a phrase of hers, "When a
man begins to make love to me I instantly see it as a stage performance." Their brief love affair came to
an end because "she got bored." '

[4] The man with a stutter was possibly Joseph Hone.

[5] WBY and the Belfast-born Roberts evidently lacked an appreciation of demotic Dublin humour.
The first Irish novel published by Maunsel & Co. was *Dan the Dollar* (1905) by Shan F. Bullock (1865–
1935), a prolific Irish author, best known for his *Thomas Andrews, Shipbuilder* (1912).

[6] This phrase does not appear in *Cathleen ni Houlihan*, but the line 'Oh, Kathleen Ní Houlihan, your
road's a thorny way' occurs (with variations) twice in Ethna Carbery's much-quoted poem 'The Passing
of the Gael', published in *The Four Winds of Eirinn*, which had gone through numerous editions since its
publication in 1902. 'Ethna Carbery' was the pseudonym of Anna Isabel Johnston (1866–1902).

now—Miss Walker a delight and Fay as Wise Man very varied and powerful.[7]

The caller has come so—

Yours ever

W B Yeats

Printed copy. Bax, 52–3; Wade, 450–1.

## To A. H. Bullen, 22 June 1905

18, Woburn Buildings, | Euston Road,

June 22nd, 1905.

My dear Bullen,

I called today to see Sidgwick but found him away on his holidays, so must needs write.[1] I want to know the result if any of your correspondence with Elkin Matthews. It has just struck me that there is a way out of the difficulty. In the ordinary course of nature Elkin Matthews' period with 'The Wind among the Reeds' comes to an end when Unwin's period ends in 1907. Now I think it very likely that you will not want to publish 'The Wind among the Reeds' separately. In 1907 both you and I will want to bring out a collected edition of my poems in say two volumes. It is for this alone that you will want the Elkin Matthews book. What do you think of offering Matthews if we cannot get his assent on cheaper terms, an extended term of years on the condition of his assenting to the inclusion at once of 'the Wind among the Reeds' in a book containing everything I have written in verse from 1895 to the present moment. I believe this large

[7] Mary Elizabeth Walker (1884–1958), who adopted the Irish form of her name, Maire nic Shiubhlaigh, had begun acting in the Fay's Ormond Dramatic Society in November 1901, and was a founding member of the Irish National Theatre Society in 1902. She was to leave the Company later this year, following a disagreement with WBY, but she returned from time to time. She married Eamon Price in 1928, and her reminiscences, *The Splendid Years*, appeared in 1955. She played the Angel in this production with George Roberts as the Fool. The *Freeman's Journal* (see p. 112, n. 2) noted that 'Mr. F. J. Fay, as the Wise Man, rose above even the high level we expect from him.'

[1] Frank Sidgwick (1879–1939) joined Bullen's firm in October 1901, after coming down from Cambridge, and became his junior partner six months later. From May 1904 to March 1905 he moved to Stratford to start the Shakespeare Head Press, the record of which is preserved in *Frank Sidgwick's Diary* (1975). The partnership was dissolved in 1907, and in October 1908 he joined R. Cameron Jackson to found the firm of Sidgwick & Jackson. Sidgwick had published an article on WBY in the *English Illustrated Magazine* of 29 June 1903, reprinted in the *Gael* (NY) August 1903. He was evidently not taking his holiday in Sligo: in his poem 'When My Ship Comes In', published in the *Cornhill Magazine* in January of this year, he proclaimed (53) that when his ship came home he would 'follow no poet to Innisfree, | For I don't much care for the honey-bee's hum, | And a clay-wattled cabin is not for me: | But I'll bid farewell to the life of a clerk | And third-floor lodging in Battersea Park.'

volume to be essential for my reputation just now. Of course you may by this time have got round Matthews. Let me know about the matter anyway. If he agrees you can have copy for the book immediately.[2] I saw Roberts in Dublin, he showed me a list of books of mine which they were offering to the new firm.[3] I raised no question about the matter in principle indeed it was hardly my business but I would just like to know if you are "remaindering" The Celtic Twilight or not. I do not recollect the price, but certainly I cannot see any reason why it should be sold at remainder prices. It is complete. I do not want to change it any way, and your collected edition being so much more expensive would hardly make the cheaper volume unnecessary. Roberts will agree I know to your proposal, but I said Wait until I had asked you about this.[4] Roberts has, I believe, got his way and is a partner in the new firm.

Yours sincerely<br>
W B Yeats

TLS Kansas.

## To Maud Gonne, [*late June 1905*]

Mention in letter from MG, 'Sunday' [? 2 July 1905].
Asking how her case is proceeding,[1] and whether she liked Colum's play.[2]

*G–YL*, 207.

---

[2] Although Lane was causing particular difficulties over the American rights, Elkin Mathews was guarding the English publication no less tenaciously if less obtrusively. In the event, Bullen did not publish the poems from *The Wind Among the Reeds* in *Poems, 1899–1905* (see p. 65, n. 5).

[3] Apart from publishing five of his plays in 1905 in the Abbey Theatre series, Maunsel also issued editions of WBY's *The Secret Rose, Ideas of Good and Evil*, and *The Celtic Twilight*.

[4] Bullen had published 2,000 copies of the revised *Celtic Twilight* in July 1902 at a price of 6 shillings. He subsequently sold some sheets to Macmillan for an American edition, and in August 1905 disposed of a further 400 copies to Maunsel & Co. which issued them with a new title page and at a reduced price for sale in Ireland only.

[1] MG repeated that the hearing of her divorce case was fixed for 26 July (see p. 113, n. 2), adding that her lawyer was 'quite certain of success but thinks it probable that MacBride & his 5 lawyers will obtain an enquete which will drag things on till the autumn'.

[2] MG replied that she liked 'Colum's play very much but I think he will do better work than that yet'.

## *To Lady Gregory,* [*24–25 June 1905*]

18 Woburn Buildings | Euston Road. | London.

My dear Lady Gregory: I shall amuse Masefield, who is coming to dinner, with your account of Oldmeadow.[1] M^rs Emery dined here last night & I made what are I hope my last corrections of 'The Shadowy Waters'. I added yesterday some new lines for Dectora which I think good.

> "What can the eagles of the undying do
> But harry us with hopes that come to nothing
> Because we are not proud, imperishable,
> Alone & winged; O hide me from the eagles.
> I am a woman. I die at every breath."[2]

---

[1] Ernest James Oldmeadow (1867–1949), a former Nonconformist minister, author, editor of the *Dome* (1897–1901), and sometime owner and proprietor of the Unicorn Press, which published many fine books, including W. T. Horton's *A Book of Images, Beltaine*, and a collection of essays by Irish authors, *Ideals in Ireland*, edited by AG. AG, WBY, and Bullen had all suffered from Oldmeadow's financial sharp practice (see II. 597–9, III. 379–80, 382), and in a letter dated 'Tuesday Evening' (June 1905; Berg) AG had given an extended account of chancing upon his latest enterprises. On a trip through Co. Galway she arrived in the village of Carna '& my car driver informed me it was a place that had been let to an English gentleman, but he had been evicted for non payment of rent. This was Oldmeadow! My car driver was eloquent as he had gone off owing him £3—He owed money in the shops—& to a poor man who worked in his garden. In fact the only money he had paid was to a police constable, £5—& when the cheque was sent in there were "no assets" & the constable threatened to arrest him, and he then provided money—"He was a sort of a lad that would always be dodging"—Looked like a clergyman "but there is no church would have a use for one of his sort"—He made some inadequate excuses for not paying rent, but the Congested District Board sent him a notice to quit, by the police, and he hurried off before the shopkeepers & other creditors knew of it or could seize his goods, which were chiefly books & a piano—He had imported some flat bottomed boats from England & had not paid for them, but sold them before he left—He had his misses with him, taller than himself, fair hair, clear complexion. He had amused himself by fishing & shooting—This was the car drivers account, but I stopped to lunch at the Carna Hotel & the landlady . . . said poor Mr. Oldmeadow had been a riddle—& she pitied him very much, feeling sure he had seen better days. He had not done her out of money, except that he persuaded her to have pictures taken of the neighbouring lakes, saying he would have them reproduced as cards which would bring swarms of people to the Hotel, & she spent £5 on the pictures & gave them to him, & has heard nothing of him or the cards—He said, when his cheque was dishonoured, that he had a partner called Crossland, who had spent all the money, but that his father-in-law, Mr. Dawson could pay everything—He attended mass regularly & told some man he was out with, that he had been a clergyman, but that one morning as he was washing his hands in a basin of cold water, it came upon him that he should turn Catholic. His wife though not a Catholic also attended mass. When we left my car driver said the reason this woman spoke kindly of him was that she had got a bargain on the flat bottomed boats. . . . If Oldmeadow makes anymore demands on Bullen, tell him to say there are people at Carna who will be glad of his address.'

[2] An amended version of these lines was included in the 1907 acting version of the play but all except the last line were omitted from subsequent editions (*VPl*, 337–8).

The sailors are good, & Aibric fair but I fear Forgael will be pretty bad. They are all the men I mean over emphatic & he especially. I wish I had trusted my own judgement about him. He played Herod in Salome & Symons & Max Belbohm [*for* Beerbohm] & everybody praised him. I had as a feeling that he *seemed to play* Herod but in reality *was* <all himself> exactly what he showed on the stage. He gave an impression of weakness, & childish petulance that suited the part & in real life he is the decadant of tradition—feminine, emotional & histrionic. You cannot play Forgael without nobility or any of my verse without pride & he has neither.[3] M[rs] Emery will however be very fine. She has more passion than is usual with her.

Sunday.

I spoke last night at 'The Lyceum Club' dinner. The Club is a new & very large club of women <just in Picaddily> close to Hyde Park Corner. I had a great success. The[y] applauded for a good time after I had finished. I had to reply for art—Lavery who was there being too shy—& I congratu-lated the club upon its movement for the destruction of the Home which I described as the source of all bad art. One woman, whom I do not know lent over the table & said 'Your speach is the finest peice of sarcasm I have ever listened to'. I found that she & a great many others thought that I was really mocking at the club itself so incredible did they find my real meaning. The young women alone seem to have thought I was in earnest. I think it was a good speach, audacious & laughing.[4] They had just been bored by Ryder Haggard, who had wandered on at great length urging them to do something for British agriculture—I wonder how many of them ever spoke

---

[3] Robin de la Condamine (1878–1966), an actor of Spanish extraction, who used the stage name of Robin (Robert) Farquharson, began acting with the Stage Society in 1900. He played Herod in the New Stage Club production of *Salome* in May 1905 (see p. 90, n. 7), and again in July 1906 when the play was revived by FF's Literary Theatre Society, of which WBY was a committee member. Arthur Symons dedicated his play *Cesare Borgia* to Farquharson in 1920. Aibric was played by Jules Shaw.

[4] The Lyceum Club, then at 128 Piccadilly, W1, was conceived by Constance Smedley in November 1903 and inaugurated in June 1904 'to focus the work of women in art, literature, science, medicine, music, public service, journalism, drama, and other important directions'. It included among its members Jane Barlow, Katharine Tynan Hinkson, Dora Sigerson, Nora Chesson, Martin Ross, Charlotte Shaw, and Alice Meynell, and at weekly dinners, held for the discussion of literary, artistic, and social questions, entertained many prominent men and women of the day. The dinner at which WBY spoke was a special one, to mark the Club's first anniversary, and, according to the *Evening Standard* of 26 June (5), he created a 'mild sensation' by expressing 'his sympathy with the object of such ladies' clubs as the Lyceum, for they aimed at abolishing an institution which did more than anything else to degrade British art, British literature, and British music. "I need hardly add," continued Mr. Yeats, "that I allude to—the home." It was some moments before the startled audience laughed.' In *Aut* (484) WBY was to remark that he had 'certainly known more men destroyed by the desire to have wife and child and to keep them in comfort than I have seen destroyed by drink and harlots', and in rewriting *On Baile's Strand* this year he sharpened the contrast between Cuchulain's wildness and Conchubar's domesticity.

to a farmer or ever will.[5] Before that a certain Justice Darling had drifted from joke to joke, some of them not in good taste.[6] I began by telling that Lavery, when he was a Scots man would have made them a speach but that he had grown too serious since he became Irish—England & Scotland being the nations of humour.[7]

Miss Horniman makes no difficulty about guarranteeing the actors pay. She puts at our disposal she says £400 a year—this inclusive of rent & taxes Etc—. I imagine that her present liabilities are about £200 a year & I suppose the 'building next door' will add something.[8] Some of this money comes back in 'lets' & more & more should do so. I think she is going to let us sell tickets at a reduced price to trades unions, schools Etc.

Madam Troncy has made that pastel a little less offensive.[9]

Yrs ever

W B Yeats

ALS Berg, with envelope addressed to Coole, postmark 'LONDON.N.W. JU 26 05'.

[5] Henry Rider Haggard (1856–1925), the English novelist who achieved fame with *King Solomon's Mines* (1885), was also an expert on agricultural and social conditions in England, and his *The Poor and the Land* was going through the press at this moment. His talk was largely on a farm colony scheme he had been studying in Canada, and his knighthood in 1912 was in recognition of his agricultural rather than his creative writings. Haggard submitted a play, *The Star of Egypt*, to WBY in 1910 for production at the Abbey, but it was turned down.

[6] Charles John Darling, 1st Baron (1849–1936), a High Court judge, had earlier been a journalist on the *St James' Gazette*, the *Pall Mall Gazette*, and the *Saturday Review*, and for ten years before his elevation to the Bench in 1897 sat as Conservative MP for Deptford, his opposing candidate in 1888 being Wilfrid Blunt. He later told AG (*70 Years*, 446) that 'he made a point of never speaking to any of the Irish members the whole time he was in Parliament'. He was famous—or notorious—for his relentless jokes and witticisms in court; in July 1916, in somewhat less humorous circumstances, he was to preside at Sir Roger Casement's unsuccessful appeal against the death sentence for treason.

[7] John Lavery (1856–1941), knighted 1918, a painter influenced in his early work by Whistler, became best known for his portraits of women, particularly of his beautiful second wife Hazel, whom he married in 1910 and whose portrait decorated Irish bank notes from 1923 to 1977. At this time he was vice-president of the International Society of Sculptors, Painters, and Gravers. Although born in Belfast, he had moved to Scotland as a young man and became a leader of the 'Glasgow School'. In 1904, however, he had given paintings for the Irish section of the St Louis Exhibition, and was represented at Lane's London exhibition of Irish art. Although politically uncommitted, he was later to paint a number of the leaders of the Irish struggle for independence.

[8] On 12 June AEFH wrote to WBY (NLI) offering to guarantee the Company's salaries if difficulties should arise in meeting them. In return for a £600 annual guarantee she was also to ask that the Society become a limited liability company to protect her against serious financial loss. The 'building next door' was the house at 27 Lower Abbey Street, which AEFH was negotiating to lease to make space for a scene dock and a green room. The house was acquired on 18 Nov of this year at a cost of £1,250 and a ground rent of £70 per annum.

[9] AEFH's friend, the Parisian painter Mme Laura Troncy, had done a portrait of WBY in black chalk in January 1903 and a profile in colour. At first WBY was delighted, telling AG that she was 'really a fine artist', and her portrait 'the best yet' (see III. 296), but he seems to have changed his mind subsequently and there was now some question of whether the picture should hang (as AEFH wished) in the Abbey vestibule. Mme Troncy later married the artist Robert Anning Bell (1863–1933) as his second wife.

## *To George Roberts, 25 June 1905*

18 Woburn Buildings, | Euston Road, | London.
June 25<sup>th</sup>,/05.

*Dictated.*
My dear Roberts,

I send you that letter of Miss Horniman's which I mentioned at the General Meeting. It was necessary that I should show our balance sheet to Miss Horniman that she might withdraw the letter if necessary; she however still holds to it; so please put it in the Archives & keep it carefully.[1]

I return the balance sheets.

Yrs sny
W B Yeats

[*With enclosure*]
*Official*

H1 MONTAGU MANSIONS, | PORTMAN SQUARE. W. | London.
June 12<sup>th</sup>,/05.

To the President of the Irish National Theatre Society.
Dear Mr Yeats,

It is a matter which gratifies me intensely, that the Society should be now able to free certain of its members so that their whole strength and energy should be given to the theatre & its needs, practical as well as artistic. We must all have a little patience with the public and in time the theatre will become part of the natural life of the community. If a time of difficulty should arise and there should be anxiety as to continuing these payments, I will now try to minimise this anxiety by offering myself as security. I will undertake to make up the salaries to the sums agreed on, when any deficiency occurs; but when more people are freed I must be informed first so as to know the extent of the liability.

Please give my hearty congratulations to the Society on the artistic results of their first Season at the Abbey Theatre.

Yours sincerely
A.E.F. Horniman

Dict AEFH, signed WBY; Harvard.

---

[1] WBY had cited AEFH's letter of 12 June at the General Meeting of the INTS on 18 June and now wanted it put on record. The Meeting, which was attended by WBY, AG, W. G. Fay, F. J. Fay, Colum, Starkey, Frank Walker, Ryan, Roberts, Miss Walker, Miss Allgood, Miss Garvey, AE, T. Keohler, and Miss Laird, passed unanimously the resolution that the committee would pay certain members, should the necessary financial aid be forthcoming.

## *Agreement with the Macmillan Company (New York), 26 June 1905*

AGREEMENT, made the 26th day of June 1905 between W. B. Yeats, Esq. of 18 Woburn Buildings, Euston Road, London, W.C., England and THE MACMILLAN COMPANY, of the city of New York, Publishers.[1]

1. Said W. B. Yeats hereby grants and assigns to THE MACMILLAN COMPANY a work, the subject or title of which is the right to print and publish a collected edition of the author's Poems and Plays in two volumes with all translations, abridgments, selections, and rights therefor of said work, or parts thereof, with exclusive right and power, in its own name, or in the name of said W. B. Yeats to take out copyright thereof, and any renewal of the same, and publish said work during the term of said copyright in all languages the United States of America. The said W. B. Yeats guarantees that he is the sole owner of said work and has full power and authority to make this contract; that said work is not a violation of any copyright and contains no scandalous or libelous matter; that he will defend, indemnify, make good and hold harmless THE MACMILLAN COMPANY against all claims, demands, suits, actions or causes of action made or brought against said Company, and against all loss, damage, costs, charges and expenses that the said Company shall sustain or incur on account or by reason of any scandalous or libelous matter contained in or alleged to be contained in said work, or any violation or alleged violation by said work of any copyright.

2. THE MACMILLAN COMPANY agrees to publish said work at its own expense, in such style as it deems best suited to the sale of the work, and to pay said W. B. Yeats, his (And see Section 9) representatives or assigns, ten (10) per cent. on its retail price for each copy by it sold. And THE MACMILLAN COMPANY shall render always, annual statements of account, in the month of July, and make settlements in cash four months after date of each statement. In case an edition of the work shall be sold at a reduced price for export, the percentage to be paid thereon to said . . . . . . shall be . . . . . . per cent on the export price.

3. THE MACMILLAN COMPANY may publish, or permit others to publish, such selections from said work as it thinks proper to benefit its sale, without compensation to the grantor herein, but the compensation for translations and dramatizations shall be subject to agreement between the parties hereto.

4. Alterations in type, plates, or otherwise in the work, after delivery of copy to THE MACMILLAN COMPANY, which exceed . . . . . per cent. of the cost of original composition, shall be at the expense of said . . . . . . and any

---

[1] This, at last, was WBY's agreement with the Macmillan Company of New York for *The Poetical Works of William B. Yeats*, negotiations about which had begun early in 1904 (see III. 503–5, 555, 558).

~~index that may be required by THE MACMILLAN COMPANY for said work shall be prepared by said . . . . . or at . . . . . expense.~~

5. If the plates or type forms be rendered valueless by fire or otherwise THE MACMILLAN COMPANY shall have the option of reproducing them or not, and if it declines to do so, then, after the sale of all copies remaining on hand, it shall reconvey the copyright and all rights herein granted to said W. B. Yeats, his heirs or assigns, and this contract shall terminate.

6. If, at any time after two years from the date of publication, THE MACMILLAN COMPANY shall be satisfied that the public demand does not justify the continued publication of the work, or if for any other cause it shall deem its further publication improper or inexpedient, then it may offer in writing, to said W. B. Yeats, his heirs or assigns, the plates and any original engravings or illustrations to said work at half cost, and all copies then on hand at cost, and said W. B. Yeats, his heirs or assigns shall have the right within sixty days to take and pay for the same, and shall thereupon become sole owner of the copyright herein named, and THE MACMILLAN COMPANY shall thereupon transfer such copyright, but if said offer be not accepted and such payment made within sixty days, then THE MACMILLAN COMPANY may destroy the plates, and sell all copies then on hand free of percentage to said W. B. Yeats, his heirs or assigns, and this agreement shall thereupon terminate, the copyright reverting to said W. B. Yeats, his heirs or assigns.

7. This contract may be assigned by either party, and the assignee thereof shall have all the rights and remedies of the original parties hereto, but only as a whole, and neither party shall assign any part interest therein.

8. Six copies of the complete work will be furnished on publication to said W. B. Yeats by THE MACMILLAN COMPANY without charge.

[*remainder of contract typed*][2]

---

[2] The rest of the contract is specially typed because WBY and Watt had insisted on considerable changes to the original terms. On 17 May of this year Watt had written to George Brett (NYPL) that if, as he expected, he retrieved the rights to *The Shadowy Waters* and *The Wind Among the Reeds* (see pp. 64–6), 'one or two minor alterations' would have to be made to the draft agreement so that Macmillan would have rights to use them only in *The Poetical Works* 'and not any exclusive right such as it seems to me the present wording of your agreement would convey to you'. He suggested therefore 'that in Clause 1 the words "hereby grants and assigns to the Macmillan Co. a work, the subject or title of which is a collected edition" etc., should be altered to "hereby grants and assigns to the Macmillan Co. the right to print and publish a collected edition of the Author's poems and plays in two volumes" (I understood you to say when you were here that you would have no objection to adopting Mr. Yeats' proposal that the plays should be published in one volume and the poems in another.)'. Watt also thought it necessary 'that the words "that all abridgments, selections and rights therefore of the said work or parts thereof" should be deleted and also that the remaining portion of Clause 3 should be deleted'. He also confirmed that WBY wished to delete clause 11, as agreed with Brett the previous October. He asked Brett to send him a new copy of the agreement incorporating these changes, which he would at once submit to WBY for his signature. Brett made the alterations and returned the agreement to Watt on 29 May pointing out that Macmillan had made the changes requested 'excepting that we have not stricken out the first part of

9. After the sale of five thousand (5000) copies of said work The Macmillan Company agrees to increase the royalty provided for in Section 2 to fifteen percent (15%) on any further copies sold thereafter.

10. The increase in percentage of royalty provided for in Section 9 of this agreement is to apply also to the two books by the author entitled "Where there is Nothing" and "The Hour Glass" already published by The Macmillan Company under a separate agreement dated March 24 1903, such increase of royalty to take effect on the further sales of each volume after the sale of such volume has reached five thousand (5000) copies.

11. No other complete or collected edition of the works of said W. B. Yeats shall be published in the United States, and no separate editions of the works included in this collected edition, excepting of those already published, shall in future be published in the United States, excepting through The Macmillan Company.

12. Said W. B. Yeats hereby authorizes and empowers his agents, Messrs. A. P. Watt & Son, of Hastings House, Norfolk Street Strand, London, W.C., England, to collect and receive all sums of money payable to said W. B. Yeats under the terms of this agreement and declares that Messrs. A. P. Watt & Son's receipt shall be a good and valid discharge to all persons paying such monies to them. Said W. B. Yeats also hereby authorizes and empowers The Macmillan Company to treat with Messrs. A. P. Watt and Son on his behalf in all matters concerning this agreement in any way whatsoever.

THE MACMILLAN COMPANY.
George P. Brett President

Printed doc. Watt.

Section 3 as this is intended only to cover permission for the use of selections to be printed in school books, anthologies, or even in press notices and reviews in connection with the exploiting of the book and all such questions are decided with a view to the possible enhancement and widening of the knowledge of the author and his works in this country, and we think it much better to leave this section of the contract in; but if you prefer it taken out we are quite willing to have it taken out.' Watt forwarded this letter to WBY on 21 June, with the advice that they should 'avail ourselves of Mr. Brett's permission to delete the remainder of clause 3 as if we leave it in and he publishes or permits others to publish selections from, say "THE SHADOWY WATERS", we might thereby become involved in difficulties with Messrs. Dodd, Mead & Co., from whom we are asking and shall not obtain anything more than the right to include that poem in the collected edition'. He also pointed out that clause 11 as now drafted by Brett was 'quite new', and that while he had 'no objection to the first two lines of the clause', he did 'not see how you can agree with Mr. Brett that no separate editions of the works included in this collected edition, excepting those already published, shall in future be published in the United States except through the Macmillan Co.' He therefore advised WBY to delete the remainder of clause 3 and everything in clause 11 from 'and no separate editions of the works'. WBY obeyed the first of these instructions but, whether by intention or oversight, left clause 11 unamended, so giving the Macmillan Company greatly increased rights in his American publications. At this stage both Brett and Watt expected that both volumes would be issued in October of this year.

## To Patrick D. Kenny, [*late June 1905*]

Mention in following letter.
Saying that WBY will join his syndicate as soon as Kenny can produce a list of names which mean good work, and telling him that names which merely have the value of the usual Irish letter of recommendation will not do.[1]

## To Lady Gregory, *29 June 1905*

18, Woburn Buildings, | Euston Road,
June 29th, 1905.

My dear Lady Gregory,
I send you a card for the sake of the address. An effect of your book.[1] I wired to-day for that unlucky store number which I have lost for the second time. As I have not had an answer I suppose you are away. I shall go to the Stores and give your name, which I hope will suffice.[2] I am going to the theatre tonight with Mrs. Emery. The play is Pinero's "Cabinet Minister". She has orders.[3] I am afraid Forgail is going to be very very bad I am going to ask Mrs. Emery tonight if I dare get him by myself and set him speaking on a note. He has all the usual faults in an aggravated degree. He rushes up and down the scale merely because he thinks he must have variety, or because he cannot control his voice. I dont know which.[4] I have had further letters from

---

[1] Patrick D. Kenny (1864–1944) had emigrated from Mayo as a youth to become a labourer in England, but had put himself through a university course in economics, and returned to Mayo in 1901, where he quickly grew impatient with the political, social, and religious conformism he found there. In 1903 he became editor of the *Irish Peasant*, published in Navan, Co. Meath, and founded by James McCann, a wealthy stockbroker interested in industrial and agricultural development. After McCann's death in 1904 Kenny's editorial policy became more radical and secularist, following Michael Davitt's line that the Irish labouring classes should make common cause with the British working class. This was antagonizing the local priests and, increasingly, the Irish hierarchy, and Kenny was now evidently trying to establish a syndicate, composed of influential Irish men of letters, to back a new literary weekly magazine which would be more intellectually consequent and internationally orientated than the *Leader* and the *United Irishman*, and independent of clerical interference. Although wary of this initiative, WBY was apparently intrigued by the prospect of a sympathetic Irish journal at a time when the Dublin press was growing increasingly hostile towards him. In the end, Kenny was unable to raise enough financial support to launch the magazine.

[1] The card is untraced, but was presumably a complimentary reference to *Gods and Fighting Men*, published early the previous year.

[2] AG was arranging for a summer suit of undyed sheep's wool to be made for WBY through the Army and Navy Store, at which she kept a running account. She told him on 30 June (Berg) that Robert Gregory was 'going to send colour for your tie'.

[3] Sir Arthur Wing Pinero's four-act farce *The Cabinet Minister*, first produced in April 1890, was revived at the Haymarket Theatre from 1 June to 15 July. In this gentle satire on British class attitudes, the extravagant Lady Twombley falls into the clutches of a money-lending vulgarian and his social-climbing sister, but manages to save her reputation and the family fortunes by speculating on inside government information she has gleaned from her husband, the cabinet minister of the title. FF's 'orders' were complimentary tickets.

[4] See p. 118.

Kenny. He is very anxious to have your name for his Syndicate. He had thought when I saw him in Dublin that your version of "The Lay of the Great Fool" would be quite suitable.[5] I wrote saying that I would give him my name as soon as he could show me that he had a list of names which meant good work. I said that names which merely had the value of the usual Irish letter of recommendation would not do. He now writes that his not having my name would make it much more difficult for him to get such people as I would approve of. I think I shall have to give it to him on his own terms, not for the sake of his syndicate which I dont much believe in, but for the sake of his other projects. He tells me—this I imagine is private—that Mary Butler tried to hurry the project when he had only names of people like herself and tried also to keep the good writers out.[6] There was a row whether about this I do not remember—and he got her off the Committee and got himself into entire literary control. I will not make up my mind about what I shall do until tomorrow. I will write to him then, and let you know what I say.

Yours sny<br>W B Yeats

TLS Berg, with envelope addressed to Coole, postmark 'LONDON. W.C. JU 29 05'.

## To John Quinn, 29 June 1905

18, Woburn Buildings, | Euston Road.<br>June 29th, 1905.

My dear Quin,

I have been meaning for some days to write and thank you for your large share in the gift of the Chaucer. The book is a very great pleasure coming as it does just when I am setting out to read Chaucer. I have always thought it the most beautiful of all printed books.[1] The pictures have already raised

---

[5] AG was evidently contemplating a translation of the anonymous 17th-century Gaelic poem 'Laoidh an Amadaín Mhóir' ('The Lay of the Great Fool'), in which the valiant hero, who has gained his nickname because of his penchant for fighting armed men with his bare hands, and who has distant affinities with Sir Gawain of Arthurian legend, undergoes a test of fidelity to his host, who turns out to be his bewitched brother. AG would have found the Gaelic text and an English translation in John O'Daly's edition of *Fenian Poems, Second Series* in volume six of Transactions of the Ossianic Society (Dublin, 1861) and in the third volume of John Francis Campbell's *Popular Tales of the West of Ireland* (Edinburgh, 1862), but she did not persevere with the project.

[6] Mary Ellen Lambert Butler, later Mrs Thomas O'Nolan (1872–1920), journalist and short-story writer, was a regular contributor to the *Irish Homestead* and edited a column 'Eire Og' for the *Irish Weekly Independent*. Her popular collection of Irish stories *A Bundle of Rushes* appeared in 1901, and her one-act pastoral play *Kithe* was published in the *Weekly Independent* in May 1902. Although a cousin of Sir Edward Carson, she became a Daughter of Erin and a protégé of MG, and suggested the name of Sinn Fein to Griffith for his political movement.

[1] In late spring of this year AG and John Masefield had invited 'friends of Mr W. B. Yeats and appreciators of his work' to contribute £1 each towards the purchase of 'a book he has long wished to possess', the Kelmscott Press edition of *The Works of Geoffrey Chaucer* (1896). Their circular (Berg)

images of stage scenery, and one of them has made an important change in the setting of the Deirdre play.[2] I am busy rehearsing the Shadowy Waters for a performance under Mrs. Emery's direction at the Court Theatre. The Theosophists are paying the Piper as it is to be one of the entertainments at their Annual Convention. Of course this does not identify me with them in any way. They get the play from me as might any other manager. Mrs. Emery is to be Dectora, and will play it very beautifully. The Forgail is Farquharson who made a success as "Herod" in Wilde's "Salome". I am afraid he is going to be bad. He is over emphatic, and shoots his voice up and down the scale in a perfectly accidental way. I long to get him by myself and make him speak on a note day after day till he had got rid of accidental variety but I cannot do that as he is playing for nothing, or rather for the advertisement's sake, and would think he knew as much about it as I do. I have consented to the performance not because I think it a play I would like to be judged by, or because I thought it could be well played, but because it gives me a chance of making a lot of changes and testing them. I missed the rehearsals of the play or most of them when it was done at first, through being in America, and besides I did not know as much then as I do, now I want to get it right for Brett's edition, and for an edition here which I am trying to arrange.[3] I got your telegram and for that too thanks, but I got it in Ireland, where I had gone for the performances of "the

revealed that a 'fine copy (Mr Wickham Flower's) was bought at a recent sale, for £49, and is being kept for the purpose in the hands of Mr S. C. Cockerell'. As well as AG, Masefield, and Cockerell, other subscribers included the Hon. Maurice Baring, Una Birch, Wilfrid Blunt, A. H. Bullen, Lord Castletown, the Countess of Dufferin, Edmund Gosse, Robert Gregory, AEFH, Hugh Lane, C. G. Lawrence, Elkin Mathews, Mrs Alberta Victoria Montgomery, Gilbert Murray, William Orpen, John Quinn (who subscribed £10), Charles Ricketts, William Rothenstein, Charles Shannon, Cornelius J. Sullivan, the Duchess of Sutherland, Arthur Symons, R. C. Trevelyan, and Miss Williamson. The book (*YL*, 377) was for WBY's fortieth birthday on 13 June, and was presented at a small ceremony in which the Duchess of Sutherland, AG, Blunt, Symons, Rothenstein, Bullen, and Gilbert Murray took part. AG had informed Quinn in a letter of 28 June (NYPL) that she had given WBY 'the Chaucer in time for his birthday, & it was received with great joy & appreciation. I told him how large your share in it had been.'

[2] The Kelmscott Chaucer was lavishly illustrated with eighty-seven woodcuts after designs by the Pre-Raphaelite artist Sir Edward Burne-Jones (1833–98). Burne-Jones tended to choose the more noble and chivalric incidents in Chaucer's work and many of his drawings position the figures in carefully blocked architectural or formal settings, which, with flat back walls, short side walls, and wide floors, are often reminiscent of stage sets – their echoes of the shallow perspective of Quattrocento Tuscan painting coinciding further with the shallow Abbey stage. The illustration which caused WBY to alter the setting of *Deirdre* was probably that placed at the beginning of 'The Book of the Duchess', which depicts the narrator with Dame Fortune who is seated on a settle playing chess and leaning on a large wheel. The chess-playing scene in the play was to give WBY particular trouble, and he was to change it again in 1907 (see *VPl*, 353–8, 391–3).

[3] When WBY took Frank Fay to a dress rehearsal of *The Shadowy Waters* on 8 July, Fay, as he reported to AG on 10 July (Berg), warned him 'that I did not think its performance would benefit him or the play. Mrs. Emery frankly I did not like at rehearsal so well as Miss Walker, but I should have liked to see her performance. She was of course the only one in the picture. The others did not believe in the play and spoke the musical lines with colloquial inflection, and I was amazed to find them all "fluffy" (i.e. not knowing or unsure of their words).' The first production of the play had taken place in Dublin from 14 to 16 Jan 1904, while WBY was in America, although the INTS had revived it for him in a special performance on 26 Apr 1904. A revised version of the play was included in *Poems, 1899–1905*.

Land".[4] I imagine I wrote to you about that play and told you how beautifully played it was. The heroine's character is very unsatisfactory, and that mars the play a good deal, for its construction develops from her character. Colomb thinks he is getting that right now, but I doubt if he knows enough about the mind of women to do that for some years to come.[5] The play has been well liked and better praised though, this largely for non-artistic reasons, than anything we have done, except "Kincora". The people are not yet sufficiently deep in their new artistic education to understand what temperament is. The very elements in Synge, let us say, which make him a man of genius repel them and they like Colum for what is his defect. He has not yet much temperament. He does not pass the people through his imagination and creates the main elements of his art more out of the critical capacity than out of the emotional or imaginative. I felt rather the same about a good deal in Lady Gregory's Kincora. You felt that it was a wonderful tour de force a wonderful achievement of dramatic logic, considering the stubborn historical incidents that had to be brought together. You did not feel as one did in her <comedies> "Spreading the News" or as one will feel about a play she is writing now,[6] that only one mind could have made it and that everything has a colour and form and sound of that mind. Mrs. McBride writes to me that her case comes on definitely on the 29th July, but she doubts if it can be kept from dragging on till October.[7] Her husband has caused the delays, hoping I suppose that delay might give him a chance of some unexpected evidence. She seems to be quite easy in her mind and to have recovered her old serene courage. I imagine that this case will break up the old United Irishmen Group and I cannot say I am sorry.[8] I am hoping that by the mere force of circumstances she will be put into the centre of some little radical movement for personal freedom. The woman's question is in a worse state in Dublin than in any place I know, and she seems naturally chosen out by events to stir up rebellion in what will be for her a new way. I am always hearing stories of

[4] Quinn had telegraphed WBY on 13 June, congratulating him on his birthday. In a letter of 17 June (Himber, 75) he said he hoped it had reached WBY at 'the "psychological moment," I mean at your apartment at about ten o'clock in the evening, surrounded by certain of your friends and after you had had about two good drinks of Irish whiskey.'

[5] *The Land* dramatizes the effects of the Wyndham Act of 1903, which gave Irish tenant farmers the opportunity of purchasing their land, but suggests that emigration is caused not so much by the impoverishing effects of landlordism as by the dullness and harshness of Irish rural life. Ellen Douras, the heroine, 'slightly built, nervous, emotional', wants to emigrate to America for the excitement and opportunities it offers, and persuades her fiancé Matt Cosgar, the son of a neighbouring farmer, to go with her. Thus the land, won at last after years of agitation and sacrifice, loses its ablest inheritors.

[6] *The White Cockade*, a three-act comedy, first produced at the Abbey Theatre on 9 Dec 1905. Its plot centres on the farcically ignominious behaviour of James II after his defeat at the Battle of the Boyne, including his hiding in a barrel to escape enemy soldiers.

[7] In fact, the hearing was to take place on 26 July, as MG had informed him a few days earlier (*G–YL*, 207), although she correctly anticipated that things would drag on until the autumn (see p. 113).

[8] i.e. the group associated with Griffith and his paper the *United Irishman*, which MG financed and of which she was a director (see II. 510).

women who are bound in a worse way than where the clerical conception of life is less strong than in Dublin to drunken husbands. Fay comes in to me with tales of households where the chief effect of religion seems to be the duty of bearing as many children as possible to a man besotted with drink who hands his besottedness on in the blood. I think we are going to have a very active time in the next year or two in Dublin, and I count this case as one of the causes of disturbance. Of course I dont know in the least what she is thinking in this matter. I mean on the general question, but I think I know her well enough to be certain that she is thinking and that something will come of her thoughts. After all most powerful convictions have their roots in personal suffering. A man came to see me the other day with a proposal for a weekly literary paper of an advanced kind, but that project wont be ripe for discussion for some time and I am trying to make up my mind about him, and making—you will laugh—the necessary astrological calculations. Whether I throw my lot in with him depends at this moment on the view I take of a certain opposition of the Moon to Neptune.[9]

Yrs sny<br>W B Yeats

TLS NYPL, with envelope addressed to 120 Broadway, New York, postmark 'LONDON W.C. JU 29 1905'. Partly in Wade, 451–2.


## To *J. B. Yeats,* [c. *29 June 1905*]

Mention in letter from JBY, 1 July 1905.
Telling him that he is revising and condensing JBY's lecture into the form of an article,[1] and quoting from a letter from Arthur Symons praising Jack Yeats's illustrations.[2]

NLI.


[9] The caller was Pat Kenny (see previous letter). WBY wanted to see whether Neptune, which governs poetic inspiration, would be strengthened or weakened by the opposition to the moon and the houses, signs of the zodiac, and other planetary aspects which accompanied the opposition. The charts would determine whether throwing in his lot with Kenny at this particular time boded good or ill.

[1] This may have been JBY's Royal Hibernian Academy lecture on 'The Art Instinct', which WBY had attended on 29 Dec 1904 (see III. 691).

[2] Symons's letter is untraced, but evidently expressed his admiration for Jack Yeats's illustrations to Synge's series of articles 'In the Congested Districts', which were currently appearing in the *Manchester Guardian* (see p. 108). The editor of the paper, C. P. Scott, was also delighted with the series, and told Synge on 6 July (TCD): 'You have done capitally for us and with Mr Yeats have helped to bring home to people here the life of those remote districts as it can hardly have been done before.' Most of the fifteen sketches Jack Yeats drew for the articles are reproduced in Hilary Pyle's *The Different Worlds of Jack B. Yeats* (Blackrock, 1994), 129–33.

## To Henry G. O'Brien, *3 July 1905*

18 Woburn Buildings, | Euston Road. | London. | W.C.
July 3$^{rd}$,/05.

Dear M$^r$ O'Brien,
    I am very sorry, but I shall miss you, for I go to Ireland next Monday. I shall be back in the Autumn & hope to see you then.[1]

Yours sincely
W B Yeats

Dict AEFH, signed WBY; Pierpont Morgan.

## To Sydney Cockerell,[1] *[6 July 1905]*

18 Woburn Buildings
Thursday

My dear Cockerell,
    I know you will excuse my dictating this letter, but I have to spare my eyes all I can. I do not know how to thank you for the trouble you have been put to about the Chaucer. It is a book I have longed for for some years, indeed ever since it was made. To me it is the most beautiful of all printed books.[2] It is especially valuable to me just now, for I am to start reading Chaucer right through. I have never read him since I was a boy, and then not thoroughly. Just as one gets at certain times a desire for a certain kind of food or drink which the body needs, one desires things that the mind needs.

---

[1] O'Brien had evidently replied in a letter now lost to WBY's letter of 15 Feb, trying to arrange a meeting (see pp. 40–1). In fact the two men never did manage to meet.

[1] Sydney Carlyle Cockerell (1867–1962), former secretary to William Morris, was from 1900 to 1904 a partner of Emery Walker (1851–1933) in a process-engraving firm in Clifford's Inn. WBY had met him occasionally at William Morris's house in Hammersmith in the late 1880s, and the two became reacquainted on 25 May 1902, when he advised WBY on the setting up of the Dun Emer Press. The acquaintanceship turned into friendship in June of the same year (see II. 202), and WBY often turned to Cockerell for advice on the design of his books.

[2] On 29 Jan 1905 AG had commissioned Cockerell, who had been secretary of the Kelmscott Press from 1891 to 1896, to buy a copy of the Kelmscott Chaucer (see pp. 125–6): 'The truth is (*private*) I have never known W. B. Yeats wish for anything so covetously as for that book, and I think of getting 40 or 50 of his friends and admirers to give £1 each and give it to him (I buying it in the first place). I have given him no hint of this. His birthday is in June and I should at any rate by that time have made up the number. It would be a better compliment, I think, than a few large sums from a few' (*Friends of a Lifetime*, 268). To have found a copy for £49 was canny: in March 1901 a copy had fetched £80 at auction, quadrupling its issue price.

Three or four years ago, I had the need of Spenser and read him right through. Now it is Chaucer, a much wiser and saner man.[3]

Yours sincerely

W B Yeats

TS copy Indiana. *Friends of a Lifetime*, ed. V. Meynell (1940), 269.

## *To John Millington Synge, 8 July 1905*

18, Woburn Buildings, | Euston Road.
July 8th, 1905.

My dear Synge,

I shall know much more about the matter in a week or two as I have a German of my own on hands and have referred him to A. P. Watt. This German who is not your man, wants your one act plays but I suppose he will write presently.[1] There are one or two rules which you ought not to depart from. First and foremost you ought to give him a period of time, during which he must secure a publisher. John Murray makes it a rule and I believe only gives a few months, but my German asks for two years. He is however undertaking a big work for he wants to translate a number of plays, and arrange for their performance together. You, Hyde, Lady Gregory, myself Colum, in fact anybody whose name I give him is on the list.[2] I should think that six months while perhaps adequate to get a publisher in is inadequate to get a theatre in. The permission lapses should the translator fail to get a publisher. If he get a publisher I should give him a

---

[3] WBY had read the works of Edmund Spenser (*c.* 1552–99) intensively in the autumn and winter of 1902 while editing his anthology *Poems of Spenser*. This reading caused him to place Spenser at a moment of transition, when he conceived English culture and society as moving from a joyous Anglo-French inspiration to a sombre, moral and allegorical Puritanism. Geoffrey Chaucer (*c.* 1345–1400), unlike Spenser, WBY placed in the old medieval world, and in his radio talk of 1936 'Modern Poetry' he recalled (*E & I*, 491–2) praying as a youth 'that I might get my imagination fixed upon life itself, like the imagination of Chaucer'.

[1] Synge had written to his would-be translator Max Meyerfeld on 14 June along the lines suggested by WBY (see p. 108), and was now seeking further advice since on 3 July Meyerfeld replied (TCD) that he had reread *The Well of the Saints* 'and told its plot to the Manager of a Berlin theatre who seems to be willing to perform it'. He had 'also found already a publisher for the book', and now only lacked Synge's 'consent to the translation'. Meanwhile, WBY was negotiating with Dr Frank E. Washburn-Freund (b. 1878), playwright, art critic, and translator, about plays for a proposed German playbill. On 12 Sept Synge was able to write to WBY (*JMSCL* I. 130) that Meyerfeld had a publisher and that the play had been accepted by the Deutsches Theater, where it was produced on 12 Jan 1906 as *Der Heilige Brunnen*. On the following day it was published by S. Fischer Verlag.

[2] Freund did, in fact, seek rights in Synge's *In the Shadow of the Glen* and *Riders to the Sea* as well as WBY's plays, but the translations and productions never materialized.

term of years, say five—and I should ask for half profits, or a royalty that might be reasonably be expected to give you half profits. A royalty is always much the best arrangement but there may be difficulties in working it out, in a case of this kind.

I am looking forward to your new play with great expectations. There are very stirring rumours about your first act.[3] My poor play comes on tonight, Mrs. Emery is fine but the Forgail despicable. He made a success in Wilde's Herod, I did not like him, I thought he was not acting at all, but merely exaggerating personal peculiarities. I did not however like to put my opinion against that of Simmons and Max Beerbohm. I let Mrs. Emery engage him, and now I find that I was right. He exaggerated himself in Herod and in Forgail he merely abates himself. I think he is the most despicable object I ever set eyes on—effeminate, constantly emphatic, never getting an emphasis in the right place, vulgar in voice and ridiculous with a kind of feeble feminine beauty. The very sign and image of everything I have grown to despise in modern English character, and on the English stage. He is fitted for nothing but playing the heroine in Stephen Phillips' plays, a sort of wild excited earth-worm of a man, turning and twisting out of sheer weakness of character.[4]

Yrs sny<br>W B Yeats

P.S. Of course acting rights <as well as translating rights> should fall to the ground if translator fails to get a theatre.

TLS TCD. Saddlemyer, 69–71.

---

[3] i.e. *The Playboy of the Western World.*

[4] WBY had just seen Stephen Phillips's play *Almyer's Secret*, which, as Frank Fay (who accompanied him) reported to AG on 10 July (Berg), was performed by the Benson Company as a curtain-raiser to their production of *The Comedy of Errors*. Phillips (1864–1915), dramatist and poet, was born in Oxford. He studied for the civil service, but from 1885 to 1892 became an actor in the company of his cousin Frank Benson. He gained a sudden and resounding reputation in the late 1890s with his poem *Christ in Hades* (1897), and *Poems* (1898), and with his very popular poetic drama *Paolo and Francesca* (1900), which was followed by *Ulysses* (1902) and *Nero* (1906). His popularity disappeared almost as quickly as it had grown, and, although WBY was always sceptical of his talent, Rothenstein reports (*Men and Memories*, 283) that when he invited the two men to lunch, 'Yeats was in one of his best moods, and he and Phillips sat and talked for hour after hour until I, who had a dinner engagement, had to break up the party. In Phillips there was little of Yeats' nonsense, and but little of Yeats' poetic sense; but he had admirers, and his popularity made Yeats curious to meet him.'

## *A. P. Watt to Hodder & Stoughton, 12 July 1905*

12th July 1905.

Messrs. Hodder & Stoughton,
      27, Paternoster Row, E.C.

Dear Messers. Hodder & Stoughton,
    I am just in receipt of a letter from Mr. W. B. Yeats in which he writes:—
    "I want you to give notice to Messers. Hodder & Stoughton that I shall take back The Shadowy Waters at the conclusion of their term of years, that is to say early next year. I want you to find out how much they want for plates etc. and also how much they want to permit me to include the poem in my book with Bullen."
    In referring to the book with Bullen Mr. Yeats is I understand alluding to a complete edition of his books in several volumes which he is arranging to publish with Mr. A. H. Bullen and in which he wishes to include "THE SHADOWY WATERS".[1]

                I am,

                            Yours sincerely,

TS copy Watt.

## *To Florence Farr, 15 July [1905]*

at Coole Park, | Gort, | Co. Galway.
July 15

My dear Mrs Emery: I meant to write yesterday, for I have been afraid that I did not seem sympathetic enough about your accident. I had hoped to have some talk with you on Monday evening, or to get out to you on Tuesday and so learn how you were, but both became impossible. Please write and tell me for it must have been a great shock and I have been afraid that you may have been more shaken than you thought.[1] I brought the book

---

[1] Hodder & Stoughton had published *The Shadowy Waters* in December 1900, and held the English rights for five years from 1 Jan 1901 (see II. 577–80). They were, however, happy to surrender the book at once, as they made clear in an accommodating reply on 18 July (Watt): 'we shall be willing to let you have the stereotype plates and the stock (150 quires and about 40 cloth) of "Shadowy Waters" for the sum of £10. 10*s*. and are willing to deliver these to your order at once without waiting for the expiration of our terms of publication.' Watt strongly advised WBY to accept this offer.

[1] FF, despite her accident (the causes of which remain obscure), had apparently recited to the psaltery at WBY's Monday Evening on 10 July.

of Johnsons poems with me that I might send it to you. Shall I send it while you are away from home or wait till you get there again? One of the covers has got a little soiled, on the journey as I think, but I shall get a vellum cover put on it when I get to London again.[2] I am at work on *Shadowy Waters* changing it greatly, getting rid of needless symbols, making the people answer each other, and making the ground work simple and intelligible. I find I am enriching the poetry and the character of Forgael greatly in the process. I shall make it as strong a play as *The King's Threshold* and perhaps put it in rehearsal in Dublin again. I am surprized at the badness of a great deal of it in its present form. The performance has enabled me to see the play with a fresh eye. It has been like looking at a picture reversed as in a looking glass. When you went, Maclaggan, after another thrust at Narcissus (who "spoke the lines about holding a woman in his arms as if he were murmuring of his experiences in Piccadilly,") said "it was worth while having the play done well, well worth while, because Mrs. Emery was a delight. It was a great joy to hear her." Or some such words, even stronger words I think, which I cannot remember.[3] There is a good notice of the play—very well written—in 'To-day' where Synge and myself and Shaw are enumerated with Ibsen and Maeterlinck as great dramatists, you are commended for "fine imaginative power", and after you, Jules Shaw is praised with evident enthusiasm for his Aibric.[4] Lady

---

[2] *Twenty-One Poems* by Lionel Johnson, published on 21 Feb 1905 by the Dun Emer Press; see p. 49. FF had known Johnson, and she and WBY had used his poems when performing for the psaltery.

[3] Presumably the conversation about the performance took place at WBY's Monday Evening on 10 July; evidently WBY and his friends had given the unsatisfactory Farquharson the nickname 'Narcissus'. He would have spoken the lines about holding a woman in his arms in the character of Forgael (see *VP*, 749, ll. 53–5), although WBY was to cut them from the revised version of the play. Piccadilly was a notorious haunt of prostitutes. The reviewer in *Black and White* of this day (86) preferred the acting to the play, praising Farquharson as 'a strikingly magical Forgael', and adding that 'Miss Farr, whose charm of voice and manner are less familiar to London playgoers than they ought to be, delighted me as Dectora. Frankly, I am not particularly anxious to see The Shadowy Waters again.'

[4] In 'Drama: Ibsen and W. B. Yeats', the critic in *To-Day* of 12 July (328) stated that 'Every great dramatist, or dramatic poet of to-day—Ibsen, or Maeterlinck, or Bernard Shaw, or J. M. Synge, or W. B. Yeats—embodies a creed, an oracular pronouncement on life, in every play he writes.' He went on to say of *The Shadowy Waters* that 'this exquisite play, with all its tremulous and shadowy beauty, leaves us with the same tragical emotion as we obtain in "Hedda Gabler". Only, like a great religion, it leaves us with more hope. Miss Florence Farr, as Dectora, expressed with fine imaginative power the tumultuous warfare that is waged by the kingdoms of the world with the kingdoms of the next.' Julius ('Jules') Shaw (1882–1918) was the youngest brother of the musician and composer Martin Shaw (see III. 52 n., 326 n.). Although intended for the Church by his parents, he left Cambridge after a year to go on the stage, and was struggling to make his name with provincial fit-ups and occasional London appearances. He took secondary roles in plays produced at the Court Theatre from 1904 to 1907, appeared briefly with AEFH's Gaiety Company in Manchester, and on 11 Nov 1909 played Michael Byrne in the first production of Synge's *The Tinker's Wedding* at His Majesty's Theatre during a short engagement with Beerbohm Tree. His return to the West End, as the Detective in *Raffles* at Wyndham's Theatre, was cut short by the outbreak of the First World War; he joined the United Arts Rifles and rose

Cromartie[5] was I think really delighted with the Psaltery and when she comes here, which she does in August, I shall find if she could arrange for the Duchess of Sutherland to hear you.[6]

Yours ever
[*Signature torn off*]

Printed copy. Bax, 38–40; Wade, 453.

## To Florence Farr, [? *19 July 1905*]

at Coole Park, | Gort, | Co. Galway.
Wednesday.

My dear M[rs] Emery: I am glad you are so much better—you spoke to the Psaltery very well but I was afraid—not because you did not hide it—that you were worse than [you] pretended to me. I am changing *The Shadowy Waters* on almost every page and hope you will be able to play the new version—I think if you investigated however you would find that 'the beautiful poetry' was whenever you spoke and 'the irrelevant drama' whenever Farquisson did.[1] I am making Forgaels part perfectly clear and straightforward. The play is now upon one single idea—which is in these new lines—

from private to second lieutenant before being killed in the German offensive of March 1918. The critic for *To-Day* thought that his performance as Aibric 'was impressive and heroically delightful in its earnestness, its vigour, and its poetical suggestiveness'. Martin Shaw described him in *Up to Now* (1929) as 'a struggling actor who spent two-thirds of his time resting' (58) but also as a 'strong, impressive actor and a simple nature', who 'threw himself into all his parts and performed every stage action at rehearsal as completely as "on the night", so that anyone playing to him had to be very much on the *qui vive*' (10).

[5] Sibell Lilian, Countess of Cromartie (1878–1962), the niece of the Duchess of Sutherland, was an author whose works reflect her interest in the occult. In 1899 she had married Major Edward Walter Blunt-Mackenzie of Castle Leod, Strathpeffer, Ross-shire, and in 1902 she became a member of the Celtic Association. Her first book, *The End of the Song*, a collection of twelve Highland tales, appeared in 1904 (*YA4*, 282). She occasionally attended WBY's Monday Evenings, and he was to be her guest in Ross-shire in January 1906.

[6] Lady Millicent Fanny Leveson-Gower, Duchess of Sutherland (1867–1955), was an author, humanitarian, and friend of AG. One of the most fashionable of London hostesses, WBY frequented her salon during these years, and her patronage would have been of considerable advantage to FF. In 1904 WBY had contributed 'Old Memory' (*VP*, 201) to her anthology *Wayfarer's Love* (see III. 421–2).

[1] In a now lost letter, FF had evidently defended her protégé Farquharson against WBY's and his friends' censure.

"When the world ends
The mind is made unchanging for it finds
Miracle, ecstasy, the impossible joy
The flagstone under all, the fire of fires,
The root of the world."[2]

There are no symbols[3] except Aengus and Aedane and the birds[4]—and I have into the bargain heightened all the moments of dramatic crisis— sharpened every knife edge. The play as it was came into existence after years of strained emotion, of living upon tip-toe, and is only right in its highest moments—the logic and circumstances are all wrong. I am going to make some fine sleep verses for Forgael when he enchants Dectora and I have done a good bit where he sees her shadow and finds that she is mortal.[5] I have got into my routine here—always my place of industry. After breakfast Chaucer—garden for 20 minutes—then work from 11 till 2 then lunch then I fish from 3 till 5, then I read and then work again at lighter tasks till dinner—after dinner walk. To this I have added sandow exercises twice daily.[6] Today I break the routine sufficiently to bicycle over

---

[2] These lines, slightly amended, appeared in *Poems, 1899–1905* (*VP*, 227, ll. 100–4).

[3] The rewriting of *The Shadowy Waters* marks a significant stage in the shift in WBY's aesthetic away from the sometimes esoteric symbolism of the 1890s to the more Apollonian and objective style of his middle years (see III. 369–70, 372). In a letter to AE of 17 Aug 1899 he had stressed the symbolic nature of the play, believing that he might 'be getting the whole story of the relations of man & woman, in symbol,—all that makes the subject of "The Shadowy Waters"' (see II. 443). As he explained in the *Arrow* of 24 Nov 1906: 'I began *The Shadowy Waters* when I was a boy, and when I published a version of it six or seven years ago, the plot had been so often rearranged and was so overgrown with symbolical ideas that the poem was obscure and vague. It found its way on to the stage more or less by accident... and it pleased a few friends, though it must have bewildered and bored the greater portion of the audience. The present version is practically a new poem, and is, I believe, sufficiently simple, appealing to no knowledge more esoteric than is necessary for the understanding of any of the more characteristic love-poems of Shelley or of Petrarch. If the audience will understand it as a fairy-tale, and not look too anxiously for a meaning, all will be well.'

[4] The play was prefaced in its earlier and later poetic versions with an introductory poem, 'The Harp of Aengus', which retold the mythological story of Edain, her husband Midhir, and the Danaan god of love Aengus Og, who was accompanied by four birds formed from his kisses. Aengus rescues Edain, who is being persecuted by Midhir's first wife Fuamach, and builds her a house filled with flowers and with invisible walls. But Fuamach finds her and turns her into a fly, and for seven years she is blown about through Ireland. Forgael also tells this story in the body of the earlier versions of the play, as a symbolic parallel for his own quest for a transcendent love (*VP*, 749–50, 757, 762–3), but in the new version WBY allocates it to the sailors, thus diluting its symbolic significance into choric narrative (*VP*, 224, 228).

[5] In the early versions of the play Forgael's harp-playing enchants Dectora to a sleep in which she forgets her recently murdered husband (*VP*, 760–1), but in the revised version, although enchanted into forgetfulness, she does not actually fall asleep. In both versions Forgael is disappointed that Dectora is a human, not an immortal love, but in the later version this realization comes immediately (and more dramatically) after she has entered, when Forgael asks: 'Why do you cast a shadow? | Where do you come from? Who brought you to this place? | They would not send me one that casts a shadow' (*VP*, 235).

[6] Fred Muller, pseudonym Eugen Sandow (1867–1925), studied anatomy in his native Germany and resolved to perfect his muscular development on a scientific basis. After arriving in London in 1899, he defeated Samson, billed as 'The Strongest Man in the World', at the Aquarium and established a

to Edward Martyn's and dine there—I have therefore given up my fishing hour to writing.[7] M[rs] Ladenburg—the American who heard you on Monday week[8]—recited some of Brownings *Saul* after you left to show it would do for you. She thinks you should try it. You might do it something like the Homer. It would be a change with its resounding masculine music.[9]

I have sent you the Johnson.

Yours always<br>W B Yeats

Printed copy. Bax, 42–4; Wade, 454.

successful school of physical culture. His first book, *Physical Strength and How to Obtain It*, appeared in 1897. In the 'Calypso' chapter of *Ulysses*, Leopold Bloom resolves (II. 119) that he 'Must begin again those Sandow's exercises. On the hands down', and in the 'Ithaca' chapter the catechistical narrator describes the exercises (III. 1495), 'which, designed particularly for commercial men engaged in sedentary occupations, were to be made with mental concentration in front of a mirror so as to bring into play the various families of muscles and produce successively a pleasant rigidity, a more pleasant relaxation and the most pleasant repristination of juvenile agility'.

[7] Edward Martyn (see p. 46) lived in Tillyra (sometimes Tullira or Tulira) Castle, Ardrahan, situated about 4½ miles from Coole Park. Tillyra retained its Norman keep, but, to WBY's regret, the rest of the house had recently been 'improved' in a 19th-century Gothic style (see II. 43 n., 49).

[8] Mrs Emily Louise Stevens Ladenburg (1865–1937), the socially prominent widow of Adolf Ladenburg, a wealthy New York banker who was lost from a ship at sea in 1896, was a friend of AG. A horsewoman of note, she entertained extensively in London, where she was a favourite at the smartest social functions during the closing years of Victoria's reign.

[9] The dramatic monologue 'Saul' by the English poet and playwright Robert Browning (1812–89) is based on 1 Samuel 16: 14–23 and was first published in its complete form in *Men and Women* (1855). In the poem, the harpist David cures King Saul of an evil spirit through his music, and the fact that much of the poem is supposedly spoken to harp accompaniment no doubt suggested it as suitable for recitation to the psaltery. WBY evidently thought that it might provide a counterpoint to FF's rendition of William Morris's translation from *The Odyssey* 21. 419–23, the setting of which FF included in *The Music of Speech* (1909), accompanied by a description (12) of her recitation by H. V. Barnett: 'Her method of treating a fragment of Homer . . . began on a descending scale from the dominant in a minor mode, first enunciating the theme on the psaltery, and then uttering the noble syllables . . . to approximately the same notes; so the verse moved in drama and in tones whose lines of music really reproduced in sound the gravity and grace of an antique frieze until, at the close, the original theme reappeared, and with an intensity and beauty of effect that cannot be described the speaking song was replaced with by the veritable singing song. Than this, nothing could be more impressive.'

## To an unidentified correspondent, *19 July* [*1905*]

Coole Park, | Gort, | Co. Galway.
July 19

Dear Sir—
I send you a little scrap of verse, I generally get £2 for such a thing.[1]
Yrs sny
W B Yeats

Dict AG, signed WBY; Fales.

## To William Robertson Nicoll, *22 July* [*1905*]

Mention in following letter.
Discussing the terms whereby Hodder & Stoughton will surrender their rights in *The Shadowy Waters*.[1]

---

[1] This probably refers to 'Do Not Love Too Long', which WBY had originally intended for the *Green Sheaf* (see p. 48, n. 5). Now that that magazine had folded, he took the opportunity of sending it to the *Acorn*, which was being planned as a illustrated magazine, devoted to literature and art. Because the poem was slight, and left unexpectedly on his hands, and since the *Acorn* was a new and struggling publication, issued by the Caradoc Press which had published his *Cathleen ni Houlihan* in October 1902 (see III. 183, 236), he may have kept the price down to the fee he was charging six years before (see II. 420). It appeared in the first number of the *Acorn* in October 1905, but the magazine folded after its second number in February 1906.

[1] Dr (later Sir) William Robertson Nicoll (1851–1923), clergyman, publisher, and man of letters, had been literary adviser to Hodder & Stoughton since 1886. After giving up his Free Kirk ministry in Kelso in 1885 he came to London, and the following year founded the *British Weekly*, a Nonconformist journal which soon built up a wide circulation, and in 1891 the *Bookman*, a literary monthly aimed at the general reader. He had a high opinion of WBY, who reviewed regularly for him from 1892 to 1898: 'Mr. Yeats is a great genius, and everything he writes merits the attention of all true lovers of poetry. He is so original, so wonderful, so profound, that he cannot be analysed.... I remember the pride with which I published in the "Bookman" ... some of his finest lyrics, along with not a few of his subtle criticisms.... Mr. Yeats has his own way. He is too kind to despise anyone. He listens to advice with the utmost patience, but he follows his star' (*Irish Book Lover*, Oct–Nov 1919, p. 16). In 1900 Nicoll and WBY negotiated about the possibility of Hodder & Stoughton taking over all WBY's books, but in the end the only book of his that they published was *The Shadowy Waters* (see II. 528, 545, 556–7). This had not been an overwhelming success, and WBY was seeking to regain copyright so that he could transfer it to Bullen. In fact, the letter to Nicoll was unnecessary, since Watt had already received a very reasonable offer from Hodder & Stoughton about the surrender of the book (see p. 132, n. 1).

## *To A. P. Watt, 22 July [1905]*

Mention in letter from A. P. Watt, 24 July 1905.
Enclosing a letter to William Robertson Nicoll,[1] discussing the terms whereby Hodder & Stoughton would surrender their rights in *The Shadowy Waters*, discussing whether he or Watt should deal with the Society of Authors in the dispute with John Lane over *The Wind Among the Reeds*, and asking Watt to send him the correspondence with Lane and Mathews over the book.[2]

TS copy Watt.

## *To A. P. Watt, 28 July [1905]*

Coole Park | Gort, Co Galway
July 28

Dear Mr Watt,
I have just received your letter of the 18th sent on from my London address. I should not have written to Dr Nicoll if I had seen it. It seems to me a very fair offer, and if you still think I should close with it please do so. Am I to send a cheque to you or to Hodder and Stoughton?[1]

Yr siny
W B Yeats

[1] Watt replied that 'So far as I am aware, there is no reason why your letter to Dr. Robertson Nicoll (by the bye, he spells his name without an h) should not go on and, presuming you would wish me to do so, I have accordingly posted it to him this afternoon.'

[2] WBY had evidently suggested that Watt should negotiate with the Society of Authors in the dispute with John Lane over *The Wind Among the Reeds*, but Watt replied: 'I think, however, it would be better for you to deal with them direct in the John Lane affair and, under these circumstances, and in accordance with your request, I send you herewith all the papers of yours which I have here and which so far as I can see have any bearing upon the matter.' He also advised WBY not to 'bother about applying again to Lane. I think the sooner the Society of Authors are instructed to deal with him the sooner the matter will be settled to your satisfaction.' WBY had known John Lane (1854–1925), antiquarian and publisher, since the late 1880s, shortly after he set up the Bodley Head with Elkin Mathews in 1887. The firm published the two Rhymers' Club anthologies and many of WBY's contemporaries, and, after the partnership broke up in 1894, Lane kept the Bodley Head imprint. He opened a New York office in 1896, and had the American rights to *The Wind Among the Reeds*.

[1] For the misaddressed letter of 18 July, from Watt see below, p. 141. It informed WBY that Hodder & Stoughton were willing to sell him the plates and stock of *The Shadowy Waters* for 10 guineas.

[*In other hands*]
What answer was sent to this?
You asked Yeats to send you a cheque on July 30 & he answered that
Mr. Bullen would send it.

TLS Watt. Date-stamped 'A. P. WATT AND SON ?29 JUL 1905 LONDON'.

## To A. H. Bullen, 28 July [*1905*]

Coole Park | Gort, Co Galway
July 28

My dear Bullen,
    I have just had the enclosed from A. P. Watt sent on from London. To
save time I have told him to close with it, and that I will advance the money
(£10.10). If you think it is a fair sum I hope I shall get it back from you.[1]
Possibly we might put the old copies on the market through the new Dublin
firm.[2] I have practically re-written the Shadowy Waters. I have simplified it
greatly and strengthened the character motives. I should say that another
couple of weeks will suffice to get it and probably the rest of the material
ready for the new book. I suppose you have got the arrangement with Elkin
Matthews into black and white by this time. Sidgewick told me you agreed
to it.[3]
    I wont do the Shakespeare article for you. My mind is not on Shakespeare
at present, and I might very possibly have to upset all my habits to get it
there.[4] A chance such as seeing the historical series of plays which Carr is
going to bring out might set me thinking of Shakespeare, but one cant
count on such things.[5] I imagine I'll be reading nothing but Chaucer for

---

[1] See previous letter. Bullen offered to pay the 10 guineas direct to Hodder & Stoughton.

[2] Maunsel & Co. did not, in fact, issue *The Shadowy Waters*.

[3] Negotiations between Bullen and Mathews over *The Wind Among the Reeds* (see pp. 115–16) were
far further from settled than WBY supposed, and those with John Lane even less advanced.

[4] Bullen had evidently asked WBY to contribute to his ten-volume *Stratford Town Shakespeare* (see
p. 88, n. 7), the last volume of which contained essays by Shakespearian scholars.

[5] Philip Carr followed up his policy of reviving Elizabethan and Jacobean drama (see pp. 3, 90) by
announcing a cycle of Shakespeare's History Plays, but there is no evidence that these productions were
ever mounted.

A Burne-Jones illustration for the 'Wife of Bath's Tale' in the Kelmscott Chaucer.

some time to come. By the bye I dont think I ever thanked you for your share in giving me a big Kelmscott book. I like it all, it is a delight, even 'The picture of the Wife of Bath', which by the bye is not the Wife of Bath at all but a person in her story, 'the loathly damsel' of the folk-lorists, and very good at that.[6]

Yrs sny
W B Yeats

[6] In Chaucer's *Wife of Bath's Tale*, a squire is saved from execution by an ugly crone in return for a promise of marriage, but when he offers her 'mastery' in the marriage she turns into a beautiful young woman. Burne-Jones drew three illustrations for the tale: two depict the old woman as emaciated and wrinkled, with straggling hair and tattered clothes; the third shows her transformed into a naked and beautiful young woman. Bullen evidently found the first two drawings distasteful and had erroneously taken them to represent the Wife of Bath herself, whom Chaucer describes as ample in figure and flamboyantly dressed: 'Bold was hir face, and fair, and reed of hewe. . . . and on hir heed an hat | As brood as is a bokeler or a targe; | A foot-mantel about hir hipes large.' WBY may have first come across the wide-spread motif of the 'loathly lady', the hag who transforms into a beautiful young woman when the hero sleeps with her, in the Irish tale of 'Niall of the Nine Hostages', in which the encounter also wins Niall the High Kingship of Ireland.

[*With enclosure*]

18th. July 1905.

W.B. Yeats Esq:
  18, Woburn Buildings,
    Euston Road, N.W.

Dear Mr. Yeats,
    As the result of my further negotiations with Messrs. Hodder & Stoughton you will be interested to know that I am this morning in receipt of a letter from them in which they write:—
    "With reference to your letter we write to say that we shall be willing to let you have the stereotype plates and the stock (150 quires and about 40 cloth) of 'Shadowy Waters' for the sum of £10. 10 s. and are willing to deliver these to your order at once without waiting for the expiration of our terms of publication."[7]
    Personally, I think this is a proposal which you would be well advised to accept and on hearing that you agree with me I will write to Messrs. Hodder & Stoughton accordingly.
    With kind regards,
                    Believe me,
                              Yours sincerely,
                              A. S. Watt[8]

TLS Kansas. Partly in Wade, 456–7.

## *To Stephen Gwynn, 30 July* [*1905*]

at | Coole Park, | Gort, | Co. Galway.
Sunday. July 30

My dear Gwynn: I am very sorry but I dont like your play. It makes me doubt very much if power as a novelist often goes with dramatic power. You struggle—as it seems to me—to do something which your very talents

---

[7] See p. 132, n. 1. Bullen offered the copies to the Irish market, splitting the profits with WBY, but in January 1907, 140 copies of this 'exceedingly attractive book' were still being offered to the trade at 2*s.* a copy, and in June 1907 Bullen (Bodleian) tried to sell the remnant to Elkin Mathews at 1*s.* a copy, although the deal fell through when Mathews refused to offer more that 7*d.* a copy.
[8] Alexander Strahan Watt (d. 1948), A. P. Watt's son and a partner in the agency.

unfit you for doing. It is all too scattered—the first act is not even essential—It merely tells the audience what they all know & there is little new in the way of telling—your imagination is hampered by an unfamiliar medium.[1] Worst of all there is no characterization—Emmet might be any young man[2] & Sarah any young woman[3] while MacNally is a bundle of external tricks of mind & one unexplained purpose. He would do for a minor character, though he would not be good, but when he is made a principal, we want to know why he was an informer—how he explained things to himself. It should be his play for the rest are shadows & would have to be born again to be anything else.[4] Think what Browning would have done with

[1] Stephen Gwynn (see p. 87), who had already published a number of novels, including *The Repentance of a Private Secretary* (1898), *The Old Knowledge* (1900), and *John Maxwell's Marriage* (1903), had turned his hand to playwriting. Perhaps as a result of this letter, he wrote no more plays, but went on to produce further novels, numerous biographies, and books on Irish travel, literature, and society, as well as a volume of *Collected Poems* (1923) and an autobiography, *Experiences of a Literary Man* (1926). In 1940 he edited *Scattering Branches*, a tribute to the memory of WBY.

[2] Robert Emmet (1778–1803), United Irishman, was born in Dublin and educated at Trinity College, where he was a friend of the poet Thomas Moore. He was forced to leave Trinity in February 1898 because of his association with the United Irishmen, and he went to Paris where he met Talleyrand and Napoleon, the latter persuading him that a French invasion of England was imminent. He returned to Dublin, where he collected arms and built up an impressive organization, which was to mount a rising in collaboration with the French. An accidental explosion at his ammunition factory on 16 July 1803 led to the rebellion beginning prematurely, and, without the planned assistance, it collapsed in less than a day. Emmet avoided capture, but refused to leave Dublin until he had seen his fiancée Sarah Curran, and he was captured on 25 Aug. His speech from the dock at his trial—which concluded 'When my country takes her place among the nations of the earth, then and not till then, let my epitaph be written'—became one of the most famous and influential Irish patriotic speeches of the century. He was executed on 20 Sept 1803.

Emmet was a popular subject for Irish and Irish-American playwrights (see the *Irish Book*, Spring 1963, pp. 53–7); as early as 25 July 1902 Frank Fay had told WBY (*LWBY* I. 101) of 'the *necessity* for having a play on "Robert Emmet"', and said that he had suggested the subject to Colum. The 'necessity' was the centenary of Emmet's execution, and although Colum did not oblige, the Cumann na nGaedheal had produced Henry Connell's specially commissioned *Robert Emmet* with WBY's *Cathleen ni Houlihan* on 2 Nov 1903. Although Gwynn's play, which he began in the summer of 1904 (see III. 600), was never published or produced, his historical novel *Robert Emmet* appeared in 1909, the year in which the Abbey staged *An Imaginary Conversation* (between Emmet and Thomas Moore) by Norreys Connell. Further plays about Emmet performed at the Abbey include Lennox Robinson's *The Dreamers* (1915) and *Summer's Day* by Maura Molloy (1935).

[3] Sarah Curran (1782–1808), daughter of the lawyer and orator John Philpot Curran, was secretly engaged to Emmet, but was disowned by her father when the romance became known. Their tragic love story is the theme of Thomas Moore's lyric 'She is far from the land'.

[4] Leonard MacNally (1752–1820), playwright, editor, lawyer, and informer, was one of the first members of the Society of United Irishmen, and appeared in court in defence of Tone, Emmet, Tandy, and other leaders, only to receive large sums from the British government to betray them. Although his betrayal of Emmet was never proved, he was given a secret service pension of £300 per annum from 1798 to his death, and Gwynn portrayed him as an informer in his novel *Robert Emmet*, confessing in a note (330) that this was his own invention: 'Who gave to the Castle the secret of his [Emmet's] hiding-place is not known and perhaps never will be. The reward of £1,000 was paid on Nov. 5th to Finlay & Co., for the account of Richard Jones. It has been conjectured that the name (which certainly is an *alias*) hides MacNally: I have simply made a theory of how MacNally could have acquired the knowledge. This much is certain: Government contemplated bringing forward MacNally.'

him.[5] Not only is he not characterized but you yourself are left out of the play. It is a series of external events. There is no psychological principle—no subject in the artistic sense. Try & forget it is history—say this is a story I have invented & then ask yourself why you invented it. What is the Universal idea it has been made to express. Think of it as a fable told to a child & you will find that the fable as you tell it is nothing. Then the patriotic bits at the end do not seem to me to me dominated by any artistic purpose—they are merely political. Probably you have allowed yourself too many plans, too many people & have there[fore] not got to any one unifying idea. I am very sorry to write all this & I wish you would send the play to Synge & ask him what he thinks. You need not tell him my opinion but beg him to be perfectly sincere.[6] Of course if you like I will send it on to the Committee but it seems to me that you may wish—should Synge not like it let us say—to withdraw it 'for revision' or on some other excuse. As it stands it would not do you credit or us credit, & I would have to vote against it.[7] I had a great desire for it for the subject I thought would help a play of the kind to a perhaps great popular success—but after reading it very carefully I am certain that all I can do is write to you very candidly as I hope you would write to me under similar circumstances.

Yrs ev

W B Yeats

ALS Private.

[5] Robert Browning was famous for his interest in the intricacies and contradictions of psychological motivation, as he himself acknowledges in the final lines of his poem 'A Light Woman'. As a young man WBY had been moved by his 'air of wisdom' (*Aut*, 81), and in an obituary notice praised him for his 'dramatic method' (*LNI*, 27), which he put down to his interest in life: 'To Browning thought was mainly interesting as an expression of life. In life in all its phases he seems to have had the most absorbing interest; no man of our day has perhaps approached him there.' WBY had recently been reintroduced to Browning's poetry by Mrs Ladenburg (see p. 136).

[6] Gwynn evidently took WBY's advice, for *c.* 21 Aug 1905 Synge described the play to WBY (*JMSCL*, 125) as being 'too near the conventional historical play and has too much conventional pathos to be the sort of thing we want'.

[7] The Reading Committee of the INTS comprised six members and vetted all plays proposed for performance. No play could be performed unless it had been recommended by the Reading Committee, but the final acceptance or rejection of any play thus recommended rested with the members of the Society, 'to whom such plays shall be read at meetings summoned for the purpose, when a three-quarters' majority of those present shall decide'. After these rebuffs from WBY and Synge, it is unlikely that Gwynn submitted his play to the Reading Committee.

## *To Arthur Symons,*[1] *3 August 1905*

Coole Park | Gort. Co Galway
August 3. 1905.

My dear Symons,

I have been awaiting with a great deal of expectancy your Wagner Essay and would be very much obliged for the proofs if you still have them.[2] I have asked Heinemann to send you a little volume of translations from Petrarch by a Miss Tobin that I met in San Francisco. I think them very delicate, very beautiful, with a curious poignant ecstasy, and would have written about them but for my ignorance of Italian. One feels a sort of pathetic interest in books of good poetry, as if they were waifs in the street with tragic stories. One wishes to send them to some benevolent home where they will get a little encouragement. Miss Tobin did another book from Petrarch a year ago, and that too was beautiful. Of course there are bad lines, one may read through a whole poem and find very little now and then but there is nearly always a line or a half line with the true ecstasy.[3]

I am rewriting the Shadowy Waters, every word of it. I let them play it in London and an execrable performance it was except for Mrs Emery, and

---

[1] Arthur William Symons (1865–1945), poet and critic, had been a fellow-member of the Rhymers' Club, and dedicated his influential study *The Symbolist Movement in Literature* (1899) to WBY. He became WBY's best friend during the mid-1890s and the two shared rooms in the Temple during the winter of 1895–6. WBY greatly admired Symons's literary judgement, and the two remained close until Symons's severe breakdown in September 1908.

[2] 'The Ideas of Richard Wagner' appeared in the *Quarterly Review* for July 1905 (73–108) and was reprinted in Symons's *Studies in the Seven Arts* (1906). In an extended review of Wagner's *Prose Works*, biography and letters (thirteen volumes in all), Symons argued that the German composer's fundamental ideas are contained in two early essays, 'The Art-work of the Future' and 'Opera and Drama'.

[3] Agnes Tobin (1864–1939), poet and translator, was the daughter of a prominent banker in San Francisco, where WBY had met her in January 1904, a meeting he recalled with pleasure in his article 'America and the Arts' (*UP* II. 338–42). On that occasion she sent him her first book of Petrarch translations, *Love's Crucifix* (1902), introduced by Alice Meynell, who 'discovered' her in 1895, and which WBY described in a letter to her of 7 Feb 1904 as 'full of wise delight — a thing of tears & ecstacy' (III. 546). Her new book of translations from Petrarch was *The Flying Lesson*, published by William Heinemann in May 1905; WBY had seen the MS and suggested emendations to two of the poems (MBY), but she did not adopt them. Heinemann evidently sent *The Flying Lesson* to Symons at once, and on 14 Aug he wrote to his friend Henry Hutton (Harvard) about her. He was to meet her at a garden party given by Violet Hunt in the summer of 1906 when she paid a visit to England and the two became close friends; on 13 Nov 1908 she said that she had 'loved him as if he were my own child' (Beckson, 261). In his *Confessions* (1930) he describes her (60–2) as 'bright, warm-hearted, very talkative, very amusing; she had an extraordinary charm. And wherever she went, her attraction was so curious that she was not only at home, but that one always felt at home with her.... She was very dainty; she had a droll way of telling stories; she was full of joy and laughter, she was very capricious.'

another, that I might find out what was wrong. Farquharson who seemed good in Herod was unendurable as Forgael. One friend of mine who came to the dress rehearsal said 'What is wrong with that man. I want to rush out of the theatre'. A part of the wrong was that he tried to play as if he were a woman, with little airs and graces, and an affectation of feebleness, standing with his knees together and so on. For the first time in my life I shuddered as I suppose the ordinary man shudders at everybody and everything that is called decadent. It was the Greek Hermaphrodite with a very Cockney voice. I told the company that I thought Farquharson would show himself very especially gifted if he would play the heroines in Stephen Phillips' plays.[4]

I believe I am making a really strong play out of the Shadowy Waters and am certainly losing no poetry. It is the worst thing I ever did dramatically and partly because it was written when I knew very little of the stage and because there were so many old passages written or planned before I knew anything that the little I did know could not pull it into shape.[5] We are going to have a fine season at our theatre here. Lady Gregory has done a very original play, at once merry and beautiful, and Synge is finishing a long and elaborate work.[6]

Yours always
W B Yeats

*[In WBY's hand]*
Remembrances to M^rs^ Symons—[7]

TLS Texas. Wade, 458–9.

---

[4] WBY knew that Symons admired Farquharson (see p. 118), and this perhaps accounts for the insistence of his denunciation. The heroines in Stephen Phillips's plays tended to be highly strung, attitudinizing, and histrionic; apart from *Almyer's Secret*, which he had just seen (see p. 131, n. 4), WBY had also attended a performance of Phillips's *Herod* in December 1900. He was fully aware that Symons despised Phillips and had provoked a public controversy by denouncing his poems and plays in the *Quarterly Review* of April 1902, where he asserted (498) that 'this work is neither original as poetry nor genuine as drama' (see III. 190–1). The friend at the dress rehearsal was Frank Fay (see p. 126, n. 3).
[5] See pp. 102–3, 106, 126. WBY had begun *The Shadowy Waters* in the mid-1880s, long before he had any experience of the stage. He took it up again after the production of *The Land of Heart's Desire* in 1894, but it went though many versions before its first publication in 1900 and, as this letter indicates, was substantially altered thereafter. The tortuous history of its composition has been admirably traced in *Druid Craft*, ed. M. J. Sidnell, G. P. Mayhew, and D. R. Clark (Dublin, 1972).
[6] *The White Cockade*, see p. 127, n. 6. Synge was working on *The Playboy of the Western World* (see p. 28, n. 5), not produced until 1907, which he described to Max Meyerfeld on 12 Sept 1905 (*JMSCL* I. 130) as 'an ironic comedy about a man who kills his father I will send it to you when it is finished as I would only give you a false idea of it if I told you the plot'.
[7] Symons married Rhoda Bowser (1874–1936), daughter of a Newcastle shipbuilder, on 19 Jan 1901, and they were now living at 134 Lauderdale Mansions, Maida Vale. Most of Symons's friends (including WBY) found her extravagant and difficult (see II. 586–7).

## *To A. P. Watt, 3 August [1905]*

Coole Park | Gort, Co Galway
August 3

Dear Mr Watt,

I have had a letter from Mr Thring of the Society of Authors[1] in which he says 'There is an additional document which is doubtless obtainable viz a letter from Elkin Matthews to Mr Watt of 27 Jan 1902—but it may be unimportant'.

Have you got this letter.[2]

Bullen has offered to pay the £10-10 for Hodder and Stoughton and I am writing to him to send it to you.

Many thanks for the accounts which I shall send back in a couple of days.[3]

Yrs sny
W B Yeats

TLS Watt, date-stamped 'A. P. WATT AND SON 5 AUG 1905 LONDON'.

[1] George Herbert Thring (1859–1941) had been secretary of the Incorporated Society of Authors since 1892. His letter is untraced, but refers to the tortuous agreements over *The Wind Among the Reeds* (see II. 114–16, 156–8; III. 151–2, 550–1, and p. 65) which had been a three-way source of dispute between WBY, John Lane, and Elkin Mathews.

[2] Watt had, as he reminded WBY in his reply to this (Watt), included Mathews's letter of 27 Jan 1902 in the batch he had sent on 24 July (see p. 138). The letter in question read: 'This book—together with "The Shadowy Waters" was promised to me in 1894 (shortly after Mr. John Lane left me) and I included both in my Autumn Catalogue of that year as "In preparation"; and they continued to be announced in this way until 1899 in the Spring of which year I published "The Wind Among the Reeds", having agreed to give up "The Shadowy Waters".' Mathews went on to say that at 'this late date (1899) an Agreement was drawn up and approved by Mr. Yeats and it was posted him for his signature, however, he wrote to say that he had lost or mislaid it'. WBY's carelessness was now costing him dear, especially since Mathews alleged that he had only advanced a few brief notes of the transaction which indicated that WBY should receive £12 in advance, that he should get a royalty 12½% and half profits in the American rights, and that the agreement was 'to hold for *5 years* from date of publication'. He maintained that these were the terms originally agreed upon in 1894, and that WBY had endorsed them on publication of the book in 1899. He further pointed out that there were 'more than two years of the term to run', at the end of which he 'might be willing to increase the royalty'. Mathews's 'notes' were evidently inadequate, since he misrepresented the draft agreement—which had probably been sent to WBY in early May 1897, not 1899 (see II. 114–16)—in a number of ways. This agreement (Reading) gave Mathews the 'exclusive right' to print and publish the book 'in Great Britain its colonies and dependencies, in the United States . . . and in English on the Continent of Europe', with a royalty of 12½% on the published price and half profits in the American rights. Apart from excessive proof corrections, Mathews was to bear all the costs of production, publication, and advertisement. WBY could not transfer the rights of translation without Mathews's consent, accounts were to be rendered every six months, and the copyright was to remain WBY's property. Significantly, the agreement was to hold for three years from the date of publication and could be renewed in three-yearly periods, while either party could give three months' notice of its termination at the expiry of any such period. Besides dating the agreement two years late, Mathews also, conveniently, noted that it was to run for five years, not the three years in fact stipulated. This draft agreement was never signed by WBY, and was superseded by the arrangement he made with Lane to print the book in America and to supply sheets to Mathews for the English edition (see II. 156–8).

[3] These are untraced.

## *To Charles Elkin Mathews, 3 August* [*1905*]

Coole Park | Gort. Co. Galway

Aug 3

My dear Matthews,

I have received the enclosed letter from the Society of authors,[1] and also another which says:—'assuming that Elkin Matthews told John Lane what his contract with the author was, which he doubtless did, John Lane's term expired when Elkin Matthews did'. You are my sheet anchor, and I will be very much obliged if you would write to Lane for the accounts. You will see that not only did A. Watt but the Society of Authors consider that you are the fitting person to do this, the agreement being with you. I will be very much obliged if you will do this at once, as I want to get my collected American edition out in the autumn. Please return me the Society of Author's letter.

Yrs sny

W B Yeats

TLS Leeds.

## *To A. H. Bullen, 3 August* [*1905*]

Coole Park | Gort, Co Galway.

August 3.

My dear Bullen,

Certainly I never meant those words 'I wont do the Shakespeare Essay' to be rude, I wrote as if I was talking to you, forgetting that what is a friendly petulance when spoken becomes when the tone of the voice isn't there mere brusqueness. I dictated at a great speed walking up and down the room, and forgot that you weren't there listening to me. I should like to have done it for you, but I have Samhain notes ahead of me and some other things, and my imagination is getting so deep in Chaucer that I cannot get it down into any other well for the present.[1]

---

[1] See previous letter. Both letters from the Society of Authors are untraced. Mathews was reluctant to write to Lane, not only because they had quarrelled more than ten years before, but also because it was in his own interest that Lane should retain the rights to the book for as long as possible, so that he could continue to issue English editions. Poems from the book were finally included in vol. 1 of the Macmillan edition of *Poetical Works*.

[1] See p. 139; Bullen's letter of remonstration is now lost, but in April 1929 WBY recalled the incident when writing to Lennox Robinson (Southern Illinois): 'I dictated to somebody in Museum Street a letter to A. H. Bullen, and received a letter from him a few days later asking what had changed me so,

I am very much obliged for what you say about the Hodder and Stoughton arrangement. You say 'if you like I'll pay the ten guineas to Hodder and Stoughton and go half profits with you over the stock'. Would you mind sending the ten guineas to A. P. Watt. They are making the arrangements. I shall be contented with anything you do about the stock.[2] There are a certain number of bound copies. Lady Gregory would like a dozen of these, but you should let her have them at the ordinary shop discount. She says she wants to give them to "admirers of mine who come to see the seven woods".[3]

I am still going through that heavy marsh, the Shadowy Waters.

Yours always
W B Yeats

TLS Kansas. Partly in Wade, 457.

## *To George Russell (AE), 3 August [1905]*

Coole Park
Aug 3.

My dear Russell,

Fay has written to me about his conversation with you upon the Theatre. I think the scheme he sketches out with you seems to be a workable basis. I wish you would go into it more fully with him and make a clear draft.[1]

that hitherto I had been a very polite person but now etc, etc. I remember writing to him very vehemently that he must not mistake the great cheerfulness which comes to a man who dictates for mere vituperation.' The 1905 number of the occasional theatre review *Samhain* was to appear in November of this year, and contained eleven pages of notes by WBY, which, like the offending letter to Bullen, were dictated in a hurry, and, as WBY thought, with something of the same consequences: 'A few years ago . . . my eyesight got so bad that I had to dictate the first drafts of everything, and then rewrite these drafts several times . . . but this time I am letting the first draft remain with all its carelessness of phrase and rhythm. I am busy with a practical project which needs the saying of many things from time to time, and it is better to say them carelessly and harshly than to take time from my poetry. . . . After all, dictation gives one a certain vitality as of vehement speech' (14; reprinted in part in *Expl*, 201).

[2] See p. 139. Hodder & Stoughton had originally published *The Shadowy Waters* in two editions (1900, 1901); the revised version was published in vol. II of *Poetical Works* (1907).

[3] The play in its 1900 and 1901 editions had been prefaced by WBY's poem 'I walked among the Seven Woods of Coole' (*VP*, 217–19).

[1] W. G. Fay's letter is now lost, but indicated that the implementation of the reforms decided upon at the INTS meeting of 18 June (see p. 120) had begun. In the end they were to lead to the radical

Anything that you and he agreed on would I have no doubt be acceptable to Lady Gregory and myself, and it would be far more likely to pass than if I had had a hand in it. You could let us see it, and we could go to Dublin for the General Meeting that would decide upon it.[2] The essential thing is to get some sort of scheme which will enable Miss Walker and Frank Fay to be paid.[3]

Lady Gregory has been hoping to hear you were coming here, and asks me to say she still hopes to see you. Is there any chance you could come this or next week when some disciples of yours, Lady Cromartie and another will be here?[4] I am so glad you and Fay seem near a solution of this question. I think it would be a pity to go bungling on through another Session, with the constant chances of friction that arise.

Yrs sny

W B Yeats

TLS Indiana.

## *To Florence Farr,* [? *4–5 August 1905*]

at Coole Park, | Gort, | Co. Galway.

Friday night.

My dear M<sup>rs</sup> Emery: I was about to write to you to-day, when I was sent off to catch perch for some catholics who are to dine here to-night—a fast day.

restructuring of the Society, and to the secession of many of its original members (see Appendix). The attempt to establish a permanent company after the acquisition of the Abbey Theatre, and the desire to mount British tours, had put a strain on what was still an amateur society, and WBY, AEFH, and W. G. Fay were convinced that the existing rules would have to be revised to produce a clearer division of responsibilities and to permit the payment of some of the leading players. AE was less certain about W. G. Fay's part in the Company and, marking his reply of 4 Aug '*Private & Confidential*', began by imploring WBY to 'regard this letter as confidential & not to be shown to any other member of the Theatre Society except Lady Gregory. My last conversation with you was repeated to Fay with the usual row at committee following.'

[2] AE, who had drawn up the original *Rules of the Irish National Theatre Society* in 1903, and who was more popular than WBY among the actors, was reluctantly persuaded to revise the constitution, leading to the registration of the new Limited Society on 24 Oct 1905. He took a more radical line than WBY and in his reply revealed that he had 'come to the conclusion that if the actors are to be paid the whole society must be put on an entirely different basis'.

[3] Maire Walker worked for Yeats's sisters at Dun Emer Industries in Dundrum. Frank Fay was a clerk in a firm of Dublin accountants.

[4] For Lady Cromartie see p. 134. Lady Margaret Sackville (1881–1963), daughter of the 7th Earl De La Warr, was a poet and dramatist whose first volume, *Poems*, had been published in 1901. Encouraged by Wilfrid Blunt and WBY, in 1903 she edited the *Celt*, a short-lived magazine 'Devoted to Irish Interests'. WBY met her frequently in London, and in 1909, influenced by WBY's theories of verse-speaking, she founded the Poetry Recital Society.

Isn't that a medieval way of getting a meal?[1] I stayed out till I had caught six fish, enough for a dinner—and now the mail has gone. I am very sorry about your hurts—I am afraid you must have suffered a great deal and I think it was heroic of you to play the Psaltery that night. I am making a new play of 'the Shadowy Waters'. It is strong simple drama now, and has actually more poetical passages. Aibric is jealous of Forgaels absorption in his dream at the outset and ends by being jealous of Dectora. Instead of the sailors coming back drunk at the end Aibric comes to appeal to Forgael to go back to his own land but on finding that he is taken up with Dectora bursts out in jealousy. Forgael bids Dectora chose whether she will go back to her own land or not and she chooses to go on with him—then Aibric cuts the rope and leaves them. This gives me a strong scene at the end.[2] I wish you could get a good verse speaker who is a man. I wish I could persuade you that you are mistaken over Farqusson. I have been taken in in the same way more than once myself. When a young man has even a slight vulgar element—and it is not slight in Farquson—one thinks it will leave him as he grows older I thought that about Le Galleon—who had what seemed like genius. It never leaves them, but when the enthusiasm of youth is over it gets much stronger till finally all else has left them.[3] I have never known an exception. Apart from all else Farquson is a man who always requires to be explained. M[rs] Shakespear[4] for instance thought his

[1] Not a special fasting day; Catholics were forbidden to eat meat on any Friday.

[2] The end of the new version of *The Shadowy Waters*, in line with the changes that WBY had made to the rest of the play (see pp. 133–5, 145), is more dramatic. In the early version (*VP*, 765–9), Aibric makes a brief final appearance but does not address Dectora or Forgael. After he has left to board the captured galley for home, Forgael urges Dectora to follow him, but she insists on remaining and cuts the ropes between the two ships. The revised version is as WBY describes here (see *VP*, 247–52).

[3] Richard Thomas Le Gallienne (1866–1947), poet, essayist, and novelist, was an original member of the Rhymers' Club and a frequent contributor to the *Yellow Book*. He had left England for America in October 1903 and from 1930 settled in the south of France. He was to give his own account of the 1890s in *The Romantic '90s* (1925). With the looks of a matinée idol, and a facility for artificial romantic verse, he had enjoyed great popularity in the early 1890s, when WBY had cultivated his acquaintance (see I. 249, 320–1, 346, 400–1), but his novel *The Quest for the Golden Girl*, with its coy hints of sexual improprieties and petticoats, is the product of naughtiness rather than decadence. As a reviewer for the *Star* and reader for the Bodley Head, he also exercised considerable literary power, and WBY had been careful to keep in with him; in February 1938, however, he was to tell Edith Shackleton Heald (Harvard) that 'Le Galleane was an over sexed sentimental goose, with no taste'. WBY's nickname for Farquharson (see p. 118) may have been suggested by this association of types, for Le Gallienne had published *The Book Bills of Narcissus* in 1891.

[4] Olivia Shakespear, née Tucker (1864–1938; see I. 511–12), married Henry Hope Shakespear in December 1885, and met WBY in 1894, through her cousin Lionel Johnson. During his brief love affair with her in 1895–7, WBY wrote 'He Bids his Beloved be at Peace' and other poems to her, and she appears as 'Diana Vernon' in *Aut*. After a period of estrangement they had become friends again in 1900

manner was personally very offensive to you off the stage. He is really impossible as an artist. I had to use the greatest self control over myself all through those rehearsals. Only my fear of making things difficult for you kept me quiet.

I want you to try and get me Paget's model for the *Shadowy Waters* scene. I will probably work out a scene for Dublin, which could be used by you if necessary. Our stage is nearly as big as the Court. I can probably get that harp made too—we have carpenters and so on of our own now.[5] We are in all likelihood to have a large scene dock next door this winter and will be able to work things out very perfectly.[6] You must come over some time and see our scenery, when the show comes off. You will I think prefer it to Craig. It is more noble and simple.[7]

Saturday.

I have an idea for a bicycle trip when I get back. I have my imagination full of Chaucer and would like to hire a bicycle and go the journey of the Canterbury pilgrims from Southwark and Greenwich to Canterbury through Rochester. I do not see why we should not go with some harmless person to keep up appearances.

Tell me if you try *Saul* and if you try *The Daughters of Jerusalem*. I doubt of the long grave poems like *Dark Angel* having enough internal movement

(see II. 529), and she had recently collaborated with FF on two Egyptian plays (see III. 121, 177). Her daughter Dorothy married Ezra Pound in 1914, and her brother Henry Tudor Tucker married Mrs Edith Ellen Hyde-Lees, whose daughter George became WBY's wife in 1917.

[5] Henry Paget had designed FF's production of *The Shadowy Waters* (see p. 95), but the revised version of the play was not produced at the Abbey until 8–15 Dec 1906, when it was designed by Robert Gregory. The Abbey stage was 15 feet deep, but its working space was restricted by badly placed beams. For the glowing harp, which was included in the revised version (*VP*, 239), see p. 95 and p. 102.

[6] Plans had been in hand since June to convert the old City Morgue, which adjoined the Theatre, into a much needed space for storing the accumulating scenery (see p. 119) and the architect Joseph Holloway worked on the project throughout the autumn.

[7] WBY did not long persist in this view. Edward Gordon Craig (1872–1966; see III. 697–9), illegitimate son of the architect Edward William Godwin and the actress Ellen Terry, was an actor, producer, author, editor, and stage designer whose symbolic scenes and lighting effects were greatly to influence WBY's dramaturgy. He had first seen his work in the Purcell Society productions of *Dido and Aeneas* and *The Masque of Love* in April 1901, and praised it in the *Speaker* of 11 May 1901 as 'the first beautiful scenery our stage has seen'. WBY's admiration continued, and in 1911 he was to commission Craig to make special screens for the Abbey Theatre to replace more conventional scenery. Since August 1904 Craig had been working in Berlin, where he was making a considerable reputation— Max Reinhardt and his assistants visited his studio to gather ideas for the Deutsches Theater—and where he published *The Art of the Theatre* later this year. Distressed by the contemporary state of London stage design, he was working on the new methods that he was to expound in *The Artists of the Theatre of the Future* and *The Actor and the Uber-Marionette* in 1907, and in his periodical the *Mask*, which he launched in 1908.

for the Psaltery.[8] One wants changes of voice—even different speakers at times—and choral bits for singing. The danger of the Psaltery is monotony. A thing the antients were more alive to in all arts than we are—Chaucer for instance follows his noble *Knight's Tale* with an unspeakable tale told by a drunken miller. If Morris had done the like—everyone would have read his *Earthly Paradise* for ever.[9] By the by Chaucer in that same unspeakable tale calls a certain young wife 'white and small as a weasel'. Does it not bring the physical type clearly to the minds-eye? I think one wants that sort of vivid irresistible phrase in all verse to be spoken aloud—it rests the imagination as upon the green ground.[10]

I have had a cold for some days and that is why my writing is so bad and my spelling.

Yours ever
W B Yeats

Write soon. Lady Cormartie and Lady Margaret Sackville arrive next week. I will find out what can be done for the Psaltery.[11]

Printed copy. Bax, 40–2; Wade, 455–6.

[8] For Browning's 'Saul' see p. 136. Lionel Johnson's 'Christmas', in which 'daughters of Jerusalem' is a recurring phrase, appeared originally in *Ireland with Other Poems* (1897) and was included in WBY's recent selection of *Twenty-One Poems*, which he had sent to FF (see p. 136); Johnson's most celebrated poem, 'The Dark Angel', from *Poems* (1895), was also included there.

[9] Chaucer's *Knight's Tale* is a story of courtly love, in which two squires joust to the death for the love of Emelye according to the chivalric code. In the bawdy *Miller's Tale*, an Oxford undergraduate convinces a carpenter that a great flood is imminent in order to seduce his wife but is branded on the backside by another of her admirers. The Pre-Raphaelite poet, artist, and craftsman William Morris (1834–96) had published his long poem 'The Earthly Paradise', based on Greek and Norse legends, in 1868. Writing of Morris in *Aut* (142), WBY asserted that his lack of verbal vitality was the fault of the age: 'if style and vocabulary were at times monotonous, he could not have made them otherwise without ceasing to be himself. Instead of the language of Chaucer and Shakespeare, its warp fresh from field and market—if the woof were learned—his age offered him a speech, exhausted from abstraction, that only returned to its full vitality when written learnedly and slowly.' Morris had admired Chaucer throughout his life and, addressing him as 'Master' at the beginning of Book 27 of his poem 'The Life and Death of Jason', acknowledged the inferiority of his own poetic gifts: 'Would that I | Had but some portion of that mastery | That from the rose-hung lanes of woody Kent | Through these five-hundred years such songs have sent. . . . O Master, pardon me, if yet in vain | Thou art my Master, and I fail to bring | Before men's eyes the image of the thing | My heart is filled with.'

[10] WBY's slightly inaccurate recollection of Chaucer's description of Alison, the young wife in *The Miller's Tale* (ll. 3233–6): 'Fair was this yonge wyf, and therewithal | As any wezele hir body gent and smal. | A ceynt she werde, barred al of silk, | A barmcloth eek as whit as morne milk.'

[11] WBY was hoping to persuade Lady Cromartie to interest her socially influential aunt, the Duchess of Sutherland, in taking up FF and her recitations to the psaltery.

## To George Russell (AE), 7 August [1905]

Coole Park | Gort, Co. Galway
August 7.

My dear Russell,

   I think your scheme is very workable, if all the actors will agree to become associates or honorary members.[1] This will leave in the Society proper Lady Gregory Synge, myself, yourself, Colum, Keller, Norman, Ryan, Miss Layard (unless she counts as an actor) & S. Gwynn[2] which gives us more than enough for the purposes of the act.[3] I feel strongly however against any obligatory filling up of vacancies. I have been thinking over names, and the more I think of them the more undesirable does it seem to increase what would necessarily be the least efficient element in the Society. One might add one or two, possibly Boyle for instance if he goes on well,

---

[1] AE's letter of 4 Aug (see p. 149, n. 1) had put forward far-ranging proposals for reforming the INTS: 'Roughly the plan is this. The actors of the future should cease to be members. They may be put in a class as associate members elected & reelected yearly. They will have no votes. The Society will consist of authors and such people as may be admitted up to the number of twenty. We will have to consider how this can be done later. The reading committee as at present will have full powers of considering plays, accepting rejecting & fixing the order of production. A new executive committee of three will be appointed to have sole charge of the business & financial side of the society's work.' He went on to explain that these changes were essential because the business of the Society was 'abominably managed': 'Minutes are not signed, letters not attended to, accounts abominably kept. This must all be changed. I suggest a paid secretary & bookeeper, who might either be an actor if any one of them was found competent, or else an accountant in Dublin who might like to add ten shillings or seven shillings weekly to his salary. The latter for preference if it could be managed.'

[2] This division between actors and non-actors in fact masks a social distinction; those whom WBY mentions here were all from the middle or professional classes, whereas most of the actors were working-class. Thomas Goodwin Keohler (1874–1942), solicitor, poet, theosophist, and a member of the Society since 1901, was, like H. F. Norman and Helen Laird, among those who were to secede from the Abbey in December 1905 and form the Theatre of Ireland in 1906. His *Songs of a Devotee* (1906) was second in the series of Tower Press booklets (1906–8), and AE had dedicated *The Divine Vision* (1904) to him. His account of 'The Irish Theatre Movement' appeared in the Dublin *Sunday Independent* of 6, 13, and 20 Jan 1929. Henry Felix Norman (1868–1947) edited the *Irish Homestead* from 1899 to 1905 and was a member of the Dublin Theosophical Lodge. He was a close friend of both AE and Keohler, whom he introduced to each other. Frederick Michael Ryan (1873–1913), rationalist, socialist, agnostic, and journalist, acted as secretary of the National Theatre Society from 1903 to 1904 and treasurer from 1904 to 1906. His Ibsenite play *The Laying of the Foundations* had been produced on 29 Oct 1902, and in 1904 he co-founded the magazine *Dana* with 'John Eglinton'; see p. 295. Helen S. Laird (1874–1957) was a teacher at Alexandra College, and a founding member of the INTS, for whom she acted under the name of 'Honor Lavelle'. She played Maurya in the first production of Synge's *Riders to the Sea* in February 1904, and later this year she was to marry Constantine Curran (1874–1957), the friend and intimate enemy of James Joyce. For Colum and Gwynn see pp. 28, 87–8.

[3] The INTS was registered as a Specially Authorized Society under the Friendly Societies Act of 1896, and at this point AE was attempting to amend the rules in accordance with that Act. When this proved unworkable, the Society was turned into a limited company, and radically new rules were drawn up under the Industrial and Provident Societies Act of 1893. These were later amended to comply with the Companies Consolidated Act of 1908.

but more probably not.[4] We could not add anybody unless we were quite sure they would leave us independent as to politics and religion. Meanwhile I am not quite satisfied with the list of names as they stand. You say you are anxious to resign so we cant count on you.[5] I think you will agree that Synge, Lady Gregory and myself and Colum are the four whose interests are most involved and who are putting most of their lives into the work, and who know most about it. You saw yourself however that Colum is too impressionable at present to make his opinion of much value. This leaves only Ldy G. Synge, myself, with perhaps Stephen Gwynn, face to face with Miss Layard, Keller, Norman, Ryan, with a possible Colum. This will probably mean irritating discussion and a balance of power in favour of the least efficient. If we could think of people to add with the normal amount of education (this really very important) and an abnormal interest in the theatre, it would set things right. But I cant think of anybody at the moment except Robert Gregory, who ought to be on as scenic artist. If Miss Layard and Norman and Keller would agree to become honorary members or associates like the others, that would go near giving us a capable body. I am not really afraid that the workers wont get their own way in the end under any arrangement, but what I do shrink from is the waste and worry of continual discussion, I doubt very much if the suggestion made in your postscript is workable. I understand your postscript to mean that only the actors who are paid should become associates or honorary members.[6] I see two objections to this. First, it makes an invidious distinction between amateur and professional, as if there was something

---

[4] William Boyle (1853–1923) was born at Dromiskin, Co. Louth. He began his career as a teacher, but subsequently joined the customs and excise department of the civil service, and spent his working life in Britain. He was a member of the Irish Literary Society, London, and in 1904 submitted a three-act comedy, *The Building Fund*, to the Abbey Theatre, where it was produced on 25 Apr 1905 (see p. 40). Although WBY disliked Boyle's work, his three plays, including *The Eloquent Dempsy* and *The Mineral Workers*, both produced in 1906, were among the most popular at the Abbey. Boyle withdrew them after the *Playboy* riots in 1907, but he returned to the Theatre in 1909. He was never a member of the INTS.

[5] Although, following the success of his play *Deirdre* in 1902, AE planned to write further plays, little came of it and in August 1902 he wrote to WBY (Denson, 43) that he had 'escaped from my brief folly of play writing'. He had declined the presidency of the INTS in 1903 in favour of WBY, although he agreed to become one of the vice-presidents, an office he resigned in April 1904 after a disagreement over the rights to his work (see III. 576, n. 2), although he remained as an ordinary member of the Society until later this year. In his letter he told WBY that if the ideas he proposed were not carried out he would resign from the society, that he had too much other work to attend to, and that he had nearly resigned a year ago but stayed on at Fay's urging.

[6] In a postscript to his letter AE had suggested that 'a rule might be put stating that any actor who is paid or any official who is paid should cease to be a member but would be eligible for associateship. This would obviate the difficulty of asking them to resign & as they could all be paid a small sum after a performance they would all be shifted in to associateship and the society fill their places by carefully selected people like Stephen Gwynn who might turn up from time to time. Please let me know what you think.'

disgraceful about being paid. Second, it would be precisely those who are most in earnest about their art and who know most about it who would accept payment. Those who are only trifling with it would keep on their other occupations, and be therefore under no compulsion to accept it. This would swamp us with the inefficient when any matter came up for a vote. I doubt of your ever getting all the actors to accept some kind of nominal payment, and even if you did it seems a pity to base their retirement from authority on their being paid. I think it would be better for everyone if they would retire for the sake of the great work itself. Of course one might be able to muddle on as we are for another year or so. But it is a serious thing to make any of our people give up their present settled way of living without assuring as far as possible the stability of the body they take service under. If we can only get the thing right Miss Walker and Frank Fay will be put into the way of earning their living at work they are supreme in instead of drifting through life ingloriously at work they do not care for, or sacrificing their health by trying to do both.[7] If we are to go to the country, and that is most necessary, we must free others, and this cannot be done without putting the theatre on a business foundation. One must bear in mind the end in view in any change we make. One can only get efficiency in any organization by as rigorous an application as is compatible with the circumstances, of the old saying 'the tools to him who can use them'.[8] Every ineffective or unnecessary member is like flesh where there should be muscle. I am greatly obliged to you for taking so much trouble in a matter where you are not vitally interested. You have so much influence over several of our members that nobody else can set things right.

Yours snly
W B Yeats

TLS Indiana.

[*A TLS fragment of a first draft of the above letter is among the Lady Gregory Papers in the Berg Collection*]

[7] See pp. 120, 149. AE himself had long been worried by the state of Maire Walker's health, and on 21 Apr of this year had reported to AG (Berg) that her doctor thought her on the verge of a breakdown and that she could either continue working at Dun Emer Industries or in the theatre, but not both. 'You might consult with W.B.Y', he suggested, '& see if the funds of the theatre could stand Miss Walker being employed at some salary which would release her from the necessity of work during the day.... She is too important a member of the company to lose through ill health. There is nothing immediately serious but Dr Maguire told me she would certainly break down if she went on.'

[8] WBY may have come across this saying in Carlyle's essay on 'Sir Walter Scott' (*Critical and Miscellaneous Essays* [1838]): 'To the very last he [Napoleon] had a kind of idea; that, namely, of *La carrière ouverte aux talents*, The tools to him that can handle them'. Or he may have found it in *What the World Wants* by the would-be playwright Grace Moore, with whom he had recently corresponded (see p. 57): 'The tools fall to him who can handle them' (96).

...in the hands of the literary element. But this would be a counsel of despair. Can you suggest anything else? The present method leads to constant annoyance and quarrelling. These quarrels seem to me to originate with the least efficient elements, but they spread to the others. It may be necessary to cut off the least efficient, and to take others in their place who will not be members at all, till they have gone through a probationary period. This would put us again into a bad period, for some of the less efficient have still their uses. Roberts for instance will never be a good actor, but he is sometimes a useful one. My belief is that the efficients if the others were not there to excite them would always put up with Fay's roughness for the sake of his great qualities.[9] Everything in life is had at a price. The pity is that if we can only get the thing right Miss Walker and Frank Fay will be put into the way of earning their living at work they are supreme in instead of drifting through life ingloriously at work they do not care for, or sacrificing their health by trying to do both. If we are to go to the country, and that is most necessary, we must free others, and this cannot be done without putting the theatre on a business foundation.[10] I agree with you that the constitution you drew up for us was the only one possible under the circumstances, but the circumstances are now quite different.[11] If the members would give up their objections to the actors paying themselves &c we could muddle on as we are for a bit with possibly some change in the business committee. But I dont think it could be anything else but muddling. Three or four people should be in control if there is to be efficiency. It is a serious thing to make Frank Fay let us say, give up his present settled way of living without assuring as far as possible the stability of the body he

---

[9] Both Fays had a reputation for bad temper and aggression, partly based on their temperaments and partly because their insistence on professional standards seemed mere bullying to the less committed members of the Company. AE, present at a row during a rehearsal of his *Deirdre*, prophesied that 'the National Theatre Society will go down in a sea of fists' (*Dublin Magazine*, Oct–Dec 1949, p. 16); on 25 Oct 1905 Holloway remarked (NLI) that Frank Fay was 'like a bear with a sore head when out of temper', and on 4 Jan 1908 W. A. Henderson told him that Willie Fay was 'very hard to get on with': 'his uneven temper was the cause of all the actors' troubles since the beginning of the Company. He lacks tact, and is too rough of tongue at times to be tolerated. Such is the general opinion of those who worked under him in the company.' In his letter AE insisted that 'Fays duties must be strictly defined in an agreement. If I had confidence in him I would not insist on the executive committee from whom he must take instructions & to whom he will be responsible. But I find he uses his position as stage manager to bully people who don't agree with him. For example because Miss Walker voted against something he wanted he told her he would give her no more parts. Now that sort of thing must be put down.' He pointed that Fay could only rely on the support of his brother Frank and Sara Allgood in the society, and that he did not think 'besides these any of the actors would sign an agreement which left them artistically in his hands. The business committee & executive will be the court of appeal in case of disputes or the President & Vice Presidents could act in this way. The present committee is hopeless.'

[10] It had always been one of WBY's ambitions to tour plays in the country districts of Ireland and in 1901 he had seriously considered founding a touring company (see III. 69, 72).

[11] i.e. the constitution of 1903; see Appendix.

takes service under. I am very much bothered over the whole thing, not seeing any solution at the moment except the violent one from which one shrinks a great deal. Once we have a stable nucleus however small, those who want to act or to write will attach themselves to it. We are at the beginning of a great task which will take years but at the same time it would be very hard if we lost the result of past work through an actor or two dropping out. I cant imagine any other mind but your ingenious and practical one getting us out of the hole.

Yrs snly<br>
W B Yeats

[*In WBY's hand*]
PS. I have re-read your letter & notice for the first time the significance of this sentence "They could all be paid a small sum . . . . & could all be shifted into associateship". I see therefore that you have not contemplated making an 'invidious distinction'. This seems to me a solution if all would agree 'to accept' payment & if we were not bound to fill up vacansies except very slowly.[12]

TDS Berg.

## To George Russell (AE), [9 August 1905]

Coole Park | Gort, Co Galway<br>
Wednesday 9th

My dear Russell.

I am in full agreement with your general plan. I think the business committee might be four which would work all right with the Chairman's casting vote.[1] As a matter of fact things very seldom come to a division at all on a small committee. The committee I should like would be Gwynn, Keller, and Starkie and myself. Starkie is a man in [whose] personal

---

[12] The proposal that 'certain members' should be paid was passed unanimously at the General Meeting of the Society on 18 June 1905 (Harvard), and finally all the acting members were paid, although jealousies over pay differentials contributed significantly to the split in the Society.

[1] Under the 1903 rules the Management Committee consisted of seven members, elected at the Annual General Meeting, and controlled the business arrangements of the Society, including all 'questions relating to the payment of money and the terms on which engagements may be entered upon'. The stage manager was, ex officio, a member of the Committee. Under AE's proposed amendments the Management Committee was reduced to five, of whom the president (but not the stage manager) was to be one. In the final version the Management Committee was replaced by a Board of Directors of not less that three or more than five.

character I have the greatest possible trust;[2] and if one had somebody like Keller or Ryan to help one out with actual business information <he> would be a valuable member. I should particularly like Starkie because he is a highly educated man. It is agreed on all hands Stephen Gwynn is the best secretary the Irish Literary Society ever had. He was very energetic and careful when he had the charge of our London visit.[3] I dont think I should like both Keller and Ryan, though I should be quite happy with either, but that is a detail and not a vital one. I quite agree with you that the members have all put their time and work into the society, but just in so far as they have done so they will feel that the prosperity of the movement is a vital matter and they will be ready to sacrifice themselves for it. I think they will all see that it would be very unfair when the Fays sacrifice themselves by giving up executive power for the good of the movement, executive power being very dear to William Fay, for Roberts and Miss Garvey to remain in a

---

[2] James Sullivan Starkey (1879–1958), poet, editor, and essayist, wrote under the pseudonym of Seumas O'Sullivan (his mother's maiden name). Born in Dublin, the son of a pharmacist with literary tastes, he was educated at Wesley College, Dublin, and spent a year at the Catholic University, but, failing his examinations in medicine, left to work in his father's shop. He was a founding member of the INTS, and took over P. J. Kelly's parts after the latter's expulsion from the Society in 1904, although he never considered himself a good actor. On 30 Sept 1904 he joined the Theosophical Society, and in the same year revived the Dublin publishing firm of Whaley, through which he published AE's *The Mask of Apollo*, and his own first book of poems, *Twilight People*, which appeared early in 1905. In February 1905 Gogarty wrote to G. K. A. Bell (*Many Lines*, 72) that 'Yeats thinks well of Starkey's book', and Arthur Symons wrote to praise it on 19 Feb (TCD). Starkey remained a lifelong bibliophile, and in 1905 became editor of The Tower Press booklets series, in which he published his own *Verses: Sacred and Profane* (1908). In 1923 he founded the *Dublin Magazine*, which he continued to edit until it folded in 1958. He published two collections of literary and biographical essays, *Essays and Recollections* (1944) and *The Rose and Bottle* (1946), the second of which contains an essay on the early days of the INTS. He and WBY were to fall out at the end of this year. In his reply of c. 10 Aug (Berg), AE pointed out that, although he admired Starkey as much if not more than WBY, he was not eligible to sit on the business committee: 'He has been an actor & on the proposed change would if he continued an actor become an associate & it is part of the scheme that no actor Fay or anyone else should be on any Committee of Management though their presence might be advisable at times for their views. We cannot make exceptions as it would lead in time to the old state of things. Separate actors, authors & business.'

[3] Stephen Gwynn had been secretary of the Irish Literary Society, London, from 1901 to 1904 (when he returned to Ireland), and in that capacity had helped organize and financially guarantee the immensely successful INTS visit to London on 2 May 1903, when it produced five plays at a matinée and an evening performance at the Queen's Gate Hall. Although suffering from ill-health, he also played a major part in arranging the visit of March 1904 to the Royalty Theatre, on which, largely through his efforts, the Company made a profit of £80. AG wrote to George Roberts shortly afterwards (Harvard) that he and Gwynn must feel rewarded for all their organization: 'What a splendid success last Saturday was: I feel quite elated at my belief in the Company being so fully justified, & the dignity of Ireland having been materially helped by the strong quiet, convincing work of its play writers & actors.' As a mark of its gratitude, the Society arranged a *conversazione* for Gwynn on 25 April 1904 at which they played *The Kings Threshold* and *The Shadowy Waters*. That autumn WBY suggested that Gwynn (who had signed the letter of the INTS accepting the Abbey Theatre from AEFH) should be elected a vice-president of the Society as 'a well deserved compliment'.

position to supervise the action of the Fays.⁴ I am sure if you put this to them they will do what is right. We have really a very great movement on our hands, and they would be the last people not to do what seemed right in its interests. Of course after a few years things may be different.

It is a very complicated business and requires a great deal of tact, that is why we are leaving it to you. I am just going out fishing.

Yrs sny

W B Yeats

TLS Indiana.

# *To J. B. Yeats,* [c. *10 August 1905*]

Mention in an undated letter from JBY, 'Friday' [? 11 August 1905]. Asking for details of the latest crisis at Dun Emer,¹ enquiring about the relationship between ECY, Evelyn Gleeson, and Dr Henry,² and

---

⁴ Roberts's energy as secretary of the Society made his position tantamount to that of a business manager. He had done a great deal to organize the London tour of 1904 and was assiduous in liaising with AEFH. Maire Garvey was one of the original members of the INTS, an accomplished actress, and a forceful personality. She was to marry Roberts in 1910, and they were already evidently working as a team.

¹ JBY had evidently written to WBY in a letter now lost, asking for help in bailing out Dun Emer, the Irish craft centre set up by Evelyn Gleeson, Dr Augustine Henry, SMY, and ECY in 1902. The project, in which ECY was responsible for printing, SMY for embroidery, and Miss Gleeson for weaving and carpet-making, had been beset by financial difficulties and personality clashes since its inception; it was split into two autonomous 'co-operative societies' in September 1904, and, after four further years of increasing acrimony, the partnership was formally ended in July 1908. WBY had apparently replied to his father's letter by asking for a clearer account of what was going on, and in his letter of 11 Aug JBY explained: 'It was at the commencement of the week at Dun Emer, & Miss Gleeson was obviously drinking, & we thought that to this was due many things, her queerness over money & business, & her explosions of violent temper—Dun Emer seemed to be in peril. What was to be done?—Lollie was in constant correspondence with D Henry—he was Miss Gleesons friend & Lollies & friend to Dun Emer—. He guaranteed their salaries & paid the salaries (ultimately he did not lose)—so she wrote to him—but at the time she had not as regards Miss Gleeson a single disloyal thought—very much to the contrary.'

² Evelyn Gleeson (1855–1944) was born in Cheshire, the eldest daughter of Edward Moloney Gleeson, an Irish doctor, and at the age of 8 moved with her family to Ireland, where her father set up the Athlone Woollen Mills to stimulate local employment. She subsequently studied painting in London and Paris, and first met the Yeatses through the ILS, of which she was for a time secretary. Dr Augustine Henry (1857–1930), a medical doctor, had got to know her through her brother, who was a university friend. From 1881 to 1898 Henry had served with the Imperial Maritime Customs Service in China; there he took up botany as a hobby, a study in which he eventually became a world expert. Shortly after the turn of the century he offered Evelyn Gleeson financial support in establishing 'The Settlement', a centre for Irish crafts, and in January 1902 invited ECY and SMY to join the enterprise, providing £500 to cover their salaries for the first two years. At first Henry had been impressed with ECY, but her constant quarrels with Miss Gleeson and unbusiness-like methods were now alienating him, and he refused to provide the Yeats sisters with any further loans.

apparently telling JBY that he has dropped affection from the circle of his needs.[3]

NLI.

## To Florence Farr, [c. *13 August 1905*]

Coole Park, | Gort, | Co. Galway.

My dear Florence Emery: Get the harp mended and I will pay the amount. I shall leave the harp with you for the present at any rate but I may want it in Dublin some time. If on the other hand you would prefer to have it altogether then do as you suggest—I will give it you with pleasure—but I think you had better let it be mine and have the use of it.[1] I have dreamed of you several times lately. Last night you had a friend who, as you phrased it "meddled a little with crime". His name was 'Jehovah Cutthroat'. I distinctly remember being jealous and thinking it just like you. Lady Cromarty and Lady Margaret Sackville are here, and this has made life much more [?]hurried as it means various entertainments. It leaves me little time after my work is over but *Shadowy Waters* is getting gradually finished— doubled in beauty. Lady Cromartie is as simple as a child and as innocent. She remembers a past life and her present is utterly over-shadowed by it. She remembers people so beautiful looking that the people now seem ugly and trivial. This past is intensely vivid and has appeared to her since she was a child—long before she knew of incarnations. She was at Tara and describes curious details of that old life. She is less clever but has more nature than Lady Margaret.[2] There has been a tea party, that the county may have a glimpse of these birds of paradize, and I am tired out after two hours strained conversation. One lady, who is boycotted so that nobody is

---

[3] JBY put WBY's attitude down to his reading of Nietzsche (see III. 284, 313) and asked him, as he had 'dropped affection from the circle of your needs', whether he had 'also dropped love between man & woman—. Is this the theory of the overman, if so, your demi-godship is after all but a doctrinaire demi-godship.' He added that WBY's words were 'idle—& you are far more human than you think.—You would be a philosopher & are really a poet.... The men whom Niet[zs]che's theory fits are only great men of a sort, a sort of Yahoo greatness. The struggle is how to get rid of them, they belong to the clumsy & brutal side of things.' He also revealed that he never showed WBY's letters to his sisters: 'Women are always apt to treat every utterance as if it was something final—& I dont think anything you say at present or for some [time] to come if *ever* is to be treated as final—you are haunted by the Goethe idea, interpreted by Dowden, that a man can be a complete man—it is a chimera—a man can only be a specialist.—'

[1] i.e. the glowing harp used in *The Shadowy Waters* (see pp. 102, 151).

[2] On meeting Lady Cromartie in April 1907 Nevinson described her (Bodleian) as 'a young witch ... who looked very wicked & sorceress'. She had been haunted since a child by the vision of an ancient king of Ireland, with whom she believed she had been in love in a previous incarnation.

allowed to work in her garden but the village idiot, was my share of the festival. She had a little intelligence, the others were as dull and as healthy as cabajes. I have been waiting to answer your letters until I could send you a long passage out of *Shadowy Waters*—the first meeting of Forgael and Dectora, but Lady Gregory is too tired with entertaining for me to dictate it for the present.[3] Write again soon.

Yours ever<br>W B Yeats

I think the Paris affair is going all right but it goes very slowly.[4]

Printed copy. Bax, 44–5; Wade, 457–8.

## *To Cornelius J. Sullivan,*[1] *14 August* [*1905*]

at | COOLE PARK, | GORT, | CO. GALWAY.<br>August 14.

My dear Sullivan: I have not had time to write & thank you for your share in giving me the Chaucer—all my work has been in arrears & I am getting

---

[3] See *VP*, 234–9. WBY had first described some of his revisions to this passage on 19 July (see pp. 134–5).

[4] WBY kept FF apprised of MG's marital difficulties, and when Nevinson visited her on 23 Aug (Bodleian) she was able to bring him up to date: 'Went to Mrs. Emery. Told me of Maud Gonne's longing for children, & how she had two by Millevoi, the first dying. How she married MacBride to keep Millevoi away from the house: how McBride in drunkenness ravished the servants & even the little girl. That great, fair woman! Yeats is rather disgusted now at her past. For 10 years he possessed the romantic love—now he shudders at it & is terrified lest it come again. Yet it was the secret of his power. He dare not marry for fear of Miss Horniman, Lady Gregory, & the terrors of money.' In her latest letter (*G–YL*, 208–9), MG had told WBY that MacBride was denying all her charges against him, and had suddenly demanded that the case should be tried according to Irish, not French law, as Irish law 'does not admit divorce only judicial separation'. This application was likely to delay the case for six months, but that 'if by judicial separation I can secure complete control of my child I would be inclined to tell my lawyer that I am willing to accept Irish law administered by French Judges & judicial separation with complete control of my child will please me as much as divorce—but I have got to be very sure what I am accepting first'.

[1] Cornelius J. Sullivan (1870–1932), a prominent New York corporation lawyer, was a native of Holyoke and graduated from Amherst College (of which he later became a trustee) in 1892. He met John Quinn at the Harvard Law School in the mid-1890s, where the two began a lifelong friendship. Sullivan, who traced his ancestry to Kerry and the 16th-century chieftan Donal O'Sullivan Beare, was an enthusiastic supporter of Irish culture and sponsored Eoin MacNeill and James Stephens on their visits to the USA. Like Quinn, he was also a collector and patron of modern art, and in 1917 married the art teacher Mary Quinn Sullivan (1877–1939), who became one of the founders of the New York Museum of Modern Art in 1929. Sullivan served as legal counsel for the Museum until his death in 1932, and he and his wife also built up their own impressive collection, for which they acquired works at the posthumous auction of Quinn's collection. In 1926 the Irish Senate thanked him officially for returning six portraits of leading Irish writers, including WBY, to Ireland.

out collected editions on both sides of the water.[2] Chaucer with the Morris
Burne Jones decorations is I think the most beautiful of all books—a mirror
of health & simple joy.[3] I have not read Chaucer since I was a boy & I had
just got to him in my reading when this book came.[4]

Again thanking you

I am yrs snly
W B Yeats

ALS Private, with envelope addressed to 31 Nassau St, New York City, USA, postmark
'ORANMORE AU 14 05'.

## To John Millington Synge, 15 August [1905]

Coole Park | Gort | Co Galway
August 15

My dear Synge,

Boyle's play came here last week,[1] and I have no doubt it will be sent to
you almost immediately. Both Lady Gregory and myself think that it is
impossibly vulgar in its present form, though there is a play somewhere
sunk in it. I wrote and suggested to Fay that Colum be asked by the
committee to report on necessary revision and afterwards to go to London
to help Boyle at the task, and represent us. I enclose Fay's answer. I was
anxious for diplomatic reasons as well as others to get Colum into the
business of revision. I still think he could do it all right for it is largely a
question of clearing out vulgarity, and he will be a useful ally as against the
'Catholic Laymen'. I dont want good taste to be suspected of a theological
origin. This Colum proposal is quite unimportant at the moment. What is

---

[2] i.e. the Kelmscott Chaucer (see pp. 110, 125–6). Sullivan had subscribed £2 towards the book on 25
Apr, at the instigation of John Quinn, and this letter of thanks was also prompted by Quinn who told
AG on 26 Apr (NYPL) that he thought 'Sullivan would appreciate a short line from Yeats to him when
Yeats comes around to it'.

[3] Sir Edward Burne-Jones had designed the illustrations for the book (see p. 126, n. 2, 140) and
Morris was responsible for the fourteen large borders, eighteen frames for pictures, twenty-eight large
initial words and numerous decorated capital letters, all of which were cut in wood.

[4] See p. 125. In *Aut* (47–8) WBY recalls that when a child JBY had read him 'the story of the little
boy murdered by the Jews in Chaucer [i.e. The Prioress's Tale] and the tale of Sir Thopas, explaining
the hard words, and though both excited me, I had liked Sir Thopas best and been disappointed that it
left off in the middle'. He also recalled that when he began to write in his teens, he 'began to pray that
my imagination might somehow be rescued from abstraction and become as preoccupied with life as had
been the imagination of Chaucer' (*Aut*, 188).

[1] Boyle's three-act comedy *The Eloquent Dempsy* satirizes the desperate and duplicitous attempts of
Jeremiah Dempsy, a small-town politician and publican, to keep in with both the nationalists and, in the
hope of gaining a magistracy, the unionists.

important is, if you agree with us about the vulgarity of the play, that you protest as strongly as possible. It will need vehemence, for Russell and the two Fays are evidently for it.[2] It is most likely Colum will vote for it through love of popularity and that we shall be beaten in the voting.[3] I take a very serious view of the matter indeed, partly because I am not at all sure of the effect of a play of this kind on Miss Horniman who has spent four thousand pounds on us already. The only condition she makes is that we shall keep up the standard.[4] I dont mind going against her where I know we are right, but if we produce this our position will be perfectly indefensible. When the revision of the constitution is through those of us who know will be in authority. The danger at this moment is that Fay wants his opening programme settled. Lady Gregory and I propose Moliere's Doctor in Spite of himself or another of Moliere.[5] Miss Horniman has found a fine eighteenth century translation.[6] If you agree to this please let us know at

---

[2] In an undated fragment (*JMSCL* I. 126), evidently in reply to this letter, Synge agreed that the play 'sets one's teeth on edge continually, and yet I think it is certainly worth revising and playing. It hovers over being a good picture of the patriot publican, and yet it is never quite right and it is very often quite wrong. Your brother and I saw something of these kind of people when we were away for the *Manchester Guardian*. They are colossal in their vulgarity, but their vulgarity is as different from cockney vulgarity as the Mayo dialect is from the Cockney. Boyle does not seem able to distinguish between the two and sticks in English Music Hall vulgarity of the worst kind. I rather agree with Fay that you would be more likely to get Boyle to put it to rights than Colum. Boyle would be sure to resent in his heart having Colum appointed to direct him, besides Colum seems never to know his own [mind] and if Boyle was sulky Colum would give in at once.'

[3] The six members of the Reading Committee were WBY, Synge, AE, the two Fays, and Colum.

[4] In fact, AEFH had a qualified admiration for Boyle and on 10 Dec 1906 told WBY (NLI) that 'Boyle has a certain virility (I don't know what else to call it, it has nothing to do with the quality of his work) which is missing in Yeats & Synge work; Lady Gregory has it too. It makes a barrier which has a very good side—it forces the actor into a certain character & keeps him there.'

[5] WBY had been thinking of producing the plays of the French dramatist Molière (stage name of Jean-Baptiste Poquelin, 1622–73) for some time, and had written to AG on 9 Nov 1903 (III. 462) that he had 'been reading Molière all day long. . . . You should look through him again. Some of his more farcical comedy is pure "folk" in its way of seeing life. He is full too of stage tricks one could adapt to our kind of material.' His appetite had been further whetted by Coquelin's June production of *Les Précieuses ridicules* (see p. 111). AG herself was to begin the translation of Molière into Kiltartan dialect in November of this year, and the Abbey produced her adaptations of *The Doctor in Spite of Himself* on 16 Apr 1906, *The Rogueries of Scapin* on 4 Apr 1908, and *The Miser* on 21 Jan 1909.

[6] Probably *The Mock Doctor; or, The Dumb Lady Cured* by the novelist and dramatist Henry Fielding (1707–54). The play was first produced by His Majesty's Servants at the Theatre Royal, Drury Lane, in 1732 and there were editions in 1753, 1762, and 1771. Fielding also adapted Molière's *L'Avare* as *The Miser* in 1733. Both plays had recently been republished in volume ii of a new edition of *The Works of Henry Fielding, Esq.* (1902; originally 1762). Synge would have had no objection to Molière; as early as August 1895 he told Thérèse Beydon that he had read 'plusieurs comédies de Molière que j'aime beaucoup' (*JMSCL* I. 30), and in the preface to *The Tinker's Wedding* wrote (*JMSCW* II. 3) that 'the best plays of Ben Jonson and Molière can no more go out of fashion than the blackberries on the hedges' (see also *JMSCL* II. 232). He also cited Molière in his satire 'National Drama: A Farce' as an example of a national dramatist who nevertheless dealt with the vices of his countrymen (*JSMCW* III. 222–3). He was to praise AG's translations of the plays, and in April 1908 directed her version of *The Rogueries of Scapin* at the Abbey (*JMSCL* II. 144).

once. Or will you agree to a Moliere play in principle? We could settle what play afterwards. The moment you have got Boyle's play and have read it please write to Fay very strongly.[7]

Yours siny<br>W B Yeats

[*In AG's hand*]
Dear M<sup>r.</sup> Synge—

I was very glad of your letter, you seem to be having a very good time[8]— I do envy you being able to get away so completely—I am 'serving tables' & giving up all my own time & thought for the sake of guests, most of whom have invited themselves, so it is well I had got through with my play. I think Boyle dreadful—It is very awkward for us playwriters having to criticize other plays—but it must be done—

Yrs siny<br>A Gregory

[*With enclosure*]

Abbey Theatre

Dear Mr Yeats

I have just heard from Russell that he passes Boyle's play and am writing to Colum. I certainly dont agree with you in reference to this piece. It is vulgar there is no doubt, but if a play is about the most substantially vulgar people in the country I dont quite see how it is to be done any other way. Maybe I am mistaking the particular sort of vulgarity you refer to. I think that Colum as an adviser to Boyle will make a glorious hash of the piece, for Colum can barely mend his own piece and I reckon wont be much use to help Boyle out of his difficulties can you not suggest yourself what you want done and get him to do it. I think that class of play want another sort of point of view to the general run of our pieces. Its plain on the face of it that it is intended for burlesque sarcasm bordering on farce, and I would not look deeply into the literary value of that sort of work, I should reckon on how it would go with an audience and this I think is quite safe. I think its a bit better than the Building Fund and quite safe to go well. Its on a topical subject and I dont think any worse than Laying of the Foundations for writing but of course thats not in my line so I dont put up to be an

---

[7] Synge wrote to Fay on 8 Sept (NLI) that he thought the play had 'a great deal of vitality but it is not possible in its present state, though I think a little revision would make it possible'. It was finally produced on 20 Jan 1906 in a much-revised version.

[8] On 11 Aug Synge had written from Dingle, Co. Kerry (*JMSCL* I. 120–1), that he was about to leave for the Great Blasket Island, off the Kerry coast: 'It is probably even more primitive than Aran and I am wild with joy at the prospect.'

authority.[9] I write this just between ourselves as to what I think and I certainly dont think it well to start Colum correcting Boyle. In the first place I dont think Boyle would like it considering he has lived ten years in the country for Colum's one and knows it, and secondly between ourselves I dont think Colum is competent enough to do that sort of work for others till he is able to do it for himself. I will see Russell towards the end of the week to arrange the new proposals and have them in rediness for the general meeting. We must certainly decide an opening programme at the general meeting, it should be in rehearsal at the present time, and it will keep us back in our season having to wait so long. I cant get these dear delightful people Ryan and Roberts to settle Miss Horniman's lighting account for last six months this is the third time of asking as they say in Church it should have been paid July the first as per agreement.[10] Let me have a line as to what upon think of these things and I think I would look over Boyle again and wait till we get all the verdicts and then advise him yourself, dont you think a blue pencil might help it a lot.

Yours faithfully<br>Will Fay

TLS TCD. Saddlemyer, 74–5.

## To Maud Gonne, [c. 15 August 1905]

Mention in an undated letter from MG, [? August 1905].
Describing the Countess of Cromartie's memories of having been a slave girl at Tara.[1]

*G–YL*, 209–10.

---

[9] Boyle's three-act comedy *The Building Fund* had been produced by the Abbey Theatre on 25 Apr of this year (see p. 40, n. 9), although WBY had initially doubted its artistic merit (see III. 599). Frederick Ryan's Ibsenite play *The Laying of the Foundations*, on the theme of municipal corruption in building contracts, had been produced by the Cumann na nGaedheal at the Antient Concert Rooms on 29 Oct 1902, and by the National Theatre Society at the Camden Street Hall in December of the same year. On first seeing the play, WBY described it as 'excellent... a really very astonishing peice of satire' (III. 232), and it was produced frequently in Dublin and taken to London. By July 1904, however, WBY's view was more circumspect; he now thought it 'a very witty though rather rambling attack on municipal corruption of a lightly socialistic tinge' (III. 623). According to a letter from Frank Fay to WBY of 15 Dec 1902 (NLI), the play 'was practically built up at rehearsal'.

[10] In her letter of April 1904, announcing the gift of the Theatre, AEFH had stipulated that the company could 'have the building rent free whenever they want it', but that they 'must pay for their own electric light and gas' (see III. 573). Fred Ryan as treasurer of the INTS, and George Roberts as its secretary, would have been responsible for paying these bills. Fay's allusion to the Church refers to the requirement of calling marriage banns on three successive occasions.

[1] See p. 160. MG was also susceptible to such visions, including one (*Mem*, 48–9) of 'a past personality of hers, now seeking to be reunited with her. She had been priestess in a temple somewhere

## To Charles Elkin Mathews, [*17 August 1905*]

at | COOLE PARK, | GORT, | CO. GALWAY.
Thursday

Dear M^r Mathews: I forgot to thank you the other day for your share in giving me the big Chaucer. It is a great joy & Robert Gregory has designed a lectern to hold it.[1] I am reading in it everyday & I find that the spirit of the rhyme is in the drawings & above all in the borders.[2] Morris had always as an artificer a very Chaucerian delight in health & in a kind of May day content. In his own poetry he often got far from it for then a little of the modern burden of ideas fell on him—it was as though his hands & his instincts for activity in life belonged to an older time than his deliberate & conscious thoughts.[3] I have not read Chaucer since I was a boy & have just come to him in my reading, working back from Spenser, when this book, which has always seemed to me the most beautiful of all decorated books came to me.

Yr ev
W B Yeats

ALS Texas, with envelope addressed to Vigo St, Regent St, London, postmark 'ORANMORE AU [1] 7 05'.

in Egypt and under the influence of a certain priest who was her lover gave false oracles for money, and because of this the personality of that life had split off from the soul and remained a half-living shadow.' Part of MacBride's case against the veracity of her evidence was that MG believed 'in past incarnations' (*G–YL*, 208). She found WBY's account interesting and was 'longing to hear the whole story' (*G–YL*, 209).

[1] In a letter of *c.* 18 July 1905 to AG (Berg), John Masefield announced that he was going to see WBY the following day 'to do reverence to the lectern. I am taking him the silver tobacco box he liked, for I have found that the pirates always exchanged tobacco boxes when they wished to express a mutual esteem.' In *Some Memories of W. B. Yeats* (Dublin, 1940) he recalled (7) the 'big, dark blue lectern, on which his Kelmscott Chaucer stood, between enormous candles in big blue wooded sconces. These candles stood about four feet and were as thick as a ship's oar. The dim dark blue of the lectern was the most noticeable colour in the room. He added curtains to match it.' The lectern, which was based on one of Burne-Jones illustrations in the book, was a necessity rather than mere ornamentation: the book measures 11⅜" by 16⅝" and weighs nearly 13½ pounds. In his poem 'Presences' (*VP*, 358), WBY dreams of women standing 'between | My great wood lectern and the fire'.

[2] Morris had designed the numerous borders and frames in the book (see p. 162, n. 3), mainly in patterns of vine leaves and flowers and leaves, so conveying a luxuriant sense of vernal abundance.

[3] See p. 40. At the conclusion of 'Literature and the Living Voice', published in October 1906 (*Expl*, 220–1), WBY wrote that Morris 'who did more than any modern to recover mediaeval art, did not in his *Earthly Paradise* copy from Chaucer—from whom he copied so much that was naive and beautiful—what seems to me essential in Chaucer's art. He thought of himself as writing for the reader, who could return to him again and again when the chosen mood had come, and became monotonous, melancholy, too continuously lyrical in his understanding of emotion and of life. Had he accustomed himself to read out his poems upon those Sunday evenings that he gave to Socialist speeches, and to gather an audience of

## *To Charles Elkin Mathews, 2 September* [*1905*]

COOLE PARK, | GORT, | CO. GALWAY.

Sept 2-

My dear Matthews

I enclose a letter from the Society of Authors which explains itself. I dont know whether Lane is in America or in London—If London, he has certainly had time to reply—

I cannot recollect when you wrote, but think that even if in America, you should have had an answer by this. If that is so, will you please do as the Society of Authors advise—It is for you, not for me, to put the matter in their hands, according to the decision of their legal adviser.

Yr sny

W B Yeats

Dict AG, signed WBY; Leeds. Marked at the top of the first page in another hand: 'No letter enclosed'.[1]

## *To George Russell (AE), 3 September* [*1905*]

Coole Park | Gort, Co Galway

Sept 3

My dear Russell

Ever since I came down here I have been trying to get a moment to write to you.[1] It is very important to get it through as quickly as possible, as I dont suppose we can make definite arrangements about anything or cast our plays for London and Oxford finally until the actors who are to be paid have come to a definite arrangement with the new executive. I think it was Roberts who impressed upon me when I was in Dublin that a fortnight's notice must be given of the general meeting to pass the new constitution, and that the notice paper has to contain the proposed resolutions. He asked me to write to you and remind you of this. Have you been able to arrange

average men . . . he would have been forced to Chaucer's variety, to his delight in the height and depth, and would have found expression for that humorous, many-sided nature of his.'

[1] See p. 147. Since WBY forgot to enclose the letter from the Society of Authors (which is now lost), Mathews could not act on it, although the letter was apparently sent on to him later. At this point WBY was unclear as to whether the delay in communication with John Lane about *The Wind Among the Reeds* was caused by Mathews's reluctance to write or Lane's reluctance to answer.

[1] WBY had made a brief visit to Dublin in mid-August.

things? We shall have to be in working order somehow by the end of the month, or we wont have time for rehearsal. <As it is our choice of plays to open with is rather hampered, as they must come out of our London programme. It does not seem wise> I shall have to go to Dublin I suppose for the new meeting, and I would like to know when it is likely to be.[2] I am sorry to give you all this trouble, but it means getting things permanently right, and so long as they are in the present state one's power of doing anything is rather paralysed.

Jack saw your pictures passing through, and thinks you have 'come on a lot'.[3]

Yrs sny
W B Yeats

TLS Indiana.


## To W. P. Ryan,[1] [early September 1905]

Mention in letter from Ryan, 24 September 1905.
An 'interesting letter' praising Ryan's play,[2] but suggesting that its construction is faulty, and proposing that they might meet and discuss this.[3]

---

[2] The General Meeting to discuss the reorganization of the INTS was called for 22 Sept.

[3] AE had joined with Percy Gethin (1874–1916) and Casimir and Constance Markiewicz to mount an exhibition of paintings in the Leinster Lecture Hall, Molesworth Street, from 22 Aug to 2 Sept. The opening coincided with Horse Show Week and the *Irish Homestead* of 26 Aug (650) reported that the 'pictures are attracting considerable attention, and we learn that a great many have been sold already'. On 2 Sept it singled out AE's *The Dry Lake* (664–5) as 'a picture full of natural magic'. Jack and Cottie Yeats stayed at Coole for the first two weeks of September.

[1] William Patrick Ryan (1867–1942), Irish journalist and novelist, had spent most of his working life in London, where he wrote for a number of English and Irish papers, was a member of the Irish Literary Society, and secretary of the Gaelic League. He had written sympathetically of WBY in *The Irish Literary Revival* (1894), but after the turn of the century had attacked him in the *Leader* and the *Freeman's Journal*. WBY thought that these attacks had been provoked by George Moore's failure to acknowledge a play Ryan had sent to the ILT, and that this was 'a pity for Ryan has all his life lived under a sense of wrongs' (see III. 10–11).

[2] Perhaps Ryan's *The 'Wake' of the People/ 1847*, a tragedy set in Famine times, which appeared in the Christmas number of the *Weekly Freeman* on 14 Dec 1901 (26), and was reprinted in *Plays for the People* (1904). Ryan's playwriting was put on one side when he became editor of the *Irish Peasant* in January 1906.

[3] Ryan was pleased by WBY's praise and accepted his criticism: 'I was surprised and pleased to find that you thought so highly of the play. I quite agree with you as to the errors in construction. . . . Certainly I would be greatly pleased to discuss the matter with you some time, as you kindly suggest. I intend to re-cast & rewrite the little play.'

## To George Russell (AE), 7 September [1905]

Coole Park | Gort, Co Galway
Sept 7

My dear Russell,

I have hardly a comment to make upon your rules, neither Lady Gregory nor myself find anything to disagree with, except one or two details. One of these is that you fix the number of the reading committee as five. If you yourself were remaining on as a member I mean a general member, this would be the right number, being the old committee without the two Fays. William Fay I understand is ex-officio member and should not therefore I suppose be numbered among the elected members. Perhaps I am muddling things, and you mean four elected and one ex-officio member. We cant have more than four elected members of the committee at present. There is nobody competent except Synge Colum Lady Gregory and myself.[1] The next most likely person would be Stephen Gwynn, and we have no knowledge of the value of his opinion about a play. Synge has written to me opposing a suggestion of mine to make Gwynn one of the officers of the Society on the ground of Gwynn not being a practical worker.[2] This brings me to another point. Both Lady Gregory and myself think that Norman and Miss Layard should become honorary members.[3]

---

[1] See Appendix, pp. 896, 912. As first constituted the Reading Committee, which was responsible for reading and recommending the plays to be performed by the INTS, had comprised six members, but at the meeting of 11 Aug 1905 it was decided to raise its membership to seven. Under AE's amendments, this was reduced to five. In his reply to this letter (Denson, 52) AE agreed to alter the rule to read 'shall not be more than five in number', and explained that this would leave WBY 'to elect one or two if you like'. He thought it better 'not to make W. Fay an ex-officio member but to request his attendance at meetings as I have done in rules. The secretary also attends but merely to record and has no vote.'

[2] Synge's letter is now lost. He was still at Glenbeigh in Kerry and on 8 Sept told Nathalie Esposito that 'it is a great thing to get clear away and forget all about the Abbey affairs for a month or two in the year' (*JMSCL* 1. 128). His view of Gwynn may have been coloured by having just read his play on Emmet (see pp. 141–3). In his reply AE dismissed Synge's suggestion, 'as if Gwynn is elected on business committee and will work he is practical enough. You can't restrict the society merely to authors or actors unless you want to have a business smash.' And he demanded: 'What the dickens do you know about accounts, or Synge, or Colm or Lady Gregory? . . . not one of you could say whether a statement of accounts was correctly made out or not.'

[3] Under the old constitution members of the Society were divided into two categories: the ordinary members, made up of the eight founders and those who had been elected subsequently by a three-quarters majority of votes cast at meetings called for the purpose; and associate members, who paid an annual subscription of 10s., but who had no say in the selection of plays, or in the running of the Society. AE's amendments increased these two categories to three: general members, elected on a three-quarters majority, who were not to number more than twenty, and who were to control the Society; actor members; and honorary members, who would be admitted by the general members in recognition of services to Irish culture, but who would play no part in the business of the Society. In the final version of the new constitution there was only one category of membership, since all members were shareholders, and could be admitted to the Society only if their application for shares was approved by the Directors.

They cannot object to follow your example in this matter, and it is really of some importance. If you would speak to them about it it would be a very great service. Norman is quite harmless my objection to him is one of principle. He is not a worker, but his connection with the Society gives him a right to honorary membership. The objection to Miss Layard is more serious. She is looked upon by the Fays as a centre of gossip and the gathering point for grievances. This may not be true, but we want to make everybody feel that we have got things stable at last. There is also a very great objection to her in principle. Fay's objection to her will keep her from ever getting parts. She will therefore always remain an inactive member.[4] In course of time some one or other of our really prominent players may become inactive through marriage, illness or the like. All we can do for this member will be to make him an honorary member. It will not be fair that his possible years of work must count for less than Miss Layards few months of service. As an honorary member will always have free admission to the performances we confer upon Miss Layard a practical advantage, and take nothing from her except the attendance at an annual meeting. I dont want to leave any centre round which futile discussion can gather. As it is the general members will be (I exclude Miss Layard and Norman for purposes of discussion) Lady Gregory, Synge, Colum, myself, Stephen Gwynn, (as vice-president) Ryan, Keller, with the possible early addition of Starkie and Roberts. One never knows what way Colum will vote, and I am only certain of Lady Gregory Synge and myself on a question of dramatic policy. I'm not so much afraid of an adverse vote as of irritating and wasteful discussion. Above all I dont want any possible vehicle through which the ordinary Dublin opinion, of the sort that dislikes Synge, to annoy us. I want a strong solid centre to the Society, one not only exempt from useless discussion but so manifestly beyond its reach that nobody will try and raise it, or to bring pressure upon anybody else to raise it. Besides, no work, no vote, helps salutary discipline. Lady Gregory feels very strong objections to the clause about Fay being appointed by the actor members, but will not object if Fay agrees. I personally do not think the point important, as I cannot imagine the right ever being exercised. Lady Gregory thinks it wrong to grant a merely nominal right, as she knows we could not accept any other stage manager. I however do not think the right nominal as it would enable the actor members to block our work, they

---

[4] On 18 Mar 1903 Frank Fay had complained to WBY (Private) that Helen Laird (see p. 153, n. 2) was 'not primarily interested in acting at all', and had 'no delivery nor deportment'. In his reply AE promised to speak to Norman and Miss Laird 'but not now': 'Norman is away for three or four weeks and I dont think Miss Laird is inclined at present to resign. I have not spoken to her about the changes but after they are through she may feel she is rather out of it and may volunteer. I will sound her later on and suggest it to her. I cant think either of them will ever bother about the Society in the future.'

refusing our man, we refusing their man, which would of course lead to negotiations. I would object if I thought this would ever arise. If Fay agrees and the actor members accept this privilege I dont see why they should not have it. If you can get them to give it up, so much the better, for the less opportunities for discussion we have in what is now a business organisation, the better. The natural check upon Fay is the usual check upon all stage managers; if he is objectionable beyond a certain point he loses valuable actors. This is the right check for efficiency, for it leaves the power of protest to the efficient who can be trusted to make their own combination. The objection to a vote is that it creates a power of protest in the inefficient. Of course there is no use bringing the rule forward at all if Fay objects to it.[5]

My sister sends me a proposed list of poems for your book. I haven't been through them yet, but certainly it will be a beautiful book, and should be a help to them.[6] I have been pressing Roberts to get an essay from you for his proposed annual.[7] I am writing to Roberts to summon the general meeting.

Yrs sinry
W B Yeats

TLS Indiana.

## *To George Roberts, 7 September 1905*

Mention in previous letter.
Arranging the date of the General Meeting of the INTS.

[5] AE had drafted a clause proposing that the 'stage manager shall be elected by a vote of the actors members but his election shall be subject to the approval of the business committee'. Hitherto the stage manager had been appointed by the Management Committee, and Fay objected strongly to the new arrangement (see below). In his reply AE said he would 'alter the rule about the stage manager being appointed by the actors': 'I don't feel very strongly one way or the other about it. Of course what you say about never accepting another stage manager is nonsense. If you found anyone better you would want him.' And he pointed out that WBY would now have to distinguish clearly between the duties of the stage manager and the secretary if he wanted to avoid endless conflict.

[6] The Dun Emer Press published AE's *By Still Waters: Lyrical Poems* in December 1906. AE was immediately suspicious of WBY's interest, replying defensively that this was 'a rough list', which he 'might alter as I did it in a hurry', and he hinted that he 'might possibly find better poems if I looked over what I have more carefully'. AE listed his selection for the volume in an undated letter to ECY (Emory), commenting: 'I would prefer my own selection to any W.B.Y. would make and would prefer no correspondence at all with him over it. He likes the poems I like least and I am sure we could not agree.'

[7] AE contributed 'Art and Literature', a lecture he had delivered at the Watts Exhibition in the Royal Hibernian Academy, to the first number of the *Shanachie* (1906).

## To W. G. Fay, [*7 September 1905*]

Mention in letter from Fay, 8 September 1905.
Asking Fay to help AE with the new INTS rules,[1] and eliciting his views on the proposal that his position as stage manager be by election.[2]

NLI.

## To Maud Gonne, [*early September 1905*]

Mention in letter from MG, 30 September [1905].
Telling her that Edward Martyn is troubled by the religious aspect of her petition for a divorce.[1]

G–YL, 210–11.

---

[1] The Fays were contemptuous of AE's attempts to restructure the INTS, although they acknowledged the need for urgent reform, and W. G. Fay was particularly incensed by the proposal that his position should be dependent upon annual election. In his long and exasperated reply he told WBY that he did 'not feel the slightest inclination to help Russell with his rules. They were introduced first of all by him under protest from me for I knew quite well that in a business like this there can be no democracy. But at the time I thought it would tide things over.' He now thought that 'this further tinkering at them will be only temporary and I dont feel any anxiety to dabble in them'.

[2] 'About the voting of my position', Fay replied, 'I have stated my position which is strictly in accordance with theatrical usage. If I don't suit a fortnights notice concludes my engagement at any time and as for this voting Russell may be reliable on creameries but he hasnt the Ghost of an idea about the managing of any business as far as I can see.' He pointed out that without him and his brother 'there would never have existed any acting society to produce these plays and if these people that we have made dont think we are competent we are both ready to leave them to do as they like when they can elect & vote and play round till further notice. . . . I am just fed up with this crowd of incompetent gas bags that we have here, and they have had all the rope I intend to give them. Ive put up with more insolence & impertinence from them than I ever put up with from anyone breathing before. . . . I am either fit to do this work or not. If I am not, well then the sooner I am got rid of the better for the place.' But, he intimated, there was no one else in the Society capable of doing the job and that, in any case, had AE 'from the start impressed these friends of his that there is nothing to be got in this world without plenty of hard work, instead of listening to all their little squabbles it would have help[ed] us more materially than all his drafting of rules'. He concluded that the situation required 'very gentle handling to prevent a bad rupture', and that it was 'very necessary to see that we are not overpowered in the general body'. The offending clause was deleted, and in the final version the appointment and dismissal of the stage manager was left entirely to the Directors.

[1] Martyn's religious scruples were undermining his initial support for MG (see p. 46). In her reply (not written until 30 Sept because she had been occupied nursing the feverish Iseult), MG said that when she met Martyn she would be able to 'console him on the religious side of the divorce question' by revealing that her confessor, Canon Dissard, had originally been opposed to the step 'but when he heard all the facts & my reason for asking for a divorce he said he could no longer advise me against it — it was a case where legal divorce was necessary'.

## *To John Millington Synge, 9 September 1905*

Coole Park | Gort, Co Galway
Saturday 9th Sept 1905

My dear Synge,

Where are you?[1] It is really of great importance for you that you can be at the General Meeting of Soc. Friday 22nd. You must weigh this importance against your other occupations. The way things stand is this. Everybody is in a highly excitable state, owing to the necessity of turning the Society into a business organization with paid actors. Fear of responsibility, various irritations against Fay, are working upon one side. Upon the other is the incontrovertable fact that we can neither go to London nor Oxford this year, not to speak of any country place, without paid actors. I think everybody is agreed on the necessity of the change, and the necessity of a change of constitution to make it possible. The whole future of the Society in all probability depends upon the decision of the twenty-second, certainly the whole immediate future. If we get things through in the form in which Russell proposes them at present, I think we will have quiet and a workman-like Society. To get them through it may be necessary for you and I and Lady Gregory and the Fays to stand in together, having come to a previous agreement. Lady Gregory suggests you should if possible come here either Saturday next or Monday to talk things over, and you and I could go on to Dublin together. She will not be able to come. I hope you will be able to do this. Order in the Society is as essential to you as to me.[2]

Bring if you can, or have sent to me, the M.S. of the *Tinkers*. I want to see if it would do for SAMHAIN, if you dont object, and also to see whether we can discuss it for our winter Session. We are rather hard up for new short pieces, and you have such a bad reputation now it can hardly do you any harm. But we may find it too dangerous for the Theatre at

---

[1] Since 7 Aug Synge had been in Co. Kerry, visiting Dingle and the Great Blasket Island, and was now at Mountain Stage, Glenbeigh, happily trying to 'forget all about Abbey affairs' (see p.169, n.2).

[2] In response to this letter, Synge wrote to AG on 12 Sept (*JMSCL* I. 130–1) that he would arrive in Gort at 7.20 p.m. on Saturday, 16 Sept.

present.³ Also bring the Satire on your enemies, and indeed anything you have.⁴

Yours sny
W B Yeats

TLS TCD. Saddlemyer, 78–80.

## To Charles Elkin Mathews, 10 September [1905]

COOLE PARK, | GORT, | CO. GALWAY.
Sept 10

My dear Matthews

Please send me a copy of the Wind Among the Reeds & put it down to my account—What have you done about Lane? You will have received the letter of the Society of Authors by this time—¹

Yrs sny
W B Yeats

Dict AG, signed WBY; Leeds, with envelope in AG's hand addressed to Vigo St, London, postmark 'ORANMORE SE 12 05'.

---

³ In his reply of 12 Sept (see above, n. 2), Synge reported that he could not 'bring or send you the Tinker MS. I am sorry to say, as I have not got it with me, and I am afraid to set my pious relations to hunt for it among my papers for fear they would set fire to the whole. I can give it to you in Dublin if that will be time enough.' In the event, *The Tinker's Wedding*, a rambunctious two-act comedy, did not appear in *Samhain*. It was published by Maunsel in December 1907, but not produced until after Synge's death, and even then in an English production so unsatisfactory that WBY walked out of the first performance on 11 Nov 1909. It was not staged in Ireland until 1963.

⁴ 'National Drama: A Farce', first published in 1968 in *JSMCW* III. 220–6. This fragmentary sketch satirizes the notions of Irish national drama as debated by a group of narrow-minded nationalists, one of whom states (222) that Irish drama 'shines throughout with the soft light of the ideal impulses of the Gaels, a drama in short which contains the manifold and fine qualities of the Irish race, their love for the land of their forefathers, and their poetic familiarity with the glittering and unseen forms of the visionary world'. Jameson, Synge's spokesman, replies (225) that the 'national element in art is merely the colour, the intensity of the wildness or restraint of the humour, but the other matters that have been suggested have nothing to do with Nationality as the word is and can only be used in the arts'.

¹ See p. 167. Prompted yet again by WBY, Mathews at last wrote to Lane, who replied on 13 Sept (Leeds) that he would write at once to the managing director in New York and pointing out 'that until to-day I had heard nothing of the matter. A query came from you to the Counting House I find asking for a copy of the agreement, but nothing further. . . . Of course the matter now rests with the John Lane Company.'

# To Arthur Symons, 10 September [1905]

Coole Park | Gort, Co Galway
Sept 10

My dear Symons,

The Wagnerian essay touches my own theories at several points, and enlarges them at one or two, but that must wait till we meet. I have spent the entire summer rewriting Shadowy Waters. There are not more than about thirty lines of the old left—just the few moments of lyric verse where the smoky flame burnt pure. I have made I think a strong play of it, and have got dramatic suspense throughout. In one way finding it so bad has been a comfort, for it shows me how much I have learned by watching rehearsals in Dublin and by altering my plays and other people's for the stage. In one place your Wagner essay helped me. A certain passage had always seemed wrong to me, and after I had rewritten it several times it was still wrong. I then came on that paragraph where Wagner insists that a play must not appeal to the intelligence, but by being, if I remember rightly, <so much> a piece of self consistent life directly to the emotions. It was just one of those passages which seemed to have no very precise meaning till one brings actual experience to their understanding. Your essay is a substitute for more volumes than anything of the kind I have seen, and has I believe greatly pleased Ashton Ellis. At any rate I know it has Miss Horniman who I think speaks as his voice.[1]

I am getting ready the one volume edition of all my poems since '95, and if you have in your memory any misdoings of mine, please tell me of them that I may put them right. You will hardly recognise not only the Shadowy Waters but Baile's Strand and a good deal of the King's Threshold. They have all been rewritten after rehearsal or actual performance, and the King's Threshold has been changed and rehearsed and then changed again and so on, till I have got it as I believe a perfectly articulate stage

---

[1] In 'The Ideas of Richard Wagner' (see p. 144), Symons quotes the passage from *Richard Wagner's Prose Works* II. 209: 'In drama, therefore, an action can only be explained when it is completely justified by the feeling; and it is thus the dramatic poet's task not to invent actions but to make an action so intelligible through its emotional necessity that we may altogether dispense with the intellect's assistance in its justification. The poet, therefore, has to make his main scope the choice of the action, which he must so choose that, alike in its character and in its compass, it makes possible to him its entire justification by the feeling, for in this justification alone resides the reaching of his aim' (89). Symons's article was an extended review of three monumental translations by Ashton Ellis: *Richard Wagner's Prose Works*, 8 vols. (1895–9), C. F. Glasenapp's *Das Leben Richard Wagner*, 4 vols. (1900–4), and *Richard Wagner and Mathilde Wesendonk: Tagebuchblätter und Briefe* (1905). William Ashton Ellis (d. 1919), MRCS, LRCP, had been a member of the London Lodge of the Theosophical Society and was the foremost British Wagnerian of his generation. He was a friend of AEFH, who shared his occult and musical interests.

play. I have learned a great deal about poetry generally in the process, and one thing I am now quite sure of is that all the finest poetry comes logically out of the fundamental action, and that the error of late periods like this is to believe that some things are inherently poetical, and to try and pull them on to the scene at every moment. It is just these seeming inherently poetical things that wear out. My Shadowy Waters was full of them, and the fundamental thinking was nothing, and that gave the whole poem an impression of weakness. There was no internal life pressing for expression through the characters.

We hope to bring the plays over in November, and I believe we are going to Oxford as well as London.

I see by an old post card that you asked me for Joyce's address.[2] I don't know it, but care of Oliver Gogerty, 5 Rutland Square Dublin might reach him.

Yrs ev<br>W B Yeats

TLS Texas. Wade, 459–61.


## To Frank Sidgwick, 15 September [1905]

Coole Park | Gort, Co Galway<br>Sept 15

My dear Sidgewick

I am not in London as you see, and will not be there till late October or early November. The reason why you have not that manuscript before this, is that I have been busy every day since I left London, re-writing the Shadowy Waters. It is finished now, or all but finished, and a clean copy is being made. I may therefore any day send you the M. S. for the book.[1]

Yrs sry<br>W B Yeats

TLS Texas.


[2] From 1 May 1905 to 24 Feb 1906 Joyce's address was Via San Nicolo 30 II, Trieste, Austria. He had lived with Gogarty in a Martello Tower in Dublin the previous summer (see p. 42, n. 3), but the two were now estranged. Symons probably wanted to consult him about plans for publishing *Chamber Music* and *Dubliners*; see p. 42, n. 3.

[1] See p. 106, 115. Sidgwick & Bullen were preparing WBY's *Poems, 1899–1905*, published in October 1906, which included the new version of *The Shadowy Waters*.

## To Dudley Digges, [mid-September 1905]

Mention in TS interview, 1936.
Giving Digges a letter of introduction to Arnold Daly, who is producing
*John Bull's Other Island* in New York.[1]

NLI.

## To John Quinn, 16 September [1905]

Coole Park | Gort Co Galway
Sept 16

My dear Quinn,

Many thanks for the magazines which have just come. Fiona's articles I
had not seen, which probably accounts for my having had a rather cantankerous letter from William Sharp. He had probably expected some gratitude. The articles are curiously bad, so bad that it is hard to understand
how any practised writer can have escaped getting a little simplicity by this
time. They are well meant however and I must write some thanks to that
phantom Fiona.[1]

---

[1] Dudley Digges (see p. 78), currently employed as a clerk in a wholesale clothiers in New York, was
eager to return to the stage. When he saw an announcement that the American actor-manager and
enthusiastic Shavian Arnold Daly (1875–1927) was producing *John Bull's Other Island* at the Criterion
Theatre, he 'wrote immediately to W. B. Yeats, and asked him to give me a letter of introduction to
Arnold Daly, which he did' (NLI). WBY's recommendation did the trick; Daly gave Digges the part of
the overbearing miller Barney Doran, but he proved unsuitable, and subsequently took the post of
assistant stage manager. The play, which opened on 10 Oct 1905, was a resounding flop—Shaw's first
failure in America—and the show ran for only two weeks. Digges then spent a fruitless period haunting
the agencies, before landing a part with Ben Greet's Shakespearian company.

[1] Quinn had sent Fiona Macleod's two-part article 'The Irish Muse', published in the *North
American Review* of November and December 1904. A rambling and portentous meditation on Irish
poetry, apparently occasioned by Rolleston and Brooke's anthology *A Treasury of Irish Poetry*, it is
saturated in the Celtic Twilight clichés that WBY was coming to despise. Macleod described WBY
(911) as 'the finest artist now using verse as his means of beautiful revelation: there can be little question
that his verse, at its best, is on a higher level of beauty than is that of any contemporary. Nevertheless,
those of us who thus greatly value his work look beyond anything he has done.' 'Fiona Macleod' was the
alter ego of William Sharp (1855–1905; see I. 24), poet, novelist, biographer, and editor, whom WBY
had met in late June 1887 and who, after initial dislike, had grown to be a friend. Although WBY had
long known that Sharp and Macleod were one and the same (see II. 244–5, 287), Sharp kept up the
pretence of the dual personality. His 'cantankerous letter' is untraced, but evidently WBY did not reply
to it until 4 Nov, and in early December Sharp admonished him for his neglect: 'Frankly, I have been
much hurt by your continuous and apparently systematic ignoring of any communication from me, and
had made up my mind to keep silence henceforth.... I thought that in the course of more than a year,
and after letter-after-letter, you wd. have sent even a P.C.—or, what seemed simple, dictated a message
through Lady Gregory or some other friend.'

The little books that you have copyrighted look fine.[2] Synge's play is showing itself worthy of your care, for he writes that it has been accepted for immediate performance by what his translator calls the principal German theatre.[3] The Shadow of the Glen has been put into Czech by somebody connected with the National Theatre there, but nothing definite has been arranged as to its performance.[4] Synge's foreign success is worth more to us than would the like success of any other of our people, for he has been the occasion of all the attacks on us. I said in a speech some time ago that he would have a European reputation in five years, but his enemies have mocked the prophecy.[5] I think we have seen the end of the democracy in the Theatre which was Russell's doing, for I go to Dublin at the end of the week to preside at a meeting summoned to abolish it. If all goes well Synge and Lady Gregory and myself will have everything in our hands, indeed the only practical limitation to our authority will be caused by the necessity of some sort of a permanent business committee in Dublin. We are too often away to do that part of the work, or at any rate Russell who is urging on the changes thinks so. It has been a long fight, but the change could not be made until the old method had discredited itself and until three or four people had got some sort of natural leadership. We are not out of the wood yet, but I think we are practically so. We start the autumn by playing the revivals that we are bringing to London in November, and on our return from London we start our new work with Lady Gregory's White Cockade, a very fine thing. Then we shall have new plays by Boyle and

---

[2] See pp. 17, 28. A parcel containing the plays Quinn had copyrighted in America had just arrived at Coole and AG also wrote to him on this day (NYPL) with a 'thousand thanks': 'what a wonderful present to receive! It is like having two children return from a wash with their clothes changed by the fairies! And in my turn, I shall find such a pleasure in having these charming little volumes to give to my friends, who should all be grateful to you, not me.' Quinn, as he had explained to WBY on 24 Feb 1905 (Himber, 64), took some care with these publications, having them 'printed from lynotype ... bound in paper covers and an edition of fifty of each struck off'. He had done editions of *Kincora*, *Spreading the News*, *The Shadow of the Glen*, and *The Well of the Saints* in this way, and had evidently only just got round to sending them to Ireland.

[3] See pp. 108, 130.

[4] Pan Karel Mušek (1867–1924), actor and stage manager of the Royal Bohemian National Theatre in Prague, translated Synge's play into Czech as *Ve Stinu Doliny* in the summer of 1905 and produced it on 22 Aug 1907. The barrister R. J. Kelly had told Holloway on 12 July that Mušek was translating the play, and Holloway had apprised Synge of this on 17 July (NLI), sending him later that day (TCD) Mušek's address in Prague. Mušek visited Synge in Dublin in July 1906 and at the end of the same month was AG's guest at Coole, where he met WBY. He subsequently translated *Riders to the Sea*, *The Well of the Saints*, *The Playboy of the Western World*, and *The Aran Islands*.

[5] WBY had made this statement on 8 Apr 1905 in his speech before the Literary and Historical Society of University College (see p. 77, n. 9), and it had been mocked by, among others, Maurice Joy (1884–1944) in the July number of the *New Ireland Review* (258): 'while I admire the splendid friendship which has impelled him into his petulant defences of Mr. Synge, I am entitled to smile at his prophecies. ... at the retributions which time is to thunder on Mr. Synge's critics. I hope that Mr. Synge is to have a European reputation, but I still await the evidences of it.'

Synge and I hope Colum's new version of broken Soil.[6] He has made it altogether anew, and put good common speech upon it which will be a great sorrow to those admirers of his who thought that his little confusions and muddinesses were a profound knowledge of human nature. Gatty came to 'The Land', and was very melancholy over it, a great falling off from Broken Soil he thought it, a symptom doubtless of the communications of heretical minds.[7]

I have altogether re-written my Shadowy Waters. There is hardly a page of the old. The very temper of the thing is different. It is full of homely phrases and of the idiom of daily speech. I have made the sailors rough as sailors should be, characterised all the people more or less, and yet not lost any of my lyrical moments. It has become a simple passionate play, or at any rate it has a simple passionate story for the common sight-seer though it keep something back for instructed eyes. I am now correcting the last few lines, and have very joyfully got 'creaking shoes' and 'liquorice-root' into what had been a very abstract passage.[8] I believe more strongly every day that the element of strength in poetic language is common idiom, just as the element of strength in poetic construction is common passion.

I am beginning to be afraid you are not coming over this year. It will be a disappointment to the company too, who have planned a special show for you. You are to choose what you like out of the repertory.

Yrs sry

W B Yeats

TLS NYPL, with envelope addressed to 120 Broadway, New York, postmark 'GORT SE 16 05'. Wade, 461–2.

[6] Of these three plays only William Boyle's *The Eloquent Dempsy* was in fact produced at the Abbey in the coming season. Synge's *The Playboy of the Western World* was not ready until January 1907 (see p. 28, n. 5), and Colum's *The Fiddler's House*, a rewriting of his *Broken Soil*, was first produced by the Theatre of Ireland in the same year.

[7] Probably Charles Tindal Gatty (1851–1928) who as a lifelong friend of George Wyndham (1863–1913) visited Ireland frequently after Wyndham became Chief Secretary in 1900. He was also a close friend of Wilfrid Blunt and had been a member of the Crabbet Club since 1891. He lived in Liverpool and catalogued the Joseph Mayer Collection of paintings as well as issuing the Annual Reports of the Liverpool Art Club. Apart from his interest in art, Gatty was a devout Catholic, his *The Revival of the Catholic Faith in England* having gone into its fifth edition by 1910, and was evidently suspicious of WBY's supposed influence on the Catholic Padraic Colum. He had himself published a play, a parody based on Sheridan, *The Mixed Critics; or, A Comedy Reversed* (Cambridge, 1899).

[8] The 'creaking shoes' and 'liquorice root' appear in the 1906 version of the play, *VP*, 228 (l. 128) and 227 (l. 116b).

## *To George Russell (AE), [16 September 1905]*

Coole Park | Gort
Saturday

My dear Russell
   Roberts has sent me a copy of the rules. I have only noticed one additional point. You say that the stage manager should be appointed by the business committee.[1] He should be appointed either by the reading committee or by the reading committee and business committee in consultation, probably this last. The reason is that the whole artistic policy of the Society so far as acting is concerned depends on this appointment. We have gained at least half our reputation from the peculiar methods of stage management, and from the methods of acting which arise out of these. I have seen a good many stage managers now, and seen them at work. I know what the difference between our method and theirs is. I cant imagine it ever coming to a clash between the two committees, but one may as well be logical from the outset. I notice that the rule about the reading committee to consist of five has not been changed into 'Not more than five', but I suppose Roberts had the old form of words and that the new were not in time.[2]
   I shall be up on Thursday at latest. Your picture (Lady Gregory's) has come, looking very well.[3]

Yrs ever
W B Yeats

TLS Indiana.

## *To George Russell (AE), 17 September [1905]*

Coole Park
Sept 17

My dear Russell.
   Synge is here, and has gone carefully through the rules. He thinks the scheme is a good working compromise, but raises one or two points.

---

[1] Having deleted the clause on the election of the stage manager (see pp. 170–1), AE had replaced it with the rule (Harvard) that the 'stage manager shall be nominated by the business committee'.

[2] AE's drafted clause read: 'The Reading Committee shall be five in number and they shall consider all plays proposed for performance by the society and their decision as to the acception or rejection of a play shall be final.'

[3] AE's oil on canvas portrait of Lady Gregory is reproduced in *Pictures at the Abbey Theatre* [Dublin, 1983], 40.

One is obvious the moment it is stated. The rule as to a dispute between stage manager and author being arbitrated upon by a person appointed by the business committee is open to the same objection as is the appointment of the stage manager by that committee. It is not a business question at all, and the appeal should be to the reading committee who can appoint an arbitrator at their discretion or settle it otherwise.

Synge however considered that the one matter of supreme importance is to put it in his own words 'that those who are giving their lives to the work must have a working majority among the general members'—He considers that we on our side should not accept the whole constitution at all unless we have this. Lady Gregory is strongly of the same opinion, and so am I.[1]

I have been inclined to think that it would be possible to leave the Norman and Miss Laird question over to be settled by the first meeting of the new executive. Synge is of opinion that it must be a part of the settlement itself, and Lady Gregory supports him. This is no slight to them, it is merely because it is necessary from the outset to have the control in the hands of the workers. Synge thinks that it will cause less ill feeling to do this as a part of the general settlement than to have to do it immediately afterwards.[2] The all important thing is the selection of the names of those who sign the rules. With Miss Layard and Norman off this will be, unless Starkie and Roberts cease to be actors, will be Lady Gregory, Synge, Colum, Ryan, Keller, S Gwynn, and myself, which gives those who have taken it for their life work a sufficient majority. Later on if Starkie and Roberts become general members, it will leave us four working members

---

[1] The rule in question read: 'The stage manager and author shall have the sole right to decide on questions as to how a scene shall be acted or what actors shall be selected for the performance. In case of dispute on the latter point the business committee shall appoint <a third> one of <its own> the members of the society to arbitrate. His decision shall be final.' Synge's objection to the clause was probably hardened by the knowledge that the Fays found it obnoxious. Frank Fay had told him on 14 Sept (TCD) that his brother was 'greatly disgusted at a rule, which gives the *final decision* (in the case of a dispute between the stage manager and author, as to how a scene is to be acted) to a member of the Business Committee. Of course this is a rule drawn up by a person who has little practical experience but I hope people will be put on the Business Committee *because of their fitness for transacting business*, and not for deciding artistic questions.'

[2] Again, Synge's views on the necessity of giving authority to the workers in the Society had probably been strengthened by Frank Fay's letter of 14 Sept (see above): 'The whole thing it seems to me is simple. The desire to act and the desire to write plays, among a number of people, gave birth to this Society. Do these people desire, as keenly, to pursue their hobbies seriously, as one would go in for music or painting, to make a profession of them, or do they wish to go on *en amateur*? What is in danger of disabling the Society, if not smashing it up, is just this and nothing else. . . . How do they expect the public to take them seriously when they don't take themselves *seriously enough*? The real trouble is the lack of strong desire, except among the authors, and people must get it into their heads that this is going to be our *life work!*' Although AE's new constitution

in a possible minority, but there is no very serious risk of it.[3] I write this at once, because the more clauses we can have agreed to before the meeting the less time will be wasted in discussion. Neither Miss Laird nor Norman can be offended at being made honorary members when you are being made one by your own desire, and as part of the general settlement.

Yr sny
W B Yeats

TLS Indiana.

## To George Russell (AE) 19 September [1905]

Coole Park | Gort
Sept 19.

My dear Russell,

I said this scheme was a compromise because the only quite satisfactory way of carrying on a theatre is to adopt the system of organisation which has grown up under the ordinary stress of business. I thought you understood that we would always prefer to take the ordinary business scheme used in ordinary theatres and work on that. A director, acting manager, stage manager and so forth, and these responsible to no one. It would be an ungracious thing to propose this unless absolutely driven to it, and there is no need for doing so. The present scheme is from the very nature of things a compromise arising out of the local circumstances.[1] You say we could always bring any combination to an end by stopping our plays and stopping

concentrated power in the hands of the 'general members', there could be no long-term guarantee that the majority of those members would support WBY's party—despite his attempts at gerrymandering here. He was soon to realize that only a more radical restructuring could assure his power over the Society.

[3] WBY's calculations are precarious: it was unlikely that Helen Laird would have accepted the powerless 'honorary' membership, or that James Starkey and George Roberts would have remained as actor members. Both were venturing into publishing, and Starkey was already thinking of giving up acting after a bad performance in *Kincora* in March of this year (see p. 227). WBY himself was to put Roberts out of the part of Conchubar in November because he thought him not up to the role.

[1] This is a reply to an exasperated letter from AE, evidently written the previous day (Berg), in which he demanded: 'Why the devil do you talk of the new rules as a compromise? What do you want. If you want anything else why dont you say so at once & dont be agitating later on for more changes.' Although

the theatre. That is the last thing in the world we could do.[2] What I want to avoid is the kind of thing that happened this summer. After the principle of paying the actors was accepted by a general meeting a long delay arose through the hesitation of the business committee.[3] The result of this has been to throw back the work of the society. We should have gone to

they had early seen the necessity for a radical reform of the INTS, WBY and AG were still trying to square the circle by grafting more businesslike rules onto the comparatively unexacting terms of the 1903 constitution. AE's letter had pointed out that this would almost certainly lead to ambiguous lines of authority, which would offer continuing occasions for disputes: 'I am indifferent about who appoints an arbitrator between the author & stage manager. I suggested the business committee because they are on the spot. You & Synge & Lady Gregory could not come up to Dublin to consider a row between let us say Colm & Fay over who should act a certain character. The delay would be absurd & the business committee should be quite competent to nominate some one on the spot for the purpose. There is no use having rules which would become inoperative afterwards if secession arose. However this can be done as you please. I dont care. I am only suggesting rules for the future work of a society I shall have no further part in, and it is for you to consider whether you want the rules to be practical or not. I am of the opinion that the stage manager, as well as business manager, secretary, and all paid actors should be bound to the business committee by agreements. I think your difficulty could be got over by a clause stating that the Reading Committee must approve of the appointment, but the actual performance of duties must, if your society is not merely to play about in the old way, be seen to by the business committee. To make exceptions would be a great mistake. I think you should be satisfied by the reading committee having to pass the appointments.' Since 30 Dec 1903 the INTS had been registered under the 1896 Friendly Societies Act, which gave non-profit societies certain rights and privileges concerning the holding of land and property, insurance, bankruptcy, and freedom from stamp duties. After the present reorganization it was to be reregistered on 24 Oct 1905 under the Industrial and Provident Societies Act of 1893 (see p. 153, and Appendix).

[2] AE had argued in his letter that WBY's obsession with the politics of faction was misplaced in that his 'side' held the ultimate power: 'Do you mean that you would prefer to go on in the old way when you say that "we on our side should not accept the whole constitution at all unless we have this". What other side are you talking of. Who on earth is there to oppose you. Can the general members carry on the society without you or Synge or Lady Gregory?'

[3] The motion (proposed by AE, seconded by AG) that W. G. Fay, Frank Fay, Maire Walker, Sara Allgood, and Frank Walker should be paid for their exclusive services had been carried with ten in favour at the General Meeting of the INTS on 27 Aug 1905. Since seventeen members were present, there had evidently been a large dissenting minority, and according to Maire Walker it was the proposal to pay the players which began the break up of the original INTS: 'The motion had a mixed reception. Some members supported it; others pointed out that the suggestion that players turn professional was premature, since it had already been agreed to continue on an amateur basis for at least another year, independent of exterior support. Regarding the suggestion that the company as a whole should be subsidised by Miss Horniman, it was pointed out that the old Irish National Theatre Society had been founded in 1902 on the understanding that its independence as a national movement was to be secured only through the efforts of its members. It would be contrary to these ideals to accept a subsidy from an independent source. If such a subsidy was accepted the individual character of the movement would be completely destroyed.' It was also argued, she recalled, that the subsidy was unnecessary since the members were prepared to continue working as they were until the company became self-supporting, but 'Yeats was adamant. He stubbornly supported the motion. "Miss Horniman offers to subsidise us; we will accept her offer." The discussion went on. There was some fiery talk; a number of opinions were aired. The meeting split into two opposing factions—the directorate and some of the members on one side strongly advocating the acceptance of the subsidy; over two-thirds of the original Irish National Theatre Society members on the other. Eventually, on the strength of shares, the motion was carried in favour of the directorate. Since most of the original player-founders were opposed to the decision, the inevitable happened. There was a secession of members' (Nic Shiubhlaigh, 71–2). This account elides

Galway, and might probably have gone from that to some other place, but as things are now we have lost for perhaps a considerable time to come our chance of beginning in the country at all. Under the new arrangement of paying actors we, the authors—I have just heard today that some of those we are paying insist on their contracts being signed by us[4]—are responsible for a sum of nearly three hundred a year.[5] We cannot undergo the risk of arrangements made in our presence being upset or delayed in our absence. So long as we have not a working majority among the general members this may happen.

The Miss Layard-Norman question ought to be settled as part of the general settlement. It is much more civil to them to settle it in that way, and it starts us on the new arrangement with a sense of possible finality. I dont say that she ought to be voted out, but that they ought to be spoken to while the melting pot is still bubbling.[6]

You hadn't told me anything about the legal difficulty, it is one of the penalties we have to pay for the Friendly's Act, which has, I suppose, some counterbalancing advantage. However there is a saying about a coach and four.[7] I dont for one moment however believe that anything of the kind is

---

several different meetings and telescopes the split in the Society; it also disguises the fact that Miss Walker herself was a willing beneficiary of the new system.

[4] W. G. Fay had warned WBY on 8 Sept (see p. 172): 'I expect that the Walkers wont except [*for* accept] of the guarantee. Moire has suddenly developed an extraordinary interest in her brother and thinks he ought to be offered more money. I said I have know [*for* no] objection to him getting more & that I stated the sum as a starting basis to see how he would get on. I dont know of course whether he would settle down to work or not. I will hear tonight & then let you know.' He duly reported the following day (NLI) that he had 'had an interview with Moyra Walker last night and she is willing to take the moneyed engagement, but reckoned that her brother was worth more than 10s. and of course I think they are all worth more but we are too hard up to give it. But as she seemed very anxious that he should be along with her I said that I am sure we could promise him the 15s. the same as the others' . Fay's assurance was evidently not enough, and the paid players were insisting on binding contracts.

[5] This was made up of AEFH's subsidies and receipts from productions, and is an understatement.

[6] The anomalous position of Helen Laird and Harry Norman, and their potential for tipping the balance of power in the new Society in what he considered undesirable directions, had preoccupied WBY for some weeks (see pp. 154, 169–70, 181–2). His plan was to neutralize them by altering their status from general to associate or honorary membership, although as they were not actors this was unconstitutional, a fact that AE forcefully pointed out in his letter: 'About Miss Laird & Norman. I think I already told you that the united vote of all the members would have no power to remove them from their position as general members unless on a charge of misconduct brought before a special meeting of members. The Friendly Societies Act has guarded the rights of members most carefully. And of course this applies also to the actors. If they or any of them refuse to change from general to actor members you cant force them. I assume that they will accept the change. I told you I would suggest to these two after the rules were passed to resign but if you bring it before the meeting you will be only doing what you have no power legally to do if they object, and I believe if you mentioned it a good many of Miss Lairds friends would object also & you would not be able to carry it.'

[7] 'A coach and four may be driven through any Act of Parliament': WBY is suggesting that AE could surely find large loopholes in the Friendly Societies Act.

necessary. Norman is I understand quite ready to do anything we want. I dont believe Miss Laird will make difficulties. But I wish very much Miss L[ai]rd could act again, and making her an honorary member would keep this a possibility.

Synge & I will go up tomorrow, by the train which reaches Dublin between 7 & 8.

Yes of course I have no tact, and bully people. That is why I am leaving the whole matter to you. I can only threaten the body, but you can put the soul in uncomfortable places.[8]

Yrs ever<br>W B Yeats

TLS Indiana.


## To Charles Elkin Mathews, [*19*] *September* [*1905*]

COOLE PARK, | GORT, | CO. GALWAY.<br>Sept 20.

My dear Matthews: I enclose a letter from Thring. Please do as he suggests. It will save us both trouble.[1]

Yrs sny<br>W B Yeats

APS Texas, with envelope addressed in AG's hand to Vigo St Dublin, redirected to London; postmark 'ORANMORE SE 19 05'.[2]


[8] AE evidently levelled these charges towards the end of his letter, which is now missing, but something of his tone and sentiments are recoverable from an undated letter he wrote to AG at this time (Berg): 'I feel sure that there would be no use in my continuing to negotiate in this matter, so long as Yeats interferes. He would wreck anything he is concerned with by his utter incompetence to understand the feelings or character of anybody he is dealing with. With you and Synge anyone might arrange a compromise but if W.B.Y is to act as diplomatist then I see nothing for it but a row and publicity of the whole business, and it will certainly do neither W.B.Y or the drama any good.... Every time I meet W.B.Y I feel inclined to throw him out of the window when he talks business. He has no talent for anything but writing and literature & literary discussions. Outside that he should be fined every time he opens his mouth. If I was autocrat of Ireland I would give him twenty thousand a year if at the end of a year he had written two hundred lines of poetry. If he opened his mind on business or tried to run any society I would have him locked up as dangerous to public peace.'

[1] See pp. 146–7, 167, 174. The letter from Herbert Thring, secretary of the Society of Authors, has not survived, but presumably suggested that Mathews should put more pressure on John Lane to resolve the question of rights in *The Wind Among the Reeds*.

[2] On the flap of the envelope, but not in WBY's hand, is written: 'The Wind Among the Reeds'.

## To Lady Gregory, [21 September 1905]

Nassau Hotel | Dublin

My dear Lady Gregory: All is going better than well—as Morris' people say.[1] Russell has himself proposed a limited liability company with you I & Synge as directors.[2] Miss Horniman is behaving very generously I spoke to her about it to day & said she would not go into the company, as Russell proposed, as if she did she would be King Stork & thought King Log the better part.[3] She will however hand over to one of us—Synge I think—enough money to run the company & give us full power—the others will receive a few shares each to connect their names with it without giving power. Her money will be given as a personal matter which will she says free her from the responsability for our acts which she would feal, if she was herself a shareholder. I think no serious objection will be made—Robert[s] & Miss Laird agree. The preliminary will take a couple of weeks & we will then have to be on the spot to arrange details. Oct 2 is the date of the first performance of the theatre.

I think Jacks show is good—the best he has had—I have picked in consultation with Russell & my father two pictures, both very good. George Moore has bought a little picture. He praised one of those I have got for Quinn.[4] Poor Miss Horniman said this morning "It is no compliment for Lady Gregory to ask me to Coole. She does that because she likes me personally but it is a compliment to be disliked by the Gaelic League. They do that because of my public position".[5] She is really behaving very well

---

[1] In *The Well at the World's End* (1896), II. 158, Richard of Swevenham tells Ralph of Upmeads that his marriage to Ursula is 'better than well, and better than well' because he is leaving a fairy Celtic bride for a real one. In *Aut* (152) WBY revealed that the characters in this legend were 'always, to my mind, in the likeness of Artemisia and her man'.

[2] AE's attempt to reach a compromise by revising the rules of the INTS under the Friendly Societies Act having reached an impasse, he now suggested the far more radical step of reconstituting the Society as a limited liability company. This was probably the most far-reaching step taken in the history of the Abbey Theatre, and entirely altered its power-structures and policies. In her reply (Berg), AG confessed that she did not 'know anything about L.L. Companies but as you & Synge & Fay & Miss H are satisfied no doubt it is all right, & it is a comfort having got rid of those clumsy rules'.

[3] In Aesop's fable 'The Frogs Desiring a King', Jupiter first gives the frogs a log as king, but when they complain of its passivity, sends a stork which devours them.

[4] Jack Yeats's exhibition 'Pictures of Life in the West of Ireland' was held in the Leinster Hall from 19 Sept to 4 Oct, and there were forty-five items on show. Holloway noted on 21 Sept (NLI) that his prices ranged from 3 to 15 guineas, and that many of the pictures had already been sold. Moore bought *Micky Mack and John Devine*, and WBY bought *A Political Meeting, County Sligo* and '*There was an Old Prophecy found in a Bog*' for Quinn.

[5] The Gaelic League, fearing that a powerful Irish literature in English would undermine its attempts to revive the Irish language, often attacked the Abbey Theatre, but AEFH seems to have got its criticisms out of proportion and Padraic Colum recalled in the *Dublin Magazine* of Jan–Mar 1950 (24) that 'some of us felt harassed by Miss Horniman who had come over to Dublin and annoyed some of us by her repeated declarations that the Gaelic League was out for her blood'.

however over this company. She said to me this morning 'You have had experience of me in one society is not that enough'.[6]

Yrs ev
W B Yeats

ALS Berg, with envelope addressed to Coole, postmark 'DUBLIN SE 21 05'.

## To Frank Sidgwick, [c. 23 September 1905]

Mention in Sotheby catalogue.
Brief ALS to the publisher Frank Sidgwick, enclosing the preliminary verses for *The Shadowy Waters* and informing him that 'the verses about the Seven Woods come first'.[1]

Sold Sotheby's, 21 February 1978, catalogue 'Cadmus', item 469.

## To Lady Gregory, [24 September 1905]

Nassau Hotel.

My dear Lady Gregory: The Theatre has agreed to the company in principle but we arnt out of the wood yet as the very essance of the new scheme is that the capital invested may give the directors an over mastering influence. Ryan is fighting for democracy & at first asked that everybody no matter how many their shares might have but one vote. Synge & I rejected this & his present proposal is that their predominance should be limited to 'one third'. I think all will be well.[1]

Sherard the biographer of Wilde is here.[2] He came to see me this morning & told me an amusing story about a man called Bryan Leighton who has a big house some where in England. He was staying with this man,

---

[6] i.e. the Golden Dawn, which AEFH had joined in January 1890 and WBY in March of the same year. They had both been involved in controversies in the society following the rebellion against MacGregor Mathers's leadership in 1901 (see III. 29–34, 36–40, 42–7).

[1] These were for *Poems, 1899–1905* (see p. 176).

[1] A General Meeting of the INTS was held at the Abbey Theatre on 22 Sept, attended by WBY, AE, J. M. Synge, Fred Ryan, W. G. Fay, F. J. Fay, Maire Walker, Helen Laird, Vera Esposito, Sara Allgood, Dossy Wright, James Starkey, Frank Walker, George Roberts, and Thomas Keohler. AE proposed and Synge seconded a motion to form the National Theatre Society Ltd., and this was passed with fourteen in favour and one against. It was also agreed that WBY, Synge, and Fred Ryan should draw up the articles of association.

[2] Robert Harborough Sherard (1861–1943), author, biographer, journalist and great-grandson of Wordsworth, had published *Oscar Wilde: The Story of an Unhappy Friendship* in 1902, hoping that the

& spoke of Leighton. Bryan Leighton made very little of Leighton 'yes a member of the family but just a painter' & brought him to the hall & pointed to a peice of armour & said 'now there is the breast plate of an ancestor who died fighting for his king in Ireland against James II—there is the hole made by the bullet that killed him'. Sherrard said 'yes that i[s] not the breast plate, thats the back peice'. The man was very indignant & said the bullet must have richetted (is that spelt right.). Sherard says however that it was a straight hit in the back.[3] I cant get away from this yet—I hope I wont be kept here till Oct 2.[4] I am writing to M[rs] Emery for information about 'the articles of association' of the ordinary theatres.[5] Fay has had a delightful model theatre made for building scenes in. I have ordered one at a 20/- and will bring it to Coole. Robert should have one & I should have one in London. It is one inch to foot & has all the various details of a stage. I am sending a note which please send on to Miss Monsell—it is about the posters we want more & at once.

Yrs ev<br>W B Yeats

discreet private printing would 'be accepted as deference to its opinion by that section of the public who, because in a man of genius the allied madness once got the upper hand, would consign him and the works which that genius created to the eternal night of eternal oblivion'. His *The Life of Oscar Wilde* appeared in 1906, and subsequent works included *The Real Oscar Wilde* (1912) and *Bernard Shaw, Frank Harris, and Oscar Wilde* (1937). In his autobiography *My Friends the French* (1909), Sherard recalls meeting WBY at the Contemporary Club during a trip to Ireland. He was impressed (71) with WBY's 'striking appearance.... Winning voice devoid of affectation and ... evident fund of thought and knowledge'. Holloway recorded his impressions of this opening meeting of the Contemporary Club, which took place on 23 Sept (NLI): 'Mr Robert H. Sherard, who is over here looking up materials for a life of Oscar Wilde, was the guest of the evening & Oscar Wilde formed the subject of discourse. His literary side was scarcely touched upon by the speakers, but many personal reminiscences of exceptional interests were told by W. B. Yeats & others. His "great sin" & how his biographer should deal with it was the subject of a long debate in which C. H. Oldham, the Chairman [Jack O'Connell], Mr Walker, W. B. Yeats, & John O'Leary were the chief speakers.' Holloway records that there were twenty-three people present, including AE, Synge, and JBY ('who jotted down a profile of John O'Leary in his note book').

[3] Major Sir Bryan Baldwyn Mawddwy Leighton (1868–1919), a JP for Shropshire, fought in the Spanish-American War, the South African War, the Russo-Japanese War, the Balkan War, and the First World War. The family manor was at Loton Park, Shrewsbury. Frederick Leighton (1830–96), Lord Leighton of Stretton, the popular Victorian painter, was president of the Royal Academy for the last eighteen years of his life. Although both Leighton families originated in Shropshire, Sir Bryan and Lord Leighton were not related.

[4] The next productions by the INTS, revivals of *The Building Fund* and *The Land*, were scheduled for 2 Oct. In fact, WBY was obliged to remain in Dublin until the beginning of November.

[5] It is unlikely that WBY did write to FF at this point, as his letter of 6 Oct (which does not mention articles of association) assumes ignorance on her part about the restructuring of the INTS. Since negotiations went better than he had anticipated, he would not have needed further information about articles of association.

Miss Monsells address is in my address book which is [in] my room or in drawing room.[6]

ALS Berg, with envelope addressed to Coole, postmark 'DUBLIN SE 24 05'.

## *To Lady Gregory, 25 September 1905*

NASSAU HOTEL, | D U B L I N.
25th Sept. 1905.

My dear Lady Gregory

All is going intolerably well. Ryan, Russell and Synge come in to-night to discuss details. The principal question is the distributing of the votes. Ryan at first wanted the voting power to be equal, that is to say, that the holder of a hundred shares would have no more votes than the man who had one. Synge and myself of course rejected this. Ryan then proposed various other devices to limit the director's voting power to one quarter of the whole. He then proposed one-third. I think this would be workable as it would give us the majority if we could always be certain of five votes in addition to our own. The worst of it is, it does not leave much for accidents, as I calculate there are just five people who are taking the work entirely seriously.[1] The rest are likely to drop out as better people join us. The permanent satisfactoriness of this arrangement would depend on our power to make new efficient people shareholders from time to time.[2] I have now put the matter

[6] WBY wanted a new batch of Abbey posters (see p. 30) to advertise the productions beginning on 2 Oct. At this time Elinor Monsell was living at 95 Elm Park Gardens, in Hendon, north-west London.

[1] See p. 181, n. 2. AG was not at all pleased by this proposal and replied in some anxiety on 26 Sept (Berg): 'Your letter today rather alarms me—It does not seem worth all the trouble of forming a Company if we are still in danger of being over-ruled. Until it is formed, we have it in our power to break up the present Society & start one of our own—but if we have once made this new Company, we shall be tied to it for ever. I dont know anything about LL Companies—but I should like to be sure the adding of new shareholders is not unlimited. . . . I thought the object of forming a company was that the Directors shall have the power—If we have not got it, I dont think Miss Horniman ought to part with her money. It seems to me that the practically useless element are trying to exploit the valuable property created by the work of a few authors & actors & by Miss H capital. If we give in to this now, we have but little chance of getting free again. I feel sure there must be some reason for your accepting only a one third chance of power, since you, or we, will have practically all the responsibility & all the blame will fall on us if things go wrong.' The five workers were WBY, AG, Synge, and the two Fays.

[2] The 1906 constitution put control of the Society's membership exclusively in the Directors' hands. Rule 25 read: 'Applications shall be considered by the Directors at the next ensuing meeting, and notice of admission or otherwise shall be sent to the applicant within one week after the meeting of Directors at which the application is considered.'

into Russell's hands who has just seen Miss Hornaman.[3] She is a very valuable ally just now as she is insisting upon such arrangements as will give her security for the successful employment of her guarantee and of the capital she is about to invest. Russell is supporting us thoroughly. I don't think we can get to London with the Company until November 25th owing to difficulties of getting a hall.[4] What change this will make in our programme I don't quite know, but it will mean rehearsing "White Cockade" before London and performing it early in December. This morning Fay and Synge and myself considered the tinker play with a view to performance and publication in Samhain but decided that it would be dangerous at present.[5] Synge is taking the re-organisation very much in earnest and will, I think, make a good director. He has a plan for bringing a Gaelic Company from the Blasket islands which Miss Hornaman does not object to. We will have to consider it presently. Synge would stage-manage it himself. Fay is very doubtful of it however, as he thinks we would not be able to do the plays better than the League.[6]

When do you come up? I suppose you are coming for the plays on October 2nd. We will want you for the Meeting that is to ratify or reject our new arrangement, which has only been accepted in principle. That meeting will come, I imagine, towards the end of next week.[7] I can't

[3] Probably as a consequence of this visit from AE, AEFH wrote a formal letter to WBY the following day (NLI), insisting that voting power should exactly match the shares held (see below, pp. 236–7).

[4] The London productions took place on 27 and 28 Nov at St George's Hall.

[5] See p. 173. In *The Tinker's Wedding* a young tinker's attempt to marry the man she has been living with for several years is thwarted by an avaricious, worldly priest and the amoral, drunken mother of her intended husband. It was 'dangerous' because its theme and outspoken language would have certainly intensified the charges of immorality and anti-Irishness levelled at Synge since the production of *The Shadow of the Glen* in 1903, and which had been repeated at the beginning of this year (see pp. 25–7, 31–3, 34). Another controversy would have been particularly unwelcome at a time when WBY and Synge were engaged in delicate negotiations over the future of the INTS, and hostility to Synge was always latent in Dublin: on 10 Nov Holloway, describing him in his diary (NLI) as 'another writer puffed into existence by the log-rolling of Yeats', maintained that he looked at 'Ireland through the glass of non-moral Paris Bohemia, which makes all Irish folk rub their eyes . . . on beholding his puppets deport themselves in the same non-moral way, though labelled Irish & set in an Irish background'. A few weeks later WBY failed in an attempt to get Maunsel to publish the play in the same volume as *The Aran Islands*, the canny George Roberts informing Synge on 8 Dec that 'W.B. suggested we should put your tinker play in the Aran but I think that one play is enough for this publication — for other reasons I think they would be better in a seperate [*sic*] book.'

[6] Synge had written to Nathalie Esposito on 8 Sept (see p. 169, n. 2), describing his August visit to the Great Blasket Island: 'Every evening twenty or thirty men and girls used to come up into our house to dance and amuse themselves in the kitchen so that we had great festivities. The worst of that sort of place is that I feel so miserably lonely for weeks after I leave it.' This 'Gaelic company' impressed Synge with their 'peculiar attractiveness', but they never appeared at the Abbey Theatre. Apart from the logistical difficulties of bringing a company from Aran, the Keating branch of the Gaelic League was mounting regular and successful performances of Irish plays in Dublin.

[7] The meeting took place on 9 Oct. AG replied (Berg) that she was uncertain about her movements: 'I don't know when I can go up. . . . I think certainly I can't go up till end of next week — just for last night of theatre.' In fact she arrived in Dublin on the afternoon of Saturday, 7 Oct, in time to see the last night of the plays.

possibly get away from here till these negotiations are over. I am trying to do a little work and worked on the "Shadowy Waters" for about an hour yesterday.

I think I told you about Fay's model Theatre for building scenery on. I have ordered one, partly, because there's a carpenter who has to be kept busy till we can definitely engage him.[8] Fay had got his made for this reason in part. I think we should have one of these stages at Coole and another at my rooms in London. They are much more elaborate things than that little model of mine, and will make it possible to judge of the effect of a scene before making it on a large scale.

I am writing to Harry Padget to try and get his model for the "Shadowy Waters" scene that Fay may set it up in his model stage.[9] I am afraid I must ask you to send me some of my shirts as I am staying on so much longer than I expected.[10]

Ys ever
W B Yeats

TLS Berg, with envelope addressed to Coole, postmark 'DUBLIN SE 25 05'.

## *To Harry Paget, [? 26 September 1905]*

Mention in previous letter.

---

[8] Seaghan Barlow (1880–1972), a friend of the Walkers, contributed reminiscences of his thirty-year association with the Irish players, as handyman and stage carpenter, to Lennox Robinson's *Ireland's Abbey Theatre* (1951), 69–76. Although he took minor roles in AG's *Spreading the News* and Boyle's *The Mineral Workers*, it was, as Robinson recalls (66), 'in all other ways that he has shown his genius for the stage. He knows everything in scene-making and prop-making, but, sullen over his cocoa and his Greek, he states he can do nothing. An hour later, everything is done to perfection.' Sara Allgood corroborates this impression in her unpublished 'Memories' (Berg), describing Barlow as 'a curious young man, hardly ever smiled, taciturn, rather bad tempered. He would be asked to make a chair or a table for a scene and every difficulty in the world he would make as to why it could or should not be made the way it was wanted; till finally the Fays or the Directors would give up in despair and leave him, and then to their complete surprise, at the appointed time, up would come the article in dispute, beautifully made, and ready for what it was wanted for.' Gordon Craig had built WBY a miniature stage in 1902 (see III. 185, 201), but this new model theatre was probably the more elaborate one described by Ernest Rhys in *Everyman Remembers* (1931): 'a most ingenious little toy with small electric lights and other contrivances' (70).

[9] For Harry Paget see p. 95. WBY wanted to take the London scenery as a model in reviving the play, rather than that used in the production at the Molesworth Hall in January 1904. On 13 Oct he told Holloway (NLI) that the London staging 'was a well defined galley & was effective. Mr Synge thought the scene used at the Molesworth Hall too gloomy for anything & Yeats agreed with him'—presumably hearsay on WBY's part as he had been in America at the time of that production.

[10] AG replied that she was 'sending shirts', and the following week sent the rest of his clothes as 'I dont suppose you will want to come back here so late' (Berg).

## *To Lady Gregory, 26 September 1905*

NASSAU HOTEL, | D U B L I N.
26th Sept. 1905.

My dear Lady Gregory
    Russell and Ryan and Synge came in last night to go on drawing up rules. We have decided to hold out for an absolute majority. Synge I think <is> a little doubtfully, but Russell, strange to say, is strong for it. Of course Synge wants it if we can get it but seems inclined to make concessions if they are insisted upon. Fay wants us to have absolute majority and so does Miss Hornaman. We are drawing up the Articles of Association in such a way as will give us this. Ryan is helping us but will oppose us when we put them to the Society.[1] I am very glad to have your letter on the subject as it strengthens our position.[2] I am sorry London is coming on as the necessity of having enough peace to get there <rather weakens our hand> makes it necessary to be cautious. I agree with you however that we must get a final settlement now while we have Fay and the more earnest members thoroughly upon our side.
    I am going to have the Meeting called for next Monday week. <If I find that the afternoon of Saturday week is impossible for Russell.> Russell told me last night that he couldn't come on afternoons and that Sunday Meetings were illegal. I will ask him if he could make an exception for Saturday afternoon [*added later in WBY's hand*: he is away so Monday it must be] that we may be through as quick as possible—I don't suppose it greatly matters however as we will all have to be in Dublin to settle up things under the new arrangement for a few days. We can do a certain amount before hand, coming to an understanding between ourselves as to the distribution of the officers, etc. Koeller and Ryan are the chief difficulty. They are neither actors or dramatists, and feel therefore that the Society is only of service to them as an illustration of their public principles. Last night Ryan went back to his original proposal of everybody, no matter how much capital they had in the Society, having but the one vote. I wish he'd stick to that as it would make his position absurd, but he won't. The controversy will be between the absolute majority proposal and the one-third proposal. We must leave things as much as possible to Russell who now advocates

---

[1] See p. 187, n. 1.
[2] On 24 Sept AG had written (Berg): 'I read Robert what you said, & he thought like me that it sounded very unsatisfactory, if the directors get so little power—& are dependent on diplomatising and picking up outside votes. I feel it should be put plainly, we & Colum are giving plays, the Fays are giving acting, at a low rate of pay—Miss Horniman is giving the theatre—what is anyone else giving?'

everything we insisted upon in our correspondence with him. All those arguments came out last night in his discussion with Ryan.

Let me know when you are coming up.

Synge and myself are going thro' Boyle's play. We have finished the first act and have crossed out quantities.[3] I have settled the date of my Aberdeen lecture and Lady Cromartie has asked me to go and stay with her afterwards. I am trying to arrange a lecture in Edinburgh thro' a friend of Miss Hornaman's.[4] By the by Miss Hornaman entirely misunderstood us about the "Shadowy Waters". She was under the impression that you or I had told her at Coole that I had definitely given "Shadowy Waters" to Mrs. Emery. This came out when she said "I couldn't feel any interest in the play. It is Mrs. Emery's play."[5] I am rather in difficulties over the scene where Forgail wakes Dectora.[6] I wish you were here to help me with it. I am going to have a try at it to–day.

[*Remainder of letter in WBY's hand*]

Fay asks me to ask Robert to send him a design for Forgaels harp at once. He says he must have six weeks experiment.[7]

Yrs ever

W B Yeats

TLS Berg, with envelope addressed to Coole, postmark 'DUBLIN SE 26 05'.

[3] i.e. *The Eloquent Dempsy*, see p. 162.

[4] During this trip to Scotland WBY lectured in Edinburgh on 10 Jan 1906 on 'Irish Heroic Poetry', at Dundee on 11 Jan on 'Literature and the Living Voice', a talk he repeated the following day at the University Literary Society in Aberdeen, with Professor Herbert Grierson (1866–1960), the 17th-century scholar, in the chair. He then went on to visit the Countess of Cromartie at Castle Leod, Strathpeffer, Ross-shire. The Edinburgh friend of AEFH's was probably the painter James Paterson, who was later to lend valuable assistance during the Abbey Theatre's visits to the city.

[5] AEFH had evidently purported to believe that WBY, in allowing FF to produce the play for the Theosophical Society, had assigned the rights permanently to her. She and FF had fallen out over the Golden Dawn in 1901 (see III. 25–7, 29–34, 36–40, 42–7), and WBY's now intimate relationship with FF (see pp. 112, 114) no doubt added to her jealousy.

[6] In the revised version of the play Forgael, while enchanting Dectora with his harp-playing into forgetting her previous life, does not, as previously, send her to sleep, and so there is no awakening scene (see pp. 135, 161).

[7] FF had evidently failed to send the now broken harp used in her production (see pp. 95, 102, 151), and the problems with it finally proved insurmountable, as WBY explained in his notes to *Poems, 1899–1905*: 'the stage carpenter found it very difficult to make the crescent-shaped harp that was to burn with fire; and besides, no matter how well he made the frame, there was no way of making the strings take fire. I had, therefore, to give up the harp for a sort of psaltery, a little like the psaltery Miss Farr speaks to, where the strings could be slits covered with glass or gelatine on the surface of a shallow and perhaps semi-transparent box; and besides, it amused one to picture, in the centre of a myth, the instrument of our new art' (*VP*, 815–16).

## To Lady Gregory, 27 September 1905

NASSAU HOTEL, | D U B L I N.
27th Sept. 1905.

My dear Lady Gregory

There is something in your letter which I don't understand. You say "Robert doesn't go till 30th and I could go up that day and see the last night of play and stay for Meeting". But the plays don't begin till October the 2nd. They go from Monday the 2nd to Saturday the 7th and the Meeting has been summoned for Monday 9th. The essential thing is that you are up for the Meeting, but of course the sooner you come the better pleased I shall be.[1]

The Company is going to London at the end of Nov. and it is, I am afraid, imperative that "White Cockade" be put into rehearsal immediately Colum's play is finished.[2] The alternative is a very bad programme of revivals. You can, however, see the opening rehearsals and the final ones which will I suppose, be sufficient. One can only really chop about at the beginning. The play should be performed about the 11th or 12th November. I am afraid you wanted it later than this but it is our only chance of a good programme.

Fay suggests putting either "Spreading of the News" or "Riders to the Sea" or "Bailey's Strand" with it.[3] I think "Bailey's Strand" had better go with Boyle's play which we propose to start on Boxing Night. Fay sends this day the model stage by passenger train, as though this is slightly more expensive, it is much quicker.[4] It is very important for us to have the scenery for "White Cockade" as soon as possible. I think Robert may be able to work out model scenes which can be copied pretty easily, especially if he can come to Dublin for a few days to put the last touches on them. Fay is, however, very urgent about having designs for scenery and costumes at once.[5]

---

[1]  In a letter of 28 Sept (Berg) AG explained that she had 'made a slip of the pen in saying "30th" — it is 7th I go up. Robert will I think come with me, & stay to do any scene-painting necessary.'

[2]  Colum's *The Land* finished on 7 Oct, but, although *The White Cockade* was rehearsed during October, it had to be postponed until 9 Dec, as extra time was needed to prepare the plays to be taken on the English tour, a decision which, as Holloway noted on 3 Nov (NLI), further exacerbated the ill-feeling in the Company: 'The Walkers seem very annoyed over the postponement of the monthly performances at the Abbey this month — sacrificed for the sake of London! The Irish National Theatre Society has been turned into a limited company under the title of *The National Theatre Society Ltd* lately, & if omens are to be trusted, it is an ill one that made its first act the boycott or abandonment of this months Dublin shows for the sake of those to be given in London at the end of the month. All eyes are on London just now at the Abbey.'

[3]  When it was finally staged, the play was produced by itself.

[4]  This was true: in her reply of 28 Sept (Berg) AG announced that the 'model theatre has just arrived. I wonder where you will find room for one in Woburn Buildings!' In fact, according to Rhys (see p. 191, n. 8) WBY kept it in the stuffy attic where he slept.

[5]  Robert Gregory's watercolour costume designs for *The White Cockade*, placed in an album compiled by AG, were sold at auction at Sotheby's in December 1982 (lot 189). They were generally

Now about the Company,—the directors reserve the right to refuse transfer of shares and nobody but the directors can allot shares. The directors will be absolutely supreme in everything. They will appoint all Committees and all Officers and decide on the programme of plays etc. It was avowedly because of these powers that Ryan fought for a limitation upon the votes under their personal control. We have however, refused this limitation. I think we will carry the thing through but it was very doubtful last Saturday when we did not yet know how far Russell would go in his support of us. The power to allot shares would, in any case, have given us authority in the end of an absolute kind. We are all now, however, quite resolute about making no concessions.[6]

Fay is nervous about the front scene in "White Cockade", but confident about the rest.[7] I think he is only nervous about the front scene because it is one, and that he is wrong. Miss Hornaman has just bought Jack's picture of the old Mechanic's Institute Theatre to hang up in the Entrance hall.[8]

Boyle's play, except for the last few pages, gets sufficiently right by the mere cutting out of passages. You will be surprised when you see it again, it has a genuine energy. He has made a lot of revisions but has not sent over his revised version. We are writing for this and will make a text ourselves and give him a seniero [ *for* scenario] probably for the swampy bit at the end.

Now that we are going to have a position of so much more authority we needn't be so diplomatic. However, we can get Colum to explain our

admired at the first production, and Holloway remarked on 12 Dec (NLI) that 'quite a series of beautiful historical pictures were exhibited to your gaze during its progress. The costumes and scenery had been designed by Robert Gregory with an eye to harmonious colouring, and the grouping of the various characters was arranged so as to realise to the full the colour scheme of the youthful artist. "Charm" is the only word to adequately sum up the result of this combination.'

[6] See p. 189 and Appendix. Rule 27 of the new constitution stated that transfers of shares 'may only be made with the consent of the Directors'. Rule 44 stipulated that all questions at general meetings 'shall be decided by a majority of votes, and each individual member shall have one vote for every fully paid up share held by him', with the exception of proposals about expulsion of members, appointment of new directors, and amendment of the rules, when a policy of one-man-one-vote operated. This, as WBY says, gave the Directors absolute power, and rules 46 and 47 confirmed their right to appoint and remove any of the Society's employees, including the secretary and stage manager.

[7] Act II scene i of *The White Cockade* takes place in a wood and has to be played in front of a curtain hiding the inn setting that is used in Act I and Act II scene ii. W. G. Fay's objection was, however, more fundamental: in *The Fays of the Abbey Theatre* (1935) he complained (185) that the play 'lacks dramatic movement' so that the actors suffered 'from having to play a series of short scenes none of which has enough emotional scope for anyone to show his quality'.

[8] Jack Yeats's watercolour *'Willie Reilly' at the Old Mechanics Theatre* was on show at his current exhibition and depicts a scene from James Whitbread's melodrama based on William Carleton's popular novel of 1855, *Willy Reilly and his Dear Colleen Bawn*. On 21 Sept 1905 Holloway noted in his diary (NLI) that the picture (which is reproduced in colour in *Pictures at the Abbey Theatre*, 15) was 'probably intended for the Mechanics before it became the Abbey, but is not a bit like it was. The audience, however, are happily characterized.' In her reply (see above) AG said that she was 'delighted Miss Horniman bought that picture of Jack's—we all but cheered for him at breakfast!'

changes still. I have been disappointed however to find that he had cut out hardly anything out of the copy of the play that he had left here for me.[9]

Please get Robert to make that design for a harp, as Fay says he will be 6 weeks experimenting before he gets the electrical part right,[10] both Fays like the new "Shadowy Waters" very much.

Yrs alway<br>W B Yeats

TLS Berg, with envelope addressed to Coole, postmark 'DUBLIN SE 27 05'.

## *To Lady Gregory, 29 September 1905*

NASSAU HOTEL, | D U B L I N.<br>29th Sept. 1905.

My dear Lady Gregory

I have no particular news. The Articles of Association are being drawn up by Ryan, and when they are finished we will meet again, that is to say, Synge, Ryan Russell and myself will meet and put them into what seems to us a final shape. A public auditor is looking through our books to find out how much money we have on hand, he will finish that part of his work to-night; he will then, in consultation with Roberts and Fay, value the costumes and scenery. The Hornaman costumes, the raw material of which Miss Hornaman has estimated at £70 or £80 I think, will be accredited to me.[1] The costumes and scenery of "Kincora" will be accredited to you and any other odds and ends which you may have paid for. The rest of the costumes and scenery will be accredited to the Company as a whole. In this way the number of shares each member is entitled to will be estimated. It will probably work out to about £100 for the Company, exclusive of you and I, who will have about £100 worth of shares between us. Miss Hornaman will then put in about a £100 more distributed in such a way that you I and Synge will have about equal voting power.[2] I think

[9] Colum had been detailed to help with the rewriting of *The Eloquent Dempsy*, but the Fays' and Synge's reservations about this (see pp. 162–3, 164–5) had evidently been confirmed.

[10] See p. 193.

[1] AEFH had bought the material and made the costumes for the first production of *The King's Threshold* in October 1903, and for *The Shadowy Waters* and *On Baile's Strand* in 1904.

[2] Owing to the break-up of the Society, the Directors finally took the controlling number of the shares. A draft 'Allotment Sheet' dated 26 Oct (NYPL) allocated one share each to the Fays, Wright, Sara Allgood, Vera Esposito, and Colum, and 63 each (raised from an original 10) to WBY, AG, and Synge.

this will give us ample capital to work on for the present, as we have her guarantee for all salaries. I have just seen Russell, he thinks he has talked over Starkie who was very much opposed, he tells me, to capital having its full share of votes. He thinks he has talked round or will succeed in talking round all the others. Colum, I am rather sorry to say, is coming up for the Meeting, but Russell will see him before it begins. Russell rather wants us to make Colum a director but I have objected to this. He says that Colum's popularity would help us with the propaganda papers. I have based my objection on the difficulty we would have in consultation. You I and Synge can easily keep in communication with one another and we can talk out all weightier matters at Coole, but the addition of Colum would just have the effect of turning us into a sort of Committee which would have to be got together at stated intervals. There are, of course, other objections, but I thought this one would carry most weight with Russell.

The sooner we get the whole thing settled the better for I can see little signs of returning grievances against Fay etc. in Russell's mind. I shall suggest when the directors get together, if you think well of the idea, that Synge be made Managing Director for (say) the next six months. His business will be to be here on the spot and supervise the other officers and see that they carry out the duties laid upon them by the directors. I think we had better make Frank Fay Secretary, Roberts Advertising Manager, Keoller, Business Manager, and for the present at any rate, limit William Fay strictly to stage management.[3] None of these people will mind being responsible to Synge, while they would very much mind being responsible to one another. When we have got a regular routine of work it will need less close attention, and if Synge wants

---

[3] Hitherto George Roberts had been secretary to the Society, and Keohler had audited its annual accounts, but both were to secede. AE had warned WBY on 6 Sept (Berg) of the need 'to define clearly the rules of stage manager and secretary in the future. Under the rules the secretarial duties are those required of any secretary under the Act, but in a small society like yours where there is a lot to do and few paid people you must have some private understanding as to the *execution of business.* I have provided for the election of a *business manager* which office may be united either with the stage managership or the secretaryship. There is a great deal of work which Roberts used to do, like getting advertisements for programmes, seeing about printing, posters, getting bills in, arranging advertisements none of which are strictly secretarial work. Roberts complained that Fay would never do any of these things. . . . I have about ten years experience of the rows between managers and secretaries in eight hundred societies and I tell you the only way to get things done is to define the work of each in an agreement. Otherwise each will be laying the blame for things not attended to on each other as Roberts and Fay do now. I have heard them complain about each other for hours. Dont let their work depend much on each others work or there will be more.'

to be away out of Dublin, you or I can take the post coming here from time to time to look after it.

I am very glad that you don't mind the "White Cockade" coming on at once. It will give us the best possible start.[4] The impression I myself gather from the countenance of members is, that the anti-Fay party has more sorrow than fight in it and that all will go pretty well. Owing to the bad state of the business management, I am expecting very thin audiences on Monday, something has gone wrong with the advertisement. Holloway, who is not very popular, with some member or other said to that member that they should advertise in the Leader, Nationist, etc. Because he said that it has not been done.[5]

I am trying to get <on> with the "Shadowy Waters" and did a fair day's work to-day and yesterday. I have read it to Fay and there is still some re-casting to be done. I wish you would send me my address book and also that book of Mystic Manuscript, which is in the drawer of my writing table. Please don't look at it for that is against the regulations, but let me have it for it ought to have gone home long ago.[6] There is also a book which I was to autograph for my sister, I left it on the little table in the Library where I generally forget things. If you could sen[d] it me I could get it sent to its owner.

One of the letters you sent on to me was from Miss Carmichael, we forgot to send her the Irish version of "Kathleen Ni Houlihan" which we promised and she asks for it. She has invited me to stay with them when I

---

[4] In her letter of 28 Sept (see p. 194, n. 1) AG wrote that she did not 'mind much if White Cockade comes on in November, as I have to go to Dublin in any case'.

[5] WBY was right in supposing that there would be poor audiences. Sherard, who evidently attended the performances (see the following letter), wrote in *My Friends the French* (72) that the 'patronage of the Dublin public is very poor, and after the first night or two of a new piece the house is practically empty'. Holloway also commented on the thinness of the audiences and on 2 Oct (NLI) was 'beginning to wonder if the Dublin playgoing public will ever find out the National Theatre'. He put down the neglect to various causes—the fact that the two plays were revivals, and that they were too similar in theme and decor—but stressed 'haphazard' business methods as the chief problem, and on 10 Nov asserted that what 'the Society wants most is a person with business tact (having no connection with the Society as actor or dramatist) to manage the commercial side of the theatre. The present people at the head of affairs are too stupidly independent, & egotistical to cater to the interest of the public.' The handling of advertisements and publicity was to be better organized in the new year.

[6] This was almost certainly a Golden Dawn ritual. Following the schism in the Golden Dawn in 1903, WBY had joined R. W. Felkin's Stella Matutina faction (see 1. 488 and 11. 300–1) and was studying sporadically for the grade of Theoricus Adeptus Minor (to which he was admitted in January 1912). For this he was required, among other things, to study rituals on the Enochian System and on the Vibration on the names of Adonai. The Ordinances of the Order directed that all its communications and materials must be 'protected from the view and investigation of all outsiders'.

am in Edinburgh[7] but I think I am promised to some friend of Miss Hornamans.[8]

Yrs alway
W B Yeats

TLS Berg, with envelope addressed to Coole, postmark 'DUBLIN SE 30 05'.

## To R. H. Sherard, 29 September 1905

Nassau Hotel, | Dublin.
Sept. 29th,/05.

Dear M[r] Sherrard,
If you are still in Dublin next Monday, I wish that you would come to the first performance of the new season of the Irish National Theatre Society. We have as you know our own theatre, the Abbey Theatre, Marlborough Street. It begins at 8 o'clock, ask for me & I will get you a seat.[1]

Yours sinly
W B Yeats

Dict AEFH, signed WBY; NYU.

[7] Elizabeth Catherine Carmichael, afterwards Watson (d. 1928), was the daughter of Alexander Carmichael (1832–1912), a Scots scholar, a leader of the Celtic Association, and author of *Carmina Gadelica* (1900). WBY had met them both at the Pan Celtic Conference in Dublin in August 1901 (see III. 110–11), since when Elizabeth had become editor of the *Celtic Review* in 1904, and lectured to the National Literary Society on 'Celtic Folklore' in December of the same year. WBY did stay with them during his visit to Edinburgh, and Alexander Carmichael presided at his lecture on 'Irish Heroic Poetry' at the Philosophical Institution on 10 Jan 1906. The friend of AEFH's was probably the artist James Paterson.

The Revd Thomas O'Kelly's translation of *Cathleen ni Houlihan* into Gaelic (*Caitlin Ni Uallacàin*) had appeared serially in the *United Irishman* from 11 Feb to 11 Mar 1905. It was published shortly afterwards by M. H. Gill & Son, and produced with Hyde's *An Tincéar agus an tSidheóg* at the 1905 Oireachtas on Monday, 14 Aug. An enthusiastic review in *An Claidheamh Soluis* on 19 Aug (7) claimed that Fr. O'Kelly had 'produced an Irish version which does not suffer considerably by comparison with Mr. Yeats' beautiful original. The rhythm and the melody of the English prose are wondrously preserved in the Irish, which, however, has all the excellence of an original.' However, it went on to admit that 'the actors to whom the performance was entrusted did not give so beautiful an interpretation of the play as the interpretation of the English version given by Mr. Fay's company. Probably no actors could.' The Theatre of Ireland revived this version at the Molesworth Hall, Dublin, on 2 and 3 May 1912.

[8] See p. 193, n. 4.

[1] The INTS opened its autumn season on 2 Oct with performances of *The Land* and a revised version of *The Building Fund*. Sherard evidently took up this invitation for he commented upon audiences at the Abbey Theatre in *My Friends the French* (see above, n. 5), where he also noted that WBY's 'autocracy in the matter of selection of plays and general management, very fortunately, remains undisturbed'.

# *To Lady Gregory,* [*4 October 1905*]

Nassau Hotel, | DUBLIN.

My dear Lady Gregory

I have not written to you, because I have been knocked up with a bad cold. I caught it in the Theatre last Saturday, it is practically gone now, but it has left me rather exhausted.[1] I have not been able to write anything since I had the cold, except a few letters and a prose sketch for part of shadowy waters and a couple of hours verse this morning. The articles of the Association are now finished. I hope to get a legal opinion on them to morrow. Russell thinks that Koeller will oppose us at the meeting. It looks as if we were [*for* are] going to have something of a fight. I am quite confident however of winning. Even if what is very unlikely happens, and Miss Walker wavers again, we must go on. We are entirely certain of a perfectly sufficient group of actors going with us whatever happens. I have been impressing upon everybody concerned that if we are defeated on the vote I shall adjourn the meeting, and go on the form of company, which they can enter or not if they like.[2] I mean that I am getting our supporters to understand this for they won't waver so long as they are quite certain that a make shift is impossible. I am putting the worst possible; for the probable result will be that we shall carry our proposal by say, 10 to 4. And we only require a bare majority. Perhaps it might be as well if you got Stephen

---

[1] WBY had probably been attending to business matters at the Abbey Theatre early on Saturday, 30 Sept, but he may have gone to the amateur variety concert put on there that evening by the employees of Hely's Ltd.

[2] This in fact happened. His typed address to the meeting of 9 Oct (see p. 190, n. 7), reveals (Berg) that WBY began by denying that the Society had become a commercial enterprise, went on to call for goodwill (since 'everything has to be done by mutual agreement'), and then devoted most of his speech to explaining why the Society's financial resources could not in fairness be shared out in equal proportions: 'When the Abbey Theatre was opened a sum of I think about £20 was brought into it from the Molesworth performances, and when the session closed there was about £70 to the credit of the Society. Now in measuring out the different portions of this sum due to the activity of different members one comes to one indisputable fact. Mr Frank Fay and Mr William Fay did a larger share towards earning it than any other players. They are with the new Society. All the playwrights also had a share in earning that money. They are with the new Society. The Society was helped also from time to time with sums of money. The Society could not have gone on at all had not a friend of mine in America sent a sum of fifty pounds, to be expended by myself and Lady Gregory on the benefit of the Society as we chose. Other sums were given to the Society, £20 by Lady Gregory, £20 by myself. There were other small sums given from time to time which I cannot recall. Before Abbey Street was open at all, my plays were staged by Miss Horniman at an expense of some fifty or sixty pounds. Lady Gregory's Kincora was staged by her at an expense of thirty pounds for costumes and scenery, and her son gave his time and labour for nothing. If the present directors of this theatre carried on their work in a commercial spirit, they would have had these sums put down in the books of the society, and instead of closing with a profit of £70 last session would have closed with a very large deficit. I need not also remind you that you had not to pay rent for any performances since last January Miss Horniman asking nothing in return

Guinn to come. Yet on consideration do not do anything about this until I see you, it might cause ill-feeling to bring him down just for this one occasion, he never having voted before.[3] We can write to him at the last moment if it is absolutely necessary. We are getting fair audiences for Columns play.[4] Now another matter, I have just had a letter from Mrs Mc'Bride, she has been recommended by Sir William Geary to get an Irish Council's opinion on the question of her husband's domicile. He is claiming Irish Domicile. Her solicitors do not know who to write to, she asks our advice. Please write to me at once, if you have any ideas on the subject. I shall make what enquiries I can.[5] She tells me by-the-by that she

but that the document signed by all should be remembered by you all and its obligations carried out.' After prudently omitting the warning that he had taken legal advice on the matter, and assuring the potentially dissident members that their work was not undervalued in that each of them had 'helped with devotion and self-sacrifice to do work for the intellectual life of this country that will be remembered in history', he adjourned the meeting for a quarter of an hour 'that you may come to an understanding among yourselves as to the amount of the money which you think the individual members to be entitled to'.

[3] In her reply on 5 Oct (Berg) AG thought that if Harry Norman came 'we ought perhaps have Gwynn, but otherwise I am not much for having comparative outsiders'. In fact, neither turned up at the General Meeting of the INTS on 9 Oct, which was attended by seventeen regular members: WBY, AG, Synge, AE, Colum, W. G. Fay, F. J. Fay, Fred Ryan, Maire Walker, Helen Laird, Vera Esposito, Sara Allgood, Dossy Wright, James Starkey, Frank Walker, George Roberts, and Thomas Keohler.

[4] This was not the view of Sherard or Holloway (see p. 198, n. 5), nor of Martyn and others, although when Holloway visited the Abbey on 12 Oct (NLI), W. G. Fay assured him that the 'receipts for the recent season equalled those for June last'.

[5] On 30 Sept MG had written (*G–YL*, 210–11) that she might 'have to get the opinion of an Irish Council as to the question of MacBride's right of claiming an Irish domicile & Irish Nationality. My French Solicitor would of course write to him the exact legal points he would want opinion on — but he will ask me what Council to write to & I thought perhaps you or Lady Gregory could advise me who it would be best to consult. Sir William Geary wrote me most kindly & gave me his opinion unofficially, but he said if it came before the French Courts the opinion of an *active council* of the Irish bar would be necessary.' The question of MacBride's domicile was complicated since technically he was not allowed to return to Ireland on pain of arrest for high treason, having fought for the Boers in the South African War. MG was eager to challenge his claim to Irish domicile because Irish law did not allow divorce but only legal separation. At the hearing in Paris on 26 July MG's lawyer had argued that 'in a divorce it is the law of the country of domicile of the parties, not the law of their native country which must be appealed to. I affirm that Mr. MacBride can no longer appeal to English law, as he was a naturalised citizen of the Transvaal by a decree of President Kruger, and was not only appointed a Major in the Irish Brigade but also a special Justice of the Peace.' He went on to claim that MacBride could not deny this 'as he had the documents signed by President Kruger, framed and hung in the dining-room' (*Irish Independent*, 27 July 1905, p. 5). For his part, MacBride, whose return to Ireland had been ignored by the British authorities, was to assert in an affidavit in the Irish High Court on 1 Jan 1906 that he had not lived in Paris since November 1904, when he returned to Ireland permanently, and that he intended to remain in Ireland permanently.

Sir William Nevill Montgomerie Geary, 5th Baron (1859–1944), barrister-at-law, Inner Temple, and politician, was the author of *The Law of Marriage and Family Relations* (1892), a copy of which he presented to AG who had advised MG to seek his advice (see p. 18, n. 1). He was a long-time friend of George Moore, Edward Martyn, who shared rooms with him in the Temple in 1882, and George Bernard Shaw, with whom, in 1904, he published a manifesto and stood for election to St Pancras County Council. In her reply to this letter (Berg), AG advised WBY to consult Whitney of Whitney & Moore, who 'wd know who is good counsel on questions of domicile', but thought a better bet might be Mr Carton, 'who would tell you for nothing who would be a good man for the London solicitors to write & get the opinion from'.

has the full approval of her French confessor for her action in connection with the divorce. He has even unasked sent her a formal letter of approval, and advised her to show it to Bishops and Priests in Ireland. He came to Paris specially to try and arrange a settlement, but on hearing the facts told her that he considered divorce the only possible step.[6] She is very grateful to Sir William Geary, with whom she has been in correspondence again.

Miss Horniman has been perfectly angelic, she has not lost her temper for a moment, and she has been very practical all through this theatre business. I think she must have been ill at Coole. She goes away to-morrow. Cave praises my brother's pictures, he said "the drawing is sometimes magnificent".[7]

The Exhibition closes to-day, I wish you could have seen it. For the first time since she [*for* he] started these exhibitions, there is real advance I think. John Shawe Taylor and his wife were at the Theatre, and she talked of buying one of the pictures, I do not know whether she has done so.[8]

Yrs ever<br>W B Yeats

TLS Berg.

[6] MG describes her first meeting with Canon Dissard in Royat in *SQ* (330–4): 'I was combining a rest, after a strenuous lecture tour, with meeting a few of "*La Boulange*"; among them was a young priest, l'Abbé Dissard, a fervent Nationalist whose hero was Napoleon.' He later became a canon and was chaplain to a Carmelite convent in Laval, where he received her into the Church and 'stood firmly by me when I sought the civil dissolution of my marriage. He knew all the circumstances, which others did not.' Her letter to WBY (see above, n. 5) told WBY that Canon Dissard had in fact come to Paris to ask her to 'be content with judicial separation' rather than a divorce, but on hearing the facts said 'it was a case where legal divorce was necessary'. She also disclosed that Dissard had written her a letter to 'show to any priest or Bishop justifying my demand for legal divorce', and refuting the plea that 'MacBride's conscience as a Catholic forbade him accepting the divorce & saying that I had turned protestant because I asked for it'. Dissard also suggested that MG should write to the papers refuting the statement '& stating my position in the matter, but as I have decided on not writing to the papers or correcting any lies until the whole affair is ended I have not done so'.

[7] William Wilfred Cave, figure and landscape artist from Bramborough, Cheshire, studied at the Slade from 1901 to 1903 and exhibited 1908–32. He was a friend of Robert Gregory, who described him to AG in January 1904 (Emory) as 'the most graceful draughtsman at the Slade at present but some of his drawings rather want vigour'. He had shared a house with Robert in Delamore Terrace, London, since January of this year, and had been staying at Coole through the autumn. AG got him to bring WBY's clothes up to Dublin in early October.

[8] Jack Yeats's exhibition (see p. 186) ran until 4 Oct. John Shawe-Taylor had married Amy Eleonora, daughter of Gerard Norman of Bromley, Kent, on 12 July of this year. AG generally helped to arrange Jack's exhibitions, but had been unable to attend this one, and on 28 Sept told WBY (see p. 194, n. 1), 'I am very sorry I can't see Jack's show but it can't be helped.'

## *To Florence Farr, 6 October 1905*

Nassau Hotel, | Sth. Frederick St, | Dublin.
6th Oct 1905.

My dear Florence Emery

I am dictating this because I have had an influenza cold for the last week and anything of that kind always affects my eyes and makes writing a much greater labour. I imagine I shall be over in London in a week or so but cannot say for certain. I have been kept all this while and am still kept by the affairs of the Theatre Society. We are turning it into a private Limited Liability Co. in order to get control into a few hands. If all goes well Lady Gregory, Synge and myself will be the Directors in a few days and will appoint all Committees and have more votes between us than all the other Shareholders. I have foreseen that something of this kind was inevitable from the first, but it has come rather sooner than I hope[d] for. I am pretty confident that we have the majority of the members with us in the change. It has been a very slow business winning their confidence, but I think we have it now. We have all the really competent people with us certainly. Hitherto the democratic arrangements have made it impossible to look ahead and settle dates and all that kind of thing. There were always too many people to consult. We started on our Autumn Session last Monday and are holding our audiences very well. This gets rid of my last anxiety for I had been sometimes afraid that our last year's people came from curiosity and would fall off. I am now entirely certain that we will make a great Theatre and get an audience for it.

Did I tell you that the *Well of the Saints* has been accepted by a principal Theatre in Berlin? It is a great triumph for us here as I foretold European Reputation for Synge at the Catholic College and have been mocked for the prophecy.[1] All the incompetentness united in making little of that play and now its German acceptance comes just in time to prepare for the production of his new play an even wilder business.[2] He is a great man and I wish you could get a chance of playing him. I am still in the abyss over *Shadowy Waters*, it is not yet finished and my perplexity is as nothing to Fay's over that shining harp. He and the stage carpenter are at this moment working away boring holes in the half of an old wooden bicycle wheel which is to

---

[1] See pp. 77, n. 9, 178.
[2] i.e. *The Playboy of the Western World.*

play a mysterious part in the instrument. There are to be wonderful effects prepared for months beforehand, burning jewels on the harp and twinkling stars in the sky, but I imagine that both stars and jewels will slowly dwindle and fade as the night of performance gets near. Fay has just given me a good deal of pleasure by telling me that the players discussed last night in the Green Room whose plays drew the best and decided that mine did. I should not begrudge it to anyone if his plays drew more than mine, but it gives one more than a personal pleasure to find that anything so difficult as poetry can, under modern conditions, even hold its own against comedy in prose. Of course a good deal of this popularity comes from the fact that my name is better known than that of the others, but it does mean that I have a small genuine following as a dramatist. I think myself that in the long run Boyle and Lady Gregory will be our most popular playwrites. Her new play *The White Cockade* is a beautiful, laughing, joyful extravagant and yet altogether true phantasy. I have noticed by the by that the writers in this country who come from the mass of the people,—or no, I should say who come from Catholic Ireland, have more reason than fantasy. It is the other way with those who come from the leisured classes. They stand above their subject and play with it, and their writing is, as it were, a victory as well as a creation.[3] The others—Colum and Edward Martyn for instance, are dominated by their subject, with the result that their work as a whole lacks beauty of shape the organic quality. They are never really gay though they can sometimes write about people who are. I wonder if this is true everywhere of the man of the people as contrasted with the man of traditional leisure. Of course Edward Martyn, on the father's side is one of the oldest families in Ireland, but he always seems to have more of his mother's temper, and besides he has taken the habit of his mind from the mass of

[3] In March 1909 WBY was to elaborate this observation into a critique of Catholic education in Ireland: 'The education given by the Catholic schools seems to me to be in all matters of general culture a substituting of pedantry for taste. Men learn the dates of writers, the external facts of masterpieces, and not sense of style and feeling for life. I have never met a young man from an Irish Catholic school - who did not seem to me injured by the literature and the literary history he had learned at it. The arts have nothing to give but that joy of theirs which is perhaps the other side of sorrow. They are always an exhausting contemplation, and we are very ready in our youth, before habits have been formed, to turn from it to pedantry, which offers to the mind a kind of sensual ease. The young men and women who have not been through the Secondary Schools seem to me upon the other hand much more imaginative than Protestant boys and girls and to have better taste. My sisters have the same experience. Catholic education seems to destroy the qualities which they get from their religion. Provincialism destroys the nobility of the Middle Ages' (*Mem*, 187).

the people.[4] But philosophic generalisations are bad things to set out on at five minutes to six with the type writing office about to close.

Write to me, but I daresay I shall write again in a day or two for I am not quite certain that a typewritten letter is a letter at all.

Yours ever

W B Yeats

Printed copy. Bax, 49–52; Wade, 462–4.

## To W. G. Fay, 12 October [1905]

12 October.

My dear Fay: I have a telegram from Miss Horniman which must be acted on at once.[1] Please come & see me at Nassau. I shall be here at 2. I shall then have to go on to theatre.

Yrs snly

W B Yeats

ALS NLI.

---

[4] The Martyns of Galway claimed descent from the Crusader Sir Oliver Martin, who had come to Ireland with Richard, Earl of Pembroke ('Strongbow'), in 1170 as part of the original Anglo-Norman invasion, and who was later granted arms in the Holy Land by Richard I. In 1857 Edward Martyn's father John Martyn married Annie May Josephine Smyth (1830–98), the daughter of a Galway peasant who had amassed a large fortune through land speculation; she reputedly bringing a dowry of £20,000 and her own weight in gold as a personal fortune. Martyn had no recollection of his father, who died in 1860, and his mother, a devout, austere Catholic, continued to exert a dominant influence over him until her death. In *Salve* George Moore, describing her as having 'some good looks, a distinguished appearance, many refined tastes', reports that Martyn was 'prouder of the Smiths than the Martyns, attributing any talent that he may have to his grandfather, John Smith of Masonbrook' (Cave, 326). In *Aut* WBY observed that Edward Martyn's 'father's family was old and honoured; his mother but one generation from the peasant. Her father, an estate steward, earned money in some way that I have forgotten. His religion was a peasant religion; he knew nothing of those interpretations, casuistries, whereby my Catholic acquaintance adapt their ancient rules to modern necessities' (388).

[1] The telegram has not been traced, but may have referred to arrangements for the coming tour of Oxford, Cambridge, and London, or to work on the annexe to the Abbey, which was being converted by the architect Joseph Holloway. Holloway records in his diary (NLI) that on this day he 'saw W. G. Fay at the Abbey on business in connection with the Annex'.

## To Maud Gonne, [*mid–October 1905*]

Mention in letter from MG, 24 October [1905].

A series of letters and a telegram, arranging an Irish counsel for MG in her divorce proceedings, and suggesting Serjeant Dodd.[1] One letter expressing exasperation with things and people in Dublin.[2]

*G–YL*, 211–12.

## To George Roberts, 16 October [*1905*]

Nassau Hotel | Dublin
Monday 16 Oct

Dear Roberts: I should like to see you to morrow with those papers you forgot to bring last time.[1] I must also see the requisition calling the special meeting.[2] Please come before 12.

Yrs sinly
W B Yeats

ALS Harvard.

[1] In her reply, MG thanked WBY for 'all the trouble you have taken in getting me names of Councils & for your letters & telegram—I think Sergeant Dodd would be the best. He defended me in the action I took against Collis of the Dublin *Figaro*. Things legal move so slowly here that my lawyers have not yet decided on writing to him. My charges against John MacBride they say will have to be proved before the question of nationality is gone into.' Serjeant William Huston Dodd (1844–1930) was called to the Irish Bar in 1873, appointed QC in 1884, and serjeant in 1892. He represented Tyrone North as a Liberal MP from 1906 to 1907, when he became a Justice of the King's Bench Division of the High Court of Ireland, a position he held until 1924. He had appeared for MG in her successful libel suit against Ramsay Colles in May 1900 (see II. 525).

[2] WBY had evidently told her of his problems in trying to restructure the INTS, and in her reply MG wrote that he 'seemed exasperated with things or rather people in Dublin—I know one does get exasperated sometimes for it's aggravating to have to waste time & energy in little struggles over details—but after all no-where else does one find people as capable of enthusiasm & devotion & work as in Ireland only we want a few energetic & practical wills to prevent all this devotion & enthusiasm being wasted on trifles', sentiments that WBY may have recalled in writing his poem 'The People' (*VP*, 351–3).

[1] Roberts was still secretary of the INTS, but apparently getting slack in his duties following the conversion of the Society into a limited liability company. His inefficiency persisted, and on 2 Nov AG reported (Berg) that the 'Business Committee was to have sat Tuesday, but Roberts arrived without the Minute books.... Last night it came off—but Roberts again arrived without the Minute books!' On 10 Nov Holloway noted (NLI) that 'Roberts & F Walker are not pleased with the new turn things have taken & are most likely to secede'.

[2] Roberts, as secretary, had been responsible for notifying members about the special meeting of 9 Oct. WBY was eager to have evidence that this had been done according to due process, since this was a legal requirement (see p. 167) and he evidently wanted no quibbles about the constitutional legitimacy of such an important meeting.

## *To George Roberts, [23 October 1905]*

Nassau Hotel
Monday

My dear Roberts:

Please come round to morrow (tuesday) about one. I have something important to say—I may as well tell you the truth—I dont like your Concobar & I must make a change. I think I should tell you that both the Fays are against my taking you out of the part but I am afraid it must be done.[1]

Yr ev
W B Yeats

ALCS Harvard, addressed to 19 St Patricks Road, Drumcondra, and postmark 'DUBLIN OCT 24 05'.

## *To A. H. Bullen, 2 November 1905*

18, Woburn Buildings, | Euston Road.
Nov. 2nd, 1905.

Dear Mr. Bullen,

After seeing Matthews today[1] I thought over the whole matter again. I have come to the conclusion that it would be unwise to accept his proposal. If we agree to make the book 8/6 and not less than 7/6 for five years after 1907 we tie our hands very seriously when the times comes for you to have all my books. It would make any kind of a popular edition impossible. It would be better I think either to buy out Matthews which I daresay you wont think worth while, or to publish the present book without the lyrics

---

[1] Roberts had played the role of Conchubar in *On Baile's Strand* since the opening performance of the Abbey Theatre, but he was replaced by W. J. Tunney for the performances in Oxford, Cambridge, and London from 23 to 28 Nov. According to Holloway (*Abbey Theatre*, 67–8), it was this demotion which accelerated Roberts's secession from the INTS later this year: 'Roberts was sore over his being ousted out of the role of "King Concobar" in *On Baile's Strand* for the English trip, and also Colum cast him for the role of "Matt" in *The Land*, and Yeats would not have it so.' Although Roberts got reasonable reviews, Fay considered him, like Starkey and Helen Laird, 'not primarily interested in acting at all' and complained of his delivery and bearing (NLI).

[1] WBY had returned to London from Dublin the previous day, as AG informed Quinn in a letter on 1 Nov (NYPL): 'WBY left for London this morning. His stay at Coole was shortened by some weeks, and his work thrown back by all this and we are determined that shall not occur again. He has really finished Shadowy Waters—it is very rich and beautiful but I wish he could have got on to Deirdre.'

from the "Wind among the Reeds" volume at say 5/-.[2] It would be practically a volume of new work, none of the "Seven Woods" lyrics or longer poems have been published in England before and the three plays have all been greatly re-written. The "Shadowy Waters" is entirely new. Nothing remains of the old except a few stray passages imbedded in new writing. The first half of "Baile's Strand" is entirely new. Five shillings is a much better price than 8/6. And it will be a great matter to have an entirely free hand in 1907.

Yrs sly
W B Yeats

TLS Harvard. Wade, 464–5.

## Lady Gregory to George Roberts, [? 2 November 1905]

Nassau Hotel
Friday

Dear Mr Roberts

Mr Yeats asks me to say that he will feel obliged if you will let him see the Minute books, a proof of the new rules before they are finally printed—& the letters refusing shares in the new company.

Yours sincerely
A Gregory

ALS Widener.

## To Lady Gregory, 3 November 1905

Mention in letter from AG, 5 November 1905.

Telling her that AEFH is wearing him and herself out addressing envelopes,[1] that there is trouble over the visit to Cambridge,[2] that AEFH

---

[2] *Poems, 1899–1905*, published in October 1906 at a price of 6*s.*, did not contain any poems from *The Wind Among the Reeds* under the erroneous supposition that Mathews still held the English rights. Bullen did however republish the poems in the 1908 *CW* and in *Poems: Second Series.*

[1] The envelopes were for publicity leaflets and letters concerning the forthcoming tour of the INTS. In her reply of 5 Nov (Berg) AG commented: 'I am very sorry to hear about Miss Horniman, we must make her go away after the plays. It is provoking that besides the things she does well she takes on her shoulders things that are tiring and that others would do better. She ought not, nor ought you, to have anything to do with addressing envelopes.'

[2] WBY had evidently told her that an INTS visit to Cambridge would be impossible on this tour. She replied that she thought they were 'better without' Cambridge this time.

has suggested an extra London matinée on 30 November,[3] and that he may have to omit *The Wind Among the Reeds* from his next book.[4]

## To F. J. Fay, 4 November 1905

18, Woburn Buildings, | Euston Road.
Nov. 4th, 1905.

My dear Fay,

I have asked the lady who is typing this to look after that typewriter. She will hear by Monday as to whether it is still unsold and if it is will get an expert to look at it. If this falls through she knows of another place where they can be got. We should get one quite cheaply for it is, she says, an old machine now. I went to "The Merchant of Venice" the other night and disliked the stage management even more than I expected. I found that as usual for a Shakespeare Play nothing moved me except the scenes of prolonged crisis. The Trial scene was moving but owing to the stage management the rest was broken up. Shakespeare had certainly intended those short scenes of his to be played one after the other as quickly as possible and there is no reason that they should not, if played in this way, keep the sense of crisis almost as living as in the long scenes. The stage management however never lost an opportunity of increasing the breaking up caused by changes of scene by bringing in gondolas, crowds, masqueraders etc. One kept asking oneself "what has brought me to this childish peepshow?" That wonderful succession of passages beginning "On such a night as this" was cut out. It is almost the most beautiful thing in the whole play but they cut it out because there was nothing in it for the eye, no peepshow. I think the whole of our literature as well as our drama has grown effeminate through the over

---

[3] AG was against this, and reported that 'Fay says it would not do to have a London matinee 30th as Miss H suggested as possible. He says it is always a mistake not to stick to one's programme.' Fay's view prevailed and there was no extra matinee on 30 Nov.

[4] AG replied that she was '*furious* about Wind Among the Reeds. Do get it in if possible. It is wanted, partly because of being in another mood—and there are not enough lyrics without it.'

development of the picture making faculty. The great thing in Literature above all in drama is rhythm and movement. The picture belongs to another art. I thought Bourchier good in the quiet parts but merely an Old Father Christmas in a rage when he came to passion.[1] One thought of Irving at every moment.[2]

Yr ev

W B Yeats

TLS Private. Wade, 465–6.

## To Lady Gregory, 4 November [1905]

18, Woburn Buildings, | Euston Road,

Nov. 4th, 1904.[1]

My dear Lady Gregory

I cannot find my address book. I think I must have left it behind in Dublin. It may be somewhere among my things but if you have it please send it. There is also a little pamphlet belonging to me at the Nassau. I think it is somewhere on that sideboard. It is an old pamphlet of Russell's. If you havent read it do so, for it is a very fine bit of writing here and there, and then send it on to me. It is rather a treasure, a thing that collectors will value greatly. It is bound in a little black cover without any name on it.[2] I have written to Fay about the typewriter, and as it may take a few days getting him one hadnt he better hire one for the present instead of keeping

---

[1] Arthur Bourchier (1864–1927), actor-manager and lessee of the Garrick Theatre since 1903, produced *The Merchant of Venice* from 11 Oct 1905 to 20 Jan 1906, with himself playing Shylock. For the omitted 'wonderful succession of passages' see v. i. 1–22.

[2] See p. 82. Henry Irving had died on 13 Oct of this year.

[1] An error by WBY's typist.

[2] This may have been *The Future of Ireland and The Awakening of the Fires* (1896), but was probably the more rousing, defiant, and focused *Ideals in Ireland: Priest or Hero?* (1897). Both were in the same series and comprised articles that AE had published in the *Irish Theosophist* from January to May 1897. They were originally issued in uniform grey wrappers with the title and name of author, and so it may even be that WBY had had both pamphlets dressed together in an unlettered black case. Written at the time of AE's most exuberant Celtic enthusiasm, both works urge the Irish to reject the twin tyrannies of

you out of yours? I find that we can apparently get one quite cheap, but it cannot be done under a few days. I went with Robert last night to Rickett's and Shannon's studio. There are some new pictures by Ricketts that moved me more than anything I have ever seen of Shannon's. They have an amazing intensity of originality, an intensity in no way less than Blake's though different. Hitherto they have puzzled me, but last night I was puzzled no longer. I felt as I think I have felt about no contemporary painting, "Here is absolute genius. And the rarest kind of genius, for it is the romance not of the Woman but the romance of the Man, and hardly anybody but Michael Angelo and Blake and Albert Dürer have done anything in that."[3] One felt that the whole active nature, the capacity for movement, organisation, command, all that makes up a man's life took fire in a sort of passionate contemplation. I wonder what Robert thought of them. I dont suppose they are really as great as I think them. They probably moved me for some personal reason. I would feel more certain, that I am right about them if it were not that I was only moved in this way by a couple of the pictures. It may be of course that I have not yet understood the others for the same man made them, the same quality must be there.

Yrs ev
W B Yeats

TLS Emory.

materialistic modernity and intellectual repression by the Catholic Church, and to seek their true freedom in an idealism based on a contemporary version of the nature worship and hero worship of ancient paganism. When answering an enquiry by WBY on 11 July 1921, AE described *Priest or Hero* as 'a blazing piece of rhetoric, quite good rhetoric'. In her reply on 5 Nov (Berg) AG told WBY that she had 'found the pamphlet and will send it. I am almost sure you have your address book but will send the old one.'

[3] Ricketts's recent paintings included *The Betrayal of Christ, Christ before the People*, and *Moonlight Deposition*. On 3 Nov 1905 he recorded in his diary (*SP*, 126) that WBY called in the evening 'full of his Irish Theatre. He said one thing about my work which I liked: "You *paint* the tragedy of Man, most people only understand the tragedy of Woman, or the pitifulness of their tragedy".' WBY owned a reproduction of *The Betrayal of Christ*, now in Carlisle Museum. In *E & I* WBY quotes Blake (120) on the need for bounding outline: 'Raphael and Michelangelo and Albert Durer are known by this and this alone. . . . How do we distinguish the oak from the beech, the horse from the ox, but by the bounding outline?' WBY meditated further on these questions in 'The Death of Synge' (*Aut*, 500–2).

## To William Sharp, 4 November [*1905*]

Mention in letter from Sharp, late November 1905.[1]
Asking if Sharp has sent anyone to him 'on a veiled mission',[2] hoping they might be able to meet,[3] and telling him of developments at the Abbey Theatre.[4]

## To Lady Gregory, 5 November 1905

Mention in letter from AG, 5 November 1905.
Agreeing with AG's suggestion that the INTS should present flowers to Douglas Hyde during the demonstrations to mark his departure for America.[1]

[1] In his undated reply (*LWBY*, 155–7) Sharp told WBY that his 'letter of the 4th' had reached him 'in Sicily some 9 days later'. He and his wife were visiting Alexander Nelson Hood near Taormina in the Sicilian mountains, where he was to die on 12 Dec of this year. Since WBY describes Sharp's reply as being written 'a few days before his death', and since WBY's letter had taken nine days to reach him, it must have been written in November 1905.

[2] WBY had corresponded for many years on occult matters with Sharp, who was also helping him with the rituals for the Celtic Mystical Order (see II. 663–9), but a good deal of Sharp's reply was devoted to upbraiding WBY for not replying to his letters (see p. 117), and he also disclosed that for many months of this year he had been at the point of death. He went on to say that he was 'unfortunately not in a position to say anything definite on the matter which you broach. If we meet, we may speak of what cannot well be written about. I may add, however, that neither I nor any person *personally* known to me "sent" any one to you on a veiled mission. <At the same time that a certain person sought you and that you did not recognize the person, the occasion, or the significance.> As you know, we are in a crucial period of change in many ways, and there are circles within circles, veiled influences and good and evil (and non-good and non-evil) formative and disformative forces everywhere at work. Obscure summons, obscure warnings, meetings & partings, veiled messages, come to us all.' He conceded that all this sounded 'very absurd, or mysterious, or conveniently vague. However, you'll understand. Also my present silence.'

[3] Sharp replied that he would remain in Sicily until Christmas and would then go to the French Riviera for three months, so that there was 'little likelihood of our meeting till after Easter'. He also revealed, presumably as the result of his clairvoyant gifts, that WBY was likely to be in Paris in April or May (although WBY perhaps knew 'nothing of any such likelihood, and it may be mere wildfire of supposition'), so that they might 'possibly meet *there*'.

[4] Sharp hoped 'the dramatic undertakings will be a success, above all in reaching the psychic nerves, the living thought, of those to whom their appeal is made'.

[1] This telegram is now lost but was apparently in answer to one that AG had sent him earlier in the day. Its occasion, as she explained in her letter, was that the procession to be held on 6 Nov from the Gresham Hotel to King's Bridge station to mark Douglas Hyde's departure for a fund-raising lecture tour in America on behalf of the Gaelic League would pass close to the Abbey Theatre, and she, Fay, and Roberts wondered whether the INTS should, like many other associations, join in. They 'thought Miss Walker in costume might give him a bouquet or branch or some such thing' but then, given AEFH's implacable dislike of the Gaelic League, 'began wondering if Miss Horniman would make a commotion if she saw it in the papers, and I sent wire, but was afraid to put her name. I am sure we ought to do something, Hyde being or having been a Vice Pres.' WBY's telegram evidently agreed with this initiative. AG went to the reception at the Gresham Hotel, at which Hyde spoke, and reported that he 'had a gr. send off, the torch light procession a most impressive sight'. The following day she noted (Berg) that their presentation of flowers had been mentioned in the *Freeman's Journal*. Hyde, accompanied by his wife, travelled from Dublin to Cork and sailed for the USA on 8 Nov.

## To George Bernard Shaw, 6 November 1905

Mentioned in following letter and in a letter to George Roberts, 8 November 1905.
Trying to make an appointment with Shaw for the following day, or for 8 November.

## To Lady Gregory, 6 November 1905

18 Woburn Buildings, | Euston Road.
Nov. 6th 1905.

My dear Lady Gregory

I have only just found the Postscript to your letter this very instant when I was beginning to dictate. I shall go to see Murray to-morrow if possible.[1] I am inclined to suggest subject to your decision that he print 500 at 6/- and get a certain number of copies put into paper covers (the book going into 2 volumes) and sell these for a reduced price in Ireland. The objection to waiting until a new 6/- edition is sold out is that your books at a moderate price would be of great advantage to the movement at its present stage. On consideration I think I shall wait till Wednesday as this would give you a chance of writing what you think upon this point. If I find however that Wednesday looks like being filled in, I shall go to-morrow and see Lawrence and discuss the matter generally with him without getting things definite. I wonder would Murray object to working off his cheap edition through Maunsell & Company. The two volumes could be "The Gods and Fighting Men Volume 1 and 2" and sold separately. I would have more to say about the matter probably if I had not overlooked that postscript.[2] I am going to

[1] Plans were in hand for a second edition of *Gods and Fighting Men*, AG's version of the Fenian tales, and WBY and AG were sounding John Murray out as to the possibility of a cheaper Irish issue through Maunsel & Co. In a postscript to her letter of 5 Nov (see p. 208, n. 1) she passed on a letter from Murray, and asked WBY to see him 'as soon as you can, for if there is a new edition, it should be out for Xmas. I am inclined to say print 500 of the 6/- edition, and after a while when both that and the remaining Cuchulain copies are sold out, split both vols. into two, at 1/- or 1/6 each, to try and get to a popular sale here. I don't think 2/6 is more likely to sell than 6/-. But it will be a great help if you will go and settle with them—and urge Murray because of Xmas.'

[2] In her reply to this, on 7 Nov (Berg), AG said that she thought 'the point of Murray's letter was that Ireland is the principal consumer of G. & F. Men, and if he published a cheap ed. for Ireland, I don't suppose he wd bring out a 6/- one for England. I think the adv of a 2nd edition wd sell off a good many of the 6/- 500. However, you and Lawrence can talk it over.' Charles Edward Lawrence (1879–1940), John Murray's literary editor and reader since 1897, was AG's long-time friend and publishing adviser, once describing himself to her as 'an Englishman whose heart is Irish' (*Journals*, 1. 130). A playwright and novelist, he was also joint editor of the *Quarterly Review* and reviewed for the *Daily Chronicle* from 1904 to 1918. Murray published a new edition of *Gods and Fighting Men* in February 1906, priced once again at 6s. The book was not issued by Maunsel.

Cambridge on Thursday to see people about our visit there. We shall have to give two performances in two different halls there which is a nuisance.[3] Miss Horniman says she won't listen to Fay on the subject of the Matinee. She says it won't be given unless there is a real demand—places all sold out and so forth—and that it is quite usual in London and about the best advertisement there is.[4] We had better let her have her head about everything at present, for if we object she will only worry and make herself more ill than she is.[5] I have got the authority of Miss Owen[6] who is acting as nurse not to tell her about the music but we shall have to tell her sooner or later. As £6 a week during performances will of course take so much away from the money that would otherwise go to making her guarantee unnecessary, I don't think she will mind as the only thing she will care about is that the music shall be good.[7] I shall tell her in a few days but she is being overworked in spite of everybody at this moment. Everybody tells one that we are to have a big success. I am sorry that you are having so much trouble over Boyle's play.

[3] See p. 208. W. G. Fay explained the reasons for this in *Fays of the Abbey Theatre* (179): 'I wrote to the manager of the Oxford theatre asking if he could offer us a date with Cambridge to precede or follow, for at that time the same management controlled the theatres at both places. I had a very curt refusal saying that he did not want to book any Irish plays. . . . Now, Miss Horniman is not easily beaten, and she had made up her mind that Oxford and Cambridge were to see us. She wasted no time in regrets, but went down to Oxford herself and booked the Corn Exchange Hall for two performances on November 23rd, and then went on to Cambridge, where she took the Victoria Assembly Rooms for the evening of November 24th and the small Guildhall for a matinée on the same day.' In fact, the matinée at the Small Guildhall took place on Saturday, 25 Nov, at 2.30 p.m.

[4] WBY had evidently told AEFH of Fay's opposition to an extra London matinée on 30 Nov, as AG had reported in her letter of 5 Nov (see p. 209, n. 3).

[5] WBY had arranged for music to be played between the acts of AG's *The White Cockade*, evidently at the insistence of the company who, as AG reported on 7 Nov (Berg), 'think people are indignant & stay away because of the want of it'. Certainly Holloway, noting on 2 Oct the silence and cheerlessness at the Abbey between plays and scene changes, thought (NLI) that a 'little music would get over all the feeling of gloom & the sweet sounds would make others break the silence also', and when, on 13 Oct, 'W. G. Fay hinted to me that the intervals would be enlivened by Hilles' Orchestra in future . . . I suggested that the innovation should be proclaimed from the housetops'. On alternating nights Arthur Darley and Mr and Mrs Kenny played traditional Irish folk music on the violin and pipes, while on the final night Ralph Burnham and Miss Bourke Irwin were to have played selections from Grieg on violin and piano but were indisposed. Darley (1873–1929) continued to play for the company at the Abbey and on tour until the summer of 1906, when G. R. Hillis became music director. Although Mrs Kenny, a native of Galway, had won three first prizes for the violin at the Feis, the annual Irish music festival, Joseph Holloway did not think her performance 'enlivened the entertainment very much' on 9 Dec (NLI) but on his next visit to the play, on 12 Dec, he was entranced by Darley who 'played six Irish airs with his soul in the interpretation of each & the audience instantly awoke to the great artistic treat provided for them. . . . W B Yeats came before the curtains to introduce him, & said "There were two kinds of music in theatres, the music that one wished to hear & that which was merely played to drown the stage noises & the conversation of those behind us. Mr Darley's was of the former class as they would soon discover & he hoped they would keep silent while he played.'

[6] Mary Price Owen was a singer, actress, and a close friend of AEFH. She had appeared as the Poisoner in Beerbohm Tree's production of Stephen Phillip's *Nero* from January to March 1905, and later acted with AEFH's Gaiety Company in Manchester.

[7] In her letter of 5 Nov AG said that, having made enquiries about a small orchestra for the Theatre, 'I don't think we could do it much under £6'.

Had you not better leave it alone until you are quite well? Hating it as much as you do I can well understand it becoming a sort of nightmare when you were ill. You are probably altering it too much. Nothing will ever give it distinction. Go on making all inquiries of course about the music—I don't foresee any difficulty with Miss Horniman but what you say about the £6 made me feel that it would not be right to definitely make a permanent arrangement until she had been consulted. What do you think about the point? I don't think I should mind if she were well but when she is ill I don't like getting into her head that we are taking any serious step of the kind without telling her. Her nerves seem to be all right, she is merely weak but one never knows. I hope you will be soon well. I don't think I ever remember your being kept to the house by a cold for so long a time. You say in your letter that Fay came back to consult about play and that "we decided it ought to stop at the public meeting but then should the magistracy rejection come before that. For what reason should he refuse". My idea was that when the militia captain asked for a subscription for the Hunt Club or the Foxhounds or whatever it was Boyle's hero should offer not say the £10 he was asked for but £20, £30, £50 even, in his excitement; this money to be given the moment the commission of the peace was handed to him. I think the commission of the peace should be handed to him after the public meeting that he being generally discouraged should think of that £50 and refuse. And that the curtain should go down upon his building up a new character for patriotism, a new fit of self-delusion on the foundation of that refusal. However don't bother about the thing for the present.[8] I hope your headaches are well by this time. I am rushing hither and thither. I went to see Shaw this morning, it was the very first morning I could but he was at his rehearsals of his new play at the Court. I have written for an appointment for to-morrow or Wednesday. I am afraid this delay will upset Roberts but it

---

[8] WBY, Synge, and W. G. Fay had attempted to put Boyle's three-act comedy *The Eloquent Dempsy* into shape (see p. 196), and now AG was lending her reluctant assistance. In her letter of 2 Nov (see p. 206, n. 1), she told WBY: 'Boyle I have been through, & have gone through with Fay . . . I think it is *very* much improved by the cuts you & Synge made & that your idea of hunt subscription will do—I suggest his leaving out drink altogether—& making Mrs Dempsys motive for getting D away his propensity to treat first one side, then the other, so squandering his substance—This wd come out of character, & enrich the play besides getting rid of the rum.' But in her letter of 5 Nov AG revealed that the problems had not been solved, and that she had 'never left the house since you left—first it seemed a heavy cold; then the other ev, Fay who had taken away Boyle's play came back with it at 9:00 and said his head was whirling and he wanted to consult about it. We decided it ought to stop at the public meeting—but then, should the magistrate's rejection come before that? For what reason should he refuse? What should be final tableau? We gave it up at last—and I entered upon 2 days and 2 nights of violent headache, and am not right yet. I am not sure how much was Boyle and how much influenza, however I am very sorry for myself and for all this waste of time.' In the final, much-revised version, the contrivance of the Hunt Club subscription is dropped, as is the drinking, and Dempsy, unmasked when he signs petitions both for and against a proposed visit to the town by the Chief Secretary, redeems himself in the eyes of the people by publicly rejecting the magistracy he has been scheming for. The play opened on 20 Jan 1906.

can't be helped.[9] I went out to Mrs. Emery yesterday to read her Shadowy Waters. She made a few useful criticisms of detail and I have altered a line or two. She likes the first part immensely but the middle not so well, she likes the end however. She thinks the play as a whole greatly improved but that the improvement is principally in Forgael's part. I read it to Arthur Simmonds later on and he thinks it all much richer. Bye-the-bye Mrs. Emery put the last touch of tragedy to the McBride affair by telling me that she has heard from Mrs. Clay that the McBride child threatens to be an epileptic.[10] I am afraid nothing can be done about "the Wind on the Reeds" as it would be unwise to tie ourselves, as Matthews wants, not to publish any book containing it at a less price than 8/6 for the next two years or a less price than 7/6 for the five years after that. I may want to issue a volume of Selections at a moderate price for Ireland.[11] The little wretch has behaved very badly but there is nothing to be done. Do you remember my writing to him and asking him to put the John Lane matter into the hands of the Society of Authors. I thought he had done this as he replied that he would do what he could. He had done nothing whatever and I had to stand over him until he wrote the letter.[12] I brought it away with me for the better security and sent it on to the Society of Authors myself. I have had a letter from Boland's brother saying that a proof of my evidence before that Royal Commission has been sent to Coole. It is evidently pressing as I am to write and say if I have received it.[13] I hope the Miss Quins won't squirrel it.[14]

Yrs ev

W B Yeats

TLS Berg, with envelope addressed to Nassau Hotel, Dublin, postmark indecipherable; second postmark on back of envelope 'CORK PACKET 2.30 AM NO 7 05'.

[9] Shaw's *Major Barbara* ran at the Court Theatre for six matinée performances on Tuesdays and Fridays from 28 Nov to 15 Dec. WBY wanted to ask him to permit George Roberts to include one of his stories, 'The Miraculous Revenge', in the *Shanachie*, a new Irish literary magazine being planned by the Maunsel Press.
[10] Séan MacBride (see p. 7, n. 2). Mrs Clay's diagnosis was incorrect.
[11] See p. 88.
[12] Mathews had evidently not acted upon the latest letter from the secretary of the Society of Authors; see p. 185.
[13] On 13 Oct 1905 WBY had given evidence at Leinster House to a committee appointed to inquire 'into the Work Carried on by the Royal Hibernian Academy and the Metropolitan School of Art, Dublin', and this was subsequently published in the Committee's *Report* (*Parliamentary Papers* xxxi, Cd. 3256 [1906], 60–1). John Pius Boland (1870–1958), MP for South Kerry and a strong supporter of the Irish language movement, wrote the minority report. His brother, H. P. Boland of the Board of Works (Ireland), was secretary of the Committee. WBY, who had been a student of both schools, was particularly anxious to point out 'that the contrast between the two schools was a contrast between a system on the one hand and the influences of individuals upon the other. The whole system of teaching at the Metropolitan School of Art was, in the opinion — I do not say of myself merely, but of all the students who had to go through with it — boring, and destructive of enthusiasm, and of all kinds of individuality. . . . I was bored to death by that routine, and in consequence I have left Art, and taken to Literature' (60).
[14] The daughters of a local Gort family who were evidently forwarding mail while AG was in Dublin.

## *To George Roberts, 8 November 1905*

18, Woburn Buildings, | Euston Road,
Nov. 8th, 1905.

My dear Roberts,

I called on Shaw on Monday but he was not in. I wrote to him but he did not answer. I saw him yesterday however and he gives leave about the story. He says you are to say however, that it was written about a quarter of a century ago.[1] Shaw, as I daresay you know, was a land agent in Ireland for a year or two before his twentieth year.[2] You might work up some sort of a biographical note saying that the story was written when he had Ireland fresh in his mind and so turn an acknowledgement of immaturity into an assertion of superior knowledge.[3] The story is really brilliant and should be the making of your annual.

Yr ev
W B Yeats

TLS Harvard.

---

[1] Shaw's story 'The Miraculous Revenge', first published in 1885, had been announced as the second publication of the Dun Emer Press, but did not appear. It was reprinted above its original date, but without WBY's suggested note, in the first number of *Shanachie* (Spring 1906), which also contained two of WBY's lyrics, 'Against Witchcraft' (from *On Baile's Strand*) and 'The Praise of Deirdre' (from *Deirdre*). The story involves the investigation by an English aesthete, Zeno Legge, of a miracle in rural Ireland whereby, according to a local priest, a nuns' graveyard has moved location rather than entertain the burial of a reprobate there. Zeno finds this to be true, but, slighted by the priest and his beautiful niece, he takes revenge by reburying the reprobate in the new location, whereupon the graveyard reverts to its original position. A Protestant committee sent to verify the miracle thus finds it invalid and the disgraced priest is suspended from his duties. WBY had given a brief variant version of this story in *Fairy and Folk Tales* (214). By late May 1930 Shaw could no longer remember where he had placed the story and enlisted AG's help in finding it, telling her (*Journals*, II. 529): 'I seem to recollect that it was printed in an Irish Magazine with a barbarous name — *Samhain* or something like that, probably pronounced O'Shaughnessy — which was connected with Abbey St. Could I buy, beg, borrow, steal, or otherwise obtain access to the number containing my story, if it really appeared there?'

[2] In 1871, aged 16, Shaw was appointed junior clerk in the Dublin estate agency of Charles and Thomas Townshend, and quickly became a very successful land agent, remaining on the staff until he left Dublin for London in 1876.

[3] Roberts did not take up the suggestion of a biographical note, WBY's wording of which may have been prompted by a desire to vindicate his rejection of Shaw's later Irish work in the form of *John Bull's Other Island* (see p. 79).

## *To Lady Gregory, 10 November 1905*

18 Woburn Buildings | Euston Rd
Nov. 10th 1905.

My dear Lady Gregory

I have a great many things to say, but first I have just seen Laurence, I could not get to him before for yesterday I was at Cambridge and the day before the lid was coming off the kettle among other things. Laurence couldn't do anything and evidently did not wish to discuss the matter at the moment. Murray is away and has the estimate with him, and I am to call next week when he is back.[1] Robert is in communication with Philip Carr and Miss Horniman and is seeing about scenery costumes etc. The type-writer has been bought but has gone back to the seller for a slight repair. It will be sent to Dublin addressed Frank Fay Abbey Theatre immediately. It cost £4.10s which I have paid. Fay need not have I think any anxiety about the audience being confused at Cambridge through our going from one hall to another. One of the don's wives assured me that it is quite a common thing there. The halls are within 50 yards of each other.[2] In any case I could not have interfered. When I went round to Miss Horniman the day before yesterday I found Miss Owen in a great state of agitation.[3] Miss Horniman who has never been told how ill she has been and is, had got into her head that we were keeping things back from her and that authority had been taken from her in the matter of the English tour and put in my hands. She had confused matters over the countermanding of the printing and thought that I had given the order. I had really shown her every scrap of writing I had received from Fay and told her every message that came through you, but it was quite a long time before she was quieted. That she was quieted at all is owing to Miss Owen who rouses both my admiration and my sense of humour. Miss Owen got it into her head that Miss Horniman might permanently quarrel with me and that this might upset the whole theatre project. The result was that she tried to take responsibility for the change about the letters on to her own shoulders. She is going about with her lips compressed and an air of determination. She has been very good tempered with her patient but says at intervals such things as "She will have to apologise to me as soon as she is well again". I dont know what has happened but I can imagine. I made a speech in Newnham College yester-

---

[1] See p. 213.
[2] On 7 Nov (see p. 213, n. 2) AG had written that W. G. Fay 'nearly got a fit, especially about the two halls—said it wd be impossible to change the fit-up in the time! besides looking bad in the advertisements'.
[3] Miss Owen remained a close friend of AEFH.

day at the house of one of the teachers to an audience which included the Principal of the College,[4] a number of other teachers, some Cambridge dons and their wives. Not a large audience but influential. I gave the history of the Company and characterised the playwrights. I said of you among other things "she has two things it has been said no woman ever has,—humour and style". O'Donovan complimented me very much on my speech—but I forgot to say I brought him down with me and set him organising at one end of the room while I took the other.[5] The speech was at tea but we had already lunched with a large party got up in our honour by the Professor of Arabic at one of the colleges.[6] There is a likelihood of my being asked to lecture to the Newnham students. After my speech a committee was formed to entertain the whole lot of us. We were to be boarded out, you and I Synge and the company. We shall be fetched by various don's wives. I am convinced that we will have a great reception in Cambridge but unfortunately the halls are very small. I have been asked to lecture to an Oxford undergraduates club on the day before the Oxford performances[7] and I lecture here in London to a dramatic Society of which Grein is President the day before the London performances.[8] There was also a proposal that the Marquis of Townsen[d] should be asked to invite a distinguished audience of some sort to his house here in London, that I might speak to them about the project.[9] This has however been postponed for later

---

[4] This may have been the house of FF's friend Jane Ellen Harrison (1850–1928), one of the most influential authorities on Greek religion and myth of her period. Mrs Eleanor Balfour Sidgwick (1845–1936), from 1892 to 1910 the principal of Newnham College, founded in 1871 for the higher education of women, was the sister of the Rt. Hon. Arthur James Balfour (1848–1930), Prime Minister of Britain from 1902 to 1905. She had married Henry Sidgwick (1838–1900), Professor of Moral Philosophy at Cambridge, in 1876, and was an active member of the Society for Psychical Research.

[5] Gerald (formerly Jeremiah) O'Donovan (1871–1942), former administrator of Loughrea parish, had recently left the priesthood and Ireland, and moved to London.

[6] Probably Edward Granville Browne (1862–1926), Sir Thomas Adams Professor of Arabic at Cambridge since 1902, and a lifelong friend of Wilfrid Blunt. He was a Fellow of Pembroke College. There is no evidence that WBY gave a further lecture at Newnham, but, as AEFH informed Synge on 8 Nov (TCD), the Company was honoured at Cambridge since the young women at Newnham 'are never let out after 10 except for Greek plays—but you & Mr. Yeats & Lady Gregory are to be treated like Aeschylus & Sophocles'.

[7] After the Oxford performances on 23 Nov, WBY was entertained by Sidney Ball, Senior Tutor of St John's College, who had presided at his lecture to the College's Essay Society in May 1902 (see III. 185). The Society may have invited him to give a further lecture, but there is no evidence of his having done so.

[8] WBY lectured on 26 Nov at Frascati's in Oxford Street to the Dramatic Debaters' Society, founded by J. T. Grein in 1903. Grein's wife Alix (writing under the pseudonym 'Michael Orme') recalls in her *J. T. Grein: The Story of a Pioneer 1862–1935* (1936), 215, that he spoke on '"the Drama as it is and what it might be" to a group of people who each and separately knew what it ought to be, or thought they did'.

[9] After their marriage on 9 Aug 1905, John James Dudley Stuart, 6th Marquess Townshend (1866–1921), an aspiring poet and author, and Lady Townshend (b. 1884) let the family home at Raynham Hall, Norfolk, and took a house in Brook Street. Before her marriage Lady Townshend, then Miss Gladys Ethel Gwendolen Eugénie Sutherst, had held frequent at-homes in imitation of John Todhunter's gatherings at Bedford Park.

consideration. Miss Horniman has broken loose so completely that she is going to Oxford and Cambridge in spite of her illness. She seems incapable of resting but how she is to get to either place I dont know as she is very weak. The doctor seems to have consented from the point of view that she wont rest here and may be forced to there if she can be kept from taking any introductions with her or doing any business except certain definite things about scene shifting, licensing etc. I saw her this morning, she was up and in good humour again but had to go and lie down before I left, having talked herself out of her strength. I am writing to the Leeds people[10] and to Boyle to ask him to dinner to discuss that play which has just come from Wm Fay.[11] Did you see the letter he has written me or have you any suggestion independent of that? Dont bother about it if your head is still aching however. I wish I knew how you really were, I do not like your being ill for so long, you must have tired yourself out and would be better over here where even if you wished to you could not get into a new whirl for a few days at any rate.

Yr ev<br>W B Yeats

P.S. I have wired to cut out that paragraph about Gaelic plays. It has served its purpose now that the two Fays have seen it, but even if it had not, I would not like to put in to Samhain anything they disapproved of.[12] I have come to the conclusion that the best thing for me to do is to submit to you and Synge, my fellow directors, a written statement as to the arguments for the establishment within a reasonable time of a Gaelic Company. You can then show this statement to the Fays and I will give Miss Horniman a copy. It will crystallise our ideas and give us a basis for discussion. It is a thing I have already talked over with Miss Horniman several times and I pretty well know her mind upon the subject. I have no very strong conviction myself and cannot have until we have seen where the difficulties lie. I will know that very much better when I have your comment upon the statement

---

[10] The Leeds Arts Club had enquired whether the Abbey Company could visit Leeds after their forthcoming performances in London.

[11] i.e. *The Eloquent Dempsy.* Fay's letter is untraced, but he thought Boyle's sense of theatre redeemed the elements of vulgarity in his work. WBY was presumably inviting Boyle to dinner to persuade him to accept the radical rewriting to which his play had been subjected.

[12] WBY had evidently prepared a paragraph for *Samhain* criticizing in detail the form and propagandist content of the Irish plays he had seen at the recent Gaelic performances at the Abbey by the Keating branch of the Gaelic League (see p. 190). In an undated letter, probably written on 9 Nov (Berg), AG had told him that W. G. Fay did 'not like your note about the Gaelic plays—thinks it will weaken our position & offend Gaelic Leaguers who wont like to be told they have no plays—I am glad he is strong about it, for I felt in reading the notes that from a literary point of view it weakens them.... So I think you may let it slip for this year.' In the end WBY contented himself with observing that 'the typical Gaelic League play is essentially narrative and not dramatic', and that such plays were 'obviously propagandist' (*Expl*, 189, 198), but, rather than letting the matter 'slip' altogether, wrote the statement on the possibility of an Abbey Gaelic company printed below (see pp. 222–6).

and Synge's comment. I shall begin dictating that statement at once and may get it off to you by to-night's post—

Yrs ev
W B Yeats

TLS Berg.

## To Lady Gregory, 11 November 1905

18 Woburn Buildings | Euston Rd
Nov 11th 1905

My dear Lady Gregory

I enclose that statement. Show it to Synge if he comes to see you & Fay if you like but if he does not it can wait. There is no immediate hurry. I have merely written it now because my mind happened to be on it. I have no particular news—no proof sheet yet.[1] I went out to Mrs Emery's last night to meet Hughes the musician. I wanted him to do a little scrap of music for the Fools Patter in Baile's Strand.[2] His eager interest in the music of the theatre reminded me that we had asked him on Synge's recommendation to look after our music for us. An impulsive act which may or may not embarrass us now. I must say that he talks very intelligently and is full of what sound like good and practical ideas as to what an orchestra should play and what sort of music you would have in the country and so on. He is of course a professional musician and if his own music is good we may have done the right thing. Mrs Emery admires a little song of his greatly, the words are by Colm. It is called the Moon child.[3] On the other hand Miss Horniman thinks that Hughes has been rude to her and does not like his music. I imagine he has done a certain amount of hack music to earn a living as he spoke of accepting the paid secretaryship of the Irish Literary Society as a substitute for working for the commercial music publisher. If Synge comes over and if he and Robert think Hughes a competent man it might be

---

[1] Presumably the proofs of *Samhain* (1905).

[2] See p. 56, n. 3. The Abbey Theatre programme for the opening performance of *On Baile's Strand* on 27 Dec 1904 credits 'Music by Herbert Hughes and Florence Farr', and WBY states in *Poems, 1899–1905* that Hughes had 'written the music for the Fool's song in the opening dialogue, and another friend a little tune for the three women' (*VPl*, 526). FF had earlier set the Fool's song, but Liam Miller suggests in *The Noble Drama of W. B. Yeats* (Dublin, 1977), 118, that for this performance WBY had Hughes set the song, 'probably because Florence Farr's setting was outside Willie Fay's range'. FF's setting was printed in *Plays in Prose and Verse* (1922).

[3] In 1905 Colum wrote several poems for traditional airs collected by Hughes, but there is no record of one entitled 'The Moon Child'. WBY had possibly confused his quatrain 'The Moon Cradle', later published in *Wild Earth* (1907), with Fiona Macleod's poem, 'The Moon Child', which had appeared in *The Hills of Dream* (1897).

of great advantage to leave our music wholly to him. He would take pride in it and as he cares for very little except Folk songs would make it as Irish as possible. At the present moment he is drifting into violent politics of the united Irishman sort. There is a new organisation here called the Dungannon Club. It is spreading from Belfast and is responsible for the antienlisting propaganda. Hughes is deep in this which makes one a little distrustful of his music, but if his music is right his association with it would be rather a help to us than otherwise.[4] I like him personally, and I have no doubt could smooth things with Miss Horniman.

[*In WBY's hand*]

When do you come over—I shall be very glad to hear that you are coming & still more glad to hear that you are well again[5]

Yrs ever

W B Yeats

Miss Horniman wants the dog registered as a trade mark at once.[6]

[*With enclosure*]

Reasons for and against the Establishment of the Gaelic Co.

———

I have a conviction that if we are ever to establish a Gaelic Company we must do it during the next year possibly during the next few months. I cannot analyse very successfully the facts that give me this feeling, but I am pretty confident that almost immediately some more or less permanent Gaelic company will be created by some Gaelic league branch. The Keating Branch may for instance be drifting on towards it. If this company is formed it will become a centre for all the Gaelic league opposition to us. Ever[y] person who dislikes us because we have ideas or for any other reason will point to this Gaelic company and say this is the true national theatre.[7] They will even deny our right to use the name and their own

---

[4] In March 1905 two Ulstermen, Bulmer Hobson (1883–1969) and Denis McCullough (1883–1968), a leader of the Irish Republican Brotherhood, founded the Dungannon Clubs because they thought the Cumann na nGaedheal too quiescent. The Clubs, named after the 1782 Volunteer Convention at Dungannon, Co. Tyrone, were established in Ireland and London to discourage recruitment into the British Army, to promote enlistment into the Irish Republican Brotherhood, and to work for Irish independence. In 1906 the Dungannon Clubs and Cumann na nGaedheal united to form the Sinn Fein League.

[5] On 12 Nov AG told him (Berg) that she had intended to cross on the night of 11 Nov, but that Robert Gregory had turned up unexpectedly that morning to discuss the design of scenery with Fay and that she now hoped to cross with him on 13 Nov.

[6] i.e. Elinor Monsell's Irish wolfhound design, used on Abbey posters and stationery; see p. 30. AEFH was no doubt eager for registration to prevent its being appropriated by the secessionists from the Theatre.

[7] WBY's concern with Gaelic plays at this time was prompted by recent productions by the Keating branch of the Gaelic League and the National Players' Society. On Saturday 28 Oct WBY

performances will be sufficiently bad to keep their audiences from getting any interest in the theatre of an artistic kind. This opposition will be a very serious thing for us when we go to America a couple of years hence. We wil[l] always have enemies and these enemies will be always anxious to find some reason which will seem convincing to popular feeling. If they can say "these people call themselves a national theatre although that name belongs by right to the theatre established by the Gaelic league, these people are really Anglicisers etc." then they will be able to hide from themselves and others the fact that they really dislike us because we have intellect and culture. In England the Philistines attack the morals of a writer in Ireland he attacks his nationality. It would be wel[l] if we could apply [*for* reply] to the critic "A national theatre must reflect the dramatic activity of a nation." You believe that Ireland is going to give up talking the English language and to transact all its business in Irish. Well, what if that be so, "At present the majority of Irish people can only hear and understand and write through English. The majority of our plays are in English but you will also hear in our theatre the best plays that are written in Irish. If the country is going to give up English then our theatre will do so, but gradually. When half the people think and speak in Irish then in all probability there will be enough dramatic activity in Irish for half our plays to be in Irish. And so on, until all the plays are in Irish when all the country is speaking Irish." Now this would give us an irresistible logical position and it is worth paying something for that but one might pay too dear. We have to calculate the price. We could form a small company of native Irish speakers who should be all paid that they may be under proper discipline. This company should have all its bills in Irish that they may not be confused with our English speaking company and they should perform on different nights from our company. They should either have a few days to themselves at some time of the month when we are not performing at all—or they should if this was not likely to cause too much confusion perform one night in each of our weeks. They should be all native speakers for this would prevent any of our

and AG attended the second night of a Gaelic concert given at the Abbey by the Keating branch, in the course of which Fr. Patrick Dinneen's *Creideamh agus Gorta* ('Faith and Famine') was presented. The following week the National Players' Society put on plays in Irish and English at the Molesworth Hall for the Cumann na nGaedheal's Samhain Festival from 30 Oct to 4 Nov, billed as 'A Great Week of National Plays'. WBY and AG saw Hyde's *Teach na mBocht* (*The Poorhouse*) there on 31 Oct, and another of Hyde's plays in Irish, *An Pósadh* (*The Wedding*), was produced on 30 Oct and 1 Nov. The Society continued to give occasional performances over the next few years but its acting and production were so poor that it never rivalled the Abbey Theatre, and although it made another attempt to establish an Irish-speaking company in March 1907, backed by Martyn and Colum, nothing came of the plans. The Keating branch, based in Dublin, was not part of the National Players' Society, but was one of the most vigorous sections of the Gaelic League. It had provided the actors for the ILT's production of Hyde's *Casadh an tSúgáin* (*The Twisting of the Rope*) in October 1901, and its energetic drama group frequently mounted plays in Dublin and its environs. Despite this memorandum, the Abbey theatre did not establish a Gaelic company.

own people from joining them and they should as soon as William Fay can train a stage manager, be handed over to a stage manager of their own. In other words they should be made as distinct as possible so far as the practical working goes, from our English speaking company. Of course if Fay were to insist on stage managing them throughout, we should have to agree, but I think that he will want all his imagination for the English work. The great point is where would this company get plays? It would be essential to play the few good plays that there are in Irish, and I cannot see any plays except Dr Hyde's and unfortunately Miss Horniman objects to these because we have not the copyright. I dont think however that she would make this a vital question, especially as the main body of the plays would for some time have to be translations.[8] These translations should not I think be from great classics like Moliere so much as the plays belonging to various national movements similar to that of Ireland. Miss Horniman for instance, has suggested Flemish. Count Lutzow told me that the Bohemian

---

[8] WBY had attempted to be as encouraging as possible about plays in Irish and mentioned productions of those by Douglas Hyde, Fr. Peter O'Leary, 'An t-Athair Peadar' (1839–1920), and Fr Patrick Dinneen (1860–1934) regularly in *Samhain*. Of the three he preferred Hyde, although he thought Gaelic plays in general too rambling and too narrative, noting in 1903 (*Expl*, 98) that the 'play-writing, always good in dialogue, is still very poor in construction, and I still hear of plays in many scenes, with no scene lasting longer than four or six minutes, and few intervals shorter than nine or ten minutes, which have to be filled up with songs'. Hyde had worked with the ILT and was elected a Vice-President of the INTS, until his resignation in September 1903 over the production of Synge's *In the Shadow of the Glen*. His one-act *Casadh an tSúgáin* (see above, n. 7) was based on a scenario by WBY, and published in Gaelic and in AG's English translation in *Samhain* in 1901. He subsequently wrote a number of one-act plays in Gaelic, many from scenarios provided by WBY or AG: *Teach na mBocht* (1902), produced by the Abbey in AG's English translation as *The Poorhouse* in April 1907; *An Naomh ar Iarraid* (1902), translated by AG as *The Lost Saint* and based on WBY's story 'Where There Is Nothing, There Is God'; *An Pósadh* (1902), translated by AG as *The Marriage*, first produced on 20 Aug 1902 at the Connacht Feis, Galway; *Dráma Breithe Chriosta* (1902), translated by AG as *The Nativity*, performed in Sligo in February of this year, but not at the Abbey (and then in English) until January 1911; *An Tincéar agus an tSidheóg* (*The Tinker and the Fairy*), privately performed in George Moore's garden on 19 May 1902, and published in the *New Ireland Review* in May 1902; *Cleamhnas* (*Matchmaking*), first produced at the Galway Feis in 1903; *Rig Séumas* (*King James*), published in 1904; and *Pleusgadh na Bulgóide* (*The Bursting of the Bubble*), a satirical skit on the anti-Gaelic dons at Trinity College, Dublin, based on a scenario by AG, and produced at the Molesworth Hall on 2 Nov 1903 by Cumann na nGaedheal. Hyde was eager that his plays should be performed as widely as possible, as part of his attempts to popularize the Irish language, and so he waived all his production rights in them. He was also wary of associating himself too closely with the Abbey, which he criticized during his American tour of 1905–6. Among Dinneen's plays were *Creideamh agus Gorta* (*Faith and Famine*), which WBY described in 1901 (*Expl*, 79) as the 'best Gaelic play' after Hyde's *Casadh an tSúgáin*, and *An Tobar Draoidheachta* (*The Magic Well*), which WBY thought (*Expl*, 90) 'probably the best' Gaelic play of 1902 after Hyde's *An Pósadh*. In the 1901 and 1902 numbers of *Samhain* WBY had criticized Peter O'Leary for excessive changes of scene, finding his *Tadg Saor* (*Tadhg the Smith*) 'vivid and picturesque, though far too rambling dialogue' (*Expl*, 78), and asserting (*Expl*, 91) that his plays were unlikely 'to have any long life on our country stages'.

The debate about the performance of plays in Irish continued over the coming years, with sporadic public controversies as to whether plays of slight merit should be produced merely because they were in Irish. The only Gaelic play to be produced by the NTS before 1938 was Hyde's *An Tincéar agus an tSidheóg*, given on 15 Feb 1912.

plays were poor, but there may be one or two amongst them which are good enough.[9] There may be Hungarian plays, probably every national movement has produced one or two plays. I dont think there will be any great difficulty about translations, one can generally find somebody who knows any particular language one wants, and whoever turned the play again from English into Irish, could put the style right. Possibly some Gaelic writer with a dramatic talent and no construction would care to adapt some of his plays, giving them an Irish environment. Then comes the question of an audience—the Keating branch drew I think about £15 audience on each night. This audience ought to have been much bigger, and if spread out for a week would be about what we ourselves have done at our worst. On the other hand, the Keating branch is not I am told very popular in the league at present, the most serious question is this very question of audience, and we should not do anything till we have some idea as to what audience we may count on.[10] There would be no difficulty about the money, Miss Horniman's only condition being I understand that there can be no outside guarantors. If we do decently well on tour, we could afford the necessary capital and I begin to think that we are going to do very well indeed. A very serious question however is this—If we had a small Gaelic company would this give the Gaelic malcontents an opportunity of crying out every time we sent our English company on tour "Why dont they send their Gaelic Company" or would Gaelic league opinion recognise that we would send it for our own sake whenever it was possible. This applies to the whole scheme, would there be a perpetual cry for an artificial pushing of Gaelic? Whether we could get native speakers easily is another matter, but this will have to be found out by enquiry. I dont consider that this company if formed would be propangandised in the sense in which Frank Fay uses that word. It would be an attempt to meet a demand which already exists in a more artistic way than the propagandist societies can meet it, and to give the opportunity for the present writers of Gaelic grammar to develop into artists. We possess a theatre, a knowledge of drama, and we would, under these circumstances place these at the service of an already existing enthusiasm. Our own company at the start consisted very largely of people—Miss

---

[9] Count Francis Lützow (1849–1916) was English on his mother's side, and spent half the year in London, where he was well known and popular. He was a Chamberlain of the Austrian Emperor and had been a member of the Austrian Parliament, 1885–9. A native of Bohemia, he took an active interest in its history and culture, publishing a *History of Bohemian Literature* (1899) and *The Bohemian Historians* (1904). He lectured at Oxford and a number of American universities, and was a patron of the emergent Bohemian dramatic movement.

[10] Holloway had commented upon the thinness of the audience at the Irish plays given on 28 Oct by the Keating branch (NLI): 'So much for all the talk about the need for plays, etc., in the Irish tongue. The people who clamour for them, & abuse all other artistic efforts in the English language, never attend when an opportunity arises like to-night or last night.'

Quinn and Walker for instance—whose interests were predominantly propagandist.[11] A more serious objection to the whole thing is that we will be training and creating rivals to ourselves, but against that one may put the fact that every person who has a genuine interest in drama, and good art would create this, will care for our work.

In 92 the National Literary Society contained within itself a number of very ignorant wrongheaded and fanatical Gaelic scholars. I had always meant to work them in as a wheel in the machine. Hyde was then our President and it would have been easy. We had a good deal to give for we had the ear of the public at the time. While I was away they started with no very great hopes, the Gaelic league. I have always thought that if the National Literary Society had got them into its mechanism, the whole attitude of the Gaelic movement towards the Anglo Irish literary movement, would have been different.[12] I have no doubt they would have eaten up the National Literary Society, and maybe changed its name in the end, but that would not have mattered. A Gaelic company could not eat us up for a decade or two at any rate.

[Unsigned]

TLS Berg, with envelope addressed to the Nassau Hotel, postmark 'LONDON.W NO 11 05'. Enclosure TS doc NLI.

[11] Both Maire Quinn and Maire Walker had come into the dramatic movement through MG's political organization Inghinidhe na hEireann ('The Daughters of Ireland'). In January 1909 WBY was to write (*Mem*, 144) that 'Politics had made them sterile. They could not work seriously at their art, and they could not see it with pure eyes and love it for its own sake.'

[12] The Gaelic League was founded on 31 July 1893, less than a year after the National Literary Society, when about a dozen enthusiasts met at Martin Kelly's house in Lower Sackville (now O'Connell) Street. Hyde was elected president, John MacNeill secretary, with a council comprising P. J. Hogan, Martin Kelly, C. P. Bushe, J. M. Cogan, Patrick O'Brien, T. O'Neill Russell, and Fr. William Hayden SJ. Hyde and T. O'Neill Russell were members of the National Literary Society and other members soon joined the new organization, including George Sigerson, David Comyn, the Revd Eugene O'Growney, and T. W. Rolleston. Of these the most 'wrongheaded' was Thomas O'Neill Russell (1826–1908), a travelling salesman and language propagandist, described by an acquaintance as 'that Prince of Cranks' and even by the emollient Hyde as 'obstinate' (Dominic Daly, *The Young Douglas Hyde* [Dublin, 1974], 198). In the late 1880s he had conducted an extended quarrel with John Fleming of the *Gaelic Journal* over the use of the genitive case in Irish, and as recently as 22 Oct 1905 berated the INTS in a lecture because it had turned down a play of his. On 5 Dec 1909 Holloway (NLI) recalled him saying, with WBY in mind, that he would 'run twenty miles with a sore heel to avoid a mystic poet'. David Comyn (1854–1907), though less obstreperous than O'Neill Russell, spent a good deal of energy in the 1880s attacking the Society for the Preservation of the Irish Language, from which he had seceded in 1879 to set up the Gaelic Union. In its early days the Gaelic League actually met in the rooms of the National Literary Society in College Green, but its growing popularity took even its founders by surprise, and it quickly outstripped the NLS in numbers and influence.

## *To Charles Elkin Mathews, 11 November 1905*

18 Woburn Buildings | Euston Rd
Nov. 11th 1905.

Dear Mr Matthews,

I enclose a letter which I have received from one of our actors in Dublin who is editing under the inspiration of AE an Anthology of contemporary Irish poetry.[1] He is an unimaginably bad actor, but quite an amiable person and I dont want you to charge him anything for the right to include these poems.[2] You will remember his name possibly, as one of the poets in an Anthology edited by Russell a while back.[3] Please write to him.

We have decided not to include the "Wind among the Reeds" lyrics in my new book at all. That is I think fairer to every body—[4]

Yrs ev
W B Yeats

TLS Leeds.

## *To T. Fisher Unwin, 11 November 1905*

Mention in following letter.
Forwarding a letter from Starkey asking for permission to include WBY's poems in an anthology of Irish poetry.

[1] Seumas O'Sullivan (James Starkey) was preparing an anthology of Irish poetry, and WBY had already asked for permissions from A. H. Bullen, who replied to Starkey on this very day (TCD): 'Mr. Yeats tells me that you are printing at a private press some 200 copies of an anthology of Irish verse, and that you would like to include a couple of pieces from his forthcoming volume. I have much pleasure in saying that I freely give my permission & wish every success to your venture.' John Lane and Macmillan also gave permission for AE's poems, but plans for the anthology collapsed when Starkey took on the joint editorship with James Connolly of the Tower Press booklets (see p. 153, n. 2), the first number of which was AE's *Some Irish Essays.*

[2] Starkey agreed with this estimation, and in *The Rose and Bottle* (Dublin, 1946) wrote (28) that he 'was, as I still think, one of the very worst actors that ever encumbered the stage'. Nevertheless, he appeared in a number of minor roles 1903–5, including a pupil in *The Hour-Glass,* the Chamberlain in *The King's Threshold,* the Helmsman in *The Shadowy Waters,* and the Blind Man in *On Baile's Strand.* After playing Maelmora in AG's *Kincora* on 25 March 1905, he 'heard a criticism ["that dreadful man who played Maelmora"] of my performance as an actor which completely cured me of any further desire to shine in that difficult art'. Although Maelmora was his last role for the Abbey, he continued to take minor parts as a player for the Theatre of Ireland.

[3] Starkey had been a contributor to AE's anthology *New Songs* in 1904 (see p. 87, n. 3) and WBY had picked out his contribution 'The Twilight People' for particular mention (see III. 576–7).

[4] Although WBY had given up his attempts to publish these lyrics in *Poems, 1899–1905,* he did make sure that they were included in the first volume of the American *Poetical Works,* published only a month later.

## *To James Starkey, 11 November 1905*

18, Woburn Buildings | Euston Rd.
Nov. 11th 1905

My dear Starkie,

I have sent your letters on to Elkin Mathews and Unwin. I shall have to ask Bullen's permission as the Seven Woods is now passing through his hands and will be out in a couple of weeks.[1] You need not write to him however, I will do that.

Have you done anything about those miracle plays. I think you will find particulars in [G]ratton Floods History of Irish music. I am very anxious to know about them. They would have a small but perfectly certain and lucrative sale—[2]

Yrs ever
W B Yeats

TLS Texas.

## *To Holbrook Jackson,*[1] 11 November 1905

THE NATIONAL THEATRE SOCIETY, LIMITED,
| ABBEY THEATRE, DUBLIN.
18 Woburn Buildings | Euston Rd
Nov. 11th 1905.

Dear Sir,

Mr Fay has sent on to me your kind letter—It is as I daresay he has told you impossible for us to send the company to Leeds at this moment. They

---

[1] *In the Seven Woods* had been published in a limited edition by the Dun Emer Press in August 1903. It was not reissued as such by Bullen, but was included as a section of *Poems, 1899–1905*, which was delayed until October 1906.

[2] William Henry Grattan Flood (1859–1928), organist of Enniscorthy Cathedral, Irish correspondent of the *Tablet*, and vice-president of the Irish Folk Song Society, had published his *A History of Irish Music* in March of this year. In this he mentions various miracle and morality plays performed in Ireland from the 14th to the early 17th centuries, but few particulars are given. WBY may have been deceived into thinking there was more about them in the book by Flood's letter on the mystery plays of Ossory quoted in the *United Irishman* on 28 Jan 1905, next to his own letter on Synge (see pp. 25–7). Starkey did not publish a collection of miracle plays.

[1] Holbrook Jackson (1874–1948) was an editor, biographer, and author of *The Eighteen Nineties* (1913), where he describes WBY (152) as 'the fullest expression of the intellectual Celt-poet, mystic and patriot—expressing himself in an imaginative propaganda which has affected the thoughts and won the appreciation of the English-speaking world'. At this time Jackson was co-founder of the Leeds Arts Club (see p. 220) with A. R. Orage (1873–1934), who had been teaching for the Leeds County Council.

will have to be back in Dublin for the production of a new play there very soon after London performances. We think however of sending them to England during Lent of next year and hope to arrange for visits both to Manchester and Leeds. The assistance of a club like yours would be the greatest possible help and when the time comes near I will write to you again.[2]

Yr sny
W B Yeats

P.S. Is there any objection to Lent performance in your town or any objection that would seriously interfere with us. If there is not you need not write but tell me if there is—

TLS Colgate.

## *To Ernest Rhys,*[1] *11 November 1905*

THE NATIONAL THEATRE SOCIETY, LIMITED, | ABBEY THEATRE, DUBLIN.

Nov. 11th 1905
18 Woburn Buildings | Euston Rd.

My dear Rhys,

Can you send me tickets for your Guinevere for either Tuesday or Wednesday of next week.[2] If these days are full up I will make any other day of the week but Monday suit me. Wolves do not prey upon wolves, and I think the Managing Director of a Celtic theatre has a right to be on your free list—

---

[2] The Abbey Company performed in Leeds on 27–8 Apr 1906. In May 1907 Jackson and Orage moved to London to become editors and joint owners of the periodical the *New Age*, 'a Weekly Record of Christian Culture'.

[1] Ernest Rhys (1859–1946; I. 507–8) was born in London of Welsh extraction, and took up a literary career after a period as a mining engineer. He wrote fiction and poetry but is best known for his work on Everyman's Library, which he edited from 1892 to 1914. He had met WBY in May 1887, when he arranged the publication of *Fairy and Folk Tales of the Irish Peasantry* (1888), and in 1890 he helped WBY found the Rhymers' Club. The two remained friends throughout life.

[2] Rhys's *Gwenevere* (1905), a lyric play written for music, played at the Coronet Theatre from 13 to 18 Nov, with music by Vincent Thomas. The libretto was described in *The Times* of 15 Nov (14) as 'a fairly successful effort to get three scenes from the main current of Arthurian legend into the compass of one evening; it is not devoid of poetical words. It has, however, two fatal defects as an opera book—first, that the action does not tell the story, so that some familiarity with the legend is absolutely necessary to the hearer's enjoyment; and, secondly, that its rhythmic structure is nearly always the same.' The *Stage* of 16 Nov agreed (17) that Thomas's 'maiden effort in grand opera' was 'somewhat lacking in ... dramatic spirit'; 'written in too minor a key', it came at times 'perilously near to the monotonous', but was 'hampered by a weak and undramatic book'.

[*In WBY's hand*]
I send a copy of this through Symons as I am not sure of your address.[3]

Yrs ever
W B Yeats

TLS BL.

## To F. J. Fay, *13 November 1905*

18 Woburn Buildings | Euston Rd
Nov 13th 05

Dear Fay
I enclose a postal order for 10s, being the amount due to you for copying that play.[1] Many thanks. I found when I went down to Cambridge that our organiser there thought that a flute would do instead of a trumpet to announce the entrance of Cuchullain's son. Imagine a herald with a flute. I of course put the matter right.[2] I think we have good prospects here and should make a pot of money.

Yours ever
W B Yeats

TLS Private.

## To Maud Gonne, [*mid–November 1905*]

Mention in letter from MG, 'Tuesday' [21 November 1905].
Two letters saying that nothing can be done about her exclusion from election for office in Cumann na nGaedheal on the grounds that she is English not Irish;[1] and telling her that he is to give a lecture in Oxford.[2]

*G–YL*, 214–15.

[3] Rhys was living at Derwen Cottage, Hermitage Lane, in the Hampstead district of London.

[1] Presumably the revised version of William Boyle's *The Eloquent Dempsy*; see p. 215.

[2] In the early versions of *On Baile's Strand*, a herald's trumpet is heard just before the entrance of Cuchulain's son and the stage directions instruct that the '*great door at the back is flung open; a young man . . . stands upon the threshold. Behind him are trumpeters. He walks into the centre of the hall, the trumpeting ceases*' (*VPl*, 496, 498). In the revised version of the play, published in 1906, the heralds and trumpets were cut and Cuchulain's son, now solitary, knocks upon the door to gain admittance (*VPl*, 499, 501).

[1] Cumann na nGaedheal had been founded in September 1900 by Griffith and William Rooney as an umbrella organization for a number of small anti-British institutions and was shortly to merge into the Sinn Fein party. MG, like MacBride, had been a vice-president since its foundation, but at the recent annual convention her nomination for re-election was ruled inadmissible because she was not of Irish birth or descent. Deeply pained by this snub, she had written to WBY, and on 17 Oct to John O'Leary (NLI), to see if anything could be done about it, but in her reply to this letter conceded that he was right: 'I was very pained at the time but I am very philosophical over things generally. I worked for Ireland for Ireland's sake, not for my own. . . . I will never under any circumstances enter on a personal fight or campaign.'

[2] See p. 219.

## To Hugh Lane, [*16 November 1905*]

18 Woburn Buildings | Euston Road
Thursday

Dear Lane

I am afraid I must be at Oxford & Cambridge with the Abbey Company all next week. I am sorry.[1]

Yr ever
W B Yeats

ALS Private.

## To Lady Gregory, *20 November 1905*

18 Woburn Buildings | Euston Rd.
Nov. 20th 1905

My dear Lady Gregory

I send you two letters one of Synge's and one of Fay's.[1] I think you told me that you sent Fay £50 but I am not quite sure, and therefore send you this letter by special messenger. "Where there is Nothing" is beginning to shape itself in my mind.[2]

Yr ever
W B Yeats

[*With enclosure*]

31 Crosthwaite Park | Kingstown
Sunday

Dear Yeats

Thanks for invitation for tomorrow evening, I will turn up if I get across all right. My neck is much better, but I have been so unwell in my stomach the last few days that I began to fear I would have to drop the trip altogether. However I have decided to start tomorrow for London and if

---

[1] Lane had presumably asked WBY to a reception or to dinner.

[1] Fay's letter is untraced but evidently complained that he had insufficient funds for the expenses of the English tour which AEFH had agreed to subsidize.

[2] WBY was unable to reshape *Where There Is Nothing* until 1907, when he and AG together rewrote it as *The Unicorn from the Stars* (1908). He described the new play, first produced at the Abbey Theatre on 23 Nov 1907, as 'almost wholly hers in handiwork, which I can read . . . and recognize thoughts, a point of view, an artistic aim which seem a part of my world'(*VPl*, 712). WBY's heavily revised proof copy (Emory) contains his alterations in over seventy places.

I am not well enough for the Oxford and Cambridge round, I will go out and stay with a cousin in Surrey till you all come back to London.[3] I do not know whether I am wise to go, but I will see if I am better or worse for the day's travelling tomorrow and make my plans accordingly.

Yours sincerely

J. M. Synge

TLS Berg, with unstamped envelope addressed in another hand C/o the Honble Mrs Goldman, 34 Queen's Anne's Gate, W.[4]

## To Edmund Gosse,[1] [20 November 1905]

18, Woburn Buildings | Eustn Rd

Dear Mr Gosse

I have tried to get to you both yesterday and the Sunday before that. I wanted to remind you that our plays are coming on at the St George's Hall on Monday and Tuesday next. I want you to try and see my play on Baile's Strand, which is played on both evenings and I wish you could see The Well of the Saints by J. M. Synge, an extraordinary dramatist as I think. If you come either Monday afternoon or evening you will see Lady Gregory's "Spreading the News" a most gay extravagant, wise farce. I have such a rush of things to do and such a crowd of people to see or I should have told you of these things myself—

Yr ev

W B Yeats

TLS Leeds. Dated by Gosse 'Nov 20th 05'.

[3] Synge stayed with a favourite cousin, Edward Millington Synge (1860–1913), an artist, who lived at Clare Cottage, West Byfleet, Surrey, before joining the Company at Cambridge on 24 Nov.

[4] The Hon. Mrs Agnes Mary Goldman, née Peel (1869–1959), a daughter of 1st Viscount Peel, had married Charles Sydney Goldman (1868–1958), an industrialist with interests in East and South African mining, in 1899. She was a lifelong friend of AG's, who often stayed with her in London, and her brother William Robert Wellesley, 2nd Viscount Peel (1867–1937), Secretary of State for India 1922–4 and 1928–9, and 1st Earl Peel, was to support AG during the 1920s in her campaign to have the Lane pictures returned from London to Dublin.

[1] Edmund William Gosse (1849–1928), critic, minor poet, and author of the celebrated autobiography *Father and Son* (1907), was now an important figure in the British literary establishment. Although he had an active professional life in the civil service, he wrote prolifically on English and European literature, acquiring a particular reputation as an authority on the Scandinavian writers. Although WBY had described him in 1886 as an 'altogether trivial' English poet (*UP* 1. 92), he responded to his praise in 1895 (see 1. 476), and, apart from some coolness in the early 1920s, they remained good, if not close, friends. Gosse had contributed to the Kelmscott Chaucer (see p. 125, n. 1), and helped WBY, among other things, to raise money for the Abbey Theatre and to secure a Civil List pension. Gosse was knighted in 1925.

## To Lady Gregory, 21 November 1905

18 Woburn Buildings | Euston Rd
Nov. 21st 1905.

Dear Lady Gregory,

Miss Horniman, who seems very excited and broken down again, is not going down to Oxford until Thursday and probably not at all to Cambridge. Synge and I will go to Oxford to-morrow by the 12–10 train from Paddington. Can you come with us?[1]

Yours ev
W B Yeats

TLS Berg, with envelope addressed to 34 Queen Anne's Gate, Westminster, postmark 'LONDON No 21 05'.

## To A. B. Walkley,[1] [c. 25 November 1905]

Mention in letter to Padraic Colum, 18 December 1905.
Asking him to go to the afternoon performances of the INTS productions on Monday, 27 November, rather than in the evening, so that he can see Synge's play.[2]

---

[1] AG had sufficiently recovered from her cold to go to Oxford, and while there she and WBY inscribed a copy of the 1905 *Samhain* (Private) 'to John Quinn from W B Yeats & Augusta Gregory — at Oxford, Nov 23 — just before the 1st performance of the plays'.

[1] Arthur Bingham Walkley (1855–1926), drama critic of the *Star* for twelve years before he moved to *The Times* in 1900, was one of London's most influential reviewers. He had welcomed the first visit of the INTS to London in May 1903 in a lengthy and detailed review in the *TLS* on 8 May (146), which set out 'to record the keen pleasure which an afternoon with the Irish National Theatre has afforded us, and to do our best to analyse that pleasure'.

[2] In fact, Walkley attended both the matinée and evening performances on the opening day and discussed them in his unsigned review in *The Times* on 28 Nov (10). Though he found *The Well of the Saints* 'just as much English as Irish', he thought it 'a fresh, natural, and imaginative little story, and a very well written play'.

## *To Mrs Patrick Campbell,*[1] *[26 November 1905]*

18 Woburn Buildings | Euston Road
Sunday

Dear M[rs] Campbell: I have just got back from Cambridge—where we have had a great success—[2]& found your letter. I enclose two seats—I dont think there are any boxes at the St Georges Hall.[3] I am in a great rush— heaps of letters some waiting an answer for days.

Yr ev
W B Yeats

ALS Fales.

---

[1] Beatrice Stella (Mrs Patrick) Campbell, née Tanner (1865–1940), the celebrated English actress, had known WBY since late 1900, when she negotiated with him and George Moore over the possibility of her producing *Diarmuid and Grania* (see II. 602, 606, 609, 614–16, 618–20, 622–3, and III. 8, 20–1, 126). Although this production never took place, she and WBY kept in touch, and she was to star in a special performance of his *Deirdre* in November 1908.

[2] The INTS had performed *In the Shadow of the Glen, On Baile's Strand*, and *Spreading the News* at the Victoria Assembly Rooms, Cambridge, on the evening of 24 Nov, and *The Well of the Saints* and *Cathleen ni Houlihan* at the Guildhall on the following afternoon (see p. 214, n. 3). Reviewing the evening performance, the *Cambridge Daily News* of 25 Nov remarked on the 'distinguished audience', and reported (3) that 'the hall proved too small for the numbers that desired to make the acquaintance of Mr. Yeats and his friends, and hundreds were unable to attain admission. The anticipations of those who were fortunate enough to secure seats were more than realised. Each of the three plays presented gripped and held the interest of the audience in a striking fashion.' After praising each of the three plays, and the acting in them, the notice concluded: 'Altogether, the performances were most successful, and those who were present feel they owe the Society a debt of gratitude not only for the excellent entertainment provided, but for the glimpse into Irish life, past and present, that the various plays afforded, and for the opportunity of making a personal acquaintance with the Irish Literary Renaissance.' In an interview on the same page, WBY said he 'was delighted with the enthusiastic reception of the Society in Cambridge. "It is a pleasure to play," he said, "where one is appreciated."' The players shared WBY's pleasure, and, immediately after his return to Dublin on 30 Nov, McDonnell, who acted under the name Arthur Sinclair, told Holloway that he 'was delighted with the reception of the company at Oxford & Cambridge. . . . They were treated like princes in both towns.' McDonnell also mentioned that *Cathleen ni Houlihan* had 'proved a prime favourite in the university towns', but that during its performance in Cambridge 'one of the audience cried out "That is treason!" & then sank back into his shell again without creating any disturbance' (NLI). The *Cambridge Review* of 30 Nov considered (120) that the play 'demands a very lively sympathy with native Irish sentiment to be altogether impressive'.

[3] St George's Hall, also known as the Matinee Theatre and later as Maskelyne's Theatre of Mystery, 4 Langham Place, Marylebone, held an audience of 1,000, and the stage was 50′ × 49′, but there were no boxes. It was regularly used by amateur groups.

## *To Maud Gonne,* [c. *30 November 1905*]

Mention in an undated letter from MG, [*c.* 1 December 1905].
Apparently asking whether the affidavits collected by John Quinn are admissible in the French court,[1] expressing disappointment with the thought of the masses,[2] and telling her that the INTS's English tour has been a success.[3]

G–YL, 221.

## *To Holbrook Jackson,* 1 *December 1905*

18, Woburn Buildings | Euston Road,
Dec. 1st 1905.

Dear Sir,

I did not reply to you before as I have been desperately busy for the last ten days or so owing to my having been with our players, who have been to Oxford and Cambridge and London, and can now begin to think again. I could either lecture to you myself at the time of the Plays or could give a lecture to you in conjunction with Miss Farr on speaking to musical notes. You could call this "Literature and the Living Voice" or some such title.[1] On the very few occasions I have lectured with her we have drawn good audiences, at Manchester a very large audience—we took sixty pounds at the door, which was I think divided between us and the local people, or else the profit was divided, I cannot recollect.[2] I think the double lecture is the better sport, but I suppose it would largely depend on whether you have any way of getting at the general public. We have had a very

---

[1] There had been a problem about the affidavits as to MacBride's drunkenness in New York (see pp. 76, 96–7) because Quinn had initially been given the wrong dates for MacBride's time there, but evidently this had been resolved since MG replied that 'as Mr Quinn had had them all legally taken down before the French consul in New York', she did not think they could be contested.

[2] WBY had perhaps complained about the behaviour of the members of Cumann na nGaedheal towards her and the ill-will being generated in the INTS over the reorganization of the Society, situations which may have led him on to comments similar to those at the end of his letter of 6 Oct to FF (see pp. 204–5). However, in her reply MG told him: 'I only part agree with it, there is more good than you admit in the unconscious thought of the masses of the people.'

[3] MG replied that she was 'so glad the theatre tour has been so successful'.

[1] See pp. 228–9. Under the auspices of the Leeds Arts Club, WBY lectured on 'Poetry and the Living Voice' in the Philosophical Hall on 14 March 1906, with A. R. Orage presiding. FF illustrated the lecture with the psaltery.

[2] WBY had lectured on 'Speaking to the Psaltery', illustrated by FF, in the Whitworth Hall of Owens College, Manchester, on 18 May 1903 in connection with the Owens College Women's Union (see III. 374). In the course of a long and appreciative review on the following day, the *Manchester Guardian* noted (7) the 'large audience'.

considerable success here and at Oxford and Cambridge with our players and are very anxious for a Lenten tour—[3]

Yours sny
W B Yeats

TLS Colgate.

## *To George Roberts, [early December 1905]*

THE NATIONAL THEATRE SOCIETY, LIMITED,
| ABBEY THEATRE, DUBLIN

Dear M^r Roberts: I got the enclosed from Miss Horniman some time ago: I thought she had written to someone else but I find that you as sec had not received a copy. This is as you will notice sent to me in my official capacity, please see that it is entered on the minutes.

Yrs sy
W B Yeats

[*With enclosure*][1]

Standard Hotel, Dublin.

Dear Mr. Yeats.

I have already spent nearly £4000 in the Abbey Theatre and it is now proposed that I should aid in making the society into a Limited Company. I am most willing to do this but I consider that the value of the shares should

---

[3] The INTS performed *On Baile's Strand*, *In the Shadow of the Glen*, and *Spreading the News* at a matinée in Oxford on 23 Nov, and *The Well of the Saints*, *Cathleen ni Houlihan*, and (by special request) *Spreading the News* at an evening performance on the same day. The *Oxford Times* of 25 Nov (12) reported that the Company 'met with a cordial welcome from large audiences', and that during the interval in the evening performances WBY thanked the audience 'for their appreciation of the work of the Society', and 'pointed out that it was their effort to take out from Irish life some element that had not yet been put upon the stage'. The *Oxford Chronicle* of 24 Nov 1905 (12) regretted that the plays had to be produced in 'the comfortless Corn Exchange [see p. 214, n 3], where many of the audience found it difficult to see what was going on on the stage', and that it had been impossible to bring adequate scenery, but reported that 'despite these drawbacks the performances were very enjoyable'. It described *On Baile's Strand* as 'one of the best of Mr. Yeats's short plays—a play for the study, where its fine poetic diction may be best appreciated, but a play also for the stage, impressive with the shock of elemental passions and with a highly dramatic catastrophe, led up to with great art'. The acting also came in for praise: 'They speak poetic language. . . . with its proper musical accent, and in comedy they are wonderfully natural and singularly happy in humorous interpretation. . . . the main attraction in the acting of the Abbey Theatre Company is not found in its individual parts, but in the general high level attained. It will be a good thing if the visit of these clever Irish Players leads our audiences to look less to the "stars" and more to the *ensemble* in the theatre.'

[1] See p. 190. This letter is now in the Roberts papers at NLI. It was written on 26 Sept of this year.

bear an exact proportion to the voting power. I have always been accustomed to this in the Companies in which I already hold shares and in these Companies I obviously hold a position with a very small voting power.

Yours sincerely,

A. E. F. Horniman

ALS Harvard. Enclosure NLI.

## To John Quinn, 5 December 1905

THE NATIONAL THEATRE SOCIETY, LIMITED,
| ABBEY THEATRE, | DUBLIN.
5th December 1905

My Dear Quinn,

I enclose a note which explains itself. You will remember that we talked over my next tour, and you suggested my going to Pond. You will also remember our interview with Pond's representative about Mrs. Emery.[1] It is a long time ahead to be making arrangements; but apart altogether from Mrs. Emery's hurry, I want to have my dates definite.[2]

With good luck I might have the company out there at the same time, and we would all advertise each other.

I dont write any more now, as the same steamer that brings you this will have brought you a more personal letter. I am sending this to Mrs. Emery that she may put the circulars into it.[3]

Yours ever

W B Yeats

*[With enclosure]*

[1] WBY was planning a lecture tour of America with FF. James Burton Pond (1889–1961), lecture-manager, inherited the Pond Lyceum Bureau upon the death of his father Major James Burton Pond (1838–1903), who had acquired the business in Boston in 1874, and moved it to New York in 1879. As head of the firm for over thirty years, Pond managed the American tours of, among others, WBY, AE, Lord Dunsany, John Masefield, and Rabindranath Tagore. At this time he was only 16 years old and the business was being run by his representatives.

[2] Quinn discouraged WBY from accompanying FF (whom WBY had introduced to him in November 1904) on a joint tour, writing circumspectly on 13 July 1906 (Himber, 77): 'Now for a confession: I did not show your letter to the Pond Bureau. It wouldn't do for you and Miss Farr to come here together. This is after all a provincial people. You are now known in a most dignified way, favorably known, and can lecture here again, especially at the Women's Colleges. But coming here with a woman it would be entirely different. Your position here now wouldn't stand it. Others have tried it and failed. She alone or you alone, yes. . . . But you two to come, no, it is too risky, too easily misunderstood. I feel sure that you will understand exactly what I mean.' In the event, FF's American tour was delayed until January 1907, when she spent four months there (unaccompanied) lecturing on 'Speaking to the Psaltery', and when, in spite of his wary advice here, Quinn almost certainly became her lover.

[3] FF added two circulars: the testimonial sheet prepared for the psaltery lectures in 1903 ('Lectures by Mr. W. B. Yeats on Poetry and the Living Voice. Illustrated by Miss Florence Farr'; see Appendix,

THE NATIONAL THEATRE SOCIETY, LIMITED,
| ABBEY THEATRE, DUBLIN.
5th December 1905

Dear Sir,
    I went to Major Pond's office with Mr. John Quinn in the early Spring of 1904, and discussed with his representative certain Lectures. I suggested that Miss Florence Farr be invited to deliver Lectures or rather Recitations, and spoke of her in connection with my own work. Major Pond's representative seemed to think that she would be a success, but the matter fell through afterwards. I had myself, at the time, just finished a Lecturing Tour in the United States which was from my own point of view, and I hope from the point of view of the audiences, successful. One of these Lectures had been arranged by Major Pond or his representatives, but my Lecture Tour, as a whole, had been organized by my friend, Mr. John Quinn (120 Broadway, New York).[4] I am anxious to go to the States again in the Autumn, Winter, or Spring of 1906–7. It is difficult, so far ahead, to describe, very precisely, the subjects of my Lectures; but they would be Literary and Dramatic. If possible, I should very much desire that Miss Florence Farr should be engaged in conjunction with me, or for some Lectures in conjunction with me and for others on her own account, to illustrate my theories by recitations of poetry to musical notes. The little dramatic company of which I am at present Managing Director might possibly go to America about the same time; if not, it would follow me.
    The reason why I write so far ahead is that Miss Florence Farr has been offered a ten months' engagement by Mrs. Patrick Campbell, and as part of this engagement would take her to the United States, it would, in Miss Farr's opinion, take away some of her value for Lecturing purposes by giving her name an association of a totally different kind with the public.[5] If, under the circumstances, you care to consider a Lecturing Tour in which I should lecture partly in association with Miss Farr, I should be glad if you would let me know as soon as possible. Miss Farr is not absolutely essential to me; but her help would be, I believe, of the greatest possible advantage. I

pp. 885–9), and a new one advertising her choric chanting in Gilbert Murray's translations of Euripides ('The Chorus of Classical Plays to the Music of a Psaltery'; see Appendix, pp. 889–91). The letter also printed testimonials from WBY, Gilbert Murray, Jane Ellen Harrison, a lecturer at Newnham College (see 219, n. 4), and Miss Dorothea Beal, Principal of her old school, Cheltenham Ladies' College, where she had returned to speak to the psaltery in the summer of 1903.

    [4] The Pond Bureau had commissioned WBY to give a lecture at Bridgeport, Connecticut, on 25 Feb 1904. On 26 Jan 1904, Quinn wrote to tell him that they had also just enquired 'what your rates would be for another lecture at Hartford, Connecticut', but there is no record of his speaking there.

    [5] In fact, FF had decided on this very day that she would not visit America with Mrs Campbell. On 2 Dec Shaw had written to her (Bax, 30), 'Mrs. P.C. is a clever and lovely child of about 13. By all means

enclose a circular containing explanations and Press Opinions upon our Lectures, and another giving an account of the application of the method of speaking to notes as it has been applied to the performances of Mr. Gilbert Murray's translations of Euripides. [*In WBY's hand*] I found a constant difficulty while I was in America in making audiences understand certain things I said about recitation to a musical instrument, a constant need for Miss Farrs help. She has a most wonderful voice & method.

[*Typewritten on a separate sheet*]

I am sure that Mr. Quinn will answer any question as to the measure of success my own Lectures met with when I was in America.

Yours faithfully<br>W B Yeats

TLS NYPL, with envelope addressed in FF's hand to 120 Broadway, New York, postmark 'WESTMINSTER DE 6 05'.

## To John Quinn, 6 December 1905

ABBEY THEATRE, | ABBEY STREET, | DUBLIN<br>6th December 1905

Dear Quinn,

I think you will get a letter from me this post which will explain itself. I sent it to Mrs. Emery to add circulars to.

We have got back from our tour at Oxford and Cambridge and London. We roused a lot of enthusiasm at Oxford and Cambridge and made about £100 in London. We were entertained at Oxford and Cambridge by professors and their wives and the whole company were put up in private houses. They gave us a supper in one of the halls at Oxford.[1] At London we lit on rather a bad season of the year. Our own audience which is a

---

tour with her.' In her reply of 5 Dec (BL) FF announced that she had 'just arranged to associate myself with Sturge Moore & Ricketts in organizing a little theatre for Poetry.... So I shall not go to America with the "clever & lovely child of 13" after all.'

[1] Reviews in the Oxford and Cambridge papers were enthusiastic (see pp. 236, n. 3, 234, n. 2), and in *The Fays of the Abbey Theatre* (181) W. G. Fay recalled that the 'reception was amazing. Down to the Corn Exchange came everyone of note in Oxford from all the colleges.... It was the first time we had played to a cultured audience of this kind . . . For the first time in our experience no subtle point in any of the plays went unnoticed, and *The Well of the Saints* in particular was appreciated in a way that was in striking contrast with its reception in Dublin. Everybody was most hospitable, too. We were shown the principal sights, and tasted the very best from college cellars. Both artistically and financially the players came through with flying colours. At Cambridge.... the audiences were thoroughly representative. They filled both halls in every part and there was once more the understanding and sympathy that made

particularly fashionable one is only there during the meeting of Parliament, and we fell on the rather flat general public; but they came in very considerable numbers, which is the great point.[2]

We are going to tour in Ireland very shortly, in January if all goes well, and then some time in Lent, when we can do little here, we will go to Leeds and Manchester and some neighbouring towns. The editor of the Manchester Guardian, the most powerful of all the provincial papers, has urged us to go there, and we have an invitation from the Arts Club in Leeds.[3]

Lady Gregory's "White Cockade" is coming out on Saturday. You will get a copy of it, I have no doubt, in a few days. It is a fine play as a whole, but I doubt if it has got into its final shape yet.[4] It takes a long time making out a new dramatic form. It isn't so difficult to take some writer, some French writer, let us say, and copy his form, and that is the way most dramatists begin; but, for some reason or other, every current dramatic form looks curiously foreign when you try to put Irish material into it. After seeing the performance of "Baile's Strand" I made Bullen stop the publication of my new book which was half printed that I might work on the play again. It had already been re-written twice since its publication in the form you know. I think I am getting it right this time.[5] Edmund Gosse told me on Sunday that Ibsen rewrote all his earlier plays, but that he rewrote no more when he got to "Brand".[6] I hope it will be that way with us. I noticed

it a delight to play to them.' At Oxford WBY and the Company were entertained by Sidney Ball, Senior Tutor of St John's College, and at Cambridge WBY made a brief speech after the performances, thanking the audience for their interest and support. In a letter of 19 Dec (NLI) AEFH remarked to Holloway: 'I wonder if Dublin believes that an Oxford don sold sixpenny programmes in his enthusiasm & imitated Cuchullain's "little mutterer" speech to the sword [see *VPl*, 510], walking home along the street in broad daylight?' In the same letter she revealed that the Company had made a net profit of £135 on the tour, and on 20 Dec she wrote to Synge (TCD): 'I presume the cheque for £135 arrived as the Managing Director referred to it. . . . I wish it had been more, but I did my best.'

  [2] McDonnell had told Holloway on 30 Nov (see p. 234, n. 2) that the 'afternoon performances were not well attended in London, but the evening shows drew considerable houses'. However, on 12 Dec Holloway discussed 'the cause of the unfavourable notices in the London press' with George Roberts, who accounted for them (NLI) 'by the novelty of the style of plays and players having worn off'.

  [3] The NTS played in Wexford in February and Dundalk in March 1906. On 23–4 Apr they opened at the Midland Hall, Manchester, the first stop on a tour that took in Liverpool and Leeds. Charles Prestwich Scott (1846–1932) was editor of the *Manchester Guardian* from 1872 to 1929 and governor of Manchester University from 1895 to 1906. He remained a friend of the Abbey Theatre and in 1910 arbitrated in the dispute between AEFH and the Directors over the withdrawal of her subsidy.

  [4] As well as receiving a copy of the play, published by Maunsel & Co. as vol. VIII in the Abbey Theatre Series, Quinn also acquired the manuscript of *The White Cockade*, marked 'Finished Aug. 1, 1905'. He published an edition of thirty copies of the play, with AG's *The Travelling Man*, on 29 Dec of this month to protect the US copyright. AG did not revise the play, which was well received.

  [5] See p. 90. A new version of *On Baile's Strand* was published by Bullen in *Poems, 1899–1905*. After meeting the Company on their return from London on 30 Nov, Holloway reported in his diary (NLI) that '*On Baile's Strand* was not understood and W. B. Yeats is thinking of again tinkering at it'.

  [6] Gosse was to make this point in his book *Ibsen*, to be published shortly in 1907. Ibsen had had little theatrical experience before his appointment as stage manager of the theatre in Bergen in 1851. Here,

in London that the commoner sort of critic and theatre-goer liked our work best when it was really worst, when it was most like the machine play— Colm's second act, for instance[7]—I think it will take a couple more years before the five of us—Lady Gregory, Synge, Colm, Boyle and myself—get a mastery of our different forms, or at any rate get a mastery of them for any kind of ambitious purpose. The little one act plays are all right, I think: but I dont think anything else is. What delights me in "The White Cockade" is that Lady Gregory is there working towards a new form, a form as much her own as that Synge is working out.[8]

You must be overwhelmingly busy with Dr. Hyde on your hands; but are very evidently making a great success of him. All manner of echoes of the Irish American cheers get into the Irish papers.[9] If he captures Irish-America, it should make a great difference this side of the water. For, hitherto, the Irish Member of Parliament, who had a bundle of old agrarian speeches in his head, could always escape from Gaelic Leagues and the like by crossing the Atlantic. I think the most interesting events here lately have been that a young man called Kettle founded a rather advanced little paper called "The Nationist" a few weeks ago; but has been put out of it because of some purely historical articles on Liberal Catholicism in France and a mild article asking for lay control of the University College, Stephen's Green.[10] It was presumably our friend Finlay that put

---

and at the Norske Theatre in Kristiania (now Oslo), which he directed from 1857 to 1863, he learned his craft as a dramatist, writing mainly historical dramas. A travel grant and pension allowed him to settle in Rome and write what he wished, and *Brandt* (1866), the first product of this new freedom, was written with more spontaneity and mastery than any of his earlier works, so placing him, Gosse argues (102), 'at a bound among the greatest European poets of his age': 'It was . . . during the summer and autumn of 1865, that *Brandt*, which had long been under consideration, suddenly took final shape, and was written throughout, without pause or hesitation. In July the poet put everything else aside to begin it, and before the end of September he had completed it.'

[7] On 30 Nov McDonnell had told Holloway (see above, n. 2) that in London Boyle's play *The Building Fund* 'took best & Colum's play "The Land" also went remarkably well', but that they 'played the *Spreading the News* without a laugh in the afternoon'. Later W. J. Tunney and William Boyle were to allege that the Directors had been jealous of this success.

[8] In her notes to the play (*CPLG* II. 303), AG recalls that when *The White Cockade* 'was first produced I was pleased to hear that J. M. Synge had said my method had made the writing of historical drama again possible'.

[9] Quinn was extremely busy organizing Douglas Hyde's visit to the USA, which took place from November 1905 to June 1906 (see p. 212). It was, as WBY suggests, a great success, and Hyde collected over $64,000 for the Gaelic League.

[10] Thomas Michael Kettle (1880–1916), journalist, politician, and the son of one of Parnell's most loyal lieutenants, had been a friend of Joyce's at the Royal University. In May 1899 he signed the students' letter of protest against *The Countess Cathleen*, and was later to take the chair when the Abbey seceders formed the Theatre of Ireland. He was called to the Irish Bar in 1905 and in 1906 became Nationalist MP for East Tyrone. In 1909 he tried to help Joyce obtain a lectureship at University College, and later in the year married Joyce's childhood sweetheart Mary Sheehy. He became Professor of Economics at the National University in 1910, but his promising public career was cut short when he

him out.[11] But I dont know for certain. Also a man called Kenny who had doubled the circulation of "The Irish Peasant" an important provincial newspaper, and done this in a few months, has been driven from his chair by nothing more important than the umbrella of a parish priest.[12] It is a pity for he was coming up to Dublin to run a weekly paper, more or less in the service of the intellectual movement.[13]

Your snly<br>W B Yeats

[*In WBY's hand*]
This is Fays paper, his choice & design!![14]

TLS NYPL, with envelope addressed to 120 Broadway, New York, postmark 'DUBLIN DE 6 05'; New York postmark 'DEC 14 1905'; and 'DUE 10 CENTS'.

was killed in action with the British Army on the Somme in 1916. Robert Hand, a character in Joyce's play *Exiles* (1918), is largely modelled on Kettle. On 21 Sept 1905 he and Francis Sheehy-Skeffington (1878–1916) began the *Nationist*, which, despite its sympathy for the Parliamentary Party, described itself (4–5) as an organ of 'complete independence'. Like Kenny's *Irish Peasant* (see p. 124), it advocated progressive Catholicism, and its regular contributors included Thomas Keohler, Padraic Colum, Joseph Campbell, Herbert Hughes, Maurice Joy, William Buckley, and Robert Elliott. Kettle was not 'put out of the editorship' at this time, but remained in charge until publication ceased on 5 Apr 1906, a failure caused as much by insufficient financing as clerical opposition. Maurice Joy's four-part article 'Catholic Democracy in France', which ran from the first issue to 12 Oct, was an enthusiastic account of *Le Sillon*, the French lay Catholic movement which advocated a blending of democratic Republicanism and Catholicism. Joy urged that Ireland could learn much from its combination of Catholic and progressive ideals; from its awareness of modern conditions; and from its doctrine of brotherhood. 'The New Scholarship', an unsigned article on 21 Sept, pointed out that in effect the funding of University College rested upon the salaries of six Jesuits which produced a combined income of over £1,500 p.a. The writer argued that this financial power gave the Jesuits virtual control of Catholic higher education in Ireland and, at the same time, rendered the system incapable of extension and proper development.

[11]  The Revd Thomas A. Finlay SJ (1848–1940), former rector of Belvedere College (1882–87), was editor of the *New Ireland Review* and lecturer in Mental and Moral Philosophy at University College, Dublin. The *Nationist* had been set up in part as a more intelligent, radical, and internationally orientated rival to the *Leader*, whose owner and editor, D. P. Moran, was a great friend of Finlay. Like Moran, Finlay was deeply suspicious of WBY and had attacked him bitterly in America in 1904 (see III. 539).

[12]  Although he had doubled the circulation in a few months, clerical pressure persuaded the proprietors to remove Kenny from the editorship of the Navan-based *Irish Peasant*, and replace him with W. P. Ryan. In a defence of his editorial policies, published in the *Nationist* of 14 Dec (204), Kenny alleged that he had provoked clerical hostility by quoting the Pope's teaching that Catholics should show 'complete deference to the priest of all things of religion, and complete independence from him in all things else'. Reviewing the whole controversy in the *Shanachie* of March 1907 (51–3), he noted that he 'had for some time been preaching undeniably sound Catholicism, as against obviously heretical Parochialism.... the local bishop [Gaffney], apparently recognising the merit of a man who knew how to quote the Pope, drew the attention of the whole nation to me. He caused a whole issue of the paper to be burnt.... His Eminence [Logue] caused me to be relieved from the stress of working a newspaper.' After his dismissal he was allowed to continue his column, 'Patriana', provided that he did not live in Navan. W. P. Ryan gives an account of the subsequent history of the paper in the introduction to his *The Pope's Green Island* (1912).

[13]  See pp. 124, 125.

[14]  The short-lived letterhead contained a grotesque, winged, serpentine figure with arms and a frog-like head in the top left corner, hovering above the three oversized capitals of Abbey Theatre, Dublin,

## To Holbrook Jackson, 6 December 1905

THE NATIONAL THEATRE SOCIETY, LIMITED,
| ABBEY THEATRE, DUBLIN.
6th December 1905

Dear Mr. Jackson,

I am very sorry to trouble you, but I would be greatly obliged if you could advise us as to what time in Lent it would be best for us to go to Leeds and as to what theatre you think best. We could then write to the theatre and pencil our dates.[1] We did very well at Oxford and Cambridge and London and are now setting out on our work here which will include some Irish country touring. I send you a copy of Samhain which you may not have seen. I enclose also a circular about Miss Farr's Speaking to Notes as I am rather inclined to think that I forgot it when writing last.[2]

Yours faithfully
W B Yeats

Holbrook Jackson Esq.
The Arts Club,
18 Park Lane, Leeds[3]

TLS Colgate.

---

highly doodled in Beardsley-baroque letters with excessive twirls, dots, and deformations. Abolishing this design had been one of the first actions of the new administration and WBY was evidently using up old stock. In writing to Quinn on more restrained Abbey notepaper on 1 Nov (Berg), AG expostulated: 'If you could but know the amount of worry and wasted time the securing of above heading has cost us! But already we begin to feel the advantage of being able to make plans without having them upset by irrelevant people. The Directors have absolute power.'

[1] Following WBY's lecture in March (see pp. 235–6), the National Theatre Society played at the Albert Hall, Leeds, on 27–8 Apr 1906 under the auspices of the Arts Club.

[2] See p. 237.

[3] The Leeds Art Club was founded in 1903 by A. R. Orage and Holbrook Jackson with the aim of 'reducing Leeds to Nietzscheism'. For twenty years the Club, open to men and women by election, prospered as the most avant-garde club of radical thought and experimental art outside London. It popularized the introduction of Nietzschean philosophy, fostered Guild Socialism, Fabianism, theosophy, and women's suffrage, held exhibitions of Impressionist and post-Impressionist paintings, architecture, sculpture, and photography, and hosted musical recitals and demonstrations. In addition to Yeats and Farr, its many lecturers included G. B. Shaw, G. K. Chesterton, Hilaire Belloc, Richard Cobden-Sanderson, Edward Carpenter, and Wyndham Lewis. Even after Orage and Jackson left Leeds in 1907 to edit the *New Age*, they returned regularly to support the activities of the Club, which merged with the Playgoers' Society in 1923.

## To Ernest Rhys, 6 December 1905

THE NATIONAL THEATRE SOCIETY, LIMITED,
| ABBEY THEATRE, DUBLIN.
6th December 1905

My Dear Rhys,

I wish I could be with you on Monday 11th but we are producing a new play here on that day.[1] I shall hope to see you when I get back to London, which will probably be about Christmas—unless we work ourselves up to the heroic effort of a play on Boxing Night.[2]

Yr ev
W B Yeats

TLS Kansas.

## To Maud Gonne, [c. 6 December 1905]

Mention in letter from MG, 'Dimanche' [? 10 December 1905].
Asking about the progress of her divorce hearing;[1] telling her of the clerical opposition to Thomas Kettle, and of the devastating effect of this on him.[2]

G–YL, 218–20.

[1] The nature of Rhys's invitation is unknown, but WBY occasionally dined with him and his wife Grace, and Rhys probably wanted to hear his opinion of *Gwenevere* (see p. 229). *The White Cockade* actually opened on Saturday, 9 Dec, but ran though the following week.
[2] The National Theatre Society had hoped to produce Boyle's new comedy *The Eloquent Dempsy* on Boxing Night, but it was delayed until 20 Jan 1906.

[1] In her reply of Sunday, MG complained of another 'hideous day of listening to MacBride's friends perjuring themselves', in the course of which they had insinuated that she was a morphine addict, and that her half-sister Eileen Wilson was her daughter. 'The strain of the last month has worn me thin as a shadow. It was such a nightmare work having to sit in court day after day listening to my witnesses describing the hideous things I knew of. . . . Day after day I had to listen to MacBride's witnesses perjuring themselves & contradicting each other . . . all the time at the bottom of my heart was the sickening fear that the name of my innocent little Iseult would be dragged into the sea of mud.' This, she revealed, had finally happened, when, against the advice of his lawyers and the protest of the judge, MacBride 'insisted in calling his brother Dr MacBride to go into the whole affair, he ended by saying it was his belief that I & the British Government had concocted this to get rid of his brother'. In consequence of this, she had been obliged to recall a number of her witnesses, although she refused to call Iseult.
[2] See p. 241. MG was astonished 'that clerical censor or any censor should break a man up so much. I am afraid Kettle can't be very strong, but I am glad you are seeing him, it will be good for him & help him get back his balance for even if he is not strong, an active brain capable of original thoughts is always valuable.'

## To George Roberts, 7 December 1905

THE NATIONAL THEATRE SOCIETY, LIMITED,
| ABBEY THEATRE, DUBLIN.
7th December 1905

My Dear Roberts,
    Please send or bring the Free List of the theatre to Abbey Street to-morrow (Friday). It is important that we get this early in the day that we may get off the Press tickets etc. before the evening rehearsal.[1]

Yrs sny
W B Yeats

TLS Harvard.

---

[1] Another example of Roberts's increasing slackness as secretary of the NLT (see p. 206), following the reorganization of the Company and his dismissal from the part of Conchubar (see p. 207). It was already very late to send out free press passes for *The White Cockade*, which was to be staged in only two days' time, and as a result the play enjoyed fewer reviews in the Dublin papers than normal, being entirely ignored by the *Irish Times* and *Irish Independent*. The *Freeman's Journal* of 11 Dec (6) described it as 'in the nature of a comedy. It is unconventional in many respects. There is no romantic love affair such as is usually found in historical plays, and it is not a drama in which, as is the vogue in such work, there is a story having for its kernel the historical event.' The reviewer thought that the character of the 'Poor Lady' was 'strikingly pathetic': 'The great dignity of the sorrow-laden lady who has lost her estates, her ever-buoyant hopes expressed in stirring and poetic pathos, are magnificent features of the play, which raise it to a high level in the dramatic art.... As to the cast, it was well chosen. Foremost in it stands Miss Maire Nic Shiubhlaigh, who took the part of the Old Lady. There was a ring of pathos in her voice, and she treated the part with much grace and dignity. Mr. Arthur Sinclair was allotted the part of James. It is a difficult role to fill, but it was fully done justice to. The comical gestures expressing fear, and the undignified attitude in the barrel scene, were admirable.' The review also recorded that at the final curtain 'the audience called for the author, and Lady Gregory bowed her acknowledgements'. The Dublin *Daily Express* on 11 Dec noted (6) that AG's presentation of King James II 'does not possess any feature of attractiveness', but on the same day the *Evening Mail* insisted (4) that Arthur Sinclair 'was worth coming a long way to gaze at, for his resemblance to the portraits of the Stuart King is quite startling, while his changes of expression from terror to relief, and his assumption of dignity while uttering the most ridiculous bombast could scarcely have been better.' An extremely brief notice in the *Evening Herald* of 12 Dec (5) merely commented that 'the piece was staged skilfully by the well-known company of the National Theatre Society'. The lack of press coverage was presumably one of the causes for the thin audiences: on the opening night Holloway noted (NLI) that a 'goodly crop of the usual first-nighters...was present, but very few of the ordinary public put in an appearance'; the following Tuesday he lamented 'a meagre house', and even on the final night the turnout was still 'wretchedly poor'.

## *To Maud Gonne,* [c. *10 December 1905*]

Mention in letter from MG, 'Monday' [? 11 December 1905].
Telling her that he is checking the papers for reports of her divorce case to send to her,[1] and asking for the latest news on its progress.[2]

*G–YL*, 192–3.

## *To Maud Gonne,* [c. *14 December 1905*]

Mention in letter from MG, 16 December [1905].
Sending her a copy of AG's *The White Cockade*, and praising it.[1]

*G–YL*, 221.

---

[1] The hearings in Paris were attracting wide coverage in the Irish and British press, and this, as MG disclosed in her reply, had obliged her to subscribe to a press-cutting agency, '& the bundle of cuttings I receive every day are surprisingly large & require a certain amount of resolution to read, however I always prefer to know exactly the facts & the dangers to be faced'. She noted that the English papers expatiated on the allegation that she was an Englishwoman who only converted to Catholicism to marry MacBride and had now become a Protestant to divorce him, but reported that she had 'quite decided to reply *nothing* until the divorce is quite over & I have a judgement in my favor'.

[2] MG thought that her case was proceeding favourably, and said her lawyer advised that she 'need have no anxiety'. Nevertheless, she feared that the 'enquête will probably have to go through & through, it is painful & will make a long delay', although this would be for the best in the long run 'because if ever the question of the custody of the child is raised in the future by the English Courts it will be better that all my charges against MacBride are fully & separately proved'.

[1] MG wrote in her reply that she had 'just read the *White Cockade*. Indeed you did not say too much about it! It is wonderful to read, & must be wonderful to see acted.' She added that AG 'knows the soul of our people & expresses it as no one else does. Through the surface of triviality, of selfish avarice, of folly which often jars on one, she never ceases to see & to express in her writing that deep passion which *only heroic* action or thought is able to arouse in them, & when once aroused makes them capable of sacrifice for ideals as no other people on earth are. It is a play that will live & I know I shall often have the opportunity of seeing it, which consoles me little for missing its first production. It is a play that will be popular...such plays are needed for your work & for the public.'

## *To Maud Gonne,* [c. *17 December 1905*]

Mention in letter from MG, 'Monday' [? 18 December 1905].
Thanking her for a picture of Iseult Gonne;[1] discussing the progress of her divorce proceedings and their repercussions in Ireland;[2] asking if it is correct to address his letters to her as 'Madame Maud Gonne';[3] telling her that he is going to Scotland after Christmas;[4] and evidently mentioning William Sharp's death.[5]

*G–YL,* 222–3.

[1] Earlier in the month MG had promised to send him 'a little drawing of Iseult I have done—I shall send it by my cousin Miss Gonne who is going to London for Xmas. It is Iseult with her hair twisted up for the bath, it is like her but makes her look older than she is.' She sent the picture on 16 Dec, and was delighted with his admiration for it: 'I am so glad you like the little drawing of Iseult. It is very like her except that having her hair twisted up gives her a grown up air she has not got. She is only 11 & though very tall, is a real child. She will be very beautiful I think & she has a wonderful imagination & a love of art remarkable in a child & she would always rather go to a picture gallery or to see beautiful things than to the circus.' This letter has a proleptic irony, since WBY was to propose to Iseult in 1916 and 1917.

[2] In her reply MG revealed that Henry Dixon had revived his idea of a compromise between her and MacBride (see p. 33) and that this had 'crystalised into an offer to Ella Young to try & settle matters (*this is private*) Dixon practically admitted I was likely to gain my case in France through technicalities whatever that may mean & that he knew I would never consent to any arrangement which did not give me complete control of the child & he felt could undertake this should be conceded. He added that he was acting independently of MacBride, but he felt MacBride would take his advice.' MG replied to these overtures by sending translations of the evidence on both sides to see whether Dixon 'still would advise compromise' after reading it. She claimed that there was 'not a single thing against my character in all the evidence produced by MacBride' except the fabrication that she was a British agent, 'whereas the evidence against MacBride is overwhelmingly terrible & complete—I thought it was good that Dixon who according to his lights is an honest man should have a chance of reading the evidence for though he witnessed for MacBride I am certain they did not show him the evidence of the other witnesses. If he & his friends continue to support MacBride once they have read this evidence they can no longer support the theory, which is one they love—of Irish intolerance of immorality—Of course there is no possibility of compromise now—After all that has been said a public verdict is the only possible ending to this miserable business.'

[3] 'You are quite right to address my letters to Madame Maud Gonne', MG told him in her reply, 'In France I have always been Madame Maud Gonne before & since my marriage so the divorce makes no difference in this respect.'

[4] See p. 193.

[5] See p. 177. William Sharp had died in Sicily on 12 Dec. In her reply MG asked whether the death of Sharp inevitably meant the end of Fiona Macleod.

## *To George Roberts, 18 December 1905*

THE NATIONAL THEATRE SOCIETY, LIMITED,
| ABBEY THEATRE, DUBLIN.
18th December 1905

Dear Roberts,

I write this to remind you that there is a share awaiting your acceptance. It is waiting for you quite apart from any decision you may make as to whether you go on with us as a player or not. I hope you will do so and I write this with the full concurrence of William Fay. You will not care, I dare say, to tour with us as a regular thing, for we will have to go here and there about Ireland a good deal and to places where your books would get no sale;[1] but I hope you will sometimes give us a hand. There will always be some part cropping up that you can do better than any other available person.

Please let me know in a couple of days. I think you had better let the question of the books stand over for a short time, but if you feel this is putting you in any wrong light with Hone, I will see him about it.[2]

Please summon a meeting of the business committee of the Irish National Theatre Society for some time this week. There are a number of bills to settle; most of them are now in. There is, for instance, an account with Miss Horniman.[3]

Yours sny
W B Yeats

TLS Harvard.

---

[1] This was an attempt to keep Roberts in the reformed National Theatre Society, Ltd. (NTS), but to dissuade him from acting (see p. 207). Roberts had permission to sell volumes of the Abbey Theatre series (see pp. 29, n. 6, 99) in the Abbey and in theatres used by the Company when on tour.

[2] Roberts was also evidently afraid that his secession from the NTS might endanger his right to sell the Abbey Theatre series in the Abbey and that this would compromise his already fraught partnership with Joseph Hone in Maunsel & Co. (see p. 91, n. 1). In the event, AEFH reconfirmed his rights.

[3] These were presumably expenses connected with the recent British tour. Although he was secretary, not treasurer of the Society, AEFH had used Roberts in many of the Theatre's day-to-day financial affairs (Harvard).

## *To Holbrook Jackson, 18 December 1905*

THE NATIONAL THEATRE SOCIETY, LIMITED,
| ABBEY THEATRE, DUBLIN.
18th December 1905

Dear Mr. Jackson,

Very many thanks for your letter of 8th instant. I have not had time to reply to it until to-day, for I have been lecturing in Cork,[1] and there has been a new play running here, and between one and the other, I have been pretty busy. I thank you very much for your information, and will probably write to you again when we feel able to fix a date. We will probably have to send somebody in any case to look at the halls for us.

Yrs sy
W B Yeats

TLS Colgate.

## *To Padraic Colum, 18 December 1905*

THE NATIONAL THEATRE SOCIETY, LIMITED,
| ABBEY THEATRE, DUBLIN.
18th December 1905

My dear Colm,

Is there even an act of your play in a state for reading. We shall have to start touring very quickly and must have a number of plays before us.[1] One can make so much better arrangements if one make them a good time ahead. I saw Russell on Saturday and he told me that you had complained to a number of people that we had treated you badly about the place we gave you in the London programme.[2] I dont ask you to deny this for I am sure it

---

[1] Jackson's letter has not been traced, but was clearly a reply to the queries WBY had raised in his letter of 6 Dec (see p. 243). WBY lectured on 'What is a National Theatre' to the Cork Literary and Scientific Society on 14 Dec.

[1] In his reply to this letter (*LWBY* I. 151) Colum wrote that 'I will have some of the play finished soon after I get back.... I am determined to finish "Broken Soil." I find the material difficult.' *Broken Soil* was rewritten as *The Fiddler's House* and produced by the Theatre of Ireland on 21 Mar 1907 in the Rotunda, Dublin.

[2] This complaint had been voiced in the *Nationist* on 7 Dec (183): 'We regret also that what is probably the best — and certainly the most characteristically Irish — play in the Company's repertory should have been obscured. We refer to Mr. Colum's play, *The Land*, which was only produced at one matinee, and this on the second day in London, when Mr. Bernard Shaw's new play was also seeking the verdict of critics. This treatment of such a play is, we submit, not quite fair, considering that Mr. Yeats's

is not true. I never bother my head about Dublin rumours but in case people may speak to you of it, I may as well tell you how the programme was arranged. Miss Horniman asked in return for her guarantee that she would have the right to name the plays and place them in the programme. She did however tell me why two of the plays were placed where they were. She put Synge in the afternoon of Monday because the critics came to the matinee rather than the evening when we were in London last year. She thought that it was better for them to see Synge than me this year as I had been longer before the public and was therefore less in need of the advertisement. I wrote personally to Walkley asking him to go on Monday afternoon and see Synge as he had not seen him the year before.[3] He was an exception to the general rule, according to Miss Horniman and had gone in the evening. Miss Horniman told me that Boyle had asked for Tuesday evening as that was the best evening for his friends.[4] That was all I knew about the programme. I imagine that the other parts of it followed from these two decisions; but I don't know. When somebody asked me the order of the

*On Baile's Strand* was played on each night in London. One night certainly might have been given to *The Land*.' The belief that the Directors pushed their own work at the expense of others was a recurrent source of ill-feeling at the Abbey, but, in his reply, Colum denied that he had been upset by the scheduling of the programme: 'Of course it's not true that I blamed the society's arrangements about "the Land". It's quite true that I expressed my disappointment that the matinee would prevent many of my friends being present. I expressed it to Miss Horniman herself. But I knew it was due to inevitable circumstances. As a matter of fact I am almost indifferent to the show I got in London, and anyone who knows me, knows this. I wouldn't have come to London at all only Lady Gregory asked me to play. I am very distressed about the matter being spoken of. I see a reference to it in the "UI". I would have written to Griffiths, only I know from a somewhat bitter experience that this would be no use. It may be that I am not so intensely interested in the artistic side of the movement as you are, but I can assure you that you can always reckon on my loyalty to you personally & to my school.' Despite this, there was a strong feeling in Dublin that Colum had been badly treated. On 21 Sept 1906 W. J. Tunney described to Holloway (NLI) 'the terrible state the Fays were in after the great success of Colum's *"The Land"* in London, & the way Willie Fay laughed with derision when he heard him congratulate Colum on its success.... The failure of Synge's *The Well of the Saints* soured all the worshippers at the shrine of Yeats & Synge & made them doubly bitter against the triumphs of Colum & Boyle.' This suspicion continued to rankle and, writing to D. J. O'Donoghue on 17 Jan 1908 (NLI), Boyle recalled that during this London visit WBY and AG 'kept back *The Land* and *The Building Fund* till the day of a first performance of a Shaw play at the Stage Society knowing well the critics would be at Shaw's play and the newspaper space occupied with it. They also put off *The Building Fund* from the place they had assigned it on the programme to the very last item of their engagement—apparently for the same reason. Fortunately they did not succeed—the favourable notices it got probably preventing them from staging *Dempsy* on their next English, Welsh, and Scotch tour.' As a draft programme in her hand shows (Harvard), AEFH did, as WBY claims, draw up the programme and was responsible for scheduling *The Land* as a matinée.

[3] Walkley attended both the matinée and evening performances on the opening day and discussed them in *The Times* on 28 Nov (see p. 233, n. 2). As well as discussing Synge's *The Well of the Saints*, he also praised *On Baile's Strand* for its 'strange and terrible atmosphere', and 'the contrasts [which] are Shakespearian in their violence'. He mentioned that Colum's play was to be produced 'this afternoon' but did not subsequently review the performance.

[4] Boyle's *The Building Fund* played on the evening of 28 Nov with *On Baile's Strand* and *Cathleen ni Houlihan*.

plays, I had to look them up in an advertisement and was very much puzzled because the Stage Society advertisement contradicted the others. I need hardly say that Miss Horniman knew nothing about "Major Barbara" being on Tuesday afternoon and the Stage Society on Monday afternoon when she arranged the programme.[5]

Personally I am convinced that we were perfectly right, considering all Miss Horniman has done for us, to let her arrange our programme and that considering one thing with another, she arranged it very well. If I had thought about it, I would probably have seen to it that "Baile's Strand" wasn't given twice, but I didn't think about it.

Yours sny
W B Yeats

TLS Berg.

## *To Maire Garvey,*[1] *18 December 1905*

THE NATIONAL THEATRE SOCIETY, LIMITED,
| ABBEY THEATRE, DUBLIN.
18th December 1905

My Dear Miss Garvey,

I want to remind you that there is a paid up share in the new company awaiting your acceptance.[2] I hope you will still continue one of our players; but the share is for you whether you do or not, if you care to accept it. If you will come on with us as a player, we shall be able to find parts for you that you can do better than anybody else. I have just put three women into

---

[5] See p. 216, n. 9. On Sunday 26 and Monday 27 Nov the Stage Society produced E. F. Benson's three-act comedy *Dodo* at the Scala Theatre. MacDonnell told Holloway on 30 Nov (see p. 234, n. 2) that most of the Abbey Company had attended the Sunday performance. The INTS had evidently advertised their plays in the Stage Society programmes.

[1] Maire Garvey, 'Maire Ni Gharbhaigh' (d. 1946), was one of the signatories of the letter accepting AEFH's original terms for the gift of the Abbey Theatre (see III. 596). She first appeared as an extra in *Riders to the Sea* on 25 Feb 1904, and thereafter played a variety of minor roles, including Delia Cahel in *Cathleen ni Houlihan*, and Bride in *The Well of the Saints*. She eventually declined the share in the NTS and joined the Theatre of Ireland. Her loss was a considerable blow, and in a memorandum of December 1906 WBY described her as 'a verse speaker of . . . feeling even with some slight touch of passion, though a very narrow range', adding that since her and Maire Walker's departure 'there has been no good speaking of verse among the women of the company'.

[2] An actor–shareholder in the limited liability company could be paid a salary, which the directors were now offering to selected members of the NTS.

"Baile's Strand"³ and there is "Deirdre" coming on,⁴ and I hope we will have the chance of casting you for verse parts again, as well, of course, as for prose. Please let me know in a day or two.

Yrs ever
W B Yeats

TLS NLI.

## *To Frank Walker,*¹ [c. *18 December 1905*]

Mention in Joseph Holloway's diary, 19 December 1905.
Offering him a salary of 15*s.* a week for his services as an actor in the new National Theatre Society.²

---

³ WBY was making further alterations to *On Baile's Strand*, following its London production (see p. 240), including an elaborate new scene in which three women perform the rite which accompanies Cuchulain's oath of allegiance to Conchubar (*VPl*, 489–501).

⁴ Although WBY had been working on *Deirdre* since July 1904, it was not finished until over two years later, and first produced on 24 Nov 1906.

¹ Francis Joseph ('Frank') Walker (1879–1960), who acted under the Gaelic form of his name Prionnias MacSiubhlaigh, was the brother of Maire Walker. He had first appeared with the INTS in Fred Ryan's *The Laying of the Foundations* on 29 Oct 1902 and subsequently took parts in WBY's *The Hour-Glass*, *The Shadowy Waters*, and *On Baile's Strand*, AG's *Twenty-Five*, *Spreading the News*, and *Kincora*, Colum's *The Land*, MacManus's *The Townland of Tamney*, and Synge's *The Well of the Saints*, giving his last performance at the Abbey as Owen Kelleher in AG's *The White Cockade* on 9 Dec of this year. He was to be associated with the Theatre of Ireland over the next few years, but never became a professional actor, and remained a printer until his retirement.

² Holloway recorded in his diary on 19 Dec (NLI): 'Had a chat with F. Walker, M'Donald & Tunney on my way home. Walker told us that he intended severing his connection with the National Theatre Society & we tried to persuade him not to. He showed us a letter he had received, signed W B Yeats, asking him to decide today as to his becoming a salaried member (15/- a week was the sum proposed to give him for his services) & he had not replied to it. M'Donald was offered £1.0.0 per week for his services. The new Company seems to have given general dissatisfaction to the members of the troupe, other than those at the head of affairs ... & I fear there will be a smashup of the company as at present arranged.' The differential in the salaries being proposed no doubt annoyed Frank Walker as much as it did his sister, especially since he had originally been offered only 10*s.* a week. In a letter of 9 Sept, W. G. Fay told WBY that Maire Walker reckoned her brother was worth more than 10*s.* and that he had assured her that 'we could promise him the 15*s.* the same as the others' (see p. 184, n. 4).

## *To Lady Gregory,* [c. *18 December 1905*]

Mention in letter from AG, 'Wednesday' [20 December 1905].
Forwarding MG's letter in praise of *The White Cockade*,[1] and passing on gossip about Ralph Burnham.[2]

Berg.

## *To the Editor of the* Cork Constitution, *21 December* [*1905*]

Dublin,
21st December.

Sir,—A correspondent says in your issue of 20th, "In the course of his address, Mr Yeats, speaking as the head of the National Theatre Company, Limited, disowned all connection with the Cork National Theatre Society, and referred to it as one of the small societies which his movement has given rise to. Why did Mr Yeats go out of his way to disown the local body?"[1] I am distressed to think that even one of my hearers so utterly misunderstood my meaning. I stated that the Cork National Theatre Society was not officially connected with us, for it is only right that they should have the credit of their admirable initiative. I do not think I described them as "small," but if I did it was not to make light of a movement that has

---

[1] See pp. 127, n. 6, 194. In her reply AG thanked him for sending MG's letter, 'one is always glad of appreciation'.

[2] Ralph Burnham, who was booked to play the violin in the interval during the final performance of *The White Cockade*, but who failed to appear (see p. 214, n. 5). As Holloway reported (NLI): 'After act I W B Yeats came before the curtain telegram in hand & announced "with regret that the violinist engaged for the evening was unwell & that even the pianist who was to have accompanied him had not turned up, but if any one has a pianist he would feel grateful if they sent him on". The poet's joke amused, & the search for a "piano thumper" filled up the interval good humouredly.' Evidently Burnham's absence had been caused by something more piquant than illness, and AG replied: 'How amusing about Burnham! The Shawe Taylors say that when they were at the Hibernian he gave a large dinner party to which he asked the manager of the hotel & even the clerk from the office. Sometimes Ld Limerick entertains his guests, & sometimes Ldy Fargale.' AG may have destroyed WBY's letter to keep the gossip private.

[1] The correspondent, 'Diarmuid', went on to suggest answers for his own question: 'Is it because it is not sufficiently imbued with the Ibsen spirit, and that it is striking out on lines of its own? or, is it because it retains the word "Cork" in its title and has not deleted it, as the "school" of Mr. Yeats has done to the word "Irish", which originally appeared in its name?' 'Diarmuid' asserted that, in contrast to WBY's 'strange dramas' and his 'Commercial' theatre, 'the Cork National Theatre Society is doing much more National and practical work in giving to the public plays replete with the National idea and of a propagandist nature' (3). This was not the first time that WBY had ruffled local Cork patriotism (see I. 342), but the protests were misplaced: in December 1913 he told AG (Berg) that the Abbey was 'getting all our dramatists from Cork, because they are free from propagandist ideas and Dublin gossip. It makes me think that my instinct of twenty years ago was right. We should have started in Cork.'

great promise for Irish intellectual life. I have read every report I could get of the work of your Cork Society, and I have questioned everybody I could about it, for I think that the rise of societies of this kind is essential to any proper understanding of dramatic art in Ireland. People learn to appreciate things fully by doing them, and by finding out what measure of joy and difficulty they contain. I have only this day received a letter from a London friend, upon whose critical capacity I have considerable reliance, which says of a play called "The Enthusiasts," produced by the Dungannon Club Dramatic Company, a body very similar, I think, to the Cork National Theatre Society, "The writer of it has a better gift of construction than any of the Irish dramatists, at least that is my opinion, and every word of it told, and the hall was full of keen discussion afterwards." I have never seen the play and know nothing of its author, but if it is as good as my correspondent says, the seeing or reading of it will be one of the few pleasures that one values deeply.[2] There is no pleasure, I think, quite so great as meeting fine work in an art, to which one has devoted one's own life. For one knows, as no other can, how great are the difficulties.

If your correspondent really wants to know what I think about Ibsen, and about the need for local dramatic societies, he will find a good many pages on the subject in "Samhain," 1901.[3]—Yours truly,

W B Yeats

Printed letter, *Cork Constitution*, 23 December 1905 (6).

[2] Lewis Purcell's *The Enthusiasts*, first produced by the Ulster Literary Theatre in Belfast from 4 to 6 May 1905, was performed with Colum's *The Saxon Shilling* by a dramatic group from the London branch of the Dungannon Club (see p. 222, n. 4) at the South Hampstead Club Hall on 9 Dec. The 'enthusiast' of the play, James McKinstry, the son of a Protestant farmer in Antrim, tries to persuade his family and neighbours of the benefits of agricultural co-operation, but a public meeting he calls to preach these new ideas breaks up in sectarian violence, and he abandons his crusade in the face of obdurate Orange bigotry. The play had been published in the Belfast literary journal *Uladh* in May 1903. There was a lively discussion after the plays, and *Inis Fail* of January 1906 reported (2) that Padraic Colum 'declared from the stage when the play was over, that "The Enthusiast" was "an immoral play" because it showed no door of hope opening to the idealist and his dreams', but the reviewer praised the play and pointed out that Purcell was 'a satirist'. Colum himself wrote in the *Nationist* on 11 Jan 1906 (253) that it 'was well staged in London, and the ending, which I had barely noticed in reading, became very marked.... An idealist fails. His effect on the community is not merely negative, it is positively harmful. After his fiasco there is drinking and Orange drums.... It is a piece of social satire, and the weariness of the idealist is satirised as much as the prejudice of his neighbours.' WBY's 'London friend' may have been Stephen Gwynn, but the letter does not survive. 'Lewis Purcell' was the pseudonym of David Parkhill, an architect of independent means, who had helped Bulmer Hobson found the Ulster branch of the Irish Literary Theatre in 1903. WBY did, in fact, know something of him, and had written to him in May 1904 about the production of *Cathleen ni Houlihan*, as a result of which the Company decided to commission its own plays and changed its name to the Ulster Literary Theatre (see III. 597–8). Purcell subsequently emigrated from Ireland, but a play of his, *Cobblers Go Halves*, was produced by the Company as late as 1931.

[3] 'Diarmuid' was mistaken in ascribing an admiration of Ibsen to WBY (see above, n. 1). While WBY's lecture had pointed out the historical parallels between the beginnings of the dramatic

## To Lady Gregory, 21 December 1905

THE NATIONAL THEATRE SOCIETY, LIMITED,
| ABBEY THEATRE, DUBLIN.
21st December 1905

Dear Lady Gregory,

Ryan has been in and gone through all the accounts, and advises that the way to manage the apportioning of shares in return for costumes is by a system of exchange of cheques. I send you herewith a cheque for £60. being the value a Directors' meeting (Synge and myself, that is) put, in consultation with Ryan, upon "The White Cockade," "Kincora" and other costumes. There is no reason for working out a very exact calculation. In return for this, you are to send us a cheque for the same value. We pay this cheque into the Bank. In this way, all our shares will represent actual capital. I am of course doing the same.

You will be amused about what has happened about Maire Walker. I got a note saying that she wanted to see me, but could not get away from Dun Emer for some days. I went there yesterday. She had nothing to say about one man vote or anything of that kind. What she wants is a slight nominal increase of salary which she promises to keep a profound secret, she wants to feel, she says, for her own satisfaction that she is getting more than Miss Allgood.[1] She sticks to this with a most unsmiling face, and is in deadly earnest. I first told her that, though I could not give any promise, I thought it possible it might be managed. I saw Fay and Synge last night, and Fay is of opinion that the fact of it would come out the first time Miss Walker fell out with Miss Allgood. After that "the Affaire Walker" would be succeeded by "the Affaire Allgood". I saw Miss Walker again to-day, and told her we would not give the increase. She said that she would not give me any

---

movements in Norway and Ireland, he had little time for Ibsen's realism, although he thought his technique a useful model for inexperienced or undisciplined young Irish dramatists. The 1901 *Samhain* was much occupied with possible successors to the ILT, and WBY discussed proposals for travelling Irish stock companies, since he was sure that there was a wealth of local dramatic talent in Ireland that should be fostered, and no less sure that it must be disciplined: 'there is no chance of our writers . . . doing good plays of any length if they do not study the masters. If Irish dramatists had studied the romantic plays of Ibsen, the one great master the modern stage has produced, they would not have sent the Irish Literary Theatre imitations of Boucicault, who had no relation to literature. . . . Let us learn construction from the masters, and dialogue from ourselves' (*Expl*, 80–1).

[1] Sarah Ellen (Sara) Allgood (1880–1950), a student of Frank Fay, joined the company in 1903 and first appeared in the Horse Show performances in August and in WBY's *The King's Threshold* in October of that year. She quickly became Maire Walker's rival as the Company's leading lady and stayed on until 1913, playing major roles. In 1914 she joined the Liverpool Repertory Theatre, but she returned to the Abbey in 1923 to play Juno Boyle (her favourite part) in O'Casey's *Juno and the Paycock*. She took up a film career in 1929, moved to Hollywood in 1940, and became an American citizen in 1945. She played Molly Byrne in the first production of *The Well of the Saints*.

decision there and then as to what she would do; but would consult her mother. She is to let me know by to-morrow morning. If it is a refusal, as I rather suspect it will be, it will be a refusal for touring, not for Dublin. I shall then, I think, see her mother and offer an additional 2s. a week not for acting but for looking after the wardrobe. Miss Walker can then represent this to her own imagination as proof that she is really leading lady, but, owing to diplomatic difficulties, has to accept the larger salary with a pretence that it is really not all given her for acting. I said to her, "would it meet the case if we gave you both a little more?" She said "No. No matter how much you gave us. I should always want to get a little more than Miss Allgood."[2]

The cup for Miss Horniman has come and looks very nice. I have brought it down to the theatre and as soon as it has been properly seen, will send it off.[3]

Yr ever<br>W B Yeats

[*In WBY's hand*]
Frank Walker wont join.
[*On back of envelope*]
Forgot to post this—all right about Moira—two long interviews today.[4]

TLS Berg, with envelope addressed to Coole, postmark 'DUBLIN DE 22 05'.

[2] In a letter of early January 1906 (TCD) Maire Walker recounted to AG the course of events leading up to her rejection of the contract and repeated her complaints about Sara Allgood: 'I reminded Mr Yeats that I expected to be placed in the position next to the two Mr Fays and not on an equality with Miss Allgood, having been acting with them for a longer period. Mr Yeats considered Miss Allgood a more popular actress but said he would see the directors and ascertain what could be done in the matter. Next day he saw me at Dun Emer again and said it was impossible—that they were afraid of Miss Allgood's very bad temper (perhaps if I was possessed of this attribute my position would have been made better). Mr Yeats also reminded me that Miss Allgood had joined the new Company without pressure (which was to her advantage) he then said that there was only one way out of it, namely that I should look after the wardrobe (*Ladies* I understood) for which he offered me 2/6 of an increase. I then signed the document.... The question of money did not enter into the matter <at all> as position as I had been acting for four years without any thought of money and I had thrown up in the beginning a profession which might have been more remunerative, and the fact of asking me to look after the mens and women's wardrobe instead of giving me the station I believe I am justly entitled to, takes away from me that which I ask, the "ordinary duties of a wardrobe mistress" are not I think the ordinary duties of an actress, and one only learning too.'
[3] The Company had subscribed towards a silver cup in gratitude to AEFH for her generosity in buying and endowing the Theatre. Visiting the Abbey on 12 Jan 1906, Holloway noted (NLI) 'a letter from Miss Horniman thanking the members of the Company for their nice Christmas gift & hoping the New Year might bring them & her good luck'.
[4] In her reply (Berg) AG wrote: 'Your letter today was an enormous relief, for I had but little hope of Marie. I suppose there was a struggle going on in her mind that last day. F. Walker will be a loss for a while, & I liked him personally, but I daresay in the end it will be for the best. Marie will be independent of him. It is very amusing her scruples having ended in jealousy of Miss Allgood. One forgets what a baby she is in intellect.'

## To Maire Walker, 23 December [1905]

Nat Theatre Soc
Dec 23.

Dear Miss Walker,

Many thanks for contract. I write in the name of the Directors to say that we have appointed you Wardrobe Mistress for which we will give you 2/6 a week. Your duties will be to see that the wardrobes in the men's and women's dressing rooms are in good order not out of repair, not eaten by the moths, and to set them out before performances; in other words you will be responsible for the wardrobe being in good condition. These are I understand the ordinary duties of a wardrobe mistress.

I need hardly say I am very glad that you have seen your way to come on with us. It is the best thing both for you and for us. I am sorry I was so emphatic with you last night; but I have been waiting so many days on in Dublin to get the thing settled, that I did not look forward with much pleasure to another period of wasted time.[1]

Your sincerely
W B Yeats

TS copy Berg.

## To Lady Gregory, [23 December 1905]

Nassau Hotel

My dear Lady Gregory: The agreement is signed but it has been a job. I got rather angry last night. I had seen her in the morning & she had promised to sign last night—last night she would not without the leave of the old society (business committee of which was meeting). I told her if I did not get agreement signed this morning we would engage somebody else at once. I got it this morning[1] the committee (which was for all that very gloomy &

---

[1] The previous evening WBY and William Fay had gone to the Abbey to ask Miss Walker to sign her contract. WBY became angry when she refused to do this on the spot, though she agreed to sign and send it by morning. She kept her promise, but the present letter, far from closing the matter, led to a further and final rupture, for, as Synge explained to AG on 6 Jan 1906 (*JMSCL* 1. 149), 'apparently the irritation he felt with her went into the tone of the letter.... When Miss W. got it she said to herself, "the Fays have turned Mr. Yeats against me too. They are all against me now. I wont have anything to do with them".'

[1] Synge described the sequence of events to AG in a letter of 5 Jan 1906 (*JMSCL* 1. 149): 'Miss W. was not very eager to come to us—because she is afraid of the Fays, and their theory is that we are all absolutely in the Fays' hands!—however she started negotiations with W.B.Y ... and all went well till

cross) had given her leave. Tunny has been in & will join us for good & all in two weeks if a certain negociation of his fathers breaks down. It is either a new public house & no acting for ever or else he will turn actor for good & at first without salary.[2] We are to have Macdonald's decission in a few minutes—he wants 25/- shillings. We offer 20/-.[3] Fay has some hope of getting Alton a good Amateur[4]—So things are looking up. I had Kettle to dine last night. Kenny has it seems scored. After the news of his dismissal got out so many people wrote & called to protest that they only took the paper for his sake that he was engaged, not as editor but as contributor, with Kettle says three times his origornal salary. W P Ryan to be nominal editor to pacify the priests. Whether Kenny is as free as he was he did not know. I should think that the increased salary probably means that he is not. Kettle thinks Kenny is as free.[5]

Friday night Dec. 22nd. That evening I dined at the Nassau [Hotel] with W.B.Y Kettle and Fay. After dinner W.B.Y. and Fay went to the Abbey T. to meet Miss Walker and get her to sign her contract, as she had agreed to do, while I discoursed [with] Kettle. When they came back I thought there was storm in the air, and after Kettle went, it turned out that Miss W. has refused to sign on the spot but promised definitely to sign and send it in before morning. W.B.Y. added that this new vacillation had made him loose [*sic*] his temper with her, for the first time, and he was rather excited about the whole thing. He thought she was not going to sign at all and he began planning a vehement letter that he would write her the next morning when he found the contract had not arrived. I tried to put oil on the waters but it was no use. That night I got cold so that I was not in again. I heard barely that Miss W. had signed and then nothing more till Fay turned up on the 31st with her resignation.'

[2] William James Tunney played minor roles in numerous Dublin amateur productions from 1897 to 1905, appearing in James Duncan's *A Gallant of Galway* (24 Mar 1902), AE's *Deirdre* (13 Apr 1903), James Cousins's *The Sword of Dermot* (20 Apr 1903), and in the Players' Club production of Martyn's *An Enchanted Sea* (18 Apr 1904). He had recently made a local success in *My Friend the Prince*, and on 2 Sept told Holloway (NLI) 'that the Royal [Theatre] folk were inclined to become nasty over their playing at the Abbey.... I was pleased to hear that he intended taking part in some of the coming productions of the I.N.T.S.' Tunney acted with the NTS on the tour to Oxford, Cambridge, and London in November 1905, but thereafter appears to have abandoned his professional acting career. On 19 Dec he had tried to help Holloway persuade Frank Walker not to leave the National Theatre Society (see p. 252, n. 2).

[3] Francis Quinton McDonnell (1882–1951), known among friends as 'Mac' and on the stage as Arthur Sinclair, was born in Dublin and began work in a law office but joined the INTS for the opening productions of the Abbey Theatre in December 1904. At first he played a number of minor parts, but had earned good notices for his performance as Dan McSweeney in *The Building Fund*, and had recently scored a palpable hit as King James in AG's *The White Cockade* (see p. 245, n. 1). He remained with the NLS and became one of the Society's leading actors until 1915, when he led a mass resignation over the management of St John Ervine. A dandy and an egotist, he was best known for his comic roles in the plays of William Boyle and AG, although on 20 Aug 1917 he told a friend (NLI) that his favourite part was Martin Doul in Synge's *The Well of the Saints*. His marriage to Molly Allgood (Maire O'Neill) in 1926 was not a success, but he toured with her and Sara Allgood in his own company.

[4] Probably Frank D'Alton (1850–1935), a well-known Irish character actor who had influenced W. G. Fay, and the young Sean O'Casey, whose brother Isaac was a great friend. Frank Fay described him as an 'admirable and versatile actor' (*Towards a National Theatre* [Dublin, 1970], 18) and in *Fays of the Abbey* W. G. Fay wrote (52–3) that 'Frank Dalton had ... that great gift ... of holding your attention every second he was on the stage'. D'Alton did not join the Society, and in the *Freeman's Journal* of 2 Nov 1906 (8) was to criticize its productions and choice of plays at length. His son Louis D'Alton (1900–1951) was to become one of the Abbey's most successful playwrights from 1937 to 1947.

[5] Although at this stage Ryan (see p. 168) was a staunch Catholic and had written anonymously for the sectarian *Leader*, he was not as orthodox as those appointing him supposed, and Kenny recalled in

I think all is in good order here now—we have paid all our bills, & I got the old society to get its committee to geather last night to pay its bills. Boyle has signed his 'will'[6]—I shall try Colum next

Yrs ever<br>W B Yeats

PS. Please put enclosed in book. I have written to contradict last letter.[7]

ALS Berg, with envelope addressed to Coole, postmark 'DUBLIN DE 23 05'.

## To Sarah Purser,[1] [c. 23 December 1905]

Nassau Hotel

My dear Sarah Pursur: no it was not information I got in your office but the information that brought me there,[2] & some of that was got by a friend of

his *Shanachie* article (see p. 242, n. 12) that his 'successor, Mr. W. P. Ryan, a pious journalist, fresh from Fleet Street, E.C., kept well up to the interesting situation created for him'. This Ryan did by giving the paper a Sinn Fein bias and by airing the views of the modernist movement in the Catholic Church to such effect that Cardinal Logue denounced it as 'a most pernicious anti-Catholic print', and successfully persuaded the proprietor to suspend publication in December 1906. Ryan however relaunched the paper in Dublin in February 1907, first as the *Peasant* (1907–8) and then as the *Irish Nation* until publication ceased on 24 Dec 1910. Ryan's accounts of these journalistic struggles appear in his novel *The Plough and the Cross* (1910), and in *The Pope's Green Island* (1912). Kenny remained as a columnist on the paper, but left before the move to Dublin.

[6] The Directors were asking the playwrights to assign the Irish rights in their work to the NTS for a period of five years. WBY describes this as a 'will' because it was designed to protect the Society's interests in the case of an author's death.

[7] i.e. the correspondence in the *Cork Constitutional* over his lecture (see p. 253), to be placed in AG's press-cutting book.

[1] Sarah Henrietta Purser (see p. 72, n. 2) had helped change the course of JBY's career by organizing a Dublin exhibition for him in the autumn of 1901, and later that year, with the help of Edward Martyn, began planning an Irish stained-glass industry, An Tùr Gloine (The Tower of Glass).

[2] While discussing Irish opposition to sincerity in the arts in the recently published number of *Samhain*, WBY had given as a proof that the 'bourgeois mind is never sincere in the arts', the fact that a 'Galway convent a little time ago refused a fine design for stained glass, sent from Miss Sarah Purser's studio, because of the personal life in the faces and in the attitudes, which seemed to them ugly, perhaps even impious. They sent to Miss Purser an insipid German chromo-lithograph, full of faces without expression or dignity, and gestures without personal distinction, and Miss Purser, doubtless because her enterprise was too new, too anxious for success, to reject any order, has carried out this ignoble design in glass of beautiful colour and quality' (10). In *Today We Will Only Gossip* (1964) Beatrice Lady Glenavy (née Elvery), who worked in An Tùr Gloine, explains (41) why Miss Purser suspected that WBY had obtained his knowledge from her own office, since, when he and AG went there to inspect her design for the windows for Gort Convent, they 'looked at my drawing but said nothing. I began to explain that it was not quite the way I would like to have dealt with the subject but I had to do it the way the nuns wanted and showed them the pictures that the nuns had left with me.... The next edition of [*Samhain*] appeared with an article by Yeats saying that Miss Purser's Stained Glass Works was going the way of all artistic ventures in Ireland.... Sarah read this and came flying to me in a terrible rage—what had I been saying to Yeats and Lady Gregory? I told her, and I heard afterwards that she demanded a denial of the statement in the article, an apology and, I think, the extermination of the entire review. She said, "I don't interfere with your Abbey Theatre. Keep off my Stained Glass Works!"'

mine straight from the nuns & it was all got round Gort.[3] The matter is common knowledge owing to the agitation kept up by Edward Martyn & others against Father Fahey[4] & the nuns before you got the order at all. I should not wonder if I know more about the whole thing than you do yourself. I did not take you seriously when you said you liked the design—I thought & still think that banter.

Yr ev<br>
W B Yeats

ALS NLI.

## To John Millington Synge, [c. 28 December 1905]

Mention in letter from Synge, 31 December 1905.
Asking him to take charge of the key to the Abbey,[1] making a proposal about the £50 claimed by those defecting from the INTS.[2]

*JMSCL* I. 140–1.

## To Maire Walker, 29 December 1905

Mention in letter to AG, 30 December 1905.
Telling her that if she does not retract her letter resigning from the NTS, the Directors will place the matter in the hands of their lawyers, and direct them to take the usual steps to enforce the contract.[1]

---

[3] Presumably AG, who kept on friendly terms with the Sisters of Mercy at St Patrick's Convent.

[4] The Rt Revd Monsignor Jerome Fahey (see p. 93, n. 1), the parish priest of St Colman's Church, Gort. An antiquarian and local historian, he had published *Antiquities of the Diocese of Kilmacduagh* (1893), which included a history of the Gregory family, and contributed a study of the antiquities of Oranmore and Kilcogan to the *Journal of the Royal Society of Antiquities of Ireland* (1901). He had conservative views on ecclesiastical art, which clashed with those of his neighbour Edward Martyn.

[1] In his reply of 31 Dec (*JMSCL* I. 140), Synge wrote that he had not been able to get to the Abbey because he was suffering from a cold, but that he was to meet Fred Ryan on 3 Jan 1906 'to see how things are going on, and I will then take over the key'. The key was to the Directors' box, which contained important legal documents and correspondence.

[2] Synge replied that WBY's 'proposal about the fifty pounds is I think a good plan, but I doubt that it would be worth while putting the £100 into Deposit till we see how our expenses go when we are touring'. The £50 was the sum owing to the seceding members of the Society, and WBY had presumably suggested that this should be secured in an interest-earning deposit account prior to its repayment.

[1] Upset by the tone and terms of WBY's letter of 23 Dec (see p. 257), Maire Walker had informed him that she was withdrawing from the NTS. He, therefore, wrote her the 'vehement' letter he had, according to Synge, planned out on the evening of 22 Dec (see p. 257, n. 1).

## *To Vera Esposito,*[1] *29 December 1905*

Mention in letter to AG, 30 December 1905.
Offering her 15 *s.* per week if she would join the NLS as an actress, and evidently inviting her to dinner on 1 January 1906.

## *To W. G. Fay, 30 December 1905*

DE 30 05

| Handed ⎱ in at ⎰ | Euston at 3.7 p m | Received ⎱ here at ⎰ 3.26 |
|---|---|---|

To {        W Fay Abbey Theatre
Miss Walker backing out engage MacDonald immediately urgent writing
Yeats

Telegram Berg.

## *To W. G. Fay, [30 December 1905]*

Mention in letter from Fay, 31 December 1905.
Sending letters from Maire Walker, suggesting legal action against her for breach of contract,[1] and telling him that he is negotiating with Vera Esposito to take Maire Walker's place.[2]

Berg.

---

[1] Vera Esposito (b.1883), daughter of the musician and composer Michele Esposito, acted under the stage name of 'Emma Vernon'. She had joined the INTS in February 1904, and played Norah, the younger daughter, in *Riders to the Sea*, Mrs Tully in *Spreading the News*, Mary Doul in *The Well of the Saints*, and Mrs Grogan in *The Building Fund*. She was now in London, looking for an opening on the English stage, although she was subsequently to abandon her acting career. WBY had known her for some time; on 6 Feb 1908 her mother told Holloway (NLI) that he had paid the family a visit 'when Vera was a little girl playing with a catapult in the garden & Yeats took it from her & began to explain he always made them with a bigger pocket & began to fire with it & what is more had a good shot'.

[1] WBY had followed up his wire to Fay with a letter which is now lost. In his reply Fay expressed perplexity at Maire Walker's conduct, but also his opposition to legal proceedings (see below, pp. 272–3).

[2] In his reply Fay expressed reservations about Vera Esposito, warning that 'it would be as well not to close with her till we are quite sure what is to be done, for she is just as Kittle Cattle as Miss Walker and wants very careful handling'.

## *To Sarah Purser, [30 December 1905]*

18 Woburn Buildings

Dear Miss Pursur: your letter[1] has reminded me of one thing that I very much regret—in the haste of writing or rather dictation[2] (-I have made quite an interesting set of enemies since I took to dictating letters -) I forgot that I had seen the cromo I spoke of—which it seems is not German—at your studio. I think that I took the fineness of the old design on some body else's testimony—I certainly might have done so for I heard enough about it (I may however have seen it). I am very sorry about the whole thing (a hasty sentence in the midst of an argument on another matter) &, if you will send me a statement of the facts, I will make the only amends I can—write a letter to the press withdrawing my statement where yours contradicts it. The root of the matter <from the point of view of the general public> I suppose is what use if any was made of that design? (German or otherwise) & whether you were made to do less artistic work by the influence of the nuns. Of course you can contradict it yourself but if I do <it> it may probably put the matter more completely at rest—I having made the original statement. My impression is that your design shows what looks like an influence from the German glass, which we are all fighting—I did my share in America. I have often found it a hard thing writing in Ireland to remember clearly at the moment of writing where certain facts have come from—we have no critical press to set the seal of publicity on certain facts & to exclude others. This happens to be a matter which interests me deeply—I am constantly in Lebanne Chapel—where your work is with Images old saints & that 'Elizabeth'—& have long had in my head an essay or impression of the glass & of what the country people think about it—its folk lore as it were.[3] Your art criticism would probably be as limited as mine would be, or almost, if we were confined to the churches we worship in &

---

[1] Sarah Purser's letter, a reply to WBY's of *c.* 23 Dec (see pp. 259–60), is now lost, but WBY gives a résumé of its main charges in this letter, and in the following letter to AG.

[2] i.e. dictating the offending passage in *Samhain* (see p. 259, n. 2), not his letter to Miss Purser.

[3] When in 1900 Edward Martyn wanted to commission five stained-glass windows for his local parish church, St Teresa's of Labane, Co. Galway, he discovered that English and Continental factories had a monopoly in the artwork bought by the Irish Catholic Church. He therefore employed the English designers Christopher Whall and A. E. Child to train Irish assistants in the craft, and to design and execute the windows in an Irish studio. The windows, erected in 1900 and still intact, commemorate members of the Martyn family, and depict St Anne, St Robertus, Naomh Eils (St Elizabeth), Naomh Peadar (St Peter), and Naomh Andris (St Andrew). Selwyn Image may, as WBY indicates, have helped design some of the windows, but the work was executed by Child and his assistants, one of whom was Sarah Purser. The success of this work led to commissions at Loughrea Cathedral, and to the establishment of An Tùr Gloine in January 1903. WBY did not write his impressions of the windows, but was to use Labane as the setting of *The Cat and the Moon* (1926).

the works we subscribe for. M<sup>r</sup> Martyn agitated in a most effective way by refusing to subscribe, as he told me, if you did not get the window.

Yr ev<br>W B Yeats

ALS NLI.

## To Lady Gregory, [*30 December 1905*]

18 Woburn Buildings | Euston Road.<br>Saturday.

My dear Lady Gregory: your letter has just come. I wrote last night but did not send the letter—I was tired & worried & wrote in that spirit.[1] I had just got an angry letter from Moira Walker saying that nothing would ever induce her to act for us, that my letter appointing her wardrobe mistress was an insult. She had accepted the appointment before I wrote but I suppose showed the letter to somebody, & was told some nonsense or other. I thought over the thing very carefully & after writing various letters & tearing them up I wrote to say that if I did not receive a retraction of her letter we would place the matter in the hands of our lawyers, & direct them to take the usual steps to enforce the contract. I did this, which I thought to be my duty as managing director, after consulting Miss Horniman. If done at all it would lose effect if not done at once. I also wrote to Miss Esposito offering her 15/- a week, & hope to have her answer on Monday when she dines with me, & to Fay to engage Macdonald at once, even if he had to give a little too much. I hope you will not mind all this but I feal that there is nothing else for it. Once let them play fast & loose with contracts & all will be up, & yet at the same time there will be such a row over what will seem this harsh action that the sooner everybody has signed on the better. I warned Miss Horniman that this might mean added expenses but that I thought anything was better than more delay, a loss every week of so many pounds & no chance of getting to the country. I feal myself that this

---

[1] AG had written on the previous day (Berg) wondering at not having heard from him, and still assuming that Maire Walker had joined the new NTS. She asked him to tell her his 'plans and doings', and hoped that the New Year would be 'the best you have ever had', reflecting that '1905 has not been altogether a good one for you—the MacBride worry and the Theatre worry took too much of your time and thought—and as to rewriting, it may be necessary, but I hope it is all over, and that the New Year may be given to production. . . . I am ready to help you in any way I can—but I do feel you must use "a little hardness to yourself" and make some plan of work and stick to it. You can do a great poetical drama, and it has to be done, and in my mind it all depends on one thing, the getting the prose scenario right.'

uncertainty takes too much out of life. A stern action of this kind will I am certain stop the vagueness & drifting. I sent Moira Walker's letter to Fay to show to Synge. I dont want you to think I was in a temper—I acted quite deliberately. I wish I could be at Russells to see the dove cot rocking. M$^{rs}$ Walker said to me 'I should perhaps have taught my children a trade & made them independent but I preferred that they should associate with nobody if they could not associate with those above them in station'—this in that dirty room of hers.[2] Hence this futility. The duty of a wardrobe mistress is I wrote 'to see to the setting out of the clothes in the dressing rooms before performances, to see that they are not moth eaten & to get them repaired when wanted'. I took these words down from Fay. Moira must I suppose have become convinced that this is a menial task—though one that her mother would have taken joyfully. I suppose Miss Allgood will take it over now. It is a miserable business[3]—I had rather thought that Moira was playing with us on the Friday & was surprized to get her contract the day after. We are fighting Dublin futility & it is like fighting the sea.[4] One can only go on logically—we will have an efficient theatre in the end but I see it will have to be a paid theatre—enthusiasm is to[o] self-regarding a thing to count upon. To add to the general activity (- I wonder what my Stars are at -) Sarah Pursur has just seen that passage in Samhain & written to break off my acquaintance. I will send you her letters when I am done with them. I have never seen anything quite like them— her design was 'conventional & commonplace' she says but to describe it as 'ignoble' is 'dastardly' & so on. I have written to say that if there are mistatements of fact in the paragraph I will, if she wishes, write a letter to the papers setting the facts right—but I took no notice of her abuse. She really has not troubled me at all but Moira is another matter. I thought of every kind of way of dealing with the matter peacefully &

---

[2] The Walkers ran a newsagent's shop at 18 High Street, Dublin, and Mrs Mary Anne Walker, née Doherty, Maire's mother, also acted as a dressmaker, as Seaghan Barlow recalled: 'I was often in the Walkers' house at this time, and saw a good deal of the work that was done behind the scenes by Mrs. Walker, who, assisted by Mrs. Martin, made most of the costumes used at that time; they were nearly all made of hessian, as that was the cheapest and most serviceable material for costumes such as were used in *The Hour-Glass*, *The Shadowy Waters*, etc. In some cases, indeed, hessian was even used for costumes in peasant plays' (Robinson, 70). In a letter of 8 Jan (MBY) ECY told AG that she thought 'the house the Walkers live in is unhealthy but I do not think that she is badly fed, or that she drinks too much tea—she only has tea twice a day—I *do* think that she needs more care & much more rest, & a more regular life, early to bed when possible, I dont think her mother knows the importance of this—& unless she is actually ill she sits up to all hours'.

[3] Maire Walker's resignation was unhappy for everyone. Recalling AG in a letter to Holloway of 30 June 1932 (NLI), she confessed: 'I was very fond of her and I think she was very fond of me at times although she never forgot I left the Abbey Theatre and I never forgot it either for I know I made a very great mistake it upset my whole life.'

[4] WBY associates himself and AG with Cuchulain, the hero of his *On Baile's Strand* and her *Cuchulain of Muirthemne*, who is bewitched by Druids' spells into fighting the sea.

could think of none. It was obvious from the tone of her letter that she was going to leave us & that being so the only thing was to administer this shock and tonic to the whole enterprize. Even if we do not get Miss Esposito we can go ahead with Miss Allgood & Miss Dempsey for some time.[5]

Yours sny

W B Yeats

ALS Berg.

## *To Witter Bynner, 31 December 1905*

18 Woburn Buildings, | Euston Road, | London. W. C.

Dec. 31$^{st}$,/05.

*Dictated.*

Dear M$^r$ Brynner,

I have suddenly come upon your letter of I know not how many months ago, asking for a copy of "Never give all the Heart". You must have thought it very rude of me but your letter came in a great rush of work & went clean out of my head. I send it to you now & hope I am forgiven.[1]

Yours sincly

W B Yeats

Dict AEFH, signed WBY; Harvard.

---

[5] Brigit (Anna Bridget) O'Dempsey (b. 1887), the daughter of a Wexford solicitor, began to act with the NTS in early 1906. She was to marry W. G. Fay in October 1906, but her family disapproved of the match, and at one point Fay, as he told AG (Berg), had a fight with her brother Michael, who had struck him with a cane.

[1] Witter Bynner (see p. 105, n. 11), the American poet whom WBY met on his American tour (see III. 552, n. 2), was assistant editor of *McClure's Magazine* from 1902 to 1906. Quinn had sent Bynner's letter on to WBY on 17 Mar (see p. 105) but Bynner, despairing of WBY, had evidently got hold of another copy of the poem from Quinn, for *McClure's Magazine* had already published 'Never Give All the Heart' in its current December number.

## *To Eric Maclagan, 31 December 1905*

18 Woburn Buildings, | Euston Road, | W. C.
Dec. 31$^{st}$,/05.

*Dictated.*

My dear Maclagan,

I am back in London but only for a few days. Can you come in to-morrow evening (Jan 1$^{st}$) & bring Russell if he can come?[1]

Yrs sny
W B Yeats

Dict AEFH, signed WBY; Private.

## *To John Masefield, 31 December 1905*

18 Woburn Buildings | Euston Road, W. C.
Dec. 31$^{st}$/05.

*Dictated.*

Dear Masefield,

Will you be in town to-morrow? If so come & see me in the evening. We have not yet been able to settle anything about Manchester I'm sorry to say.[1] I thought we could get things definite day after day, but something always delayed us. We are trying to form a paid touring company & it is very hard to get the exact people we want.

Yrs sny
W B Yeats

Dict AEFH, signed WBY; Texas.

---

[1] i.e. Archibald George Blomefield Russell (1879–1955), a close friend of Maclagan (see p. 57) from Oxford days, and co-editor with him of works by William Blake. WBY met him often in London, and in 1903 had helped him and Maclagan with their edition of Blake's *Jerusalem* (see III. 407). In 1906 he was to publish an edition of Blake's letters, and, after a temporary appointment in 1918–19 as a secretary at the British Embassy in Madrid, became Lancaster Herald in 1922, a post which he held until his death.

[1] See p. 240, n. 3. Masefield, who had contacts in Manchester through his work on the *Manchester Guardian*, was trying to help the Abbey's tour there. On 29 Nov he had informed AG (Berg) that he was 'writing to some friends in Manchester asking them to tell me of the Manchester Arts Club, of their rooms and general influence. I am also asking whether the people would object to Lenten performances. I will get the measurements of the rooms available.' The Abbey Company first performed in Manchester on 23 and 24 Apr 1906, after Lent and in the Midland Hall.

## To Emery Walker,[1] 31 December 1905

18 Woburn Buildings | Euston Road, | W. C.
Dec. 31ˢᵗ,/05.

Dear Mʳ Walker,

I send back that document to you. I am sorry, but I really don't know anything about the question & besides I am Irish & not English. Until I got your letter I hardly knew that there was any trouble between England & Germany; & at this moment I don't know what it is about.[2]

I am sorry to refuse to sign anything you have asked me to sign, for you have been very kind to my sisters.[3] If I were to sign this, it would be taken in Ireland as a proof of Anglicisation.

Please excuse my dictating this, but I have to dictate almost everything because of my eyesight.

Yrs sny
W B Yeats

Dict AEFH, signed WBY; Bucknell.

[1] Emery Walker (1851–1933), process engraver, antiquary, and typographical expert, whom WBY had first met at William Morris's, advised the Kelmscott, Doves, and Dun Emer Presses about book production. He became master of the Art-Workers' Guild in 1904 and was knighted in 1930.

[2] Anglo-German relations were dangerously strained over the Morocco question and the revelation that Lord Lansdowne had promised British military and naval support to France in the event of a German attack. Alarmed by these developments, and by inflammatory statements in the press of both countries, Harry, Count Kessler (1868–1937), a patron of the arts, who had an Irish mother, and was often in London, wrote to William Rothenstein and Emery Walker to find out whether an equal number of Englishmen would respond if twenty distinguished German intellectuals published a letter insisting upon the solidarity of British and German civilization. The two letters, each with forty-one signatories, were published together in *The Times* on 12 Jan 1906, and in the German press. The English letter declared (15) that a 'war between the two Powers would be a world-calamity for which no victory could compensate either nation: and we emphatically declare our belief that the levity with which certain journalists discuss such a possibility is the measure of their profound ignorance of the real sentiments of the nation'.

[3] Walker had given invaluable help to SMY and ECY when they were setting up the Dun Emer, later the Cuala, Press. See III. 192, n. 4, 335, 336.

# 1906

## To W. G. Fay, [1 January 1906]

Mention in letter from Fay, 2 January 1906.
Discussing the action to be taken against Maire Walker,[1] asking how negotiations are going with McDonnell over his terms of employment,[2] enclosing a letter from Vera Esposito,[3] and remarking that both she and Maire Walker 'owe a great deal' to the Company.
Berg.

[1] Like Synge and AG, Fay was not in favour of suing Maire Walker, and replied (see pp. 282–3): 'About Miss Walker I am still of opinion the best thing to do is let the matter drop, it will be most dignified I would not even send a lawyers letter, for we cant use her if she comes now, and if we dont want her whats the use of wasting time considering her at all. Of course as you say I think both girls owe a great deal to us but if they dont recognize that themselves there is nothing further to be said. I think the best thing we can do is to set our minds down to get this new crowd into fighting trim as soon as possible & go on with our work as if nothing had happened. It is useless wasting our time over people who are not coming right on with us.'

[2] For McDonnell see p. 258, n. 3. Fay informed WBY that he had spoken 'to MacDonald last night but could not get any farther reduction in terms but told him that if he agreed to take complete charge of the wardrobe I would think him worth the money. I agreed to these terms but no contract to be made till we had quite settled up and were ready to start, but I promised I would see he got something for each show he played in until we make a start touring.' AG was particularly eager to retain the services of McDonnell (who had just had a triumph in her play *The White Cockade*), and told Frank Fay on 6 Jan (Berg) that the 'only thing I am really anxious about is the securing of McDonnell, because he is the most useful when you have trained his voice. He has a gift of natural gesture.'

[3] Vera Esposito (see p. 261) had remained in London after the Abbey visit in November to try to find work as a professional actress, and WBY was trying to entice her back to Dublin as a replacement for Maire Walker. She had evidently replied to these overtures with some hauteur, and in his reply Fay wrote that he found her attitude 'very humourous not to say comical'. In a letter of 7 Nov 1905 (Berg), AG warned WBY that she had 'found Miss Esposito, rather grumpy of late, & went to ask her mother what was the matter; and she said "She wants to be paid." Mrs. Esposito herself doesn't care if she is paid or not or if she acts or not, but "hopes she will marry a man with plenty of money".' In fact, WBY had serious reservations about her acting, and in a letter to Synge of 21 Aug 1904 (see III. 638) had commented that, while she was 'not without cleverness', he had 'no real hopes of Miss Esposito, though she certainly works very hard, and has made the company believe in her'. On 12 Jan 1905, Holloway recorded in his diary (NLI) that 'she is also lost to the Company'.

## *To S. M. and E. C. Yeats,* [*2 January 1906*]

Mention in next letter.
A 'blood curdling letter to my sisters' about Maire Walker.[1]

## *To Lady Gregory,* [*2 January 1906*]

18 Woburn Buildings

My dear Lady Gregory: Fay & Synge are against legal proceeding –
<I suppose I must be wrong & that I am [indecipherable] without knowing
it. But I hope> What I would like to do is this. Send a lawyers letter & then,
if there was no apology, bring her into court—explain that this girl has by
preventing us touring lost to us a large sum (London accounts & my
correspondence with Kilkeny would prove *bona-fides*) & then ask nominal
damages—a shilling.[1] We want to make an example of Dublin futility that
is all. If you decide with Synge & Fay that nothing is to be done I would be
greatly obliged if you would write to Miss Walker & say that I was over
ridden by my fellow directors, out of consideration for her past services or

---

[1] Maire Walker was working at Dun Emer Industries, and had many friends there, including WBY's
sisters and his father, who invited her to stay with them and sided with her during this crisis. AG wrote
to WBY on 3 Jan, 'I am glad she is with your sister, militant as that sister is, it is better than being in that
fluffy stuffy household' (Berg). Miss Walker left Dun Emer soon after this in order, according to
Holloway (NLI), 'to be able to abuse [WBY] more fully'. On 4 Jan Synge met JBY, and, as he told AG
(Saddlemyer, 91–3), 'heard the other side of the story—Miss Walker is staying with them, so that one
can now see pretty well what happened'.

AG also wrote at this time to ECY, who, in her delayed reply of 8 Jan (see p. 264 n. 2), agreed that it
was 'the very greatest pity that the company should lose Máire—Lily and I have all along counselled
Máire to keep with the company'. She also placed the blame squarely on WBY's shoulders. Maire
Walker was, she insisted, 'quite a reasonable girl, indeed very much wiser and more reasonable than
other girls of her age—but she finds just as Lily & I, (and even Papa, feels) that it is quite useless trying
to talk reason to Willie, who can never see any side of anything but his own, & who if at all opposed at
once becomes overbearing & rude—I know—we all know—this from out own experience.... I don't
think the prosecution idea knocked Máire up at all—indeed she did not seem to mind it—but the
worry that went before was very bad for her.... I do not think it was so much what Máire was asked to
agree to, as all the various offensive things said—I know Willie came out here & wasted two of my &
Máire's afternoons to no purpose—his manner was sneering and offensive—& Máire would discuss
nothing. Willie kept on telling her that she was "a beginner" & had much to learn & so on—& at the
same time spoke the whole time of Mr. Fay & Miss Allgood & the others as if they were finished actors &
actresses—then he talked in a silly way about what he called "The affair Allgood".'

[1] The NTS, with Maire Walker, had made a net profit of £135 on their recent British tour (see
pp. 239–40, n. 1). The Society had been planning a country tour in Ireland, including visits to Kilkenny
and Cork, but these had fallen through owing to the unsettled state of the Company. As early as 24 Dec
1905 AG had warned WBY that she was 'getting very anxious about the country programme... we must
not risk failure. We should look on it as quite as important an occasion as London. Once we have got the
ear of country towns we can bring anything that is handy, but if we once get the name of being scrappy &
amateurish, we shall be thrown back for a long time. It wd even be better to wait till we can get a cast
together and then put our money into it & risk it.'

what you will, but that she has treated us very badly—or write to her mother.[2] She may then show you the letter which she chooses to take as an insult.[3] She has behaved like Miss Quinn only much worse. I wrote a civil note to Miss Quinn & got an insulting answer[4] & Moira after our doing everything for her, giving her teaching, & changing all our plans that she might be paid first keeps us waiting weeks & weeks & then breaks her contract. What I dont want her to think is that I made a threat & did not mean to carry it out. I had meant if I had not heard by next Thursday from her to have instructed Whitney & Moore[5]—I had asked Miss Horniman to see us out with expenses—How would it do if you asked Miss Walker to let you see the letter she calls insulting? I enclose Fays letter from which you will see he is as puzzled as I am about the insult. You can tell if you like that I am pressing my fellow directors strongly for prosecution.

Yrs ever<br>W B Yeats

PS.
I wrote a blood curdling letter to my sisters—in hopes that it may get round.[6] Between ourselves I merely want to get it into these peoples heads

---

[2] AG did write to Maire Walker on 4 Jan (Berg) that WBY was 'about to take the legal proceedings that are usual in such a case' but that she had written to dissuade him: 'I would not sanction it, because if you have been vacillating and over-ready to take offence, I believe it is because your health has not been good and that you have been over-worked and over strung, and I feel that so much of that work was helpful to the enterprise we have at heart, besides a great personal pleasure to the writers whose work you interpreted, that you should be treated with great gentleness and consideration. I cannot believe Mr Yeats' letter was "an insult" I think you must have misread it. . . . He is impatient sometimes—all men are so, they have a different nature from ours; we are born with a capacity for the nine months child-bearing,—for the endless child-rearing. But I think you will confess you tried his patience—indeed you must have tried it very much to drive him to the intention of a lawyers letter.' She concluded: 'Whether you go on acting with us or not, I should like to see you some day in our Seven Woods, making friends with squirrels and the birds.'
[3] i.e. that of 23 Dec 1905, offering to make her mistress of the wardrobe; see p. 257.
[4] In September 1903 Maire Quinn and Dudley Digges, then the leading actors in the INTS, seceded with MG from the Society in protest at the proposed production of Synge's *In the Shadow of the Glen* and attempted to set up their own company. Miss Quinn then claimed the rights in WBY's *Cathleen ni Houlihan* as well as the ownership of a number of stage properties, and WBY had written to her about this (see III. 431–2).
[5] The Dublin firm of Whitney, Moore & Co. (later Whitney, Moore & Keller) were the Abbey Theatre's solicitors.
[6] WBY's blood-curdling letter does not survive; see p. 270. AG replied to this letter on 3 Jan (Berg), opposing legal action since 'the cry would have been that you were bullying a poor weak girl! I am not taking her part at all; I think her conduct has been extraordinarily irritating, & that the real insult lies in her having dared to take up so much of your time with her silly waverings. But I do think you made a mistake in the threat. If nothing else she can boast we felt her loss so much.' And she added that she 'took very much to heart the thought of seeming to side with Fay & Synge against you'.

that we are dangerous—that one director at any rate has an awful temper—
we are not fighting Miss Walker but the combination behind her.[7]

I am good friends with Sarah Pursur again. She has written a quite nice
letter—accepts my regrets at an error of fact (I think an unimportant one) I
am not for heavens sake to write to the press to correct it—as that will draw
more attention—& I am not to be too hard on a young industry that cannot
yet bear criticism. It has been a drawn battle, I think.[8]

Yrs sny

W B Yeats

Am doing good work on play

[*At top of first page*]

PS. A prosecution for breach of contract would ruin her chances on
professional stage.

[*With enclosures*]

Croswaithe Park | Kingstown

Sunday

Dear Mr Yeats

Your letter with enclosure to hand which I have just shown to Mr Synge.
I am rather puzzled to know what the insult referred to was, as I can
remember no letter except the Contract you sent her for Wardrobe Mis-

---

[7] WBY suspected that Maire Walker had been influenced by James Starkey, George Roberts, and
others who wished to secede from the reconstituted INTS and set up a new theatre society. Information
gathered by Joseph Holloway (NLI), suggested that the schism was caused by a mixture of *amour propre*
and proper *amour*. When he visited the Abbey Theatre on 12 Jan, Frank Fay told him that Colum had left
the Society 'because the company would not play to a sixpenny audience. He wanted to appeal to a popular
audience and much more in the same strain. Swelled head shows strongly in the mutineers' action. Roberts
was sore over his being ousted out of the role of King Concobar in *On Baile's Strand* for the English trip &
also Colum cast him for the role of Matt in *The Land* & Yeats would not have it so, Miss Garvey followed
Roberts as a matter of course as they both are in the "marrying" stage of the world's progress. Frank
Walker got the hump at being offered the paltry sum of 15/- a week, & of course his sister followed &
Starkey did the same as Miss Walker & he are in the same stage of love's young dreams as Roberts & Miss
Garvey.' The following afternoon, Holloway met Frank Walker in College Green, who suggested that
swelling hearts rather than swelled heads had caused the split: 'The affection of Miss Garvey was the
original fountain head of the whole affair. . . . Frank Fay sought for it, but George Roberts obtained it, &
consequently things did not run smoothly with the rivals & the latter's room was denied to his company by
the former, but when the latter "took his hook" Miss Garvey was found attached to it. Starkey's case with
Miss Walker was precisely the same. Mr. Walker told me they (who looked upon themselves as the Irish
National Theatre Society) did not intend joining any other company but of starting out on their "own", &
including Gaelic plays in their programmes. George Russell (AE) & P Colum are on their side.'

[8] See pp. 259–60, 262–3. Sarah Purser's letter has not been traced. In her reply AG said, 'I am glad
S. Purser is getting sense, & it is no good having enemies just now.'

tress. As tho she is evidently still on the warpath and both Mr Synge and I think legal proceedings would be just so much waste of time for if we gained the case (which I very much doubt as the contract did not come into operation till the 9th of January) she is no good for damages. If on the other hand we forced her to come she will be worse than useless to us, in fact if she withdraws that resignation, I would be in favour of giving her a fortnights notice from the 9th January as in her present mood she would be quite useless and only make mischief in the crowd.

As the new people dont know anything about her and what old people we have dont care, upsetting her would have no influence on them whatever. What terms have you offered Miss Esposito[9] for it would be as well not to close with her till we are quite sure what is to be done, for she is just as Kittle Cattle[10] as Miss Walker and wants very careful handling and my own feeling is that until such time as she makes up her wants to be an actress and nothing else it would to [*for* do] only pay her for show. There is so much to settle up. I would not be in a very violent hurry to add more salaries to the present ones. And in continuation of my letter of last night,[11] I would suggest that the Directors decide how many people they are prepared to pay. How much to each, and let them all start together. If MacDonald is to get 25/- he must do something else beside act, or it will make our scale of payment seem unreasonable.[12] Compared for instant [*for* instance] with Miss Allgood at 15/- Mac having the same line of business for 25/- would not seem right.[13] Mr Synge has read this letter and agrees with what I have put in it.

Yours faithfully
W G Fay

31 Crosthwaite Park | Kingstown
Dec. 31st/05

   [9] WBY had offered Vera Esposito 15*s.* a week (see p. 261).
   [10] People or animals that are capricious or erratic.
   [11] This untraced letter was evidently written on 30 Dec 1905, shortly after Fay had received WBY's telegram about Maire Walker's defection. It apparently went into the logistics of building up what was now virtually a new Company, and addressed the vexed question of pay differentials. It probably raised the questions to which Fay returned in a letter of 4 Jan, after the Maire Walker crisis had been resolved (see pp. 300–2), particularly the need to plan a programme to match the range of the actors available.
   [12] McDonnell had been wooed by the seceders for some time, and was to be invited by Frank Walker to join the new company (see p. 301).
   [13] The salaries of the various Abbey actors and actresses were to be a chronic cause of dispute, although a generous intervention by AEFH was to solve this particular problem, and within a few months both McDonnell and Sara Allgood were getting 30*s.* a week.

Dear Yeats[14]

I got your letter a day or two ago. I have not been able to get into the Theatre yet, as the weather has been very bad and my cold is still hanging about, though nearly gone. It has not got into my chest which is the great thing. I am to meet Ryan there on Wednesday to see how things are going on, and I will then take over the key. Your proposal about the fifty pounds is I think a good plan, but I doubt that it would be worth while putting the £100 into Deposit till we see how our expenses go when we are touring.

Fay has been out here with your letter about Miss Walker. It is annoying but I think it would be worse than useless to take proceedings. We could only proceed against her, I suppose, for damages for breach of contract, but she has left us a fortnight—from the 28th to the 9th—to fill her place, and in any case she can leave us at a month's notice so that we are not in a strong position. The only loss we could sustain would be on our January show the profits of which judged by our last show—the accounts would of course have to be produced—would be nil, and we would be hooted out of court! All the same great capital would be made out of it by the enemy so that we would be considerably more unpopular than ever. On our side meanwhile we have absolutely nothing to gain. If Miss Walker comes back for the month against her will, she will be utterly useless and demoralizing to the rest of our people, while we pay her, her wages for making mischief.

I suppose you feel more than I do that she should be made an example of, but we would be so obviously punishing ourselves more than we could punish her, that we would lose more prestige than we could gain. That at least is how I feel about it, and I am inclined to think that this is a sort of case in which the *three of us* should be of one mind *before* a definite line of action is taken up. Fay is not excited about the matter, but he has some theory that proceedings are out of the question, because she has not actually taken up her contract. That, however, does not sound very convincing. For the rest he is in the best of spirits, and is evidently pleased with the new people he has seen.

He is bargaining with McDonnell and it is better to let him make a good bargain as he can, for there is no fear of losing the man altogether. If we begin giving 25/0 weekly to those that ask it we'll have Miss Esposito asking it before long.

We must be careful not to let our next show clash with the General Election. That would mean another empty week.[15]

Yours sincerely

J. M. Synge

ALS Berg, with envelope addressed to Coole, postmark 'LONDON W JAN ?3 06'.

[14] It is evident from the following letter that WBY sent this letter to AG.
[15] A General Election had been called for 13 Jan.

## *To John Millington Synge, [2 January 1906]*

18 Woburn Builds, Euston Road.

My dear Synge: you & Lady Gregory can of course out vote me—please write to her—I have sent your letter[1] & Fays but you may as well write as she has the deciding voice.[2] I would, left to myself, give Moira to next Thursday & then instruct Whitney & Moore. We could easily prove that she has caused a long delay first by vacilation, & then by promises to sign & after delaying her signing, crying off after five more days & that this delay prevented touring—our London accounts & my letter from Kilkenny would prove *bone fide*. I would prove many pounds worth of loss but only out of consideration & youth Etc only ask nominal damages—1/- say. I would give evidence on Dublin futility—if it could be brought—& that beautiful Allgood-Walker story would add to the general happiness.[3]

Now I wont give way unless I am definitely out voted—you & Fay & Lady Gregory will have to quiet me down. I have come to under stand that this Theatre must have somebody in it who is distinctly dangerous. I am at present "seeing red"—or what ever suitable phrase occurs to you—I shall have to be very delicately managed you understand. If I dont get a distinct opinion from both directors I go on in the mood I am in.

Yr ever
W B Yeats

Masefield read a magnificent play last night. Your craft applied to English peasants.[4]

ALS TCD, with envelope addressed to 31 Crosthwaite Park, Kingstown, Dublin, postmark 'LONDON W.C. JAN 2 1906'. Saddlemyer, 88.

## *To A. E. F. Horniman, [c. 2 January 1906]*

Mention in following letter.
One or two dictated letters, telling her of the dispute with Maire Walker.

[1] i.e. Synge's letter of 31 Dec 1905, printed above.
[2] Synge did write to AG, but waited until 5 Jan (*JMSCL* 1. 148) 'as there has been nothing definite to say'.
[3] i.e. the account WBY had given AG of Maire Walker's insistence that she must be paid more than Sara Allgood as a matter of principle (see p. 255). Their jealousy was to persist and cause trouble again in the summer of 1910, when Miss Walker returned temporarily to the Abbey.
[4] i.e. *The Campden Wonder*, produced at the Court Theatre on 8 Jan 1907. See below, pp. 287–8.

## To John Millington Synge, [? 3 January 1906]

THE NATIONAL THEATRE SOCIETY, LIMITED,
| ABBEY THEATRE, DUBLIN.

My dear Synge: Lady Gregory has sent me your letter.[1] No—I am acting on nobodies opinion but my own—of course I have spoken to Miss Horniman as this might involve us in more expense—in two or three ways. I would ask damages on the ground of delay to our touring. You can only give notice when engagement *begins*—not when it is signed—& a month is the time not a fortnight (see agreement). We have lost a fortnight (say) during which we might have been getting pieces up for touring. I have never however thought of asking more than nominal damages—say a shilling. Our purpose would be to establish the binding nature of a contract & to show our people that we mean to insist on their legal obligations being carried out as carefully as we will carry out ours. The moment I got Moira's letter I had a kind of illumination—I was not angry but I was dead certain that something must be done to show people that we are not to be played with. I am writing to day to Russell telling him that I am pressing you & Lady Gregory to take legal action & why. In life one has at times to act on something which is the reverse of scient[if]ic reasoning or scholourly reasoning & this is why sedentary reasoning is dangerous. Instead of merely deducing ones actions from existing circumstances, one has to act so as to create new circumstances by which one is to be judged. It is all faith. We have to lift this enterprize int[o] a different world. I dont much mind whether Moira is prosecuted or not if we can get it into the heads of our people that we are dangerous to play with. Somebody must press determined action upon you & I propose to do so. I have dictated one or two letters in connection with the matter to Miss Horniman because I want people to understand that we have her resources behind us—that will make them feal I am in earnest. Remember "There is always a right & a wrong way & it is always the wrong way that seems most reasonable."[2]

Yrs ev
W B Yeats

PS. Do grasp the situation. If Moira is to be got off it must not be on grounds of policy but because Lady Gregory or somebody is to[o] good

---

[1] This letter is now lost; nor did WBY preserve many of Synge's letters to him, although on 5 Jan Synge told AG (*JMSCL* 1. 148–9) that 'Yeats and I have been corresponding rather vehemently all the week'.

[2] This quotation occurs in Act II of George Moore's *The Bending of the Bough*, first produced by the ILT on 20 Feb 1900. WBY had helped Moore with the play (a rewriting of Martyn's *The Tale of a Town*) and provided him with the words he quotes here.

hearted to prosecute. If you want to stop the thing do it in this way. Somebody must be a devil.

ALS TCD. Saddlemyer, 88–90.

## To Lady Gregory, 3 January 1906

18 Woburn Buildings, | Euston Road, | London.
Jan. 3$^{rd}$, / 06.

*Dictated.*
Dear Lady Gregory,

Miss Horniman asks me to say that she can give us a guarantee of £400 a year for salaries without serious personal inconvenience. She could even if it were necessary, increase this by £50.[1]

Now about Miss Walker—I wrote to my sisters saying why I thought her prosecution desirable & I am about to write to Russell saying that I am pressing it upon my fellow directors. Your "goodness of heart" etc. stands in the way. I am pretty confident that we will have both her & her brother back in the course of a few months, but we will have no peace with them, if they don't get it into their heads that we are ready to take things into Court. I need hardly say that I infinitely prefer not to have all the bother of the Police Court business, but I want them to feel that if Moira gets off this time, it is only by good luck. A trial of this sort, as she may probably know, would in all likelihood ruin her chances with Barker.[2] I wish that this could go around in some way. We must get these people afraid of us. I am really rather enjoying the game.

Yrs sny
W B Yeats

[1] This guarantee greatly eased the quibbling over salaries (see p. 273), but AG told Synge on 6 Jan (Saddlemyer, 95) that she had 'written a letter to W.B.Y. about Miss Horniman's guarantee saying that before or in accepting it he ought to say we must be left absolutely free as to actors and writers. She is developing such a virulence against members of the Gaelic League, and against Colum in particular, that she may interfere some time against them, for she has been I think inclined to interfere more of late. However I tore up the letter, and thought we had better accept the money, and chance it, but just keep a watch that we dont get into bonds.'

[2] i.e. the actor and playwright Harley Granville-Barker (see p. 23, n. 4), who had been director of the Stage Society, and was now managing the Court Theatre with John E. Vedrenne (1868–1930), making it the focus of a dramatic revival. Maire Walker never acted at the Court Theatre, and in her memoirs, *The Splendid Years* (Dublin, 1955), recalled that although 'for most of us who took the course of secession, the action meant the finish of any progress we might have been making individually towards international distinction as Irish players—in my own case it virtually meant the end of a career on the stage which might or might not have taken me away from Dublin altogether in the years that followed—I doubt if many of us had any regrets at the time. For myself, I can only say that at that period I had no desire to act, professionally or otherwise, with any theatrical project unlike the one I helped to launch in 1902.'

[*In WBY's hand*]
Have written the lyrical bit for Bailes Strand.[3]

Dict AEFH, signed WBY, Berg; with envelope addressed to Coole, postmark 'LONDON. W. JAN 4 1906'.

## To George Russell (AE), 3 January 1906

18 Woburn Buildings, | Euston Road. | London.
Jan 3rd, / 06.

*Dictated.*
My dear Russell,
 You must have heard that I am pressing my fellow directors for the prosecution of Moira Walker for breach of contract & you may as well know my reasons. If I can get over Lady Gregory's good nature, which is a difficulty, I shall ask only nominal damages, 1/- let us say. I can prove however that she prevented us from touring, kept us back for about a fortnight & that this means so much loss. I mean that this will be the case in Court. You may take it that I have not gone this far without being pretty sure of my legal ground. In reality of course the loss she has occasioned us, by her long vacillations is very much greater—it is a loss that ultimately falls upon Miss Horniman. The reason why I think it necessary to make an example, is, that we must get our people to understand that the old vague fluctuating incoherent Dublin way is over so far as we are concerned; & that the management of the new Company is not going to be trifled with. We have been disgracefully treated by the old one. Moira Walker left us after shewing absurd jealousy of Miss Allgood & because she took offence at the written statement of an offer which she had accepted in conversation. An offer by the bye, which has since been <joyfully> accepted by another member of the company.[1] I think I understand her, I am certainly not in the least angry, I know why Dublin has grown to be the cloudy place it is, I have however to deal with facts & to get the clouds out of my own house. The fundamental fact of all business is—*contract*. I have written to Lady Gregory & Synge & to Fay most urgently upon the subject. I need hardly say I don't want Moira back—for she would come in a most insubordinate

---

[3] This was part of the chant sung by a chorus of woman as Cuchulain binds himself by an oath of obedience to Conchubar (*VPl*, 495–7, ll. 393–432). WBY added to this chorus over subsequent months and it was first performed in the production of the revised play on 16 Apr, and appeared in *Poems, 1899–1905*, published later this year.

[1] i.e. McDonnell (see p. 269).

mood, but everything is impossible unless we have discipline & the Police Court may be the way there. Miss Horniman is writing this for me, but I think that you will recognise the attitude of mind as sufficiently characteristic for you not to make her responsible.

Yr ev

W B Yeats

Dict AEFH, signed WBY; Indiana.

## *To Padraic Colum, [4 January 1906]*

18 Woburn Buildings

My dear Colum: Go & see Fay & you will find that the movement is flourishing—rehersals going on actively—several new men & women, who promise well, & that we have greatly increased monetary resources.[1] We are getting ready to tour & for January show. Dont bother about Dublin gossip, which, or rather one small part of it, is probably excited just now because I in a spirit of perfect amiability have been playing at tiger to scare people into understanding that to keep one's contracts is law as well as honesty. I proposed proceeding against Miss Walker but have been over ruled by my fellow directors as I rather expected. I would have merely asked a shillings damages or some other nominal sum. The Society is now a business, run on the ordinary lines of a business & people must get this into their heads. We are artists & are therefore content with little profit or none but the obligations are the same as those in any other company. I am sorry of course to lose the Walkers—they are the only loss that matters but young Walker was so insubordinate that it was necessary & his state of mind & Starkies made Miss Walker impossible.[2] She left us because she wanted to be paid more than Miss Allgood—we could not grant this in the form she wanted it, but arranged to give her a little more on condition that she took charge of the wardrobe (we adopted the same method in 3 other cases)—she accepted this offer & signed her papers, but drew back when she saw the offer in black & white—I mean the wardrobe part of it which I had put in a seperate paper (another member of company has now accepted it). No compromise is possible—if you got them back all would be brought to a stand still by bad fealing. I have seen a good deal of societies & I am certain that when radical

---

[1] For Colum's letter of 3 Jan, which prompted this reply, see below.

[2] James Starkey (see p. 272, n. 7) was having an affair with Maire Walker, and influencing her to break with the Abbey. JBY told AG in an undated letter of this time (Berg): 'Of course Starky knows that if she goes on acting she is lost to him.'

differences arise the sooner the sectaries part the better. Our new people understand the conditions. They have joined to learn to act & to be paid for it. They will do what they are told. There will be no opposition theatre—for there is no place for our rivals to play in, no possibility of enough plays, no money to tour or pay actors—it would merely be Mary Quinn over again. We have everything in our <head> hands. The old people can join us—but it must be on our terms, which they know. I am just off to Scotland so if you have anything to say please see Synge, who is in my place in Dublin. I shall be going from town to town lecturing for some little time.

Yr sy<br>W B Yeats

Miss Esposito is quite friendly—dined with me Monday—is trying to get on London stage but if fails in this will join us at end of Feb.

A re-united society would be "five wild-cats struggling in a bag."

ALS Berg.

## To W. G. Fay, [4 January 1906]

Mention in letter from Fay, [4 January 1906].
Telegram telling him that he has decided not to proceed against Maire Walker.[1]

## To John Millington Synge, [4 January 1906]

Mention in letter to Lady Gregory, 4 January 1906.
Telegram telling him 'painted devil back in his box'.[1]

## To George Russell (AE), [4 January 1906]

18 Woburn Buildings | Eust Rd

My dear Russell: Have dropped idea of legal action as directors are against me out of consideration for Moira's good support of society in the past.

---

[1] In his reply (see below, pp. 300–2) Fay said: 'Telegram to hand. I think that is very wise for we could do nothing dignified in the matter and we could do nothing that would make her any use to us under the circumstances.'

[1] See *Macbeth* II ii: ''tis the eye of childhood | Which fears a painted devil'. On 5 Jan Synge wrote to AG (see p. 275, n. 2) that WBY had sent him 'a humourous and pleasant telegram last night which I take to mean that he has come to our view about the proceedings'.

I shall be in Dublin for our Jan Show probably some days before 25 when I lecture.[1]

Yr ev<br>W B Yeats

ALS Indiana.

## To J. B. Yeats, 4 January 1906

Mention in letter to Lady Gregory, 4 January 1906.
Telling him that he is not proceeding with the prosecution of Maire Walker.[1]

## To S. M. and E. C. Yeats, [4 January 1906]

Mention in letter to Lady Gregory, 4 January 1906.
Telling them that he is not proceeding with the prosecution of Maire Walker.

---

[1] WBY was to lecture on 'The Ideal in Art' at the Royal Hibernian Academy on 25 Jan, in a series to which AE also contributed.

[1] JBY had, like his daughters, taken Maire Walker's side in her dispute with WBY. Synge, as he informed AG on 5 Jan (see p. 275, n. 2), had met him on 4 Jan and heard that 'Miss W. told him what was in the letter, word for word, and that it was very scolding and annoying in tone. When Miss W. got it she said to herself, "the Fays have turned Mr Yeats against me too. They are all against me now. I wont have anything to do with them." ' And he added that it was 'rather serious the way people are misrepresenting all our doings in Dublin. Mr Yeats had everything by the wrong end and was quite hostile, but when I explained everything to him, he quite came over and urged me again and again to write out a plain statement of what we had done and send it round to everyone—he added "to Russell for instance." —!!!'

AG also wrote to JBY, as she told Synge on 6 Jan: 'I have written old Yeats a long letter this morning, explaining our position for he talks so much, and so many of our enemies bring their complaints to him in order that they may come round, that he might as well be kept posted. It is extraordinary the animosity there is against anyone who is doing anything' (Saddlemyer, 95). But on 9 Jan she reported (Saddlemyer, 101): 'I am a little disheartened today, because having spent a morning writing a long statement of the case to old Mr Yeats, he writes back that "the mad poet is in the hands of vulgar intriguers" (Dont repeat this to the Fays)!'

## To Lady Gregory, [4 January 1906]

18 Woburn Buildings | Euston Road.

My dear Lady Gregory: I wired to Synge to day 'painted devil back in his box' so that is over. When I found that it could not be done I merely went on long enough to make our friends understand that I had been in earnest & that henceforth we were not to be trifled with. I wrote to my sisters, my father & Russell. After a long period of wasted time & worry I thought I could change things by a sudden action. But no more of that. I send Fays last letter. Did I tell you that I got that money from Hyde—after the relations have had their share we will have about £50. I shall put it aside unless I hear to contrary for staging etc—for incidental expenses.[1] Miss Horniman says if absolutely necessary she could add another £50 to her guarrantee for saleries—making it £450. I enclose a letter which I have had from Colum—I have said that a re-united society would be 'five-wild cats struggling in a bag' & that I was off lecturing & would have no certain address for some time & that he had better see Synge. I dont think he will give trouble, but I dare say he will do something to show that he is everybody's friend. I go to Edinburgh on Sunday night. I have done good work on Bailes Strand but find it hard to get on with it—with lectures & things to get ready. I have done the lyrical bit in rhyme—quite short but sufficient.[2]

Yrs affectionly
W B Yeats

[*With enclosures*]

THE NATIONAL THEATRE SOCIETY, LIMITED,
| ABBEY THEATRE, DUBLIN.
2 January 06

Dear Mr Yeats
Your letter to hand I think that enclosure of Miss Espositos very humourous not to say comical. They are of course very young very green and think that they were so good we told them lies in order to keep them

---

[1] This was the legacy from the bequest of Dr Charles Murray, a surgeon, born in Donegal, who had emigrated to California in 1900, and who died shortly after hearing WBY lecture in San Francisco in 1904. In his will, he left money to WBY and Douglas Hyde to be spent on 'Gaelic propaganda' (see III. 609–11).
[2] i.e. the Three Women's Song; see p. 278.

with us and for fear Mr Tree or Forbes Robertson would swoop them up on us.³ I saw Signor Esposito on Sunday and he was vexed at her throwing up her chance with us, but I thi[nk] Sub Rosa the girl wants to get loose & have her fling and was too much cooped up at home. But that is none of our affair.⁴ About Miss Walker I am still of opinion the best thing to do is let the matter drop, it will be most dignified I would not even send a lawyers letter, for we cant use her if she comes now, and if we dont want her whats the use of wasting time considering her at all. Of course as you say I think both girls owe a great deal to us but if they dont recognize that themselves there is nothing further to be said. I think the best thing we can do is to set our minds down to get this new crowd into fighting trim as soon as possible & go on with our work as if nothing had happened. It is useless wasting our time over people who are not coming right on with us. I spoke to MacDonald last night but could not get any further reduction in terms but told him that if he agreed to take complete charge of the wardrobe I would think him worth the money. I agreed to these terms but no contract to be made till we had quite settled up and were ready to start, but I promised I would see he got something for each show he played in until we make a start touring.

The two new men turned up last night and I have shoved them into Riders to the Sea to walk on and cast Molly Allgood for Cathleen in that piece.⁵ Boyle play is going all right and I will finish the scene for it

---

³ Vera Esposito's 'comical' letter is now lost, and she was briefly to join the rival theatrical group. Both Fays had low opinions of the Company's histrionic skills, and after a conversation at the Abbey on 12 Jan Holloway reported in his diary (NLI): ' "Few of the Company know how bad they act!" was one of Frank Fay's great thoughts.' Tree and Forbes-Robertson were two of the leading actor-managers on the London stage. Herbert Draper Beerbohm Tree (1853–1917), a half-brother of the novelist, essayist, and drama critic Max Beerbohm, made his professional debut in 1878; his company was based in Her Majesty's Theatre in the Haymarket, which he opened in 1897, and where he mounted spectacular productions of Shakespeare's plays, which WBY detested. He was knighted in 1909. Johnston Forbes-Robertson (1853–1937), who was knighted in 1913, acted with Sir Henry Irving and Mrs Patrick Campbell, and was famous for his romantic performances in Shakespeare. Both he and Tree made regular tours to Dublin.

⁴ Michele Esposito (1855–1929), an Italian pianist, composer, and music teacher, had been Professor of the Pianoforte at the Royal Irish Academy of Music since 1882, and conductor of the Dublin Orchestral Society since its founding in 1899. He had composed the music for Hyde's *An Tincéar agus an tSidheóg*, performed in George Moore's garden in May 1902, and his one-act operetta *The Postbag*, written in collaboration with A. P. Graves, had been played at the Gaiety Theatre, Dublin, and by the Irish Literary Society, London, in 1902. Her parents were perhaps over-regulating Vera Esposito's social life because they wanted her to 'marry a man with plenty of money' (see p. 269, n. 3).

⁵ A Mr Anderton, from the north of Ireland, and Joseph H. Dunne. Anderton did not remain with the Company beyond these performances, and Dunne, who took minor parts in the Society's productions in 1905 and early 1906, did not become a permanent member, but continued to help out intermittently with walk-on parts before emigrating to Buenos Aires in May 1910. In October 1905 he had made a spirited defence of the Abbey against T. O'Neill's charges that it was anti-national (*Weekly Freeman*, 28 Oct 1905, p. 9), but on 4 Apr 1907 he complained to Holloway (NLI) that he 'was not wanted since they began to pay the members of the co. He was welcome when there was hard work & nothing to get!' *Riders to the Sea* was next revived on 20 Jan.

tomorrow. I am afraid we will have tough work getting our repetoire right again for there is no piece left complete not even the "Pot of Broth", wc is rather distressing, but I will make all the haste I can.

When will you be back to us for we want to see what way we will get up the touring pieces and keep the monthly shows going at the same time.

I am

faithfully yours
Will Fay

Shall I send Miss Esposito letter to Lady Gregory[6]

30 Chelmsford Rd | Ranelagh
3 Jan 1905

My dear Mr. Yeats,

As you are aware I voted for the establishment of a limited liability Co in order to save the Society from a disastrous split. I come back to Dublin and I find the Society hopelessly shattered. The one thing to be done is to re-unite the Society. Until this is done the dramatic movement is hung up. I appeal to you—I earnestly appeal to you to take steps to re-unite the group.[7]

Please write to me at once and let me know what steps you are about to take.

Yours sincerely
Padraic Colum

ALS Berg, with envelope addressed to Coole, postmark 'LONDON W. JA 4 05'.

## To Padraic Colum, [4 January 1906]

18 Woburn Buildings

My dear Colum: I forgot to say when writing this afternoon that I want you to see Synge about quite another matter. Lady Gregory, Synge, Boyle & myself have all signed a paper granting the Irish rights of our plays to the National Theatre Company. Synge will show you the form—& you can talk over other matters at the same time. We have signed for 5 years the term of

[6] There is no evidence that Fay sent Vera Esposito's letter on to AG.

[7] Colum had stayed on in London after the November tour but had returned to Dublin in late December. On 1 Jan he wrote to Starkey (TCD) that he would 'never go over to Yeats' party as it is at present. I want to make our party so strong as to force Yeats back. This is the only policy I shall commit myself to. If the production of "The Land" would strengthen our society I shall be willing to produce it. But I shall keep out of personal quarrels.' In her reply to WBY, AG commented that Colum's letter was 'amusing': 'he stayed away until he thought everyone satisfied, and came back to find nobody was!'

the patent. If you write to Synge who has the key of the Directors box he will show you the form—it is necesary chiefly in case of our deaths.[1]

Yr ev

W B Yeats

ALS Berg.

## To John Millington Synge, [4 January 1906]

18 Woburn Buildings

My dear Synge: to day I got a letter from Colum asking what steps I was going to take to re-unite company. I replied that a re-united company would be 'five-wild cats struggling in a bag' & that all was going well & I referred him to you. I have just had this wire from fay 'Write Colum secure Irish rights of his peices writing Fay'. I have again written to Colum asking him to see you. I strongly advise you to concede nothing—a rival theatre would only show the power of ours. Colum will be chaos without us & his actors chaos without Fay.[1] We have now £400 a year to spend on salaries & a fine theatre—all we have to do is to hold firm.

Yr ev

W B Yeats

ALS TCD. Saddlemyer, 90–1.

## To Maire Walker, [4 January 1906]

Dear Miss Walker: I am very sorry that you are ill—It is probably a much harder thing than any of you know carrying on the work of a theatre & one's own work as well & perhaps in the fight one sometimes forgets that those one strikes at suffer. If I have added trouble to your illness beleive me I am very sorry. I for my part was a little hurt that you should think I could offer a 'deliberate insult' to you or any body. Before I got your letter to-night

[1] This was the 'will' which WBY, Synge, AG, and Boyle had already signed (see p. 259), but Colum refused to waive his rights. On 13 Jan 1906 Holloway reported (NLI) that Colum had been asked 'to sign an agreement "only to write for them for the next five years", which he refused, adding that he did not belong to them at all'. In fact, almost immediately on receipt of this letter Colum applied to copyright *The Land* at Stationers' Hall, naming himself as 'the Proprietor of the Sole Liberty of Representation or Performance'. He was granted copyright on 8 Jan 1905.

[1] This was true: Colum's play was badly acted and he was discontented with its translation into Irish, which he confided to Holloway on 13 Sept (NLI) made it 'too heavy and & without humour'. He was careful to keep up his association with the Abbey, and allowed *The Land* to be performed there in 1907.

I had already written to Lady Gregory & Synge to withdraw my proposal.[1] I need not trouble you now that you are ill with the reasons that made me think of it, but I want you to beleive that though I was very angry with a certain member of the company who plays Moira Walker's parts I was not angry with Moira Walker herself, or not very angry.

[unsigned]

PS. The damages I had meant to ask for were—one shilling.

A copy Berg.

## *To Lady Gregory, [4 January 1906]*

18 Woburn Buildings | Euston Road<br>Thursday

My dear Lady Gregory: I enclose a letter which I have just received from Moira & my answer, which is probably foolish but I begin to think first thoughts are best.[1] Now that it is all over I dont mind saying that I have no doubt I was wrong (I shall not say this to Synge or Fay).[2] I was very tired out—this theatre row has been a good deal of a strain. When I got her letter I was very angry that she should think I could 'deliberately insult her'. I wrote a letter to you leaving the matter in your hands & Synges as I felt that I could not stand the strain any longer—I felt too that I had perhaps done wrong in letting Miss Horniman spend so much money on these inconsequent people then the idea formed of giving them a fright. I put the idea away but it came again next day—just before post time. Moiras letter has really made me sorry.

I dont think Miss Horniman is particularly down on the Walkers—she praises young Walkers acting a good deal but she certainly is on Colum. Something he said to her.[3] I have, by the by, just had the enclosed from

---

[1] See pp. 280–2.

[1] See previous letter.

[2] Synge did not need to be told that WBY was in the wrong. On 5 Jan he had remarked to AG (*JMSCL* I. 150): 'One moral from the story is that W.B.Y. must not be the person to deal *directly* with the actors, as he is rather too impetuous.'

[3] In her letter of 3 Jan (see p. 270, n. 1) AG alleged that AEFH had 'been dying to get rid of the Walkers & is now firing her animosities on Colum'. AEFH had been incensed by Colum's request that he and the new company should be allowed to use the Abbey and, as she informed Synge on 9 Jan (TCD), had written to tell him 'that he could not have the theatre'. On 6 Jan she warned AG (Berg): 'Colum writes that he wants things to be patched up; he does not see as Fay does that the whole split was dishonest. I feel as if he would give us future trouble.' She took to referring contemptuously to the

Fay.[4] I have written to Synge & Colum about the matter but imagine from Colums letter early in the day that there is something up. I have of course urged Synge to be quite firm. We cannot concede anything. We have now £400 or 450 to pay actors & are masters of the situation.

I will talk things over with M[rs] Emery but she has some plays coming on in March & besides Fay seems quite confident. However one may as well know her terms.[5]

Yr affecly\
W B Yeats

[*With enclosure*]

56 High Street | Dublin\
January 3rd 1906

Dear M[r] Yeats

I shall not withdraw my letter of the 28th & if you wish to 'place the matter in the hands of your Lawyers' you can do so.

I would remind you, however, that I am, as you know without means.

Let me add that my going on with your company, would not have been of the least use to you as I had fully determined to hand in, with my contract, a months notice of resignation. I am at present too ill to take part in any work of the kind. I do not intend to act at all for some time to come.[6]

I have written Lady Gregory to the same effect.

Sincerely Yours\
Maire nic Shiubhlaigh

ALS Berg, with envelope addressed to Coole, postmark 'LONDON W. JA 5 06'.

seceders as 'the Columbines', and in May 1907 assured A. H. Bullen (NLI) that as 'the leader of the black-mailers' Colum was 'a good riddance', and that his talent was the sort 'that is over & gone by the age of 27'.

 [4] Evidently the telegram cited in WBY's letter to Synge; see p. 285.

 [5] In her letter of 3 Jan AG told him that she had suggested to Fay that the Company should try 'to get Mrs. Emery to help us for a bit. He wouldn't like to put Miss Allgood's nose out of joint, but I think it might get us through, & it wd have a good effect on Miss Horniman.' Although FF was prepared to come, if needed, she was engaged to play Mrs Stockmann in a revival of Ibsen's *An Enemy of the People* at His Majesty's Theatre, London, on 18, 19, and 20 Jan. Subsequently, she was occupied rehearsing for the part of the Nurse in a production of *Hippolytus* at the Court Theatre in late March, and for Phaedra in the Literary Theatre Club's performance of Sturge Moore's *Aphrodite against Artemis* on 1 Apr. Although W. G. Fay was worried by the defection of so many key players, he had advised WBY on 2 Jan (see p. 283) that the best thing was to get the new people 'into fighting trim' as soon as possible.

 [6] In fact, Maire Walker played an active part in the organization of the Theatre of Ireland later this year, and played a major role in its production of Cousins's *The Racing Lug* on 7 and 8 Dec.

## To Holbrook Jackson, 4 January 1906

18, Woburn Buildings, | Euston Road,<br>Jan. 4<sup>th</sup>, / 06.

*Dictated.*

Dear M<sup>r</sup> Holbrook Jackson,

How would it do if I went to Leeds some little time before the Company. I could lecture there in the third week of February, on "Literature and the Living Voice", that would cover all I want to say. There is just a possibility of the touring of the Company being a little delayed.[1] We have lost one of our actresses & we have to train somebody to take her place.

Yrs sny<br>W B Yeats

Dict AEFH, signed WBY; Colgate.

## To John Masefield, 4 January 1906

18 Woburn Buildings, | Euston Road,<br>Jan 4<sup>th</sup>, / 06.

*Dictated.*

My dear Masefield,

I have been thinking over that wonderful play of yours & the more I think of it, the more certain do I feel that the letter business is a mistake. It spoils the simplicity of the last act & distracts attention from the characters. Why should not the missing man's wife come in the moment the chaplain has gone out with John Perry. She is looking for the chaplain, she heard he was there, perhaps he is in the inner room, she must find somebody, where is Tom Constable? She had found her missing man sitting by the fire, come home as if nothing had happened. Chaplain comes in, she patters on about her husband, been away boozing all the time, hadn't asked him where he had been, hadn't time, been with Mrs Ebsworth for certain, now Richard Perry can go home to his children etc, learns that she is too late. It would be necessary to keep this scene from being in any way a repetition of close of Act III; it is an opportunity for a fine scene. It's ghastly humour would take away the feeling of depression while deepening the tragedy.

---

[1] This is what happened: WBY lectured at Leeds with FF on 14 Mar, and the NTS performed there on 27–8 Apr.

I told this idea to M$^{rs}$ Emery, she thought it better than the letter business.[1]

Yrs ever

W B Yeats

Dict AEFH, signed WBY; Texas. With sketches of ships' masts, probably by Masefield.

## To Henry G. O'Brien, 4 January 1906

18 Woburn Buildings, | Euston Road.

Jan. 4$^{th}$, / 06.

*Dictated.*

Dear M$^r$ O'Brien,

By an extraordinary chance your letter of some months ago has only just reached me.[1] It was amongst a number stolen while going through the post by a dishonest post-office clerk in Galway. He is now on his trial & it has been sent <back> to me by the Post Office.[2]

I am very sorry that I have only just got it, as I am leaving London again in a few days. I will ask you to come & see me when I get back.

Yrs snly

W B Yeats

Dict AEFH, signed WBY; Pierpont Morgan.

[1] In *The Campden Wonder*, set in rural Gloucestershire, and based on an incident which had occurred in Chipping Campden in the seventeenth century, a ne're-do-well farm labourer, John Perry, confesses to the murder of his employer William Harrison, and implicates his mother and envied and exemplary younger brother Dick in the crime. Despite the absence of a body, and the known proclivity of the supposed victim for prolonged drinking sprees and a certain Mrs Ebsworth, Perry convinces a gullible parson, the law officer, Tom Constable, and later a judge and jury, of his family's collective guilt, and in a final scene they are all hanged. Immediately after the hangings, the 'victim's' wife arrives at the jail to say that her husband has reappeared. In the original version a letter revealed that Harrison was still alive, but Masefield evidently took WBY's advice, and rewrote the last scene.

[1] O'Brien, who was now training for the priesthood at St Mary of the Angel, Bayswater, London, had evidently once again written to try to arrange a meeting with WBY; see pp. 40–1, 129.

[2] Seventeen-year-old Terence Vincent Brady, who was employed by the Galway post office as a 'paid learner', had been arrested on 15 Nov 1905 and found to be in possession of gold rings, a watch, postal orders, cheques, American bank drafts, seventy-eight postal letters, and a set of false teeth. After preliminary hearings at the Petty Sessions, he was brought before the Galway Quarter Sessions on 22 Jan 1906. The *Connaught Champion* reported on 27 Jan (9) that the boy had pleaded guilty and co-operated with the authorities from the time of his arrest. Testimony revealed that he was earning only 6s. a week after two years' service, that his father had recently died, and that he and his mother were destitute. The judge deplored the meagre wages paid by the Post Office, which had helped to open the door to temptation, and remarked that this was 'as sad a case as he had had before him for a long time'. In light of the extenuating circumstances, he sentenced Brady to six months' imprisonment, rather than twelve.

## *To George Russell (AE), [6 January 1906]*

18 Woburn Building | Euston Road

My dear Russell: many thanks for your letter, which I understand as it was meant.[1] My sister will tell you whether I got Miss Walkers consent by 'threatening' or the like as she & she only was present. I was indignant when I found Miss Walker wavering after having wasted a week of my time but not till then. As for the more general questions. I desire the love of very few people, my equals or my superiors. The love of the rest would be a bond & an intrusion. Those others will in time come to know that I am a fairly strong & capable man & that I have gathered the strong & capable about me, & all who love work better than idle talk will support me. It is a long fight but that is the sport of it. The antagonism, which is sometimes between you & me comes from the fact that though you are strong & capable yourself you gather the weak & not very capable about you, & that I feal they are a danger to all good work. It is I think because you desire love. Besides you have the religious genius to which all souls are equal.[2] In all work except that of salvation that spirit is a hindrance. I know quite well—I knew when Synge wrote his first play—I will never have the support of the clubs, but I will beat the clubs. I am trying for the general public—the only question with me (& it is one I have argued with Synge & Lady Gregory) is whether I should attack the clubs openly.[3] Our small public at the theatre is I am glad to say almost entirely general public. I have no objection to a rival theatre by the by nor can the old society give me any serious annoyance—if

[1] In a long undated letter, written in reply to WBY's letter of 3 Jan (see pp. 278–9), AE had reviewed WBY's position in the Irish Literary and Theatre movements, and warned him that his dictatorial behaviour was losing him support among the younger Irish writers (see below, pp. 292–8). He went on to accuse WBY of bullying Maire Walker, and urged him to seek the affection of the Irish people.

[2] WBY placed AE in Phase Twenty-Five of *A Vision* (see *AVB*, 172–6), one of those born to 'the arrogance of belief.... He must eliminate all that is personal from belief; eliminate the necessity for intellect by the contagion of some common agreement.... He has but one overwhelming passion, to make all men good, and this good is something at once concrete and impersonal.' In a letter to Dorothy Wellesley, written on 26 July 1935 just after AE's funeral, WBY told her that AE's 'ghost will not walk. He had no passionate human relationships to draw him back. My wife said the other night "AE was the nearest to a saint you or I will ever meet. You are a better poet but no saint. I suppose one has to choose".... I constantly quarrelled with him but he never bore malice & in his last letter, a month before his death, he said that generally when he differed from me it was that he feared to be absorbed by my personality' (Wade, 838).

[3] In his letter AE had pointed out 'the very insecure hold' WBY had on the old Society, and warned that if he irritated the members they would vote him out of office, and he would lose most of his actors to the political clubs, which would denounce him for his lack of national spirit.

it observes its obligations to Miss Horniman which it will do I have no doubt.

Yr ev

W B Yeats

ALS Indiana, with envelope addressed to 25 Coulson Avenue, Rathgar, Dublin, postmark 'LONDON. W.C. JAN 6 [o]6'. Partly in Wade, 466.

## *To Lady Gregory,* [*6 January 1906*]

18 Woburn Buildings

My dear Lady Gregory: I enclose a characteristic letter from Russell—a curious struggle between his desire to be fair & generous & his desire to say all the disagreeable things he knows. His notion that I got Miss Walker to consent by 'threats' is evidently the official account. I was not even very urgent. But after she consented she began to waver, as I thought, this on Friday night when she came to the theatre with Starkie & I said 'You will ruin your career.' I dare say Russell is right in a good deal. I wish I could keep from calling people 'poultry' but I cant.[1] I have written to him to say that 'I want the love of a few equals & superiors' but that the love of the others could only be 'a bond & an intrusion', but that I hope in time that they will understand that I am fairly 'strong & capable' & value my work. I suppose it is because Russell thirsts for love, like a single woman, that he fills his window with canary birds.

I thank you very deeply for writing that letter to Moira, a wise beautiful letter.[2] When I meet you I can explain my own action better than by letter. It has had one good effect—Miss Horniman has given us £200 a year more. We can go on now whether we have audiences or not which we could not on the smaller sum. M$^{rs}$ Emery could come if we wanted her but I doubt if we will, Fay is delighted with his new people. He writes that our enemies are boasting of having drawn Colum away, for a new company. I doubt it but

---

[1] AE deplored WBY's dismissal of Dublin writers as ' "singing canaries" and "poultry gardeners" ', and complained that there was 'probably not one of the younger people of whom you have not said some stinging and contemptuous remark' (see below). WBY responded defiantly to this in his poem 'To a Poet, who would have me Praise certain Bad Poets, Imitators of His and Mine' (*VP*, 262).

[2] See p. 271, n. 2.

Synge will see him. It might be no harm for a bit. He would learn much in the Molesworth Hall— about himself & others.[3]

Yours sny
W B Yeats

My address after Sunday will be '28 Viewforth, Edinburgh'.
PS. In the morning—I think I was right about Moira—right I mean to make the threat—in the evening I agree with you. You wont understand what I mean until I can talk it all over with you. It is often very hard to know why one did a thing—I find so at least. I sometimes find that one acts because one sees clearly a number of detached pieces, which one never sees again. Looking back afterwards one either doubts or affirms the act, but not from reason in either case. Miss Hornimans mood certainly came into my calculation. One thing I am quite clear about—I am very sorry for poor Moira.

[*On back of envelope*]
Just received wire "Enemy rehearsing Land; author present, letter to-night Fay" So much the better in the end. WBY

[*With enclosure*]
25 Coulson Avenue | Rathgar

My dear Yeats
I heard you wrote to Miss Walker but have not seen her or spoken to her about the matter. The only time I spoke to her on these points since the new company was formed was a little afterwards when she came up to me to ask my advice. I advised her to join you then & never advised her in any contrary way since. I told Roberts, who mentioned about Miss Walkers refusal to go on with the arrangement made, that she would have no ground unless you on your side had broken through some understanding and if not she must go on whether she liked it or not. I did not imagine that you were in earnest anyhow, and of course you may be acting in the best way, but I am inclined to think it is unwise considering the very insecure hold you have on the old society. If you irritate the members they will certainly elect a new President & Vice Presidents at their next meeting and you Lady Gregory & myself who are not members except ex officio from our position

---

[3] Colum's *The Land* was produced by the Theatre of Ireland, which did not come formally into being until May of this year, on 9 Aug 1906, and then in an Irish translation. Cumann na nGaedheal had performed at the Molesworth Hall, and WBY assumed that the new Society would do so too; its first season was in fact staged there, but subsequent productions took place at the Rotunda and, later, the Abbey Theatre.

will drop out & have no grounds for interference.[4] Synge was elected a member & will remain, but if they adopt this course, with whatever new President or Vice Presidents they may elect, the voting power will give the old society completely into their hands. In all "resolutions" a three quarters majority is necessary, but an election will go by majority of votes. I myself thought I was elected a member of the old society but I found I only can act ex officio and if I was not renominated as a Vice President I would be out, so would you & Lady Gregory. The books contain the list of members formally admitted. I believe the rules have been submitted for a legal opinion on this point. Of course if you are prepared to let the old society go you can act regardless of any irritation you may arouse. I think if you do you will lose Dublin completely. You have managed to upset the nerves of all the younger people who write in the U.I. the Nationist and other papers. You will get no defenders in the press here, however matters may stand in London where of course your reputation will carry a weight which it would not in Ireland. What I think is wrong about your way of getting a movement to work is that all movements need volunteers and you cannot afford to pay everyone, and when you talk in Dublin about "singing canaries" and "poultry gardeners" it all comes back to the people for whom it was intended, and with very vivid exaggerations. There is probably not one of the younger people of whom you have not said some stinging and contemptuous remark. They may have been justified. But if you wish to lead a movement you can only do so by silence on points which irritate you or by kindly suggestions to the people.[5] A man without followers can do nothing and you have few or no friends in Dublin. Their irritation leads them to tear to pieces everything you write until they persuade themselves that it has no merit at all. Of course if an angry man read Homer he would see nothing in it and would describe it as a series of brutal rows. You are committing the

---

[4] Since AE had drawn up the original rules for the INTS in 1903, he is, unsurprisingly, correct on these points. Rule 3 (c) stated that 'The President, Vice-Presidents, and Secretary shall *ex officio* be members of the Society', and rule 4 (3) stipulated that the president, vice-presidents, Committee of Management, Reading Committee, auditor, and treasurer should be elected at the Annual General Meeting of the Society, 'held during the months of April or May in each year'. Since WBY, AE, and AG were not founding members of the Society their membership depended upon the offices they held.

[5] In an unpublished draft of his autobiographical fragment 'The Sunset of Fantasy' (Texas), written in 1934, AE recalled this estrangement from WBY: 'I think I was one of his most intimate friends in youth. Later we were both friends and enemies for we saw different eternities and our intimacy ceased thirty years ago, that is I never spoke to him about anything but what lay on the surfaces. He had the least spiritual manner of anyone I ever met, and would interrupt with some scornful or blighting remark for he did not know by what gentleness by what affection and how delicately the soul [feels] its way into mysteries.... And as nature has given to many lovely flowers their thorns so it gave him an arrogant manner which killed real intimacy except by those few whose imaginations mixed harmoniously with his own like Lady Gregory.... I had some work of my own to do and [parted] from him except as an acquaintance halfway through my life. It is best for us to balance our diversities and remain at peace. We cannot come to any deep life with a companion who gets angry & scornful when we differ from him.'

great mistake of so many people about Ireland "the twenty years of resolute government" theory.[6] Irish people will only be led by their affections. Wake their affection and they will move heaven & earth to help you. Look at Hydes power compared with your own and you have twenty times his ability.[7] Fall out of the circle of their affections and they will turn on you like Healy on Parnell.[8] You may lose all your present actors who are not paid, as they will probably meet continually the young men in the clubs[9] who will say you are confessedly not a Nationalist, and if a new company was formed it would get all the old group of actors except the two Fays, Miss Allgood and Wright. I am giving you the situation as it appears to me. Remember there is Martyn, Moore, Colm who is young and who may be swept from you by the tide of popular resentment & the Gaelic League which has no affection for you, and an amalgamation of all the dissentients with a Gaelic dramatic society associated with it would leave you Synge,

[6] Lord Salisbury's Conservative and Unionist administration, elected after the defeat of Gladstone's first Irish Home Rule Bill in 1886, was dedicated to the idea that what Ireland needed was not independence but 'twenty years of resolute government'. This was put into effect through the Chief Secretary, Arthur Balfour, who brought in a new Crimes Act in 1887 and made extensive use of coercion acts. The policy backfired; not only did Parnell's popularity in Ireland soar, but English liberal sympathy for the Irish maltreatment led to the 'Union of Hearts' and the election of Gladstone's Home Rule government in 1892.

[7] Douglas Hyde had achieved immense popularity through his presidency of the Gaelic League, as had been spectacularly demonstrated on 6 Nov 1905, when a vast procession had escorted him to Kingsbridge Station on the first stage of his tour of America (see p. 212). A poll of 15,000 readers in the *Irish Independent* on 1 Nov 1905 had returned him (3) as the fourth most popular man in Ireland (after John Redmond, Cardinal Logue, and Archbishop Walsh). But AE's argument cut no ice with WBY, who believed that Hyde had bought popularity at the cost of his creative work: 'He was to create a great popular movement, far more important in its practical results than any movement I could have made, no matter what my luck, but... I mourn for the "greatest folklorist who ever lived", and for the great poet who died in his youth.' WBY argued that under the influence of doctrinaire nationalists Hyde sacrificed his style to 'common English... and took for his model the newspaper upon his breakfast-table, and became for no base reason beloved by multitudes who should never have heard his name till their schoolmasters showed it upon his tomb. That very incapacity for criticism made him the cajoler of crowds, and of individual men and women... and for certain years young Irish women were to display his pseudonym, "Craoibhin Aoibhin", in gilt letters upon their hat-bands' (*Aut*, 218–19). In his poem 'At the Abbey Theatre' (*VP*, 264–5) WBY calls on Hyde as 'most popular of men' to advise him how to please the protean Abbey Theatre audience.

[8] Timothy Michael Healy (1855–1931), a powerful but maverick politician, had been a loyal follower of the Irish leader Charles Stewart Parnell (1846–91; 1. 503–6), dubbing him 'the uncrowned king of Ireland' in March 1880, but became his bitterest opponent after his involvement in the O'Shea divorce case (see 1. 237, 242, 503–6). It was Healy who brought matters to a head during the tense debate over Parnell's leadership in Committee Room 15 in December 1890. When John Redmond suggested that the anti-Parnellites were making Gladstone the 'master of the party', Healy retorted: 'Who is to be the mistress of the party?', and in the uproar that followed Parnell denounced him as 'that cowardly little scoundrel there, who dares in an assembly of Irishmen to insult a woman'. Healy continued to attack Parnell in pamphlets such as *Under Which Flag? or Is Parnell to be Leader of the Irish People* (Dublin, 1890), and in the *Nation* and the daily *National Press*. In a letter to *United Ireland* of 30 Dec 1893 WBY denounced Healy's 'underbred and untruthful articles and speeches' (see 1. 373). Healy was now MP for North Louth, and eventually became the first Governor-General of the Irish Free State, 1922–8.

[9] i.e. small, radically nationalist political societies such as the Celtic Society, the Young Ireland Societies, and the Dungannon Clubs.

Lady Gregory, & Boyle with yourself and none of these have drawing power in Dublin. The others will get tremendous houses as the National Players did crammed to overflowing.[10] Griffiths, Ryan of the Nationist, Moran of the Leader would all welcome another society.[11] You who initiated the theatre movement in Ireland will be out of it. You irritated the Cork people, the Belfast people would work with a new nationalist society & get them good houses there. You will be as out of everything in Ireland as Dowden & with as little influence.[12] Your last Samhain did you endless harm it was so badly written and more patronising in its references to other writers than the quality of thought or writing displayed by yourself allowed.[13] I imagine you get few people to tell you the truth because you are too ready to fly in a rage, they have not your vehement power of language and while they remain quiet, they go away to work against you. There have been greater artists in literature than yourself but it is not always recorded that their position impelled them to speak contemptuously of everyone not

[10] The National Players' Society had performed at the Molesworth Hall during the Samhain festival from 30 Oct to 4 Nov 1905 (see p. 223, n. 7), and at the same venue on 26 and 27 Dec 1905 presenting plays by Seumas MacManus, Fr. Peter O'Leary, and Lady Gilbert.

[11] All three journalists were hostile to the Abbey for different reasons. Griffith, editor of the *United Irishman*, attacked its supposed lack of nationalist commitment (see p. 25), while Fred Ryan (se p. 153, n. 2), a regular contributor to the *Nationist* and former secretary of the INTS, thought its plays too mystical and unrealistic. David Patrick Moran (1869–1936) was born in Waterford, and worked from 1888 to 1898 as a journalist in London, where he was active in the ILS and the Gaelic League. In these years he developed his own form of the 'Irish-Ireland' philosophy—that Ireland should be Irish-speaking, Gaelic, and Catholic, and that the country's greatest need was self-criticism and the development of individualism. He had formulated these ideas in the *New Ireland Review* during his editorship, 1898–1900, and disseminated them more widely by moving to Dublin and setting up the *Leader*. Moran's belief in the necessity of criticism soon led him to attack all nationalist movements other than the Gaelic League, and he constantly used his paper to disparage and sneer at WBY's cultural aims and intentions.

[12] This was a calculated barb since Edward Dowden epitomized for WBY all that he disliked in unionist and cosmopolitan Victorian criticism. Dowden (1843–1913; see I. 482–3), Professor of English Literature at Trinity College, Dublin, established his reputation with *Shakspere: A Critical Study of his Mind & Art* (1875) and consolidated it with further Shakespearian studies and his biography of Shelley. WBY had challenged his attitudes in a number of public controversies (see I. 430–1, 448–50). In December 1915 WBY told JBY (Wade, 602–3) that Dowden was the 'image' of 'certain Victorian ideals' against which JBY and WBY had been in revolt.

[13] The November 1905 number of *Samhain* had been a defence of personal vision and individual extravagance in the arts, as opposed to realism and politically or ideologically committed literature. In the course of arguing this case, WBY had criticized Gaelic League plays (see p. 220, n. 12), and the writings of Wilde, Shaw, and George Moore. He had also expressed reservations about the plays of William Boyle and Padraic Colum in comparison with those of Synge and AG: 'the speech of their people shows the influence of the newspaper and the National Schools. The people they write of, too, are not the real folk.' He suggested that Synge's 'sarcasm' was more original than Boyle's satire, which he characterized as the satire 'such as all men accept; it brings no new thing to judgement. We have never doubted that what he assails is evil, and we are never afraid that it is ourselves.' He also dismissed Colum's social purpose as immature: 'He is still interested in the reform of society, but that will pass.' Another aspect of the magazine that evidently irritated WBY's critics was the uncompromising tone in which it laid down the aesthetic policy of the Abbey: 'So long as I have any control over the National Theatre Society it will be carried on in this spirit, call it art for art's sake if you will; and no plays will be

their equal. The fact is the position you wish to hold of general autocrat in literary, dramatic and artistic matters in Dublin or Ireland is a position accorded through love and cannot be assumed and without a press to back you up or a band of energetic propagandists to carry your opinions about, you may be as right as God Almighty is in his secrecy but with as little influence in the lives of men. You may say you dont want a popular influence. You only want the educated intellectual opinion on your side. But you know Dublin and are Magee,[14] Moore, Colm, and the small crowd of young people like Starkey, Kettle, Joy with you. I dont think they are. There is society but there are strong social influences against you and I doubt whether anything but a recantation of your Queen's letter would help you much with them.[15] You must not take this letter as written in a spirit of

produced at it which were written, not for the sake of a good story or fine verses or some revelation of character, but to please those friends of ours who are ever urging us to attack the priests or the English, or wanting us to put our imagination into handcuffs that we may be sure of never seeming to do one or the other.' This issue of *Samhain* is repetitious and lacks WBY's customary elegance, largely because he had dictated it in a hurry. He himself was painfully aware of its shortcomings, as he openly confessed in a concluding paragraph: 'I have had very little to say this year in Samhain, and I have said it badly.... this time I am letting the first draft remain with all its carelessness of phrase and rhythm. I am busy with a practical project which needs the saying of many things from time to time, and it is better to say them carelessly and harshly than to take time from my poetry. One casts something away every year, and I shall, I think, have to cast away the hope of ever having a prose style that amounts to anything.'

[14] The Dublin-born William Kirkpatrick Magee (1868–1961) wrote under the pseudonym 'John Eglinton'. After a distinguished career at Trinity College, Dublin, he became an assistant at the National Library, and drew many of his ideas in literature and ethics from Emerson, Thoreau, and Wordsworth. He had known WBY since their days at the High School, and became firmer friends with him and AE in the early 1890s. WBY had published mainly sympathetic reviews of his collections of essays, *Two Essays on the Remnant* (*UP* 1. 356–8) and *Pebbles from a Brook* (*UP* 11. 255–62). Although they had different views on individualism, nationalism, and modernity—as evidenced in their 1898 controversy in the Dublin *Daily Express*, over the nature of Irish drama (see 11. 289, 293–8)—the two men respected each other. Eglinton's accounts of WBY appeared in *Irish Literary Portraits* (1935), and in the *Dublin Magazine* (July–Sept 1953), where he echoes AE's criticisms here by recalling (25) that 'there was a certain malicious vein' in WBY's nature, and that 'his worst personal fault was a lack of ordinary good nature. No one could say that he was without humour, but it was a saturnine humour, and he was certainly not one who suffered gladly the numerous people whom he considered fools.' In a copy of *Some Essays and Passages*, inscribed for James Healy in July 1938 (Stanford), WBY wrote of him: 'Eglinton was the sceptic of our movement, always for the individual against the race. We lived in our better moments.'

[15] In March and April 1900 WBY had denounced Queen Victoria's state visit to Ireland in the Dublin press (see 11. 502–4, 507–9), and this had made him *persona non grata* among the Irish upper classes, who were predominantly unionist and loyalist. *The Times* reported on 3 Apr 1900 that Professor William Lecky had withdrawn his support from the ILT in protest against the 'recent discreditable language of Mr. W. B. Yeats, Mr. George Moore, and others who are prominently associated with that movement', and on 3 Apr the Dublin *Daily Express* noted that other unionist guarantors were following suit (2). In December 1900 Sir Richard Henn Collins and Sir Charles Stanford resigned from the Irish Literary Society, London, telling A. P. Graves (NLI): 'They can't have this Yeats on the Committee if they wish to be considered non combative and nonpolitical' (see 11. 620–1). In fact, WBY was later to regret his 'Irish propaganda' of these years: 'I never met with, or but met to quarrel with, my father's old family acquaintance; or with acquaintance I myself might have found, and kept among the prosperous educated

antagonism. I have had no particular reason to support you and many good reasons to fight you if I wished to do so. But I have always recognized your genius as a poet, and have always fought for you there where I could. I have felt for some years past that the old friendship between [us] was worn very thin.[16] But at least you are one of the few people in Ireland who have done something and are still trying to do something, and I do not wish to fight you unless your track of action interferes with my own, and a question of principle arises. I have always tried to avoid any friction, and have decided that as I did not wish to write plays myself I should not interfere with you who did. I have no doubt I have been represented as always thwarting your views but as a matter of fact I have lost a great deal of my influence among the young men by defending you. When the society was started you may not be aware of the fact that I was unanimously elected President, and it was with some difficulty I induced them to put you into that position.[17] I mention this merely to show you that I did not wish to take any position which I felt rightly belonged to you. There was I think hardly a time since then when if I wished actively to oppose your views I could not have carried the society with me. I have a kind of honour of my own and did not think because you went round sneering at "Deirdre" as a bad & popular play and at my opinions as valueless, that that was any reason why I should try to upset your work.[18] Of course I do not deny that I have laughed at most of

class, who had all the great appointments at University or Castle; and this I did by deliberate calculation....I chose Royal visits especially for demonstrations of disloyalty, rolling up with my own hands the red carpet spread by some elderly Nationalist, softened or weakened by time, to welcome Viceroyalty; and threatening, if our London society drank to the King's health, that my friends and I would demonstrate against it by turning our glasses upside-down....I thought many a time of the pleasant Dublin houses that would never ask me to dine; and the still pleasanter houses with trout-streams near at hand, that would never ask me upon a visit....Yet it was in those pleasant houses, among the young men and the young girls, that we were to make our converts' (*Aut*, 233–4).

[16]  In his article in the *Dublin Magazine* (see above, n. 13) Eglinton remembered that even at the beginning of their friendship WBY and AE 'soon began to indulge privately in rather acrimonious comments on one another'.

[17]  This was true: at the founding meeting of the INTS on 9 Aug 1902 AE was first asked to become president of the new Society. He declined, and proposed that WBY (who was not present) should be elected instead; this was then unanimously agreed.

[18]  AE's two-act play *Deirdre* (see p. 94) had been produced by the Fays' dramatic company with WBY's *Cathleen ni Houlihan* at St Teresa's Hall, Dublin, from 2 to 5 Apr 1902, and the success of these performances had led to the setting up of the INTS (see III. 162–9). From the first WBY had had doubts about it, and in January 1902 told AG (III. 148) that the play 'rather embarrases me. I do not believe in it at all. If it is offered to us I shall have to vote against it', and on 5 Apr he described it to her as 'thin & faint but it has the effect of wall decoration. The absense of character is like the absense of individual expression in wall decoration' (III. 167). In January 1903 he described the play as 'lacking in invention', and in April 1904 apologized to AE for his and AG's disparagement: 'Please forgive me for giving expression to some of my general exasperation...& making Dierdre the scape goat. I was foolish enough to quote a phrase of Lady Gregorys <about Deirdre> which must have annoyed you....I myself sometimes give unbridled expression to my dislikes moved perhaps by my knowledge of the strength of my likings & my loyalty to them' (III. 576). And he told John Quinn that the

your dogmas, and have never disguised my opinion that in trying to write plays you are deflecting a genius which is essentially lyrical & narrative from its best manifestation and that your want of logical constructive power unfitted you for dramatic writing, at least for the stage.[19] You spoke once to me of two courts of appeal the "popular" and the "intellectual". Neither one or the other have awarded you any other position than as a writer of beautiful verse, and I think it a mistake which later on you may regret that you should lose time managing a business bringing endless annoyance with no added influence. As a poet you could and would exercise an immense influence on your contemporaries, as a dramatist you lose influence. The few dozen people who come to the Abbey Theatre are a poor compensation for the thousands who would read another Wind Among the Reeds or another Usheen or work like that.[20] However as you have begun it and tied the Theatre round your neck you must go on with it, and my advice to you is let Miss Walker alone and do as little as you can to irritate those who are against you, or you will find that a man with no friends and many active enemies may for all his genius have less influence on his time than some person of one half his abilities. This is my advice. Ask yourself whether you did not bully and worry Miss Walker into joining you against her own wish and whether as a gentleman you are right in trying to bully and threaten her into remaining whatever your legal rights may be.

Yours sincerely
Geo. W. Russell

ALS Berg, with envelope addressed to Coole, and postmark 'LONDON JA 6 06'. Enclosure MBY.

characters in the play were more like phantoms than heroes, and in his briefing for the Abbey patent hearing that summer said that *Deirdre* was 'by a dear friend and a charming writer, but I do not consider it a good play'. Commenting on AE's letter to Synge on 10 Jan (Saddlemyer, 107), AG identified this as the motive for his attack of WBY: 'the real cause comes at the end "you went about sneering at Deirdre and saying it was a bad & popular play"! I am sure he never said it was popular!'

[19]   AE's disparagement of WBY as playwright was done privately rather than in print. In April 1904 he had assured WBY that his plays were 'of more importance than mine'.

[20]   It is significant that AE, who always preferred WBY's earlier poetry, cites here *The Wanderings of Oisin*, published in 1889, and *The Wind Among the Reeds*, most of the poems for which were written in the mid-1890s. In 1901 and 1902 he had annoyed WBY by republishing his early poems (see III. 274, 276), explaining that 'I love your early work'. AE's son Diarmuid Russell recalled in the *Atlantic Monthly* of February 1943 how his father 'used to chuckle over the fact that once, when Yeats had been rather scorning his own early poems, he had recited a number of them to him. Yeats was excited and pleased over the poems and asked who wrote them—and was displeased when he was informed that he himself was the author' (56).

## *To John Millington Synge, 6 January 1906*

18, Woburn Buildings, | Euston Road.
Jan. 6th, 1906.

My dear Synge,

I have had a wire from Fay "Enemy rehearsing land author present letter tonight, Fay." I am delighted. This is far better than a vague feeling of irritation. Everything they do would only reveal the superiority of our work. The Land without the two Fays will be a miserable thing. If you see Colum be firm with him, he is with them now for all his works and if he comes back to us he comes back with all his work. They will either collapse after a performance or two or they will become more and more crudely propagandist playing up to that element in the country. That too will be a gain for it will show the division that underlies all the petty disputes the division between those who want good play writing, and those who do not. We will lose none of our people in that battle, for the few hundreds of supporters four or five hundred at the most, three hundred to the worst I am judging by sale of programmes are from the general public and they care no more for clubs than we do. The whole quarrel will now become open. We can carry it on in the Freeman's Journal if we like and it is a quarrel in which we are bound to get the support of the ordinary theatre goer. At the present moment I am inclined to carry out that idea of ours and substitute a little newspaper for the programme. We might call it the Fan in imitation of a German thing of the kind, and in this little newspaper to keep up the fight I am going to make the suggestion to Lady Gregory.[1] It must to some extent depend upon my getting a little quiet to write in, from Sunday my address will be C/o A. Carmichael Esq. 28, Viewforth, Edinburgh, on Thursday I go to Dundee, on Friday I lecture in Aberdeen and after that I shall go to stay with Lady Cromartie in some wild place far north for a few days.[2] If Lady Gregory approves of the idea I can write a little essay there. My spirits have been raised by Russell telling me that last Samhain made a lot of enemies, by as far as I can make out its insistence on sound doctrine by what they call "art for art's sake." He says in his letter that I irritated people by my lecture in Cork, well, I never before was quite so successful with an audience. Two correspondents in one of the local papers afterwards confirmed my own impression on that matter, but I fought your battle

---

[1] WBY finally called his occasional periodical the *Arrow*, the first number appearing on 20 Oct 1906, when the name caused some comment in the Dublin press. The *Leader* of 1 Dec 1906 (226) thought it 'an ominous name anyway, suggesting at once wounded deer and British convicts'.

[2] WBY had met Scots Celtic scholar Alexander Carmichael in August 1901 (see p. 199, n. 7). For the Countess of Cromartie see p. 134.

against the Clubs, that was the irritation.[3] The fight will evidently now become public. The only thing one regrets is the waste of time. The Fan would have the advantage of limiting that waste to one page a month.

Fay expects to have Boyle ready by the 20th. I forgot to put on my notes in Directors Box "to write or help Frank Fay to write a number of preliminary paragraphs for papers and get these published during week before a show".[4] Boyle gives a fine chance for such things his story is so topical.[5] I enclose a letter of Fay's.

Yr ev<br>W B Yeats

[*With enclosure*]

Abbey Theatre

Dear Mr Yeats

Telegram to hand.[6] I think that is very wise for we could do nothing dignified in the matter and we could do nothing that would make her any use to us under the circumstances.

---

[3] WBY's lecture, 'What Is a National Theatre', given to the Literary and Scientific Society in Cork on 14 Dec (see p. 249, n. 1), had provoked a correspondence in the *Cork Constitution* over the following days on two particular counts: his support for Synge and his comparison between the Irish dramatic movement and that of Ibsen. On 19 Dec S. de Maistre, while acknowledging (8) that 'Mr. Yeats' personal magnetism and . . . plausible sophistry, carried all before him, and enthused an audience, who sat down cold and unemotional', censured his praise for the 'hideous taint' of Ibsenism. The following day 'Diarmuid' (see p. 253) wrote to support and amplify de Maistre's criticisms, but 'Cham' rallied to WBY's support, pointing out that he had held up Ibsen and the Norwegian drama as a historical parallel, not as a model to be imitated. On 23 Dec 'D.C.' wrote in support of the artist's freedom to express things as he saw them, rather than as according to political or social stereotypes, and, although he condemned *The Well of the Saints*, he did so on aesthetic grounds rather than those of authenticity. On 30 Dec 1905 Daniel Corkery attacked WBY's remarks on Synge in the *Leader* (313–14).

[4] It seems that Synge failed to help Frank Fay, who confessed to WBY on 16 Jan that 'my pars are crude, stiff things'—a sentence that WBY annotated with the reproachful 'I asked Synge to help him'. However, unlike the publicity for *The White Cockade*, the advertising for the new season was comprehensive, and in his letter Fay reported: 'Last Saturday we had an inch in the Times, Freeman, and Independent, and pars in the Herald and the Telegraph, and the Telegraph par appeared in Monday's Freeman. I also sent a par to the Times. . . . The theatre bills are up on the boards here since Saturday last; crimson and black, and Allens are posting their hoardings on Thursday. Mr Darley has arranged about the music and his name is large on all the advertisements and bills, and is mentioned in the pars. Last night we sent advt. to Leader, U.I., Nationist and Claidheamh, for one inch.'

[5] i.e. Boyle's comedy *The Eloquent Dempsy*. Dealing with the machinations of a venal politician, it was topical because of the General Election which was to begin on 13 Jan. In his letter of 16 Jan (see above), Fay lamented that his inability at writing publicity paragraphs had prevented him making the most of this: 'a great deal more could be made out of the election side of The Eloquent Dempsy than I have been able to make out of it. We are right in the middle of the elections—municipal and others—and if this could be brought out properly in the pars, it might help to draw good houses.'

[6] i.e. that of 4 Jan, telling him that WBY no longer intended to prosecute Maire Walker for breach of contract (see p. 280).

Boyles play is going all right likewise the Riders to the Sea. Are we to run 6 nights or seven for next time[7] and if things go all [?]gay I expect the pieces to be ready for the 20th Jan. and onwards.

The problem I am trying to solve is how to get the Repertoire right and still not miss the monthly shows, for we have the caste of no piece complete.[8] I can get these two new as I told you for 18/- a week the pair they will of course be raw, but anyone we get will be that.[9] What I think would be best would be to lie up for lent & get things right but that means present salaries going on till then or else get at them after this show & start all the contracts from then. It [is] a thing wants a bit of thinking out no matter what way its done. And I think you ought to have a discussion on it. Frank Walker met MacDonald the other night and invited him to join the new Company they were getting up. What ho? What a nice new company that will be. I have the postcards in hand for next show.[10]

M<sup>c</sup>Donald as King James & very well he looks.[11] I am glad in an way that we have at last seen the end of the emigrants and know what we have to do. I have Molly Allgood play Cathleen in Riders to the Sea and shes not at all bad.[12]

[7] The bill ran for seven nights in all, starting on Saturday, 20 Jan, and playing from Monday to Saturday inclusive on the following week. The productions were revived on 21–2 Feb.

[8] The basic pattern at the Abbey had been a new show every month, but this had been broken by tours, and was to be even more disrupted over the coming months for the same cause.

[9] i.e. Anderton and J. H. Dunne (see p. 283, n. 5). Holloway commented in his diary for 20 Jan (NLI) that Dunne was 'adequate' as Mike Flanagan, a working man in *The Eloquent Dempsy*.

[10] The Abbey was publishing publicity postcards to advertise forthcoming productions.

[11] McDonnell had made a success in the role of King James in AG's *The White Cockade* in early December 1905 (see p. 245, n. 1), and was to revive the part in late February 1907.

[12] Molly Allgood (1887–1952), the younger sister of Sara Allgood, took her stage name, Maire O'Neill, from her maternal grandmother. She had been a member of the Daughters of Erin, and was like her sister a french polisher before taking this her first Abbey part. She went on to rival her sister as the Abbey's leading lady. Synge was to fall in love with her later this year, and they became engaged shortly before his death in 1909. She remained with the Abbey until 1911, when she married G. H. Mair. Shortly after his death she married Francis McDonnell, and toured with him, although the marriage was not a success. In later life she worked mainly on the London stage and in film and radio. The part of Cathleen, Maurya's daughter in *Riders to the Sea*, had previously been played by her sister, who now replaced 'Honor Lavelle' (Helen Laird) as Maurya. Holloway noted in his diary for 20 Jan (NLI) that Miss O'Neill 'shewed great promise as Cathleen', and, after seeing the production for a third time on 27 Jan, commented that 'Maire O'Neill's Cathleen was ever & always attuned to the scene. The pathetic stops in the voice, & subdued demeanour of resigned sadness were present in her interpretation.'

I think you will like Mr Dempsys Dining room.[13] Will you send me the sketch of boats for Shadowy waters also model.[14]

Wishing you

Many Happy New Years

I am sincerely yours

Will Fay

TLS TCD. Saddlemyer, 98–9.

## To Elizabeth A. Sharp,[1] 6 January [1906]

18 Woburn Buildings | Euston Road

Jan 6.

Dear M^rs Sharpe: I want to tell you how much I sympathize with you in your great trouble.[2] Your husband was a man of genius, who brought something wholly new into letters & thousands will feal his loss with a curious personal regret. To me he was that, & a strange mystery too & also a dear friend. To talk with him was to feal the presence of that mystery, he was very near

[13] In fact all three acts of *The Eloquent Dempsy* take place in the drawing (not dining) room above Dempsy's shop. The stage directions call for 'Doors C. and L. Windows L. An easy chair, some other chairs, a stool and a sofa. A side-table. A cabinet.' This would have been the first elaborate drawing room scene designed for the Abbey, and so something of a challenge to Fay and Seaghan Barlow. Boyle had written to F. J. Fay on 29 Dec 1905 (NLI) with elaborate suggestions for the dress of the characters, but had said nothing about the scenery.

[14] The model was presumably that from Henry Paget (see p. 95), but Robert Gregory was now designing the production.

[1] Elizabeth Amelia Sharp (1856–1932), who had married Sharp in 1884, was an energetic woman of letters, who apparently acquiesced in his various amours, including his long-standing relationship with Edith Rinder. She translated selections from Heine, including his *Italian Travel Sketches* (1892), and edited several anthologies of poetry, among which were *Songs and Poems of the Sea* (1888), *Women Poets of the Victorian Era* (1890), and *Lyra Celtica: An Anthology of Representative Celtic Poetry* (Edinburgh, 1896), which included three poems by WBY. In 1910 she published a memoir of William Sharp and edited his *Collected Writings*, 7 vols. (1909–11). On 28 Dec 1905 she forwarded a letter from her late husband (*LWBY*1. 157–8) with a covering note explaining that he 'wished that you should receive the enclosed immediately on his death. Unfortunately I found it today only. As you will see, he and he only, was, and wrote as, Fiona Macleod.' In his letter Sharp said: 'This will reach you after my death. You will think I have deceived you about Fiona Macleod. But, in absolute privacy, I tell you that I have not, howsoever in certain details I have (inevitably) misled you. Only, it is a mystery. Perhaps you will intuitively understand, or may come to understand. "The rest is silence." Farewell. . . . It is only right, however, to add that I, and I only, am the author—in the *literal* and literary sense—of all written under the name of Fiona Macleod.' He had written in identical terms to AE (Indiana). Although WBY and AG had long known the truth, Sharp had kept up the pretence that Fiona Macleod was a separate person to the very end, and in his last letter to WBY asked whether he had 'heard of or from Miss Macleod? If I can get a copy . . . I'll send you a copy of her new Tauchnitz volume of revised, augmented, and selected matter called "The Sunset of Old Tales". . . . If in the course of a week or two one does not reach you, write to Miss Macleod who wd. like you to have one.'

[2] William Sharp, who suffered from diabetes, had died in Sicily on 12 Dec 1905.

always to the world where he now is & often seemed to me to deliver its messages. He often spoke to me of things of my personal life that were unknown to him by the common channels of sense.[3] I knew he was ill—but never knew how ill. I had a letter from him only two days before I saw his death in the paper.[4] I had been looking forward to seeing him again very shortly.[5] I feal now that one of the Gates of Wisdom has been closed for much as I admire his writing he was, as a man should be, more than his writing.[6] What must you feal at so great a loss. You must however know that one, who was so often as it seemed out of the body while he lived, cannot have undergone any unrecognizable change or gone very far away. Blake said of death that it was but going into another room.[7]

He was certainly the most imaginative man—I use the word in its old & literal sense of image making—I have ever known, not like a man of this age at all.

Yrs sny
W B Yeats

ALS Private.

[3] A number of entries in WBY's 'Visions Notebook', kept in the late 1890s, give instances of Sharp advising WBY of occult influences on his life and well-being. On 2 Feb 1900 he had warned him that 'great powers of evil' were against him ('Visions Notebook', 12 Feb 1900), and on 15 Apr of the same year he told WBY that a flute-playing spirit he had seen in a trance announced that he was 'going to play the tune of his [i.e. WBY's] destruction'. When asked what that was, he replied: 'Maud Gonne, Maud Gonne, Maud Gonne!' ('Visions Notebook', 4 May 1900). Sharp had given WBY a great deal of help with the Celtic Mysteries (see p. 212, n. 2), and even in his very last letter had recounted an elaborately symbolic dream he had recently had about WBY. In *Mem* WBY wrote that he felt that he had 'never properly used or valued this man, through whom the fluidic world seemed to flow, disturbing all.... To look at his big body, his high colour, his handsome head with the great crop of bristly hair, no one could have divined the ceaseless presence of that fluidic life' (128–9).

[4] Sharp had written from Sicily in early December 1905, complaining that WBY had not answered his letters, and answering a query about a 'veiled mission' (see p. 212). His death was reported in the London *Morning Post* on 15 Dec (7). In his last letter, Sharp had told WBY that for 'many months this year I was ill—dying—but there were other than physical reasons for this, & I survived thing after thing and shock after shock like a swimmer rising to successive waves—& then suddenly to every one's amazement swam into havens of relative well-being once more. But the game is not over, of course: and equally of course is a losing game. Nevertheless I'm well content with things as they are, all things considered.... I have much on hand, but for long I have had to do little. Now, if the Gods permit, I hope to recover some lost ground.'

[5] In his last letter to WBY Sharp had suggested that they might meet in France 'after Easter' (see p. 212, n. 3).

[6] WBY made this tacit reservation about Sharp's writing more unambiguously elsewhere, remarking to Sturge Moore on 24 Aug 1916 (Bridge, 26) its 'looseness and redundance.... Fiona Macleod ... had matter but only very occassional style. If Fiona had style through out the best of the stories would have been masterpeices.'

[7] William Blake made this observation when Henry Crabb Robinson brought him news of the death of his old friend John Flaxman on 7 Dec 1826, and WBY would have come across it in the enlarged 1880 edition of Gilchrist's *Life of William Blake* (1. 397): 'I had just heard of the death of Flaxman, a man whom he admired', Robinson recorded in his diary, 'and was curious how he would receive the intelligence. He had been ill during the summer, and he said with a smile, "I thought I should have gone first." He then added, "I cannot think of death as more than the going out of one room into another".'

## *To Sarah Purser, 6 January* [*1906*]

18 Woburn Building | Euston Road.
Jan. 6.

My dear Sarah Pursur: of course I wont write [to] the papers—no body withdraws their own statement for the mere sport of the thing.[1] I was ready to put right any error of fact in my paragraph that was all. As for the rest, whatever criticism I write will I hope be helpful to the fame & name of work I so greatly admire. My Ardrahan essay, if it gets written, will be less criticism than an impression like those in the Celtic Twilight.[2]

Yr ev
W B Yeats

ALS NLI.

## *To W. G. Fay,* [*7 January 1906*]

My dear Fay: This is I should think the calculation of our friends.[1] They think that nobody can get a resolution passed in the old society & know that they control the business committee. They are mistaken I think. I as president am the principal executive officer & can act at a moment of emergency. I can instruct Whitney & Moore to get out an injunction— obviously a matter of emergency—& they can only stop me by a ¾ majority at a special meeting.[2] Under normal circumstances the President & Sec would act but in this case the Sec is in a conspiracy with certain

[1] On 30 Dec 1905 WBY had suggested he might write to the press (see p. 262).

[2] WBY had envisaged an essay on the reaction of the local people to the windows in the chapel at Ardrahan, and the way the images related to local folklore, but he never wrote this (see p. 262). The first edition of *The Celtic Twilight* had appeared in 1893, and another, much revised and expanded version, in 1902.

[1] This is a reply to a letter from W. G. Fay of 5 Jan (Berg) in which he told WBY that the seceding members were rehearsing *The Land*, and intended to perform as the INTS: 'The latest information from the front is that there was a rehearsal in Walker's in High St. last to which MacDonald was invited to attend. Colm was there, and the "Land" was in rehearsal—Roberts as Matt you will be glad to hear, Miss Garvey, Miss Laird, Frank Walker, and Starkey. They gave MacDonald to understand that he could have whatever part he liked and that they were also in communication with Mr Power and that it was their intention to perform the piece as The Irish National Theatre Society. What is to be done in the matter. Of course, up to the present, we have but hearsay to go upon; but it is as well to sharpen your battle-axes before the battle.'

[2] 'As far as I can make out', Fay had written, 'this performance could not legally be carried out without consulting us as per rule 13, for we would certainly dispute it.' He went on to say that it was also illegal under rule 7, and asked whether WBY thought it 'wise to act on his rumour, though it is scarcely such as MacD. was present at this rehearsal and told Dunne who told me. Mr Synge, who is here, says it might be well to consider writing to Roberts or Colm to ask for an explanation; but I suppose we would

members to act outside the rules.[3] They would meet this in the first case by a resolution of business committee: I would however declare this resolution illegal as no society can break its own rules & be legal at the same time. Show this letter to Synge & if he thinks well he can consult Whitney & Moore & at a wire from him I will send letter of instructions—for them. If we get out an injunction I would propose at same time that our dispute with old society be submitted to arbitrators not necessarily members of society & that both sides abide [to] agree to what ever arbitrators decide about name, money, continuance in present form etc *provided their decision did not interfear with Miss Hornimans pattent rights.* It is possible that our friends would accept arbitration without injunction but I doubt it. Synge should consider this. Possibly if Lady Gregory could come to town & see them individually she could get them to do it.

An obvious course is to submit the whole matter to register but he might possibly disolve the society as the simplest way out & so damage our position under the patent.[4] Synge (& I think you should go with him) had

not say from what source we got the information. Better not to act too hastily in the matter; but let us first make quite sure our legal position in the matter, and then act straightforwardly on it.' The legal position on both sides was far from clear, particularly as the status of the Patent was involved. The Committee of Management, or Business Committee, was the most important executive committee in the old Society (see Appendix). With a membership of seven, elected at the Annual General Meeting, it had control of the business arrangements of the Society, including all 'questions relating to the payment of money and the terms on which engagements may be entered upon'. Decisions made by the Committee had to be communicated to the Society as a whole, and, if one-fifth of the members objected, they could call a Special General Meeting, at which a three-quarters majority would decide the matter. The president's powers were more vaguely drawn than WBY here suggests. In adopting the name Irish National Theatre Society the seceders were signifying that they rejected the new limited company and asserting their legitimacy as the original Society. Under the old 1903 constitution, rule 13, 'Settlement of disputes', stipulated that 'Any dispute arising between the members or officials of the Society shall first of all be referred to the Committee, and, if their decision be not accepted, it shall be brought before a Special General Meeting of members, whose decision shall be final.' Rule 7 related to the powers of the playwright and stage manager in the choice of plays: 'The Stage Manager and Author shall have the sole right to decide on questions as to how a scene shall be acted, and the choice of actors shall be left to the decision of the Stage Manager in consultation with the author' (see Appendix).

[3] Padraic Colum was appointed secretary when the seceders constituted themselves the Theatre of Ireland on 18 May 1906, but Fred Ryan, who had been secretary of the INTS, may have been standing in for the time being.

[4] The INTS had been registered under the Friendly Societies Act, and its conduct was ultimately monitored by the Assistant Registrar for Ireland, whose offices were in Dame Street, Dublin. The dissolution of the Society was governed by rule 14: 'The Society at any time may be dissolved by the consent of five-sixths of the members, testified by their signature to an instrument of dissolution in the form provided by the Treasury regulations in that behalf.' Originally the main seceders (Starkey, Laird, Keohler, Ryan, and Frank Walker) had asked Roberts (Harvard) to call a Special Meeting to 'consider the dissolution declared passed by the Chairman on October 9th [see pp. 200–1] but which had not the ¾ majority necessary under Rule 4 of the Society'.

better discuss the whole question with Whitney & Moore. He can show this letter. I am sending copy to Lady Gregory.

Yrs Etc

W B Yeats

Write first to Colum & get intentions in writing.[5]

ALS copy Berg.

## *To Lady Gregory, 7 January* [*1906*]

18 Woburn Buildings | Euston Road

Jan 7.

My dear Lady Gregory: I enclose my answer to a letter of Fays, of which you have a copy.[1] I have said you might go to town to settle it, but dont think I want to press that. I want you to act on your own opinion. My inclination is for a consultation with lawyers first—it may be that the register is the way out. If not my temprement says first an injunction then negociation. We are a business now & besides it is hard to negociate with these vague people—negociation means hours of wasted time. They have no leader to settle with unless one could take Russell as that.[2] I doubt if he would help us. Do not however take me as *voting*. I am too far away—& cannot be consulted quickly enough to take the responsibility.

One joy is the Boyle, with the Fays in it, will end Colum for a bit. I would be inclined to leave things alone but that would mean a petty newspaper dispute as to which is the society etc. Far better a clean stroke & have done with it—even though it costs a little money. I am writing to Miss Horniman

---

[5] Fay did write to Colum, who replied on 9 Jan (Berg), and AG also wrote to him on 7 and 9 Jan. In his reply to Fay Colum denied an allegation (made in a letter to him from AEFH) that he was 'a leader of the malcontents'. Having thought through the situation, he had come to the conclusion that the Society must reunite if it wanted to retain an audience in Dublin. He insisted that he had 'not committed myself in any way to the old society', although he was aware that they were rehearsing *The Land*. He would not withdraw the play from them as that 'would be to declare against the old society and so injure the policy of re-union'. He said that his ideal was 'a people's theatre', and he warned that 'to split up, to change the title of the society would be against the terms of the contract we all signed'.

[1] That of 5 Jan (see previous letter), in the course of which Fay said he and Synge were 'sending copy to Lady Gregory'.

[2] In her letter to Colum of 9 Jan AG tried to clear up these points: 'Can you say definitely who is the responsible speaker for the other side? Can you say or can he say what we are asked to do? If I knew that, I should know whether negotiations were possible or if they would lead to further waste of time.'

who is away.[3] This rival society is no new plan & they have always wanted the name. If we mean injunction we must be silent about it.

Yr ev

W B Yeats

PS I reopen the envelope to say that Fay wants Roberts design for 'the Shadowy Waters scenery' as soon as possible.[4] I enclose end of Russells letter which I had forgotten. I told him in my letter that the whole reason why [I] found that my work & his were opposed was that he though strong & capable got about him the weak & incapable, & that my friends were all strong & capable. Only I put this more politely than I can here—I spoke of his religious genius that makes him think all souls equal I replied to little else. This was really the Kernel of the nut, the pip of the orange.

ALS Berg, with envelope addressed to Coole, postmark 'LONDON. N.W. JAN 8 '06'.

## *To A. E. F. Horniman, 7 January 1906*

Mention in letter to AG, 7 January 1906.[1]
Telling her of Colum's equivocations and the formation of a rival drama group.[2]

---

[3] AEFH was in Paris, and WBY's letter is now lost.

[4] *The Shadowy Waters*, designed by Robert Gregory, was postponed until 8 Dec 1906.

[1] Although this and other letters have not survived, WBY evidently kept AEFH abreast of the volatile situation following the schism in the Society, and she helped stabilize the situation by formally giving the Abbey Theatre to WBY's new company (cf. *LWBY* 1. 158). She also sent a copy of this letter to Synge, to whom she wrote on 9 Jan (see p. 286, n. 3), warning him against his too accommodating attitude to the seceders, telling him that they 'must know where we stand quite clearly', and setting out her 'personal position': 'I gave a theatre for a certain scheme—changes were made in the government for the benefit of the scheme—I approved of it—the objectors completely ignored me and their own signatures to a letter of 1904—they have never lodged any complaints with me nor have they given me any reason for their actions.... I never made the slightest pretensions to any political sympathies and the objectors knew this quite well when they accepted the use of the theatre. If they had asked me before signing the letter it would have been much better.... If anyone thinks that "Irish" or "National" are anything to me beyond mere empty words used to distinguish a Society, merely a title for convenience, they are much mistaken.... The theatre was given for the carrying out of Mr. Yeats's artistic dramatic schemes and for no other reasons. These patriots are all jealous of *Art*, they want to keep the standard down so as to shine themselves. "In the Kingdom of the Blind, the one-eyed man is King."' She concluded by urging him to 'have patience and show a bold front', even if the audiences diminished.

[2] AEFH had already begun to demonize Colum (see p. 286) and on receipt of WBY's letters wrote to him, accusing him of being the leader of the seceders (see p. 306, n. 5).

## To F. J. and W. G. Fay, 7 January 1906

Mention in letter from F. J. Fay to AG, 7 January 1906.
Telegram telling the Fays that he is leaving for Scotland, and that his
address will be 28 Viewforth, Edinburgh.[1]

## To H. J. C. Grierson,[1] [c. 9 January 1906]

c/o A Carmichael | 28 Viewforth, | Edinburgh

Dear M<sup>r</sup> Grierson: your kind letter has just reached me sent on from
London. I have of course great pleasure in accepting your kind invitation—I do not yet know what train I shall go by.[2]

Yr sny
W B Yeats

ALS NLS.

## To Lady Gregory, [12 January 1906]

7, King's Gate, | Aberdeen.

My dear Lady Gregory: Have just got letter—extract from patent which
please keep dark alters situation.[1] We must make terms—but not I think

---

[1] In his letter to AG, F. J. Fay wrote (Berg) that WBY 'goes to Edinburgh to-day or to-night. (He
wires his address as 28 Viewforth, Edinburgh and we have asked him to keep us posted in his Scotch
address).'

[1] Professor Herbert John Clifford Grierson (1866–1960), the celebrated 17th-century scholar, was
educated at Aberdeen and Oxford Universities, and held the Chair of English at Aberdeen from 1894 to
1915, when he was appointed Professor of Rhetoric and English at Edinburgh University. His *The First
Half of the Seventeenth Century* was to appear in September of this year, and his influential edition of
John Donne's poems in 1912. He wrote an article comparing Yeats's and Shakespeare's fairies in *Dublin
Review*, April 1911, and sections on WBY's poetry in *Lyrical Poetry from Blake to Hardy* (1928), and in
*A Critical History of English Poetry* (rev. edn. 1950).

[2] Grierson's letter is untraced, but evidently invited WBY to stay with him when lecturing in
Aberdeen on 12 Jan. In its report on the lecture, the *Aberdeen Daily Journal* of 13 Jan reported (3)
that Grierson, 'whose guest Mr. Yeats had been', took the chair, and 'referred to Mr Yeats's intrinsic
merit as a poet, and to his eminence as the leader of a great and inspiring movement in modern
literature'.

[1] AG had sent WBY an extract from a newspaper account of the Patent, dealing with the relation
between the Society and the continuation of the Patent, which radically altered the balance of power in
the present dispute in favour of the seceders:

Synges terms except at last emergency. The thing is to get them if possible to leave old society to us. If they would do this I would be inclined to concede everything else they could want—the £70² the name—which they

> The patent shall only empower the patentee to exhibit plays in the Irish or English language written by Irish writers on Irish subjects, or such dramatic works of foreign authors as would tend to interest the public in the higher works of dramatic art; all foregoing to be selected by the Irish National Theatre Society under the provision of Part 6 of its rules now existing and subject to the restrictions therein contained, a clause to be inserted against the assignment of rights to any person or persons other than the trustee for Miss Horniman her executors or assignees, the patent to cease if the Irish National Theatre is dissolved.

This was a compressed but basically accurate version of the terms of the Patent, the comparable passages of which gave AEFH and AG permission 'publicly to act represent or perform or cause to be acted represented or performed all Interludes, Tragedies, Comedies, Plays in the Irish or English language written by Irish writers or on Irish subjects and such dramatic works of foreign authors as would tend to educate and interest the Irish public in the higher works of dramatic art and as may be selected by the Irish National Theatre Society under the provisions contained in part six of the Rules of the Irish National Theatre Society'. Rule 6 of the INTS governed the way plays were to be selected through the Reading Committee (see Appendix, p. 896):

> (a) The Reading Committee shall be elected at the Annual General Meeting of the Society. The Members shall be eligible for re-election on the expiry of their term of office.
> (b) The Reading Committee shall be six in number; and they shall first consider all plays proposed for performance by the Society. No play shall be performed until it has been recommended by the Reading Committee. The final acceptance or rejection of any play thus recommended shall rest with the Members of the Society, to whom such plays shall be read at meetings summoned for the purpose, when a three-quarters majority of those present shall decide. The author shall not be allowed to be present when a vote is taken.
> (c) No official of the Society shall have power to accept a play on behalf of the Society, or to reject one which shall have been accepted and passed in accordance with the foregoing rules.
> (d) No play shall be accepted or rejected on political grounds solely, and the literary, dramatic, and acting merits of the play shall primarily be considered, and no objection raised to a play on the ground that its performance would antagonize any political party shall be valid unless it should be considered that there is any degradation of National ideals in the work submitted.

This now presented a major legal difficulty, in that the majority of the Reading Committee were seceders who could block the machinery for selecting new plays. Even more worrying for the Directors was the other condition, which stipulated that 'in the event of the said Irish National Theatre Society being dissolved during the term of these Presents then on the happening of these events these Presents and every grant privilege and immunity hereby given or granted shall become null and void to all intents and purposes whatsoever'. This gave the seceders a considerable lever. Since they were the majority of the original INTS, they could legitimately claim that their secession was in fact a dissolution, and that the Patent was consequently void. Ironically, WBY himself may have alerted them to this stipulation; in a letter to George Roberts of 29 Sept 1904 he had told him: 'Remember that if the society were to split and the governing authorities were not able to carry a certain percentage of the members with them, our patent would lapse. Please show this letter to all who it may concern' (see III. 655).

² This sum was the credit balance left in the accounts of the old INTS. As WBY had explained at the General Meeting of 22 Sept 1905 (see p. 200, n. 2): 'When the Abbey Theatre was opened a sum of I think about £20 was brought into it from the Molesworth performances, and when the session closed there was about £70 to the credit of the Society' (NLI).

could use if they did not incorporate under act of parliment & we do not object—& leave to hire theatre.[3] I mean to concede all this if we cannot get society cheaper. Synges plan too dangerous—they might split up at any time & patent be lost.[4] It is a most complicated situation. You will have to come to Dublin & so shall I—I go to Lady Cromarties to-morrow but doubt if I should—however a little delay may be no harm—we must not seem anxious & we must keep the reason of our anxiety to ourselves. I recognize defeat & see there is nothing for it but terms—if we had been in the position I thought—& I had Whitney & Moores opinion—they never saw that paragraph—fighting to the end would have been the best plan I think. An Alternative Scheme would be Synges plan *plus* enough people in old society to keep it from disolution.

I go to Lady Cromartie's, Leod Castle, Strathpeffer tomorrow but if you wire will go to Dublin at once.

Yrs ev
W B Yeats

[*On back of envelope*]
We must soothe other side—
W B Y—

ALS Berg, with envelope addressed to Coole, postmark 'ABERDEEN JAN 12 '06'.

---

[3] In fact the seceders did not seek incorporation and chose to call themselves the Theatre of Ireland (see p. 292, n. 3). And although AEFH, much to the Directors' embarrassment, vigorously opposed their requests to use the Abbey Theatre, they were permitted to mount productions there in December 1907 and in May and November 1908.

[4] Synge had wanted to patch up the quarrel with the seceders, and hoped, like Colum, that the two sides could work at least in tandem. On 5 Jan 1906 he had told AG (*JMSCL* I. 150), 'I don't see that we can do anything but quietly live things down and explain ourselves in a friendly way to anyone we can.' He put this view into a more formal proposal, which is now lost but which he sent to AG before 10 Jan as on that day she thanked him for his 'letter re an arrangement, for I think all we can hope for is an amicable separation' (Saddlemyer, 106). His proposal evidently wished to avoid lawyers and to allow the seceders access to arbitration and to continue to enjoy rights under the Patent. On 11 Jan Synge again wrote to her urging caution: 'I have not heard what Yeats thinks of the arrangement I proposed to you, so it is too soon to do anything yet' (*JMSCL* I. 151).

## *To Lady Gregory,* [*13 January 1906*]

CASTLE LEOD, | STRATHPEFFER, | N.B.

My dear Lady Gregory: I have been thinking over the situation. I dont like Synges solution at all.[1] It leaves us in their power & gives them a victory that will only make them the bitterer. This is the way we are circumstanced. We are like a band of men who have tried to divide & take different roads but have found that they must go togeather after all. It is essential that we get rid of bitterness. Colums idea of re-union wont work because it would lead to more fighting still. Not being able to fight them as I should like I now propose a scheme so generous that it will as I think help us with the public as well as in the long run bring back everybody we want. Let us ask them in the first instance to agree to reduce the old society to seven persons[2] nominated by Miss Horniman or you & kept togeather merely for reasons of the patent—a mere 'licensing' committee as it were. Let this committee give a written undertaking to pass all our rivals plays. Let us then say to them "Colum wants 'a popular theatre', we dont beleive it possible but we are willing that you try it under the most favourable circumstances. You have no endowment therefore we give you the £70 *minus* a nominal sum to keep the remnant of old society—in tecnical existance. You Being original members of that society we will urge Miss Horniman to grant you for one year the same rights as our selves on same terms. We will lend you costumes & give you share of those that once were property of old society. You are bound as we are to do your best to keep up artistic standard but are other wise free to do what plays you like. In any case we will not & cannot interfear. We must both ho[we]ver undertake not for one year to take actors from each other. At the end of year members of both companies shall be invited to choose. You must form a distinct society & we can decide on names for ours & yours that will not confuse the public (I would give them the word national if they wished). We are to publish statement in U I & "Nationist" as to this settlement." This arrangement will let them test their plan & that will be all to our advantage. They will get no plays and they will act badly & that & our good behaviour will please our audience. The difficulty will be Miss Horniman but I think I can talk her round in any case we can prove our *bona-fides* by a correspondence with her which we can

---

[1]  See previous letter.

[2]  The INTS initially consisted of seven members, the signatories to the original rules—W. G. Fay, P. J. Kelly, Frederick Ryan, Helen Laird, Maire Walker, James Starkey, F. J. Fay, and George Roberts. Of these, Kelly had been expelled in 1904, and Frederick Ryan was withdrawing from the dramatic movement in disgust at the recent quarrels, while the two Fays were now members of the new limited liability company.

show. Fay will not like it but you & I & Synge can get him round. We could not but for that paragraph in patent.[3] They do not know about that paragraph but even if they did this settlement is so logical that it cannot but end the dispute (unless they are only bluffing & really want "re-union" & in that case it will break them up.)

I feal very strongly that I am right. To fight was logical & it was not worth fighting unless we could fight strongly—To make peace is logical & it is not worth doing unless it is done strongly & completely. This is not change of point of view—facts have changed that is all. Please send this to Synge & if you agree urge it on him.[4] We can then go to Dublin for Boyles play, first summoning a meeting of old society & settle the whole thing which should be done in consultation with lawyers.

If they want 6$^d$ seats I should be prepared to join them in asking that of Miss Horniman—she would grant it.

I have just arrived here & write to catch post. Lady Cromartie is rolling a ball on the floor for her baby[5]

Yours alway

W B Yeats

ALS Berg.

## *John Synge to Whitney, Moore & Company,* [c. *15 January 1906*]

### Letter to W & Mo.

Gentlemen

Mr W. B. Yeats and Lady Gregory are out of Dublin at present for a week but they both join me[1] in asking if you would kindly give information on the following points in connection with the working of the National Theatre Society.

1st.   You are doubtless aware that the National Theatre Company Limited has been formed by certain members of the Irish National Theatre Society in the hope of carrying on the work in a more efficient way. A considerable

---

[3] See p. 308, n. 1.

[4] This was evidently done, for it forms the basis of the following letter from the Directors to Whitney, Moore & Co.

[5] Lady Cromartie's first son Roderick had been born on 24 Oct 1904, and she was to give birth to a second son later this year. In an edition of *Discoveries*, inscribed for James A. Healy in July 1938 (Stanford), WBY revealed that he had used her as the model for 'The Guitar Player' in that book.

[1] Although written by Synge, this is evidently the work of all three Directors, and sets out the questions raised by AG's discovery of the Patent's clauses dealing with the Reading Committee and the dissolution of the INTS. It also follows closely WBY's new strategy as outlined in the previous letter to AG.

number however of the other members of the I.N.T.S. however has decided
for various reasons [not] to take part in the new company. We are now
informed that these members are rehearsing one of the plays of the repertoire and intend to play in public as the Irish National Theatre Society. This
rehearsing and—performance if it takes place—break the Rule [on page]
seven of the Rules of I.N.T.S. which reads as follows[2]—as Mr. Fay, the
stage manager, was given no notice of the rehearsals and not consulted. Now
we wish to know if we decide that these performances will tend to do us
harm in any way [indecipherable] what steps could be taken to restrain them.
Would the breaking of rule seven enable us to get an injunction against them
for instance if we thought the matter sufficiently serious?

2nd.   We understand that the patent gives Lady Gregory power to carry
on a well-conducted theatre in the Abbey Theatre, quite independently of
the I.N.T.S. except in regard to foreign masterpieces—which it is stated
I believe, must be chosen by the reading committee of the I.N.T.S.[3] In the
newspaper version of the patent however a clause is given as follows—
After speaking of the I.N.T.S. it says the patent shall cease if the Nat T is
dissolved. Could you tell [us] if that clause is in the patent, and if so whether
the dissolution of the Irish National Theatre Society would endanger our
patent.[4]

3.   We are most anxious to leave the members of the I.N.T.S. who have
not joined the new company perfectly free to go on acting as they seem to
desire so long as they do not compromise us or endanger our patent. If I am
right in the reading of the patent with regard to foreign masterpieces do you
think it would be possible to draw up some agreement with the old
company which would guarantee our rights for the foreign [plays] and
the patent, and leave us—who are in New Company free to resign out of
the old and continue our work independently. Do you think the following
would put us in a safe position. If the Irish N.T.S. would sign agreement to
appoint a nominal sub-reading committee which would be empowered to
give us or any of Miss Horniman's tenants the necessary authorisation to
play any foreign masterpiece we decided to produce. Then if seven of the
members would further agree to keep the old I.N.T.S. in legal muster

---

[2] The rule in question (Appendix, pp. 895–6) was not copied into the draft letter, but stated that 'Any
acting member taking part in any performance other than those given by the Society, shall give notice of
such engagement to the Secretary, who shall submit same to the Committee, who shall decide whether or
not such performance is prejudicial to the interests of the Society. If, against the decision of the
Committee, any such acting member should take part in performances other than those given by the
society, the Committee shall have power to suspend any such person from membership until the matter
has been brought before a Special General Meeting of Members, whose decision shall be final.'

[3] In fact, the Patent makes no distinction between foreign and Irish plays: every play had to be passed
by the Reading Committee (see p. 309, n. 1 and Appendix, p. 903).

[4] For the clause in question (which did confirm that dissolution would end the Patent) see p. 309, n. 1.

during the serving of our present patent. Then all of us who are in the New company would resign out of the old and leave the members free to carry on their work their own way. A simpler way would of course be for the old members to form a new Society and leave old one to us with the patent, but it is feared they do not wish to adopt this course.

I shall be greatly obliged if you can let me have your opinion on these points. I believe Mr. Yeats will be back in Dublin shortly and then we wish to come to some understanding as the present state of things is unsatisfactory in many ways and confusing for the public.

Yours faithfully
J M Synge

Draft MS TCD. *JMSCL* 1, 153-4.

## To Padraic Colum, [*15 January 1906*]

C/o The Countess of Cromartie | Castle Leod, | Strathpeffer, N.B.

My dear Colum: I shall be in Dublin for Boyle's play & we can discuss things then. I simply dont know what your friends want. I made an offer to them at a general meeting which might have been a basis for discussion. They said nothing at all. I asked if they had anything to suggest. Dead silence. I asked if they had any complaints. Dead silence. Life cannot stand still & we have gone on with our work.[1]

Yr ev
W B Yeats

I have just re-read your letter.[2] Even if Lady Gregory & myself leave old society your friends will not be near a working majority—The Fays, Wright, & Miss Allgood are alone enough to stop that. Furthermore there is in the long run no worthy way to be popular except good plays. At the same time I am ready to consider anything you suggest provided it does not weaken discipline or delay the work in any way. Remember it is we who are in the strong position. We are quite ready for any reasonable concession but cannot conceed any thing that will make the work commoner or the discipline worse. My dear Colum in long run popular support is not got by concession to it, but by strength—by the quiet doing of ones work. Of the demagogue Ireland has

[1] This was at the General Meeting of the INTS held on 9 Oct 1905; see p. 200, n. 2.

[2] Colum had written to WBY from Ranelagh, Dublin, on 7 Jan (see below, pp. 317-18), urging him to reunite the INTS, and warning him that otherwise he and AG would be forced out of the Society. WBY was now using the letter as a pretext for making more accommodating overtures to the old Society.

enough. By the by I never advocated a 'free gallery' & the peoples theatre[3] I want must be one of all classes—peer & peasant if that be possible but certainly not one class, like the theatre of 'the National players'.[4]

ALS Berg.

## To Lady Gregory, [15 January 1906]

CASTLE LEOD, | STRATHPEFFER, | N.B.

My dear Lady Gregory: I send you a letter that I got from Colum some days ago. I have pointed out that the Fays & Miss Allgood & Wright are quite enough to keep his friends from getting a working majority (they would need twelve votes which they cant get). I have pointed out that we are in the strong position not his people—thank God they have no copy of that patent—that we will listen to any thing he suggests but cannot delay work or weaken dicipline.[1] I want that proposal about which I feal strongly to come, as it will seem from our strength. If we can lack the bitterness that holds them togeather & make all easy for them they will break up after a performance of Colum & Dierdre.[2] The very proposal will show how little

---

[3] In September 1903 WBY had toyed with the idea of instituting inexpensive INTS performances, modelled on Bruno Wille's Die Freie Volksbühne of Berlin, which provided theatre for working people who could not afford commercial prices. He suggested to Frank Fay (III. 432–3) 'that we give a special free performance of our most popular plays or at any rate of our most patriotic ones, and invite to this performance the members of the Dublin Working men's organization and also if it seems advisable to the society members of certain other clubs. I would charge no one for admission to these performances all seats would be by invitation. We might announce on the invitations that a plan would be laid before those present for the formation of a national Theatre, at very popular prices or a plan for a series of special performances at popular prices. One might use the word a People's Theatre in this case.' Colum, whose ideal was a people's theatre (see p. 306, n. 5), had been impressed with these plans.

[4] WBY presumably meant the urban lower middle class, from which at this time Sinn Fein drew most of its support. The National Players, more usually known as the Players' Club, had mounted occasional performances of plays by Ibsen and other realist dramatists of the middle classes, since the late 1890s. It produced *The Heather Field* and *A Doll's House* at the Queen's Theatre in June 1903, and Martyn's *An Enchanted Sea* in April 1904. From 1905 its programmes became more nationalist and Irish, and WBY and AG had attended its performances at the Cumann na nGaedheal Samhain Festival in 1905 (see pp. 222–3, n. 7). Its most recent productions, at the Molesworth Hall on 26 and 27 Dec 1905, had been dominated by revivals of undistinguished plays, mainly by Seumas MacManus, and included his farces *The Resurrection of Dinny O'Dowd* and *The Lad from Largymore* as well as two longer pieces by him, *The Leadin' Road to Donegal* and the *The Hard-Hearted Man*. Other familiar plays on the same bill were Fr. Peter O'Leary's *Tadg Saor* (see p. 224, n. 8), Rosa Mulholland's 'minature comedy' *Boycotting*, and Colum's one-act melodrama *The Saxon Shilling*. Maud Gonne had been elected president of the Society in November 1905, with Seumas MacManus, Edward Martyn, and Arthur Griffith as vice-presidents.

[1] See previous letter.

[2] It was supposed that the new company would begin with productions of Colum's *The Land* and AE's *Deirdre*.

we fear their 'popular theatre'. Re-Union is impossible, but it will keep Colum out of mischief to try it.

A lady in Edinburgh has given me a beautiful pendent made of enamel by M^rs Traquair.[3] I saw M^rs Traquair her self. She talked of the Dun Emer embroider & thought just as you do that it was not large & bold enough. She offered a design & said she would like to have my sister to stay with her presently to show her things & talk over the whole question. She likes the printing & Miss Gleesons work.[4]

My lectures were a great success—just like America—the people are more emotional than in England—the Academic people I mean.[5]

Yrs ever

W B Yeats

[3] Mrs Phoebe Anna Moss Traquair (1852–1936) was born in Dublin and trained at the Metropolitan School of Art there before marrying Dr Ramsay Heatley Traquair (1840–1912), Keeper of the Natural History Collection at the Royal Scottish Museum, in 1873 and moving to Edinburgh. She did a great deal of book illustration in a Pre-Raphaelite style, became a key figure in Patrick Geddes's Social Union, and in 1884 began mural work in Edinburgh, painting frescoes in the Children's Hospital, in St Mary's Cathedral, and in the Catholic Apostolic Church (now the Bellevue Reformed Baptist Church). Besides painting, she also worked in enamels, metal, embroidery, and bindings. WBY was to visit her studio on 16 June of this year. He was given the pendant by the Edinburgh-born medievalist and anthologist Grace Warrack (1855–1932). In sending it to him on 10 Jan 1906 (NLI), she explained that she would 'like this little enamel of Mrs Traquair's to go to the country that she comes from, and I should like it to be yours since you care for it', and added that she had 'put it inside a poor little old frame. . . . I thought that in a frame it would be most convenient for you & that it would make a little picture easy to take about if you liked.'

[4] The printing was done by ECY. Evelyn Gleeson (see p. 159, n. 2) had returned to Ireland from London in 1902 to establish the Morris-inspired Dun Emer Industries in Dundrum for the production of hand-woven carpets, tapestries, embroideries, and hand-printed books. She had a volatile temper, and relations between her and WBY's sisters were often strained, and in an undated letter to Rosa Butt (Bodleian) JBY described her as 'the always detested Miss Gleeson'. In September 1904 the enterprise was divided into two separate but connected co-operative societies, the Dun Emer Guild, under the control of Miss Gleeson, and Dun Emer Industries run by the Yeats sisters. The partnership was to break up in 1908, when ECY moved Dun Emer Industries from Runnymede House to Lacken Cottage, Churchtown. She later surrendered the name Dun Emer to Evelyn Gleeson and continued trading as Cuala Industries.

[5] WBY had lectured under the auspices of the Celtic Union on 'Irish Heroic Poetry' before 'a numerous company' in the Hall of the Philosophical Institution on 10 Jan. The *Scotsman* of 11 Jan (6) reported that WBY, 'chief of the younger school of Celtic poetry', had argued that Cuchulain and Finn were created by different races at different epochs. Of his lecture in Dundee on 11 Jan, the *Courier and Argus* (Dundee) reported (7) that WBY had brought 'the magical glamour of Erin' to 'the prosaic precincts of a college classroom. . . . Our guide through this fairy region was Mr. W. B. Yeats, the eager, idealistic young Irishman. . . . It is seldom, indeed, that Dundee, the practical and commercial, loses itself so utterly, as some hundreds of its citizens did last night, in listening to the inspired and inspiring utterances of Mr. Yeats.' The reporter noted that it was 'when Mr. Yeats begins to speak that one loses sight of the man in the poet—his eyes now soft, now flashing fire his musical voice, his whole being radiating enthusiasm and eagerness. . . . Indeed, one might just as soon attempt to chronicle the sparkle of a star or the changing cadence of a Beethoven symphony as to transcribe on paper the words we listened to last night.' On 13 Jan 1906, the *Aberdeen Daily Journal* (3) reported that in his lecture on 'Literature and the Living Voice' WBY had deplored the loss of popular culture and popular memory: 'If we had produced a political democracy we had lost the spiritual democracy to which the troubadours sang . . . just as in all the arts machine-made articles were driving out the old hand-made things, so it was with thoughts. . . . Music was the great popular art. Narrative, lyric, dramatic poetry, spoken to simple

It is important to have a good opening audience for Boyle—as the rumour of our quarrel will keep some away—Do you think you could get Harvey & Alibastair to help us.[6] Would it do for you to write to Moran & say it is a play after his own heart 'a Leader play' in fact.[7]

WBY—

[*With enclosure*]

30 Chelmsford Rd | Ranelagh
Sun 7|*1*|06

My dear Mr. Yeats,

I shall work with no one who does not work for the re-union of the Society. Have you considered what will happen if this re-union does not take place? Lady Gregory and yourself cease to be members in April. The

---

notes was the change Mr Yeats wished in art. He would like to set our poets writing plays and narrative poems. William Morris made the things in use in ordinary life beautiful, and now we require a movement for applied art in literature.' George H. Mair, an undergraduate at Aberdeen, who was on the platform, and who was later to become a useful supporter of the Abbey, wrote in the university magazine *Alma Mater* on 17 Jan: 'Mr. Yeats has come and gone: we are all enthusiasts for the "Celtic Revival" now.... the Debating Hall was crowded... to the back of the galleries by an audience which hung on the words of the Lecturer, and went away at the end feeling that they had... turned a corner on the highroad of culture, and found a new world open to their view.... It was no mere argument we were listening to, it was a rhapsody transcending argument, a declaration by a poet and an artist of the high dignity of his calling and its pre-eminence in the world.'

[6] The Revd Thomas Arnold Harvey (1878–1966) was educated at Trinity College, Dublin, and had spent a good deal of time at Coole in the late 1890s while acting as Robert Gregory's private tutor. He was ordained in the Church of Ireland in 1904 and was currently a curate of St Stephen's Church, Dublin. In 1908 he was appointed Rector of Lissadell, Sligo, and subsequently held parishes in Portrush and Booterstown, Dublin. He was to become Professor of Pastoral Theology at Trinity College, Dublin, 1929–34, served as Dean of St Patrick's Cathedral, Dublin, 1933–5, and was appointed Bishop of Cashel and Waterford from 1935 to 1958. He was a frequent visitor to the Abbey Theatre and was present at the opening performances of the winter season on 13 Oct this year.

Edward Percy Alabaster (b. 1870) was an assistant keeper at the Science and Art Museum, Kildare Street, from 1892 to 1908, and contributed chapters to the Museum's *General Guide to the Art Collections* on Japanese Lacquer (Dublin, 1905) and Ivories (Dublin, 1910). He was also a member of the committee of Hugh Lane's Gallery of Modern Art. P. L. Dickinson describes him in *The Dublin of Yesterday* (1929) as an amateur publicist: 'an eccentric and odd personality he stood out as a prominent figure in certain circles in Dublin life.... He held a position in the Irish National Museum... and was an authority on Japanese bronzes.... He wrote semi-serious letters to the papers on all sorts of subjects—mainly those dealing with ingenious methods to improve the amenities of life. Some were very sound, some hare-brained, all were clever' (70–1). There is no evidence that he did write to the press about Boyle's play, but Holloway records (NLI) that he was present at the first night.

[7] This was a canny move on WBY's part since the *Leader* devoted many column-inches every week to attacking the Irish party and other professed nationalists for hypocrisy and flunkeyism. Its editor, D. P. Moran, took the bait; he attended the first night of *The Eloquent Dempsy* on 20 Jan and it became one of his favourite plays. In a review in the *Leader* of 27 Jan, unsigned but evidently by him, he reported (382) that he could recommend the play to his readers, that it was 'a great advance on the same author's "Building Fund" ', and that it was certainly 'very entertaining and is well worth seeing'. Characteristically, the only fault he could find with it was Dempsy's self-awareness in his double-dealing: 'In our view

other people will have a working majority. They get the funds, they can elect new members and continue the work of the Society, getting popular support. You will be forced into more unpopular courses. As you are aware I am interested only in a people's theatre. I cannot go with anyone who would bring me into direct conflict with that ideal.

For the present I remain apart. The old Society, I understand, is rehearsing "the Land", but I have neither arranged a cast nor attended rehersal. I shall *not* withdraw the play. But I am not going with them. I shall work with no one unless on the basis of re-union.

The policy of the Society has been a long series of disappointments to me. I have seen it get further & further away from my ideal of a popular ideal. I voted for the resolution establishing it on a new basis because I thought that was the only way to avoid a split. I made application for a share because I thought the resolution legally carried. I have regret[ted] the vote & the application ever since. I remember how you once talked of a people's theatre, a free gallery &c. It was that more than anything else that made me study & work to be of use to the Society. Remember, you are definitely going against that ideal if you do not strive for a new arrangement. Dublin will not go to Miss Horniman's theatre when the facts become know[n]. None of us have standards for a country audience. None of us would write for an English audience. I will not write for twenty people in the stalls.

I would give all the plays I am thinking of—I would remain silent for years if we could work together. However, I shall not go with you into the wilderness. My mind is made up and nothing can move me now.

Yours
P Colum

ALS Berg, with envelope addressed to Coole, postmark 'STRATHPEFFER JA 15 06'.

the heart of the real comedy of Anglo-Irish urban life is the self-conscious *patriotism* of the humbugs and double-dealers, and not the self-conscious *double-dealing* of some patriots. You considerably distort the real comedy of Irish life when you put up the Mr. Dempseys [*sic*] as conscious hypocrites and double dealers. The cunning worldly wise Irish wobbler, convincing the people that he is a pure-souled patriot, and ever occupied . . . in the endeavour to keep himself in a state of being convinced of the same thing, is the heart of the comedy of Anglo-Irish public life. Possibly Mr. Boyle, in making his play less of a comedy, has made it more droll and amusing to the average audience.' Favourable extracts from this review were published in the programme when the play was produced in Wexford on 26 and 27 Feb this year.

# *To Lady Gregory, [18 January 1906]*

CASTLE LEOD, | STRATHPEFFER, | N.B.[1]
Thursday

Dear Lady Gregory: I shall get to Dublin on Saturday. I hope very much that you will be there—I want to see you very much & there is so much to settle that cannot be settled by letter. I now think that the words from the solicitor generals speach are not in the patent. That was a later composition but we must know definitely.[2] If they are not I dont think much concession is possible even if desirable. Both Fay & Miss Horniman will have to be consulted. We can still, if lucky get a committee in our own hands to pass foreign masterpeices probably in return for that £70 or part of it (if as I think they are all wrong in their notion of how they can capture the society) on that too I want legal opinion. If the passage is in patent then I am for what I proposed and nothing else. I will <have> nobody in your place,

---

[1] Castle Leod, a five-storey, L-shaped, turreted tower house, was built in red sandstone in 1606 by Sir Roderick ('Rorie') MacKenzie on the site of an earlier castle and ancient Pictish fort, and became the home of the earls of Cromarty (later Cromartie) and seat of the Clan MacKenzie; it was restored and expanded in the 19th century, and partially rebuilt in 1904. The Castle stands close to the small town of Strathpeffer, situated near the head of the Cromarty Firth, 11 miles north-west of Inverness in the north of Scotland, and a popular spa in the late Victorian and Edwardian periods, noted for its sulphur and peat baths.

[2] According to notes taken by R. N. Keohler, an assistant solicitor and brother of Thomas Keohler, the Solicitor General (J. H. Campbell KC), in hearing the application for the Abbey Patent on 4 Aug 1904, 'considered the appltion favourably but desired Counsel on both sides to see if they could not draft a clause which wd limit the Patent for the Special purpose for which Miss Horniman required it & safeguard the rights of the existing theatres'. The new restrictive clause was drafted by counsel on 5 Aug 1904, and put before the Solicitor General on 20 Aug in the library of Dublin Castle. Keohler, acting for Whitney and Moore, recorded the occasion in the office book (NLI):

> Suggested Restrictive Clause in full, accepted by Solicitor General on 20 Aug:
> 'The Patent shall only empower the Patentee to exhibit plays in the Irish or English language written by Irish writers or on Irish subjects, and such dramatic works of foreign authors as would tend to educate and interest the public of this country in the higher works of dramatic art, all the foregoing to be selected by the Irish National Theatre Society under the provisions of part 6 of its rules now existing and subject to the restrictions therein contained.
> Clause against assignment to any person or persons other than a trustee for Miss Horniman, her executors or administrators.
> Patent to cease if the (Irish National Theatre) Society is dissolved.
> No enlargement of the Theatre (so as to provide for a greater number of spectators than it is capable of holding at present).
> No Excise Licence to be applied for (or obtained)' On 20 August the Solicitor General delivered judgement stating he would recommend his Excellency to grant a Patent subject to the restrictions which he mentioned.

Contrary to WBY's recollection, these new clauses were incorporated into the Patent, and the proceedings were reported with varying degrees of accuracy in the *Daily Express* and in the *Irish Daily Independent* on 22 Aug 1904 (see p. 308, n. 1).

so far as I am concerned <as director &> I will resign if you do. As Patentee you must be a director & the objections to Colum are as great as ever.[3]

I start to morrow—there is no other guest here—there was one but she got tooth ache.[4] Lady Cromartie seems to me in perfectly good health now—the old nervous putting of her hand to her forhead gone & she seems full of energy. She has asked me to tell you this. I have done well at 'Bailes Strand' since I got here—I have at last got a grip of the thing—[5]

I suppose that speach is in the Theatre Book, perhaps you had better bring it if you come. I shall have so much to tell you.[6]

This is a most lovely place—an old castle with wooded hills all round & a ravens rock where there are still ravens. They got the habit the people say in the time when there were so many fights at it—it is at the head of a pass.[7]

　　　　　　　　　　　　　　　　　　　　　　　　Yr sy

　　　　　　　　　　　　　　　　　　　　　　　　W B Yeats

ALS Berg, with envelope addressed to Coole, redirected to Nassau Hotel, Dublin, and postmark 'STRATHPEFFER JA 18 06'.

## *Abbey Directors*[1] *to Thomas Keohler*, [c. *20 January 1906*]

I hear that some of those acting with you have an impression that they can get rid of Mr. Synge, Lady Gregory, and Mr. Yeats, and of those members of the old Society who are playing for the new by an ingenious application of the rules. Messrs. Whitney & Moore and the Registrar have both been consulted by us on this question. We understand that some of those who are opposed to us are under the impression that they can suspend

[3] On 16 Jan AG wrote (Berg) that she had written to JBY and Colum with proposals for negotiation, one of which being that she 'offered to resign my Directorship in favour of anyone chosen by the other side, and accepted by my co-Directors'.

[4] The guest who got toothache is unidentified.

[5] The revisions to *On Baile's Strand* were continuing (see p. 240, 251–2). Lady Cromartie had been at Coole the previous summer, when her nervous behaviour had evidently alarmed AG.

[6] i.e. 'The Play, the Player, and the Scene', a speech given by WBY on 8 Oct 1903 at the opening of the INTS autumn season, and which AEFH regarded as the manifesto for the Abbey Theatre (see p. 15, n. 3).

[7] Castle Leod is situated on a small green hill, in an extensive estate wooded with ancient chestnut, hazel, and Wellington trees. Raven's Rock, at Achterneed above Strathpeffer, provides a dramatic panorama of the scenic transformation as the lowlands rise into the highlands: on one side are green plains and grazing fields that stretch to the Cromarty Firth; on the other, lochs, hills, and the rich woodlands of a rocky landscape. WBY would also have been attracted by the Gaelic and Norse folklore that inform local stories about Raven's Rock: here was to be found physical prowess, victory in battle, second sight, and the gift of prophecy. An old Gaelic curse, 'a raven's death to you', derived from the belief that the young birds killed their parents on Easter Day, and it was from the captured King of the Ravens that the Gaels first learned the secret of 'mouth music' played at their annual festival on Raven's Rock.

[1] Although initialled by AG, this is a joint letter from the Abbey Directors, as the use of plural pronouns indicates.

our players under rule 5, section K.[2] We are advised by our lawyers that Mr. Yeats will be entirely right in quashing any decision of the kind, on the ground that rule 5 section K must be taken in connection with rule 3 section H.[3] The word acting member in the first mentioned rule, which occurs nowhere else, must also be taken as signifying a distinction between those actually engaged in playing for the Society and its ordinary members.[4] Mr. Yeats' decision upon this question would be final. The rules are vague in their expression; but the most natural construction to put on them is that rule 5 section K defines the punishment for rule 3 section H which by its very nature implies the power to punish. It is no more possible for those in opposition to us to get rid of their President and Vice Presidents. The plan is, we understand, to declare that they are no longer members of the Society when the impossibility of their getting a three-fourth majority in April shall have made their election as impossible as the election of anybody else. It is considered that they are only ex officio members of the Society and that they would cease from it on ceasing from office. We have taken legal opinion upon this point and find that Presidents or Vice Presidents remain in office until the appointment of their successors.[5] We should, if necessary, be prepared to test this question in a Court of Law, as we consider ourselves bound to take every step necessary to preserve Miss Horniman's patent in the hands for which she intended it.

AG

TLS Harvard.

[2] This rule (see p. 313, n. 2) forbade acting members of the Society from performing with other companies without formal notice and the express permission of the Committee. Breaches of the rule resulted in immediate suspension and the strong possibility of expulsion at a General Meeting called specifically to adjudicate on the infraction. It was under this rule that P. J. Kelly had been expelled from the Society in April 1904 (see III. 568), and that the Fays were to be ousted in March 1908 after leaving the Abbey earlier that year.

[3] Rule 3 (h) read: 'The Committee shall have power to give a retaining fee to any member or actor if it seems desirable. If a retaining fee is given to a member he or she shall engage on his or her part not to act in any play not produced by the Society during the period for which the retaining fee is given, without the permission of the Committee.'

[4] This distinction is less clear in the 1903 constitution than it is in AE's revision of the rules in 1905 (see pp. 153–4, 169–70).

[5] According to the rules, the president, vice-presidents, and secretary were ex officio members of the Society. Other members (apart from the seven founders) had to be elected by a three-quarters majority at a meeting called for the purpose. A member could be expelled only by the vote of two-thirds of the members present at a Special General Meeting, if due notice had been given in writing. The present split in the Society was such that neither faction could muster a two-thirds majority.

## *To Sydney Cockerell, 22 January 1906*

Abbey Theatre
Jan 22nd, 1906

My dear Cockerell, Thank you ever so much for the promise of that book, which I am most curious about. I have heard about it from Lady Gregory; but I have not seen it. I should very much like to have it while I am here, as I have very little to read.[1] I have always felt that Byron was one of the great problems, the great mysteries—a first-rate man, who was somehow not first-rate when he wrote. And yet the very fascination of him grows from the same root with his faults. One feels that he is a man of action made writer by accident, and that, in an age when great style was the habit of his class, he might have been one of the greatest of all writers. His disaster was that he lived in an age when great style could only be bought by the giving up of everything else.[2]

Yours ever
W B Yeats

Text from Wade, 467.

[1] Cockerell had offered to send *Astarte; a fragment of truth concerning George Gordon Byron, sixth lord Byron, recorded by his grandson, Ralph Milbanke, earl of Lovelace,* privately published by the Chiswick Press in December 1905. Ralph Gordon Noel Milbanke, 2nd Earl of Lovelace (1839–1906), had written the book to vindicate his grandmother Lady Byron from aspersions of hypocrisy and treachery, and to set the record straight on Byron's incestuous relationship with his half-sister Augusta Leigh (whom Byron had named Astarte in his poetic play *Manfred*), which precipitated the break-up of the Byrons' marriage. Lovelace, the brother of Lady Anne Blunt, was a friend of AG, and had discussed the preparation of the book with her as early as March 1897 (Pethica, 135). It had originally been intended for publication by John Murray, but Lovelace withdrew it as he 'didn't want to publish scandal at all — Murray thought the public wd be disappointed if there were none . . . & Lord L. doesn't want all to be published, at least during his lifetime' (Pethica, 303). AG had written to WBY on 29 Dec 1905 (Berg) that she had just got Lord Lovelace's book and thought 'he is right to have set the question at rest. It seems to have been an extraordinary passion—he thinks that if A. Leigh had gone away and lived openly with him, Byron might have been an almost normal character, and perhaps never have written poetry. . . . It is beautifully printed at the Chiswick Press—it "has been formally published and a few copies have been sold, but the greater number of a strictly limited impression are not intended for the market." I see at the end of the book Lord Lovelace takes a brief for Paganism versus Christianity — the old world against the new. You must meet him some time.' Since so few copies were for sale the book was difficult to acquire, but Cockerell had close contacts in the Chiswick Press through his association with William Morris and the Kelmscott Press (see p. 129).

[2] WBY, who had purchased the *Selected Letters and Journals* of Lord Byron (1886) in Dublin in 1887 (*YL*, 323), spent some time in trying to pluck the heart out of this mystery (see *UP* 1. 270–1 and *Mem*, 203), finally suggesting in *A Vision* that, as a man of Phase Nineteen, Byron may have been 'torn in two' by a desire for Unity of Being which he knew in his case was impossible, and a compensatory escape into wilful but fragmentary self-dramatization. While this self-dramatization may 'have great permanent value as the expression of an exciting personality', it may also, out of phase, become 'tyrannical and capricious'. In or out of phase, however, such a man 'is doomed to attempt the destruction of all that

## To Holbrook Jackson, 22 January [1906]

THE NATIONAL THEATRE SOCIETY, LIMITED,
| ABBEY THEATRE, DUBLIN.
22nd January 1905

Dear Mr. Jackson,

Your notes followed me to Scotland, where I was lecturing. I thought each day I could reply; but could not until it was too late. (Your last note however was not sent on to me in time to have done anything with it). Just when I was about to settle the date, I got a letter from Dublin, telling me about a complicated legal difficulty in connection with the theatre. I thought every day would clear this up; but it remained until this very day when I saw our lawyers. I am very sorry that for some time it looked as if it might have been quite impossible for me to settle any date outside Dublin for weeks to come. I am not quite through the trouble; but am almost so. You will probably not care to arrange anything for so uncertain a person; but on the chance that it may be still possible, if not for February, for early March, I will write to you in a few days. I am sorry to have given you so much trouble uselessly.[1]

Yr ever
W B Yeats

TLS Colgate.

## To the Editor of the Daily Express (Dublin), [23 January 1906]

Dublin, January, 1906.

SIR—We beg to inform you that, in accordance with a desire which has been generally expressed amongst those interested in the Gallery of Modern Art, a small Committee, consisting of the undersigned members, has been formed for the purpose of arranging for a presentation to Mr. Hugh P. Lane, the Honorary Secretary of that Gallery.[1]

breaks or encumbers personality, but this personality is conceived of as a fragmentary, momentary intensity', and his fate is 'enforced failure of action', although 'many at this phase desire action above all things as a means of expression' (*AVB*, 147–51).

[1] In fact WBY's and FF's lecture did take place, as did the Abbey tour to Leeds (see pp. 229, n. 2, 235, n. 1).

[1] The Committee was to commission a portrait of Hugh Lane from the American-born painter John Singer Sargent, and this was presented to Lane in January 1907.

We believe that some public acknowledgement of Mr. Lane's services in the cause of modern art should be made, and that suitable recognition should be shown, not merely of his indefatigable and disinterested labours in the face of much opposition and criticism, as Secretary of the proposed Gallery of Modern Art, but also of the resource and energy he has displayed in connection with the promotion and organisation of the various Art Exhibitions which have taken place during the last three years in Dublin.[2] It will, we think, be generally admitted that the increasing interest in, and the better knowledge of art which is now being evinced in this country, is largely due to Mr. Lane's spirited action and efforts.

Should any of your readers desire to associate themselves with us in making this presentation they should communicate with Dermod C. Trench, Esq., 22 Lincoln place, Dublin, to whom subscriptions may be sent.[3] A considerable number of subscriptions, ranging from one shilling to £10, have already been promised.—Yours etc.,

DROGHEDA,[4] MAYO,[5] W. HUTCHESON POE,[6]
GEO. W. RUSSELL, W. B. YEATS.[7]

Printed letter, *Daily Express* (Dublin), 23 January 1906 (6). This letter was also published in the *Irish Times* (8) and the *Freeman's Journal* (9) on the same day.[7]

[2] As part of his campaign to establish a gallery dedicated to modern art in Dublin, Lane had organized an exhibition of Old Masters in Dublin in 1902, a well-attended exhibition of Irish artists in the London Guildhall from 30 May to 23 July 1904 (see III. 564), and a Loan Exhibition of Modern Art, based on the Staats Forbes-Collection, in Dublin from 21 Nov 1904 to March 1905.

[3] Samuel Richard Chevenix Trench (1881–1909), was educated at Balliol College, Oxford, where he met Oliver Gogarty. He became a fervent Gaelic Leaguer, taking the name Dermod by deed poll in 1905. He was now working for the Irish cause with Horace Plunkett in the IAOS, which at this time had offices at 22 Lincoln Place, near the back gate of Trinity College. In 1904 he had shared the Martello tower at Sandycove with Gogarty and James Joyce, who portrays him in *Ulysses* as the troubled Englishman and Gaelic enthusiast Haines. He committed suicide at the age of twenty-seven.

[4] Ponsonby William Moore, 9th Earl of Drogheda (1846–1908), had been a civil servant, and succeeded to the title after his cousin's death in 1892.

[5] Dermot Robert Wyndham Bourke, 7th Earl of Mayo (1851–1927), had succeeded his father in 1872 and took an active interest in the agricultural and industrial welfare of Ireland, as well as in the development of Irish art.

[6] Lieutenant-Colonel Sir William Hutcheson Poe (1848–1934) was born in Co. Down and joined the Royal Marine Light Infantry in 1867. He had a distinguished military career, before wounds received at the Battle of Metemmah in 1885 led to the amputation of his right leg. He subsequently served as a member of Naval Intelligence, before retiring from the services in 1888. An extensive landowner in Co. Tyrone, he stood unsuccessfully as Unionist candidate for the Ossory Division of Queen's Co. in 1895, having served as High Sheriff of Queen's Co. in 1891 and of Co. Tyrone in 1893. He was a member of the Irish Land Conference held in Dublin in 1902 on the initiative of AG's nephew Captain John Shaw-Taylor, and he became a governor of the National Gallery of Ireland in 1904. In 1912 he was created 1st Baronet and served as a Senator of the Irish Free State from 1922 to 1925.

[7] In the version of this circular published in the *Freeman's Journal* WBY's name appeared as 'J. B. Yeats'.

## *To Joseph Holloway,*[1] *23 January 1906*

Nassau Hotel
Tuesday | Jan. 23 1906.

Dear M[r] Holloway: I would be very much obliged if you could come & see me at the Abbey Theatre to-night, or to-morrow night. The cold last night was frightful & yet I hear the fires were lighted very early[2]—I find to[o] that owing to structural change involved in the work next door the protecting bar has been taken from that trap door.[3] Some temporary protection is essential. I dont know what is to be done about the cold but I would like to have a talk over it.

Yr sny
W B Yeats

ALS NLI.

[1] Joseph Holloway (1861–1944) was born in Camden Street, the son of a master-baker, and studied at the Dublin School of Art before becoming an architect. He designed and oversaw the conversion of the Mechanics' Institute into the Abbey Theatre in 1904, and was consulted on all subsequent alterations and developments. He was a dedicated theatregoer, and his diaries and scrapbooks are an invaluable source for the history of modern drama in Ireland.

[2] Holloway probably saw WBY on this evening, when he attended the Abbey's current production of *The Eloquent Dempsy* and *Riders to the Sea* for the second time. The problem with the fires persisted (see below, p. 801).

[3] Improvements and enlargements to the Abbey Theatre continued over several years. On 18 Nov 1905 AEFH had purchased the house next to the Theatre in Abbey Street, and work was in progress on building a green room in its yard, at the total cost of £1,250 (see p. 119, n. 8). On 19 Dec 1905 she had written to Holloway (NLI) to say that she was glad to hear that work on Abbey was going well, and reported that 'Mr. Fay wants something, done in regard to bringing the musicians into the theatre from behind the scenes. Please try and manage this somehow.' On this very day she had written to tell him (NLI) that it might be necessary to enlarge the Theatre further, and asking him what was needed. She said that the leading lady must have a room for herself, and enquired about the cost and suitability of the adjoining stable for this purpose. On 9 May of this year Holloway commented in his diary (NLI) that WBY 'seems to reside in the theatre since the additions were completed', and on 27 Jan he made the following sketch of WBY's chagrin at the popular success of the despised *Eloquent Dempsy* by Holloway's great friend William Boyle.

"The Eloquent Dempsy"
amuses the pit.
Expression is everything.

W B Yeats
Abbey Theatre
Sat. Jan 27. 1906.        Dublin

## To Holbrook Jackson, [c. 25 January 1906]

THE NATIONAL THEATRE SOCIETY, LIMITED,
| ABBEY THEATRE, DUBLIN.

Dear M^r Jackson: your last note saying that the dates were still open has hunted me from London, to Scotland from that to the West of Ireland & then here.[1] I am still rather in a difficulty here—a few days may set things right or it may not.[2] I can however definitely undertake to lecture on any date in March before the 20th that you may pitch upon. How much do you think we would be likely to take? I suppose I should send some rough estimate to Miss Farr & ask her if she will come. I accept for myself of course in any case. I am sorry to give you so much trouble, but if March will suit you I will keep whatever arrangement you make for me.[3]

Yours sny
W B Yeats

ALS Colgate.

[1] Untraced.      [2] See p. 323.
[3] Jackson passed this letter on to A. R. Orage (1873–1934), co-chairman with him of the Leeds Arts Club, who responded, 'I saw Crowther: & fixed up *definitely* the date, *Wednesday, March 14th*. So unless you know any just cause or impediment, you can write Yeats at once.' WBY and FF lectured on 'Literature and the Living Voice' in Leeds on 14 Mar (see p. 235, n. 1).

## To Florence Farr, [c. 25 January 1906]

Nassau Hotel, | South Frederick St. | Dublin.

My dear Florence Emery: thank you for your hint about the theatre—I will never mention it again.[1] There is by the way a pretty scandal about—but I forgot I am not to speak of it. I want to see *Lady Inger* at Stage Society but though I should see it at any cost I have not enough resolution to go over as I must return at once. If you can give me Tuesday morning afternoon or evening, or at worst Wednesday morning or afternoon or both I will come over on Monday see the play and return after having had a little of your company.[2] I have to be here for a week or so after that as—but I forgot I have sworn. I have written to the Leeds man (from whom I heard) again[3] asking for a date for us both in March and to know how much we can expect. I shall also write to Edinburgh where I go for two more lectures in March—or rather one there one at St. Andrews—and see if you can come.[4] I want to see you very much now and it will always be a great pleasure to be with you. I have such a fine book to show you. Lord Lovelace's privately printed book about Byron and Mrs. Leigh, his half sister.[5] A very vivid

---

[1] FF, in letters now lost, had evidently complained of WBY's preoccupation with theatre business. Their affair finally ended because 'she got bored' (see p. 114, n. 3).

[2] The five-act historical drama *Lady Inger of Östrat* (1857) was one of the few Ibsen plays of which WBY approved and he had sent Padraic Colum a copy of it in January 1903 (see III. 293). The Stage Society production at the Scala Theatre, Charlotte Street, took place on 28 and 29 Jan, but was, according to the *Stage* of 1 Feb, something less than a palpable hit: 'One cannot imagine what possessed the authorities of the Incorporated Stage Society, who have so much excellent material at their disposal, to select for performance such a dull, lugubrious, depressing, tedious, antiquated play' (16–17). The *Pall Mall Gazette* of 30 Jan took a more charitable view (2): 'this early melodrama, now more than half a century old, is not trotted out without an apology.... The play is certainly no masterpiece, but it is just the sort of thing that a workmanlike house-dramatist would nail together for popular audiences.... There was a very large audience, which was doubtless interested in this raking up of Ibsen's "past".' Although WBY is not reported as attending any of the performances, he may have seen one of them: on 13 Feb he informed Bullen that he had recently had to go to London and back 'two or three times' (see below, p. 338).

[3] i.e. Holbrook Jackson; see previous letter.

[4] These proposed lectures in Edinburgh and St Andrews did not take place.

[5] i.e. *Astarte*; see p. 322. Augusta Leigh (1783–1851) was Byron's half-sister and five years his senior; he met her while a schoolboy and they became close friends. He saw less of her after her marriage to her cousin Colonel George Leigh, but they remet in 1813 and even planned to elope together; it is possible that he was the father of her daughter Meldora, born in April 1814. Augusta, troubled by the relationship, advised him to marry Annabella Milbanke (1792–1860) and persuaded him not to break the engagement off when he wished to do so. Although very different in temperament and outlook, Byron married Annabella on 1 Jan 1815 but the new bride's suspicions were aroused by his familiarity with his half-sister when they went to stay with Augusta that March and, following his increasingly erratic behaviour after the birth of their daughter in December of that year, she left him on 15 Jan 1816. She drew up a list of her husband's offences, but did not mention his affair with Augusta, with whom she was still corresponding, but in February 1816, fearing that he might claim custody of their child, told her lawyer of the incest, and gossip about it circulated in London society. Byron's friends professed to be baffled by the reasons for the separation, and his first and influential biographer, the Irish poet

powerful book and not to be bought. I have been sent a copy and will bring it over. You cannot think what a pleasure it is to be fond of somebody to whom I can talk—as a rule any sort of affection annihilates conversation, strikes one with a silence like that of Adam before he had even named the beasts. To be moved and talkative, unrestrained, one's own self, and to be this not because one has created some absurd delusion that it all is wisdom, as Adam may have in the beast's head, but not in Eve, but because one has found an equal, this is the best of life. All this means that I am looking forward to seeing you—that my spirits rise at the thought of it.[6]

Synge—but I forget he is a part of what I have sworn off—well I cannot help it. His play was done in Germany in association with a play in one act by Wilde called I think *Florentine Nights*.[7] I don't think it has been even published in England. Why not get it and play it at your new theatre.[8]

Do help me to get over to the play. I won't go if you are not kind.

Yours ever
W B Yeats

Text from Bax, 53–4. Wade, 467–8.

Thomas Moore (see p. 38, n. 3), suggested that it might have been nothing more than 'some dimly hinted confession of undefined horrors, which, though intended by the relater but to mystify and surprise, the hearer so little understood him as to take in sober seriousness' (*Letters and Journals of Lord Byron* [1830], II. 791). Publicly, Lady Byron kept silent about the affair (a point stressed to her credit in *Astarte*), although privately she seems to have discussed it with a number of people, including Harriet Beecher Stowe, who gave a garbled version of it in her *Lady Byron Vindicated* (1870). Lovelace's intention in writing *Astarte* was to present an accurate and documented account of the episode and by so doing refute earlier claims that his grandmother's behaviour had been arbitrary and vindictive. He himself took a broad view of the incest: 'Men need not be forbidden to think that the love of sister for brother is infallibly pure and sexless; it is often wise and just not to search for undiscovered sins; but it is neither noble nor even expedient to fabricate false righteousness' (33).

[6] See Gen. 18–22. WBY was to use the same allusion, amplified, as a central theme in his address to the British Association on 4 May 1908 (*Expl*, 241–3). WBY's long friendship with FF had developed into a sexual relationship (see p. 112).

[7] Max Meyerfeld (see p. 108, n. 2) had translated Synge's *The Well of the Saints* as *Der Heilige Brunnen* for production with Oscar Wilde's *A Florentine Tragedy* at Max Reinhardt's Deutsches Theater in Berlin. The first performance was on 13 Jan 1906, but as Meyerfeld later recalled (*Yale Review*, July 1924, p. 690) it 'had no success at all. After some six or seven performances . . . it was withdrawn'. He wrote to Synge on 13 Jan 1906 (TCD): 'Just a line to tell you that the Well of Saints was not a great success, but some of the papers are full of compliments for you. I'll send you a few cuttings in a day or two.' This he did, and on 26 Jan Synge sent translations of them to AG (*JMSCL* I. 156–7): 'The German cuttings are hard to make anything out of their style seems so outrageous in translation.' WBY had perhaps confused the name of Wilde's play (which was produced on 16 Jan) with *Florentine Nights*, the title under which S. A. Stern had translated Heinrich Heine's *Florentinische Nächte* in 1873.

[8] In December 1905 FF, Sturge Moore, Ricketts, Shannon, Binyon, W. A. Pye, and Gwendolyn Bishop revived the Literary Theatre Club as the Literary Theatre Society, Ltd. (see III. 722–3, 724). The first production by the new Company was Sturge Moore's *Aphrodite against Artemis* on 1 Apr of this year; it did not stage *The Well of the Saints*, but in June 1906 gave two performances of *A Florentine Tragedy* with *Salome*. In 1907 the Company merged with the Stage Society.

## To Maud Gonne, [late January 1906]

Mention in letter from MG, 15 February [1906].
Asking for news about the progress of her divorce proceedings,[1] and telling her that he is unpopular in Ireland,[2] but that he is content with a small, discriminating audience.

G–YL, 224–5.


## Lady Gregory[1] to Thomas Keohler, 30 January [1906]

ABBEY THEATRE, DUBLIN
Jan 30

Dear Mr. Keohler

In reply to your letter of 28th January,[2] containing draft agreement, the three main points are: (1) Use of Theatre; (2) Proposed division of the funds, costumes etc., (3) The preservation of Miss Horniman's rights in the Patent.

Now, as to use of Theatre. If you will refer to Miss Horniman's letter to Mr. Yeats, published in Samhain 1904, offering the Theatre, you will find that she says in the opening paragraph "I have a great sympathy with the artistic and dramatic aims of The Irish National Theatre Company, as publicly explained by you on various occasions. I am glad to be able to offer you my assistance in your endeavours to establish a permanent Theatre in Dublin". This makes it entirely plain that the Theatre was given to carry out Mr. Yeats' dramatic projects. No one not acting in

---

[1] MG did not answer this letter until 15 Feb, as she wanted to wait until she 'had some news of my affairs — The date is at last settled for the final trial — the 28th of this month. It is likely that Major MacBride's lawyers will obtain a week or a fortnight's delay, as delay has been all along their tactics but this will be the limit of delay now possible I think — I shall not have to be present at this trial — & if it were not for my anxiety lest Labori will, to satisfy his client's desire for vengence, drag Iseult's name into it I should be fairly indifferent.'

[2] 'Why are you rejoicing in unpopularity?' MG asked. 'I know our people are full of prejudices many of which get on one's nerves & hinder work greatly, but many of these prejudices, wrong in themselves, spring from a good source & their intensity show a capacity for feeling & action which is hopeful.... Why I am sorry, if what you say about unpopularity is true, is that the people who *need* your movement & the theatre will not benefit by it. The National Theatre *ought* to be *crowded* & it *might be* but we can talk of all this better than write of it.'

[1] This letter was signed by AG but written on behalf of the three Directors of the National Theatre Society Limited. Presumably she had been asked to sign it as the most diplomatic and socially distinguished of the Directors.

[2] This letter has not been traced.

association with him, least of all any one who is in revolt against those projects, has any moral right to expect the Theatre free.[3] The Directors, however, are prepared to advise her to permit those in association with you to hire the Theatre, provided we can come to an agreement upon other points. They are not prepared to ask her to grant the Theatre free, and they are confident that she would not do so, under any circumstances likely to arise.

Now, as to the distinction of money, clothes etc. In strict ethics, we do not consider that the share falling to those in whose interest you write would be large. There is a sum of about £70 or £80 standing to the credit of The Irish National Theatre Society, and there are debts against it of about £20. We are not sure of the exact sum in either case. The accounts are in Mr. Roberts' hands, who is acting with you, not in ours;[4] the first sum is probably greater than we say. Upon the other hand, the Society would have been bankrupt but for a sum of £50 given to Mr Yeats by an American friend to be used as he thought fit for the advantage of the movement.[5] This sum was not given to the Society but given to him, and the Society would have been under great difficulties, if a considerable portion of the money had not been expended in paying Mr Roberts for his work as Secretary.[6] Other portions of the money were spent on posters, costumes etc. Another sum of £45 was paid by Mr Yeats and Lady Gregory, one giving £20 and one giving £25, towards the payment of the Stage Manager, the use of whose entire time was found necessary for the work of the Society in the Abbey Theatre.[7] In addition to these sums, Lady Gregory paid for a good many of the costumes, besides those of her own plays, and Miss Horniman

---

[3] For AEFH's letter see III. 572–3, 596. The seceders put a very different construction on this letter and in their reply (NLI) maintained that AEFH's 'words, to anyone taking them in their most palpable construction, and to us who believed, as we did at the time, that our President was acting not in his own interests, but in those of the society, would have but one meaning viz that the theatre was given, *not to Mr. Yeats, but to the society for which he stood.* Your interpretation of Miss Horniman's words, as conveyed in the surprising sentence which follows is one which you will find it very difficult to make any unprejudiced person accept.... We may tell you frankly that had we known at that time that such was the meaning, that instead of giving the theatre to the I.N.T.S., Miss Horniman gave it to one member "to carry out Mr. Yeats's dramatic projects"—we would most certainly have refused the offer.'

[4] Many of these accounts, relating to the period from 1904 to 1905 when Roberts was secretary of the INTS, are now at Harvard.

[5] On 12 Apr 1903 Quinn had written to WBY (NYPL) that he would 'be very glad to pledge £20 a year for the theatre if you will let me'. He went on to say that he hoped to persuade another friend to put up another £20 per annum, '& perhaps between us we can get a third person to add the remaining ten' to make it up to the £50 W. G. Fay thought necessary to the continuation of the Theatre. In the end Quinn had made a one-off contribution of £50.

[6] George Roberts received £1 a week as secretary of the INTS.

[7] AG's and WBY's subvention enabled W. G. Fay to give up his job as an electrician to become full-time stage manager at the Abbey shortly after the purchase of the premises. The arrangement was put on a more permanent footing when AEFH agreed to meet the costs of paying key members of the Company (see pp. 119, 120).

for others.[8] The actual amount of money carried into the Abbey Theatre was extremely small, and certainly would not have kept the Society from bankruptcy without the £95 paid by Mr Yeats American friend, Mr Yeats and Lady Gregory. And the amount of money made in the Theatre would have been much smaller or would have been nothing if Miss Horniman had charged a rent, or if the performances had to be given with the old disadvantages; nor could the Society have made any of this money under any circumstances without the work of the Dramatic Authors, the majority of whom are now acting with The National Theatre Society, Ltd., and none of whom are, as far as we know, acting with those who desire the distribution of the money. We are however prepared to grant a generous share of it to those acting with you. Our proposal is that all debts incurred by The Irish National Theatre Society, up to the formation of The National Theatre Society, Limited, be first paid, and that the fund then remaining shall be divided in proportions to be agreed on hereafter. It has been suggested, for instance, that if two-thirds of the members decide on a particular course, they may, on their resignation from the Society, have two-thirds of the money, each receiving his share individually. The exact form in which this is given may have to be submitted to the Registrar; but this is only a technical point. This seems about the most reasonable way of working. We certainly do not consider it strictly just, but we are not anxious to press that point. If we get the main points agreed upon, we can discuss in detail the distribution of costumes, properties etc.

We are sure that you are as determined as we are that no damage shall be done to Miss Horniman's right under the Patent.[9] She has behaved with great generosity, and no one, whether they agree with her or not, desires to put her to further expense. Some months ago, we were advised by Messrs. Whitney & Moore that it was absolutely essential to preserve the old Society in legal existence, and that the proper way of doing this was to reduce it to a nominal membership. It will then become a very small body, existing exclusively for the formalities made necessary by the nature of the Patent. The resignation of those not working in association with us from active membership is therefore the first essential, and we do not see our way to consider any proposals that do not contain it.[10] We do not consider that

---

[8] AG's expenses were for the costumes for *Kincora* and *The White Cockade*, and AEFH's for dressing *The King's Threshold* and *On Baile's Strand*. See p. 196.

[9] See pp. 308–10.

[10] In their reply (see above) the seceders were, or purported to be, affronted by the suggestion that they should resign: 'Your demand, or proposal, that we the members of the I.N.T.S. who have been all through—and still are—loyal to the original objects of that society, should resign our membership, in order that a few people may for private interest take to themselves the advantages of a society which we, and we *only*, have preserved in its original form, is simply an outrage, and under no circumstances

proxy voting would be in any way a sufficient protection of Miss Horniman's rights. We are of course prepared to undertake to make no use of the name of the Society, except for the formalities of the Patent. Should those working with you desire to keep a nominal connection with the old Society, they can become Honorary Members.

The formation of The National Theatre Society, Limited, was, let me remind you, a necessity, as the monetary responsibility was too heavy a burden for us to continue under. Under the old Society, those of us who had private means of any kind, were liable for all we possessed, and it was impossible to go on in that way, when the business of the Society was growing into larger proportions. Every other change followed logically from this first one, and there is recorded in the books of the old Society a vote showing that about two thirds of the members voting were at the time in favour of the formation of such a Company, and that all the members of the old Society were offered fully paid up shares in the new Company.[11]

To summarize therefore, we offer to urge Miss Horniman to permit you the hire of the Theatre upon the ordinary terms; to grant you a fair proportion of the funds of the old Society; you upon your part agreeing to resign from the old Society or to become Honorary Members. We consider this last essential to the safety of the Patent, and for the avoidance of future disputes.

May I ask you to kindly let me know who you are acting for? I do not know how many of the members of the old Society, who have not joined the new Company, have joined in making these demands.[12]

Believe me yours sincerely

Augusta Gregory

P.S. Since writing above, I have had a letter from Miss Horniman in which she mentions that she had already informed Mr Colm that

---

whatever will we forego what we have for so long striven to keep in existence. It is, believe us, with the utmost regret we now find that our trust was utterly misplaced. We worked, and without remuneration of any kind, let us remind you, with the idea that we were carrying out the objects of our society. We now find that we have been simply used to forward the interests of one man.'

[11] In fact the resolution to form the National Theatre Society Ltd. at the General Meeting of 22 Sept 1905 (see p. 187) was passed with fourteen in favour and only one against.

[12] The reply was signed by Honor Lavelle (Helen Laird), Frank Walker, Emma Vernon (Vera Esposito), Seumas O'Sullivan (James Starkey), Maire Garvey, and George Roberts. Apart from their absolute refusal to agree to resignation, the reply was strong on outrage but short on practical suggestions.

those acting against Mr Yeats would not be allowed to use the Abbey Theatre "because I had made that Theatre for the purpose of carrying out Mr Yeats' published ideas. Mr Fay has a letter to be given to Cramer in case of necessity."[13]

TLS Roberts Papers, Harvard, and TS copy NLI. Marked '*Important*' in another hand.

## *To Holbrook Jackson, 31 January 1906*

Nassau Hotel, | S. Frederick St., | Dublin
31/1/'06.

Dear Mr. Jackson/

A great many thanks for your letter which I have sent on to Florence Farr.[1]

If I am going alone then we can share profits and arrange the proportion presently, but if, as I hope and believe, she is coming with me, would it be too much to ask you to let us have the whole profits? I am going to Leeds partly to make things straight for my Theatre,[2] but she has no such object. When we went to Manchester we had a great meeting. Then, I think, we shared with some local club, but I doubt if your audience will be so large.[3] I feel bound to get as good terms for her as I can.

---

[13] For AEFH's letter to Colum see p. 306, n. 5. In order to undermine the seceders' position, AEFH had written an 'official' letter on 9 Jan to WBY in his capacity as president of the INTS (NLI): 'I am informed that various of the members of the Irish National Theatre Society, yourself amongst them, have formed a Ltd Co called the National Theatre Society, *Ltd.* so that the promises made to me in the letter of 1904 can be better carried out. I highly approve of this for as I have spent so much time & money on my side I consider it to be fair that every precaution should be taken by the members towards carrying out the objects as announced by you. I hereby transfer my gift of the free use of the Abbey Theatre (on the same conditions as before) to the National Theatre Society, Ltd. as I consider that the *Ltd.* Co will honestly carry out my intentions. Those members who have not followed you, have completely ignored me & so I have no reason to believe that they wish for my further help in any way. They have never formally protested to me against your new plan & so under whatever name they may choose to call themselves, I can have nothing to do with them. The theatre is a means for carrying out a certain theatrical scheme & as long as you continue in the same path, the theatre is at the disposal of you & your friends under whatever title you may choose to use.' She also sent a copy of this letter to Synge. Cramer, Wood, and Co. were ticket agents for the Abbey Theatre.

[1] Untraced, but presumably conveying Orage's suggestion that the lecture should take place on 14 March (see p. 326, n. 3).

[2] See Matt. 3: 3. The Abbey Theatre played at the Albert Hall, Leeds, on 27-8 Apr 1906 under the auspices of the Leed's Art Club.

[3] i.e. WBY's and FF's lecture on 'Speaking to the Psaltery' at Owens College, Manchester, on 18 May 1903 (see p. 235).

We have no posters, but I think Miss Farr has some of those notices of which I sent you one.[4]

Yrs ev
W B Yeats

TLS Colgate.

## To Florence Farr, [6 February 1906]

Coole Park, | Gort, | Co. Galway.
Tuesday.

My dear Florence Emery: I have sent *Ideas of Good and Evil* to Mrs. King,[1] so I hope I shall be forgiven, by you too, my too great preoccupation with your self. Mrs Patrick Campbell, on whose tail I have not succeeded in dropping salt, should receive a copy of the new *Shadowy Waters* with a devout letter, but not yet.[2] I myself—though I am still at Nassau Hotel—leave for Coole today to spend a couple of weeks of most unwilling industry—so great is your power.[3] I think you may take the Leeds lecture as settled—but I have had to delay about Edinburgh until I get some other dates right. We shall have to make our own way in lecturing—one lecture will lead to another—we have not the advantage of the sort of popular subject which advertises a lecture by itself—our reputations are too esoteric for the general public outside certain university towns. We shall make our way by our faculty, not by our subjects or fame. This was what happened in my own case—I was refused by the agencies and then made hundreds of pounds. The second week in April would suit me for Oxford or Cambridge lectures.[4]

I have been speaking here lately—I at least find that I can move people by power not merely—as the phrase is—by 'charm' or 'speaking

[4] See pp. 243, 340.

[1] Perhaps Helen Ashe King (née Jacob), who had married the Irish literary journalist and lecturer Richard Ashe King (1839–1932) in April 1898. The Kings were friends of WBY, and Richard Ashe King, an enthusiastic member of the Irish Literary Society, London, had given him a number of good reviews (see I. 100, 248, 271, II. 98, 29–31). WBY dedicated his *Early Poems and Stories* to Ashe King in 1925. The copy of *Ideas of Good and Evil* may have been one of those published by Maunsel in August 1905 from the now nearly exhausted second English edition (*Bibl*, 63–4).

[2] The new text of *The Shadowy Waters* was first published in *Poems, 1899–1905* in October 1906, and Bullen issued a 'Theatre Edition' early in 1907. The first performance of this version took place at the Abbey Theatre on 8 Dec 1906.

[3] i.e. the rewriting of *On Baile's Strand*.

[4] WBY lectured in Glasgow and Edinburgh in June but did not lecture in Oxford or Cambridge this year. His very successful American tour of 1903–4 had been overwhelmingly organized by Quinn rather than professional lecture agencies (see pp. 237–9).

beautifully'—a thing I always resented.[5] I feel this change in all my work and that it has brought a change into the personal relations of life—even things seemingly beyond control answer strangely to what is within—I once cared only for images about whose necks I could cast various 'chains of office' as it were. They were so many aldermen of the ideal, whom I wished to master the city of the soul. Now I do not want images at all, or chains of office being contented with the unruly soul.[6] I think you have changed too—is it that those eastern meditations have freed you—made you free of all but the holy church[7]—now alas steering its malignant way, I suppose, through the Indian Ocean—a sort of diabolical Aengus carrying not a glass

---

[5] WBY had lectured on 'The Ideal in Art' at the Royal Hibernian Academy on 25 Jan, spoken in the discussion after AE's lecture, 'Art and Literature', also delivered at the Royal Hibernian Academy on 1 Feb, and to George Sigerson's paper 'The Irish Peasantry and the Stage', delivered to the NLS at 6 St Stephen's Green on 5 Feb. 'The Ideal in Art' was part of a series of lectures arranged in connection with an exhibition of the paintings of the English artist George Frederick Watts (1817–1904), mounted by Hugh Lane at the Royal Hibernian Academy. According to the Dublin *Daily Express* of 26 Jan (7) WBY lamented the fact that Watts thought it was his duty to be popular but, finding no myths or resonant religious symbols in modern England, turned instead to moral zeal and 'took moral legends and maximums [*for* maxims] for his pictures—things that could be explained to a child or an imbecile.' In this too deliberate moral intent, Watts was, WBY argued, betraying the true artistic mission, since 'one could not in art do anything deliberately, consciously. Nature was the mother of the artist.... She gave nothing to self-control; everything to self-surrender.' Speaking to Sigerson's paper of 5 Feb, the *Freeman's Journal* of 6 Feb 1906 (8) reported WBY as saying that 'Ireland had for centuries been in two attitudes of mind, both of which were destructive of literature and the habit that created literature— Ireland had been forced into continued attack and on the other side into continued defence.... The Ireland of the present day, in its relation to literature, was the most abjectly material nation in the world because of its absorption in history, owing to its tendency to be always believing itself in the dock, always calling up its virtues from the past, always looking upon history as the brief handed it for its defence. It endeavoured to enslave the artistic mind and to lay down that he should not try to express what was in himself, the thing that came from eternity, but that his business was to express accidental forms taken by life under the cover of material circumstances.'

Not everyone agreed that WBY's effect came from power rather than melodious delivery. Holloway, who attended the lecture on 'The Ideal in Art', stressed (NLI) his 'flowing lyrical method of speaking & easy flow of beautiful poetic language ever & always interests though often you cannot follow the drift of his monstrously musical speech. You are sort of hypnotised by the charm of his strong personal magnetism & strange crude gesticulation as he chants beautifully expressed ideas without hesitation in a kind of weird monotone.... W. B. Yeats is a wonder & as a talker his command of language is second to none, while the quality of it is precious & beautiful:—he speaks in poetry!' Holloway also noted a similar discrepancy between medium and message in WBY's contribution after Sigerson's lecture, describing 'his enthusiastic bursts of eloquent talk signifying nothing on the whole—a flood of words beautifully put. He gesticulated wildly & walked up & down as he chanted his litany of poetic phraseology.'

[6] WBY had been increasingly conscious of this change since the turn of the century, and had described it (in different imagery) on the publication of *Ideas of Good and Evil* in 1903 (see III. 369–70, 372).

[7] FF recorded her Eastern meditations in a diary (Private) begun in July 1902 (see p. 113, n. 4). Her spiritual quest seems to have been inspired by a mid-life crisis and her joining the theosophical society. Initially she attempted to reconcile Christian and Eastern thought, but rapidly focused on Indian religious texts, with the aim of seeking freedom from the 'illusions' of self, space, and time, noting that 'when freed from all bonds of thought, which are fetters of flesh, the spirit is observed to be without bounds, limitless, absolutely pure'. She contrasted her path to enlightenment with 'half baked people like Yeats & Shaw', who had 'tremendous influence & yet they only tell half truths; they only see half truths. They are thorough as far as they go & I see further than I can be thorough.' A number of the articles she published in the *New Age* in 1906 and 1907 were based on her meditations, and these interests were to lead her in September 1912 to emigrate to Ceylon (Sri Lanka), where she immersed herself in Tamil religious thought.

house for Etain—as did the Irish one—but a whole convent, alter lights, vegetarian kitchen and all.[8]

I have myself by the by begun eastern meditations—of your sort, but with the object of trying to lay hands upon some dynamic and substantialising force as distinguished from the eastern quiescent and supersentualizing state of the soul—a movement downwards upon life not upwards out of life.[9]

Yours ever

W B Yeats

Printed copy; Bax, 55–6, Wade, 468–9.

## *To Holbrook Jackson,* [*7 February 1906*]

Coole Park, | Gort, | Co. Galway.

Dear M^r Jackson: Miss Farr will come with me on March 16 if it is all right about terms—she has not answered about circulars but I am writing to her again on the subject.[1]

Yr sny

W B Yeats

APS Colgate, with envelope addressed to The Arts Club, 19 Park Lane, Leeds, postmark 'ORANMORE FE 7 06'. Marked in another hand '*not 19. Try 9*'.[2]

---

[8] In the ancient Irish tale of Midhir and Edain, Aengus, the god of love, rescues Edain, the second wife of Midhir, after she has been driven away from her husband's house by spells put upon her by Fuamach, his jealous first wife. Aengus, as AG recounted in *Gods and Fighting Men* (1904), 'made a sunny house for her, and put sweet-smelling flowers in it, and he made invisible walls about it, that no one could see through and that it could not be seen' (89). WBY refers to the myth in a number of poems and plays, including 'The Wanderings of Oisin' (*VP*, 5), 'Baile and Aillinn' (*VP*, 195), and 'The Harp of Aengus' (*VP*, 219–20), and two pieces he had been working on recently, the choruses from *Deirdre* and 'The Shadowy Waters' (*VP*, 224): 'wild Aengus . . . carried Edain off from a king's house, | And hid her among fruits of jewel-stone | And in a tower of glass (see p. 135).' In the present letter he inverts the image to attack the influence of both Western missionaries and, in the reference to vegetarianism, cults such as theosophy, which had attracted him in his youth.

[9] WBY was to develop this idea in his series of brief essays 'Discoveries', which he was to begin in March of this year: 'There are two ways before literature—upward into ever-growing subtlety . . . or downward, taking the soul with us until all is simplified and solidified again' (*E & I*, 266–7). He later elaborated this metaphor in his writings on the 'Condition of Fire' (see *Myth*, 356–7, 364–6) and it underpins the oppositions in his later poem 'The Statues' (*VP*, 610–11).

[1] See previous letter.

[2] Although WBY had put '19' not '18' Park Lane, the letter reached its destination (despite being redirected to the wrong address), since it is among Jackson's papers.

## To Holbrook Jackson, [8 February 1906]

at | COOLE PARK, | GORT, | CO. GALWAY.

Dear M^r Jackson: I wrote yesterday to say Miss Farr would come, if the terms suited you, but put a wrong number. I therefore write again. I have written to her about circular etc & will let you know if she has any.

Yr ev
W B Yeats

ALS Colgate, with envelope addressed to Leeds Arts Club, 18 Park Lane, Leeds, postmark 'ORANMORE FE 9 06'.

## To Hugh Lane, 8 February [1906]

at | COOLE PARK, | GORT, | CO. GALWAY.
Feb 8

My dear Lane: I am very sorry that I cannot be at your meeting to-morrow—It is generally wise to give people what they want—though I think academic & official Ireland thinks otherwise—and I am certain that if you get this gallery, being the indefatigable man you are you will make it one of the great galleries.[1]

Yr ev
W B Yeats

APS NLI.

[1] A widely advertised public meeting to discuss Lane's proposed Dublin Gallery of Modern Art took place in the Large Hall at 6 St Stephen's Green at 3.30 p.m. on 9 Feb, and was extensively reported in the Dublin press the following day. This letter was evidently written to be read out at the meeting, and the *Freeman's Journal* of 10 Feb (3) quoted such letters of support from the Lord Mayor of Dublin, J. Hutchinson, William Hutcheson Poe, and T. W. Rolleston, as well as noting that similar communications had been received from many others. But WBY's letter with its disparagement of academic and official Ireland might have been thought too undiplomatic to be read aloud at a gathering attended by the Lord-Lieutenant, as well as many other representatives of the Irish unionist and nationalist establishments, and numerous members of the Royal Irish Academy. The meeting was chaired by the Earl of Mayo, who gave an account of the progress towards the gallery, praised Lane as 'the life and soul of the present movement . . . notwithstanding the ill-natured sneers and criticisms in the Press', and remarked that while the 'student who visited the National Gallery saw the best of the past . . . what they wanted him to see also was how painters of the present day were expressing their ideas'. Lord Aberdeen, the Lord-Lieutenant, speaking 'from the point of view of the general public', called for pictures not only of 'the highest skill and talent' but also of 'the highest tone and the most elevated character', those 'which can be understood by the general mass of mankind' since 'they are characterised by that human sympathy . . . that finds a response in all minds'. The first resolution, put by Count Plunkett, 'That this meeting is of opinion that a Gallery of Modern Art is wanted in Ireland', was passed unanimously. After a speech by Count Markiewicz, giving a European perspective on the scheme, Sir Walter Armstrong's proposal that 'definite steps be immediately taken to provide a gallery' was adopted. The proceedings were subsequently published as a pamphlet entitled *Proposed Gallery of Modern Art for Dublin. Report of Proceeding at the Public Meeting held 9^th February 1906* (Dublin, 1906).

# *To A. H. Bullen, 13 February [1906]*

Coole Park | Gort, Co Galway
Feb 13

My dear Bullen

You must have thought it very bad of me leaving that Baile's Strand so long unrighted, but I have had the devil of a time with it. I have had two or three times to go to London and back: I have been in Scotland lecturing, and I have had some odds and ends of the influenza, with the result that though I worked pretty constantly at the play I could not get it done. As soon as I got a few passages right I had to go away, and so the mood was broken, and some considerable scenes written which had no proper coherence. At last I asked Lady Gregory to let me come down here; and now having been for a week out of all distractions I have almost finished. Nothing remains but a little work on the prose opening, and a few words here and there to knit the old to the new. The big scene is done including thirty lines of a lyric chorus. I shall go to Dublin next Saturday and by that time all shall be done.[1] I shall give Sidgewick the completed M.S. and proofs in the middle of next week.[2]

What I write to you about is this: Would it be worth making another attempt to get the Wind among the Reeds out of Matthews? I dont think it is any use Sidgewick going for he has a quarrel on with Sidgewick about some book of I think Bliss Carmen's.[3] I am disinclined to go again,

[1] WBY had been revising *On Baile's Strand* since shortly after its first production in December 1904 (see p. 240) and Bullen now needed it urgently for *Poems, 1899–1905*. The most extensive revisions were in the first half of the play, where WBY completely rewrote 313 lines and added a further 154. This involved the recasting and lengthening of the first scene between the Blind Man and the Fool, making Cuchulain's entrance far more dramatic, his debate with Conchubar more cogent, and introducing a theatrically effective oath-binding scene (see pp. 251–2). In a note in *Poems, 1899–1905*, WBY explained (*VPl*, 526) that he had made some alterations to the play in 1905 but after the British tour in November 'entirely rewrote it up to the entrance of the Young Man [Cuchulain's son], and changed it a good deal from that on to the end.... It is now as right as I can make it with my present experience, but it must always be a little over-complicated when played by itself.'

[2] Frank Sidgwick (see p. 115, n. 1) joined Bullen's firm in October 1901, after graduating at Cambridge, and became his junior partner six months later. From May 1904 to March 1905 he moved to Stratford to start the Shakespeare Head Press, the record of which is preserved in *Frank Sidgwick's Diary* (1975). Their partnership was dissolved in 1907, and in October of 1908 he joined R. Cameron Jackson to found the firm of Sidgwick & Jackson. Sidgwick had published an article on WBY in the *English Illustrated Magazine* of 29 June 1903, reprinted in the *Gael* (NY), August 1903.

[3] The poet and literary journalist Bliss Carman (1861–1929) was born at Fredericton, New Brunswick, and was related to Ralph Waldo Emerson on his mother's side. He was educated at the University of New Brunswick and Edinburgh University, and in 1885 went to Harvard, where he met Richard Hovey with whom he wrote three volumes of *Songs from Vagabondia* (1894, 1895, 1897). Settling in New York, Carman published a number of books of verse, while keeping himself by journalism, and in this year he became editor of the *Reader*. Mathews had published two of his earlier books in England, *Low Tide on Grand Pré* (1894) and *Songs from Vagabondia* (see 1. 405), and when he visited London in the early summer of 1896 he gave Mathews's office as his postal address. However, once in London he was poached by Lawrence & Bullen, as he delightedly reported to the American poet Louise Imogen

as the failure of my last negotiation rather spoils my chances, but we could try him with A. P. Watt. Some months have now passed since I saw Matthews with Sidgewick, and Matthews's term with the book is so much nearer its end.[4] It occurs to me that we might offer him whatever sum he is accustomed to make in a year of it & something more—. This sum to be calculated on the average of the last three years, like the Income tax people. I suppose he would be content to estimate his own profits as the same amount I get out of the book. The sum isnt very considerable and we could let him go on selling the book. If you think well of it I will see A. P. Watt when I get to London. I think Matthews is striking at his own interest to some extent out of spite over the Bliss Carmen book and because he is cross at my book passing out of his hands at all. A letter from A. P. Watt might persuade him to look at the matter from a business point of view alone.

My book with Unwin is now bringing me about thirty-five pounds a year, and if we got the same proportion of lyrical work into this new book it ought to sell at least as well.[5] At first when I wrote to you about it I was inclined to think that the Wind among the Reeds poems were in a mood so different from these later poems that they would be no great help, but so many people have asked me will it contain those lyrics that I suppose I was wrong. I dont want to press the point but I would like your opinion upon it.

Guiney: 'I met Lawrence and Bullen, to whom I took a great fancy, and who treated me royal. I thought them princes of publishers' (*Letters of Bliss Carman*, ed. H. Pearson Gundy [Montreal, 1981], 109). Bullen contracted for a selection of his work, using some of the material from the books issued by Mathews, although this did not appear (as *Ballads and Lyrics*) until 1902. In fact, Bullen would have been better off not thwarting Mathews, since Carman's book did not sell and on 8 May 1905, on his orders, Sidgwick offered it (Bodleian) to the dealer A. B. Sloan in a list of remainders: 'All offered 1/- net in quantities if you can get them. The long and short of it is, we want to get rid of as much of the above as we can, and know you will do your best for us.' Carman had been introduced to WBY's work by Guiney and the aesthete Fred Holland Day (1864–1933), and during his London trip of 1896 Arthur Symons took him to Woburn Buildings: 'Dark alley, near midnight, silent door, loud knock, moment of silence, footsteps groping down stairs, rattle of key in lock, door opened—and there, lamp held high above his head, stands your dark Celtic velvet inspired W.B.Y. himself, the William Blake of this smaller generation' (*Letters of Bliss Carman*, 109–10). From 1903 Carman's main British publisher was John Murray, and he edited the *Oxford Book of American Verse* in 1927.

    [4] WBY and Sidgwick had seen Mathews shortly before WBY left London for Coole in early July 1905 (see p. 139), when Mathews had evidently told them that he could only act after consulting John Lane. WBY's attempt to build on this over the summer of 1905, and subsequently, had failed (see pp. 115–16, 146, 227). At this time WBY believed that Mathews's rights in *The Wind Among the Reeds* expired in 1907.

    [5] *Poems* was first published by Unwin in 1895, and revised and reissued regularly thereafter, most recently in June 1904. It was WBY's main source of income from his publications, and he wrote in a copy of the 1929 edition (*Bibl*, 154): 'This book for about thirty years brought me twenty or thirty times as much money as any other book of mine—no twenty or thirty times as much as all my other books put together.' In fact, *Poems, 1899–1905* had a far larger proportion of dramatic verse to lyrics than *Poems*, largely owing to the enforced absence of the poems from *The Wind Among the Reeds*. It published new versions of *The Shadowy Waters* (together with two introductory poems), *On Baile's Strand*, and *The King's Threshold*, as well 'The Entrance of Deirdre' from *Deirdre*. There were only twelve lyrics in all, ten of which were taken from *In the Seven Woods* (1903), from which WBY also included two narrative poems. In contrast, *Poems* contained only two plays but thirty-seven lyrics and ballads, as well as the long narrative poem 'The Wanderings of Oisin'.

Lady Gregory has asked me to get her some copies—a dozen—of the old edition of Shadowy Waters, she wants them to give to friends who have stayed here among the Seven Woods.[6] What are you selling the old edition at?[7]

I was dining with Symons when I was in London, and Mrs Symons said you are the most delightful man she ever met.

Yrs ever
W B Yeats

TLS Harvard. Wade, 469–71.

## *To Holbrook Jackson, 13 February* [*1906*]

Coole Park | Gort, Co Galway
Feb 13

Dear Mr Jackson,

I enclose a note which Mrs Emery has asked me to send to you. It explains itself. Please let me know if you agree to what I have said about terms. I am merely anxious for enough to make it worth while for her to come from London. She has not my propagandist fire, having no theatre on her hands.

Yrs sny
W B Yeats

[*With enclosure*]

107½ Holland Road. | Kensington, W

Dear Sir

If you will let me know how many posters you would like I can send you a few double crowns with this Beardsley design on them & a blank space at the side for printed matter.[1] Also how many of the press cuttings notices would you like. I have pinned one example to this letter.[2]

Yours faithfully
Florence Farr

P.S. I have not very many about 100 perhaps of the Press notices.

[6] This edition of the play, which Bullen had taken over from Hodder & Stoughton (see pp. 137–9, 141), was prefaced with the poem 'I walked among the seven woods of Coole' (*VP*, 217–19), dated September 1900, and celebrating the demesne. The poem was not included in the new 'Acting Edition' of the play, published early in 1907, but did appear in *Poems, 1899–1905*.

[7] Both Arthur and Rhoda Symons (see pp. 144, 145) liked Bullen, and writing to her in May 1911 (*ASSL*, 218–19) Symons described 'a splendid time with Bullen. He was his old self, the same charm, walking, drinking, smoking, talking, and reciting verses of immense length. . . . We talked incessantly— on every sort of thing.'

[1] The posters were based on the Aubrey Beardsley design for the first production of *The Land of Heart's Desire*, which FF had stage managed at the Avenue Theatre in 1894. The now obsolete paper size 'double imperial' was used for posters, 20″ × 30″.

[2] WBY and FF had had a circular of press-cuttings printed explaining and publicizing his lecture 'Poetry and the Living Voice' (see Appendix). The circular comprised mainly C. H. Herford's article in the *Manchester Guardian* of 9 May 1903, with shorter extracts from *The Times*, the *Academy*, the *Daily News*, and a further extract from the *Manchester Guardian* (see *YL*, 661).

[*On back of envelope*]
By 'expenses' in my letter of some days ago I of course meant your expenses. We naturally pay our own.[3]
                    WBY.

TLS Colgate, with envelope addressed to The Arts Club, 18 Park Lane, Leeds, postmark 'ORANMORE FE 14 06'.

## To Florence Farr, [*16 February 1906*]

at Coole Park, | Gort, | Co. Galway.
Friday.

My dear Florence Emery: I enclose a letter from Leeds and have written to say that you will write direct about posters etc. Don't you think that we should get some more of those hand bills or circulars about the "chanting" printed?[1] I will now try and arrange for Liverpool and Edinburgh but had better wait till I get exact dates in Dublin where I go tomorrow.[2] I have done magnificent work here. I have a sketch of a strange little play about the capture of a blind Unicorn,[3] and I have written a choral ode about witches which contain these lines—suggested in some vague way by your letter, only suggested I mean in phantasmal exageration of some sentence.

> Or, they hurl a spell at him
> That he follow with desire
> Bodies that can never tire
> Or grow kind, for they anoint
> All their bodies joint by joint
> With a miracle working juice,
> That is made out of the grease
> Of the ungoverned unicorn;
> But the man is thrice forlorn
> Emptied, ruined, wracked and lost

[3] See p. 333. Although WBY had asked for the 'whole profits' from the lecture, he expected the Leeds Arts Club to cover their expenses out of this sum first, and intended to take his and FF's travelling and accommodation expenses out of the overall fee, rather than claiming them in addition.

[1] FF acted at once on receiving WBY's letter, and wrote to Jackson on 18 Feb (Chapel Hill) telling him that she would 'send you off 50 blank posters with the Beardsley design & 50 press cutting notice tomorrow morning by 12 o'clock'.

[2] WBY and FF gave a lecture in Liverpool on 15 Mar, the day after the Leeds lecture. They did not go on to Edinburgh, but WBY was to lecture there alone in early June of this year.

[3] This was evidently an early scenario for *The Unicorn from the Stars*, which WBY quickly began to see as a rewriting of his earlier play *Where There Is Nothing*. It was composed in close collaboration with AG, and grew into three acts. In *Where There Is Nothing* blindness is seen as conducive to apocalyptic vision (*VPl*, 1139), but in both plays unicorns are associated with clear, blue eyes.

That *they* follow, for at most
They will give him kiss for kiss
While they murmur "After this
Hatred may be sweet in the taste."
Those wild hands that have embraced
All his body can but shove
At the burning wheel of love
Till the side of hate comes up.[4]

The hero had been praising an indomitable kind of woman and the chorus sing of her evil shadow.[5] The Unicorn in the little play is a type of masterful and beautiful life but I shall not trouble to make the meaning clear—a clear vivid story of a strange sort is enough. The meaning may be different with everyone.[6]

I shall get you to teach me meditation. My difficulty is that I get partly hypnotized at once and that a sleepy calm makes it very difficult to get the mood of fiery understanding which must represent the spirit which is,

---

[4] These lines, slightly revised and incorporated in a longer chorus, were added to *On Baile's Strand*, where they are sung by the Three Women as part of Cuchulain's oath-binding ceremony. They were printed separately in Spring number of the *Shanachie* later this year under the title 'Against Witchcraft', and also appear in *VP* (775–6). In the final version of the play, WBY instructed that these lines were to be sung '*in a very low voice after the first few words so that the others all but drown their words*' (*VPl*, 495), explaining in a note: 'Very little of the words of the song of the three women can be heard, for they must be for the most part a mere murmur under the voices of the men. It seemed right to take some trouble over them, just as it is right to finish off the statue where it is turned to the wall, and besides there is always the reader and one's own pleasure' (*VPl*, 526).

[5] At this point in the early versions of the play Cuchulain recalls Aoife, the warrior Queen of the Hebrides. After defeating her in a fierce fight, Cuchulain begets a son by her on the battlefield. When the son has grown she sends him to challenge Cuchulain to single combat and, although reluctant to fight, Cuchulain finally kills him, only to discover his identity as he is dying. Throughout the play Cuchulain is haunted by the memory of Aoife and her wild self-sufficiency, and Conchubar reminds him of his boast that 'although you had loved other women, | You'd sooner that fierce woman of the camp | Bore you a son than any queen among them' (*VPl*, 487).

[6] The unicorn became a compelling symbol for WBY at this time. Paul Ruttledge, the hero of *Where There Is Nothing*, has a vision of a beast 'with iron teeth and brazen claws that can root up spires and towers', which he identifies as 'Laughter, the mightiest of the enemies of God' (*VPl*, 1099), but he also dreams of 'a great many angels riding upon unicorns, white angels on white unicorns.... And then they laughed aloud, and the unicorns trampled the ground as though the world were already falling in pieces' (*VPl*, 1132). In *The Unicorn from the Stars* the vision of the apocalyptic beast is subsumed more coherently into the symbol of the unicorn and given occult and biblical resonances. The hero of the play, Martin Hearne, is carried in a trance to vineyards by horses which 'changed to unicorns, and they began trampling the grapes and breaking them' (*VPl*, 659), and in a later vision sees a 'shining vessel . . . broken with a great crash; then I saw the unicorns trampling it. They were breaking the world to pieces' (*VPl*, 669).

WBY probably first came across the symbol of the unicorn in the GD; on advancing to the Grade of Practicus ($38° = 88°$), which he had achieved by early 1891 (see 1. 486–8), he was given the mystic title 'Monocris (or Monoceros) de Astris' (i.e. 'The Unicorn from the Stars'). He would have found further information about the unicorn in Johann Valentin Andreas's *The Chymical Marriage of Christian*

according to the old definition, 'that which moves itself.' I have never got this mood except in absolute trance at night.[7]

Yours always, shall I say affectionately or would that arouse too much scorn.

W B Yeats

I shall be back in London next week.

Printed copy; Bax, 56–7, Wade, 471–2.

## To Holbrook Jackson, 16 February [1906]

at | COOLE PARK, | GORT, | CO. GALWAY.
Feb 16

Dear M$^r$ Jackson: many thanks I have sent your note to Florence Farr (M$^{rs}$ Emery) & asked her to write direct. My address for the next few days will be Nassau Hotel, South Fredrick St, Dublin. I then go to London (18 Woburn Buildings).

Yr sny
W B Yeats

ALS Colgate, with envelope addressed to The Arts Club, 18 Park Lane, Leeds, postmark 'ORANMORE FE 16 06'.

*Rosencreutz*, a translation of which was included in A. E. Waite's *The Real History of the Rosicrucians* (1887), and more particularly in Waite's edition of *The Hermetic Museum* (1893), a translation of *Musaeum Hermeticum* (Frankfurt, 1678). This included 'The Book of Lambspring', a series of alchemical emblems, the third of which pictured a unicorn and a deer in a forest, signifying the Spirit and Soul in the Body (I. 280–1). These emblems were given further iconic force in WBY's imagination by Gustave Moreau's painting *Ladies and Unicorns* (*Les licornes*) which remained one of his favourite paintings, and by W. L. Bruckman's illustrations for the endpapers to the *Dome*, a quarterly to which WBY contributed regularly from 1898 to 1900. In 1915 he commissioned Sturge Moore to design a decoration of a unicorn leaping from a star-filled sky for the frontispiece to the Cuala edition of *Reveries of Childhood and Youth* and used this device in several of his subsequent books issued by Cuala, explaining to William Maxwell on 21 Sept 1932 (Texas) that the 'leaping Unicorn, "Monoceros de Astris" is a symbol of the descent of spirit'. In an earlier letter to ECY (Wade, 662) WBY told her that the unicorn was 'a private symbol belonging to my mystical order', and (apparently confusing the emblematic significance of deer and unicorn) that it stood for 'the soul'.

[7] Aristotle defines the soul as that which moves itself in *De Anima* (II.4), and WBY was to quote him on this topic again in his article 'Compulsory Gaelic' (*UP* II. 448). WBY may also have come across the idea in *Immortality of the Soul* (1659), where the Cambridge Platonist Henry More (1614–87), lists the human soul and the spirits which animate angels as manifestations of the 'finite spirit': 'that can move itself, that can penetrate, contrast, and dilate itself, and can also move and alter the Matter.' FF knew of the concept and in her spiritual diary (see p. 335, n. 7) gave it an occult inflection, as well as the musical notation of a mantra: 'For the present think of nothing but the sentence – *I am the One without motion, giving motion to all things* – Whenever you are alone or working at mechanical work . . . repeat that'.

## *To Lady Gregory,* [*18 February 1906*]

Nassau Hotel | Dublin.
Sunday

My dear Lady Gregory: Fay had no news—he had heard nothing of any meeting, but this morning Synge came in looking for news from us for he had met my sister who had said "Moira tells us that she has been to a meeting where they agreed to sign something which will put fear into you all"—whether Moira was in joke or earnest I dont know but my sister seems to have thought earnest. I should not wonder if it was all a joking disguise for Moiras usual Thur[s]day evening with Starkie.[1] Synges play is to be done in London by the German company Fay says.[2] He also says that our company is in great humour & already takes great airs & looks down on all amateurs. Synge says my new bits in 'Bailes Strand' are magnificent.

I have just been at my fathers studio. Harrington sitting as usual but no news.[3]

Fay has made upper windows for Hyacynth[4] & the new house next door is almost finished—plenty of room.[5]

My sister according to Synge says "Moira is selfish & idle & that one reason why she wont join in is probably that she saw in the couple of weeks

---

[1] i.e. Maire Walker, who was having an affair with Starkey (see pp. 272, n. 7, 279). Unofficial meetings of those seceding from the INTS took place frequently during the early part of the year, but the first formal initiative to set up a new theatre society, later to become the Theatre of Ireland, was on 9 May 1906. The legal and definitive break occurred at the General Meeting of the NTS on 25 May.

[2] This was not the Deutsches Theater (which appeared regularly in London from 1901 to 1907), but a German company which was based in London, and gave weekly performances on Friday and Saturday at the Great Queen Street Theatre under the direction of Hans Andresen. It planned to stage productions of Meyerfeld's translations of *Riders to the Sea* and *The Well of the Saints* (*Der Heilige Brunnen*) in June 1907, but seems to have folded before this. Synge wrote to Meyerfeld on 10 Mar 1906 (*JMSCL* 1. 162–3): 'There is a rumour here that the German Company which plays in London are going to do the "Well of The Saints" there next year... have you heard anything of it?'

[3] The Rt. Hon. Timothy 'Tim' Charles Harrington (1851–1910), Parnellite, barrister, and MP for the Harbour Division of Dublin since 1885, had been Lord Mayor of Dublin in 1901–2. The founder and editor of the *Kerry Sentinel*, he had been an architect of the Plan of Campaign in 1886, a counsel for Parnell during the Parnell Commission of 1888–9, and a member of the first Committee for the Municipal Gallery when the Corporation of Dublin passed a unanimous resolution in support of it in March 1905. He had supported the ILT and appeared on behalf of the Abbey Theatre in its application of a Patent in July 1904. A public subscription had been got up for his portrait, and JBY's oil now hangs in the Mansion House, Dublin. In an undated letter, AG later reported to WBY that 'Robert & I went to the Academy & were delighted with yr fathers portrait of Harrington—a fine piece of colour, very vivid & dignified, I think far beyond Orpen, the only other painter there, & it makes the feeble attempts of poor Markievicz & D. O'Brien seem ridiculous'.

[4] The play is set outside the post office and the butcher's shop in the town of Cloon, and both the postmistress, Mrs Delane, and the butcher, James Quirke, are required to call down from the upper windows of their establishments on various occasions during the action.

[5] Work had finished on the new green room (see p. 119).

after London that it was going to be very hard work". She seems to have called Moira all the names.[6]

Yrs ev
W B Yeats

ALS Berg, with envelope addressed to Coole, postmark 'DUBLIN FE 18 06'.

## *To Holbrook Jackson, 20 February* [*1906*]

18 Woburn Buildings | Euston Road | London.
<Friday> Feb 20

Dear M^r Jackson: May I introduce Miss Horniman who is going to Leeds to arrange about the visit of our company.[1] She gave us our little theatre as I dare say you know, & is now arranging our English tour.

Yr ev
W B Yeats

ALS Colgate.

## *To F. J. Fay, 22 February* [*1906*]

Nassau Hotel.
Thursday | Feb 22

My dear Fay: I write to you as managing director to ask you to undertake classes in voice production & verse speaking. At first these classes are to be confined to the company but afterwards we may admit others. We propose to pay you extra for this work—that is to say 10/- a week extra.[1]

---

[6] i.e. ECY, whose enthusiasm for Maire Walker (see p. 270) had evidently cooled considerably.

[1] See p. 243. AEFH worked with her customary zeal in publicizing this tour and on 18 Apr told WBY (NLI) that to 'please your blessed country-men I'm arranging for a portrait of Kathleen Ni Houlihan to go in to that paper & also in the Leeds edition with an article built up from the Times'.

[1] This brought Fay's weekly salary up to £2, and put a long-standing arrangement onto a formal and financial footing.

I always look upon you as the most beautiful verse speaker I know[2]—at least you & M^{rs} Emery compete togeather in my mind for that[3]—& I know nobody but you who can teach verse speaking.

Yr sny<br>W B Yeats

ALS Private.

## To John Millington Synge, [*? late February 1906*]

My dear Synge: I have sent your letter to Lady Gregory.[1] F Fay has complained to me about his 'Hour Glass' clothes[2]—please look into matter & do anything you think right & in any case come to your own conclusion & let us know for next time. Ask F Fay about it.

Yr ever<br>W B Yeats

ALS TCD. Saddlemyer, 114.

## To Lady Gregory, [*2 March 1906*]

18 Woburn Buildings | Euston Road.

My dear Lady Gregory: I am in entire agreement with you & was only waiting to see Miss Horniman before writing to say so—on Tuesday I went

---

[2] Frank Fay had started collecting books on the theatre from an early age and gained a detailed and scholarly knowledge of acting styles, productions, and verse-speaking techniques. He trained the Irish players in what he understood to be the French acting tradition, and attacked most of the current English companies for their lack of training, and their reliance on 'business', spectacle, and tricks instead of vocal modulation and articulation. He repeated with approval Coquelin's opinion that articulation was 'at once the ABC and the highest point of art', and his own acting and tuition was based upon this view. In a letter to the *Academy* in May 1903 (III. 374) WBY said that Fay knew 'more than any man I have ever known about the history of speach upon stage', and praised him two years later as 'our best speaker of verse and our teacher of elocution' (see p. 80). In *Poems, 1899–1905* he dedicated *The King's Threshold* 'To Frank Fay | Because of his beautiful speaking in the | character of Seanchan'.

[3] WBY had a similarly high regard for FF's 'one great gift, the most perfect poetical elocution', recalling that 'her voice was among the most beautiful of her time, her elocution, her mastery of poetical rhythm incomparable', and he kept her performance as Aleel in the first production of *The Countess Cathleen* 'among my unforgettable memories' (*Aut,* 280, 407, 417).

[1] Synge's letter is now lost.

[2] *The Hour-Glass* had been produced in a triple bill with *Cathleen ni Houlihan* and AG's *Hyacinth Halvey* on 19–20 and 23–4 Feb. Frank Fay played the part of the Wise Man.

to the type writer to dictate a letter on the subject but put it off.[1] I have had a letter from Synge, which I have sent to Miss Horniman—she is in Leeds or Liverpool.[2] It is the most serious matter we have yet had to deal with— we must be firm & I think refuse to surrender our own right to play Kathleen or anything else we think good should she be inclined to make a general rule against propaganda.[3]

I am going to stay with Lord Howard de Waldon from Saturday to Monday—a motor car calls for me to morrow & takes me into the country.[4] I have been dining out a great deal but of all these things later—when I can type what I have to say.

I enclose a letter of Lilys which will interest you, especially the PS.[5]

Yrs ev

W B Yeats

This is so short because there is something wrong with my pen.

ALS Berg, with envelope addressed to Coole, postmark 'LONDON. N.W. MAR 2 06'.

---

[1] AEFH had caused further difficulties in the delicate negotiations between the NTS and the secessionists, by insisting on vetting all plays to be produced at the Abbey, and reserving the right to refuse its use to those she considered propagandist. Since the Directors had just agreed to the secessionists using the theatre, this put them, as AG wrote to WBY on 28 Feb (Berg), in a 'very awkward' position, for, if they banned plays after booking them, it would seem bad faith, but to ban them in advance would lead to accusations that they were being dictated to by AEFH.

[2] Evidently the now lost 'long letter' Synge mentioned to AG on 1 Mar 1906 (*JMSCL* 1. 160), 'saying that, I, for my part, refuse to negotiate with the opposition if they are kept in the dark about this point, and that if they are told they will refuse to make terms. If you agree with me you had better write to him to that effect also to strengthen his hand in dealing with her.'

[3] i.e. *Cathleen ni Houlihan*, which the seceders were eager to retain and to which they thought they had the rights (see III. 429). Not only did AEFH think the play too propagandist, she was also adamant that nothing in the Abbey repertoire was to be given to other companies, and on 10 Nov this year admonished WBY that 'I will not permit *anyone* to play *anything* from our repertory at the Abbey Theatre. . . . If Colum & Co. object they must be told the fact that I treat them as I do anyone else—that I will not allow Kathleen ni Houlihan to be done by amateurs as I've seen it burlesqued in London.'

[4] Thomas Evelyn Scott-Ellis, 8th Baron Howard de Walden (1880–1946), had succeeded his father in 1899. A soldier and a racehorse owner (he and his horse Zinfanden are mentioned in *Ulysses* 1. 367), he also composed operas and took an active interest in the arts. Binyon described him to Ricketts later this year (BL) as 'quite young, races horses & motor-boats, fenced at the Olympic games & nearly lost his yacht in Charybdis, admires Yeats, & aspires to write verse plays himself'. He was the sole financier of Craig's Theatre School in the Arena Goldoni, Florence, giving £5,000 in 1913 to get the School going and £25,000 to cover the running costs over the two following years. He lived at Audley End, Saffron Walden, a magnificent Jacobean mansion built from 1603 to 1616 and remodelled in the mid-eighteenth century.

[5] SMY's letter is now lost, but probably contained comments on Maire Walker and the other secessionists. JBY had written to AG that Maire was a different person since she had spoken to her.

## To John Millington Synge, 9 March 1906

Mention in following letter.
Telling Synge that he will not reply to the attack in the *United Irishman*, and agreeing that they should hurry the meeting with the secessionists.

## To Lady Gregory, [9 March 1906]

My dear Lady Gregory: You will have seen the U I—Starkie I should think—the malice of a weak will & weak body & that is the worst malice.[1] Synge very rightly wants to hurry on meeting to settle things—I have said

---

[1] The *United Irishman* for the week ending 10 Mar had published an unsigned letter fiercely critical of new arrangements at the Abbey Theatre, and attacking WBY personally. The correspondent asserted that the members of the new limited company 'in nowise represent the Irish National Theatre Society which was registered on 30 Dec 1903, for the purpose of producing dramatic work which would have a definite bearing upon the National aspirations of this country', and that the new company was 'a secession from the original society, representing those members who had definitely abandoned the possibility of producing good dramatic performances on broadly-defined national lines. . . . Mr. Yeats is now the leading spirit in the seceding members. The National Theatre Society Ltd is a body run in the interests of one person, Mr. W. B. Yeats, who has proved himself capable of absorbing for his own personal ends the disinterested work of a large number of people given on the understanding that they were aiding in a work which was devoted primarily to the development of the highest interests of nationality in this country. . . . The plain fact then remains that Mr. Yeats is trying to foist a purely literary movement upon the people of Ireland as a national one . . . anyone supporting the performance of the National Theatre Society, Ltd., under the impression that he is thereby supporting the cause of nationalism, is labouring under a grievous misapprehension. Mr. Yeats took particular pains when founding the new society, by numerous consultations with his lawyers, to ensure that his power in the society would be predominant. This he has secured by having it registered as an industrial society, in which every member has a vote for every share he holds.' Griffith prefaced this letter with the editorial comment that 'the attempt to convert the Abbey Theatre into a "Theatre of Commerce", has led to the strenuous opposition on the part of the bulk of the members. However, the commercial minority has secured possession of the theatre, and is now about to proceed through the country, arrayed in the plumes of their opponents. It is this last injustice which has impelled our correspondent to place the position of affairs in regard to the Abbey Theatre before the public.' A further editorial note at the end of the letter commented: 'Everybody will be sorry for the conversion of our best lyric poet into a limited liability company.' Starkey's recent behaviour, capped by this article, changed the high opinion that WBY had entertained of him up to the previous autumn (see pp. 157–8), and Starkey was aware that WBY disliked him. Austin Clarke reports (*A Penny in the Clouds*, 73) that some years later, while travelling on top of the Rathfarnham tram, 'a young intoxicated painter swayed and spewed' on Starkey's shoulder. 'I have known W. B. Yeats for twenty years', Starkey complained, 'and he never did that to me.' He for his part attacked WBY in 'To a Poet', published in *Verses: Sacred and Profane* (1908):

> I too, with Ireland, loved you long ago
> Because you sang as none but you could sing,
> The cause we hold the dearest; now I know
> How vain your love was, and how mean a thing.

> And not to you whose heart went anywhere
> Her sorrow's holy heritage belongs.
> You could have made of any other air
> The little, careful, mouthfuls of your songs.

the sooner the better—we will have to go to town for it.[2] I try to think of Starkie, as a great ostrich feather that I carry upon my head—I think the final falling of the 'borrowed plumes' rather wants 'an arrow' to celebrate it.[3] Would it not be well to prepare a statement putting clearly the question of literature or politics?[4] I can go to Dublin any time after my lectures at Leeds & Liverpool that is after next week.[5] When would you be there—I might even run down to Coole if it seems worth taking notice of a wish on Synges part not to see me until the day before the meeting for fear I might <interfear with> fight with Russell. I have been staying with Lord Howard de Walden in a great feudal looking house, & am going to M^rs Ladenburgs & perhaps Lady Cunard between this & Monday.[6]

Yrs ev<br>W B Yeats

I begin to wonder if that paragraph was by Walker—has probably not agreed to go off and is not a party to negociation.[7]

ALS Berg, with envelope addressed to Coole, redirected to 22 Dominick St., Galway, postmark 'LONDON.W MAR 9 06'.

[2] Although Synge's letter to WBY is now lost, he told AG on 10 Mar (*JMSCL* 1. 162) that he had written to him as soon as he saw the *United Irishman* attack 'advising him not to answer, and I have just heard from him to say that he agrees and will not . . . I think it is doubly important however to hurry on our arrangements, so I will try and arrange with Russell tonight about drawing up the agenda paper for the meeting.'

[3] WBY is echoing the image used by Griffith (see above, n. 1), which evidently provoked him to name his new theatrical publication the *Arrow*; he had earlier thought of calling it the *Fan* (see p. 299). Recalling Elinor Monsell's Abbey trademark (see pp. 24–5), he suggested in the first number that the *Arrow* would be a monthly and hoped 'that the queen with the wolf dog has one in her quiver for every month'. In Aesop's *Fables* a jay disguises himself in the borrowed plumes of a peacock; see also the 'great cock's feather' in 'The Statesman's Holiday' (*VP*, 627).

[4] This was not done in any formal way.

[5] i.e. on 14 and 15 Mar (see p. 341, n. 2). The lectures went well: according to Mary Gawthorpe (*Uphill to Holloway* [1962], 196) when FF recited the 137th Psalm, 'By the Waters of Babylon', Orage was 'visibly moved by the sad strains, holding back his tears with difficulty', and the *Leeds and Yorkshire Mercury* reported on 15 Mar (6) that 'Mr. Yeats and Miss Farr are clearly on the right track, and should be encouraged to proceed'.

[6] For Mrs Ladenburg see p. 136, n. 8. Melton Mowbray in Leicestershire is a centre of hunting, and she was a dedicated and courageous rider to hounds. Lady Maud (Emerald) Cunard, née Burke (1872–1948), was born in San Francisco of an Irish-American father. After affairs with the property speculator Horace Carpentier and George Moore, she married Sir Bache Cunard, a grandson of the founder of the shipping line, and in 1895 they took up residence in his house Nevill Holt, Market Harborough, Leicestershire, an extensive low building in yellow and grey stone with crenellated towers, walls, and cloisters. Here she set out to become a fashionable hostess, and numbered among her guests at this time politicians, artists, musicians, and writers, including Lord Howard de Walden, through whom WBY's invitation may have come (although there is no firm evidence that he took it up). In 1911 Lady Cunard began a serious relationship with the orchestral conductor Thomas Beecham, separated from Sir Bache, and set up her own household in Cavendish Square, London.

[7] For Frank Walker see p. 252, n. 1. In his letter of 10 Mar (see above, n. 1) Synge told AG, 'Russell does not know who is at the bottom of U. I. business He says he will try and find out', but in a letter dated 'Friday', and probably written on 23 Mar 1906 (Berg), AG informed WBY that Dublin rumour suspected Seumas O'Connolly, later honorary secretary of the Theatre of Ireland, to be the author as he 'lives with Starkie and hears his & all Russell's views'. For his part, AE told AG (Berg) that the 'letter was written without the knowledge of most of the members'.

## *To Maud Gonne,* [c. *9 March 1906*]

Mention in letter from MG, 'Tuesday' [? 13 March 1906].
Telling her of George Birmingham's 'absurd' novel *Hyacinth*, and offering
to send her a copy,[1] discussing her drawing,[2] telling her that the theatre
audiences are improving, and asking for news about the final hearings in her
divorce proceedings.[3]

*G–YL,* 225.

[1] MG is lampooned as Augusta Goold in George Birmingham's novel *Hyacinth* (1906), a satire and
*roman-à-clef* in which Hyacinth Conneally, a naive young man from the West of Ireland, becomes
embroiled in extreme nationalist politics in Dublin. Here he meets the beautiful agitator Augusta Goold,
described as 'a remarkable woman both physically and intellectually. It was her delight to emphasize her
splendid figure by draping it in brilliant reds and yellows. To anyone who cared to speculate on such a
subject it seemed a mystery why her clothes remained on her when she walked.... Similarly it was not
easy to see why her hair stayed upon her head. It was arranged upon no recognized system, and
suggested that she had perfected the art, known generally only to heroines of romances, of twisting her
tresses with a single movement into a loose knot. That she affected white frills of immense complexity
was frequently evident, owing to the difficulty she experienced in confining her long legs to feminine
attitudes. Her complexion put it in the power of her enemies to accuse her of familiarity with
cosmetics.... She had great brilliant eyes, which were capable of expressing intensity of enthusiasm
or hatred, but no one had ever seen them soften with any emotion like love. Her attitude towards social
conventions was symbolized by her clothes. In the old days, when the houses of "society" had still been
open to her, she was accustomed to challenge criticism by fondling a pet monkey at tea-parties. Since
she had lost caste by taking up the cause of "Independent Ireland" the ape had been discarded, and the
same result achieved by occasional bickerings with the police. She was an able public speaker, and could
convince her audiences for a time of the reasonableness of opinions which next morning appeared to be
the outcome of delirium. She wrote ... incisive and vigorous prose. Occasionally even the Castle officials
got glimmerings of the meaning of one of her articles, and suppressed the whole issue of the *Croppy* in
which it appeared' (42–3). The novel also gives an account of her part in a riotous public meeting,
evidently based on the fracas that occurred when MG led a deputation to an Irish Parliamentary
Fund meeting at the Rotunda on 18 May 1903, to protest against the possibility of a loyal address
being presented to the King (see III. 377). John MacBride also appears in the novel as the unscrupulous
opportunist Captain Albert Quinn from Mayo. In her reply MG asked WBY to send her the book:
'Even if absurd I would like to see it & it won't worry me. I am too indifferent.' T. W. Rolleston, writing
to Birmingham in February of this year remarked that 'Augusta ought to be grateful; you've made
her a much more interesting person than she is' (C. H. Rolleston, *Portrait of an Irishman* [1939], 40).
George Birmingham (1865–1950) was the pseudonym of the Belfast-born James Owen Hannay, a
Church of Ireland clergyman turned novelist, who was at this time rector of Westport, Co. Mayo, John
MacBride's home town. *Hyacinth* was the second of many comic novels, and WBY owned Hannay's
first book, *The Spirit and Origin of Christian Monasticism*, which he had published under his own name
in 1903.
[2] MG was contemplating a series of drawings to illustrate the life of Cuchulain, and had begun with
one of his mother Dectora, which she promised to send to WBY. As she explained in her reply it 'was
done entirely without models so of course the figure drawing is not good—If ever I intend to carry out
my ideas for the illustration of the life of Cuchulain I shall have to get models—these I am doing now
are merely ideas not worked out—'
[3] In her reply MG told him she was 'still uncertain of the date of the final trial of my divorce case & of
my plans after—I certainly shall go to Dublin immediately after, but whether alone & only for a short
time, or whether with my family & to stay there is still uncertain.'

## To Lady Gregory, [*12 March 1906*]

THE LODGE, | MELTON MOWBRAY.

My dear Lady Gregory: I am here till to-morrow—a very pleasant place in a flat dull country.[1]

I write chiefly to enclose a letter of Synges I should have sent before & for the sake of the words I have underlined. We want a number of names I can only think of Robert, Harvey, Carton, & at a pinch my father.[2] That will not be enough of them if the others should refuse to resign. Or rather it would be just enough to give us a majority of 3/4 & a quorum with no margin of a workable sort. We want half a dozen or more I think. If however only two remain we can get on with just enough to give us a quorum (10) at one meeting at which we can reduce the quorum to (say) 7.

I may have to go to Dublin sooner than Synge wants to talk to Harvey & Carton Etc.

Dont you think we had better reply to 'U I' in the 'Arrow', even though we never wrote another number.[3]

Yrs ev
W B Yeats

I go to Leeds & Liverpool on Wednesday & return Friday.

[*With enclosure*]

57 Rathgar Road
March 7th

Dear Yeats

Every thing will go smothly, if we give Roberts the right to sell books during our shows,[4] and agree that the new society shall be treated exactly as other tenants if they want the theatre. Miss Horniman wrote practically

---

[1] See p. 349, n. 6. Egerton Lodge, originally called Park House, stood in 300 acres and boasted a coach house, stabling for forty horses, as well as an equine Turkish bath. It was the centre of hunting society and in the mid-nineteenth century was visited regularly by royalty. In the 1880s the Lodge was owned by Viscount Grey de Wilton and then Arthur Pryor and Countess Wilton.

[2] Synge urged WBY and AG to draw up a list of the new members who would give the NTS a majority and quorum (see below). They were thinking of Robert Gregory, his sometime tutor T. Arnold Harvey (see p. 317), and 'Carton', probably Joseph J. Carton, a barrister and librarian of King's Inns (see p. 201, n. 5). In a letter of 8 Apr (Berg) AG advised him to 'make Robert [Gregory] a member, & yr sister—names that will seem a natural & reasonable choice'.

[3] By the time the first number of the *Arrow* appeared on 20 Oct 1906 the attack in the *United Irishman* (see p. 348) was all but forgotten and the Abbey audiences had picked up again. WBY explained that the new magazine was 'not meant as a substitute' for *Samhain* but would 'interpret or comment on particular plays, make announcements, wrap up the programme and keep it from being lost, and leave general principles to Samhain'. It did however reprint adverse press comment on various Abbey plays to show the perverse and contradictory nature of the criticisms.

[4] In May 1905 AEFH had given Roberts permission to sell the Abbey Theatre series in the Theatre itself (see pp. 99, 248). Roberts was worried that this concession might be withdrawn under the new

saying she would agree to anything we thought necessary. I have told Russell that she will let to them as to anyone else and that satisfies him.[5] *Now you and Lady Gregory had better draw up a list of* the new Members that are to go in to give us a majority and quorum. Russell and I will draw up an agenda paper of the matters that are to go before the meeting, and he will show it to his friends individually and get their agreement to it. Then at the meeting he advises—I think wisely—that there should be no speechmaking what ever. The resolutions can be put one after the other and carried straight off. When can you come over? We cannot play till Easter Week in Dublin (April 16) but I think it would be unwise to let the matter hang on, now that things are agreed on. Heaven knows what new difficulty might turn up in the next five weeks. You might come over to see how Baile's Strand is going, and then we could fix off everything. It would probably be best for you to come the day before meeting so that Russell may not have time to fight with you.

Yours

J. M. Synge

Of course I will send you and Lady G. a copy of agenda paper when it is drawn up.

ALS Berg, with envelope addressed to Coole, redirected to Euston Hotel, London, postmark 'MELTON MOWBRAY MR 12 06'.

## *To Florence Farr,* [c. *13 March 1906*]

can I get out of Blighs[1] Lady Gregory passing through. Wants to do Electra.[2]

Yeats

A draft telegram Berg, addressed to 'Emery, 107½ Holland Road, Kensington'.

arrangements; on 1 Mar Synge told AG (*JMSCL* 1. 160) that most of the seceders had promised to resign from the INTS if the terms were satisfactory, but that 'Roberts will not resign...or let his friends resign unless he gets an agreement about the books to *himself personally*, he says that this agreement is the one asset on which his claim to partnership [i.e. of Maunsel & Co.] is based'.

    [5] The Directors evidently acted upon this assumption, and on 9 Mar AG wrote to WBY (Berg) that she 'was relieved to get Miss Horniman's saying she was giving in to "blackmail" '. But the compromise was to rankle with AEFH, and on 1 Feb 1909 (NLI) she reproached WBY: 'I much regret that I did not see the letter you wrote making promises on my behalf before you sent it. I consented much against the grain that these people should even be allowed to hire the Abbey Theatre.... I know that it was only after some good time that you mentioned that Roberts alone might supply the books sold in the Abbey. I believe that this was part of a contract.'

    [1] Possibly Andrew Bligh, who was a member of the Irish Texts Society. The Blighs attended WBY's Monday Evenings intermittently.

    [2] Gilbert Murray's translation of Euripides' *Electra* had been given a matinée production at the Court Theatre on 16 Jan, and it was revived for a two-week run of evening performances at the same theatre from 12 Mar. AG was making a sudden visit to London in mid-March, 'instead of after Easter', as she informed WBY on 9 Mar (Berg), 'to get through the necessary dentist & dressmaker'.

## To Lady Gregory, [c. *13 March 1906*]

My dear Lady Gregory,

I cannot get off from Blythes[1]—somebody to meet me—but I will be at that little resteraunt at end of play.[2] Very sorry.

Yrs ev

W B Yeats

I am in great joy at your being back here.[3]

ALS Berg, with unstamped envelope addressed to 'Lady Gregory'; and engraved 'Euston Hotel, London'.

## To George Brett, *13 March 1906*

18 Woburn Buildings, | Euston Road.

March 13th, / 06.

Dear M[r] Brett,

I have received the enclosed letter from the solicitor of the Society of Authors.[1] I will write again to you in a few days.

Yrs sny

W B Yeats

Dict AEFH, signed WBY; NYPL.

---

[1] i.e. the Blighs (see above).

[2] Probably Spiers and Pond's refreshment rooms, situated two doors away from the Royal Court Theatre in Sloan Square, London.

[3] The trip also did AG good, and she wrote on 23 Mar (Berg), immediately after her return to Ireland: 'I am so well, quite a new creature. That little trip was like a trip abroad, no responsibilities or duties. I am ready for any amount of work now.'

[1] WBY was once more attempting to gain repossession of the rights to *The Wind Among the Reeds* from Lane and Mathews, but Brett was reluctant to become involved, thanking him on 21 Mar (NYPL) for sending the letter from the Society of Authors but firmly returning it with the comment, 'I shall do nothing further in the matter until I have received your further instructions in relation to it.' He went on: 'I shall be very glad indeed if the solicitor can settle this matter to your satisfaction without our having anything further to do with it, as my offer to you was only in order that the matter might be expedited by the attention of someone actually on the spot: my anxiety being both in your interest and in our own, to have the books published and on the market in complete form at the earliest possible date.'

## To the Treasurer of the Stage Society, *17 March 1906*

18 Woburn Buildings | Euston Road,
March 17<sup>th</sup> / 06

Dear Sir,
I enclose my subscription for the current year for the Stage Society.[1] But please take my name from the list when it is exhausted. I am so little in London that I have been able, I think to attend only one performance since I joined.[2]

Yrs sny
W B Yeats

Dict AEFH, signed WBY; Private. Stamped by Stage Society 'No 4508 / Rec'd 19/3/06 / Ans'd 19/3/06'.

## To Maud Gonne, [*mid-March 1906*]

Mention in letter from MG, 'Tuesday' [27 March 1906].
Sending her a copy of *Hyacinth*,[1] asking for news about the progress of her divorce proceedings,[2] and discussing her drawings.[3]

*G–YL*, 226–7.

---

[1] The treasurer of the Stage Society in 1906 was W. Hector Thomson, who did a great deal of the Society's administration and who remained on its council for many years. The entrance fee was 1 guinea, and the annual subscription was also a guinea.

[2] WBY applied for membership of the Stage Society on 7 Aug 1904, and was elected ten days later. Since then he had seen Brieux's *The Three Daughters of M. Dupont* on 13 Mar 1905. He had seen more performances of the Society as a non-member, as the guest of FF or AEFH: e.g. Fiona Macleod's play *The House of Usna*, produced with Maeterlinck's *Interior* and Alfred Sutro's *The Death of Tintagiles* on 29 Apr 1900, and Ibsen's *When We Dead Awaken* on 25 January 1903, besides which the Society had produced his own *Where There Is Nothing* on 26–9 June 1904 (see III. 604–7, 613–15).

[1] See p. 350. In her reply MG thanked WBY for sending her a copy of the book, saying that it 'was not *so abominable* as I expected, of course a great deal is absurd & grotesque & evidently written by a man who doesn't know me at all — what vexed me most in it was the infamous calumny on the Irish boys who went out to fight for the Boers, with one exception they were very fine young fellows, who were absolutely unselfish and patriotic.'

[2] In her letter MG complained at the unnecessary delay over her divorce proceedings, caused by her husband's lawyer refusing to appear until after elections in which he was a candidate: 'My lawyer says there is no hope that the case will be heard now, till the *middle of May*, as when the Lawyers don't agree the Judge cannot fix a date out of turn.'

[3] MG had been diverting herself during the strain of the divorce proceedings with painting (see p. 350). On 15 Feb (*G-YL*, 224) she told WBY: 'I am working steadily at painting all day & every day — As you like my work I am sending you another little pencil sketch — my master Granié says it is the best thing I have done, the model is rather old & worn but the drawing I think will interest you — In my

## *To Godfrey W. Mathews,*[1] *20 March 1906*

18 Woburn Buildings, | Euston Road, | London.
March 20th, / 06,

Dear Sir,

I don't know of any book on prosody of the kind you speak of & I don't think that I ever read one. For the most part, all one can do, for anybody who wishes to write it, is to tell them to read as much good poetry as possible, and the older the better; plenty of Elizabethen <song-ma>[2] & Jacobian lyric writers.

Yours sny
W B Yeats

Dict AEFH, signed WBY; Bodleian. *Notes and Queries*, 203 NS 6, June 1958, pp. 260–1.

## *To Alexander Theodore Brown,*[1] *21 March 1906*

18 Woburn Buildings | Euston Road, | London.
March 21st, / 06.

*Dictated*
Dear M[r] Browne,

I find from O'Donoghue's Life of Mangan, that he first used the pseudonym Clarence in 1832.[2] He published in the Dublin Penny Journal a few poems which he pretended were the work of an Italian who lived in

spare time in the evenings I am working at illustrations for the Cuchulain Saga & have got some rather interesting studies but they all want being worked out with models & having no studio of my own it is rather difficult to manage so I am for the present leaving them in the state of projects rather than finished drawings.' She sent the sketch, 'an illustration of the wedding cup of Dectora', in early March, asking him to tell her 'just what you think of it', and explaining that she was 'working very hard. Drawing has been a great comfort to me & helped me to get through this awful time. I am quite happy when painting and have no time to worry over troubles.' WBY evidently criticized the drawing, for in her reply MG agreed that 'What you say about the *weakness* in my drawing is probably right. I feel it myself, & in all the work I do at the *Académie Julian*. I fight against it by using brushes the size of house painters & steadily ignoring fine detail—it is only in the little pencil drawings like those I sent you that I let myself follow my love of delicate line & detail.' And she also revealed that she was 'very dependant on my model'.

[1] Godfrey William Mathews (b. 1868) lived in Liverpool and had probably been present at WBY's recent lecture there (see p. 341). He published two volumes of verse, *The Search for Pan* (Liverpool, 1919) and *A Legend of Paradise* (Liverpool, 1927), as well as studies of Walt Whitman, Pirandello, Edward Fitzgerald, and John Drinkwater.

[2] Presumably WBY was going to write 'song-makers'.

[1] Alexander Theodore Brown, a minor poet, contributed a biographical sketch of the author to Alexander Anderson's *Later Poems* (1912), and published his own book of verse, *In City Streets and Country Lanes* (Glasgow, 1913). WBY had evidently met him after his recent lecture at Liverpool.

[2] This letter is tipped into WBY's anthology *A Book of Irish Verse* (1900), and on p. 59, at the end of Mangan's poem 'Siberia', there is a note, initialled 'ATB': '15.3.06 W. B. Yeats at Liverpool University

Clarence Street Liverpool; immediately after this he became Clarence.[3] I have an impression that I read what I told you, in some biographical pamphlet, published some fifteen years ago, but either I or the pamphlet may have been mistaken.[4] It does not seem likely from O'Donoghue's biography that Mangan's mother was in Liverpool shortly before his birth.[5] It is quite possible however.

Yrs snly
W B Yeats

Dict AEFH, signed WBY; Private.


## To Alberta Victoria Montgomery,[1] 24 March 1906

18, Woburn Buildings, | Euston Road, | W. C.
24-3-'06

Dear M^rs M.

I shall come on Thursday at 4–30, that being the nearest hour that you name. I have been wondering what had happened to you all this time. Thank you for the "Rushlight": I am glad to have it. I have seen Mac

tells me that Mangan was named after Clarence Dock, Liverpool, his mother having sailed from it shortly before his birth. But Clarence Dock was opened not till Sept. 1830, see Annals of Liverpool—Gore's Directory.' WBY had told Brown the fable that the Irish poet James Clarence Mangan (see p. 38) had taken his second name from the Clarence Basin in Liverpool, a canard he was to repeat over a decade later in *Reveries over Childhood and Youth*: 'When I arrived at the Clarence Basin, Liverpool (the dock Clarence Mangan had his first name from), on my way to Sligo for my holidays I was among Sligo people' (*Aut*, 49). In fact the story was spurious: Mangan adopted the name in the 1820s, before the Clarence Basin had been constructed, and was perhaps associating himself rather with 'false, fleeting, perjured Clarence' of Shakespeare's *Richard III*, or the protagonist of Maria Edgeworth's *Belinda*, Clarence Hervey.

[3] Mangan used numerous pseudonyms and aliases in his writing, and contributed to the *Dublin Penny Journal* under the persona of 'Clarence', an Italian residing in Liverpool, starting on 15 Sept 1832 – some years after he had first assumed the name Clarence.

[4] The biographical pamphlet was John McCall's *The Life of James Clarence Mangan* (Dublin, 1883; see 1. 46–7). McCall does not associate 'Clarence' with Liverpool, but merely notes (19) that Mangan adopted the name while writing for the *Dublin Penny Journal* in 1832.

[5] There is no evidence that Mangan's mother had been in Liverpool at any time. She was the daughter of a Dublin grocer, and married Mangan's father in 1798. Mangan, her second child, was born in 1803. D. J. O'Donoghue's *The Life and Writings of James Clarence Mangan* was published in 1897.

[1] Alberta Victoria Montgomery (*c.* 1864–1945) of Grey Abbey, Newtownards, Co. Down, wife of Major-General William Edward Montgomery (1847–1927), of the Scots Guards. Her mother, the Hon. Mary Elizabeth Ponsonby, had been maid of honour to Queen Victoria, who was Alberta Victoria's godmother and attended her wedding in 1891. Mrs Montgomery became a member of the GD (Independent and Rectified Rite) in 1910 as Veronica. She published two collections of poems: *The Rose and the Fire* (Cranleigh, 1908), which displays an obsession with the mystic rose, and which borrows a passage from 'Rosa Alchemica' as head-note to 'The Unknown God'; and *Angels and Symbols*, published by Elkin Mathews in 1911. She had met Joseph Campbell at Alice Milligan's house in Bangor, Co. Down, in September 1905, and the two had an intense relationship, from 1906 until shortly

Catmaol's[2] work in the papers from time to time.[3] He has got down to imaginative material, which is more than our young poets in Ireland have done for the most part. They seldom get deeper than rhetoric. Still, judging by what I have seen, for I have not yet had time to read this book, his thoughts are like well-dressed and light-limbed dancers, but they are standing. The dance has not yet begun. The only one of the young men who get them to dance a little is Colum, and he has only done it once or twice.[4] Your friend, however, is very promising, and as I have no doubt young enough to have a future. Irishmen develop very slowly. An Irishman of 30 is at the most where an Englishman gets to at 20. That is, because all the traditions in Ireland are undeveloped, and we have to find out everything for ourselves. The "Rushlight" is very well got up, and that, too, is a new thing in Ireland.[5]

before his marriage in 1911. He dedicated his book of poems *The Gilly of Christ* (Dublin, 1907) to her, while she kept notebooks of his earlier poems, his pictures and letters, and they renewed their affair in the early 1920s. She knew WBY through their common interest in folklore and magic (see 11. 558–60).

[2] Joseph Campbell (1879–1944) was born in Belfast and from 1902 began contributing poems and articles to the *United Irishman*, the *All-Ireland Review*, and later the *Nationist*. In 1904 he collaborated with Herbert Hughes on *Songs of Uladh*, and subsequently became associated with the Ulster Literary Theatre, which produced his play *The Little Cowherd of Slainge* in May 1905. Early that year he published his first book of poems, *The Garden of the Bees* (Belfast, 1905), and, after a short stay in Dublin, he moved to London in 1906, where he taught in a state school, served as secretary of the ILS, and worked with the Irish Texts Society. He joined T. E. Hulme's Imagist Group in 1909, the year in which he published one of his best-known books of verse, *The Mountainy Singer*. He was to fall in love with Nancy Maude while they were rehearsing WBY's play *The Hour-Glass* for a performance at the ILS in November 1909, but her parents did not approve of the match and refused to attend the wedding in May 1911. Immediately after the marriage Campbell and his new wife returned to Ireland, where his play *Judgment* was produced at the Abbey Theatre on 15 April 1912. He fought on the Republican side during the Irish Civil War and was interned for eighteen months. After his release his marriage deteriorated and in 1925 he emigrated by himself to America, where he lectured on Irish culture at Fordham University and founded a New York 'School of Irish Studies'. He returned to Ireland in 1939, spending his last days in seclusion in Wicklow. WBY included one of his poems, 'The Dancer', in *OBMV* (192–3). *The Rushlight*, Campbell's second collection of poems, was published under the Gaelicized form of his name, Seosamh mac Cathmhaoil, by Maunsel on 1 Feb 1906. The book was dedicated to Mrs Montgomery, and the copy in WBY's library (*YL*, 1170) was presented to him by A[lberta] V[ictoria] M[ontgomery]. A prefatory verse explains the significance of the title: 'Here is the chapbook of my dreams: | I made it in the candle-light | (The lowly symbol of my dreams).'

[3] i.e. in the *United Irishman*, the *All Ireland Review*, and the *Nationist*.

[4] Campbell was in fact a close friend of Padraic Colum, whom he had first met in June 1902 at an Ulster feis, and, as Colum recalled in *Rann* (Autumn 1952, p. 11), they saw a good deal of each other in 1905, when Campbell was living in Dublin: 'in those days we were a great deal together. . . . We used to have great talks about poetry—about drama too, for the Abbey Theatre was then opening.'

[5] Handsomely printed by Davidson & McCormack of Belfast, the cover, title, and dedication page, as well as the margins of all forty-two poems, were illustrated with woodcuts by Campbell himself under the pseudonym 'Ceann-Maor' or the initials 'C. M.' Priced 3*s*. 6*d*., the book is a tribute to the style and production values of the new Irish publishing house Maunsel & Co., and in particular to its most active director, George Roberts.

Please excuse my typing this, but I have eyes that soon get tired.

Yours<br>W B Yeats

MS copy in Campbell's hand of TLS[6] Berg.

## To John Singer Sargent,[1] 24 March 1906

Mention in following letter.
A letter on behalf of the Dublin Picture Committee, commissioning Sargent to make a drawing of Lane.[2]

## To Hugh Lane, 24 March 1906

18, Woburn Buildings, | Euston Road, W. C.<br>24/3/06.

My dear Lane,

I enclose the note for Sargent, you have not given me his address,[1] and you put the wrong address on your letter <to me>, with the result that it only came this morning. I have written his name on the envelope but without his initial which you must add. Probably you had better not write the address yourself as I suppose this is to be considered a spontaneous act

---

[6] Campbell had obviously borrowed the original letter, which is untraced, from Mrs Montgomery to make this copy.

[1] John Singer Sargent (1856–1924), the American-born painter, studied in Florence and with Carolus Duran in Paris. He had settled in London in 1885, and became one of the most celebrated portrait painters of his time. His portrait of WBY appears as the frontispiece of *CW* 1.

[2] Lane's friends on the Dublin Picture Committee had raised a public subscription 'in recognition of his invaluable services to Irish art and in commemoration of the founding of a permanent collection of Modern Art in Dublin', and WBY was writing, evidently in collusion with Lane, to see if Sargent would accept a commission for a drawing of him (see pp. 323–4).

[1] Sargent, whose address was 31 Tite Street, Chelsea, London, undertook the commission, and, although the money subscribed was only enough for a drawing, decided to execute a portrait. As Lane explained to AG, 'Sargent has a fancy for ears that stick out, and mine stick out. And he has a fancy for red ears... and mine are red. So he took his brush instead of a pencil and began working in colour, and went on, and after a while when a sitter came who had an appointment he was put off, and he went on with me. Then he told me to come again the next day, and after another long sitting it was finished' (*Hugh Lane*, 72–3). The half-length portrait, which now hangs in the Municipal Gallery, Dublin, shows Lane aged 31, dressed in a blue overcoat, white stock, and striped waistcoat, and holding a pair of leather gloves in his left hand (Plate 000). The finished portrait was presented to Lane at a special ceremony in the Hibernian Hotel, Dublin, on 11 Jan 1907, with the Earl of Mayo presiding. At the presentation ceremony, the subscribers to the portrait were represented by AE, AG, Orpen, Alabaster, and Ellen Duncan, and WBY was named in the printed list of subscribers.

of the Committee. Which reminds me that it is highly irregular and you must make my peace with Russell and the rest <for me>. I am writing in their name without any authority to write. I am very glad however, to be able to do it for you.[2] Miss Horniman was in great delight over your note on the visiting card.[3]

Yr ev<br>W B Yeats

TLS Southern Illinois.

## To Mabel Washburn,[1] 25 March 1906

18 Woburn Buildings, | Euston Road, | London.<br>March 25th / 06

Dictated
Dear Madam,
    You may certainly play the Hour Glass for the Convent & need not pay royalty. When we play it in Dublin we drape the stage with plain sacking dyed of a dull peacock green, and dress the characters in colours chosen to harmonise with it, purple predominating.[2]

Yrs sny<br>W B Yeats

Dict AEFH, signed WBY; NYPL.

[2] Lane was a great admirer of Sargent, and, according to AG, was wont to say that if he ever married it would only be so that 'my wife's portrait may be painted by Sargent' (*Hugh Lane*, 72). Knowing this, WBY was clearly approaching Sargent without the knowledge of AE and other members of the Committee.
    [3] Untraced.

[1] Mabel Washburn (b. 1876) was a teacher in Worcester, Massachusetts. She later married the playwright, art critic, and translator Frank E. Washburn Freund (see p. 130), and herself translated German drama; she and her husband collaborated in 1917 on an adaptation of Keyserling's *The Grasshopper* with Padraic Colum, and this was produced at the Abbey on 24 Oct 1922.
    [2] See III. 270. Sturge Moore's stage setting for *The Hour-Glass*, after a sketch by Robert Gregory, is reproduced with written instructions in Liam Miller's *The Noble Drama of W. B. Yeats* (Dublin, 1977), 80–2. In an accompanying letter Sturge Moore suggested that 'a raw undyed material would be best for the walls and ceiling', and WBY later noted in *CW* IV. 238–9: 'We always play it in front of an olive-green curtain, and dress the Wise Man and his Pupils in various shades of purple. Because in all these decorative schemes one needs . . . a third colour subordinate to the other two, we have partly dressed the Fool in red-brown, which is repeated in the furniture. There is some green in his dress and in that of the Wife of the Wise Man who is dressed mainly in purple.' Maire Walker, who played the Angel in the first production, recalled in *The Splendid Years* W. G. Fay's original set for the play: 'In pursuit of a remote poetical effect in keeping with the character of the play, he threw away realism altogether. The scenery, such as it was, was calculated to centre the onlookers' attention principally on the dialogue and action.

## *To Lady Gregory,* [*27 March 1906*]

18 Woburn Buildings | Euston Road. | London.

My dear Lady Gregory: it was very good of you to send me that money I had but I found on going to the Bank £3 left. You have always done everything for me & I thank you.[1] I am anxious to get to D[e]irdre & could go to you after the Dublin Show or else I might go north & give another Edinburgh lecture—what do you think? Would it be convenient for you to have me.[2] I am really working hard just now—I have rewritten a lot of my Spenser & sent off a lot of proofs.[3] Lord Mayo have [*for* has] rejoiced Miss Horniman by writing to her for that £25,000 but I think the theatre is going to get it.[4] This private—O if only I had got that business of the costumes over![5] She talks of putting a sentence to her will leaving it to me 'for a public purpose' & has said we might 'want it for pensions' for our people. She is in great spirits just now. T P O'Connor ask[ed] her to come & see him & is writing a lot of letters for us to Liverpool.[6] I may go to Dublin at once after

A background of dark-green tapestries; a rough desk, bearing a heavy book, open to show an illuminated text; a tasselled bell-pull and a wrought-iron bracket holding the hour-glass; these were the only properties employed. Costumes merged into the background, only those of two of the ten characters having tints of warmth in them. The dark austerity of the colour-scheme heightened the effect of the piece as nothing else could have done. It was an outstanding example of that classic simplicity of decor which is so often sought on a stage but seldom achieved. It was undoubtedly one of the most satisfactory settings for which Fay was responsible during his association with the theatre, and was probably never surpassed, although several attempts were made to improve on it through the years' (33–4).

[1] On 23 Mar AG had written from Dublin (Berg) that she was 'going to the bank, & will enclose what will make things easier for you till you are in yr summer quarters'.

[2] On 25 Mar AG had written (Berg), 'Don't put off Deirdre too long; we have at present only the certainty of Synge's new play for next season—if that is certain.' On 28 Mar, after receiving this letter, she replied: 'You can come here at any time—I am inclined to think you ought to get to Deirdre as soon as you can, and do a prose scenario that cd be read on the stage. Perhaps in middle or end of May you might lecture somewhere if it suited, & then be ready for Deirdre here again in June. It may not take you long doing the scenario, but it would be good to keep at it without a break, & then have a run.'

[3] WBY had completed his selection for *Poems of Spenser* in early 1903 (see III. 294), but the book had been postponed. The publishers had now at last sent him proofs and he was taking the opportunity of revising his introduction.

[4] Dermot Robert Wyndham Bourke, 7th Earl of Mayo (see p. 324). He had chaired the public meeting to discuss the setting up of a Dublin Gallery of Modern Art on 9 Feb (see p. 337, n. 1), and, hearing of AEFH's legacy had apparently asked her to donate it to that cause.

[5] WBY had the delicate task of telling AEFH that they had asked Robert Gregory to redesign the costumes she had made in 1904 for *On Baile's Strand*, a revised version of which was to be produced on 16 Apr.

[6] Thomas Power ('Tay Pay') O'Connor (1848–1929) was born in Athlone and educated at Queen's College, Galway. He moved to London in 1870 and after a period as a sub-editor on the *Daily Telegraph* went on to become one of the most successful journalists of his time, founding and editing the *Star*, the *Sun*, the *Weekly Sun*, *MAP*, and *T.P.'s Weekly*. He was appointed a Privy Counsellor in 1924, and wrote several biographies and parliamentary reminiscences. He represented the Scotland Division of Liverpool as MP from 1885 until his death, the only member of the Irish party to be elected to Parliament by an English

Sturge Moores play—which is next Sunday[7]—it will depend on Fay to whom I am sending music.[8]

I will write a longer letter at typewriter.

Yrs ev

W B Yeats

ALS Berg, with envelope addressed to Coole, postmark 'LONDON.W.C MAR 27 06'.

## *To W. G. Fay, 27 March 1906*

Mention in previous letter, and in letter to Lady Gregory, 29 March 1906. Sending him FF's music for the Fool's song in *On Baile's Strand*, but asking him to wait for Hughes's music unless he is in a great hurry,[1] and enquiring whether he thinks a week before the performance would be soon enough for WBY to come to Dublin. Also outlining a scheme for increasing the efficiency and expansiveness of the Abbey work.[2]

## *To Sydney Cockerell, 28 March 1906*

18 Woburn Buildings

March 28th, 1906

My dear Cockerell, I have been in a dream, rewriting a play[1] and have awoken out of it to find that it was last Sunday I should have gone to you to see *Lancelot du Lac*. I am very sorry. May I come out a little later on, after my return from Dublin where I go in a few days?[2] If you were in town on Monday I wish that you would come in, in the evening. I have asked Sturge Moore, but don't know whether he is coming.

constituency. As such, he was in close touch with the large Irish community in Liverpool, and his help in raising support for the forthcoming visit of the Abbey Theatre would have been invaluable.

[7] Sturge Moore's *Aphrodite against Artemis*.

[8] i.e. the music for *On Baile's Strand*.

[1] When WBY met Hughes with FF in November 1905 (see p. 221) he arranged that he should compose 'a little scrap of music for the Fools Patter in Baile's Strand'. Hughes had evidently not yet delivered this, and in the end FF's setting was used in the new production of the play.

[2] WBY was obviously softening Fay up for the new proposals being advanced by AEFH.

[1] i.e. *On Baile's Strand*, see pp. 338, 344.

[2] Cockerell spent much of this year cataloguing illuminated manuscripts for the collector and bibliophile Henry Yates Thompson, and temporarily had in his possession *Lancelot du Lac* (now in the Pierpont Morgan Library), which he described as 'one of the finest copies now in existence of the Arthurian romance'. It was written in north-eastern France *c.* 1290–1310, and Cockerell worked on it from April to September. He evidently re-invited WBY to see it on the following Sunday, for on 1 Apr he recorded in his diary (BL): 'W. B. Yeats came in the afternoon and was intensive as usual.'

*Astarte* is a fine book, a vehement confident book and that is a rare thing today, when Science has robbed us of our courage. It has a quality of personal exaltation about it, coming from I don't know what.[3] It is I suppose the meditations of a lifetime.[4] What a subject for a play the whole story is, but no English audience would endure it.[5]

Lady Gregory brought me to see Lord Lovelace, but he was very unlike the man I had expected.[6] How did that little short stumpy man ever get that hidalgo air that he puts on when he writes? I think that both as a man and as a writer (for I had some talk with him) he underrates Byron's imaginative

[3] Cockerell had sent WBY a copy of the book in January (see p. 322), and WBY had found its lofty, disdainful tone congenial. Lovelace explained in the preface (pp. vii–viii) that the book was 'placed together in obedience to two duties': 'to preserve a minimum of truth and justice . . . and . . . to testify how deeply the sources of literature were poisoned by Byronese traders.' To preserve the truth and confound the 'traders', he announced that he had used only 'authenticated' family documents and had 'not sought for information outside the papers held on this fiduciary tenure. Of all the books about Lord Byron, I have referred only to those which date far back. I am not familiar with things published about him for some fifteen or twenty years past. Nothing has appeared that I should have sanctioned or condoned. In the absence of acknowledged power to prohibit, I did not care to examine. My duties are not to search for information from sources I mistrust; and it is unnecessary for me to investigate the character of books made up by strangers with uncertain ingredients; therefore I do not read them.' He concluded the preface on the same unyielding note (p. xi): 'I do not think I have made any statements likely to admit of specific modification. Opinions and inferences have been formed and stated with care and sincerity; whether they find favour everywhere is of minor importance. . . . I put on record certain facts and repudiate those deceptions which I ought to notice. Having done so, nothing is further from my mind than to take part in discussion; and I shall adhere in silence to what I have written.'

[4] On 1 Sept of this year, shortly after Lord Lovelace's death, his brother-in-law Wilfrid Blunt told AG that *Astarte* 'was the result of fifty years of agitation and ten or twenty years of labour. . . . I don't think he would ever have written another' (*70 Years*, 477). Lovelace himself refers several times in the book to the arduousness and length of the chore he had set himself: 'It would have been betrayal of a trust to be silent, and I was driven virtually unaided to discover as best I could by a process of failure how to execute a difficult and thankless task. . . . The crudest and weakest places might perhaps be considerably amended, even at my hands, if it were worth while or practicable to undertake so heavy a labour over again' (pp. x–xi).

[5] The core of *Astarte* is the first authentic account of the passionate affair between Byron and Augusta Leigh and his brief, stormy marriage to Annabella Milbanke (see p. 327, n. 5). The story is told largely through letters, journals, and memoranda, and illustrated with quotations from Byron's play *Manfred*, which the relationship inspired. Incest was still a taboo subject on the British stage, as WBY had discovered when he was contemplating a translation of *Oedipus Rex* (see p. 22, n. 2), and his recent experiences of the false morality of the audiences at *Mice and Men* and *His House in Order* (see pp. 364–5) did not inspire confidence.

[6] AG had presumably introduced WBY to Lord Lovelace during her recent visit to London, since he had evidently not met him as late as January this year (see p. 322, n. 1); the meeting was just in time as Lovelace was to die on 28 Aug.

power,[7] certainly he underrates his letters.[8] He has come to see in Byron the grandfather and not the poet.[9]

Yours sincerely
W B Yeats

Text from Wade, 472–3.

## *To Hugh Lane, 28 March 1906*

18 Woburn Buildings, | Euston Road, | London.
March 28<sup>th</sup>, / 06

*Dictated.*
Dear Lane,
    I have the enclosed from Sargeant so that's all right.[1] Please send it on to the Committee.

Yours snly
W B Yeats

Dict AEFH, signed WBY; Southern Illinois.

[7] Lovelace thought Byron's poetic gift fitful, arguing that 'literary composition was not natural to him', and that he was 'a true poet only on subjects identified with himself'. He maintained that even by 1830 his 'literary influence was a "light of other days"—distant moonshine' (32), and that the 'breath of pagan and sensuous melancholy which vibrated in Byron has little or no significance to the present age'. He believed that Byron's reputation had been manufactured out of a spurious legend concocted for commercial reasons by Thomas Moore and John Murray, but that they had in fact done much to impair his gift: 'Lord Byron's style was sometimes of the highest beauty, but it was greatly influenced by his subject and by his associates, these last too often of the lowest order.... Great deterioration of Lord Byron was produced by his intimacy with Moore ... who imparted something of his mean, vapid varnish of conceit to everyone who suffered him to approach them' (24–5).

[8] Lovelace had particular scorn for the letters quoted by his *bête noire* Thomas Moore in his *Letters and Journals of Lord Byron* (see pp. 327–8, n. 5): 'The worst of his letters that could be begged or stolen were included. There were juvenile letters in which, having nothing to tell, he made up crude unrealities into idiotic nonsense for idiots to read.... Lord Byron's memory was vilely gibbeted upon the refuse of his correspondence.... The immature letter-writer ... cannot write with that total and absolute sincerity on which literary beauty must be founded' (23–4).

[9] In his letter to AG of 1 Sept (see n. 4), Blunt observed that Lovelace 'was too much wrapped up in his family history to have time to work seriously at anything else'.

[1] Presumably a letter accepting the commission to execute a portrait of Lane; see p. 358, n 1.

## To Lady Gregory, 29 March 1906

18, Woburn Buildings, | Euston Road,
29/3/06.

My dear Lady Gregory—

I have told about the costumes, and have had rather a bad evening of it. But that is over and she is quite amiable. She said she did not mind our changing them, but that she had bitter recollections of the unpleasantness that arose out of them, and so on.[1] She is really very amiable just now and, I think, in good health. I wrote to Fay for such a scheme for increasing the efficiency and the expansiveness of the work and I rather hope it will come pretty soon, while the mood lasts. I went to Pinero's new play yesterday and was nearly as much annoyed by it as by "Mice and Men".[2] I never realise I have a conscience except when I go to the Theatre to these virtuous plays.

---

[1] See p. 360 and III. 687. AEFH had made the costumes for the first production of *The King's Threshold* on 8 Oct 1903, and hoped that dress design would be her creative contribution to the Irish dramatic movement, writing to WBY on the following day (NLI): 'I am so anxious to help effectually as best I may and it seems as if it were already ordained. . . . Do you realize that you have given me the right to call myself "artist"? How I thank you!' Her many letters to George Roberts in 1903 and 1904 (Harvard) are obsessive in their concern with the details and measurements of her costumes, but others found her work over-elaborate and lacking in style, and her dressing of *On Baile's Strand* in 1904 caused an open rupture with WBY. Holloway records (*Abbey Theatre*, 49–50) that at the first rehearsal on 16 Dec 1904 some of the costumes 'were found to border on the grotesque or eccentric, and at the conclusion of the play the entire company was recalled on the stage, and an exciting and amusing exchange of difference of opinion took place between author Yeats and designer Miss Horniman. . . . Yeats likened some of the kings to "extinguishers", their robes were so long and sloped so from the shoulders. Father Christmas was another of his comparisons. He wished the cloaks away, but the lady would have none of his suggestions. Then commenced a lively scene. . . . Candidly I thought some of the costumes trying, though all of them were exceedingly rich in material and archaeologically correct. "Hang archaeology!" said the great W. B. Yeats. "It's effect we want on the stage!" And that settled it!' Nevertheless, Holloway preferred AEFH's efforts to the new designs, recording in his diary on 16 Apr (NLI) that 'on the whole Miss Horniman's original scheme gave me more artistic pleasure', although the *Freeman's Journal* of 17 Apr (9) thought the play 'was admirably mounted'. In a letter to WBY of 31 Mar (Berg) AG said that she was 'delighted' he had told AEFH about the new costumes: 'She would have found out some time we had been working at them without telling her, and might have had it in for us.'

[2] WBY had seen Madeleine Lucette Ryley's four-act historical comedy *Mice and Men*, commissioned by Charles Frohman and described by the reviewers as 'a pure and innocent play', in Dublin in 1903 and denounced its false morality at length in *Samhain* of that year (*Expl*, 112–13). The plot concerns the attempt by Mark Embury, a jilted middle-aged bachelor, to select a young girl from a foundling home and train her in such a rational way as to fit her to be his wife. She however falls irrationally in love with his wild young nephew George Lovell, who throws over his married mistress for her and, after numerous complications and misunderstandings, gains Embury's blessing on their union. WBY took particular issue with the incident in which Lovell, with the author's and evidently the audience's approbation, ends his relationship with his mistress by tossing away one of her love-letters so carelessly that her husband discovers their affair: 'Men who would turn such a man out of a club bring their wives and daughters to look at him with admiration upon the stage, so demoralising is a drama that has no intellectual tradition behind it. I could not endure it and went out into the street and waited there, until the end of the play.' The play, which had been first performed at the Lyric Theatre, London, on 27 Jan

The situation at the close of the Third Act is this. It has been found out that the hero's first wife who has been dead some years had a lover and that the child was the lover's child. The lover is an old friend, and is devoted to this child who is devoted to him. At the end of the act to the entire and demonstrative approval of the audience, the lover is told, not by the husband, but by the husband's brother that he must leave England and never return, and the child is given five minutes to say goodbye. It sounds absolutely incredible, such plays give one the sensation of looking down into some sort of pit of <devils> worms.[3] One thinks of the end of Madame Bouverie and how the husband and the lover become friends because the husband is always longing for someone to whom he can talk about the woman he had loved.[4] I really came away from this play of Pinero's in a state of depression that I did not get over for hours, with the sensation of having been at a monstrous spectacle, and yet I suppose Flaubert's scene set upon the stage would shock an English audience and empty the theatre.

I have sent Fay some music for those lines by Mrs. Emery but have asked him to wait for Hughes' music unless he is in a great hurry.[5] I dont think I would gain anything by going over before Sturge Moore's play. I have asked Fay if he thinks a week before the performance would be soon enough. If not, I will go over next Tuesday, and that will give me a fortnight, all but a day. I am doing a round of theatres. Tonight "Hypollitus", tomorrow night "Nero", tomorrow afternoon something else, Sunday Sturge Moore, and if Fay does not want me on through next week in much the same way.[6] I think Mrs. Emery must be very fine in the "Hypollitus" she is the Nurse and I have heard her do it a couple of times when she was

---

1902, was revived in Dublin in October 1907 by Forbes-Robertson's touring company. WBY had had a life-transforming affair with a married woman, Olivia Shakespear, in the mid-1890s (see 1. 511–12).

[3] Arthur Wing Pinero's four-act comedy *His House in Order* had opened at the St James's Theatre on 1 Feb and enjoyed a long run. In the play Filmer Jesson, an earnest and fastidious MP, has recently married the young and disorganized governess Nina, three years after the death of his apparently perfect and efficient first wife. Unable to endure his new bride's lackadaisical ways, he invites the glacial and domineering sister of his first wife to run his affairs and 'keep my house in order', and his relationship with Nina reaches crisis point when his disapproving former in-laws come to stay. Nina thinks she has gained the upper hand when she discovers letters revealing that her paragon of a predecessor had in fact had a long affair with her husband's close friend, and that her stepson Derek is their illegitimate child. Jesson's brother Hilary, an urbane diplomat, persuades her not to broadcast this scandal and, at the beginning of the fourth act (not the end of the third as WBY states), orders the lover to leave the house for ever, giving Derek, who has formed a close friendship with him, only five minutes to say goodbye. In the remainder of the final act Hilary shows his brother the letters to induce him to disentangle himself from his in-laws and treat Nina with more understanding.

[4] After the death of the adulterous Emma in Gustave Flaubert's *Madame Bovary* (1857) her widowed husband Charles discovers and reads the letters from her two lovers. Meeting one of them by chance a little later, he goes for a drink with him, glad to be near someone who has been associated with his wife.

[5] See p. 361.

[6] Gilbert Murray's translation of Euripides' *Hippolytus*, which had been produced in May and October 1904, was revived at the Court Theatre on 26 Mar 1906 with a number of changes to the

learning the part. She has learned how to act without losing her beauty of speech, instead of trusting to the speech alone a little too much as she used to. Did I tell you I lunched at T. P. O'Connor's and met Prince Christian there, looking like an old dowdy City merchant.[7] O'Connor has been very good about the plays, he saw Miss Horniman last Monday and arranged to write a number of letters to Liverpool. I have had a letter from Maud Gonne about 'Hyacinth', the only thing she complains of is the attack on the character of the young men she sent out to Africa. She says that with one exception they were unselfish and self sacrificing and of high character.[8] Her case is postponed again. It cannot come on before the end of May.

Yrs ever

W B Yeats

TLS Berg, with envelope addressed to Coole, postmark 'LONDON W.C. MR 30 06'.

## To Lady Gregory, 30 March 1906

18 Woburn Buildings | Euston Road.

March 30th 1906

My dear Lady Gregory

I think that that is a very possible idea about the novel, at the same time the habit of construction is too deep in me, for me to make it a mere bundle of opinion. I shall have to complete the present form of it, very much as it is sketched out, but condensing it, and perhaps bring this out by itself as Michael's mystical life and then start another book about his literary life. It will become a kind of spiritual autobiography. I shall bring it over but I a little shrunk from actually starting on it. I know how absorbing anything of that kind becomes.[1] I shall be more inclined to get rid of my opinions by every afternoon for half an hour (say) dictating to you a certain number of

cast. Stephen Phillips's four-act poetic spectacular *Nero* had opened at His Majesty's Theatre on 25 Jan with Beerbohm Tree in the leading role, and Robert Farquharson and Mary Price Owen in the cast. Despite qualified notices it ran until late May. For Sturge Moore's *Aphrodite against Artemis* see p. 371, n. 10.

[7] His Royal Highness General Prince Frederick Christian Charles Augustus of Schleswig-Holstein (1831–1917) had married the third daughter of Queen Victoria, Princess Helena (1846–1923), in 1866. They lived in Schomberg House, Pall Mall, and Cumberland Lodge, Windsor Park. He was actively interested in drama and opera, and was president of the Rehearsal Club.

[8] See p. 354, n. 2. In the novel George Birmingham has Augusta, the character based on MG, admitting that 'if her men weren't more or less blackguards, she wouldn't expect them to go out to South Africa' (136).

[1] In a letter dated 'Thursday' (29 Mar 1906; Berg) AG had proposed that WBY should adopt a new approach to his unfinished novel *The Speckled Bird* by making it 'a sort of framework for opinions, a setting for ideas, sermons & conversations. . . . You could put practically everything into it. Michael cd go to a London theatre & criticize it, & he & friends could plan out what a theatre should be, & so with other subjects. It would . . . have a much larger sale than essays. You might bring it over with you when you come.'

detached paragraphs if you can make time—I have a great many odds and ends to say.[2] Miss Horniman is rather anxious that I should go to Liverpool and Manchester and Leeds with the company at the company's expense. I believe Synge is going, which should I think be sufficient, but in any case it would only be a few days and I could go to Coole after that. I am very anxious to get to Dierdre. I want to put into practice the technical knowledge I have got lately.[3] I think I was a little disappointed with Mrs Emery's performance as the nurse in Hippolytus but this may only be that I know her so well that I cannot realise any characterisation she assumes upon the stage. She tried to play as an old woman, and I never found it convincing and the old voice robbed me of her own beautiful voice.[4] I expect to like her a great deal better on Sunday, when there will be no characterisation, except a selection among passions, the only sort possible to the principal character of poetical drama.[5] The chorus is still quite good but every now and then one saw signs that she was no longer teaching them, in some one or other of the women who would sing a big round note, soft and foolish like a raw egg—the usual sort of modern singing, sounding very strange in the midst of the really articulate voices of the others. There was one big fat woman that roused one to fury, the usual mechanical wind instrument on two legs.[6] I imagine that the Irish Literary Society is going to collapse or join with the Gaelic League or something of that sort. I have not had a talk

[2] These were to grow into *Discoveries*, when published in book form by the Cuala Press on 15 Dec 1907, and subsequently became part of *The Cutting of an Agate* (1919). WBY took the name from Ben Jonson's *Timber; or, Discoveries* (1641), a commonplace book of observations and thoughts over thirty years 'Made upon Men and Matter: as they have flow'd out of his daily readings; or had their refluxe to his peculiar Notion of the Times'.

[3] WBY did not accompany the Company on this tour, preferring to get on with *Deirdre* at Coole, but he was to attend the more extended summer tour intermittently.

[4] In the earlier productions of *Hippolytus* FF had been leader of the chorus, but both Granville-Barker and Murray were discontented with her performances and had conducted a lengthy correspondence on the matter during the summer of 1905, during which Barker had revealed: 'I don't really want to get rid of Miss Farr at all—at the very least I want her psalteries. But I want someone to replace her jejune harmonies with something better, and her muddling with a little real training of the chorus' (C. B. Purdom, *Harley Granville Barker* [1955], 51). Giving her the part of the Nurse was no doubt a diplomatic way out of the problem, and on 29 Mar the *Stage* reported (14) that Edyth Olive's Phaedra 'had fairly good support from Miss Florence Farr who, formerly responsible for the music and for the control of the choral work, took up on Monday the *role* of the Nurse . . . who prompts Hippolytus to gratify her stepmother's desire. Miss Farr proved scarcely as strong in the part as was either Mrs. A. B. Tapping or Miss Rosina Filippi.'

[5] On Sunday 1 Apr FF was to play Phaedra in Sturge Moore's *Aphrodite against Artemis*.

[6] The new leader of the chorus was Gertrude Scott, whom WBY had probably seen while she was under contract to F. R. Benson's Company from 1903 to 1905. She performed in a series of Greek plays at the Court Theatre 1905–6, and was to appear in *Tristan and Iseult* at the Adelphi in September of this year. She married the Scots actor and director Norman McKinnel (1870–1932) on 2 Nov 1907. The chorus comprised Amy Lamborn, Vera Longdon, Violet Myers, M. Saumarez, Elaine Sladdell, Hazel Thompson, Penelope Wheeler, and Gladys Wynne, but reviewers were too gallant to reveal which of these was the 'big fat woman'.

with any member of it, but I notice from the balance sheet which has just come, that they had a deficit of seventy pounds last year and that there is a resolution down for the general meeting about coming into communication with the executive of the League to find out how they can come into "closer touch" "with that great organisation"—I heard some time ago that all the young were joining the League and that the Society was feeling the life ebbing out. It has no real raison D'etre for it has no ideas and if you haven't ideas you may as well join the League which can teach you to be patriotic without them, at least I suppose that is about the state of the case.[7] I dont think you need mind about Miss Horniman's letter—she has said that kind of thing to me for some time, but accepts for all that the situation, she knows that we are going on with decorative scenery and with nothing else.[8] We must say as little about it as we can, but make decorative scenes to tour with assuming that all she wants is good scenes and not the sort of thing we had to put up with at St George's Hall.[9] She said something to me about the girls jackets in Synge's play at Oxford but I laid the blame on the stays which, by the bye, shouldnt be allowed.[10]

I have just finished dictating the new version of the Spenser essay[11] and write this as I find I have a few minutes to spare—

Yrs ev

W B Yeats

TLS Berg, with envelope addressed to Coole, postmark 'LONDON W.C. MR 30 06'.

[7] There was, in fact, already a considerable overlap in the membership of the ILS and the London branch of the Gaelic League, although, as WBY says, many in the latter organization found the ILS's proceedings too cautious and dull. In its February number of this year, *Inis Fail*, the monthly mouthpiece of the League in London, criticized the way discussion had been suppressed after a controversial lecture by Stopford Brooke at the ILS and asked (6): 'Why is it that the lectures of the Irish Literary Society so often leave behind them a peculiar sense of respectability, rarely obtained at other Irish gatherings? One can figure mediocrity amid the charm of that exquisite entourage.' In the event, the ILS did not amalgamate, and survives to this day.

[8] In an undated letter, probably written on 27 March (Berg), AG had informed him: 'I had rather a cracky letter from Miss H. . . . She says she wants money to have us properly set up with actors and canvas another time; & that Well of the Saints & Spreading the News were spoiled by that "conventional" scenery—(the wood curtain)—& must have "proper" scenery in future. Poor woman; it was only Baile's Strand that suffered by its staging.'

[9] The NTS had appeared at St George's Hall on 27 and 28 Nov 1905 (see pp. 233–4) with rudimentary scenery, although the reviewers had been as generous as possible about this. The London *Evening Standard* of 28 Nov 1905 reported (11) that on 'a stage as poverty stricken as Ireland is reputed to be, under stage management that bore all the signs of inexperience and sometimes of laxity, a company of earnest performers attempted the difficult interpretation of four as ambiguous dramatic compositions as could very well be gathered together'.

[10] This was in Synge's *The Well of the Saints*, performed as part of the evening programme at Oxford on 23 Nov 1905 (see p. 236). The *Oxford Chronicle* of 24 Nov 1905 (see p. 236, n. 3) regretted that it had been impossible for the company to bring adequate scenery on tour, but said nothing about the costumes.

[11] The proof of the introduction to the shortened version of WBY's selection from Spenser, stamped 'Ballantine Press', is dated 23 June 1906.

## To George Brett, *31 March 1906*

18 Woburn Buildings | Euston Road. | London.
March 31 | 1906

Dear M^r Brett: Please act for me in the way you suggest, in the matter of my poems 'The Wind Among the Reeds'. I shall be very glad if you can get them transferred to yourself—provided I suffer no financial responsability in the matter <John Lane had intentions of [indecipherable]>[1]. I shall send you the MSS of the poems out of my various books in a few days.[2]

Yr sny
W B Yeats

ALS NYPL.

## To Harley Granville-Barker, [c. *1 April 1906*]

Mention in letter to Lady Gregory, 4 April 1906.
Praising Masefield's play *The Tragedy of Nan*, and presumably urging Barker to recommend it for production.[1]

## To John Millington Synge, [*4 April 1906*]

Mention in following letter.
Announcing that WBY was crossing to Dublin that night, and inviting him to dinner on 5 April.

---

[1] See p. 353. Brett replied to this letter on 9 Apr (NYPL), telling WBY that he had 'already communicated with the Lane Company here, and I am sorry to say that they show a disposition to shift the responsibility back onto John Lane in London. At any rate, in response to my application they tell me that they have written to Mr Lane in London full particulars from their standpoint in relation to the matter and that they cannot give me a reply until Mr. Lane replies in the course of the next three weeks or thereabouts.' He promised 'not to lose sight of the matter' and to get in touch with WBY again at that time.

[2] For the forthcoming edition of *The Poetical Works of William B. Yeats* issued by Macmillan's of New York on 27 Nov 1906.

[1] Granville-Barker was extremely complimentary about the play (see p. 372), and was to put it on at the Court Theatre for eight performances from 8 Jan to 1 Feb 1907. He and Masefield subsequently became close friends.

## *To Lady Gregory, 4 April 1906*

18, Woburn Buildings, | Euston Road, W.C.
4/4/06.

My dear Lady Gregory.

I am crossing tonight, and have just written to announce the fact to Synge, and to ask him to dine tomorrow.[1] I meant to have crossed over last night or this morning, but remembered at the last moment that I had forgotten two wigs Fay wanted from Clarkson.[2] I am afraid Miss Horniman is getting knocked up again. When I went there yesterday she was out but her servant told me that she thought she was getting knocked up and should be kept as far as possible from over-exerting herself. I did not of course mention this to her but arranged to go to Liverpool in her stead in the middle of next week. There has to be an application there for our license on the 12th and she was to have made this, but now I am to go in her stead.[3] It will be a great nuisance but wont so much matter from the point of view of rehearsals as Fay apparently intends to spend next week rehearsing the English programme. This week is to wind up "Baile's Strand" I hope Robert will be up a good time before our first night as I imagine that Fay is already looking forward to saying There will be no time for one thing and another.

He has dropped out Hughes' music and taken some musical notes of Mrs. Emery's instead as time was running short.[4] I expect to have a struggle with him over the singing of that song. I have begged Miss Horniman not to come to Dublin and I think she will not. This may save us all from another breakdown of hers. She has now, I think, definitely, decided to reserve that £25,000 for the purpose at some time, perhaps a good many years hence, helping to endow an English National Theatre.[5] I think, however, that she

---

[1] WBY had gone to Dublin with a certain reluctance, as he had wanted to attend the production of Symons's play *The Fool of the World*, mounted by the New Stage Society at the Bijou Theatre, Bayswater, on Thursday, 5 Apr, in a double bill with Villiers de l'Isle Adam's *La Révolte*. In her reply (Berg), AG said that she was 'sorry you had to miss Symons' play after all, but I am sure you were right to come'.

[2] Clarkson was a major theatrical costumier and perruquier and had recently moved to 41 and 43 Wardour Street, off Shaftesbury Avenue. The wigs were probably wanted for the rewritten and redesigned *On Baile's Strand*; Holloway had considered 'the long, streaky hair' in the 1904 production 'to border on the grotesque' (*Abbey Theatre*, 49–50).

[3] The NTS needed a special licence for their performances in Liverpool on 25–6 Apr because they were appearing at St George's Hall, rather than a regular licensed theatre.

[4] See p. 361. Although WBY stated in *Poems, 1899–1905* that 'Mr. Herbert Hughes has written the music for the Fool's song in the opening dilaogue, and another friend a little tune for the three women' (*VPl*, 526), both pieces (as well as the second Fool's song) were composed by FF and they are reproduced and credited to her in *CW* III, 225–7.

[5] In the end AEFH used the money to establish the Gaiety Theatre in Manchester.

will expend a part of the income on the Irish work. I know that she is going to write immediately to Robert sending him a definite sum to be expended on duplicating scenery for touring purposes. She sends it to him as he is in charge of the scenery. She wants him to get out of Fay or out of someone else a complete working set of "fit-up" scenes for the plays we are to tour with.[6]

I imagine she will do other things of the same kind but I dont think we can get anything definitely arranged except this for a few weeks <at any rate>. I dont know how much she is going to send for the scenery, not I am sure a large sum; as for the other improvements I imagine that we shall have to submit a scheme before we get any definite decision which reminds me that Fay has written wanting an increase of pay for Miss Allgood. I shall tell him when I see him that I must consult you and Synge. If we give an increase it would, I should think, be better to increase it by 5/- than by 2/6 as it must come to that <sooner or later> very soon and we may as well do things as handsomely as we can.[7] Miss Horniman, on whom I suppose the expense will fall, thinks that we should give it. The chief trouble is that if we get Miss Walker back as a permanency, she will make a struggle for the same amount. I dont see that she has any moral right to it, but that wont make any difference. We might get out of the difficulty by paying her by shows.[8] Miss Esposito is back in Dublin and we shall have to consider her relation to the Company.[9]

Poor Sturge Moore's play was a failure. It had imaginative moments, but was made intolerable by a whole series of mistakes. I saw it with the greatest sympathy, for there were gathered together all the mistakes I had ever committed myself. I read the thing years ago, and evidently knew nothing about the business when I did read it, for I thought it was going to succeed. On the night of the performance I made off as soon as I could to avoid having to pay him insincere compliments. He came in Monday evening, but had been so much abused by the papers that he took all my criticisms and proposed changes with a docility I did not think him capable of[10] I think he

---

[6] There is no trace of any letter of this time from AEFH to Robert Gregory, and scenery was hired locally during the forthcoming British tour, but for the prolonged summer tour AEFH provided £50, telling WBY on 12 June (NLI): 'I have written to Lady Gregory to say that the £50 for the fit-up is ready at the Bank, that I told Mr. Gregory about it & have waited for the bills. But I refuse to send it to Fay to be dribbled away without any account being rendered to me.'

[7] See p. 273; AG already knew of this, and had reported on 30 Mar (Berg) that 'Miss Allgood seemed very low — W Fay is anxious to give her another 2/6 or 5/- a week, I don't know if he thinks this will make up for her wounded feelings.' Miss Allgood's feelings were hurt because W. G. Fay had transferred his affections to Brigit O'Dempsey.

[8] See pp. 255–6.

[9] See p. 269, n. 3. In fact, she was now a convinced member of the new rival company and did not rejoin the Abbey.

[10] *Aphrodite against Artemis*, a one-act play based on the Phaedra–Hippolytus story, had been published in August 1901, when WBY wrote to assure Sturge Moore (see III. 104–5) that it 'should

will make a playwright in the end, if he can keep his Dramatic Society alive long enough for him to learn the business, and that is very doubtful.[11] On the other hand Masefield's play has delighted Granville Barker. I wrote him a very eulogistic letter about it, and Barker replied "All you say of it is true"—He wrote to Masefield himself "It has come down by some queer crooked road from the Elizabethan", which is good criticism. He has sent it to Vedrenne so I suppose its production is likely. It is really a wonderful thing. I forget whether you heard it, but its gloom! Synge is perpetual sunlight beside that.[12] I hope after all you will be able to be more than one day in Dublin. I suppose we are to have some of the English programme in the middle of the week, and it will be a pity if you cannot see Miss Allgood in Miss Esposito's shoes as well as the Moliere and my play.[13]

I went last night with Miss Horniman to Anstey's play "The Man from Blankley's". Miss Horniman was in the greatest spirits as she recognised <or pretended to recognise> various relations of her own on the stage and wound up with "Dont you think I am very tolerable considering the bringing up I had".[14] On Sunday I went out to see Cockerel at Richmond.

act admirably. . . . I think you have done the best play of the kind there is', and that all the characterization was good. It was produced at the King's Hall, Covent Garden, on 1 Apr, and Charles Ricketts, who designed the scenery, reported in his diary (BL) that 'though it was bad, it was not so bad as the Rehersal [*sic*] had led me to expect. . . . The bad portions stood out in livid patches underlined by atrocious acting, the hurried entrance and funny intonation of the Theseus set me off into a fit of convulsive laughter which nearly killed me.' All the reviews were bad, but the most damning was that by William Archer in the *Tribune* of 2 Apr (4), which began: 'Many strange things have been done in the name of Art, but few so weird as the performance of "Aphrodite against Artemis".' He noted that Moore had some reputation as a lyric poet 'but after last night's exhibition, he may be urged, and even implored, to hold aloof from drama. . . . Of the absurdities of a grotesque presentation I shall say nothing. These are accidental and corrigible; what is fundamental and incorrigible is the feebleness, tactlessness, and ever-recurring vulgarity of the play itself.'

[11] See p. 328, n. 8. The programme for *Aphrodite against Artemis* said that the performance was for 'the Members of the Literary Theatre Club on the occasion of their first meeting together'.

[12] See p. 369. This was *The Tragedy of Nan*, like *The Campden Wonder* a rural melodrama in which a beautiful but harshly treated peasant girl kills her lover and commits suicide. The play was produced by Granville-Barker on 24 May 1908. In July 1938 WBY, inscribing Masefield's *John M. Synge: A Few Personal Recollections* (Dublin, 1915) for James A. Healy (Stanford), wrote that 'Synge had much influence on Masefields dramatic work. I think especially of Masefields Nan.' Masefield dedicated the play 'To W. B. Yeats'.

[13] During the week beginning 16 Apr the NTS alternated the programme comprising AG's new version of Moliere's *The Doctor in Spite of Himself* and WBY's *On Baile's Strand*, with one made up of *In the Shadow of the Glen*, *The Building Fund*, and *Spreading the News*, three of the plays they were taking on their forthcoming tour to Manchester, Liverpool, and Leeds. Sara Allgood had taken over Vera Esposito's parts as Norah in *Riders to the Sea*, Mrs Tully in *Spreading the News*, and Mrs Grogan in *The Building Fund*. On 16 Jan Frank Fay had written (cf. *LWBY* 1. 159) that she promised 'to beat Miss Esposito' as Mrs Grogan.

[14] *The Man from Blankley's* by the humorist, novelist, and dramatist F. Anstey (pseudonym of Thomas Anstey Guthrie; 1856–1934) had first appeared in *Punch*, to which Anstey was a regular contributor. Adapted for the theatre in April 1901, it was currently enjoying a very successful revival at the Haymarket Theatre, with Charles Hawtrey and Weedon Grossmith in leading roles. A satire on

He has been ill and unable to go out. He abused Tonks and the Slade, described him as one of those people Morris said should keep silent in general company. He meant that he is a sectary and mistakes an emphasis for the normal of art, and therefore needs always a special audience. He thought the Slade influence destructive but good if one got out of it after learning to draw. He tells me that he lives by describing old manuscripts and buying them on commission.[15]

I shall stop now and write to Quinn, to whom I have not written this long while.

Yours

W B Yeats

TLS Berg.

## To John Quinn, 4 April 1906

18, Woburn Buildings, | Euston Road, | W.C.

4/4/06.

My dear Quinn,

It is a long time since I have written to you. I dont expect to hear from you till Hyde is on the high seas.[1] I am crossing over to Ireland tonight and dictate this in an odd half hour, between a visit to a theatrical wigmaker and my dinner. On the 16th we produce "Baile's Strand" all rewritten and all

---

bourgeois pretensions, it mocks the snobbishness and then toadying of a suburban dinner party when a young nobleman, Lord Strathpeffer, is mistaken for a hired agency guest. As the daughter of an upwardly mobile Nonconformist family, AEFH may have recognized relatives in the aggressively radical Gabriel Gilwattle, who, despite his avowedly egalitarian principles, fawns on Strathpeffer; in the relentlessly snobbish hostess Mrs Tidmarsh; and perhaps in the dully conventional guests the Ditchwaters.

[15] WBY was a reasonably regular visitor to Cockerell, and had last seen him about the MS of *Lancelot du Lac* (see p. 361, n. 2). Henry Tonks (1862–1937) gave up a successful medical career to study art at the Westminster School under Frederick Brown, becoming his assistant at the Slade, and succeeding him as Slade Professor in 1919. The Slade School of Fine Art had been founded in 1871 as part of University College London. Its style was set by the French Realist Alphonse Legros (1837–1911), who was appointed professor in 1876 and who based his teaching on French academic ideas, and most notably training in draughtsmanship, in which he stressed contour rather than outline and hatching to convey three-dimensional form. Tonks, with his professional knowledge of anatomy and inventive use of lighting, carried on this tradition. The Slade's influence on British art was considerable; among those who studied there were Augustus John, William Orpen, David Bomberg, Wyndham Lewis, and the Bloomsbury Group.

[1] Quinn had spent months personally organizing and supervising Douglas Hyde's successful American tour on behalf of the Gaelic League, which ran from mid-November 1905 to mid-June 1906 (see p. 212). Hyde did not sail for home until 15 June.

restaged with what I believe is going to turn out beautiful schemes of colour.[2] In the same week we shall play "Le Medecin malgré lui" translated by Lady Gregory and revive the "Building Fund" and "Shadow of the Glen". We had a great audience in Dundalk every seat taken and people standing up[3] and have been invited to play for a week at the Munster Exhibition and at various parts of Ireland besides. Immediately after the Dublin show we have a short English tour so we are very active. John Eglinton is translating for us OEdipus the King[4] and a meeting summoned for a few days hence in Dublin will I hope get rid of our internal enemies.[5]

My book with Macmillan has been delayed by the trouble with John Lane but I daresay that will wind itself up now as Brett is dealing directly with the Lane Co. in America.[6]

You, I hope will be over in the summer[7] I shall have plenty of news of all sorts and I hope a finished play "The House of Usna".[8] I imagine that Lady Gregory has told you about Colum's waverings and wanderings. He has the horoscope of the kind of pretty woman who never grows up.[9] I know an old

---

[2] The *Freeman's Journal* of 17 Apr reported (9) that the 'piece was admirably mounted, the oath scene being weirdly grand'. Holloway in his diary (NLI) described the beginning of the play, 'the darkened stage with the vivid expanse of blue sky seen through widely opened double doors', and, although initially critical of the new design, conceded on his third visit to the production on 21 Apr that 'Robert Gregory's colour scheme grows on one, & gives many moments of high artistic pleasure'.

[3] On 17 Mar the Abbey Company had performed *The Pot of Broth*, *The Eloquent Dempsy*, and *Cathleen ni Houlihan*, in Dundalk Town Hall under the auspices of the Young Ireland Society. Synge wrote to AG on 19 Mar (*JMSCL* I. 164) that they 'got a tremendous House in Dundalk—the largest we have ever played to in Ireland', but added, 'our resception [*sic*] was not very good. The Pot of Broth, failed absolutely and there was no applause at all when the curtain came down', although the other plays were better received. One of the plays that went better—in his home town—was William Boyle's *The Eloquent Dempsy*, as W. G. Fay explained in *Fays of the Abbey*: 'the house was crammed with people eager to spot if they could the original of Dempsey [*sic*]. We had no reason there to complain of lack of enthusiasm, and Boyle had had the happy thought of putting in a few local touches which meant nothing to us but were rapturously applauded by the audience' (191). The *Dundalk Examiner* of 24 Mar thought *Cathleen ni Houlihan* 'the play of the night' (4), but regretted that none of pieces was in Irish. Seaghan Barlow later recalled (Robinson, 72–3) the difficulty of mounting a one-night show on the national holiday. After leaving Dublin by a 6.30 a.m. train he had to fit up the scenery himself ('I tried to find some idle labourer who wanted a day's work, but nobody wanted to work on St Patrick's Day'), and 'had the stage set for *Cathleen ni Houlihan* when the company arrive about 3 o'clock ... After the show I had to get all the stuff out again and back to the station, but this time I had the help of Ambrose Power and one or two others; but when I got to the station I found it in darkness, and nobody but an old night man, who, instead of helping to load the truck, grumbled and abused me for dragging a man out to work on St. Patrick's Day.' The Munster and Connacht Industrial Exhibition was held in Limerick in the first week of July 1906, but the Abbey Company was on tour in England at that time.

[4] See p. 22, n. 2.

[5] i.e. the General Meeting of the INTS which actually took place on 25 May.

[6] See p. 369.

[7] The illness of his brother Jim (who died in March) and pressure of business meant that Quinn did not make a trip to Europe in 1906. On 1 Aug he left Alexander and Colby to set up for himself; this greatly increased his workload, and he moved to offices in the National Bank of Commerce Building at 31 Nassau Street, where he remained until end of his career.

[8] i.e. *Deirdre*.

[9] AG had frequently complained about Colum to Quinn. She had received the latest letter from him only a few days before, and quoted its 'columesque' qualities to WBY on 31 Mar: 'You have said you hope the Society will come together again. I will never do anything to make that difficult. At the same

lady of title, who at an immense age keeps all the little mincing ways of what has been charming, and, in her case, slightly scandalous five and twenty. I am sure the stars had in all things except the scandal a like record at her birth as at Colum's.[10] I have had wonderful letters from him, and so too has Lady Gregory. He is turning in every direction, always trying to butter somebody's parsnips anew,[11] and will not have a friend left in about six months. Synge's new play is not finished even yet, but will, I think be a fine thing—three acts but as energetic as "Shadow of the Glen".[12] It was generous of Hyde to say all those fine things about the movement and about myself. Did you see them? An interview in a San Francisco paper[13]— I am going down to Coole for a little while after the Dublin show to get at Deirdre and am looking forward very much to a new start after all this re-writing of old work. Lady Gregory has a new comedy on hand that will be as amusing as her last.[14] I had a <terrible> gloomy encounter with a Boston lady the other day of a sort I never met in America. She is very wealthy and has wholly given up to Bridge, motors and horses. She asked to go and stay from Saturday to Monday and I refused giving as my reason that I was quite certain that I could not stand any of the three. She then promised me that there would be only appropriate subjects of conversation, and appropriate guests. There was no one there but a young man whom she considered wanted educating. She read out to me all Saturday Browning and read it out to him all Sunday—In the evening she attempted to read it

time if a more popular theatre is started I shall work for it.' Holloway also commented on Colum's immaturity in his diary for 15 Apr (cf. *Abbey Theatre*, 71): 'He certainly is a strange boy with all the manners of a little child! When he gets sense what will be the result? Ah, what!'

[10] Probably Lady Dorothy Fanny Nevill, née Orford (1826–1913), a celebrated hostess and an old friend of Sir William Gregory. When in London, she lived at 45 Charles Street, Berkeley Square, where she had entertained among others Oscar Wilde and Frank Harris. WBY had met her through AG, and had lunched with her on 19 Dec 1897 and 27 Mar 1898 (see II. 161, 202). As a young, unmarried woman Lady Dorothy had been discovered in a compromising situation in a summer house with the gifted but notorious George Augustus Smythe, 7th Viscount Stranford (1818–57), close friend of Disraeli, one of the founders of the Young England Party, and the model for Coningsby. The scandal sheets broadcast this indiscretion as 'a summerhouse folly', and, although speedily married off to Reginald Nevill, she was banished from Queen Victoria's court for ever. Smythe, who fought the last duel in England, died prematurely of his excesses, hastened by tuberculosis and a persistent if incautious intake of brandy, but she lived on to enjoy a robust and flirtatious old age, posing at the age of eighty-six in revealing décolletage for a photograph in *Vanity Fair*.

[11] 'Fair words butter no parsnips', an English proverb from the 17th century.

[12] i.e. *The Playboy of the Western World*.

[13] An interviewer in the San Francisco *Bulletin* of 18 Feb 1906 told Douglas Hyde that when 'Yeats came out he read us your "Twisting the Rope"... and spoke of you as the pioneer of modern Irish drama'. Hyde commented, 'That was very nice of him, I'm sure. But it isn't true. Yeats himself is the moving spirit of the whole dramatic movement in Ireland. Yeats is the beginning and the centre of the theatre there. Beyond his lyrics even, Yeats's greatest gift to Ireland is that he has called her attention to the possibilities of a national drama.' Asked to name WBY's best play, he replied that 'to me the most pleasing personally is "Countess Cathleen"; but possibly the most popular is "Kathleen-ni-Houlihan", and his delightful bit of comedy "The Pot of Broth".'

[14] AG's latest comedy, *Hyacinth Halvey*, had been produced on 19 Feb, and she was now at work on *The Jackdaw*, the first performance of which was delayed until 23 Feb 1907.

out to him again, but he went to sleep first and then she herself gradually closed the book and slept. She woke first and kept the poor young man apologising and timidly caressing her sleeve when he thought I could not see for the rest of the evening.[15] I could see he could not make out what had happened to his Egeria to make her so terrible without notice.[16] I could see that Boston had awakened under a deep loam of the fashionable rush & noise—and pushed up through it and had a brief flowering of some twenty four hours. When I left her she was still reading out this time to her daughter.[17]

Yours sny
W B Yeats

TLS NYPL, with envelope marked '*Personal*', addressed to 120 Broadway, New York, and postmark 'LONDON W.C. AP 4 06'.

## To Lady Gregory, [6 April 1906]

THE IRISH NATIONAL THEATRE SOCIETY, | ABBEY THEATRE, | DUBLIN.

My dear Lady Gregory: William Fay is going to marry Miss Dempsey but Synge is quite cheerful about it. I said to Fay 'Its all right Fay if your family is not too big' & Fay said 'There'll be none'. He asks us to give Miss Dempsey when the marriage takes place 10/- a week & that, & what he gets, will be enough for them.[1] Both he & Synge think it necessary to give Miss Allgood a rise but we can talk of that when you come up. Fay thinks it will be necessary to get two new men at 20/- a week & I know Miss Horniman wont object—he has failed to get them in the old way.[2]

---

[15] Evidently Mrs Ladenburg (see p. 349, n. 6), who was actually born in New York, but whose mother came from Massachusetts.

[16] Egeria, a 'woman counsellor or adviser', named after the mythical companion and adviser of Numa, legendary second king of Rome. WBY may have recalled Chasuble's description of Miss Prism in Act II of Wilde's *The Importance of Being Earnest*: 'But I must not disturb Egeria and her pupil [Cecily] any longer.' When Miss Prism corrects her name, Chasuble replies, 'A classical allusion merely, drawn from the Pagan authors.'

[17] Eugenie Marie (1895–1975).

[1] See p. 265, n. 5; the two married in October of this year. AG replied (Berg) that she thought Miss O'Dempsey 'may on the whole be better than Miss Allgood, who would have mastered him'.

[2] It had been the Fays' practice to bring in minor supporting actors on a part-time basis, but this was now proving impossible. Holloway also noticed the need for more actors to replace those lost during the recent split, commenting in his diary on 16 Apr (NLI) that 'the company really needs a few competent

He will however try for Digges brother at 10/-.[3] I have seen the latter half of Moliere & think it goes finely. The chief trouble is that there should be no wait between scenes. Fay would like to play the first scene as well as the second in the wood scene & to merely drop the curtain between—This would enable him to set the first scenes inside the interior for last scene & have no waits.[4] I have got the song to go well in 'Bailes Strand'[5] but Fay wants to know what is to hold the fire & suggests a gilded skillet pot 'hung between chains' if that will suit Robert's scheme he should write & say as if we are to get a bowl turned we shall have to get it done at once.[6] The clothes are to be finished by Wednesday—& Fay is anxious to have Robert here, as long beforehand as possible, he says.[7]

Fay is not to be 'engaged' until June & very few know of his purpose & I have asked leave to tell you.

Yrs ev

W B Yeats

male players for youthful parts, of the stamp of Digges, Kelly or Walker'. Part of the problem was the Fays' reputation: W. J. Tunney told Holloway on 21 Sept of this year (NLI) that he had been asked to join the Company, but refused on the grounds that while the Fays had 'a genius for stage managing which no professional possesses', it was 'mighty hard to pull with them, their tempers are so vile at times, & they treat those under them like dogs frequently'. The situation was not eased until the autumn of this year, when J. A. O'Rourke and J. M. Kerrigan joined the company.

[3] Dudley Digges, the former INTS actor who was now in America (see pp. 78, 177), was the eldest of three brothers. The one referred to here is the youngest, Ernest (b. 1887), who was later to become a member of Alexander Marsh's Shakespearian Company with Frank Fay, and who took part in a radio production of *The Land of Heart's Desire* broadcast by the BBC National Service on 13 Mar 1928. Neither he he nor his brother James West Digges (b. 1884) appeared in any plays at the Abbey.

[4] The first scene of *The Doctor in Spite of Himself* takes place in Sganarelle's and Martha's cottage, the second in a wood. The final two acts are set in a room in Geronte's house.

[5] AG had been worried about this when she saw the play in rehearsal on 31 Mar, informing WBY that although the play was now 'splendid', the 'only real blot at present is the song & it is very bad—the three women repeat it together, their voices don't go together, one gets nervous listening for the separate ones—No one knows how you wish it done, everyone thinks the words ought to be heard.' In fact, WBY gave instructions that the song should not be clearly heard (see p. 342, n. 4).

[6] The fire was needed for the ritual oath by which Cuchulain binds himself to obedience to Conchubar. This incident was picked out by a number of reviewers; the *Freeman's Journal* of 17 Apr (9) found it 'weirdly grand' and Holloway (NLI) thought 'The Three women of the cups of burning fire looked well, & their chanting had a peculiar fascination for me'.

[7] In a letter which crossed with this AG told WBY that Robert Gregory hoped not to go up to Dublin until Easter Saturday, but would put the finishing touches to the scenery then and the following days: 'Of course, if necessary he will go sooner, but you will know this. I will go with him, and stay for Monday and Tuesday, we come back here then.'

What drove Fay to marriage seems to have been that his relation with whom he lodged turned him out because of the dog.[8]

ALS Berg, with envelope addressed to Coole, postmark 'DUBLIN AP 6 06'.

## To Lady Gregory, [7 April 1906]

THE NATIONAL THEATRE SOCIETY, LIMITED,
| ABBEY THEATRE, DUBLIN.

My dear Lady Gregory: (1) Galway has been secured. (2) Limerick has not as yet agreed to terms, Fay by Synges advice asked £60 for a week, two shows a day & they have replied by asking terms for three days. They have also asked for copies of proposed plays that they may 'place same before the branch of the gaelic league here'. (3) Circulars have been sent.[1] Fay says Robert should be here for Friday night as it will be impossible to give him a dress rehearsal on Saturday.[2] Synge was put out—very—because I said that I am against the revival of his 'Well of the Saints' at this moment & he is dead against the present revival of 'White Cocade'.[3] I am going off to Library to look up Shaw. 'Devils Diciple' has I am afraid to[o] big a caste will you look at 'Arms & the Man' & let me know what you think? There is

---

[8] Fay was inordinately attached to his pet dog, which he insisted on bringing into the Abbey Theatre and which, much to the annoyance of AEFH and the Directors, he took on the British tour this summer.

[1] This is a reply to a letter from AG dated 'Friday' (6 Apr 1906; Berg) in which she had asked for information on these three topics, adding that the 'Limerick engagement would be a splendid advertisement and establish us as the real national theatre'. In fact the Company did not go to Limerick (see p. 374, n. 3) but planned to take *Hyacinth Halvey*, *Cathleen ni Houlihan*, and *The Building Fund* to Galway on 18–19 Sept of this year, although problems over finding sufficient casts may have prevented this too.

[2] In her letter (see above, n. 7) AG had said that Robert Gregory hoped not to go up to Dublin until Easter Saturday, but in a subsequent letter, dated 'Sunday' (8 Apr 1906; Berg), she told him, 'Robert & I will go up Friday'.

[3] *The Well of the Saints* had not been a popular success during its first production (see p. 38, n. 2). In her letter of Sunday (see above, n. 2) AG replied, 'I am sorry about Synge. When he proposed Well of Saints I did not like to object—I dont think its revival in Dublin wd do us any particular harm, but I felt it rather waste of time & energy at this time of your [?]getting up a play that we cant tour with—But if he is set on it, I should give in.' In fact, *The Well of the Saints* was not revived at the Abbey until 14 May 1908, and *The White Cockade* not performed again until 23 Feb 1907.

also 'The Admirable Bashville' which might suit & that I shall look at in library.[4] 'Bailes Strand' went finely last night.[5]

Yrs ev

W B Yeats

ALS Berg, with envelope addressed to Coole, postmark 'DUBLIN AP 7 06'.

## To Robert Gregory, [c. 7 April 1906]

Nassau Hotel | South Fredrick St | Dublin.

My dear Robert: we tried the pot last night & it seemed too heavy & a little too small—a larger would have been all togeather too heavy.[1] Owing to easter holidays we must give directions to Shawn who is to make one of paper mache.[2] What do you think of this sketch—made out by Fay & myself? If it is all right you need not reply, as Shawn will start on it on Monday—but if you dont like it please send a design to-morrow & it will be in good time.

Yr ev

W B Yeats

---

[4] Shaw was enjoying palpable success in London at this time; his *Major Barbara* had played at the Court Theatre in February and *Captain Brassbound's Conversion* had just finished a successful run of matinées there. *The Devil's Disciple*, first produced at the Princess of Wales Theatre, Kensington, in September 1899, and set in the period of the American Revolution, culminates in the success of the New England rebels over the British army of General Burgoyne. In October 1901 WBY had told Shaw (III. 117) that he regretted not getting this play for the Irish Literary Theatre: 'It was the very play for this country—as indeed you said to me—but I did not understand.' The first production of *Arms and the Man* had been directed by FF at the Avenue Theatre on 21 Apr 1894, with WBY's *The Land of Heart's Desire* as curtain-raiser (see I. 386), and the play was first published in *Plays, Pleasant and Unpleasant* (1898). Set in a small Bulgarian town during the Serbo-Bulgarian War of 1885, the hero is an unmartial but eminently practical Swiss mercenary, who subverts the heroine's received ideas about heroism and military prowess. *The Admirable Bashville; or, Constancy Unrewarded* is a dramatic adaptation in blank verse of Shaw's novel *Cashel Byron's Profession*. Shaw wrote it in a week in late January 1901 to preserve the British copyright and it was produced by the Stage Society in June 1903. Described by Shaw as 'not a burlesque' but 'irresistibly ridiculous' (*Collected Plays* [1971], II. 486) it tells how the heiress Lydia Carew is wooed and won by Cashel Byron, a prizefighter, much to the chagrin of her butler Bashville, who is also in love with her and who turns out to be a good boxer in his own right. The play was published in October 1901 as part of a new edition of *Cashel Byron's Profession*. WBY had asked as early as December 1902 for permission to produce *The Man of Destiny* (see III. 288–90), and although Shaw refused that play, he offered the INTS a choice of *Arms and the Man*, *The Devil's Disciple*, or *Widowers' Houses* (see III. 288–9, 296, 302). In the event the Company did not stage any of these plays, and they were also unable to produce *John Bull's Other Island*, which Shaw had written for them, because it was beyond their resources (see p. 79). The first play by Shaw to be performed at the Abbey was *The Shewing-Up of Blanco Posnet* on 25 Aug 1909. In her letter of Sunday AG revealed that she was 'not inclined for Shaw just now that he is a fashionable craze'.

[5] i.e. in rehearsal.

[1] The pot was for the new oath-swearing ritual in *On Baile's Strand*.

[2] i.e. Seaghan Barlow, see p. 191, n. 8.

*18 inches*

It has to be deep enough
to keep people from seeing the
second little bowl which will
hold the fire.

Cords or chains for holding it by, when the girls
carry it between them.

There is to be dress rehersal on Wednesday. Fay says you should be up for
Friday nights rehersal—the last dress rehersal.

ALS Berg.

## To A. H. Bullen, 8 April 1906

The National Theatre Society, Limited, | Abbey Theatre, Dublin.
8th April 1906

My Dear Bullen,

I have sent you off to-day the last proofs.[1] We have been rehearsing
Baile's Strand and I find that the bit I wrote in for the three women after the
Kings go out doesn't work. I have substituted the enclosed. Now I feel
practically certain that the printers have gone beyond that part (though
I have had no revised proofs yet); but on the faint chance that they may not,
I send the new lines. They are substituted for the passage that came between
Cuchulain's last speech "Out, I say, out out!" and the entrance of the Fool

---

[1] i.e. proofs for *Poems, 1899–1905*, to be published by Bullen in October 1906. An incomplete set of
corrected galley proofs, stamped 'Wm Brendon Plymouth First Proof' and dated 'Nov 29 1905 — Jan 12
1906' is in the Berg Collection.

and Blind man. If it is too late to put it in without more expense, I will put it into a note I am writing on the stage representation of the plays.[2] The play is going very well and with more than double its old life.

Yr ever<br>W B Yeats

[*On a separate sheet*]

| | |
|---|---|
| 1st WOMAN | I have seen, I have seen! |
| 2nd woman | What do you cry aloud? |
| 1st woman | The ever-living have shown me what's to come |
| 3rd woman | How? Where? |
| 1st woman | In the ashes of the bowl |
| 2nd woman | While you were holding it between your hands |
| 3rd woman | Speak quickly |
| 1st woman | I have seen Cuchulain's roof-tree |
| | Leap into fire, & the walls split and blacken |
| 2nd woman | Cuchulain has gone out to die. |
| 3rd woman | O! O! |
| 2nd woman | Who could have thought that one so great as he |
| | Should meet his end at this unnoted sword |
| 1st woman | Life drifts between a fool and a blind man |
| | For ever, and nobody can see his death. |
| 2nd woman | Come, look upon the end of so much greatness |
| | (The other two begin to go out, but they stop |
| | for a moment upon the threshold and wail) |
| 1st woman | No crying out, for there'll be need of cries |
| | And knocking at the breast when it's all finished. |
| | They go \<out\> |

TLS Texas.

## *To Lady Gregory, 9 April 1906*

THE NATIONAL THEATRE SOCIETY, LIMITED, | ABBEY THEATRE, DUBLIN.
9th April 1906

Dear Lady Gregory,

    We have not yet definitely arranged with Limerick but I think they will have us for three days at any rate. We have put Kincora on the list and

---

[2] These lines were in time to be included in the new book and appear, with slight changes, in *VPl*, 514–15.

rather pressed it on them but asked them to choose an alternative in case "we are not able to cast it when the time comes".[1]

Fay is rather bothered through not knowing what is to be done about the costumes of the fool and blind man, and wants to know at once.[2] Are they to be played in the old costumes. It is now 5 o'c., and the panel has not arrived. I am afraid it will be necessary in order to save time to simply repeat the other pattern. So far as Fay can understand Robert's directions, Robert planned the panels for a door 6 ft. wide whereas our door cases are 5 ft wide.[3]

Yrs ever
W B Yeats

TLS Berg, with envelope addressed to Coole and postmark 'DUBLIN AP 9 06'.

## To Lady Gregory, [*11 April 1906*]

Abbey Theatre.

My dear Lady Gregory: the stage carpenter[1] came up to day to say that he had made the door this way & could not change it.

---

[1] This was done at AG's own request. After discussing the pros and cons of including *The Well of the Saints* in the Limerick bill in her letter of 8 Apr (see p. 351, n. 2), she had added: 'On the other hand, I cant help thinking the play for Limerick is "Kincora", being its own locality & that if it is ever to be acted it should be there—If this is practicable & you & all approved, I wd. start working to improve it—And if we decided on it, that wd. be a reason for doing it in Dublin in May—But of course I will not press this, it is only my suggestion.' AG's three-act historical play *Kincora*, first produced at the Abbey Theatre on 25 Mar 1905 (see p. 28, n. 3), is set mainly in Kincora, Co. Clare, close to Limerick. Its hero, Brian Boru, was King of Thomond and of Munster. With a cast of fourteen, a new production would have severely stretched the resources of the post-schism Company and, in the event, the play was not revived until 5 Nov 1908, and then in a heavily revised version.

[2] Since Robert Gregory was designing the play, his advice was essential.

[3] In a letter dated 'Saturday' (7 Apr 1906; Berg) AG informed him that Robert would 'send his panels first train on Monday'.

[1] i.e. Seaghan Barlow.

Robert wanted it to go like this

I dont know whether a change is really impossible but I can see that nerves are so upset by the general rush of work & the short time to do it in, that there'd be a scene if I insisted, especially [as] neither Fay or the Carpenter thinks it would make much difference. Robert must talk to them himself if he wants it changed. M^rs Walker has now got her directions about the Fool & Blind Man.[2]

Please bring up a copy of 'Hyacynth Halvey' to send to Miss Darragh— she has had all the other plays sent to her—[3]

Yrs ev<br>W B Yeats

ALS Berg, with envelope addressed to Coole and postmark 'DUBLIN AP 11 06'.

[2] See p. 382. Mrs Walker, the mother of Frank and Maire Walker, made costumes for the theatre; see p. 264, n. 2.

[3] 'Florence Darragh' was the stage name of Letitia Marion Dallas (d. 1917). She began her career in the Strand Theatre in 1897, and played small parts in a number of London theatres before attracting attention in May Pardoe's *Margot* in 1903, but WBY probably first saw her in July 1905, playing the title role in Wilde's *Salome* (see pp. 90, 103–4). A close friend of AEFH, she joined her Gaiety Theatre, Manchester, in 1908, and later formed the Liverpool Repertory Theatre. One of her last appearances was as Mrs Alving in a London revival of Ibsen's *Ghosts*. WBY was sending her copies of the plays in the Company's repertoire because he wanted to enlist her aid in running the Abbey Theatre; she was to help organize a tour to Longford in July of this year, and WBY was to try to establish her as an Abbey actress later this autumn. She was to take the title role in WBY's *Deirdre* on 24 Nov, and also played Dectora in *The Shadowy Waters* from 8 to 15 Dec 1906. On 16 July of this year AEFH told WBY (NLI): 'If you can get Miss Darragh to help you, you will have to support her in every way for *she* cannot be expected to put up with what I bore as long as I could.'

## A. P. Watt to the Editor of the
## Contemporary Review, *14 April 1906*

Percy Bunting, Esq
"The Contemporary Review",
11, Old Square, E.C.

Dear Mr. Bunting,[1]
     I take pleasure in sending you herewith typewritten 'copy' of a new article written by Mr W.B. Yeats, the title of which has not yet been fixed.[2]
     I shall be glad to hear that you have read this article and that you like it so well as to be willing to purchase the British serial rights for use in "The Contemporary Review" only (after which all rights will revert to the author and on terms likely to be satisfactory to Mr Yeats.
     Awaiting your early decision and trusting that it may be a favourable one.

TS Copy Chapel Hill.


## *To Holbrook Jackson,* [*16 April 1906*]

Nassau Hotel, | South Fredrick St | Dublin.

Dear M^r Jackson: many thanks for the cheque which reached me a couple of days ago, after following me for a bit. It does not matter about it being less than you thought I had a very pleasant time & am well content.[1] I am very busy here—for to night we re-open with 'Baile Strand' staged anew & very

---

[1] Thomas Percival ('Percy') Bunting (1836–1911) was editor of the *Contemporary Review* from 1882 until his death, and editor of the *Methodist Times* from 1902 to 1907. From a family of influential Methodists, he was a founder of the Forward Movement in Methodism and an energetic member of the National Free Church Council, the Social Purity Party, and the National Vigilance Association. He was knighted in 1908.

[2] This was 'Literature and the Living Voice' (see pp. 316, n. 5, 326, n. 3), which had evidently been first intended for the *International Review*. In his 'Notes' for *Samhain* (1906), where the essay was reprinted, WBY explained (3) that it 'was written shortly after the opening of the Theatre, though through an accident it was not published until October of this year, and it gives a better account than anything I have written of certain dreams I hope the Theatre may in some measure fulfil'.

[1] i.e. for the lecture he gave on 14 Mar; see p. 326.

beautifully by Robert Gregory, an Irish artist—& Lady Gregory translation from Moleire.

Yr ev<br>
W B Yeats

ALS Colgate, with envelope addressed to The Arts Club, 18 Park Lane, Leeds, postmark
'DUBLIN AP 16 06'.

## *To Frank E. Washburn Freund,*[1] *[after 16 April 1906]*

Abbey Theatre | Abbey St | Dublin

Dear M[r] Freund: M[r] Synge agrees to your doing 'Riders to the Sea' or
'Shadow of the Glenn' in proposed German bill & I send that German
translation of 'Hour Glass' to see if it will suit your purpose.[2]

We have just produced a translation from Moliere 'The Doctor in Spite
of Himself' with success.[3]

Yrs sny<br>
W B Yeats

A draft S. Berg.

[1] Frank E. Washburn Freund, playwright and translator, and husband of Mabel Washburn
(see pp. 130, 359). In an undated letter written at this time (*JMSCL* I. 165) Synge told Max Meyerfeld:
'A German gentleman who knows Mr. Yeats is getting up a bill of Irish plays...and he wishes
to include my "Riders to the Sea" or "Shadow of the Glen," but I have told him that I would not
give him leave to translate them without consulting you, as you had spoken of translating them yourself.
What do you feel about it? If the bill is made up and played I would not, of course, like my work to be
omitted.'

[2] This may have been by AEFH, who was a fluent German-speaker, but evidently did not
suit Freund's purpose since on 17 May of this year he wrote to A. P. Watt from Harrow on the
Hill (Watt), seeking permission to translate *The Hour-Glass*, *The Pot of Broth*, and *Cathleen ni Houlihan*
into German for production on the German stage. The permission was granted on condition that the
plays were performed within three years, but there is no evidence that Freund translated any of WBY's
work.

[3] AG's version of Molière's *Le Médecin malgré lui*, produced at the Abbey Theatre from 16 to 21 Apr,
was so successful that some of the audience called for the author at the end of the performance. The
*Freeman's Journal* of 17 Apr (7) reported that 'Continuous peals of laughter testified to the risibility of
the farce', and the *Irish Times* of the same day noted (6) that AG 'presented a dialogue which is easily
acted, while all the humour of the original is faithfully preserved'.

## To A. E. F. Horniman, [c. 17 April 1906]

Mention in letter from AEFH, 18 April 1906.
Telling her that she has been described as the sister of an MP,[1] that the Abbey intends to produce more plays by Molière,[2] that the audience called for the author at the end of *The Doctor in Spite of Himself*, and evidently asking about the possibility of hiring more actors.[3]

NLI.

## To Holbrook Jackson, 19 April 1906

ABBEY THEATRE, DUBLIN
19th April 1906

Dear Mr. Holbrook Jackson,
  Miss Horniman asks me to tell you that we are taking Mr. Arthur Darley, our musician, with us on tour. He will play traditional airs between the plays. He is a wonderful violinist and has made a lifelong study of Irish folk music. He always plays for us here in our own theatre.[1]

---

[1] The description did not please AEFH, and she replied with heavy humour: 'Who has been advertising me as the sister of a mere MP? Are there not many Radicals & Unionists & Irish Members & such like rag bag & bob-tail? There are several peeresses in their own right, too, *several* mark you, but only one dissenting spinster from a London suburb who subsidises a real live theatre.' AEFH's brother, Emslie John Horniman (1864–1932), had been elected Liberal MP for Chelsea in the general election held in January this year. Her father, Frederick John Horniman (1835–1906), had been Liberal MP for Falmouth.

[2] In the long run AEFH did not approve of AG's renderings of Molière into a Kiltartan dialect, but at this time she saw the plays as an element in the conquering of Irish opposition to the theatre: 'We will conquer your country in time, with the help of *mine* (it has been done before you may remember in a worse cause) & the dear sane Molière is a worthy ally.' Not understanding the waggish Dublin theatrical tradition of calling for dead authors (Molière had died in 1673), she commented: 'Dear cultured Dublin calling for Molière! If he had appeared what a shock for them & advertisement for us!!'

[3] AEFH was expansive on this point in her reply: 'Get more actors, I can screw out more than £430 per annum by various arrangements. . . . I won't have Willie Fay worried more than I can help, he is such a valuable specimen of humanity.'

[1] Arthur Darley (see p. 214, n. 5) had recently been engaged to perform traditional Irish airs between plays at the Abbey Theatre, and was mentioned as an added attraction in advertisements for the Theatre. The decision to take him on the tour to Manchester, Liverpool, and Leeds was made late; Holloway had expected to hear him play in P. J. McCall's house on Sunday evening, 22 Apr, 'but when I arrived he informed me he just had a letter from him stating that he had gone on tour with National Theatre Society & left for Manchester in the morning'. The programmes sold on the tour devoted a separate page to Darley's repertoire, announcing that on the first evening he would play 'The Snowy-breasted Pearl', 'The Blackbird and the Thrush', 'The Gaol of Clonmel', 'A '98 Marching Tune', 'Lament for Michael Dwyer', 'Going to Kilkenny: Slip Jig', and 'Lament for Father John Murphy', and on the second evening, 'The Emigrant's Farewell', 'The West's Awake', 'The Lark in the Clear Air', 'The Kerry Star: Reel', 'An Iverk Love Song', 'The Independent Hornpipe', and 'The Coolun'. The *Liverpool Daily Post* of 27 Apr (8) reported that Darley 'captivated everybody with his superb playing of national airs and jigs', and the *Leeds and Yorkshire Mercury* of the following day (4) noted that a 'feature of the performances was the splendid playing of Mr. Arthur Darley on the violin. It was marked by

We have produced Moliere's Le Medecin Malgre Lui this week and my new 'Baile's Strand': I wish we could have toured with them but that, for various reasons, was out of the question. The two plays have shown our people at their very best.[2] The performance of my play is the first thoroughly efficient performance of a verse play of mine that there has been.[3]

Yrs sy

W B Yeats

TLS Colgate.

breadth of sympathy and a melodic freshness, which added to the pleasure of the audience.' Darley also accompanied the Company, as 'Solo Violinist', on their extended tour of Britain in June and July, when the 'Illustrated Programme' described him as having 'tramped through the remotest parts of Ireland, collecting from wayfaring minstrels those legendary airs that have been handed down through generations of wandering fiddlers and harpists. This traditional music would be difficult indeed to set down, for its proper rendering depends on the sympathy and feeling of the musician, who must be able to catch those strains of sadness which beautify and distinguish all true Irish music and are heard in the merriest of tunes and liveliest jigs. . . . The usual theatre orchestra is not required when Mr. Darley accompanies the National Theatre for, out of his ample budget, comes music so characteristic and beautiful that the orchestra, however good, would only be "interfering".' In a lecture to the ILS in October 1938 (Berg), Wareing claimed that he gave AEFH the idea of including Darley on the summer tour, since to let the intervals pass 'in dead silences as in continental Theatres, would mean that after warming up their audience the actors had to begin again with a cold one. . . . It was important to create and essential to retain the suitable atmosphere and we did this by music. . . . Not only did Arthur Darley's playing keep the audience in harmony with the players, it also induced the right moods. . . . It also brought to the Theatre many lovers of music for its own sake.' Unfortunately Darley offended the Directors by giving Brigit O'Dempsey a noisy tin trumpet during this tour, and he did not appear with the Company again, although he wrote incidental music for a number of plays, including WBY's *Deirdre* and revised *Shadowy Waters*, and Blunt's *Fand*.

[2] WBY had tried to impress this view upon a reluctant Joseph Holloway on 17 Apr (cf. *Abbey Theatre*, 70–1): 'Meeting W B Yeats just outside the Greenroom, he asked me, "how I liked Moliere's farce," & I told him, "Well." He was loud in his praise of W G Fay, whom he thought richer in his humour than ever as Sgnarelle. He was tickled at the idea of the audience wanting the author out at the end of the farce, & thought Lady Gregory's translation the finest he had ever seen of any of Moliere's plays, & dilated on how easily the works of Latin countries could be translated into racily Irish surroundings, such as Lady Gregory had successfully done in *The Doctor in Spite of Himself*. Catholic peoples could always enjoy fun for its own sake, whereas people, like the English, who had more moral than religious sense always wanted their comedy with a sting in it before they could appreciate it to the full. I asked him if he had had any opinion expressed to him re the new version of his play *On Baile's Strand*, & he said he had from Colum & others & they were favourable. I frankly told him I did not care for it nearly as well as the original version, & thought it less clearly worked out, instancing that a person whom I had with me, who saw the play for the first time could not follow it. He thereon spouted something about "a poetic play must be seen more than once before it can be understood". So that settled that point.' Holloway also challenged WBY on 'the poor playing of Sinclair & Power as Concobar & Fintain', but 'he did not agree with me—he thought them very good & we parted agreeing to differ on many points in our short conversation'.

[3] Newspaper reviewers were respectful but not ecstatic about the rewritten *On Baile's Strand*, although most praised the acting: the *Freeman's Journal* of 17 Apr (9) commented that F. J. Fay's 'portrayal of the erstwhile unbending and ill-fated Cuchullain was cast in an undeniably heroic mould. Deeply effective was his frenzied declamation on learning that the youth who had so stoutly confronted him in mortal combat, and whom he had slain, was his own son. Mr. W. G. Fay did some excellent fooling in his depiction of Barach, whilst as Fintain, the blind half-seer and burly mendicant, Mr. A. Power added considerably to the success of the drama. Mr. U. Wright was rather stiff in his

## To Lady Gregory, [20 April 1906]

Abbey Theatre

My dear Lady Gregory: we had a little over £5 last night in house—a slight rise in Pit on night before—& practically the same as night before as stalls were a little less.[1] I found Macdonald working at Sandow apparatus in a desperate way. Fay had told him to do an hour a day of it (Sandow says five minutes increasing to thirty in course of time). This to improve his figure.[2] The house was wild with excitement over 'Spreading the News' last night[3] & Trees business man Waring was there. He wanted to know if I would mind if he offered Miss Allgood an engagement—she was just the actress they were looking for. I said I would mind & I dont think he is going to do it. I dont think she'd go but there is no use saying anything about this offer in any case. He has invited the company to see Oliver Twist on Saturday.[4]

Yrs ev

W B Yeats

ALS Berg, with envelope addressed to Coole and postmark 'DUBLIN AP 20 06'.

delineation of Cuchullain's son, but his make-up, so as to convey the idea of femininity, by which his father discovered in him a likeness to his mother, was unimpeachable.' The *Irish Times* of 17 Apr (6) approved of the rewriting of *On Baile's Strand*: 'The action now moves smoothly, and the dialogue is full of life and vigour. The scene between Cuchullain and Concobar is very cleverly treated, and Fintain, the blind man, is an excellent study. Mr. Yeats could not complain of the actors in whose hands his play was cast.'

[1] The disappointing audiences at the Abbey were remarked in the press. On 28 Apr, the *Leader*, under the heading 'The Deserted Abbey', commented that the Theatre seated 'five hundred and sixty-two persons. On Wednesday evening it seated sixty-two, and Wednesday was the second night of a new play . . . sixty two persons do not make a nation and unless the Abbey Theatre can attract a larger audience than its predecessor, the Coroner's Court, the movement for an Irish national theatre will remain chiefly a journalistic one.' The review went on to disparage *On Baile's Strand*, and AG's use of 'Anglo-Irish dialect' in her translation of *Le Médecin malgré lui*, which was 'fit only for a pantomime or a music-hall "sketch" '. Holloway repeatedly noted and deplored the lack of patrons (NLI) over these weeks, and on Saturday, 21 Apr, lamented that the 'audience almost reached vanishing point at the Abbey to-night—there was an air of desolation about the place', and concluded his positive account of the productions by returning to the subject: 'The very small audience gave an air of intense sadness to the entire entertainment, & W B Yeats wandered about amongst the empty seats like a lost soul seeking out someone to confide in. What will be the result of the lessening of the audience? Who can tell!'

[2] For Sandow's exercises see p. 135, n. 6. Francis ('Mac') McDonnell ('Arthur Sinclair'; see p. 258, n. 3) was the son of a draper's assistant and of a vain and dandyish disposition, famous in Dublin for his tight trousers, but unhappily prone to plumpness, so the excessive indulgence in physical exercise may have been as much his idea as Fay's. In the *Evening Herald* of 17 May 1913 W. A. Henderson admitted that 'his tight-fitting garments, his ample cravat, his raven locks parted across his forehead, his complexion, his peculiar gait as he swings a dandy cane, all suggest the stylish buck of past generations'.

[3] AG's *Spreading the News* was played on alternate nights with *In the Shadow of the Glen* and *The Building Fund*; see p. 372, n. 13.

[4] Alfred Wareing (1876–1942) had joined Sir Frank Benson's company in 1900 after nine years as a bookseller's assistant. He became Benson's manager and also managed for Sir Herbert Tree and Oscar

## *To Maud Gonne,* [c. *27 April 1906*]

Mention in letter from MG, 29 April [1906].

Enclosing a cutting from the *Freeman's Journal*, discussing John MacBride's libel case against the *Irish Independent*,[1] asking her if she is as thin and worn as she appears in one of the drawings she has sent him,[2] telling her that he is rewriting *Deirdre*,[3] and evidently asking for news of Iseult.[4]

*G–YL*, 228–9.

Asche. In 1909 he was to set up the Glasgow Repertory Theatre, and he directed the Royal Theatre, Huddersfield, from 1918 to 1933. He was currently in Dublin managing a tour of a dramatization of Charles Dickens's *Oliver Twist* by the Beerbohm Tree Company. The play had opened at His Majesty's Theatre, London, in early July 1905 and played at the Theatre Royal, Dublin, for a week from 16 Apr. Rather than Sara Allgood going to Tree, it was Wareing who joined the Abbey. As he explained in his lecture to the ILS (see p. 387, n. 1), he took the opportunity of some free time on 16 Apr to go 'across the river to look at the newly opened Abbey Theatre.... There was no one in the entrance hall to stay me and I passed through the auditorium. The curtain was up, two men were carpentering a flat, a woman was sewing canvas to go on it and another man was painting a back cloth. It was the dinner-hour and they were eating their midday meal, bread and butter, cheese bananas and tea while they worked. This should have prepared me, but all the same it was a surprise when I had introduced myself to four members of the acting company. One was Willie Fay, the seamstress was Sally Allgood, and I think Wright and Power were the names of the other two.' Wareing returned to see the productions that night, and was so impressed with the Company's performances that he crossed over with them to Liverpool, where they appeared on 25 and 26 Apr, and subsequently left Tree's company to manage the Abbey tour of Cardiff, Glasgow, Aberdeen, Edinburgh, Newcastle, and Hull from 28 May to 7 July. During this time he and his wife became friends with AEFH, and he was later to be influential in persuading her to set up the Gaiety Theatre in Manchester, which she purchased from his friend John Hart.

[1] This was evidently the article 'Major MacBride's Action' published in the *Freeman's Journal* on 21 Apr 1906 (4), giving an account of MacBride's suit against the *Irish Daily Independent* for alleged libels published in February and July 1905. In thanking him for it, MG remarked that although a press-cutting agency and friends sent news items relating to her she was 'always glad to get the news from you as often the commentaries are very different' (*G–YL*, 228). She added that 'Nothing but madness can have prompted MacBride to take a libel action against the *Independent* for having published a *very* modified account of what took place in the Paris Courts. The *Independent* up to that moment was distinctly favorable to MacBride, & used to publish all sorts of touching little paragraphs about his visits to my son, supplied by himself, & also how his name was applauded at all the meetings when it was mentioned etc.' MacBride's case did not come to court until December of this year.

[2] WBY had been worried by self-portraits that MG had drawn, but in her reply she assured him that she was 'not so thin & worn as I was when I drew the picture. I drew it at the beginning of the winter, soon after these long enquiries which were fearfully trying on my nerves. Now I am much stronger & am looking well again.'

[3] WBY had evidently told her that he was reworking his play *Deirdre*, for she said in her reply: 'What courage you have to begin a great work like Deirdre all over again—I don't think I could do that. In painting when a picture goes wrong I destroy it but seldom have the courage to begin it over again.'

[4] MG assured him that 'Iseult is very well & very charming. She is working hard at lessons I am afraid rather against the grain but with very good results.'

## *To W. K. Magee [John Eglinton], 29 April [1906]*

COOLE PARK, | GORT, | CO. GALWAY.
April 29

My dear Magee: I hope you are getting on with the Sophocles play. We shall want it before long if we are to give a good performance.[1] The Artist & musicians & players have alike to brood over it for a bit.
Company has got great praise in England this trip.[2]

Yrs ev
W B Yeats

ALS Southern Illinois, with envelope addressed to National Library, Kildare St, Dublin, postmark 'ORANMORE', date indecipherable.

## *To Frank Sidgwick, [30 April 1906]*

at | COOLE PARK, | GORT, | CO. GALWAY.
Monday

My dear Sidgewick: Bullen misunderstood me about the proofs—I meant to hurry him about the corrected ones—however with these you send I can

[1] i.e. *Oedipus Rex*, see p. 22, n. 2.
[2] The NTS had been warmly welcomed on its first tour in the north of England. The Company's repertoire comprised *In the Shadow of the Glen*, *Cathleen ni Houlihan*, *Spreading the News*, *A Pot of Broth*, *Riders to the Sea*, and *The Building Fund*. They opened at the Midland Hall, Manchester, on 23 and 24 Apr, played at St George's Hall, Liverpool, on 25 and 26 Apr, and at the Albert Hall, Leeds, on 27 and 28 Apr. The *Manchester Guardian* of 24 Apr (6) reported that at first the audience, used to conventional 'stage Irish' representations, seemed bewildered by 'the real Irishman of the new drama', but that it 'warmed fast and ended enthusiastic'. The reviewer, C. E. Montague, commented that in 'these plays the English of Elizabethan speech comes back to us from Ireland as clean and as fresh as the Elizabethan settlers left it there'. The following day (7) he pronounced *Riders to the Sea* 'the pick of . . . all the six played in the two nights', and praised the Company's actors generally for 'their grave and simple composure of movement, and their subdual of all rant and flare in elocution' which achieved an 'effect of spiritual austerity'. Summing up the two night's performances in Liverpool, the *Liverpool Daily Post* on 27 Apr concluded (8) that: 'All who have once seen this remarkable group of performers will count it a misfortune if no further opportunity is afforded of enjoying their delightful work.' The *Leeds and Yorkshire Mercury* and the *Yorkshire Daily Observer* praised both the plays and the actors, the former remarking on 28 Apr (4) on the 'deserved success' of the NTS, and commenting that the plays' 'literary flavour' was 'genuinely poetic, restrained, and quiet', and adding on 30 Apr (4) that their 'sheer musical beauty would inspire a strong sympathy in any heart'. The *Yorkshire Post* of 30 Apr (6), observing that the 'plays stand or fall by the acting and the literary standard of the dialogue', thought that 'judged by these tests they stand very high'.

make up a copy for America, with the help of an actors copy of 'Bailes Strand' from Dublin.[1] I am sorry to have put you to so much trouble.

Yrs sny<br>
W B Yeats

ALS Texas.

## To John Quinn, 1 May [1906]

Coole Park, | Gort, Co Galway.<br>
May 1

My dear Quinn,

Lady Gregory has read me your letter.[1] You have evidently had a distracting as well as busy time with Hyde's tour, and I can imagine the trouble you have had with our countrymen in patent leather boots.[2] Hyde however must have made Irishmen with you think differently of Ireland, and Americans think differently of Irishmen. He is in a certain sense the race tradition embodied.[3]

Something of what you say about the difficulties of making an art movement here is true,[4] but the subject matter of the art is here and I am

---

[1] See the letter to Bullen of 8 Apr (pp. 380–1), enclosing alterations to *On Baile's Stand*. WBY was using the proofs of *Poems, 1899–1905* as copy for the second volume of *The Poetical Works of William B. Yeats*.

[1] In a fourteen-page letter to AG of 20 Apr (NYPL), Quinn had apologized for not writing, telling her that this was almost 'the first personal letter I have sent abroad in the last three months', and that 'my next will be to Yeats'. He explained that he had 'been more or less occupied with the Hyde tour since last May, when I first sent out the circulars to the colleges, and since September I have given a large part if my time to it everyday'. The tour had begun in November 1905 (see pp. 212, 241) and was to continue until June.

[2] A large part of Quinn's letter was taken up with an attack on 'professional Irishmen' in America, whom he and Yeats had designated as men in 'patent-leather boots'. In a letter to AG of 2 Aug 1907 (NYPL) Quinn described such people as 'worse than useless' and 'mere windbags'.

[3] Although Hyde was of Anglo-Irish settler stock, WBY had always identified him with the Gaelic people. In *Aut* (216) he recalled that 'there was something about his vague serious eyes, as in his high cheek-bones, that suggested a different civilization, a different race'.

[4] In his letter Quinn told AG that he was 'beginning to regret the time that Yeats has devoted to the Theatre. . . . I am very sceptical as to the success of any art movement in Ireland. Ireland is too poor and too Catholic to produce great art.'

becoming more and more certain that new form, new technical mastery, comes more from the shock of new subject matter than deliberate effort.[5] If we can get enough of an audience here to keep our players and our play-[w]rights busy with the expression of Irish life, we shall make a great movement in the end even if it turn out that we get our best welcome in your country or in England. You would be delighted if you saw our people now after some months constant practice in the daytime, for they have no longer to work at something else during the day. Both the Fays have developed a power they never had before of building up a part, as the phrase is, of making a character change with events, and we have a really fine actress in Miss Allgood.[6] While I write they are on their way home from a tour in Manchester, Liverpool and Leeds where they have not drawn great audiences—they are not known there enough yet—but have roused great enthusiasm, as you will see by the newscuttings which Lady Gregory is sending you.[7] Waring, Tree's manager has been so impressed by them that he has arranged a tour for them in Scotland in early June.[8] Of course there

---

[5] WBY seems to have got this idea from Synge, and in *The Bounty of Sweden* wrote: ' "Is not style", as Synge once said to me, "born out of the shock of new material?" ' (*Aut*, 531). See also *Mem*, 105.

[6] While the *Manchester Guardian* of 24 Apr found (6) that W. G. Fay was 'the chief individual pillar' of the acting, it commented the following day (7) that 'the chief beauty of the acting—and it was very great, much above that of anything else the company has done here—was that of a whole', and the *Manchester Courier* of 25 Apr (10) described Allgood's study of Mrs Grogan as 'the acme of clever acting'. The *Liverpool Daily Post* of 27 Apr (8) picked out Sara Allgood's performance as Maurya as 'wonderful': 'Miss Allgood so thoroughly shows us the process of the heart-broken woman.... The subtlety of the dramatist's conception is obvious and Miss Allgood adds to it by the many startling and admirable points of her interpretation. Such an exhibition of powerful acting is rarely seen in these days.' The *Yorkshire Daily Observer* of 30 Apr (4) also reported that the 'acting of Miss Sara Allgood as Maurya was impressive and powerful, and the beautiful cadence of her voice lent intensity to the pathos of the words'. On 2 May (NLI) Holloway discussed the acting at the Abbey with James Starkey, who 'praised Miss Sara Allgood's voice & thought her greatly improved of late', and on 7 May W. J. Tunney told Holloway that he thought Sara Allgood had 'improved vastly of late'.

[7] See p. 390, n. 2. Many of the reviews of the tour commented upon the modest audiences, but all praised the plays, acting and method of production. In *Fays of the Abbey* (198–9) W. G. Fay recalled that the 'Manchester newspapers were kind and did all they could to fill the house for us.... At Liverpool we were not so successful in attracting audiences, for the hall where we played was not in a good location. However, what the audiences lacked in numbers they made up in warmth, and, as at Manchester, the newspapers were our good friends. As for Leeds, we could not have gone there had it not been for the guarantee of the Arts Club.' The difficulty in Leeds also had much to do with the venue, and the *Yorkshire Post* suggested on 30 Apr (see p. 390, n. 2) that 'it would be better on another occasion if the Society appeared in one of the local theatres and extended their visit over a week. Their repertoire would justify it ... the company would intercept that great stream of theatre-goers who in ordinary circumstances never think of gravitating to the Albert Hall, and the "Celtic revival" would make itself known to a much wider section of the public.' The tour made a loss of £199 18s. 7d., with expenses of £247 17s. 10d. and net receipts of £48 7s. 10d. The company took £28 0s. 5d. at Manchester, £14 15s. 11d. at Liverpool, and £5 10s. 11d. at Leeds (NLI). AG had probably sent Quinn reviews in the *Manchester Guardian* of 24 and 25 Apr; the *Liverpool Daily Post* of 26 and 27 Apr, and the *Leeds and Yorkshire Mercury* and the *Yorkshire Daily Observer* of 28 and 30 Apr.

[8] See p. 388, n. 4. As Alfred Wareing recalled in his 1938 lecture to the ILS (see p. 387, n. 1) he returned to England with Tree's company on the same boat that took the Abbey Company to

are moments when one desponds as to one's chances of making a really great movement here, but it really doesnt matter. Fine works of art are like curses, and all come home to roost in the end. Synge may have to find his way home through England and America. Thanks to Lady Gregory my Deirdre play has at last come right. She has kept me to the point and prevented my imagination from being in all four quarters of the heavens. It is there now the most of it, good logical story telling and with plenty of moments for poetry even lyric moments. But alas I have had to fling out of the window last years verse writing, and with it a fine hawk-like Lavarcam, and begin afresh.[9] When you get my rewritten Baile's Strand, Shadow Waters &c I think you will see I have got much out of all this re-writing. I think in about another twelve months we shall be able to see some clear results in Ireland, but not till that. We are holding our audiences and slightly increasing them, or rather we were until the brightenin[g] evenings sent them out of town on their bycicles and the like. For the moment however the withdrawal from the work of Colum, Starkey and their sort,

---

Manchester, and in the course of the voyage had a long talk with Fay, who told him 'of his many but unsuccessful attempts to get one or two of the managers of regular Theatres to give the Abbey Theatre company an engagement. Not one would give them a chance or take the smallest risk, not even the managers at Oxford and Cambridge.... As most men find who bring ideas into the Theatre Fay found the Theatre managers a reactionary body, a close corporation governing a rotten system which even then was nodding to its fall... I knew I was right when I said I believed the Irish Players had an audience waiting for them in England, and when Fay entreated me as the first real living Theatre manager to see and appreciate this work to help him break though this barrier of ignorance and prejudice I promised to help him. It was impossible to be with these people long without realising the worth of their efforts and their sincerity and I felt convinced I could urge their cause with reasoned eloquence.' W. G. Fay corroborates these recollections in *Fays of the Abbey* (197–8): 'Mr. Wareing thereupon made a proposal. The tour that he was at the moment looking after for Sir Herbert Tree was coming to an end in a few weeks, and then the company were having a holiday during which he would be free to do other work. He was sure that he could open some dates for us at first-class theatres in towns where he was known.... The upshot was that on my advice Miss Horniman got into touch with Mr. Wareing, and she made with him an arrangement that was to take effect as soon as our present short tour was finished. In the meantime he was to get as many towns booked as possible before joining us in Dublin.' Wareing attended the Abbey performances in Liverpool, and managed the extended British tour from 28 May to 7 July.

[9] See pp. 360, 389. In the legend 'The Fate of the Sons of Usnach' it is prophesied that Deirdre will be the cause of great bloodshed in Ireland and so her father sends her from infancy to a sequestered house where she is brought up by Levarcham, a wise but stern fostermother. Despite Levarcham's best endeavours the attempt to keep Deirdre hidden fails, and she falls in love with Naoise, one of the three sons of Usnach. However, Conchubar, the High King, also wants her for his wife and she escapes to Scotland with the sons of Usnach to avoid his wrath. Under Fergus's protection and against Deirdre's better judgement, they return to Ireland, where, despite his promise, Conchubar has Naoise murdered and where as a consequence Deirdre commits suicide. As he wrote the play WBY focused increasingly on the climax of the story and in the final version it begins after Deirdre and Naoise have returned from Scotland, so that Levarcham's part is completely omitted. In a note to the play (*VPl*, 389) WBY explained that the tale 'is made up out of more than a dozen old texts. All these texts differ more or less, sometimes in essential things, and in arranging the story for the bounds of a one-act play, I have had to leave out many details, even some important persons, that are in the old versions.'

has set the little gossipy barren group who look upon themselves as the official supporters of everything Irish of an intellectual sort, mewing after us.[10] It will take them a few more months to realise that they have lost us for good and all, and that we are going our own way. They will become silent and some other group will join us, and we shall have the beginnings of an intellectual Dublin, at least that is the way I see things. We shall have educated our own public a little, what following we have is fanatical. When we produced Lady Gregory's White Cockade we bought some sailors tackle ropes blocks and so on from a rope-maker on the quays.[11] We found he was an enthusiast for us, he came to all our shows, and though he was accustomed to go over to London for first nights, being theatre mad, he said we alone were on the right track[12] and would soon have the only plays there were.[13] The one night I saw an elderly gentleman ordering a drunken man to be turned out of the gallery. 'Whats this' cried the drunken man 'in the first theatre for intelligence in Ireland?'

Now about Mrs Sutherlands proposal that Miss Kauser be made agent for our plays in America.[14] From watching our plays now with quite a number of audiences I feel pretty confident that some of them would succeed. The important thing would be to begin pushing none but the little group of plays, not necessarily the best, which are most powerful with normal audiences. With one exception these are all one act plays. They are Shadow of the Glen; Riders to the Sea; Hyacinth Halvey; Spreading the news; Kathleen ny Houlihan; Pot of Broth; Hourglass; The one exception is Boyle's Building Fund, which is in three short acts. The Building Fund however, vigorous as it is, has no distinguished qualities of style, I mean that granted the right actor it will always play, but is not a play to cry up for its intellect. I mean that there are plenty of vague places, for the most part

---

[10] The *Leader* review (see p. 388, n. 1) had mentioned the split in the Abbey and the secession of Colum and the Walkers as one of the reasons for the small Abbey audiences. It also cited the cost of the 1s. seats and Dublin's preference for English entertainments as further reasons for the Abbey's unpopularity.

[11] This was first produced on 9 Dec 1905. The ropes and tackle were part of the scenery in the final act, set on the pier of the harbour of Duncannon from where James II sails for France.

[12] A great number of rope-makers had premises on the Dublin quays, but this may have been J. P. Keogh of George's Quay, with whom Holloway had numerous conversations about the theatre.

[13] The typist has repeated the words 'soon have the only'.

[14] Alice Kauser (*c.* 1872–1945), a successful theatrical agent and play-broker, was the daughter of a naturalized US citizen of Hungarian birth. She was born in Budapest, where her father was American consul, and received her education in Europe. Her cosmopolitan background (her godfather was Franz Liszt) was of assistance when she moved to New York as an agent, and she represented Sardou, Hauptmann, Suderman, Anatole France, and Arthur Schnitzler, and was said to have sent Ibsen the only royalties he ever received from America. But she was also noted for her encouragement of promising American playwrights. Evelyn Greenleaf Sutherland, née Baker (1855–1908), a journalist and playwright, had, as Quinn reported in his letter to AG, recently put on a season of Irish plays, including *The Land of Heart's Desire*, Hyde's *The Twisting of the Rope* and *The Lost Saint*, and Synge's *Riders to the Sea*, in Boston.

places out of which Lady Gregory and myself have cut conventional idealisms that were not at all vague but positive and common.[15] Boyle is a good gentle loyal soul and one hates to say these things. I believe that Synges new long play[16] will be as accomplished on a big scale as his one act plays are on a small scale, and I am feeling very confident that I have got my three latest verse plays technically efficient at last, but I may be wrong;[17] in any case the new versions are not yet in print. Lady Gregory has a new long play in her head, and will probably get that right.[18] I think her White Cockade charming on the stage, but it wants an audience who can think themselves into sympathy with a dreamy point of view. It is too loosely constructed for a normal audience, and if it were not, could not do its work, which is to make the world seem vaporous and visionary as it is in an old country song.[19] She has practically finished a one act play, The Jackdaw, a sort of parody of 'Twenty-Five', and as delightful as Spreading the News.[20] I say all this because of the possibility that the play broker may write to you. We are all learning our craft and there is no hurry. I wrote to you some months ago with a letter to forward to a lecture agency. I havnt heard anything from them but that doesnt matter,[21] as I find I cannot get out next winter, but must keep close to the Theatre here. In any case I doubt that I should go there till my collected edition with Macmillan has been out for a while, and the whole movement has a few more months growth in it.[22]

---

[15] WBY had suggested changes to Boyle on first reading the play (see III. 599) and others were doubtless made in rehearsal. Boyle's *The Eloquent Dempsy* was subjected to even more radical surgery; see pp. 162–3, 195–6, 214–15.

[16] i.e. *The Playboy of the Western World*.

[17] i.e. the rewritten *The Shadowy Waters*, *On Baile's Strand*, and *Deirdre*.

[18] i.e. *The Canavans*, first produced at the Abbey Theatre on 8 Dec of this year.

[19] See pp. 127, n. 6, 245, n. 1 for reviews and an account of the play. Part of WBY's fulsomeness may be due to the fact that AG was typing this letter at his dictation. Quinn had recently sent fifteen copies of his copyright edition of the play to AG and told her he had distributed the others among his friends.

[20] AG's one-act comedy *The Jackdaw* was not produced at the Abbey Theatre until 23 Feb 1907. Its plot revolves around the attempt of a well-to-do farmer to give his sister £10 to save her from bankruptcy without her discovering the identity of her benefactor. The village wiseacre tells her the money is from a South African mine-owner, who wants to buy her pet jackdaw; this ruse works but the whole village goes in quest of jackdaws to sell to the mythical buyer, and suspects he has been murdered when he cannot be found. In its theme of hidden benefaction it resembles, and at times even directly echoes, AG's earlier one-act play *Twenty-Five* published in the *Gael* (NY) in December 1902 as *A Losing Game*, and first produced by the INTS on 14 Mar 1903. In that play an emigrant returns from America as a rich man to marry his sweetheart but, discovering that she is now the wife of an impoverished farmer, deliberately loses to him at cards to save his farm. In a programme note for the first production of *The Jackdaw* AG wrote that *Twenty-Five* 'was especially liked in England "because it is so sentimental." I have myself a leaning towards sentimentality, and to convey it have written a parody of the old play, letting loose *The Jackdaw* to croak upon its grave.'

[21] i.e. the letter of 5 Dec 1905 to the Pond Bureau which Quinn had decided not to pass on; see pp. 238–9.

[22] The first volume (*Lyrical Poems*) of this edition was to be published in New York on 27 Nov 1906. The second volume (*Dramatical Poems*) appeared on 8 July 1907.

We have at last got things into our own hands here with the theatre. We compounded with the enemy, making a bargain with them that they were all to resign in return for fifty pounds (to which they had not the slightest claim) and costumes, to start a theatre of their own. So far from their ever having helped to earn any of this money, the society would have been bankrupt but for the money which you, Lady Gregory and Miss Horniman had put into it, but there was nothing else to be done but give it; while they were in the Society they could have stopped our work at any time, and the wear and tear on all our actors nerves was too great.[23] It is wonderful how quickly everything is decided now there are only three people to decide things.

Yrs ever
W B Yeats

TLS NYPL, with envelope marked 'Personal', addressed to 120 Broadway, New York, postmark 'ORANMORE MY ?3 06'.

## *To Maud Gonne,* [*early May 1906*]

Mention in letter from MG, 'Monday' [early May 1906].
Asking for news about the progress of her divorce proceedings,[1] enquiring when she will be coming to Ireland,[2] and suggesting that he might come to see her in Paris.[3]

*G–YL*, 229–30.

[23] The cheque for £50 was paid by 20 May 1906, when Keohler issued a receipt for it (Harvard), but it proved to be made out incorrectly and had to be resubmitted in late June. WBY's resentment at having to hand it over remained a recurrent topic of adverse gossip in Dublin for several years.

[1] In her reply MG said her lawyer 'only returns from his election campaign today', and that she was to see him the following day to try to fix a date for the final hearing. But she thought that MacBride's lawyer would ask for a postponement until after MacBride's libel case in Dublin on 6 June, and supposed that 'it will be nearly the end of June before the case is over'.

[2] MG said that she intended coming to Dublin directly her case was over 'though the lawyers have not yet decided as to whether it will be safe for me to take my son out of France — much depends on the terms of the verdict. If I cannot bring him to Ireland with me at once, my stay there will be very short as he is very delicate & I shall have to take him into the country for the hot weather.' She promised to let WBY know as soon as possible when she would be in Dublin and London 'as I should like to meet you then & there is a great deal I would like to talk to you about'.

[3] MG declined his offer to go to Paris, as she would be soon in Ireland, and because 'you have so much work, just now waiting for you'.

## *To A. H. Bullen,* [*? early May 1906*]

COOLE PARK, | GORT, | CO. GALWAY.

My dear Bullen: I dare say there is an obscurity about 'Although' but I do not feal able to alter it at present. I mean that 'Although' he had so cheerful an eye he was ragged etc.[1] You are right about the italics. 'bird' is right.[2]

When you go to A P Watt dont forget about 'Poems 1897–1906' or 'Dierdre'.[3]

Yr ev
W B Yeats

ALS Kansas.

## *To Witter Bynner, 5 May* [*1906*]

Coole Park, | Gort, Co Galway
May 5

My Dear Mʳ Bynner

I have no lyric to send because I have been buried in plays this last year. I think of nothing else, for the existence of my little company gives me an opportunity that no dramatic poet has had for generations of mastering the technique of dramatic verse. I shall have time for lyrics later on.[1]

I however send you a play, not mine but Lady Gregory's, which I think extraordinarily amusing. I know that editors have a prejudice against plays, but if there are any exceptions, they should be just such pieces of abounding merry dialogue as this. If however you cant take it, and I have an uneasy feeling it may be too long, please send it to John Quinn, 120 Broadway, who very kindly looks after the copyrighting of such things for us.[2]

---

[1] Bullen had evidently queried lines 25–30 of 'Baile and Aillinn' (*VP*, 190), to be republished in *Poems, 1899–1905*: 'They found an old man running there: | He had ragged long grass-coloured hair; | He had knees that stuck out of his hose; | He had puddle-water in his shoes; | He had half a cloak to keep him dry, | Although he had a squirrel's eye.'

[2] Bullen had perhaps questioned whether 'bird' was to be singular or plural in the line '*Let rush and bird cry out their fill*' in 'Baile and Aillinn' (*VP*, 197). The line begins the final stanza of the poem, which, like the first and two others, is in italics.

[3] As was his custom, Bullen did not sign the contracts for *Poems, 1899–1905* and *Deirdre* until both had been published.

[1] Bynner had evidently asked WBY for further poems for *McClure's Magazine* (see p. 105, n. 11). Although in October 1906 it advertised WBY as among its contributors for 1907, he did not publish in it again until 1910.

[2] WBY was sending *Hyacinth Halvey*, first produced on 19 Feb, but *McClure's Magazine* did not print it.

The little company is touring at present, and gaining much glory for itself.[3] The play I send you is one of its most successful things. I am deep in a new verse play which I think my best poem as well as my best play, and hope to be through with it in a reasonable time.[4] I have done apparently very little work for some two or three years, but really a great deal, for I have been rewriting old work stuff to make it fitting for the stage. It is just the kind of work one gets no credit from but learns most from.

Yrs sny<br>W B Yeats

TLS Harvard.

## *To T. Sturge Moore, 6 May [1906]*

at | COOLE PARK, | GORT, | CO. GALWAY.<br>May 6

My dear Sturge Moore: many thanks for name of Appias book which I have asked Miss Horniman to get.[1] I tried to join in that contraversy but nothing worth having would come though I wrote a lot.[2] My people are setting out

---

[3] In fact the Company was between tours: it had finished its tour in the north of England at Leeds on 28 Apr, and was to begin its more ambitious British tour in Cardiff on 28 May, after a one-night visit to Dundalk on 15 May.

[4] i.e. *Deirdre*.

[1] Adolphe Appia (1862–1928), stage designer, was a first-cousin of Marie, Sturge Moore's wife. His ambition was to develop the perfect *mise en scène* for Wagner's music dramas and so achieve Wagner's ideal synthesis of all fine arts. The book WBY refers to may have been *La Mise en scène du drame wagnérian* (Paris, 1895), especially as he had recently read Symons's essay on Wagner (see p. 175), but might also have been *Die Musik und die Inscenierung* (Munich, 1899), although, since no English translation appeared until 1962, WBY could not have read it. WBY had written of Appia's dramaturgy in *Samhain* 1904: 'M. Appia and M. Fortuni are making experiments in the staging of Wagner for a private theatre in Paris, but I cannot understand what Mr. Appia is doing, from the little I have seen of his writing.... One agrees with all the destructive part of his criticism, but it looks as if he himself is seeking, not convention, but a more perfect realism. I cannot persuade myself that the movement of life is flowing that way, for life moves by a throbbing as of a pulse, by reaction and action. The hour of convention and decoration and ceremony is coming again' (*Expl*, 179–80).

[2] William Archer's attack on *Aphrodite against Artemis* (see pp. 371–2, n. 10) had led to a controversy in the correspondence columns of *Tribune*. Sturge Moore showed Ricketts the article on 3 Apr, and, although Ricketts privately shared many of Archer's reservations about the play, he loyally wrote a reply, published on 7 Apr (2), complaining of Archer's 'distortion and misquotation' and insisting that Moore contributed something to the legend not found in Euripides or Racine: 'the tangle of passion and remorse, the despair of the Phaedra of Mr. Moore touches even in its range the subconscious self, where the proprieties and limits of a common sorrow or of accident are outreached; this has been done in its degree by him only.' Archer, noting that 'Mr. Ricketts' generous indignation has a little got the better of his urbanity', reiterated on the same page that he had been able to find no trace 'of dignity, restraint, tact, taste, dramatic instinct, or sense of style' in the play. Gordon Craig, in a letter published on 18 Apr (2), discriminated between literary and theatrical work, alleging that while Moore's play was 'beautiful', he knew nothing of the stage: 'each art is and must be by its nature independent of all the other arts, and

on the first regular professional engagement at the ordinary theatres, Trees manager has engaged them for an English tour[3]—they will I think however take nothing but peasant work. I am sorry you have chosen 'Salome' though 'The Florentine Tragedy' will probably make all the difference between success & failure as it will bring the old audience.[4] I think the Wild audience is limited to a few hundred, who have already been; but my real objection is that 'Salome' is thoroughly bad. The general construction is all right, is even powerful, but the dialogue is empty, sluggish & pretentious. It has nothing of drama of any kind, never working to any climax but always ending as it began. A good play goes like this

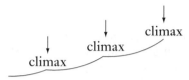

but 'Salome' is as level as a table. Wild was not a poet but a wit & critic & could not endure his limitations. He thought he was writing beautifully when he had collected beautiful things & thrown them togeather in a heap. He never made anything organic, while he was trying to be a poet. You will never create an audience with any liking for anything by playing his poetical work.[5] No good actor will ever succeed in inorganic work, & you will get

only he who is a master of the materials of the theatre can produce a work of art in the theatre.' WBY's attempts to join in the debate were probably frustrated by his serious doubts about the play (see p. 371).

[3] i.e. Alfred Wareing (see p. 388). In his ILS lecture Wareing recalled that in planning the tour 'Miss Horniman expresssed a preference for certain towns and disregarded the increased travelling expenses and the fatigue of long journeys. And so, addressing my letters from His Majesty's Theatre London and writing firmly but hopefully I was able to book the Irish Players . . . for a week at each of the following: Cardiff, Glasgow, Aberdeen, Edinburgh, Newcastle and Hull on very good sharing terms, it being understood that I was in charge of the company and would go ahead in advance to organise audiences for the visit.'

[4] Plans had been in hand since March for the production of Wilde's *Salome* and *A Florentine Tragedy* by the Literary Theatre Society, and the two plays were presented at the King's Hall, Covent Garden, on 10 and 18 June. Miss Darragh played the title role in *Salome* (after Mrs Pat Campbell had cried off), with FF as Herodias, Lewis Casson as Iokanaan, and Farquharson as Herod. In *A Florentine Tragedy* Gwendolyn Bishop took the part of Bianca and Reginald Owen that of Guido Bardi. The costumes were designed by Charles Ricketts, who was obliged to take over the direction of the two plays when the stage manager walked out two days before the first night.

[5] WBY's heavily marked copy of *Salome* is signed 'W B Yeats | Feb. 07' (*YL*, 2271). The play uses the same theme as his own *King of the Great Clock Tower* (1935), as he acknowledged ('The dance with the severed head, suggests the central idea of Wilde's *Salome*'), although the main influence was his story 'The Binding of the Hair': 'In attempting to put that story into a dance play I found that I had gone close to Salome's dance in Wilde's play. But in his play the dance is before the head is cut off' (*VPl*, 1010). WBY was fascinated by Wilde's personality and describes him at length in *Aut* (130–2) and *Mem* (21–3). In his introduction to *The Happy Prince and Other Fairy Tales* (1923), he wrote that 'when I remember him with pleasure it is always the talker I remember. . . . The further Wilde goes in his writings from the method of speech, from improvisation, from sympathy with some especial audience the less original he is, the less accomplished.' In *AVB* WBY places Wilde in the nineteenth phase, explaining in *Aut* (293) that he 'understood his weakness, true personality was impossible, for that is born in solitude, and at his moon one is not solitary; he must project himself before the eyes of others'.

your self into the hands of the amateur, of the dillitante, & of vulgar charlitans like Farquesson.[6] I have nearly as strong objections to the Hell act out of Shaws play—though different ones. That too has no real dramatic life.[7] To do anything you must have a group of players who will stick to you, & learn the business of simplicity & imagine that your present 'people' will if they get a chance, & you must write & choose such plays as will display them at their best—never on any excuse of expediency or convenience putting upon the stage inorganic work which means boredom for them & therefore bad work for them & boredom for all.

Yr ev

W B Yeats

PS: it is not in the least because of anything I say or think about 'Salome' but I wish you could put somebody else on that committee in my stead.[8] I have made a general rule of confining work to Ireland for the present & also of never making myself nominally responsible when I cannot give the time to work at a thing properly. My Irish work gets every day more exacting.

ALS Texas. Bridge, 8–9.

---

[6] For WBY's dislike of Farquharson see pp. 126, 145, 150–1. He was, apparently, as bad in *Salome* as WBY anticipated, for Max Meyerfeld, reviewing the production in *Tribune* on 12 June (4), reported that 'Mr. Robert Farquharson, whose Herod delighted us last year, has now elaborated it to the verge of caricature. He emphasizes far too much the neuropathic element, and revels in the repulsive symptoms of incipient softening of the brain.' The *Pall Mall Gazette* of 19 June 1906 noted (2) that 'Herod was an aesthetic decadent of the Nero type, strangely devoid of all kingly dignity, but often grotesquely effective'. 'Michael Field' gave a rather more sympathetic account in her diary (*Works and Days*, ed. T. and D. C. Sturge Moore [1933]): 'The Herod is a most Flaubertian study, but so individualised that it is out of the tone of the music that Oscar weaves dramatically. It is somewhat too clever; but consistent and engrossing, as the sombre eyes grow hollow and the wanton mouth grows slack under the reddest red of the rose crown. In the red of this rose crown the highest note of the scarcely emerging, yet basal blood-red of the picture is struck for us—the red that couches in the shadow of the precious blue of the moon' (250).

[7] The third act of *Man and Superman*, entitled 'Don Juan in Hell', was published in the first edition of the play in August 1903, but not produced on the stage until it was presented by itself at the Court Theatre on 4 June 1907 (see p. 99).

[8] i.e. from the committee of the Literary Theatre Society.

## A. P. Watt to the Editor of the Contemporary Review, *12 May 1906*

Percy Bunting, Esq
"The Contemporary Review",
11, Old Square, E.C.


Dear Mr. Bunting,
    I now have the pleasure of informing you that I am authorised by Mr W.B. Yeats to accept the offer of £10.10 (ten guineas) which you were good enough to make for the British serial rights wh I offered to you in the article.[1]
    I presume that you will as usual be willing to pay for the rights wh you have purchased now.
    I also take it that you will publish the article in the "Contemporary Review" within a reasonable time, say six months from date and I shall be glad if you will kindly give me not less than 2 months' notice of the exact date of pub in order that I may have an opportunity of arranging for its simultaneous pub in America.[2]

TS Copy Chapel Hill.


## To John Millington Synge, *15 May* [*1906*]

COOLE PARK, | GORT, | CO. GALWAY.
May 15


My dear Synge: Limerick cannot arrange dates until they see how their exhibition turns out—but they are anxious to have us.[1] Will send letter to Fay with some other papers. Please let us know how things go at Dundalk— I am really anxious [about] country places, so much depends on them.[2]

---

[1] i.e. 'Literature and the Living Voice' (see p. 384). On 27 Apr 1906 Bunting had written to Watt that he was 'ready to give Mr Yeats ten guineas for the use of his paper in the "Contemporary Review"'.
[2] The article appeared in the October 1906 number of the magazine; it was reprinted in *Samhain* 1906, in vol. IV of *CW*, and in *Plays and Controversies* (1925). It was not published in any American periodical, but parts of it were printed in appendix IV of the second volume of *Poetical Works* published in New York in 1907.

[1] See pp. 374, 378, 381–2.
[2] The NTS had visited Dundalk on 17 Mar (see p. 374, n. 3), and another visit took place on 15 May, when the company performed *Cathleen ni Houlihan*, *The Building Fund* (by Boyle, a native son), and *Spreading the News* in the town hall. This was a brief visit, which attracted little press attention: when Holloway called at the Abbey on the morning of 15 May W. G. Fay told him (NLI) that 'the Company

M^rs Emery writes to say that she plays Herodias in 'Salome' & has for her page a young man, who is described by Wildes executor—Ross—as his "third great passion".[3]

By the by—& this is private—Lady Gregory is dead against the admission, short of unforseen excellence of a remarkable kind, of another O Dempsey into the theatre. She thinks that if we took Miss O Dempsey's sister we could never get rid of her & it would leave Fay himself open to family pressure, more than is desirable.[4]

Yr ev

W B Yeats

ALS TCD, with envelope addressed to 57 Rathgar Road, Dublin, postmark 'ORANMORE MY 15 06'. Saddlemyer, 123.

# To Phoebe Traquair, 17 May 1906

Mention in following letter.
Informing her that James Paterson is trying to arrange an Edinburgh lecture for WBY.

---

were paying a flying visit to Dundalk this afternoon, & returning by Mail at 3 oclock in the morning'. In *The Fays of the Abbey Theatre* (192) W. G. Fay commented that these performances, and an earlier visit to Wexford on 26 and 27 Feb, had 'satisfied us that there was a future for a specially trained company that would tour the country, playing a repertoire of Irish plays of the modern kind'.

[3] The syntax is ambiguous and refers not to Wilde's but Ross's 'third great passion' (Wilde had been an earlier one). Ross was eager to enlist Charles Ricketts's help in getting his lover, whom both alluded to as 'Amico', one of the main roles in the forthcoming Literary Theatre Society's production of *Salome*. When this failed Ricketts wrote hoping that 'Amico will not have been ruffled', and assuring Ross that it had 'been arranged, *at my express wish*, that *he*, and no other should be the page of the moon'. But even here Ricketts was unsuccessful and he had to tell the now huffy Ross that all his efforts had been thwarted by the opposition of the other actors (*Robert Ross, Friend of Friends*, ed. Margery Ross [1952], 126–7). 'Amico' may have been John Moray Stuart-Young (see below, 503, n. 7), who falsely claimed to have had an affair with Wilde. In the end the role of Herodias's page was taken by Shiel Barry (1882–1916), who married the actress Dorothy Minto (b. 1892), and whose promising acting career was cut short when he was killed in the First World War. Reviewing the production in the *Speaker* on 7 July 1906 (315–16), Desmond MacCarthy thought him the one mistake in the casting, since he was 'a man almost as robust as the friend he deplores'. Robert Baldwin Ross (1869–1918), art critic and journalist, was an executor of Wilde's; he took his revenge on the disobliging members of the Literary Theatre Society in the *Speaker* of 14 July 1906, where he denounced 'the shameful stage management and the utter incompetence of the actors, whose glaring deficiencies were only emphasized by the magnificent histrionic powers of Mr. Robert Farquharson and the exquisite costumes they were privileged to wear'.

[4] In spite of AG's misgivings, Eileen O'Dempsey (b. 1884), the sister of W. G. Fay's fiancée Brigit O'Dempsey, did join the Abbey Company for the forthcoming British tour.

## *To John Millington Synge, 17 May [1906]*

Coole Park | Gort, Co Galway
May 17

My dear Synge,

Dundalk is bad, but after all it tells us nothing that we didnt know before. The country towns in Ireland are mainly animal, but can sometimes be intoxicated into a state of humanity by some religious or political propagandist body, the only kind of intellectual excitement they have got used to.[1] I should think we ought to go back to Dundalk tolerably soon when we have a spare time offering profit sharing terms to the Young Ireland Society, and avoiding race weeks when there is too much country about the country.[2] I am sorry that Limerick has postponed us, for Limerick would be an organization of some sort, but it is possible that they would accept us on some profit sharing arrangement, which would lessen their risks, but before starting on anything of that kind, we had better find out something of our chances there. The Exhibition might be drawing enough, because of the quality of the people going, to serve our purpose while not drawing enough for them to risk the whole expenses. However as we are not bound to Limerick we had better not attempt to make arrangements at this moment but let the company have their rest when they come back from England undisturbed so far as Limerick is concerned.[3] When I said the 12th for Longford I thought we might be going to Limerick the day after. I think you had better pencil any day that seems to you most suitable at about that date, seeing that you dont clash with a fair or Saturday confessions.[4] Fay

---

[1] On 20 May W. G. Fay wrote to AG (Berg) that the visit to Dundalk had 'cost us altogether about £14. . . . We had a very small audience but much nicer to play to than the crowded one on St Patrick's night. . . . We took about £7.10.'

[2] There is no evidence that the Company went back to Dundalk, although the received wisdom at this time was that provincial venues needed sustained cultivation, and in his letter of 20 May (see n. 1) Fay had told AG: 'I think it very unlikely we will make money in these sort of towns until the 3rd or 4th visit and then I think it absolutely essential that some of our own people go down in front and work things up.' The Dundalk Young Ireland Society had sponsored the performances on 17 Mar, but not apparently those of 15 May.

[3] The proposed Abbey visit to Limerick (see p. 401) had fallen through by 20 May, when W. G. Fay wrote to AG that it was 'a pity the Limerick show did not come off as it would have given us a bit of standing in the South'.

[4] The Abbey Company performed at the Temperance Hall, Longford, on 12 and 13 July of this year after the end of the British tour. W. G. Fay told AG on 20 May (Berg) that he had 'written to Longford asking particulars of the Bally Mahon street Theatre to see will the Abbey scenery fit it. . . . I reckon the Longford run will cost £20 all told . . . I doubt it will stand two nights for the population is only 5,000.' Seaghan Barlow recalled (Robinson, 74) that the stage was 'so small that we could barely manage to fix up the fit-up frame, and the contrast between it and the big theatres we had been playing in England made it seem even smaller'.

knows about these. I can then write to Miss Darragh and clinch the matter, or if there is any hurry 'wire.'

Of course she may be too hopeful in promising us so much, but she is a strong friend, and the worse we do in our direct appeals to the public here, the more necessary does one think it to hold on to anybody who is ready to do a little organizing for us.[5] My sisters are convinced that our Dublin audiences will have to be organised in the same way.

Yes you were certainly right about Flood, but one doesnt like to press things too hardly against a wastrel, who might have found his principle of order in artistic expression. His impertinence to Fay however settles the matter and he must go. If there is any possibility even by expending some more money of getting a man to take his place for the English tour—his parts cannot be very big—he should go at once. For the sake of discipline the sooner he is punished for insubordination the better, and, apart from all that, he may give us serious trouble in England, where he will look upon himself as indispensible. The other business is very disgusting, but he might excuse himself by saying that he was deceived in his friends, and besides Mac was in that, and we dont want to lose Mac who may be all right when Flood is out of it.[6]

I have had a card from Miss Horniman saying that a most advantageous offer has come from Manchester for a fortnight in the autumn.[7] I am writing to her in my private capacity for it is of course a matter for us as directors, but will send you a copy, that you may see if you agree.

I will put the copy in if I get it done before post time.

Yours ev<br>W B Yeats

[*With enclosure*]

Copy, to Miss H.

I dont quite know what to suggest about a date for Manchester, for I suppose it needs immediate reception or rejection.[8] If they merely want

---

[5] Letitia Darragh had offered to organize an Abbey tour of Ireland (see p. 383, n. 3), and was to oversee the tour to Longford in July.

[6] W. A. Flood had joined the Abbey tour of England, but, despite Fay's support, did not remain with the Company on a permanent basis. The 'disgusting' business probably involved drunken behaviour, but he remained with the Company until after the summer tour, and his dismissal was to become a point of disagreement between W. G. Fay, AEFH, and the Directors. Flood evidently continued to exert a bad influence on McDonnell during the coming British tour, when Sara Allgood accused them of 'kissing harlots out of railway carriage windows' (see p. 441).

[7] AEFH's card is untraced.

[8] The Abbey Company had performed at the Midland Hall, Manchester, on 23–4 Apr, when it presented *In the Shadow of the Glen*, *Cathleen ni Houlihan*, and *Spreading the News* on the first night, and *A Pot of Broth*, *Riders to the Sea*, and *The Building Fund* on the second. They did not return this autumn, but were to pay a further visit from 26 to 30 Nov 1907, as part of a tour to Manchester, Edinburgh, and Glasgow.

the same bill that went there this time, with the addition say of Hyacinth, a date could be got without much trouble. It would mean taking a fortnight from rehearsals. But if a new programme is in question, it will need a good deal of thought because of these rehearsals I have been trying to think what is the smallest number of monthly performances we must have in Dublin before we have a new programme ready, and before we dramatists have had our necessary dramatic lesson. I think the smallest number is three. Synge's new play[9] might come in September if hurry is essential and if it is ready. The summer is my working time and last summer I lost a good part of it over the Theatre row.[10] I dont want a performance of my work before the end of October at soonest. Lady Gregory's 'Jackdaw' could be done at the same time, she still less could get away until the autumn as she has guests. I want to have Shadowy Waters as well as Deirdre performed, and this may involve putting one or other into the November bill. And this leaves us the rest of the November programme either for a revival of the Well of the Saints with the new scenery, which must be tested before we can tour, or for a possible new play by Lady Gregory, but this is too vague to talk about. In case of Synge not having his new play ready by September, we might be able to get the Well of the Saints done then, and [try] out the new play with Deirdre.[11] I dont know if this programme is compressible in any way, but I am sending a copy of this letter to Synge, who can talk it out with Fay. I am rather afraid however of compressed programmes, for they have a way of not coming off, and if they do come off may mean bad rehearsals. These are all heavy tasks though of course the company being now all practically free during the day, makes it easier.

It will be a mistake to go on touring indefinitely with a practically comedy programme, for if we dont get an audience for the work more burdened with thought pretty early we will make our audience expect comedy and resent anything else. Comedy must make the ship sail, but the ship must have other things in the cargo.[12] It is much better for us to get through a lot of rehearsal and performance in Dublin early in the season, which would give us a large programme to choose from, instead of leaving it to the end when our touring is ending for the time being. Besides it is entirely essential that we should know as soon as possible when we may adventure London again.[13]

---

[9] i.e. *The Playboy of the Western World.*

[10] i.e. over the reorganization of the Society into a limited liability company.

[11] *Deirdre* was produced in late November and *The Shadowy Waters* in early December of this year, but *The Jackdaw* was not performed until 23 Feb 1907. Nor was *The Well of the Saints* revived until 14 May 1908. The new play by AG was presumably *The Canavans*, first produced on 8 Dec 1906.

[12] Apart from *Cathleen ni Houlihan* and *Riders to the Sea*, the bulk of the plays taken on tour were comedies, and many English reviewers described the Abbey Company as the 'Irish Comedians'.

[13] The next performances in London took place in June 1907.

I enclose a letter from Mrs. Traquair about Edinburgh which doesnt look very promising for a lecture at any rate. I have written to her to say that Mr Paterson is arranging for me.[14]

P. S. to Miss Hs letter. Of course I only write this in my private capacity, and the programme I suggest is an emergency one, intended to run through the greatest number of plays. I should prefer to put Edipus somewhere early in the winter's work, but that will be no use for touring, as the censor wont let it be played in England.[15] I should like to do it early in Dublin as it will be an immense advertisement there among the academical and scholastic people who are most suspicious of us now.

TLS TCD. Saddlemyer, 124–7.

## To George Pollexfen, 19 May [1906]

at | Coole Park, | Gort, | Co. Galway.
May 19

My dear George: The horoscope <about which I will try & write in more detail shortly> is I think right in general. The Native is The Countess of Cromartie.[1] She is a Countess in her own wright [*for* right] but not I think wealthy as such people go. She is married to a Colonel Blunt, whom she married on coming of age against her familys wish. He is probably the venus man & I rather thought while I was staying there, that she looked down on him intellectually.[2] The reason however why I asked you to work the horoscope[3] is this—& you must keep it private. She invited herself to

[14] The letter from Phoebe Traquair (see p. 316) is untraced. The Glasgow-born artist James Paterson (1854–193, n. 4; see p. 193, n. 4) went to great trouble to make the Abbey visits to Edinburgh a success. He was a friend of AEFH, and through the theatre became a friend and correspondent of Synge's. He did portraits of AEFH, Synge, and WBY (see Plate 000). He was elected to the Royal Scottish Academy in 1910, and contributed pictures and photographs of Synge to the collected edition of Synge's works in the same year. On 2 July W.G. Fay wrote to AEFH (Berg) that the Company had done 'better in Edinburgh than anywhere thanks to yr working up and Mr Patterson who seems to have put himself to no end of trouble on our account'. The Company made a profit in Glasgow and did well in Edinburgh and Aberdeen, but the audiences in Cardiff, Newcastle, and Hull were disappointing.

[15] See p. 22, n. 2.

[1] For the Countess of Cromartie see p. 134.

[2] Major Edward Walter Blunt-Mackenzie (d.1949) married Lady Cromartie in 1899. WBY had met him on his visit to Strathpeffer in January of this year (see pp. 311–12, 314–20).

[3] WBY often conducted occult experiments (see *Mem*, 75–6, and *Aut*, 258–63) while staying in Sligo with his uncle George Pollexfen (see p. 96). He also introduced him to astrology, which thereafter became, as JBY testified, 'the passion of his life... his horoscopes as many can testify were verified' (*Early Memories* [Dublin, 1923], 95–6; see also I. 428). WBY celebrates his uncle's astrological interests in 'In Memory of Alfred Pollexfen' (*VP*, 360–1) and 'In Memory of Major Robert Gregory' (*VP*, 325). WBY preserved two ledgers of Pollexfen's horoscopes (MBY) after his death. Many of them were of

this house a year ago—asked Lady Gregory if she might come—greatly to Lady Gregory['s] surprize, as it was so much out of the track of her life.[4] She was here a couple of days before she told me what she had come for. She had had an impression that I could help her in a trouble she was in. I should tell you she was <obviously> plainly seriously ill—she could only walk a very little way without fatigue. She had from early childhood been haunted by the vision of a man, who had been she beleived a king of Ireland many centuries ago. She had been his slave & had loved him, & now he was trying to draw her away. I could see that her death was quite possible. She had lost all interest in life. She leant me her diary, in which there were descriptions written down from time to time of the vision of this king mixed up with rapturous cries of love. She was obviously quite sane & as simple as a child. I was able to cure her (not of her vision but of her longing to get out of life) & now the king comes to her in meditation & without the old 'pulling' as she called it. Her health has got so much better that her <friends> relatives who do not know the reason cannot make out what to think of it. I broke off my evocations some months ago, & she is now I believe independent of them. Now what I would like to know is under what star does this king come. If I knew that I might give her some talisman that would help. This king may not have <been an incarnation> at all come out of the past, he may be a spirit clothing himself in an imaginary personality, or a part of her self, but he is certainly the vital thing in her life & apart from the 'pulling' not I think evil. He is described as very handsome, dark haired, a soldier very strong (rather a school girls ideal perhaps) but it is hard to get much detail out of her blind worship.[5] Now the ordinary details of the horoscope. She is *less* than medium size but the rest of the description is

WBY's friends, including MG, Olivia Shakespear, and AE, but he was also sent the birth dates of GD candidates to determine astrologically their fitness to enter the order.

[4] See p. 160. On 25 Nov 1926 (*Journals* II. 151), AG recalled this 'visit of Lady Cromartie who had ... "looked into crystal" or some equivalent, and was so gentle, fragile, beautiful, playing on her little violin. ... She thought Yeats could help her to some mystic knowledge.'

[5] During a visit to Lady Margaret Sackville's country house with WBY on 1 July 1906, Sidney Cockerell recorded in his diary (BL) that they 'talked of ghosts and reincarnation etc. Lady Cromartie declared that she remembered a previous incarnation and that she was a slave in Ireland and was killed by a knife aimed at the king, which she intercepted.' Perhaps at WBY's suggestion she was about to use this experience as the theme of a play, *The Finding of the Sword*, which was produced as part of a charity matinee at the Playhouse, London, on 30 Apr 1907. In the course of the two-scene play, Osra Innis, an ancient Celtic chieftan, appears to Muriel, the daughter of Lord Colmore during excavations in the north of Scotland. He then assumes the identity of a modern man and is invited to dinner by Lord Colmore, where he manifests himself in ancient dress and reveals that in olden days Muriel had been his slave and mistress, but, despite a vow, had refused on his death to accompany him to "the Country of the Young", with his horse, his hound, and sword. He has re-appeared now to regain the sword, unearthed in the recent excavations, but Muriel, the old influence renewed, implores him to take her with him. Muriel dies, accompanied by a thunderclap and a violent shaking of the Hall, and she at last accompanies him to the Country of the Young.

true. She is amiable & fond of company a good talker on a small scale with a slightly malicious wit & is certainly fond of the Arts. She writes books of Celtic stories but not very well. I know nothing of her money affairs except that I notice she has to be economical for her station & that her husband is losing money over an electric light station in his neighbourhood.[6] She married I should have said, partly to get away from her immediate relations & was forgiven by her "King" on consideration of the circumstances.

Yrs ever

W B Yeats

I have been writing much & my handwriting & spelling are worse than usual.
[*At top of first page*]
I suppose you have kept a copy of figure.
[*On back of envelope*]
On looking again at figure I notice you have put ☽ II.4 ♒. In mine it is ☽ II. ♓. I am more likely to be wrong but do look it up & let me know.[7] I have not the ephemeris at hand.[8]

WBY

[*Added in George Pollexfen's hand*]
☽ II–6 ♓
O apply to ♂
A love match


ALS Boston, with envelope addressed to Thorn Hill, Sligo, redirected to Shelbourne Hotel, Dublin, postmark 'ORANMORE MY 20 06'.

---

[6] Major Blunt-Mackenzie had invested heavily in the Strathpeffer and Dingwall Hydroelectric Company, the first commercial hydroelectric company in Britain, and the project swallowed up a large proportion of the Estate's money.
[7] WBY writes Moon 11 4° Pisces, and Pollexfen corrects this to 11–6° Aquarius. The Moon reaches 11 degrees of each zodiacal sign approximately once every twenty-eight days in its sidereal revolution, but without the complete horoscope to which these calculations refer, it is difficult to assess the significance of Pollexfen's emendations.
[8] An ephemeris gives tables of the planets' movement over the year. From the 1830s 'Raphael' issued an annual ephemeris, set on noon Greenwich Mean Time, for the coming year, and Pollexfen's collection of such ephemerides, bound in Cuala Press style, is at Texas.

## *To Susan Mary Yeats, 21 May 1906*

THE NATIONAL THEATRE SOCIETY, LTD.
| ABBEY THEATRE, DUBLIN.
May 21. 1906

My dear Lilly: please dont forget—I conclude you have had a letter from Roberts—that we want both you & Lolly at the Abbey Theatre on Thursday at 8.30 to help us with our annual meeting. It is really important[1]—It is to give us a clear 3/4 majority over young Walker & Miss Garvey who remain on as members & in the case of Roberts, who remain[s] for the present, joining them in a vote.[2] We require six in the first case & nine in the second. There will be six of us old members—Synge will be away—& with you two & Harvey & Miss Harrison we shall be ready for all emergencies, but I dont know if Miss Harrison & Harvey are coming.[3] If you can come at 8 I will explain the circumstances.

Here are some London address[es] for you—or rather of people who may be in London—

　　　M$^{rs}$ Ladenburg
　　　Melton–Mowbray

---

[1] WBY wanted SMY to attend the crucial Annual General Meeting of the INTS, held on 25 May, which was to decide the shape and direction of the Society after the recent schism. She did, in fact, attend, as did Synge, WBY (in the chair), AG, W. G. Fay, Frank Fay, Sara Allgood, Udolphus Wright, Sarah Harrison, Fred Ryan, George Roberts, and Brigit O'Dempsey. The NTS thus had more than a three-quarters majority, and the meeting was less contentious than WBY had feared, and, after the accounts up to December 1905 had been accepted, five proposals for elections were carried unanimously: that WBY be president; that AG and Douglas Hyde be vice-presidents; that WBY, AG, Robert Gregory, Wright, Synge, W. G. Fay, and Frank Fay be elected to the committee; that Synge be secretary; and that W. G. Fay be treasurer. The only disagreement was George Roberts's proposal that 'the plays registered in the name of the Society should be asigned [*sic*] to their authors as agreed upon'. Although this was finally carried by six votes to four, there was more discussion and 'Mr Yeats drafted the following resolution which was proposed by W. G. Fay and seconded by J. M. Synge. "That the secretary inform the Authors (Mr Russell Mr Colm & Mr Yeats) that the Irish National Theatre Society will never interfere with performances of their plays—A Pot of Broth, Broken Soil and Deirdre— wherever and whenever their authors may think fit and that the business committee shall guarantee the carrying out of this resolution".' This resolution was passed by eleven votes to one (see Appendix).

[2] Frank Walker and Miss Garvey did not attend, although they were still members, since their names did not appear in the list of those who had resigned membership of the NTS, i.e. Maire Walker, Helen Laird, Miss Starkey, E. R. Norman, George Russell (AE), Keohler, and Padraic Colum. Fred Ryan, the former secretary of the Society, was neutral, having confided to Joseph Holloway on 15 May (NLI) that 'he was disgusted with the whole thing. Said he had enough of it and did not intend to join any company. The bickering was awful when he was secretary. Kettle summed the situation up when he said that W. B. Yeats did more than anyone to get a theatre for Irish plays and now he does more than anyone to keep people away from it.'

[3] Sarah Celia Harrison (1863–1941) an Irish painter and friend of Lane. She was to cause WBY and AG much trouble in the dispute over the interpretation of Lane's will after his death in 1915. She did attend (see n. 1), but T. A. Harvey (see p. 317, n. 6) was not mentioned as being present.

Miss Montgomery
    10 Hans Crescent
        S W.

Miss Una Birch
    1 Old Burlington St

Hon M^rs Goldman,
    Queen Annes Gate

These are the only really rich people I know sufficiently well[4]—or think I can get you to sew for for one reason or other. If you will send me some circulars to London I will get a friend or two, who are not well enough off to buy to send them about—or I will try to. The best thing you can do however is to write to Hugh Lane & ask him to send out some for you—I know he has some friends who could buy & he is very good natured.[5]

                                  Yrs ever
                                  W B Yeats

ALS Boston.

## To George Brett, [c. *1 June 1906*]

FIELD, ROSCOE & C° | 36, LINCOLN'S INN FIELDS.
                              | LONDON. | W.C.

Dear M^r Brett: I enclose letter of Authorization.[1] I have just seen M^r Emery—who acts for Society of Authors—& he has had a letter from

---

[4] For Mrs Ladenburg and Miss Montgomery see pp. 136, 356. Una Birch (1876–1945) was the eldest daughter of Sir Arthur Birch, and both she and her family were close friends of AG. She married Ladislaus Pope-Hennessy in 1910. The Hon Mrs Agnes Goldman (see p. 232) was also a friend of AG. SMY and ECY were arranging a London exhibition of Dun Emer work, which took place in late June, and which was a success—as JBY reported to WBY on 2 July (*LJBY*, 92): 'Lolly did well in London—but their work at Dun Emer is terribly anxious. It requires huge exertions to keep it going.' However, WBY came in for censure: on 5 July AG told him (Berg) that she had received a letter from ECY 'full of complaints of you for not going to her sale, & not bringing a lady in a white satin ball dress (probably Miss Tobin)'.

[5] Lane did help Dun Emer, as AG reported to WBY on 28 June 1906 (Berg): 'Your sister Lily writes that they have made £47 in London but that their account is overdrawn by £48—but Hugh Lane comes in for a good word as he sent a lady who bought £7 worth.'

[1] WBY's letter of authorization gave the Macmillan Company the right to negotiate on his behalf in the dispute with John Lane over the American rights to *The Wind Among the Reeds* (see pp. 369, 374). The John Lane Company in New York had written to Brett on 24 Apr: 'We learn from London that Mr. Yeats is making arrangements to issue his book, "Wind Among the Reeds" under the imprint of some other publisher. It will not be within the scope of our power to grant any permission in reference to the use of this book. On the other hand, we shall not oppose any plan which you may have in view. Our

Lane saying the matter does not concern him, as it concerns 'John Lane Co
New York' who have bought from him. M^r Emery now advises me to
accept your offer but will keep up the fight that you may be able to say 'You
will get into trouble with the Society of Authors'.[2]

Yr ev<br>W B Yeats

PS.
By 'no financial responsibility'—it was your phrase—I understand that the
expense will fall on your firm & not on me.

ALS NYPL.

## *To William Brendon & Son,* [*? June 1906*]

To Printer.
I conclude that there will be "half titles" with the names of the various
sections. Please put the following dedications on the back of these
'half titles' as is already done in the case of the dedication to "Shadowy
Waters"; on back of 'half title' to "Bailes Strand" put "to William Fay
because of the beautiful phantasy of his playing in the part of the Fool" on
reverse of 'half title' to "In the Seven Woods" put "To Florence Farr, the
only reciter of lyric poetry, who is always a delight because of the beauty of
her voice & the rightness of her method"; & on the reverse of 'the half title'
to 'The Kings Threshold' put "To Frank Fay because of his beautiful

connection with the book will terminate when we have disposed of our present stock of books and our
set of plates. If you are planning to issue a complete set of Yeats' works, you might be able to utilize
our plates. If the page is the proper size we will be glad to make you an offer for the same.' Brett
sent WBY a copy of this letter on 26 Apr, explaining that it followed 'an admission on the part of the
John Lane Company that they had no legal rights in the copyright of this work at the present time,
such admission however being made only in conversation and not repeated, as requested, in the
letter enclosed herewith'. Nevertheless, Brett judged 'that it will now be quite safe for you to include
the "Wind among the Reeds" in the complete edition of your works which we recently arranged to
publish for you, and the copy for which we are anxiously awaiting', and he explained that he was
'writing to ask the Lane Company what they want for their stock and plates, and if the price is a
small one we may decide to purchase the books in order to clear the way of any possible misunderstanding in regard to the matter for the future, but before doing so of course we ought to be in
possession of copy for the work so that we should know exactly when we may be ready to publish
the book.'

[2] On receipt of Brett's letter, WBY went, probably on 1 June, to consult Frederic W. Emery, a
solicitor in the firm of Field, Roscoe & Co., who acted for the Society of Authors. On 2 June
Emery wrote to him that the letter from the John Lane Company 'does not seem to me to be altogether
satisfactory as it does not show what stock they still have in hand nor what they propose to do with the
plates if the Macmillan Company does not purchase them'. Yeats sent the correspondence on to A. P. Watt,
marking the copy of the John Lane letter 'to get Brett to find out what copies they have in stock'.

speaking in the character of Seanchan". & let me have proofs of these dedications.[1]

W B Yeats

ALS Berg.


*To Frances C. Brinton,*[1] *4 June [1906]*

18 Woburn Buildings | Euston Road,
June 4

Dear Sir: I cannot remember whether I ever wrote to thank you for your kind letter about our plays in Leeds. I am afraid I did not, but you will forgive my forgetfulness. I have drawn the attention of M^r Synge to the two points you mention.[1]

Yrs ever
W B Yeats

ALS Lincoln College. Dated in another hand '06'.

[1] These were instructions to the Plymouth firm of William Brendon & Son, Ltd., printers of *Poems, 1899–1905* which was to be published in October 1906. The volume did appear with half titles for the various sections. *The Shadowy Waters* was dedicated 'To Lady Gregory', and the printer included WBY's dedications, with minor changes of punctuation, to the succeeding sections as instructed here. The first proofs are dated 'Nov 29 1905—Jan 12 1906'.

[1] WBY had failed to make the gender discrimination between 'Francis' and 'Frances'. Frances C. Brinton lived at 16 Blenheim Terrace, Leeds, and had taken a party of friends to the Abbey Theatre performances at the Albert Hall there on both 27 and 28 Apr (see p. 390, n. 2). She had written to WBY on 8 May (TCD), to tell him how much she had enjoyed the plays and to express the hope that 'the small audiences will not discourage the company from coming here again'. She explained that all her friends had been 'delighted' with the performances: 'The whole thing is so unique, & the acting so good because so unlike "acting". I felt as if I had become invisible, & was watching a real bit of life.' She particularly liked the fact that there 'was no posing before the footlights, & "making eyes" at the Audience, as so often happens in theatres, & none of that irritating stage walk', but noted that 'the light seemed too strong in the last part of "Riders to the Sea", & unfortunately the luggage label had been left on the stretcher! But these are very little things, & it is too bad to find any fault with such an excellent performance.' Since her criticism related to the staging of a play by Synge, WBY sent on her letter to him.

## To George Brett, 5 June [1906]

18 Woburn Buildings, | Euston Road, | London
June 5

Dear M<sup>r</sup> Brett: I would be very much obliged if you would ask John Lane Company while you are negotiating with them how many copies of the Wind among the Reeds they have in stock. 'The Society of Authors' have pointed out to me that by John Lanes account, on which he has paid royalties, they should not have any copies at all.[1]

Please let me know on this point.

Yrs sny
W B Yeats

Please excuse half sheet.

ALS NYPL.

## To John Bell,[1] [c. 8 June 1906]

Mention in following letter.
Saying he has heard that theatre managements are grumbling at the Abbey Company using their own people to sell books instead of employing local programme girls, asking him to try to get leave for one of the young women associated with the Abbey to do this, and requesting that that person might be Miss Gildea.[2]

---

[1] Frederic Emery had pointed out that WBY needed this information (see pp. 410–11), but Brett had already sounded out the John Lane Company. On 27 Apr they informed him (NYPL) that they had forty copies still in stock, but the following day they rather suspiciously corrected this: 'We notice an error in the carbon copy of our letter to you of the 27th. This should read: "We have on hand approximately *400* copies of this book" ("Wind Among the Reeds") not 40, as we believe was erroneously stated in the letter.' Brett reported to WBY that 400 copies remained when he replied to this letter on 19 June (NYPL).

[1] John Joy Bell (1871–1934), journalist, author, and dramatist, wrote plays in Scots vernacular, and was creator of a series of plays dramatizing the adventures of 'Wee Macgreegor'. Wareing staged several of his plays at the Glasgow Repertory Theatre in 1910–11.

[2] Ida Gildea, described by Wareing (Berg) as 'a charming young protégée of Miss Hornimans', was a close friend of AEFH and was helping out with the tour. Her book-selling experience was to have important if unforeseen consequences: AEFH revealed that the location of her English repertoire company 'depended on which city had brought the most bound books when the Irish Players visited it', and, as Rex Pogson explains in *Miss Horniman and the Gaiety Theatre Manchester* [1952], 'the report of Miss Gildea, who had been responsible for selling the books had its influence' (22). Miss Gildea remained close to AEFH, who helped arrange her 'happy and successful' marriage to Hargreaves Heap; she acted as AEFH's travelling companion in her old age, and was with her at Shere in Surrey when she died there in August 1937.

## To Lady Gregory, 13 June 1906

18, Woburn Buildings | Euston Rd. | W.C.
June 13th 1906.[1]

My dear Lady Gregory

Wallis, Bullen's new partner was a friend of Count de Bastro and stayed with him in Ireland some years ago. It was his father who travelled in India with De Bastro.[2] He wants the address of Madame La Baronne de Montgascon. She wrote to him sending a copy of De Bastro's Memoirs, and did not give her address in the letter. Wallis wants to propose publishing an English edition.[3] I had a very busy time in Edinburgh. On Friday Miss Horniman arrived and dispatched me to Glasgow,[4] where I had to settle a complicated row or what might have been one. Bell, the business manager,

---

[1] WBY's forty-first birthday.

[2] It is doubtful whether Arthur Frederick Wallis ever became Bullen's partner in the full sense. Sidgwick's partnership with Bullen was not dissolved until 1907 and it seems likely that Wallis limited his contributions to the firm specifically to the Stratford Town Shakespeare: his name appears in the colophon of the edition as one of the proof-readers and he was present at the dinner to commemorate its completion on 21 Mar 1907. Wallis had published his four-act historical play *Stars of the Morning* with Elkin Mathews in 1903 and an article, 'Sea-Painting and Sea-Myth', had appeared in the *Cornhill Magazine* in May 1905 (652–62). He went on to write a number of mainly historical novels over the next twenty-five years. Comte Florimond Alfred Jacques de Basterot (1836–1904), traveller and ethnographer, was a cousin of Martyn, and had been a close friend of Sir William Gregory. The family had come into Galway when his ancestor Bartholomew de Basterot, president of the Bordeaux Parlement, had married the heiress Frances ffrench in 1770. AG frequently stayed with him in Paris, and he came every summer to his estate, Duras, near Kilcoran, Co. Galway, where, besides Wallis, he often entertained French literary figures, including Guy de Maupassant and Paul Bourget. WBY had first met him in 27 July 1896 (see II. 49), when de Basterot described him in his diary (Private) as 'un poète irlandais.... de Sligo; intelligent, il l'est clairement, et vif de conversation, mais sa figure est étrange, inquiétante, elle annonce certainement du sang jaune'. According to WBY (*Mem*, 117), de Basterot was 'paralysed from the waist down through sexual excess in youth', and spent 'his old age in the duties of religion and in attending chapel'. Arthur Symons described de Basterot as a 'strange, attractive figure, the traveller, the student of race, the student of history, with his courtly violence, his resolute pieties' (*Cities* [1903], 30). The date of his Indian trip with Wallis's father is uncertain.

[3] La Baronne Jeanne d'Acher de Montgascon, née Roussel de Courcy (b. 1870) was a kinswoman of de Basterot and one of his executors. She had, as AG records in *OIT* (18–19), been among the signatories of 'that sad, pompous, black-bordered document I received one day signed by those who have *l'honneur de vous faire part de la perte douloureuse qu'ils viennent d'éprouver en la personne de Florimond Alfred Jacques, Comte de Basterot'*, and may have been the unnamed 'French Countess', whom, to de Basterot's delight, WBY rendered speechless when he defended the Irish people against her charge of dirtiness (*70 Years*, 350). She had evidently sent Wallis a copy of de Basterot's *Souvenirs d'enfance et de jeunesse*, which he had printed in Paris in 1896 for private circulation. In her reply of 17 June (Berg), AG promised to 'try to get address of de Basterot's executors'.

[4] The Company played at the King's Theatre, Glasgow, 4–9 June. The *Glasgow Herald* of 6 June (6) lamented that the players had 'chosen so ill a season' for their tour: 'In summer days interest in things theatrical naturally languishes. Still, the audience... was encouragingly large, and their obvious delight in the fare provided must have been gratifying to the Irish players.' And the paper warned those 'who take an interest in literary movements will make a grave mistake if they fail to make acquaintance with

had at her suggestion, and, as he says against his better judgment, proposed "to make up" the Company. Fay had refused with indignation and yet there was no question about it but almost all "the make up" was extremely bad. I got Bell to dictate to me a list of all the errors "in make up" and of how they were to be put right and I gave this list in confidence to Synge. I then got Fay to undertake to tackle the whole question of make up himself in Aberdeen.[5] Synge is bent on his doing so so I think it will work out all right especially as everyone agreed that Fay himself makes up admirable. There was a question of principle behind the whole trouble. Fay is for the first time since he came to understand artistic things face to face with the commercial conditions of the English theatre and is horrified at them, and has a most wholesome fear of being dragged into the system. Bell is not a bad little fellow but he has no education but what he has picked up and knows nothing except the machinery of the stage which he knows very well. He has been making the most absurd suggestions (—on other questions) a grotesque gag for the "Building Fund", desirability of limelight on the heroine in the Shadow of the Glen—and the like. This last has roused Synge. Yet I think every suggestion made by Bell which did not involve some artistic idea has been sensible. Fay is finding out that it is a very humiliating thing to have to learn what to do, in necessary secondary things, from people who are wrong about primary things. I think and hope that I left them more amiable to Bell than I found them. Fay had blazed out at Miss Horniman, and of course it wont do for him to do that sort of thing, but at the same time, as I told her, if she pitches into Ireland every time she meets a member of the Company she must expect rows.[6] She

these earnest players of the National Theatre Society'. The Catholic *Glasgow Observer* of 9 June also welcomed the Company with great enthusiasm (4): 'It is no exaggeration to say that, judged merely from the standpoint of histrionic art, their visit to the city is the theatrical event of the season, if not, indeed, of our generation.... The National Theatre Company and the Irish plays they produce do not reflect nature, they ARE nature: living, breathing, moving, speaking nature.'

[5] The NTS performed at Her Majesty's Theatre, Aberdeen, from 11 to 16 June.

[6] Synge had already given AG an account of Bell's intervention in a letter of 9 June (*JMSCL* 1. 169): 'Mrs Wareing ... went off to London and they got down a Mr Bell to replace her, a profoundly self-satisfied and vulgar commercial man, that none of us can abide. He got Miss H[orniman] more or less into his hands, and at last she sailed round to Fay one evening just before the show to suggest that Bell should "make up" the company. Fay broke out forthwith, and she describes her exit as that of "a strange cat driven out of a kitchen with a broom-stick"! She complains pathetically to me that everyone knows in Glasgow that she is paying for our show, and that she feels in rather a foolish position when she has to confess that she had no authority over it!!' W. G. Fay's flash of anger cost him dear; AEFH never forgave him, and her complaint of his behaviour henceforth became a leitmotiv in her letters to WBY. Neither the *Glasgow Herald* not the *Glasgow Observer* (see n. 7) commented on the make-up, but the former noted that the NTS was 'not only a revolt against the conventional Irish drama. Mr. Yeats and his daring coadjutors also assail the conventions of the modern theatre. Actuality is the keynote of their method.' The same paper commented that the 'speech and action of the players are redolent of the soil. Some of them may lack the technique of the ordinary mummer, but all of them possess naturalness.'

is away from them now and wont meet them for some time.[7] There was another matter—which might have been very troublesome. The other Miss O Dempsey has been helping Miss Gildea to sell books—All went well while Waring was about but the day after Waring had gone she turned up in a very low cut and very dirty evening dress. She had I believe borrowed it from a ballet girl who happened to be staying at the same lodging. Further- more—she developed a profitable form of flirtation—she used to sell her autograph at sixpence each to flirtatious young men. She would write it in one of the books for them and this had the advantage of getting sixpence for herself and giving an opportunity for quite a long conversation with the young man. Furthermore, she would sometimes sell books to the young man and after a series of conversations take back the books and return the money. One had to get rid of her, but one could not tell her brother in law to be, why one got rid of her.[8] I found out that the local managements had grumbled at our having our own people selling books instead of employing their programme girls. Accordingly I wrote Bell a letter saying that I had heard this and asking him to try and get leave for one of our girls and asking that that girl might be Miss Gildea. I told Fay that I had done this, because some trouble was growing up, I did not mention what the trouble was, and he replied "it is a much more dignified position for the girl to be doing her work as an understudy and not to have books to sell." I tried to get Fay to shift Flood out of his part but could do nothing with him. I was as urgent as possible and one of the local papers has spoken of Flood as the blot on the performances. He is still very very bad but Fay does not see it or wont see it and he says if they made a change the new man might fluff and put the others out. Its not a moment to force Fay against his will. The others have all I think improved and that makes Flood seem worse than ever[9]—I have

The *Glasgow Observer* was hyperbolic in its praise of the acting: 'There are no stage mannerisms, no "playing to the gallery," no recognition of the audience in any shape or form until the curtain is rung up in response to the applause which follows every play. It is that highest form of art which effectually conceals its art. Nothing like it has been seen in this country before.'

[7] AEFH stayed in Edinburgh until the beginning of July, when she returned to London.

[8] This was Eileen (Ellen) O'Dempsey, about whose employment both WBY and AG had had serious reservations (see p. 402). On 4 July Synge complained to AG of the O'Dempsey sisters (*JMSCL* 1. 172): 'It is extraordinary how those two girls have lowered the tone of almost the whole company. Bridget O.D. by the way has greatly improved in her acting but she is one of the most silly and vulgar girls I have ever met.' In an undated memorandum listing her complaints about the tour (NLI), AEFH noted that both Miss O'Dempseys were 'tom-boys & rather vulgar' and that Eileen O'Dempsey was 'obviously impossible—flirtatious, loud & irresponsible. I think that everyone is agreed that she must never be allowed into the company again but that she has—outrageous low dresses—flirtatious and assignation with a stranger, overheard by Miss Horniman—shewn that Fay either does not know what goes on or cannot interfere where an O'Dempsey is concerned.'

[9] AEFH had already tried unsuccessfully to persuade Fay to remove Flood, and the arguments he used to her (Berg) are probably those he deployed against WBY: 'with regard to Flood, the lad is not good, but remember he has had but a fortnight to get up two parts and he is very fresh. . . . I think Flood

had a letter from Miss Horniman to day saying that Waring has got us very good terms at Limerick but not giving me particulars of either terms or dates.[10] Fay however is very nervous about the big Irish towns—In his present mood, he wants to do the small towns and not go near the big towns till what he calls the political opposition to us has died away—and until we have a greater position outside Ireland than we have won as yet. He is afraid that if we do the big towns now we may spoil them for us and make the managers afraid to give us dates later on. I would rather like to hear from you on this subject.[11] Nearly all my time in Edinburgh I was absorbed in Mrs Traquair's work and find it far more beautiful than I had foreseen—one can only judge it when one sees it in a great mass for only then does one get any idea of her extraordinary abundance of imagination. She has but one story—the drama of the soul. She herself describes it as captivity, the divine descent to meet it, its liberation, its realisation of itself in the world of spirit. This is told over and over again, with a manifest sincerity and intensity like that of Fra Angelico.[12] She is herself delightful—a saint and a little singing bird. It was very funny to watch her and her husband who is a great authority on fossil fish—years ago he tried to keep her from painting at all. He forbid her to paint, for everything that showed the artistic consciousness seemed unhealthy to his scientific mind. Some of her most beautiful work—a wonderful mortuary chapel at an hospital was done in stolen hours—painting at the greatest possible speed because the hour was short. Then he gave her leave to work on condition that she gave up her friends and of these he made a careful list thinking I suppose that they

ought in all fairness to be given his chance.' He explained that Flood had been upset by his uncle's death, and that he tried to do his best and was attentive. He complained that the real difficulty was that the Company did not have reputation or money enough to tempt people of real merit 'and so have to be content with what we can get for the present'. He pointed out that 'if Flood cannot pull it off, then MacDonald is the only alternative. . . . I spoke to Lady Gregory and Mr Yeats on the subject and told them I would settle nothing in the matter till next week, till I see if Flood doesn't improve.'

[10] AEFH had written on 12 June (NLI) that Wareing had got the NTS 'good terms at Limerick and is trying for other Irish places. It would be impossible for any of *us* to get good terms at decent theatres even where we are already a little known.'

[11] He did hear, on 17 June (Berg), when AG replied that she did not 'know anything about Irish big towns, but I hope Wareing & Miss H. are not going to rush us again. Fay said he thought it wd be a mistake having Wareing to arrange for us in Ireland, unless perhaps he went with him. We talked over possible places with Wareing, you may remember, & wrote a possible list which he was to send us copies of & didn't. It was after that we spoke to Fay & he was doubtful, & we said nothing had been definitely settled. So I hope nothing will be booked without your being consulted. . . . I would much rather not go to any Irish large town until Senchan is ready to go. Limerick is the only place I think we ought to make a rush for, while the exhibition is on.'

[12] Phoebe Traquair had modelled her work on Blake, Rossetti, and the early Renaissance artist Fra Angelico (Guido di Pietro; 1400–55), who had been a profound influence on her since 1889 when she discovered him on her first visit to Italy. She told a friend that his 'colour really belongs to the lyric, but is so purely spiritual I can't compare him, unless it be to spring flowers, or boys' voices, or birds' (*Centenary Exhibition Catalogue* [Edinburgh, 1993], p. 21). She decorated the Children's Mortuary

encouraged her. Now poor man he has surrendered and suffers daily from her celebrity. He is no one and feels himself no one, and all the evening— he dined with my hostess Mrs White—I could hear him babbling to someone in the corner about fossil fish. Some one person had always to be told off to listen—everybody else sat listening to Mrs Traquair, who, as it were, sang a little happy child like song.[13] I have come from her work, overwhelmed, astonished, as I used to come long ago from Blake,[14] and from him alone. She differs from all other modern devout painters but him in this supreme thing. The nearer she approaches the divine the more passionate become the lines—the more expressive the faces, the more vehement is every movement. To the others the world is full and the spirit empty— [*In WBY's hand*]

What did you & Robert think of Ricketts staging of that play.[15] It cost about £200, an absurd sum. M^rs Emery says she was very bad when you saw her—playing on a false conception—but better on Sunday. Moore abuses her final performance however, though he thinks she was good in his play,[16]

Yrs ever

W B Yeats

I gave one good lecture in Edinburgh & one bad one.[17]

TLS Berg, with envelope addressed to Coole, redirected to Burren, Co. Clare, postmark 'LONDON W.C. JU 13 06'.

Chapel (see p. 316, n. 3) in 1885–6, her first project outside her home. In a letter to AG written on 'Thursday' (? 28 June 1906; Berg) W. G. Fay told her that 'Mrs. Traquhair has written a charming letter of appreciation, in which speaking of Miss Allgood's Maurya she says "I never saw a figure on the stage so absolutely fine nor heard more beautiful speaking . . . the colour all through was beautiful. At one moment one of the young girls had a break in her voice which thrilled one, so slight, & so real, but to me the old woman & her speaking stands out as the most tragic figure I ever saw. She was outside station, time or circumstance, an external thing".'

[13] For Ramsay Traquair, keeper of the Natural History Museum in Edinburgh, who had married Phoebe Anna Moss in 1873 after she had drawn fossil fish for him in Dublin, see p. 316, n. 3. Jane E. Whyte, a great friend of the Traquairs, who had helped to raise audiences for the visit of the Abbey Company to Edinburgh, lived at 7 Charlotte Square, Edinburgh. On 22 June 1912 she asked WBY (NLI) whether he ever wrote 'the article on M^rs Traqhair' and invited him to 'come & visit us again'.

[14] WBY had made a similar comparison with the work of Charles Ricketts in November 1905 (see p. 211).

[15] i.e. *Salome*, which had been designed by Charles Ricketts (see p. 399, n. 4). In her reply AG refused to comment: 'I won't say anything about the Salome staging, but I hope you will see it yourself & judge who you would like for Deirdre.'

[16] FF had played Phaedra in Sturge Moore's *Aphrodite against Artemis*.

[17] These may have been private lectures, since neither was apparently reported in the Scottish press. They both took place on Friday, 8 June, and on 10 June AEFH informed AG (Berg) that 'Mr Yeats two lectures . . . went off well, especially the evening one'. Presumably they were on the Irish dramatic movement and designed to advertise the Abbey's current visit, rather in the way he had prepared the ground in Cambridge the previous year (see pp. 218–19).

## *To Stephen Gwynn, 13 June 1906*

18 Woburn Buildings | Euston Road
June 13th 1906.

My dear Gwynn,

Many thanks for the cheque which is all right. What happened about that magazine is this—Roberts saw me about it and told me that you seemed doubtful about its success—he seemed anxious for it himself. I talked over the matter with Lady Gregory and she objected to doing any thing for it on the grounds that it would be merely another Celtic Xmas, and that amateurish things of that kind were injurious to the whole movement and that so long as they didn't pay they were bound to be amateurish.[1] I then asked Roberts if contributors to it were to be paid and he said they were—I also talked out with him certain schemes as to the contents of the magazine, and gave him that story of Shaw's. I told him that Shaw had given it to me for the Dun Emer press. Roberts of course knows that we pay for everything that my sisters print. Indeed we pay a very decent price—about 15 per cent I think. Shaw does not care about money and whatever he would get for a little story like this, and it a reprint, would I daresay not seem worth having to him—but I rather think that my argument to him about this little story for I think it was I who wrote was that he would be encouraging the first Irish publication of its kind to pay contributors. I certainly drafted a letter of this sort and I believe I sent it.[2] It is possible therefore that you may have to pay Shaw—the whole thing is a mess owing to Roberts' vagueness of mind. When I saw Hone in Dublin he was under the impression that Roberts had got the various contributions, I had to do with, for nothing. I dont so much blame Roberts for the magazine itself being unlike the original scheme, or what I thought was the original scheme, or rather I dont blame him at all for such things change under the hand and I put no definite question & made no condition on the point. I think it better however to say to you that I think it too scrappy, that I think people like Alfred Percival

---

[1] Gwynn, as one of the partners in Maunsel Press, was involved in the publication of the periodical the *Shanachie*, an illustrated miscellany, which ran from spring 1906 to winter 1907, and was intended to be a vehicle for the Irish Literary Revival. The cheque was presumably for WBY's contributions to the first number, 'Against Witchcraft' and 'The Praise of Deirdre' (see pp. 341–2). JBY's pencil sketch of Gwynn appeared in vol. 2 of the magazine. AG feared that it would resemble *A Celtic Christmas*, an annual published by the *Irish Homestead* from 1897 to 1902, which printed a great number of second-rate poems and stories, and which had angered WBY by reproducing juvenilia of his own (see III. 274, 276). She must have been persuaded to change her mind, for she contributed a play, *The Travelling Man*, to the *Shanachie*'s first number.

[2] G. B. Shaw's wrote his story 'The Miraculous Revenge' in 1885, and there had been talk of its publication by the Dun Emer Press in 1903 (see p. 217, n. 1).

Graves and Starkey are most injurious. Graves especially—some three generations have yawned at him now and he is at his worst in what he sends you.[3] I do not find in the editing of this magazine any one selective mind or any one principle of selection. The little Father Peter O'Leary fragment for instance is insufficient to make a Gaelic leaguer buy it and is a wasted page for the English reader.[4] Colum has been let send what he likes, as he will I suppose be let perform what he likes in the new theatre. His little fragment is Celtic Xmas all over and I imagine that even Starkey's marshland grows some better weed than that poem about Eden.[5] I dont believe it is possible to make a good magazine without making up your mind who it is for whom you are making it and keeping to that idea throughout. I suspect that you and Roberts and Hone have all done this thing, and because you are all in it have felt no individual responsibility. Indeed Hone admitted something of the kind to me—but damn all Celtic Christ-mases now and for ever—what Dublin wants is some man who knows his own mind and has an intolerable tongue and a delight in enemies and I wish I could see you setting out upon that man's journal—

Yrs ever<br>W B Yeats

TLS Buffalo. Wade, 473–4.

---

[3] The Dublin-born Alfred Perceval Graves (1846–1931) is best remembered for his ballad 'Father O'Flynn' (1889). He began publishing in periodicals and his *Irish Songs and Ballads* appeared in 1880 and *Songs of Old Ireland* in 1882. He went on to edit a number of anthologies, and *The Irish Poems of A. P. Graves* appeared in two volumes in 1908, with a preface by Douglas Hyde. He had contributed two poems to the first number of the *Shanachie*, 'The First Winter Song' and 'The First Summer Song', renderings of Kuno Meyer's prose translations from Old Irish. In 1895 he moved to London, where he became inspector of schools in the borough of Southwark, and where he was elected secretary of the Irish Literary Society. The title of his autobiography, *To Return to All That* (1930), echoes that of his more famous son Robert Graves, *Goodbye to All That*, first published in 1929. Graves returned WBY's disparagement, and on 31 July 1922, following the serialization of WBY's *The Trembling of the Veil*, he complained to Mrs Todhunter (Reading): 'I cannot tell you how annoyed I have been at Yeats' attacks on his old friends in the London Mercury.... it is a record of self glorification as regards the Irish Literary Society for which Willie Rolleston & I worked hardest—tho' no doubt he did a good deal, though I should imagine very injudiciously, for the National Literary Society of Dublin.'

[4] Fr. Peter O'Leary, 'An t-Athair Peadar' (see p. 224, n. 8), was a Gaelic playwright, translator, and avid supporter of the Gaelic League. He had acted as a Land League organizer in various of his parishes, and he had been parish priest at Castlelyons since 1891. His most celebrated work was *Seàdna*, a folk narrative in Munster Irish first published in the *Gaelic Journal*, 1894–7, and he was to write the first autobiography in modern Irish, *Mo Sgéal Fein* (1915). WBY admired his plays in Irish for their vividness, but thought them rambling and badly constructed (see *Expl*, 78, 91). His story 'Aesop', published in Irish in the first number of the *Shanachie*, in fact extends over $2\frac{1}{2}$ pages.

[5] Padraic Colum's ten-line poem 'The Builder' also appeared in the *Shanachie* (51): 'Around me I heard the men stir in their rest, | And stir of the child that is close to the breast. || And these came before me, my father's wide lands, | And strength for the building came into my hands. || Now round me the wild-duck arise up and fly, | And here will I build to the wind and the sky. || O clay of the making that's moist in the pit; | O horses that trample the rushes through it. || For her do we build on these rough

## *To Lady Gregory, [18 June 1906]*

18 Woburn Buildings | Euston Road. | London.
<Saturday.> Monday

My dear Lady Gregory: Fay is at his wits end for <Irish costumes> country men clothes for Longford. This went out of my head when I wrote last—through my absorbtion in my own writing I am sorry to say—our enemies may claim those we have, & that man who was to have found us new ones has done nothing. Can you get some made, or what are we to do. Evidently the old clothes man is no use in a hurry. We play in Longford on the 11 & 12th & may go on to Mullingar.[1] Miss Darragh says full houses are a certainty. We have also had a letter from the Irish Institute of Journalists wanting to hire theatre & asking if we could perform for there Conference in September—we have offered to play for nothing, as this will carry our name all over Ireland.[2] I am writing away at those notes & have now got 12,000. Some of the notes are I think poetical & as one days work suggests the next there is more coherence than I had hoped for.[3] I begin each days work with a few pages of Sir Thomas Brown to keep me in key.[4]

I shall have to go to Ireland about July 6th to work things up in Longford I think—at least that seems to be Miss Darraghs plan. I found that Fay was under the impression that our enemies could claim the Hour Glass clothes.

---

heavy lands, | Where my days like white birds shall pass through her hands.' The reference to the new theatre may have been an intentional tilt at Gwynn, who had chaired the inaugural meeting to set up the Theatre of Ireland on 18 May 1906. *A Celtic Christmas* (see above, n. 1) was edited by AE and Henry Norman and became a general term of abuse with WBY and AG as representing all sentimental and flaccid writing in a pseudo-'Celtic' mode. James Starkey had contributed a sonnet entitled 'Eve and Lilith', which began: 'With Adam I have mourned for Lilith flown, | Yea, walked disconsolate in Paradise, | Through the green ways of Eden unconsoled.'

[1] The NTS played *Hyacinth Halvey, Riders to the Sea*, and *The Building Fund* on 12 July at Longford and *A Pot of Broth, The Hour-Glass*, and *Spreading the News* on the following day (see p. 403). The ownership of the costumes was a point of dispute between the company and the seceders (see pp. 311, 329, 330–1, 396), and, as this was the first Irish performance since the end of April (with the exception of one night in Dundalk on 15 May), WBY feared that they might be left without sufficient costumes. At present the costumes were looked after by Francis McDonnell (see p. 283) but in August Joseph O'Rourke was given the job. The visit to Mullingar was apparently postponed until late September.

[2] The annual conference of the Institute of Journalists took place in Dublin in the week beginning 31 Aug 1906, but although Synge negotiated with the Committee about the feasibility of putting on a special performance at the Abbey, this finally proved impossible.

[3] WBY had now written 12,000 words (not notes) of the series of short essays that he was to publish as 'My Thoughts and my Second Thoughts' in the *Gentleman's Magazine*, and, later, as *Discoveries* in 1907. See pp. 366–7.

[4] WBY was evidently reading the edition given to him by Eric Maclagan (see p. 110).

Am I not right in saying that they were paid for by you? If not please let me know at once.[5]

Yrs ev

W B Yeats

Did you hear of M^rs MacCarthys (Miss Christian's death)? She died in child-bed. Moore told Symons or Ricketts I forget which a few days ago.[6]

ALS Berg, with envelope addressed to Coole, redirected to Burren, postmark 'LONDON W.C. JUN 18 06'.


# To A. E. F. Horniman, [c. *18 June 1906*]

Mention in letter from AEFH, 19 June 1906.
Asking why he has not received a letter from Wareing she had mentioned in a previous letter,[1] telling her that Fay objects to taking the Company to Limerick,[2] discussing the Abbey tour to Longford, reminding her about the music for *Diarmuid and Grania*.[3]

NLI.

[5] Sturge Moore designed the costumes for the first production of *The Hour-Glass* in March 1903 after a sketch by Robert Gregory (see p. 359, n. 2), but AG had evidently paid for the material (see III. 225).

[6] Clara Christian (1868–1906), a painter who had studied at the Slade School and exhibited her work widely in Britain from 1885, became George Moore's mistress in 1899 and followed him to Dublin in 1901. She had ended her relationship with him in 1904, and on 11 Jan 1905 married Charles MacCarthy, the City Architect of Dublin. She retained her home, Tymon Lodge, Tallaght, after her marriage, and died there in childbirth on 7 June 1906. She appears as 'Stella' in Moore's *Hail and Farewell*, and before her death presented her painting *Meditations* to Hugh Lane's gallery.

[1] AEFH replied: 'The reason why you have not received my formal letter & the copy of Mr Wareing's, is simple—the duplicating book in which is the Leeds letter is in London & cannot be got at till the end of the tour. They all can be arranged easily.'

[2] See p. 417. WBY had told AEFH that Fay did not want to perform at Limerick, but AEFH had evidently heard differently, probably from Wareing, and in her reply complained: 'You told me that Fay objected to Limerick – to-day I hear that he is pleased.'

[3] The music for *Diarmuid and Grania* had been composed by Edward Elgar (see III. 163), and WBY evidently thought that it might be used in other plays. In her reply, AEFH wrote that the 'Diarmuid & Grania music matter shall not be forgotten'.

## To A. E. F. Horniman, [c. 22 June 1906]

Mention in letter from AEFH, 23 June 1906.
Telling her that he is to go to Longford in person to work up the Abbey
performances,[1] discussing her plans to put all the power of the Theatre into
the Directors' hands.[2]

NLI.

## To Lady Gregory, 25 June 1906

18, Woburn Buildings | Euston Rd.
June 25th 1906.

My dear Lady Gregory—
    I have just been to Bullen who happens to be in town. He wants me to
run my new book—the Book of Impressions through the Gentleman's
Magazine—He offers two pounds a thousand words which is only moder-
ately good pay but if I were to send them to the Fortnightly where one
would get three pounds a thousand words they would only take a small
amount of the book and might be a long time before they publish. I think
I shall close with Bullen. You suggested my giving the book to my sister for
a first edition but Bullen seems anxious to bring it out in book form as soon
as possible. How do you feel about it? I shall have thirty thousand words in
about six weeks and may be before the summer ends a good deal more.
I shall either publish a small book of 30,000 words or enlarge Impressions to
that amount with other essays including perhaps Extracts from Samhain.[1]
I have had some rather important letters from Miss Horniman lately—she
has marked them private as they are only suggestions for me for consideration before I see her. I think it is right however to tell you about them but
dont say I have done so. She seems to have been very upset by her trouble
with Fay at Glasgow. She says she cannot continue to do her business

---

[1] In her reply AEFH said she did not 'like you having to go to Longford to work things up, I thought
that that was to be done by those on the spot. Your time should be spent on your own work now, not
doing what would be done by others.'
    [2] Following her contretemps with W. G. Fay AEFH had resolved to adopt a less intrusive role in the
running of the Theatre.

    [1] All but four of these essays were published in the *Gentleman's Magazine* under the title 'My
Thoughts and my Second Thoughts', Sept–Nov 1906, and, with additions, as *Discoveries* by the Dun
Emer Press in December 1907. They were included in vol. VIII of *CW* and in *The Cutting of an Agate*
(1912). AG replied that WBY should 'certainly accept Bullen's offer & start your notes in his magazine
at once'.

through him. She very generously however proposes to hand over to us the guarantee—and money for the management of the theatre—and entire control of the theatre with leave to have sixpenny seats or anything we like. We undertaking merely to give her the letting money and to pay as before for electric light her idea is that we would have more influence over the company if we had the power of the purse. We will have five hundred a year to guarantee salaries. I think she is really behaving very well and very generously and that this arrangement should be the best possible so far as smoothness of working are concerned. I am a little anxious however about anything that may lessen her own interest in the project. When I see her I shall know how far she is inclined to continue in control of tours. I think it is necessary to leave some part of the work in her hands. The recent trouble has been caused I think by Fay's curiously instinctive dread of authority he does not understand. He has been afraid of her getting too much influence. The new arrangement would make him give up that fear.[2] She says however

---

[2] AEFH's series of letters (NLI) were to continue through July. On 12 June she announced that she would not send money to the Company through W. G. Fay 'to be dribbled away without any account being rendered'. On 19 June she confessed herself disappointed at the tour of England, on 21 June complained that Fay was not sending accounts directly to her and that if he 'insists on overdoing the part of the old-fashioned Prima Donna, he *must* be brought to his senses'. On 23 June she decided that since 'Fay tells you one thing & other people another thing so as to get his own way', her 'only possible course of action' was 'to resign all connection with the theatre except that I shall hand over to the Directors the money to carry it on. I have been virtually dismissed by Fay & as the performances are absolutely under his control, the only way I can practically help the Directors is by putting the power of the purse into their hands.' The following day she sent detailed proposals along these lines (cf. *LWBY* I. 161–2):

Abbey Theatre to be completely in the hands of the Directors.
A sum of £500 a year to be paid quarterly in advance to pay salaries.
A sum of £100 a year to be paid quarterly in advance to cover cost of attendants etc for my tenants.
The proposed right to sell refreshments to belong to the Directors for their profit.
Any price of seats to be charged to the public by the Directors. But tenants must charge as at present.
The money paid by tenants to Cramers to be put in my bank as at present & with it the gas & electric money from the Company. These monies with the rent from the house in Abbey Street to be used by me towards paying rent, rates, & taxes. I bear the expenses of rent, rates & taxes.
For scenery such as would be required by my tenants or useful to them, I will pay half the cost.
In case of repairs, I will bear the expense of such as are necessary when applied to by the Directors. But these matters have just been done & so should not occur again for some time.
I retain the right to forbid Maunsell [*sic*] & Co. to put plays into the Abbey Theatre Series which have not been acted by your company, if I think fit.
That the prices charged to my tenants remain as before until I see fit to alter them, also the rules in the business circular.
That no alterations nor additions be made to the Abbey Theatre in public parts without my full consent.

AG replied (Berg) that she was 'altogether for' accepting AEFH's offer 'chiefly because I honestly do not think she is sane enough for us to be indefinitely tied to—Each violent antipathy makes her a little more difficult to deal with, she is getting cross with Synge, it is a miracle she has not yet turned against me, & she will never quite trust you while she thinks Mrs MacBride a possible danger.' AG also doubted 'the possibility of working for very long with one so Anti-Irish as she is giving everyone to understand that she is—& in this last year we can see how her ideas are diverging from yours & mine'.

that we will be worried to death under this arrangement unless we engage some business man to do all that part for us. If we do this we can satisfy Fay by getting a man (if we can find one) who will undertake the work of advance agent in Ireland.[3] Such a man could also do Ryan's work.[4] He would however be a horrible expense. I dont really know what I think about the thing until there has been some chance of talking the whole matter out with you and Synge and Miss Horniman or with as many of you as can be got together. It wont do to lessen Miss Horniman's interest while she is dreaming of an English National Theatre.[5] If that comes it should grow out of our work and take its traditions from us. I wish there was some way of making use of Miss Darragh for instance—she is Irish and has I think the makings of a great tragic actress—if either that twenty five thousand came to us or was used in an English theatre where we had influence it would be possible to use people like her in the creation of a real poetical tradition of beautiful speech.[6]

I have not been writing my little essays for the last four or five days. My letters have accumulated again and my proof sheets. I have now got all the proof sheets off my hands and shall be back on the essays to-morrow.[7] I seem to have endless time on my hands owing to the fact that I now am able to begin work the moment I come down in the morning and to work for three or four hours without difficulty. I have done that practically every day since I came here from Scotland. The result is that I am even paying calls and taking exercise—Bullen wants an installment of the essays at once— my difficulty is that they contain an attack on Farquharson's acting of such unmeasured violence that I want time to tone it down. I find that writing while the impression is fresh upon one sometimes makes the impression a

---

[3] In her reply AG agreed that the new business arrgangements needed careful thought: 'we are none of us strong on questions of finance, & we have more or less had Miss H. to fall back upon & so not gone very carefully into questions of expenditure—None of us three ought I think to give the necessary time & thought to details of business, we should mainly have accounts & proposals submitted to us—I suppose however someone could be found or trained—not impossibly Dossy Wright who is steady & could be taught bookkeeping (but I wouldn't mentions his name to Miss H). He might after a little take Ryans place & act as advance agent, & look after front of house or take small parts—I think having him would, like having F. Fay, make William Fay feel his responsibilities.'

[4] Fred Ryan had acted as secretary to the INTS in its early days, and although he was now withdrawing from the dramatic movement in disillusion (see p. 409, n. 2), he was helping to oversee the Abbey accounts.

[5] AG agreed with this in her letter of 28 June: 'I saw Miss H was, as you say, making us a "career" for herself in England, & this wd inevitably lead to the loss of all our ideals—Now she is like a child that has licked the paint off its toy & cries because it is ugly.'

[6] AG did not share WBY's admiration for Letitia Darragh and the two were to disagree about her role in the Abbey Theatre. The £25,000 was a legacy that AEFH had recently been left by her father, the tea-merchant, collector of curios, and Liberal MP Frederick John Horniman, who had died on 5 Mar 1906. Father and daughter had been long estranged and in acknowledging a letter of condolence from Holloway on 15 Mar (NLI) AEFH informed him that she had 'not seen my father for years & altogether the circumstances between us were such as I hope that you will never experience similar ones'.

[7] The proof sheets were presumably those of *Poems, 1899–1905*, which appeared in October.

little heated.[8] Did I tell you that I met somebody the other day who had cried over your play in The Shanashee.[9] Mrs Emery is I think going touring with Mrs Patrick Campbell after all—she is to be away eight months.[10]

Miss Horniman writes that Waring says that Flood has greatly improved and that the make up steadily improved towards the end of the Aberdeen week.[11] I think Miss Horniman would be much less anxious from this out judging by her letters to rush the touring.

I enclose an unsatisfactory letter from Maclure and a circular from America in which you will find your books mentioned.[12] I dont think the clothes can be at the theatre as Power goes there regularly for letters etc.[13] I was not greatly impressed by the Rickett's scenery or costumes. They were much better than one sees at the ordinary theatre but they lacked as a whole in breadth of treatment. There was too much fussy detail and though individual costumes and groups were beautiful they did not compose into a powerful effective whole.[14]

Yours<br>W B Yeats

TLS Berg, with envelope addressed to Burren, Co. Clare, Ireland, postmark 'LONDON W.C. JU 25 06'.

[8] WBY had been incensed by Farquharson's performance as Forgael in the 1905 production of *The Shadowy Waters* (see pp. 126, 145, 150–1, 400), but did not, in the end, publish this 'unmeasured' attack on him.

[9] *The Travelling Man* (see p. 419, n. 1), a one-act play in which a farmer's wife fails to recognize Christ when he appears at her house in the guise of a tramp.

[10] FF did not tour in the USA with Mrs Campbell, but lectured there by herself in the spring of 1907.

[11] AEFH had written on 19 June (NLI) that 'Flood has also improved & is more in the picture', and that the '"make-up" began to improve gradually towards the end of the visit to Aberdeen & is much better now I hear'.

[12] The letter from McClure is untraced, but presumably told WBY that the magazine could not publish AG's *Hyacinth Halvey* (see p. 397). On 12 July Quinn told AG (NYPL) that Bynner had sent him the play a few weeks before as 'not suitable for publication': 'I will see whether I can do anything with it in some of the other magazines. In any event I will have it copyrighted before the autumn.... It is very funny and very well done.' On 23 Nov he cabled 'Hyacinth copyrighted Tuesday or Wednesday next'. The circular is also untraced, but was presumably a publicity leaflet issued by Charles Scribner's Sons, who had published her *Cuchulain of Muirthemne* and *Gods and Fighting Men* in America.

[13] WBY was particularly worried about the costumes for *The Hour-Glass*, which was to be produced at Longford on 13 July (see p. 421), since the seceders claimed that these belonged to them. Ambrose Power was a member of the INTS from late 1904, but at first combined his acting career with a job in the civil service. In 1907 he had a row with Willie Fay over his salary, and Fay refused to cast him in any of the plays he was then directing, although Ben Iden Payne continued to use him in his Abbey productions. After appearing in some productions of the Theatre of Ireland, he returned fully to the Abbey following the departure of the Fays in early 1908, and remained with the Company until 1911. On 21 April 1906 Holloway remarked in his diary (NLI) that there was 'the germ of an actor in A Power ... but at present he is inclined to overact & get out of the picture, & his voice has yet to be put under control & his rather flat accent modified before his work can be enjoyed.' AEFH told WBY on 26 Oct 1906 (*LWBY* 1. 174) that 'Power is a nice fellow but I don't think that he will ever be a real actor'.

[14] i.e. Ricketts's scenery and costumes for *Salome*. As Ricketts recorded in his diary (BL), he had had a great deal of difficulty with the stage manager (see p. 399, n. 4) and the scene painters in this production. On 4 June, six days before the opening, no scenery had been started, and the first night was unusually fraught: 'Turned up at 4 nailed up scenery, dressed and dined 6, placed furniture,

## To Frederick Ryan, [c. 25 June 1906]

Mention in letter from Ryan, 26 June 1906.
Sending him a cheque for £50 on behalf of the Theatre of Ireland, and asking him if this endorsement is correct.[1]

MBY.


## To Lady Gregory, [28 June 1906]

18 Woburn Buildings | Euston Road | London
Thursday

My dear Lady Gregory: I enclose a letter from Miss Horniman, which will show you the state things have got to between her & Fay. I did not realize how serious things were or I would have made a serious attempt to get him to apologize at Glasgow. He was excited & I thought I could get him to do it at the end of the tour, when he had forgotten on his side his anger with Bell & people of that kind. I was wrong—I suppose I shrank from the unpleasantness of immediate action.[1] What has happened is that Fay has been careless about a bill & has not sent it to Miss Horniman till it was pressed

supervised dresses, train of Salome lost. Dress for Bianca lost in building. M^rs Bishop walking on in a borrowed art dress, handed cakes in thro the window, rehersed [*sic*] taking of [*sic*] head with Miss Darragh who grew nervous, stood by the limelight man, the most absolute idiot I have ever met in my life.' But his efforts were not in vain, as 'Michael Field' enthusiastically recorded in her diary (*Works and Days*, 250): 'The curtain up!—At once, what we came for. Eastern luxury in moonlight. A picture painted by Titian or Delacroix. . . . no, only by Ricketts himself. Never has the stage been so wonderfully used—the picture painted by a great painter, with all the masses, lights, sparkle, glow, atmosphere of a masterpiece to set the human passion it symbolises.' She also noted that the hall was 'full of little London' and identified Thomas Hardy, George Bernard Shaw, John Todhunter, Arthur Symons, Max Beerbohm, George Moore, and Selwyn Image among the crowd, as well as three 'curious devilkins all in one place at one time—Zangwill, the finer Yeats and Bobbie Trevelyan—all dusky irritants'. Max Meyerfeld, writing in *Tribune* (see p. 400, n. 6), thought the costumes the 'most notable feature of the production . . . a marvellous harmony of blue and green and silver', but added: 'Here praise must end. The stage was left ridiculously bare, and never for a moment produced the illusion of a terrace outside Herod's banqueting-hall.' The *Pall Mall Gazette* of 19 June (2) thought that 'Salome was exquisitely staged—a triumph in harmony with blue as the predominant tone. Only an artist like Mr Ricketts could have given such a perfect setting.' In her reply, AG said, 'I knew you would not like the Ricketts scenery, just as you say, fussy & inorganic, & without nobility. It is evident he can only think of his one material.'

[1] The £50 was the settlement between the NTS and the seceders, who had now constituted themselves the Theatre of Ireland. The first cheque for this in early May (see p. 396) had evidently been invalid, presumably because the Theatre of Ireland had not at that stage decided upon its final name. WBY marked Ryan's letter of 26 June: 'Have put bank receipt in drawer of theatre papers.'

[1] See pp. 415, 423–4.

for.[2] She faught with Carr on the same ground[3] & this on top of Fays rudeness has got us at this state. I thought the Company were playing well at Glasgow but they are probably tired out by this & bored—& I dare say Edinburgh may pride itself on not following Manchester & London. The Scotsman gave us rather faint praise, I noticed.[4] It is of course true there is no dicipline & great waste of time. I am afraid it will go on so, for Synge has no influence & you & I are not enough with the company. We shall have to be rather stern. Miss Horniman will probably take up something else, & we shall have to get money for tours by guarrantiers & the like. We shall have £500 a year a free theatre & leave for 6ᵈ seats.[5] I suppose I should have foreseen the crash—where there

---

[2] On 21 June AEFH had written two letters, one formally to the Directors, the other indignantly to WBY (NLI), complaining of W. G. Fay's carelessness. The letter to the Directors explained that AEFH had 'only this morning received an account from the Irish Decorating Co. dated June 5ᵗʰ for the sum of £25–17–7. It was passed through other hands instead of being forwarded to me immediately by Mr Fay. No information as to the correctness of the account has been vouchsafed to me nor whether this is the whole cost of the "fit-up". I very much object to accounts, which are made on my credit, not being paid immediately; but until the bills are sent me it is impossible for me to pay them.' She demanded that AG should 'see this letter soon'. In her personal letter to WBY she expostulated: 'This last is too much— Fay gave the account to Mr Bell who gave it to Mrs Wareing who posted it to her husband here. It was purely a matter for me to pay out of the Abbey Theatre account, *not* the tour. Fay said he wanted it to be paid at once because the people are poor; but he did his best to keep them from getting their money soon. This has annoyed me very much indeed. I feel as if whatever we do will be frittered away unless Fay comes to the conclusion that the Directors must direct.... If what you disapprove of as "commercialism" is a desire to pay accounts at once & to get acknowledgements for money & to know how money is spent—I don't agree with you. It is that using of big terms & philosophical phrases by Fay, which is his means of blarneying you.... as things stand now—I am in the position of having been told not to interfere in a matter which I am financing. Instead of behaving decently, he kept back that account & then sent it on through people who had nothing to do with it.' She returned to the matter in a letter of 23 June (NLI), complaining that when she 'objected to wrong information being given to me in the day-bill (of which Fay had corrected a proof) I was told that it did not matter, just as if I were an errand boy. I said that it must be put right & it was done in the next lot, but it was not so much the carelessness I objected to as the denial of my right to get correct information.' This incident convinced AEFH that she should put the Abbey finances in the hands of the Directors and a professional business manager.

[3] Philip Carr (see p. 3, n. 3), had received financial help from AEFH to found the Elizabethan Stage Company, which aimed at reviving Elizabethan and Jacobean drama.

[4] In reviewing the Abbey Company's productions on 26 June (6) the *Scotsman* detected 'something of an amateurish character, though they have been playing for some time together'. It thought *Riders to the Sea* and *The Building Fund* well done, but *The Pot of Broth* 'a trifling sketch ... not particularly well acted', and *Spreading the News* 'very loosely acted', but concluded with the limp observation that the 'experiment the National Theatre Company are making is one certainly of an interesting nature'. The members of the Company were not unduly depressed by this and on 28 June Frank Fay, reporting to Holloway (NLI) that the '*Scotsman* gave us the cold shoulder', added that the 'tepid notice seems to have done us more good than harm; & after all we have had so much enthusiastic notice that we must not complain of a little Scotch coldness'. On 1 July AEFH wrote to Synge (TCD) that the drop in receipts at Edinburgh was a nuisance and must have been 'most depressing to witness', adding that she had 'written very fully to Lady Gregory about the deadness (or rather absence) of the acting. Hull won't be much better I suppose even in that way & I hope that Longford won't be suicidal.'

[5] The fact that at AEFH's insistence the cheapest seats at the Abbey Theatre cost 1s.—double that of other Dublin theatres—had been a contentious issue from its first opening (see III. 677). But in her new charter for the NTS of 24 June (see p. 424, n. 2), she had given the Directors discretion to charge any price they wished for seats, although she stipulated that all other companies hiring the Theatre 'must

was Miss Horniman on one side with her business precision & temper—& a growing fealing against her among undiciplined people on the other, & Synge, who was on the spot & might have checked it, without practical force. I am of course anxious about the acting—I have dreaded the effect of this tour upon it but thought from what I saw in Glasgow that it had done good, the company now look upon themselves as professionals & some of them Flood & Mac for instance really dont care about the acting—at least I think not. Several of the others are of course quite raw.

Yrs ever
W B Yeats

[*With enclosure*]

36 Grindlay Street, | Edinburgh.[6]
June 27th,/06.

My dear Demon,

I enclose you 40 envelopes & three dozens booklets will I hope reach you from Hull very soon.[7]

The performances on Monday night were (except those of Miss Allgood) shocking. Dead amateurs not caring for anything. Every word clear throughout the theatre but articulated by dolls.[8] During the tour there have been two rehearsals of Hyacinth & none at all of the under-studies. I spoke of this to M[r] Synge & he tells me that an under-study rehearsal will be

charge as at present'. The Directors brought the new prices into effect in the forthcoming season and the *Arrow* of 20 Oct 1906 announced that '*Henceforth there will be Sixpenny Seats in a part of the Pit*'.

[6] AEFH was staying in Edinburgh with a Miss Rimer. 'Demon' was AEFH's affectionate name for WBY, taken from his GD motto 'Demon est Deus Inversus' (see p. 993, n. 8).

[7] The NTS performed in Hull from 2 to 7 July, and the material being sent to WBY was presumably the unsold illustrated programmes to be used as advanced publicity for the forthcoming visit to Longford.

[8] The NTS had opened their visit to Edinburgh on Monday, 25 June, with *A Pot of Broth*, *Riders to the Sea*, *The Building Fund*, and *Spreading the News*. Sara Allgood played Maurya in *Riders to the Sea*, Mrs Grogan in *The Building Fund*, and Mrs Fallon in *Spreading the News*. AEFH was particularly mortified by the shortcomings in the acting because she had concentrated her most intense publicity work there and had many friends and influential acquaintances in the audience. Her disappointment, as much as W. G. Fay's rudeness to her in Glasgow (see p. 426), soured the tour for her and permanently altered her relationship with the INTS. Others found the Edinburgh performances more satisfactory: in his letter to WBY of 2 July (see p. 431), Synge pointed out that 'a number of people in Edinburgh' were 'entirely carried away by our shows', and Seaghan Barlow later recalled (Robinson, *Ireland's Abbey Theatre*, 73) that at Edinburgh they 'had at any rate intelligent audiences, even if they were not numerous'. Writing to Holloway from Edinburgh on 28 June (see above, n. 4) Frank Fay reported that the 'plays have been very successful & in Glasgow & here have drawn well: at Aberdeen we did only fairly well & the same at Newcastle. At Cardiff we didn't do very well: but it was not expected & the date was booked to get the pieces on their feet for Glasgow.' He added that in Edinburgh they were 'doing very well: all along we have had increasing houses, but here the increase is in the dearer parts of the house & hence the financial result is of course good.'

taken to-day. He never seemed to have imagined that such a thing was the ordinary custom & he argued that it was not necessary because they *see* the plays continually. I think that I have made him understand the impossibility of my continuing connected with the theatre, he had not taken my account of the Glasgow incident seriously—I had not been able to do much before last Monday to explain matters to him as I wanted to give Fay a chance. I cannot & will not behave to Fay on any other grounds than his behaviour to me. He may blarney you as much as he likes & call me "commercial"; I accept this & I claim the commercial temperament as he does the artistic. I will not allow my credit to be used to obtain goods & then for the people to be obliged to wait for their money unknown to me. It was this same thing that has made me determined to have nothing more to do with Philip Carr. I am told that the performance was better last night, but I did not get back from seeing M$^{rs}$ Cathcart until it was too late to go to the theatre.[9]

The whole affair is this—that wild fresh flavour has absolutely departed—the company have become ordinary amateurs who are not particularly interested in their work—the discipline necessary to turn them into good professionals is absent, by that discipline they might have been able to learn to *act* what was nature at the beginning. M*rs* Burry is coming to the flat.[10] I shall return on Thursday late & I shall hope to see you early on Friday.

Yours
Annie

ALS Berg, with envelope addressed to Coole, redirected to Burren, postmark 'LONDON W.C. JU 28 06'.

[9] Mrs Agnes Cathcart knew AEFH through the Golden Dawn; she had joined the Edinburgh Amen-Ra Temple of the GD on 12 Mar 1894 taking as her motto 'Veritas vincit'. She lived at Pitcairlie, Newburgh, Fife, a fishing port some 40 miles north of Edinburgh.
[10] Mrs Rose Pullen-Burry was the wife of Dr Henry Pullen-Burry (1857–*c.* 1927) of Liphook, Hampshire. They had both known AEFH through the Golden Dawn; he became a member in November 1892 ('Anima Pura Sit'), and rose rapidly to the position of Cancellarius; she joined in March 1894, taking the motto 'Urge semper igitur'. When Henry Pullen-Burry subsequently deserted his family to seek his fortune in the Klondyke gold-rush, AEFH took them under her wing, paying for the education of his two daughters Ethel and Winifrid. Mrs Pullen-Burry later remarried and became Mrs Wreford.

## *To Lady Gregory, 3 July 1906*

18 Woburn Buildings | Euston Rd
July 3rd 1906.

My dear Lady Gregory

I have had a letter from Synge in which he says that he thinks he notices that the long tour has been injurious to the acting powers of the company—he says also that Fay is playing very badly through being too excited over his love affair.[1] I have of course seen Waring's letter and am to see Waring himself on Thursday.[2] The most serious matter however is that you will see from a statement I will make out with Miss Horniman to night that the discipline of the company has got dangerously loose (on the high way to scandal I should think). We have all known that it is bad, but it is getting beyond bounds.[3] It has been strained by these convent school young women and by Macdonald and Flood. I am perfectly convinced that we must take advantage of the present upset to get the discipline permanently right. Miss Horniman seems to me very reasonable—she is in good health and quite unlike her old self but she has made up her mind not to go on in any business relation with Fay. At the same time she had made it perfectly plain that she had looked upon the English work of this theatre as supplying her with what she called a career. I never had this in so many words but have always suspected that the finding of work for her was a condition of whole hearted support. She is prepared to treat us very generously under any circumstances but if we cannot restore her relation to some part of the work however circumscribed we will probably find either that she may break with us altogether on some unforeseen issue or that all her means may be taken up with some other project just at the moment when our theatre is in want

---

[1] On 2 July Synge wrote from Hull (*JMSCL* I. 171) that he did 'not quite know how the company are acting, everything is done accurately but I sometimes fancy they are getting a little mechanical from so much playing of the same pieces to poor audiences', and that 'W. G. Fay . . . is not good, just now as he is too much occupied with his love affair'. The tour had concluded at Hull, which the Company found uncongenial, especially at the end of a long and exhausting expedition. On 9 July W. G. Fay, 'looking particularly worn & fagged out' told Holloway (NLI) that 'Hull was a rotten place to play to— the worst of the tour . . . They could not understand anything there & disheartened the players.' Wareing recalled (Berg) that financially the tour was not a success: 'I believe Miss Horniman lost several hundred pounds, but cheerfully, knowing that it was bread upon the waters. We made a handsome profit at Glasgow, and did well at Edinburgh and Aberdeen; but Cardiff and Newcastle let us down badly, and we gained nothing at all at Hull.'

[2] Wareing had written to AEFH from Hull, telling her that he had purposely not warned her or given her an account of his bad impressions of the Company at Newcastle. He followed this up with a detailed record of the faults in the productions and the misbehaviour of the Company.

[3] AEFH was collecting reports of the Company's various bouts of misbehaviour from the Wareings, Ida Gildea, and others. These, with WBY's help, she recast as a formal statement, the substance of which WBY gave in his next letter to AG.

of fresh capital. I have tried to find out how she has done the work of an
advance agent and I believe that taking one thing with another she has done
it well. She has certainly shown immense energy. Now comes the question
of how to restore her relations to the company. We must I think engage a
business man who will take all the financial business out of Fay's hands.
This man must pay the actors weekly. He must not hand the money in a
lump sum to Fay but pay each actor individually. This will make the actors
dependant upon us and give us an opportunity of insisting on the work
being done properly and on orderly behaviour. I am inclined to think that as
it is I shall have to reprimand MacDonald for drunkenness and Fay may
resent this for he looks on himself as in entire control of the actors.[4] I think
when you have read the statement you will see that it is necessary to confine
Fay to stage management and to send somebody with the company when
they go on tour. The business man I speak of would for instance pay the
stage hands the sceneshifters—and etc.—This will reduce Fay's power of
obstruction considerably—I imagine that in every business there is a
dangerous moment when some old and valued employee begins to look
upon himself as indispensable and to behave as master. At least I have been
told so and that the whole future then depends on showing him or upon
persuading him even falsely that he is not indispensable. I have asked
Dunlop who is I believe good at his own business[5] to recommend us
some young Irishman who has a business training if possible in England
and who is either now employed in Dublin or anxious to get back there. We
want some man who has a job there which leaves him free in the evenings.
We could pay him more than we pay Ryan who has not enough force or
enough firmness for the new work.[6] Of course I have not committed you
and Synge—I have merely asked for a Man's name without pledging us to
take him. I have also asked Miss Darragh to try and find us a couple of
young Irishmen with decent tradition who want to learn to act without
paying a premium. She thinks we should be able to get them at first for a
nominal wage. She has her self proposed to call on one of the Dublin
theatre managers the man at the Royal I think and find out if he knows any
stage struck young men[7]—We can then sack Flood and keep a tight hold on

[4] In her reply of 5 July (Berg) AG wrote: 'I don't think you ought to speak to McDonnell yourself –
"Why keep a dog & do the barking yourself?" my husband used to say—& none of us should put
ourselves in the way of meeting impertinence.'

[5] Daniel Nicol Dunlop (1868–1935), who had edited the *Irish Theosophist* from 1892–7, had moved to
London in 1899 and was working in the publicity department of the Westinghouse Company. WBY had
known him well from 1890–3, when he lived in the Irish Theosophical Society's lodge at 3 Ely Place,
Dublin.

[6] Fred Ryan received £1 a week (see pp. 31, n. 13, 425).

[7] The manager at the Theatre Royal, Dublin, was Frederick Mouillot (*c.* 1865–1911). Born and
educated in Dublin, he joined Janet Steer's troupe as a young man, and later H. H. Morrell's company,

MacDonald. I am rather disappointed about Synge—He is afraid of Fay and does not take trouble.[8] For instance the sound of the strangled hen was cut out of the Pot of Broth at Edinburgh and I was not told of this.[9] The weak spot in the plan of the organisation is that it leaves no one in control on tours. Miss Horniman urged I dare say by Waring has been asking if we could not confine Fay to the acting and have another stage manager—I have no doubt she would pay—but I have told her this is impossible. Of course our tours in the future will in all likelihood be much shorter and therefore a much less strain on the discipline. We can leave them aside for the present (especially as Miss Horniman has refused to guarantee anything for English tours until she is convinced that she can get better performances than the company seem to have given in Edinburgh—and till we have got rid of wooden people like Flood.) She is urgent about our refusing Manchester but makes no demand as she has cut herself off from the work.[10] The meaning of this is that we are thrown back on Ireland very luckily for months to come. I doubt if she will soon give up her conviction as to the slackness of the work and in all probability therefore (short of a guarantee got up by ourselves and rather a heavy one now that we have to go to theatres) we must give up London for about 12 months[11]—so much the better if we get things re-organised. Miss Darragh has been very useful. She strikes me as a thoroughly sensible woman and has done a great deal to

---

acting in a number of popular musical comedies. He returned to Dublin in 1897 to organize a syndicate which built the Theatre Royal, opened on 13 Dec 1897 on the site of the Leinster Hall, with Mouillot as managing director, a position he retained until his death, although he also directed the management of fourteen theatres in the provinces and in the suburbs of London, and, later, the Gaiety Theatre, Dublin.

[8] Although Synge conceded in a letter to AG of 4 July (*JMSCL* 1. 172) that 'Fay is almost wickedly [*sic*] careless about everything', he felt that there had been 'no real falling off' in the standard of the acting and that AEFH had been unduly influenced against the Company by Wareing. AG however thought Synge had grown too vain following the reception of his plays in Manchester in the spring, and blamed him more than Fay for the current problems, describing him in her reply as 'evidently quite useless, he only thinks of himself & Molly . . . & his behaviour with Molly Allgood must have helped to destroy discipline'. On the other hand, Alfred Wareing had a very high opinion of Synge, recalling in his ILS lecture (see p. 387, n. 1): 'To my great content Synge was with the company throughout the tour; head and shoulders above the others, he held sway over all without their knowing it, and because he was ever present when need arose harmony prevailed.'

[9] At the beginning of *The Pot of Broth* the wily Tramp hears the cackling of a hen as John and Sibby Coneely make protracted attempts to catch her for the priest's dinner and several stage directions culminate in the call for a '*choked cackle and prolonged screech*' (*VPl*, 237–8). In her memorandum of complaints about the tour (see n. 3) AEFH noted that at 'Edinburgh on Tuesday two young Patersons were listenening [*sic*] to hear the hen cackle in Pot of Broth & she made no sound. Her cries were very feeble on the Monday.'

[10] AEFH had herself initiated the proposal that the Abbey Company should return to Manchester (see p. 404). In her reply, AG thought that they would 'be better without Manchester next Autumn, we might take it in Lent with new work'.

[11] This was an exact estimate: the next Abbey visit to London took place at the end of June 1907.

get Miss Horniman reasonable. Miss Horniman was rather emotional at first but now thanks I think to Miss Darragh, is in high spirits. Miss Darragh has invited her to Longford to do advance work there and I think she is going. Miss Darragh has come to the conclusion now, that I owing to my political past may be rather dangerous there but that Miss Horniman's wild declarations of contempt for politics nationality and all the rest are just what is wanted. Last night Miss Horniman listened to her just like a canary bird into whose mouth somebody was putting leaves of groundsel. I am to hear from Miss Darragh who started this morning next Saturday, as to whether it will do for me to go down. I am now rather anxious to go as I want to find out what Flood is like and how the company generally are acting. If I do not go Fay will have such a mass of legends as to Flood's wonderful improvement.[12] I rather think that properly managed the present crisis will be the making of us even financially.

I hear that Swinburne has made a wild attack on me in the Athenaeum. I have not seen it and I dare say I will not as I dont mean to reply and dont want to annoy myself uselessly.[13] Ellis wrote something perfectly polite and

[12] AG urged WBY 'to see the Longford performance, if you go even for the one night—We shall never make out the truth from the stories on both sides', and he did join Letitia Darragh, who had organized the visit there with great efficiency—as is evident from an advance publicity paragraph in the *Longford Independent* of 7 July: 'We strongly advise our readers not to lose the opportunity of enjoying a most unusual treat, and at the same time showing their approval of the efforts being made to revive our National literature by a large and influential attendance. Two of the plays in its repertoire have been translated and played successfully at the Deutsches Theater, Berlin, and in Prague.' The NTS evidently had to overcome local feeling that the plays were too highbrow. On 14 July the *Longford Journal* deplored the fact (1) 'that some persons are unreasonably prejudiced against anything produced by the National Theatre Co.', and the following week warned its readers that 'they must not judge the productions of the National Theatre Co. on the same lines as the ordinary run of plays'. In fact, the Company seems to have overcome both prejudice and the season; summing up the visit on 21 July, the *Longford Journal* (1) found the turnout satisfactory: 'Considering the weather—July heat is not conductive of play going—the audiences on both nights were not small, and we feel sure that on the next visit of the company to our town they will be more liberally patronised.'

[13] The English poet Algernon Charles Swinburne (1837–1909) was bringing out a new edition of his *William Blake* (originally published in 1867), and on 30 June the *Athenaeum* quoted (798) from the 'new and powerfully written preface, in which Mr. Swinburne will discuss what he considers to be the fantastic theories concerning the meaning and value of the prophetic books which have lately been advanced. Alluding to the fact that some of these critics have claimed for Blake a Celtic origin, Mr. Swinburne . . . contends that as a matter of fact there is no Celtic literature at all of the smallest value.' The commentator then went on to quote at length from a passage in the preface in which Swinburne was clearly aiming at WBY: 'Some Hibernian commentator on Blake, if I rightly remember a fact so insignificant, has somewhere said something to some such effect as that I, when writing about some fitfully audacious and fancifully delirious deliverance of the poet he claimed as a countryman, and trying to read into it some coherent and imaginative significance, was innocent of any knowledge of Blake's meaning. It is possible, if the spiritual fact of his Hibernian heredity has been or can be established, that I was: for the excellent reason that, being a Celt, he now and then too probably had none worth the labour of deciphering—or at least worth the serious attention of any student belonging to a race in which reason and imagination are the possibly preferable substitutes for fever and fancy. But in that case it must be gladly and gratefully admitted that the Celtic tenuity of his sensitive and prehensile

just—he is a Swinburne enthusiast—in the big Blake book about Swinburne not understanding some doctrine of Blake's.[14] Swinburne thinks I am the author of this passage and now that he is reprinting his own Blake book avenges himself by a furious attack apparently upon everything Celtic. He says, Cockerell tells me, that the Celt has no imagination and puts the emotions above the reason which is a curious complaint for him. I have had a most indignant letter from my father about it, in which he tells how in the old days Swinburne could not read out one of his own poems without bursting into tears three or four times.[15] There would be no use replying for it would only lead to more violent rhetoric of the sort there is no reply to. I had a most delightful time at Miss Horner's—I spent Saturday and Sunday there— Cockerell and Lady Cromartie and Lady Margaret Sackville and young Asquith son of the politician—were the only other guests. She lives in a most beautiful Elizabethan manor house[16]—I read out Miss Toban's translations of Petrarch on the Sunday afternoon and am going off now to tell her that Cockerell thinks her as I do the finest poet of America since the death of Whitman.[17] She is very charming and simple—a strange person for a

intelligence throws into curious relief the occasional flashes of inspiration, the casual fits of insight, which raise him to the momentary level of a deep and free thinker as well as a true and immortal poet.'

[14] In discussing the failure of earlier critics to understand Blake's system in vol. I of *The Works of William Blake* (1893), Edwin Ellis described Swinburne (p. viii) as 'the one-eyed man of the proverb among the blind'. He, with Gilchrist and the Rossetti brothers, deserved credit 'for having brought Blake into the light of day', but, 'though whatever is accessible to us now was accessible to them when they wrote, including the then unpublished "Vala," not one chapter, not one clear paragraph about the myth of Four Zoas, is to be found in all that they have published'. Ellis also criticized Swinburne's ignorance on p. 338, and made other references to him on pp. 207 and 209 of vol. I and pp. 15 and 81 of vol. II.

[15] JBY had written on 2 July (cf. *LJBY*, 92–4) telling him of Swinburne's 'particularly insolent & contemptuous' reference as quoted in the *Athenaeum*, but added that it was 'not worth anger or any reply, only it makes one disgusted'. He went on to tell WBY that 'More than thirty years ago I heard many stories of Swinburne, amongst others of his reciting his ode to Mazini [*sic*] himself, & of his bursting into floods of tears, a capacity for nervous weeping is exactly what I should expect from his kind of lyricism.' On 28 June 1914 WBY told Charles Ricketts 'an amusing criticism of his father's on Swinburne, "Who had ever heard of a poet who had neither a wife, a mistress, nor a friend?—for who could call Watts-Dunton a friend?"' (*Self-Portrait* [1939], 200).

[16] WBY had spent 30 June and 1 July at Katharine Horner's country family home, Mells Park, near Frome in Somerset, a forty-bedroom Georgian manor. Katharine Horner (1885–1976), a great friend of Lady Margaret Sackville (see p. 149, n. 4), was described by Lady Cynthia Asquith in *Remember and Be Glad* (1952) as 'Tall, slender, starry-eyed, with a countenance of rare and changeful loveliness' (88), and in her *Diaries* (1968) she recalls her drifting into the room carrying 'a volume of Yeats' early poems, and she herself looks not unlike one of his fated heroines' (196). On 25 July 1907 she was to marry Raymond Asquith (1878–1916), eldest son of the then Chancellor of the Exchequer, and later Prime Minister, Herbert Henry Asquith (1852–1928), who, after a brilliant career at Oxford, had become a barrister in 1904. In his diary (BL) Cockerell reported that he had gone for a long walk with WBY and Lady Margaret after dinner on 30 June.

[17] Cockerell recorded in his diary that on 1 July 'Yeats read some very fine translations by Miss Tobin of Petrarch's sonnets—which are in proof but not yet printed off. . . . In the evening we talked of ghosts and reincarnation, etc.' WBY was an admirer of Walt Whitman (see I. 9), who had died in 1892, and

millionnaire—an Irish Catholic of a new sort. I am going through her Sonnets making little corrections—

Yr ev

W B Yeats

[*In WBY's hand*]
D<sup>r</sup> Felkin is I think still in Germany[18]

TLS Berg, with envelope addressed to Burren, Co. Clare, postmark 'LONDON W.C. JY 3 06'.

# To Agnes Tobin, [*3 July 1906*]

18 Woburn Buildings | Euston Road.
Tuesday

Dear Miss Tobin: I will come as soon after 4 as I can. I read your sonnets on Sunday to Cockerell, Lady Margaret Sackville, Lady Cromartie & Miss Horner. They have asked me to tell you how wonderful they think them. You are the greatest poet of America since Whitman.[1]

Yr ever

W B Yeats

ALS Private. *Agnes Tobin: Letters, Translations, Poems with Some Account of her Life* (76a).

whose poetry had initially been ignored in his native America. On 26 Sept Holloway reported in his diary (NLI) that 'Mr Keohler told us of W B Yeats' new find—a lady (Miss Tobin) from San Fancisco who writes poetry after the manner of Walt Whitman—& her meeeting with Colum at J B Yeats' studio.'

[18] Dr Robert William Felkin (1853–1926) had interrupted his medical studies in 1878 to become a missionary in Uganda, but returned to Scotland and graduated at Edinburgh in 1884. He then studied for an MD at Marburg, and became an expert in tropical medicine. He joined the Edinburgh Temple of the GD on 12 Mar 1894, taking the motto 'Finem Respice', but moved to London two years later, where he joined the Isis-Urania Temple, to which WBY belonged. He became WBY's medical doctor, and after the schism in the GD of 1903 took on the leadership of the Stella Matutina faction. At the time of this letter he was conducting lengthy negotiations with A. E. Waite to make peace between his and Waite's rival GD Orders. This involved elaborate questions of legitimizing warrants and authorities, and, convinced that he must either 'find out the whole truth of the matter or drop the whole of my connection with the Orders' (Howe, 259), Felkin had gone to Germany to make contact with the successors of Anna Sprengel (SDA), from whom the British temples had putatively derived their authority. On this trip, as he recalled in a statement of March 1914, he finally managed to meet 'a professor, his adopted daughter, and another gentleman near Hanover, who he believed were undoubtedly Rosicrucians'. They were, however, reluctant to give him much information, 'because they said that although they knew him as a scientific man, he was not a Mason, nor did he belong to any occult society that they had knowledge of' (Howe, 259–60). It was not until 1908 that he succeeded in getting in touch with the German occultists he was seeking. Since AG would have been unaware of the these secret occult manœuvres, her interest in him was presumably connected with her concern for WBY's health.

[1] See previous letter. The translations were to be published in November of this year as *On the Death of Madonna Laura.*

## To Lady Gregory, 4 July [1906]

*Private.*

18 Woburn Buildings, | Euston Road, | London.
July 4th. 1906.

My dear Lady Gregory,

I am writing this letter in order to place on record in some detail the various things that shew the necessity for a reorganisation of the company; a reorganisation that will make the actors individually responsible to the Directors who must have the power to enforce the contracts, as I think, by the usual system of small fines in the first instance.[1] We have all been anxious for some time, as to the effect on the "morale" of the company of the new elements and our anxiety was justified. There has been, as I think, some falling off in artistic aim; but it is hard to bring evidence of this, as one can of ordinary breaches of discipline. Both the Miss O'Dempseys are tomboys and rather vulgar.[2] The Miss O'Dempsey who was engaged for small parts is obviously impossible, flirtatious, loud, irresponsible. One need not discuss her further, but that Fay either did not know of her behaviour or knew it and did not interfere shews one the necessity of change. Her sister has naturally few opportunities for flirtation, but she is noisy. At Liverpool she was given a tin trumpet by Darley and with this trumpet made so much noise at the Trevelyan Hotel, Leeds, that the proprietress complained that she had not been able to sleep until after 2 a.m. She complained also of the noise made by other members of the company, talking and running from room to room. There would have been trumpet playing in the streets at Leeds had not Miss Horniman stopped it through Mr. Synge. Miss Horniman tells me that when she was ill during the Manchester, Liverpool and Leeds tour, she asked for reasonable silence after 11 p.m., but that the racket grew worse each night. On the way from Cardiff to Glasgow Miss O'Dempsey made so much noise with the wreckage of this trumpet through the night that in all likelihood Wareing who is deaf, was the only person who got a wink of sleep. Miss Gildea who was very tired, complained that she could not. I have been told that when the train stopped at Edinburgh between Aberdeen and Newcastle, the company hung out of the carriage windows and shouted to the people on the platform.[3]

I now come to more serious matters. At Cardiff station Macdonald was drunk, and wanted to travel through the night with Miss O'Dempsey

---

[1] The Directors later instituted a time-keeping book and a system of fines for late or non-appearance at rehearsals.

[2] See pp. 402, 416.

[3] In her undated memorandum (see p. 416, n. 8) AEFH reported that at Liverpool Brigit O'Dempsey 'came into possession of a toy tin trumpet foolishly given her by Mr Darly & with the wreckage of this

(Fay's) and Wareing put him in a compartment with the other men and took a centre compartment for himself to keep watch between the two ends of the corridor carriage. If he had not done so there would probably have been a fight with Fay. Bell has complained that on one occasion at any rate, as he passed along the compartments, he could see the stage manager in one "with his girl on his knee" and a director with another upon his. Miss Horniman is indignant because Synge sat with a young woman upon his knee in a public room at Leeds where a stranger might have entered at any moment and in her presence.[4] Miss E. Burry[5] and Miss Gildea had already complained to Miss Horniman of this in their presence. I don't want to make too much of these points; the company is very harmless and innocent, but that will not prevent their getting a bad name and a single person of an undesirable sort might get rid of the innocence. It is part of the carelessness in all details, the absence of precise habits. I need not labour the carelessness of the stage management. You and I had an understanding at Cardiff that Flood was to be changed if he was not good at the end of the week at Glasgow. I saw him there and he was not changed and he was practically as bad as ever. Understandings with Fay mean nothing because we can enforce nothing. The light was coming through holes in the scene at Cardiff and though I spoke of this and it was right for a time it was as bad as ever at Edinburgh. The frames I find were very badly made originally and the carpenter engaged for the tour was always tinkering at them. There were a great many little points, the clumsy upsetting of the basket in "Spreading the News", the leaving out the cackling of the hen in the "Pot of Broth". I dwell upon them now because I feel that just as things became ripe for dealing with the Roberts' party last Summer, they have now become ripe for a further strengthening of our hold on the company. The members of the company, the stage carpenter, the scene shifters, everybody down to Mrs. Martin,[6] should be paid by our representative and nobody engaged or dismissed without our consent. Reports as to the state of the electric light, scenery, costumes and everything should be made to us. This will liberate Fay's entire attention for his own acting and the acting of the others.

trumpet she made a frightful row between Cardiff and Glasgow. The only person in all probability who slept was Wareing who is deaf. Miss Gildea has complained that she could not, though tired out.' The trumpet survived to Leeds, where, at the Trevelyan Hotel, AEFH was 'scolded by the proprietress because she could not sleep until after 2 a.m. because of the row made by this trumpet as well as the general noise made by the company who kept running from room to room. The tin trumpet would have been played through the streets in Leeds but for Miss Horniman's objection on the railway platform, made to Mr Synge.'

    [4] Maire O'Neill, to whom he was shortly to become engaged.

    [5] i.e. Ethel Pullen-Burry (see p. 430, n. 10). The INTS had made a presentation to her in recognition of her assistance during their London tours, and in acknowledging this she told George Roberts (NLI) that she would be happy to help them whenever she could.

    [6] Mrs Martin, who superintended the cleaning of the theatre, had joined the Abbey in October 1904 as dressmaker and to sew canvas for scenery. In December of that year she was appointed caretaker at

We will probably have great objections raised by Fay, but if we are quite unyielding he will submit and all our relations with him will become smoother and his own work incomparably better. I have not had any communication with Fay and will not till we know precisely what we are going to do.

Yrs snly<br>W B Yeats

TLS Berg, with envelope addressed to Burren, Co. Clare, postmark 'London JY 5 06'.

## *To George Brett, 5 July 1906*

18 Woburn Buildings | Euston Road. | London.

*Dictated.*

July 5<sup>th</sup>,/06.

Dear M<sup>r</sup> Brett,

I got the enclosed letter from the solicitors of the Society of Authors, please return it to me & tell me what you have done about the book, that I may answer it.[1] I sent you the M.S. of the book some two months ago & would like to know if it has reached you.[2]

Yr sinly<br>W B Yeats

Dict AEFH, signed WBY; NYPL.

the new theatre, and remained there until the 1940s. Her portrait and reminiscences of the Abbey appear in Lennox Robinson's *Ireland's Abbey Theatre* (1951). In her unpublished 'Memories' (Berg) Sara Allgood recalled 'Mrs Martin, our charlady, a wonderful woman, harried to death by a ne'er-do-well husband, a large family, and very little money.... I remember her so well, rushing into the theatre in the early morning, putting on her canvas apron, dashing round with her duster, brush and pail, sweeping and washing up. In fact, I modelled my "Juno" in "Juno and the Paycock" on her. I gave her some money to get and make me a canvas apron, like she used to wear doing her work.' In his diary for 6 Dec 1918 Holloway gives as an example of WBY's absent-mindedness that one day he 'was passing through the Abbey, and seeing the charwoman at work, he said, "Good morning, Miss Allgood, that's a splendid make-up." "I'm not Miss Allgood, but Mrs Martin," said the charwoman, and Yeats, putting up his right hand palm outward, repeated as he walked away, A splendid make-up"' (*Abbey Theatre*, 199).

[1] See pp. 410–11. The second solicitor's letter is untraced, but Brett returned it on 17 July (NYPL), with a long covering letter. He recalled that when he met WBY in London (see pp. 64–6) he had offered to buy out Lane's rights in *The Wind Among the Reeds* book on behalf of Macmillan (NY), but he now discovered 'that Lane has apparently no right whatever in the matter and no right to sell or publish the book in this country, i.e. relying upon the statements made by you in regard to the contracts for this book's publication'. Given this, he thought that Lane's position might 'be safely ignored and the book included in the new edition provided you wish us to include it'. He went on to say that he proposed 'to pay a small sum to Lane for his plates and stock (in order that there might be no attempt to sell these by someone's mistake later on) but only at a merely nominal price'.

[2] Brett reassured WBY that Macmillan (NY) had 'received the copy for the two volumes which you sent and have it set up and the proofs have been sent to you, and I am surprised indeed to learn from

## *To Lady Gregory, [7 July 1906]*

18 Woburn Buildings | Euston Road,
Saturday

My dear Lady Gregory: I agree that we must try & get Fay to accept the means of better dicipline in a friendly way but friendly or unfriendly we must get those means.[1] My proposed man (with other work) is only part of <a plan <for> of getting ?some new clarity into the Company> a larger plan. I shall know more after I have seen Waring to-morrow[2]—I fear that Fay is too near the company to keep order & too much afraid of making his work unpleasent by being stern—this was why he could not change Flood. He should be able to plead that he himself is forced. I enclose a note which has just come.[3]

When will you be at Coole. I am going to Longford. Miss Horniman is not going.

You & I & Synge should consult & form a plan before seeing Fay—& we should then concede as much as possible in detail.[4] We should make the increase of dicipline essential & on this point we may find it impossible to explain our reasons to Fay—I am afraid Dossy Wright is too much Fays own man[5]

Yrs ev
W B Yeats

ALS Berg, with envelope addressed to Burren, Co. Clare, postmark 'London W. C. JUL 7 06'.

your letter of the 5th that none of these have reached you'. A set of page proofs of vol. 1, stamped 'J. S. Cushing & Co Norwood Press, Mass' and dated 'June 30—July 13 1906', is in the Berg Collection.

[1] AG was concerned that the new arrangements would alienate W. G. Fay and had told WBY on 5 July (see p. 410, n. 4): 'What I am really anxious about is Fay—He is excitable, & excited, & we *must* not lose him—Of course he must remain stage manager—& must be in our full confidence, we must consult him as to every step—At the same time we must keep some check on him, & to do this we must be under no compliment to him, we have been under a compliment while he was overworked & doing every sort of business.'

[2] The meeting with Wareing, who had just returned from Hull, was set up by AEFH, who had written to WBY that morning (NLI) that 'Mr. Wareing will call on you to-morrow morning. Late on Sunday Miss Gildea will arrive here & I should like you to see her on Monday if possible. It is only fair that you should do so, to *all* concerned.'

[3] Untraced, but perhaps AEFH's letter of that morning.

[4] In her letter AG had suggested that 'you & Synge & Fay ought to have a week together at Coole as soon as may be, we should have Fay better in hand there than in Dublin'.

[5] AG had suggested on 27 June that Dossy Wright might be appointed business manager (see p. 425, n. 3) and in her letter of 5 July was 'still inclined to think Dossy possible, directly under us & accounting to us'.

## *To Lady Gregory, [10 July 1906]*

Nassau Hotel | South Fredrick St
Tuesday

My dear Lady Gregory: I have just had a long talk with Frank Fay. I think we can get the payment of the people into our hands by offering to take "all the financial work" out of Fay's, which Frank Fay thinks should be done. Miss Allgood has complained to Frank Fay "that there is no good in the girls being careful of their reputation if Macdonald & Flood go on as they have been doing" (kissing harlots out of railway carriage windows).[1] She complained to somebody else that 'the tour of the company was not what it was' or some such phrase. W Fay had said he could not interfear. I have told Frank Fay if the theatre got a bad name we should be forced to close the theatre. I hope that will get round. I shall say the same to W Fay to morrow. I think that Synge will need very drastic treatment, so please dont get him to Coole till we have had a talk first, unless I get at him myself.

Molly Allgood is only 20 & there difference in social state and his being a director, will make scandal very quick to arise. A scandal of that sort would ruin us in Ireland. He should have kept it to himself. We shall have to try & get him to keep away from the theatre for a good long time. Frank Fay I can see thinks that his brother has been careless about rehersals of late. He said so & then pulled himself up & said he would not talk of it except in his brothers presence. I am inclined to think that the present dispute is a reversal of the old saying that men are mistaken in their denials & right in what they affirm. I think that almost all each side alleges against the other is perfectly true. I think Waring is avenging himself in part for his own mistake in starting this tour[2] by saying a great many necessary things about our people. Their retort in which they object to what he likes on the stage, or they think he likes, <has dramatic merit> is good general dramatic criticism. Warings case is that what success there has been has been a success of the plays in spite of the carelessness of the acting, <certainly an exageration>.[3] Ryan says that Fay is

---

[1] This was an allegation made repeatedly by AEFH and by Wareing in his report to her on the misbehaviour during tour. None of it was news to AG, who had been bombarded with detailed letters of complaint from AEFH throughout June and early July. AG evidently wrote to tell her of Sara Allgood's criticism of the arrangements for the tour and on 12 July AEFH replied (Berg) that any 'complaints made by Miss Allgood should have been attended to at once, she had so much on her shoulders that she deserved all consideration.'

[2] See pp. 392–3, n. 8.

[3] AEFH corroborated this view in her letter of 12 July: 'Mr Wareing assures me that though the actors have done for themselves, all the managers are delighted with the plays. I feared that we had slammed the door in our own faces, but he says that the plays have made a certain reputation for themselves & the authors which might be of great value in the future. They have stood a very hard test triumphantly.'

incapable of managing a large undertaking. His phrase was "he has neither the character nor the education needed". I should know to-morrow by the way Fay takes the suggestion of giving up the financial control whether we shall get our way without having to risk all. If I meet Synge I shall go straight to the point about Molly Allgood. I am much more anxious about the lax behaviour in public than about the stage management, which is at least good enough for us to learn playwriting by.

Yr ev
W B Yeats

ALS Berg, with envelope addressed to Burren, Co. Clare, postmark 'Dublin JY 11 06'.

## To Lady Gregory, [*11 July 1906*]

Nassau Hotel | South Fredrick St | Dublin.

My dear Lady Gregory: I have now seen Fay. He is very humble & himself asked for a business man, who will take over all accounts & wants to have nothing but his artistic work to do. He then got the company togeather & told them that there was to be no noise at railway stations Etc & is to take Flood & MacDonald aside & tell them that they will be fined if they are disorderly. In any case Flood is to be sacked after Longford & he thinks that MacDonald should be sacked as soon as we have a substitute. Flood & Mac have he says lowered the tone on the stage & off. I spoke about Synge & told Fay that I was going to remonstrate with him about Molly. He then told me that Sara Allgood had told him in confidence that Synge was going to marry Molly in November.[1] Lunacy of course but it keeps off the main danger <for the present> at the moment. He says that Synge as a director should have left the girls in the company alone and that it is a stupid marriage but that he never had any anxiety about the reputation of the company so far as that is concerned as Synge is too timid for irregular relations.

Can Synge & Fay go on to Coole after Longford as all is now ripe for the making of arrangements.[2] Fay wants to go immediately after Longford. You

[1] Because of Synge's chronic ill-health, the marriage never took place. AG strongly disapproved of the match, and it is perhaps significant that her reply to this letter has not survived.

[2] Synge, WBY, W. G. Fay, and AG conferred at Coole later this month, but Frank Fay did not join them. WBY had evidently told AEFH of the plan, but on 9 July (Berg) she wrote to warn AG against it: 'Will there not be a certain difficulty in your position as hostess if you deal with Mr Synge & Mr Fay at Coole? I don't think they will be restrained by their position as guests, because they will both be anxious to conciliate you at the moment so as to do as they choose on their return to Dublin.'

& I & Synge had better discuss things for a few minutes before we open up serious discussion with Fay so it would be better if Synge—who will not be at Longford—could go to Coole in time to be there when Fay & I arrive. We want to explain why for instance neither of us think either Dossy Wright or a woman would do as business manager & such things.[3] It is also desirable that you should hear from Synge what has really happened on tour, how far that Fay has been to blame & so on. If Fay & I arrive first you will not be so well posted for discussion.

Yr ev<br>W B Yeats

I am off to see about Oedipus.[4]

ALS Berg.

## *To George Sigerson,*[1] [c. *12 July 1906*]

Nassau Hotel

My dear D[r] Sigerson: please tell me for Lady Gregory the private address & if you know it the business address of the Hon Sec of National Lit Society

Yr ev<br>W B Yeats

---

[3] In reply to WBY's letter repudiating Dossy Wright as business manager (see p. 440), AG had written: 'Dont be too set on a business *man* for it is quite possible a woman with a business training would be easier to find, cheaper & more satisfactory.'

[4] i.e. about the progress John Eglinton had made with his translation of Sophocles' *Oedipus* (see p. 390).

[1] Dr George Sigerson (1836–1925) had studied medicine in Paris under Charcot and practised for many years in Dublin, where he was MG's physician. He later became Professor of Botany and Biology at the Catholic University, and from 1922 to 1925 a Free State Senator. Sigerson combined medicine with a literary career, publishing poems, essays, books on Irish politics, history, and society, as well as editing a number of anthologies, the most celebrated being *Bards of the Gael and Gall* (1897). His wife Hester (d. 1898) also wrote poetry, as well as novels and stories, and their house, at 3 Clare Street, was a major Dublin salon. He was president of the National Literary Society, and as such would have known the address of W. A. Henderson (1863–1927), who had been secretary of the Society from 1898. WBY knew Henderson to be a keen student of the theatre and had spoken to his paper 'The Stage Literature of Ireland', delivered to the National Literary Society on 8 Mar 1897, and published in the *New Ireland Review* in May of the same year (see II. 81). Henderson became business manager of the Abbey Theatre later this year, and was reappointed in February 1908. His volumes of scrapbooks about the theatre, now in NLI, are an invaluable source for the history of the Irish dramatic movement.

[*Written in Sigerson's hand at the head of this note*]
  W. A. Henderson
  Beldare
  Leinster Rd West
  Rathmines
Do not know business address[2]

ALS NLI.

## To T. C. & E. C. Jack, [c. *12 July 1906*]

C/o Lady Gregory | Coole Park | Gort | Co Galway, | Ireland.

Dear Sir: If you will send me copy for 'Spenser' selections to above address—where I shall be on Monday—I will condense the required amount & return it to you at once.[1]

Yrs sny
W B Yeats

I think you have selected the right poems to leave out but I am not quite sure in one or two cases.

ALS NLI.

## To Lady Gregory, [*13 July 1906*]

18 Woburn Buildings | Euston Road | London.

*Friday.*
My dear Lady Gregory: your letter of Saturday has just come with Synges enclosed.[1] I think I am glad I did not get yours before for if I had I could not have pressed the matter further. I have had to leave the matter

[2] Henderson lived with his parents at 23 Leinster Road West, Rathmines, and Sigerson evidently passed on his address as WBY wrote to him shortly after this.

[1] WBY had begun work on his selection from Spenser in late 1902, but publication had been delayed. The latest problem was the length of the book which had to conform with the other volumes in The Golden Poets series, and the publishers had evidently had to cut it on the eve of appearance.

[1] AG's letter of 'Saturday' (7 July; Berg) had evidently been held up in the post. In it AG took up a number of points WBY had raised in his letter of 4 July. She also enclosed a letter from Synge, dated 4 July (see p. 416, n. 8), in which he told AG that AEFH had taken 'a regular craze' against Fay, and himself complained of Fay's carelessness and the vulgarity of Brigit and Eileen O'Dempsey. Both AG and WBY found Synge's remarks hypocritical in that he had contributed to the general laxity of behaviour, and in her letter AG remarked that 'discipline' was 'evidently needed—& I must say Synge is the worst

to you because I am useless in <diplomacy> personal interviews. I would feal Fays moods so strongly that either sympathy or hostility would destroy my power of thinking. At the same time if you wire to me I will meet you in Dublin. I beleive that the existence of the theatre is at stake because
(1)    Getting independent of Miss Horniman is a dream <for the present> as we must apply to a new patent in association with her & we must have more capital to tour. Miss Horniman because of the very defects which make you dread her will not be influenced by any consideration for her personal interests to work with us if we refuse a manifestly reasonable demand
(2)    We had already decided to hand over all the practical non artistic work to a £100 stage manager & manager. You had said to Fay 'you must not know where a hammer is'. That is why I said 'responsible to Fay for production, to us in all else'. There is therefore nothing changed by this new proposal except that we shall get a better man & that Fay will have to give up a little a very little production. Fays objection to the new mans income must be the real difficulty—this is not an objection which should rouse us to deep sympathy though we have practically to consider it. M$^{rs}$ Emery says we could get Burchell for £200 or 300 (but I do not want to pick any body till I know more).[2] We could have an understanding that the amount of the salery is to be secret—this is usual in theatres—& we can give Fay an extra £100 a year if necessary (all the more readily if he will leave this dependent on our earning it of which I have however no doubt with tours).

I am quite aware of the danger to the theatre from the tension between myself & Fay.[3] I will not let it effect the theatre except that if we cannot agree on something <and if I can do it without putting his ?main work on you> it will be necessary for me to fade out of the practical side of the work & leave it to Synge. This is not 'huff' but knowledge of Miss Horniman & of the danger of tension between two people when one is in authority. <I cannot know anything for certain until she returns.>

Yrs alway
W B Yeats

offender, because his joining in the general disorder condones it on the part of the directors. I had a letter from him complaining, of the vulgarity of the Miss Dempseys but not a word abt Miss Molly!'

    [2] William Burchill (1874–1930) was born in Bath, and made his first stage appearance with Maggie Morton in 1897. He spent three years with the Forbes-Robertson Company, followed by six years as Mrs Pat Campbell's stage manager, during which, in 1904, he assisted with her famous production of *Pelléas and Mélisande* with Sarah Bernhardt. He subsequently toured as stage manager with Bernhardt before joining Arthur Bourchier's company in September 1905, and he was to play Lennox in Bourchier's production of *Macbeth* later this year. He did not join the Abbey Theatre.

    [3] In her letter AG had defined the 'real difficulty' as 'how to get W Fay in hand without offending him so much that he will throw us over & take an engagement elsewhere'. She conceded that he was 'certainly very hard to deal with.... But we have to get on with him somehow or break up the theatre', and hoped that WBY would make a public speech on the future of the Abbey 'for the company to hear': 'we must work on the *best* side of them if they are to put their hearts into their work, & both Fays are impressed by your public speaking.'

In light of Synges letter of manifest approval of the proposed paid director I can only look at the letter of his that you send with 'amusement'. I need hardly say I do not take Fays threats more seriously.[4]

ALS Berg.

## *To A. E. F. Horniman,* [c. *16 July 1906*]

Mention in letter from AEFH, 17 July 1906.
Telling her of the excellent acting at Longford and sending 'such full particulars',[1] discussing Fay and arguing that with all his faults he is against the commercial drama,[2] that he was disgusted by Bell's suggestion of a 'gag',[3] sending her a cheque for £11, evidently suggesting that the

---

[4] AG had written: 'What I am puzzled about is, suppose Fay sticks to his dog or any other prerogative, what threat or punishment can we bring to bear? We must consider that in making our rules—I wonder if you could get a statement of a stage managers duties from any 1ˢᵗ class company? Wareing could get it.'

[1] See p. 421. In her reply AEFH thanked him for letting her 'hear at once about Longford & then to send such full particulars', but added that it all 'makes me the more annoyed about what I witnessed at Edinburgh; the carelessness there was inexcusable because they could act well at Longford so soon after'. WBY's opinion of the Company's success was shared by the *Longford Independent*, which reported on 14 July (1) 'any lingering doubt as to the usefulness of such an institution is put for ever from our minds, as the plays are truly national in character, presenting remarkably well-drawn portraits such as were, and are, to be found in peasant life in Ireland. Nothing is exaggerated, everything is evenly balanced and nothing offensive is introduced.... we must give a word of praise to the remarkable standard of histrionic ability displayed by most of the members of this truly Irish combination of players, particularly the character studies of Mr W. J. [*sic*] Fay, and, the old woman parts so ably essayed by Miss Sara Allgood.'

[2] WBY had evidently and futilely attempted to defend Fay against AEFH's more intemperate charges, but only succeeded in stirring her to a more ferocious diatribe: 'My own personal unbiassed opinion is that Fay is absolutely unsuited to the part of Stage Manager. Your ideas against the faults of what you call the "commercial" drama have been played upon by him, so that he should be free to indulge in all slovenliness. He does not know about make-up except for the characters he plays himself & he will *not* learn & his proposals as to fines are blarney of an obvious sort. Grease paint is *not* washed off but first removed by the use of clarified lard. Chemises do not go up so high in the neck as to be in the way; that is a *lie*. Ask Marion to tell you as the servants at Coole are likely to wear the same under garments as those girls. The clean boots & tidy aprons of the peasants are purely Gaelic League vanity, this is part of how you told me that they objected to cottages looking poor & shabby. Fay cannot expect to be able to discipline Macdonald or anyone else, he talks of Mr. Synge leading him astray by a bad example, but no one accuses Mr. Synge of rowdy conduct out of a railway-carriage window. Fay hates the honest hard-working professional life and wilfully misleads you when he joins in your words against the "commercial drama"; he wants an excuse to be lazy & slovenly whilst you want even greater care & greater loyalty to Art.'

[3] In an attempt to demonstrate W. G. Fay's artistic sensibility, WBY had evidently repeated to AEFH the account of his repugnance at Bell's suggestion of a 'grotesque gag' for *The Building Fund* (see p. 415). Predictably, AEFH would have none of it: 'His disgust at Mr. Bell's suggestion of a gag is absurd—he speaks the American pig bit in Hyacinth exactly as if it were a gag & so vulgarises the little play. The clowning of his snores in Shadow of the Glen are quite different from the real sleepiness & fatigue which he represented so well when the play was first put on.'

Synge-Maire O'Neill affair was cooling,[4] telling her that AG's next play will be a three-act treatment of Elizabethan Ireland,[5] discussing the possibility of a Greek play at the Abbey,[6] and revealing that Fay has taken to his bed to terrorize AG.[7]

NLI.

## To A. E. F. Horniman, [c. 18 July 1906]

Mention in letter from AEFH, 22 July 1906.
Discussing the proposals she made in her letter of 13 July, reporting that Synge has told him that Fay 'has fallen off in his acting',[1] saying that Fay's mistakes were carelessness rather than malice, discussing the recent British tour, commenting on the administration and stage management of the Abbey Company,[2] and on Synge's relationship with Maire O'Neill,[3] and discussing Letitia Darragh's contribution to the Abbey Company.

*LWBY* 1. 162–4.

[4] 'Of course Mr. Synge is willing to give her up now,' AEFH retorted, 'three months of one girl on his knee doubtless leads him to wish for a change'.

[5] i.e. *The Canavans.* AEFH replied that she was 'glad that Lady Gregory's next play will be in three acts — what beautiful but impossible material she has at hand'.

[6] WBY had evidently told her of his hopes of putting on *Oedipus* (see pp. 390, 443), but she replied, 'I don't advise a Greek or any poetical play until you get a hold on things again. Rather begin with Boyle or Lady Gregory.'

[7] This AEFH thought 'delicious', and supposed that 'Mr Synge will gloomily wander by the lake side & threaten suicide in silence'.

[1] WBY had evidently reported Synge's observation that W. G. Fay had 'fallen off in his acting' (see p. 431). This led to an explosion of indignation from AEFH: 'yet he objected to my presumption in seeing it for myself! . . . It was an impertinence of Mr. Synge to write about me to you as he did, now it is *impudence* to avow an opinion as his own, which he had not the courage to express until he found that *I* had support. Perhaps cowardice is the root of what I call impudence. I don't mind people disagreeing with me & opposing me, but I do mind being virtually told that I'm too great a fool to judge for myself, especially by one who should know that my opinion was founded on a patent fact.'

[2] WBY had presumably told AEFH of his proposal to keep discipline by levying 'small fines' (see p. 437), but she maintained that Fay was so ignorant of basic theatrical skills such as make-up that fines 'on that matter would be absurd unless the people learned what to do & who should judge the matter?'

[3] AEFH had been scandalized by Synge's behaviour with Maire O'Neill on the tour and had reported to AG on 9 July (Berg) that 'Miss Gildea never walked about the corridor of the carriage as she says that if she had seen Mr Synge there with Mollie Allgood on his knee she could never have spoken to him again. One of the sisters sat on his knee before *me* at Leeds. Miss Gildea & Miss E. Pullen-Burry went into the public drawing-room at Leeds & saw Mollie Allgood on the floor sitting between his knees & they retreated at once, so as to avoid embarrassing him.' Given this, the news that Synge intended to marry Maire O'Neill was something of a relief and she replied that the 'affair is not as serious in one way as the influence of Fay; if he marries her & she gives up acting, he will be freer from Fay; yet on the other hand he may keep close to Fay so that she shall have good parts & have in time a larger salary.'

## To F. J. Fay, [c. *19 July 1906*]

Mention in letter from Fay, 20 July 1906.
Praising Miss Darragh's acting, asserting that she has more personality than the Abbey actresses, telling him that he has been speaking to her about acting intermittently at the Abbey ('Miss Darragh, who will merely as far as I can see play for a few days'), beginning with Dectora in *The Shadowy Waters*, and predicting that this would draw full houses,[1] criticizing Sara Allgood's acting, and saying that she was over-assertive.

MBY.

## To A. H. Bullen, 21 July [*1906*]

Coole Park | Gort, Co Galway
July 21

My dear Bullen,
    I am settled here for the summer, so please send the new book when it comes to this address.[1] Now what I want you to tell me is this. If we begin the collected edition when your Press is free, or at whatever date you have in your mind, how long can we keep our hands off the prose plays? I want to make a new version of Where there is Nothing, for it is the one thing of mine that neither you nor I want in the present shape.[2] I have to reshape either the Countess Cathleen (in this case not for publication) or Where there is nothing this year. One or other is wanted by my theatre. I think they would prefer Countess Cathleen,[3] but it must be Where there is

---

[1] Although Letitia Darragh occasionally played comedy, she was best known for her portrayal of 'modern' passionate and even neurotic women. The *Stage* of 9 Nov 1905 (16) commented that her performance in Alfred Sutro's *The Correct Thing* 'showed again the fine sensibility and coaxing *calinarie* that mark her performances of ladies with a past'.

[1] *Poems, 1899–1905*, not published until October.

[2] In fact, work on *CW* was postponed until the following summer as the financial arrangements were still far from settled. WBY had been dissatisfied with *Where There Is Nothing* since its first hurried publication in the *United Irishman* on 1 Nov 1902 (see III. 238, 241) and began to revise it almost at once (III. 245, 254, 257, 263, 264–5). He thought out a new scenario of the play after seeing it produced by the Stage Society in late June 1904 (III. 614–15), but was not to begin a full-scale revision until the summer of 1907, when he asked AG to collaborate with him; with her help he rewrote the play as *The Unicorn from the Stars*, which was first produced at the Abbey from 21 to 23 Nov 1907 and published in *CW* in 1908.

[3] In the second appendix ('The Dates and Places of Performance of the Plays') of *The Poetical Works of William B. Yeats*, II: *Dramatical Poems* (New York, 1907) WBY wrote that '"The Countess Cathleen" was revived in New York about a year ago... by Miss Wycherley, and will probably be played next autumn, a good deal altered for technical reasons, at the Abbey Theatre' (*VPl*, 177). Despite these plans, WBY did not revise the play until the summer of 1911, in preparation for Nugent Monck's production at the Abbey Theatre on 14 Dec of that year.

Nothing if you are in a hurry. You will have The Secret Rose, Ideas of Good and Evil and the Celtic Twilight to start off with (The Secret Rose however wants some slight revision)[4] and sometime next spring, all the poems, including a long new one.[5] The Pot of Broth, Hourglass, Cathleen ni Houlihan and Where there is Nothing will make a volume of prose plays, but I dont want to get at them till I have to. Even the small plays require some little revision.

Mrs Pat Campbell has seen my new play and wants it, but I dont know whether I can arrange with her or not, as she cannot have the Irish rights.[6]

Yrs ever
W B Yeats

TLS Kansas.

## To J. B. Yeats, 21 July [1906]

Coole Park, | Gort, Co Galway
July 21

My dear Father,
    Thank you ever so much for your letters about Swinburne. I have seen nothing of his criticism, except one rather absurd sentence quoted I think by the Sketch. I did not get the Athenaeum as I did not intend to reply.[1]

---

[4] WBY made some insignificant changes of punctuation and wording to *The Secret Rose* for its republication in the seventh volume of *CW*.

[5] Because it turned out that WBY had a shorter time than he supposed to prepare the text for *CW*, revision to the 'small plays' was very light. There were no changes to *The Pot of Broth*, very few to *Cathleen ni Houlihan*, and slightly more to *The Hour-Glass* (the most important of which was the addition of a four-line song for the Fool [608]). The most radically altered play was *Where There Is Nothing*, which was rewritten as *The Unicorn from the Stars*, but this had already appeared in three American editions before its publication in the third volume of *CW*.

[6] Mrs Pat Campbell had probably been shown a version of *Deirdre* by FF, with whom she was on friendly terms. She was interested in WBY as a dramatist and in 1901 had come close to producing his and George Moore's *Diarmuid and Grania*, while he, eager to keep up the association, had invited her to the Abbey plays in late November 1905.

[1] JBY had followed up his letter of 2 July (see p. 410, n. 4) with two others, dated 'Tuesday' (3 July 1906; NLI) and 'Saturday' (7 July 1906; Texas). In the letter of 3 July he said that he detested 'the kind of man Swinburne is. . . . Had his humanity been exercised by a various life his verse would not be so turgid and so monotonous. . . . I call Swinburne's insolence by that name, not merely because of its venom, but because of a *certain smack of self-complacency*—a sure mark of intellectual underbreeding and of an inferior kind of pride, tho' a quick passport to success with the kind of readers we are pestered with. Take any line you like of Swinburne's and it is three-parts journalism—there is always a something that savours of the great newspaper.' In his letter of 7 July he complained that he was 'disappointed at your not taking any notice of my two letters. I was very much perturbed at Swinburne's attack, and the source of my perturbation was hot zeal and affection for you.' The *Sketch* on 11 July 1906

The passage about him in the Blake book was by Ellis, and was entirely just and civil. I am not at all surprised at Swinburnes attitude for one practically never converts anyone of a generation older than one's own. One's readers are one's contemporaries, or the generation that comes after them. Andrew Lang was hardly civil when I sent him my first book, and was very uncivil indeed when he reviewed the Rhymers Book. Two years later he wrote a very generous article of apology. He excused himself by saying that new work was very difficult to him, and that when he first read Verlaine's poetry he thought it no better than one finds in the poets corner of a country newspaper.[2] Swinburne is a delight. Ellis said he didnt understand "the doctrine of the four Zoas" a most intricate thing that we had spent four years working out; and fourteen or fifteen years after that criticism and because he thinks I wrote it Swinburne is still so excited that he denies both reason and imagination to Ireland. Mrs Patrick Campbell has asked for my 'Deirdre', which she has seen though in somewhat incomplete form. She wants to produce it in the autumn and to take it on tour in America. I am not quite sure however whether I can let her have it, as my own theatre has first claims. And besides there is a new actress, a Miss Darragh who may want it for England, and I am inclined to think that Miss Darragh has more intellectual tragedy in her. She is an Irishwoman, and played Leah in the

had summarized the *Athenaeum* report (434) and also quoted Swinburne's 'amazingly clumsy' sentence beginning 'Some Hibernian commentator' (see p. 434, n. 13), adding that 'Mr. Yeats, I believe, has seen occasion to modify some of his theories. But Mr. Swinburne irresistibly recalls the famous observation . . . "your expressions are coarse and your meaning is obscure".'

[2] Andrew Lang (1844–1912) the Scottish scholar, classicist, folklorist, and poet had given up an Oxford fellowship to become a prolific literary journalist. He was perhaps responsible for the anonymous and dismissive review of *The Wanderings of Oisin* in the *Scottish Leader* of 20 June 1889 (2). His review of *The Rhymers' Book* is untraced, but he began to make amends in his notice of *The Celtic Twilight* in the *Illustrated London News* on 23 Dec 1893 which began: 'For a pleasant, pathetic, charming view of the Irish people and Irish manners, no modern writer is to be matched with Mr. Yeats.' An even more handsome apology was proffered in his review article 'The Young Men', which appeared in the *Contemporary Review* in February 1894 over the pseudonym 'A Fogey'. Here Lang explained that he had made a determined attempt 'to find pleasure in the multitude of new poets' but that it was not very easy to do this: 'For example, I once bought a batch of Monsieur Verlaine's poems, a lot of little books. I read right through them, and, at the end, had a general sense that they were fair magazine poems, many of them . . . and this proves how difficult it is for a fogey to accept the poetry dear to *les jeunes*' (178). He returned to this theme in speaking of WBY's poetry (186): 'we can never appreciate a poet till we have lived with his verse. A first reading may captivate us, but does not reveal all its qualities, and thus we can never criticise a poet truly, unless he both captivates us at first and then constrains us often to renew our intimacy with him. There is certainly something that captivates us in Mr. Yeats's verse. It really has the distinct and indefinable Celtic quality, the yearning note, and the confused memory of things ancient and wonderful.' He picked out 'The Man who dreamed of Faeryland' as having 'the same unique note' as 'the old Irish heroic tales' and other primitive legends, but wondered whether 'Mr. Yeats's Muses have matter enough for long endurance'. WBY admired Lang and had corresponded with him about folklore (see II. 280).

Walls of Jericho.[3] She gave a magnificent performance of 'Salome' the other day.[4] I am inclined to think, though I have not seen enough of her yet to be quite certain, that she is the finest tragedian on the English stage. I feel that a change is taking place in the nature of acting; Mrs Campbell and her generation were trained in plays like Mrs Tanqueray,[5] where everything is done by a kind of magnificent hysteria (one understands that when one hears her hunting her monkey and her servant with an impartial fury about the house).[6] This school reduces everything to an emotional least common denominator. It finds the scullion in the queen, because there are scullions in the audience but no queens. It gives the scullion grace and beauty, but it must be the grace and beauty that the scullion dreams of. A new school of acting is now growing up under the influence of the various attempts to create an intellectual drama, and of changes deeper than that. The new school seizes upon what is distinguished, solitary, proud even. One always got a little of this in Mrs Emery when she was good, and one gets a great deal of it in Miss Darragh. Both miss their climaxes as yet, for they are the reaction and the old school missed everything else at least in tragedy. Besides they are interested, the best of them anyway, in building up character bit by bit. I feel these things rather vaguely, as one feels new things; the problem

[3] WBY or his typist had evidently misheard 'Alethea' as 'Leah'. Miss Darragh, who had been born in Limerick, took over the part of Lady Alethea in Alfred Sutro's popular social satire *The Walls of Jericho* shortly after it transferred from the Garrick Theatre to the Shaftesbury in October 1905. The languid and sophisticated daughter of a marquis, Lady Alethea marries a forthright, self-made Australian millionaire, Jack Frobisher, but encourages overtures from a would-be lover and, accusing her husband of 'tedious virtue', endorses the easy morals and idle ways of her Mayfair set. Frobisher finally denounces the English upper classes and resolves to return to Queensland. At first Lady Alethea refuses to accompany him, and there is a separation, but she relents and the couple are reconciled just in time for the final curtain.

[4] Actually on 10 and 18 June (see p. 399, n. 4).

[5] Mrs Campbell had made her reputation as Paula in Arthur Wing Pinero's 'problem' play *The Second Mrs. Tanqueray* in 1893, although according to an interview in the *San Francisco Examiner* on 31 Jan 1904 WBY had never seen her in it:

'A fine technician, a master of stage-craft, I'll grant you that—but no personality. . . . Pinero has not what Arnold calls the literary conscience.'
'You've seen many of his plays?'
'Some comedies, and I read, or rather I should say I failed to read his "Second Mrs. Tanqueray." I had to give it up.'
So much for Pinero. I told Yeats that he should have seen Mrs. Patrick Campbell play Paula Tanqueray, and he regarded me kindly through his gold-framed glasses, as much as to say, 'Drama, my dear boy, should be bigger than its mimes.'

The play was to be produced at the Gaiety Theatre, Dublin, in mid-September of this year.

[6] Apart from an excessively indulged lapdog called Pinkie Panky Poo, Mrs Campbell's household at 33 Kensington Square, London, included 'the children': a black monkey named Venus, a parrot, and a Siamese cat. On 29 Nov 1909 WBY was to regale his father with a graphic account of an attempted play-reading at her house, which was punctuated by her tumultuous rows with her musician and dressmaker and which lasted from 1.15 p.m. to the early hours of the following morning (Wade, 539–40).

with me just now is whether as I am rather inclined to, to leap at the advertisement of a performance by Mrs Pat, or to keep to my own people and my own generation till they have brought their art to perfection.

Yrs ever<br>W B Yeats

TLS Boston. Wade, 474–6.

## *To Henry Meade Bland,*[1] *21 July* [*1906*]

Coole Park | Gort, Co Galway<br>July 21

Dear Mr Bland,

I have no photograph near me that is not very bad, but I send you a reproduction of a drawing by my father.[2] I am at this moment revising the proofsheets of a complete edition of all my poems, plays and all, which is to be published by Macmillan in the autumn in New York.[3] I shall also have a new verse play ready for the stage and for publication some time in the winter.[4] My company has just finished a six weeks tour in England & Scotland, and has now scattered for a holiday. It was very well received everywhere, and papers in Wales and Scotland are calling out of [*for* for] a national drama of their own on the same lines.[5] When the holiday is over, that is to say in about three weeks, they will start rehearsing again. This winter they will produce a three act play about a returned Irish American by William Boyle;[6] a three act play called the Playboy of the western world,

---

[1] Henry Meade Bland (1863–1931), poet and Californian regional writer, was a Professor of English at San Jose State Teachers College. He had been on the platform for WBY's lecture at Santa Clara College on 29 Jan 1906 (see III. 536), and had evidently entertained him that evening. In 1905 he founded the Pacific Short Story Club, which made WBY an Honorary Member in 1907. As editor of its journal, the *Pacific Short Story Magazine*, and as a regular contributor to the San Francisco *Town and Country Journal*, he kept his Californian readers up to date with WBY's publications in numerous articles and reviews.

[2] The drawing by JBY was probably that used as the frontispiece for the seventh volume of *CW* (see Plate ooo).

[3] For the American edition see pp. 64–6, 121–3.

[4] i.e. *Deirdre*.

[5] WBY himself had apparently been assiduous in promoting this idea, and, according to the *South Wales Daily News* of 31 May (7), introduced the topic during an address at a luncheon given for the INTS at the Royal Hotel, Cardiff, on 30 May, where he 'dwelt upon Celtic characteristics and national theatres', and said he 'was glad to be alive to the necessity of moving in this direction, for at the Carnarvan National Eisteddfod a Welsh play would be produced from the pen of the ardent nationalist, Mr. Beriah G. Evans. He was very glad the Eisteddfod had taken the matter up, and thought much good would result.'

[6] i.e. *The Mineral Workers*.

a wild fantastic thing by Synge; a three act historical fantasy by Lady
Gregory; a new long one act play by myself, Deirdre; a translation of
Edipus by John Eglinton, as well as two or three new one act comedies,
and the new versions of my Shadowy Waters and Kings Threshold. We
are a pretty lively school as you will see; and we will play not only in
Dublin but in various schoolhouses and temperance halls through the
country. We have a charming and very perfectly arranged little theatre in
Dublin, but it is these country halls that give us the best sport. My Pot of
Broth was encored at one of them once, and played right through a second
time.[7]

> Yrs ev
> W B Yeats

I have been seeing something of a San Francisco lady lately, Miss Tobin,
and have had thrilling accounts of the earthquake.[8] I am glad you got off so
lightly and very sorry [*for* glad] also that Santa Clara college of which I
have some beautiful memories is unharmed.[9]

TLS Bancroft.

[7] WBY is presumably thinking of the performance given in early 1903 at Foynes, Co. Limerick,
under the auspices of Lord Monteagle's Social Improvement Society, although the circumstances as
described by W. G. Fay in *Fays of the Abbey* (127–9) are not quite as WBY recalls them here. The first
performance, Fay wrote, 'felt like the hideous eternity of a bad dream. From start to finish stony
silence—not a murmur, not even the ghost of a smile. There was no curtain call.' Nevertheless, Lord
Monteagle asked them to give another performance, explaining that the audience had probably never
seen a play before and would think it disrespectful to laugh at actors from Dublin. Fay therefore went
before the curtain and gave a résumé of the plot 'and up went the curtain again. This time we had no
cause for complaint. They laughed at every line, whether it was funny or not. The scene at the fall of the
curtain was tremendous.'

[8] The great San Francisco earthquake had occurred on the morning of 18 Apr 1906, when the San
Andreas fault, which extends along the west coast, settled. The earthquake and sweeping fires that
followed destroyed 3,000 acres in the heart of San Francisco, leaving 500 dead, 300,000 homeless, and
causing damage to property over 20 square miles of over $200,000,000. During the four-day disaster,
one of the most devastating in American history, the press was filled with accounts of thrilling escapes
and heroic rescues.

[9] WBY had lectured on 'The Intellectual Revival' at the Jesuit foundation Santa Clara College in San
Francisco on the evening of 29 Jan 1904 (see III. 536–7). On 8 Sept 1911, on the eve of the Abbey
Company's first visit to the USA, he recalled that as he walked to the College he 'passed under palms
and all kinds of semi-tropical vegetation, and yet those boys were reading the same Young Ireland poets,
and thinking almost the same thoughts that young Catholic boys would have thought in Dublin' (*Irish
Times*, 9 Sept 1911 [8]). These fond memories make the mistranscription of 'sorry' for 'pleased' all the
more unfortunate.

# *To Stefan Zweig,*[1] *21 July* [*1906*]

Coole Park | Gort, Co Galway
July 21

Dear Mr Zweig,
I hope you will have heard from A. P. Watt by this time. What has happened is I imagine this. Meyerfelt wrote to me a week ago saying that he thought I should not have anything adapted for the German stage until I had a three act play ready. I sent this letter to A. P. Watt, who is now I imagine making enquiries, and making up his mind what I am to do. I told him that I left the matter entirely in his hands and would not give an opinion. At the same time I told him what you had said to me and what Meyerfelt had said.
I am very sorry about this delay, and hope very much that A. P. Watt will come to the conclusion that we are to go ahead. I am impatient to see my

---

[1] Stefan Zweig (1881–1942), poet, short-story writer, and biographer, was born into a wealthy Austrian family and, having recently completed a doctorate at Vienna University, was travelling widely in Europe. His first collection of poems *Silberne Saiten* had appeared in 1901 and his *Die frühen Kränze* was published later this year. In 1913 he settled in Salzburg and, despite his pacifist views, served in the Austrian War Office during the First World War. From 1925 he became famous for a series of perceptive biographies of writers and politicians, which were influenced by his reading of Freud. Driven into exile after the Nazi takeover of Austria, he became a British citizen in 1938 and subsequently settled in Brazil, where he and his second wife, despondent at the course of contemporary history, committed suicide in February 1942. Zweig had recently arrived in London in 1906, but was finding it difficult to make literary and social contacts. He had, however, met Arthur Symons and in his autobiography *The World of Yesterday* (1943) recalls (126–7) that Symons arranged an introduction to WBY, 'whose poems I liked very much and a part of whose delicate poetic drama, *The Shadowy Waters*, I had translated for the pure joy of doing so. I did not know that it was to be a poetry reading; a small circle of select people had been invited, we sat fairly crowded in a not very large room, and some even had to sit on folding chairs and on the floor. Finally Yeats began, after two huge altar candles had been lighted next to the black or black-covered reading desk. All the other lights in the room had been extinguished so that the energetic head with its black locks appeared plastically in the candlelight. Yeats read slowly with a melodious sombre voice, without becoming declamatory, and every verse received its full value. It was lovely. It was truly ceremonious. The only thing that disturbed me was the preciousness of the presentation, the black monkish garb which made Yeats look quite priestly, the smouldering of the thick wax candles which, I believe, were slightly scented. And so the literary enjoyment—and this afforded me a new charm—became more of a celebration of poems than a spontaneous reading. . . . It was the first "staged" poetry reading that I had ever attended, and in spite of my love for his work I was somewhat distrustful of this cult treatment. Nevertheless, Yeats had a grateful guest.'

work played, and it would be a great pleasure to have for my translator an admirable poet.[2]

Yr ev
W B Yeats

TLS Fredonia.

## To Maud Gonne, [c. 21 July 1906]

Mention in letter from MG, 22 July [1906].
Telling her that he has not been able to write lately because preoccupied with the difficulties and worries over theatre affairs,[1] hinting that her stars are ominous,[2] asking about the progress of her divorce suit,[3] and discussing his revision of *Deirdre*.[4]

*G–YL*, 231–2.

[2] Although Zweig had undertaken the German translation of *The Shadowy Waters* out of 'pure joy', he was now evidently thinking of possible publication and production. He had been working on the project since at least the end of May, when he described the play in a letter to Ellen Key as 'ein kleines Versstück' (*Stefan Zweig Briefe*, 120). He may have abandoned the translation because Watt had already entered into negotiations with Frank E. Washburn Freund for the German rights of WBY's plays (see pp. 130, 385), but more probably because he had become fascinated with Blake: 'the actual poetic discovery that came to me in London did not concern a living poet, but an artist who at that time was very much forgotten—William Blake, that lonely and problematical genius who, with his mixture of helplessness and sublime perfection, still fascinates me.... For days and weeks I tried to penetrate more, deeply into the labyrinth of that soul, at once naive and yet daemonic, and to reproduce some of the poems in German' (*The World of Yesterday*, 127).

[1] WBY evidently apologized for not having written lately, and explained that he had been occupied with the difficulties arising from the Abbey's British tour. MG was sorry that he had 'had so much worry about the theatre affairs & hope things are satisfactorily arranged, for though your theatre is not quite the theatre I wanted, still it is beautiful & there is room for both—you will be able to make it much more popular if you have got complete control. Popular in Ireland does not mean the same as popular in England or in most other countries—for in Ireland it is the *people* who guard the ideal & who will sacrifice & strive for it.'

[2] In her reply, MG asked WBY to tell her 'what you see in the stars & don't be afraid of telling me, *I want to know*'.

[3] WBY had apparently asked MG about the latest developments in her divorce proceedings, and she replied that she had 'been working very hard' at it: 'The more I see of lawyers the more I learn that one must do all the work for them if one wants it well done.' She explained the judge had refused to allow MacBride's lawyers to delay the case any further, and that there would be hearings on 26 July and 1 Aug, with the verdict given on 8 Aug: 'Major MacBride is relying entirely on the point of International law that if he can prove Irish domicile the French Courts cannot grant divorce only separation but I think he will find it hard to prove Irish domicile.' And she promised to let WBY 'know the result at once'.

[4] MG replied that she wanted 'so much to hear your Deirdre & I hope to when I am in Ireland this autumn'.

# To J. L. Rutledge,[1] 22 July [1906]

Coole Park | Gort, Co Galway
July 22

Dear Mr Rutledge,

I am nothing of a novel reader,[2] or rather have read nothing of any novel for some years now, written later than Gil Blas.[3] I think the last modern novel I read was about half of Huyssmanns En Route, five or six years ago.[4] I should think that the novel will flourish most in countries where it finds new forms of life. In England and France it is, my friends tell me, threatening to die out in philosophy and essay writing. The United States have all the old delight in it and have great numbers of people that write stories, and that must be because they are very curious about themselves, and have so much life that has never come into literature. Here in Ireland

---

[1] Joseph Lister Rutledge (1885–1957), journalist, short-story writer, and historian, was born in Winnipeg, Manitoba, and was at this time reading History at Victoria College, University of Toronto, where he was literary editor of the college magazine, *Acta Victoriana*. After graduating in 1907 he joined the staff of the London *Advertiser* and was subsequently editor of *Maclean's Magazine*, the *Canadian Magazine*, *Liberty*, and the *Canadian Author and Bookman*.

[2] Rutledge was eliciting the views of 'a number of eminent authors' on 'the value of the present-day novel' ('Whither is it tending? What will be its ultimate form?') for a compilation on 'The Future of the Novel', which appeared in the 'Christmas and Book Number' of *Acta Victoriana* (Dec 1906, pp. 140–4). WBY's letter was reproduced verbatim over a facsimile of his signature (142), and Rutledge prefaced it with the comment that: 'Few men are in a better position to express an opinion in regard to this than the leader of the Celtic movement, William Butler Yeats. As a dramatist and a novelist he is likely to speak with authority as to the comparative merits of the two.' The other authors who contributed were the American man of letters John Kendrick Bangs (1862–1922), whom WBY was to meet in 1914, the folklorist, novelist, and poet Andrew Lang (see p. 450), the English novelist 'Anthony Hope' (1863–1933), the American novelist and short-story writer Hamlin Garland (1860–1940), the popular American novelist Winston Churchill (1871–1947), the English-born Professor of Literary Theory at Chicago University Richard Green Moulton (1849–1924), and the Irish academic and critic Edward Dowden (see p. 295). Most of the commentators saw a future for the novel, but were reluctant to prophesy what it would be. Moulton thought that 'the experimental side of human science fiction' would 'become the dominant literary form', while Garland, like WBY, preferred drama to fiction: 'It will not supersede the novel, but it may come to subordinate it.'

[3] The immensely popular picaresque novel *L'Histoire de Gil Blas de Santillana*, by the French playwright, novelist, and translator Alain-René Le Sage (1668–1747), was published in four parts from 1715 to 1735. WBY, who owned a four-volume translation by Henri van Laun, published in 1896 (*YL*, 1107), had also read his *Le Diable boiteux* (1707) in translation, and cites it in *E & I*, 242, 272.

[4] *En route* (1895), a novel of spiritual pilgrimage by the French prose writer Joris-Karl Huysmans (see p. 77, n. 9), marks a significant stage in his transition from naturalism to mysticism. WBY would have read it in the English translation published in 1896. On 25 Mar 1904 WBY had told an interviewer in the *Pall Mall Gazette* (6) 'with sharp emphasis' that he 'read no modern novels. . . . At least, none except Mr. Meredith's. I never open one of them, and so I cannot tell whether they are good or bad.'

we are taking to playwriting, because we are curious about ourselves & yet not good readers.

Yrs ever<br>W B Yeats

TLS Toronto.

## To F. J. Fay, [c. 23 July 1906]

My dear Fay,

I full[y] agree with you it would be a most highhanded proceeding to ask Miss Allgood to surrender even for a few nights a part at which she had worked so hard.[1] Your brother however told me that Miss Allgood had no

---

[1] This is a reply to Frank Fay's extremely long and plaintive letter of 20 July, defending Sara Allgood against what he saw as WBY's unfair partiality for Letitia Darragh (see p. 448): 'Miss Allgood has never asserted herself; she has too much modesty and ability to do so. . . . You must pardon me if I ask you to wait till I see Miss Darragh act before I know whether she deserves the words you use. Even if she be what you say, she is not our product and has a different way of doing things. Suppose she is what you say and draws full houses for a week, how will it be when she is not with us. It is no answer to say that Miss Allgood will play many times the part or parts Miss Darragh plays first. The original player of a part is rarely effaced in the memories of those that saw him or her. . . . It seems to me an actress should be judged by how she acts. You have seen what the newspapers thought of Miss Allgood. You have had professional opinion upon it. . . . You don't care about acting—you must let me say this—at the bottom of your heart you prefer Irving because of some personal traits you admire and you don't like Coquelin. . . . You want oratory and peculiar personal qualities, what you call distinction and so forth. . . . I am in no way upset over the matter except as regards Miss Allgood's position. I have trained her: she has been the one success I have had. She has earned the position of leading actress here by ability and hard work.' He denied AEFH's allegation that they had 'given up trying' as a 'lie', and warned WBY that what he what he proposed was 'dangerous to the company and dangerous to the movement'. He also challenged WBY's contention that 'Miss Darragh . . . will merely as far as I can see play for a few days', on the grounds that this would still give her first crack at all the leading parts, and the publicity that went with this. Later on the same day Fay also wrote to AG (Berg): 'I am very disappointed over Mr. Yeat's action. I am not afraid to play with Miss Darragh whom I liked, so far as one can like or dislike on a moment's talk; but I would rather he had taken a part from me than from Miss Allgood, whose support is so vital to us; who has been so loyal; & whom I don't want to see made appear small before our audience or the "intellectual" lady who, as far as they could snubbed her when they were in the company. I am the more angry because she has worked so hard for me & has given back tenfold every bit of teaching I gave her. You will have read my letter to Mr. Yeats, & this only repeats what I have said in it. It seems obvious to me that my brother acted hastily, & if Miss Darragh must get Dectora, it seems to me that Miss Allgood should get Dierdre. Mr Yeats should be careful lest he drive a very valuable talent away from us. If Miss Allgood went, my interest in the show would be precious slight. . . . I don't care how I am treated but I care a great deal how Miss Allgood is treated. Surely the natural thing in these cases is to write to the person concerned.' Fay's support for Sara Allgood was not merely professional. As she recalled in her unpublished memoirs (see p. 191, n. 8), 'I think it was on the second or the third tour that poor Frank wrote me a letter asking me to marry him. Apparently he had fallen in love with me. . . . He used to give me lovely presents, such as a first edition, signed, of Synge's works, W. B. Yeats poems, the first edition printed at the Cuala Press. . . . Well, the letter asking me to marry him was a cause of great distress. I told Brigit O'Dempsey of it. . . . I cried all afternoon. . . . Finally I wrote to Frank, telling him I could not marry him because I did not love him. He wrote me back, saying he would wait, because he would rather have "Hell with you than Heaven without you"'.'

objection, he said this most sympathetically. Miss Darragh is a great tragic actress and she is Irish, and it will be of importance for us this winter to get a element of attraction as well as of permanent importance to us to draw into our work a new powerful Irish talent. This theatre should become the centre in course of time for all Irish Dramatic talent. I will have *Deirdre* finished before the autumn,[2] and I can give that to Miss Darragh instead of *Shadowy Waters* if Miss Allgood will prefer it. It is in either case merely a question of having Miss Darragh play for a few days if our work goes on as I believe it will for years, and if the plays succeed Miss Allgood will play many times oftener is both parts than Miss Darragh, who will merely as I can see help us for a few days this Autumn. It is a partly a question of generosity between artists and I feel quite certain that neither you nor Miss Allgood will be less generous to a new acting talent in our movement than Synge or Lady Gregory or myself would be to a new dramatic talent.

Yours sincerely
W B Yeats

TLS Private

## To Robert Ross, [*late July 1906*]

at | COOLE PARK, | GORT, | CO. GALWAY.

Dear M^r Ross: May I introduce you to a very distinguished actor & stage manager, M^r Musek of the National Theatre of Prague. He wants to produce one of Wilde[s] plays, does not know where to get a copy.[1]

Yr ever
W B Yeats

ALS Private.

[2] The play was not in fact finished until mid–November and WBY made revisions in late 1907.

[1] Ross was Wilde's literary executor (see p. 402) and would have been able to give Mušek translation rights as well as an actual copy.

## *To Katharine Tynan Hinkson,*[1] *30 July* [*1906*]

Coole Park | Gort, Co Galway
July 30

My dear Mrs Hinkson,

I want to make a selection from your lyrics for the Dun Emer Press. It will be quite a little book, but I want to read through everything, and I havnt much time to do it in, as my sisters want the book by the 15th August.[2] I know from what my sisters tell me that they have had some correspondence or conversations with you about it. Probably you have settled the business side of the matter but if not they will no doubt write to you about that.

Can you get your publishers to send me the books? Are the poems in your own hands or have we to get leave from the publishers? and will it be better for you to ask or for us?[3]

I am looking forward very much to making this selection. It will be a great personal pleasure to have a little book of just those poems I care most for to put beside the Allingham and the Johnson.[4] I am hoping that

---

[1] Katharine Tynan Hinkson (1859–1931; see I. 516–18), poet, novelist, and journalist, whom WBY had first met in June 1885. She remained one of WBY's closest friends and confidantes until her marriage in 1893, and he reviewed several of her books in this period. After her marriage she and her husband settled in London, where she produced a great number of romantic novels and a stream of journalism. Although there had been some coolness between her and WBY over disparaging remarks he made about an anthology, *Dublin Verse*, edited by her husband in 1895, this had passed, and in his essay 'Poetry and Tradition', originally entitled 'Poetry and Patriotism' in *Poetry and Ireland* (1908), he counted her, himself, and Lionel Johnson as the triumvirate who had begun 'to reform Irish poetry', seeking 'to make a more subtle rhythm, a more organic form, than that of the older Irish poets who wrote in English, but always to remember certain ardent ideas and high attitudes of mind which were the nation itself, to our belief, so far as a nation can be summarized in the intellect' (*E & I*, 247–8).

[2] *Twenty One Poems* by Katharine Tynan, selected by WBY, was published by the Dun Emer Press on 6 Aug 1907 in an edition of 200 copies. Mrs Hinkson had paid a visit to Dublin in late July, and probably discussed the possibility of a book with ECY then. The business arrangements were characteristically casual, and on 11 Mar 1908 she wrote to Frank Matthew (Manchester): 'The Dun Emer series is not paid for: and I don't think they have ever published any book that was. To my amazement they sent me a £7 odd cheque for the book of mine the other day. The idea of a cheque signed by a Yeats nearly made me faint.'

[3] Kegan Paul, Trench & Co. published Katharine Tynan's first two volumes of poetry, but, after a brief move to Elkin Mathews, she had now transferred to Bullen, apparently bringing the rights to her earlier verse with her. The only acknowledgement in *Twenty One Poems* was to Bullen, and, although WBY selected poems from a number of her earlier books, he could have found the text for all but four of them in her collected *Poems*, published by Lawrence & Bullen in 1901.

[4] WBY's selections of Lionel Johnson's *Twenty-One Poems* and William Allingham's *Sixteen Poems* had been published by the Dun Emer Press on 21 Feb and 27 Nov 1905 respectively.

this series may in time become known for containing the best of our Irish work.

Yrs sny

W B Yeats

TLS Harvard.

## To Elizabeth Corbet Yeats, [c. 30 July 1906]

Mention in an undated letter from JBY, [3 August 1906].
A stern letter, attacking her commissioning of a two-volume selection of AE's poetry, and insisting upon his absolute authority in the selection of books for the Dun Emer Press.[1]

NLI.

## To George Brett, 2 August [1906]

Coole Park | Gort, Co Galway

August 2

Dear Mr Brett,

I have received your letters of the 17th and 20th July; they arrived today, sent on from my London address.[1] I sent you a complete Manuscript of all the poems and plays in verse I cared to preserve. I never understood that this edition was to contain any prose, and could not at this moment arrange for an edition to contain prose, as the prose plays of mine which you publish need a complete revision, and I have not time to give it to them at this moment.[2] I received some time ago the proofsheets of the poems and plays

---

[1] WBY's always strained relations with ECY had reached breaking point owing to a dispute over a proposed book by AE. WBY and he had collaborated on a Dun Emer selection of his poems, *The Nuts of Knowledge*, in 1903 (see III. 370, 493–5), and ECY had now contracted to publish a further selection, *By Still Waters*, without consulting WBY, although he was officially literary adviser to the Press. On receiving the MS he sent her an uncompromising letter, refusing to sanction the book and threatening to resign as adviser. Although this letter is now lost, it caused deep offence in the Yeats family. Writing to Emery Walker on 3 Oct 1906, ECY reported (MBY) that 'Lily said [it] was like the British Government during the Boer War — "full of threats & ultimatum & last words" — so I felt that *then* I could not give in'.

[1] Brett's letter of 20 July is untraced, but that of 17 July (see p. 439, n. 1) had reviewed Lane's legal position with regard to *The Wind Among the Reeds*, expressed alarm that WBY had not received the proofs for *The Poetical Works of William B. Yeats*, and then confessed that they were 'in a quandary here as to whether you wish to include in this collected edition the books of yours which we ourselves have published, as no copy for these was included in the collected copy which you sent us. As I understand the matter however everything of yours was to be included in this new collected edition which had been hitherto published and which you wished to preserve.' He ended by begging WBY to 'at once let me know if you have yet received the proofs which we have sent, and . . . also to advise me immediately as to whether I am right in supposing that the collected poems and plays which we are publishing for you is indeed, as we have always supposed, complete to date'.

[2] Both volumes of the New York *The Poetical Works* have prefaces, and that to the first volume, which contains a generous selection of his poems (including thirty-seven from *The Wind Among the*

up to the middle of the second act of the Countess Cathleen. I returned all the poems, that is to say the first volume and sent you a preface for it. I shall send you a preface for the second volume and what proofs of it I have received in a few days.[3] I am a little puzzled by your letter, and it is just possible that when you say the two volume edition does not contain all my poems and plays, that you mean that some part of the Manuscript is missing. I know that I sent it all, but if any of it has gone astray, will send you that part again the instant I hear. The verse plays you publish have been so completely revised by me that the plays I sent you were practically new plays. The complete second volume will contain The Countess Cathleen, The Land of Heart's Desire, The King's Threshold, On Baile's Strand, and The Shadowy Waters. These are the only verse plays I have written. This will be my address for all this summer.[4]

Yrs ever

W B Yeats

### PS.

Since writing the above I have re-read your letter of July 20. You say 'Will you kindly let us know if we should include in the volume of plays those plays which we have published here, which are not embraced in the list of contents.' I see by this that you do mean the prose plays. I could let you have a revised version of the three small plays and will if you like. But I have no hopes of having a revised version of 'Where there is Nothing' for a year or so, as I shall have to revise it on the stage, and rehearse every alteration. I dont think these three small prose plays would go well with the verse plays, but you are welcome to them if you like, I would recommend you however to keep them back to make a volume together with the revised 'Where there is Nothing' a year or so hence; and to advertise this present book as what I intended it to be, a collected edition of my lyrical and dramatic poetry.

WBY

TLS NYPL.

---

*Reeds*, is dated 'July 1906'. The second volume, published on 8 July 1907, collects his poetic drama, but no plays in prose, although a series of appendices give prose accounts of the legendary background to the plays and poetry, and a statement of the principles upon which the INTS was founded.

[3] See p. 452.

[4] Brett had enquired about the plays already published by the Macmillan Company: *Where There Is Nothing* (published as the first volume of Plays for an Irish Theatre in 1903) and *The Hour-Glass, Cathleen ni Hoolihan* [*sic*], and *The Pot of Broth* (published as the second volume of Plays for an Irish Theatre in 1904). Since the title of the present collection was *The Poetical Works of William B. Yeats*, WBY was reluctant to include slight works in prose, and he may also have been influenced by the fact that all four plays were to various degrees collaborative. Brett took his advice and issued a separate volume of prose plays in May 1908, comprising the rewritten *Where There Is Nothing, Cathleen ni Houlihan*, and *The Hour-Glass*, under the title *The Unicorn from the Stars and Other Plays*. AG's name appeared on the title-page as co-author of *The Unicorn from the Stars*, and in his preface WBY acknowledged her contribution to the writing of the other two plays.

## To Charles Elkin Matthews, 3 August [1906]

Coole Park | Gort. Co Galway
Aug 3

My dear Matthews,

I have received the enclosed letter from the Society of authors, and also another which says:—"assuming that Elkin Matthews told John Lane what his contract with the author was, which he doubtless did, John Lane's term expired when Elkin Matthews did"...You are my sheet anchor, and I will be very much obliged if you would write to Lane for the accounts. You will see that not only did A. Watt but the Society of Authors consider that you are the fitting person to do this, the agreement being with you. I will be very much obliged if you will do this at once, as I want to get my collected American edition out in the autumn. Please return to me the Society of Author's letter.[1]

Yours sincerely,
W B Yeats

TLS Leeds.

## To Field, Roscoe & Co, [? 3 August 1906]

Mention in letter from Field, Roscoe & Co, 5 September 1906.
Sending on a letter from George Brett about the rights in *The Wind Among the Reeds*.[1]

---

[1] These were letters about *The Wind Among the Reeds*; see pp. 410–11, 439. Matthews had written to John Lane earlier in the summer, but to no avail. Lane had replied on 10 July (Texas) quoting his New York manager to the effect that 'Last April Macmillan Company informed us that they intended to issue a complete edition of Yeat's work. The Macmillan representative suggested that they might be able to utilize our plates in their new complete edition. We made them an equitable offer for these plates, which they did not accept. Nothing further was done in the matter' (see p. 410, n. 1). Lane added unyieldingly that 'Mr. Yeats cannot remove the book without he makes some provision for my interest in it, consequently the matter is still in abeyance'.

[1] Frederic Emery, the Society of Authors' solicitor, did not read WBY's letter, which also enclosed George Brett's letter of 17 July, until 5 Sept, when he returned from his summer holiday, but WBY had almost certainly sent Brett's letter on to him shortly after it arrived in early August. Emery returned Brett's letter with his reply of 5 Sept, and commented (Watt) that he was 'glad to find that the Macmillan company are able to take up the position that they will republish the book without regard to Lane's al[l]eged claim. It is not often that publishers will take this courageous line and if they adhere to this and republished the book I do not think the Lane company will dare to reprint again and if so the matter may be considered to be working satisfactorily. You will of course not hold any communication with the Lane company and if you hear anything about them from Mr Brett or otherwise you will no doubt write me further.'

## To J. B. Yeats, [5] August [1906]

Coole Park | Gort, Co Galway
August 3.[1]

Copy

My dear Father,

I do not think you quite understand my relation to the Press.[2] I have unfortunately been so little able to help my sisters in other ways that I have done my best to help them in trying to make it a real and permanent success. The printing though very good and very creditable cannot compete with the printing of hand presses which employ the experienced labour of men under the supervision of connoisseurs of printing. It is not so good as the Dove Press for instance, nor as good as the Vale Press—this however was not a hand press but used on the other hand specially designed types, and yet the Vale Press has had to close.[3] The one chance of making the Dun Emer Press a permanent success and of making it in the long run a valuable property was to get the books a reputation for fine literary taste and

---

[1] Although dated 'August 3' in this typed version, the copyist may have misread WBY's '5' for a '3', since this is clearly an answer to a letter from JBY of 'Aug. 3rd, 1906'.

[2] WBY's imperious letter to ECY about AE's proposed book (see p. 460) provoked an angry letter from JBY on 3 Aug (NLI) to which this is a reply: 'Why *do you write such offensive letters?* There is nothing fine in a haughty & arrogant temper.... You treat Lollie as if she was dirt—She is as clever a woman as you are & in some important respects much cleverer.... When you advise about choice of books for the Press, it should be advice, & not haughty dictation backed up by menaces—After all *the press is Lollie's business*, & it means our means of living, & she has often other things to consider besides the literary excellence of a particular book—there are questions of convenience & commercial expediency & policy, matters for tactful consideration, not to be decided offhand, by a literary expert.... I think you ought to write a frank apology—If you want to withdraw from the business of advising, it is easy to do so in a temperate & kindly letter. This letter if not recalled *leaves a cleavage between you & Jack & Lolly & Lilly*—I appeal from Philip drunk to Philip sober.... My own impression is that it would be best for all parties if you withdrew altogether from the position of literary adviser.... A haughty temper is closely connected with personal vanity—its virtues are theatrical & unreal. It is a brigand among the other qualities that make up the human family. It is a cut throat trying to pass itself off for a gentleman.' JBY was relieved by the tone of this reply, and on 6 Aug wrote (NLI) to thank WBY 'for taking in such good part what I wrote. I have had many anxious moments since I wrote. I still think that what I wrote was in the main the truth, but I thought possibly my manner of putting it might be very irritating.'

[3] The Doves Press had been founded at Hammersmith in 1900 by Thomas Cobden-Sanderson and Emery Walker. Its type, designed by Walker, was based on a 15th-century model, and its most celebrated publication was a five-volume edition of the Bible (1903). The partnership broke up in 1909, but Cobden-Sanderson carried on until, badly hit by the First World War, the Press came to an end in 1916, and he threw the type into the Thames to prevent its being used for inferior work. The Vale Press (see p. 110, n. 4), operated by Charles Ricketts and Charles Shannon with the help of T. Sturge Moore, ran from 1896 to 1903, its most important publication being *The Works of William Shakespeare* (1900–3) in thirty-nine volumes. On its closure, Ricketts destroyed the types, which he had designed, and like William Morris and Cobden-Sanderson threw his punches and matrices into the Thames.

to associate them in the mind of students with what was finest in our movement. In this way there was a possibility of the fame of the Press growing with the growth of the movement itself. I have not spared myself trouble in doing my part of the work as perfectly as possible. The selection from Lionel Johnson for instance meant a great deal of very careful thinking and weighing of poem against poem, and waiting upon one's own permanent taste. I have also spent a considerable time over books that did not in the long run prove suitable, and with my bad eyesight this has meant a very considerable amount of trouble. It was only for instance after I had practically made my selection from De Vere and had a great deal of correspondence through Lady Gregory about the copyright, that I found out that De Vere, beautiful as his best work was, had not done a sufficient amount of beautiful work to make up a volume of sufficient size.[4] I have suggested books to people, some of which may still be done, and there has always been a possibility that the work available might grow both in quantity and quality with the movement. I need hardly remind you and Lollie that I can get permission from publishers and authors that Lollie alone would find it difficult to get. The one thing necessary for success was that the standard should be high, and that Dublin inefficiency should be kept at a distance. So long as I have had the usual rights of an editor or literary adviser, that is to say the certainty that nothing would be included in the series I disapproved of, I could ensure this. Lollie should have recognised that my power to exclude was her protection for she could always shelter herself from local pressure by making me responsible. Lollie has never professed to have any particular point of view in literature and I have always supposed that I was free to take my own point of view. I spent last Sunday going through Russell'[s] books with the list of his selections. I found to my deep disappointment that they did not seem to me good. This so upset me, seeing as I did the complication in my own personal relations with Russell that a refusal might cost, that it brought on a headache. I said to myself, it is possible that I may be deceived, and I took up the old book of selections and found it as beautiful as ever. Russell has done more of beautiful poetry than

---

[4] Aubrey de Vere (1814–1902), Irish poet and man of letters, was a Catholic convert, and a friend of Wordsworth, Tennyson, Carlyle, and Browning. WBY published four of his poems in *BIV*, and chose *Selections from the Poems of Aubrey De Vere*, ed. G. E. Woodberry, as one of his 'Best Irish Books' in 1895 (*UP* 1. 387), praising 'The Bard Ethell' for its 'perfect marriage of meaning and form' and 'The Little Black Rose' for being 'quaint and beautiful' (*UP* 1. 381). But he told Katharine Tynan on 12 Mar 1895 (1. 451) that, while De Vere had 'done three or four wonderful things', he had 'no copious stream of beauty', and later that year (*UP* 1. 381) maintained that he was 'seldom master of the inevitable words in the inevitable order', and that his works were 'but slightly related to the Irish lyrical movement of to-day'. AG was an old friend of De Vere, who was the first person she approached for a subscription towards the ILT (*OIT*, 21). The idea of the anthology was revived in the summer of 1908, when the Cuala Press separated from Dun Emer Industries and advertised *A Selection from the Poems of Aubrey de Vere and Sir Samuel Ferguson*, chosen by WBY at 7s. 6d., but this never appeared.

De Vere, but not enough for two volumes of selections. I asked Lollie to postpone the book, giving as an excuse that it would give Russell the opportunity of writing more poems to select from. Lady Gregory wanted me to give way for the sake of peace but it would have been going against every instinct I possess to do so.[5]

There are only two things possible, one that I should have the usual control of an editor, and the other is that Lollie shall do the work herself or get some person she can trust to do it.

I have had the same fight over our plays. I have been pressed to consent to do inefficient work for various popular reasons. I have made enemies by holding out against it, but the result is we are already getting the credit of being the only creative school of drama. We have a long way to go yet, but we have gone far enough for the Stage Manager of the National Theatre of Bohemia (subsidised by its Govt to the amount of £12,000 a year) to have been sent to find out particulars and report upon the plays. He left here two or three days ago.[6] Ireland is inefficient in all forms of life, and it is not possible to make her efficient in any of them without making any enemies. Hugh Lane has made quite as many enemies as I have, but his exhibition has shown the advantage of the selection being made by a mind that admits no consideration except artistic excellence as it appears to an individual imagination. Besides is there not the old saying 'One bad general is better than two good ones'.[7]

I shall have a large volume of poems out in a few days, not absolutely new, but old work so revised to be practically new.[8] I have not quite decided

---

[5] WBY's relationship with AE was at a difficult stage, the temperature of their cooling friendship having dropped even further after the Maire Walker dispute (see pp. 291–8). In her letter to Emery Walker of 3 Oct, ECY gave her version of the dispute, explaining that 'Willie & AE quarelled' over the selection of the poems for AE's book, and that 'now Willie wants to fight with me also—I had to take AE's selection of his own poems—for one thing because I had already waited for Willie to settle it, & the book or some book had to be done at once—also—it is a very good selection a good many new poems—& it is quite clear that it is a good book to do as quite a number of people have already written to ask me to keep copies for them—Willie of course says AE has only written three or four good poems.'

[6] Pan Karel Mušek (see p. 178, n. 4) visited Coole from 27 to 31 July. He had arrived in Ireland on 17 July, visited the Abbey on 22 July, and saw a good deal of Synge in Dublin, who reported to AG on 24 July (*JMSCL* 1. 181) that he had asked permission for the Czech National Theatre to produce *The Shadow of the Glen*, that they 'have £12,000 a year *and* all scenery and light from the government so they can afford to do things well', and that he had recommended *Cathleen ni Houlihan* and *Spreading the News* to Musek. On 5 Aug he reported (185) that he had 'packed Musek off last night; he was very much pleased with his visit to you'. Mušek's visit to Coole was noticed in the *Lady's Pictorial* on 18 Aug (204) in a paragraph presumably inspired by AG. In a note written in August 1929 (Private) WBY recalled him as 'a vivid energetic man' and was 'inclined to think that Musek's visit was the first important sign that our movement was recognized on the continent'.

[7] It is possible that the typist mistranscribed WBY's 'mad' as 'bad', and that he was thinking of George II's retort to the Duke of Newcastle, who had complained that General James Wolfe was mad: 'Mad, is he? Then I hope he will *bite* some of my other generals'.

[8] i.e. *Poems, 1899–1905*, not in fact published until October.

about Mrs Pat. I can honestly say it is the advantage of the Theatre I am thinking of on both sides of the question, and there is much to be said on both sides.[9]

W B Yeats

TS copy Boston.

## To J. B. Yeats, [7 August 1906]

Mention in letter from JBY, 8 August 1906.
Agreeing to write a more temperate statement to ECY, setting out his views on the Dun Emer Press and his association with it,[1] and saying that he thought the Press should be made a kind of literary principality.[2]

MBY.

---

[9] See pp. 449, 450. In a letter dated 'Friday' (? 27 July 1906) JBY had asked 'What are you going to do about Mrs Pat Campbell. I think it is a difficult question—no doubt the ideal thing is to keep the play for the Irish theatre & we all & you especially ought to do ideal things—it might also be the prudent thing—the theatre is a very *serious product* of the Irish National movement.... Giving it your best play will give you a considerable accession of position & authority with such people as *John Quinn*—& besides all this, it is a dignified thing to do.... you should not forget that you are a public man in the Irish movement, & its leader in all literary & philosophical movements—& that your influence here is really more important to you than anything else & *dearer to you*—& more important than anything else to other people as well.'

[1] WBY had evidently followed up his letter of 5 Aug with a formal statement, setting out his views on the Dun Emer Press and his conditions for remaining as literary adviser, but JBY found its tone too critical. In his letter of 6 Aug (see above, n. 2) JBY revealed that 'Lilly & Lollie don't know of this correspondence, nor have I shown them yr statement ... because of your disparaging criticisms about her printing. *On this subject she has no delusions*, but she won't take any criticisms from you, they at once rouse her pugnacity, & her obstinacy.... *She knows her faults far better than you can point them out.*' He went on to explain that because of this WBY's criticisms would be counter-productive since ECY was 'far *too prone to see her shortcomings*' and 'to see the worst side of things, & to lose hope' and he asked in conclusion: 'If I send you back the statement could you not revise it, leaving out the criticisms on the printing, as to which Walker of London constantly advises her.'

The present letter was a reply to these remonstrations, which WBY evidently accepted, since he agreed to rewrite his statement, and in his response of 8 Aug (NLI) JBY advised him on what to say. He suggested that WBY should not take credit for the Press, should not discourage ECY about the printing, and should not 'say anything about your own trouble & time & exertions'. On 9 Aug he wrote again (NLI) to suggest that WBY should also point out that good books were as crucial to the success of the Press as good printing, and explain that this was the reason 'you thought that you ought to have been granted an absolute dictatorship—but that you have known all along that this rested with Lollie herself—Of course obviously it is so—& you think still you ought in the interests of Lollie herself to have this dictatorship—but that if Lollie preferred it you were willing to confine yourself to the mere giving to advice.'

[2] In his reply of 8 Aug JBY agreed with WBY that to make the Dun Emer Press a success 'it must be made a kind of literary principality', and to this end urged him to make peace with his sisters and treat AE and John Eglinton 'with great respect', admonishing him to 'keep strictly to *advising*—otherwise you wreck everything'.

## To W. A. Henderson, [c. 7 August 1906]

Mention in letter to Synge, 17 August 1906.
Assuring Henderson that his duties as business manager of the Abbey Theatre could be so arranged that he would be able to take off the nights he wished to attend the National Literary Society, and also conduct his literary work at the National Library.[1]

## To A. E. F. Horniman, [c. 12 August 1906]

Mention in letter from AEFH, 14 August 1906.
Telling her that he feels in good spirits about the theatre, that they have a business manager for the Abbey in view,[1] that there is a proposal that authors should direct their own plays,[2] discussing his dispute with ECY over the publication of AE's book at the Dun Emer Press because of his 'real passion for good work',[3] wondering why there are no 'lets' to visiting companies at the Abbey.[4]

*LWBY* 1. 165–7.

---

[1] WBY was conducting what turned out to be prolonged negotiations with W. A. Henderson over the terms of his employment as business manager at the Abbey (see p. 443). Henderson was secretary of the National Literary Society, and deeply involved with its running and management.

[1] WBY had written to AEFH, who was in Bayreuth for the Wagner Festival, to tell her that he was negotiating with W. A. Henderson to become business manager at the Abbey. In her reply AEFH said she was 'glad that you feel in good spirit about the theatre & have got a Business Manager in view', adding that he was 'a necessary person', but that better training and greater efficiency of the Company was also necessary.

[2] AEFH replied that she quite understood 'the idea of the authors stage-managing their works; this is quite right when practicable, but something must be done to make it certain that their orders will be carried *out in their absence*. Until this is done all your toil is just making ropes of sand! Fay will never do this, his carelessness & slovenliness are *not* unreasoned I am certain.'

[3] AEFH was indignantly on the side of WBY in this dispute: 'You authors (some of you) *really* care, but Russell does not care & if your sister makes a mess of the status of Dun Emer, *she* does not care. You know perfectly well that your "real passion for good work" gets no sympathy from the emotional people. It is this worship of sentiment & emotion which is used as means of keeping down the artistic standard; it is *sloth* on the part of those who want to keep on top with the least possible trouble.'

[4] In her reply AEFH wondered if this was due to the 'absurd' canards circulating in Dublin about the exorbitant fees charged by the Abbey: 'Fay told me at Cardiff very gaily that there were "no lets for June." I shall be very suspicious if no cheque comes in October, it will be serious if there is a complete stop to the letting. But that won't stop us, I'll hold on as long as you & Lady Gregory think it worth while.'

## To W. A. Henderson, 13 August 1906

Mention in following letter and in letter from Henderson, 15 August 1906. Telling Henderson that the Directors could not expect him to make the financial sacrifice that coming to the Abbey would apparently involve.

## To John Millington Synge, 13 [August 1906]

Coole Park | Gort, Co Galway
Monday 13

My dear Synge,

We have been negotiating with Henderson, but I doubt being able to arrange with him. We may wire to you to see a man called Sanders who is recommended by Oldham.[1] Fay is put out evidently at our making the business man pay the actors, but he forgets that Miss Horniman added this money for a business man, on the understanding that all business of this kind, this business in particular, shall be in his hands. This argument is sufficient for Fay, who I dont think in any case is likely to cause trouble in the matter. I look upon it as essential upon other grounds. If we cannot get the stage carpenter, the man responsible for the electric lights, &c under our direct control, there will be all kinds of evasions and difficulties.

There has been a more serious difficulty. You will remember our talk about Miss Darragh playing in Shadowy Waters, and Fay's statement that Miss Allgood would not object. A week or so after you left this, I got a letter from Frank Fay, saying that he wouldnt play with Miss Darragh and threatening to resign. I answered him arguing the matter out, and saying that judging from what he said—he had spoken of his months of training of Miss Allgood for Dectora—it might be better to give Miss Darragh Deirdre. He replied by another letter of indignation, to which I replied stiffly, saying that it was a matter for the stage manager and the directors. That ended it so far as he was concerned, and I dont see any reason to take seriously his threats of resignation. Even if he had meant them, we would have had to hold on, even if it meant the bringing of an actor from London for the sake of the discipline of the company.[2] Yesterday Lady Gregory got

---

[1] AG had written to Synge on 6 Aug to tell him that Henderson was to become business manager at the Abbey at a salary of 30s. a week, but negotiations over terms continued until 17 Aug. Oldham was at this time Principal of the Rathmines School of Commerce and thus had a professional knowledge of the abilities of numerous commerical clerks in Dublin. Sanders is unidentified, but may have been a poor relation of Robert Massy Dawson Sanders, whose firm, R. & C. Sanders, Land Agents, had offices at 32 Nassau Street, Dublin.

[2] In Longford, and apparently in Dublin (see pp. 457–8), W. G. Fay had asserted that Sara Allgood would not mind the leading female roles in *The Shadowy Waters* and *Deirdre* being given to Miss

a long letter from William Fay, typewritten by F. Fay, of an incoherent nature, owing to William Fay's endeavour to stick to his own statement about the desirability of Miss Darragh playing Shadowy Waters, and to stick also to his brother's objections. So far as I can make out though I am really very uncertain, he doesnt object to Miss Darragh playing in Shadowy Waters, though he dwells on all the grievance of Miss A having learned the part, but does object to her playing Deirdre.[3] Now one thing is entirely certain, that as we Directors arrived at a decision and asked Miss Darragh, she has got to play something or other if we are ever to get our way in anything. I also want to explain my own point of view to you before asking your advice. You and Lady Gregory and Boyle can look forward to good performances of your plays from the present company and from the people who will join it in the natural course of things. You are already getting better performances than you could get from any English Company. I am getting it of course also with my prose plays. But I am essentially a verse writer. At this moment in spite of Frank Fay's exquisite speaking, I could get a much better performance taken as a whole in England of a play like Deirdre. Mrs Campbell is anxious for the play, but the more I think over it the more do I feel that we should keep all our plays in the hands of our company. This is the one way of making it a great company, but to do this I must get good performances. It will be easiest for me to do this by gradually bringing in actors who need not be a permanent part of the company, at first at any rate, but who can come over for special parts. I require for Deirdre for instance an emotional actress of great experience. Miss Allgood is I think essentially a character actress, but even if she is not, there has been nothing in her experience to prepare her for this most

Darragh, and Miss Darragh had been invited to Coole to arrange terms. On 1 Aug Dorothy Carleton, who was staying with AG, reported to W. S. Blunt (Fitzwilliam Museum) that 'this afternoon a Miss Dallas, one of the Irish actresses is expected. She is in a way on trial to see whether she will agree to do all they want—so there will be more theatre talk—' In the meantime Frank Fay had written to WBY on 20 July (see p. 448) complaining of the treatment of Miss Allgood. He repeated his objections and threats in a letter to AG on 23 July: 'It seems obvious to me that my brother acted hastily, & if Miss Darragh must get Dectora, it seems to me that Miss Allgood should get Deirdre. Mr Yeats should be careful lest he drive a very valuable talent away from us. If Miss Allgood went, my interest in the show would be precious slight.'

[3] W. G. Fay's 'incoherent' letter is now lost, but he repeated the nub of his complaint in an explanatory letter of 14 Aug (see below, p. 471, n. 1). Many years later he gave a more considered analysis of Miss Darragh's acting: 'The public and the Press voted her magnificent. She was manifestly a highly trained professional, the like of which was not among us. But in my eyes it was just this manifestness that ruined the show. It did not fit with our technique, which, for all its lack of obviousness, had been slyly planned so as to get a special effect out of special material. It was like putting a Rolls Royce to run in a race with a lot of hill ponies up the Mountains of Mourne, bogs and all. The ponies, knowing each inch of the way, could outpace the Rolls every time. On the one hand, Miss Darragh made our company look young and simple, and, on the other hand, their youth and simplicity made her look as if she were over-acting' (*Fays of the Abbey*, 208).

elaborate part, where there is a change of emotion in every few lines. Miss Darragh is I think a great tragic actress, and she is Irish. It will probably be necessary, though there is no need to speak of this at present, to add a man of equivalent power, if he can be found. I certainly do not see him at present. Any objection raised by the present company to this process of development will be very shortsighted. We shall sooner or later have to go to America, and we cannot go there without players with the full range of emotion of the very highly developed American stage. With a proportion of say one romantic or verse play to every three peasant plays, and that one play passionately played we shall sweep the country and make enough money to make ourselves independent of Miss Horniman. We have also to think of the possibility of playing several weeks in London each year. The alternative to this is the giving of my plays to English companies, for if I am to be any use even in Ireland, I must get good performances. Till I get that I shall be looked on as an amateur. If Miss Allgood possesses the power of playing these passionate parts, she will hold her own against Miss Darragh, who will only come for occasional performances. Deirdre has grown in complexity since you were here and is very much more outside the range of Miss Allgood than the part of Dectora (in which by the bye she was passably good but not more in rehearsal).[4] Now what I propose to do is to write to Fay and say "Deirdre is now so complicated that it requires the work of an experienced emotional actress. If I let Mrs Campbell have it, Miss Allgood can play it in Dublin, in that case, Miss Darragh will do Shadowy Waters. If I do not give it to Mrs Campbell, I will ask Miss Darragh to play in it, and Miss Allgood can have Shadowy Waters." Of course it is always to be understood that Miss Allgood understudies Miss Darragh for performances when she is not available. In this latter case, we will bring both plays to London, and both Miss Allgood and Miss Darragh will have parts there.

You had better let us know what is happening, and what Miss Allgood herself thinks. Of course when I say that I am pressing Miss Darragh for my own work, I am not hiding from myself or you that there may be occasions when she will be necessary for work of yours or Lady Gregorys, but I suppose we can leave that to the future. After she has given a successful performance the company will begin to take pride in her and it will be easier to find parts for her. In a company like ours one emotional actress is a necessity. Would you mind returning me this letter, as I have taken some trouble putting my case, and may want to copy it for Fay.

---

[4] Rehearsals of *The Shadowy Waters* had taken place in the autumn of 1905 (see pp. 198, 203–4).

Colum's little tract is a rag; the printing, the paper, typical in its penury and lack of taste.[5]

Yrs ev
W B Yeats

[*In AG's hand*]
Forgot to say there is a good part for Miss Allgood in Deirdre, leader of chorus & all the choruses to give—
[*In WBY's hand*]
On consideration I have written to Fay a long letter on the Darragh question saying what I have said in this letter I would say but also putting the general argument. I thought delay would look like hesitation.

WBY

TLS TCD.

## To W. G. Fay, 13 August [1906]

Coole Park | Gort, Co Galway
August 13

My dear Fay,
Lady Gregory has read me your letter. I cant understand it, as you first tell us that you are very glad that Miss Darragh should play Shadowy Waters, but do not like the idea of her playing Deirdre, and then go on to argue against her playing Shadowy Waters.[1] I think I recognise your brother's voice as well as your own. I know of course that it was Shadowy Waters that we discussed when you were here, but I got such strong remonstrances from your brother about the waste not only of Miss All-good's time but his, that I saw the matter in a different light, especially as

---

[5] This was a leaflet distributed at the performances given the previous week at the Oireachtas, the annual festival sponsored by the Gaelic League. Among the plays presented was a Theatre of Ireland production of *An Talamh*, a translation by 'Torna' of Colum's *The Land*. Synge had attended the performances on 9 Aug and sent a copy of the leaflet to AG on 12 Aug.

[1] Fay replied to this letter with a certain exasperation on 14 Aug (cf. *LWBY* 1. 186): 'I am sorry my bad composition made my letter hard to understand, but I will try again. You asked me in Longford to get Miss Allgood to let Miss Daragh have Dectora. Act 2. Lady Gregory wrote me in Enniscorthy that you wished Miss Allgood to have her choice of Deirdre or Dectora. Act III. You write this morning & say Miss Daragh must have Deirdre. Now what am I to make of it. I don't care a red cent which of them plays either part but is Dectora now finally to be rehearsed by Miss Allgood. Ive got to keep down rows here but I cant if we change about week by week. I dont see any means of comparing Miss Daragh with Miss Allgood but they are certainly not equal in experience. I dont mind a bit how much of Miss Daragh you want its no affair of mine but i[t] will be no use losing any of what we have for something we might possibly get in the future.'

Deirdre contains an excellent part for a woman as well as the title part. I think this is the fairest way to put it. If I decide to give Deirdre to Mrs Campbell, about which I am growing very doubtful, then Miss Darragh will play Dectora on its first production, and Miss Allgood Deirdre in Dublin. If on the other hand I keep the play for the Abbey Theatre, Miss Darragh must play Deirdre, and Miss Allgood will play Dectora. Since you were here the part of Deirdre has grown so complex, so full of continually changing emotion, that nobody could play it adequately except an emotional actress of great experience. If I got a fine London performance an inadequate Dublin performance would not matter so much. I feel however that I cannot establish my reputation as a poetical dramatist with quite the same cast as is sufficient for a peasant play. Your brother is of course more delightful to my ears than any player I could get in England, and your performance in Baile's Strand was of course a masterpiece.[2] But you can see yourself as well as I do or better, that the performances of my verse work have imperfections that one does not find in the peasant work. Neither Synge nor Lady Gregory could ever get anything like so good a performance in any other theatre, but the training that perfects an actor or actress for peasant work does not perfect them for tragedy in verse. Miss Darragh is a tragedian, tragedian and nothing else, born to it as you are born to comedy, as Miss Allgood is born to certain kinds of character work. The moment I thought of her for Deirdre I began to write better, I thought of moments of her Salome, and ventured and discovered subtleties of emotion I have never attempted before. Miss Allgood may discover a tragic personality for verse, but she has to be tested, and no one is denying her that test. She will not lose but gain from understudying a fine tragedian, and if I am wrong and prove herself the better, no one will suffer in the long run. Miss Darragh is not likely to play more than occasionally for us, at least not unless we were to make a great success. If she gets another engagement she might not play for us this winter at all. This is the issue. Can I get sufficiently good performances of my work from the National Theatre to refuse it to all other English speaking companies? Lady Gregory and myself have been inclining more and more to the opinion of a London manager (not Waring) that we should keep all plays in the hands of the theatre.[3] This is especially important with a view to our ultimately going to America, our one chance of making a large sum of money. It is also very probable that if we can hold to our whole mass of plays and give adequate performances of them we may get very good offers for London shows. When we go to America, one quarter let us say of the work or one third, would be romantic

[2] W. G. Fay played Barach, the Fool, in *On Baile's Strand.*

[3] Probably Granville-Barker, of whom WBY had seen a good deal this year (see p. 369).

and poetical. We will have to do that work not only finely but finely enough to compete with emotional acting of players of very great reputation. By emotional acting I mean acting which arises out of the expression and definition of passion as distinguished from character. It will be enormous service to us to have got a powerful actress who is Irish, used to our method. The choice before us is the choice that comes before every sort of movement. We have all to choose between a narrow view of the interests of our little community, and a generous and far seeing view. Every player in the company though he may get slightly less to play increases his chances of a big reputation and a decent income with every new player who increases the efficiency of the company. Miss Allgood is a most admirable actress, powerful, moving and sincere, one of the best actresses within her limits that I have ever seen, a great possession to the Theatre, but remember the finer the artist the more definite the limits. You cannot do everything though you have been years upon the stage, and she cannot do everything. Besides I long to see her measured against an equal, whose limits will just because she is a good artist be as precise and as narrow.

I have a few slight alterations to make in the text of Shadowy Waters, but you will have them in good time.[4]

[*No signature*]

TS copy MBY.


## To John Millington Synge, [*17 August 1906*]

Coole
Friday

My dear Synge,

About the autumn's work. The changes in Boyle will cause some little delay before we put that into rehearsal.[1] We must therefore make up our minds at once, for I suppose they are now back or all but back from the holidays, what we are to set them at.

The first performances will be according to the programme we talked out here, country performances in September. Fay is very doubtful of getting a cast that can tour White Cockade, and if he cannot get it Galway had better be put off, as Lady Gregory doesnt want us to go there till we have

---

[4] The scene in which Forgael wakes Dectora was still giving WBY trouble (see pp. 135, 161, 193).

[1] The Directors wanted changes made to *The Mineral Workers*, which was not produced until 20 Oct of this year. The plot involves the attempts of a successful returned emigrant from America to establish a mining industry in a conservative Irish rural community.

historical or romantic work. In any case it is probably too late, for if we were going there we should have decided in time for Lady Gregory to have worked it up during Feis time. Fay's doubt prevented her doing this. We may therefore decide on giving up Galway for the moment, which leaves us Mullingar Athlone, and possibly Tuam. (Tuam however had probably better be worked from Galway.) We could do two nights at Mullingar and two nights at Athlone.[2] <I dont like the idea> I think it better not to send the English programme pure and simple to these places. It is very scrappy, and the company would be better for a change, Lady Gregory and I favour the following:—One night Building Fund, Hourglass, and Spreading the News. The other night Cathleen, Doctor in Spite of himself and Spreading the news or Hyacinth. What do you think of this? It will give us a costume play each night, and it will be most interesting to try Moliere on country people. My own belief is that he will go extremely well with them. Besides, he touches the educational interest. We will want the Moliere certainly during the season in Dublin for a mid week revival, and if there is any delay over Boyle, it will give the company something to do working at Moliere with the business out of the French book.[3]

Now for our first Dublin programme. Boyle may seem a little sordid to people, a little too near their ordinary life. I think we should revive the White Cockade as a mid week revival, more especially as this will give Miss Allgood, whose part in Boyle is rather uninteresting, an opportunity of playing the Old Lady, and will get the piece up for a winter visit to Galway. There will be so much work to do this winter that I doubt a later chance of reviving the play. White Cockade however is not long enough to fill an evening bill, but I think though I am not sure that Hyacinth has not yet had a revival in Dublin. I think Hyacinth would go therefore with the White Cockade. I am personally very anxious for this, as with O'Rourke[4] or Power as the policemen it will give Lady Gregory an opportunity of judging whether a change of structure is necessary. Boyle's play, the first act of which will have I think to be slightly cut in rehearsal will not be specially with the alterations in the third act, too long for a short play with it. Lady Gregory and I suggest the Poorhouse, (I think we decided on this when you were here) with Mac and Frank Fay as the two old men. This will be taking advantage of Hyde's present popularity, and will add a new name to our

[2] Although planning continued for some weeks, it is unlikely that this country tour took place (see p. 378), and no visits by the Abbey company in September are recorded in the local newspapers.

[3] The company were using a prompt copy acquired from the Comédie-Française.

[4] Joseph A. O'Rourke (1884–1937) joined the Abbey Theatre Company in 1906 and played second-string and comic parts until 1916 when he seceded with Arthur Sinclair to found the Irish Players. On 14 Aug 1906 W. G. Fay had asked WBY (cf. *LTWB* 1. 186) whether O'Rourke was 'to go on the pay list at 10/- a week'.

list, and save the piece from the enemy.[5] The company can therefore if you agree with us, begin at Moliere, White Cockade, Poorhouse, and the policeman part of Hyacinth without waiting on Boyle. I think also Miss Allgood and Fay might go on with Shadowy Waters, provided they leave alone the bit before Forgael wakes, as I have some alteration to make there. There will also be an alteration of three or four lines in the speech of one of the sailors at the harp-playing. I have written to Fay and told him that I was writing you on all these matters. I have also said that we shall have to develop in the future the tragic and romantic side of our work more than in the past. The company is as good as one can desire in peasant work. Robert Gregory is inclined to translate the Antigone for Miss Allgood, and we shall have to think out a big tragic programme. You see if I give up Mrs Campbell I have got to set my mind to making the poetical and tragic side of the work as good as the peasant. It will be necessary to find or translate enough plays for constant practice.

Henderson has accepted and will probably call on you.

Yr ev
W B Yeats

TLS TCD. Saddlemyer, 141–4.


## To W. G. Fay, [*17 August 1906*]

Mention in previous letter to Synge, and in letter from Fay, 18 August [1906].

Discussing the introduction of sixpenny seats,[1] O'Rourke's position in the Company,[2] and the arrangements for cleaning the windows at the Abbey,[3] agreeing with the points raised in Fay's previous letter about

---

[5] After his triumphant American trip (see pp. 212, 372, 391), Hyde was at the height of his popularity in Ireland. He received a tumultuous welcome back to Dublin on 24 June, when he addressed a thronging crowd in O'Connell Street, and in his poem 'At the Abbey Theatre' (see p. 294, n. 7) WBY apostrophizes him as 'most popular of men'. *The Poorhouse* was an English version of his play in Irish *Teach na mBocht*, but was not produced at the Abbey until 3 Apr 1907; see p. 224, n. 8.

[1] In his letter of 14 Aug Fay asked if the Abbey was 'to have 6[D] seats this Autumn for we could spend it a bit if we are'. The Directors had arranged with AEFH in June that sixpenny seats should be introduced, and they were advertised for the autumn season (see p. 424).

[2] Fay had asked whether O'Rourke was to get a regular salary of 10s. a week (see p. 474, n. 4), and on 18 Aug told WBY (*LWBY* I. 187) that he had 'given O Rourke a start and put him on to wardrobe which I think he will look after better than MacDonald [*sic*]'.

[3] Fay had informed WBY on 14 Aug that the 'Window cleaning people want 8 or 9 shillings a month for keeping the place clean' and asked if he should accept the offer. On 18 Aug he said that he had 'closed with Window cleaning can they start Monday'.

Sara Allgood and Letitia Darragh,[4] telling him that John Eglinton is working on a translation of a Greek play for the Abbey,[5] and that they must develop the poetic and Romantic side of their work,[6] asking if costumes sent on from Coole have arrived safely,[7] and whether the Company's holidays have ended,[8] revealing that William Boyle has had to return to England with the MS of the *The Mineral Workers*,[9] and that Robert Gregory has made a model stage.[10]

*LWBY* I. 186–7, where it is dated '1907'.

## To W. A. Henderson, 17 August [1906]

Coole Park | Gort, Co Galway
August 17

Dear Mr Henderson,

I understand from your letter that you accept, and I am of course very glad. Perhaps the simplest thing would be for you to see Synge, who is at Glendalough House, Glenageary, Kingstown. You might write to him and arrange a meeting. If after talking things over with him there is still anything to discuss with me, Lady Gregory asks me to say she will be happy to see you here, for a day or two. I am sure you will be a great help

---

[4] Fay was relieved to hear that WBY at last understood his position over Letitia Darragh, replying on 18 Aug: 'I see by your letter you have got my meaning about Miss Algood and the crowd. My objections were not to Miss Daragh but we must get more varied work and keep our best people in good parts for I don't see much possibility of increasing salaries for a good while to come and if we can't pay in money we can in parts.'

[5] Having failed with Gilbert Murray and Gogarty, WBY had now turned to Eglinton for a translation of Sophocles' play (see p. 390), and on 17 Oct 1906 AG was able to tell Quinn (NYPL) that 'John Eglinton has translated "Oedipus the King". WBY was also trying to persuade Robert Gregory, who had read Classics at Oxford, to translate Sophocles' *Antigone*, the production of which was announced later this autumn. In his reply Fay commented: 'I think the translation of Greek play would help us & I hope we will get the Oedipus as well from Eglinton.' In fact neither Eglinton's nor Gregory's translation was produced at the Abbey.

[6] WBY's letter had told Fay that he was arranging for more poetic and tragic plays at the Abbey, and in his reply Fay warmly endorsed this policy: 'I am very glad there is a prospect of us getting more poetic work & Romantic, for we have a fine stock of peasant plays even at present time.'

[7] AG was sending costumes from Gort by rail and on 18 Aug Fay acknowledged: 'The clothes to hand all right and will send P. O.'

[8] Fay replied on 18 Aug that the Company's holidays had finished on 13 Aug and that they 'have all been here last week rehearsing White Cocade' [*sic*].

[9] On 14 Aug Fay had asked for a copy of *The Mineral Workers* 'as soon as possible', but WBY's letter informed him that it had had to be returned to Boyle for revision (see pp. 473–4).

[10] In his letter WBY had evidently told Fay that Robert Gregory had made a model of the staging for *The Shadowy Waters*, and in his reply Fay enquired whether the scale of the model was 2 inches.

to us, and that you on your side will find the work pleasant and not too heavy.

Yrs sny

W B Yeats

TLS NLI.

## To John Millington Synge, [*17 August 1906*]

Coole

Friday

My dear Synge,

I have written to ask Henderson to arrange to see you. The sooner he gets instructed in his duties the better. I think we are probably lucky in getting him, but at the same time it is only right to tell you that he has been a little intriguing in the negotiations. In his first letter he said that he was giving up his present occupation in November to get more time for literature, but could not accept our offer as it would take too much of his time as well as making it impossible to do his work at the National Literary Society.[1] Oldham[2] who had recommended him wrote to say that what Henderson wanted was some time during the days for research work at the library, and strongly recommending us to take him. I wrote to Henderson saying that we could arrange to let him off duty on National Literary Society nights and that I thought he could arrange his hours so as to do his work in the

---

[1] In *Life in a Wooden O* (New Haven, 1977), Ben Iden Payne described (75) Henderson and his literary research: 'a reserved and shy man, rarely appeared at the theatre except briefly in the morning and at the performances. If I suggested that he do anything except pay salaries and enter the receipts of the performances in a ledger, he behaved like a frightened rabbit. I gathered in conversation with him that most of his time was occupied in "literary research." The research consisted in counting the number of times that Shakespeare used the words father and mother, respectively, throughout his plays. By this statistical analysis, he expected to prove that Shakespeare had loved his father a certain percentage more than he loved his mother. The balance so far as he had progressed was on the masculine side.' By 1915 Henderson claimed (NLI) that he had written 'over 300 articles, reviews, travel sketches etc., for various papers and periodicals' and 'close on 150 notes and articles to "Notes and Queries" (1892–1902)'. At that time he was contributing a series of articles on Arthurian romance to the *Athenaeum*, and had 'given several years to the study of the Tristan and Isolde Romances, and hope to publish a book on the subject'. Henderson was manager of a firm in Thomas Street, and D. J. O'Donoghue informed Holloway on 1 Aug (NLI) that the 'pay there was better but he'll have more time for literary pursuits as Secretary to the Abbey Theatre. At any rate the work will be more congenial.' On 3 Jan 1909 Holloway and a group of friends discussed Henderson's writing (NLI): 'McCall thought his style rather laboured & scarcely suitable for journalism. Curtis told us he left a job of £170 a year to take the present one up. He was a slow writer—a fact greatly against his success as a journalist—a calling he would like to follow.'

[2] Charles Hubert Oldham (1860–1926), economist and barrister, had helped to found the Contemporary Club, the *Dublin University Review*, and the Protestant Home Rule Association.

library. To this Henderson replied by asking us to increase the pay to £2 a week as he would be giving up for us a post in which he received £170 a year. He had forgotten his first letter. I replied that under the circumstances we could not of course think of asking him to make such a sacrifice, and sent Henderson's two letters to Oldham. Oldham has probably seen Henderson, for we have received the enclosed. In arranging with Henderson I think you should arrange for him to come every day at ten or eleven o'clock whatever time the actors will be there, to teach them punctuality as well as himself. He can then make time for himself for his library work. He should probably always call in again about five or so. In my letter I asked him to take the work for a few months as an experiment, for none of us really knew how much work there was. Of course one is inclined to give Henderson rather more rope than one would a younger man about whom one knew less. We have Oldham's very strong recommendation of him. He is popular with members of the Literary Society and should be able to bring them in. Dont mention to Fay his having been a bit slippery, it is a quality he shares with others. In my letter of today I suggested Moliere for the two country towns, but as I thought it would be an advantage for you to be able to show the letter to Fay I did not give you my whole reason. I dont think it is wise to let Fay go round with that old farce programme. He has got to despise it and to play with it, to overact abominably. His doctor is one of his finest parts and he is still sufficiently new to it not to play tricks. From the one point of view I am sorry at even Spreading the News having to do.[3] But there is nothing to put in its place, and it is most certain success with country audiences. He is all right in the Building fund. But I think Spreading the News should be repeated both nights instead of Hyacinth going. This programme will leave him nothing to play tricks with except the News.

Yours ever
W B Yeats

[*With enclosure*]

Beldare | Leinster Rd West | Rathmines | Co Dublin
15/8/06

Dear M^r. Yeats.

I am in receipt of yours of the 13^th inst. I fear my hastily penned epistle has conveyed an impression, which I did not intend. My attention has in

---

[3] AEFH had been harping on these complaints in her letters to WBY, and he had evidently seen for himself that they were true during the performances of *Hyacinth Halvey*, *The Building Fund*, *A Pot of Broth*, and *Spreading the News* at Longford. Fay went on gagging and overplaying in *Spreading the News*, and Holloway reported (NLI) not only his own disgust at this during the autumn season, but also that of many other Abbey patrons.

the past week been wholly centred in my sister's wedding, which has taken place.[4]

On consideration, I now feel inclined to accept your offer. You are very flattering in your estimate of my influence, and of course, if I did undertake the work, I would do my utmost to make the theatre a success.

As I stated in my first letter, I had purposed leaving my present occupation in September or October. The work has been uncongenial, and I wanted more leisure for literary work.

This course I had definitely decided on, some months ago. One however is irresolute in severing a connection of 27 years.

There are some details, which I think could be satisfactorily arranged between us.

As M[r]. Synge is on the spot, would he be available? or will you wait till you are next in town when we could arrange an interview?

Believe me

Yours sincerely
W A Henderson

To
W.B. Yeats Esq
Coole Park
Gort.

TLS TCD. Saddlemyer, 144–5.

## *To W. G. Fay,* [c. *19 August 1906*]

Mention in letter from Fay, 20 August [1906].
Discussing the dates and programme for an Abbey Company tour to Galway,[1] asking Fay to look after WBY's friends the Keoghs,[2] sending

---

[4] Henderson's sister Margaret Jane married the widower and stationer James Gilchrist on 11 June 1906.

[1] See pp. 378, 473–4. Fay replied that the best dates would be 'Galway 18, 19, travel on 17th Monday, Mullingar 20, 21st', and he thought it wise to stick to one programme, suggesting *The White Cockade* and *Spreading the News* on one night, and *Hyacinth Halvey, Cathleen ni Houlihan,* and *The Building Fund* for the second night in both towns. He also asked if they could provide music, as the shows 'drop flat without it'.

[2] Judge Martin Jerome Keogh (1855–1928), Irish-born justice of the Appellate Division of the New York Supreme Court, was one of John Quinn's closest friends, and a generous benefactor to all things Irish. WBY had met him on his first American tour, in November 1903 (see III. 467–8). Judge Keogh, his wife (née Emmet, a collateral descendent of Robert Emmet), and their son Martin were on an extended visit to Ireland.

him an article from the *Morning Post*,[3] and discussing costumes and ward-robe.[4]

*LWBY* I. 188, where it is dated '1907'.

## To Karel Mušek, 24 August [1906]

Coole Park | Gort, Co Galway
August 24

Dear Herr Musek,[1]

It was very good of you to take so much trouble for us, I am afraid it must have taken you a very long time summarizing that play, and above all writing that detailed account of your theatre which tells me exactly what I want to know and will be most useful.[2] The treatment of the Diarmuid and Grania story departs further from the legend than we would dare to in a play, for here the legend is of course very well known. Indeed one of our troubles is that they always want the whole legend and nothing else. It is just possible however that if I ever come to write on that story again I will find that this version may help me to forget my own old one and begin over again.[3]

---

[3] WBY would have sent the *Morning Post*'s retrospective article of 15 Aug, 'Past Theatrical Season', which gave (3) an account of the plays, adaptations, and visiting companies which had been seen on the London stage: 'Another set of visitors not to be forgotten are the Irish comedians. Of the plays they presented two—"The Well of the Saints," by Mr. J. M. Synge, and "The Building Fund," by Mr. William Boyle—were of a very high class. In each Mr. W. G. Fay was superb.'

[4] Fay advised that they should 'finish the Wardrobe right out now for we never know the minute we may want it. Things always come in a rush so with us.'

[1] See p. 178, n. 4.

[2] WBY had evidently asked Mušek for an account of the Bohemian National Theatre which, like the Abbey, was a product of nationalist aspirations. It had first been suggested in 1844 but not until 1851 was a public subscription organized, and a site, on the Vltava river, was purchased the following year. The opposition of the Austrian authorities dampened any further substantial progress until May 1868, when foundation stones from all over the country were laid and construction in a neo-Renaissance style began under the direction of the architect Josef Zitek. The Theatre was first opened on 11 June 1881 in the presence of the Austrian Crown Prince Rudolph, but later that year it was severely damaged by fire. Another public subscription was immediately launched and the Theatre quickly rebuilt by Josef Schulz, who adapted and amplified Zitek's original plans. The reconstructed building was opened in November 1883 with a performance of Smetana's opera *Libuše*, composed for the occasion. The Theatre was home to opera as well as drama in the Czech language, and from the start it was superbly equipped technically, with electrical lighting and a steel frame stage. The motto of the Theatre was 'narod sobe' ('the nation itself'), and a number of the plays performed there were based on heroic stories from the Slav epics in the Královodvorsky and Zelenohorsky Manuscripts. Mušek had sent WBY an account of one of these with affinities to the Irish legend of Diarmuid and Grania.

[3] WBY's and George Moore's play, based on the legend of Diarmuid and Grania, was produced at the Gaiety Theatre from 21 to 23 Oct 1901 (see III. 117–18, 126), and WBY had long planned to revise

Lady Gregory tells me that she asked you to call on Miss Horniman who is in Prague. Miss Horniman seemed anxious to make your acquaintance. She had written once or twice. She gave us our theatre and has been very generous to us.[4]

We have decided to play Antigone this winter, and Robert Gregory has begun a translation.[5] We will play it in prose, and with an Edipus will make a brave show. With a great many thanks.

Yr sny

W B Yeats

Dear Herr Musek, I have been typing this for Mr Yeats, and I must add a few lines to thank you so very much for the beautiful account of Bohemian Art you sent me, it is most interesting, and has taught us a great deal, my son is especially interested in it. I hope you found Madame Musek well, and your little daughter, and that you had lost your cold when you got back to Prague, and were none the worse for so long a journey. It was a great pleasure having you here, and we all felt it a great encouragement that you who are doing such good work at home should take an interest in us, who are so to speak at the edge of the world.

[*In AG's hand*]

With remembrances from my son I am

Yours sincerely

Augusta Gregory

TLS Private.

the play. It had been fiercely attacked by some Irish critics for allegedly deviating from the legendary sources (see III. 126–7, 133, 141).

[4] On 4 Aug 1906 AEFH had written to tell WBY (NLI) that she hoped 'to see the National Theatre at Prague where I go on Aug. 21st & perhaps Dr. Musek as well. . . . He may be very useful in advising master-pieces, but Prague is not Dublin, fortunately for Prague.' She visited Prague later that month and on 30 Aug wrote to WBY from Dresden that she had 'seen the National Theatre at Prague, every part of it, & been behind during a performance & seen part of a rehearsal. Before meeting Dr Musek I saw Gounod's "Faust", it was a good *provincial* performance in every way. . . . All was done with the perfection of the Antoine Company. Then I saw a legendary *play* at the National Theatre & that was charming. The "make-up" was especially good in all cases. I went about a good deal with Dr Musek & came to the conclusion that in Bohemia the *people* wanted the drama for itself, not merely as a means of propaganda. His theatre was crowded for Gounod's Faust, the very sort of thing—(nationalities of Goethe & Gounod & sort of tale) that the Irish spirit would detest, as far as I know. The people were exactly of the same class as those I saw in Dublin enjoying Mignon, a work of the same calibre; the fashionable people were of course away from Prague. How you would love to meddle with that elaborate lighting apparatus! There was a pleasantly lighted back sheet without any of that shuddering effect I object to so much & the colour of the moonlight was good.' AEFH kept up a correspondence with Mušek after this.

[5] See p. 476, n. 5. Robert Gregory did not get far with his translation, and on 19 Oct AG told Holloway (NLI) that he had only 'just started translating *The Antigone*'. Although *Antigone* was advertised for production in early 1907, it was not produced at the Abbey.

## *To Katharine Tynan Hinkson, 24 August [1906]*

Coole Park | Gort, Co Galway
August 24

My dear Mrs Hinkson,

Since I wrote to you[1] I have had a difference of opinion with my sister, which has resulted in my ceasing to be literary advisor to the Dun Emer Press. It was merely about the merit of a book they proposed to put in the series, but I couldnt go on unless I had authority to reject books as well as to choose them. I have no doubt they will write to you shortly and tell you who is to be their new editor.[2] They may very probably ask you to make your own selection; I had looked forward very much to choosing from your work. The way I have hitherto at least the way I did with Russell's book was that we more or less did it together.[3] If you think I could be of any use to you it would be a very great pleasure to read through your work and make suggestions. If you wish me to do this however please do not mention it to my sister, as there is just a possibility that she may change her mind, and she will certainly not do so if she thinks she can have me on her own terms. She would like me to go on editing various books, she on her part to put in others when the fancy pleased her, and this I wont have, as it means I know the gradual lowering of the standard of quality until it is like that of most Dublin publications.

I have taken a great deal of trouble up to this and made things easy for her, and she wont know till she gets to the work or tries to get another unpaid editor to do it, what a job it is.

Yrs sny
W B Yeats

TLS Southern Illinois, with envelope addressed to Pine Cottage, Blechingley, Surrey, postmark 'ORANMORE AU 24 06'.

[1] i.e. the letter of 30 July, asking her to make a selection from her lyrics for the Dun Emer Press; see pp. 459–60.

[2] In her letter of 3 Oct (see p.470, n. 1) ECY told Emery Walker that 'AE is willing to be adviser— but he would do some things well—Katharine Tynan—he would do well—but his Knowledge of literature is hardly wide enough'.

[3] See pp. 460, 463–5. WBY is referring to AE's earlier Dun Emer publication *The Nuts of Knowledge* (see p. 460, n. 1), not to *By Still Waters*, which was the occasion of the present dispute but which was to be published by the Dun Emer Press on 14 Dec of this year.

## *To W. G. Fay,* [c. *24 August 1906*]

Mention in letter from Fay, 25 August [1906].
Sending a revised programme for the Abbey's tour to Galway,[1] discussing
the difficulty of finding children for *The Hour-Glass*,[2] and saying that he
and AG think it important to make every effort to make the tour to Galway
a success.[3]

*LWBY* 1. 189–90.

## *To Katharine Tynan Hinkson, 28 August* [*1906*]

Telegram mentioned in the following letter.

## *To Katharine Tynan Hinkson, 28 August* [*1906*]

Coole Park | Gort, Co Galway
August 28

My dear Mrs Hinkson,
    I wired to you this evening on getting your letter,[1] because I want you to
help me if you can in this business which is giving me a great deal of trouble

---

[1] Fay was finding it difficult to acquire a cast for the tour to Galway and Mullingar (see pp. 473–4). He
had written to WBY on 22 Aug (*LWBY* 1. 188–9) to alert him to 'More trouble in Ireland': 'The man I had
playing Carter struck yesterday for money he wanted to be paid, he said. I pointed out the fact that he
could not speak English and didn't know how to act and asked him to think it over, so this morning he
came in & said he couldn't go on as he had a job to go to. Thats Carter off. The genius I had playing the
Soldier has not turned up either so theres no chance of getting White Cocade to Galway by the 17 sept. I
dont know where the Dickens to look for people. You see it got round town we are paying people, & that
we did well on tour, so that every sundowner that turns up expects to be paid, and its perfectly absurd the
cheek they have. They cant speak Kings English walk or do a thing One has to begin at the very beginning
with each of them & waste the time of our own people Im short even for Spreading the News. . . . What is
to be done.' He estimated that they needed 'at the very least two more men'. In his reply to this letter, Fay
said he thought WBY's suggested bill for Galway 'all right only I will put the First night Hyacinth
Cathleen & Building Fund so as to make the length of each program the same'. He thought it would 'be
necessary to get some sort of music for Galway & Mullingar I think to keep the show up', and that, since
he was still looking for a man for *Spreading the News*, he had not yet booked the Galway theatre.
[2] The difficulty of finding children for *The Hour-Glass* had hitherto deterred the Company from
taking it on tour, but in his reply Fay said that he would get one of the actor J. H. Dunne's children.
[3] In his reply Fay affirmed that he was 'quite with both you & Lady Gregory about the importance of
making every possible effort to make the Galway show a success so there is no use my booking the dates
till I can be absolutely sure of a caste for Spreading the News'.

[1] KT's letter is untraced, but evidently expressed her concern and disappointment that WBY was not
to edit the Dun Emer selection of her poems.

and anxiety. My sister knows very little about literature, and she has no chance of making a success of the Dun Emer books unless properly guided. It is very important for her to succeed in them as the Dun Emer industry generally is her means of livelihood. I have taken the greatest trouble about these books and the present difficulty is a piece of temper upon her side, complicated by old endeavours of mine to improve various matters in the Industries.

Now what I want you to do is this. I want you to write to Lolly saying that you want me to edit the book, and will not give it otherwise. Now I know this is a hard thing to ask, and you may very fairly say to me that you know nothing of the merits of the dispute, but after all you do know something of my mind and of my purposes, and I hope what you do know may be a guarantee that I have not done anything capricious or illtempered. What I am afraid of is that Lollie acting on her own ignorance may put into the series various books which will pull down its reputation and make it useless for me to go back to the editing when she has learned her lesson. Now if you were to refuse, or even to insist on postponing the book for a few months till you saw if things were patched up between her and me, she will have to give in at once. I have a book of Lionel Johnson's Essays for instance, his Irish Essays, ready for her, I had meant it to follow yours. I had asked Synge to start on a book, a translation, and I had hoped to bring out with her selections from my own lyrics.[2] I have one or two other books in my mind. She started into this editing idea without understanding the difficulties in the least, I want her to understand them as soon as possible. I think you said that Bullen was the publisher of your Innocencies; I am sure I could get leave to select from it.[3] I had a letter from Bullen yesterday, not invited in any way, saying that my ceasing to edit would bring down the standard, and that the subscribers would very quickly find it out. He said in his letter 'There is too much imitative poetry being written in Ireland' and it is precisely this imitative poetry I want to keep out. The sort of thing you may see coming out in the Tower Press, and read in the Celtic Christmas.[4] The chief objection to fighting the fools is that by sheer clamour they influence some who should be naturally on one's

---

[2] The Cuala Press (the name under which the Dun Emer Press continued from 1908) published *Poetry and Ireland*, essays by Lionel Johnson and WBY, on 1 Dec 1908, and Synge's *Poems and Translations* on 5 July 1909. In her letter to Emery Walker of 3 Oct (see p. 460, n. 1) ECY complained that WBY wanted her to 'do a book of Johnson's Essays' instead of AE's poems but that 'no one will buy Essays—& besides he had not the book ready for me'. Although no anthology of WBY's poems appeared until *A Selection from the Love Poetry of W. B. Yeats* in July 1913, Dun Emer published his *Discoveries* on 15 Dec 1907, and Cuala *The Green Helmet and Other Poems* in December 1910.

[3] KT's collection of poems, *Innocencies*, had been published by A. H. Bullen in December 1905, and it was also issued by Maunsel & Co. in Dublin.

[4] WBY had long despised the *Celtic Christmas*, the literary supplement to the December numbers of the *Irish Homestead* (see III. 274, 276). The Tower Press booklets, issued by the Maunsel Press under

side. Our Theatre has made endless enemies in Dublin through our refusal of bad work, our insistence on artistic standards only, and on hard work among our actors. Some day I will be able to tell you the whole preposterous story. My sister is right in the midst of all these animosities, and it is very hard to resist the atmosphere in which you live. I would gladly edit this book of yours as you ask me, and make that my farewell to the Press, I might even do so logically as I asked you for it. But I am not dealing with logic but with three very emotional people, my sisters and my father. My father wrote begging me to go on acting as literary adviser, but to give up the claim to reject work, which is the essence of my dispute with my sister. He wrote several letters and was very much troubled at my refusal. If I were to edit your book he would not like my doing for you what I had refused to do for him. And Lolly would take it as a sign that I was giving in.[5] You will remember my old battles in Dublin and you will understand that this is vital to me, vital to keep a series that is associated with my name, if it were nothing else, from drifting into the amateurish Dublin way.

[*In WBY's hand*]

I am working very hard at my play 'Dierdre'. M^rs Campbell saw my prose version & asked for the play but after a struggle with temptation I decided to keep it for my own people. I think it is my best play. I remember you were the first person, who ever urged me to write a play about Ireland—I had showed you some wild thing I had called Spanish.[6] After I have done a couple of little plays wanted to complete the cycle of plays on Cuchullan I have planned I shall go back to lyric & narrative poetry for a bit. This dramatic work has been a great joy. Small as our audiences are they are Irish & well pleased. We had an audience at Longford that would have stirred your imagination—shopkeepers & lads of the town who smoked and all delighted I think. I wonder if I had this dream of an Irish Theatre when at Whitehall—I had it very soon after I know—in 1892 certainly.[7] I am

the joint editorship of James Starkey and James Connolly, published two series of small paper-covered books of poetry and essays from 1906 to 1908. Among those contributing to the twelve-volume project were AE, George Moore, T. G. Keohler, John Eglinton, Frederick Ryan, and Starkey himself, whose *Verses: Sacred and Profane* (1908) contained 'To a Poet', an attack on WBY. KT had in fact told Bullen that WBY was severing his ties with Dun Emer.

[5] JBY had followed up his outraged letter of 3 Aug with more conciliatory communications on 6, 8, and 9 Aug (MBY). These letters conceded the validity of WBY's position, but urged him to be more diplomatic with ECY, to confine himself 'to the mere giving of advice', and reminded him of the disastrous financial consequences to the Yeats family if the Press foundered.

[6] Probably *Mosada*, a poetic drama set in 15th-century Spain (*VP*, 689–704), which first appeared in the *Dublin University Review* in June 1886. WBY published an offprint edition of 100 copies later that year, and KT reviewed it in the *Irish Monthly* in March 1887 (166–8).

[7] Whitehall, Clondalkin, was KT's family home (see 1. 43), a farmhouse south-west of Dublin, and WBY was a frequent visitor there from June 1885 to 30 Apr 1893, when he paid a final farewell visit on the eve of KT's departure to be married in London. In 1892 WBY had helped establish the National Literary Society in Dublin, which he hoped would sponsor a touring theatre company.

breaking my 'Deirdre' work with a curious impressionistic book on the work here—almost a spiritual diary.[8]

Yrs ever
W B Yeats

TLS MBY and Harvard. Partly in Wade, 476, and McHugh, 147.


## To A. E. F. Horniman, [c. *28 August 1906*]

Mention in letter from AEFH, 30 August 1906.
Telling her that he is busy working,[1] and that he has decided not to give his *Deirdre* to Mrs Pat Campbell.[2]

NLI.


## To Katharine Tynan Hinkson, *1 September* [*1906*]

Coole Park | Gort, Co Galway
Sept 1


My dear Mrs Hinkson,

I thank you very much for what you have done. It has been very kind of you and very generous. I know how much generosity it requires to let oneself be drawn into other people's quarrels.[1]

I should like very much to have a talk with you about our young writers, and hope I may do so some day. It is not easy to write fully about their work, but I will tell you roughly what I think of it.[2]

---

[8] i.e. the short essays published in 1907 as *Discoveries*; see pp. 366–7.

[1] In her reply AEFH, who was in Dresden, said, 'I quite comprehend how your time must be taken up.'

[2] This decision did not please AEFH, and she continued to complain about it in letters throughout the autumn. In her reply to this letter she said that she was 'sorry that you settled to refuse Deirdre to Mrs Pat because I do not think that any "sacrifice" you make will have the slightest effect on Fay, he has got so used to being petted & humoured that he takes everything as a matter of course'.

[1] See pp. 483–5. KT had evidently written to ECY asking that WBY should make the selection from her poems.

[2] As KT explains in *The Middle Years* (1916) she was eager to write an article publicizing the work of the new school of Irish poets: 'I wrote to Seumas O'Sullivan and he gave me a list of names and addresses. Maunsel sent me the books. All was in train; but the poets themselves would not answer my letters' (353). She therefore wrote to AE and WBY, who did answer her, and, although the article was never written, she evidently used some of her material in a lecture to the ILS entitled 'The Younger Irish Poets' on 6 Nov 1909. As the *Irish Book Lover* for 1909 reported (56–7): 'Mrs Hinkson's lecture was most interesting, including reminiscences of her early days in Dublin with their literary

The best thing about them is that they show some increase of culture in the country, and nearly all their faults arise out of the newness of that culture. They are vague, self conscious, literary; the reverse of the young poets of our young days who were not literary at all,—I remember getting into trouble for calling them electioneering rhymers.[3] It is no longer possible to say that. They have not however yet learnt how to work at a poem. They play with words and have no organic structure. In other words they are not yet worth talking about, except here and there, when what seems accident makes a poem, just as what seems accident made rhetoricians of the old sort [of] poets on occasion.

Colum has written a couple of little poems The Ploughmen and the Poor Scholar which are charming, though not all charming;[4] and Boyd who is no good as a whole has one really fine thing, 'Ballyvourney'.[5] The Rushlight

associations, and illustrated by many extracts from the Irish poets of the present generation, such as Padraic Colum, Ethna Carbery, Alice Milligan, and Seosamh MacCathmhaoil. Her criticism of these and other writers, and the beautiful intonations with which she rendered the passages from their poems were much appreciated by the audience.'

[3] In the 1890s WBY made many efforts to break the influence of the Young Ireland school of poets over the Irish imagination (see p. 27, n. 9), and is probably recalling here both the controversy in *United Ireland* over the deleterious effect of politics on Irish literature following Richard Ashe King's lecture 'The Silent Sister' (see I. 369–74), and also the public outcry in the Dublin press in February 1899 after he had described Thomas Davis's poem 'The Battle of Fontenoy' as 'a clever imitation of Macaulay . . . very useful in its way; but after all . . . mere journalistic and rhetorical poetry' (see II. 387–9).

[4] Colum's poem 'The Plougher', a poetic apostrophe to a ploughman, apprehended as an elemental figure at nightfall in a savage landscape, was included in his major collection *The Wild Earth* (Dublin, 1907). WBY had praised his 'A Portrait', subtitled 'A poor scholar in the 'Forties', in January 1903 as 'a real achievement' (see III. 293). The poem, first published in the *United Irishman* on 1 Nov 1902, is a monologue in which a hedge schoolmaster, a man of contemplation, meditates upon the thanklessness of teaching classics in the west of Ireland at a time of political agitation. Colum used a phrase from the last line as the title for *The Wild Earth*, in which it was included under the title 'A Poor Scholar of the Forties'. Given his strictures on Young Ireland, WBY would have been engaged by the confrontation in the poem between scholarly disinterest and political commitment:

> 'You teach Greek verbs and Latin nouns,'
> The dreamer of Young Ireland said.
> 'You do not hear the muffled call,
> The sword being forged, the far-off tread
> Of hosts to meet as Gael and Gall.
>     What good to us your wisdom store,
>     Your Latin verse, your Grecian lore?'

Both poems had appeared in AE's anthology *New Songs* (Dublin, 1904), but WBY included neither of them in his selection from Colum for *OBMV*.

[5] Thomas Boyd (1867–1927), a journalist, had recently published his only book of verse, *Poems* (Dublin, 1906), containing the elegy 'Ballyvourney' which begins: 'He came from Ballyvourney and we called him "Ballyvourney," | The sweetest name in Erinn that we know, | And they tell me he has taken now the last, the last long Journey, | And it's young he is, it's young he is so very far to go.' Boyd, who was secretary of the ILS, had himself just taken a long journey, decamping with £285 of the Society's money; as D. J. O'Donoghue explained to Holloway on 29 Sept (NLI), he had been instructed 'to

man knows better than the others what a poem is, though not a very interesting sort of poem, but he has not written it yet.[6] On the other hand I dont care at all for the people who imitate Russell or myself, that is to say Starkie (Seumas O'Sullivan) Keohler and Miss Young, or Roberts, and Miss Mitchell. This little group are always imitative and subjective and sentimental. They never see anything clearly or think anything clearly. Starkie has some cultivation and scholarship and I feel this occasionally in his use of words, but he has never enough energy to make the words poetry. Miss Mitchell is quite a good comic poet, but I am only talking of the serious work. I do not think anything will come out of this group, because I do not feel any genuine inspiration amongst them, and they havn't as the more objective people have the inspiration of the Irish tradition.[7] I once hoped a great deal from George Russell's influence, but I have come to think of it <as a pose that so> so far as it is a literary influence as opposed to everything I care for. He has the religious genius and it is the essence of the religious genius, I mean the genius of the religious teacher, to look upon all souls as equal. They are never equal in the eye of any craft, but Russell cannot bear anything that sets one man above another. He encourages everybody to write poetry, because he thinks it good for their soul, and he doesnt care a rush whether it is good or bad.[8] When we started our theatre he actually avowed this about plays, and tried to persuade Lady Gregory and myself to keep it a small amateur theatre that various interesting souls might be given the opportunity of dramatic expression, for the soul's health. He grew quite excited against the idea of creating a theatre that would have an elaborate technique and therefore the exclusiveness of

remove the Society's funds from one bank to another, owing to the one in which it was lodged having refused to receive cheques signed in Gaelic, & drew the amount in gold & has never been heard of since. Drink alas was the cause of his degradation!' Nevertheless, WBY was to include his poem 'The King's Son' in *OBMV*.

[6] i.e. Joseph Campbell (see p. 357, n. 2), who became secretary of the ILS in place of Boyd.

[7] For James Starkey, George Roberts, Thomas Keohler, and Ella Young, see pp. 158, n. 2, 24, 153, n. 2, 44, n. 3. Susan Langstaff Mitchell (1866–1926), poet, wit, and editor, had been born in Carrick-on-Shannon but lived as a paying guest with the Yeatses in London from late 1897 to 1899. She joined the *Irish Homestead* in 1901 as assistant editor, and spent the rest of her career working with AE on this magazine and its successor, the *Irish Statesman*. Her best-known book was a collection of satiric verses, *Aids to the Immortality of Certain Persons in Dublin: Charitably Administered*, which appeared in 1908, the same year as a book of mystical and religious verse, *The Living Chalice*. She published a further book of satires and parodies, *Secret Springs of Dublin Song*, in 1918, and in 1916 a study of George Moore, one of her favourite butts.

[8] KT had also written to AE, asking for his opinion of the younger poets, and he replied in an undated letter (Southern Illinois) that 'Colum, Seumus O'Sullivan and Campbell are the best', and also mentioned James Stephens (of whom he had 'great hopes'), Susan Mitchell (some of whose serious poems he thought 'very good'), Paul Gregan ('full of promise'), and Eva Gore-Booth (who 'writes too much, but she has flashes and splendid lines occasionally'). In a further letter on the same subject, AE confessed that the 'greatest pleasure I find in life is discovering new young poets' (*The Middle Years*, 355).

an art. He is just the same in painting, he urged upon a friend of mine last year the getting up of an annual exhibition of painters, the point of which was that nobody was to be bothered about drawing. I dont suppose you remember but years ago somebody attacked me in a debate in the Nat Literary Society with the phrase 'Literature is not a thing of technicalities and calculated cadences, but comes from the inspiration of God'.

I replied that I believed that until I got to Ireland, but that I found that there being inspired by God was a profession that was full.[9]

It is just the same now, and Russell is the arch inspirationist. He gets support from everyone who dislikes discipline, and from others that like him but do not understand the issue. He very nearly wrecked our theatre, and it is he who has influenced my sisters at this moment. When Starkie seceded from the Theatre where his acting was worse than his poetry he brought out with him a charming young woman who embroiders for my sisters,[10] and this has kept them more or less in the midst of the discussions. It is all really one dispute. I have no doubt my sisters will learn before very long that I am right about the books as they have learned that I was right about the theatre. The trouble is that Russell in himself is perfectly charming, and all the more charming because he suffers fools gladly. His very mischief is a logical expression of his genius. The idea that my sisters should permit me to exclude good worthy people from their series of books merely because they write badly fills his soul with horror. He even pressed upon us the production of a play the hero of which was a giant eight feet high, rather than hurt the feelings of a friend.[11]

[9] WBY made this point towards the end of his lecture on 'Nationality and Literature', delivered to the National Literary Society on 19 May 1893 (see *UP* I. 266–75). In this lecture WBY insisted that Irish literature must keep its energy, but must also learn to achieve style though unremitting concentration and dedication, and condemned the idea of pure inspiration: 'How often do I not hear in this country that literature is to be achieved by some kind of mysterious visitation of God, which makes it needless for us to labor at the literary art. . . . When I hear this kind of talk I am inclined to say that being inspired by God is a profession that is full, so many men have I met who have held themselves to be thus visited. Alas, the inspiration of God, which is, indeed, the source of all which is greatest in the world, comes only to him who labours at rhythm and cadence, at form and style, until they have no secret hidden from him. This art we must learn from the old literatures of the world' (*UP* I. 274). KT would not have remembered the occasion as she had moved to London a few weeks before, where she married Henry Hinkson on 4 May.

[10] i.e. Maire Walker; see pp. 272, n. 7, 279.

[11] This may have been a play by Edward McNulty. In a letter published in the *Irish Times* of 25 Oct this year he recalled (8) that about 'three years ago G. Bernard Shaw in a private letter asked me to write a humorous play for the Abbey Theatre, stating that Yeats had no sense of humour, and that George Moore, in presence of a joke, assumed a pained and bewildered expression'. Subsequently AE also urged him to contribute a play to the INTS and so he wrote 'a three-act comedy which Mr. Russell . . . delightedly forwarded to his committee. I waited a year for a response, but none came. Eventually, after some letter writing and several visits to the theatre, I got my MS. back without comment.' Matthew Edward McNulty (1856–1943) was a schoolfellow and lifelong friend of Shaw, who described him in youth as 'a genius . . . a corpulent youth with curly black hair' (*BSCL* I. 7). He served as an official in the

His own work shows you how little criticism he has, it is sometimes magnificent and sometimes very like Koehler.

I'll go out and see you the very first thing when I get to London, but that will not be for some time.

Yrs always

W B Yeats

*[In WBY's hand]*

PS. I have plans for improving our new poets myself. I want to get them to write songs to be sung between the acts. Herbert Hughs will set them & we have a fine singer in Miss Allgood. I hope to begin with two groups of songs—one selected from 'The Rushlight Man', Colum & so on & one chosen from Johnson, you & myself. I will get them sung so as to make the words as expressive as possible. I am not quite sure that the time has come yet but I shall get one or two things set as a start.[12] One has to go slowly, perfecting first one thing & then another. We have got our peasant work very good now, & are starting on our verse work, & on getting things like the 'make up' right.[13] By the by have you read Lady Gregorys books? She has a beautiful book 'Saints & Wonders' coming out with my sisters in a few days.[14]

TLS Harvard, with an envelope addressed to Pine Cottage, Blechingley, Surrey, postmark 'ORANMORE SP 2 06'. Partly in Wade, 476–8.

Bank of Ireland for over forty years and published four novels of Irish life and several plays, including a three-act comedy, *The Lord Mayor*, which was produced at the Abbey in March 1914.

[12] This plan, which WBY had mentioned to MG in March 1905 (see p. 52), was not implemented, but is in line with WBY's lifelong desire to make poetry a spoken and public art.

[13] This had been a long-standing defect (see p. 415). The *Cambridge Review* of 30 Nov 1905 commented (120) that the make-up in all the plays performed on the Cambridge tour 'was crude and unsatisfactory', and that 'the pallor of Kathleen was so much overdone as to be merely ghastly and repulsive; so that it was always a relief when her face was hidden in her cloak'. The poor quality of the make-up had been one of AEFH's complaints during the previous summer's tour and she told WBY on 17 July (NLI) that Fay did 'not know about make-up except for the characters he plays himself & he will *not* learn'. However, AG, as she told WBY on 4 June 1906 (Berg), sympathized with Fay when he told her that it was impossible to make up four plays in one evening.

[14] The Dun Emer Press published AG's *A Book of Saints and Wonders* on 10 Sept 1906.

## *To A. E. F. Horniman,* [c. *1 September 1906*]

Mention in letter from AEFH, 3 September 1906.
Enquiring about the quarterly subsidy since they need to pay the actors and staff,[1] telling her that Synge has gone on holiday,[2] discussing Miss Darragh's possible influence on the Company,[3] and informing her that Henderson has been engaged.[4]

NLI.

## *To T. C. & E. C. Jack, 11 September 1906*

LONDON, 11th September 1906. RECEIVED from Messrs T. C. & E. C. JACK, Publishers, Edinburgh, the sum of Fifteen pounds sterling which with Twenty pounds already paid makes up the amount, viz., Thirty five pounds, payable for MS of Introduction and passing through the press of a volume of the Poems of Spenser in virtue of which payment the absolute copyright becomes the property of the said Messrs T. C. & E. C. JACK.[1]
£15: -: -.

TS Doc NLI.

[1] AEFH assured WBY that she would have paid £200 into the Abbey account before he received her reply to this letter, 'so you can pay the people all right'. She added that the 'next £200 shall go in on Dec. 1st unless something very extraordinary happens', but she pointed out that under the present arrangements the Company was being 'paid for doing nothing for three weeks out of each month & that this is ruinously extravagant if they don't tour'.

[2] Having savaged Fay in her recent letters, AEFH was now working up a dislike of Synge, and WBY marked this letter 'Synge "No good"'. She was particularly incensed to learn that he was taking a holiday in Kerry: 'As to Mr Synge—he too has proved himself to be of no good. Any holiday can be put off for a few days when necessary.' And she maliciously enquired whether he had had 'the courage to take Mollie Allgood with him? Or has he gone to escape from her? Is the man content with what he has done already or does he think that he can get along without the help of the theatre?'

[3] WBY had evidently told AEFH that he hoped the arrival of Miss Darragh would have a beneficial effect on the Company's acting technque, but she doubted whether 'one or two appearances by Miss Darragh can have much effect on the company; she won't have long enough experience of them to be able to manage to impress them. They will despise her as being "commercial" & "made in London".'

[4] In fact, Henderson's contract did not officially begin until the beginning of October, but AEFH commented: 'Poor dear Henderson, he does not know what is before him.' Holloway's reaction on learning of the appointment (NLI) was similar to AEFH's: 'Says "he must have a free hand." Well we shall see what we shall see!'

[1] This was the final payment for WBY's selection from Spenser (see pp. 368, 444).

## To John Millington Synge, [14 September 1906]

Coole
Friday

My dear Synge,

The only thing I can suggest is that Lady Gregory's Canavans followed by her Gaol Gate shall take the place in which you had put your play; that Deirdre followed by her Jackdaw come on the 10th Dec; and that your Playboy come on the 31 December.[1] It is possible that Deirdre and Jackdaw may not make a bill, but we can add something at the last moment, say the Workhouse. Lady Gregory cant be in town after beginning of December, so her things have to be played early. She is not so anxious about Rising of the Moon but must rehearse the others. Dec 31 is a very good time, you remember the theatre opened then, so you will come well out of the business. We must chance Advent, and really I dont think it matters with our public[2]—White Cockade was in Advent and it made more than anything else—or that it will matter until we begin to draw the general public. I have no copy of your list here but as a general principle it is well— this did not occur to me when I was writing—to put as little new work as possible on revival nights as it means putting new work on for one night only instead of for the week needed to test it and to make the players perfect. If Henderson does not think it detrimental to his subscribers idea it might be well to repeat one or two of the one act pieces. I leave this entirely to your discretion. Our second series of ten Saturdays will have to repeat out of the first ten nights in any case. What you have to consider is whether it is well to spoil the subscribers, if spoil them it will, by giving too much, or whether it is better to try and make each set of ten nights free from repetition within itself. Please consider all this as mere musing aloud for the sake of helping you to a decision.[3]

---

[1]  This letter is evidently an answer to one from Synge, now lost, which told WBY that he had still not managed to finish *The Playboy of the Western World* (see p. 28); on 18 Sept Synge was to write to Maire O'Neill (*JMSCL* I. 205) that he was 'getting very unhappy about it as it wont come out right. . . . I am at my wits end with it'. AG's *The Canavans* was first produced on 8 Dec 1908, but her one-act comedy *The Jackdaw* was postponed until 23 Feb 1907. WBY's *Deirdre* was produced on 24 Nov.

[2]  In 1904 WBY had feared that Advent, a period of restraint and spiritual exercise in preparation for the birth of Christ during the four weeks before Christmas, might have an adverse effect on Abbey audiences in Dublin (see III. 676), but *The White Cockade* had finally done reasonable business in December 1905, despite a lack of publicity (see p. 245). *The Canavans* did even better during the coming Advent, taking £56 8s. 5d., the largest amount (apart from *The Playboy*) in that season. In a letter of 4 Oct (*JMSCL* I. 212) Synge was also unsure that 'Advent makes much difference'. The revised version of *The Shadowy Waters* was produced with *The Canavans* during this December, but in the following years the Company toured in Britain during Advent.

[3]  Part of Henderson's remit was to improve the size of the audiences at the Abbey, and Synge had told AG on 30 Aug (*JMSCL* I. 197) that he thought he would 'be very energetic in working up an

Now here is something I want you to set Henderson at. The lighting of Shadowy Waters is extremely important. Dossy Wright has charge of the electric light and was to have made a report every month to Fay as to the quantity of lamps &c. We are now Miss Horniman's representatives and so the report should be made to us. At the same time I dont want to hurt Fay's feelings more than necessary. Would you mind as managing director in my absence getting Wright to find out in consultation with Fay or not as you may think right how many lamps there are, how many are required. We will want a very considerable number of amber lamps and if we are short a stock of plain lamps will have to be laid in and proper stuff for dipping them got from electricians. I absolutely refuse to countenance any more makeshift stuff made up at the local oilshop. Somebody will have to be set to dip them, we all require these amber lamps, but I for my own purposes require a large number of blue and green lamps. During the playing of the harp the light upon the stage is green. During the rest of the play there will have to be blue ground rows. We have I think but we cannot be satisfied with suppositions, blue and green glasses for the limelight. If all these lamps are not in when I go up I wont be able to get the lighting of Shadowy Waters in order and the whole effect depends on the lighting. Robert Gregory is coming up to work at that and the scenery though a little later than me.[4] I want Henderson, you or he having got this information, to send me a letter on the subject stating that he has the lamps or that they have been written for. This information may take a day or two but please ask Henderson without waiting for this to find out if all the costumes properties &c are ready or in hands for Shadowy Waters. I cannot recollect what was said and done about the backcloth. It will be necessary to have all these things before we work on the lighting. I would also like to know as a matter of curiosity whether Fay finds that he can work the limes from the bridge all right.[5]

audience, an important part of our work that we have rather neglected'. He had set about the task at once, and proposed that the Theatre should offer subscription tickets for ten consecutive Saturday nights at a cost of 1 guinea, so attracting a regular stalls audience. This was put into place with great success during the coming season, but complicated the arrangement of the programmes.

[4] For the production of the revised version of *The Shadowy Waters* on 8 Dec (see n. 2) Robert Gregory designed the set and supervised the lighting effects. Joseph Holloway (NLI) considered that Gregory was 'to be complimented on the staging and lighting . . . and many memorably and poetic pictures resulted during the progress of the play', although the *Irish Times* of 10 Dec (8) commented simply that the 'play was appropriately staged'. WBY put great store on the staging of the play as contributing essentially to its overall effect, and particularly sought the harmonization of greens and blues in the costumes and *mise-en-scène* (see p. 90).

[5] As Seaghan Barlow explained (Robinson, 71), there was so little room on the right-hand side of the Abbey stage that the 'builders had put in a narrow wooden bridge across the back of the stage'. At first this bridge was too high, but Barlow was asked to lower it.

Henderson had better begin getting advertisements for the Arrow I will send you materials in two or three days. It will be quite a little thing.⁶

Lady Gregory is anxious to know what the programmes cost either for one month or for the season.⁷ We hope to get our publishers to put advertisements of our books and when she asked Murray he asked what we would charge. If we knew what the programmes cost we might make a rough calculation of what each publisher should be asked to give, that they might together cover the cost of printing.

Yrs ever<br>W B Yeats

TLS TCD. Saddlemyer, 155–7.

## To A. E. F. Horniman, [c. 18 September 1906]

Mention in letter from AEFH, 19 September 1906.
Asking if she has had a letter from Miss O'Dempsey.¹

NLI.

---

⁶ Since the *Arrow* was a less substantial publication than *Samhain* there were fewer advertisements. As AG's main publisher, John Murray took space to advertise her books in the forthcoming number, and Maunsel & Co. listed WBY's *Poems, 1899–1905* and Synge's *The Aran Islands* among its other Irish books. Another Dublin publisher, M. H. Gill & Son, advertised new Irish historical novels, and Hely's, the printing and stationery contractors, and Marks Brothers, a firm of painters who decorated the Abbey Theatre, also took out advertisements.

⁷ WBY is not referring to the price of individual programmes (which were usually 1*d.*) but the production costs of printing the whole batch.

¹ This was apparently an error by WBY who had meant to write 'Miss Darragh'. In her reply, AEFH told her that she had received 'no letter from Miss O'Dempsey & do not intend to enter into any correspondence with any member of the Company except through the Directors'. In the light of her remarks in her previous letter, WBY was evidently worried that AEFH might dissuade Miss Darragh from acting at the Abbey (see p. 491, n. 3), and wrote to ask her not to do this. AEFH replied: 'If "O'Dempsey" is a mistake for "Darragh", all I can say is that I shall not see her until Friday afternoon & that I feel myself free to tell her as much as I choose. You need not think that I shall tell her anything of the personal reasons involved in my great relief at being no longer obliged to visit Dublin; indeed I am too ashamed that any friend of mine should have acted as you did, that I should pain myself by repeating it. I shall make it perfectly clear to her that as long as Fay remains Stage Manager that I shall not countenance any important touring & give her my simple reasons—first that I cannot afford the money, secondly that I will not risk a repetition of my Edinburgh experiences. Maybe she does not accept my written words as serious but I will not mislead her.'

# To A. H. Bullen, 21 September [1906]

Coole Park | Gort, Co Galway
Sept 21

My dear Bullen,
I am groaning over the task of copying the next instalment of Thoughts and Second Thoughts, and you shall have it by Monday, no, by Tuesday. The first instalment which reached me today sent on from Woburn Buildings looked very well.[1] I wish you would let me know without crying 'Wolf' at me, what is the real day for sending in. I didnt know that you were a middle month magazine till I found myself late last time. I also wish you would tell me when the poems are really coming out. I keep telling people that they are just coming, and the Bohemian Stage Manager not getting his copy thinks, I hear, that I have forgotten him altogether.[2] If they are not coming for another month, let us say, I would like to know it. Besides I should stir up Masefield and one or two others to get it for review.[3] This is the first number of the Gentleman's Magazine that I have seen, and you have kept the old fashioned leisurely air very well.[4]

---

[1] WBY published 'My Thoughts and my Second Thoughts' (see p. 367, n. 2) unsigned in the September, October, and November numbers of the ailing *Gentleman's Magazine*, of which Bullen had become editor in February.

[2] i.e. Pan Karel Mušek.

[3] *Poems, 1899–1905* appeared in October but was not widely reviewed, and Bullen actually wrote to the *Academy* on 20 Oct 1906, complaining (389) that it had been unduly neglected because the reviewers erroneously regarded it as merely a reprint. There is no evidence that Masefield noticed it; other reviewers tended to give most attention to the plays in the volume, and a number complained of the book's Celticism and obscurity, although 'M.B.' in the *Morning Post* of 19 Nov 1906 (2) praised WBY as one of those 'who have wandered in the secret places of nature . . . full of the shadows of dead kings and beautiful witches and of heroes. . . . Mr. Yeats lives in this country, and by the strain of his mysterious harp summons up for us the holy vision, the wizard glimpse.'

[4] The *Gentleman's Magazine* had been founded in 1731 as a review of contemporary political and cultural events. In the later part of the 19th century it had become more antiquarian and architectural in orientation, and the outgoing editor, Joseph Knight, was also editor of *Notes and Queries*. On being appointed editor by Lord Northcliffe, who had acquired the magazine earlier this year, Bullen immediately set about changing its style, and improved the quality of the paper and printing. In the February number, the first under his direction, he announced (3) that he hoped to restore it 'to the position that it held in the first half of the last century': 'The events of the month will be succinctly recorded, and contemporary literature will be reviewed; but much space will be given as of old to literary and antiquarian research.' Priced 1s., and containing over 100 pages, the front cover announced that it was 'Published in the Middle of the Month'. Apart from publishing WBY's essays, the magazine also frequently reviewed his and AG's books. However, Bullen's editorship was short-lived, coming to an end in December of this year under circumstances that he described in a letter to KT of 16 Dec 1906 (Manchester): 'People had warned me that I should find Lord Northcliffe a fickle and unsatisfactory chief. It was all honey when I last saw him . . . but his subordinates did their best to thwart me, and succeeded. The poor magazine was tardied from pillar to post and never had a ghost of a chance. . . . I shall miss the work (and the cash) sadly.' The magazine finally folded in 1912.

I am deep in Ben Jonson, and have tried to buy your Marston in vain. I have a great desire upon me to read the Satiromastik of Dekker, and got the Mermaid Dekker, but it is not in that. Can you tell me where I can get it, or can you lend it to me?[5] I am thinking of writing something on Ben Jonson, or more likely perhaps upon the ideal of life that flitted before the imagination of Jonson and the others when they thought of the Court.[6] The thought grows out of my Spenser Essay which is just out.[7] I would send it to you but they have only given me one copy, (being Scotch). It is published by Jacks.

[5] WBY succeeded in acquiring Bullen's three-volume edition of *The Works of John Marston* (1887), although most of the pages in his copy remain uncut (*YL*, 1238). If WBY cut the pages himself, he would have done so to read *The First Part of Antonio and Mellida* and a quarter of *Antonio's Revenge* in the first volume and half of *The Dutch Courtezan* in the second volume. None of the pages in the third volume have been cut. He already owned *Thomas Dekker*, four plays edited for the Mermaid series in 1894 by his old friend Ernest Rhys (*YL*, 503), and also possessed several editions of Ben Jonson's plays and writings (*YL*, 1028–33). Jonson's influence on him at this period is felt in his current plays and poetry, and in his adoption of the Jonsonian title 'Discoveries' for his 'My Thoughts and my Second Thoughts'. Jonson had quarrelled with John Marston (1576–1634) who, he believed, had lampooned him as Chrysogonus in *Histriomastix* in the summer of 1599, and retaliated with satirical portraits of Marston and Thomas Dekker (?1570–1632) in a revised version of his play *The Case Is Altered*. Marston replied with *Jack Drum's Entertainment* early in 1600, Jonson counter-attacked with *Cynthia's Revels* that autumn, Marston came back with *What You Will* in the spring of 1601, and Jonson rushed out *The Poetaster* in the early summer. Dekker brought this *Poetomachia*, or War of the Theatres, to an end (after Jonson had been arraigned before the Lord Chief Justice over it) in the autumn of 1601 with *Satiromastix*, which gave a withering picture of Jonson as the Roman poet Horace, a role he had arrogated to himself in *The Poetaster*. WBY referred to *The Poetaster* in one of the 'Thoughts' he was currently writing (see *E & I*, 278) and he borrows lines from the 'Apologitical Dialogue', with which Jonson concludes the play, in his poem 'Notoriety' (*VP*, 321, ll. 5–6).

[6] WBY admired Jonson as a writer who actively resisted the spread of a dreary uniformity he associated with the rise of capitalism in the early 17th century. He particularly esteemed his delight in aristocratic *sprezzatura* and 'Promethean fire' (*E & I*, 278), his 'cold implacability' (*Expl*, 445), and his contempt for the dull and second-rate. He relished Jonson's description of a contemporary (WBY hoped it was Shakespeare) as 'So rammed with life that he can but grow in life with being' (*Aut*, 480), and recollected something of what he understood by Jonson's 'ideal of life' at this time when he encountered the Swedish Court during the presentation of his Nobel Prize in 1923 (*Aut*, 545–6), recalling that he had been wont to repeat to himself 'what I could remember of Ben Jonson's address to the Court of his time, "Thou art a beautiful and brave spring and waterest all the noble plants of this Island. In thee the whole Kingdom dresseth itself and is ambitious to use thee as her glass. Beware then thou render men's figures truly and teach them no less to hate their deformities, than to love their forms. . . . Thy servant but not slave, Ben Jonson".'

[7] In his introduction to his selection from Edmund Spenser's poetry (see pp. 360, 368), WBY proposes that Spenser was caught between the 'Anglo-French' medieval world of 'Merry England', and the earnest zeal of a reviving Anglo-Saxon influence, arguing that the poetic part of Spenser responded to the medieval impulse, and that 'though a joyless earnestness had cast shadows upon him . . . [he] was of the old nation'. He also insisted that Spenser's allegory is least disruptive 'when he sets before us some procession like a Court pageant made to celebrate a wedding or a crowning. . . . He should have been content to be . . . a Master of the Revels to mankind' (*E & I*, 365, 368). He thought that Jonson, although of a later generation, carried on this tradition, not least as a noted writer of masques and Court revels.

Is there any possibility that Jonson meant Shakespeare not Chapman by the character of Virgil in the Poetaster?[8] I find it hard to believe that the few not too lively plays written by Chapman before that date could have made Jonson say as he does that whatever event of life came upon one, one could find appropriate words for it in the writings of 'Virgil'. I havnt read the Elizabethans for fifteen years, except Shakespeare and Spenser, and find myself drifting about a good deal. Is there any book that would tell me about the various people the plays are dedicated to, and the various ladies

---

[8] Jonson's *The Poetaster* is a satire on late Elizabethan literary life transposed to Augustan Rome and champions the authentic poetic tradition of Virgil, Ovid, and Horace against the invasive pretensions of vulgar, ill-bred, and uneducated poetasters. The loose-knit plot culminates with the trial of Crispinus (Marston), a tedious poetaster and plagiarist, and Demetrius (Dekker), a down-at-heel 'dresser of plays about the town', for calumnies on Horace (Jonson). Virgil, appointed to judge the case by Caesar, orders the accused to desist from their slanders and libels on pain of being committed to Bedlam. The play hails Virgil as the supreme poet of the period, particularly in the lines that WBY paraphrases here: 'That, which he hath writ, | Is with such judgement, labour'd, and distill'd | Through all the needful uses of our lives, | That could a man remember but his lines, | He should not touch at any serious point, | But he might breathe his spirit out of him.' A number of late 19th-century critics were tempted, like WBY, to suppose that Jonson must be alluding to Shakespeare here, and when William Poel produced the play in London in April 1916 he actually (and anachronistically) made up and costumed the actor playing Virgil to look like Shakespeare. In fact, although Jonson was later to celebrate Shakespeare's genius in famous dedicatory lines to the First Folio and to confess in *Discoveries* that he 'loved the man, and do honour his memory, on this side of idolatry', in 1601 he was enraged with the Chamberlain's Men, Shakespeare's company (which he satirized in *The Poetaster* and which, he knew, was planning to perform Dekker's *Satiromastix*), and, according to some contemporaries, with Shakespeare himself. Moreover Shakespeare had not yet written the works for which he is most remembered and so the terms in which Virgil is praised were not yet appropriate to him, nor did Jonson at any time think of Shakespeare's verse as 'labour'd, and distill'd', but rather too much the reverse. The idea that Virgil represents the older poet and playwright George Chapman (?1559–1634) has also received some critical support, especially since he was a friend of Jonson's and enjoyed a considerable contemporary reputation as a poet and scholar. However, the qualities that are ascribed to Virgil's work and character do not match those associated with Chapman, and Jonson actually parodies some of his lines in the play. WBY had long recognized the want of dramatic interest in Chapman's plays, but thought this proved the superior taste of Elizabethan and Jacobean audiences over their modern counterparts, pointing out in July 1891 that they 'were popular in their day, and yet there are pages on pages in them of sheer poetry, long speeches that have no dramatic justification of any kind except their beauty' (*LNI*, 111), and lamenting in 1894 that the modern world could not produce the kind of audiences 'who tolerated so great a poet, so poor a dramatist as Chapman' (*UP* 1. 325). He admired both 'Ben Jonson's Masks' and 'Chapman's *Bussy D'Ambois*' for their 'set passages of poetic oratory' and 'audacious metaphors' (*LNI*, 113), and in his preface to Oliver Gogarty's *Wild Apples* (Dundrum, 1930) celebrated Chapman's 'sense of a hardship borne and chosen out of pride and joy'.

one lights upon in Ben Jonson's Masques?[9] I have been dipping into Clarendon.[10]

Yrs ever<br>W B Yeats

TLS Kansas. Wade, 478–9.

## To A. E. F. Horniman, [c. 21 September 1906]

Mention in letter from AEFH, 22 September 1906.
Suggesting that they should talk things out since her recent letters have pained him, complaining of her attitude to the theatre, hinting at a conflict between his work and ambitions and her ideas,[1] protesting against her repellent attacks on his national feeling,[2] saying that Letitia Darragh agreed with her in thinking that a light green costume would have been better for the Angel in *The Hour-Glass*, and that the play had been a success,[3] telling her that Mrs Pat Campbell is thinking of taking his *Deirdre*,[4] hinting that

[9] WBY owned Henry Morley's edition of Jonson's *Masques and Entertainments* (1890; *YL*, 1032).

[10] Edward Hyde, 1st Earl of Clarendon (1608–74), was a staunch Royalist and shared Charles II's exile during the rule of Cromwell. After the Restoration of Charles in 1660 he was created an earl and appointed Chancellor, but was subsequently impeached, and in 1667 fled to France, where he wrote a celebrated history of the English Civil War, the profits from which enabled Oxford University Press to set up the Clarendon Press. He also wrote a *History of the Civil War in Ireland*, which was published posthumously. None of Clarendon's works would have given WBY much help with identifying characters in Jonson's masques.

[1] WBY had evidently been surprised and worried by the animosity and reproaches of AEFH's letter of 19 Sept (see p. 494), and had written that they should meet to discuss their positions. She replied on 22 Sept 'There is absolutely nothing for us to talk out, I wrote nothing fresh to you, I only repeated what it was necessary to impress upon you so as to force you to believe that my "letter to the Directors" is genuine in its fullest application. I did not want to pain you more than was absolutely needful, indeed I was foolish enough to imagine that you would be glad to know how much relieved I feel at the ceasing of the continual sources of disagreement between us. I don't remember ever having wished to sacrifice your work or ambitions to any personal idea of my own; only when worn out & obstructed I got cross from mental & physical fatigue.'

[2] 'I know that my intense distaste for any manifestation of "national feeling" is unpleasant to you, that you are repelled by it & so I have tried to keep it in check. I accept "national feeling" as part of your nature but you cannot accept as part of my nature what is personal to me.'

[3] In an attempt to mollify her, WBY had evidently told AEFH of Miss Darragh's suggestion that the costume of the Angel in *The Hour-Glass* (which had been revived at Longford in July (see p. 421), should be light green, the colour that AEFH had preferred when she was in charge of designing the costumes for the INTS. This information did indeed please her, and she replied: 'Yes, I'm gratified that Miss Darragh thought that light green would have been better for the Angel, but your text demanded red. That poor halo, how carefully it was made, with a device to hairpin it on exactly! I always did my best & it was only after a fight against too heavy odds that I found my incapacity. I'm very glad that the people had the sense to like "The Hour Glass."'

[4] AEFH was desperate that WBY should allow Mrs Pat Campbell to produce *Deirdre* (see pp. 449, 450), and replied: 'If Mrs Pat Campbell will take Deirdre I *beg* you to raise no obstacles in any way. A play

the authors might donate their Irish royalties to the Company,[5] and praising her for acting finely towards the Irish theatre.[6]

*LWBY* 1. 167–70.

## To Letitia Darragh, [c. 21 September 1906]

Mention in letter from Darragh, 22 September 1906.
Telling her that the writing of *Deirdre* is going well,[1] that AG's play is progressing, that everything is going smoothly in Ireland, and asking her about AEFH's state of mind and her attitude towards the Irish theatre.[2]

*LWBY* 1. 170–2.

by you, toured over England & taken to the Theatre Royal Dublin would indirectly help the Abbey Theatre most powerfully. It would shew your work to the class of people who would not be seen coming down Marlborough Street. It would prove to them in the clearest way that the work was not political; & because a well-known actress had paid you for it, there was most likely some merit in your other works. . . . To *beg* Mrs Pat Campbell to play your Deirdre in Dublin would be wise policy.'

[5] The Directors had arranged for the Abbey playwrights to receive royalties for the performance of their works, and WBY had evidently asked AEFH if she would have any objection to these royalties being ploughed back into the Company. She replied that 'If any of you choose to give the royalties gained by your plays in Ireland as a donation to the Ltd Company, no one can prevent you. As they would be paid (or reckoned) by the week it would be quite simple to arrange.'

[6] In an appeal to her better nature, WBY had apparently reminded AEFH that she had acted altruistically in her benefactions to the Irish dramatic movement, and in her refusal to use this financial power to influence the artistic policies of the Abbey. In her reply AEFH accepted WBY's praise and tried to explain the motives that lay behind her behaviour: 'I only try honestly to act uprightly, partly because of my own feeling of self-respect. I don't care about money for itself but I have a great sense of responsibility & just because of that strong feeling I will not be really foolish even in regard to small sums. . . . It was as soon as I realised the unwisdom of the divided authority that I saw that my right to interference of any sort must cease at once.' But she went on to complain that WBY's refusal to speak out against the attempts to associate George Moore with the INTS (see III. 630), although he knew that Moore was personally abhorrent to her, had revealed that her '*personal* feelings would never be considered, but I never let that come in the way of energies & my efforts. . . . Yes—in one way I did act "finely," that I did not let a personal matter stop what I knew to be the right course. But when I saw after Glasgow that subservience to Fay would not be "fine" but would eventually ruin the scheme I saw that I must go.' And she added that she had 'always felt myself to be an outsider amongst you & it was a very painful position to be in'.

[1] In her reply Miss Darragh said: 'I'm so glad "Deirdre" has risen & is in full flight & that everything your side is so smooth.'

[2] WBY was eager to ascertain as accurately as possible the grounds of AEFH's increasingly volatile attitude towards the Abbey, and Miss Darragh obliged with a detailed account of her current feelings: 'she lunched with me on Tuesday & in her own words burst into song from 1.30 to 5. So I listened & said about 6 sentences. . . . Of course she is in a state of seething fury about the whole thing and says she hates everything and nearly everyone apparently concerned with the Irish Theatre. However thro' it all she has a tenacious hankering after it partly hatred and partly to prove herself right in her judgement of art and acting—her views are perfectly sound & in the main she is right. . . . Fay is of course her obsession & one that will remain too—till he is put in the position of a paid leading actor & producer *only* of peasant plays I doubt her doing anything more for the Co. I think her difficulty could be solved later on by having a Stage

## To A. E. F. Horniman, [c. 25 September 1906]

Mention in letter from AEFH, 26 September 1906.
Telling her that illness has interfered with the completion of *Deirdre*,[1] that he intends to keep that play for the Abbey and not give it to Mrs Patrick Campbell,[2] suggesting that she should delay her holiday in France until they had had an opportunity to talk things over,[3] sending a paper praising Frank Fay's verse-speaking,[4] hoping that her renewed friendship with Helen Rand would not lead her to drift into A. E. Waite's occult group,[5]

manager and let Mr Fay be Producer. But the long & the short of it is she is dissatisfied because the theatre has neither made money nor acquired reclame from the public. — If the audiences can only be worked up this winter & some money got in *and* the *General public* — I underline it because she made so much point of it — tho' she might not be willing to pay for a season in London & tour she would be certainly be more likely to contemplate it — her idea is simply to make the Dublin Theatre the nucleus — the factory — the school — for an international Theatre. Irish plays & Ireland she really now cares nothing for — but I quite see she is willing for the Irish plays legendary & otherwise to be played sandwiched in with French ones & others. I don't think the situation is desperate if taken in hand now & worked up gradually.' Miss Darragh went on to advise WBY to correspond more frequently with AEFH about theatre affairs, and to appoint an energetic American manager at the Abbey.

[1] WBY had apparently told AEFH that illness, which had impaired his eyesight, was delaying the completion of *Deirdre*. In her reply she hoped 'that by this time you feel well again & are able to go on & finish Deirdre'.

[2] AEFH thought this a mistake, and replied that she was 'most sorry that you think fit to bury it at the Abbey Theatre, for I do not honestly think that any good can come of your sacrifice on the altar to Fay. He is hardened to incense & offerings.'

[3] WBY had evidently asked AEFH to postpone a planned holiday with a friend in France until after he had returned to London and spoken with her, but this she refused to do, replying that her travel arrangements had already been fixed: 'Miss Fletcher will arrange all about our trip....I do not think that we should be away more than a month, starting about Oct. 8th. I am not going to ask her to alter any of her arrangements unless it be absolutely necessary. This may surprise you, but if you think back a little you may remember that I may well be a bit tired of having all my affairs at the beck & call of other people.'

[4] Since AEFH had been much agitated by what she perceived as a falling off in the Abbey acting (see pp. 447, 491), WBY had evidently sent a press cutting praising Frank Fay's verse-speaking. In her reply AEFH said that she would show the paper to Miss Darragh, and remarked that quality of work was 'really more important than quantity. Frank Fay can train people to speak verse beautifully & it seems a pity that he should waste his time on anything else.'

[5] WBY had evidently heard that AEFH had resumed her friendship with Mrs Helen Mary Rand, a former co-member of the GD, who had succeeded her as Sub-Praemonstrator after her resignation in 1896. After the split in the GD in 1903 Mrs Rand ('Vigilate') joined A. E. Waite's faction, 'The Independent and Rectified Order', rather than remaining with the Stella Matutina group to which WBY belonged, and he was worried that AEFH might now be contemplating joining Waite's order. However, in her reply AEFH reassured him: 'I saw Helen Rand at Bayreuth & she came to see me yesterday & will most likely come again. Miss Spencer was here but even if we had been alone I do not think that any mention would have been made of the reasons which have kept us apart for so long. I shall treat her just as if she had been out of the country for many years & we had not been able to write. As I have a horror of any occult body with a low standard of morals you need not imagine that I shall drift into belonging to one again. If the resumption of my friendship with her were a source of acute misery & public insult to even an acquaintance, I should be very sorry & should do all I possibly could to mitigate the pain I was causing. I want you to understand that what I have been through myself makes me very anxious to cause as little suffering as possible.' AEFH did not join any occult group, but Helen Rand remained a close friend and was appointed literary executor in her will.

trusting that her animosity towards the Abbey would not cause her to harm its reputation in public,[6] and thanking her for a gift of the cigarette case.[7]

NLI.

## *To A. E. F. Horniman, 29 September 1906*

Mention in following letter and in a letter from AEFH, 1 October 1906. A conciliatory letter, asking about her disapproval of W. G. Fay's engagement to Brigit O'Dempsey, and of their elopement (with Lady Gregory's approval) to England,[1] telling her that there will be a delay in reopening the Abbey,[2] taking up her criticisms of his behaviour over George Moore,[3] evidently comparing the Abbey to the Court Theatre, revealing that Miss

[6] WBY was afraid that AEFH's excitable temperament and obsessive hostility to the Abbey might lead her to damage the Theatre's reputation through incautious talk. In her reply AEFH tried to lay these fears to rest by telling him that she did 'not rush about telling everybody that I've washed my hands of the theatre. I simple say that you have "Home Rule & a subsidy" because Fay managed to get rid of me & that I hope that you & Lady Gregory will be able to carry it on to a successful issue. . . . I shall not say anything to anyone which will damage you & Lady Gregory's efforts, that would be most foolish and undignified on my part.'

[7] On 22 Sept AEFH revealed that she had failed to find the 'chrysophrase & gun-metal cigarette case' she wanted for him, but sent a less elaborate one to be going on with, which would 'do quite well for when you go out fishing for the servants' Friday dinner'.

[1] WBY had evidently told AEFH that Brigit O'Dempsey's family disapproved of her relationship with W. G. Fay, and that, since she was too young to marry without her father's consent, she had eloped to England, where Fay was to join her shortly. AG, who had corresponded with the father on her behalf without result, had sanctioned the elopement. In her reply on 1 Oct AEFH had pointed out that 'What I "don't approve of" is obvious—I don't think you do either. I feel that the aid given (or rather countenance shewn) to the elopement by a woman of Lady Gregory's age & position will be damaging.'

[2] Nor did AEFH approve of the delay in reopening the Abbey, which she looked on 'as a plan to shunt Miss Darragh who *I am certain* will not be welcomed'. However, in strict accordance with her policy of non-interference, she declined to comment further on these matters.

[3] In her previous letter AEFH had complained of the way her dislike of George Moore had been disregarded in 1903 and 1904, and WBY's letter had evidently defended his response to Moore's article 'Stage Management in the Irish National Theatre' in the September 1904 issue of the Dublin periodical *Dana* (see III. 630, 639). The article enraged AEFH less for its criticisms of the acting and direction in INTS productions, than, as Holloway recorded in his diary (Hogan and Kilroy III. 230), because of its comment that 'at last W. G. Fay had found an admirer in Miss Horniman', which AEFH took to mean 'that they were "carrying on," as the saying goes. . . . Probably Moore never meant anything of the kind. The lady had her own thoughts on the matter and loathes Moore ever since. Refusing to be introduced to him and all that sort of thing.' WBY had apparently pointed out that he had brought pressure to bear on Moore to write a letter of apology to AEFH, and reminded her that she had refused to receive this. However, in her reply AEFH alleged it was not the *Dana* article that had most angered her, but that, prior to this, AE, who knew of her antipathy to Moore, supported a proposal to elect him a vice-president of the INTS: 'That under the circumstances was most unfitting—if I had openly taken it as a publicly expressed desire to insult me & had refused to sign the agreements, the rows would have come on at once & by this time there would be a solid company. I have never to my knowledge sacrificed the good of the theatre to my own feelings—can you honestly think that if I had allowed myself to know that person that it would have done anything but harm to our status? I leave the Dana affair quite on one

Darragh will not play Dectora in the production of the revised *Shadowy Waters*,[4] and asking when precisely AEFH is leaving for France.[5]

NLI.

## To Florence Farr, 30 September [1906]

Coole Park, | Gort, | Co. Galway.
Sunday Sept. 30.

My dear Florence Emery: as a correspondent you are prompt but meagre—your last was anyway—four lines I think. I have been meaning to reply these two weeks past, but have been absorbed in *Deirdre*. What I wanted to do was to suggest your sending circulars and lectures to 'Hon. Sec, Philosophical and Literary Society Cork.'[1] I was also going to give you the name of the sec. of an Aberdeen society which has invited me but on looking up his letters I find he has written from a French hotel and that I have neither the name of the society or the address.[2] I shall have to find out these from a professor I know in Aberdeen.[3] I have had a bad time with Miss Horniman, whose moon is always at the full of late, but hope a letter yesterday has quieted her. Miss Darragh is trying to play her for the chances it may lead to: but Fay is doing quite the reverse for he has just encountered an enemy and they have fought with fists and with a result about which each is confused for each seems to mix up what he did with what he had hoped to do. In other words each claims that he has licked the

side; my refusal to receive the letter was necessary—I could not have anything to do with a man who had insulted me in the public street without any justification.' In fact, AEFH had no need to fear that Moore had designs on the Abbey: in a letter to Synge of 11 Nov 1906 praising his writing (TCD), he went on to ask: 'Why do you never come to see me. And why dont Yeats come. The dose of Gregory powder is so frequent at the theatre that I dont go. But do you come here.'

[4] Predictably AEFH regretted 'that Miss Darragh is not to do Dectora as she likes the part so much'.
[5] AEFH promised to send him 'a telegram as soon as I hear when I am going away', but that she would 'not be certain until Wednesday at the earliest'.

[1] In fact, the Hon. Sec. of the Cork Literary and Scientific Society, to which WBY had lectured on 14 Dec 1905 (see pp. 249, 253–4), and with which the Cork Philosophical and Literary Society had merged almost a century before.
[2] This was George Tullock Bisset-Smith (1863–1922), honorary secretary of the Franco-Scottish Society of Aberdeen, and a civil servant in the Department of the Registrar-General for Scotland. He was arranging for WBY to address the Society on 'The Heroic Poetry of Ireland' on 25 Jan 1907. Introducing Yeats on that occasion, Professor Grierson remarked that 'no society was doing more for Aberdeen in the way of excellent lectures than the Franco-Scottish. The lectures in French which had hitherto been delivered, had been themselves a boon and had been of a very high order' (*Aberdeen Free Press*, 26 Jan 1907, p. 3). WBY had lectured to the Aberdeen University Literature Society on 12 Jan 1906 (see p. 316, n. 5).
[3] i.e. Professor Herbert John Clifford Grierson (see p. 308).

other and Fays enemy says he will attack him next time 'before the public on the stage.' Fay meanwhile writes that the enemy 'will be sorry before he (Fay) has done with him.' I think after careful investigation that Fay had slightly the better for he was dragged off while imploring to be let finish. It is all about a young woman. Do not talk about it just now as I don't want it to get round to Miss Horniman's ears that people know about it. I have not time to interfere but I think, for certain reasons, they will have to fight it out.[4] No signs of my book yet and only an advance copy of my *Spenser* but you will have both in good time. Miss Tobin is back in London—she is a charming talker—gave Synge and the principal players a dinner and was delightful[5]—but well if I should cross to London in the next month it would not be for her sake. I am getting restless—as the swallows do at this time of the year—but *Deirdre* has me tied to the table leg. I enclose some lines I wrote this morning. They are Deirdre's words spoken to the Musician in expectation of death.[6]

I have just been sent an absurd book—very expensively got up—called Osric and largely an account in bad verse of Oscar Wilde. At the end are several poems by the author in his own person—one to Robert Ross, very emotional and one to a negro boy whose 'lips like cupid's bow' are celebrated. There is an illustration of the author with a benign smile pointing to the negro boy, who is quite hideous, and looking much like a young missionary with his first convert.[7]

Yours ever  
W B Yeats

---

[4] Fay had fought his fellow-actor 'Arthur Sinclair' (Francis McDonnell), who was also a suitor for Brigit O'Dempsey's hand. On 23 Mar of this year AG reported to WBY (Berg) 'a little unpleasantness between Fay and MacDonell yesterday, Fay sharp & Mac impudent. . . . the root cause was, that Mac had taken Miss Dempsey to Dalkey, & Fay called half an hour later to take her for an outing & she had gone.' During the recent British tour, as AEFH had noted disapprovingly (NLI), McDonnell 'was drunk at Cardiff station & wanted to travel with Miss O'Dempsey. Mr Wareing objected, & put him in a compartment at one end & the girls at the other & took a central one himself.' Fay was also challenged to a fight by Miss O'Dempsey's brother, who however apparently backed down when Fay accepted.

[5] This was after the special performance for Judge Keogh and his family, which Agnes Tobin also attended (see p. 479). On 18 Sept Synge had accompanied her on a visit to Waterford.

[6] These lines were not finally used in the play.

[7] John Moray Stuart-Young's *Osrac, the Self-Sufficient* had been first published by the Hermes Press in October 1905, and was reissued this year in an enlarged edition of fifty numbered and signed copies in full vellum, stamped in gold for presentation to friends and selected writers. Entitled *An Urning's Love (Being a Poet's Study of Morbidity), Osrac the Self-Sufficient and Other Poems*, this edition contained 'Remembrance' (71), dedicated to Robert Ross: ' "Forget, forget, | And ne'er regret," | Cries to my heart the bird of night; | If mad dreams at eve and regrets by day, | If all the anguish a soul can pay, | Are price that has purchased a sorrow's blight, | I will forget.' Also published in this edition is 'A Glimpse' (140) dedicated 'To Ibrahima', an African youth glimpsed by the poet on a speeding ship: 'Ai, there in tunic clean, | White from the neck, with feet that peep below, | And soft brown shoulders, gleaming teeth, red lips, | (Of honey'd sweetness, shaped like Cupid's bow,— | I know them well!) and undulating hips!' A picture of Stuart-Young and Ibrahima, dressed in a knickerbocker suit and stockings, faces the poem.

[*With enclosure*]
DEIRDRE

> There's nothing here for tears—a king and queen
> Who've been true lovers are about to die.
> And what is that? What is't but putting off
> What all true lovers have cried out upon—
> The too soon wearying body, barriers
> That are not broken when lip touches lip,
> And all those changes that the moon stirs up,
> Or some worse star, for parting lip from lip
> A whole day long. I'd have you laugh with me.
> I am no more afraid of losing love
> Through growing old, for temporal change is finished
> And what I have I keep from this day out.

Text from Bax, 45–8. Wade, 479–81.

## *To Elizabeth Corbet Yeats, 1 October* [*1906*]

Coole Park | Gort, Co Galway
Oct 1

My dear Lollie,
I conclude from your letter that you are ready to grant me my terms, which are the usual terms of an editor under the circumstances.[1]

Stuart-Young (b. 1881) was born John Young in humble circumstances in Manchester. Although he had never known Wilde, he identified himself with one of his supposed young lovers, and forged inscriptions and letters from him.

[1] This is a reply to a letter from ECY of 'Sunday' (30 Sept; NLI), asking WBY which of KT's poems he had chosen for the Dun Emer selection (see pp. 459–60, 482). Although ECY made no mention of accepting WBY's terms for continuing as literary adviser to the Dun Emer Press (see pp. 482–5), he forced the issue by interpreting this as a tacit surrender to his wishes. In this he was premature: ECY sent his letter on to Emery Walker immediately on receiving it, and begged for Walker's advice as to 'whether you think our Press could possibly get on without having W. B. for literary advisor for *every book*—? Jack says we will never have any peace if we go on allowing Willie to boss the whole thing—he has just come from Coole Park, & so can judge & he is very keen on my not giving in. You see at Coole it is a regular mutual admiration society.... If I could get hold of something of Bernard Shaw's or something like that I could print it—& by *that time* Willie would probably have come to his senses, especially if he is away from Coole for a while—he generally comes round all right in the end—I don't want a dictator for my Press—but a literary advisor—Have you any advise [*sic*] to give—I have not answered Willie's letter at all.' She added that 'Willie thinks he cannot be done without, that is just it— this letter is polite compared to most I get from him & it is so worrying'.

You would never have thought I was treating you unfairly if I had carried out my first intention of getting A. P. Watt to arrange the whole thing. You will remember that he did arrange the terms for us about the Seven Woods.[2] My difficulty about the editorship was that I did not see how to pay him his percentage where you paid me nothing. He is supposed as you know to arrange all my affairs, every article I publish, every book I edit. I am ready to resume editorship on the condition that you give me a written statement that you will accept the following proposal, which can be put in legal form while you are in America.

1st. I to be sole editor, no books to be published of which I disapprove. I do not however claim the right to put in a book you object to.

2nd. You to pay me for the editorship such annual sum as A. P. Watt shall consider sufficient to give him his percentage.

I on my side will give you a written undertaking to return to you the annual payment minus A. P. Watt's percentage so long as the agreement holds good. I need hardly point out that I will have no reason to press for a large sum, the whole thing will probably cost you at the utmost a couple of £ a year, <and I thin> and this will be a small price to pay to save us both from a great deal of worry. You will know that I am not treating you badly, and I will feel secure on my side.

You can go to America quite easy in your mind about trusting the matter to Watt, whose business is to be on terms with both authors and publishers. Once before in a dispute between myself and a publisher both agreed to accept A. P. Watt's decision.[3]

I think you should do very well in America with your work once you get started there, and you cannot be in better hands than Mrs Ford's, who I imagine rather likes running things.[4]

Yr affecly
W B Yeats

TLS Bucknell.

[2] The contract between WBY and ECY for *In the Seven Woods* was drawn up by Watt on 7 Jan 1903, although WBY then took a hand in redrafting it, and did not sign it until September of that year (see pp. 1015–17).

[3] WBY is probably referring to his dispute with Elkin Mathews over *The Wind Among the Reeds* (see pp. 138, 338–9, 462). Watt had helped persuade Mathews to come to terms over the matter, although he firmly declined to deal with John Lane.

[4] Mrs Ford (see p. 66, n. 1), a patron of the Cuala Industries and the Dun Emer Press, had invited ECY to accompany her back to New York as her guest and the two sailed from Queenstown (now Cobh) aboard the *Cedric* on 5 Oct. Although WBY suggests that this was a business trip, ECY explained to Emery Walker on 3 Oct that it was 'a visit of pleasure.... I expect indirectly it will be good for business—although it is not a business visit'.

## *To Katharine Tynan Hinkson, 1 October* [*1906*]

Coole Park | Gort, Co Galway
Oct 1,

Dear Mrs Hinkson,

I never wrote to thank you for your beautiful book,[1] I wanted to write you a long letter, and I have been so overworked of late trying to get through all I can before I leave this for Dublin that letters to friends have been all but impossible. Even today I can only write on business. You will see from the enclosed letter that the crisis has arrived. I have written to my sister reaffirming my claim to be sole editor, and asking to have the matter referred to A. P. Watt. I have no idea whether she will agree or not, but hold out if she writes to you.[2] I hardly know which I wish so far as my personal feelings are concerned but I am certain that if I dont hold out for that editorship the Press will sink to the general Dublin level. On the other hand it gives me a great deal of trouble and responsibility and not a little general annoyance; of course I do not ask to be paid for my work, or rather I ask for only one payment, the right to keep the Press good.

Yrs alway
W B Yeats

[*with enclosure*]

Gurteen Dhas, | Churchtown, | Dundrum, | Co. Dublin.
*Sunday*

My dear Willie

I wrote to Lady Gregory first & so I have told her all about my great surprise—The American Trip—so I won't write it all again to you—You know Mrs Ford, when she was here last year she took a great liking to me— of course she had often written to me too before we saw her at all—& then when she was here she often said, 'You must come & stay with me', but I never thought it would come about—Luckily AE's book is *all set* up ready to print—& he is here on the spot if anything unexpected turns up while I am away so the girls can print it[3]—the bother is I will not like to take my

---

[1] Evidently her *Innocencies* (see p. 484), two copies of which WBY had in his library (*YA4*, 289).

[2] There is no evidence that Watt took any hand in the dispute, which was settled by John Quinn and AE himself, who, according to a letter from ECY to Quinn of 25 Nov (NYPL), drew up 'a little agreement on a half sheet of paper'. This, although it contained only 'a tenth of the words' in WBY's letter of 1 Oct, evidently resolved the matter so satisfactorily that both sides thought they had won.

[3] i.e. *By Still Waters*. Since this was the book at the centre of the dispute between them, ECY is trying to present WBY with a *fait accompli*. After further negotiation, it was finished by Dun Emer in November and published on 14 Dec 1906.

months salary from the Industry while I am away as it is too hard up an industry to pay a manager who is away amusing herself in another continent—Do you think you could select Katharine Tynans poems while I am away? because we will want the book to set up when I come back—in the middle of November—I dont like to write to her as I dont know what you & she settled upon—& I would like it settled before I leave on Wednesday night (I may be here till Thursday)—I expect I will get subscribers for Hanrahan & Saints & Wonders in America[4]—& so after all the visit may help the Press indirectly. When is your big book to be out?[5]

Yours affectionately Lolly Yeats

TLS Harvard, with envelope addressed to Pine Cottage, Blechingley, England, redirected to 9 Longfield Road, Ealing,[6] postmark 'GORT OC 1 06'. ECY letter NLI.

## *To John Millington Synge,* [*2 October 1906*]

COOLE PARK, | GORT, | CO. GALWAY.<br>Tuesday

My dear Synge: I think Lady Gregory will have to go to Dublin to-morrow to look into the Fay Dempsey business[1] & if she goes I will let her know & you can see her & arrange program. I quite agree about programs containing the new work but is it to be the last or first night of that work? Is it vital for it to be the first? It would be better to have Monday first nights as we should have sixpenny seats always on Saturday & it is a pity to give the sixpenny people first night peices—Our first nights should in the end pay very well on the full prices. On the other hand to have shilling seats on some Saturdays will confuse the public. What do you think.[2]

[4] i.e. WBY's *Stories of Red Hanrahan*, published by the Dun Emer Press in May 1905 (see p. 78, n. 1) and AG's recently issued *A Book of Saints and Wonders* (see p. 490).

[5] i.e. *Poems, 1899–1905*, which was published later this month.

[6] KT and her family had been living at 'Wrentham', 9 Longfield Road, Ealing, in west London since 1900, but she had evidently last written to WBY from a summer holiday address at Blechingley in Surrey, and he persisted in using this address.

[1] William Fay's stormy courtship of Brigit O'Dempsey (see p. 376) was reaching a crisis. There was a rumour that she had resigned from the Company, and she did go Glasgow and subsequently to London. Fay was planning to marry her under the more permissive Scottish laws since her father withheld his consent, and, as she was under the age of 21, this was legally required in Ireland and England. On 29 Sept Synge had written to AG (*JMSCL* 1. 209) that it would 'be impossible to get any good of Fay till his private affairs are arranged'. Brigit O'Dempsey's father had been in correspondence with AG about the situation.

[2] Planning the Abbey programmes had been complicated by the introduction of the cheaper 6*d.* seats and by Henderson's scheme for 1-guinea subscription tickets (see p. 492). In replying to this letter on 4 Oct (*JMSCL* 1. 211), Synge told WBY that he had proposed 'to have productions always full price, revival Saturdays always six penny seats, but perhaps it is too complicated, so let us work as you suggest beginning on Mondays'.

I agree that much hangs by this winter—the future of our theatre in its present form probably depends on it.

I will g[o] up for 'At Home.'[3]

Yrs ever

W B Yeats

Program sent with the following in their proper places will do but show it to Lady Gregory or send proof[4]

Oct:   Shadowy Waters & Mineral Worker
Nov:   Play Boy
Dec:   Deirdre & The Canivans
Jan:   Oedipus or Antigone

ALS TCD. Saddlemyer, 150–1.

## To John Millington Synge, 3 October [1906]

Coole Park | Gort,
Oct 3

My dear Synge,

We cannot have first nights on Saturdays unless we bring down the price of the pit on the other nights to sixpence. You cannot charge sixpence for your first night and a shilling for the second. It will confuse the public horribly upon the other hand if we have a shilling some Saturdays and not others. <If the new subscribers want> The simplest thing is to have our first nights on Mondays. A great many of Henderson's subscribers would I should think be quite glad to go the last night of a play when it is at its best, but some will probably desire to be there the first night. Could the tickets be drawn up in such a way as to be available for any night of a new play? Or else it could be marked upon them that they could be exchanged at the box office for another night.[1] I now deal with your list on the assumption that first nights come upon Monday. The great difficulty is that it is

[3] A 'Conversazione and Concert' to mark the commencement of the winter season were arranged at the Theatre on 13 Oct 1906. The *conversazione* was held in the Annex at 8.00, and the concert began in the Theatre at 8.45, with an address by WBY. This was followed by a programme of songs, recitals, and readings, and among the performers were F. J. Fay (who recited WBY's 'The Death of Cuchulain' and 'The Host of the Air'), Sara Allgood, Arthur Darley, Vera Esposito, and Joseph Holloway. Holloway greatly enjoyed the event and it was widely reported in the Dublin press.

[4] This programme was considerably altered in the event (see Appendix, pp. 856–7).

[1] Although in his reply Synge assented to the idea of beginning on Mondays (see above n. 2), first nights at the Abbey continued to be held on Saturdays in the new season.

impossible to have Deirdre so late in the month, as Robert Gregory who is doing the scenery must be there to supervise it and he cant at that time of the year, furthermore Lady Gregory has helped me very much with the scenario and it is necessary to have the play performed at a season when she can see it, besides we have been calculating on putting her new play the Canavans with Deirdre. If you can by any possibility have your play finished earlier so that it could be performed on Monday 19th instead of 24th, and let me have Monday Dec 10 for Deirdre and the Canavans, I would be very much obliged.[2] It only puts you five day[s] earlier. <As it is> I might possibly not be ready—<this is very unlikely, but it will be unlucky in a good many wa> If I am not something will have to be substituted, and we have something in our head. The point is that it is extremely important to get all our proposed London programme through before Christmas as we will have to go [to] London next year at our own expense and cannot run risks.[3]

Furthermore we have arranged with Miss Darragh after a talk with Fay who suggested early December for Deirdre that she is to be in Dublin in November for rehearsals. Looking down the rest of your list Cathleen ni Houlihan or something ought to be played with Eloquent Dempsey. Riders to the Sea was with it last time and helped to save our reputation. The play is harsh and ugly and wants a companion. Rising of the Moon and Kings Threshold wont make a bill, something must go with them. I suggest Lady Gregory's Jackdaw.[4] Dont put the Antigone by itself but give Edipus as an alternative, or we may offend Magee. On the other hand it wont do to put Edipus by itself because Magee's elaborate style may not prove vocal, or if you dont like putting the alternatives put Edipus by itself.[5] I think that is all the list. I see nothing but the Deirdre problem. Lady Gregory would prefer to solve the first night question by

[2] In his reply Synge agreed that the 'Deirdre matter is a puzzle' but confessed that *The Playboy of the Western World* 'though in its last agony, is not finished and I cannot promise it for any definite day'. In the end, *Deirdre* was produced on 24 Nov, and *The Playboy of the Western World* so far from being 'finished earlier' was postponed until the new year. On 19 Oct Synge told Holloway (NLI) 'that he was putting the finishing touches to his play', but difficulties with the second act and his subsequent ill-health delayed its completion further.

[3] Under the new financial arrangements, AEFH was giving the Theatre a fixed subsidy, and no longer providing the special touring allowances that had made the 1906 visits to Britain possible. The Abbey were to appear at the Great Queen Street Theatre, London, in mid-June 1907, having previously visited Glasgow, Cambridge, Birmingham, and Oxford.

[4] In his reply Synge revealed that 'Kathleen was omitted from list (with Demsey) by oversight, so was the Jackdaw from the Kings Threshold week.' In fact, neither *The King's Threshold* nor *The Jackdaw* was produced with *The Mineral Workers* on 20 Oct (see Appendix).

[5] Neither *Antigone* nor *Oedipus* was produced at the Abbey (see p. 476, n. 5), although both were advertised in the *Arrow*. On 18 Oct Synge had an 'OEdipus dinner with Magee', evidently to discuss progress on the play, and brought an MS of the play to WBY on 8 Nov (*JMSCL* 1. 218, 230).

altering all the shilling seats to sixpennys for every night, but it seems to me if we take that big leap we should do it on its merits and not to get out of a momentary difficulty.

I dont suppose you got a letter I sent you yesterday. You had put Glendalough instead of Glendalough House on the letter and so I put that and Co Wicklow on the envelope, having looked in an Irish Cyclopedia to find what county it was in.[6]

Lady Gregory is relieved by getting a telegram from Fay, as she need not go to Dublin.[7] She cannot possibly be in Dublin before 18th or 19th having business here, but I will be up for the At Home. I return Henderson's provisional list.

Yr ever
W B Yeats

TLS TCD. Saddlemyer, 151–3.

## *To A. E. F. Horniman,* [c. *13 October 1906*]

Mention in letter from AEFH, 15 October 1906.
Complaining about Fay,[1] discussing the division of parts between Sara Allgood and Letitia Darragh,[2] sending her the circular about subscription tickets and the programme for the opening *conversazione* at

---

[6] The Irish Post Office's sense of place was superior to WBY's and the letter (see above) had been delivered. Glendalough is the site of monastic settlement in Co. Wicklow, founded by St Kevin in the 7th century. WBY was to know it better; he mentions it in 'Under the Round Tower' (*VP*, 331) and uses it as the location of his poem 'Stream and Sun at Glendalough' (*VP*, 506).

[7] Fay's telegram to AG has not been traced, but evidently concerned his forthcoming marriage to Brigit O'Dempsey in Glasgow. AG had written to Synge on 2 Oct confessing (Saddlemyer, 150) that she was 'worried to death about this Fay-Dempsey affair. If we cld. get the family to consent to marriage that wld. be best, & if not, I incline to Scotland.' She offered to come up to Dublin 'if absolutely necessary' to try to resolve matters, and in his reply to the present letter Synge asked WBY to tell her 'that I got her letter and saw Fay last night. Scotland seems to be all right so that matter will be arranged easily enough.'

[1] WBY was keeping AEFH, who was in France, up to date with the preparations for the new season at the Abbey and had sent her two letters on theatrical affairs. She replied on 15 Oct that his 'second letter reached me this afternoon so I'll answer both now. You have had a pretty severe lesson now about "wool-gathering". I know you don't intend to be unkind, but it hurts dreadfully sometimes when one is very serious & you show openly that you are horribly bored. In that matter I quite understand how Fay felt that he could act just as he chose instead of insisting on your attention against your wills.'

[2] WBY had evidently informed AEFH of the latest manœuvring between Sara Allgood and Letitia Darragh. AEFH hoped 'that you will see fit to tell Miss Allgood exactly how matters stand, it is a confidence which I am sure she deserves. Fay cares far more for his power over the company than the position of the company towards the public.'

the Abbey,[3] and mentioning the possible return of Vera Esposito to the Company.[4]

NLI.

## To John Millington Synge, [*15 October 1906*]

COOLE PARK, | GORT, | CO. GALWAY.
Mond

My dear Synge: yesterday I left all material for 'Arrow' with Fay & asked to have proof if there was time. If not I said you would correct proofs. Please arrange to do so as there are one or two French words that Henderson is sure to get wrong.[1] Please also see that there are not too many kinds of type used Etc. & that the list of plays is clear & any advertisement of ours is [in] good taste. I dont quite like Hendersons circular about the 'Saturdays.' 'Rare oppertunity' is a little common, there are too many types, & there is no mention of our monthly seven night shows—this has misled the Freeman leader writer.[2]

---

[3] WBY had sent AEFH the circular about subscription tickets, and the programme for the opening *conversazione* at the Abbey, organized by Henderson on 13 Oct (see pp. 492, 508). Unlike Holloway and most of the Dublin press, WBY found fault with the singing and the choice of songs, which included settings of poems by Thomas Moore and Todhunter, pieces by Del Riego, Benedict, and Tosti, as well as a violin solo of Gaelic airs, recitations of WBY's poems 'The Death of Cuchulain' and 'The Host of the Air' by Frank Fay, and readings from Dion Boucicault by Joseph Holloway. The programme was comprised in fact of favourite party pieces by popular Dublin amateur singers such as Raymond Victory, J. C. Doyle, Emilie Martyn, and Alicia Keogh, but AEFH gleefully took up and amplified WBY's criticisms: 'The choice of music was "*common*" in the extreme. And there is an ignorant error too, the title of an opera is put down as a musician's name. The whole is a vulgar pandering to narrow-minded, patriotic ignorance. I don't for one moment believe you when you call the singing "second-rate", it must have been far worse than that.' She returned to this theme in her next letter: 'The "at home" programme was a most *common* selection of music chosen to please a vulgar ignorant "patriotic" taste. Mr Darley is an excellent violinist but his worship of archeological *scraps* has prevented his judgment from being of any value.'

[4] Vera Esposito (see p. 261), who had returned to Dublin, was making a success in a number of local productions, and WBY had thought of offering her a place in the Abbey Company, a thought which, as she told him, had already occurred to AEFH: 'By some telepathy I too was thinking of the possible return of Miss Esposito. The roughness of her voice & style do well in Spreading the News, they give more value to Miss Allgood. Also she would do much better than Mollie Allgood in Kathleen (or whoever is the old woman now) for the same reason.' Miss Esposito did not rejoin the Abbey, but was to play Agnes in the fourth act of Ibsen's *Brandt*, produced by the Irish National Players' Society in early December this year.

[1] Apart from 'Arc de Triomphe', the only French words in the 1906 *Arrow* occur in the note on AG's version of Molière's *The Doctor in Spite of Himself*: 'Molière', 'Comédie Française', and 'Sociétaire'. Unlike WBY and, apparently, Henderson, Synge was a fluent French speaker.

[2] The circular, which sports a variety of font styles and sizes, is dated 12 Oct but was in fact posted to subscribers on 11 Oct. It announced the series of plays to be given on 10 Saturday evenings from 20 Oct

On thinking over things I think it will be well to keep Miss Esposito friendly if we can do it without hurting Miss Allgood but I dont think that at this moment Miss Allgood should be asked to give up any part.[3] We may be able to put her into 'Heather Field' as it is not yet caste into the part of Lady Shule (I think that is the name) & possibly something else.[4] If she would be content with rather small parts for the moment she would get her chance later on. I conclude that Miss Allgood has either rehersed or been offered 'Mary Dhoul'.[5] Queen Maive showed her self a true organizer when she said of her lovers 'I have always one man in an others shadow'.[6] Besides we want variety—& we may sometimes want to reherse two plays side by side only repeating the minor parts. I dont beleive that 'Pleaders' will be done this three months & something will have to be put into its place that will be less of a tax & therefore can be played as an extra (say) in early January or in Dec for a week (not including Sat) & repeated on the Saturday 'Pleaders' is down for.[7] This is all vague & only means that there may be an oppertunity.

Yr ev<br>W B Yeats

ALS TCD. Saddlemyer, 157–8.

1906 to 26 Jan 1907, and proclaimed that the list afforded 'a rare opportunity to all lovers of the Drama of studying new Plays by Authors whose works have received high commendation from competent critics; have been successfully toured in Ireland, Scotland and England, and some of which have been played in Germany, Bohemia and America'. The circular also announced (in capital letters) the special subscription tickets devised by Henderson 'AT A CONSIDERABLE REDUCTION' (see p. 492, n. 3). Mentioning the circular on 13 Oct 1906, the *Freeman's Journal* announced (9) 'the issue of subscription tickets at a greatly reduced rate for ten Saturday nights', but gave the impression that these performances would be one-off and not part of the new arrangement whereby each programme would extend over seven days.

[3] See previous letter; Vera Esposito did not act again with the Abbey Company and by 1909 had given up acting altogether.

[4] Lady Shrule is the worldly and conventional wife of a neighbour of the hero, Carden Tyrrell, and a friend and abetter of his shrewish wife Grace Tyrrell. In fact, Edward Martyn's play *The Heather Field*, although mentioned as forthcoming in the *Arrow* of 20 Oct, was not revived at the Abbey until 15–17 Apr 1909, when Maire O'Neill played Lady Shrule and Sara Allgood took the part of Grace Tyrrell.

[5] Mary Doul, a blind beggarwoman, is the main female role in Synge's *The Well of the Saints*. The part had been performed by Vera Esposito under her stage name 'Emma Vernon' at the first production in February 1905. The play was not revived until 14 May 1908, when the part of Mary Doul was played by Sara Allgood. In January 1909 Sara Allgood told Holloway (NLI) that Miss Esposito had been 'asked to play Mary Doul in her absence in London, & refused to do so under £5.0.0. Miss Allgood started at 15/- a week. Miss Esposito was offered the same & refused the offer.'

[6] Maeve was a legendary Queen of Connacht and wife of the ageing Ailell. Apart from her martial prowess, she was famous for her amorous propensities, characteristics WBY celebrates in his poem 'The Old Age of Queen Maeve' and in *The Death of Cuchulain*, where she is alleged to have 'had three in an hour' (*VPl*, 1062). In AG's *Cuchulain of Muirthemne* Maeve tells Ailell (142) 'it would not be fitting for me to be with a husband that would be jealous, for I was never without one man being with me in the shadow of another'.

[7] Although advertised in Henderson's circular for presentation on Saturday, 19 Jan 1907, Jean Racine's comedy *Les Plaideurs* (1668), based on Aristophanes' *The Wasps*, was never produced at the

# To A. H. Bullen, [c. 21 October 1906]

Nassau Hotel, | Sth. Frederick St., | Dublin.

My dear Bullen,

I send you the third instalment of my "thoughts and second thoughts".[1] I am not sure that I have got the number of paragraphs right, as you never sent me the Gentleman's Magazine containing the last. Please get it sent. I want you also to send me six more copies of my book, putting them down to my account of course.[2] We have turned the corner here in Dublin with the Theatre and the receipts are now going up.[3] I have finished my new Play,[4] but won't let you have it to print until I have got it right in performance, for I am tired of rewriting. I forgot to tell you that the "Crown of Melodious Diamonds" which roused your mockery is from a prayer <to> by the Gnomes published at the end of the seventeenth century or early eighteenth.[5] It is probably much older, you evidently thought it came out of your enemy Walter Pater.[6]

Yrs ever
W B Yeats

---

Abbey. On 19 Jan 1907 a bill of revivals, *Hyacinth Halvey, In the Shadow of the Glen, Spreading the News*, and *Cathleen ni Houlihan*, was substituted instead.

[1] This instalment of 'My Thoughts and my Second Thoughts' (see p. 495) appeared in the *Gentleman's Magazine* in November 1906, and contained sections XI–XVII.

[2] i.e. *Poems, 1899–1905*, published this month. WBY evidently wanted them for presentation copies, and he gave copies to FF (see p. 517), W. G. Fay (NYPL), MG (Princeton), AEFH (see p. 524), and JBY (Anne Yeats).

[3] Henderson's subscription system and the cheaper 6*d.* seats had successfully boosted the Abbey audiences, and a rapturous Holloway noted in his diary on 20 Oct: 'Has the era of success dawned at last for the National Theatre Society? To judge by the crowded house to-night at the Abbey, one would be inclined to say so! A rainstorm flooded Dublin all the afternoon and evening, and yet the stalls were better attended than any night save the opening ones of the theatre. The new sixpenny seats were crowded to overflowing, and some who sought shilling seats had to be accommodated in the balcony. This was all very refreshing to those who have followed the fortunes of the little company through thick and thin, and Mr. Henderson, the new secretary, must feel very proud that his untiring exertions met with such instant success.'

[4] i.e. *Deirdre*.

[5] In his essay 'Personality and the Intellectual Essences', published in *Discoveries*, WBY figures (*E & I*, 267) the bifurcation of modern consciousness as upward, 'the way of the bird', or down 'to the market carts': 'That is the choice of choices—the way of the bird until common eyes have lost us, or to the market carts; but we must see to it that the soul goes with us, for the bird's song is beautiful, and the traditions of modern imagination, growing always more musical, more lyrical, more melancholy . . . are, it may be, the frenzy of those that are about to see what the magic hymn printed by the Abbé de Villars has called the Crown of Living and Melodious Diamonds.' The Abbé de Villars (1635–73) was author of *Le Conte de Gabelis; ou, Entretiens sur les sciences secretes* (Paris, 1670).

[6] Walter Horatio Pater (1838–94), critic and aesthete, spent most of his life as a Fellow of Brasenose College, Oxford. He made his name with *Studies in the History of the Renaissance* (1873) and a historical novel *Marius the Epicurean* (1885), both of which set the agenda for the Aesthetic Movement in England.

[*In WBY's hand*]
I send you an ill corrected MSS with 3 written pages among the typed but I
cant help it—I am desperately over worked just now.

TLS Kansas.


## To A. E. F. Horniman, [c. *21 October 1906*]

Mention in letter from AEFH, 26 October 1906.
A 'most welcome letter' informing her of the success of AG's *The Gaol
Gate* and Boyle's *The Mineral Workers* on 19 Oct,[1] and that people had to be
turned away because the theatre was full,[2] telling her of the subscriptions
scheme at the Abbey,[3] that AG has finished her new play,[4] that MG was

---

Pater was a potent influence on WBY's early prose; in *Aut* (321) he reveals that Pater influenced his *Rosa
Alchemica*, and describes *Marius* as 'the only great prose in modern English' (*Aut*, 302–3), and yet
wondered (477) whether 'the ideal of culture expressed by Pater can only create feminine souls. The
soul becomes a mirror not a brazier.' The more robust Bullen had little time for Pater.

[1] As Holloway recorded on 20 Oct (cf. *Abbey Theatre*, 72–4) *The Gaol Gate* and *The Mineral Workers*
had been palpable successes: 'Everything worked admirably & the two new pieces proved successes. The
audience was attentive, alert, & enthusiastic.... Lady Gregory's tragic incident, *At the Gaol Gate* [*sic*]
impressed by the excellence of the playing rather than by the excellence of its dramatic quality.... Miss
Sara Allgood as Mary Cahel, the mother, & Miss Maire O'Neill as Mary Cushin, the wife, entered the
spirit of the terrible situation, & made the intense grief of the women appear almost real to us.... The
figure of The Gate-Keeper (F. J. Fay) in the gloom of the open gate with the faint light from the lantern
which he carried cast upward on him, was most impressive, & the actor hit off just the right tone to keep
the unmoved, matter of fact official in the picture. The grouping of the three figures at the point when
he hands out the clothes was very fine & worthy of a great artist's brush. The lighting of the gloomy gate
& high repellent wall just suited the scene enacted & added to the pathetic grandure [*sic*] of the tragedy
in humble life. Rounds of applause followed, & the actors took these calls in artistic attitudes in keeping
with what had gone before.... *The Mineral Workers*, caught on from the first & the applause increased
after each act until on the final fall of the curtain the whole house became enthusiastic & calls for
"Author" were heard from all parts of the house.' The Dublin press uniformly praised *The Mineral
Workers*, but split along political lines in the notices of AG's more nationalist play. The Conservative
*Irish Times* of 22 Oct thought it 'a rather unconventional, not to say unconvincing, piece of work', and
the more extreme unionist *Daily Express* dismissed it as 'a work of mournful type', while the nationalist
*Freeman's Journal* found that 'into that one act is thrown an all but infinity of the deepest pathos'. AEFH
replied that she was 'very glad indeed that you are so happy about the success on Saturday night'.

[2] The Theatre took more money on this evening than any other, with the exception of its very first
night, and, although numbers fluctuated thereafter, they were well up on previous seasons, Saturdays
being particularly successful. In her reply AEFH hoped 'that the people turned away will return another
night'. Holloway commented in his diary (NLI) that success 'would continue to shine on this theatre if
W B Yeats was kept from making speeches or writing on the theatre. His writing always reminds me of
the poetic way of saying to people they are quite incapable of forming an opinion of their own. And
nobody likes to be told that!'

[3] The scheme greatly appealed to AEFH's business instincts, and she replied that she looked on the
arrangement 'as excellent': 'If anyone new offers of course they can be given extra tickets for the missed
Saturdays. If the "corner be turned" we must not drift back again.'

[4] i.e. *The Canavans*. In her reply AEFH sent many congratulations to AG on the new play, and asked
to read it 'as soon as it is printed please'. In fact the play was not published until 1912.

hissed on her visit to the Abbey,[5] sending her a copy of the *Arrow*[6] and a newspaper article on the Abbey Theatre,[7] saying that Sara Allgood may attempt the part of Mrs Walton,[8] discussing the new actors and the acting in the latest performances,[9] telling her that AE is hostile,[10]

[5] MG was back in Dublin after an absence of nearly two years, and Holloway (NLI), noticing her among the 'notabilities' present at the opening performances, reported that as the theatre was clearing at the end of the evening 'some in the pit raised "Cheers for Major Mc Bride" to which some responded'. He remarked that this 'was scarcely an Irishman's way of treating a lady', but in her reply to this letter AEFH suggested that it was the consequence of the cheaper seats: 'I am going to write a very polite note to Mrs Mc'Bride to say how sorry I am that the audience behaved in such a manner in my theatre. Why were they such cowards as to stop until the end? They are afraid of the police . . . I consider myself to be pitied for having prophesied a fuss with 6[d] seats & Mrs Mc'Bride on a Saturday night. . . . She knows what "patriotic" manners are like so she knew what to expect; but for my own credit's sake I am sorry that such low behaviour should happen in my theatre.' The pit had evidently been in ebullient mood and on 22 Oct Holloway heard (NLI) that after the performances 'a man in the pit asked for "three cheers for the fools on the stage", & a oncer on the jaw landed him on the floor by way of reply'. AEFH did write to MG but WBY ignored her remarks and on 10 Dec she commented (NLI): 'You naturally made no remark when I said that Mrs Mc'Bride got what she deserved when she came to the theatre. In a case like that your silence is quite right — you know that it is true but of course you object to saying so.' On 27 June AG had warned WBY (Berg) that AEFH 'will never quite trust you while she thinks Mrs MacBride a possible danger'. Mary Colum gives an account of the hissing of MG in *Life and the Dream* (Dublin, 1966), 124.

[6] A thousand copies of the *Arrow* had been distributed by post on 20 Oct, but WBY had evidently sent a special copy to AEFH with his letter, which she said she liked 'very much'

[7] WBY had sent AEFH a copy of the *Irish Times* of 23 Oct which quoted (8) a paragraph from a London paper asking why the INT had never produced Shaw's Irish play *John Bull's Other Island*, and suggesting as a reason that 'the blinding flashes of naked truth in that outburst of an English valet would so enrage all Nationalist auditors that they'd rise as one man at it, and burn the house down'. In fact, the INTS had commissioned the play, but were unable to stage it in 1904, not through cowardice, but because of inadequate resources (see p. 79 and III. 660–3). In her reply AEFH, while assuring WBY that the views 'of the valet are mine most assuredly', urged that 'the real reason of our refusal of "John Bull" should be made known. . . . I hate the thought that we should be considered cowardly.' In fact, this had already been done: at the Directors' instigation, Henderson wrote to the *Irish Times* at once, and his letter, which appeared on 24 Oct (8), pointed out that the only reason the play had not been produced at the Abbey was that it had proved impossible 'for our company to find an actor amongst them to play the English Liberal politician, who is Mr. Shaw's principal character'. On the same day Henderson confided to Holloway (NLI) that the letter was 'signed by him (but not written by him or approved of)'. Nor did it close the matter and suspicions about the Abbey's treatment of Shaw were to persist in Dublin.

[8] In fact Sara Allgood did take the part of Mrs Walton, the lively and forward-looking widowed sister of Sir Thomas Musgrove in *The Mineral Workers*. This part, of an assured, upper-class woman, was a new departure for her, since her previous roles had been of women of the people. AEFH commented in her reply that she did not think 'that "Mrs Walton" would be a really "intolerable part" in the hands of an experienced actress, *not* a girl. But the mere attempt will do Miss Allgood good.' The reviewers gave the performance brief and respectful notices, but devoted more space and praise to her portrayal of the tragic aged mother Mary Cahel in *The Gaol Gate*.

[9] In response to WBY's news that W. G. Fay was scoring a resounding success in the part of Boyle's Dan Fogarty, AEFH remarked that the 'better Fay is now the worse I think of his insulting the public at Edinburgh'. Of Arthur Power, who took the part of Ned Mulroy, she commented that he was 'a nice fellow but I don't think that he will ever be a real actor.'

[10] WBY's criticism of AE's poems (see pp. 460, 464–5) had worsened their already deteriorating relationship (see pp. 291–8), and AE's 'at-homes' had become a focus of those who resented WBY's

and that his own speech at the theatre has received one good newspaper notice.[11]

LWBY I. 172–4.

## *To George Brett, 3 November 1906*

Mention in letter from Brett, 31 November 1906.
Telling Brett of his 'new play' and asking whether it will be possible to add it to the second volume of *The Poetical Works*,[1] and also commenting on the cover design for the book.[2]

attitudes and influences. In her reply, AEFH put this latest surge of hostility down to the fact that WBY had announced a play on the Irish heroine Deirdre, who had also been the subject of AE's play *Deirdre*, performed in 1902 (see III. 166–8): 'Of course Russell is savage, no wonder considering the title of your next play. He is absolutely a *Philistine*, one of those who fear Art & hate it because of that fear. I think that you should have chosen another title unless you want to defy him & defying Russell is rather like teasing a very woolley sheep.' AEFH may have been right in this analysis: when it was produced, WBY's *Deirdre* was compared unfavourably both publicly and privately with AE's treatment, and there are hints of conspiracy in these attitudes. Holloway had spotted AE at the first night of *The Mineral Workers* (NLI), hobnobbing with Edward Martyn and 'looking quite remarkable with his long untidy hair & reddish beard'.

[11] This was the speech given at the *conversazione* and concert on 13 Oct (see p. 508, n. 3). As the *Freeman's Journal* reported on 15 Oct (6), WBY 'delivered a little address on the progress so far made by the Society, and described what it hopes to do in the immediate future'. Recalling various plays that the Abbey had produced, he suggested that they differed 'from the Irish plays of earlier generations' in that they tried 'to get nearer to the actual life of the people'. Drawing an analogy with 19th-century Irish writing, he maintained that the Abbey was in the tradition of William Carleton, whose novels and stories gave 'authentic pictures of Irish life', rather than that of Dion Boucicault and Charles Lever, whose plays and novels had established the false caricature of the stage Irishman. Because of its refusal to pander to vulgar taste, the clientele of the Abbey had remained, he said, small, but its audience was discriminating and growing, and he concluded by listing the new plays to be performed in the coming season. AEFH replied that she had 'not received my paper with your speech', but was 'very glad that you got even one good report'.

[1] WBY had evidently written to ask Brett to include *Deirdre* in the second volume of *The Poetical Works*. In his reply (NYPL) Brett assured him that 'we should be very glad to add this new play to the collected edition of your plays which we now have in preparation, publishing the volume containing the poems and holding the volume of plays until you are able to let us have copy for this new play, as kindly suggested by you'. He added that if WBY would 'send us the copy as soon as it is ready we shall be glad to submit proofs and publish the volume of plays immediately thereafter'. In fact, whereas the first volume of *The Poetical Works* appeared on 27 Nov, the second was not published until 8 July 1907. It did contain *Deirdre*.

[2] In his reply Brett noted 'what you say about the cover design submitted by us and I am referring this part of your letter to our manufacturing department for attention'. Both volumes of *The Poetical Works* were issued in dark blue cloth with the same gold design by Althea Gyles on the spine as that used for the second edition of *Poems* (1899).

## To John Millington Synge, [6 November 1906]

Mention in letter from Synge, 7 November 1906.
Postcard asking him to come to a meeting about theatre business.[1]

*JMSCL* I. 230.

## To Florence Farr, [11 November 1906]

Nassau Hotel | South Frederick St. | Dublin.
Sunday

My dear Friend: It is a long time since I heard from you. Isn't the debt on your side—I think I sent you my book[1]—I am a little anxious (I have become so since so long has passed without my hearing). You spoke of being 'seriously' out of sorts and then of being all right 'in a week.' I assume that it was only a passing upset. Do write and tell me how you are. I have been overwhelmingly busy and thoroughly overworked. The theatre is now a success, if it goes on as it is now we are through all our troubles. Last night for instance was a revival of *Doctor in Spite of Himself*, *Hyacinth Halvey*, *Riders to the Sea* and the house was full. People standing up both in gallery and pit. The audiences have been steadily going up and this is the best yet.[2] At this rate with our

---

[1] In his reply, Synge said that he would come in to see WBY on the afternoon of 8 Nov, and reminded him that they had to discuss two matters postponed from the previous meeting so that they could take advice from Fred Ryan, the previous secretary of the INTS and an efficient adminstrator (see pp. 153, n. 2, 425): 'He was to advise us as to Miss Horniman and the minutes the form of the notice we are to send Bank about Henderson and the I.N.T.S. money.' And he concluded that they would 'have to come to some arrangement with Ryan, I think, as to his overseeing of the accounts for the present'.

[1] WBY had sent FF a copy of *Poems, 1899–1905* inscribed 'Florence Emery from her friend the writer', and again on the back flyleaf 'To Mrs Emery from her friend the writer. Oct 1906' (Private).

[2] *The Doctor in Spite of Himself*, *Hyacinth Halvey*, and *Riders to the Sea* were revived on 10 Nov. Like WBY, Holloway was delighted with the size of the audience, and in a diary entry of 10 Nov (NLI) gave the credit for this to Henderson: 'W. A. Henderson is truly a magician. It is little over a month since he became officially connected with the Abbey Theatre & he has pilotted [*sic*] the thought to be sinking ship into the smooth waters of success & hopefulness for its future seaworthiness. . . . To see the audience pouring in a continual stream—filling up pit, balcony & stalls was a sight to behold & rejoice in. . . . the National Theatre Society have had a long & patient wait for the happy time to arrive. I think it has come at last . . . At all events the audience tonight was enough to gladden any players heart—it was appreciative & most enthusiastic & listened with wonderous attention to every word spoken on the stage.' As he was leaving the theatre Holloway had 'a word with W B Yeats . . . he said "Hyacinth Halvey" never went better", & I added "Every point was taken up splendidly", & passed on. A red-letter night in the annals of this theatre, Miss Horniman's generous gift is likely to bear fruit at last.'

present expenditure we are making a profit[3]—but of course we must raise salaries.[4]

Since I wrote the above sentence Fay and Mrs. Fay (they eloped and got married a week ago) have been in and Fay 'I have come round to crow.'[5] Both Lady Gregory and I have been building castles in the air with you for one of their inhabitants. We mean to get you over to play for us presently. Miss Darragh is I notice not popular with the company. She says such things as 'Why do you not get that caster screwed on to the table leg,' instead of making enquiries and finding out that that caster cannot be screwed on because the woman who washes the floors and the stage carpenter have quarrelled about it—and the stage carpenter would sooner die than screw it on. She is considered to lack tact and the finer feelings—at any rate she has got them into the right state to welcome you. I think she will be very useful to us in a number of parts, but there are a number of others that neither she or our own people can touch.[6] I do believe I have made a great play out of Deirdre—'the authors are in eternity' etc.—most

---

[3] When Holloway called at the Abbey on Monday, 12 Nov, he found Henderson (NLI) 'like the King in the nursery rhyme, in that he was sitting in his room, counting out his gold after Saturday night's success. He beamed as he told me of the receipts being over £30.' The takings were in fact £31 2s. (NLI) and this figure was surpassed on the two following Saturday nights. But the season as a whole showed a loss: total expenditure from October 1906 to May 1907 was £1,432 0s. 11d. while the total receipts were £763 19s.

[4] Salaries were not increased during this season and from 19 Oct 1906 to 7 May 1907 the cost of salaries amounted to £782 16s. 11d. In *Ireland's Abbey Theatre* Udolphus Wright reported (92) that the 'first person to go on salary was W. G. Fay. I don't think his salary was more than £3 a week. Frank Fay was not getting salary until some time afterwards. Then Frank Fay and Sara Allgood started at about £1. Then O'Rourke and myself did not get anything until we came right in to the Theatre. When we were on tour I would get a tour allowance, which was £1 a week, plus my home salary, that was about £2. Arthur Sinclair came about that time and was getting about 30s. . . . and when I came in permanently—about 1908—I started with £2 a week. The highest salary at that time was £3 a week and on tour one got £1 for lodging and when the Company went to London they got 7s. 6d. extra.'

[5] W. G. Fay and Brigit O'Dempsey had married in Glasgow on 29 Oct, having left Dublin on Saturday, 27 Oct, after the final performance of *Spreading the News*, in which Fay played Bartley Fallon. In *Fays of the Abbey*, he recalled (210) that at the 'end of October I managed to dash over to Glasgow for a week-end, and in Shamrock Street of happy omen was married to Brigit O'Dempsey'. In fact they had chosen Scotland because under English and Irish law the bride, aged nineteen, was still young enough to need parental consent (see p. 501, n. 1). On 1 Nov Holloway was visiting the Abbey Theatre 'when the bride and bridegroom (Mr & Mrs W. G. Fay) arrived in the Green Room to receive our hearty congratulations. They were married in Glasgow on Monday & returned to Dublin this morning. Mr Henderson made a presentation on behalf of the members of the Company, including myself, & everyone seemed quite happy. A call to rehearsal broke up the little gathering' (NLI).

[6] On 9 Nov 1906 Holloway recorded '"O (Ough) I know that", I have it on the authority of Sara Allgood, is what Miss Darragh says to everything she is told when rehearsing. The actresses of the company have made it a sort of "gag" amongst them.' And on 1 Jan 1907 Henderson confided to Holloway (NLI) that 'Miss Darragh was not popular with the company & she was partly herself to blame. At first she sort of sneered & looked down on them as mere amateurs, & they naturally resented the slight & gave her the cold shoulder in return! . . . Her engagement was not popular with the patrons of the theatre either, & did much to lessen the audience.'

powerful and even sensational.[7] I will get a copy made and send it to you I think, as it may be some time before it is printed.[8] The first musician was written for you—I always saw your face as I wrote very curiously your face even more than your voice and built the character out of that.[9] I am a prisoner here until Dec. 15 but shall go over then and see you before you go to America.[10]

Yours ever

W B Yeats

We very nearly wired to you to come over and play 'first musician.' Lady Gregory went so far as to put it to Fay—but our players woke up then. I don't think you would have liked to come but we would have been very urgent.

Text from Bax, 48–9. Wade, 481–2.

# To A. E. F. Horniman, [c. 12 November 1906]

Mention in letter from AEFH, 14 November 1906.
Telling her of the success of the plays on Saturday night,[1] of nationalist opposition to Synge's plays,[2] discussing the production of Molière and Edward Martyn's views on it,[3] telling her that a new management is

---

[7] This quotation, which WBY also cites in his essay on 'Magic' (*E & I*, 36), is taken from William Blake's letter to Thomas Butts of 6 July 1803 in which he describes his poem *Milton* (1804) as 'a Sublime Allegory, which is now perfectly completed into a Grand Poem', adding, 'I may praise it, since I dare not pretend to be any other than the Secretary; the Authors are in Eternity' (Geoffrey Keynes, *Complete Writings of William Blake* [1966], 825).

[8] *Deirdre* was not published until August 1907.

[9] See III. 653. In the stage directions to the play, the First Musician is described as 'a comely woman of about forty'.

[10] WBY had to remain in Dublin until the last day of the Abbey's autumn season. FF left for the USA on 30 Jan 1907.

[1] AEFH replied that she was 'extremely glad that Saturday night was such a success'.

[2] AEFH retained her hard line on this, and admonished WBY that he 'must not on any account "kow-tow" to the "patriots" by dropping Mr Synge. The 6ᵈ seats are quite enough of a climb-down to their desires.'

[3] AG's version of *The Doctor in Spite of Himself* had been revived on 10 Nov, but AEFH disapproved of the production of Molière at the Abbey, and brushed aside Martyn's apparent approval of the performance: 'I am sorry that what I expected to be the case has been confirmed professionally about Molière. Edward Martyn's opinion on such a subject is valueless, he would only know that words were said & "business" done, *not* the way they were carried out. Molière requires most finished delicate art or else he is only old-fashioned farce.'

operating the tea bar,[4] criticizing O'Rourke's performance in *Hyacinth Halvey*,[5] and telling her that they intend to produce *Antigone* soon.[6]

NLI.

## To T. Fisher Unwin, [c. 14 November 1906]

Mention in letter from Unwin, 15 November 1906.
Telling Unwin that although his firm has done well by him and his books, he now wishes to get all his British publications into the hands of one publisher, and that he is therefore transferring those issued by Unwin to Bullen.[1]

*LWBY* 1. 175–6.

[4] A new tea bar, under a separate management, had been set up in the Abbey foyer (the Theatre did not have a licence to sell alcoholic drinks), and in her reply AEFH hoped that they might 'make something by it eventually'.
[5] A number of commentators remarked upon the nasal and sometimes monotonous delivery of J. A. O'Rourke, and WBY had evidently found fault with the lack of direction in his performance as the Policeman in AG's *Hyacinth Halvey*. AEFH fell eagerly upon his criticisms: 'What you say about O'Rourke (whose nasal voice must be cured if he is ever to be of any good) as the policeman fits in with my great objection to the Fay system, which is to use merely the material already in the *amateurs* not to increase and broaden them into *professionals*; & so learn to *act* not merely to *be*, as life has taught them only. *That is not Art* at all.' Holloway found this lack of art a virtue, noting (NLI) that 'J A O'Rourke as the active-minded Sergeant with a turn for improving the people took nature for his model & copied his subject with scrupulous accuracy'.
[6] WBY had evidently informed AEFH that the NTS had advertised *Antigone* (see p. 509) as beginning on 26 Jan 1907, but this filled her with foreboding: 'I wish that you were not going to risk "Antigone" so soon, who will teach the men not to look foolish in the costumes? And their "make-up" will look far worse than in modern plays. But these things are not my business now—THANK GOODNESS. The bored audience won't be very happy but they will feel "superior".'

[1] WBY had long wished to get all his books into the hands of one publisher, but this letter, as Unwin told him in his reply, caused 'considerable surprise and indeed regret. I have never imagined that there would be an ending to our literary and professional connection.' He went on to point out that matters were 'not quite so easy, neither is it so simple, as practically I hold if not the copyright, I have certain publishing rights in connection with one or more, so it seems to me that I have, shall I say prior rights, if not legal (and I dislike that word), professional rights as your first publisher, and so why not have your other works transferred to the publisher whom you tell me has done well by you and your writings? It would surely be simple to transfer the one or two from the other house to my firm, and I must ask you therefore to consider this suggestion.'

## To A. E. F. Horniman, 19 November 1906

Mention in letter from AEFH, 26 November 1906.

Discussing the hanging of his portrait by Mme Troncy,[1] telling her that the Abbey audiences are cultured and intelligent,[2] that he is making more alterations to *Deirdre*,[3] commending W. G. Fay's acting,[4] disclosing that Martin Harvey has been asking after her,[5] revealing that he is thinking of

---

[1] AEFH's friend, the Parisian painter Mme Laure Richard-Troncy, later Mrs Robert Anning Bell, had loaned the portrait of WBY that she had executed in 1903 (see p. III. 296) to the Abbey. It was hung in the green room in 1904, but AEFH thought it should have been placed in the vestibule and in her letter of 14 Nov gave WBY an ultimatum: 'If you will not allow the M^me Troncy portrait of you to hang there please let me know because it is *her* property & not mine & so (not being mine) it must not be injured by being knocked about or hung in a hidden place. I don't like snubbing her by sending it back, but I won't injure her property. Personally I like it much better than the other portraits; but, as you know I will never put any stress on my own feelings in regard to such matters. But I must be told what has become of it.' In her reply to this letter she told him that it was 'all right about the portrait if it hangs in a safe place & you shall not be troubled about it any more'. Holloway agreed with AEFH's estimation of the portrait, and on 14 Jan 1909 noted (NLI) that the 'clever pastel of Yeats by a French artist now hangs in the Manager's room. It is a speaking likeness of the poet.'

[2] In an attempt to set AEFH's mind at rest about any possible deterioration as a result of the cheaper 6*d*. seats, WBY had evidently stressed the good taste and intelligence of the new Abbey audiences. She replied that she was 'glad that a decently dressed audience behaved in a fittingly respectful manner to the serious plays'.

[3] WBY had told her that he was revising parts of *Deirdre* (see p. 503), and she hoped that for 'the long-suffering Bullen's sake . . . you will finish Deirdre before it is printed'. On 11 Nov W. J. Lawrence told Holloway (NLI) that Frank Fay had been complaining 'that Yeats was chopping & changing each day *Deirdre* until the players are almost becoming distracted. . . . They would say nothing against him although he is worrying the life & soul out of them over his play.'

[4] W. G. Fay had played James Quirke, the seller of dubious meat, in the recent production of *Hyacinth Halvey*, with, as Holloway reported, 'humour that there was no resisting', and he also made 'a very droll Sganerelle' in *The Doctor in Spite of Himself*. Holloway judged that he portrayed Bartley in *Riders to the Sea*, in the same programme, 'with commendable restraint resulting in naturalness'. On 17 Nov he made a great success in the title role of *The Eloquent Dempsy*, keeping the audience 'in the best of good humour . . . every phrase he uttered went home to those who listened'. AEFH grudgingly conceded that 'No one with any sense could doubt Fay's capacity as an actor when he takes the trouble to act nor his real power when he cares to let the audience hear what he is saying.'

[5] WBY had apparently told AEFH that the actor-manager Martin Harvey, whose company was performing in Dublin, had been asking about her, and discussing the demonstration at his production of Rosamund Langbridge's one-act play *The Spell* at the Theatre Royal on 19 Nov. In the play a Galway peasant girl falls in love with a boy who has a superstitious dread of her red hair. The girl's mother puts a spell on the boy so that he will return her daughter's love as long as she does not reveal that he has been bewitched. But the girl tells him of the spell on their wedding night and he kills her in superstitious terror. The theme of the play was reminiscent of an actual event which had caused horror and embarrassment in Ireland, the witch-burning of Bridget Cleary near Clonmel in March 1895, although Holloway maintained that the protest was caused not by the plot but by the melodramatic writing and overacting, so that, as he noted (NLI), 'what purported to be tragedy turned out farce & the supreme moment of the play was received with laughter instead of dread', while Harvey's 'acting was distinctly bad & quite legitimately earned the ridicule it received'. AEFH would have none of this and replied that she had 'sent a note to Martin Harvey (saying who I was) to thank him for his interest in me & I told him why The Spell caused a "row". Everyone else will tell him a variety of causes—the people did not like being reminded that an old woman was burned at Clonmel as a witch some ten years ago!'

new schemes to improve the management of the Abbey,[6] and suggesting that a raise in pay in the form of a bonus will increase the powers of discipline.[7]

NLI.

## To A. H. Bullen, [*23 November 1906*]

Nassau Hotel | South Fredrick St | *Dublin.*

My dear Bullen: 'Shadowy Waters' will be played here to-morrow two weeks I have made a stage version partly prose & about one third shorter than old version. Will you bring out stage version for sale in theatre?[1] Play will probably go to London as well as be revived here as all my plays are.[2] We have now good audiences—already two thirds of our stalls booked for tomorrow (Dierdre)—Audiences are encreasing steadily. Please wire. Could be printed here in time I think—could see printer myself. We will turn away people from all parts of house to-morrow.

Yrs ev
W B Yeats

[*In Bullen's hand*]
Print Shadowy Waters thirty two pages like sixpenny Pot Broth. Thousand copies. Keep type standing Bullen

ALS Kansas.

## To A. E. F. Horniman, [c. *25 November 1906*]

Mention in letter from AEFH, 26 November 1906.
A 'welcome epistle', telling her that the Abbey continues to be packed,[1] discussing Maire O'Neill and discipline, saying that they have withdrawn

---

[6] See below, p. 524. AEFH looked forward to hearing 'all about your new schemes when you come to London'.

[7] The Directors were thinking of raising the players' salaries and introducing a system of bonuses, and AEFH agreed that an 'increase of pay in the form of bonus or anything else will, as you say, increase the powers of discipline'. A special 'Christmas Bonus' of £40. 10s. was divided among the Company on 17 Dec.

[1] As the note in his hand suggests, Bullen brought out an 'acting version' of *The Shadowy Waters*, partly in verse and partly in prose, 'As First Played At the Abbey Theatre, December 8th, 1906', early in 1907.

[2] *The Shadowy Waters* was produced in Oxford and London during the Abbey's 1907 British tour, but it was not revived in Dublin.

[1] The dramatic rise in Abbey audiences had continued, and on 17 Nov Holloway noted (NLI) that the 'people came pouring in until the little theatre could hold no more. Long may the National Theatre Society remain on the crest of the wave of popularity now that it has weathered the stormy seas of

*The Canavans* because it is not ready,[2] reporting that O'Rourke has been substituted in a Frank Fay role unannounced,[3] discussing criticism of Letitia Darragh's acting as 'wooden',[4] noting that *The Building Fund* is dragging[5], complaining about the lack of enterprise of Walter Saville at Cramers, the Abbey's ticket agents[6], mentioning rehearsals of *The Shadowy*

neglectfulness.' AEFH was suitably cheered 'to hear of the Abbey being "packed", I can hardly realise how it must look.'

[2] This was the true explanation, but not the one given to the Abbey patrons. The first production of AG's *The Canavans* had been announced for Saturday, 24 Nov, but, when the audience arrived at the theatre, they found a notice announcing that it had been postponed at the last moment owing to the illness of one of the players (O'Rourke), and as Holloway reported (NLI), 'Mr Yeats came before the curtain & explained that it was five oclock that evening when they heard of the illness of one of their actors & as their company was a small one & no substitute available, *The Canavans* would be postponed until Dec 8th & *The Building Fund* advertised for that date substituted.' Holloway was suspicious of this explanation and almost got Henderson to confess that they could have mounted the play on 24 Nov, surmising that perhaps O'Rourke's 'illness was prearranged. Who can say!' AEFH told WBY that if the play 'was not ready you were most wise to withdraw it. Lady Gregory's work must be well treated—she is the best "draw" of the lot of you. I am so proud of her because she makes the people laugh in a witty manner.' AG had told Holloway on 19 Oct that she 'had completed her play *The Canavans*, but had to revise it, & touch it up'.

[3] O'Rourke had evidently taken over the title role in *Hyacinth Halvey* for one or more performances during its recent run, without the audience being informed. AEFH insisted that when such substitutions occurred, 'the public *must* be told. I will not have the Directors follow Willie Fay's idea that "it does not matter".'

[4] Opinion on Letitia Darragh's acting differed widely (see pp. 425, 457–8, 518), and discussion had been revived by her appearance in the title role of WBY's *Deirdre* on 24 Nov. Most critics found her performances not so much 'wooden' as affected and artificial because of her use of professional mannerisms, and contrasted these with the more natural delivery of the regular Abbey actresses. Holloway thought that the difference between her acting and that of Sara Allgood was that the 'former acts, the latter lives her parts'. AEFH did not agree, and in her reply to WBY's letter expostulated that 'No one could see Miss Darragh & think her at all wooden; "excitable" is what is necessary as long as the will is able to control the manifestation', and she asked WBY to please let her know 'how she gets on after a day or two'. The problem was compounded by the fact that Miss Darragh was not at ease in the role, and confided to Henderson (as he told Holloway on 8 Dec) that she 'never cared for the part' of Deirdre. The Dublin press felt that the fault lay with the play as much as with her. The *Irish Times* of 26 Nov praised its 'poetic feeling' and 'highly cultivated imagination' but complained that these did not compensate 'for the absence of . . . dramatic elements'. The *Irish Independent* of the same day also considered that it lacked 'certain of the essentials of a successful stage production', and the Dublin *Daily Express* found it 'too heavily weighted with grandiloquent melancholy'. In June of this year Max Meyerfeld (see p. 108, n. 2) had described Miss Darragh's performance as Salome as 'impossible': 'She lacked nearly every thing required by this complex character. The Dance of the Seven Veils was executed with all the propriety of a British governess.' Nevertheless, her performance in WBY's play picked up over the week and on 1 Dec Holloway recorded (NLI) that she 'entered fully into the spirit of Deirdre tonight, & became most impressive frequently . . . indeed, once she almost became quite melodramatic in her actions and delivery'.

[5] This was evidently a personal opinion as, according to Holloway, the rest of the audience enjoyed the play. However, AEFH used WBY's reservations to take another shot at Fay: 'I think that Fay is tired of Building Fund & that made it drag. It went excellently with the Glasgow audience, stalls & all. That is the sort of case where I see the necessity of a strong stage-manager—I mean for performances, quite apart from production.'

[6] Walter Saville was a clerk with Cramer, Wood, & Co., who acted as the Abbey's ticket agents at 4 Westmoreland St. In her reply AEFH said, 'I know that Saville is a stick, my first interview was enough; but I had to go to Cramer & Wood because you told me that they already sold your tickets for the

*Waters*,[7] discussing the timing of the reorganization of the Company[8] and the arrangements for paying bonuses,[9] sending her a copy of his new book.[10]

NLI.

## To A. E. F. Horniman, [c. *30 November 1906*]

Mention in letter from AEFH, 3 December 1906.
A typed letter telling her there has been no open row and that he is quite hopeful about everything,[1] discussing the new schemes for development and a stage manager, suggesting that they may put on *The Heather Field*,[2] apologizing for the trouble over a copyright performance at the Abbey,[3] reporting JBY's views on Miss Darragh's acting,[4] mentioning that the

Molesworth Hall performances. I will on no account employ Fay again—he could not expect it.' On 16 Nov she had complained to Holloway (NLI) that she had 'received nothing from M^srs Cramer & Wood for six months' for the letting of the Abbey to other companies.

[7] AEFH replied that since WBY had referred to ' "Shadowy Waters" rehearsals' she supposed 'that that is to be put on soon'.

[8] The controversy over Letitia Darragh had brought home to WBY the need for a different kind of acting and production for his poetic plays, and it was also evident that the expanding theatre needed managerial and administrative skills superior to those possessed by W. G. Fay. AEFH agreed with this, but in her reply reminded him that there was 'no hurry about re-organisation, what is necessary to be done will gradually shew itself to you'.

[9] AEFH thought the 'bonus arrangement is quite right' on profits and on particular plays: 'What I objected to was any "*presents*" in the old way.'

[10] WBY had sent AEFH a presentation copy of *Poems, 1899–1905*, inscribed to 'To Miss Horniman from her friend the writer. Oct. 1906.' In thanking him for the book, she revealed that she 'had already given away one copy (in France) & now I've sent one to Ethel Burry in Natal'.

[1] WBY was keeping AEFH abreast of developments in the dispute with W. G. Fay, and she wrote that she 'gathered from your typed letter, which arrived on Saturday night, that there had been no open "row", & that you personally were quite hopeful about everything. The whole of your new schemes for development & a stage manager & everything else depend on one thing alone—who runs the show? Miss Allgood I know learned much on the tour, none of the rest condescended to do the same. Fay will use her to get rid of Miss Darragh if he can.'

[2] WBY had discussed the planned Abbey production of Edward Martyn's *The Heather Field*, which had been announced in the *Arrow* of 20 Oct (see p. 512, n. 4). AEFH opposed the production on a number of grounds: 'I'm sorry if you put on Heatherfield—it is dull, immoral & false to human facts of life & besides needs some actors who can look like gentlefolk. Where would you get the little boy?' In fact the play was not revived at the Abbey until April 1909.

[3] WBY had apparently defended himself against the difficulties that Fay had put in the way of a copyright reading of a play on mesmerism by Agnes Tobin, which was given at the Abbey in late September of this year. On 29 Sept Holloway heard that the play was 'not effective', and that the 'usual notice with guinea admission was placed outside the door during the performance'. AEFH assured WBY that she 'never thought that *you* had been troublesome about that copyright performance—I know quite well how messages are forgotten on purpose & Fay would not mind involving you & me in a quarrel to please the Markievitcsh people or anyone else he had a fancy for.'

[4] WBY had asked his father for his opinion of Letitia Darragh's acting and had evidently sent JBY's remarks on to AEFH. JBY had set out his views in a letter dated 'Saturday' (? 24 Nov 1906; NLI) 'not

Abbey dressing rooms are now inadequate,[5] telling her that he cannot accompany her to Algeria for the winter,[6] and discussing the takings over the previous week.[7]

NLI.

## To Katharine Tynan Hinkson, 1 December 1906

Nassau Hotel, | South Frederick Street, | DUBLIN.
1st Decr. 1906.

Dear Mrs. Hinkson,

Lolly has capitulated and has signed an Agreement giving me a veto.[1] They are to publish nothing I object to, and put in no illustrations I object

because I think my opinion of any importance, but because you asked for it'. He thought that 'in her present form she is a bad actress and the worst possible for your play. She is an actress born, an actress genius, possibly a great actress. But her present style is altogether too florid, what is called too stagy. She should not always be so intensive and so impressive—it is monotonous. There were moments when she reached extraordinary levels of passionate sincerity; let her keep these moments and let the rest be ordinary speech. She has wonderful transitions . . . in voice and gesture, and her lowest whisper must have been audible in every corner of the theatre, but in good acting as in good painting emphasis must be employed sparingly. Thrift is the great principle in style—as we all know, you especially.' JBY then turned to 'a delicate matter': 'she should cover up her neck more. Deirdre was not a Cleopatra. Altogether she should be gentler, *more cloistral* till the moment comes for passion and nature, that at any rate is the Irish idea of heroic womanhood.' He thought it 'unfortunate that Miss Darragh's acting "shows up" too glaringly the faults of the others—she has too much style. They hardly any. . . . I think Deirdre far the finest play you have written and *I think Miss Darragh the BEST PIECE OF LUCK yet come to you*—only, she must prune her luxuriance.' In her reply AEFH was unconvinced by this judgement: 'Your father's sentiments are much stronger than his critical faculty—he taught me this when he struck me dumb by his admiration for Moira Walker's (non-existent) figure, especially her (invisible) shoulders. If he liked Miss Darragh he would see no faults, I daresay that she has modified her performance, let it ripen in fact & would do it perfectly in a fortnight. But by that time the rest would be weary of their parts & are not artists enough to care to hide the fact.'

[5] AEFH replied that she was 'very sorry that there are difficulties about dressing-rooms. If things prosper we may need to spread a little further up the Lane as I fear that the annex walls would not bear another story. Soon you must have a man who will need a dressing-room to himself, either a stage-manager or a man for heroic parts.'

[6] AEFH was about to set out for an extended trip to Algeria, and had evidently invited WBY to accompany her—an offer he had declined. She replied: 'I'm sad that you are not to fight camels in Algeria. As I may start early on Dec 21st do try & let me see you first.' WBY was not to visit Algeria until early July 1930, when the boat bringing him home from Italy made a fleeting stop in Algiers.

[7] WBY had sent AEFH the receipts for the run of *Deirdre* and *The Mineral Workers*, which totalled £84 17s. 11d., including £8 13s. 3d. taken at the matinée on Saturday, 1 Dec. In her reply AEFH thought the 'improvement (even minus the matinée) in the week's takings is hopeful', but could not resist adding tartly that 'the difficulty will be to keep people's interest up when you put on long classical plays with dead fish in most of the roles'.

[1] This 'Agreement' was presumably the brief one drawn up by AE in consultation with Quinn (see p. 506, n. 2). ECY was confident that it gave her, not WBY, victory, and she informed Quinn on 25 Nov (NYPL) that he had 'signed it like a lamb'.

to. On Monday morning I shall get to work at your poems and they will begin printing at once. I would have written to you before, but I have had a desperate three months of it, writing for the theatre and doing its business. We are beginning to get audiences. Last Winter we played to almost empty houses. A sprinkling of people in Pit and stalls. Now, we have big Saturday audiences. Last Saturday we turned away people from all parts of the house. My Play "Deirdre," after leaving me doubtful for a little is now certainly a success.[2] It is my best Play, and the last half of it holds the audience in as strong a grip as does Kathleen ni Houlihan, which is prose, and therefore a far easier thing to write. The difficulties of holding an audience with verse are ten times greater than with the prose Play. Modern audience has lost the habit of careful listening. I think it is certainly my best dramatic poetry, and for the first time a Verse Play of mine is well played all round. I think the Irish accent in Blank verse is rather a shock to what whatever ordinary Theatre goers find their way to us, but they will get used to it. Miss Darragh, an Irish star on the English stage who is playing for us, says that our pit is a wonder; she never knew a pit listen to tragedy with such silent attention. I think that we are gradually working down through the noisy and hypercritical semi-political groups to a genuine public opinion, which is sympathetic. I am rather repentant over something I wrote to you, I think, about Ella Young's poetry. I took up the book the other day, and found a charming little song, in which a child, imitating somebody I daresay in Stevenson's child's garden, or whatever he called it, wonders if the moon is cold in the sky. I have not seen the book since, but that is really a poetical idea.[3] I have been reading your old letter and I agree with what you say about Nora Chesson, and the way our Irish Fairyland came to spoil her work, but there is one exception. There are a couple of lovely verses

[2] Holloway's diary on this day (NLI) confirms WBY's confidence. When he arrived for the evening performance, Henderson told him that 'the matinee was a success—over £9 was taken at the doors & that last night was the best receipts of the week.... To-night the pit was full & the balcony & stalls fairly sprinkled. The audience was most appreciative, & both pieces were excellently played.' He remarked that *Deirdre* was 'listened to in deathlike silence, & the applause was generous & sincere at the end'.

[3] On 1 Sept WBY had mentioned Ella Young as one of a 'little group [who] are always imitative and subjective and sentimental' and without genuine inspiration (see p. 488). Her poem 'Bed-Time', which appeared in her collection *Poems*, published this year by Tower Press booklets, begins (36): 'At night when I am tired of play | The sun shuts up its house of gold, | And all the stars that sleep by day | Steal out like sheep that leave their field | O little moon, so far away | In the dark sky, are you a-cold?' Robert Louis Stevenson had published *A Child's Garden of Verses* in 1883, and Miss Young's poem may have reminded WBY of 'Escape at Bedtime' included in it.

inspired by it in the King of Ireland's son.[4] I am writing to Bullen about Innocencies.[5]

Yrs ever
W B Yeats

TLS Harvard, with envelope addressed to Pine Cottage, Blechingley, Surrey, redirected to 9 Longfield Road, Ealing, postmark 'DUBLIN DEC 3 06'. Partly in Wade, 482–3.

## To the Directors of National Theatre Society, 2 December [1906]

Dec 2 1907[1]

The National Theatre Society has reached a stage in its development which makes some change necessary. This has partly come from increasing work making it more and more hard for two or three people to do all the work of management and teaching, but to a still greater extent from the necessity of enlarging the capacities of the Company and increasing the number and types of plays available for performance, and of training our audience to accept many different forms of art. At the present moment the theatre is extremely accomplished in the performance of Irish peasant comedy and in nothing else. It cannot run indefinitely on peasant comedy for to do that

---

[4] The poet and novelist Nora Chesson, née Hopper (1871–1906), had died on 14 Apr of this year, leaving an invalid husband and three small children. KT's letter is now lost, but she had always had reservations about her (see I. 423–7). Her poem 'The King of Ireland's Son' was first published in *Under Quicken Boughs* (1896), but WBY is more likely to be thinking of the lines which appeared in her prose sketch 'Daluan' in *Ballads in Prose* (1894), and which he quoted in a note in *A Treasury of Irish Poetry* (1900): 'I got *Ballads in Prose* when it came out . . . and it haunted me as few new books have ever haunted me, for it spoke in strange wayward stories and birdlike little verses of things and of persons I remembered or had dreamed of. . . . Even now, when the first enchantment is gone . . . I cannot go by certain brown bogs covered with white tufts of bog-cotton . . . without remembering the verses her Duluan—a kind of Irish Pan—sings among the bogs; and when once I remember them, they run in my head for hours—

> All the way to Tir na n'Og are many roads that run,
> But the darkest road is trodden by the King of Ireland's son.
> The world wears on to sundown, and love is lost and won,
> But he recks not of loss or gain, the King of Ireland's son.
> He follows on for ever, when all your chase is done,
> He follows after shadows—the King of Ireland's son.'

[5] Bullen was the publisher of KT's *Innocencies* (see p. 484, n. 3), and WBY wanted to ask him for permission to reprint four poems from it in his Dun Emer selection: 'An Old Song Re-sung', 'Nymphs', 'Blessings', and 'The Doves'.

[1] This memorandum, although dated 1907, was written on 2 Dec 1906. A copy in the Synge papers at TCD lacks the emendations WBY made to the present version.

will be to tire its audiences out and to come to an end for lack of plays. The popularity of the Theatre at this moment depends upon two writers Mr Boyle and Lady Gregory; I do not say that individual plays by other writers have not assisted them but these are the only two writers who can be counted upon to draw audiences. There is no indication of their creating successors and in all probability the next dramatic imagination will be a complete contrast, for the imagination works far more by reaction than imitation. If they produce imitators the imitators will be bad. Ireland is not sufficiently large sufficiently well educated to supply a theatre of one specialized activity with plays or an audience for them. On the other hand my work will hardly draw large audiences for a considerable time, and though verse drama might well create a school of very varied temperament there is certainly no sign of another verse dramatist. Just in so far as the Theatre widens its capacities of performance, will it appeal to different temperaments, and multiply its chances of creating writers. The natural means for it to do this is to perform selections from foreign masterpieces chosen as much for a means of training as for anything else, and to add to its players and if necessary to its teachers as opportunity offers. We should keep before our minds the final object which is to create in this country a National Theatre something after the Continental pattern. This Theatre should be capable of showing its audience examples of all great schools of drama. It was of a Theatre of this kind that I was thinking when I said in the first number of the Arrow that we could not accomplish our work under ten years.[2] Such a National Theatre would perforce keep in mind its educational as well as its artistic side. To be artistically noble it will have to be the acknowledged centre for some kind of art which no other Theatre in the world has in the same perfection. This art would necessarily be the representation of plays full of Irish characteristics, of plays that cannot be performed except by players who are constantly observing Irish people and things. It might very well happen also that a beautiful representation of plays in verse would be an art it had the mastery of, but this must depend on individuals, there is nothing in the conditions to bring it about of necessity. Such a Theatre must however if it is to do the educational work of a National Theatre be prepared to perform even though others can perform them better representative plays of all great schools. It would necessarily look to a National endowment to supply it with resources before its work could be in any way completed upon all sides. If however we are

---

[2] In the first number of the *Arrow*, which had appeared on 20 Oct 1906, WBY had written that as they wished 'our work to be full of the life of this country our stage manager has almost always to train our actors from the beginning, always so in the case of peasant plays, and this makes the building up of a theatre like ours the work of years. We are now fairly satisfied with the representation of peasant life, and we can afford to give the greater part of our attention to other expressions of our art and of our life.'

working towards this end we must keep it in mind and see that our activities lead it towards it however slowly.

I now come to the immediate future, to the next step, or steps. The whole Theatre at this moment depends upon its executive side upon one overworked man, and upon a group of players who are necessarily and must necessarily so long as the Theatre remains as it is be chosen for their capacity in a single highly specialized form of work. Every course I should suggest will be founded therefore upon the necessity of adding other forms of personality and activity.

(1)   The natural course as it will occur to the mind of an ordinary business man is to get more capital and to engage some actor or actors whose imaginations will express themselves in other forms of work with the same ease and abundance with which W Fay's imagination expresses itself in comedy. He is not a romantic actor, he is not a tragic actor, he is a very clever man and can do not badly many things that are not his natural work, but the other side of the Theatre—I am trying to speak as the hypothetical business man—requires the entire time and thought of a different sort of actor or teacher. We might say to this business man should he come, or to Miss Horniman let us say if she were to find him, "We only understand the Irish comedy; there we can have no interference; Mr Yeats must of course retain the rights natural to the only verse writer in the Theatre over the production of work in verse. As to these things we want the principles of Samhain 1904,[3] but as to the rest we are ready to accept any efficient professional help that can be found. We are ready to employ any efficient teachers you can find us; our comedy people must be properly paid, but if you want to develop the Theatre on the other side and we can agree on some scheme of work that is educational or sufficiently educational not to sink us below a Continental Municipal Theatre, why you are our benefactor and may do what you like. Our interest is to preserve the Irish base, and that is our whole interest". I dont know whether Miss Horniman would be willing or able to supply this capital but if she were or if she be willing to supply it at some future time, I can imagine that she would engage some old actor, if Hermann Vezin were a little younger he would serve

---

[3] The 1904 number of *Samhain*, published to coincide with the opening of the Abbey Theatre, deals more extensively than any of the other issues of the magazine with the principles behind the INTS, but WBY is thinking particularly of his article 'The Play, the Player, and the Scene' (Expl, 164–80), expressly commissioned from him by AEFH 'to go more into detail as to my own plans and hopes than I have done before'. The article set out three principles: (1) that the Abbey plays 'must be literature or written in the spirit of literature', (2) that such a drama would require 'an appropriate stage management', and (3) that the new Theatre 'must have a new kind of scenic art'.

her turn[4] and put him in charge of the non Irish work or of some portion of the non Irish work, legendary plays for instance which does not require Irish knowledge. She would then select or rather this man would select, one or two young actors and would set out to train these and such of our own people as did not desire to specialize for comedy of Irish life only, for the production of representative masterpieces. Both William Fay and this hypothetical man would have their time entirely occupied without interfering with each other for such a Theatre would of course play continuously.[5] I do not pretend that this scheme is practical in its details. I give the details to define the scheme not to show its working. The scheme in essence simply would be more capital, new actors, selected from the professional Theatre to stiffen our own company with non comedy elements, and some mind in control of the new element to which romance and tragedy are a natural means of expression. It is hardly necessary to add that such a theatre would probably require a paid managing Director to correlate all its activities. It would be expensive but not too expensive if Miss Horniman desired it and if our own audiences go on improving for a little while. I do not however think that Miss Horniman would be ready for a scheme of this kind at the present moment. I can see William Fay's face as he reads this sentence. It will brighten like the face of a certain old Fenian when Mrs Mac Bride's Italian revolutionist wound up a detailed project for a rising in Connacht with the sentence "I see no chance of success before this course."[6] I think however that this scheme will come of itself in course of time. We will want more capital, we will get it from some quarter, it is obviously artificial to confine our non Irish work to actors of Irish birth. It will grow more absurd as time passes; and it becomes possible to pay at ordinary rates we shall be

---

[4] Hermann Vezin (1829–1910) was born in Philadelphia, and destined for the law, but abandoned this career owing to bad eyesight and, against his father's wishes, went to London where Charles Kean gave him a start in a pantomime company. He made his first appearance in London at the Princess's Theatre, under the management of Kean, in 1852, and thereafter became a prolific actor in the provinces and in London, particularly noted for his Shakespearian roles, and for creating in 1876 the part of Dan'l Druce in Gilbert's play of the same name. He was famous for his speed in delivering Shakespearian verse, and his rapid, crisp, and incisive articulation. In later life he became a teacher of elocution, and in February 1901 had vehemently opposed WBY's theories of verse-speaking (see III. 41), although earlier this year, as the *Stage* reported on 7 June (3), he had recited at a concert with Anna Mather, whom WBY had frequently used to illustrate his lectures on speaking to the psaltery. His wife committed suicide in April 1902, but he kept acting to the end of his life, and shortly before his death played old Rowley in Tree's revival of Sheridan's *The School for Scandal*. Frank Fay, as he told WBY on 31 July 1901 (NLI), admired Vezin as belonging to what he termed 'the old school', actors who gained their effects though oratory and declamation: 'With them, it is not so much what they do as what they say that is of importance.'

[5] Currently the Abbey was played on Saturday nights and for the following week when they had a new production, in a season that extended from October to April.

[6] The old Fenian was presumably John O'Leary (1830–1907; I. 503) and the Italian revolutionist was Amilcare Cipriani (see pp. 11–12).

more inclined to take the best available talent, it will be more and more impossible for one man to do all the teaching.

(2)   This larger scheme is certainly impossible for the present and the consideration of it is not vital at the moment. But a smaller scheme which is a gradual development towards it in all probability is pressing. William Fay must be freed from all work except his artistic work, that the comedies may be as fine as possible, instead of consciously enlarging our work which we cannot do without more capital than we are likely to get, we must perfect what we have and that is principally comedy, and be content to add other elements very slowly. We must see that William Fay's own work which should be the chief attraction of all our comedies, is given the opportunity to develop. If he has to do the work of <an Assistant> Stage Manager as well as that of a producer and actor, in a years time people will begin to talk of the monotony of his acting. He will be satisfied to express his personality instead of creating self consistent personalities & the teaching will grow careless. <He will have less and less time for teaching.> The business side of the Theatre and the non artistic side of the stage work must be put into other hands. This will ensure the efficiency of the comedy. I must ask for certain measures to <ensure> improve the efficiency of the other side of the work. Frank Fay is a born teacher of elocution up to a certain point, but people come from his hands certainly with great clearness of elocution, with a fine feeling for both line and passage as units of sound with a sufficient though less infallible sense of accent, but without passion without expression, either in voice or gesture. William Fay has in comedy a most admirable understanding of gesture <and of course of acting> & expression, but his ear for verse is very defective, only experiment can say whether the two men together can teach verse speaking. I am doubtful, for verse expression is essentially different from prose expression. Something can be done I know. If William Fay were to take in hand let us say Miss Allgood he would certainly make her a useful speaker of verse, but I doubt if any combination of two contrary talents can be relied upon to create fine speakers of verse. I hope that it may be possible by some such plan as the suggested elocution classes to make an annual visit of Mrs Emery to Dublin for teaching purposes, self supporting. I am most anxious that my work shall not cost the Theatre more than it is worth to them in the long run. I must however ask more than this. The verse speaking at the Theatre through the exclusive development of the comedy side has not improved. Maire Walker had no passion or power of characterization in verse, but she had considerable rather delicate expressiveness. <She also alone among the women who have played for us in verse had the tragic note.> Miss Garvey was a verse speaker of more feeling, even with some slight touch of passion, though a very narrow range. Since they have gone there has been no good speaking of

verse among the women of the company. I do not regret Starkie though he could get through a quiet passage creditably, but what is more serious is that Mac Donald has not advanced upon his performance at the opening of the Theatre. I got Power to speak a few lines to me the other day, and I saw that he could not be relied on to speak a passage with force and simplicity. Frank Fay is always beautiful to listen to, but he is not improving, I am not quite sure that he is as good as he was. I do not want to add acting in the sense of movement as he thinks, but I have always asked for a degree of expressiveness in voice, not less but more than that required for prose drama. From the first day of the Theatre I have known that it is almost impossible for us to find a passionate woman actress in Catholic Ireland. I remember saying that to somebody when we were playing in Molesworth Hall. I must therefore have the right to bring in a player or players from without when I can do so without burdening the finances of the Company more than my work is worth. To do this it will be necessary that he or she sometimes play in other work than mine. I mean that my work may not in its present immaturity and in the immaturity of our audiences be able to be self supporting. For instance we might find at some future time that the Vikings of Heligoland, I merely give it as an illustration, might succeed with our audience, and make it profitable to bring in a player who would enable me to get a competent performance of some play of mine.[7] The company would not lose by this as the other work chosen would necessarily be chosen from its possible popularity or from some other definite value to the company. In this scheme everything remains as at present, except that some experienced man is engaged to take non artistic work off Fay's shoulders, and Miss Darragh or Mrs Emery or some equivalent is brought in occasionally and some foreign masterpiece chosen. Some re-arrangement of dressing rooms is implied.

W.B.Y.

TD NLI.

## To John Millington Synge, [2 December 1906]

PRIVATE I have made number 1 proposal with the following private knowledge.

---

[7] *The Vikings of Helgoland* was one of the few Ibsen plays of which WBY approved (see III. 326–7, 352–3), but it was never produced at the Abbey Theatre.

Miss Horniman I know has always had before her the German municipal Theatre as an ideal.[1] She has stated to one or two people and almost in so many words to myself, that she has £25,000 for the development of the Company under certain circumstances.[2] She has also stated to one or two people that if the company goes on on its present lines she will not continue the subsidy longer than the patent period.[3] In four years and a half we shall therefore very possibly find ourselves face to face with the necessity of a new application possibly seriously opposed for a renewal of the Patent, and with neither Subsidy or Theatre. In fact I dont see how we can apply for a renewal of the Patent without her co-operation. It is possible that she might agree, though stopping the subsidy, to allow us free use of the Theatre. It would be her interest to do so or at any rate her interest if we did not require a too constant use of the Theatre, as the value of her property depends on the Patent to some extent. But considering how little she thinks of her interest in comparison to her feelings the position is one of the greatest possible peril. We might hire the Theatre but I know no Theatre in any English speaking country which is able to consistently perform intellectual work. Every English and American dramatic critic of standing has claimed that a conditional subsidy is necessary to keep intellectual work on the stage. But subsidy or no subsidy I cannot at this moment think of a Patent which depends upon friendly working as in other than extreme danger if we permanently quarrel with her. The scheme marked Number 2 will I believe keep her for a time friendly for the appointment of a stage manager of the kind I suggest has been her one condition. I believe that I have it in writing that she would use the £25,000 for our English and presumably our American tours if we had a permanent Stage Manager, and I know that I have it in writing that she is prepared to leave William Fay producer (we owe this to Miss Darragh's friendliness as she has insisted in talking to Miss Horniman on Fay's paramount

---

[1] AEFH had been introduced to drama by her German governess, who told her of the central role played by municipal theatres in German towns, and she paid frequent visits to Germany to attend plays at such theatres. In August and September of this year she had seen a number of plays and operas in Bayreuth, Dresden, and Prague, and commended the taste and professionalism of their productions (see p. 481, n. 4).

[2] The £25,000 was the legacy from AEFH's father (see pp. 386, n. 1, 425, n. 6), and her shares in the Hudson Bay Company and the Canadian Pacific Railway were rising sharply at this time.

[3] As early as 16 July of this year, AEFH told WBY (NLI) that she had 'completely lost all confidence in the future of the company as at present constituted', and, although she agreed to continue the subsidy while playing no role in the running of the Abbey, her carping continued and on 17 Jan 1907 she was to warn him (NLI) that after 'the Patent is up any further application would be ridiculous unless we had some real success to show behind us.... No one could expect me to continue the subsidy uselessly after four years more.'

importance).[4] It possesses the disadvantage that it will leave the National Theatre Society many opportunities for Miss Horniman to quarrel with it; every tour would be an opportunity. She is now very anti-Irish. Number 1 proposal should be considered in connection with the possibility of securing support granted to us with proper legal safeguards for a number of years. I am supposing that the other element if it came into the company would insist upon a period of time during which the arrangement was to hold good. Whatever man she in consultation with us put in control of the non-Irish work, would necessarily come to us for a lesser income because a permanent income than he was getting from the existing Theatres. After a possible probationary period or with some substantial penalty for breach of contract he would necessarily expect a legal guarantee of some sort. I mean that we have received a guarantee that she will go on with her payment for four years [and] a half. The new element would require a similar guarantee. I certainly would not be prepared to go in for it unless I could say "we have now given you your full desire, You have in control of each department the most competent people obtainable. In return for that we require the certainty that the scheme shall be fairly tried for so many years."

W.B.Y.

TL TCD.

## Lady Gregory to the Directors of the National Theatre Society, 6 December [1906]

Dec 6 About a week ago Yeats asked me to give him a free hand in making some proposals to Miss Horniman. He said it was of vital importance to do so at once, as Miss Darragh had said we should lose the subsidy at the end of four years unless we took some such course, and that her own approaching termination of engagement would go against us very much with Miss Horniman. Miss Darragh had suggested when she came to Coole last summer that she herself should practically 'Run' the company for a

---

[4] As Letitia Darragh had explained in her letter of 22 Sept (see p. 499), she was taking some trouble to temper AEFH's growing displeasure with the Abbey Theatre and W. G. Fay: 'Now as to Miss Horniman—she lunched with me on Tuesday & in her own words burst into song from 1.30 to 5. So I listened & said about 6 sentences which resulted in her asking me to go and see her on Monday to meet a Miss Spencer who would tell me more grievances etc. She is dining here on Thursday so you see I am paying her all those ridiculous little attentions which she values so much and which she has firmly fixed in her mind none of the Irish Theatre have paid her.... The mistake has been not to pay her more attention in the business point of view answering her letters, consulting her etc. In fact a little tact & diplomacy from Fay but now of course nothing he would or could do would alter things till he takes *apparently* a back seat ... you know I think if you had an enterprising clever American manager who ran the whole thing & got it into ship shape a man who would put money into it arrange everything & yet be clever enough to let you all have your way as to the plays & stage etc it would be so much better.'

while, bringing over friends of her own to act with our actors, and using tours and advertisements largely. This we had refused to accept. She now suggested that Hermann Vezin should be put in permanent charge of its non peasant side bringing in what actors were necessary and that the work of the Company should be considerably widened.

I refused to consent to this idea, and in talking things over with Yeats we arrived at a practical agreement, at least I think we have done so. I asked him to write down his original scheme and his present one. My comments or reasons for resistance are these:

1)    Miss Horniman has not enough money if she had the desire to carry out so large and expensive a scheme, as that of putting Vezin in charge and bringing in other English actors of repute. If however we admitted the principle of someone from without being put in charge of one side of the work, she might probably send some nominee who would come for a comparatively small salary, some actor or actress. Such a person might have quite different ideas from those 'laid down by Mr Yeats in Samhain and elsewhere' & which we have been trying to look out and might also probably think more of showy parts for him or herself than of the ultimate good of the work. Her nominee might soon tire of Irish audiences, and would, with Miss Horniman, wish for tours. Verse not bring[ing] an easy success would probably be put aside for more popular plays with a tragic or melodramatic side to balance the comedies, and the distinction of our work would be lost.

The verse work was put aside last spring for the tour, and but for my opposition another London tour was to have been arranged in which verse was to be dropped altogether.

(2)    I am against the taking up of too many types of play. We have already decided on doing Greek and other masterpieces. I would choose these as a part of our scheme of development. We have acted Moliere because a part of our comedy is influenced by him, and I would have some Greek plays because their performance will help to an understanding of Yeats work. Ibsen's heroic plays are not far outside our limits but I would not have his social plays, or any drawing room plays that we know of at present, for they have been better done in England than we can hope to do them, and there is already a reaction beginning against them in England. I may have been wrong in pressing the Heather Field, but it is anyhow of our own country and gets some distinctive quality from that. Racine may also come into our scheme, but while gradually increasing the number of foreign plays I would limit the type. We are only sure of four years in which to complete our experiments, and this is little enough time in which to perfect two forms, the peasant and the poetic or heroic play.

(3)    I entirely agree that an Assistant Stage Manager (independent of Fay) is wanted to take charge of all mechanical and business parts of the work. If we had money enough we should engage one at once. As it is we must wait and see if Miss Horniman is inclined to pay for one, and on what terms.

(4)   I agree that Yeats should from time to time and for fixed periods bring in such players as he thinks necessary for his own work on the condition (that of not putting the Company to undue expense) he mentions. The right of first production of Yeats work is our chief distinction, and we must do our utmost for its success. I do not think a player should be brought in for work outside his without a decision of the Directors.

(5)   My own plan or idea, or hope is, to develop the beautiful speaking of verse, in which we have practically the field to ourselves, and had a little time ago made a considerable advance. We lost ground through the split, which took away the Walkers and Miss Garvey, and through the neglect of verse during the English tour. We have Frank Fay as a speaker and voice producer as our foundation, but he cant get on very far without more material to work upon. I propose that Mrs Emery who has done so much to work out Yeats theories, should be employed, if she will come, for a month or six weeks to hold classes in verse speaking together with Fay, and to be carried on by him. This should bring in new voices and give us the opportunity of choosing from among them.

Other teachers might be brought in from time to time, and these teachers might take parts while with us, if thought desirable, as a part of their teaching. I think Yeats agrees with me on these points.

AG

TS Doc Berg.

## To A. E. F. Horniman, [c. 9 December 1906]

Mention in letter from AEFH, 10 December 1906.
Discussing Abbey politics,[1] criticizing O'Rourke's acting in *The Canavans*,[2] and telling her that the Theatre of Ireland is producing Act IV of *Brand*.[3]

NLI.

[1] WBY had evidently discussed the problems in trying to reorganize the Abbey Company, and AEFH lost no time in reminding him that the 'root of the matter is what I have often said—these people have been so flattered by politicians that they are demoralised & no Art flatters. This applies to both Snarlers & Sulkers who have both been fed on flattery ceaselessly by politicians.'

[2] *The Canavans* was produced with *The Shadowy Waters* from 8 to 15 Dec, and WBY had criticized O'Rourke's performance as Anthony Canavan, the hero's troublesome brother. In her reply AEFH said, 'I don't believe that O'Rourke will ever be of much good even if he does learn to use his nose properly & it is a great pity that The Canavans had to suffer. When you revive the play I hope that you will be able to put in someone else.' In his report on the first night of the show Holloway also noted that 'J. A. O'Rourke's way of speaking is terribly monotonous & wearies the ear after a while', and the *Freeman's Journal* of 10 Dec (10) commented that 'Mr. J. A. O'Rourke is a little too mechanical in demeanour and monotonous in expression, which is a pity, for he evidently has a keen sense of humour'.

[3] In a letter of late October (NLI) AEFH had asked whether Vera Esposito was rejoining the Company (see p. 511) and WBY had evidently replied that she was performing in the Theatre of

# To A. E. F. Horniman, [10 December 1906]

Nassau Hotel | South Fredrick St | Dublin.

My dear Miss Horniman: This is to ask you to go to Woburn Buildings & find there a volume of a several volume Chaucer, which contains a 'glossary.' It is a large dark volume.[1] The lender Clement Shorter, 16 Marlborough Place, Marlborough Road, wants it back.[2] I know this is a big trouble but I dont like leaving it until next week. I send my keys which please return or I shall be shut out on Monday when I expect to arrive (I shall dine with you Monday if I may). Miss Darragh considers 'Shadowy Waters' a great success—her friends are delighted & are returning—or some of them—to see it again. She was admirable & most moving & charming. The papers, which Henderson will have sent you, are better than I expected. The newspaper critics are slow to care for work that does not appeal to the ordinary interests. The Freeman man—if as I think it was Bradyn himself—came in after my play was over & reviewed it from the acting edition.[3] I got the impression I got from Dierdre's first night of a fair success which will take time to grow but Miss Darragh got the impression

---

Ireland's production of the fourth act of Ibsen's *Brand*. Although AEFH was an admirer of Ibsen, she was contemptuous of this initiative: 'Brand is trying even with a highly trained company & a large stage, it is so long that the necessary cuts leave it only a succession of scraps. But I suppose that the Columbines did only the bit about the baby-clothes; that is not even one complete act or scene even.'

[1] This was volume VI of *The Complete Works of Geoffrey Chaucer*, edited by Walter W. Skeat and issued in dark blue cloth by the Clarendon Press in 1894. Initially the final volume in the set, it contains a general introduction but is mainly taken up with a glossary (1–358), followed by a series of indexes. WBY had presumably borrowed it while reading the Kelmscott Chaucer (see pp. 129–30, 135, 139–40), which contained no glossary.

[2] Clement King Shorter (1857–1926), editor and journalist, was the biographer of the Brontës, Mrs Gaskell, and others. Editor of the *Illustrated London News* from 1891 to 1900, he was the founder editor of the *Sphere* (1900) and the *Tatler* (1903). In 1896 he had married Dora Sigerson (1866–1918), Irish poet and daughter of the Dublin physician and man of letters George Sigerson, and WBY was a frequent dinner guest.

[3] As with previous productions of the play (see III. 540), the critics found *The Shadowy Waters* unsuitable for the stage. William Henry Brayden (1865–1933) had been editor of the *Freeman's Journal* from 1892, and in April 1903 described WBY as 'a dangerous man' (see III. 342). Much of the paper's unsigned review on 10 Dec (10) could have been written from the book alone, but concludes with comments on the acting in this particular performance: 'Miss Darragh is a stately figure, who speaks fine verse with fitting exaltation of style, and her Dectora was an impressive creature. Mr. F. J. Fay spoke his lines with real poetic feeling. His Forgael was as dreamy and, indeed, as aery as the poet willed. Mr. Arthur Sinclair tried to enliven Aibric, but even the sailor who panted for the skin of all could not pull down the piece from the clouds. A thing of beauty it is, but not a play.' Indeed, the notice was largely taken up with variations on this last theme, arguing that WBY was so much the poet 'that one may doubt ... whether he will ever become a genuine playwright. ... Mr. Yeats will scarcely condescend to poor human nature, and thereby this beautiful fantasy is heard without emotion on the stage. His people do not come forth from the side wings, but from other worlds; they cannot live in an atmosphere of the earth, earthy; their language is not ours.' While conceding that 'Mr. Yeats plays his fancy with exquisite delicacy', and that the elements of the play constituted 'a picture painted in colours ethereal, yet intense', the reviewer insisted that they were 'pervaded with a cool warmth which cannot stir the blood,

of a <great success> triumph. I hope she is right. I know one thing I have done all I can with the play & think it will make its way as Maeterlinck has done.[4]

Yrs ev
W B Yeats

ALS Rylands. Marked in AEFH's hand 'Dec 10th/06'.

## To Clement Shorter, [*10 December 1906*]

Nassau Hotel | South Fredrick St | Dublin.

My dear Shorter: your book is in London & I have sent my keys to a friend & asked her to send it to you if she can find it. In any case I get back next week. I must apologize for not having written before but I have been very busy with the theatre—a new play was produced last Saturday & I have got desperate about my correspondence. I am very sorry about the book.

We have trebled our audience here and are paying our way—even without our subsidy—but must increase salaries. We play every Saturday night & in addition a week whenever we have a production.

Yrs ev
W B Yeats

ALS BL.

but must heat the imagination. The picturesqueness of the situation . . . the uncommon imagery, the harmony of expression, the deep sway of emotion, make one wish to read the ideal love poem alone; but it is devoid of that kind of action and exhibition of character we seek upon the boards, and thus performed it is, at best, a costume recital. As such the programme had high merits.' The Dublin *Daily Express* of 10 Dec agreed (6) that the play had 'great literary merit, but for stage representation it lacks dramatic body and strength', and commented that if it 'did not actually bore, it went pretty nigh to bewildering those who listened to it'. *Sinn Fein* of 15 Dec was characteristically more terse in its dismissal (3) of both '*The Shadowy Waters* by Mr. W. B. Yeats, and *The Canavans* by Lady Gregory': 'The first-named is described as "a play in verse," and the second as "a comedy in three acts." It was, however, somewhat difficult at times to discover the "play" in the first item, or the "comedy" in the second.'

[4] As one of the most symbolist of WBY's plays, even after the latest revisions, *The Shadowy Waters* had a good deal in common with Villiers de l'Isle Adam's *Axël*, and with the plays of the Belgian symbolist Maurice Maeterlinck (see p. 77), whom in 1897 WBY had hailed as belonging to the same movement: 'M. Maeterlinck has called himself a disciple of Villiers de L'Isle Adam . . . but he has carried his master's revolt farther than his master, and made his persons shadows and cries' (*UP* II. 52).

# *To A. E. F. Horniman,* [c. *11 December 1906*]

Mention in letter from AEFH, 12 December 1906.

Asking if she is 'out' with him,[1] discussing the prospect of the Company touring,[2] evidently speculating on the possibility of Mrs Pat Campbell playing Deirdre,[3] speaking of the sensation made by Miss Darragh's dress in *Deirdre*,[4] telling her that W. J. Lawrence, the critic of the Abbey, was

---

[1] In her letter of 10 Dec (see p. 536) AEFH had accused WBY of snubbing her and warned him that when he returned 'I must have a number of questions answered, I'll remove all reading matter from within reach & you will have to give me your full attention whether you are bored or no. You have been too much petted of late years until you have taken to use that crushed pained & distressed look of misery as a means of terrorising Lady Gregory & me whenever we object to anything. . . . you might remember that continual snubbings when kindly feelings are expressed may in time not only stop their expression but blunt their vitality or even at length destroy them. Yet, as I ought to know well, writing (& even speaking) makes no difference to you when you wish to abstract yourself from life, as I'm not at all cross & trying not to be sad & I certainly will not worry you, for I have my own dignity to consider.' On receiving WBY's complaint about this, she replied on 12 Dec: 'I'm so "out" with you for a traditional reason; our interests are like Tweedledee & Tweedledum & they fought a renowned battle.'

[2] AEFH replied that while she would do nothing to prevent the Abbey touring, she would 'have nothing to do with it until I feel assured that it will not damage us'.

[3] The recent production of *Deirdre* had evidently led WBY to broach the possibility of Mrs Pat Campbell acting the title role, and in her reply AEFH reminded him that she had 'done all I could to urge that Mrs Pat Campbell should have Deirdre & even now I consider that if she would still take the play that any conditions she might offer should be accepted. My point of view being that the sacrifice of one play of yours would be an enormous gain to the whole scheme.'

[4] Miss Darragh had played Deirdre in what a number of the audience and reviewers considered too low cut a dress, but in her reply AEFH was suspicious and contemptuous of this prudishness: 'Now don't mistake the real cause of the out-cry against Miss Darragh's dress. This is touching loyalty on the part of Moira Walker's admirers—her skinny chest & shoulders are impossible for exhibition & so they want to cover up everyone elses!' Dublin's objections to Miss Darragh were in part based on the fact that she had replaced local actresses and on 27 Nov Holloway told Henderson (NLI) that it was 'a big mistake to get Miss Darragh to play Deirdre when such as Miss Walker could be had in Dublin.' But Miss Darragh's décolleté was the focus of a more general fear of sexuality, and it was felt that WBY's version of the legend was too sensuous. On 1 Dec *Sinn Fein* compared the play unfavourably on these grounds with AE's *Deirdre*, and, after seeing the play, Lawrence (who also 'fancied he would like Miss Walker better in the part') told Holloway that 'some of Yeats' lines [were] not too nice in tone'. Holloway himself complained (NLI) that WBY's 'thoughts got entangled in the bed curtains of a bridal chamber until the play was fairly strangled in bed clothes talk. This sort of thing grates on the ear, especially when put into the mouth of women! Clean love-talk makes good poetry as well as the sort of thing talked by Deirdre, Concobar, & the First Musician in Yeats' play!'

hissed by the audience,[5] and informing her that there are 'complaints' about Fay's carelessness in acting.[6]

NLI.

## To Florence Farr, [c. 12 December 1906]

My dear Friend: just a word to say we had a success with 'Shadowy Waters' on Saturday—I am very busy working again on 'Deirdre' Etc but will write in a day or two. I cross over early next week.

I was delighted with the New Version of Shadowy Waters on the stage— I thought that granted interest in the subject matter I could not have made it more perfect. Miss [Darragh] was fine & quite different from you (Lady Gregory sighs for you in the part she says) passionate & human where you were lofty & divine—Fay was fine as Forgael though a little too frenzied.[1]

---

[5] The Belfast-born drama critic William John Lawrence (1862–1940) had attracted a good deal of opprobrium in Dublin as a result of a violent attack on WBY and the Abbey following Colum's lecture on 'Our National Theatre' to the NLS on 10 Dec. Even Lawrence's great friend Joseph Holloway described his onslaught (NLI) as 'a slashing, intemperate speech': 'he canonized the poet by styling him "St Yeats", attacked Miss Darragh's style of acting as "watered down Bernhardt", objected to the low-necked costume she wore as Deirdre . . . spoke of *The Canavans* as "the first pantomime of the season" & generally speaking ran amok of the Irish theatre.' By contrast, WBY's 'fine, well reasoned reply in the defence of the policy of the National Theatre movement wiped the floor with the detractors, & said that the limitation to Irish subject matter in their plays was necessary for the present. So long as plays dealt with Ireland they had a chance of getting them better acted than they could be acted anywhere else. The end, if they succeeded, would be the creation of a theatre in Dublin like the municipal theatres in Germany, where all plays could be produced.' On 13 Dec Holloway met Miss Garvey, who thought 'Lawrence's remarks were in very bad taste', but that WBY's speech 'was great', and the following day another of his friends complained that Lawrence had been 'intemperate' because those 'behind him goaded him on, and he got his temper up'. A tight-lipped report in the *Irish Independent* of 11 Dec (6) noted that Lawrence's intervention 'was not received with unanimous approval', and gave more space to WBY's speech. AEFH was not unhappy to hear of Lawrence's discomfort at the Abbey, commenting in her reply that he was 'evidently jealous of you & your efforts & I am delighted that he was hissed'.

[6] AEFH replied that she had 'never hesitated in my opinion that Fay has a genius for acting, but his carelessness I remarked on to you when I saw him for the first time & did not hear enough of what he said in "Twenty-five" to gather the meaning although I sat in the second row. You say that there are already "complaints" so I suppose that things are beginning to be noticed more carefully. What would be passed over & forgiven in beginners cannot be excused now.'

[1] FF had taken the role of Dectora in her own production of the old version of *The Shadowy Waters* in July 1905 (see pp. 126, 133). The Dublin press had been complimentary about Letitia Darragh's and Frank Fay's acting in the new production, although reviewers stressed her decorum and elocution rather than her human passion. Apart from the *Freeman's Journal*'s description of her as 'a stately figure, who speaks fine verse with fitting exaltation of style' (see p. 537, n. 3), the Dublin *Daily Express* reported on 10 Dec that she 'made a dignified Queen, and she spoke her lines with faultless elocution', and on the same day the *Irish Times* noted (8) that 'Mr F. J. Fay and Miss Darragh . . . gave an excellent rendering of the verse'. On 12 Dec Holloway commented (NLI) that 'Miss Darragh's Dectora was dignified & queenly in bearing, & despite her mannerism of extending her arms outward with palm of hands downwards, (a Sarah Bernhardt trick) she was often very graceful & imposing in her attitude.' None of

The scenery was magnificent—an actor from the Cyril Maude Company says it was the most wonderful stage scene he ever saw[2]—it was like the boat of Osirus—[3]

Yrs ev

W B Yeats

ALS Texas.

## To Lady Gregory, [20 December 1906]

18 Woburn Buildings

My dear Lady Gregory: Miss Horniman was told by Waring, I think, (he was here when I arrived) that the proposal I made was unworkable.[1] She has sent you another proposal, with which I (and Waring) have had nothing to do.[2] As I have considered myself bound to press upon her nothing out side the compromise we talked over (& to press nothing else upon you & Synge)

the reviewers thought Frank Fay 'too frenzied', but on 8 Dec Holloway complained that in his speech before Dectora's entry he 'sang his words too much, & entered the region of melodrama in his looks & manner'. However, on 12 Dec he found him 'vastly improved since the first night'.

[2] The actor-manager Cyril Maude (1862–1951) had been co-manager of the Haymarket Theatre 1896–1905, and had just rebuilt the Playhouse in Northumberland Avenue, London, of which he was to be manager until 1915. He and his company were on tour in Dublin from 3 to 8 Dec, playing at the Theatre Royal in *Her Son* by Horace Annesley Vachell and *Olivia*, an adaptation of Oliver Goldsmith's *The Vicar of Wakefield*. Joseph Holloway (NLI) also waxed ecstatic over the scenery: '"A thing of beauty is a joy for ever," & certainly Robert Gregory's setting & lighting of *The Shadowy Waters* is very beautiful indeed. The poet has dreamed a strangely-lovely dream & put it into words, which the actors have committed to memory, but they could not give this the shadowy substance necessary to make the dream & living picture for us, were it not for the really poetic, artistic, & hauntingly beautiful setting conceived by the artistic minded young Gregory . . . were it not for their poetically-conceived surroundings Forgael & his queen Dectora would have appeared a pair of lovers talking fool talk:—the former inclined to have a "slate off". As it was, tableau followed tableau, until the eye & the imagination were filled with the sense of delight & repose that only the really beautiful things of earth give.'

[3] In ancient Egyptian mythology Osiris was cut into pieces by his evil brother Seth but restored by his consort Isis. He became the god of fertility and of death and by means of his boat brought the dead to the sun god Ra. There was a strong Egyptian influence in Golden Dawn, particularly in the 0°=0° and the 5°=6° rituals, and FF had been particularly drawn to Egyptology and the study of Egyptian magic in the 1890s.

[1] See pp. 527–32.

[2] On 17 Dec AEFH had written formally to WBY (NLI), directing him to engage a managing director: 'He should be fairly young, of good manners and such a temper as will make the position possible for him. He must have practical stage experience as well as experience in stage management of all classes of plays. He would need to be able to stage-manage anything and be competent to produce all plays except those treating of Irish peasant life. I should like this engagement to be made as soon as possible and this letter is to be taken as pledging me to guarantee the money.' In the letter to AG of 19 Dec, to which WBY refers, AEFH elaborated upon this proposal, telling her that the present state of affairs 'should not continue', and that the 'following proposition has not been suggested by Mr Yeats',

I shall remain silent. I do not think she is cross with Fay as a man I heard her telling some body that he was 'such a little gentleman'. She is in good spirits but very determined. She leaves to-morrow.[3] Miss Tobin had arranged a party for the theatre the night I went to see her & seems full of nothing but her work. I have not yet seen M^rs Emery (or indeed anybody except Miss Horniman & Miss Tobin & Sidgewick). Miss Horniman made such objections to our engaging M^rs Emery because of her "carelessness" Etc that I shall let that matter sleap until the new arrangements have been made if they are to be made. I shall talk the matter over with M^rs Emery & tell her the difficulty. I think however that she is going to America—she is wavering but has an offer of some kind.[4] I shall see her tomorrow evening. Sidgewick lunched with me to-day. They have sold already 800 copies of my poems & will be ready for new editions with 'Wind Among the Reeds' by Easter.[5] This is the quickest sale I have had. I lost my fur-rug on my way over—left it on the boat & am trying to recover it through the railway company. I have had an ecstatic anonimous letter from somebody in Dublin, who goes to all our plays it seems and "everywhere I speak".[6]

Yrs ever<br>W B Yeats

ALS Berg, with envelope addressed to Coole, postmark 'LONDON.W DEC 20 06'.

and was for 'a majority of the Directors to accept or refuse': 'I propose that they should engage a Managing Director at a good salary (say £400 or £500 a year) who would be able to stage manage all the plays and produce such as would be performed, except when the Directors wished to do them themselves or to leave them in the hands of an artist; Fay to retain the production of all Irish peasant plays and to have nothing to do with the rest except his own parts. This would free him from much wear and tear and allow him to perfect himself in his own lines.' She added that the 'engagement of this Managing Director would of course be under the control of the Directors and he must be recommended by some one of known theatrical position. This would remove my objection to touring under the present state of affairs and would I believe be extremely advantageous to all concerned.' She emphatically repeated that she would have nothing to do with hiring the new man 'and he would be responsible to the Directors and I would pay the money for his salary to you. I leave this offer open until my return on Jan 21 but as time is of value, if you accept it, Mr Yeats holds a formal letter authorising such an engagement immediately. Will you kindly communicate this to Mr Synge as I should like all the Directors to accept this; but as in the case of the subsidy a majority is sufficient, Mr Synge never having accepted it.'

[3] i.e. for North Africa (see p. 525).

[4] AEFH had fallen out with FF over the Golden Dawn in the late 1890s (III. 26, 31–4), and on 2 July 1907 informed WBY that while she 'would not wish to injure Mrs Emery, yet on the other hand I would not be mixed up in anything connected with her'. FF did go to America in late January 1907.

[5] i.e. of *Poems, 1899–1905*, which had been published in October. The sales were impressive, given that the book had received very few reviews (see p. 495, n. 3). *The Wind Among the Reeds* had not been included because of the dispute over the rights with John Lane, but the proposed new edition was superseded by plans for the *Collected Works*.

[6] This letter is now lost.

## *To Ernest Rhys, 21 December 1906*

18, Woburn Buildings, | Euston Road, W. C.
21/12/06.

My dear Rhys,[1]

I dont think I ever answered your note of October 27th.[2] It came when I was desperately busy, more busy than I ever have been in my life, trying to do my own writing and manage the Abbey Theatre at the same time. When would you want the contribution for the new magazine?[3] I have a queer sort of a little dirge out of a new play (I suppose a whole one act play as long as Baile's Strand would be somewhat outside your limits). The dirge is one of the choruses in the play and there is also a love lyric, separable from its surroundings.[4] I have nothing else at the moment and am feeling rather overworked and disinclined to start anything for a little while. I have just got back to London and after I have finished off some odds and ends shall make holiday for a bit.

Yrs ever
W B Yeats

TLS BL.

## *To Violet Hunt,[1] 21 December 1906*

18, Woburn Buildings, | Euston Road,
Dec. 21st, 1906.

Dear Miss Hunt,

Your note was sent on to me in Ireland. I wish I had been in London to accept your invitation. I wonder have you some day when you are at home.

Yrs sy
W B Yeats

TLS Berg.

[1] For Rhys see p. 229, n. 1.     [2] Untraced.
[3] The new magazine is unidentified and apparently never appeared.
[4] Both passages are from *Deirdre*. The dirge is that sung by the Chorus of Musicians as Deirdre pretends to bid farewell to the murdered Naoise, but in fact commits suicide over his body (*VPl*, 387, ll. 733–7). The 'separable' love lyric, beginning 'Love is an immoderate thing | And can never be content', is also sung by the Musicians, as Naoise and Deirdre play chess together, knowing that they have been betrayed and waiting for Conchubar's assassins (*VPl*, 375, ll. 474–85). Since Rhys's magazine never appeared, WBY published both pieces in F. T. Marinetti's *Poesia* in 1907.

[1] Isobel Violet Hunt (1862–1942), novelist and biographer, was the daughter of Alfred William Hunt (1830–96), the Pre-Raphaelite watercolourist, and the novelist Margaret Raine Hunt (1831–1912). She had first met WBY in the 1880s at Mrs Anna Bryce's, and had re-met him on 23 Dec 1900 at the

## *To George Brett, 22 December* [*1906*]

18 Woburn Buildings | Euston Road | London.
Saturday | Dec 22.

Dear M$^r$ Brett: I have got rid of all my work except the revision of play & proofs etc & shall I hope let you have all with[in] a couple of weeks at most.[1] There will be preface, appendix with illustrations for stage purposes of one of the plays etc.[2]

Yr sny
W B Yeats

ALS NYPL.

## *To Lady Gregory,* [*22 December 1906*]

18 Woburn Buildings | Euston Road | London.
Saturd

My dear Lady Gregory: there is an unexpected embarresment over 'Dierdre' & M$^{rs}$ Campbell. M$^{rs}$ Emery has written a play herself & a very good one & offered it to M$^{rs}$ Campbell to fill the vacant place with 'Electra'. I cannot offer my new play through M$^{rs}$ Emery that is certain, & a little hesitate about offering it at all—I suppose I shall but I am not sure. I should not like to oust M$^{rs}$ Emery.[1] I hear—it is private—that Howard de

Shorters', where he put her into a trance (see II. 361). She described him in her diary (Cornell) as looking 'rather like a gipsy's baby', and thereafter frequently invited him to social functions. She made her house, South Lodge, 80 Campden Hill Road, Kensington, a salon for writers and artists; from 1910 to 1915 she was to live there notoriously unmarried to Ford Madox Hueffer (1873–1939) after his unsuccessful attempts to divorce his first wife.

[1] These were for vol. II of the American edition of *The Poetical Works*, the first volume of which had been published on 27 Nov. In his reply of 3 Jan 1907 (NYPL) Brett wrote that notwithstanding 'the disadvantage which has come about through the publishing of the volume of Poems separately, I am glad to be able to report to you a satisfactory sale for it up to the present time, and I look forward to a renewal of interest in the whole matter just as soon as the volume of Plays, in uniform style is ready'. He was, 'accordingly, very glad to learn from your letter of the early despatch by you of the additional material . . . I trust that this may reach us in time for early spring publication'.

[2] The preface to the second volume of *The Poetical Works* was dated 'December 1906', and it contained four appendices: the first gave 'The Legendary and Mythological Foundation of the Plays and Poems', the second 'The Dates and Places of Performance of the Plays', the third the 'Acting Version of "The Shadowy Waters"' (see p. 522), while the fourth was a shortened version of WBY's essay 'Literature and the Living Voice' (see pp. 316, n. 5, 384) under the title 'The Work of the National Theatre Society at the Abbey Theatre, Dublin: A Statement of Principles'. There were, however, no illustrations.

[1] WBY had been prevaricating over whether he should offer *Deirdre* to Mrs Pat Campbell (see pp. 449, 452, 469), and, now that he had given it to the Abbey for its first production, felt able to

Walden has given Binyon a large sum to produce a play called 'Atilla' with Ashe as principal character.[2]

This is only to wish you a merry Xmass—for I must get on with my proofs for America

Yrs affectly
W B Yeats

ALS Berg, with envelope addressed to Coole, postmark 'LONDON.W.C. DEC 22 06'.

## *To Lady Gregory, [24 December 1906]*

My dear Lady Gregory: as I understand Miss Hornimans offer[1]—the managing director would have no vote—perhaps he should be called manager. Waring, who takes a much more serious view of Fays character than Miss Horniman said something which put it into Miss Hornimans head—M$^{rs}$ Waring being equally emphatic as it seems—that a £2 a week stage manager would be in a false position, and that she could not conscientiously put him there. My own view is that for every body['s] sake we should induce Fay to accept. (1) It would leave him free to devote himself to his acting & to the production of peasant work—including Moleire I conclude (2) it would free us from much vexatious work & give us more time to write (3) If we do not we shall have to pay a stage-manager out of the takings & so reduce everybodies chance—Fays included—of a decent income as well as making a London tour very difficult (4) We have to recognise that almost everybody who has had personal dealings with Fay of a business kind has ended in furious exasperation & this whether he be right

approach her. FF's unpublished play may have been a revised version of *The Mystery of Time: A Masque*, which had been produced at the Albert Hall theatre on 17 Jan 1905; she evidently hoped that Mrs Campbell would play it on the same bill as Hugo von Hofmannsthal's *Electra* (1904). In her reply of 24 Dec (Berg) AG, who was less enthusiastic about Mrs Campbell, told him: 'I feel you cannot interfere with Mrs Emery's play by offering yours at the moment. I should think however you might tell her about it, in case there is another chance. I do not thirst to see Mrs Campbell as Deirdre, but I think you have for the moment lost faith in your own most beautiful and distinguished work, and feel the want of the stimulus of a popular success'.

[2] For Lord Howard de Walden see p. 347. The poet, dramatist, and art historian Robert Laurence Binyon (1869–1943) was an assistant in the Department of Prints and Drawings at the British Museum, where he became Keeper of Oriental Paintings and Prints in 1913. WBY had got to know him in the late 1890s and had praised his poem 'The Death of Tristram' in 1901 (see III. 6–7). The Australian-born actor Oscar Asche (1871–1936) produced and played the title role in the first public performances of Binyon's *Attila* in September 1907.

[1] See p. 541, n. 2. AG wrote to WBY on 22 Dec 1906 (Berg) that she did not find AEFH's letter of 19 Dec 'quite clear': she did not understand the different meanings of 'stage manage' and 'produce', and was not sure whether her adaptations of Molière came 'under the head of "Irish peasant plays"'. . . . At present I dont feel that I can give a definite opinion. The one thing I hold to is that the Fays should not be put out either by forcible or gradual means. I dont know by the wording of the letter if the proposal is one that we ought to advise him to accept. . . . Would the Managing Director have a vote equal to Synge's and mine? And there are questions as to division of office &c you would have to talk over with Fay.'

or wrong is a continual danger to the whole project. If we are firm & united we can secure his future with that of the project. He should for his own good be forced to give [up] all that he is unfit for.

I should say that I faught hard to leave in Fays hands all production as distinguished from stage management (production being the complete setting of a play on the boards as distinguished from the necessary attention after it has been got there) including verse work (though I doubt his capacity for this). I thought he should be given a trial, but Miss Horniman would not hear of it. She used such arguments as 'how could he stage Racine. What does he know about it. I wont be made ridiculous'. If we agree to this she talks of reserving a further £500 a year for our tours—that is to say we have the income on the £25,000. I am personally inclined to think that we could get <somebody perhaps> Foss[2]—who is obtainable I think—who is genttle & reliable for less than £500, but Vedrenne or Benson might not think him good enough as a producer. I rather hesitate about that Benson man I spoke of—we could I have no doubt get him for the money—as he struck me as rather a confident <dominating> ambitious man who might fight with Fay.[3] Fay would get on with Foss. I should be more anxious to get a good business man capable of stage management than an artist like Phillip Carr (Miss Horniman would refuse him). Miss Horniman agrees with me that this manager should if possible be Irish. (This might rule out Foss). The chief trouble is the large income the new man must get but as this does not come out of earnings Fay may not object. I should say that M[rs] Emery does not think Foss good enough if we want a producer. All depends on the man. The right man would free us from all anxiety and from all theatrical work except writing. He would look after Henderson & every body else. In any case we propose to free Fay from all but his playing & from production & it is hardly worth fighting to keep in his hands verse production & the classic plays—a small part of our repetoire—As for the rest—getting of actors in time, management of the building, fines etc, it is better that we put this in the hands of an educated, well bred man earning a good salery than into the hands of some inferior man at £2 a week (without Miss Horniman we can hardly afford more) above all better for Fay. If we are firm & unanimous he

---

[2] George R. Foss (1859–1938), producer and actor, toured extensively in the 1880s and 1890s before devoting himself to producing plays. He was stage manager and producer at the Avenue Theatre, where he played Father Hart in the 1894 production of WBY's *The Land of Heart's Desire*, and where he directed FF and Mrs Campbell in Ibsen's *Little Eyolf* in 1896. As stage director of Henry Neville's Dramatic Studio in Oxford Street he directed students in a production of WBY's *The Pot of Broth* 20–2 Dec 1905. He later became a producer at the Old Vic.

[3] This may have been Henry Jalland (1861–1928), a member of the original Benson company, who became business manager when Benson opened at the Globe Theatre in 1889. Thereafter he was associated with Benson, and managed the company in 1900, when it took the Lyceum Theatre, London, for a season.

will agree, if we are uncertain he will fight us. We should all if possible advise him the same way.

Yr ev
W B Yeats

No sign yet of rugg but I can hardly hear I suppose till after Xmass. I have no note paper & no envelope on me—A stamped & directed one from some autograph hunter.

ALS Berg, with envelope addressed in another hand to <?Miss Lorna Johnston, Louden Park, Bridge of Weir, Renfrewshire>, heavily cancelled and redirected to Coole by WBY; postmark 'LONDON.N.W. DEC 24 06'.

## *To A. E. F. Horniman,* [c. *26 December 1906*]

Mention in next letter and in a letter from AEFH, 31 December 1906. Sending her a letter of Synge's about the running of the Abbey.[1]

NLI.

## *To John Millington Synge,* [c. *26 December 1906*]

18 Woburn Building

My dear Synge: I am altogeather in agreement with you & had actually gone to the typewriter to type a letter on the subject but decided to wait on Miss Hornimans return here. I have sent her your letter, which is admirable.[1] I shall be away till Monday but I think that is for the best as your letter will influence her at this moment more than I could.

Yr ev
W B Yeats

ALS TCD.

WBY had known him at least since 1901 (see III. 95, 98). Ben Iden Payne, who was eventually to be appointed to the Abbey post, had also been a member of Benson's company, but WBY had not yet met him.

[1] i.e. Synge's letter of 24 Dec; see below.

[1] Synge had written to WBY on 24 Dec (*JMSCL* I. 265–6) putting forward the modifications to AEFH's 'excellent' proposal that WBY adumbrates in the following letter to AG, with the addition of a sixth: that AEFH should understand that the Company would limit its tours 'as we have seen so plainly that except in a few centres of culture our time and energy is thrown away'.

## *To Lady Gregory, [26 December 1906]*

18 Woburn Buildings | Euston Road | London
Wednes

My dear Lady Gregory: Synge writes a letter of conditional acceptance which I have sent on to Miss Horniman. He thinks "the arrangement would be an excellent one for us all" if (1) Managing director has no vote (2) If he cannot engage or dismiss actors without us (3) If Fay "produce" all dialect work (this to include work like 'Canavans' and 'Eloquent Dempsey' (4) *If we are not bound* to give verse work to new [man] till we have tried him (5) If 'Arrangements be such as Fay can cooperate in cordially'.[1]

If Miss Horniman agree[s] to Synges conditions & I see no difficulty about any—the early ones are part of her scheme—though the last may need some such plan as testing him on a round of carefully chosen plays, I think we should all three make up our mind about scheme & urge Fay to accept.[2] If you hold out Fay will be suspicious. I mean by hold out if you seem out of sympathy. I do not think he can reject it in any case—the alternative being our paying a stage manager out of earnings & he may as well accept with an easy mind[3]—we should have the whole scheme in black & white & then I should see Vedrenne. I beleive that it may be the making of the whole work as well as of our peace of mind. We might possibly give Fay a rise—say £25 a year to him as producer.

Yr ev
W B Yeats

ALS Berg, with envelope addressed to Coole, postmark 'KENSINGTON W. DEC 26 06'.

[1] See above. Synge had also copied the letter to AG at the same time, and she told WBY in a letter of 26 Dec which crossed with this one (Berg) that 'Synge sent me his six reasons—fair enough, & very cautious!'

[2] AEFH did not agree to Synge's conditions and wrote both formally and privately to WBY about them from Algiers on 31 Dec (see below, p. 550, n. 1).

[3] In her letter of 26 Dec (see n. 1), AG enclosed one that she had written to W. G. Fay 'for you to give him or not, as you think best'. She added that she thought Fay would accept the proposals for the new manager 'for I talked the matter over and over with him, but I would rather see the whole theatre come to an end for the time being than have you looked upon as kicking down the ladder by which, as a dramatist, you had risen, and that is what many of those who care most for you would feel'.

## To Lady Gregory, [27 December 1906]

18 Woburn Buildings, | Euston Road

My dear Lady Gregory: no sign of Fay & as I conclude he must reherse to-morrow I shall hardly see him.[1] I am afraid you & Synge will have to talk or write the thing out with him.[2] I certainly do not want to wrong Fay—I give the case against him to you but his case to Miss Horniman. The reason of her present proposal is I beleive that when Waring objected to my proposal of a stage manager on the ground that Fay would make the post of an equal impossible (he put it in worse form) she suggested putting the new stage manager in control (with power to act in our absense). I thereon quite deliberately flew into a passion, & said that any proposal of the kind—to subordinate Fay to a £2 a week manager—was preposterous & that I would resent any attempt to put any man in control—if he could take any important act without direction from us as a most unwarrantable inter-fearence with the power of the directors. I then said "if you will pay £500 & get a thoroughly good man I dont mind putting Fay & everybody under his direction—he being subject to us". I never thought she would do it—but now she wont do anything else. I think she is right—except that Fay should have been given a fair trial as producer of verse. It is no kindness to Fay to let him go on doing work he is unfitted for & thereby destroying the fame of his good work by the fame of his bad. If we dont now while he is inclined to do as we wish get him to give up work—where he merely makes enemies (I am entirely certain that another year of the present management would create another split—peacable as all seems now among the actors—there is always quibling—, or rather the loss to the ordinary theatre of our best people). It will be hard for him to see a man better paid than himself in general control, but it is essential if he is [to] create a great position for himself in the long run. I dont beleive that anybody but you can make him accept the situation. I proposed to Miss Horniman appointing the new man merely long enough to train our own people but she insisted on his being engaged for long enough to

---

[1] In her reply AG agreed that it was 'strange' that Fay had not called on WBY while he was in London: 'perhaps he did while you were at the Museum—It is a great pity—for your knowing Miss H's point of view could have talked the whole thing out with him.' Fay had evidently avoided WBY on purpose at this highly charged time, and on his return to Dublin advised Sara Allgood (*JMSCL* 1. 269) 'to save up some money as he thought the Abbey Company was in a very shaky state'.

[2] AG had anticipated this request, and had already sent WBY a letter she had written to W. G. Fay (see above, n. 3), in which she enclosed AEFH's letter of 19 Dec (see p. 541, n. 2), and assured him (MBY) that she 'would not sanction any putting out of you and your brother either by force or gentler means'. She recounted the reasons for accepting the scheme as put forward by WBY in his letter of 24 Dec, with which she said she was 'inclined to agree', and concluded: 'I know you will trust me in any advice I give, that is why I have been slow in giving it. Mr Yeats will be able to explain his own point of view to you, so I need say no more about it, but I dont think your views will really clash. You & he & I are all working for the same end, I dont think there is a selfish thought between us –.' In her reply to this letter of WBY she supposed that 'you will not send him my letter—it was only to help you if he was suspicious'.

make it worth the while of a thoroughly good man coming to us. If we had Fay['s] acceptance—I doubt if he will accept by letter—I could—without waiting for details to be arranged look out for possible man—I have just heard of a man who was with M^rs Campbell & should be good & would I hear be cheap.³ We should have a man in our mind before Miss Horniman returns (on Jan 21) at latest. The new man must certainly not be an actor—that will always leave Fay his position unassalable because he will be our chief representative in the eyes of the public.

Another matter. I dont [think] M^rs Emery will come this Spring even if Miss Horniman would stand (I dont care our negociations are over). She says she d come for 'Phedre' but quibles about the other things. Miss Darragh wanted to know before the New Year. What should we do.

No news yet of rug but will go to station to morrow. The museum bell has just rung for closing—I am writing there.

Yrs ev<br>W B Yeats

[*On back of envelope*]
I notice that Griffith was at that corporation meeting—*Shin Fein* anti-culture at work I have no doubt. He was suspicious of Lane.⁴

ALS Berg, with envelope addressed to Coole, postmark 'LONDON W.C. DEC 27 06'.

## *To John Millington Synge, 28 December 1906*

18 Woburn Buildings | Euston Rd. | W. C.<br>28th Dec. 1906.

My dear Synge,
I sent your letter on to Miss Horniman but have not yet heard—I have been waiting to hear or I should have written to you before.¹ I dont think she ever intended that the new man should have a vote. I dont think there is any point at issue between you and her except possibly about the verse work.

---

³ Mrs Campbell's man was William Burchill (see p. 445).

⁴ Arthur Griffith was a member of the Public Libraries Committee of Dublin Corporation, which had recently been charged with conducting the Corporation's negotiations over Hugh Lane's proposed gallery. The Committee, with Griffith's support, was suggesting conditions which Lane found unacceptable, and in her letter to WBY of 22 Dec 1906 AG had enclosed 'a plaintive bleat' from *Sinn Fein*.

¹ i.e. Synge's letter of 24 Dec, outlining his six proposals (see p. 547, 548). AEFH, who was in Algiers, did not reply until 31 Dec, when she wrote both formally and privately to WBY repudiating Synge's suggestions. In the formal letter she insisted that she could not 'alter my offer in any way, it was carefully considered at the time and no new evidence has been laid before me. Any modification on Mr. Synge's lines would simply be the undoing of my intentions.' She then went on to make three detailed observations on Synge's proposals about the new manager:

What I said to her was this: "It is necessary for our sake and for Fay's sake that all work except acting and production be taken out of his hands. He is an artist not a business man and should not be made to do things which anybody else or somebody else could do as well or better. He should produce but the work should go from his hands to a stage manager." These were not my exact words b[ut] the[y] were the sense of them. I expected that she would give us a stage manager at two or three pounds a week. Waring who was there made difficulties of a practical kind about the divided control. I refused to hear of any authority of any important kind being given to the kind of man we would get at this price. Next day she proposed getting a first rate man and paying him four or five hundred a year and making him managing Director in my stead. I should have said that I had told her that not only was it very undesirable that Fay should be allowed to go on worrying with all sorts of things which had nothing to do with his work as an artist but that sooner or later (I supposed it would be very much later) we directors should have to be freed from the bother and anxiety of business management and left free to write our plays. I tried to get her to give to this new director only so much right over the artistic side of the work as we would have given to the two pound a week man. I said something like this—"It is obvious that there is no other man whatever who could produce the peasant work besides Fay. I am not yet certain that he has any special faculty for verse work but considering what he has done for the theatre he should be tried in this. He should be given a definite period during which he could show what capacity he had when freed from other bothers in the production of verse plays." I held out for several hours on this point though I made no secret of the fact that he had not yet shown remarkable capacity that way. I pointed out that various failings of various verse plays were failings of stage management not production. Finding I could not carry my point with her (I imagine that she has had very decided reports about Fay in that capacity (not I think from Miss Darragh)) I proposed the new man should be engaged for a time—a year let

1.) The right of voting on your board is not a matter in which I can interfere.

2.) He must be free to engage or dismiss actors; if not supported by the board (or a majority) he must go. In this case *I* should have to decide whether I should authorise you to engage a new man. If he were unsuitable we could try another; but if otherwise suitable & yet not supported by the directors, things would return to their present position.

3.) I carefully left it open for a play *at the wish of the author*, to be put in the hands of any Director or artist instead of the new man; if an author chooses Fay, let him take the risk. But only the author can choose the producer; where the author is not at hand, it must be done by the new man. If the 'Samhain Principals' [*sic*] are to be stretched into an intention to go in every way against the rules of the ordinary stage *where these rules are right & necessary*, I have been under a serious delusion. At present my position is 'false and absurd' in the eyes of the public & I naturally object.

In her 'Private' letter, AEFH warned WBY that 'Mr. Synge wants Fay to run the show, he is too lazy to care about anything except his own plays and too cowardly to fight for the whole. Unless Lady Gregory will decide you will be obliged to give in and Fay will only permit a cheap man whom *he* can virtually dismiss to be engaged. Over and over again the road has forked before you; at this moment Fay, in the form of Mr. Synge, points one way, and I and your interests point in the other.'

us say—with the object of his teaching our people and training some less expensive man to do the work. This she refused on the very reasonable ground that we could not get a thoroughly good man unless he had an opportunity sufficiently great to attract him. She made great use of the necessity of Racine being produced by a man of wide theatrical knowledge.[2] All through the discussion she insisted that only through a man of this kind could I get the principles of Samhain 1904 carried out. They are always implied in all these arrangements.[3] If I had had a more innate conviction of Fay's capacity for verse work I might have carried the point—though I doubt it very much. I believe she had been thinking the whole thing out for a long time though it was some chance sentences of Waring's and of mine that launched the project. When I am talking to you and to Lady Gregory I put Fay's limitations (when I have a point to carry) but I assure you I put even more strongly his genius when talking to Miss Horniman. His enemy is not Miss Horniman but the Warings who are very bitter. I heard Miss Horniman telling someone the other day that he was "such a gentleman". I do not think that Fay need fear for his position indeed I believe he need only fear for it if he shrinks from this change and tries to go on in the old way. If he does not consent we shall have to pay a stage manager out of the earnings of the theatre and this will lessen the money there is for everyone and make tours impossible for we wont have the money for them. The new man will not be an actor and the necessity of his having general capacity, rather than particular, will in the long run leave Fay even if we ourselves did not intend to keep our grip, the principal producer as well as actor. The liberation from other worries will give Fay the opportunity to become in reality a great actor instead of a great actor in promise. It will end all these nerve wasting disputes, and give us enough money for tours and make all pretty smooth for America.

The first volume of my collected edition in America is out and I have just finished a preface and appendix for the second volume which is to contain the plays. I wind up the preface by a sentence of praise to Frank Fay for having made the beautiful speaking of verse on the stage again possible, and there is a long essay in the appendix on the work and principles of the Abbey Theatre—all this to prepare our way for America—[4]

Yrs ever<br>W B Yeats

[2] The Directors had discussed the possibility of presenting a number of plays by Racine, and *Phèdre* had been announced as forthcoming in the *Arrow* of 20 Oct. Agnes Tobin was also translating *Les Plaideurs* for the Abbey at this time, although this, also, was never produced.

[3] See p. 529. In her formal letter of 31 Dec AEFH repeated that the Directors were 'free to carry out their own ideas as long as they are in harmony with the "Samhain Principals" [*sic*]'.

[4] WBY ends his preface (dated 'December 1906') to vol. II of *The Poetical Works of William B. Yeats* (see p. 544) with an account of his and his Abbey fellow-dramatists' attempts to 'restore the whole ancient art of passionate speech', and concludes that the 'labour of two players, Miss Florence Farr and Mr. Frank Fay, have done enough to show that all is possible, if the summer be lucky and the corn ripen' (*VPl*, 1294).

P. S. Private—I have written you rather a long letter that you may have my arguments at hand should it be necessary for you to put the matter before Fay. I personally think that if Lady Gregory would do it or could do it— that would be the best way. You may already have been discussing it however. Lady Gregory has written me a letter for Fay stating the proposal and urging him to accept, this she did under the belief that he was to be in London this Christmas and that I could talk it out with him. It is important to get the matter settled in principle that I may enquire more definitely about available men. It will be much pleasanter for Fay to work with a well bred, well educated, knowledgeable man than with some two pound a week Bell.[5] I imagine the change will be a considerable relief to the company once they get over the discomfort of novelty. Fay is thoroughly unfitted for the management of people. Two or three years ago Fred Ryan came to me privately and said this—That if only somebody else could be put into control there would be no trouble (this was at the time of the first split). He said the same to me when we came back from the tour.[6] Miss Walker's various reasons for not rejoining us always in the end got down to Fay's management. For obvious reasons he awakens suspicions in all directions. I have seen him telling the truth and have known by the look upon his face that he did not know that it was the truth. He is precisely what his training in little fitup shows and the like was bound to make him and in addition to that he has the excitability of the artist.[7] You and I and Lady Gregory have the same excitability though in very different ways. None of us are fit to manage a theatre of this kind and do our own work as well. Lady Gregory's work this autumn would have been twice as good if she had not the practical matters of the theatre on her mind. Several times in the last two or three years the enormous theatrical correspondence has been the chief event both of her day and mine. Many and many a time we have had to go to the typewriter the first thing after breakfast with the result that our imaginations were exhausted before we got to our play-

---

[5] i.e. John Joy Bell (see p. 413).

[6] Fred Ryan had helped AE draw up the new constitution for the NTS in 1905, and shared AE's doubts about W. G. Fay's temperament and efficiency (see p. 156, n. 9). He told Holloway on 15 May of this year that the 'bickering was awful' when he had been secretary of the INTS (see p. 409, n. 2).

[7] W. G. Fay had begun his theatrical career in his late teens by touring Ireland with the theatre-manager J. W. Lacy and his wife Maud Randford, in their travelling (fit-up) company. He worked for them as an odd-job man and advance agent, but graduated to playing small parts. He subsequently toured Scotland with Lacy and, when that company went broke, joined Whitbread's company which took *The Irishman* to Irish and English towns. He subsequently toured with R. B. Lewis in *Uncle Tom's Cabin*, with H. E. Bailey's company (in a repertoire of melodramas), and with Lloyd's Mexican Circus. He did not share WBY's disparaging view of this experience, arguing that at least some of the knowledge he gathered 'was to be of practical value to me afterwards, when I had to produce, at the Abbey Theatre, plays written about many different parts of the country from Galway to Cork' (*Fays of the Abbey*, 91).

writing. Every little question has often to be debated in correspondence when we are away.

W B Y

TLS TCD, with envelope addressed to the Abbey Theatre, postmark 'LONDON DE 28 06'. Saddlemyer, 187–90.

## To Edmund Gosse, 28 December 1906

18 Woburn Buildings | W.C.<br>
Dec 28th 06.

Dear Mr Gosse,

I got back from Ireland a week ago and have found awaiting me here your invitation for Monday. I should have written long ago and I hope you will forgive me. I would like to come very much but unfortunately my friends will expect to find me at Woburn Buildings that night for I am always there on Monday evenings. I tried to get to you last Sunday but it was not possible—I want to give you a beautiful book by a friend of mine and as I dont think I can get to you next Sunday I send it with this. It is full as I think of wonderful things. Read the long Canzone, beginning on page 104. There are more beautiful things among the sonnets but I have not my own marked copy and do not know where to look. There are wonderful lines— of real poetical intensity. I met the author in San Francisco and she is translating Phedre for my Dublin theatre which looks like prospering at last.[1]

Yr ever<br>
W B Yeats

TLS Leeds.

[1] WBY was sending Agnes Tobin's translation of Petrarch's *On the Death of Madonna Laura* published the previous month. 'Canzone VI' (104–6), a translation of Petrarch's 'Quando il soave mio fido conforto', begins: 'When my most constant comforter and stay, | To heal my weary heart that long has bled, | Sits down upon the left side of my bed | And talks to me in the old dear tranquil way; | White with great awe and yearning, low I say: | "Whence comest thou now, O happy soul so calm?"' She had published another version of this canzone in *Love's Crucifix* (1902), and WBY had picked it out for particular praise in his first letter to her on 7 Feb 1904 (see III. 553–4). Miss Tobin had begun translating Racine's *Phèdre* in 1905, at the suggestion of Mrs Pat Campbell. Although the Abbey intended to stage it, and Mrs Campbell planned 'the most sumptuous production I can make', the play was never produced, but was eventually published as *Phaedra* in San Francisco in 1958. A typescript of the play, with WBY's holograph emendations, is at MBY.

## *To Lady Gregory, [?31 December 1906]*

Dear Lady Gregory

I enclose a letter I had forgot (I have not answered it)[1] & also a copy of my note on your books for American edition. I have no time to write.

Yr ev<br>W B Yeats

[*With enclosure*]

The Legendary and Mythological Foundation of the Plays & Poems.

---

Almost every story I have used or person I have spoken of is in one or other of Lady Gregory's "Gods and Fighting Men" and "Cuchulain of Muirthemne". If my present small Dublin audience for poetical drama grows and spreads beyond Dublin I shall owe it to these two little books, masterpieces of prose which can but make the old stories as familiar to Irishmen everywhere as are the stories of Arthur and his knights to all readers of books. I cannot believe that it is friendship that makes me weigh these books with Mallory and feel no discontent at the tally or that it is the wish to make the circumstantial origin of my own art familiar, that would make me give them before all other books to Irish boys and girls. I wrote for the most part before they were written that all or all but all is there "Oisin's wandering" "Cuchulain killing his son and fighting the sea, Mave and her children, Baile and Aillin, Angus and his fellow mortals, all literally translated though with much condensation and selection from the old writings. A few of my stories are not hers also, I took

[*Remainder missing*][2]

ALS Berg, with envelope addressed to Coole, postmark 'London W Dec [?]31 [?]06'.

---

[1] This has not been traced.

[2] The full, revised, version of this note was printed as appendix 1 in vol. 11 of *The Poetical Works of William B. Yeats*, published by Macmillan, New York, on 8 July 1907, and is reprinted in *VPl*, 1282–3. WBY has sent the part referring to AG's plays, but not bothered with the remainder, which went on to give the sources of other poems and plays.

# 1907

## To Elizabeth Corbet Yeats, [early January 1907]

Mention in letter to AG, 21 January 1907.

A letter, which WBY hoped 'was quite civil', 'saying that it was rather a delicate matter, but I would like to know if she was paying her writers as it would render my position very difficult as the Editor if she were not. I put a rather hasty phrase, I am sorry to say, in the letter which I was dictating. It was this "I know you haven't paid myself or Lady Gregory, this last an unfortunate omission".'[1]

## Memo re Managing Director,[1] [early January 1907]

(1) Managing director to have no vote
(2) No power to dismiss actors without directors
(3) Fay to produce dialect work. No hard and fast rule. Eloquent Dempsey not dialect. Historical play.[2]
(4) Not bound to give verse if the man does not suit.
(5) 'What ever arrangement is arrived at it must be of such a kind as Fay will be able to co-operate in it cordially. We owe this to him as he has in reality built up the company.'

A Doc NLI.

[1] AG had published *A Book of Saints and Wonders* with the Dun Emer Press on 10 Sept 1906 (see p. 490), and, as she informed WBY on 24 Dec 1906 (Berg), ECY had written to tell her there were 'only 30 copies of "Saints" left—She is in gt good humour because I sent cheque for copies of Russell book I got, instead of leaving it against my royalties—which she gives many good reasons for not being able to pay at present.'

[1] This one-page memorandum, based on Synge's letter of 24 Dec (see p. 548), was presumably an aide-mémoire for WBY in his correspondence with AEFH.

[2] *The Eloquent Dempsy* was a contemporary political satire in the accent of Dundalk rather than a historical play, but WBY evidently wanted to get it out of the hands of W. G. Fay.

## *To Lady Gregory,* [*2 January 1907*]

My dear Lady Gregory: I have had a letter from Miss Horniman showing she hopes I may have engaged the new man before her return—it might be as well to be free in the choice—though there is something to be said on the other said [*for* side].[1] Certainly I would like to get in re-commendation. I beleive we could get Burchill, who staged managed for M^rs Campbell when she played 'Pasadas & Memesande' of Materlinck with Sarah Barnett. He did not produce it, but has been in the best possible school.[2]

I have also just got enclosed from Synge. Please do as you think right about Fay—perhaps you may think it well to get him down to Coole at end of the week (Mineral Workers runs a week) or you may think Synge had better speak.[3] Fays point of view is only another proof of the need of some well trained man—we are all excitable artists & all fitted [?*for* unfitted] to manage this complex thing & do our own work at the same time—that alone being wasting enough for the nerves.

I dont beleive that Fand is possible without some one highly trained actress—I mean that it will be a very amateur thing without, & upset Miss Horniman & our good repute with our new audience. But I have no objection to its being put off, & our work limited to what we can do. Moira can speak blank verse, though not act it & may be able to speak the Alexandrine & the two Allgoods cannot speak either well enough for their long parts—though Molly may learn in time.[4] I would agree to leaving the

---

[1] AEFH had written from Algiers on 28 Dec 1906 (see below, pp. 569–70), reiterating her belief that a professional manager was essential for the Abbey Theatre and concluding that on her return she would 'like to hear that you have engaged the new man already'.

[2] For William Burchill see p. 445, n. 2. A special matinée performance of Maeterlinck's *Pelléas et Mélisande* had been staged in French at the Vaudeville Theatre on 1 July 1904, with Sarah Bernhardt as Pelléas and Mrs Patrick Campbell as Mélisande. The success of this cross-gender production led to three more special performances on 18 and 19 July also at the Vaudeville, and to a subsequent British and Irish tour. Mrs Campbell and Sarah Bernhardt's portrayal of the lovers as if they were a pair of children enhanced WBY's opinion of the play (see III. 614), although one Dublin critic wrote: 'Last night Mme. Bernhardt took the part of Pellèas and Mrs. Campbell played Mélisande, and both are old enough to know better' (Margot Peters, *Mrs. Pat: The Life of Mrs. Patrick Campbell* [1984], 260).

[3] Synge had written to AG on 2 Jan (*JMSCL* I. 278) that he would see W. G. Fay that afternoon and talk things over with him. William Boyle's *The Mineral Workers* ran from 29 Dec 1906 to 5 Jan 1907, with Fay playing the part of the cantankerous, opinionated, and reactionary farmer Dan Fogarty.

[4] Although AG was eager to see the production of Wilfrid Blunt's play *Fand*, based like WBY's *Only Jealousy of Emer* on the Gaelic legend 'The Sickbed of Cuchulain' (see p. 80, n. 2), the fact that it required three strong actresses stretched the Abbey's resources, especially as she was reluctant to employ Letitia Darragh, whose style she disliked. She had written on 29 Dec 1906, suggesting WBY should tell Miss Darragh 'that as everything is so uncertain, she had better make her plans independently of us', and that it would be 'better to put off M^rs Emery' until the new manager had 'tried his hand'. In the same letter she revealed that 'Maire Walker sent me a Xmas card, & I wrote a

matter [to] the new man—but I dont like making him judge of verse speaking much, till I know more of him. I may have to keep our opinion final on that—Benson's man I could trust I think.[5] The best way will be to drop 'Fand'. With good speach it will be a real help to us & it is a fine thing it self but without that a great blow to us.

Yr ever

W B Yeats

I think Fay should be definitely dropped or else some proffesion[al] actress & Moira Walker engaged for it (both are essential).[6] With three good speakers & players it will be safe enough. I quite see your point of view[7] & another of my own—they double expense.

Ever so many thanks about the rug—you are good as always—but I am still hoping to get the old one out of the steamer company.[8]

---

day or two ago asking definitely if she w. take a part in Fand—& saying "probably one or two of your old parts that have not been filled up, will be coming on"—I said nothing about money, & did not urge her but I think it will be well to know where we are.' On 17 Aug 1906 Blunt had recommended to AG that the Abbey should engage Lady Margaret Sackville for one of the parts, and she had played Eithne in a private performance of the play at his home, Newbuildings, Sussex, on 24 Sept 1906. Although the *Arrow* of 20 Oct 1906 had announced that *Fand* would be produced on 26 Jan 1907, it was postponed; however, despite WBY's hesitations here, it was finally produced on 20 and 27 Apr of this year. In the end Maire O'Neill took the title role, Sara Allgood played the part of Emer, and, since Maire Walker had declined AG's offer, another seceder, Maire Garvey (see p. 251), was brought back to play Eithne.

[5] See p. 546.

[6] AG had kept up good relations with Maire Walker after her departure from the Abbey (see n. 4) and on 25 Mar 1906 told WBY that 'Maire came in with Mrs Walker, nothing to say, but just to see me—& I said nothing but that I hoped we should be making costumes for her again before long' (Berg).

[7] In her letter of 29 Dec, AG had said: 'If we get our new man, I think it would be better to let him start on our own people without any outsiders, because if we had any outsiders, he would think that was the standard we are aiming at—I would rather let his imagination work on the permanent material.'

[8] See p. 542. WBY had lost a travelling rug while crossing from Ireland, and in a letter of 26 Dec (Berg) AG had offered to buy him a new one as a Christmas present. With her letter of 29 Dec 1906 she had enclosed an order to the Army and Navy Stores for 'one fur rug' to be chosen by WBY and charged to her account. In her letter she explained that whenever she looked 'at the snow I think of you without your rug! I hope you may have got it, but if it is really lost please take enclosed to A & N Stores & get a new one—I think the old was £7 or thereabouts—but you may go up to £10—I haven't given you anything "worth while" for a long time, except annoyance, obstinacy, exasperation & their kin—so let me wind up the old year with something better.'

[*With enclosure*]

Glendalough House | Kingstown
Dec. 31st/06

Dear Yeats

Thanks for your letter, with which I am practically in agreement.[9] I have not said anything to Fay as it would be better for Lady Gregory to speak to him if possible. I will do it of course if you and she think it advisable. Fay said to me on Saturday, that he was not going to make any further objections to anything that was proposed. We—or you—might appoint anyone we liked and if we got the whole place into a mess it would be our fault not his. Then he went on to say that he thought the time would come when we would find it necessary to have some independent person to manage the place, as we would find that a Board of Authors was nearly as unworkable as the old committee of actors. What he wants, I suppose, is someone to have charge of the bills and put on plenty of Boyle. He is depressed, I think, and when he came home he took S. Allgood aside and advised her to save up some money as he thought the Abbey Company was in a very shaky state. All this of course IS PRIVATE between ourselves and Lady Gregory. I do not think he will oppose new proposal. If I am to break it to him I suppose I should tell him the salary that it is proposed to give. Let me hear what I am to do.

Yours
J M Synge

£10 in house on Saturday.[10] Both Fays got good round of applause on their entries in the Mineral Workers.[11] The Hour Glass went well, except that F.J.F's cloak was too long and put him out a good deal.[12]

ALS Berg, with envelope addressed to Coole, postmark 'LONDON JA 3 07'.

[9] i.e. that of 28 Dec 1906 (see pp. 569–70).

[10] The exact takings were in fact £10 11s. 9d., a very reasonable sum considering that, as Holloway reported (NLI), the weather in Dublin was 'terribly cold & snowy, seated in front of a big fire even cannot keep out this intense cold'. Nevertheless, he noted 'a fairly good house considering the coldness of the night'.

[11] Holloway commented that *The Mineral Workers* was '*the* play of the theatre up to the present. Everyone likes it, & it has won more patrons for the Society than any other piece as yet produced at the Abbey.' He noted that the play 'was followed with rapt attention & every point punctuated by applause'.

[12] Holloway thought *The Hour-Glass* was 'very impressively played. . . . a beautiful little play lovingly interpreted alround'. He picked out the performances of Sara Allgood and W. G. Fay for particular praise, but, without mentioning the cloak, commented that 'F J Fay's "Wise Man" was a sound, consistent study, just lacking in the touch that makes reality of a stage portrait'.

# To Lady Gregory, 3 January [1907]

18, Woburn Buildings, | Euston Road,
Jan. 3, 1906.

Private
Unless you care to send it to Synge.
My dear Lady Gregory

Miss Horniman's letter is merely a controversial petulance the new Director or Manager is to be under the vote of the Directors. She has repeated this again and again. He can do nothing without their authority. Even if I were to try and support *her* ideas you would have two votes against me.[1] It is quite true that she never felt any interest in the Irish side of our work as such. She helped us because she thought that we would do work of universal artistic interest.[2] Furthermore she explained to me at the very start that she was personally not greatly interested either in peasant work or verse drama. She would prefer a theatre putting on the stage what she described as "people like herself" that is to say plays like those of Haupmann.[3] <You will understand her letter better if I try and summarise the conversation that led to it> She recognises, however, that we can only work in our own way but she does demand the work done in our own way shall, both in the writing (and with this part she is satisfied) and in the production

---

[1] On 26 Dec 1906 AEFH had written a long letter to AG from Algiers to 'put my point of view' on the hiring of the new manager. This letter, which was provoked by what she construed as Synge's resistance to her ideas (see p. 550, n. 1), pointed out that the Irish aspect of the Abbey was extrinsic to her, and that her interest in the Theatre was entirely bound up with WBY's plays. She alleged that Fay's 'absolute incapacity' and the 'scandalous carelessness of the stage-management' were making her and the Abbey 'ridiculous in the eyes of cultivated strangers' and hampering the development of WBY's dramatic art. She therefore urged AG to support WBY against Synge in the proposal to appoint a new manager. Since the letter contained accounts of conversations with WBY, and a number of enigmatic and tendentious remarks, AG sent a copy to WBY on 2 Jan, confessing herself 'rather bewildered': 'Miss Horniman seems to be making claims we never heard of when we accepted the theatre or the subsidy. She says her proposals are "in distinct opposition" to Synge's views . . . and that you feel strongly for their acceptance. Do you wish to oppose the views in Synge's letter? You said at the time you would accept the compromise we agreed to.' She went on to ask whether, if they agreed to the proposal of a manager, they were not 'in honour bound to carry out Miss Horniman's views now for the first time hinted at by her? I must show Synge the letter, but would rather hear from you first. I don't want a complete change of policy to be caused by a side wind like this appointment. I am quite sure you are not betraying us, but you must write me a definite letter for Synge to see . . . I am in great trouble about the matter.'

[2] AEFH always insisted that she had established the Abbey to assist WBY's work, and she reiterated this point several times in her letter to AG, describing Dublin as extrinsic to her plans, and nothing more to her than 'a mere geographical detail'. She also alienated AG permanently by describing the Abbey as 'an Irish *toy*'.

[3] AEFH's ideas on drama were based on the German municipal theatres (see p. 533), and she was an admirer of Ibsen and of the social realist German playwright Gerhart Hauptmann (1862–1946).

and acting be sufficiently good to interest people outside Ireland and to have an universal art value. When she speaks of the "fact of the theatre being in Dublin" and "the local circumstances and people" being to us intrinsic and to her extrinsic she put the whole thing very accurately.[4] I am probably more in agreement with her than you are though not more than Synge is really so far as this point is concerned, for I think that if the Movement does not rise to a standard of excellence universally accepted it will help to keep Ireland provincial. She was too impatient to listen to Synge's letter properly. This was always one of the possibilities but it was better for her to fall foul of him than of you and it really doesn't matter. I read her my statement and his reply in the presence of the Warings.[5] I told her that I of course did not agree with Synge or the compromise but would do nothing against it. She flew into a temper, she said she had given the theatre to carry out my ideas, I asked for chapter and verse. She brought down Samhain, 1904 and read out that the theatre was given to carry out my ideas as expressed in articles and speeches upon different occasions. I insisted that there was nothing in Synge's letter that was not legitimate interpretation of my words, she denied this and said that no interpretation but my own was legitimate. I said that she had not made any demand for a doctrine of progressive development in our church and that Samhain 1904 being the books of the Early Fathers could be interpreted by private judgment or some such words. She was too angry to listen. I think, by the bye, that you and Synge had better look up that Samhain to be ready for future battles. She chose to interpret Synge's letter to mean that everything was to be sacrificed to the peasant side of the work, Fay being only

---

[4] In her letter AEFH, picking up Synge's dismissal of the 'extrinsic reasons' for altering the Abbey (see below, n. 6), had said: 'As you know well *I* am extrinsic to *your* scheme not intrinsic; I mean that the fact of the theatre being in Dublin and the limitations of patent etc. are impediments to me and my ideas. The local circumstances and people which to you are intrinsic, are extrinsic to me.'

[5] This was Synge's letter to WBY and AG of 13 Dec 1906 (*JMSCL* 1. 260–2), which commented on WBY's statement of 2 Dec 1906, and which WBY had shown to AEFH. In it Synge claimed that WBY's and AEFH's proposals to turn the Abbey Theatre 'for what are to some extent extrinsic reasons' into 'an executive movement for the production of a great number of foreign plays of many types would be . . . a disastrous policy'. He suggested that foreign plays were worth doing 'because they illuminate our work but for that reason only', and recommended that the Directors should 'keep our movement local'. He also insisted that any arrangement through which AEFH exercised direct control over the Theatre would be unworkable. While acknowledging the desirability of a new assistant stage manager (mainly because it would free W. G. Fay to concentrate on his acting), he suggested that it was a mistake to look to 'the English stage for the people that are needed', and disparaged in particular the acting of AEFH's favourites, Letitia Darragh and Mrs Campbell. He concluded with the conviction that it would be 'our wisest policy to work on steadily on our own lines for the term of the Patent'. This letter, which ran counter to all AEFH's ambitions, fanned her growing dislike of Synge into an intensity which approached her hatred of W. G. Fay, and she complained to AG that 'Mr. Synge's letter made me really angry; it carried this to my mind — let us have a theatre where foreign classics and other plays may be used to train actors to play Synge, let the other authors go hang! . . . Fay is necessary to Synge himself but neither are anything but extrinsic to my root idea.'

competent on that side and the present company only competent on that side. I need hardly say that I gave her no support, but that is the meaning of her letter to you. She looks upon herself as appealing to you in my interest as against Synge.[6] She has probably got it into her head that Synge will play into Fay's hands and get the new Managing Director project refused. She considers this man necessary for the production of my work as well as for the production of the foreign masterpieces which are, of course, a part of the original scheme, the Samhain 1904 programme. Whatever her own personal point of view is we will get the advantage as well as the disadvantage of her very literal fanatical loyalty to formulae and printed words. She will never ask us to go outside that programme but she will never be satisfied until all the parts of it are carried out as well as possible. The meaning of the passage you put the marks of exclamation at is, as I told her, that on the night Robert Gregory left control of the scenery and scenic arrangement of 'Shadowy Waters' the lantern was not lighted, there was only one torch instead of three, the sailors missed their cue and the lighting of the harp went wrong. I did this because I was impressing upon her that a stage manager must be engaged at once.[7] There is no use trying to deceive her about the facts. If she were to think that I was keeping back facts about Fay she would grow suspicious of everything I said in his favour. So far from my departing from the compromise I refuse[d] to write you her proposal about the managing director for fear you might think that I was going back upon it. I told her she must write it herself and would not let her say more about my opinion of it than that I would accept it if you and Synge did. I should say that in asking for a stage manager I said that if it were not

    [6] In her letter AEFH had told AG that it was 'much to Mr. Yeats's advantage that you should accept' the proposal, and that he 'was much relieved in mind' when he understood that she wanted to appoint as manager 'an educated man who would lift a great burden off his and your shoulders, and who would be able to help his plays to worthy representation'. She went on to comment that since her ideas were 'in distinct opposition to Mr. Synge and as presumably you have the casting vote, the whole depends on you. It is so much to Mr. Yeats's advantage that you should accept it (and promptly too) that his sense of delicacy may prevent him from urging it as strongly as he feels it.'

    [7] AG had penned exclamation marks by a passage in the letter in which AEFH had demanded: 'What is the use of Mr. Gregory's artistic help if as soon as his back is turned he is to be insulted? *I* resent this as having happened to an artist in an institution for which I am at any rate somewhat responsible in the public eye.' Attending the penultimate performance of *The Shadowy Waters* on 14 Dec, Holloway noted (NLI) that the 'lighting . . . was dimmer & more shadowy than at the two previous performances I had witnessed, &, perhaps, not quite so effective on that account. . . . One likes to see the principal figures in this dream more clearly defined. The harp at the end failed to be lit up & remained in deepest darkness, & the Queen, as she watched Aibric cut the ropes . . . became scarcely even a shadowy outline, instead of being a dimly-lighted vision of ecstatic beauty.' He erroneously supposed that this was deliberate, and complained that this 'constantly experimenting in presence of an audience is a mistake, especially when the lighting (as in this strange play) has won general eulogy. Had I seen it for the first time to-night I would have been unfavourably impressed with the gloom. . . . Much of the action was carried on in black night-like gloom, & voices came out of the darkness only. . . . This was a mistake & bored the audience visibly.'

granted now Fay must be allowed to return to the full control he had at the beginning as at present his authority was shaken and that there must be some authority in the theatre either that of proper organization or of his disorderly personal methods. I should, under the circumstances, retire from the managing directorship unless I found that my doing so would shake Miss Horniman's faith in the scheme too much. I believe that a continuation of the present system or anything like it will have the result of you, I, Fay, Synge and Miss Horniman being all at each other's throats in six months. Your letter to Fay is charming and will, in all probability, carry its point. I should have been more drastic I should have said "we are convinced that your future and the future of every person in the theatre probably in the immediate future, but certainly at the end of the patent term depends upon your acceptance. If you refuse the whole company must be got together, players and authors—Boyle must be brought over and the vote of the majority taken" that, I believe is the only refusal a Director should accept.[8] I recognise our obligation to Fay but our obligation to the

---

[8] Since WBY had not after all seen W. G. Fay in London he could not pass on AG's letter of 26 Dec 1906 (see p. 548, n. 3). She therefore wrote another letter to Fay on 1 Jan 1907, and sent a copy of this to WBY on the same day, with the comment: 'You may not think I write strongly enough, but, first, I want him to tell me his views frankly—&, 2, I don't want him to give notice in a temper—I am on the whole anxious to accept, but also determined not to do so, or promise to do so, till I know if Fay has objections, & what they are.' In her letter to Fay she enclosed a copy of AEFH's proposal and WBY's comments on it in his letter of 27 Dec (see pp. 549–50). She continued: 'I am very anxious to have your views. You and I had talked the matter over pretty fully as you know, and I think the thing we were agreed upon was that a new business man was absolutely necessary to take the burden of business off you.' She went on to say that she had come to the conclusion that they ought to accept AEFH's offer if Fay had 'no insuperable objection', and pointed out that AEFH had given them liberty in choice of the new manager 'so we should be free to change one that did not suit. I do not believe the plays would gain by his production and stage management, for the mixing of methods is probably a mistake, but Mr Yeats can look after his own, which are our principal stock in trade, and our audience dont want too many foreign masterpieces any more than we ourselves do. The high pay is annoying in a way, for you who have worked so long and so hard at the creation of this theatre deserve it better, but on the other hand it may enable us to get a man who you can respect and learn from. The more you learn the better fitted we shall be to make our own way in the future, if ever that day comes when we can be independent. Though I do not myself care so much for the peasant work as for Mr Yeats verse, we know it is more popular and has more attention, so your side will always be sure of full appreciation, even outside your own acting. Now as summing up, I think I may ask you to give the scheme a fair trial. The only alternative is, to pay a business man ourselves, about £100 a year, to do extra work to try and pay him, (which it will not be easy to do with Miss Horniman against our tours), and in the end to find that the brunt of the business falls on you again, for he would not be likely to have sufficient authority.' She urged him 'not to refuse the offer in a hurry; and above all not to speak of it until you have decided. If you make up your mind to accept you should let the whole company know that it is by your own wish, indeed almost by your suggestion, for you said more than once to me that a Managing Director would be the right solution. If they think the arrangement has been made with grudging assent from you it will lessen their respect for you, and if Miss Horniman thinks she has forced it upon you it will lessen her respect. If we accept it, I am going to write to her as if it was just the thing we are "thirsty for" . . . and I will keep in mind the old saying that "a defeat can always be turned to a victory". I am not afraid, I am sure with more time for you and for the writers we shall do great things and in the end sweep the foreigners into the sea.'

others is very considerable and no personal obligation, however great, can exist for one moment if it runs counter to the supreme object of the Movement, the creation of great dramatic art in Ireland. Every member of the organization should be made to feel that, no one has a right in it except in so far as their presence there serves that object. You and I and Synge have also to consider that if this theatre goes on consuming our time on controversial follies and business details we had better leave it for we have all other ways of expressing ourselves than playwriting. I have practically lost this day, necessarily lost it, I admit, because of a <personal> dispute <for that is what it is> that has arisen simply out of the exasperating side of Fay's character and this dispute is drawing us all in. Exactly the same thing happened when Mrs. Emery's very similar temperament (the same evasions, the same struggle to keep Authority, the same chrisses) broke up a society established for many years and set lifelong friends against each other (I am not suggesting that anything of that sort will arise here).[9] But I do mean that it would be better for us all to end the whole thing than leave Fay in control. I daresay I am writing a little strongly, perhaps more strongly than I mean but you know what dictation is. One writes as one talks and forgets that the written word is weightier than the spoken. I have no time to re-dictate or weigh my words for if I don't get some of Dierdre written I shall miss the American mail.[10] I do hope Fay will decide soon or somebody decide for him, for the man must be got at once and there is no time to waste. Burchill sounds like a piece of luck as he must have the very best tradition there is, for the Maeterlinck play was a beautiful piece of quiet, stately arrangement, the best I have seen after the French Phaedre.[11] [*Remainder of letter in WBY's hand*] I would sooner in some ways get a man from Vedrenne as Miss Horniman seems set on that.[12]

Yr ev<br>
W B Yeats

TLS Berg.

[9] A reference to the disputes in the Golden Dawn in early 1901, when FF's attempts to retain her heterodox 'Sphere' group caused a serious convulsion in the Order (see III. 25–7, 29–34, 36–40, 42–7).

[10] See p. 516.

[11] For Maeterlinck see p. 558, n. 2. WBY had seen Sarah Bernhardt in Racine's *Phèdre* when she performed it in French at the Garrick Theatre, London, on 20 June 1902 as part of a three-week repertory season, and the production was seminal in showing him an alternative to conventional contemporary acting, as he recalled in 'An Introduction for my Plays' (*E & I*, 527–8): 'I wanted to get rid of irrelevant movement—the stage must become still that words might keep all their vividness—and I wanted vivid words. . . . It seems that I was confirmed in this idea or I found it when I first saw Sarah Bernhardt play in *Phèdre*, and that it was I who converted the [Irish] players.'

[12] This is finally what happened. In a letter of 28 Jan 1907 to the Directors, AEFH said that she had 'asked Mr Vedrenne to advise Mr Yeats', and this led to the appointment of Ben Iden Payne.

## *To Lady Gregory,* [*3 January 1907*]

PS. to letter of to day.
I have just remembered a fact which may be working in Miss Hornimans
mind causing her excitement about Synges letter. The theatre was given to
carry out according to Samhain letter ideas in 'essays & *speaches*' of mine!
The one speach that had significance for her—*the one that made her give the
theatre*—was that on the first night of 'The Kings Threshold'. 'The Independent' had attacked me among other reasons because I wanted to produce
foreign masterpeices which it thought 'dangerous'. I appealed for help to
the audience particularly on this point. You might look up speach the next
time you are near theatre book, which is at Abbey St. If my memory is right
we must consider their production as an important part of our charter & make
our plans accordingly. I never thought of the thing to this moment & when
Miss Horniman quoted her letter wondered what she meant by 'speaches'.[1]

Yr ev<br>W B Yeats

ALS Berg, with envelope addressed to Coole, postmark 'LONDON JA 3 07'.

## *To Lady Gregory,* [*4 January 1907*]

18 Woburn Buildings | Euston Road

My dear Lady Gregory: It occurs to me that you may have thought Miss
Hornimans letter a reply not to Synges answer to my "statement" but to his
recent letter about the new man. It was a reply to the 'statement'—as
I know from her letters to me.[1] There is no need to re-discuss policy with

---

[1] The *Irish Daily Independent and Nation* (4) had attacked the INTS on 8 Oct 1903 (see III. 444),
condemning particularly the Society's proposal to produce foreign masterpieces: 'we mislike the
importation proposal because of its dangers, though these could be obviated were those charged with
the selections of plays persons on whose taste or judgement reliance could be placed.' WBY had replied
to this attack in a speech given on 8 Oct 1903, the first night of *The King's Threshold*, and widely reported
in the Dublin press. This speech impressed AEFH so much that it finally persuaded her to purchase a
theatre for the INTS, and she asked WBY to expand on it in the 1904 number of *Samhain*, where it
appeared as 'The Play, the Player, and the Scene' (see *Expl*, 164–80). Thereafter she treated the
principles adumbrated there as non-negotiable, and in a letter from Algeria of 31 Dec 1906, which
WBY may already have received, told him (NLI): 'I leave the Directors free to carry out their own ideas
as long as they are in harmony with the "Samhain Principals" [*sic*].' She warned him in the same letter
that if 'the "Samhain Principals" [*sic*] are to be stretched into an intention to go in every way against the
rules of the ordinary stage *where these rules are right & necessary*, I have been under a serious delusion. At
present my position is "false and absurd" in the eyes of the public & I naturally object.'

[1] Besides his letter of 13 Dec 1906 reflecting on WBY's statement of 2 Dec (see p. 562, n. 5), Synge
had also written to WBY on 24 Dec commenting on AEFH's 'very generous offer' of 17 Dec (see p. 547),

her. We are bound to carry out the ideas in my 'essays & speaches' before her public letter. It may be desirable to summarize these for new man in some compendious form but that is for us. The essence of those ideas is that it must be a theatre of general artistic interest—but Synges letter—except possibly that the foreign side of the work should be taken more seriously—is as legitimate a deduction from my written word as my 'statement'. On the other hand if 'Fand' is to be done I dont see any body but Miss Darragh & she must be got at once. I dont think M$^{rs}$ Emery will come at present—she certainly wont promise to do so as she is trying to arrange for America, and her play, & as I said some time ago her engagement would be deeply resisted by Miss Horniman (who thinks her another Fay) & this would make negociating about new man much more difficult.[2] I on my side will oppose as strongly as possible any attempt to perform any play in verse with a considerable passionate part in verse for a woman with any of our own people—including Moira.[3] I have no objection to putting all such plays off indefinitely. If we get the right man his decissions may be satisfactory but we must get him first & unless we secure Miss Darragh now—we cannot be certain of having anybody for the part unless of course she can on being asked leavi[ng] us another two or three weeks delay—she said she must know by Jan. 1. I have no objection but every wish for M$^{rs}$ Emery but not till negociations are finished. We cannot give Colums people sixpenny seats; & without knowing how they can act & act the particular play & what that play is like cannot I think give him a Saturday at the Abbey—as they would be taken as part of our programme. This however I may be wrong about but the seat question is a hopeless barrier—Miss Horniman would never give way.[4]

Yr ev<br>W B Yeats

but this letter, which WBY sent on to her (see p. 550), would hardly have reached her in Algeria by this time, and her letter to WBY of 28 Dec 1906 (enclosed with this letter) makes it clear that she is objecting to Synge's letter of 13 Dec.

[2] For *Fand* see p. 558. This is an artful move by WBY, as he knew AG was eager to have the play by her great friend and former lover Wilfrid Blunt produced soon and well by the Abbey. He also knew that AG and Synge disliked Letitia Darragh (see pp. 558, n. 4, 562, n. 5). They had both, however, been in favour of bringing FF over (see pp. 558, n. 4 and *JMSCL* I. 262), but AEFH had fallen out with her during the dispute in the GD in 1901 (see p. 548, n. 4).

[3] i.e. Maire Walker; see pp. 558, 559. WBY constantly complained that Abbey actresses lacked the passion of their English and French colleagues, and on 28 Sept 1904 had informed John Quinn (III. 650) that the 'company want Kincora, but we are afraid that the part of Gormleith, a very big passionate part, overtakes Miss Walker's somewhat narrow range of emotions'. According to Mrs Martin, the Abbey caretaker, 'Mr. Yeats called Maire [Walker] the Virgin actress. He said she possessed Virginal Beauty and Charm' (*Ireland's Abbey Theatre*, 68).

[4] The Theatre of Ireland had hoped to take the Abbey in early February of this year for productions of Colum's *The Fiddler's House* and Alice Milligan's *The Last Feast of the Fianna* (see II. 483–4, 487). However, although AEFH had permitted the Abbey Company to lower its cheapest seats to 6*d.*, she

M^rs Emery has given me a charming gold & platinum ring that belonged to York Powell.[5] I hope to read her revised 'Dierdre' on Sunday.

I have just found this letter & put numbers to what seems important. She has clearly that speach of mine in her head I think in a vague way & looking on the Foreign classics as "intrinsic". That the proposal to get them up under Fay is to sacrifice what is "intrinsic" to his "vanity" & to subordinate them to our creative work is to sacrifice them [to] Synges "Egotism" (he having put this point of view in letter answering my "statement"). The new "producer" should put us in the right in this matter. I have only Theatre book No 1—by the by & so cannot make out the "charter" clearly.[6] We are certainly bound by that "charter" what ever it is. I know I am right about speach after "Threshold".[7]

[*At top of first page*]

I have begged Miss H— to write no more letters to Ireland two negociators are intolerable.

[*On back flap of envelope*]

I have just heard from M^rs Emery. She leaves for America on the 18th (it is now by certain). Wants you to be one of her "patrons". Quinn says she must have "patrons".[8]

---

insist that other companies hiring the Abbey should continue to charge a minimum of 1*s.* (twice the price of other Dublin theatres), and this proved such a deterrent that the Theatre of Ireland plays were finally staged at the Rotunda on 21 Mar 1907.

[5] York Powell (1850–1904) had been a close friend and neighbour of the Yeatses at Bedford Park from 1887 to his death. An expert on the Nordic sagas, and upon folklore generally, he was Regius Professor of Modern History at Oxford from 1894 until his death, and served as president of the Irish Texts Society. He was a particular friend of Jack Yeats, but had also encouraged WBY, and written enthusiastically about his poetry. As a resident of Bedford Park, he had been a neighbour of FF's relations the Pagets.

[6] 'Theatre book No 1' seems to have been the first in a series of compilations of documents relating to the setting up and administration of the Abbey Theatre; none of the series appears to have survived the Abbey fire of July 1951. The 'charter' was presumably the letter AEFH had sent to the INTS in April 1904, setting out the conditions under which she was offering them a permanent home, and instructing them 'to make a powerful and prosperous Theatre, with a high artistic ideal' (see III. 573), although she may also have been thinking of the clause added to the Patent on 20 Aug 1904, which restricted the Abbey repertoire to plays 'written by Irish writers on Irish subjects, or such dramatic works of foreign authors as would tend to interest the public in the higher works of dramatic art' (see III. 640, n. 5).

[7] i.e. 'The Play, the Player, and the Scene'; see p. 529, n. 3.

[8] AG did not become an 'official' patron, but in a letter of 11 Jan (Berg) told WBY that she would 'be proud to help Mrs. Emery in any way'.

[*With enclosure, the interpolated figures '(1)', '(2)', and '(3)' in WBY's hand*]
<Hotel Oriental, | Algiers.>
You are to write to *Poste Restante, Tunis*
*up to Jan. 12<sup>th</sup>.*
Dec. 28<sup>th</sup>/06.

My dear Demon,

How it rains! We have had some lovely weather, but now it comes down in sheets. I had not expected to find such a beautiful white city in such a beautiful situation. This is far more European than Tunis & there are no camels. But the beggars are a joy, they are so picturesque. I had a charming letter from Lady Gregory; she seems to understand that my offer was well-meant, but she does not want to decide at once. I wrote her a long letter giving my own personal views on the subject & saying that I consider it necessary to take action at once, so as not to lose any of the advantages of the present growth of the audiences. I told her how I understand that I am *ex*trinsic to the Irish idea, but that on the other hand, all that side is *ex*trinsic to my scheme itself. But maybe she will send you the letter to read.[9] I did not mention nor refer to Miss Darragh at all. That is a matter in which I must not interfere. The more I think of it, the better I like the idea of a professional hand on the reins. I dread more & more the scheme of letting Fay (1) practise on classics & so to make us ridiculous in the eyes of the few who matter. It comes to this— why am *I* to be sacrificed to Fay's (2) vanity & Mr Synge's (3) egotism? That is the root of the whole difficulty. They would "miau" loudly enough if I wanted you to produce an Irish play written by me, wouldn't they? *That* would be damaging the whole scheme to please me & not any worse, if as bad, as wanting to insult Sophocles to please Fay. The posts are not daily so my card about the dandelion won't have given you any help.[10] The "properties" ought to be kept ready always, for *all* plays in the repertory, so as not to have a rush at the last moment. A few bits of white wool & some wire & a bit of artificial green stalk and some ingenuity could easily make what is wanted.

Miss Tobin has a good review in the Saturday. I hope that she had the decency to acknowledge your help in the preface, even if not mentioning your name.[11]

---

[9] i.e. that of 26 Dec 1906; see p. 561.

[10] AEFH's card has not been traced, but presumably advised WBY on how best to make a stage property for *The Hour-Glass*, which was produced at the Abbey from 29 Dec to 5 Jan. At the beginning of a crucial scene between the Wise Man and Teigue the Fool, Teigue blows a dandelion-head to find what time it is (*VPl*, 628, 630). WBY retained this incident in his revised version of the play in 1913.

[11] Agnes Tobin's translation of Petrarch's *On the Death of Madonna Laura*, published in November 1906 (see p. 554), had been admiringly reviewed by her friend Arthur Symons (see p. 144) under the

On my return I'll come & put your papers tidy. Could you manage, I wonder, to remember to keep old foreign stamps for me? I should like to hear that you have engaged the new man already.

Yours<br>Annie

ALS Berg, with envelope addressed to Coole, postmark 'NORTH WEST GPO JA 4 07'. Enclosure NLI.

## To A. E. F. Horniman, [c. *4 January 1907*]

Mention in letter from AEFH, 10 January [1907].
Telling her that there is still a loophole left,[1] criticizing her attitude to W. G. Fay, censuring her description of the Abbey Theatre as an 'Irish Toy',[2] telling her of the imminent production of Masefield's play,[3] and expostulating that her letter to AG did harm.[4]

NLI. Misdated by AEFH '1906'.

title 'A Woman's Petrarch' in the *Saturday Review* of 22 Dec 1906 (776). Describing the book as 'one of the most beautiful volumes of English verse' Symons claimed that it was 'not only more human but more imaginative than Petrarch': 'It is Petrarch as if seen through the veil of the Portuguese sonnets, a man's formal and checked sorrow interpreted and set to gush forth though a woman's tears. A quality of piercing tenderness, of homeless pathos, comes into and alters the severer convolutions of the original. Body and sense are given to sentiment. . . . It is difficult to praise individual excellence where almost all is good in its own way, where almost everything is re-seen, relived, and altered again in a new, unlikely, beautiful way.' WBY had helped her with the book, and she had asked for both WBY's and Synge's assistance in correcting its punctuation and proofs. WBY's name does not appear in the book, which had no preface.

[1] WBY was still seeking a compromise in the dispute over the proposed new Abbey manager, and in her reply AEFH said that she was 'very glad that there is still a loop-hole left'.

[2] WBY had pointed out that AEFH's relentless hostility towards W. G. Fay and gratuitous belittling of the Abbey in her letters to AG were giving offence and creating unnecessary difficulties. She, however, justified her position, replying that she had written to AG (see p. 561, n. 1) 'simply to explain my own views of the matter. It was only right that she should know them. If I thought Fay "capable" why should I offer to pay another man? "An Irish Toy" is I consider the right name for what now exists, but I ask no one to agree with me. This is not a case for "diplomacy" as I cannot fight Fay with his own weapons; he is so unscrupulous in his vanity & Mr Synge is under his thumb.' She added that she was 'dreadfully sorry that my letter did harm, but I was anxious to let Lady Gregory know how my feelings on the matter justify such a further outlay. You yourself *know* that Fay is not capable & that the scheme is only a *toy* at present. The public agree voicelessly, let the other Directors say what they may. That I want him left to do what he is capable of doing should shew that I have no spite against him.'

[3] Masefield's three-act tragedy *The Campden Wonder* (see pp. 288–9) opened at the Court Theatre on 8 Jan and received eight performances between then and 1 Feb. In her reply AEFH hoped 'that Masefield's play will go well & be a success'.

[4] AEFH repudiated WBY's insistence that she should try to be more diplomatic (see n. 2): 'If you only get the new man accepted by "diplomacy" he won't be allowed to be of any use & will simply cause a waste of money.'

## *To A. E. F. Horniman,* [c. *5 January* [*1907*]

Mention in letter from AEFH, 12 January [1907].
A 'short letter' discussing AEFH's and Miss Darragh's views on the Abbey Company,[1] W. G. Fay's avoidance of him in London,[2] AEFH's recent letter to AG, and the appointment of a stage manager.

NLI. Misdated by AEFH '1906'.

## *To Lady Gregory,* [*5 January 1907*]

18 Woburn Building

My dear Lady Gregory: I think Fay has sacrificed his fellow workers & the future of the theatre to himself & deserves no sympathy or support but there is no use cry[ing] over spilt milk.[1] I shall not go to Dublin unless you wire that you have demanded with me a vote of whole crowd, authors, actors & all (Boyles expenses to be paid). Failing this I shall see Vedrenne on Monday & engage as soon as possible a stage manager at £100 a year to manage all under us except that he is to obey Fay in production. I am not quite sure whether I shall continue as managing director. I do not beleive theatre can succeed on present lines & may think it better to wait some future chance to re-construct without responsibility for a failure. We cannot get independent of Miss Horniman without her

---

[1] This letter was evidently written before WBY had received AG's telegram telling him that Fay had rejected AEFH's offer of £500 for a new manager. In her reply AEFH said: 'I got both your letters this morning & read the short one first. It is useless to fight a radical Tarot—Miss Darragh & I have seperately [*sic*] done our best to save your scheme. . . . I accept the decision of the Directors in silence, mostly because I see that they are sacrificing the scheme, your repute & my feelings to Fay's vanity. There is no other reason that I can see & it is a great pity. Fay himself would gain by being properly stage-managed himself but he cannot see this.'

[2] AEFH said that she thought Fay's 'avoiding you in London is *abominable* at this moment, no amusement nor social matter should be allowed to stand in the way of such a real duty. How can Synge's play win fame out of Ireland under such circumstances? I know that he has a certain greatness in him, but his *cowardice* will destroy him unless he grows out of it.'

[1] On Saturday, 5 Jan, AG had wired WBY (Berg): 'Fay refuses Synge relieved My instincts with them but most unwilling to go against you ought you to see them.' This meant that Fay had refused to accept AEFH's offer of a managing director to take charge of verse and non-Irish work at £500 a year (see p. 541, n. 2). On receiving this letter AG wrote to Synge: 'I had, as I expected, an angry letter from Yeats this morning—however I think from it he wld give Fay better terms.'

capital in the [?]initial stages. I doubt if we can draw even Dublin with present arrangements—we cannot get to America or probably to England. What do you mean by wiring that your instinct supports Fay & that Synge is "releived". I hope you will not write this to Fay—Synge thought it would be a 'capital' thing for us all—& you both urged him to accept. I really look on this as closing the theatre in the end & do not pretend that I will accept this decision except as a necessary evil for a time. <One of the reasons why I think that I had better leave the Management is that Fay will> I shall let the company know Fays decission on the first opportunity—as I beleive it wrecks their careers. If Fay had accepted I should have been prepared (so far as I am concerned) to add to his income a part of what we must pay the stage manager or all if he had pressed—but I dont think this last would have been fair to the others—now they loose 1 hundred a year the chance of good teaching, large capital to build up our independence & get nothing in return except the blessing of a very careless & often very unjust rule, and all that Fay may keep empty position & the production of verse work (remember all that we were to give to the educated & distinguished man we might have had is now to be handed with the exception of <our work> a little production to a £2 a week stage-manger) for which I think him unfit—but I forgot your instincts are with him & that you only urged him to accept to please me. Synge is now probably telling Fay that his decission is 'capital'. I wont go to Dublin because if I went now I should make a scene with Fay, which would make the future more difficult—and it is difficult enough—they will hardly have done much more than touch £40 or £45 last week.[2] You & I & Synge & Miss Horniman have done as much as Fay for the theatre, & he knows that his will <will> [?]prevail against us. I do not think he will do better in the future because of this, or that our authority has enough dignity to last. If I find that is so I shall leave things to go their own way without me & wait the wreck to re-construct.

Yr sny  
W B Yeats

ALS Berg, with envelope addressed to Coole, postmark 'LONDON.N.W. JA 5 07'.

---

[2] The Abbey played *The Hour-Glass* and *The Mineral Workers* from 29 Dec 1906 to 5 Jan 1907, and took in all £46 6s. 7d.

## To A. E. F. Horniman, [c. 5 January 1907]

Mention in following letter, and in letter from AEFH, 12 January [1907]. A long 'very angry', blotted letter about Abbey affairs[1] and Miss Darragh's connection with the theatre,[2] and evidently endorsing AEFH's view of W. G. Fay.[3]

NLI. Misdated by AEFH '1906'.

## To Lady Gregory, 8 January 1907

18, Woburn Buildings,
Jan. 8, 1907.

My dear Lady Gregory,
There must be something wrong with the post.[1] I have received no letter about Fay's decision except yours to-day containing proposals A and B.[2]

---

[1] This letter was evidently written shortly after WBY had received AG's telegram about Fay's rejection of AEFH's offer and conveyed the sentiments expressed in the above letter to AG. In her reply AEFH wrote 'Your last letter, dear Friend, is very angry, the blots tell their own tale. But maybe by the 21st the other Directors may see their mistake.'

[2] AEFH replied that Miss Darragh had 'written clearly that she is *not* returning to the Abbey Theatre, she will be in London at the end of January looking for an engagement. Her help or that of some other finished artist is *necessary* for classical plays, you know this as well as I do. Faults & mannerisms are small things compared to a solid knowledge of the business required. Anyone able to hold her own would arouse the same antagonism under these circumstances. She certainly means what she writes, but I shall see her in London.'

[3] AEFH felt that her attitude towards Fay had been entirely vindicated by events: 'I did *not* ask Fay's consent, but that of the Directors & so now my rude remarks about his "assuming the whole show" are perfectly justified. Don't let them think that I take this as a personal snub, it *is* one; but the point that pains me is the way in which your interests & those of your scheme are being sacrificed.'

[1] There was something wrong: on 9 Jan AG told Synge that, puzzled by the lack of replies to her letters, she had had the Kiltartan postbox opened '& it was stuffed with letters from before the New Year! They are all going now.' WBY was perplexed because she had written to him on 'Monday' (7 Jan; Berg) saying that he would 'have had my letter and Synge's by this'. In fact, Synge did not write until 9 Jan, and he apparently felt that her earlier letter (presumably written on Saturday evening or Sunday, 5 or 6 Jan) had been superseded by that of 7 Jan, and so did not bother to send it on after retrieving it from the Kiltartan box.

[2] With her letter of 7 Jan she enclosed two proposals, which she had also sent to Synge:

PROPOSAL A

We agree to work with the new man for six months as cordially as possible. Whatever foreign masterpieces our own people are thought fit for can be put on. Mr Yeats can bring in anyone he likes for his own plays, according to compromise, and in the case of Phedre can bring in Miss Darragh as he had promised it to her.

At the end of six months if any of the Directors are dissatisfied with the new methods, a meeting to be called. If any of the actors wish to leave they are naturally free to do so; if any of the authors wish to

I have also received nothing from Synge[3] and no "Irish Peasant" which you mention having sent.[4] The proposal B is unworkable for reasons which I will give, but proposal A is perfectly satisfactory as I think and I believe that I am within my rights in accepting it in Miss Horniman's name. The only point I must raise is this that there shall be no reference to the Company as a whole unless demanded by either side after a vote of the Directors. In other words I believe that we should accept responsibility. In Miss Horniman's letter in reply to Synge's proposals which only reached me, I think, on Saturday she says: That we are perfectly at liberty to dismiss the Managing Director in which case she adds "I should have to decide whether I should authorise you to engage a new man." I thought this was understood from the beginning, furthermore she says "I carefully left it

leave they must be allowed to take their plays with them, their agreement to leave them with the Society for the term of the Patent being cancelled.

PROPOSAL B

We cannot with self respect, and looking at the list of plays produced and the notices of them, accept Miss Horniman's statement that we are "in the public eye an Irish toy". We cannot accept her statement that our stage manager having had "his chance to carry out what he could" has "proved his absolute incapacity". To accept the new man would be to accept these statements.

We claim six months in which to work in our own way. We claim the right of taking our work to London and elsewhere before the end of that time, that "the public eye" may judge what we can do while still working by ourselves.

At the end of six months, should Miss Horniman renew her offer, we should hold a meeting of authors and actors and make our decision.

If this proposal is accepted I would ask leave to re-organise at once, engaging a new man at say £2 a week to help business side, and I would give all possible time to the theatre during the next months.

In her covering letter AG explained that she had spent 'a good part' of Saturday night 'thinking things out': 'I tried how near I could go to your wishes, and wrote proposal A. Then I tried to think what was the right, just and straight thing to do, and I wrote proposal B. I think A is weak, and would have too much uncertainty. I think B is the right and logical course. I hope you will be able to accept it. I should write it to Miss Horniman as nicely as I could, and in my belief she would respect us the more for adopting it.'

[3] If there was a letter from Synge, it is untraced.

[4] WBY had long been sympathetic to the editorial policies of the *Irish Peasant*, a Navan weekly which had made a stand against what it considered undue clerical interference in Irish life, particularly education, and he had considered joining an editorial syndicate in the summer of 1905 (see p. 124, n. 1). The paper was now in the middle of a crisis: in December 1906 Cardinal Logue wrote to its proprietor, John McCann, alleging that under the editorship of W. P. Ryan it 'was becoming a most pernicious anti-Catholic print', and threatening to suppress its 'poisonous influence' by denouncing it publicly and prohibiting it throughout his archdiocese. Ryan printed the letter and started a spirited controversy over it, but the McCann family took fright and decided to close the paper down. Ryan thereupon resolved to continue to publish it independently from Dublin, and AG was almost certainly sending WBY the issue for 29 Dec 1906, in which, under bold headlines, Ryan proclaimed: 'The *Irish Peasant* has ceased to exist. The *Peasant* takes its place. . . . We bring out the present issue to explain the situation, and our plans, to Irish-Ireland.' While accepting that the clergy should 'have entire control of religious education', and a 'liberal share in the management of secular education', he argued that in any 'really national' system 'intelligent and interested laymen should have part in the direction and control of secular education', and announced that the paper would continue to advocate this policy when it moved to Dublin. He relaunched the paper (as the *Peasant*) in Dublin on 9 Feb of this year.

open for a play *at the wish of the author* to be put in the hands of any
Director or artist instead of the new man; if an author chooses Fay let him
take the risk. But only the author can choose a producer, where the author
is not at hand it must be done by the new man."[5] I don't think it would be
wise to ask her straight to allow the word author to include translator. I
know she would refuse this, but a clause empowering Fay to produce all
Dialect work would enable you to give Fay Moliere. Her object is to place
out of Fay's hands what, one may describe, as the more or less international
work. I had not understood her original proposal to permit the author to
give work to Fay, my work for instance. I do not say that I would give it to
him, for I should be inclined to experiment with the new man. As I am very
doubtful of Fay's capacity for poetical work, though far from certain that he
has it not, I should certainly try him again, when I knew more and he knew
more. As I imagine this proposal makes all well it is hardly worth discussing
proposal B. Miss Horniman would not accept it because Waring has
impressed upon her mind very strongly that Fay would not give an equal
or subordinate to whose appointment he objected a fair chance.[6] I am afraid
you will find your chance of making Fay accept more difficult now than if
you had approached him sternly at the outset. He will have taken up a
certain position before the others and find it hard to recede. You may have
to be very stern indeed, even to the point of accepting his resignation which
he would never stick to. It may be a question of risking all for all. It is better
however for me to recapitulate my argument. I feel that our obligations are
very heavy to the Company as a whole and less to Fay who, if he left us
tomorrow, would be in a better position than if he had never joined us, than
to the others who could not no not even Sarah Allgood get regular work in
the commercial theatre except perhaps Mac,[7] for they are only fitted for

[5] On 31 Dec 1906 AEFH had written WBY two letters from Algiers. One was a formal reply to the
Directors' response to her offer of 19 Dec, and stated that she could not 'alter my offer in any way. . . . Any
modification on Mr. Synge's lines would simply be the undoing of my intentions.' While undertaking to
leave the Directors free to carry out their own ideas as long as they were in harmony with the principles set
out in the 1904 *Samhain*, she insisted that the new manager must 'be free to engage or dismiss actors' and
that if his decisions were not supported by the majority of Directors 'he must go'. While conceding the
right of an author to select any producer he wished, she stipulated a further proviso: 'only the author can
select the producer; where the author is not at hand it must be done by the new man.' She was also
adamant that her offer 'must be accepted or refused finally by January 21ˢᵗ'. In an accompanying letter,
marked 'Private', she urged WBY 'to resume your literary & practical work, go on writing plays, get them
produced wherever you can & only trouble about the Abbey Theatre when it is to your own advantage'.
[6] Embarrassed by the shortcomings of the Abbey tour of 1906, which he had instigated, Wareing was
quick to place the blame on W.G. Fay (see pp. 431, 433, 441). He and his wife continued to see a good
deal of AEFH in London in the autumn of 1906, when they helped reinforce her antipathy towards Fay
(see pp. 545, 549, 551).
[7] Arthur Sinclair (see p. 258, n. 3) was now one of the leading actors at the Abbey and his range of
parts was wider than that of the other players. W. A. Henderson commented in the *Evening Herald* on 17
May 1913 (6) that as 'an exponent of flamboyant Irish character he stands beside Boucicault, Charles

Irish dialect work, or like Frank Fay have temperamental limitations.[8] We are fitting them for our theatre and for no other. Now if we quarrel with Miss Horniman at the present stage of development we leave ourselves no chance except one to which I shall recur presently of becoming independent of her. We know that for the sake of Fay's art we must appoint this new stage manager and if we have to give him a £100 a year out of our profits we shall have no capital for development, we may, though I doubt it, get to London for a day or two and perhaps make £70 or £80 and that would be the end in all probability. Miss Horniman will have an extremely bitter feeling and to get over that our success when the application for a new patent arises will have to be very great indeed before she admits it. No matter how financially independent we may have become and I have no belief in our becoming so we shall be dependent upon her goodwill before we apply for a new patent. The present one was not given until the Corporation had made certain reports, if I remember rightly, about the Abbey theatre and I know that it is dependent on the existence of that theatre and that no Patent is possible without a theatre and without the concurrence of the owner of the theatre.[9] Furthermore we shall be in the worst possible position for negotiation. In all probability with an only slightly enhanced reputation we shall have to bargain with the neccessity of procuring a livelihood for our people. Our obligation to people like Kerrigan who will have been taken from the chance of getting some sort of a lucrative trade will be overwhelming.[10] Miss Horniman will have set her imagination on something else. Furthermore she reminded me the

Sullivan, O'Grady and others, and he is greater than them, for he can impersonate characters which they could not touch.'

[8] Frank Fay had always been noted for moodiness, and lately this trait had grown noticeably worse. When Holloway called into the Abbey for a friendly chat on 29 Dec 1906 (NLI), Fay told him that 'were he not a coward he would end all, life wasn't worth the candle. And a lot more in the same despondent strain, I tried to reason it out of him but to no avail. I have noticed him getting strange & distant to everyone for the past year, & as he says himself he always wishes to be alone for then he cannot be deceived by false friends.' Later that morning Sara Allgood told Holloway that she 'was pleased I had spoken to Frank Fay as I did & hoped it would do him good. He had got very strange & distant in his manner recently.'

[9] The Patent granted to AEFH applied to the theatre rather than to the company which occupied that theatre, and so the INTS could not have sought its protection had it moved elsewhere (see Appendix). Moreover, a special restrictive clause, sought by the Dublin Corporation, forbade AG, who was AEFH's Irish agent, from assigning its rights to any person or persons other than a trustee appointed by Miss Horniman, her executors, or administrators. See pp. 308–9, n. 1.

[10] Joseph Michael Kerrigan (1885–1965) joined the Abbey Theatre Company in October 1906, after a short career in journalism, and made his first appearance in WBY's *Deirdre* on 24 Nov. In April 1907 he confided to Holloway (NLI) that 'he had never acted until he took part in *Deirdre*, nor never seen the N.T.S. play until shortly before that'. Nevertheless, he gained rapid prominence as an Abbey actor, and appeared regularly until 1916, when he joined the Irish Film Company. In 1920 he emigrated to the USA, where he did stage and film work.

other day of something I had forgotten, she tells me that when she gave this money, or I think when she gave some large increase of money I promised her to let her do what she liked with my plays at the end of the Patent period.[11] Now what does Fay gain by refusing? besides vain pomps, nothing except the right to produce a very small number more plays. To get that he gives up the leisure that would have made him an artist, his one opportunity and all likelihood of concentration a £1000 a year for the theatre. All that has made the reputation of the theatre the dialect work remains in his hands in any case. I believe that his position is indefensible and I cannot understand how anyone would support him for one moment. I think we are all to blame and I believe that I have the right to demand that in one serious matter we should put ourselves in the right. We have allowed him to suppose that we think him fit to manage the theatre and that if some other means could be found of saving his time and of lightening the pressure of Miss Horniman we should leave him in that position. I know that both you and Synge think that not only his undisciplined character but that his very genius which makes him excitable and capricious unfits him for the work. I think I have a right to ask that should he show hesitation you should say to him, no, I think that you should say to him in any case "even if we become financially independent of Miss Horniman we will not make you manager of the theatre. We think you too excitable, too hot-tempered, too unfit for the post in half a dozen ways, if you like, too much of an artist." Let it be put as agreeably as you like but let it be put. A great deal of our difficulties with Fay, mine expecially, is that he has always been struggling for an authority which he believed to be not only his right but his right in our eyes. In our anxiety to spare his feelings we have helped to create the present situation. I will just write a word to Miss Horniman to say that I think the matter will be arranged and when I have heard from you again put my understanding of her letters in writing so that there can be no mistake. It was my sense of obligation to the Company that made me say that if Fay refused I thought it undesirable to take any further active part in management. I should keep myself as a moderator on Miss Horniman for the reconstruction at the end of the three years and a half. I had almost forgotten that I do see one chance of becoming financially independent of Miss Horniman without more of her capital, though no way of getting round the difficulty of the new Patent. Frohman is to be in Dublin in two months and through Mrs Meakin and Miss Tobin I am trying to get a promise that he will go to the

[11] AG was aghast at what she termed this 'secret treaty' and wrote indignantly on Thursday (10 Jan; Berg): 'this "promise" business has upset everything. I am paralysed by it as to business, & indeed physically for I had a very bad night.' She reported that she had sent on the letter to Synge to 'see what he thinks about the "promise"—I don't think I am exaggerating its importance & the break up it wd mean.'

theatre.[12] We shall have to arrange a special programme. But here again there is a difficulty Frohman is a very stern master and Fay would have to submit absolutely to his authority. If he did any of the things about make-up and the like or kept the lax discipline which he did on tour we should have him dismissed in no time. It would be far better for him to go to America with some man in control who would be responsible to Frohman.

Yr ev<br>W B Yeats

P.S. I am not inclined to enter into any discussion of Miss Horniman's petulancies about an "Irish toy" or the like, we cannot base public action on private petulance.[13] [*In WBY's hand*] I have written to her say[ing] what I think of her diplomatic methods.

TLS Berg, with envelope addressed to Coole, postmark 'LONDON.W.C. JA 8 07'.

## To George Brett, 9 January [1907]

18 Woburn Buildings | Euston Road.<br>Jan 9th

Dear M[r] Brett: I have not finished Dierdre but it is not my fault the affairs of my theatre have drawn me away from the work again & again & I am in despair. I can only suggest this—if you do not get the MSS by this day week go on without it cutting out the paragraph at end of Appendix B about its performance in Dublin & publish it seperately.[1]

Yr sny<br>W B Yeats

ALS NYPL.

[12] Charles Frohman (1860–1915), the American theatrical manager and impresario, had a controlling interest in numerous theatres and companies in the USA and Britain. His first London success was with Charles Klein's *A Night Out* in 1896, and he subsequently collaborated with the Irish-born theatre manager George Edwardes and the playwright James Barrie. He lived for a great part of the year in London, where his main base was the Duke of York's Theatre, although at one time he had interests in four other theatres there, and he took a great number of London and European productions to the USA. He had been interested in Irish drama since June 1903, when he made enquiries about producing plays by WBY and AG (see III. 388). Violet Charlotte Meeking, née Fletcher (d. 1921), was the widow of Captain Bertram Meeking of the 10th Hussars, whom she had married in 1893 and who died in 1900. She was a London hostess, a philanthropist, and friend of Agnes Tobin. In 1912 she was to marry the stockbroker Herbert Johnson, and in 1921 sponsored a lecture by WBY at her house in Portman Square in aid of the Abbey Theatre. WBY and Synge dined with her on 11 June 1907.
[13] AEFH's description of the Abbey Theatre as being 'in the public eye an Irish toy' (see p. 570, n. 2) continued to rankle with AG and she had referred to it in 'Proposal B' (see above, n. 1).
[1] Brett would stand for none of this temporizing and, in his reply of 17 Jan (NYPL), urged WBY sharply to finish the play: 'I should be very sorry indeed to omit "Deirdre" from the second

## *To Lady Gregory*, [c. *9 January 1907*]

[*Starts at page 9*]

Miss Horniman has not refused us leave for M$^{rs}$ Emery but I sense that, owing to her dislike, to press that matter now would be tactless & make negociation more difficult. After the new man is in I am most anxious for M$^{rs}$ Emery or anybody else we may think necessary for our art.[1] Miss Horniman ment by 'diplomatic sulking' her refusal to pay for tour.[2] Let the new man have a fairly free hand, but, if we cannot get him, then we must do our best with Miss Darrah and the £100 a year stage manager—that is the way I see things. This is logical for none of our women have passionate dramatic power or passion in them but if I get a good man—I now agree with you that he should be left to judge of this. The stage manager is essential & Fay agreed to it in Dublin—we have always said we must get him ourselves if Miss Horniman wont or Fays genius is lost to us. That genius is our chief possession.

If you wish even now that we are in agreement, as I think, to be able to withdraw your plays I shall not hold you to that old bargain[3] but I think you had better leave the thing as it is, for if we can dismiss the man when we please all is in our hands.

I am sorry to have to press these things but I beleive the existence of the movement is at stake—& that I am bound by my obligation to the

---

volume, as we have made a public announcement that that play is to be included in the volume. I think that under these circumstances that our customers (your readers and admirers) would have reasonable ground for complaint. I shall accordingly hope that you will send me the copy for the play as soon as possible and permit me to include it in the book, as has been intended and announced.' *Deirdre* was finally included in the volume, which also printed the brief paragraph about the play's cast and first performance on 27 Nov 1906. Macmillan did not publish a separate edition of *Deirdre*.

[1] In her proposals of 6 Dec 1906, AG had suggested that FF should come to the Abbey as a verse-teacher (see p. 536). AEFH had not mentioned this in any of her letters, and AG interpreted this silence as a refusal.

[2] AG had, understandably, found this phrase (in AEFH's letter of 26 Dec; see p. 561, n. 1) perplexing. In the letter AEFH had explained that she believed 'that many of our difficulties which arose through Mr. Russell and his lambs came from his instinctive feeling of deeply felt opposition to *my* aim—the Art to be for its own sake, and to be done as well as possible. During all my long time of diplomatic sulking I was as you know most carefully watching events. I did my best out of my income to aid you to conquer a Dublin audience, knowing quite well that success in this would be *to me* a side-issue.'

[3] i.e. that they would invest the rights of their plays in the Abbey Theatre.

movement, to Miss Horniman & above all to the company as a whole[4]—our young people have no future but with us—to press them.

WBY

Masefields play very fine but coldly received.[5]

AL Berg.

## To Hugh Lane, [9 January 1907]

Wed

In haste
My dear Lane:
I shall see Holroad at once & write you result.[1]
I meant to go to you yesterday but Masefields play was not over until 5.45 and it would have been after six before I got to you.[2]
Hold out against corporation for the present—you can say Tate is considering question.[3] I will write a letter to committee, which they can

---

[4] See pp. 571–2.
[5] Masefield's tragedy *The Campden Wonder* (see pp. 288–9, 570), which had opened on 8 Jan. The production was not a success, partly because Barker (whose first production at the Court it was) paired it with Cyril Harcourt's *The Reformer*, a superficial comedy of manners in which a young widow's attempts to reform a rakish nobleman lead to contrived complications.

[1] Sir Charles Holroyd (1861–1917) had been knighted in 1903 and was director of the British National Gallery from 1906 to 1916. Lane wanted WBY to sound him out about the possibility of the Gallery making a room available for Lane's pictures, which would be loaned as a collection until the matter of the Dublin gallery had been resolved. When Charles Ricketts met him on 6 July 1905, he described him (BL) as 'a full blown specimen of the born official who lives on art, not by or for it'.
[2] See previous letter.
[3] Negotiations between the Committee for the Municipal Gallery and Dublin Corporation had begun in February 1905, when the latter placed on record its appreciation of the gift of paintings by Hugh Lane and others. At first gallery matters came under the jurisdiction of the Estates and Finance Committee, which allocated the project a maintenance grant of £500 per annum, and which, on 11 June 1906, was charged with hiring temporary premises pending the erection of a permanent building. In November 1906 gallery business was transferred to a subcommittee of the Public Libraries Committee, of which Arthur Griffith was a member. The question now at issue concerned the terms under which the pictures were to be presented to the Corporation. Its law agent advised that, legally, the Corporation could not give a grant to the gallery unless the pictures were made over absolutely to it; Lane and his Committee were unwilling to do this unless recognized artists and art historians were guaranteed places on the Gallery Subcommittee, and unless there were clear indications that the commissioning of a suitable temporary and satisfactory permanent gallery was going forward. (The Corporation had suggested the old Turkish Baths in Lincoln Place as a temporary venue.) In an attempt to achieve these goals, Lane now contemplated bringing pressure to bear on the Corporation by threatening to lend the pictures to English galleries, including the Tate and the National Gallery. It was not until 6 Sept 1907 that the Corporation adopted a recommendation from the Public Libraries Committee to acquire Clonmell House as a temporary home for the pictures, and accepted a compromise whereby certain of the pictures were donated absolutely and others on loan, in return for which Lane's nominees would

use if I get a chance.⁴ The trouble is that 'corporation' does not beleive we are in earnest—think it all 'bluff'.

Yr ever

W B Yeats

excuse paper & blots

ALS NLI.

*To Hugh Lane, 10 January 1907*

18, Woburn Buildings,

Jan. 10, 1907.

Dear Lane,

I saw Holroyd to-day, but only for a few minutes. I got there at five minutes to twelve and he had to inspect Rubenses on what sounded like a club roof in the neighbourhood of Whitehall.¹ I walked so far with him and poured out my thoughts with a good deal of vehemence and heard his. I dare say he said all or the most of all to you on Tuesday but as I was not there I can do no more than repeat them. There is a difficulty about room in the National Gallery as he is applying for an extension and does not want to compromise his case but in spite of that he is anxious for some of the pictures if he can talk over the Trustees who object to loans. Macoll is to see Lady Tate who objects to foreign pictures in the Tate Gallery and to get her

---

serve on the subcommittee. However, the battle over sites for a permanent building dragged on for many years, and on 5 Nov 1912 Lane finally forced the issue to a crisis, writing to the Town Clerk of Dublin that his collection would 'be removed from Dublin at the end of January 1913, if the building of a new and suitable gallery is not decided upon; but, if the provision of a Gallery is definitely arranged for, the pictures and sculptures will remain on loan until it is built, when they will be given to the city.'

⁴ It is unlikely that WBY wrote to the Committee of the Modern Gallery, but presumably he would have urged them to hold out against what he saw as the Corporation's attempts to take control of the running of the gallery.

¹ The Flemish painter Peter Paul Rubens (1577–1640) was one of the greatest artists of his time, and also an influential diplomat. During a diplomatic mission to London in 1629 he found time, amid political affairs, to paint a number of major pictures and also to begin work on canvases for the ceilings (rather than roof) of Inigo Jones's Banqueting Hall in Whitehall, work that he completed in 1634. Jones had built the Hall, the first Palladian building in England, between 1619 and 1622 and the nine pictures by Rubens were commissioned by Charles I to celebrate the reign of his father James I, with the central panel, *The Apotheosis of James I*, depicting the glorious ascension of the King into heaven. Ironically, on 30 Jan 1649 Charles took his last walk beneath the ceiling on his way to the scaffold, which had been constructed on the north side of the Hall. In 1893 Queen Victoria granted the Hall to the Royal United Services Institute, which remained there until 1962.

to permit a loan there.[2] He said that he would raise the matter but whether at the National Gallery or Tate I do not know, at a Board Meeting on February 2nd.[3] At first he said I will do it privately so that no one will know the result, meaning, I conclude, that no one might know who could use it against you if the result was a refusal. He then said "Lane had better write me a letter, offering <some of the> pictures to the Tate and National Gallery, and if I have to refuse I will write him a letter saying how fine the pictures are." I should think that a letter of this kind would make an end of all suspicion of the pictures that mattered. He had seen Miss Harrison[4] and she had spoken of the Corporation putting on to the Committee of Selection in case of their getting control say three of our people, but he had pointed out to her that this was no guarantee for the future as no man could say of the next generation what the Corporation will do. There is nothing, I am persuaded, between Corporation control with all the usual results and full artistic control (secured by what legal subterfuge you will) and to get this one must fight and fight with a sort of vehement patience. If you surrender the whole Cause of artistic intellect in Ireland is damaged for a generation, if you give up and scatter the pictures there is no man can blame you, but we in the times to come shall be the poorer for it. You have taken like everybody who works in our damned undisciplined country something of Atlas's job upon your shoulders and all one can say is one gets used to it.[5] If you decide to give in to the Corporation please let me know in good time that I may resign and send my letters to the papers, this will do you no harm but a little good for it may put the Corporation on their mettle.

[2] For MacColl see p. 21. The problem was not caused by Lady Tate alone: the Tate Gallery, which had opened at Millbank in 1897, was at this time subordinate to the National Gallery, and was intended only for the exhibition of modern British paintings, for which there was not room in the parent institution. It remained dedicated to British paintings until 1915, when the Curzon Committee recommended that a Gallery of Foreign Art should also be formed there, and that its administration should henceforth be independent of the National Gallery. Since Lane's own collection of paintings, and those purchased from the Staats-Forbes Collection, contained many examples of modern European art, they were unsuitable for the Tate. Lady Tate, née Amy Fanny Hislop (1850–1919), had married Sir Henry Tate (1819–99), founder of the Tate Gallery, as his second wife in 1885.

[3] The matter was raised at a Board Meeting of the National Gallery on 2 Feb 1907 but no firm decision was taken.

[4] i.e. Sarah Harrison; see p. 409, n. 3.

[5] In the end a compromise was worked out (see above). The pictures were divided into two groups: Class A, comprising the thirty pictures purchased from the Forbes Collection by subscription, and Class B, comprising eighty-four pictures which artists were prepared to present to the gallery and Hugh Lane's own collection. The pictures in Class B were vested unconditionally in the Corporation, those in Class A were loaned to the Corporation for an indefinite period. In return the governing Committee of the gallery was to include two members nominated by the Royal Hibernian Academy, two members nominated by the Irish National Gallery, and four members nominated by the Modern Art Gallery Committee. Such an arrangement ensured that the views of artists and art critics would prevail on the Committee.

I had almost forgotten to say that Holroyd said just as we parted and when it was too late to discuss the matter further that if he could not take the pictures for the National Gallery or the Tate he would make private enquiries as to some important provincial gallery that could do so. I said that you were anxious to keep the pictures together as much as possible, and he said that he understood that.

[*unsigned*]

P.S.

You said to me something about fearing that some of your artists might object to fighting if their pictures could not be hung conspicuously[6] meanwhile but I am certain that you are wrong there or the case should be put to them that is all and if I can do anything by going on a deputation or anything of that kind, please make use of me. This is not your battle only but all our battle. Why should not an artist have as strong bones as a politician and show his objections to being kicked in the usual way? They will fight a Corporation with joy and think you the better man for calling them to the work.

TS copy NLI.

## To Lady Gregory, 10 January 1907

W.B.Y. London Jan. 10 1907.

I send you a copy of a letter I have just sent to Lane thinking it may overtake you and give you something to talk over with Lane.[1] I believe that it will indirectly help us considerably if he decides to fight as a good deal of the mischief comes from Arthur Griffith's people.[2] One has to get into the people of intellect of Dublin a belief that they can hold their own in the long run. I am counting on the fact that at the end of the five years which will be the period of the loan[3] we may have won our battle and be in a position to

---

[6] These were the artists represented in Class B, and included among others JBY, Jack Yeats, AE, William Rothenstein, Charles Ricketts, Charles Shannon, William Orpen, Nathaniel Hone, John Lavery, Dermod O'Brien, and Augustus John.

[1] AG was travelling from Coole to Dublin.

[2] Griffith had long been suspicious of Hugh Lane and incensed WBY by 'hinting at a preposterous scandal' against him in the *United Irishman* as early as 17 Dec 1904 (see III. 688). Griffith was to be appointed to the Libraries Committee on 23 Jan 1907, so joining three other directors of *Sinn Fein*: Alderman Thomas Kelly (the Committee's influential chairman), Alderman Walter L. Cole, and Councillor Henry Dixon. Griffith's close friend P. J. McCall was also a member.

[3] In the end those pictures that were not vested outright in the Corporation were loaned to it indefinitely, and for at least twenty years.

help him considerably. New journalistic forces will have arisen amongst the young men for the very cultivated generation who are now coming from University College will have put itself in the place of the present self-educated one in the weekly papers which reminds me that I have just had a letter from a man who is I believe the auditor of the seceding majority of University College Debating Society complaining that people are smoking in the pit of the Abbey Theatre.[4]

TS copy NLI.

## To Lady Gregory, [*10 January 1907*]

Mention in letter from AG, 11 January 1907.
A telegram assuring her that he had not entered into a 'Secret Treaty' with AEFH over his plays.[1]

Berg.

## To Elizabeth Corbet Yeats, [c. *10 January 1907*]

Mention in letter to AG, 21 January 1907.
A letter, which WBY hoped 'was quite civil', telling ECY 'that when she wanted delay in payment she had better merely say "I am hard up" or some phrase of that kind and not go into a lot of detail'.[1]

[4] i.e. Francis Cruise O'Brien (see p. 77, n. 9), the auditor of the Literary and Historical Society at UCD. The singing of the British National Anthem at the conferring of degrees had long been a contentious issue with the students of the Royal University and UCD, and on 26 Oct 1906 a protest meeting was broken up by the police on the order of Fr. Delany, the president of the College. The following week the Committee of the Literary and Historical Society, claiming that the Society represented student opinion, passed and forwarded to the president a motion censuring his action, although a number of Committee members later wished to rescind this. On 13 Nov 1906 the Council of the College announced that Cruise O'Brien was rusticated for a year, and that he could therefore no longer be a member of the Society. Although the Committee split 4 : 3 over the repudiation of this judgement, an extraordinary general meeting of the Society on 17 Nov passed a resolution refusing to recognize the jurisdiction of the College authorities to expel any member from the Society, or to deprive an officer of the Society of his position. A majority of the Society then seceded from the College and met for the remainder of their term of office (until late May) elsewhere, including the Oak Room of the Mansion House.

[1] WBY had wired on getting AG's letter of 10 Jan, expressing her distress at the supposed 'Secret Treaty' between him and AEFH (see p. 577, n. 11). On receiving the wire AG wrote: 'Your telegram about "Promise" the greatest possible relief! I had been *miserable* about it.'

[1] This was the latest round in WBY's battle over ECY's failure to pay AG (see p. 557).

## *To Lady Gregory,* [*11 January 1907*]

18 Woburn Buildings | Euston Road

My dear Lady Gregory: I have just re-read your letter. I had thought that you meant that our man—the one we talked of last Autumn—was to be paid by Miss Horniman instead of the more expensive man. I now see that you meant that we should pay Fay out of the <four hundred her> £500. I admit that this is just but I doubt if she will do it though I am prepared to urge it—if I get the new man for £200 or £300 but in any case we can give Fay £100 extra. It does not really matter much whether we give it or she does as we must make more than that on tours.[1] I am certain from my knowledge of her that once get a removeable man between her & Fay we will have her quite amicable & even generous for the patent period if I can get the right man—that is the real problem & that is I think the point you should watch. The wrong man might be what Fay fears but the right man (apart from Miss Horniman) an indescribable releif to us all. I want business not artistic ambition & that is one reason why I want to see Vedrenne before the 21st. We have had rows from the first days of the theatre & I dont suppose you will beleive me but the Fay personality has been a principal cause (Miss Walker for instance complained bitterly & gave it as a chief reason for leaving us)[2] & we want a quiet, good tempered man who will co-ordinate a mass of activities. I need hardly say that I do not take Fays threats of the Music Hall seriously. He is alarmed at the unknown that is all. I am much more anoyed with Synges assumption that I am doing

[1] In a letter of 8 Jan (Berg) AG told WBY that she would try to arrange the engagement of a stage manager if he would authorize an extra £100 for W. G. Fay out of AEFH's £500, and if he agreed to cancel the arrangement whereby the rights in Abbey plays remained with the Company rather than the playwrights. WBY evidently wired his agreement, and AG went to Dublin on 11 Jan for a meeting with Synge and Fay, at which, as she reported to WBY immediately afterwards, they had decided that the playwrights should 'have leave to take plays into their own hands after 6 months if they find it impossible to go on with new arrangement. . . . Fay to get £4 a week—that is an extra £104 per an— This if possible to be got from Miss H—but if not paid out of Company funds.' In return they were 'all to receive new man "as if we ourselves had asked for him"'. A formal statement from Synge, written on the same day (*JMSCL* I. 282), restated these points and added four more: that WBY was to work out a scheme of duties for the new man and submit it to the other Directors; that the modifications to AEFH's proposal suggested by Synge on 24 Dec 1906 (see pp. 547–8) should be adopted; that Fay should have a written contract defining his duties and giving him control of dialect work; and that the new man 'should be thorough theatrical *business* man, if possible an Irishman'.

[2] See pp. 75, n. 4, 156. On 5 Jan 1906 Synge reported to AG (*JMSCL* I. 149) that Maire Walker was 'not very eager' to remain with the Abbey Company 'because she is afraid of the Fays, and their theory is that we are all absolutely in the Fay's hands!' He added that when she received WBY's 'scolding' letter about her contract (see p. 257, 281, n. 1) 'she said to herself, "the Fays have turned Mr Yeats against me too. They are all against me now."' In *The Splendid Years* Maire Walker recalled more tersely (73) that W. G. Fay 'disagreed completely' with her decision to leave the Company, and that she only ever saw him once again – and this thirty years later.

all this for the sake of my own plays—he judges me by himself. They have not consciously influenced me—or anything but the theatre as a whole.[3]

Yr ev

W B Yeats

It might be well if you could be here when I get recommendation to see stage manager before he is accepted and to join me in giving instructions. I think this would probably somewhat lessen Fays fears.

ALS Berg, with envelope addressed to Coole, postmark 'LONDON.W.C. JA 11 07'.

## To A. E. F. Horniman, [c. *13 January 1907*]

Mention in letter from AEFH, 17 January [1907].

Repeating that her letter to AG and her offer to replace W. G. Fay have caused much trouble, and that AG and Synge suspect there is a 'Secret Treaty' between AEFH and him.[1]

NLI. Misdated by AEFH '1906'.

## To Letitia Darragh, c. *14 January 1907*

Mention in following letter.

Asking her if she said offensive things about him while at the Abbey.

---

[3] The supposed pushing of their own work by AG and WBY was a constant theme of theatrical gossip in Dublin, and his recent engagement to Maire O'Neill (see p. 442) was causing Synge to review his position in this respect. He had already contemplated moving to London (*JMSCL* 1. 249), and on 9 Jan he had implored WBY (*JMSCL* 1. 281): 'Please *do not* bring or send over new man till the playboy is over as it is *absolutely* essential that Fay should be undisturbed till he has got through this big part.' On 18 Mar of this year his discontent was to boil over when he learned (*JMSCL* 1. 316) that his plays were to be underrepresented during the visit of the American impresario Frohman (see pp. 557–8): 'they are showing Frohman ONE play of mine "Riders", five or six of L G's and several of Yeats. I am raging about it. . . . It is getting past a joke the way they are treating me.' At about this time he wrote Frank Fay 'a letter (which, *at his request*, I burnt) in which he said a Yeats–Gregory Theatre would be no use to anybody' (*Abbey Theatre*, 156).

[1] AEFH replied that she was 'most sorry that my well-meant offer should have raised so much trouble', and explained that she had 'put matters clearly about the future—once we both felt things were rather hopeless & *in case of shipwreck* I said, "Let me have the plays (implying after the Society is dead) to do what I can with & you said 'yes'." Then more lately I reminded you of this & said "*after the Patent has lapsed* I'll try in another way, promise me yours". . . . Please let everyone know that there was no "secret treaty"; merely a desire on my part to salvage that part of the cargo which is of real importance.'

## *To Lady Gregory, 14 January 1907*

18, Woburn Buildings, | Euston Rd., N.W.

Jan. 14, 1907.

My dear Lady Gregory,

I saw Vedrenne[1] to-day and gave him the note of introduction from Miss Horniman. In this note she told him that we wanted an Irishman if possible but the great thing was to get a good man. I told him that business capacity was the essential thing though he would have to do a small amount of production and be able to stage manage. Miss Horniman had said in her note that his production would be of classical and romantic work. Vedrenne said he would take trouble about it as he admired the work of the theatre so much. I said we don't want a theatrical speculator of all things and that he must have a good temper. He said that he had a very good man in his mind but wasn't quite sure if he didn't want him himself, but his difficulty was, the man he had in mind was fitted for the first whereas he could only in his own theatre offer him the second place.[2] He said that he would not recommend us anybody who had not worked under himself. I asked if he knew Burchell who is Mrs. Emery's selection. He said he did not but that Barker did and that he would ask Barker about it.[3] I told him that the great thing for me was to get somebody he felt he could recommend as this would not only satisfy us but Miss Horniman. I am to hear from him in two or three days. I think we should take his recommendation unless we have some strong reason to the contrary. If the man is not Irish we cannot help it. If the choice is between filling our country's stomach or enlarging its brains by importing precise knowledge I am for scorning its stomach for the present. No paper is likely to attack except Sheinn Fein and that has done us all the damage it can.[4] I hope, of course, we can find an Irishman but merely because that is the course of least resistance not because I accept the principle. He says we should offer £5 a week and prospects. If we can get

---

[1] The manager of the Court Theatre; see p. 23, n. 4.

[2] This was Ben Iden Payne.

[3] i.e. Harley Granville-Barker; see p. 23.

[4] Arthur Griffith had reconstituted the *United Irishman* under the name *Sinn Fein* in May 1906, but the change in title did nothing to dampen its attacks on the Abbey. Reviewing WBY's *Deirdre* on 4 Dec 1906, the paper commented (3) that the piece was 'of course, no nearer to being a play than any of his previous attempts. The devices and general shifts of his stagecraft (or want of it) are as palpable and futile as ever,' and it had scorned the double bill of *The Shadowy Waters* and AG's *The Canavans* on 15 Dec 1906 (see pp. 537–8, n. 3). On 24 Nov (3) it alleged that 'a little examination' of his plays 'show[s] that Mr. Yeats's ideas about drama are of the most superficial and trivial nature possible....He cannot—at any rate he does not—conceive things and think them out naturally after the manner of drama.'

the man for that I have hopes of getting Miss Horniman to pay Fay a £100. I shall use the argument that it should be Fay's advantage to make the arrangement work and that if she pays the £100 he will know that an unjustified quarrel with the new man would stop it. I should also appeal to her better side and urge her to show that she has no grudge against him. I had an instinct that there was a crisis on with her of some kind and I heard last Saturday, though I cannot give my informant and I have a reason for asking you to keep the fact very private, that Miss Darragh having despaired of working with us was getting up a performance of Salome with Courtney Thorpe at Manchester and that Miss Horniman was to be invited to this and asked to finance the scheme.[5] My informant[6] thought that Miss Horniman had agreed to go there but if that is so, we have certainly stopped it, for she definitely told me that what she called her public money is now earmarked for us. Which reminds me that I have done what I believe to be the only honest thing when one hears that any person one has been working with has spoken against one in a serious way I have written to Miss Darragh and asked her if she said the things attributed to her.[7] Now about Fand. I had forgotten Miss Garvy and had thought of the play with the two Miss Allgoods and Miss Walker. You will get at least if you give Miss Garvy

[5] Courtenay Thorpe took leading parts in a number of Ibsen plays produced by the Independent Theatre Company and the Stage Society in the 1890s, and adapted Kipling's *The Light that Failed* for the London stage in 1898. Shaw thought him 'a clever character actor' but noted 'his curious effeminacy' (*BSCL* 11. 271). Letitia Darragh had played the title role in *Salome* in June 1906 (see p. 399, n. 4), and AEFH, who greatly admired her style of acting, and her views on the theatre, subsequently asked her to join the Gaiety Theatre, Manchester.

[6] Evidently FF; see below p. 608.

[7] AG and WBY disagreed fundamentally about Miss Darragh's talents: WBY believed she possessed a passion lacking in the regular Abbey actresses, but AG thought this merely sensuousness, while the regular actresses, as Holloway reported on 16 Nov 1906 (NLI), found it merely risible: 'She is fond of riggling [*sic*] in her movements, & she is likened to a jelly on that account by some of the company.' On her trip to Dublin on 11 Jan AG discovered (as she gleefully relayed to WBY the same day) that 'Miss Darragh told "the company" that you were a dreadful bore, bored her to death with yr attentions "trotting all over the theatre after her like a little dog"—& "so vain, thinking every woman was in love with you" !!!... Synge says he has never come across such a mischief maker, thinks she set all the company against you for the time being, making little of you, although they all dislike her, except possibly Mac—.' On her return to Coole the following day, AG elaborated on her reasons for not wishing Miss Darragh to return to the Abbey. While she judged her competent as Dectora, she thought she had 'emphasised so much the less noble parts' of *Deirdre* as to 'overbalance' it. 'You say we want passion, but she has not got that. She has as Synge wrote "*emotion* without distinction or nobility"....As to her speaking it does not bite, she makes a mash, a bog, of it, one can never remember a line of a passage....(she told Mac that "Yeats verse is nothing but *miffle*", I think that is the word, it means "rot") and she certainly in both plays spoke of it as if that were her view.' In a third letter, written the following day (13 Jan; Berg), AG took the opportunity of correcting some of what she had related, although her emendations were hardly calculated to cheer WBY: 'It was *piffle* Miss Darragh called your work, not *miffle*. I think I put a gloss of my own by saying you bored her "by your attentions". Synge said "she used to tell them he was such a bore, he bored her to death by running after her all over the theatre" Etc, but it may have been only your conversation.'

Emer and get Molly Allgood, not her sister, sufficiently taught to be able to take the smallest of the three parts a show that will not disgrace the theatre, though I still think a show that will spoil the play.[8] I will not press this however, but I would be rather glad if you would allow me to register this opinion in the Minutes of a Directors' Meeting. We can hold a meeting when I am in Ireland. I want this because later on Fay or somebody may be inclined to make me responsible for any failure of policy in the matter of verse. Please don't think that I am fighting you on the point. If you are bound to produce the play in February I don't well see what can be done for there is no other play we could get up near to it, as neither you nor Robert would like Miss Darragh for the Antigone[9] and we could not afford to import an actress for one play alone, especially if we have to pay Fay ourselves. Of course the new man may be in in time to judge but one cannot be sure of that. If there were no real objection to a postponement it might be worth waiting till we had his opinion and if he thought our people inadequate putting it off till we could do a group of plays and had decided upon an actress. Which reminds that I wish you would look at Polyeucte of Corneille and let me know whether you think it would better suit our audience than Phaedre. Mine own inclination is rather for Phaedre but I feel the strong religious nature of Polyeucte might possibly be of advantage to us.[10] I have got so far in the letter without thanking you for all you have done to smooth over the whole thing and get Fay's consent. We are certainly at peace now and I only got so far without thanks because there is something lively and heartless about dictation which isn't in writing. I don't think Mrs. Emery goes until the 30th of the month but she has now definitely decided to go and has taken her berth.

[8] AG was eager to have Blunt's *Fand* put into production (see p. 558) and in her letter of 12 Jan suggested that they should 'put the new man at Fand. I asked Fay to try and get Maire, Miss Garvey, and one of the Allgoods to work on it, and we could see what the result is.' Maire Walker was not recalled and when the play was finally produced, on 20 Apr of this year, the part of Cuchulain's wife Emer was taken by Sara Allgood and that of the enchantress Fand by her sister Maire O'Neill, while Maire Garvey played Eithne, Cuchulain's mistress (see p. 80, n. 2).

[9] Robert Gregory had begun translating Sophocles' *Antigone* in October 1906 (see p. 481, n. 5), but, as AG reported, had abandoned it by 16 Jan.

[10] *Polyeucte* (1642), was the third of a series of seven Roman tragedies by the French playwright Pierre Corneille (1606–84). The play's involved plot explores the working of divine grace in the human soul when Polyeucte, a pagan Armenian warrior, is converted to Christianity during a secret mission. Although Christianity is proscribed and persecuted throughout the Roman Empire, he repeatedly rejects the pleas of his wife Pauline and her father Félix, a Roman governor, to abjure his faith, even in the face of execution. But his martyrdom causes the miraculous conversion of Pauline and Félix, and Sévère, Pauline's former admirer who is now a powerful adviser to the Emperor, is so moved by their conversion that he vows to use his influence to end the persecution of the Christians. The suggestion that the Abbey should play it had probably come from AEFH, who had seen it at the Comédie-Française the previous autumn and reported to WBY on 26 Nov 1906 (NLI) that she was 'not at all bored, rather to my surprise'.

Her address is 21, Warwick Chambers, Pater Street, Kensington and she would very much like the book.[11] I should have said but [*for* that] I told Vedrenne that good temper was essential and he said the man he had recommended was a vegetarian and that Bernard Shaw says that vegetables are wonderful for the temper.[12]

Masefield's play has horrified everybody. They are all as Vedrenne said raving against it. I thought it extraordinarily powerful but too lacking in redeeming beauty not to be too harrowing.[13] I would like to know a little more in detail how you think the Play Boy acted but I forget you only saw the last act.[14] Have they cleared many of the objectionable sentences out of it? I am wondering whether it might not be rather a good thing for us to make a sort of compact with "The Peasant" I don't suppose it will become so anti-clerical as to be a dangerous ally but that is rather the point. I wonder if I could get Miss Horniman to take a few shares. If we were sure of editorial support we might drop the Arrow next season and reply to our critics there.[15]

Henderson keeps writing to me about the February programme and the

---

[11] FF had asked AG to act as her patron in the USA, and in her letter of 11 Jan AG told WBY that she would 'be proud to help Mrs. Emery in any way' (see p. 568). She also asked for her address so that she could send her *A Book of Saints and Wonders*, in case it contained anything she could use in her recitals.

[12] Ben Iden Payne does not appear to have been a vegetarian, although his slight figure may have given Vedrenne this impression. Shaw, as he told Joseph Teleki in November 1910 (*BSCL* 11. 953–4), had 'been a vegetarian since 1880', adding that some people were 'extraordinarily the better for it — especially gouty, rheumatic, neuralgic people. It improves the temper and nerves of irritable people.'

[13] i.e. *The Campden Wonder* (see pp. 288–9, 580). The play had scored a *succès de scandale* because its melodramatic theme was thrown into stronger relief by the frothiness of Harcourt's *The Reformer* (see p. 580, n. 5). On 9 Jan 1907 Masefield had written to AG (Berg) that he 'never saw a more hopeless failure', and Shaw complained to Masefield (Bodleian) that the pairing of the comedy and tragedy was an 'aberration'. The *Stage* of 10 Jan reported (16) that the curtain had fallen on the play 'amid solemn silence, the audience having been harrowed.... The subject ... is really quite unsuited for dramatic treatment, and in his handling of an unutterably horrible theme John Masefield has shown little sense of the stage.... *The Campden Wonder* is too gruesome a production to gain general acceptance.'

[14] In her letter of 12 Jan AG reported that while in Dublin she had attended a rehearsal of *The Playboy of the Western World* and that it would 'be very fine indeed, though I only saw the last act.... It did make me a little sad as I watched Playboy to think how easily that sort of work comes to our players, and how long it will be before your plays can go as well all round.'

[15] See p. 574. The first number of the new series of the *Peasant* appeared in February 1907, and despite threats, opposition, and limited funds, the paper, which became the *Irish Nation* in 1909, survived until 1910. There was no compact, and publication of the *Arrow* continued, largely because, as he recalled in *The Pope's Green Island* (1912), the editor W. P. Ryan had reservations about the Abbey's policy (304–5): 'While we devoted a great deal of attention to the Abbey and its work ... I was not one of those to whom it represented the beginning and the end of art and literature in Ireland; it was one of several new interests, and it seemed to me at times to be more restricted and less promising than some others; it certainly had not their colour and character. There was a sense of posing or strain about a few of its writers on occasion, what they took for reality was only a fraction of reality, and they harped on peasant Ireland, seen at a peculiar angle, almost to tedium.'

Arrow.[16] Would you mind settling the programme with Synge, for I can only recollect what we talked over quite lately and there is no use complicating matters by having three people to consult and Synge can speak for Fay.

Yours ever
W B Yeats

TLS Berg, with envelope addressed to Coole, postmark 'LONDON W.C. JA 14 07'.

## To Maud Gonne, 14 January 1907

18, Woburn Buildings, | Euston Road,
Jan. 14, 1907.

My dear Friend.

I was unable to write to you when I got your letter[1] for I was up to my eyes in business. I am putting a professional theatrical manager at a fair salary in charge of the Abbey Theatre and it has been a huge fight. Do not tell this in Dublin for I imagine that everybody except Synge has been more or less in tears. Fay struggled hard to keep his authority threatened even to go on the music hall stage but it is done now, I mean it is agreed to, and everybody seems quite content, even I think a little relieved. Battles of pride are like that, it is a cloudy thing and when the battle is over people know they have fought about clouds. I have asked the Manager of the Court Theatre, the only intellectual theatre in London to recommend a good man certainly and an Irishman if possible. We will take whatever man he recommends for I have great reliance in him and if he be an Englishman and know his business, well, I shall be sorry, but I prefer to enlarge the brain of my country where it is weakest in expert knowledge, than to fill one Irishman's stomach and think myself the better patriot for the choice. Fay is to produce all the Irish plays but the new man is to stage manage them as distinct from production and to produce classical and romantic work, which is outside Fay's knowledge. I always knew this would have to come, for Fay is far too excitable and hot-tempered for management. I know you will agree with me in that though you won't like the Englishman, if English he

---

[16] Henderson's letters have not been traced, and the February programme was to be overshadowed by the dispute over the *Playboy*. *The Doctor in Spite of Himself*, *Cathleen ni Houlihan*, and *A Pot of Broth* played on 9 Feb, and *The White Cockade* and *The Jackdaw* from 23 Feb to 2 Mar. AG wrote to Synge on this very day to discuss the February programme, the success of which she saw as crucial to their becoming independent of AEFH (Saddlemyer, 205).

[1] MG's letter, evidently written in early January 1907, has not been traced.

is to be.[2] I saw Mrs. Sharpe the other day and know a great deal more now about the Fiona Macleod mystery. It is as I thought. Fiona Macleod was so far as external perception could say a secondary personality induced in Sharpe by the presence of a very beautiful unknown woman whom he fell in love with. She, alas! has disappeared from everyone's sight, no one having set eyes on her except George Meredith who says she was the most beautiful woman he ever saw.[3] Whether there was more than this I do not know but poor Mrs. Sharp, though generous and self-sacrificing as I can see does not want to enlarge that unknown woman's share. A great deal, however, which Sharp used to give in letters as an account of Fiona's doings were she insists a kind of semi-allegorical description of the adventures of his own secondary personality and its relation with the primary self. For instance in one letter to me he had said "I will leave your letter where Fiona will find it when she wakes," and by this he meant that the secondary personality when it awoke in him would answer the letter which it certainly did in a much more impassioned way than that of the rest of the letter.[4] I don't think there would be much of all this in the official biography for when I said to Mrs. Sharp that she should tell the whole truth, she answered "How can I! Other people are so much involved." She never talked quite openly about things, except it being a secondary personality, but told things in a series of hints and yet, at the same time, quite clearly. I noticed that each time she said this personality was awakened in him by a beautiful person she would add as if to lessen the effect, "and by beautiful scenery."[5] She was evidently very fond of him and has sent me his birth date and her own to find out how their horoscopes interlocked.[6]

---

[2] In her reply of 21 Jan 1907 (*G–YL*, 235–6) MG said she was 'almost sure you are making a great mistake in getting a manager from England for the theatre, of course I won't mention it to anyone'.

[3] See pp. 177, 302–3. The very beautiful woman was Edith Mary Rinder, née Wingate, who had married the art critic Frank Rinder (1863–1937) in 1890. Sharp fell in love with her the following year, and she became his mistress and the inspiration behind Fiona Macleod, once posing as Fiona for the benefit of George Meredith. Mrs Sharp knew of the relationship and tolerated it.

[4] On 5 May 1898 Sharp had written from Dover '*In strict privacy*' to tell WBY (see II. 219–20 and *LWBY* I. 36–7) that 'my friend Miss Macleod is here just now. . . . She was sleeping when your letter came, but I left the enclosure for her at her bedside—& if she wakes before the post goes she will doubtless give you a message through me, unless she feels up to writing herself.'

[5] In her biography of her husband, *William Sharp (Fiona Macleod), a Memoir* (1910), Elizabeth Sharp does not mention Edith Rinder, although she does mention Frank Rinder.

[6] Elizabeth Sharp had written to WBY on 9 Jan (*LWBY* I. 176–7) that she had obtained particulars from Sharp's mother, so that WBY could cast his horoscope: 'William Sharp was born on Wednesday the 12th September 1855. She cannot tell me the exact time, but thinks it was about midday. She writes that bells were ringing and she was told it was because Sebastopol was taken. She thinks it was about 12 o'clock. *12* seems to be a number that has some special significance for my husband's life—as it was the 12th December on which he passed out of this life. Moreover, I went to Iona this summer—to perform a little rite for him myself there—in St Oran's chapel—and it chanced to be the 12th September, at 12 o'clock. . . . Now, would it be possible also to have *my* horoscope cast? I should greatly like it; because I want to see in what way the two horoscopes suggest the touching of our two lives. And to that end may I give you the necessary particulars.'

I would be rather glad if you would keep this letter, for I am fresh from seeing Mrs. Sharp (I saw her a week ago) and this will be a record. Put it in some safe place and I may ask you for it again some day for it is a fragment of history. She told me that the morning William Sharp died she heard visionary music and indeed a good deal of one sort and another about the supernatural side of his talent.[7]

I should think that your husband must have been badly damaged by that Dublin cross-examination and will gradually sink and disappear now.[8] You never told me what happened at the Convention of Cuman-Na-Gael. How was the temperance resolution met,[9] and is there any likelihood of your being in Dublin in time for Synge's play on the 25th of this

---

[7] Elizabeth Sharp does not mention hearing visionary music in her description of Sharp's death, but recounts several visionary experiences that Sharp had prior to his death. Her description of the day of death is given on p. 419: 'On the morning of the 12th—a day of wild storm, wind, thunder and rain—he recognised that nothing could avail. With characteristic swiftness he turned his eager mind from the life that was closing to the life of greater possibilities that he knew awaited him. About 3 o'clock, with his devoted friend Alec Hood by his side, he suddenly leant forward with shining eyes and exclaimed in a tone of joyous recognition, "Oh, the beautiful 'Green Life' again!" and the next moment sank back in my arms with the contented sigh, "Ah, all is well."' Elsewhere (425) Elizabeth Sharp recalls a number of Sharp's visions: 'I remember from early days how he would speak of the momentary curious "dazzle in the brain" which preceded the feeling of all material things and preluded some inner vision of Great Beauty, or Great Presences, or of some symbolic import—that would pass as rapidly as it came. I have been beside him when he has been in trance and I have felt the room throb with heightened vibration. I regret now that I never wrote down such experiences at the time. They were not infrequent, and formed a definite feature in our life.' She did, however, record 'two or three dream-visions belonging to his last summer' that he had noted down in brief sentences for future use. One was 'The Lily of the World, and its dark concave, dark with excess of light and the stars falling like slow rain', and the other was headed '"Elemental Symbolism," "I saw Self, or Life, symbolised all about me as a limitless, fathomless and lonely sea".'

[8] This was during MacBride's action against the *Irish Independent* on 12 Dec 1906 for alleged libels published by the paper on 27 and 28 Feb and 26 and 27 July 1905 (see p. 389). In the course of his cross-examination, the counsel for the *Independent*, Mr. J. H. Campbell KC, using evidence from the French hearings (see p. 42, n. 1), held MacBride up to ridicule for styling himself the 'greatest living Irishman', for his chronic drunkenness in Paris, for his alleged illiteracy, and for his squandering of 75,000 francs given to him by MG. In his final address to the jury, Campbell also took the opportunity of airing the far more serious allegations not mentioned in the *Independent* reports: 'the fact was that in mercy to Mr. MacBride much that was of strong comment on him had been omitted—that which related to obscenity, infidelity, and immorality. The French court said that the charges of drunkenness had been proved to the satisfaction of the judges, and they said that MacBride's public conduct in that way contributed what they called "une grave injure"—a deadly injury—to his wife, and they decreed that they could not give her a complete decree, but that they would cut the link that bound her to this man.' Although MacBride won the case on a technicality, he was awarded only £1 in damages and had to bear the costs of his action himself. After the verdict the presiding judge, Mr Justice Gibson, observed that 'the best thing he could do was to enter it as a verdict for the plaintiff, though it was doubtful if it was a verdict for the plaintiff', and the *Independent*'s counsel replied, 'I don't think it is, my lord, but we will not claim it. Let him have his £1 and pay the jury. The verdict does not carry costs.'

[9] MG's friends had made a fruitless attempt to have her re-elected to the Cumann na Gaedheal, from which she had been ousted in November 1905, and to get them to adopt a resolution pledging members to abstinence from alcoholic drinks.

month, it runs for a week.[10] We are still doing rather well. We have matinées now, which are bringing us quite a new audience.[11]

[*Remainder of letter in WBY's hand*]

I have such great heaps of letters that I must dictate even when writing to you.

Yr ever
W B Yeats

TLS White.


## To Elizabeth Corbet Yeats, [c. *14 January 1907*]

Mention in letter to AG, 21 January 1907.

A very careful and civil handwritten reply to a 'very fiery letter indeed', telling ECY 'that when people had worked for her she ought to thank them'.[1]


## To W. G. Fay and John Millington Synge, *15 January 1907*

Mention in following letter.

Pressing them to produce AG's *The White Cockade*[1] and to replace his *The Pot of Broth* with AG's *Gaol Gate*.[2]

---

[10] MG was in Paris at the time of the production of the *Playboy* but heard of the disturbance and told WBY in February (*G–YL*, 237), 'as I don't see the same as you over it I don't want to go into the matter'.

[11] The series of Abbey matinées which had been instituted at the Abbey from 1 Dec 1906.

[1] See pp. 557, 584.

[1] During her visit to Dublin on 11 Jan, W. G. Fay had told AG that her play *The White Cockade* was almost ready, but she thought Synge was reluctant to have it produced. In fact, as she subsequently discovered, it was less prepared than Fay had led her to believe (Saddlemyer, 207).

[2] AG had written on 13 Jan (Berg) to complain that Synge had put WBY's *Pot of Broth* on the same bill as *The Playboy*. She was opposed to this as she believed that the contrast between the two would be to WBY's disadvantage, and on 19 Jan assured him she was determined 'that Synge should not set fire to your house to roast his own pig'. She had also written to Synge on the same day to say she was 'entirely against the Pot' (Saddlemyer, 207). Although the playbills had been printed, the play was withdrawn and replaced not with AG's *Gaol Gate* but Synge's *Riders to the Sea*.

# To Lady Gregory, 15 January 1907

18 Woburn Buildings | Euston Road
Jan 15th 1907.

My dear Lady Gregory,

I have written to Fay and Synge that is to say a letter addressed to either, pressing "White Cockade" very strongly and the "Jail Gate" instead of "Pot", and pressing Darley instead of "Spreading the News" but less strongly, as they may object to change their announcements.[1] I dont very much care about anything except getting "White Cockade" and "Jackdaw" while you are in Dublin, and able to learn from seeing them and to rehearse the second. I was not shown the programme, but Synge as Director in my place, may have felt himself justified, and I daresay was justified. Burchell is out of the question as he wont leave London—I am not really sorry, as I am inclined to think he was probably too considerable a man for us and would have been ambitious and I am really doing my best to get somebody who will leave Fay alone, and do his day's work for his day's pay without dreaming too many dreams. I am also anxious to take Vedrenne's own choice as he really knows what we are doing and wont recommend anybody he does not know all about. Besides that will do more than anything else to put Miss Horniman's mind at rest. I shall tell Miss Tobin to go on with Phedre, I consider the theatre, assuming the translation to be well done, just as much bound to it as we are to Fand.[2] It will be a splendid thing for

---

[1] AG felt that four one-act plays on Saturday, 19 Jan, made too long and too dislocated a programme, and suggested that one of the plays might be replaced with a performance by Arthur Darley (see p. 386) on his violin. In fact, the full programme went ahead with AG's *Spreading the News* and *Hyacinth Halvey*, Synge's *In the Shadow of the Glen*, and WBY's *Cathleen ni Houlihan*. Holloway commented in his diary (NLI) that 'triple bills' were fairly frequent, 'but "quadruple bills" are very rare—in fact unknown in Dublin until the National Theatre Society introduced them at the Abbey today at matinee & evening performances'. Nevertheless, a 'splendid audience assembled at the evening show & enjoyed each of the pieces immensely to judge by their repeated laughter & enthusiastic applause at the fall of the curtains after each little play'. The bill had been improvised to cover the withdrawal of Racine's *Les Plaideurs* (see p. 512).

[2] WBY had asked AG to read *Polyeucte* as a possible alternative to *Phèdre* (see p. 589), but on 14 Jan she reported that 'it would be a very interesting performance for convent schools, in the original French, but I don't think our audience would be anything but bored by it. Those long speeches are out of date, and in blank verse would be very dull.... I think Phedre will be about as much as our audience will stand, and we are lucky if it doesn't put them off verse altogether.' She felt, too, that WBY's own plays should be preferred over other verse plays, and also feared that he might use the play as a pretext for bringing Miss Darragh back to the Abbey, writing to Synge on 14 Jan (Saddlemyer, 205–6) that it was 'far more Pauline's play than the hero's.... I dont see why we should go out of our way to find parts for a great tragic actress just the thing we havent got. And in any case I think those immensely long speeches are out of date, especially when done into mediocre blank verse.' In her reply to this letter on

practice in verse speaking and being non-Shakesperian will be a fine
training for our audience. Masefield play is still a standing horror here.
I said to him last night, I heard people crying and he replied "Oh so
did I, but that's nothing, a lady in the upper circle was sick."[3] I lunched
with Miss Hepworth Dixon to-day at the Lyceum, and was next Lady
Cromartie.[4]

Yr ev

W B Yeats

I have an uneasy feeling that we may have arranged a quartette for next
Saturday ourselves. I remember we had a great difficulty in knowing what
to play, but if we did I imagine that the "Pot" was one of the four. My mind
is very vague on the subject. When you are arranging a February programme with Synge for the Arrow you wont find it very easy as it is to get
extra Saturdays. It is a misfortune in some ways that neither of my verse
plays could be revived on a Saturday, I mean the new ones, but if "Pot" and
"Spreading the News" are saved they will give the nucleus for one evening,
and I imagine that "Riders to the Sea" and the "Jackdaw" are both
revivable, and Moliere. Of course I would like either "Bailie's Strand" or
"The King's Threshold" to be done, perhaps you will be able to put on one
or other the same week, with Fand.[5] How about Antigone? I suppose that is
for March.[6]

TLS Berg, with envelope addressed to Coole, postmark 'LONDON W.C. JA 15 07'.

---

16 Jan (Berg), AG told WBY that she had not understood 'you thought of Polyceute instead of
Phedre—I thought it was to be done also—I don't think there is much to choose between them, as
far as the audience goes—what I feel is, that we must not put our audience off verse by giving what
won't really interest them—it would be better to put off for a bit.' WBY had intended to use Agnes
Tobin's translation of *Phèdre* (see p. 554, n. 1).

[3] See pp. 580, 590. Masefield had attended WBY's Monday Evening on the previous day and W. T.
Horton, who had also been there, wrote to WBY on 20 Jan (*Y & H*, 115): 'John Masefield is on a very
powerful & restive dark horse. Keep his hands down, elbows in, a firm rein & gripping knees—let him
be master & not the horse or it may take the bit between it's teeth & take Masefield to what might be a
disaster.'

[4] Ella Nora Hepworth Dixon (d. 1932), novelist and journalist, was the daughter of William Hepworth Dixon (1821–79), editor of the *Athenaeum*. Her autobiography *As I Knew Them* appeared in 1930.
For Lady Cromartie and the Lyceum Club see p. 134 and p. 118.

[5] For the Saturday programme see n. 1. *Baile's Strand* was produced on Saturday, 16 Mar, but *Fand*
was postponed until 20 Apr.

[6] On 16 Jan AG revealed (Berg) that 'Robert is laying aside the Antigone for the present' (see p. 589,
n. 9), and it was not performed.

## *To Ben Iden Payne,*[1] *16 January* [*1907*]

18 Woburn Buildings | Upper Woburn Place | London
January 16

Dear Sir,

I want a managing director or manager for the National Theatre Society of Dublin & am able to give £5 a week as a beginning. Mr Vedrenne of the Court has given me your name.[2] I should want a man who can stage manage & who can produce a certain amount of classical & romantic work— Antigone Oedipus & a fine translation of Racines 'Phedre' are on our list. All Irish peasant plays & all plays needing special Irish knowledge are produced by Mr William Fay—& these are the larger part of our work at present. The whole work of the theatre, subject to the three directors, Lady Gregory, J. M. Synge & myself will be under the control of the manager. If you see your way to consider the matter I would like to see you as soon as possible. I go to Ireland next week & want to get all settled before that.[3]

I should have said that we have our own theatre, and a subsidy from Miss Horniman which leaves us independent of public support to a very great extent. We are I think the only English speaking subsidized theatre and have steadily increasing audiences, though they are still small.

Yrs sny
W B Yeats

ALS NYPL.

---

[1] Ben Iden Payne (1881–1976) spent more that seventy years in the theatre in England and America. He was born in Newcastle upon Tyne but brought up in Manchester and joined Frank Benson's company shortly after leaving school, taking small parts from 1899 to 1902. Since then he had toured with various repertory companies, combining acting with stage management, and was at this time in Ireland with Ian Maclaren's company. Following his managership of the Abbey he joined AEFH's Gaiety Theatre in Manchester, but resigned in 1911. In 1913 he went to Chicago to direct a short season at the Fine Art Theatre, and this led to his settling in the USA in 1914. He directed for several years on Broadway, working for the Shuberts, Alf Hayman, and the Theatre Guild. In the early 1920s he took a post in the Drama Department of the Carnegie Institute of Technology in Pittsburgh, but in 1934 moved as director and actor to the Goodman Theatre in Chicago. In 1935 he returned to England to become general director of the Shakespeare Memorial Theatre at Stratford-upon-Avon, but his unconventional ideas on the production of Shakespeare (influenced by William Poel) did not find favour with the critics and in 1943 he went back to America, where he devoted himself to teaching drama, mainly at the University of Texas.

[2] In his engaging but not always accurate *Life in a Wooden O* (written in his nineties), Payne recalled that he had 'been recommended for the position by Granville Barker'.

[3] WBY did not know that Payne was at present on tour in Ireland (see n. 1), and sent this letter to his home address in Norwich, so that it apparently did not reach him until after the two men had met.

## *To Lady Gregory, 17 January 1907*

18, Woburn Buildings, | Euston Road,
Jan. 17, 1907.

My dear Lady Gregory,

My letter wasn't as naive as all that. You had said that she had "destroyed my influence in the Company for a time", this was a very serious thing indeed, so there was nothing for it but to tax her with it.[1] I don't really greatly care, as it does not affect the value of her acting but it is just as well that I should check it if she were speaking against me before she plays for us again. She probably talked in the reckless sort of way the majority of us talk among our equals and forgot that it was quite a different thing to talk that way before people like Mac and the Allgoods, who have, more or less, to look up to us if we are to keep any kind of discipline. I happen to know that she is rather given to this kind of thing, and it is I imagine one of the reasons why she doesn't get on and why she has the reputation for being a devil. There is generally some explanation when you can get an actress of her <reputation> position to play for nearly nothing and so one must put up with it. She has an abyss of hysteria in her which people don't realise because of the air of efficiency and self-possession which covers it up.[2] The hysteria inspires the actress in her to some absurd display of self-glorification with every new audience. The Blighs say of her that she is always "bluffing" and they are her great friends.[3] I wrote to her because one is bound to give a person a chance of defence. <I am not sure that you should have told me all that ?she says, but as you did I had to write and> I think Russell should have written to me when he heard that I had accused him of jobbery.[4]

[1] See pp. 586, 588. On 15 Jan AG told WBY (Berg) she thought it 'very amusing your writing to ask Miss Darragh if she really thought you a bore! I should be sorry to ask any of my friends that, except maybe you yourself, in a good humour.'

[2] This was more generally recognized than WBY supposed (see pp. 524–5, n. 4, 588, n. 7). On 24 Nov 1906 Holloway had noted 'an undercurrent of intense subdued emotionalism' in Letitia Darragh's playing of Deirdre. In a conversation on 28 Dec 1906 with Henderson and Sigerson her name came up again, the former remarking (NLI) that he 'did not know whether Miss Darragh had left the country or not, but he hoped so. He agreed with D$^r$ Sigerson that she was not a draw here. Her style did not dovetail into the National Theatre Society's methods, although he was of opinion no one could have played Dectora better. D$^r$ Sigerson wanted to know did she dress in tights for the part as her form was so sharply defined through her closely clinging costume? Henderson thought not!'

[3] See p. 352. Andrew Bligh was a member of the Irish Texts Society and he and his wife had been at WBY's Monday Evening on 14 Jan.

[4] AE had accused WBY of this on 24 Feb 1905 (see p. 45). In a journal entry of 11 Aug 1909 WBY reflected that his penchant for gossip might 'be innocent enough, except for its indiscretion: and the malice of another may pervert it, as when my telling Lane that Russell would not do for a selector of pictures, because when he liked a man he over-rated his talent out of measure, came to Russell in the form that I accused him of jobs' (*Mem*, 227). AE was perhaps predisposed to believe the worst since as early as 1887 he had noted WBY's habit of saying 'such hard things of your friends' (Denson, 6).

I rather agree with you about Oedipus.[5] The immediate difficulty is that we require some programme for the Arrow, and I am at my wit's end to know what to write. I am trying to work out some sort of a leader, apologising for our not sticking to the old one. I wonder if we could substitute for a programme an indefinite paragraph saying something like this: "Owing to changes in the Company we find it impossible this month to announce more than the plays that will immediately follow "Play Boy", but these plays will be followed by a selection from the following . . . . . . . . We shall give a definite list on the same page with the programme" or "on the back of the programme on the first night of the Jackdaw and the White Cockade." In any case I must leave the matter to you, it is I should think pressing as it will take several days to print the Arrow and I am too far off for consultation.[6] I have written to the Manager Vedrenne recommends and asked him to come up from Norwich where he lives and see me.[7] If you could be in Dublin early next week and if he were free and could join us as soon as that I might send him over on Monday or Tuesday to arrange programme, if you think this would do any good but I doubt his being able to arrange anything until he knows more about our work. In fact I cannot see anything that he could do except say whether Play Boy is sufficiently up for a few rehearsals to be spared for the White Cockade and Fay might look upon this as an interference at the very outset with his prerogatives. It wouldn't be, for after all, he is to be Manager and must, I suppose, judge matters like this, but it might be taken as so. However we may possibly smooth that over. It might be a good thing to have him in Dublin as soon as that but my own idea is to get him to meet me there after my Aberdeen

---

[5] In her letter of 16 Jan, telling him that Robert was laying aside his translation of *Antigone* (see p. 596, n. 6), AG had added: 'I am inclining towards Magee's Edipus, in prose as it is—*not* verse, because as I say we mustn't overdo verse, & we must have King's Threshold & Baile's Strand this spring—I dont like Magees style, but he gives a scholarly translation which it would be dangerous to meddle with—If we decide on it, we should bring him to the theatre & make him read it from stage & correct if necessary—It wd be something to set the new man at.'

[6] In fact, plans for the next number of the *Arrow* were radically altered by the need to respond to the attacks on *The Playboy of the Western World*, and the main article, 'The Controversy over the Playboy', was a defence of artistic freedom. In her letter of 15 Jan AG enclosed one from Fay 'that you may see how impossible it would be to settle Feb programme by writing. I proposed Cockade for the 6 days 4–9—& he says he wd get it up for Saturday 9th when it would not run on, & I don't want it for one night only—And we can't settle about Fand without knowing what choice we have—I am wiring to say I will consent to Spreading the News, as the printing is out—but I hope nothing will make you consent to Pot of Broth –'

[7] Payne married the Irish actress Mona Limerick in 1906, and they had settled in Norwich, where she was expecting their first child. Since Payne was touring in Ireland the letter was delayed in reaching him.

lecture.[8] [*In WBY's hand*] What do you think. I cannot go over as I have to see Miss Horniman on the 22nd.[9]

Yr ev<br>W B Yeats

[*Typewritten*]
P.S. Since I dictated the above I have written the enclosed series of notes to the Arrow. I pass them entirely into the hands of your discretion. I have sent a copy to Henderson but said that if you did not put Oedipus into the programme that sentence could go out and that if they are too long the paragraph about Sentiment could go out. If you object to the notes in any way write and stop them with Henderson for he won't print for twenty-four hours. If you are doing the programme perhaps you might correct the proofs of these with the rest, if that will save any time. You may have made changes in the notes which I may not know of and I am quite satisfied to accept them, and if so the simplest way will be for you to get the proofs.[10]
[*On back of envelope*]
I think after all I had better see the proofs.

TLS Berg, with envelope addressed to Coole, postmark 'LONDON.W JAN 17 07'. No enclosure.

[8] WBY had agreed to lecture in Aberdeen on 25 Jan.
[9] AEFH was to return to London from North Africa on 22 Jan and had insisted that negotiations over the new manager should be settled by then.
[10] In a letter dated 'Friday' (18 Jan; Berg) AG returned these notes because of their references to Miss Darragh: 'I can't like them—for though very good in their way you couple with the great name of passion—on which we should fight together—the name of an actress who I never heard objected to because she put passion into her parts, but because she put something mean, ignoble & sensual—something never seen in any play of yours. . . . I will not write Henderson, you can do as you like—If I wrote I should suggest putting off Arrow till we have something definite to announce.' On 19 Jan she amplified her objections to the notes: 'I didn't like your making so much of Sinn Fein, and the other matter [i.e. his remarks on Miss Darragh] would have landed us in controversy which I have no objection when we have a clear case and definite issue, but which was muddled up between a play that is a permanent part of our organism and the acting of it which is not. Indeed I would rather have Deirdre be forgotten for a while, and then come with a new atmosphere. I don't know if you will agree with me, but you asked me to say or alter what I thought fit, and I didn't like to alter so much as I should have had to do to be able to support your argument.' The following day she told Synge (Saddlemyer, 207): 'I didnt think Yeats notes wise just now, they would irritate and raise discussions and when we go into a quarrel or even a discussion we should be on sure ground, and dont think the acting of "Dierdre" is very sure ground, it was not passion that was objected to in the representation.' Synge agreed with this. In the event, these notes were crowded out of the *Arrow* by the controversy over *The Playboy of the Western World* (see above, n. 6).

## *To W. A. Henderson, 17 January 1907*

Mention in previous letter.
Sending him a copy of a series of notes for the *Arrow*, telling him that if AG does not put *Oedipus* into the programme that sentence can be omitted and that if they are too long the paragraph about Sentiment can go out.

## *To John Millington Synge, 18 January 1907*

Mention in following letter, and in letter from AG, 20 January 1907. Telegram telling Synge 'I object to Pot'.[1]

## *To Lady Gregory, [18 January 1907]*

18 Woburn Buildings | Euston Road
Fri

My dear Lady Gregory:
    I think you had better write to Miss Horniman (touching contraversy very lightly if at all). I have had a letter a little grieved at not hearing.[1]
    I have wired Synge.

Yr ever haste
W B Yeats

I cannot find Act V of poor Jessops play. Do please look in my room—brown paper, red tape stitching back, type written.[2]

---

[1] This telegram does not survive, but urged Synge not to play *The Pot of Broth* with *The Playboy of the Western World* (see p. 594, n. 2). On 16 Jan AG had told WBY that she had not 'heard from Synge about Pot of Broth or Cockade'.

[1] AG was so angry with AEFH that she found it hard to write to her, and had asked for WBY's advice on 15 Jan: 'I am in a difficulty about writing to Miss Horniman accepting the offer—It may seem discourteous not to, but I could not do so without protesting against her calling us "an Irish toy"—& that might be dangerous—so tell me what to do?' On 12 Jan, AEFH had written to WBY from Tunis (NLI): 'My letter to Lady Gregory was merely a necessary statement of my personal point of view, as she does not agree nor answer I shall simply let things alone now. I've done everything possible for the scheme & now must leave matters.'

[2] George Henry Jessop (1852–1915) was born in Ireland and studied at Trinity College, Dublin. In 1873 he emigrated to America, where he became a journalist and began to write stories, plays, and libretti. He had a popular success with his play *Sam'l of Posen*, and a London triumph in 1903 with the operetta *My Lady Molly*. None of Jessop's plays was produced at the Abbey. On 19 Jan AG wrote, 'I have searched your room and can't find Jessop's play....I never read it at all.'

I have just got a most passionate denial of saying any 'injurious thing'—a most vehement & I should think sincere letter.[3] I dare say what ever she did say had not lost before it got to your ear. Nobody ever repeats anything without changing it.

[*On back of envelope*]
Have got the old furr rug back safe—[4]

ALS Berg, with envelope addressed to Coole, postmark 'LONDON.N.W. JAN 18 07'.

## To Miss Stone,[1] *19 January 1907*

18, Woburn Buildings, | Euston Road,
19th January, 1907.

Dear Miss Stone,
I shall come on the 23rd inst with pleasure at about 9 o'clock. Please forgive for not having answered before.

Yrs ever
W B Yeats

TLS Texas.

## To W. A. Henderson, *19 January 1907*

Mention in following letter.
Asking him to postpone the publication of the *Arrow*.

## To Lady Gregory, *19 January 1907*

18 Woburn Buildings, | Euston Road,
Sat | 19th January, 1907.

My dear Lady Gregory,
I send you three articles by Elton which may interest you. He is a friend of Kuno Meyer which accounts for the unsatisfactory paragraph about your book.[1] When I bring out my next book of essays I shall probably include one

---

[3] i.e. from Miss Darragh; see pp. 586, 588.
[4] See pp. 542, 559. AG replied on 19 Jan: 'I am delighted to hear the poor old rug is back.'
[1] This may have been Melicent Stone, a close friend of Mrs Pat Campbell.

[1] Oliver Elton (1861–1945) was an old friend of JBY and King Alfred Professor of English Literature at Liverpool University from 1900 to 1925. He had contributed a series of articles on Irish

of those introductions, in which case if you will help me with material, I will write a note on that Quarterly Review article. I think it is rather necessary to kill it, or at any rate to put those who quote it on the defensive.[2] I will not know about my publishing plans till I get back from Ireland as Bullen is down in Stratford. A difficulty has arisen over the expense of collected edition. It has been a piece of enthusiasm on the part of Bullen and his two partners are against it on the grounds of America being blocked to it at present.[3] However, the collected edition of the poem[s] will come out in March.[4] I went to see Ricketts last night. He said that he had had the same fight that I have had to get recognition for Miss Darragh. He says that he admits that the artistic public dislikes her and that the wrong people like her, and yet he is convinced that she has the making of a great tragic actress. He says she wants the confidence of many performances before she can make the most of herself, and get rid of certain habits formed through the accident of beginning her life in the height of a Sarah Bernhardt epoch.[5] He says that he

literature to the *Manchester Guardian* and the *Tribune*, which were collected in his *Modern Studies* published in October of this year. In 'An "Irish Malory"' he refers (297) to an anonymous critic's 'grave criticism' of AG's *Cuchulain of Muirthemne* for her choice of version, alterations, and omissions. The critic was Kuno Meyer (see p. 26, n. 5), who made this charge in his review 'The Sagas and Songs of the Gael', which had appeared in the *Quarterly Review* in July 1903. Elton was more kindly disposed towards AG, describing *Poets and Dreamers* as 'a book of value, the best book she has written, which tells us, better than many elaborate histories, of the indwelling fancy of the Irish folk, of their faculty for dreams and their power to see the fairies, and also of their natural turn for ballad and satire'. But while conceding that her work 'has a distinct niche of its own . . . it may have to be done over again, for the sake of letters and not merely of scholarship, in a different and stricter spirit; since, after all, the old Irish tales are classics, and we must have them . . . reproduced, by someone with a competent knowledge of the old language and with a genius for style, in a style that will recall their own.' In a letter dated 'Friday' (21 Jan; Berg) AG thanked WBY for the articles with the remark, 'I owe what he says good of me to you'.

[2] WBY had written enthusiastic introductions to both AG's *Cuchulain of Muirthemne* and her *Gods and Fighting Men*; he republished these in vol. VIII of *CW* in 1908, and they were later included in *Expl*, but he did not add a note about the criticism in the *Quarterly Review*.

[3] These problems were solved in March of this year by AEFH's offer to underwrite the venture financially. WBY had signed a contract with the Macmillan Company of New York, giving them exclusive American rights to his works (see pp. 121–3), and they were now in process of bringing out the two-volume *Poetical Works of William B. Yeats*. The firm consistently refused to handle *CW*.

[4] With the apparent collapse of plans for *The Collected Works*, WBY and Bullen were planning a new, cheaper edition of his poems, which they hoped would initiate a more modest collection of his works, but AEFH's intervention saved the more ambitious edition.

[5] Miss Darragh had begun her acting career in the Strand Theatre in 1897, at a time when Bernhardt's reputation was at its height in London and Paris. Sarah Bernhardt (1845–1923) had made her debut at the Comédie-Française in 1862 and began to make a name for herself from 1872. Her first appearances in London in 1879 and in New York in 1880 gave her instant successes in those cities, and she made frequent returns to London. She left the Comédie-Française in 1880 to open the Théâtre Sarah-Bernhardt. Noted for the musicality of her voice, Bernhardt had also developed a repertoire of acting techniques and mannerisms, some of which Letitia Darragh had imitated. On 10 Dec 1906 W. J. Lawrence had attacked her acting as 'watered down Bernhardt' (see p. 540, n. 5), and Micheal O Conaire wrote in *Sinn Fein* on 4 Dec 1906 (4): 'She has almost everything that the modern players' art can teach her. No trick is missing from her repertoire. Her exit was as fine as gesture and facial expression and the superficial art of the player could make it.' Miss Darragh had appeared in Ricketts's production of *Salome* the previous June (see p. 399, n. 4).

is entirely supported in this opinion by the admiration of Signora Duse for Miss Darragh's performance in Salome. I asked him if he had Signora Duse's opinion in writing. He said Mrs. Stillman had quoted it to him verbally, but that he had a letter of Mrs. Stillman's, giving a much less strong version of Signora Duse's words.[6] I got him to give me an extract from that letter. Here it is, I should say that Signora Duse dislikes Farquesson greatly.[7] "Madame Duse admired her interpretation extremely, especially at the end, and her trance like voice, but it seemed to me she did her part with so much more conviction than the first time and she looked lovely all the while, every moment was so picturesque."[8] He said he could only account for the dislike of Miss Darragh by there being something evidently not perceptable to him in her personality. He added, "my liking for her person-ally, is perhaps rather a sign of there being something to repel women about her, for I dislike all women as you know, but get on quite well with her." He told me that there was some kind of a quarrel between Mrs. Emery and Miss Darragh during rehearsal, and that undoubtedly she made difficulties for herself. He said he would have her back again, but that he would have to fight all his people.

[6] Marie Spartali Stillman (1844–1927), a Pre-Raphaelite painter, was born in London, the daughter of a Greek merchant. She modelled for Dante Gabriel Rossetti and was a pupil of Ford Madox Brown. In 1871 she married William James Stillman (1828–1901), an American painter, journalist, and art critic. The Stillmans had sat behind the famous Italian actress Eleonora Duse (1859–1924) at the first performance of *Salome* and Marie Stillman called on her the following day to discuss the performance (see *SP*, 137).

[7] For WBY's intense dislike of Farquharson see pp. 126, 145, 150–1, 425. In her letter of 18 Jan AG had made a direct comparison between Darragh's sensuality and that of Farquharson: 'she put something mean, ignoble & sensual — something never seen in any play of yours.... Farquarharson may have done the same with Forgael & you have spoken of Farquarharson quite as frankly as I do abt Miss Darragh — & I have never said "that is because he is a man" — or given any unkind explanations.' Nor was AG convinced by WBY's and Ricketts's defence of Miss Darragh, replying on 21 Jan: 'We are I am afraid still out of agreement about Miss Darragh. You forget that I thought her decidedly good in Salome, & that I agree she is competent & not offensive in Shadowy Waters. I don't think Ricketts in spite of his appreciation of her & of Tree & of music halls would have liked her in Deirdre. But I have found my formula — She is my Farquharson.' She went on to say that it was 'a great pain' for her to oppose WBY, and she asked him to consider what his feelings would be if she insisted on casting Farquharson in leading roles in her plays and tried 'to force him on, into other parts & permanent relations with the company'.

[8] In her reply, AG said that she 'honestly & most heartily wish I could see her as Mrs Stillman does. I did my very best to believe in her till the Deirdre rehearsals began. I very seriously considered then whether I ought not to leave Dublin, feeling so strongly as I did against her impersonation.... This is my difficulty; ought I through personal friendship & affection for you & for my own ease to accept — (& when I accept I must do it entirely) — an actress who I look on as you do on Farquharson & who I believe will lead to the deterioration of all our work & our ideas? On the other hand, ought I by opposing you to possibly lessen your interest in our Irish Theatre & drive you to make experiments in London, *to the great loss of Ireland*? Ought I to thwart you and have you always believe you had lost a great opportunity? ... What I want you to do is not to give up your own way to please me — that I want least of all — but to help me to find the right.'

I have written to Henderson asking him to put off the Arrow. Please show the part of this letter which is about Miss Darragh [*remainder of letter in WBY's hand*] to Robert.[9] By the by she could not have said that I would put in a manager at £500 a year I never thought of such a thing until Miss Horniman proposed it.[10]

Yr ever
W B Yeats

TLS Berg, with envelope addressed to Coole, postmark 'LONDON. W.C. JAN 19 07'.

## To John Millington Synge, 21 January 1907

Mention in letter to AG, 21 January 1907.
Telegram telling Synge 'Much prefer Riders of the Sea'.[1]

## To Elizabeth Corbet Yeats, 21 January 1907

Mention in following letter.
A 'long' but 'civil' dictated letter about Dun Emer finances and the necessity of paying authors' royalties promptly.[1]

## To Lady Gregory, 21 January 1907

18, Woburn Buildings, | Euston Road, N.W.
Jan. 21, 1907.

My dear Lady Gregory.

I have had a letter from Synge this morning asking me to wire whether it was to be The Pot of Broth or Riders of the Sea. I wired "Much prefer Riders of the Sea." I now remember my letter to him. I advised strongly

---

[9] In her letter of 21 Jan AG said, 'I will show Robert your letter. He is away & I am alone.'

[10] On the flap of the envelope containing her letter of 11 Jan AG had written, 'no need to break news to company Miss Darragh having told them some time ago you were engaging London manager at £500 per ann', thus further indicating Miss Darragh's untrustworthiness.

[1] i.e. *Riders to the Sea*, as curtain-raiser to *The Playboy* (see p. 601). This telegram had been prompted not only by Synge's letter, but also by a wire from AG. She had been against presenting *A Pot of Broth* before *The Playboy*, but Synge had evidently told her that WBY had previously consented to this, and she now thought it was his duty to stand by this undertaking. In telling Synge about her telegram on 20 Jan (Saddlemyer, 208–9), she added: 'I should certainly prefer Riders, but you may have some objection to it. Anyhow, Yeats wire will decide.'

[1] See pp. 557, 584, 594.

against "Pot of Broth" but did not like to forbid it, not being on the spot. I thought I would hear his reasons for wanting the Pot but I did not. My telegram as you see doesn't absolutely forbid it, but I wired on Saturday when I heard from you "I object to Pot".[1] The explanation of my new controversy with my sister is this. On hearing from you that she hadn't paid the royalties I wrote to her saying that it was rather a delicate matter, but I would like to know if she was paying her writers as it would render my position very difficult as Editor if she were not. I put a rather hasty phrase, I am sorry to say, in the letter which I was dictating. It was this "I know you haven't paid myself or Lady Gregory, this last an unfortunate omission." The phrase was ill-chosen but I don't like her getting into the habit of not paying promptly, she replied by a long financial lamentation and with a sentence which I must say exasperated me a great deal, objecting to paying my royalties at all, somebody or other had laughed when she mentioned them, Bullen, I believe, and she read into this laugh a hostile criticism of me for having asked for them. Now I can't do her books unless I am to be paid, for it means keeping them out of Bullen's hands where they would help to make up a possible income. This letter made me picture rather vividly the "several" reasons which she had given you for not paying. I wrote a letter which I hope was quite civil saying that when she wanted delay in payment she had better merely say 'I am hard up' or some phrase of that kind and not go into a lot of detail. This produced a very fiery letter indeed about my meddling, I replied very carefully and civilly, but at the same time saying that when people had worked for her she ought to thank them. This letter which I wrote with a pen was, I know, all right. I got the enclosed today. I had complained of the tone of the letters she had written you but had done this on my own knowledge of the letters not on anything that you said. I have just dictated a long letter and God knows what will happen now. I hope it's all right, but I haven't time to go over it very carefully. I know it is civil. I foresee that this controversy is going to enlarge itself in all directions in the usual way and to entirely lose sight of its original origin, but it is difficult to stop when once one starts.[2]

You were probably right about the Arrow, but Henderson has been urgent for some time.[3] The new man is at Cork and I am writing to him

[1] In fact he had sent this telegram on Friday, 18 Jan (see p. 601). On 26 Jan Synge told AG (*JMSCL* 1. 284), 'Yeats wired in favour of Riders so it goes on with Playboy though I think the Pot would have made a better bill.' On 23 Jan Holloway met Henderson 'looking gloomy' (NLI) and 'soon learned that Yeats had withdrawn "*The Pot of Broth*" from the bill on Saturday next, — he refused to let it be played in conjunction with Synge's new play *The Playboy*. He sent his refusal by telegram when all the printing had been done.'

[2] The letters between ECY and WBY are untraced, and were presumably destroyed.

[3] AG had advised against publishing the notes WBY had sent for it partly because the programme it was supposed to announce had not been settled, and because she found fault with WBY's remarks on Miss Darragh and on the criticisms levelled against the Theatre by *Sinn Fein* (see p. 600, n. 10).

to come to Dublin and see us there on next Sunday.[4] I hope you will be there then. I enclose a letter which he wrote to Vedrenne, I confess it was rather a shock to me to find that he was an actor, for I suppose Frank Fay will get it into his head that he is to be superseded or something of that kind.[5] At the same time as he was apparently ready to take some sort of minor managerial post with Barker, and as Vedrenne never mentioned his acting he is not likely to be ambitious as an actor.[6] If he is a competent actor without ambition he may be very useful. He may make The King's Threshold, for instance more of a possibility. As he can't play in peasant work the very small amount of acting he could at the very best do for us would not interfere, I daresay, with his stage management and business management. That is a matter for experience. It has been quite different with Fay, who is in almost every play we produce and playing principal parts. I don't suppose Synge sympathised with your telling him that you cared most for my work.[7] I really don't think him selfish or egotistical, but he is so absorbed in his own vision of the world that he cares for nothing else, but there is a passage somewhere in Nietzsche which describes this kind of man as if he were the normal man of genius.[8] A woman here the other day[9] told me that she said to Synge 'So and so thinks you the best of the Irish dramatists,' to which he replied, with a perfectly natural voice as if he were saying something as a matter of course "That isn't saying much." In some way he is as naive as Edward, but Edward's naivete came not from absorption but stolidity of nerve.[10]

---

[4] In *Life in a Wooden O* Payne recalls that he was with Cyril Keightley's company at this time, but he was in fact still with Ian Maclaren's Shakespearean and Old English Comedy Company when WBY contacted him. That company played at Cork from 14 to 19 Jan, but WBY may not have written to Payne there, as he went down personally to Wexford to interview him.

[5] Payne's letter to Vedrenne has not been traced. At this time he 'still thought of myself primarily as an actor' (*Life in a Wooden O*, 73), although he had done a good deal of stage management.

[6] In *Life in a Wooden O* Payne writes (64–5) that in the course of a short interview in a London café Barker told him 'he had nothing to offer at that time but he would bear me in mind', and that he was consequently surprised to discover that he had recommended him to the Abbey, especially since this one brief meeting was the only contact he had had with him.

[7] AG informed WBY on 18 Jan (Berg) that during an argument over whether *The Pot of Broth* should be put on with *The Playboy*, 'I told Synge I cared more for your work than for his, but he doesn't see things in that way.' This repeated a letter she had written to Synge on 5 Jan (Saddlemyer, 197), in which she said that she thought WBY's work 'more important than any other (you must not be offended at this) and I think it is our chief distinction'.

[8] In 'The Death of Synge' WBY was to comment that Synge 'had that egotism of the man of genius which Nietzsche compares to the egotism of a woman with child. . . . He had . . . a complete absorption in his own dream' (*Aut*, 511–12).WBY is apparently thinking of part 11 of 'Of the Higher Man' in *Thus Spoke Zarathustra*: 'In your self-seeking, ye creating ones, there is the foresight and foreseeing of the pregnant!'

[9] Probably Mrs Bligh, who had been at WBY's Monday Evening on 14 Jan (see p. 598, n. 3), and who knew Synge.

[10] i.e. Edward Martyn (see p. 46, n. 2).

I have just been in at Bullens, arranging with Sidgwick about the new issue of my Poems. They are not going to do the expensive collected edition at 10/- a volume but a cheaper uniform edition, they will probably begin with two volumes of poems and Secret Rose. A little later will come a new volume of Essays containing the various theatrical essays and this book should have illustrations by Robert, if he cares for the work. Sidgwick thinks they can do these in colour and would like to talk to Robert about them. He also wants a design for the cover, I mean the same design for each volume and I recommended Robert. He wants to talk to Robert about this. Of course Robert will be paid for this work.[11]

I have a frightful cold and I daresay it is getting into my controversy with my sister but were it ten times as bad I couldn't attain the heights of indignation of her letters. I wonder am I going to resign again—somewhere about the middle of next week.

Yr ev

W B Yeats

I enclose a letter from Miss Horniman which explains that vague "secret treaty".[12] She doesn't yet know that the new man is really accepted though she has had a letter saying that there were hopes he would be. Last week I got a very nice letter from her written on the supposition that he was not to be accepted. She proposed to keep £25,000 out at interest to do the best by my plays if the Dublin scheme fell through.[13] I was therefore wrong in supposing there was any understanding with Miss Darragh it was evidently pure speculation on Miss Darragh's part. Mrs. Emery who was not a friendly witness where Miss Darragh is concerned, tells me that Miss Darragh has been talking about Miss Horniman as if there was an understanding already arrived at. If this is true it is only one of her pomps and vanities.

[*With enclosure*]
[Marked by WBY "Secret Treaty"]

Tunis.
Jan 17th/06. [*sic*]

My dear Demon,

I am most sorry that my well-meant offer should have raised so much trouble. I put matters clearly about the future—once we both felt things

---

[11] These arrangements were overtaken by AEFH's offer to fund the full *Collected Works*. For Sidgwick see p. 115, n. 1.

[12] See pp. 576–7, n.11, 584.

[13] AEFH's 'very nice letter' was probably the now incomplete letter of 12 Jan 1907 (see p. 601, n. 1), which began with complaints against Fay, but in which she apparently undertook to keep her word over Abbey finances and her promises to WBY.

were rather hopeless & *in case of shipwreck* I said, "Let me have the plays (implying after the Society is dead) to do what I can with & you said "yes". Then more lately I reminded you of this & said *after the Patent has lapsed* I'll try in another way, promise me yours"—& I made some joke about bullying you for the royalties "which I earnestly hope that you will soon be receiving". Please let everyone know that there was no "secret treaty"; merely a desire on my part to salvage that part of the cargo which is of real importance.

My last offer was made to try to avoid the shipwreck. I had no idea of injuring anybody.

After the Patent is up any further application would be ridiculous unless we had some real success to shew behind us. I think that you should all be glad to feel that I shall try to save the plays, even a few of them, if you smash up in four years. No one could expect me to continue the subsidy uselessly after four years more.

Fine weather here after a wonderful two days in a motor. Someday I *must* take you to Karionan, a city in a vision & then to El-Djein, a great Roman ruin in an immense plain.[14]

Yours<br>Annie

TLS Berg; enclosure NLI.

## To Ben Iden Payne, 21 January 1907

Mention in previous letter.
A letter to Payne at Cork, inviting him to come to Dublin and see the three Abbey Directors there on Sunday next.

---

[14] Both Karionan (or Kairouan) and El-Djein (or El-Jem) are in the Sahel district of central Tunisia. Kairouan is the holy city of Tunisia, and the fourth holiest place in the Islamic world. It was here in the 7th century that Islam first gained a foothold in the Maghreb, and the impressively austere Great Mosque, situated in an atmospheric Medina, includes the oldest minaret in the world. The city is also the site of several celebrated shrines, the Bir Barouta, constructed round a sacred well, and the Mosque of Three Doors. El-Djein, built on the ruins of the prosperous Roman city of Thysdrus, is dominated by a huge colosseum, thought to have been built between AD 230 and 238 and estimated to have seated 30,000 spectators. There is also an earlier ampitheatre, some impressive mosaics, and the site of a number of Roman villas.

## To William T. Horton, 21 January 1907

18, Woburn Buildings, | Euston Rd.
Jan. 21, 1907.

My dear Horton,
   Is the fair person whose schemes I am to beware of man or woman?[1]
Yr sny
W B Yeats

TLS Texas, with envelope addressed to 6 Cheyne Row, Chelsea, postmark 'LON-DON.N.W. JAN 21 07'.

## To Ben Iden Payne, 23 January 1907

Mention in following letter.
Putting off Payne's meeting with the Abbey Directors for a week.

## To Lady Gregory, 24 January 1907

18, Woburn Buildings, | Euston Road, N.W.
Friday[1]—| Jan. 24, 1907.

My dear Lady Gregory,
   I got a letter last night, or some time yesterday from Professor Grierson
with whom I am to stay in Aberdeen[2] asking me to stay over Sunday to

---

[1] Horton (see p. 14, n. 4) had attended WBY's Monday Evening on 14 Jan (see p. 598, n. 3), and 20 Jan had written to warn him, 'You are going on a journey. Be careful how you listen to schemes & plans of a fair person. Be careful.' Replying to the present letter on 22 Jan he said: 'I could not tell you before—or I should have done so. On opening your letter & reading it I saw a fair *man* &, now I am writing, I see there is a woman with dark brown, or darkish hair, connected with the matter in some way. Both *seem* tall & slim & he the younger' (*Y & H*, 115, 116).

[1] This has been added in WBY's hand and is an error: 24 Jan fell on a Thursday in 1907.

[2] H. J. C. Grierson (see p. 308) took the chair at WBY's lecture on 'The Heroic Poetry of Ireland' at the Imperial Hotel, Aberdeen, on 25 Jan under the auspices of the Franco-Scottish Society. The *Aberdeen Daily Journal* for 26 Jan 1907 (5) reported that Grierson told 'a very large attendance', where 'even standing-room was at a premium', that they 'could have no better representative to tell them about those stories than a poet himself, who had studied the literature that had been for so long the glory of the Celtic peoples in Scotland and in Ireland'. In his lecture WBY claimed that 'it was almost impossible to over-rate the importance of legend to the world', and then addressed the question of how myth and folklore were to be rendered for a modern audience. He pointed out that modern scientific folklorists had rescued Celtic legends from James Macpherson's 'wonderful, vague eloquence that hid them from men's minds and altered them out of all recognition', but argued that modern pedantic translations could distort the originals in a different way. He read

meet some friends there.[3] Miss Horniman was with me and was convinced
that I couldn't get on from Aberdeen at all on Saturday because there were
no Sunday trains in Ireland.[4] It didn't seem possible to get any definite
information about trains and I was rather afraid of renewing my cold by a
long journey immediately and so wrote to Payne putting him off. As he
is busy in Limerick all next week, presumably playing we will not be able
to see him, until I should think next Sunday week.[5] My typewriter thinks
that I could have reached Dublin on Sunday morning and I am feeling
rather remorseful. I had thought of asking him to see you on Sunday and
Miss Horniman seemed willing for this. It then occurred to me that it
would be a mistake for if he should be unsuitable in any way she would
be more ready to trust to a decision of mine on this particular matter than
anybody else's. I think it would be putting both you and Synge in an unfair
position, if you were to see him without me. I think it necessary that you
should see him but we should both do so. If it were necessary to hurry the
matter on I might even go to Limerick. I am rather expecting to get a
telegram from him. My sister's affairs bother me a good deal. There are
moments when I think I should insist on seeing the books and being
allowed to get thorough mastery in so far as my ignorance of business
makes possible of the state of the affairs. I have a kind of feeling that
I should know all or nothing but at the present moment I am constantly
being bothered with financial reasons for one thing or another and I have
no way of knowing whether I should regard them or not. I feel between
two risks. I may either be really rather unfeeling through prolonged habit
of ignoring letters of this kind, or I may by taking notice of them allow them

---

extensively and approvingly from AG's books of folklore, analysed the characters of various Celtic
heroes, and concluded with a peroration on the imaginative power of legends 'in guiding the life
of a people', insisting that 'there was a memory of the race as well as an individual memory'. The
*Aberdeen Free Press* of the same day also gave extensive coverage of the lecture (3) and commented upon
the large audience. Mrs Sharp was particularly pleased that WBY had praised her late husband in
this lecture.

    [3] In 'J. M. Synge and the Ireland of his Time', WBY recalled (*E & I*, 311) that on 'Saturday, January
26, 1907, I was lecturing in Aberdeen, and when my lecture was over I was given a telegram which said,
"Play great success." It had been sent from Dublin after the second act of *The Playboy of the Western
World*, then being performed for the first time. After one in the morning, my host brought to my
bedroom this second telegram, "Audience broke up in disorder at the word shift." I knew no more until
I got the Dublin papers on my way from Belfast to Dublin on Tuesday morning. On the Monday night
no word of the play had been heard.'

    [4] From Aberdeen WBY would have returned to Ireland by way of the Stranraer–Belfast ferry, and
taken the train from Belfast to Dublin.

    [5] The Ian Maclaren company (see p. 597, n. 1) had moved from Cork to the Theatre Royal, Limerick,
where it performed from 28 Jan to 2 Feb. On 29 Jan the drama critic of the *Limerick Chronicle*
praised Payne's performance in William Muskerry's popular comedy *Garrick* as 'one of the best
Alderman Brackson's I have ever seen, being natural and effective . . . and looked the character to the
life' (4).

to drift into a very slack and amateurish way of treating their authors. And also of getting them into the habit of never giving me myself any royalties at all. At the present moment Lolly writes a letter, in so far as I can understand it, means that she wants a book of lyrics and will pay for it, but doesn't want to pay at all for Hanrahan.[6] From my point of view this is all wrong because their having Hanrahan for so long has meant a definite loss of mine, whereas, they could really have a book of lyrics of mine without my ordinary book containing the same poems being injured. Then I have to think that if I give them the Lyrics free it may be the beginning of the same sort of treatment of the other people and all the time for all I know they may be in a most flourishing financial condition, for Lolly's temperament is so excitable that passing worries hide from her realities. I can make nothing of her letter.

I have no answer to make about Miss Darragh except that all I want is a competent actress for my work and I believe her competent but I am perfectly content if her equal can be found. At any rate I don't propose to go any further into that matter at present.[7] As the great thing is to let the new man have a chance to take stock of the company and that will take him some little while. I don't think he will permit <Phaedre> Fand when he sees the company but I shall be entirely delighted if he does. What I am afraid of is that our women are good background but no use as foreground. Even if you were willing I would not now propose Miss Darragh for foreground as I don't wish to cause any more trouble which would only make things more difficult for the new arrangement to work. We may find somebody else necessary, however. Have you seen January *Century* with Roosevelt's article? I should think it ought to sell copies of the book in America.[8] I rather wonder if you have given the American rights to

---

[6] ECY's letter has not been traced. The Dun Emer Press had published the revised *Stories of Red Hanrahan* on 16 May 1905 in an edition of 500 copies. The next book of WBY's they issued was not a book of lyrics but *Discoveries*, published on 15 Dec of this year.

[7] On 21 Jan (Berg) AG had repeated and amplified her objections to Miss Darragh, comparing her attitude to her to WBY's feelings of disgust for Farquharson (see p. 604, n. 7).

[8] Theodore Roosevelt published an article on 'The Ancient Irish Sagas' in the *Century Magazine* in January 1907, pp. 327–36, illustrated with paintings by J. C. Leyendecker. He gave a lengthy description of the Cuchulain tales, naming AG among the recent popularizers, and regretted 'that America should have done so little either in the way of original study and research in connection with the early Celtic literature, or in the way of popularizing and familiarizing that literature, and it is much to be desired that, whenever possible, chairs of Celtic should be established in our leading universities'. A lengthy passage from AG's *Cuchulain of Muirthemne* (Findabair's report of the arrival of the Champions) was quoted in an editorial note in the same issue (336–7). In *Recollections of a Happy Life* (1924), Maurice Egan, Roosevelt's friend, records (209) that Roosevelt handed him the manuscript of the article in the middle of the 'Brownsville Crisis' in the Senate:

Murray. If not you might possibly be wise to get a distinct American publisher.[9]

My address in Aberdeen will be c/o Prof. Grierson, 7, King's Gate, Aberdeen.

Yrs sny<br>
W B Yeats

TLS Berg, with envelope addressed to Coole, postmark 'KILBURN JA 24 07'.

## To Lady Gregory, 26 January 1907

Mention in letter from Synge to Maire O'Neill, 27 January 1907.
A telegram asking her to go to Dublin to discuss the appointment of Payne and the February theatre programme with Synge.[1]

*JMSCL* 1. 285.

## To the Editor of the Evening Telegraph[1], 6 February 1907

The National Theatre Society, Ltd., Abbey Theatre, | Dublin.<br>
February 6th, 1907.

Dear Sir—My attention has been called to an interview with a Telegraph representative in which I am reported to have said:—"Mr. Boyle's own

---

'There,' he said, 'do as you please with that. It's my paper on the Celtic Sagas; you put the idea into my head and I worked it out.'

I was astonished. 'Do you mean to say, Mr. President, that with all this strife on your mind, you found serenity enough to write this article?'

'Oh, yes,' he said, 'the work took my mind off the caterwauling in the Senate.'

I gave the manuscript to Mr. Gelder [editor of *Century*], who paid the President $1,000 for it.

[9] AG's books of Irish myths and legends were published in America by Charles Scribner's Sons.

[1] It was owing to this telegram that AG was present at the tumultuous first night of *The Playboy of the Western World*; she had intended to remain in Coole. In his letter to Maire O'Neill of 27 Jan Synge told her that despite a 'splitting headache' he had 'to go in and talk business with Lady Gregory half the day. She got an important wire from Yeats, so she came up in a hurry last night and we have to talk today. There is nothing new, only details of what we had on hand before. If I get an opportunity I think I'll tell her about *us*.'

[1] This was a skirmish in the sustained campaign WBY was mounting in the Dublin press in support of *The Playboy* and of artistic freedom (see Appendix). Henderson told Holloway on 26 Oct this year (NLI) that he would 'never forget the excitement of Yeats' on his return to Dublin: 'He rushed into the theatre exclaiming "We must have columns & columns in the newspapers & 30 or forty sandwidge [*sic*] men to advertise the play" & then dictated what he wanted inserted about "the freedom of the theatre" etc.'

plays were treated in the same way as 'The Playboy' by the Abbey Theatre audiences when they were first produced." I did not say this, but spoke of attacks upon them by certain journalists, which resembled the attacks upon "The Playboy," and the many objections made to them by individuals among our audiences.[2]

Yours faithfully
W B Yeats

Printed letter, *Evening Telegraph* (Dublin), 6 February 1907 (3).

## To A. E. F. Horniman, [c. 10 February 1907]

Mention in letter from AEFH, 11 February 1907.
A 'long letter' telling her about the hiring of Ben Iden Payne as manager at the Abbey, asking if they could give the Free Libraries £16 to buy Ibsen plays,[1] telling her that Power regrets hissing from the Abbey stage during

---

[2] William Boyle had written to the *Freeman's Journal* on 1 Feb 1907 (6), announcing that: 'As the writer of plays recently produced at the Abbey Theatre, I beg to say that I have written to Mr. Yeats to-day withdrawing my sanction to the performances of any play of mine in the future. This is my protest against the present attempt to set up a standard of National Drama based on the vilification of any section of the Irish People, in a theatre ostensibly founded for the production of plays to represent real Irish life and character.' In his letter to WBY of 31 Jan (NLI), Boyle said he regretted 'to be obliged to write to withdraw my three plays – The Building Fund, The Eloquent Dempsy and The Mineral Workers from the repertoire of the National Theatre Company, as a protest against your action in attempting to force, at the risk of a riot, a play upon the Dublin public against their protests of its being a gross misrepresentation of the character of our western peasantry.' Questioned about this on 2 Feb in an interview in the *Evening Telegraph* ('Mr. Yeats Talks Again | To An Evening Telegraph Man'), WBY suggested (5) that 'Mr. Boyle evidently did not know the facts about the new play; and, besides, he added, Mr. Boyle's own plays were treated in the same way by the Abbey Theatre audiences when they were first produced.' When asked whether it would be possible for Boyle to reconsider his fundamental objection to *The Playboy*, WBY responded that he was 'the last man who should take up such an attitude; for his own admirable plays have by no means been approved of by the class of critics who are so antagonistic to Mr. Synge. . . . I know, for instance, that we lost a great many friends in connection with "The Building Fund," which was called a libel on Irish character; and, strange to say, he added, to-day a man gave me a copy of the Christmas number of a certain Dublin weekly which had been about the bitterest opponent of "The Playboy," containing an article on our plays, which says that "The Building Fund," "The Eloquent Dempsy," and "The Shadow of the Glen," should be hissed off the stage, and especially the two former, which are both by Mr. Boyle.' WBY was to reinforce this point later this spring by republishing Irish press attacks on Boyle's plays in the next number of the *Arrow*. Apart from his objection to the *Playboy* as such, Boyle had been further alienated by a triumphal letter from AEFH, and W. G. Fay, who had been sent to London expressly to retain his support, wired to AG on 4 Feb: 'Tabby [i.e. AEFH] completely upset Boyle. No use waiting here.' On his return to Dublin the following day Fay told her (as she reported to Robert Gregory) that he 'could do nothing with Boyle. Says it was temper roused by Miss Hornimans letter of cock-crows that roused him to write first, but now he wont withdraw unless Yeats will make a public declaration that we made a mistake in putting on the Playboy. Fay said of course that was impossible and Boyle wont give in. He seems to have no reason but Fay thinks had an uneasy feeling he didnt know where we might be leading him' (Emory).

[1] The £16 was the profit on the admission money to a public meeting called at the Abbey Theatre to discuss the production of *The Playboy*; AG had told Synge on 5 Feb (Saddlemyer, 210) that the 'theatre

the *Playboy* riots,[2] informing her that they are adapting Molière rather than using a translation,[3] and asking what she had written to Boyle.[4]

NLI.

---

was crammed, all the seats had been taken at Cramers. (We made £16.).' In her reply AEFH agreed to this proposal: 'Yes, let the Free Libraries have the £16 to buy Ibsen, the readers will be so disappointed to find his plays decent. The money left over might purchase some other plays, such as Maeterlinck, or Shaw for the lovers of all that is Irish.' In fact the money went to the National Library and for books on drama rather than play texts; on 11 Oct of this year Lawrence told Holloway (NLI) that he had been asked by the National Library to advise on the spending of the £16 and had named German books he had recently discussed with William Archer.

[2] On 1 Feb AEFH had written to the Abbey Directors (NLI) saying that Hugh Lane had informed her 'that low behaviour (I mean hissing) took place *from* the stage & that this hissing was political. Now I am of course aware that everyone was in a great state of excitement that night & maybe got carried away. But it must be clearly understood that I will not allow my theatre to be used for political purposes & the actors must be informed that hissing the drunken vulgarity of the stalls is just as bad as the patriotic vulgarity of the pit. I am fighting for us to stand above all low political spite on either side. I make this protest at once, it is a matter of honour that the Directors should do their best to prevent conduct in the actors which would justify my closing the theatre. From the very first & ceaselessly I have held firm to the position that *I will have no politics*. I should despise the idea of buying peace by bowing low to the Castle, you know that by my suggesting Kathleen for next week.' In this reply, WBY evidently told her that the guilty actor was Ambrose Power, who played Old Mahon in the play, but that he now regretted his outburst, for she replied that she was 'very glad indeed that Power regrets that he hissed, that clears it all away. I feared that you would find a knot of them glorying in their patriotism & objecting to any discipline on the stage just when it was much needed.'

[3] AEFH disagreed with AG's method of rendering Molière in a Kiltartan brogue and setting, but in her reply stated that she had 'made my protest against *adapting* Molière instead of using a good translation, so I have no more to say on the matter', before, characteristically, going on to say a great deal more: 'The absurdity of people with French names talking with a brogue reminds me of the plays I saw in the "seventies". You may trust me to remain silent on the point — I'm not likely to tell people unnecessarily that the Directors approve of making Molière into a sham Irishman. But I will not countenance it being brought to England on any pretence, I consider it to be most undignified from the literary point of view however many such adaptations may have been made; turning Red Indians . . . into Welshmen or Spaniards into Scandinavians etc. etc.' She also complained that she had only seen a programme of the Molière play by chance.

[4] AEFH had alienated Boyle with her letter about the production of *The Playboy*, although in her reply to WBY she said that she did not 'remember writing anything to Mr Boyle beyond an assurance that I was not going to draw back & that I was glad that the Directors were standing firm & that the societies & leagues had at last publicly shewn their wish to destroy us. It was written in such a friendly spirit that I quite expected that he would come & see if I had further news. So it only made him act more quickly as I could never have concealed from him my intense satisfaction that the stigma of being supposed to belong to any league or society has gone from us. It is better that he should go at once than remain a little & then make a new split.' In his reply to her letter, dated 31 Jan 1907, Boyle had told her (NLI): 'I regret I cannot share your satisfaction with the course of events at the Abbey Theatre, Dublin. I am extremely pained and disappointed that, in the first place, such a disgusting and untruthful picture of Irish life should have been produced by the National Theatre Company, and, in the second place, at the method taken to force such a production on an unwilling public. I have written to M[r] Yeats to withdraw my plays from the Company's repertoire.' In October 1928 Padraic O'Conaire told Joseph Holloway that he had been 'present when Boyle wrote the letter withdrawing his plays from the Abbey after the production of *The Playboy*. I tried to prevent him from sending on the letter, as he had not seen or read *The Playboy* at the time. But he, being ever and always headstrong, insisted on doing so. He had read the comments on the play, and that was enough for him' (*Joseph Holloway's Irish Theatre* [Dixon, Calif., 1968] 1. 40). In 1908 Fay told Holloway (NLI) that AG 'was fiercely jealous of Boyle, and was

## To H. J. C. Grierson, [*11 February 1907*]

Nassau Hotel | South Fredrick St | Dublin.
Monday

My dear Grierson: This is almost the first moment of leisure I have had for when the row was over I had to go to Wexford upon theatre business,[1] & found various things to do when I got back. We won in the fight for gradually our party grew until the play was received with enthusiasm.[2] I notice that nobody seems anxious to claim the credit of the attempt to keep the play from being heard. We wound up with a debate on the Monday night in which the whole opposition turned up—but I got a hearing & spoke my mind quite plainly.[3] The educated public is delighted,

greatly relieved by his secession. On the Monday after the production of the *Playboy*, I saw her in the morning and she said to me "that's a rotten branch gone".' He repeated this charge in a letter to W. J. Lawrence of 27 Oct 1907; see *Abbey Theatre*, 156.

[1] This was to interview Ben Iden Payne. Payne, confusing Waterford with Wexford (where the Maclaren company appeared at the Theatre Royal from 4 to 9 Feb), recalls in *Life in a Wooden O* (65) that 'one night, in a dingy old theatre in Waterford, the theatre manager came backstage and told me that "a gentleman from Dublin" wished to see me. I was playing a part in which I had long waits between my scenes, so I suggested that he bring the visitor around. The gentleman turned out to be a tall, dark man who looked, in his coal black suit and the dim light behind the scenery, so like a priest that for a moment I thought he was one. In fact, only the rather large, loosely tied black bow tie contradicted this assumption. He introduced himself by saying, "My name is Yeats." Naively I blurted out, "Not the poet?" "Yes," he replied gravely, "I am William Butler Yeats. I suppose you might call me a poet." I later discovered that Yeats had a frank and disarming smile when he was amused, but I saw no hint of it during this formal introduction.' The two men met after the performance at WBY's hotel, and Payne was surprised when WBY 'explained, over a glass of Irish whiskey, that he had made the journey down from Dublin especially to see *me*. They were looking, he said, for a stage director at the Abbey Theatre.... He proposed that I travel up to Dublin to look the situation over and meet his fellow directors of the Abbey Theatre, Lady Gregory and J. M. Synge. This seemed to be a sensible suggestion, especially as the Irish National Theatre was little more than a name to me.' Writing nearly seventy years after the event, Payne had evidently forgotten that WBY and Vedrenne had been in correspondence with him over this matter for some weeks, and so WBY's offer could not have come as such a surprise (nor does WBY's coyness at owning the soft impeachment of being a poet ring true). Indeed, Payne had visited the Abbey on 28 and 29 Jan as the new manager, and WBY's negotiations in Wexford were presumably to sort out the details of his contractual arrangements rather than to offer him a post he had already accepted. Payne went to Dublin on Sunday, 10 Feb, and saw AG and Synge the following morning.

[2] See Appendix. WBY had been staying with Grierson when AG's telegram 'Audience broke up in disorder at the word shift' arrived (see p. 611, n. 3), an incident which Grierson recalled in a letter to Synge of 28 Aug this year (TCD): 'M^r Yeats was with us at the time that [*The Playboy*] appeared & he sent us from Dublin papers about the trouble you had. I hope that is all over now. I have read the play very carefully since & with great pleasure. It is [a] very artistic & subtle piece of work. But apart from prejudice & patriotism— about wh. of course I know nothing—I can imagine that so fine a piece of work & in parts so searching would not at once please [a] popular audience. I trust you will not be discouraged from going on to write more plays for there is no one producing anything like them. We have read them all repeatedly.'

[3] A version of this speech was printed in the *Arrow* of 23 Feb 1907 and the closing paragraphs are quoted in *Expl* (226–8). WBY had not managed to get back to Dublin until 29 Jan and Ben Iden Payne

& I think our own audience pit & all. The opposition came largely from without.[4] On Saturday night last we played a triple Bill "Pot of Broth" "Doctor in Spite of Himself" and "Kathleen-ni-Houlihaun". The audience called the players after "Kathleen" three times & then called me, & gave me a wonderful reception, what the newspapers would call "an ovation". This was ment to show approval of our fight.[5] "The Play Boy"

recalls in *Life in a Wooden O* that he was fired up from the first by the disturbances at the Abbey: 'I have a vivid recollection of my next interview with the directors. Yeats had been absent at the opening of *Playboy*, but at this meeting he was the dominant figure. Most of the talk was about the trouble at the theatre. Synge very tentatively suggested that they throw in the sponge by stopping the run of the play, though it had been advertised to last for a week. Yeats would not hear of it. His manner was high-spirited, even elated. The fire of combat lighted up his eyes as he said they must at all hazards give the play its full allotted time. If they gave way to clamor, he said, they would ever afterward be at the mercy of the whims and prejudices of their audiences. The play must go on, he said, even if they had policemen stationed by every row of seats to throw out the disturbers.'

[4] Although there was an organized claque on the second and third nights of the performances, this is a simplification: many Abbey habitués, such as Holloway, O'Donoghue, and Lawrence, were vehemently opposed to the play and a number of them (although not Holloway) also attended the meeting. Over the following years Holloway recorded in his diary meeting dozens of Abbey patrons who no longer went there because of *The Playboy*. AG gave Robert Gregory a long account of the meeting on the following day (and sent a copy of it to Synge): 'The meeting last night was dreadful, and I congratulate you on not having been at it. The theatre was crammed, all the stalls had been taken.... Before it began there was whistling &c. "Pat" made a good chairman, didnt lose his temper and made himself heard but no chairman could have done much. Yeats first speech was fairly well listened to, though there were boos and cries of "What about the police?" &c, and we had taken the precaution of writing it out before and giving the reporters a copy. No one came to support us, Russell (A.E.) was in the gallery we heard afterwards but did not come forward or speak. Colum "had a rehearsal" and didnt speak or come. T. W. Russell didnt turn up. We had hardly anyone to speak on our side at all, but it didnt much matter for the disturbances were so great they wouldnt even let their own speakers be well heard. Lawrence was first to attack us a very poor speech, his point that we should have taken the play off because the audience and papers didnt like it.... But he bored the audience... little Beasley was the only one with a policy for he announced his intention of never entering the place again, and called upon others to do so, but the cheering grew very feeble at that point. A Dr Ryan supported us fairly well. Though it was hard to get speakers to come forward, at the thick of the riot Mrs Duncan sent up her name to the platform offering to give an address! but Pat sent back word he would not like to see her insulted! A young man forced his way up and argued with Dossy till a whisky bottle fell from his pocket and broke on the stage, at which Dossy flung him down the steps and there was great cheering and laughing, and Dossy flushed with honest pride. Old Yeats made a very good speech and got at first a very good reception though when he went up there were cries of "kill your Father" "Get the loy" &c. and at the end when he praised Synge he was booed. The last speakers could hardly be heard at all. There was a tipsy man in the pit crying "I'm from Belfast! Ulster aboo"! Many of our opponents called for order and fair play and I think must have been disgusted with their allies. The scene certainly justified us in having called in the police. The interruptions were very stupid and monotonous. Yeats when he rose for the last speech was booed but got a hearing at last and got out all he wanted to say. He spoke very well, but his voice rather cracked once or twice from screaming and from his sore throat. I was sorry while there that we had ever let such a set inside the theatre, but I am glad today, and I think it was spirited and showed we were not repenting or apologising.'

[5] Holloway recorded lugubriously on 9 Feb (NLI): 'It was with a sorrowful & heavy heart I set out for the Abbey tonight. After the mistake of last week I felt that a big change was in store for the N.T.S. The offence given to old patrons could not be easily passed over by them. Would the new people attracted to the theatre by curiosity fill their places? I found the latter to be the case. Few if any of the old familiar faces were to be seen there, but all the backers of last week's show & many of the public comfortably

was really only silenced two nights & partly silenced on one—Wednesday—& after that the majority were with us. There was a good deal of
rioting outside the theatre—here & there & we absorbed all the spare police
of the town.[6] We had great audiences twice as big as ever before.[7] We have
lost a dramatist—Boyle but I beleive we will get him back in a few months.
We had exausted his plays for the moment & would not have played him
more than for one Saturday till next winter.[8]

Yrs ev
W B Yeats

ALS NLS.

## To Rosamund Langbridge,[1] [*11 February 1907*]

Nassau Hotel | South Fredrick St | Dublin.
Monday

Dear Miss Langbridge: I have not had time till this moment to thank you for
your kind note.[2] We won the fight. On Tuesday & Monday no word of play
was audible, on Wednesday most of the play was heard & the rest of the week
the majority of the house, even the majority of the pit was on our side. On
Saturday there was enthusiasm. We will revive the play in due course &

filled the stalls & pit.... There was an air of dead calm about the house that was depressing. The
electricity of the old audience was absent. I being used to it felt its absence sorely! The literary theatre
audience was gone & in its place was an uninteresting claque created to blot out freedom of opinion.'
Holloway thought the plays successful, however, especially the 'ever-thrilling & beautifully weird little
play of *Houlihan* [which] created quite an impression as it always does. Sara Allgood's pathetic
impersonation of the "poor old woman" was superbly touching & stilled the audience into the stillness
of death. It is a glorious performance!...Loud applause followed the fall of the curtain, & calls for
"author" from the inspired ones in the pit brought the actors & ultimately the author (who hurried
round as fast as he could) on the stage to bow acknowledgment. There was a lack of sincerity about the
whole evening. The police were absent, as were the old patrons!'

  [6] For an account of the disturbances see Appendix.
  [7] For the week of 26 Jan to 3 Feb the Abbey takings were £158 10s. 1d., over three times the normal
weekly receipts, and the two shows on 9 Feb netted £24 17s. 11d.
  [8] See p. 614, n. 2. In fact Boyle did not return his plays to the Abbey until 1910.
  [1] Rosamund Grant Langbridge (1880–1964) was the second daughter of the Revd Frederick Langbridge (1848–1922), Canon of Limerick, and, like her father, was a prolific writer of novels, poems, and
plays. She subsequently married J. S. Fletcher, author, local historian, and journalist, and lived in the
latter part of her life in Dorking, Surrey.
  [2] Untraced, but evidently enquiring about *The Playboy* riots. Miss Langbridge would have been
particularly interested in the riots over the *Playboy* as her own play, *The Spell*, had received like
treatment from a Dublin audience the previous November.

it will become a permanent part of our repetoire.[3] Last Saturday I was called before the curtain after 'Cathleen' by a house evidently anxious to show that they approved of our action. Mondays debate was very stormy as you can imagine, so stormy that I know of several who came there thinking me wrong to have called in the police & went away saying that we did right. But for the police there would have been an attempt to rush the stage—this was the plan of the organized troop of about forty who led the attack.[4] The whole row has done us good—we had twice the audience we ever had & I dont think our regular audience has fallen off in any way.[5] The only serious thing is that it may stop our country tours & my Irish American lecturing for a bit.[6]

I doubt if Harvey—being English—could have made the same fight. It is more easy for us to do it because they cannot say we are producing plays that we cannot judge not being Irish. At the same time I dont think Harvey should have altered deliberately made public announcements. We have had to suffer because he & others have given way to popular demand. If we had not made this fight we would have been slaves of the mob for ever but now that the fight has been made it will be better for others—Harvey included. The trouble has come partly because theatre managers do not take themselves seriously as artists but think of themselves as "public entertainers"—this is a tradition very hard to break perhaps impossible to break for a man in Harveys position.[7] It can only be changed gradually & the fight must be made by people like us, who can exist without the help of the vast conventional public.

[3] *The Playboy* was taken on tour to Oxford and London later this year, but it was not revived in Dublin until May 1909. Thereafter it was played at regular intervals, but was to cause bitter controversy on the first Abbey tour to the USA in 1911–12.

[4] See Appendix. The protest seems to have been spontaneous on the first night, but was more orchestrated on the following evenings.

[5] This was wishful thinking; in fact the audiences at the Abbey did fall away over the coming months.

[6] Although there were protests against the play throughout rural Ireland, this did not inhibit country tours, and a very successful tour took place in August this year. WBY did not have the opportunity to return to America until September 1911, but this was not because of *The Playboy* controversy.

[7] i.e. John Martin Harvey (1863–1944), the English actor-manager, who had produced Miss Langbridge's *The Spell* at the Adelphi Theatre on 2 Nov 1906, and was to stage her *A Tragedy of Truth* in June 1907. He was particularly sensitive about Irish audiences: when he brought *The Spell* to Dublin in November 1906, it caused such a disturbance that it had to be taken off after one night (see p. 521, n. 5), a surrender which AG compared unfavourably in *OIT* (116) with the resolution of the Abbey Directors over *The Playboy*: 'In Dublin, Mr. Martin Harvey, an old favourite, had been forced to take off after the first night a little play because its subject was Irish belief in witchcraft.... We would not...allow any part of our audience to make itself final judge through preventing others from hearing and judging for themselves.' In his *Autobiography* (1933) Harvey recalls (355–7) that the demonstrations marked a watershed in his previously enthusiastic reception in Dublin: 'The atmosphere had changed. The little rift in the lute which we refused to hear had broadened out to expel a hurricane, and Dublin was never quite the same again'. In September 1912 he was to enrage WBY by publicly abandoning plans to tour *The Playboy of the Western World* when threatened with protests.

It was your friend Matty Bodkin, who wrote the Freeman leader, which started the row on a big scale.[8]

Yr sny

W B Yeats

We played through the eight performances announced, & having got a hearing were content. Had a hearing been refused we would have played on indefinitely.

ALS Emory.

---

[8] Matthias M'Donnell Bodkin (1850–1928) was born in Co. Galway and educated at Tullabeg Jesuit College, and the Catholic University, where he read law. He was called to the Bar, and represented North Roscommon as an Anti-Parnellite MP from 1892–5. He wrote a number of popular humorous stories and historical novels, including *Poteen Punch* (1890), *Lord Edward Fitzgerald* (1896), *Shillelagh and Shamrock* (1902), *In the Days of Goldsmith* (1903), and *Patsy the Omadhan* (1904), as well as a volume of memoirs, *Recollections of an Irish Judge* (1914). He regularly contributed leaders to the *Freeman's Journal*, but later this year was to cause the paper embarrassment when he was appointed a County Court judge for Co. Clare by a warrant of the Lord-Lieutenant: not only was this a crown appointment, but it was suggested that he had been angling his editorials for some time in the hope of such preferment. He was apparently responsible for the editorial in the *Freeman's Journal* of 29 Jan 1907 (6), which intensified the inflammatory reception of the play already established by a review of the previous day (see Appendix, pp. 866–7, 670): 'With an audacity worthy of a better cause, "The Playboy of the Western World", was produced again last night in the theatre in Abbey street that styles itself Irish and National. . . . It is impossible to understand the reason that prompts this continued outrage not merely on National feeling, but on truth and decency. It is not too much to say that no traducer of the Irish people ever presented a more sordid, squalid, and repulsive picture of Irish life and character. It is calumny gone raving mad. Why it was written, why it was accepted and rehearsed and produced, and why the management insist on reproducing it in the teeth of all protest, are problems for which it is impossible to hint a solution. The Abbey Theatre has often declared its mission is to elevate the Irish drama, to banish the stage Irishman from the theatre. But the stage Irishman is a gentleman in comparison with the vile wretch whom Mr. Synge presented to an astonished Irish audience as the most popular type of Western peasant.' Citing the reaction to the play in the Unionist press, he went on to hint that the play was politically motivated: 'Let us remember this calumny runs on old and familiar lines. It has ever been the custom of traducers of the Irish people to charge them with sympathy with all forms of crime. Over and over again this same lie has been made the justification for Coercion.' He concluded by reminding his readers that the Abbey had declared as its mission 'to banish the meretricious stage, and give, for the first time, true pictures of Irish life', and demanded to know 'if the production of "The Playboy of the Western World" is a fulfilment of that pledge. . . . Do those who insist on its production claim that it is true to Irish life? . . . The production of the play might be pardoned if it were promptly withdrawn. But persistence in reproducing it commits all concerned with the Theatre to approval of this very gross and wanton insult to the Irish people.'

## *To Agnes Tobin*, [c. *11 February 1907*]

Mention in letter from Agnes Tobin, 12 February 1907.
Telling her of the success of *Cathleen ni Houlihan*,[1] sending her the Musicians' lines at the end of Deirdre,[2] mentioning the engagement of Payne,[3] and that his wife was an actress,[4] telling her of Synge's illness,[5] and sending her a copy of *The Playboy*.[6]

---

[1] Agnes Tobin was glad to hear of the success of the play (see pp. 617, 619), and urged him (*LWBY* 1. 177–8) to 'let Synge's play drop, now — I hope he will not publish it in America, it would do nothing but harm to him & everybody and everything else.'

[2] WBY had evidently sent her the final chorus from *Deirdre* which he had recently completed and which he was to send to Marinetti in a few days. In her reply she declared that the lines were 'as fine as any verse ever written in any language living or dead'.

[3] Agnes Tobin took an active interest in the Abbey Theatre and did her best to promote its interest but, like MG and several other of WBY's friends, she thought he was sacrificing to drama gifts he should have devoted to poetry and in her reply told him that she could 'not but hope this stage manager will take a good deal off your hands — I do grudge your giving so much time to the theatre'.

[4] i.e. Mona Limerick (see p. 599, n. 7). Miss Tobin replied: 'I wonder if you will find a good actress, or the makings of one, in the stage manager's wife — it would be strange.'

[5] Synge had been taken ill shortly after the first night of *The Playboy* with a series of ailments including bronchitis, laryngitis, influenza, a chronic cough, and 'a sort of dissentry' (Saddlemyer, 251); he was to be convalescent until early April. Miss Tobin, who had met Synge the previous year, hoped that he was better: 'he is such a dear, charming fellow.'

[6] WBY had promised to send her an advance copy of *The Playboy of the Western World*, provided she did not show it to others. In fact, a letter from her to Synge of 30 Jan suggests (TCD) that she had seen an earlier version of the play in MS, but she replied that she was 'most anxious' to read the final text, and that she would 'not lend it or speak of its being in my possession'. On reading the play, she commented (*LWBY* 1. 179) that she 'was much interested' in it: 'it is splendid the way he gets the vivid effects of speech & character: but it seems a pity to lavish all that on a thing that has about as much connection with real life as a Chinese mask. There are one or two speeches with lovely lyric effects in them — but it seems to me he deliberately perverts his imagination. It is a curious phenomenon to watch — the way he uses his singular powers.' On 13 March she wrote to Synge himself (TCD), telling him that WBY had sent her an early copy of *The Playboy* 'and of course I enjoyed your power & vividness even shown under such a guise'. But she went on to wish that he would write only poetry in future.

## *To Cornelius Weygandt,*[1] *13 February* [*1907*]

18 Woburn Building | Euston Road.
Feb 13

My dear Weygandt: may I introduce Miss Florence Farr (M$^{rs}$ Emery) of whom you have heard me speak.[2] She speaks verse more beautifully than [any]body in the world.

Yrs ever
W B Yeats

ALS Ann Weygandt, with unstamped envelope addressed to the University of Pennsylvania, The College.

## *Contract with W. G. Fay, 15 February 1907*

### MEMORANDUM OF AGREEMENT

Between the National Theatre Society of the Abbey Theatre Dublin, and William G. Fay, hereby Mr W. G. Fay in consideration of the sum of two pounds (£2) per week consents to play such parts as may be alotted to him, and in consideration of a further sum of £100 per annum produce all the plays of the Society which are in Irish dialect and such other plays as he may be specially selected to produce. His production not afterwards to be interfered with in any essential.

---

[1] Cornelius Weygandt (1871–1957), an American journalist, academic, and critic, had worked on the *Philadelphia Record* and the *Philadelphia Evening Telegraph*. He claimed to have been the first journalist to introduce WBY, Davidson, Kipling, Watson, and Francis Thompson to American readers. In the autumn of 1897 he returned to the University of Pennsylvania to teach English, and remained there until his retirement in 1942. His numerous books include *Irish Plays and Playwrights* (1913) and *The Time of Yeats: English Poetry of Today against an American Background* (1937). He visited Coole in 1902 (see III. 216–17), and WBY stayed with him in Philadelphia in 1903 (see III. 472, 479). Weygandt gives accounts of his meetings with WBY and other Irish literary figures in *Tuesdays at Ten* (Philadelphia, 1928) and *On the Edge of Evening: The Autobiography of a Teacher and Writer* (New York, 1946).

[2] FF had sailed from Liverpool on the *Baltic* on 30 Jan, arriving in New York on 7 Feb, where her niece Dorothy Paget (see II. 395–6) advised her about her itinerary. During her three-month tour she recited and gave lectures at numerous venues, including Radcliffe College, the University of Toronto, the Albright Gallery in Buffalo, Hull House and the Fortnightly Club in Chicago, and various private homes in Boston, Philadelphia, and other major cities. Although there is no hard evidence that she performed at the University of Pennsylvania, she lectured at nearby Bryn Mawr College, and in his *Irish Plays and Players* (1913) Weygandt records (25) that she spoke WBY's 'dramatic verses in a "half chant" and his lyrical verses, many of them, to a definite musical notation, on her American tour of 1907'.

This agreement to be terminable on &lt;one&gt; three months' notice being given by either of the parties. Dated 15th day of February 1907.[1]

As witness the hands of the parties
On behalf of the National Theatre Society.
W B Yeats
William G Fay

TS Doc NLI.

## To Agnes Tobin, c. 15 February 1907

Mention in letter from Agnes Tobin, 16 February 1907.
Telling her he must remain in Dublin to look after the Theatre,[1] and discussing which plays might appeal to Charles Frohman for an American tour by the Abbey.[2]

## To Filippo Tommaso Marinetti,[1] 16 February–4 March 1907

Nassau Hotel | Dublin,
Feb 16 1907

Dear Sir,

I must apologise to you for having left your letter so long unanswered, but I left London immediately after getting it and on arriving here found a

---

[1] This contract apparently settled the question of Fay's duties, and his extra payment, but was cancelled after Payne left the Abbey this summer. WBY initialled the autograph alteration of 'one' to 'three'.

[1] In her letter of 12 Feb Miss Tobin mentioned that Mrs Mond had asked her to take her to another of WBY's Monday Evenings, but WBY had evidently told her that because of Synge's illness and the convulsions after *The Playboy* disturbances, he would have to stay in Dublin for the foreseeable future. She was 'sorry you are to be so long away—but I think you are right to finish things off for this bout! You have worked hard for the theatre the last few weeks.'

[2] In her letter of 12 Feb (see p. 621) Miss Tobin told WBY that she was going to see the American impresario Charles Frohman on 13 Feb about an American tour for the Abbey. In his reply WBY had evidently discussed the plays and players that might suit him, and in her letter of 16 Feb she gave her reflections on these suggestions: 'I am afraid The Building Fund would be too bitter for America—The Mineral Workers struck me as being very interesting to the Irish American mind, though.... Keep The Shadowy Waters for the last—it might baffle Frohman. I do hope you will find a Deirdre. It is so splendid that Baile's Strand and The King's Threshold are well within the company's range. I spoke to him of O'Rourke's acting in The Mineral Workers—he was much interested: couldn't you put O'Rourke on in the Lost Saint (is that the name of the play of Hyde's you told me about?)?'

[1] Filippo Tommaso Marinetti (1876–1944), Italian poet, author, and journalist, was born in Alexandria and educated at a French school there, before returning with his family to Italy in 1894. He studied law at the universities of Pavia and Genoa, but spent much of his time writing poetry (in French) and visiting Paris, where, under the guidance of Gustave Kahn, he published widely and became a

very stor[m]y time before me, as a satirical play was causing riots at the Theatre I am connected with.[2] I send you a photograph of myself and the only poem which I have that has not been published. It is a dirge spoken by two singers after the death of the heroine in my play Deirdre. Deirdre has gone to kill herself upon her lover's body.[3]

I thank you for the honour you have done me in asking me to join such distinguished collaborateurs.[4]

Yrs ever<br>W B Yeats

*[remainder of letter in AEFH's hand]*

Postscript.                                 March 4th/07

You will [see] by the above that I tried to answer you some time ago, but the tumults in my theatre had so many after consequences, that the letter was never posted and it went out of my mind .

I have enclosed a second poem, also a chorus out of the play.

*[with enclosure]*

recognized member of the Symbolist movement. His first book of poems, *La Conquête des étoiles*, was published in Paris in 1902, and a more avant-garde collection, *Destruction*, followed in 1904. Impatient with what he saw as the old-fashioned and parochial state of Italian poetry, he established the poetry review *Poesia* in 1905. Although run from his apartment in Milan, the magazine cultivated an international set of contributors, and was intended to effect a renaissance in Italian poetry by introducing new currents in European writing. An enthusiastic disciple of Nietzsche, Bergson, and Sorel, Marinetti abandoned Symbolism and declared himself the founder and leader of Futurism in 1909, making *Poesia* the mouthpiece of the new movement which, dedicated to the bombastic destruction of tradition and worship of the machine, had no appeal for WBY.

[2] WBY may have mentioned this because he knew of Marinetti's four-act 'satiric tragedy' *Le Roi Bombance*, which had been the subject of controversy when it was published in 1905. There were to be disturbances (if of a contrived nature) when Aurélien Lugné-Poë produced it at the Théâtre de l'Œuvre in Paris in March 1909.

[3] This dirge is sung as Deirdre goes, so Conchubar thinks, to bid farewell to the murdered Naoise, but in fact to commit suicide over his body. The copy text is a page taken from a typescript of the play, and both WBY and Marinetti have crossed out the speeches of Fergus and Conchubar, and these, like WBY's picture, did not appear in *Poesia*. Apart from some minor emendation in the punctuation, these lines appeared unaltered in the published version of the play (*VPl*, 387, ll. 733–7).

[4] Marinetti had invited WBY to contribute to *Poesia* as long ago as December 1904 through the French man of letters Henry Davray, but WBY, although eager to do so, regretted that he had 'been so long writing poetical dramas, for my little theatre here in Dublin, that I have only done two lyrics in the last year' (III. 686). On 10 Nov 1906 AEFH informed him (NLI) that a 'lady named Rossetti [probably Olivia Rossetti Agresti (1875–1960), daughter of William Michael Rossetti] has written for your address so as to write for permission to put some of your lyrics in to "Poesia". I answered & told her of the new book as being suitable for review.' Other 'collaborateurs' included Giosuè Borsi, Giosuè Carducci, Gabriele D'Annunzio, Georges Duhamel, Paul Fort, Francis Jammes, Gustave Kahn, Catulle Mendès, Stuart Merrill, Jules Romains, Arthur Symons, Émile Verhaeren, Francis Viélé-Griffin, and Charles Vildrac.

<A dirge over
Dierdre & Naise><sup>5</sup>
*First Musician*
They are gone. They are gone. The proud may lie by the proud
<*First Musician*
They are gone. They are gone. The proud may lie by the proud.>
SECOND MUSICIAN
Though we were bidden to sing, cry nothing loud
FIRST MUSICIAN
They are gone, they are gone.
SECOND MUSICIAN
Whispering were enough
FIRST MUSICIAN
Into the secret wilderness of their love
SECOND MUSICIAN
A high, grey cairn, what more is to be said.
FIRST MUSICIAN
Eagles have gone into their cloudy bed.
<FERGUS (L.)
Where's Naisi son of Usna and his queen
I and a thousand reaping hooks and scythes
Demand him of you.
CONOCHAR
You have come too late
I have accomplished all. Deirdre is mine.
She is my queen, and no man now can rob me.
I had to climb to the topmost bough and pull
This apple among the winds (*Open the curtain*)
That Fergus learn my triumph from her lips
(*The curtain is drawn back*)
No, no. I'll not believe it. She is not dead>
<(43)>

[*on a separate sheet*]
<During the chess the Musicians sing this song. At first the three voices, then two drop out, perhaps first one and then another. The last lines are given by a single voice hesitating over the last two, repeating or otherwise showing confusion of mind.>

---

<sup>5</sup> WBY's title has been crossed out and replaced with 'A Dirge over Dierdre e Naise' in another hand. The same hand has crossed out the First Musician's opening line (the only one in WBY's hand) and rewritten it verbatim, presumably to make it more legible to the printer.

Love is an immoderate thing
What can pity offer it
Or the changing seasons bring
To its laughing, weeping fit
All its heart is aquiline
And can never be content
Till it leap to the divine
Changeless shining element
That is fed on time's decay
And grows brighter <when> while we <are> dim
What's the merit in love play
What is there in limb on limb
What can be in mouth on mouth
All that mingling of our breath
When love longing is but <drowned> drouth
For the things come after death[6]
                                        Yeats[7]

TLS Getty.

## To John Quinn, 18 February 1907

Nassau Hotel, | Sth. Frederick Street
Feby. 18th 1907

My dear Quinn,

I think my sisters have sent you papers about the noise here, about the Playboy, and you will have the play itself by this time. I do not think Roberts by-the-by, should put you to the trouble of having to copyright it. Being a publisher, he might quite well have found out some machinery for

---

[6] A shortened version of these extracts was published in the winter 1906–7 issue of *Poesia* (2: 9–12, p. 12) as 'A Dirge over Deirdre e Naisi'. Marinetti omitted everything cancelled here, so that the chorus beginning 'Love is an immoderate thing' comes immediately after the First Musician's line 'Eagles have gone into their cloudy bed', although in the play it comes much earlier, being sung by the Musicians as Naoise and Deirdre play chess together, knowing that they have been betrayed and waiting for Conchubar's assassins. It was much revised in the final version (*VPl*, 375, ll. 474–85), where the stage directions are pared to '*During the chess, the Musicians sing this song*'. Although dated October–January 1906–7 on the cover, this number of *Poesia* contains an elegy on the death of Carducci (which took place on 18 Feb 1907) as well as another poem dated 'Marzo 1907', and did not appear until the spring of 1907.

[7] 'Yeats' is in another hand, and appears as 'W. B. Yeats' in the printed version.

doing it. However it was very good of you, and I know Synge will be grateful.[1] He is ill at this moment, and has been ever since the Play— bronchitis. It will take some time to measure the consequences of this dispute, but so far as I can judge it has done us good. It has been for some time inevitable that the intellectual element here in Dublin should fall out with the more brainless patriotic element, and come into existence as a conscious force by doing so. I think this has happened. After 'Kathleen ni Houlihan' on Saturday week, I got an extraordinary reception from the audience, which was certainly meant to imply approval of our action. The debate on the Monday after the row was an experience quite worth having. It began about half past eight, and went on till half past 11, a wild, disorderly mob, trying to make themselves as disagreeable as possible, and most of them very angry. I spoke my mind out, very clearly, and got a hearing, which was rather more than I expected. I had a section of the audience with me, but the majority, and the loudest part, was all made up of defeated patriots. A very small portion of them ever come to the theatre. They were followers of Arthur Griffith and obscure members of the Gaelic League, come down to serve their country, by attacking the culture that they fear. To these people nothing exists, but general ideas and in the service of these, fact and reason, must be for ever torn and twisted. It has been the first real defeat to the mob here, and may be the start of a party of intellect in the Arts, at any rate.[2] I am rather anxious about the presentation of the Play to America. Roberts showed me your wire, asking to have the whole play sent I told him to do nothing about publication in America till Synge was well enough to consult us.[3] Frohman is coming to see the Plays, during Easter week, and it is possible that this may lead to an American tour.[4] In any case we shall tour there before very long. The "Playboy" if taken up wrongly, by Irish Americans might upset things. If Synge agrees with me, I shall therefore send you, or get him to send you an introduction,

[1] Quinn had wired George Roberts, the publisher, for an advance copy of *The Playboy*, which Maunsel published in Dublin this month, with a view to getting it copyrighted in the USA. At WBY's suggestion, Quinn only had Act II of the play printed in an edition of twelve copies, and this was sufficient to secure the American copyright on 6 Mar of this year.

[2] Quinn did not approve of the debate and told WBY so in his letter of 23 Aug: 'I agreed about arresting the toughs who tried to break up the performance, but you made a mistake, I fear, in *debating* a question of art. Do you remember what Whistler said when a man tried to argue a question of art with him and who referred to Whistler's "*argument*"? Whistler said: "My dear man, I'm not *arguing* with you, I'm *telling* you. That is all." So I fear that the debate was a mistake.'

[3] See n. 1. Quinn's wire to Roberts is untraced, but WBY was right to be anxious; when the Abbey Company staged the play during their first American tour of 1911–12 there were disturbances in a number of theatres, and the company was arrested in Philadelphia in January 1912 (see *OIT*, 120–7).

[4] See pp. 577–8. Agnes Tobin saw Charles Frohman at the Savoy on 13 Feb to discuss the possibility of an Abbey tour to America and on 16 Feb wrote to WBY (*LWBY* 1. 179): 'Mr Frohman opens in Dublin Easter Monday. . . . I should expect him at the Abbey on Easter Tuesday and any other evening in Easter week if I were you. When you come to town I will take you to see him and you can talk it over.'

written probably by "Pat", (Author of Economics for Irishmen), explaining that the Play means that if Ireland goes on, loosing her strong men by emigration at the present rate, and submitting her will to every kind of political and religious dominion, the young men will grow so tame that the young girls will prefer any man of spirit, even though he has killed his father, to any one of them. "Pat" is a Catholic and I think, a good one, and would put this case, without seeming to attack religion.[5] He is a growing force here, although he is certainly suspected, by the reactionary section he is just the kind of man, who should be liked, by Archbishop Ireland, for instance.[6] The position needs very careful diplomacy, at least, that is the view I take of it. Miss Tobin, of San Francisco, advises not publishing the Play at all in America, except in so far as that is necessary for copyright purposes, but my own instincts are always for the bold course.[7] If we could keep the row from reaching America, we might withhold the publication, but the row must be on the way there by this time.[8] If we had once toured in America, and got our Plays known for what they are, it would not matter. I should think that reviewers of the book would be certain to draw attention to the row, and that this alone makes it necessary to state our point of view in the Preface or Appendix, or perhaps both. You will know, much better than I do what should be done. In the long run, American respect for intellect should work in our favour, amongst the Irish in America. On the other hand I should think that they will resent even more than here, any harsh picture of the country, which they see through clouds of tenderness. They may resent it less, if that picture has some obvious purpose, or assists

[5] The first American edition of *The Playboy* did not appear until 1911, when John W. Luce & Co. of Boston issued it at a price of $1.00 but without an introduction by 'Pat'. 'Pat' (P. D. Kenny; see p. 124) had written one of the few favourable reviews of the play for the *Irish Times*, and also took the chair at the discussion on 'The Freedom of the Theatre' on 4 Feb. Holloway had noticed him during the disturbances at the Theatre on 30 Jan (NLI) as 'a funny little man with an eyeglass', who 'was eagerly taking notes from the foot of the Stalls stairs'. As AG reported to Synge and Robert Gregory (see p. 617, n. 4), ' "Pat" made a good chairman, didnt lose his temper and made himself heard but no chairman could have done much.'

[6] John Ireland (1838–1918), Archbishop of St Paul, established thousands of Catholic colonies in Minnesota and played a major role in founding the Catholic University in Washington, DC. He and the Knights of Columbus had hosted a dinner for WBY before his lecture at St Paul Seminary, Minnesota, on 21 Jan 1904, and he became an example for WBY of the liberal and cultivated American Catholic prelate. See III. 475–6, 528, 530, and 534.

[7] In her letter of 12 Feb (*LWBY* I. 177) Agnes Tobin had, as an American, warned WBY against publishing or producing *The Playboy* in the USA.

[8] It was: the Irish-American papers had reprinted the *Freeman* attacks, although the text of the play was not yet available there. In a letter to WBY of 23 Aug of this year (Himber, 83), Quinn reported that he had distributed copies of the play among a number of Irish-Americans, including the old Fenian John Devoy (1842–1928), in the hope of persuading them of its value: 'I argued the matter out with John Devoy of *The Gaelic American* and gave him a copy of the play. I tried to *make* him see the humor of it. He laughed at some of the scenes. Then he took the book home, read it and in a few days said he was madder than ever, that it was an "outrage, impossible," and so on.' The controversy over *The Playboy* not only ended Quinn's friendship with Devoy (who attacked the play violently in the *Gaelic American*), it also accelerated his growing disenchantment with the Irish character. In his letter of 23 Aug he told WBY: 'I fought fight after fight over *The Playboy*. All the Irish or Catholic Irish-American papers republished *The Freemans*' attacks and it would be false to say that damage was not done by it. Damage was done.'

those who have some obvious purpose, which is nearer the truth, for the country's good. I, myself, think it a wonderful play, astonishing in idea and in dialogue. We shall play it in London very shortly I daresay.[9] The curious thing is that I do really believe Synge has had far more sympathy from the women he is supposed to have attacked than from the men. A copy of the Play went astray by some curious chance, which I cannot trace, and it alighted, above all places in the world, in a Convent school, in the neighbourhood of Dundrum. The girls lent it to one another, and read it in a sort of terrified delight. Fifteen of them made up a plan to come to the Theatre and see the play, and come round afterwards in a deputation to thank Synge, but the nuns found a letter, expounding this plan, and so prevented it coming off. My sisters have this story from one of the girls.[10] I know of another convent school girl, who was coming, but her father stopped her. The District Councils have been very busy of late, passing resolutions upon us, and the Gort Board of Guardians has passed one, to say that the Workhouse children at Gort are not to be allowed to have any more picnics at Coole Park, as a protest against Lady Gregory's share in the business. They have been picnicing there for twenty-three years. This is the only blow Lady Gregory minds.[11] She is planning out a very amusing little farce on the subject.[12]

---

[9] This was done in June of this year.

[10] There were two convents in Dundrum, but this was probably the Sacred Heart Convent in Cross Road, Mount Annville, a girls' boarding school. Female support was a propaganda boost since one of the major attacks on *The Playboy*, as on a number of other plays by Synge, was that it was a libel on the women of Ireland.

[11] The *Connaught Champion* of 9 Feb reported (3) that at its previous meeting the Gort District Council and Board of Guardians unanimously passed a resolution protesting 'most emphatically against the libellous comedy, "The Playboy of the Western World," that was belched forth during the past week in the Abbey Theatre, Dublin, under the fostering care of Lady Gregory and Mr. Yeates [*sic*]. We congratulate the good people of Dublin on howling down the gross buffoonery and immoral sugges[tions] that are scattered throughout this scandalous performance. It is an extraordinary thing that any Christian, much less an Irishman, should so grossly libel his country as to suggest that any Irish girl should be found wooing with no trace of modesty a man whose sole claim to affection is that he murdered his father. It is time that we should stop the children of this Union from partaking of the hospitality of Lady Gregory in the future, as a protest against her active participation and co-operation in the libelling of the Irish character.' M. O'Donohoe, who proposed the resolution, was reported as declaring that he had nothing to add 'but to say that it is a scandalous thing for any lady in a Catholic country to do'. AG recalled in her diary (Pethica, 315–16) that the ' "Playboy" row' led 'to the Guardians' resolutions against letting the Workhouse children come to Coole—& to the threatening notice on the gate against our own schoolchildren if they accepted the tea & cake I had promised—I have given up the school feast, it was another weapon to be used against me—' On 4 Mar 1907 AG wrote to Synge (Saddlemyer, 217) that Maurice Joy had 'been in Clare & Kerry & says all the District Councils are passing resolutions against the Playboy... & all the priests are buying & reading the Playboy'. As Blunt noted in his diary on 14 Mar (11. 172–3), AG feared that the controversy would have a long-term harmful effect on her position since 'in the provinces... the play is resented more than in Dublin.... She is going abroad for a while with her son.' AG was right: the ill-feeling against her persisted and on 17 Aug 1907 she wrote to Quinn (NYPL) that she was 'still suffering from the "Playboy" row. The embargo has not been taken off the Workhouse children, and a feeling is being nourished against me by a Sinn Fein or Gaelic League curate in Gort that I am not to be trusted, even that I am "souperising"! It is like all Irish life, a comedy to those who think, a tragedy to those who feel. It is likely that my time here is up, that I have done what I can at home.'

[12] AG did not proceed with this idea.

[*Remainder of letter in WBY's hand*]

At the second performance of Synges play a doctor said to Synge "I wish medical etiquette permitted me to go down & stand in front of that pit & point out among the protesters in the name of Irish virtue the patients I am treating for venereal disease". What drama.[13]

Yrs ever<br>W B Yeats

It is good of you to take so much trouble about M<sup>rs</sup> Emery she & Lady Gregory are my closest friends. She is a charming person, kind & gentle. I have seen a great deal of her of late especially, & it has been in part my urging that sent her to America.[14]

TLS NYPL, with envelope addressed to 31 Nassau St, New York, postmark 'DUBLIN FE 19 07'.

## To ?*Joseph J. Carton*,[1] [? *mid-February 1907*]

Nassau Hotel | South Fredrick St

My dear Carton: can you come here at 8.30 on Sunday to meet some people to plan out that "Club of the Arts" we talked of.[2] We will want the loan of your room I think for our meetings—this is only a committee meeting.

Yr ev<br>W B Yeats

ALS Texas.

[13] This incident probably took place on Tuesday, 28 Jan, or Wednesday, 30 Jan, when WBY was back in Dublin and when the disturbances were at their height, and he repeats the story in 'J. M. Synge and the Ireland of his Time' (*E & I*, 312): 'As I stood there watching, knowing well that I saw the dissolution of a school of patriotism that held sway over my youth, Synge came and stood beside me, and said, "A young doctor has just told me that he can hardly keep himself from jumping on to a seat, and pointing out in that howling mob those whom he is treating for venereal disease."' The identity of the doctor is unknown: it was probably Oliver St John Gogarty, but the description 'young' may imply a medical student, and W. J. McCormack suggests, among others, Daniel Sheehan, who was known to be present at the play (*The Fool of the Family* [2000], 323). On 4 Feb Joseph Holloway noted (NLI) that the 'Celia Street Medical Students formed part of the claque' that had supported the play.

[14] Quinn gave FF considerable help in America, both in arranging lecture venues for her and in promoting publicity on her behalf. The two began a sexual liaison while she was there, and he was eager that she should undertake a second American tour, but this never took place. Although they never saw each other after April 1907, they kept up a correspondence until her death.

[1] This was probably Joseph J. Carton, barrister and librarian, who lived at 11 Henrietta Street, and who had an office in the library at King's Inn. In October 1905 AG had suggested WBY consult Carton over legal questions arising from MG's divorce case (see p. 201, n. 5).

[2] The need for a club in Dublin to cater for writers and artists had been felt for a number of years, and the recent disturbances over *The Playboy of the Western World*, and the ongoing campaign to secure

## *To Lady Gregory, 1 March 1907*

Mention in following letter.
Telegram telling her that Shaw could not permit Abbey productions of *John Bull's Other Island* as it was to be toured in Ireland by the Court Theatre company, nor of *The Devil's Disciple*.[1]

## *To Lady Gregory, 2 March 1907*

18, Woburn Building, | W.C.
2nd March, 1907.

My dear Lady Gregory,

As I wired to you, Shaw is sending over his play with the Court Company. I asked him to let us do it, or let it be played by his Company in the Abbey, if at the last moment the theatre Royal refused to risk it.[1]

Hugh Lane's pictures, gave fresh impetus to it. In late 1906 a circular addressed 'To all Cultivated People' and signed by Ellen Duncan, Count Markiewicz, Llewllyn Meredith, AE, Dermod O'Brien, T. W. Rolleston, Lady Shaw, and W. G. Strickland, spoke of 'the foundation in Dublin of a Club combining the usual advantages of a Social Club, open to both Ladies and Gentlemen, with features of special advantage to workers in Art, in Music and in Literature. No institute of the kind exists at present in Dublin as a convenient place of resort in a central locality.' The Club, now called the United Arts Club, opened with an inaugural dinner in April 1907, and had rooms in Lincoln Chambers. WBY was formally elected a member on 28 May 1908, and on 19 Mar 1910 was one of the signatories to a memorandum registering the Club as a limited liability company. Carton, on the other hand, does not appear to have ever played a conspicuous part in the Club.

[1] Although Shaw had written *John Bull's Other Island* for the INTS, WBY had rejected it as being beyond the Company's resources (see p. 79). Now, presumably hoping to improve the post-*Playboy* audiences at the Abbey, he was trying to cash in on Shaw's recent popularity. On 9 Jan of this year the Players' Club had staged *The Man of Destiny* at the Abbey Theatre 'in the presence of a good audience', according to Holloway (NLI), but otherwise Shaw had been neglected in his native city: Forbes-Robertson had produced *The Devil's Disciple* in a short run at the Theatre Royal and an amateur company had privately staged *The Man of Destiny* early in 1906. Failing *John Bull's Other Island*, WBY had hoped for the Dublin rights to *The Devil's Disciple*, which he had been thinking of since the previous April (see p. 378), and which he considered particularly suited to an Irish audience. AG replied to this telegram in a letter of the same date (Berg): 'Your wire arrived and Payne has been here — sad — suggested Bashville [i.e. Shaw's *The Admirable Bashville*] — but I couldn't stand that!' *John Bull's Other Island* was not produced at the Abbey until September 1916, and *The Devil's Disciple* not until February 1920.

[1] J. E. Vedrenne and Harley Granville-Barker produced new plays and revivals at the Court Theatre from 1904 to June 1907, when they moved to the Savoy in the Strand. Their Court productions of his work made Shaw famous, particularly through a series of matinées of his plays, and they planned to launch their first provincial tour in October of this year with *John Bull's Other Island* and *You Never Can Tell*. The tour opened in Manchester on 14 Oct, took in two suburban London theatres, and subsequently visited Bradford, Birmingham, and Bristol, before concluding in Dublin. On 12 Nov the *Irish Times*, anticipating the company's arrival in Dublin for the week beginning 18 Nov, reported (6) that 'the tour has been a triumphal progress for Mr. Shaw's plays and the company'.

He had a double objection to our doing "The Devil's Disciple". The small size of our stage, and the fact that it is a good play for touring with ordinary touring companies, under the ordinary commercial conditions.[2] The Court people are taking "John Bull," and "You never can tell." He says they are having a hard struggle to live, and that provincial successes are necessary to them. This was to justify his keeping as much as possible for them.[3] I imagine that if we are to get a Shaw play, it will have to be one which is no use for ordinary touring. I spent the morning sorting out papers, etc. without completely dressing, and so was not able to send you a telegram till four o'clock. I consider that a really good production of "The Vikings" would be more useful to us than "The Land" at the moment, but I think it very doubtful our getting a good production in the time, and if Payne is doubtful, that settles it. I should like either "The Land" or "Scapin." Even if "The Vikings" were done at Easter, I should have wished for "The Land" on one of the April Saturdays. The announcement of Colum's rejoining us so far as to give us the play would be valuable.[4] I have had "Deirdre" typed, and will send three copies addressed to the theatre, where they will arrive first thing Monday morning. I saw Miss Tobin last night, and Miss Horniman in the afternoon, so I have various

*John Bull's Other Island* was first produced at the Theatre Royal on 20 Nov, and WBY's hope that the management might refuse to risk it was not without foundation, since Holloway noted (NLI) that the play was performed 'under police protection, the same as the notorious & unsavoury "*The Playboy of the Western World*" at the Abbey: but the lads in blue were not needed for the Shaw production. . . . Theatre going has come to a pretty pass when we must take our amusement under the eye of the force!' And he maliciously wondered 'how Yeats felt as he sat in the box with Lady Gregory & witnessed the play being thoroughly appreciated by a £300.0.0 house at least!'

[2] Hitherto, Forbes-Robertson had had the touring rights to *The Devil's Disciple*. The play was revived by Granville-Barker at the Savoy Theatre from 14 Oct, while the main company was on tour, and it transferred to the Queen's Theatre, London, for four further weeks from 23 Nov.

[3] In fact, the Court Theatre was heavily subsidized by Shaw, who found Vedrenne, who managed the business side of the project, particularly extravagant.

[4] Ibsen's *The Vikings of Helgoland* was never produced at the Abbey Theatre (see p. 532). In a letter of 1 Mar (Berg) AG wrote that she had 'suggested buying *The Land* from Colum for Easter week. . . . Payne agrees to this, is not keen about Vikings at end of season. . . . Please wire tomorrow if we should try for The Land.' However, in a letter dated 'Sunday' (i.e. 3 Mar) from Dublin (Berg), she told WBY that Colum had been at the Abbey the previous evening and refused to give them the play 'at present', as it was 'too soon' after his secession from the Abbey and *The Playboy* riots. In her reply to this letter on 4 Mar AG reported (Berg) that she had gone 'to the theatre & read yr letter to Payne without comment & he said he could not get a good performance of Vikings this season—I gave Fay first act of Scapin to start on.' Although Padraic Colum's father had been arrested for demonstrating against the performance of *The Playboy*, and although Colum himself disapproved of the play, he permitted the Abbey to revive *The Land*, but not until 17 Oct this year, when it was produced in a triple bill with *In the Shadow of the Glen* and *The Rising of the Moon*. The *Irish Times* of 17 Oct hailed the revival (8) as 'an event of considerable importance', and declared it 'unnecessary to say anything about the play. Its author is a poet and writer of rare charm, and both these qualities are to be found in "The Land," as also considerable skill in characterisation.' Holloway reported that the play, slightly altered in Act II, was revived at the Abbey with success, and that 'Loud & continued calls for author followed'. Although five

news. Miss Tobin thinks that we should have both Baile's Strand and Deirdre for Frohman, but I should think that quite impossible.[5] One advantage of "The Land" would be that it would be rather a good play for Frohman to see, if he wanted to see our longer work. The acting would impress him, while the acting of "The Vikings" might not.

French turned up this afternoon.[6] A friend of his had heard from Dolmetsch that Mrs. Emery is doing very well in America.[7] His news was very vague, however, and he is to have more definite information on Monday night. Althea Giles is, he tells me, comparatively prosperous. She is writing art notes for Frank Harris, and reviewing novels. She even does an occasional drawing, and has never been known to look upon the world with so little malice. She has quite a group of friends, but changes them completely every six months.[8] I had forgot to say that Bernard Shaw recommended me to write to a man called Norris Connell about a play of ninety-eight he has written.[9] Macnaughton has been writing the naievest

members of the original cast were in the revival, Holloway felt that 'the bloom had somewhat gone off the play & I was always thinking of the original cast in watching the new, & not always to the present company's advantage either. The only real live personage amongst them was the Sally of Miss Maire O'Neill; all the rest were shadows of their former selves.' Holloway recorded in his diary (NLI) the rumour that Colum was charging the Abbey £1 a week for the play.

[5] In her letter of 4 Mar AG warned WBY that Mrs Payne was 'still very unwell' and that it seemed very unlikely that she could attempt the part of Deirdre by 16 Mar.

[6] Cecil French (1878–1953), an Irish poet, artist, and stage designer, first met WBY in 1899. Work by him had appeared in *The Green Sheaf* (1903–4), although his first volume of poems and woodcuts, *Between Sun and Moon*, was not published until 1923. He dedicated the volume 'To W. B. Yeats | In token of what he has given to the world', and his pencil drawing 'The Rose of Dream', depicting a woman holding a rose between her lips, hung in WBY's sitting room. French was also a friend of FF, and patron of Althea Gyles, whom he had helped save from destitution in 1903 (see III. 198–9, 318–19).

[7] See pp. 622, 630. For Arnold Dolmetsch see p. 76.

[8] Althea Gyles (1867–1949; see II. 680–3), a symbolist painter whom WBY describes anonymously in *Aut* (237–8), was born in 1868 in Kilmurry, Co. Cork, into a family of 17th-century settlers 'so haughty', according to WBY, 'that their neighbours called them the Royal family'. She quarrelled with her father over her decision to study art and lived in poverty at first in Dublin, where she studied at the Metropolitan Art School with WBY, and later, in the early 1890s, in London. There she attended Pedders and, from 1893, the Slade School. She designed the covers of WBY's *The Secret Rose*, and his *Poems* (1899) and *The Wind Among the Reeds*. She suffered a breakdown after the end of a notorious relationship with Leonard Smithers, and did little more creative work, although WBY had recently reissued her spinal design from *The Secret Rose* on both *Poems, 1899–1905* and *Poems: Second Series*, and was to use that from *Poems* (1899) for *The Poetical Works of William B. Yeats* (1906, 1907). In February 1906 she had offered Grant Richards a new book she was designing, 'The Alphabet of the Wonderful Wood', and told him of a forthcoming show of her 'portraits' at the Carfax Gallery, although no record of such an exhibition survives. She was contributing to the *Candid Friend*, a periodical which Frank Harris had revived in 1905. In an unpublished memoir (Reading) Eleanor Farjeon describes Gyles in 1910 as living in a 'terribly poor, and very untidy room' off the King's Road, Chelsea. Here she 'started all sorts of projects which she never completed'.

[9] Norreys Connell's *The Piper*; see the following letter.

and most indignant letters to Miss Horniman. He wants a new committee to select plays on the grounds that we refused his, and offers to collect from Dublin amateurs, a company of educated people to play the plays so selected. Our present company, he complains is made up of peasants. The letters are really astonishing.[10]

Yours always
W B Yeats

TLS Berg, with envelope addressed to the Nassau Hotel, South Frederick St., postmark 'LONDON N.W. MAR 2 07'.

## To Norreys Connell,[1] 2 March 1907

18 Woburn Buildings, | Euston Road. W.C.
March 2$^{nd}$, / 07.

*Dictated.*
Dear M$^r$ Connell,
    It is a great many years since I met you, I think that it was in the days of the "Savoy".[2] The reason I write to you now is that Bernard Shaw tells me

---

[10] The typist had evidently misheard, or WBY misremembered, 'Macnaughton' for 'McNulty', who had already written to the *Irish Times* about the Abbey's neglect of his play (see p. 489, n. 11). On 26 Feb AEFH told WBY (NLI), 'I have had a second letter from M$^r$ McNulty (the man whose play was lost) & I don't want to answer it until I see you. All he says has some truth in it, although I do not feel attracted by his proposed remedies.' In a Reader's Report on an unnamed play by McNulty, probably this one, containing the characters 'Michael' and 'Nelly', and incorporating the idea of 'plethorism', WBY commented (NLI): 'An impossible play, & what a pity.' The rejection of his play by the Abbey continued to rankle, and Shaw wrote to him on 27 June 1908 about his literary frustrations: 'I note that you think that I could have held out a helping hand to you in literature, and that I didnt . . . . I did succeed to some extent in spreading a notion among the Irish Literary Theatre people that you were a sort of Irish Dickens; and I tried to persuade you to follow up my chatter with a play — you published the letter afterwards, confound you, without the least regard to my relations with Yeats! But you did nothing fresh; and I had to drop the subject' (*BSCL* II. 790). McNulty took his revenge with a letter to the *Saturday Review* in July 1911, attacking the Company and *The Playboy of the Western World* during the Abbey's visit to London.
    [1] F. Norreys Connell was the pseudonym of Conal Holmes O'Connell O'Riordan (1874–1948), novelist, actor, director, and playwright. The son of a barrister, he was educated at Belvedere College, Dublin, but abandoned plans for a military career after a riding accident which caused permanent spinal damage. Despite this physical disability, he went on the stage and appeared in the Independent Theatre's production of *Ghosts*. He began to write plays, and published a collection of short stories, *In the Green Park*, in 1894, followed by his first novel, *The House of the Strange Woman*, which appeared in 1895. Three of his plays were to be produced at the Abbey, and for a short period in 1908 he became a Director of the Theatre while acting as manager and producer.
    [2] Connell was not, unlike WBY, a contributor to the short-lived *Savoy*, which failed after its eighth issue in December 1896, although his name appeared in the prospectus, and he was associated with its publisher, Leonard Smithers, who issued Connell's second novel, *The Fool and his Heart*, in July 1896. In that year Connell put WBY in touch with the French man of letters Henry Davray (see II. 12).

that you have a little play about the rebellion of /98 which might suit the Abbey Theatre, Dublin. He said he thought that our people would be able to play it & that probably another company could not.[3]

We have not as yet been able to pay our authors, but we have been doing so much better lately that payment of authors must follow before very long. I would like to see your play very much if under the circumstances you would care to send it.

I have to dictate my letters in order to spare my eye-sight.

If you are sending the play you might send it c|o Miss Horniman
 H1 Montagu Mansions,
  Portman Square. W.

Yrs sinly
W B Yeats

Dict. AEFH, signed WBY; Private.

## *To Lady Gregory, 6 March 1907*

18, Woburn Buildings, | Euston Road,
March 6, 1907.

My dear Lady Gregory,

I don't think Payne has yet written to Miss Horniman suggesting May for a London tour. If he would do so to-morrow I could discuss it with her on Friday and it is better as a suggestion from him and a written one. I have prepared her to accept it by making a virtue of leaving all such questions to him. If I go round with it she may think me the original fomenter of the idea.[1] I have just seen Frohman who says that if he likes our show, he will propose a tour in America for November say. This is of course a bad time for us as it is our best Dublin season, but we can leave

[3] The play was *The Piper*, produced at the Abbey on 13 Feb 1908. The action takes place in an Irish camp after a battle during the 1798 Rebellion. Under the sardonic eye of a captured English officer, the rebels, with the exception of Black Mike and the Piper, insist that they have won a glorious victory, and take a vote to prove this. They turn against Black Mike but, while they stand bickering, the British mount a counter-attack in which Black Mike and two others are killed. The rest flee, leaving the Piper, who seizes the green flag, and waving it on high sings 'The Shan Van Vocht' before being shot dead.

[1] On 4 Mar AG had written 'Payne is keen for May in London & I told him to write to Miss H as she cd discuss it with you'. Payne recalled in *Life in a Wooden O* (75) that when he 'determined to arrange a second English tour for the company' he could expect no help from Henderson, and so 'arranged it myself through correspondence with Miss Horniman. She agreed to underwrite the project. Possibly she had already had this idea herself. Beginning at Glasgow in Scotland, we worked south through some of the principal English cities and finished in London.'

such matters till he tells us whether he approves or not. I suppose November is the best of the American season.[2] I asked him if he objected to Doublers[3] and he said I don't object to anything. He wants us to set on what we think right and as we choose, and he will judge it on its merits. He professes in the same way no opinion as to whether the plays should be long or short. I have been to A. P. Watt and started him negotiating the transference of my books to Bullen.[4] I have left the completed Deirdre to be copied again for Macmillan and Mrs. Emery, who wants to give a reading from it and for Bullen.[5] I have re-written that lyric sung at the chess-playing and made a fine thing of it,[6] and am feeling that I can do plenty more lyrics now the theatre is off my mind.[7] I think Monday is too soon to come to London, let it be Tuesday or Wednesday.[8] I suppose I shall stay on in Dublin at my rehearsals of Deirdre.[9]

Yr sny<br>W B Yeats

TLS Berg, with envelope addressed to the Nassau Hotel, postmark 'LONDON.W.C. MAR 6 07'.

[2] See pp. 577-8, 623, 627. The Company had high expectations of Frohman; on 27 Mar, shortly before his visit, McDonnell ('Arthur Sinclair') told Holloway (NLI) they 'probably would go to America in September if Frohman came to an arrangement with the Co.'

[3] i.e. actors playing more than one part in a play, to save expenses. AEFH was firmly opposed to the practice and wrote to WBY on 4 May of this year, just before the beginning of the Abbey's British tour (NLI): 'I am most anxious that you should get a fair show & that is why I will not consent to slovenly "doubling" in King's Threshold. It is quite a different matter when a play is in several acts, then it looks a make-shift for named characters; but in a company where not one of the actors can be *trusted* to "impersonate", I won't hear of it on tour.' She made the same point to Synge on 23 May (TCD).

[4] This was a temporary and preliminary measure to enable Bullen to begin publication of *The Collected Works*.

[5] i.e. the Macmillan Company, New York, who published *Deirdre* in vol. II of *The Poetical Works of William B. Yeats* on 8 July 1907 (see pp. 516, 578). FF wrote to Quinn on 19 Mar, sending him *Deirdre*, and hoping to arrange a public reading at the end of April before she sailed for England on 9 May. Her programme for the tour included 'Lyrics by W. B. Yeats' but no specific poems were listed. It is unlikely that she gave a public reading of *Deirdre*, and Quinn makes no mention of any performance when writing to WBY about the play on 28 Aug (see Himber, 86).

[6] The lyric, sung by the Musicians, beginning 'Love is an immoderate thing | And can never be content' (*VPl*, 375); WBY had recently sent a version of it to Marinetti (see pp. 623-6).

[7] In a letter of 7 Mar (Berg) AG commented that she was 'delighted to hear of your lyrical feeling coming back, we must foster it'.

[8] In a letter of 5 Mar (Berg) AG wrote: 'I am working hard at Scapin, for if I don't get away from here next Monday I never shall'.

[9] The production of *Deirdre* had been postponed because of Mrs Payne's illness, and *On Baile's Strand* was substituted instead. On 4 Mar (see n. 1) AG remarked that if *On Baile's Strand* went well '& we cd get up Deirdre for the next Saturday, we shd have them for Frohman'.

## To Norreys Connell, [6 March 1907]

18 Woburn Buildings, | Euston Road.
*Dictated.*     Wednesday.
1592 | Paddington

Dear Connell,

I have very few days in London & I am busy most of the time. Are you free this evening? And if so can you come to Miss Horniman's about 8–30. Her address is H1 Montagu Mansions Portman Square; it is quite near to Baker Street Station. Go down Baker Street to Dorset Street & then you will see the flats. I am looking forward to hearing the play this evening, as Shaw gave a very good account of it.[1]

Yr sny
W B Yeats

Dict. AEFH, signed WBY; Private.

## To Maud Gonne, [March 1907]

Mention in letter from MG, 'Friday' [March 1907].
Telling her that the theatre is likely to absorb less of his time in the near future,[1] offering to send her 'wonderful powder' to enhance visionary experience,[2] saying that he is likely to be in Paris during the spring,[3] and asking how her appeal against the verdict in her divorce case is progressing.[4]

*G–YL,* 238–9.

[1] Shaw was trying to help fellow Dubliner Connell place *The Piper* with WBY at the Abbey and another play, *Woman to Woman*, with Harley Granville-Barker at the Savoy in London. He was an impatient representative, writing to Granville-Barker on 11 Jan 1908 about the play, 'which I believe you have got. I am now told that the Stage Society want a first piece and that they have asked him for it. As we seem to want first pieces at The Savoy, you had better know what is up. Why dont you send the man back his play if you are not going to do it? If it is the thing he read out to me—a scene in a hotel in Paris—it ought to be treated with ... proper respect' (*Bernard Shaw's Letters to Granville Barker,* ed. C. B. Purdom [New York, 1957], 114).

[1] WBY had presumably told MG that he hoped Payne would take on much of the work at the Abbey, and she replied that she was 'very glad' to know 'that the theatre is likely to absorb less of your time in the near future'. She added that while the experience had taught him 'much about play writing which I should think only practical experience can teach', it had been 'taking too much of your time & energy'.

[2] MG and WBY had regularly experimented with hallucinatory drugs to aid meditation, and she urged him to 'send me some of that wonderful powder, it seems most fascinating. I will write you full description of results if I get any.'

[3] WBY intended to stop off in Paris on his way back from north Italy in late April, but pressing Abbey affairs made this impossible.

[4] On 8 Aug 1906 MG had been granted a judical separation from MacBride, not a full divorce, and he was given weekly access to his son. MG was 'very disappointed' (*G–YL,* 232), and said she would 'probably appeal against this verdict & change my lawyer'. She now replied that her 'law business' was 'going on slowly as usual' and that MacBride's decision to defend the suit 'means things will take longer than I expected, but I am hopeful of success'.

## To Lady Gregory, 9 March 1907

18, Woburn Buildings, | Euston Road,
March 9, 1907.

My dear Lady Gregory,

I enclose a letter which came to me some days ago and was forgotten. I cannot even write to apologise as I can make out neither name or address. Will you tell them that I am sorry about the delay and that it was my fault, but don't cause too much local joy by telling them I couldn't make out the Irish.[1] On getting your letter I decided after some vacillation not to go to Dublin last night. I was very sorry not to see the Rising of the Moon but I shall see that when it is revived as I see it is to be.[2] Will you come and see me when your train gets in on Tuesday? I have a lot to talk over. I have had a very powerful play given me by a hunchback called Morris Connell. It is the one, Shaw spoke of. The worst of it is that it seems to me pretty dangerous. It is a curious, grotesque study of a disorderly troop of '98 rebels who have taken an English prisoner, who tries to make them put out a sentry, because he is afraid they will be all shot including himself by the English troop. They put to the vote the question, whether they won in the last fight, or whether a certain Black Thomas is right who keeps saying: 'We were beat.' They decided it was a glorious victory, they were then persuaded to put out a sentry and because they are out with him, say that Black Thomas is to be sentry. Then they wrangle over who is to give them a musket, and while they are wrangling the enemy come upon them. Some run away and some die heroically, including one of the noisiest of them. It is a very queer thing, written with considerable sense for the Irish mind and with no sense of dialect, but this he would let us put right. I am very anxious for your opinion for this is certainly a new talent and a remarkable one. If we are to play it I think we might put it on upon that Saturday in April we had marked down for The Land or The Doctor and put something patriotic with it.[3] Connell showed it to Boyle, but Boyle sent

---

[1] The letter has not been traced but may have been from the National Players' Company which was currently discussing the possibility of forming a touring company to present plays in Irish in country districts, and perhaps hoped to enlist WBY's support.

[2] On 7 Mar AG had written (Berg) that Mrs Payne was still ill, and that 'Payne wont in any case begin rehearsing Deirdre before Monday & I doubt it then—so I dont think it will be worth your while coming over'. AG's *The Rising of the Moon* was produced on 9 Mar, and revived on 23 Mar and 1 Apr.

[3] See p. 632. In fact *The Piper* was not produced until February 1908, and then on a bill with the not conspicuously patriotic *The Man Who Missed the Tide*.

it back, saying that it was abominable and made him very angry.[4] It is in one act.

I have also got the MS. of Lionel Johnson's Essays.[5] I shall go over to Dublin next Thursday in time for the dress rehearsal of Baile's Strand. One thing that has tempted me to remain on here is that I shall get a better idea of the difference in the stage management by seeing the play towards the end.[6] I think I should have gone over but for your determination to return on Monday, for I want to talk out these questions of these essays and Connell's play, and it may be desirable for us both to see Connell. I have sent Dierdre off to America at last and rather against Miss Tobin's advice have given Mrs. Emery leave to give readings from it. Miss Tobin thought that this might forestall it, if it went over with Frohman, but one has to keep one's people in good heart, and as I shall want her to do Choruses and the like I did not like to refuse.[7] I think I told you that I saw Frohman. It is really most important to have Dierdre done for him, for I am certain that people will have to get to my work through a simple and passionate play like that before they care for a complicated thing like Baile's Strand. If Mrs. Payne is likely to be too unwell at the week's end and, if Miss Horniman will consent, it might be well to get someone else.[8] The difficulty is that Frohman wants our people to be all of the Company, but if he really cared for the play and the player, this might be

---

[4] On 5 Apr 1907 William Boyle warned D. J. O'Donoghue (NLI): 'Wait till the Norreys Connel thing is produced. It's more anti-Irish than the *Playboy* but of course not so carnal. The Wexford peasants are represented as absolute baboons & such choice Irish as "praste", "indade" &c belard it all through.' On 17 Jan 1908 he returned to the attack, informing O'Donoghue (NLI) that 'Norreys Connell's *Piper* is a horrid thing. He sent it to me two years ago and I told him then what I thought of it which vexed him. The dialect is pure English brogue of the worst sort, and the Wexford peasant of '98 represented by baboons and the English soldiers as heroes.'

[5] Having selected *Twenty-One Poems* by Lionel Johnson for the Dun Emer Press in February 1905 (see pp. 47, n. 6, 49, 132–3), WBY may now have been thinking of an edition of his essays. In fact, he settled for a single essay, 'Poetry and Patriotism', which was published by the Cuala Press in December 1908 with his own 'Poetry and Tradition' as *Poetry and Ireland*. Elkin Mathews issued a fuller edition of Johnson's essays, edited by Thomas Whittemore and Louise Imogen Guiney, and including 'Poetry and Patriotism', in December 1911 under the title *Post Liminium*.

[6] The stage management of *On Baile's Strand* was different because Payne had taken it over from Frank Fay. On 5 Mar AG told WBY that Frank Fay had seen her earlier that day 'to give notice, on the head of Payne stage-managing Baile's Strand. He had complained to his brother who had refused to listen to him. I shut him up also, & reminded him I had specially told him Baile's Strand was to be in Payne's hands; And I think he will be all right.'

[7] See p. 636. WBY had written the part of First Musician in *Deirdre* with FF in mind (see p. 519). As early as 16 Feb Agnes Tobin had asked him 'whether you gave Miss Farr rights of recitation on Deirdre' (*LWBY* I. 179).

[8] Mary Charlotte Louise Payne, née Gadney (*c.* 1882–1968), who was born in Limerick and acted under the name of 'Mona Limerick', had married Ben Iden Payne in 1906. They had three children (one of whom became the wife of the actor-manager Sir Donald Wolfit), but the marriage foundered after Payne moved to America in 1914. She had been ill for several days and AG kept WBY informed about her condition, complaining on 4 Mar that she 'won't have doctor or take a tonic', and warning in her letter of 7 Mar (see n. 2) that she was still so unwell that 'Bailes Strand is the only verse play we can be sure of for Frohman'. In a letter dated 'Sat night', which must have crossed with this one, AG was able

got over. Perhaps it would be possible for Mrs. Payne to know by the time you get this if she will be well enough to start rehersal. The week-end would be time enough for Frohman, but you may very well think that it is dangerous to put on the play for him, without first seeing it.

Yr always<br>W B Yeats

TLS Berg, with envelope addressed to the Nassau Hotel, postmark 'LONDON.W.C. MR 9 07'.

## *To Norreys Connell, 13 March 1907*

18 Woburn Buildings, | Euston Road.<br>March 13<sup>th</sup>, / 07.

*Dictated.*

Dear Connell,

I have read your play to Lady Gregory who admires it as much as I do, she thinks that we should play it without turning the Englishman into an Hannoverian, I had rather come to the same conclusion myself.[1] I have sent it to Ireland & have suggested an immediate performance, but I don't yet know how soon it can be done. I am going over to-morrow night & will let you know at once. I am keeping the letters you so kindly sent me, to shew to Fay & Lady Gregory.[2] The little play is really a master-piece, most original as well as most effective from the dramatic point of view. I withdraw practically all my criticisms now that I have been able to read it through deliberately & think the thing out as a piece of action on a stage. Your piper, for instance, is not at all conventional as I was inclined to think but a most admirable & most beautiful stage invention. I had not allowed for the effect of his song.[3]

Yrs sny<br>W B Yeats

Dict. AEFH, signed WBY; Private.

to report that 'Mrs Payne is better, but hasn't turned up yet'. Her ill-health persisted for some months, and although she did finally manage to appear in the title role of WBY's revised *Deirdre*, the production had to be postponed (see pp. 633, n. 5, 636, n. 9) and some performances in the run were cancelled because of the strain on her. As late as 4 May AEFH told WBY (NLI) that Payne had 'been much worried about his wife's illness, but she is beginning to get a little better now'.

[1] The captured English officer, Captain Talbot, is scornful of the garrulous and incompetent Irish rebels, but comes to respect Black Mike's courage and integrity, and at the play's end insists that the victorious English troops leave the green flag flying over the camp. To have changed this sympathetic character from Englishman to Hanoverian mercenary would have made the play more politically acceptable to Abbey audiences.

[2] Untraced, but presumably giving Connell's ideas on the staging and casting of the play.

[3] The Piper, whose pipes have been damaged in the battle, says very little during the play, but sings 'The Shan Van Vocht' ('The Poor Old Woman', a traditional Irish patriotic song) in an undertone. At

## To A. E. F. Horniman, [c. 13 March 1907]

Mention in letter from AEFH, 14 March 1907.
Telling her he is leaving for Dublin on the night boat train, discussing
Payne's desire to take the part of Oedipus instead of Frank Fay,[1] evidently
asking whether the Great Queen Street Theatre is free at present.[2]

NLI.

## From A. E. F. Horniman to A. H. Bullen, 14 March 1907

H1 Montague Mansions, | Portman Square, | London.
March 14<sup>th</sup> / 07.

Dear Mr Bullen,
I have considered very carefully that matter of a collected edition of Mr
Yeats' works.[1] I believe that I am right in taking your proposal like this.
1<sup>st</sup> That it will be done as well as possible, with new portraits, got up so as
not to be confused with volumes already published, the set of eight volumes
to be sold to subscribers at £4–4, and that only a limited edition will be
printed.[2]
2<sup>nd</sup> That I should give security for the sum of £1,500, that being the sum
necessary for the purpose. That you are reasonably sure of disposing at
once of 750 copies & that averaging those sold to subscribers at the full
price, those sold for £2 for Ireland & the review copies, that roughly
speaking the sum of £1,500 would be covered soon after publication.[3]

---

Talbot's request he sings the song aloud, only to be ordered to silence by the rebels, but in the final
English attack takes it up again and, despite Talbot's attempts to save him, is shot.

[1] WBY had apparently told AEFH that Payne was eager to play Oedipus (see pp. 508–9, 599). On
1 Mar AG, with Payne's backing, had suggested ending the season in April with the play and on 3 Mar
reported that Payne was working on it. In her reply of 14 Mar (NLI) AEFH pointed out that she would
'get the credit if Payne plays Oedipus of putting in an Englishman in Frank Fay's place, so as to spite
Willie Fay. This would damage all concerned. It would cause friction and if Payne has to go, a new man
would be needed for America if the Company goes there. Could you not let Payne see that taking the
part risks his post altogether? I cannot support him against the Directors nor can I make any remarks to
him. It looks to me as if he had been encouraged in the idea so as to get a *good* excuse to get rid of him.'
And she added that the 'good or bad acting of the part has nothing to do with the case.'

[2] In her reply of 14 Mar AEFH told him that the Great Queen Street Theatre was 'free at present
from end of April onwards'.

[1] Proposals for an elaborate collected edition of WBY's works had been vetoed by Bullen's partners
on the grounds that the American rights were uncertain and he and WBY had begun to make alternative
plans (see pp. 603, 608). Now AEFH had come to the rescue of the project, and it went forward in its
original form.

[2] Bullen printed 1,060 sets of the eight-volume *Collected Works*, and they were sold at a price of £4 4s. a
set.

[3] Bullen arranged with Chapman & Hall to take over 250 sets at once, as they employed a travelling
salesman and could reach booksellers outside Bullen's range. He also hoped to dispose of 50 sets to
Maunsel & Co. for sale in Ireland at a reduced price, but it is probable that less than 20 were taken in this

3<sup>rd</sup>   That you should take ⅔ the profits and that I should take ⅓ & Mr Yeats should have a reasonable royalty on sales.

----------------------------------------------------------------------

The whole should be selected on the basis of what will be of permanent interest, not on what would be suitable for a magazine. For instance matters connected with the Abbey Theatre itself or scenic experiments there would only interest very few people a few years hence.[4]

I do not want to interfere in any way between you and Mr Yeats, beyond expressing my opinion that new portraits are necessary, and it should be a matter of indifference whether they are done by an Italian or an Indian or an Irishman.[5]

In regard to that line in "In the Seven Woods" to which you so strongly object, I can only say that I dislike it as much as you do, but that my objection to it would carry no weight.[6]

I also dislike a certain unnecessary coarseness in "Shadowy Waters" but again, having already expressed my opinion, I can & will do no more.[7]

I will do all in my power to protect Mr Yeats' *time* from the theatre; in future I hope that he will get more opportunity for direct literary work. I am sending him a copy of this as well as keeping one myself.

With kind regards,
Yours sincerely
A E F Horniman

ALS MBY.

way. Bullen did not succeed in selling the whole edition and a number of sets were sold at half-price in a different binding. According to Bullen's stock books (Stratford), 364 sets still remained unsold by 17 Nov 1915, comprising 345 quires and 12 bound copies at Stratford-upon-Avon, and 6 bound copies and one unbound copy at W. W. Gittings of 18 Bury Street, London. AEFH was not taken in by Bullen's optimistic predictions and she wrote to WBY on 15 Mar (NLI): 'Of course I did not swallow the idea that you might make £500 by it, but if you make £150 that would be worth having. If I make any profit I shall spend it in a practical way. Your works will be presented to libraries, colleges & big schools in your own country. I shall give to female schools & colleges first, then to public libraries & and lastly to those places where Lords of Creation alone are admitted.'

   [4] In fact, WBY's contributions to *Samhain* and the *Arrow*, and two essays from *United Irishman* of 17 and 23 Oct 1903, appeared in vol. IV of *CW*, under the heading 'The Irish Dramatic Movement', while vol. VIII included WBY's introductions to a number of books, as well as some of his literary journalism.

   [5] *CW* included portraits by John Sargent (vol. I), Charles Shannon (vol. III), Antonio Mancini (vol. V), and a drawing by JBY (vol. VII). In a letter to WBY of 15 Mar (NLI) AEFH said: 'I don't think that you can object to my insisting on new portraits nor to my wish that the fresh ones should be chosen on their own merits not on the nationality of the artist.'

   [6] See ll. 5–7 of 'In the Seven Woods': 'I have forgot awhile | Tara uprooted, and new commonness | Upon the throne' (*VP*, 198). The attack on the recently crowned Edward VII would have offended AEFH's and Bullen's patriotic and royalist sensibilities. On 3 July of this year AEFH told WBY (NLI) that she and Bullen 'both feel alike as to the "taste" of the line about "commonness upon the throne", but there the matter ends as far as I am concerned'.

   [7] AEFH was thinking of the more earthy touches WBY had introduced in his rewriting of the play in the summer of 1905 (see p. 179), as well as the use of prose. In her letter of 3 July 1907, AEFH told WBY that Bullen 'agrees with me in my opinion that the sailor's dialogue in the Shadowy Waters should be in verse as at first'.

## To A. E. F. Horniman, [c. 15 March 1907]

Mention in letter from AEFH, 16 March 1907.
Discussing her letter to Bullen, setting out the terms under which she will underwrite WBY's *Collected Works*,[1] asking if she can get him a ticket for *The Persians*,[2] telling her that he is going to Italy with AG and Robert Gregory,[3] suggesting London theatres which might be better than the Great Queen Street Theatre for the forthcoming Abbey tour,[4] and evidently informing her that W. G. Fay thinks that F. J. Fay will not object to Payne taking the part of Oedipus.[5]

NLI.

## To Lady Gregory, [18 March 1907]

Nassau Hotel.

My dear Lady Gregory
    There is only a moment before the post goes & I have but just remembered that house wings for 'Spreading the News' & "Hyacynth" are urgently wanted—there is very little time to make them before Frohman

---

[1] WBY had evidently raised questions about AEFH's agreement with Bullen, and she pointed out in her answer to this letter that the 'copy of my letter to Bullen will shew you that I only consider the matter under the expection [*for* expectation] of a reasonable assurance of a sale of 750 copies at an average of £2 each at once on publication. This would cover the capital at stake. This evening you will get my letter of last night & I hope that your mind will be relieved.'

[2] WBY was eager to see the production of B. J. Ryan's prose translation of Aeschylus' *The Persians*, which was to be put on with Harley Granville-Barker's *A Miracle* at Terry's Theatre on 23 Mar 1907 as the final experiment of the Literary Theatre Society before it merged with the Stage Society. In her reply AEFH said: 'I ought to have a ticket for The Persians if that is the same Society of which I had to become a member so as to see "Salome". I *won't* be cheated by these ultra-refined people. If I get a ticket you can have it if you like.'

[3] AEFH approved of this trip and replied that the 'sooner you are off to Italy the better'.

[4] In her reply AEFH pointed out that London theatrical venues were not easy to find: 'The Royalty has been taken by "The Follies" who do little musical comediettas, so unless we can get Terry's we should secure Great Queen Street, as it seems as if that will be the only possible place empty in May except the old Princesses which must be a ruin & the Scala where one cannot hear without an awful effort from either pit, stalls or gallery.'

[5] This cut no ice with AEFH, who was convinced that allocating the part to Payne would lay her open to sinister Dublin accusations (see p. 641, n.1). In her reply she told WBY that she was 'still very anxious about "Oedipus" as I fear an intrigue. Payne cannot yet be expected to understand what would seem wild nonsense to him—that there are some who had rather destroy what is good than aid it or let it alone—just because the destruction would annoy ME, & although it would damage many Irish people.' And she added that W. G. Fay was 'quite capable of telling you that his brother does not mind in the least, if that would serve his own ends'.

comes.[1] Please remind Robert—I spoke of them when I saw him first in London. The "Hyacynth" street scene is all to be remade but we can work out something on the model of the old.

Yr ev<br>W B Yeats

ALS Berg, with envelope marked 'Immediate', addressed to the Euston Hotel, Euston, London, postmark 'DUBLIN MR 18 07'.

## *To A. E. F. Horniman,* [c. *19 March 1907*]

Mention in letter from AEFH, 20 March 1907.
Explaining that *The King's Threshold* had always had Frank Fay in the leading part and that therefore her objections to its being described as a 'Peasant Play' are beside the point,[1] citing *Kincora* and *The White Cockade* as being in a similar category,[2] accusing her of 'living by book',[3] telling her

---

[1] Both plays had been produced regularly throughout the year, and *Spreading the News* was to be played on 23 Mar, but WBY wanted the new wings for the week beginning 1 Apr, to impress Frohman when he visited the Abbey. *Hyacinth Halvey* was to be presented on Tuesday and Thursday, and *Spreading the News* on Monday, Tuesday, and Thursday. Agnes Tobin had told WBY on 16 Feb (see p. 623, n. 2) that Frohman 'seemed delighted when I said you had all the real Irish cottage things & the real clothes & all'.

[1] The latest question to stir AEFH's wrath was the classification of WBY's play *The King's Threshold*. Since it was in verse, it should strictly have been transferred to Payne's direction (see pp. 546, 551–2), but, as it was based on a folk story, had always been directed by W. G. Fay, and provided Frank Fay with one of his best parts, the Directors had decided to leave it with Fay, a decision which AG, as she reported to WBY, conveyed to AEFH on 17 Mar (Berg): 'I have seen Miss Horniman tonight, quite serene till it came out that Senchan had been left to Fay—then a flare-up—. However I was stiff, said I took the responsibility, I had thought it necessary at the time to ensure a peaceful entry for Payne, & I must when given business to negotiate be left free judgement. She quietened then, but if she attacks you, you had better look up that letter in which she said the author had power to decide.' AEFH did attack, and at once, writing to WBY (NLI) that very evening that she 'was horrified to hear that "King's Threshold" is to be treated as an Irish Peasant play'. He replied in the present letter, evidently pointing out that Frank Fay could not be put out of the part and, as AG had suggested, drawing her attention to her own insistence that the Abbey dramatists should have the final say in the production of their own works. These arguments were of no avail, and on 20 Mar AEFH maintained that she never intended that Frank Fay should lose the part of Seanchan, 'but I considered & still consider that it was a breach of our agreement that the stage-management of Kings Threshold should have been proposed to be called that of a Peasant Play. All that in my letter about "production" under the care of an artist is quite away from the point. The play has been produced & in the future can only be *revived*. If you choose to select Willie Fay to *produce* your next new play you are free to do so—but if you let him *revive* any of your verse plays which have already been produced, you will break the agreement.'

[2] AEFH was not impressed with these examples, replying that 'Kincora & White Cockade don't matter to me as they would not I believe be possible on tour'.

[3] In her reply AEFH defended her scrupulousness: 'You despise what you call my "living by book" but on the other hand if I had not that quality (which is a fault in your eyes) I should not have had the power to carry things on as I have. If the King's Threshold had been in actual rehearsal when Payne

that Mrs Payne promises well as an actress,[4] and apparently sending her press notices of *Interior*.[5]

NLI.


## To John O'Byrne,[1] [22 March 1907]

Dear Mr. O'Byrne—I am going to London to see a performance of 'The Persians.'[2] No lesser thing than this play, which may never be done in English again, would take me away from a discussion in which I am so deeply interested. I would ask those who speak of the Abbey Theatre to-morrow—if any do speak of it—to remember that we have produced many plays, written in all sorts of moods, and have never expected that all will be liked by all. We leave, and will always leave, our writers as free as possible,

---

arrived then I should have agreed that it was only reasonable to leave it until the following revival in Fay's hands; but it would have been only fair to tell me what was being done. There *is* a "practical issue"—it is that I must and will have agreements kept with me to the letter & in the spirit. If I go against any agreement in the letter or the spirit, I will be grateful for being checked at once in my meanness.'

[4] Mona Limerick had temporarily recovered from her illness (see p. 639) and had begun rehearsing *Deirdre*. AEFH was 'glad that M*rs* Payne promises well, a certain gentle girlishness with some acting power as well is very charming. That will replace Moira Walker most effectually.'

[5] Maeterlinck's one-act play *Interior* had been produced at the Abbey on 16 Mar. The play, the first to be directed by Payne at the Abbey, and the first foreign play translated into standard English rather than Irish dialect, centres on the pathos of an old man who has to break the news of their eldest daughter's accidental drowning on an obliviously happy family. It received excellent reviews in Dublin on 18 Mar: the *Freeman's Journal* observed (4) that it 'gripped the attention of the audience from start to finish', the *Evening Telegraph*, describing the production (2) as a 'complete and triumphant' success, urged that it 'should not be missed by anyone interested in modern drama and beautiful acting', and the *Irish Times* (10), while warning that it was 'not a play that will command itself very highly to those who look to the theatre for an unvarying picture of the brighter and happier side of life', commented that 'for those who pause to consider the realities, the "Interior" presents a picture of great fascination and extraordinary pathos. The intense human sympathy which vibrates in every phrase of the story holds the audience, as it were, spell bound.' Since AEFH valued modern European plays over the Abbey's peasant drama, she was delighted with this success, and suggested that the play should be taken on tour: 'It would do for Oxford & Cambridge & London I'm sure.'

[1] John O'Byrne (1884–1954) was secretary of the Literary and Historical Society at University College, Dublin, and had seceded with Cruise O'Brien the previous autumn, taking the records and minute book of the Society with him (see p. 584). He graduated from UCD in 1911 and was a member of the drafting committee of the Constitution of the Irish Free State in 1922. He served as Attorney-General of the Free State from 1924 to 1926, and was appointed a High Court judge from 1926 and of the Supreme Court from 1940.

[2] See p. 643. The play was designed by Charles Ricketts, and the *Stage* of 28 Mar noted (15) that his methods, which seemed 'founded on Mr. Gordon Craig's', favoured 'novel lighting and the use of rich yet sombre hangings'. Otherwise, it judged the play 'not at all successful' and thought the 'prose translation had some sadly commonplace lines'.

troubling them with no mere prudent counsels, that they may have that most beautiful of all beautiful things—a confident abundance.[3]

Yours truly

W B Yeats

Printed letter to the *Freeman's Journal*, 25 March 1907, p. 5.

## *To Lady Gregory, [22 March 1907]*

My dear Lady Gregory

M[rs] Payne certainly looks very ill & Payne says there is now no chance of Dierdre until Easter.[1] I shall therefore go back to London for a couple of days to see the "Persians." I will have to stay at Euston Hotel as Bullen has my rooms.[2]

The tour will if all goes as Fay expects last all May & not reach London till well on in June[3] so perhaps we might have all May for Italy.[4]

Yrs ever

W B Yeats

ALS Berg, with envelope addressed to Coole, postmark 'DUBLIN MR [?]22 07'.

[3] O'Byrne had invited WBY to Francis Sheehy-Skeffington's paper 'Stray Thoughts about the Modern Dramatic Movement in Ireland' presented to the Literary and Historical Society in the Oak Room of the Mansion House on 23 Mar. As the *Freeman's Journal* reported on 25 Mar (5), Sheehy-Skeffington surveyed the development of the INTS over the past eight years and concluded by noting a contradictory element in WBY's attitude to the drama: 'At times he seems inclined to throw in his lot with the folk, and to produce work likely to awake responsive echoes in the popular mind; and again he repudiates the profanum vulgus and appeals to the cultured few to help him to tame the wild horse of the people. If the latter is his ideal, he should continue to call his company a Literary, not a National Theatre.' In replying, Maurice Joy said that 'the stupidity of an Irish Audience was beyond anything he had ever met', but the chairman, T. M. Kettle (see p. 241), commenting that their discussion suggested 'they were assisting at an adjourned inquest held upon the Abbey Theatre', said he had always thought that 'Mr Yeats despised his fellow-man a little too openly to be a good dramatist', and added that when the Abbey Theatre 'committed such an indefensible sin against good taste and against ordinary sanity of judgement as Mr Synge's "Playboy of the Western World," he thought the expression of opinion against that play, and in condemnation of that play, was not one bit too intense'.

[1] See p. 639. On 19 Mar Henderson told Holloway (NLI) that 'M[rs] Payne has been in very delicate health since she came to Dublin. He did not know how the actresses would stand her being cast for *Deirdre* in the coming revival. He thought it a damned shame to treat Miss Allgood so.'

[2] WBY had probably been persuaded to lend Bullen his rooms because one of his purposes in being in London was to settle the arrangements for the *Collected Works*.

[3] See p. 635. The five-week tour began on 11 May and included visits to Glasgow, Cambridge, Birmingham, Oxford, and London.

[4] WBY left London on 10 Apr to join AG and Robert Gregory in Florence, and they remained in Italy until *c.* 21 May, going on to visit San Marino, Urbino, Pesaro, Ravenna, Rimini, Ferrara, and Venice.

## To A. E. F. Horniman, [? 28 March 1907]

Thursday:

Copy.

Dear Miss Horniman: your letter has made me extremely angry. If you had thought a moment you would have seen that the letter heding was a clerical error of Hendersons or Paynes (I never saw it or heard of it till I got your letter) & yet you write a letter assuming that those you have been associated with for years are liars & rogues.[1] It is intolerable.[2]

Yr
W B Yeats

AL Copy NLI.


## To Florence Farr, 29 March 1907

Mention in letter from FF to John Quinn, *c.* 20 April 1907.
FF told Quinn that in this letter, posted on 3 April, WBY was 'full of wanting to come to America but says he is off to Italy with Lady Gregory and Robert until the end of May[1]... he says... that they start in a few

---

[1] AEFH had received new Abbey stationery with Fay's name still listed as manager. Although this was an oversight, she immediately suspected a conspiracy, and wrote officially to the Directors and privately to WBY on 27 Mar (NLI) on the assumption that the Directors had acted behind her back: 'Let the Directors please face the question simply—a majority of them only formally accepted my offer; if a majority now come to the conclusion that it was unwise to accept the offer they must let me know & tell me that Mr. Payne has been given notice, that Fay is to lose his £100 a year as producer & that I am to cancel all arrangements for the tour. But it is only fair to tell me this clearly; not to force me into a most disagreeable position, that of ceaselessly making a row to get our bargains carried out. If Fay insists on some office or post being given to him beyond his acting parts & his producing, why was I not told? Why am I to be always the person who has to be put into difficult places?'

[2] AEFH was wholly unabashed on receiving this retort from WBY, replying on 30 Mar (NLI): 'I don't mind your being angry a bit, but you might shunt a little of your anger on to another line; such an error is likely to cause much inconvenience. I am enquiring from Mr Henderson & Mr Payne as to which saw the proof & whether it were an over-sight or a matter of ignorance.' She went on to rationalize her objection, alleging that she objected to producers being put on the letterhead 'as it removes the safeguard I have so carefully arranged for authors who desire it to choose outside artists for "production" & I see no reason why "General & Stage Manager" should not be put for Payne'.

[1] FF was in America and writing to Quinn from the Bastol Hotel, Boston. She pointed out that WBY's conflicting travel plans would cause 'a great muddle', since she had arranged for W. G. Glass, a lecture agent in the Pond Lyceum Bureau, to write to him, organizing a US trip. As she observed, WBY's sudden departure for Italy 'simply means he won't get Glass's letter & will miss the opportunity. There is no time to cable because he says on 29th March that they start in a few days.' Noting that WBY gave no address in this letter, she concluded that 'they've made

days.... He tells me the bookseller has ordered 200 copies of the new 8 volume set of his works.'[2]

## *To Agnes Tobin, c. 3 April 1907*

Mention in letter from Agnes Tobin, 4 April 1907.
Telling her that Frohman had visited the Abbey during a bad performance of *Deirdre*,[1] evidently asking after her translation of *Phèdre*,[2] and informing her that Synge is better.[3]

Ireland too hot to hold him for the moment. I certainly think that the best thing he can do is to go for the public generally.'

[2] In an undated fragment evidently written shortly before WBY left London for Italy, AEFH informed him (NLI) that Bullen had received a letter from 'a big publisher' who wanted 'to take 200 copies' of *CW*. This probably refers to Chapman & Hall's offer to take over 250 copies of the edition, an offer that Bullen was happy to take up as they employed a traveller and could thus approach booksellers unavailable to him. Chapman & Hall issued their copies with a special title page and simultaneously with Bullen's volumes (see *Bibl*, 90).

[1] Frohman visited the Abbey on 1 Apr when *The Eyes of the Blind*, *Deirdre*, *The Rising of the Moon*, and *Spreading the News* were performed. On 2 Apr Holloway noted (NLI) that Frohman, who 'went unrecognised by Yeats & Co', came in 'when Deirdre was half-over, & a person behind [him] heard him express delight at *The Rising of the Moon*'. WBY's *Deirdre* had suffered from Mrs Payne's illness, which had seriously disrupted rehearsals, and Holloway thought that the 'acting alround lacked sincerity & the audience felt it. I found the performance very wearing & tiresome.... The new Deirdre is a high-strung, hysterical actress, with a monotonous wail-like voice & restless manner.... This cheap, hysterical style of playing likes me not' (cf. *Abbey Theatre*, 91). In her reply to this letter (*LWBY* I. 181–2) Miss Tobin confessed herself 'grieved about Mr. Frohman—but I hope you are keeping that good bill on all this week, as he is almost certain to slip in again. He told me he meant to go on a night when the company was not prepared specially. If he does not go to you again in Dublin,—well—we must try to get him to come to a London performance. I can imagine his entire bewilderment at a scratch performance of Deirdre!'

[2] See pp. 554, 595–6. In her reply Agnes Tobin told him that she had instructed her typist 'to send you part of Phèdre she had typed. I have entirely finished the first act—since then—and made a start on the second. It is quite a little education for me.... I told her to leave the variants in the Phèdre—as I wanted your advice about them.'

[3] See pp. 621, 623, n. 1. WBY had called to see Synge on 31 Mar, and found that he was better than he had been since the beginning of February, although he was still suffering from a severe and chronic cough. He was also getting out more, and his health continued to rally in the coming weeks.

## To A. E. F. Horniman, [c. *14 April 1907*]

Mention in letter from AEFH, 16 April 1907.
Telling her that he caught a cold crossing the Alps, discussing his trip to Italy,[1] asking about the current Abbey tour,[2] and telling her that the papers relating to previous tours were not at Coole.[3]

NLI.

## To Florence Farr, [*mid April 1907*][1]

PALACE HOTEL FLORENCE | 7 LUNG'ARNO GUICCIARDINI

[*Salutation and approximately first ten lines missing*]
.... the [*missing*] [t]own—I forget [?the] [n]ame though I [?stay]ed in it—where a steam engine runs about the streets all night ringing a bell—yes it is there you have chosen for they like being read out to—I recommend that place. You are a beast for not writing. When you do write please write to London for you are hardly a prompt enough correspondent to catch me here where I shall be for two or three weeks more. Then I spend a few days at Ferrara & Venice & so back to London.[2] I have been intending to write for some days but have been ill, & am still weak & stupid—mere

[1] AEFH replied that he was evidently 'not properly wrapped up, that crossing the Alps is bitterly cold'. She recommended that, while in Florence, he should visit 'the Piazza Michelangelo in moonlight when the beastly cold permits & see the sun-set from Fiesole too. Don't forget to look at the queer marble windows at Sant' Onofino.' On 18 Apr she wrote to AG (NLI), hoping 'that Mr Yeats has lost his cold, a cold-nosed poet gazing on the Arno would not be a picturesque object'.
[2] AEFH kept WBY abreast of the Abbey's British tour: that Ambrose Power was too slow and monotonous as the Wise Man in *The Hour-Glass* and had been replaced by Ernest Vaughan, who had 'done extremely well in Baile's Strand & I think should be kept permanently'; that there was a difficulty in finding a theatre in Cambridge; that she and Payne had written to the Dublin press to contradict rumours that Frohman was planning to take over the Abbey Theatre, and that the *Catholic Herald* had reported the opposition of the 'London Gaels' to the production of *The Playboy of the Western World* there. An interview with AEFH about the tour appeared in the *Catholic Herald* of 29 Mar (5).
[3] On 30 Mar AEFH had asked WBY if the papers relating to the previous Abbey tour to Oxford and Cambridge, and so presumably containing useful addresses and contacts, were at Coole, as she remembered sending 'the bundle there after that tour'. He had evidently written to say that they could not be found, but in her reply she promised to 'try not to bear malice at the loss of those *tour* papers, it is a d—d nuisance but I'm managing as best I can'.

[1] This letter had evidently reached FF, who was in New York, before 4 May as on that day John Quinn wrote to his Harvard friend Townsend Walsh (NYPL): 'Yeats is at present in Italy. I read a letter from him to Miss Farr, who is here, the other day and he seemed to be rather depressed over the theatre now generally.' And he went on to tell Walsh that WBY had just finished *Deirdre*. Quinn evidently retained the letter as it became part of the archive inherited by his secretary Jeanne Robert Foster.
[2] WBY left London on 10 Apr to join Robert Gregory and AG in Florence. In *70 Years* (201) AG gives an account of their itinerary: 'We had chosen Florence and Siena; and then to please that student

cold & rheumatics but bad enough. But I have a great sense of peace in being out of the Dublin stress & worry—new anger there at our taking "Play Boy" to London—just two days before I left there was an attack of extrordinary violence in the Freeman describing the play as "obscene"—I had to get the company togeather—for they were all except Frank Fay wavering—& to win them over by speach (explaining our motives, reasons & so forth).[3] I left them very resolute. Two days before M^rs Fay had struck Frank Fay & flung a tea-cup at him in an argument on the subject & William Fay had to be put into the scene dock (that sounds very penitential) & Frank Fay locked up alone in the Green room to stave off a fight.[4] It has been a very unpleasant business & I have had no real support except from Lady Gregory but I know if I gave way the theatre would never be free. The whole thing has so far as I can judge been worked up by the section about Arthur Griffith (who has perhaps some fancied wrong in connection with Maude Gonne to avenge—he is beleived to be given to that sort of thing). It is certainly the result of years of hostility & that hostility, which has done

of Castiglione's *Courtier* we drove across the Apennines to Urbino, and descended to Pesaro and Ravenna. Yeats had also set his heart on visiting Ferrara, that is on the way to Venice.'

[3] On 2 Apr the *Freeman's Journal* reprinted an intemperate attack on *The Playboy of the Western World* by William Boyle which had appeared in the *Catholic Herald* (London) on 29 Mar (9). In his article Boyle described the Dublin disturbances over the play, gave a tendentious account of the plot, and claimed that the play was 'gross in conception, coarse beyond possibility of quotation and false to the very verge of absurdity. It shows the author absolutely ignorant of the life he assumes to portray.... Curiously enough, too, it appears when Home Rule is again prominently before the English public. As in the older calumnies, the Irish peasants are portrayed as lustful, idiotic, drunken, murderous, admiring the torture of defenceless animals, devoid of reverence or religion, and sunk in the lowest depths of savagery.' An editorial in the *Catholic Herald* of the same day (8) used Boyle's account to incite violent reactions to the play's forthcoming English production. Describing it as 'incredibly offensive and calumnious, a libel on the Irish peasantry and a travesty on Irish life', the paper maintained that those 'reading Mr. Boyle's article will not merely quite understand the heat of the Dublin public... but will feel an insatiable itching to get their fingers on Mr. Synge and express their feelings with blows and knocks neither apostolic nor restrained. The whole thing is rascally. It is a question whether the Lord Chamberlain would permit it to be produced in England.... The Dublin public didn't give it half enough, as all will agree who read Mr. Boyle's account of it.'

[4] This fight occurred on 1 Apr, the night that Frohman and J. M. Barrie (who was in Dublin to see a production of his *Peter Pan*) attended the Theatre, and WBY informed Holloway a year later (Hogan and Kilroy III. 205) that the fight had been over *The Playboy*: 'it was the first night of Miss Letts's play, *The Eyes of the Blind*, and all the company were in a very nervous state. Miss Letts's play got a very bad interpretation, but luckily Willie played in *The Rising of the Moon* excellently later on when the excitement had cooled down some what.' According to William Boyle (NLI), Frohman later asked Fay: 'Is Yeats the long black fellow who was passing continually between the audience and the footlights?' However, the visit led to a rumour that Frohman planned to take over the Abbey, a canard that was contradicted in the *Referee* of 21 Apr by both AEFH and Frohman himself, who told an interviewer (3) that it was true 'that in my recent tour around the British theatres, I visited the Abbey St. Theatre—a little back room kind of place. It is true that I thoroughly enjoyed myself there. Also that I regard this Irish national play venture as one of the most interesting affairs I have ever met. This little society has, in my opinion, achieved what has not yet been achieved by England, or even by America— that is, a kind of National Theatre.'

more than any other thing to keep the theatre empty will only come to an end, when we are known to be beyond popular influence. The row has made George Moore rather too friendly as he talks of doing us a play—which Miss Horniman would be furious at—but for the moment he is a delight as he is "telling all".[5] Do you remember that lady who followed him to Dublin & after married & died in childbed (I dont like putting names in letters). She married after Moore tired of her or she of him. He told me that she [*next nine or ten lines missing, reverse of page one, torn out*] . . . almost . . . He . . . "She was . . . woman, so kind & good and nice."[6]

I have made a few more changes in Dierdre, but not important for mere reading out I think or I would send them. I dare say the play will be published before you return—on both sides of the sea. My eight volume collected edition, with portrait by Shannon is coming off after all. It is to be sold only in sets of eight volumes 4.4.0 a set. One shop has already ordered 200 sets & promised to take more. So you see I am worth being nice to, even to the extent of being occasionally written to. Do you know I find it very hard to find out how to write to you. I want you too [*sic*] understand that I am sorry you are away & I am afraid to say it, because you get cross if one says such things & yet after all I shall be very glad when you return.[7]

M^{rs} Payne was not much of a success in Dierdre in Dublin—she is too young and inexperienced.[8] I shall want you in Dublin but you will refuse to come—so that all is no use.

[5] For AEFH's antipathy to George Moore see p. 501. The play was probably *The Coming of Gabrielle*, which Moore was writing at this time, although it was not published until 1920. According to Holloway's diary, Moore was a fairly regular patron of the Abbey at this time, and he was particularly impressed by Synge (see p. 37, n. 1), writing to him on 6 Mar (TCD) that he had just read *The Playboy*, which he admired 'very much', although he thought the 'disagreeable' ending would be improved if Old Mahon, realizing that his son is to marry a rich girl, forgot his wounds and started boasting about his son's exploits: 'To the peasant anything is preferable rather than money should pass out of the family.' He invited Synge (who had already thought of and rejected this scenario while writing the play) to call and talk all this over with him.

[6] i.e. Clara McCarthy, née Christian, Moore's former mistress and the 'Stella' of *Hail and Farewell* (which Moore was already planning); see p. 422. Moore told his brother that he had had 'no peace since her death' (see Cave, 597–603). FF tore the page at this point presumably because she wanted to lend WBY's letter to Quinn but did not want Moore's anecdote to gain wider currency.

[7] FF left the USA on the *Grosser Kurfürst* from Hoboken on 9 May.

[8] Mona Limerick's performance in the revised *Deirdre* was not widely noticed in the Dublin press. Oliver Elton, writing in the *Manchester Guardian* on 9 Apr (12), commented that she had 'a stature and face in keeping with a royal part, and played with no small measure of intelligence and passion. She appears, nevertheless, to have slight experience, and her method of saying verse is wholly wrong. Her voice was not too loud, but it was pitched too high and ill-modulated, so that she was often difficult to understand.' Holloway thought the acting 'lacked sincerity' (see p. 648, n. 1), and added that 'Yeats' tinkering of the text has not improved matters a bit. . . . In fact, Deirdre as presented by Mona Limerick (what a name, ye Gods!) was a very uncomfortable personage for poor Naisi to have to be exiled with for seven long years. Conchubar was lucky to have escaped her' (cf. *Abbey Theatre*, 91). He also commented that the 'players seemed to have little or no interest in their work. Considerable applause followed the ending of the play. How much of it was genuine, I wonder!'

I go every day to the Baptistry or to the Duomo or some such place.[9] There is always a hum in the Baptistry—I thought it was mass at first but found it was only people reading out the guide book—the old age of faith. Its literary equivalent is an analytic novel written in the old age of an epoch—which means that I am reading a novel by D'Annunzio & am bored. He can only write of weak people because the strong are mysterious even to themselves—"like wind or water were her ways" & think in sudden tumults of joy.[10] They may wander in the Wilderness but there is always cloud-capped Sinai when it is needed. What we can weigh & measure is but the sand underfoot.

Yr always but just now
a little sadly.
W B Yeats

I wonder if you got my last—written two weeks or so ago from Dublin.[11]

ALS NYPL.

## To A. E. F. Horniman, [late April to early May 1907]

Mention in letter from AEFH, 6 May 1907.
A series of postcards from Italy.[1]

---

[9] The Duomo, or Cathedral of Santa Maria del Fiore, the fourth largest church in Europe, was begun by Arnolfo di Cambio (d. 1302) in 1296 and, although consecrated in 1436, was not entirely completed until the 19th century. Apart from decoration by masters such as Paolo Uccello, Andrea del Castagno, Giorgio Vasari, and Federico Zuccari, its most distinctive feature is its vast dome, constructed to a revolutionary design by Filippo Brunelleschi (1377–1446) from 1420 to 1434. The Baptistry, an octagonal neighbouring Romanesque church, was renovated in white Carrara and green Prato marble in the thirteenth century, and is particularly famous for Lorenzo Ghiberti's set of bronze doors (1425–52), which depict scenes from the Old Testament.

[10] Gabriele D'Annunzio (1863–1938), the Italian poet, dramatist, and novelist. The novel was perhaps *L'innocente* (1892), translated by Georgina Harding in 1899 as *The Victim*. WBY had confessed to the *San Francisco Examiner* on 31 Jan 1904 that he saw 'lovely passages' in D'Annunzio's work, but that it would take him 'perhaps a long time to understand him as an artist that has influenced the whole of Europe' (see III. 273). 'Like wind or water were her ways' appears as a variant reading in *The Rubáiyát of Omar Khayyám*.

[11] i.e. the letter of 29 Mar, which she had received (see pp. 647–8).

[1] On 6 May AEFH wrote 'Many thanks for the post-cards, they gave me real pleasure.'

## To Holbrook Jackson, 2 May [1907]

Palace Hotel | Florence
May 2,

Dear Holbrook Jackson: I cannot lecture to you at the new Fabian society. I am very sorry but I shall still be out of England when May 13 (was not that the date?) comes round.[1] I am sorry but was doubtful from the first. I am taking a rest after a rather exausting winters work.

Yr sny
W B Yeats

ALS UCLA, with envelope addressed to Langley Park, Mill Hill, London N. W., postmark '?RIMINI 5 3 07'.

## To A. E. F. Horniman, [2 May 1907]

Mention in letter from AEFH, 4 May 1907.
Asking how many letters she has sent him,[1] enquiring about Ambrose Power,[2] and discussing the Great Queen Street Theatre.[3]

NLI.

[1] The *Fabian News* for April (36) and May (43) announced that W. B. Yeats (misspelled 'Yeates' in the May issue) would lecture on 'The Few and the Many' to the Fabian Arts Group at the New Reform Club on 16 May 1907. The aim of the new society, which had been inaugurated on 7 Feb under the chairmanship of A. R. Orage, was 'to interpret the relation of Art and Philosophy to Socialism' and its membership was open 'to all Socialists'. It met once a fortnight, and its early meetings were addressed, among others, by Aylmer Maude, Edward Carpenter, H. G. Wells, and, on 2 May, Holbrook Jackson. The *Fabian News* for June 1907 reported (49) that WBY had been 'unable to attend' on 16 May, as announced, and that in his place 'Miss M. Murby read an excellent paper on 'The Gist of the Arts Group Lectures', in the course of which she analysed the intellectual and ideological tendencies of the Society's lectures to date. By 1908 the Arts Group had become a discussion group, and ceased thereafter.

[1] AEFH's letter of 22 Apr had been sent on to Rimini from Florence, and WBY had evidently asked how many times she had written to him while he was in Italy. She replied that 'One letter & two post-cards are all I've sent you, I thought that you wanted a holiday & you gave no address except Palace Hotel Florence.'

[2] A disagreement between Ambrose Power and W. G. Fay over the terms for the current tour had become the focus of simmering rivalries in the Company. As Power himself explained to Holloway on 17 May (NLI), 'he had fallen out with the Fays & company over a question of salary for playing for a fortnight in Oxford & London with National Theatre Co. He asked a certain sum when Payne asked him to name his price & W Fay thought he wanted too much, —(more than any of the rest of the company) & told him [he] was suffering from swelled head & much more of a personal nature. Power told him that he had nothing to do with the matter, that it rested with Payne whether he got what he asked or not, & the conversation ended with that. His terms were accepted & he goes to Oxford & London. Fay refuses to let him appear in the peasant plays over which he has control. So he will only appear in *On Baile's Strand* & *The Shadowy Waters*.' Power's demands were not motivated by arrogance or greed: he had a regular job outside the Theatre (see p. 426, n. 13), and so needed compensation for loss of earnings while he was absent on tour; but Fay was obviously making an issue of it as part of his struggle with Payne. In her reply AEFH assured WBY that 'Power will take £3 a week & go to Oxford & London so that is all right. I too "smelt a trap" & wrote to Mr Payne & said the *invisible* cause is always the real one.'

[3] AEFH had inspected a number of theatres in her search for a London venue for the Abbey Company (see p. 643), and WBY had evidently warned her not to hire one that was too large, especially

## *To Maud Gonne,* [c. *4 May 1907*]

Mention in letter from MG, 7 May [1907].

Giving her an account of his trip to Italy, speaking of 'incense powder',[1] asking when she expects to be in London,[2] telling her that theatre affairs are still occupying his time,[3] complaining that people in Ireland have taken MacBride's part against her, and denouncing the views and outlook of the crowd.[4]

*G–YL*, 239–41.

given the uncertainty over the reception of *The Playboy of the Western World*. In her reply AEFH assured him that she felt 'just as you do about the size of the theatre', but thought it 'better to make enquiries': 'If we could get the Royalty it would be better. But don't trouble about that, I will *not* risk a big theatre under the circumstances. Mr Grein has a dislike (& as has everyone else) to the Great Queen Street.' In September of this year the Great Queen Street Theatre was leased by Lena Ashwell and renamed the Kingsway.

[1] WBY and MG had used various powders and drugs to help their divinations (see p. 637, and II. 95), and WBY had evidently offered to send her Italian incense for this purpose. In her reply she wished 'you could send me that incense powder for just now I think I might get some very interesting results. I have been having some strange sorts of dreams lately seeming to foretell some hideous war in which England & France would take part, they were strange fragmentary sort of dreams.'

[2] WBY had evidently informed her that he would return to London for the Abbey visit there, and in her reply she suggested that he should stop off to see her in Paris on his way back.

[3] WBY had explained that the Italian trip was a respite after the troubles in the Abbey Theatre and she replied that she was 'sorry the theatre affairs are still occupying you — Don't let them take too much of your time.' WBY's immersion in theatrical affairs had worried his Dublin acquaintances, and on 14 Apr Edward Dowden, Professor of English at Trinity College, Dublin, and a long-standing friend of JBY, had written to Rosalind Travers: 'We had a visit not long ago from W. B. Yeats. He gave us an amusing account of the wars of the Theatre. Learned as I thought myself in the feuds and factions of the Separatist parties, I could not follow the account of the ramifications of hostile party within party. I fear W.B.Y. is a little losing his finer self in "movements" and petty leadership. Still he smiled over the whole story, and was only half engaged in the strife. I wish that he were wholly out of it, and consulting his genius' (*Letters of Edward Dowden* [1914], 350–1).

[4] MG had been barracked at the Abbey Theatre the previous autumn (see pp. 514–15), and MacBride was later to be appointed to the post of water bailiff by the Dublin Corporation. Taking his cue from AEFH, WBY had apparently compared the Irish people's treatment of Synge and the Abbey with their preference for MacBride over MG, but she would not allow this, replying that she thought him 'quite unjust in what you say about our people at home. They have taken up MacBride because they had been told he was a hero & because they *know* he *actually* fought England & because they *believe* (here they are wrong) that he will fight England again.... If, knowing MacBride the Blackguard I know him, I thought he were a strong man capable of striking serious blows at England's rule in Ireland, as I once thought him, I should feel & say, that those in Ireland who support him against me are doing right & well, it is because *I know* him to be incapable of any strong action only a danger to the Nationalists, that I feel sad though not a bit indignant over the way they have behaved. And as to you Willie, we are such friends you will not misunderstand me when I say you have done things such as calling in the police & witnessing for the Crown that give them cause to hate you & it is a healthy sign they do.'

## *To A. E. F. Horniman*, [c. *4 May 1907*]

Mention in letter from AEFH, 6 May 1907.
Telling her that he has decided not to lecture to the Fabian Society's Arts Group after all.[1]

NLI.

## *To William Macneile Dixon*,[1] [*4 May 1907*]

PALACE HOTEL FLORENCE | 7, LUNG'ARNO GUICCIARDINI
Saturday

Dear Mʳ Dixon:
  Your kind invitation has been sent on to me here after hunting me from town to town for some days.[2] I wish very much that I were in Ireland to accept of it but I shall not return for a couple of weeks.

Yr sny
W B Yeats

ALS Glasgow University.

---

[1] The announcement in the May issue of the *Fabian News* that 'W. B. Yeates' would lecture to the Fabian Arts Group on 16 May had confused AEFH, who did not know that he had written to cancel the arrangement (see p. 653). In her letter of 4 May (see above) she had scolded WBY: 'Now I'm very cross with you for not telling me that you are going to lecture at the Fabian Art Branch on May 16ᵗʰ; you gave me permission to see if I could arrange for you to lecture before June 10ᵗʰ & if I had entered into negociations with anyone I should have looked very foolish. It was only a chance that I saw it in a Fabian magazine & as your name was spelled Yeat*es* I had to write to Mr Orage to find out if it was you.' And she implored him to let her know when he would be back and what his engagements were as she was trying to arrange a number of lectures for him. In her reply to this letter she said she was 'sorry that you have decided not to lecture at the Fabian Society after all. We need all the help that we can get, though I quite understand your reluctance to leave Italy.'

[1] William Macneile Dixon (1866–1946) had been a pupil of Edward Dowden's at Trinity College, Dublin, and taught there before becoming Professor of English at Birmingham University from 1894 to 1904. In 1904 he was appointed Regius Professor of English at Glasgow University, a post he retained until his retirement in 1935. He was a friend of H. J. C. Grierson (see p. 308), served on the board of the Glasgow Repertory Theatre, and published on Tennyson and 19th-century poetry, as well as writing a history of Trinity College, Dublin.

[2] At Grierson's suggestion Dixon had invited WBY to give a short course of lectures in Greenock.

## *To J. M. Hone, 4 May [1907]*

Palace Hotel | Florence.
May 4

My dear Hone: I am doing the essay I promised you but do not count on
it for May as I find I cannot be certain of anything in this hurried life—
going from place to place. I began it ten or twelve days [ago] but it was
a failure so I started in a quite different way this morning & am getting
on well.[1]

Yr sny
W B Yeats

ALS Texas.

## *To John Quinn, 5 May [1907]*

Republica di S. Marino
May 5

Greetings from us in the smallest Republic to you in the greatest,[1]
W B Yeats
A Gregory
Robert Gregory

APS NYPL, addressed to <120 Broadway> New York, postmark indecipherable.

[1] The essay, a further instalment of 'Discoveries', was published in the *Shanachie*, edited by Hone, in
October of this year.

[1] WBY and the Gregorys were visiting San Marino, an independent republic of 23½ square miles,
situated on the slopes of Mount Titano in north-eastern Italy to the west of Rimini, during their
excursion to Urbino, Pesaro, Rimini, and Ravenna (see pp. 649–50, n. 2). Founded in the early 4th
century by Christian refugees under the leadership of St Marinus, San Marino managed to retain its
independence through a combination of geographical isolation and skilful diplomacy. Its status was
guaranteed by the Congress of Vienna in 1815, and a series of treaties following the unification of Italy
confirmed its political sovereignty. The country is ruled by an elected Great and General Council,
which appoints an executive council, the Congress of State. San Marino lost its position as the smallest
republic in the world with the independence of Nauru in 1968.

## *To Mary Price Owen,*[1] [c. 6 May 1907]

Mention in letter from A. E. F. Horniman, 13 May 1907.
Sending his good wishes for her forthcoming repertory tour to South Africa.

NLI.

## *To W. A. Henderson, 9 May* [1907]

PALACE HOTEL FLORENCE | 7 LUNG'ARNO GUICCIARDINI
May 9

My dear Henderson: please send the enclosed lady[1] a bundle of 'Arrows' (three) & any 'Samhains' that are still in print, & a copy of sixpenny 'Shadowy Waters',[2] with bill.

Yrs siny
W B Yeats

ALS Private.

---

[1] Mary Price Owen, an actress and singer, and a close friend of AEFH, had helped WBY with his experiments with the psaltery (see III. 364–6), and done research on costumes for the Abbey earlier this year. From January to March 1906 she had played Locasta in Beerbohm Tree's production of Stephen Phillips's *Nero*, and on 3 May AEFH informed WBY that she was joining a repertory company going out to tour in South Africa. The tour, with Mrs Brown-Potter's company, started on 17 May, with a repertory including *As You Like It*, *The School for Scandal*, *Forget-Me-Not*, *The Ironmaster*, *La Tosca*, and *Camilla*. WBY had written to congratulate her and wish her well, and on 13 May AEFH wrote that she 'thanks you for letter & good wishes'. Miss Owen returned to London on 28 Nov of this year and on 27 Aug AEFH told WBY (NLI) she was enjoying herself, but found Mrs Brown-Potter a trial.

[1] The 'enclosed lady' is unidentified.

[2] i.e. the 'acting version' of the play, based on the text of the production of 8 Dec 1906 (see pp. 522, 537), and issued by Bullen in January of this year.

## To Hely's Limited,[1] [after 10 May 1907]

Mention in following letter.

Sending his and AG's articles for the new number of the *Arrow*, and informing them that Payne would send programmes or lists of plays to go into it.[2]

## To Ben Iden Payne, [after 10 May 1907]

PALACE HOTEL FLORENCE | 7, LUNG'ARNO GUICCIARDINI
c/o Lady Gregory | Ca Capello | San Polo | Venice.

Dear M[r] Payne: I have sent the articles for "The Arrow" one by Lady Gregory, one by self direct to 'Helys' Dublin but told them that you would send programes or lists of plays to go in 'Arrow'.[1] The enclosed paragraphs are to be incorporated in programes or lists under the names of

---

[1] Hely's Limited were the printers and publishers of the *Arrow*. The firm had premises at 27–30 Dame Street, Dublin.

[2] WBY was sending material for the fourth number of the *Arrow*, published 1 June 1907, which confessed, apropos *The Playboy*, that the 'failure of the audience to understand this powerful and strange work has been the one serious failure of our movement'. It also printed a note on the London productions: 'The plays we bring to London are a selection from a considerable number which have been produced at the Abbey Theatre, and sometimes we have had to choose some particular one, not because it is the best, but because it suits our players or as many as can travel. I would myself sooner have been represented by "Dierdre" or "The King's Threshold" than by "The Shadowy Waters," which may not seem a play to any but the lovers of lyric poetry, or "On Bailes Strand", which is part of a cycle of plays on the life of the Ancient hero Cuchulain.' The issue also published 'An Explanation' by AG: 'I wish to explain on behalf of myself and the players to some whose opinion we respect, why, having been attacked for the performance of "Playboy" in Ireland, we have decided to bring it to England. We would rather have given Ireland another opportunity of judging it when the heat caused by the collision of organized interruption and organized force had cooled down. But some attacks published, the latest through an English paper, have been of such an unworthy nature that we felt it would be necessary either to take the play into the Courts as the subject of a libel action or to some calm audience, and this audience we hope to find in Oxford, and in London.' The *Arrow* also printed a list of twelve plays produced by the NTS during the 1906–7 season.

[1] See above.

my two verse-plays.[2] 'The Arrow' is not essential, except for London, but had better be in time for Oxford at any rate.[3]

Please send me to Venice[4] the dates of 'Shadowy Waters' rehersals.[5] I can join you at Birmingham.[6]

Yrs siny

W B Yeats

[2] These were paragraphs on the mythological background of *On Baile's Strand* and *The Shadowy Waters*, which were part of the repertoire on the current Abbey tour. They were included in the programmes for Oxford and London, and printed, as WBY instructs, immediately below the list of players. They read:

> Cuchulain is, with the possible exception of Finn, the most famous of the ancient Irish heroes. He protected Ulster and its King, Concobar, against the forces of the other provinces at a famous ford, and was held for the son of the gods, and in the old stories passed, much as I have pictured him, from active life to visionary frenzy. I have given to the wise King and the ungovernable hero the two shadows, the fool and the blind man, and have besides gathered into one skein certain threads that will be better understood when I have finished the three other plays which are to re-tell much of the story of his life. The whole of that story is in Lady Gregory's 'Cuchulain of Muirthemne.'—W.B.Y.

and

> The Shadowy Waters though there is much incidental Irish legend here and there is not founded on any particular story and should explain itself to any auditor who can understand, say, the love poetry of Shelley. Forgael dissatisfied with an earthly love seeks, together with the woman chance or destiny has cast before him, unearthly love beyond what seem to be the limits of the world. By his magic harp he plunges her into the illusions of love, which become real, and they pass away from what seems real— W.B.Y.

[3] The Company left on 11 May for a five-week tour of Glasgow, Cambridge, Birmingham, Oxford, and London. Holloway reported (NLI) that on departure they 'were all in great spirits, & laughed & joked about what was to happen to them in London when *The Playboy* was put on'. They played at the New Theatre, Oxford, 3–5 June.

[4] In *70 Years* (201) AG recalled that they had journeyed to Venice by way of Ferrara: 'And leaving Ferrara one May morning we went by rail through fields that as we drew nearer to the Adriatic changed to reedy swamps, and passed by little towns showing traces of the architecture of their Queen City. Then taking steam-boat at Chioggia we came before the sun had set to our haven, not to the jangle and the uproar of the railway station, but to set foot first upon the very threshold of the city's beauty, the steps leading to the Grand Piazza, to the Duomo, of St. Mark.' And in a draft of this memoir (Pethica, 315) she recalled that as she left WBY on the Piazza 'he was as if entranced by the rich colouring, the strange beauty of the joyous Venetian night'. WBY and the Gregorys stayed with AG's friend Lady Enid Layard at Ca Cappello, San Polo, Venice.

[5] *The Shadowy Waters* had not been performed since the previous December, and since Letitia Darragh, who had not acted with the Company since then, was returning to the role of Dectora, it was essential that the play should be thoroughly rehearsed. AEFH was particularly adamant that this should be so, and had warned WBY in her letter of 4 May (see p. 653) that unless Miss Darragh could 'be properly rehearsed *I* won't have "Shadowy Waters" in London unless it can be done well'. On 13 Apr she told him that he would be able to rehearse the play at the Great Queen Street Theatre on 10 June. When Holloway called there on 11 June he 'found the company about to rehearse "*The Shadowy Waters*"'.

[6] The Company played at the Midland Institute in Birmingham from 27 May to 1 June, with eleven plays in the repertoire. On 29 May the *Birmingham Gazette & Express* remarked (3) that the INT 'are instructing the ignorant Sassenachs as to what Irish dramatic literature is capable of', and that 'these Irish plays and players will go far towards . . . dispelling the average farcical conception of Hibernian character'.

In writing please tell me roughly how you did in Dublin—how many pounds—the last Saturdays & of course how you do at Glasgow if you have opened there.[7] I do not know the date & only heard today from Miss Horniman the date of Cambridge.[8]

Please keep me informed of address & ask Hely to send me proofs of the entire Arrow to Venice if they can do so to find me there on 21st. If not they must let me know at once & I will send later address.

ALS NYPL.

## To A. E. F. Horniman, [c. *12 May 1907*]

Mention in letters from AEFH, 13 May 1907.

Enquiring why she was so distressed at his prolonged visit to Italy,[1] and about arrangements for the Abbey's current tour,[2] asking her to take delivery of a set of plates he was sending back from Italy,[3] asking her to check the London reviews of William Boyle's plays at various newspaper

[7] On Saturday, 20 Apr, the matinée and evening performances of *The Eyes of the Blind*, *Fand*, and *A Pot of Broth* had made £3 9s. 11d. and £9 11s. 3d. respectively; on Saturday, 27 Apr, the matinée and evening performances of the same bill had made £2 17s. 11d. and £8 5s. 6d. The Abbey company opened at Glasgow on Monday, 13 May, and visited Cambridge from 20 May.

[8] This must have been after 10 May, when AG had told Synge (Saddlemyer, 221): 'We haven't yet heard date of Cambridge.'

[1] AEFH had fired off two postcards to WBY on 11 May reproaching him for staying too long in Italy and for not informing her of his arrangements, so making her look foolish since she had been busy arranging lectures for him in Cambridge, Birmingham, and London in connection with the Abbey tour. She told him that she would write to Professor Feidler in Birmingham and J. T. Grein in London, making clear to them 'that I asked them to trouble themselves when I believed that you did not intend to play me false without telling me of your change of plans. I shall not blame you to them, only I shall apologise for the trouble I have given.' In the second postcard she complained that she thought they had 'a clear understanding that you would return at the middle of this month; free to help me in my efforts for the theatre. *You might have* taken the trouble to tell me. That is why I am so angry. I'm sending you this in an envelope as I don't want to let other people know how you have behaved.' Since WBY had had no idea that she was making these firm arrangements without consulting him, he evidently wrote asking for further clarification, and she replied on 13 May that she was 'much distressed because it seemed that you had behaved so carelessly in regard to letting me know your plans. You left London on April 10th & clearly told me & Miss Owen that you would be back in the middle of May.... It is not fair to me that I was not told by either you or Lady Gregory that you were not returning until June.... What I want you to be sorry & penitential for is the fact that even now you have never told me when you will be back in June!'

[2] WBY had evidently asked for the latest itinerary for the Abbey tour, and she supplied this on 13 May, when she also informed him that it would be possible to hold rehearsals at the Great Queen Street Theatre during the day on 6 and 7 June, but not on 8 June, although he could 'rehearse Shadowy Waters on the 10th so that will be all right'.

[3] WBY had evidently purchased a set of plates in Italy, and sent them back to London cash on delivery. In her reply AEFH told they they would 'be kept with care & paid for and I'll dun you for the money'.

offices,[4] apologizing for not being able to lecture for J. T. Grein,[5] and discussing a revival of Blunt's *Fand*.[6]

NLI.

## *To Maud Gonne, [mid-May 1907]*

Mention in letter from MG, 'Monday' [? 20 May 1907].
Sending a flower from the Apennines,[1] and arranging to meet her in Paris on his way back to London.[2]

*G–YL*, 241–2.

---

[4] WBY had asked AEFH to go to the office of the *Globe* to look up reviews of Boyle's *The Building Fund* when it played in London on 28 Nov 1905 (see p. 250). He wanted the notices to show that Boyle was denounced as anti-Irish in terms similar to those now being used (by Boyle himself among others) against Synge. On the following day AEFH reported her findings: 'Globe Nov 28th no mention of Boyle. Morning Post Nov 29th praises the play. Globe Nov 29th no mention of Boyle as the paper came out before the play was performed. Westminster Nov 29th mildly good notice of the play. Era Dec 2nd simply gives the story. Referee Dec 3rd says it "amused the audience". I will send you the two Globes as they are what you mean, but they are about *Colum's* play & I'll go to the office & see if there was another notice which was not sent to me.'

[5] WBY had evidently apologized for not be able to lecture for J. T. Grein (1862–1935), the Dutch-born founder of the Independent Theatre, who had been helping AEFH with advice about venues and press coverage for the current Abbey tour. On 22 Apr AEFH had told WBY (NLI) that Grein was trying to arrange 'an extra gathering of the [Dramatic] Debaters' Club about the middle of May for you to preach to them. He thinks very highly of you indeed & seemed anxious to have you sermonise his people.' She had egged Grein on to arrange this lecture (WBY had spoken to the Club on 26 Nov 1905 [see p. 219, n. 8]), and was now embarrassed that he could not appear. In her reply to this letter, she said that she had 'quoted that sentence in your letter to Mr Grein & have told him that I gathered that you thought that there might be an error. I have asked him to write to you direct.'

[6] Wilfrid Blunt's play *Fand* had been produced at the Abbey on 20 and 27 Apr 1907 (see above, n. 7), after WBY and AG had left for Italy, and without its second act. On 26 Apr Blunt had written to AG in Florence (Berg) complaining that the press reviews proved 'what I have felt all along wd be the case, that without the second act, the third is not quite intelligible. For this reason I think the play ought not to be acted again unless this whole is given. I hope, if you think of giving it again, you will let me know. Certainly when we gave it here, it was the second and third acts that went best.' Recording his impressions of the first performance on 20 Apr, Holloway observed that the play 'was followed with interest if not always with understanding'. WBY, no doubt at AG's instigation, was considering how the play might be revived, but in her reply AEFH advised him not to 'waste time just now about "Fand". When the London visit is over you will be free to make up your mind about many things.'

[1] In her reply MG, who was staying at Aix-les-Bains, said that she had 'been up near the snows too & saw the countless little star like flowers like the one you sent me from the Appenines [*sic*]'.

[2] WBY had evidently taken up MG's invitation to visit her in Paris on his way back to London, and in her reply she told him that she would return to Paris from Aix on 22 May 'so you will be sure to find us on the 23rd or any days soon after that. It will be nice seeing you & I have lots to talk of.' Because WBY had to return in a hurry (see p. 663, n. 6), it is unlikely that he managed to stop in Paris.

## *To A. E. F. Horniman, [c. 19 May 1907]*

Mention in letter from AEFH, 20 May 1907.

A conciliatory letter, explaining the length of his visit to Italy,[1] and the reason for retaining W. G. Fay's name on the Abbey stationery,[2] discussing the discipline on the current Abbey tour,[3] the subsidy for it,[4] and the £50 that AEFH has paid for scenery,[5] and seeking the latest

---

[1] WBY had evidently sent a long letter to AEFH, explaining that he had not been able to fulfil the lecturing engagements she had arranged because he had not known the exact timing and itinerary of the British tour. This assuaged her anger over his supposed indifference to her efforts on his behalf (see p. 660,n.1), and she replied on 20 May: 'Now I understand all about the plans; I was hurt more than cross. I told you the dates as soon as I heard that you did not know them.'

[2] WBY had also apparently explained more fully how W. G. Fay's name came to be on the new Abbey stationery, an inclusion that had caused a serious rift between them in early April (see p. 647), and which she had mentioned in several subsequent letters. Furnished at last with WBY's explanation, AEFH took a magnanimous line: 'I *accept* Fay's name on the note-paper now that I am clearly told that it is put there to please him, but I do not *approve*. I'll be civil to everyone and cause no friction.' Meanwhile, the Abbey stationery printed for the present tour had offended the Fays, and on 27 Apr Frank Fay had objected to Synge (TCD) that Payne's name now appeared with W. G. Fay's as a producer on the heading: 'The officers of the Society were re-elected, but Mr. Payne was not mentioned by Yeats at all, & the above comes as a complete surprise to me. In view of recent critiques it ought to be made clear on the programmes *for tour* who is responsible for the verse plays & who is responsible for the *peasant* plays.' He went on to claim that the term 'producer is preposterous', and asked what was wrong with 'stage manager': 'Is Mr. Payne the Society's servant or its master.'

[3] In her letter of 13 May AEFH had announced that 'if the company shew any want of what *I* consider to be proper discipline on this tour I shall refuse to finance another. I shall give my reasons to the Directors, it won't be my affair whether you think these good or not.' Given the problems over bad behaviour on the previous year's extended British tour, WBY had evidently suggested that the Company, not merely the Directors, should be warned as to their present conduct. In her reply AEFH insisted that she had 'told *you* that the discipline must be good on this tour, just because I felt it only fair to let you know my intentions in case it were bad. It would be idiotic for me to announce this to the company.'

[4] In her letter of 13 May AEFH had insisted that the costs of the Abbey tour (which she was underwriting) should be rigorously controlled: 'I want to make it clear that I hope that the Directors will see fit *not* to give bonuses or presents to the company in regard to this tour. If there are any profits they should be used for the fit-up & to produce new plays. The actors are to have all the money they have demanded for travelling allowances, especially the 10/- a week extra for London. If you give bonuses, I cannot ever find out how much they are *actually* paid & this is not fair to me.' In his reply WBY had waggishly suggested that she should spend some of the profits on entertainments for the company, and even a wedding present for her *bête noire* W. G. Fay, who had married the previous autumn (see p. 518). AEFH entered into the spirit of his raillery and answered that she was 'not going to give any belated wedding-presents, it would be a bad precedent & obvious humbug on my part. I have got that extra addition for the convenience of the theatre—it is all the "banquets & *pageants*" I can afford, you greedy old Demon!'

[5] This was a long-running matter of contention (see p. 371, n. 6). AEFH had provided £50 for scenery for tours on 12 June 1906, and on 23 June 1906 sent WBY a cheque for that sum, complaining that the 'bill included hessian hangings & a scene but there was no hint as to *which* scene that I could discover'. Nor was she to discover thereafter; the missing 'fit-up' became a motif in numerous letters to WBY and Synge, and it had been brought back to her memory now by a bill for hiring scenery for the present tour. She told WBY on 13 May that she was 'determined to have the fit-up £50 mystery cleared & when I've time I'll find the old cheque & your letter demanding the money. I'm not accusing anyone of theft, but it is absurd to have to pay £12–10 hire now for what I paid £50 to have of our own a year ago.' WBY had evidently replied that the money had probably been mixed up with the general tour funds, and she answered that she had wanted 'to find out whether the Directors knew that they were giving bonuses from a *deficit* as that £50 was for fit-up'.

information about the censor's attitude towards the performance of *The Playboy of the Western World* in Oxford and London.[6]

NLI.

## To Holbrook Jackson, [26 May 1907]

18 Woburn Build
Sunday

Dear Jackson: I wish you could come in to-morrow evening & bring Orage whose address I have not got.[1] I want your help over 'The Play Boy' business.[2]

Yr ev
W B Yeats

ALS UCLA. Dated in another hand 'May 26th 07'.

[6] AEFH had interrupted a letter to AG of 17 May (NLI) to tell her that Redford, the English censor (see p. 24, n. 8), was 'afraid of a row in London' over the production there of *The Playboy of the Western World*, and was 'consulting the Home Office & Lord Chamberlain'. She asked AG 'for letters to people who might help to make a fuss on our behalf' if the authorities refused the play a licence, and immediately began a correspondence herself with Redford over the matter. This dispute was to cause WBY and AG to curtail their Italian trip, and he had evidently asked for the latest information about it. AEFH replied: 'I have no more news of course from Redford about Playboy. I will consult with Payne which plays should replace it if the licence be refused. By this time you will have heard how he sees nothing against the play but fears a riot. If he refuses *we* must make a fuss. I shall wire "granted" or "refused" to Lady Gregory as you may have left.' In the end the play was permitted, and Payne recalls in *Life in a Wooden O* (76–7) that there 'was considerable tension in the atmosphere' on the night of its London performance: 'Because of the many Irish residents in London, the company feared protests similar to the Dublin outbreak. For a few ominous seconds, scattered shouts of indignation came from the gallery. These subsided, however, when they were drowned by equally indignant counter cries. Although the police had been alerted and waited outside the theatre, there was no need to call on their help. As I had been that first night at the Abbey, I was deeply impressed by the complete air of detachment with which Synge, sitting in a stage box, gazed up at the gallery apparently with a sort of placid interest. His face, always impassive, remained as calm as a standing pool on a still day.' He also reports that on another night 'King Edward VII came to a performance. I assume that it was considered a diplomatic necessity that the monarch patronize the Irish National Theatre. Unless his reputation belies him, ours was not the kind of entertainment that he was likely to choose for his amusement.... I wondered what he and Queen Alexandra, who looked as handsome as she did in her pictures, thought of such unaccustomed fare as our Irish peasant plays.' George Bernard Shaw also came to a performance, and 'shrugged his shoulders about the play and did not admire the acting. For some reason I spoke of the players' "Irish brogue." Shaw interjected contemptuously, "It is not a brogue, it's a Dublin accent; it would do them good to be told so." '

[1] A. R. Orage (see p. 326) had moved from Leeds to London and had just become co-editor with Holbrook Jackson of the weekly periodical the *New Age*, which they had acquired with a loan from G. B. Shaw and the banker Lewis A. R. Wallace. WBY evidently hoped to enlist his help in the protest against the possible suppression in England of *The Playboy of the Western World*. In fact, the magazine did not mention the censorship, but on 6 June (6) noted the forthcoming visit of the Company and puffed the Maunsel editions of the plays, suggesting that 'visitors to the plays will naturally desire some knowledge of the pieces they are to witness.... "The Playboy of the Western World," by J. M. Synge... is also issued by Maunsel.' The drama critic of the *New Age*, L. Haden Guest, reviewed the play with an eye to the censor in the issue of 20 June (124): 'my criticism of the "Playboy" is not that it is too terrible a revelation of sordid life and coarseness; the life, indeed, is much less coarse and sordid and much more real than that in Battersea; but that Mr. Synge has not really carried his revelation of Christie Mahon far enough.'

[2] In his letter of 17 May, Redford had told AEFH (MBY) that the play would have to be submitted to the Lord Chamberlain, who might 'take the opinion of the Home Office who advise us in cases of this

## *To John Millington Synge,* [*27 May 1907*]

18 Woburn Buildings | Euston Road
Monday

My dear Synge: I [*for* The] reason for taking off 'Play Boy' from Birmingham Bill was that we beleived after reading the correspondense with censor that if there was a row at Birmingham the censor would take back the license & we considered its being brought to Oxford & London of the utmost importance.[1] There are enough slum Irish in Birmingham to stir up a row & we are not sure of any friendly audience there to help us. We have just had evidence of organization against us.[2] The decission had to be made quickly. 'As a matter of courtesy' I think Lady Gregory & I who induced

kind, in which difficult legal and political questions are involved'. He also asked her to send him cuttings from the Dublin press 'giving an account of the disturbance in the Abbey Theatre . . . when the piece was produced'. AEFH complied at once and on 18 May he replied that her letter 'appears to confirm the impression I had gathered from the published accounts, that at the performance in Dublin there was a sort of cabal or organised opposition on the part of a section of the Audience to protest against the performance. . . . The only point with which we are officially concerned is that this same opposition may make itself felt at Birmingham, or "Any Theatre in Great Britain", and possibly lead to a similar disturbance in the Theatre. As Examiner of Plays I shall put the whole case before the Lord Chamberlain at the earliest opportunity.' On 29 May Blunt recorded in his diary (II. 179) that AG had called 'in terrible trouble about her plays. She had gone to Italy to get away from the worry . . . and had engaged to bring out "The Playboy" . . . at Oxford and London but the Censor interfered and she was telegraphed for to come back. Birrell, however, to whom the case was referred withdrew the Censor's opposition.' On the following day he wrote that AG was 'in worse trouble than ever. The Editor of "Freeman" has written threatening her with new displeasure if she persists with "The Playboy" in England, and I fear her theatre will be altogether boycotted. I advise her to submit to Irish opinion, but though she admits that it was a mistake to produce the play, she says it is too late now to withdraw it.' In his review of the Maunsel edition of the play in the *New Age* (see n. 1) Holbrook Jackson claimed that the play was 'one of the finest comedies of the dramatic renascence' and maintained that 'Mr. Singe [*sic*] has achieved a masterpiece by simply collaborating with nature. He and the Irish are to be congratulated.'

[1] Although the letter no longer survives, Synge had written to WBY on 25 May from Dublin proposing to resign his directorship of the Abbey Theatre. One of his grounds of discontent was that *The Playboy* had been withdrawn from the Birmingham programme without his consultation, which he evidently thought 'a matter of courtesy'. He had first got wind of this in a letter from AEFH of 23 May 1907, which told him (TCD) that although the censor Redford had telegraphed that the play could be staged, she believed that there were 'strong objections to Playboy being done at Birmingham so something else may be put on in its stead. I see the advisability of reserving it for London.' Next day Payne wrote (TCD) that AG and WBY, who had arrived from Italy on 22 May, were 'both strongly against putting on the "Playboy" in Birmingham, they think it will weaken our position in Dublin and so we have decided to change the bill there'.

[2] Frank Fay concurred with WBY's view of the Birmingham audience; when he met Holloway on 10 June (NLI) he 'was loud in his disgust of the Birmingham playgoers—he would sooner face an audience of Ringsend [then a slum district in Dublin] natives, he said'. As early as 22 Apr there had been warnings of organized opposition in London, and AEFH told WBY (NLI) that P. S. O'Hegarty (1879–1955) of the Dungannon Clubs and the London Gaelic League had 'written to Payne, quite kindly. He says that there will be hissing at the fall of the curtain.'

the company to promise to play the play in London Oxford & Cambridge as intellectual centers should have been consulted before it was put on the Birmingham Bill. It was also arranged with the players at their request that the caste should be exactly the same as in Dublin & I now learn with surprize that 'three or four' have been changed.[3] When we proposed to take the play off the Birmingham Bill we asked Fay if there was any reason against it & he said 'none whatever'. As he is responsible that seemed to us sufficient. As to the £50, I understand from Miss Horniman that the checque was made payable to me, & with no more financial knowledge than you have I am quite prepared for investigations.[4] While we are fighting your battles is hardly the moment to talk of resignation.[5]

Yr sry<br>W B Yeats

PS. Lawrence led the attack on the play at the debate & on the night of its production abused the actors in their dressing room for having acted in such "an abominable play".[6]

ALS TCD.Saddlemyer, 222–3.

---

[3] Four of the actors were changed for the London performances: J. M. Kerrigan replaced Ambrose Power as Old Mahon and Ernest Vaughan took his place as the small farmer Jimmy Farrell, while Cathleen Mullamphy and Annie Allgood took over the parts of Susan Brady and Honor Blake from Alice O'Sullivan and Mary Craig. Holloway, who saw the London production, commented (NLI) that the 'acting was fine as usual. Mr Kerrigan filled the role of Old Mahon with vivid realism & Mr Vaughan that of Jimmy Farrell with some humour and just a suspicion of stage Irishman in his method.... The rest, with the exception of a few of the girls, were in the picture.'

[4] AEFH had been nagging Synge as well as WBY about the need to pay for the rental of scenery for Cambridge, when she had provided £50 for the construction of such scenery the previous June (see p. 662). She had drawn his attention to the matter in letters of 16 and 23 May (TCD), and suggested that he had been responsible for overseeing the building of the scenery. On 24 May her tone became more insistent: 'Mr Yeats tells me that I may ask you to get the Pass Book from the Bank & the old cheque book & old cheques as well if possible from the Directors box. I only wish for information between June 24$^{th}$ & September 1$^{st}$ 1806 [*sic*], so as to be able to compare these papers with my own cheques & pass books. This will be necessary for me before I see the three Directors formally in London next month. Otherwise I shall be obliged to come to Dublin for the purpose and that seems unnecessary as Lady Gregory will not want to wait there. I want to have it clear in my own mind that I did not send enough money then for the theatre & that that particular £50 for "fit-up" was taken because of my omission. I ought to have been asked for more, instead of this happening.'

[5] These causes of friction were aggravated by Synge's deteriorating health, his anxiety over his relationship with Maire O'Neill, and a sense that his directorship of the Abbey imposed apparently non-stop burdens. He wrote to Maire O'Neill on 26 May (*JMSCL* 1. 357): 'it is an endless worry to me.... I do not think things can go on much longer as they are, and I think I would have a freer hand to ask for what <terms> arrangements I want made for the working of the company if I was *outside it*. I will not desert W.G.F. if he wants me to stay on, so I must consult him.'

[6] W. J. Lawrence (see pp. 539–40) was one of the Abbey Theatre's most relentless critics, and the *Freeman's Journal* on 5 Feb 1907 (6) reported that at the meeting held the previous evening to discuss *The Playboy* (see p. 617, n. 4, and Appendix, pp. 880–1) he had announced that he 'was not going to praise Mr. Yeats that night—"I come to bury Caesar, not to praise him" (laughter and

## To Maud Gonne, [late May 1907]

Mention in letter from MG, 'Sunday' [? 2 June 1907].
Telling her of the battle with the English censor over the production of *The Playboy of the Western World*, and that he and AG were prepared to go to prison to defend the right to perform it,[1] and sending her incense powder.[2]

*G–YL*, 242.

cheers). . . . There was no predisposition to damn the play. It got a fair and honest hearing. . . . At the end the protest was made on the indecent verbiage, blasphemy and Billingsgate that was indulged in . . . . Mr Yeats has won a Pyrrhic victory. This was not the first time in the history that a wrongly administered English law had violated Irish freedom (cheers). . . . If the censorship was abolished the English manager had only to adopt the method of Mr Yeats to obtrude any indecent, vulgar play on the public. Mr Yeats's action was an argument in favour of the creation of a censorship in Ireland (applause and dissent).' Lawrence continued to take every opportunity to attack the play over the coming years, and his animus against it may have been intensified by his own unhappy marital situation. Since Synge's letter of 25 May is now lost, it is impossible to ascertain the nature of his reference to Lawrence, but it may have been a sympathetic allusion, arising out of an encounter with him recorded by Holloway on 25 Apr (NLI): 'W. J. Lawrence . . . told me he met Synge in the street & stopped him, & had it out with him in a friendly chat. Lawrence told him he had no enmity towards him personally, but a principle was involved in refusing the rights of an audience which he strongly objected to. Synge said the Abbey was a subsidized theatre in which the audience had no rights. Lawrence answered back he thought they were trying to build up a National theatre & get an audience to support it, but if they only wanted to have a hole & corner sort of show, then no more need be said on the matter. They parted with a friendly shake of the hands.'

[1] WBY had written to tell MG that he had had to return to England on 22 May to resist the censor's attempt to ban *The Playboy of the Western World*. He also informed her that he and AG were prepared to defy the ban, even if it meant imprisonment. MG, who did not approve of the play, thought this reaction was out of proportion and tried to dissuade him: 'Do you consider Synge's literature of equal value to your own? Do you consider its literary value to Ireland comparable to the value of Lady Gregory's work? Do you even think the Playboy at all the best of Mr Synge's plays? & yet—for the sake of that mediocre play you & Lady Gregory are willing to go to prison for 3 months i.e. cease all chance of work for 3 months.' She denied that this was a matter of principle, and demanded to know 'what principle is involved for Irishmen breaking English Law *in England*. One breaks law to reform law, but why should Irish men want to reform English law? . . . I do so hate seeing you waste time & energy which you owe to your art & to Ireland.' In fact, WBY's heroics were unnecessary since Redford granted a licence for the play on 23 May, subject to the omission of Pegeen's reference in Act I to 'loosèd kharki cut-throats' and 'any other allusion derogatory to the army'.

[2] MG confirmed that she had 'got the incense' (see p. 654): 'I will try it in a few days when I can get quietly in the country & will write you the results.' On 15 June she reported (*G–YL*, 243) that she had 'tried the incense twice, my cousin May was with me. The first time in the drawing room here we had no result except a sort of drowsyness. I think I actually slept for a few minutes once or twice, but I could remember nothing clearly, the 2nd time I burned the incense one evening sitting close to the sea shore—I saw nothing except some wandering lights on the sea & once a pathway of light. My cousin saw this also & we both heard murmuring sounds all round us, sometimes like faint music, sometimes like the crying of a multitude, my cousin said she also heard what seemed to her like the howling or crying of animals. I didn't hear that. Again I got that strange drowsyness & kept waking with starts & trying to remember what I had heard & not succeeding, that was all. I shall try again for I felt I ought to be able to get better results with it.'

## To Lady Gregory, [*1 June 1907*]

HEN AND CHICKENS HOTEL, | BIRMINGHAM,
Saturday

My dear Lady Gregory: my Oxford address will be C/o George Herbert
Mair, Christ Church, Oxford.[1]

I am afraid the gilded cloak has been forgotten & packed up. It is not
however being used at Oxford as they find Kerrigan looks better—they
say—without it. It will be sent to Robert from Oxford.[2]

There has been trouble about fines. We should not have given it to Mac
in Dublin. He has led a general revolt on the subject & [?threatened] to go
back to Dublin to night (though Fay says he would not have carried this
out). We have had to give in for the moment, but I told them that means of
keeping dicipline would be settled at the end of the tour. I saw Fay last
night & he has made a suggestion which I am going to talk over with Payne.
It seems practical & may save stern measures. There have been two
occasions on which Mac & others have been late. Fay says Payne is too
anxious but has much improved the dicipline.[3]

Yr ev
W B Yeats

ALS Berg, with envelope addressed to Coole, redirected to the Euston Hotel, London,
postmark 'BIRMINGHAM JU 1 07'.

---

[1] George Herbert Mair (1887–1926) had been educated at Aberdeen University, and was on the
platform with WBY during his lecture there in January 1906 (see p. 316, n. 5). He was now reading
modern history at Christ Church, Oxford, and, after graduating in 1909, joined the staff of the
*Manchester Guardian*, acting as leader-writer, literary editor, and political correspondent in the London
office from 1911 to 1914. He was an enthusiastic supporter of the Abbey Theatre, especially after his
marriage to Maire O'Neill in 1911, and marshalled the influence of the *Manchester Guardian* on its
behalf. In 1914 he was appointed assistant editor of the *Daily Chronicle*, but resigned on the outbreak of
the First World War to join the Ministry of Information. In 1919 he became an assistant director in the
League of Nations Secretariat.

[2] The gilded cloak was for Kerrigan's role as the Young Man (Cuchulain's son) in *On Baile's Strand*,
performed at Oxford on 4 June.

[3] The Directors had instituted a system of fines for unpunctuality at the Abbey after the indiscipline
of the 1906 tour (see p. 437), but this was not working, and when Sinclair's salary had recently been
docked by 1*s*. AG tacitly made up the difference out of her own pocket to keep the peace. Despite this,
trouble had flared up over the matter on 31 May, when Sinclair wrote to her (Berg) asking whether it
was true that 'the previous fine imposed upon me in Dublin . . . had never been removed' and whether
the 1*s*. 'was a gift from you': 'Will you please let me know . . . as I feel very much hurt over the matter. I
have handed back the 1/- to Mr Payne.' In *Life in a Wooden O* Payne described the problem (71–2):
'Although constant preparation of new plays necessitated daily rehearsals, I found that the actors had a
most casual attitude toward them. This astonished and infuriated me, for I had always found prompt-
ness to be the rule. The actors had signed contracts that followed the long-established custom in
stipulating that the actor must attend rehearsals promptly but "with ten minutes grace for difference of

## To Lady Gregory, [*7 June 1907*]

18 Woburn Buildings | Euston Road

My dear Lady Gregory:

I enclose a letter, which I have just received from Miss Horniman. When you have read it you will understand at once that I have no choice but must resign my position of managing director or countinance a breach of faith with those in our employ.[1] I therefore resign. Please send this letter & enclosure to Synge.[2] I have no time to write more than this <but will see you at> at this moment. Her conduct is of course scandalous.

Yrs ever
W B Yeats

[*With enclosure, marked in WBY's hand:* 'Arrangement about Payne breaks down'.]

East Gate Hotel, | Oxford.
June 6th,/07.

Dear Demon,

I wish that you had told me a little more explicitly that our verbal arrangement that Fay should have a £100 a year to pay him for the production of Irish peasant plays *& to give up stage management* has proved impracticable. I was not surprised because of a remark made on Tuesday

clocks." The English interpretation of the rule was that rehearsals began at the time they were called, but, unless an actor regularly took advantage of the leeway, he could not be censured if he arrived during the first ten minutes. At the Abbey Theatre the actors' reading of the contractual obligation was different. They maintained that a rehearsal called for eleven o'clock should not begin until eleven-ten. Consequently, the actors generally began to arrive ten minutes after the hour. If they showed up, as they frequently did, at a quarter past, they claimed, "After all, we were only five minutes late!" ... After many appeals against this loss of time, I did sometimes succeed in starting rehearsals a little earlier than the previous custom, but to little avail.

[1] AEFH purported to believe that W. G. Fay was still stage managing (i.e. directing) for the Abbey, in breach of the arrangement which had led to the hiring of Payne (see p. 597). Although he had given up most of his stage-managing duties it had been agreed, as AEFH knew, that he should continue to take care of 'dialect' plays (see pp. 622–3). It is probable that AEFH had already decided to abandon the Abbey for her new theatrical venture in Manchester, and was engineering ways of cutting down her Dublin expenses and alienating WBY from his fellow Directors. Her attitude may also have been shaped by her conversations with Payne, who, as he was to tell WBY on 22 June (see p. 672, n. 1), thought the Abbey Company 'unsuited to your verse work', and that his own attempts to direct WBY's plays had been thwarted by animosity towards him, so that he had concentrated on business rather than artistic duties.

[2] AG may not have sent these letters on to Synge as he was just about to arrive in London from Devon, where he had been staying with Jack Yeats, and was himself unsure of his London address (*JMSCL* 1. 366). Since she was actively helping WBY to orchestrate this protest, the request was in any case rhetorical.

(or Monday) night by Lady Gregory in my presence which led up to what you said yesterday. I am very disappointed that your works should not get the fair chance I have tried my best to give them. Mr. Synge's plays would gain immensely if they were properly stage-managed & so would Lady Gregory's, & it is sad that they will not allow yours to have the advantage they object to for themselves.

I am not blaming you for not telling me before, indeed you said something to me before going to Italy, about some arrangement for Vaughan seeing after things "behind" when Mr Payne had to be "in front".[3] So maybe you were not clear on the subject & you were only two days in London. I don't know what the other directors imagined that Fay had that £100 for from me personally. Perhaps they did not grasp the situation.

I'm very glad that you told me in good time as those two extra salaries are not paid into the bank until the 15th.[4] Of course Fay's ceases at once now that I find that the contract could not be carried out. I fear that the other directors have put you into an uncomfortable position, but they cannot surely expect me to take any other course of action.

One point of "business" in last night's Playboy would give just grounds for offence so I have written to Mr Payne about it. I did not mention the name of the player concerned. As he was engaged as stage manager I don't see who else I should write to.

Henderson (I believe) came & spoke to me last night, I really don't know why. I let him see clearly that I would have nothing to do with him. It was an [?]embarrassing thing being alone in the stalls under the gaze of an interested pit; I did not want to afford them an extra entertainment.[5]

I had a cheque from Cramers' yesterday for £42.15.

Yours
Annie

ALS Berg; enclosure NLI.

[3] Ernest Vaughan was an old friend of the Fays; he had acted regularly in their Ormond Dramatic Society in the late 1890s, and introduced them to Dudley Digges, who recalled him at that time as a 'thrilling' reciter, 'a tall figure in a long black cloak and a large Fedora hat.... looking like the embodiment of Irving, Tree and Robertson', and who 'spoke of the stage with . . . authority and elocutionary style' (*Fays of the Abbey*, 68–9). He made his debut at the Abbey on 13 Apr of this year as Conchubar in *On Baile's Strand*, when he impressed Holloway 'by the dignity of his bearing, finish of his diction & musical quality of his full impressive voice tones'. He also performed well at Glasgow, and he was appointed business manager of the Abbey Company after the departure of Payne.

[4] i.e. the extra salary paid to W. G. Fay (see p. 622), and that due to Payne, since in AEFH's eyes the whole agreement had collapsed.

[5] W. A. Henderson had become the latest in the long line of AEFH's aversions. She had been suspicious of him from the first, and narrowly circumscribed the limits of his duties on his appointment. Thereafter she noted every minor lapse in his work, but really took against him after the inclusion of

## *To A. E. F. Horniman, [7 June 1907]*

My dear Miss H——

I have received your astounding letter.[1] You know as well as I do that Payne has my plays entirely in his hands with the exception of the two dialect ones. I am the person responsible for having brought the company into business relations with you & from the matter of your letter I feel it impossible to remain as Managing director——I have therefore written my resignation & sent it to Lady Gregory[2] asking her to forward it to Synge—— It will be for them to consider whether they will continue the theatre or not——

*[unsigned]*

AL draft, dict AG; Berg.

W. G. Fay's name on the new Abbey stationery (see p. 647), for which she suspected he was responsible. He fanned her anger by neglecting to reply to her letters on this matter, and on 25 May she instructed Payne to dismiss him from the Abbey tour, but assured WBY that, since he was employed by the Directors, his position in Dublin was not her affair. Unluckily, she was later to see an ill-advised letter from Henderson to Payne, which she thought insulted her, and she began to urge WBY to dismiss him altogether. On 26 Oct Henderson, unaware of all this, told Holloway (NLI) that the only thing he regretted 'was not making up to Miss Horniman when on tour. Want of push ruined his chance!'

[1] This is one of two drafts of WBY's response to AEFH's letter of 6 June (see above). Since it is the more coherent and succinct of the two, it is probably close to the final version. The less controlled version (Berg), also written from the Euston Hotel, but in WBY's own hand, read:

EUSTON HOTEL. | LONDON.

Dear M——

Your letter is either unnecessary or entirely scandalous. Payne has all my plays in his hands except two that are in dialect, & all arrangements have been made by him as general manager. You know <this> as well as I do. I am very surprised that you would rather find [?]dishonesty. It was [?]unfortunately through me that you came in association with the Irish dramatic movement. Considering this I have <resigned from the Society as your letter is not> sent my resign[ation] in writing to my fellow directors. I have sent it to Euston Hotel & asked Lady Gregory to send it to Synge. It will be the duty of my fellow directors to decide whether the <society> theatre is to go <on> or not.

It, too, was unsigned. The letter was not only written with AG's physical help, but apparently at her insistence. While she was staying with him in New York in 1912, John Quinn—although erroneously placing the incident at Coole and perhaps conflating it with an exchange involving Edmund Gosse (see *Mem*, 289–91)— recorded her complaint (NLI) 'that Yeats' subservience to Miss Horniman had been a disgrace; that her letters had been an insult; that she had written accusing them of cheating in the accounts, and Lady Gregory then said that Yeats would have to reply to that letter or leave her place, that Yeats was her guest. Yeats finally dictated a reply which Lady Gregory took as though to send. She said Yeats was very unhappy and finally she handed the letter back to him.' Although WBY's reply was evidently not delivered, and although he did not resign as Managing Director of the Abbey, the affair brought to a head the long-standing grievances between AEFH and the Directors, and she announced her intention of withdrawing from the Abbey Theatre as soon as she was legally able to do so.

[2] WBY had not 'sent' the letter to AG at the Euston Hotel but had been summoned there by her so that she could make sure he wrote an appropriately uncompromising response.

## *To A. E. F. Horniman, [18 June 1907]*

18 Woburn Buildings | Euston Road
<Mond> Tuesday

My dear Miss Horniman: I have thought carefully over your proposal of yesterday & have decided that it is impossible so far as I am concerned. I am not young enough to change my nationality—it would really amount to that.[1] Though I wish for a universal audience, in play-writing there is always an immediate audience also. If I were to try & find that immediate audience in England I would fail through lack of understanding on my part perhaps through lack of sympathy.[2] I understand my own race & in all my work, lyric or dramatic I have thought of it. If the theatre fails I may or may not write plays,—there is always lyric poetry to return to—but I shall write for my own people—whether in love or hate of them matters little— probably I shall not know which it is. Nor can I make any permament allocation of my plays while the Irish theatre may at any moment need my

---

[1] Much had happened since WBY's outraged response of 7 June. In a letter written to WBY on 24 July, AEFH recalled that he had come to see her with Payne on 16 June and they had suggested that she should immediately set up 'another theatrical scheme', using the Abbey 'as a "pied à terre" ': 'Next day after considering the matter I concluded that Dublin would not be suitable for the purpose & various towns were proposed, Manchester amongst them. Next day you backed out from the scheme which you had suggested yourself.' A few days later she returned to these matters, adding (NLI) more circumstantial detail:

(a) Proposal of Theatre Company with Dublin head-quarters—
I discussed this with you & Mr Payne. You started with a proposal of a "Company" & I flatly refused at once to have anything of business relations again with Lady Gregory & Mr. Synge or any other directors. I most certainly did *not* accept the idea except as a matter to think over. By the next morning I came to the conclusion that I could not ask actors with my *social* friends in Dublin to accept the obloquy of connection with the Abbey Theatre there. This was quite settled in my mind (an additional reason to the knowledge that Fay would obstruct everything) that it would be unwise to start at Dublin.

(b) Your attitude as to another town was uncertain but you seemed at the time to see difficulties. Some days *later* when Fay forbade you to permit it, you saw the facts of the case.

Now all I ask is that you inform Mr. Henderson that *you* joined with Mr. Payne in proposing that I should do something further, that it was not his personal separate idea to cajole me into it.

Next day from the above (b) came your letter saying that you were not free to help me. I never objected to that, I completely accept that you are right to follow your own conscience.

On 17 June AEFH had also announced, as AG reported to Synge in a letter of 20 June (Saddlemyer, 223), that she would have no more to do with the Abbey Theatre: 'Wld just continue the subsidy she was bound to, & open a Theatre elsewhere—in Manchester probably. She will capitalise her £25,000 & put it into this, will make Payne Manager, & asked Yeats to be a sort of Head Manager, & to assign his plays to her for a term of years.'

[2] WBY believed that this applied to all writers, and in 1901 wrote (*E & I*, 109–10) that he could 'never get out of my head that no man, even though he be Shakespeare, can write perfectly when his web is woven of threads that have been spun in many lands'.

help. At any moment I may have to appeal to friends for funds with the whole mass of plays for a bait.

[*Unsigned*]

AL NLI. Wade, 500–1.

## *To A. E. F. Horniman,* [c. *20 June 1907*]

Mention in letter from AEFH, 21 June 1907.
Discussing the resignation of Payne from the management of the Abbey Theatre,[1] telling her that his health is not good.[2]

NLI.

[1] Payne wrote to WBY on 22 June (Saddlemyer, 225–6) giving his reasons for resigning from the Abbey, a decision about which he had already informed WBY several days before: 'My chief contention is that an English manager is out of place in an Irish national theatre. I have only come to this conclusion after very careful consideration. Then, again, when engaged by you it was clearly stated that for obvious reasons the peasant plays should not come under my control, but that my energies were to be devoted to the verse plays and foreign masterpieces. My experience with the company has brought me to the conclusion that their capacities are, on the whole, unsuited to your verse work, that it should be wasting my time if I attempted to go on with an impossible task, and that it is only fair to you and your work to let you clearly understand this. In fact, my first thought of resigning at all arose from my inability to carry out the very thing for which I had been brought to Ireland. Then I must confess that I had a personal distaste to benefiting financially where there was clearly a misunderstanding between the Directors and Miss Horniman as to the extent of my functions. Finally, though my personal relations with the company have been entirely friendly, it is useless to disguise the fact that, officially, they can only feel antagonism towards an English manager, and this must have the effect of stultifying all my efforts. For some time I have practically been justifying myself for receiving my salary by concentrating my attention upon the business part of the work.' This letter, which confirmed all AEFH's worst suspicions about the Abbey, was written at her suggestion, as she told WBY in her reply (NLI): 'I have asked Mr Payne to let me have a formal reason in writing of the cause of his resignation & I said that a copy of his formal letter to the Directors would be better than one to me. I want this so that I can justify my present attitude to anyone who considers that I am about to "spoil the ship for a bucket of tar".'
[2] AEFH replied that she was 'very anxious' about WBY's health and 'very sad that circumstances prevent me from being able to help to cure you. I would wish to clear away the difficulties which come between you & the quiet & leisure needed for the fine work we have a right to demand from you. That my scheme has hampered and hindered you instead of being a help is a sorrow to me.'

## To Eveleen Myers,[1] *21 June 1907*

18, Woburn Buildings, | Euston Road,
June 21, 1907.

Dear Mrs. Myers,

I hope you will forgive having left your letter unanswered those few days. It was very kind of you to ask me.[2] I had a slight breakdown from overwork and lost grip of my letters for two or three days.

Yours sny
W B Yeats

TLS Trinity College, Cambridge.

## To W. G. Fay, *21 June 1907*

18, Woburn Buildings, | Euston Road,
June 21, 1907.

My dear Fay,

After I saw you I went through accounts with Miss Horniman. You will see that instead of taking and spending as you thought £1500 we have only taken a little over £500.[1] You will also notice that instead of the normal salary list going as you thought beyond the subsidy it does not even when Vaughan is added, with something more than Henderson's salary[2] and

---

[1] Eveleen Myers, née Tennant (1855–1937), was the widow of Frederic W. H. Myers, an inspector of schools and president of the Society for Physical Research, whom she had married on 13 Mar 1880, and who had died in 1901.

[2] Mrs Myers had invited WBY to a large dinner on 26 June, to which she had also asked the Norwegian Arctic explorer Fridtjof Nansen (1861–1930), who was currently Norwegian ambassador in London, and the American writer Mark Twain (1835–1910).

[1] On 19 June WBY, AG and W. G. Fay had held an emergency meeting to discuss policy in the light of AEFH's withdrawal from the Abbey Theatre. As AG informed Synge on 20 June (Saddlemyer, 223–6), 'we came to the conclusion that if she wld. give us the whole sum for the 2 years at once, we could if we thought well tour in Ireland, likely English places, & possibly American, & try for support instead of fizzling out. Fay assured us (on Henderson's authority) that we had made £1500 last season, & had spent it as well as our subsidy — & could not get on in a less good season with Miss H's £800.' AG went on to reveal that WBY had gone to see AEFH in the evening and 'unluckily told her Fays story about the £1500 (which on thinking over I had known to be impossible) & this did not make his task easier, as she got out the account of shows & corrected him'.

[2] Ernest Vaughan (see p. 669, n. 3) was appointed business manager of the Abbey Company after the departure of Payne, holding this post from the summer of 1907 until April 1908, although the Directors soon lost trust in him. In *Ireland's Abbey Theatre*, the long-serving Abbey caretaker Mrs Martin recalled him (68) as 'a very nice gentleman. He was very keen on the laundry bills, he would query other bills and would use his axe on the green-room bills, he failed to pay all the bills. He could not make ends meet; however his stay was brief.'

when Miss Allgood's is raised 10/- a week go beyond £728 per annum. I am assuming of course that the figures which I enclose are correct. You will see also from the note by Miss Horniman that a sum has accumulated at the bank in Dublin, equivalent to the salaries of the Company if they stayed at home for five weeks. There is a further sum of £250 which comes to us to pay for tours.[3] I want you to meet Payne and me one day next week, either Monday or Tuesday, Tuesday perhaps. Perhaps you might write to him direct and let me know or tell him to let me know as soon as possible, what time will suit you. It is necessary that we go through the whole situation together and engage Vaughan, give Henderson notice, decide when to play during Exhibition if we are to play.[4]

Yr sy
W B Yeats

[*With enclosure*][5]

| 1906. | £. | s. | d. | |
|---|---|---|---|---|
| Nov.26th to Dec.1st | 49. | 0. | 2. | |
| Dec.8th to Dec.15th | 56. | 8. | 5. | |
| Dec.29th to Jan.5th | 46. | 6. | 7 | |
| Jan.12th (two shows) | 34. | 9. | 5. | |
| Jan.19th (two shows) | 36. | 10. | 3. | |
| Jan.26th to Feb. 3rd | 158. | 10. | 1 | (Playboy) |
| Feb.9th (two shows) | 24. | 17. | 11. | |
| Feb.23rd to March 2nd | 24. | 19. | 10. | |
| March 9th (two shows) | 23. | 7. | 10. | |
| March 16th (two shows) | 16. | 2. | 2. | |
| March 23rd (two shows) | 11. | 16. | 5. | |
| April 1st to April 6th (8 shows) | 30. | 0. | 11. | |
| April 13th (two shows) | 7. | 15. | 4. | |

---

[3] AEFH had promised to send this on 21 June, 'to be used as a touring fund', but warned him (NLI) that when sending it 'I intend to add a remark that *I* consider the refusal to go on with Playboy in London as a *political* action, but that knowing the Directors' views on the subject of the cowardice of the company, I accept their views (or rather act on them) this time. But it must be kept in mind that my original proviso, that I have the right to put a stop to everything & to close the theatre if it be used for political purposes or propaganda must & will remain in force.' She was to invoke this proviso in May 1910 when the theatre remained open on the day that the King's death was announced.

[4] This was the Irish International Exhibition, opened by the Lord-Lieutenant on 4 May. It was a huge success, attracting nearly three million people before closing in November, despite a very wet summer. When Synge attended in May, he wrote to Maire O'Neill: 'there are good things in it. The Somali village especially is curious. A bit of the war-song the niggers were singing was exactly like some of the keens on Aran' (*JMSCL* 1. 343–4). The Abbey did not mount any productions there.

[5] The plays to which these receipts refer are listed in the Appendix, pp. 856–8.

| April 20th (two shows) | 13. | 0. | 11. |
| April 27th (two shows) | 11. | 3. | 5. |

|  | 544. | 9. | 10 |
| Subsidy to | 800. | 0. | 0. |
| June 1st. | | | |

|  | £1344. | 9. | 10. |

Subsidy of £200 paid
Sept. 1st, Dec. 1st., March 1st.,
June 1st., making £800 in all.

During this tour the complete salaries have been paid by me out of a separate fund and as there is a deficit I do not ask for their return. So for five weeks the general salaries have been allowed to accumulate in the bank at Dublin.

June 19th, 1907.          A. E. F. Horniman.

*Salary List on Tour, May 1907.*

|  | £. | s. | d. |
|---|---|---|---|
| W.G. Fay | 4. | 18. | 6. |
| F.J. Fay | 3. | 0. | 0. |
| E. Vaughan | 3. | 0. | 0. |
| Arthur Sinclair | 2. | 10. | 0. |
| U. Wright | 2. | 10. | 0. |
| J.A. O'Rourke | 2. | 2. | 6. |
| J.M. Kerrigan | 2. | 0. | 0. |
| J. Byrne (carpenter) | 1. | 10. | 0. |
| B. Iden Payne | 6. | 0. | 0. |
| W.A. Henderson | 2. | 10. | 0. |
| Sara Allgood | 3. | 0. | 0. |
| Maire O'Neill | 2. | 0. | 0. |
| Brigit O'Dempsey | 2. | 0. | 0. |
| Annie Allgood | 1. | 5. | 0. |
| Cathleen Mullamphy | 1. | 5. | 0. |

|  | £39. | 11. | 0. |

*Salary List.* (Subsidy)

|                    | £.    | s.   | d.  |
|--------------------|-------|------|-----|
| W. G. Fay          | 2.    | 0.   | 0.  |
| F. J. Fay          | 2.    | 0.   | 0.  |
| Arthur Sinclair    | 1.    | 10.  | 0.  |
| J. M. Kerrigan     | 1.    | 0.   | 0.  |
| J. A. O'Rourke     | 1.    | 0.   | 0.  |
| W. A. Henderson    | 1.    | 10.  | 0.  |
| Sara Allgood       | 1.    | 10.  | 0.  |
| Maire O'Neill      | 1.    | 0.   | 0.  |
| Brigit O'Dempsey   | 1.    | 0.   | 0.  |
|                    | £12.  | 10.  | 0.  |

I have put down only the Salaries which I understand come from the subsidy. Vaughan was first engaged only for tour at £3 special engagement; then he was taken on until starting at £1.1.0.
Salaries including Vaughan
£1 and 10/- more for        makes

£
14
52
28
70
£728

[*In WBY's hand in margin*] This Miss H's comment. £1 more for Vaughan is too much. I would offer 10/- more than Henderson had if he can do the work—

Orchestra, Stage bands, Gas and Light, Cleaning, Advertisements, Small repairs to be paid from receipts.

TLS NLI.

## *To Richard Ellis Roberts,*[1] *25 June 1907*

18, Woburn Buildings, | Euston Road, N.W.

June 25th, 1907.

Dear Mr. Roberts,

Your note and its enclosure came at a time when I was desperately busy, and until the last couple of days I have been unable for the most part to give any sort of serious attention to my correspondence. Of course I agree with you about the scandal of such writing as that you describe. I feel at the same time that it would be a mistake for a writer of my sort to join in such a protest as you propose. It would look too much like an attempt to ward off similar criticism from ones self. If a protest is to be it should be made by people of position who are not in the same world where Shaw is fighting his battle.[2]

---

[1] Richard Ellis Roberts (1879–1953), short-story writer and literary journalist, had been educated at St John's College, Oxford, and joined the staff of the *Pall Mall Gazette* from 1903 to 1905. He was now a freelance journalist and subsequently became literary editor of the *New Statesman* and *Time and Tide*. His *Poems* had appeared in 1906, and among his other books are a volume of short stories, *The Other End* (1923), *Reading for Pleasure and Other Essays* (1928), and a translation of Ibsen's *Peer Gynt* (1936). He reviewed Joseph Hone's first biography of WBY in the *Bookman* in August 1916, *The Tower* in the same periodical in April 1928, and *Collected Poems* (1933) in the *News Chronicle* on 24 Jan 1934 under the headline 'The Greatest Living Master in English'. WBY came to admire Roberts's journalism in the 1930s, when he became a friend of him and his wife, and invited him to his sixty-eighth birthday dinner.

[2] Roberts had evidently sent WBY a copy of 'Mr. Shaw's Antics', an unrestrained hostile review of G. Bernard Shaw's *Dramatic Opinions and Essays* by the poet and critic Alfred Noyes which had appeared in the *Bookman* of May 1907 (59–60). Maintaining that these 'two volumes of vulgarism require straight speaking from any critic who has managed to retain the slightest respect for English literature', Noyes attacked Shaw's style, shallow wit, and vanity, and his alleged contempt for actors, dramatists living and dead, the public, love, and Christianity: 'Intellectually he is beneath contempt. Artistically he appeals only to pseudo-philosophers.... Let us also be honest. Are we not all a little tired of this blatant self-puffery? Is it not time to cease echoing the empty laughter of the mentally bankrupt admirers of this clever person? We know nothing more vulgar than the crude vanity displayed in these two volumes.... He would pride himself on unmanliness and on vanity, we are quite aware.... Let him also pride himself on the fact that his reputation even for wit is rapidly on the wane; that even his feeblest admirers are growing tired of him; and that the great writers and poets on whom he has discoursed with so sublime an ignorance (admitted, of course) have no need of a guard about the lasting monuments on which he has tried to pose his own ludicrous naked statue.... it is our duty to the great and famous dead, the duty of all sincere critics with a respect for our literature, to say that Mr. Shaw's capers are vulgar, fatuous, and extremely wearisome.'

[*In WBY's hand*] Noyes[3] attacked me some years ago though not so violently.[4]

Yr ev

W B Yeats

TLS Texas.


# *To W. A. Henderson,* [*25 June 1907*]

Mention in following letter, and letter to AG, 27 June 1907. Dismissing Henderson on grounds of the need for economy and of making the post full-time,[1] reminding him 'very politely' that he had been engaged in the belief that he had a thorough knowledge of bookkeeping,[2] and asking for a full statement of the Abbey accounts, to be made out with Swayne's asssistance.

---

WBY had last met Shaw at the Abbey productions at the Great Queen Street Theatre on 12 June, when Nancy Maude saw them (TCD) 'talking together in the stalls', but Shaw had subsequently corresponded with AEFH over the future of the Abbey, and told her (NLI) that she 'should "get some one to pull that company together"'.

[3] Alfred Noyes (1880–1958), a popular and prolific poet, novelist, critic, and biographer, became the first writer since Tennyson to live by his poetry. He spent most of his childhood on the coast of Wales at Aberystwyth, and in 1898 went up to Oxford, but left without taking a degree shortly before the publication of his first book of verse, *The Loom of Years*. He is best known for his poem 'The Highwayman', his epic *Drake* (1906–8), his multi-volume depictions of the evolution of modern science, and his biography of Voltaire. From 1914 to 1923 he was Professor of English at Princeton University, after which he returned to England and was received into the Catholic Church in 1927. In October 1903 WBY had praised *The Loom of Years* (1902; *YL*, 1461), as 'full of beautiful things' (III. 455). However, in a letter to Gogarty of 2 Feb 1922 (Bucknell) WBY gave as one of his reasons for moving from Oxford that 'a woman today & in a quite respectable house recommended me to read Noyes'. In February 1937 WBY was to name Noyes in his poem 'Roger Casement' as among those who had slandered Casement, but withdrew his name and apologized after Noyes's 'noble letter' to the *Irish Press*, explaining his position. A conservative critic, Noyes had little sympathy with contemporary and modernist literature.

[4] Noyes had tilted at WBY (although not by name) in his obituary of 'Fiona Macleod', published in the *Bookman* in January 1906. Insisting that Macleod's sincere Celtic voice 'came from the same depths as a mediaeval soul', he warned (172) that it 'must not be confused with the voices of the Pseudo-Celtic revival.... There is no crystal-gazing, or alchemy, or magic, or imitation of Maeterlinck in the works of this Celt. Neither is there any description of those extraordinary ladies in Bedford Park, whose long, lank tresses—if one may trust the impression one gathers from the Celtic Revivalists—are so incessantly combed by pale young men in spectacles.'

[1] In fact, Henderson had been dismissed largely at the behest of AEFH (see p. 669, n. 5).

[2] Henderson did not accept that a knowledge of bookkeeping was part of the remit for his post, and in a letter of 4 July to AG Synge agreed (*JMSCL* II. 4) that he was 'technically right about the book-keeping as he read me Yeats' letter going through all his duties and book-keeping was not mentioned.'

## To John Millington Synge, 25 June [1907]

18, Woburn Buildings, | Euston Road, N.W.
June 25.

My dear Synge,

I had a consultation this morning with Payne and Fay, and Fay and I had one with Lady Gregory last week. A result of both consultations has been that I have just written to Henderson, giving him notice on the ground of the necessity of greater economy and of having the whole time of whoever takes up his work. We propose to give his work to Vaughan and Fay will have written to Vaughan probably before you get this. Now I want you to see Henderson and to ask him to get a complete statement of our accounts made out up to date. Liabilities and assets. Swayne should be engaged to write up books. I am sorry to burden you with this but it is absolutely essential.[1] Payne, as you know, is going[2] and we are on a fixed subsidy and must be self-supporting by the end of the patent period. You can arrange with Henderson for him to remain on until the end of the holidays when Vaughan can take up his work. There is no use making Henderson an enemy, so you might please impress upon him the inevitableness of the whole thing. I have reminded him, though very politely, that we engaged him in the belief that he had a thorough knowledge of book-keeping. I have done this merely that it may be there in the letter in case he brings it to old

[1] Swayne, Little & Company were the Abbey Theatre's accountants. In his reply of 27 June (*JMSCL* I. 372–3) Synge said that he had seen Henderson, who at first 'seemed rather sad, and inclined to think he was being very badly treated, but he rather cheered up.... As to statement of accounts he says that if a mere statement of how we stand is needed he can make it out easily himself, but if we want a ballance sheet we should have to get Swayne as you suggested. I am not sure from your letter which you want so I have told him to ask you.'

[2] Payne had formally resigned on 22 June (see p. 672). In *Life in a Wooden O* (77) he notes that the 'last performance at the Great Queen Street Theatre also saw the termination of my work with the Irish National Theatre. After I had handed in my resignation I saw no more of the directors, except Yeats. He was upset and expressed regret that I was leaving them, but he understood my reasons for doing so.' Summing up his work at the Abbey (73–4), Payne thought that little needed be said: 'In retrospect I look upon my sojourn there as a kind of interlude, for during the few months I lived in Dublin I never felt that I was striking root. I cannot say that the actors were antagonistic to my directions, but I was conscious that we were not working fully in harmony. Or rather, to put it more precisely, I felt myself inadequate in trying to express what I wanted to say in language to which they could respond. Also, I still thought of myself primarily as an actor, and obviously there was no place for me in that capacity with the Abbey Theatre company. I was in a blind alley and I knew that before long I should have to find my way out of it. Meanwhile, I worked conscientiously and, apart from producing two Yeats plays, *The Shadowy Waters* and *Deirdre*; *Fand*, by Wilfrid Scawen Blunt; and Maeterlinck's beautiful one-act play *Interior*, I was able, with some difficulty, to make a few improvements in the technical handling of the plays.' On 27 Feb 1908 WBY reported to AG (Berg) that Ambrose Power had told him 'that Fay worked the company into a state of hostility to Payne, talking to them one by one, while himself keeping civil enough. At last they would not answer on the stage when Payne spoke to them. "I often" said Power, "used to pity the poor little man" I said to Power "Payne made no complaint to me about Fay" Power said "For all that he must have known what had happened".'

Sigerson, or to Oldham.[3] Fay, I regret to say, has to go back into management with Vaughan under him. There seemed to be no other way, as there must be some person constantly on the spot to see that things are done, and as Fay now knows he is working for his own ultimate livelihood, he will keep a closer watch on things than anybody we could get for the small sum we could afford. I am the one who will suffer, as his little evasions and fits of temper exasperate me more than the rest of you.[4] I tried every kind of device in my imagination but none seemed possible.

Yours sry<br>W B Yeats

TLS TCD. Saddlemyer, 227–8.

## To Lady Gregory, 27 June 1907

18, Woburn Buildings, W.C.<br>27th June, 1907.

My dear Friend;

I don't think I shall stay much longer here. I am very anxious to get to some sort of routine work, and I imagine that theatrical things won't keep me much longer. A proposal from Mrs. Patrick Campbell to do Deirdre if Miss Horniman will help her to start a syndicate will take me a little time. I hope it won't come to anything as I think Miss Horniman would lose her money, but out of politeness to Mrs. Campbell I have to put the case. Mrs. Emery proposed it to me, and though I told her I was against it, spoke to Mrs. Campbell and invited me to meet her without giving me time to get out of it. She did this because she thought that it would make Mrs. Campbell interested in my work whether it came to anything or not. I find however, that I don't make a good intriguer and I told Mrs. Campbell my doubts and difficulties. I think at the bottom of Mrs. Emery's heart, the impulse is love of mischief. She wants to see Miss Horniman and Mrs. Campbell in partnership. She said that it would be a sight for gods and

---

[3] Both Sigerson and Oldham had recommended Henderson for the post at the Abbey (see pp. 443, 477). Synge himself, as he pointed out in his letter of 27 June, did 'not feel sure that we are wise to get rid of Henderson altogether as he was certainly of use in bringing us in audiences. From one reason or another we are all unpopular and it was a good thing to have one man in the place who was definitely popular in Dublin. However we could not keep him at his present salary or in his present position, and I suppose it would only make complications if we tried to keep him on in any sort of minor position as Master of the Ceremonies.'

[4] AG had already alerted Synge to this problem in her letter of 20 June (see p. 671, n. 1): 'The real danger ahead is the way Fay & Yeats irritate each other.'

men. Mrs. Campbell's object is to get rid of a Jewish capitalist, who wants to advance himself socially.[1]

I got Fay and Payne together last Tuesday. We went through our finances as well as we could with imperfect material. We decided upon a tour to Glasgow, Edinburgh and Manchester in advent which is no use to us in Dublin.[2] It had to be decided at once as Payne had arranged to let the theatre know within a certain number of days. Fay was very anxious for it, and both Payne and Fay thought failure impossible. I am doubtful of Edinburgh, but their figures seem conclusive. I have dismissed Henderson, leaving it to Synge to settle the exact date at which Henderson ceases to act.[3] I have asked Henderson for a full statement of our accounts — this to be made out with Swayne's assistance. Fay will have to be manager with Vaughan under him. When we went into the matter in detail, there seemed to be no other solution — at least that was Payne's view which I regretfully accepted. It will matter less because I shall have to keep out of the practical work, at any rate for a very considerable time. I think I had better make an excuse of my collected edition and say that I can take up no business work of any kind until that is finished. I was better last week, but have not been well the last few days. In addition to all that, I feel that I have lost myself — my centre as it were, has shifted from its natural interests, and that it will take me a long time finding myself again. Miss Horniman wants me to resign from the theatre entirely, but I am afraid to do that, as I think my presence in it is a protection to it against her capriciousness. I am afraid that if I were out, she might declare some play or other was political, and break her promise on its account. She has come to no decision yet about the

---

[1] WBY's hope was fulfilled and nothing came of the scheme. On 2 July AEFH wrote to him (NLI): 'I told Mrs Patrick Campbell my exact full income & said that I could not afford to run a theatre & company to support her. If she were to get capitalists together I should be the earthen pitcher floating down the stream with the bronze bowl, I wrote too. I told her that you had mentioned names I believe prompted by Mrs Emery. But I did not tell her the names. That seemed to be only fair to you. . . . You need not fear that I shall give way, if for no other reason that I would not wish to injure Mrs Emery, yet on the other hand I would not be mixed up in anything connected with her. Mrs Campbell must either be horribly hard up or else think me extremely wealthy & easily persuaded.'

[2] Advent, the period including the four Sundays before Christmas, is a time of abstinence and spiritual reflection for Catholics, and potentially meant diminished audiences for plays in Dublin (see p.492). Consequently the Abbey Company went on tour after completing their autumn season on 23 Nov with the first performances of *The Unicorn from the Stars*. They played 26–30 Nov at the Midland Theatre, Manchester, following this with successive weeks at the King's Theatre, Glasgow, and the Lyceum Theatre, Edinburgh. Their next scheduled performance in Dublin was on 26 Dec. The Theatre of Ireland had fewer qualms about Advent and performed at the Abbey on 13 and 14 Dec this year to reasonable houses.

[3] In his letter to WBY of 27 June (see p. 679, n. 1), Synge reported that Henderson had complained that 'it would be impossible for him to get anything to do at present, so that he thinks we should give him three months notice or its equivalent. We shall want him I suppose for two months, so it would probably be better to give him the extra month's salary and let him feel that he is being well treated by us.'

Manchester plan, but will not, I think again propose to me collaboration in that or any other project.[4]

I dined last night at Mrs. Myers to meet Reverend Mr. Campbell of the new theology. I was put next but one to him and should have been next him when the ladies withdrew, but luck was against it—I got no talk with him. He has a delicate, aesthetic face which interested me very much.[5] I however, got involved in a conversation about Fiona Macleod with the most elegant youth I ever set eyes on. He succeeded in looking like the young Disraeli in an old print with nothing but his waistcoat to work upon.[6] He is coming to me next Monday.

Yrs always
W B Yeats

[*In WBY's hand*]
I received the enclosed the other day. The society might well be of use to you.[7]

TLS Berg, with envelope addressed to Coole, postmark 'LONDON W.C. JU 27 07'.

---

[4] AEFH wanted WBY to leave the Abbey because she thought he was being exploited by the other Directors, a point she made very forcibly in an undated letter written at this time (NLI): 'Lady Gregory & Mr. Synge grovel at Fay's feet. They sacrifice your work & keep you a bond-slave to them because you are "touched" by that vampire Kathleen ni Houlihan. If they had wanted the theatre to become an Art Theatre they would have behaved very differently. But they only care to show themselves off to a small set in Dublin *at my expense*, without caring for anything beyond their own vanity.' AG was also concerned by the toll the theatre was taking on WBY's creativity, and told Synge on 29 June (Saddlemyer, 229), 'I am only sad about Yeats not getting his work done as he likes but we may beat out a way. I want him to do his next play in prose for acting, & put it into verse afterwards.'

[5] WBY had evidently been able to take up Mrs Myers's second invitation to dinner (see p. 673). The Revd. Reginald John Campbell (1867–1956) was descended from a line of Ulster Nonconformist ministers. He was educated at Nottingham and Christ Church, Oxford, and made his name as a preacher at Union Church, Brighton. In 1903 he was appointed minister of the City Temple in London, and remained there until 1915. He had published his most influential book, *The New Theology*, in March of this year and followed it up in 1908 with *Christianity and the Social Order*. He was ordained into the ministry of the Church of England in 1916, and in the same year published *A Spiritual Pilgrimage*. His articulation of the 'New Theology' was a response to a controversy which had broken among Nonconformists in January 1907 concerning his theological liberalism, and in *The New Theology* he explained (3–4) that he used the term 'to indicate the attitude of those who believe that the fundamentals of the Christian faith need to be rearticulated in terms of the immanence of God. Those who take this view do not hold that there is any need for a new religion, but that the forms in which the religion of Jesus is commonly presented are inadequate and misleading. . . . Its starting-point is a re-emphasis of the Christian belief in the Divine immanence in the universe and in mankind.' Campbell's account of the controversy which his book provoked, and which eventually led him to the Church of England, appears in *A Spiritual Pilgrimage*.

[6] The elegant youth is unidentified. Benjamin Disraeli, 1st Earl of Beaconsfield (1804–81), novelist, Conservative politician, and British Prime Minister in 1868 and 1874–80, was famous for his flamboyant style of dressing. WBY is perhaps thinking of one of the many prints by Daniel Maclise (1806–70), or of Kenneth Macleay's famous portrait (but now thought not to be of Disraeli), showing a young man with long black ringlets and wearing a cravat and jacket with wide lapels, or of Henry Robinson's 1840 engraving, after a portrait by Alfred Edward Chalon.

[7] The letter contains no enclosure and the name of the society is therefore uncertain, but WBY may have sent the brochure of 'The Play Actors', a dramatic club which had been founded earlier this month by members of the Actors Association to produce Shakespeare and 'other poetical dramatists without scenery or special costumes', to introduce the public to 'original plays by English authors', and to stage translations and adaptations of plays by foreign dramatists. The performances were to take place in the Bijou Theatre, off the Strand.

## *To W. A. Henderson, [June 1907]*

18 Woburn Building | Euston Road | London

My dear Henderson: I have been paying off accounts etc. My various type writer accounts are over £10 for the last few months.[1] A large part of this was dictation of letters apropos of the company, correspondence about Fay & Payne & actors parts Etc. I cannot work out the items even in actors parts as only one of the typewriters has as I asked kept accounts seperate, & in any case the dictation is mixed up. I shall not however be over charging the company if I put its share down as £5. Please let me have this when I get to Dublin but I send you this as a record

Yr ev
W B Yeats

ALS Kansas.


## *To H. J. C. Grierson, 28 June 1907*

18, Woburn Buildings, W.C.
28th June, 1907.

Dear Professor Grierson,

You wrote me a kind letter upon April 3rd, which I have never answered. I have been in Italy until three or four weeks ago, going from place to place, and finding correspondence very difficult, and since then the London visit of the theatre and various problems have brought with it have taken all my time. It was my conversation with you some time ago that sent me to Italy for it started me reading Gardners books about Ferrara, and in the end sent me to Ferrara.[1] In your letter you asked me to say a good word for a book of poems, but I have no way of saying it for I do no reviewing.[2] I am sorry that it is so, and you were kind enough to speak to McNeil Dickson about my

---

[1] WBY used a variety of typists in London, but his favourite was Miss Louise Jacobs, of the Misses Anderson & Jacobs agency, 38 Museum Street.

[1] A reference to *Dukes and Poets in Ferrara* (1904) and *King of Court Poets: A Study of the Work, Life and Times of Lodovico Ariosto* (1906) by Edmund Garratt Gardner (1869–1935), an Italian scholar who was to hold chairs of Italian literature and language in Manchester and London. Ferrara continued to hold its attraction for WBY and in his poem 'The People' (*VP*, 351–3) he articulates his longing to live 'Where everyday my footfall should have lit | In the green shadow of Ferrara wall'. AG recalled that WBY had 'set his heart on visiting Ferarra' during their Italian trip (see pp. 649–50, n. 2).

[2] Grierson had probably asked WBY to review his recently published *Poems of Tennyson*, a selection from Tennyson's work to which he also contributed an introduction.

giving a short course of lectures in Greenock.[3] Perhaps it may be possible for them to have me some day. For the moment I shall have to bury myself in revising my collected edition—eight volumes. I am feeling a good deal overworked, and am trying to cast off all practical and external activities.

Yr ever<br>W B Yeats

TLS NLS.

## To Henry G. O'Brien, 29 June 1907

18, Woburn Buildings | Euston Road, N.W.<br>June 29, 1907.

Dear Father O'Brien,

I am called away to Ireland unexpectedly and regret it more than anything else because it will make it impossible for me to meet you at present. I had thought I had a week or more in London and had brought your letter down to the typewriter in order to make an appointment when I had to change all my plans.[1]

I am glad that you were not shocked by The Play Boy.[2] I have felt that quite apart from its merits or demerits, it was necessary to get it fairly heard and fairly judged. I think it is a very powerful work myself, but even if I did not I should have fought for it just the same. We will never have serious literature in Ireland if we cannot make our people understand that they owe at any rate respect to a work which has taken three years of the life of a

---

[3] For William Macneile Dixon see p. 655. Greenock is a manufacturing town and seaport on the south bank of the River Clyde, close to Glasgow where Dixon was Professor of English. The ill-fated liner *Deutschland*, subject of Gerard Manley Hopkins's poem, had been built there in 1866.

[1] Fr. O'Brien had written to WBY on 13 June (MBY, cf. *LWBY* 1. 182–3), inviting him to lunch at St Mary of the Angels, Bayswater. In his reply to this letter on 6 July (*LWBY* 1. 184) O'Brien said that if WBY was 'in the South of Ireland between the 15th of July & the 24th of August I hope that you may be able to see me at Queenstown. The address is Weston, Queenstown.'

[2] In his letter O'Brien had written enthusiastically of the performance of *The Playboy of the Western World* which he had seen the previous Wednesday: 'I have rarely enjoyed anything better than Wednesday's matinee performance of the "Hour Glass" & "The Playboy" (though I would ask you to respect my confidence in the matter, as, being a cleric & in my own diocese my action might involve me in criticism) & I sincerely congratulate you & Mr Synge, the one for bringing tears into my eyes, the other for filling my heart with a sense of humour not unalloyed with truth & underlying sadness. That a morality play such as The "Hour Glass" may be as potent a factor for illustrating "simple faith" as many sermons I cannot doubt. I have always maintained that the natural wisdom of the simple uneducated Irish peasant is worth all the knowledge of those classes, to whom knowledge *is* wisdom, and who frequently possess not even a sufficiency of wisdom to render their knowledge of any practical use whatever.'

writer whose talent they all admit. They were free to hiss but not to silence the play.[3]

Yrs ev

W B Yeats

TLS Pierpont Morgan.

## To A. H. Bullen, 4 July [1907]

Coole Park | Gort, Co Galway

July 4

My dear Bullen,

I dont want to have anything to do with giving leave to people about translation rights. I have no way of finding out whether they are competent, and I suppose the matter is technically your concern as well as mine, or is it? Anyway its much easier for you to be a curmudgeon than for me to be so, for thats your business as publisher, whereas its a poets business to be amiable. I only met that Russian woman once in my life, and that was for a moment during the performance of the plays in London. She wrote to me about two years ago asking me if I could go and see her about the question of translation. I answered that I would, and heard no more until I met her the other day. Now you have her address, for I sent it you, and I have it not. Do you think you could write to her and ask her to write to A. P. Watt? I dont want to be bothered.[1]

I have no objection to your selling fifty sets of the collected edition to Elkin Matthews,[2] but if there is to be a slight extension to which I see no rooted objection, I should like that before it is finally ratified to come before A. P. Watt. I dont want anything done with either Matthews or Unwin

---

[3] O'Brien had declared himself mystified by the reaction of Irish audiences to the play: 'Of Mr Synge's play, I can only say that I consider the action of some of your Dublin audiences inexplicable. I see nothing scandalous in the play, & the moral is sufficiently obvious. What I like about the play is its truth. It is a clean play, such as are not many of the stupid musical comedies to which the prim & "respectable" have no objection.' He said that someone he had spoken to 'took exception to the scene "A Public House". He was Irish or supposed to be & thought "we should hide our weaknesses". I think we may leave the English to do that. Let them call Scene I The Hotel bar & we merely have an aristocratic public house. I prefer Mr Synge's variety & also his play.'

[1] Nothing came of this, and the Russian translator is unidentified. In December 1910 Gordon Craig recommended his friend G. Baltruschaitis should translate *The Land of Heart's Desire* into Russian, but this was not done.

[2] It is unlikely that this deal ever came off. For WBY's tangled business arrangements with Elkin Mathews see pp. 216, 338–9, 462. Bullen had called on AEFH on 3 July (NLI), 'to talk over that matter of getting your other books into his hands. I will write about what he says afterwards. I think that I can make

which will make it impossible for you to arrange for popular editions of my books if they are found desirable when we are through the collected edition. I suppose when you have arranged with Unwin that you will communicate my part of the matter to Watt. I want him to have the threads of my affairs. Now Elkin Matthews is telling lies about that agreement, but he wont tell those lies to Watt.[3] There is no <formal> document drawn up in a set form as there is with Unwin, but there is a letter written by Matthews three or four years ago to Watt, and stating the term of years for which he has the book, the amount of royalties &c. Acting upon this agreement which was considered by counsel to cover any arrangement made by Matthews with Lane, the Society of Authors got my book out of Lane's hands in America. Matthews may have written that letter because he wanted to hit Lane, but whats good of the dry tree is certainly good of the green. I tell you this not because I am likely to object, or that Watt is likely to object to any arrangement you make, but because there is no reason why Elkin Matthews, drunk or sober, should bully you into giving him better terms than you want to give by pretending there is no agreement. You can write to A. P. Watt and tell him that I have no objection to two years extension on the understanding that Matthews "takes fifty sets of the collected edition at half price" if he (Watt) has no objection.

Where There is Nothing is going on quickly, I am all but through a very full scenario. You will find the new version very much more to your mind than the old.[4]

Yr ev

W B Yeats

TLS Harvard. Wade, 483–4.

some sensible arrangement.' Immediately after the meeting she wrote again to WBY, telling him that she had had 'a long talk with Bullen this afternoon. . . . He gave me full particulars as to the unexpected expense of getting your works from the late firm. . . . In our original agreement the interest on the loan was to be paid out of the takings on the books. I proposed & he agreed that the interest on the sum of £700 to be used for this auxiliary purpose should be paid in full BY HIM. Bullen is most anxious that things should go on without any check.' She added that Bullen had expected to see WBY in person on 4 July 'to settle various urgent matters. It is only fair to him & to me for you to remember that delays will be at our joint expense.'

[3] Mathews was evidently in awe of Watt, who had managed to extract an account of the arrangements for *The Wind Among the Reeds* from him in 1902 (see pp. 138, 146).

[4] WBY was anxious to rewrite *Where There Is Nothing* for Bullen's *CW* and had asked AG to help him. She typed out a series of new scenarios with him (Berg), starting on 3 July, but in the end took over most of the project herself, and was credited as co-author when the completely revamped play was published as *The Unicorn from the Stars*. The 'very full' scenario was that of 3 July, which sketched out three acts in some detail, and began with a discussion between the troubled hero Paul Ruttledge and a Hermit about the nature of visionary experience. The play had first been written in a great hurry in October 1902 to thwart George Moore's threatened use of the plot (see III. 228, 232–3, 237–9), and WBY had made a number of alterations in its subsequent printings. In the radically new recasting he aimed to begin by emphasizing the contrary nature of Paul's and the Hermit's religious principles, and then in the final act show that they were in fact complementary.

## To W. A. Henderson, 4 July [1907]

Gort, | Co Galway
July 4

Dear Mr Henderson,

Your letter was delayed in reaching me, but it has followed me here.[1]

The circumstances of your engagement are not exactly as you remember them. I have the correspondence, but in London. We did not understand you were leaving your situation to take ours, we were informed that you were giving up your situation in any case. You were recommended to us by Mr Oldham as a book-keeper. But it is quite true that when we found that you were not we kept you on other grounds. We should probably not have made any change for the present but for the necessity which has been forced upon us of reorganising on a strictly economical basis.[2]

In other words I want a complete financial account made out in some form easy to understand to help in the re-arrangement of our affairs. I want to know our liabilities, if there are any unpaid bills, &c.[3]

Miss Horniman will send some address books to you. Will you please see they are taken care of, as they will be useful to us on future tours.[4]

What I want to find out from the accounts is, what I must look upon as regular and necessary expenditure, and how much we have to meet this.

---

[1] Henderson's letter is untraced. For details of his terms of employment see pp. 476–8, 678.

[2] WBY is being 'strictly economical' with the truth, since Henderson was being dismissed on AEFH's orders (see p. 669). In a letter of late June she had accused WBY of keeping Henderson on because he was 'afraid of his friends in Dublin'.

[3] Henderson replied to this letter on 20 July (NLI):

With reference to some queries in your letter of July 4th
1st   How much money in bank at end of season.   £54 8. 7
2nd  When Miss Horniman's last subsidy was paid. May 29th
3rd   What profit from tour.
        On July 18th a cheque for £78 was lodged to the credit of the Society. I expect this represents the profit.
4      How much have we in the bank? Only [? *for* on] Thursday July 18th we had a balance of £192. 8. 2
5      What unpaid Bills
        Electric Lighting account.  £11. 0. 2
        Helys.               3. 11. 6
        I will pay these next week.

He added that he would get the books audited up to date during the following week. On 25 July he sent a further set of returns to WBY (NLI) to 'give you some idea of the expenditure', and these showed expenses of £718.

[4] On 5 July AEFH wrote (NLI) that the 'set of address books will be sent to Mr Henderson as soon as they are ready & complete. I shall register the packet in case of their being mislaid & lost.'

How much if any besides deposit account money we have for working capital.

Yr ever
W B Yeats

TLS Kansas.

## To Maud Gonne, [c. *4 July 1907*]

Mention in letter from MG, 6 July [1907].
Telling her that he is unwell and close to a nervous breakdown,[1] discussing the effects of the incense powder he had sent her, and the American woman it had evoked.[2]

*G–YL*, 244–5.

## To A. H. Bullen, *5 July* [*1907*]

Coole Park | Gort, Co Galway
July 5

My dear Bullen,

I return proof which is not exactly what I wanted. I knew you could get the poem correct because you had the printed copy in the book of poems. What I wanted was a proof sheet of poem and prose together I want to be quite certain that the prose breaks the poem properly. You had better send me this proof sheet even now.[1]

---

[1] MG replied that she did not 'like to hear of you not being well & feeling like nervous breakdown. I know so well what that means for I went through it two years ago & know how wretched & undecided & unlike oneself it makes one.'

[2] This was the 'wonderful powder' WBY had promised in March and sent in May (see pp. 637, 666), and 'incense' here may be a euphemism for a more powerful hallucinogenic substance. In her previous letter MG had given an account of the effects the powder had had on her and asked whether he had obtained it from an 'American woman': 'I ask this because since I have used it once or twice, while I have been painting, I heard a voice with I think an American accent saying, not very interesting things about the painting I was doing & I cannot account for it, for it is the voice of no one I know.' WBY had evidently speculated on the identity of the woman (possibly Agnes Tobin), but in her reply MG hardly thought 'she can be the writer you describe for she seemed to me uninteresting & very crude, but of course the impressions I got were very vague—She seemed to me a woman who had realised that modern art is decadent & to be successful its decadent side must be exaggerated. This side *attracts &* *shocks* her at the same time. She would certainly try to put it into her work and put it in clumsily & heavily—I did not see her, but only heard her talking & got the impression ... & as I could not connect her with any one I knew I wondered if she had had anything to do with the incense.'

[1] The proof was of a poem, originally from a play called *The Country of the Young* (later *The Travelling Man*). The poem, first entitled 'The Rider from the North', but subsequently published as

You neednt have any anxiety about my text being ready for you, provided you always give me proper notice. I should know three weeks let us say beforehand when a new book is wanted. I should also know when you start a book how long you calculate the printing will take. It is no use your going ahead with the poems till you have a list of the proper order of them from me. I dont propose to follow the order in the American book.[2] I am not arranging any of these books on a chronological system. I had a special reason for arranging the American book in that way. I shall send you the proper order of the poems tomorrow. I conclude you will not want the preface until you are near the end of the printing.[3] I will also look through the Wind among the Reeds notes and see if they are worth reprinting.[4] Dont give me vague dates or predate things in order to make me hurry, for if you do I'll find it out and wont believe a word. I shall want to know how long the printing of the poems will take that I may have another volume ready to follow them. I think it is probable that I will have the volume of prose plays ready by that time. I think the proof sheet I have returned explains itself, but I will sumarise what I have done and want done. I have taken out as you see the chorus the second time it occurs to give a more accidental look to the poem. The prose paragraph comes after the "starry brink" and is followed by "The little fox he murmured".[5]

Yr ever
W B Yeats

TLS Buffalo. Wade, 484–5.

'The Happy Townland' (*VP*, 213–16), was published in *CW* I, but the proof here was intended for *CW* v, 242–4, where the poem is included in the story 'Hanrahan's Vision'. Hanrahan sings the song as he climbs Ben Bulben to visit Mary Lavelle, and the final chorus is divided from the rest of the poem by a paragraph describing his climb.

[2] Vol. I of *The Poetical Works of William B. Yeats*, published in New York in November 1906, contained a preface followed by *Early Poems: I. Ballads and Lyrics* ('To some I have talked with by the fire', followed by sixteen poems from *Crossways*), *Early Poems: II. The Wanderings of Oisin*, *Early Poems: III. The Rose* (twenty-one poems), *The Wind Among the Reeds* (thirty-seven poems), *In the Seven Woods* (thirteen poems), *The Old Age of Queen Maeve*, and, finally, *Baile and Aillin*. Vol. I of the *Collected Works, Poems Lyrical and Narrative*, began with *The Wind Among the Reeds* (substantially revised), *The Old Age of Queen Maeve*, *Baile and Aillin*, *In the Seven Woods* (with two additional poems), and *Early Poems: Ballads and Lyrics* and *The Rose*. WBY had evidently wanted to give his new American readers a sense of his poetic development, but felt that this was not necessary or desirable in *CW*. He had been alerted to a possible confusion over this matter by AEFH who had told him in a letter of 3 July (NLI) that she had just given Bullen 'my copy of the latest American edition as a clue to your arrangement of the poems'.

[3] WBY did not write special prefaces for any of the eight volumes of *CW*, but reprinted original prefaces to individual sections if they already existed, and he supplied a new preface for 'John Sherman', which was part of vol. VII.

[4] Some of the notes to *The Wind Among the Reeds* were omitted altogether and others revised and shortened. In the original edition the notes occupied pp. 65–108 of the book, and WBY himself was defensive about their length and copiousness, explaining to Henry Davray on 21 Nov 1898 (II. 306) that they were 'really elaborate essays. . . . They deal with Irish faery lore & mythology & are in most cases made out of quite new material. They have given me a good deal of trouble & will probably make most of the critics spend half of every review in complaining that I have written very long notes about very short poems.'

[5] The version of the poem printed in 'Hanrahan's Vision' (see n. 1) contains two choruses instead of three, and is divided by the prose paragraph in the way WBY describes here.

## To Mrs Pat Campbell, [? 5 July 1907]

COOLE PARK, | GORT, | CO. GALWAY.
Friday

Dear M^rs Campbell: I would be very much obliged if you would let me know sometime what you think of the enclosed.[1]

I wish I had been able to do better for you about that money.[2]

Yr ever
W B Yeats

ALS Private.

## To A. H. Bullen, 6 July [1907]

Coole Park | Gort, Co Galway
July 6

My dear Bullen,

Your letter has amazed me. It is the most extraordinary letter from a publisher I have ever seen. If this Library Edition is not to be carried through on the ordinary conditions I prefer that it should come to an end immediately. I will not have one word printed that I have not seen and passed.[1] Furthermore I now see that the whole arrangement must be made in detail by A. P. Watt, and I will think myself bound by nothing that is not put in those arrangements.[2] Whether you go on printing now or wait till the arrangements are completed is your own matter. I told you that I would not require to see proofs but after your letter I withdraw that. I must see final proofs of everything, and other proofs if I ask for them. This will be my

---

[1] This was probably a new passage for *Deirdre*. In his note on the play in *CW* III WBY recalled that he spent the spring of 1907 trying to rewrite the play from the entrance of Deirdre to her questioning of the musicians 'but felt, though despairing of setting it right, that it was still mere bones, mere dramatic logic. The principal difficulty with the form of dramatic structure I have adopted is that, unlike the loose Elizabethan form, it continually forces one by its rigour of logic away from one's capacities, experiences, and desires, until, if one have not patience to wait for the mood, or to rewrite again and again till it comes, there is rhetoric and logic and dry circumstance where there should be life' (*VPl*, 391).

[2] i.e. the money that Mrs Campbell hoped AEFH might use to subsidize her new theatrical initiative (see pp. 680–1).

[1] Bullen had begun to print *CW* from an unauthorized text, AEFH's copy of volume one of *The Poetical Works*.

[2] Although WBY had used Watt to retrieve his work from other publishers for *CW*, he had not asked him to draw up any formal agreement with Bullen for the edition, and nor, despite this letter, was he ever apparently to do so. In mid-March WBY had discussed arrangements for the edition with AEFH, who was also negotiating with Bullen on the matter (see pp. 641–3).

final text for many years, and I refuse to have any portion of that text settled by any person but myself. It seems to be perfectly outrageous that you should take a text which I have never authorized you to use and begin printing from that without consulting me. I enclose a list of poems in the order in which they are to be printed, and I require to see a revised proof of the proof of Hanrahan which I sent you yesterday, a proofsheet which I sent back by return of post.[3] Furthermore I object to your going to Miss Horniman and telling her you dont want coloured illustrations in the book of dramatic criticism...I insist on those illustrations which were part of our original bargain.[4] On knowing on what day you require the material for the different books I shall do my best never to keep your Press waiting. But I shall not bind myself to anything that is not in the agreement with A. P. Watt. If you had seen A. P. Watt some time ago as I asked you, this confusion between the rights of author and publisher would never have arisen.

I am sending copies of our correspondence to A. P. Watt.

Yr siny

W B Yeats

TLS Buffalo. Wade, 485–6.

## To A. E. F. Horniman, [c. 6 July 1907]

Mention in letter from AEFH, 7 July 1907.
Sending her his keys to Woburn Buildings and asking her to collect his mail and send it on,[1] discussing the authorship of the plays to be included

---

[3] See previous letter, nn. 1, 2, and 5.

[4] AEFH had discussed the colour illustrations with Bullen on 3 July, and on 5 July had sent him a memorandum of their discussion, a copy of which (NLI) she also sent to WBY. In it she recapitulated that Bullen thought they would 'not aid in the sale of the work, this of course I cannot tell. But we must remember that when the subject was first mooted there was then a chance that the theatrical scheme might become a matter of wide interest. Now events have shewn that it will become a peasant, not a widely artistic affair and so the general interest in the essay will be simply because Mr Yeats has written it.' She herself purported to be worried that if Robert Gregory became a professional artist, it would not be 'to his advantage to put his 'prentice work into such a permanent form', and (using a catch-22 argument *avant la lettre*) '[i]f he remains an amateur, I don't see why amateur work should be in the book at all'. The ellipsis is WBY's.

[1] Although there was little post to be collected, AEFH, as her reply divulged, could not resist this opportunity to take a thorough look-round at Woburn Buildings: 'There are some moths in your curtains & the books on the top shelves are absolutely filthy. I went upstairs to wash after finding these as my fingers were black. The mattresses are uncovered, the eider-down covers the blankets & that will be *filthy* very soon. The floors are littered with bits of papers, they have not been washed down since you left. I looked in & round the waste-paper basket for paper in which to send this parcel but I found none, only this card, telegram & prescription on the table. The press cutting packet was on the table in the

in the *Collected Works*,[2] debating arrangements for passing important Abbey papers from Payne to Henderson, and enquiring about the address books.[3]

NLI.

## *To A. H. Bullen, 8 July 1907*

### COOLE PARK | GORT, CO GALWAY
### JULY 8 1907

My dear Bullen,

At last I understand the situation. We have been at cross purposes, and the situation that has arisen is serious enough.

You were too hasty and I was too vague, or at any rate I did not succeed in making myself understood by you, or in understanding you. It is another warning that one must never start on serious undertakings without a very careful written business understanding. The first misunderstanding was this. You said that you hoped to be through with the whole matter in about thirteen months. I then gave 'Discoveries', part of one of the volumes, to my sister, and it will be issued by her in the autumn, and as I calculated would have run through its natural sales before you are ready to publish in the spring or the early summer of next year. I withdrew from active work in the Abbey Theatre with the purpose of devoting myself for a year to making final text of all my books. But for this I would never have consented to a collected edition at this moment, as I believe that an edition containing so much that is immature or inexperienced as there is in my already published books would do me a very great injury. Now I find that instead of printing at the rate of between six and eight weeks a volume, you are printing at the rate of about three weeks a volume. When I talked to you

sitting-room. I saw the box marked as containing my letters; I have kept your keys so that I may send anything more which may be required. If not I will return them at once.'

² WBY had apparently asked AEFH what she had been telling Bullen about his dramatic collaboration with AG in connection with the forthcoming *CW*. In her reply AEFH said she hoped WBY was 'going to make it quite clear in the Library Edition that Lady Gregory has given you certain help in peasant dialogue. I felt it only fair to Bullen to tell him what you told me some time ago, that she considers that she has a certain claim on your disposal of your work because of the help she has given you. I know no particulars, not even which plays you referred to.' AG had given WBY a great deal of help with his peasant plays in Hiberno-English, particularly *Cathleen ni Houlihan* and *A Pot of Broth*, and they were currently collaborating again on the rewriting of *Where There Is Nothing* (see p. 686, n. 4). AEFH, who despised peasant plays, was evidently eager to distance WBY as far from them as possible.

³ In her reply AEFH said that she had 'told Mr. Payne to send the pass book & old cheque book to Mr. Henderson. The address books shall follow when the latest ones are copied. Roberts has got a copy of the large London address book, so I need not send you a copy of that.'

of the volume to follow the Celtic Twilight it was in the belief that whichever volume you had it would not be required till autumn. I am accustomed to my sister's slow printing, and apart from that your words seemed unmistakeable.[1] When Hanrahan was taken out of the Secret Rose, it became very desirable to add something in its place, for two or three of the remaining stories are rather weak. I have had two stories in my head for a long time which I could add.[2] Besides this there are two volumes of plays to one of which it is entirely essential that I add a re-written Where there is Nothing, or rather a new play on the old theme. For nothing would induce me to consent to a reprint of the old play, and without it the volume is too small.[3] I am anxious to add to the other volume two short plays on the Cuchulain cycle.[4] I have mapped out my life for months to come that I may devote myself entirely to this work. All this mapping was based on the understanding that there would be six weeks between the volumes. Now I am ready to meet you half way as far as ever I can, but I cannot under any circumstances consent to the publication of what I believe to be bad work. Miss Horniman is as anxious as I am that this should be a final text, and we must all make our arrangements on this supposition.[5] Now I want to know can you interpolate any piece of printing which will give me more time? Even an additional three weeks would be of great importance to me. I am now working on Where there is nothing, and am making a powerful play of it; but it will take some little time. It is the only thing however which I cannot date the finishing of, for it is the only big task.[6] What I mean to say is that if you could interpolate some piece of printing after the poems and give me a calculation of the dates when the various books will be required, I shall be able to keep to those dates. In a fortnight from now I shall know with perfect certainty when Where there is Nothing is to be off my hands. There

---

[1] The Dun Emer Press habitually took many months to print and publish even slim volumes. The copy for *Discoveries* had been delivered to ECY earlier this spring but was only finished on 12 Sept and not published until 15 Dec 1907.

[2] The six rewritten Red Hanrahan stories, published in 1905 (see p. 78, n. 1), were taken out of *The Secret Rose* (*CW* VII) and placed in vol. V, *The Celtic Twilight and Stories of Red Hanrahan*. Two other stories from the original 1897 edition of *The Secret Rose*, 'The Binding of the Hair' and 'The Rose of Shadow', were dropped from *CW* VII, but were not replaced with any others.

[3] *The Unicorn from the Stars*, the rewritten version of *Where There Is Nothing*, appeared in vol. III of *CW*.

[4] The only new Cuchulain play was *The Golden Helmet*, published in vol. IV, although *On Baile's Strand*, published in vol. II, was the extensively rewritten version, also published separately in 1907.

[5] AEFH had revealed in an undated letter of earlier this year (NLI) the reasons why she was underwriting the *Collected Works*: 'The whole idea on my part is that it might be helpful to your status, or rather it might show more people what your real status *is*. It will be such a clear sign that you are not of the same class as the twittering imitators who are considered to be your near rivals in Ireland.'

[6] WBY and AG had made good progress on the revised scenarios; on 7 July they introduced the 'unicorn' theme, and on this day drafted a new version which opened with Paul in a religious trance. A little later Paul's name was changed to Martin and the Hermit became Fr. John, as in the final version.

are certain changes in the arrangements of the books which I can make and which will hurry things, but these changes will injure the edition. Whatever we do it is really important the arrangement should be made by Watt, and that everything is got down in writing.

[*no signature*]

TL Harvard. Partly in Wade, 486–7.

## *To A. H. Bullen, 10 July* [*1907*]

Coole Park | Gort, Co Galway
July 10

My dear Bullen

I am greatly obliged to you about what you say of putting the Press to something else for a short time. I have practically completed the notes for the present book and will send them to you tomorrow if I can.[1] It is a question of getting them typed. I do not think I will write any preface unless you are particularly anxious for one. I have written so much direct or indirect criticism of my own work for the essays that I hardly think it is necessary. I have re-written that poem about Maid Quiet and hope it is not too late for you to put it in instead of the present version.[2] I have changed it as you suggest. It is on the enclosed sheet. I forgot when sending you the list of poems that the "chorus for a play" in 'In the Seven Woods' is in the play of Deirdre. I shall be obliged therefore if you will leave it out and put instead of it the poem about the ragged hollow wood which I have taken out of Red Hanrahan.[3] That wont be enough so please put the enclosed with it. I quite recognise that I may be too late but I hope not. I shall always do my best to let you have the work in time now that it is possible for you to give me reasonable notice and not to go too fast.

Yr sny
W B Yeats

TLS Harvard. Wade, 487–8.

[1] These were the revised and abbreviated notes for *The Wind Among the Reeds* (see p. 689), and WBY also included a new note to the *Early Poems*.

[2] 'Maid Quiet' (*VP*, 171) was first published in the *National Observer* on 24 Dec 1892 as an untitled poem in the story 'The Twisting of the Rope'. It had a number of different titles in subsequent reprintings, and appeared in *The Poetical Works of William B. Yeats* as 'The Lover mourns because of his Wanderings'. WBY radically revised it for publication in *CW* I under its new title and reduced it from twelve to eight lines.

[3] 'The Ragged Wood' (*VP*, 210–11) had also been first published as an untitled poem in 'The Twisting of the Rope'; it appeared in *CW* I under the title 'The Hollow Wood'.

## To A. H. Bullen, 12 July [1907]

Coole Park | Gort, Co Galway
July 12

My dear Bullen,

I shall write to A. P. Watt tomorrow about the arrangements I want made. I need hardly say that I am as anxious as you are to get everything settled with the least possible inconvenience to everybody concerned. What I want is a chance to finish the unfinished parts of the different books. I can work the entire summer from this on to early October at getting through. I had meant to give myself a longer time still but I cannot do the necessary things in less than this time. When you have printed Poems, the first volume that is to say, you will have finished everything that has required practically no further work from me, at least unless I accept your proposed first volume of plays. Here are the remaining volumes as I see them.

A.   A volume containing Countess Cathleen, Land of Hearts Desire, Shadowy Waters (possibly all three versions) Kings Threshold, the Cuchulain cycle of plays (two of these still to be written) Dierdre.

B.   Where there is Nothing, Cathleen ny Houlihan, Pot of Broth, Hourglass (This volume to be called Prose Plays)

C.   The Secret Rose, John Sherman, Dhoya. (very careful verbal revision necessary and two new stories desirable)

D.   Discoveries (this is to be a book of essays, very largely theatrical but containing the Spenser. I have a few more pages to write for this, but a good deal of work to do in the way of arrangement.

The objection to your suggested volume of plays is that it will make the apportioning of plays between the two volumes purely arbitrary.[1]

Another arrangement besides the one I have suggested has occurred to me, which is to divide them into legendary and philosophical, but this would put Baile's Strand and the two unwritten plays into the Countess Cathleen volume. Even if I were to agree to your proposed first volume of plays, that would only postpone the difficulty as you would be through it before I was through my summer and had got a decent chance of doing the other plays.[2]

The only thing I can suggest to you is that you interpolate some other piece of printing when you are finished with the poems, and the longer it

[1] The contents and arrangement of *CW* went though further changes over the coming months. WBY had already sent Bullen copy for three volumes: vol. I (*Poems Lyrical and Narrative*), vol. V (*The Celtic Twilight and Stories of Red Hanrahan*), and vol. VI (*Ideas of Good and Evil*). The plays were eventually spread over three volumes, but *A Pot of Broth* was not included and finally the edition comprised eight volumes in all. There is no evidence that WBY wrote to Watt about the arrangements.

[2] WBY wanted to divide the two volumes into plays in prose and plays in verse.

takes the better. I dont see any way to promise to supply the printer with a volume every three weeks on the average.

If you have any other suggestion to make you might write to me about it. Remember that my original calculation was thirteen months. I enclose the notes to Wind among the Reeds, and will try and send the proofs before post, no, I have just remembered Sunday is so near, so tomorrow will do as well, and the same applies to the Notes. I will keep them back for after-thoughts. The text I sent you is correct for the new titles correspond to the Notes as they are at present.[3]

I am working very hard, and mean to work hard, but it is impossible to say how fast I can get on, that is why I was so glad to think that I had as it originally seemed ample time.

[*In WBY's hand*]

Remember I must have proofs of the book of poems.

Yr sny<br>W B Yeats

TLS Harvard. Wade, 488–9.

## To A. H. Bullen, *13 July* [*1907*]

COOLE PARK, GORT, CO. GALWAY.<br>Saturday July 13

When will 'Dierdre' be out.[1]

W B Yeats

APS Indiana.

## To A. E. F. Horniman, [c. *13 July 1907*]

Mention in letter from AEFH, 14 July 1907.
Sending his good wishes for her scheme of founding a repertory theatre in Manchester,[1] telling her about his progress on *Where There Is Nothing*,[2] and

---

[3] See p. 694.

[1] *Deirdre*, vol. v in the series 'Plays for an Irish Theatre', was published in late August of this year.

[1] The formation of the Playgoers' Theatre, AEFH's new Manchester theatrical company, had been announced on 11 July, and WBY had sent his best wishes for the venture. AEFH replied: 'Many thanks for the blessing. There has already been a long civil letter on the subject in the Manchester Guardian.'

[2] See p. 686. In her reply AEFH said she would 'be very glad when "Where there is Nothing" is done with, but do give it a fresh title to avoid confusion please.'

asking about the dates of her new company's residency in the Midland Institute.[3]

NLI.

## *To Norreys Connell, 14 July* [*1907*]

Coole Park | Gort, Co Galway
July 14

Dear Mr Connell,

I had intended to see you in London but came away unexpectedly soon. If you could manage to make those changes in your play you will be helping us very much. We are fighting a very difficult battle in Dublin, and though resolved to fight on, producing every good work we can, I confess that one grows a little weary of the fight, and we do not want more fighting than we can help. They will forgive your Englishman his virtues if they dont think you are on the English side. We are determined in any case to play it, I hope early on [in] the winter, so the sooner we get your enlarged version of the play the better.[1]

Yr sny
W B Yeats

TLS Private.

---

[3] Until she acquired a permanent venue at the Gaiety Theatre, the Playgoers' Theatre was performing at the Midland Institute, which the Abbey Company had booked for their Advent tour in Britain. AEFH assured WBY that 'the dates already settled at the Midland Theatre won't be interfered with' and the Abbey appeared there from 26 to 30 Nov 1907.

[1] WBY had presumably asked Connell to make the changes to the dialect used in *The Piper*, discussed in his letter to AG of 9 Mar and to tone down some of the scornful remarks of the captured English officer (see pp. 638–9, 640). Despite his precautions, there were disturbances in the theatre during its first production from 13 to 15 Feb 1908.

## To Ford Madox Ford, 22 July [1907]

Coole Park | Gort, Co Galway
July 22

Dear Mr Hueffer,

I am only today answering your letter of June 14, and that is a long time to leave a letter.[1] I have to take care of my eyes however, and have a way of letting my letters accumulate until I have about three days dictation, and in the country one does not always come across someone to dictate to.

I am afraid I cannot help you about the anthologies, for just now I am getting all my books into one man's hands for the sake of the collected edition next spring. I could not even let you have thirty pages of poems without his consent, and that I am afraid he would not give at present. He has not made up his mind yet in what form he will publish apart from a rather expensive collected edition. I think it is very probable he may want to publish a collection of my lyrics. A good many years ago now you recommended me to an old Irishwoman at Turnham Green, and I went to see her with Lady Gregory, who is collecting folklore together with me, and we got a most valuable piece of mythology from her.[2] Whenever your name has

---

[1] Hueffer's letter of 14 June is untraced, but he was writing on behalf of Walter Jerrold, whom he had persuaded to edit an anthology of poems entitled *The Book of Living Poets*, published in December 1907. Hueffer, who contributed four poems to the volume, was also writing weekly 'Literary Portraits' for the *Tribune* and on 28 Dec recalled (2) that at the beginning of 1907 'when all was hope and busy stir I suggested to a friend that he should gather together — in the hope of proving that poetry is not yet dead — an anthology of modern verse'. Now that the book (*The Book of Living Poets*) lay before him he noted that an 'incredible deal of it is given up to the Eternal Celt.... When I consider the selection from my own verse I am bound to say that it is as derivative and un-modern as anyone else's.' Among the contributors were Jane Barlow, Laurence Binyon, Edmund Gosse, A. P. Graves, Thomas Hardy, Rudyard Kipling, Andrew Lang, John Masefield, T. Sturge Moore, Henry Newbolt, Alfred Noyes, Seumas O'Sullivan, Ernest Rhys, Dora Sigerson Shorter, Algernon Swinburne, Arthur Symons, John Todhunter, and Katharine Tynan. In his introduction Jerrold described the anthology as 'a wonderful body of poetry of a peculiar richness' and 'doubted whether at any other period there could have been gathered within one cover representative work from so many sterling poets all living at the same time as the present' (pp. viii–ix). When Hueffer eventually included WBY in one of his 'Literary Portraits', for the *Outlook* on 6 June 1914, he declared (783–4) that 'Mr. Yeats's figure has always singularly intrigued me.... I must confess to having for seven-eighths of my life... regarded Mr. Yeats as almost a grotesque.... I hated, and still do hate, people who poke about among legends and insist on the charms of remote islands. All that I read of Mr. Yeats's work was *The Countess Kathleen* ... and a poem which began, "I will arise and go now." ... I have certainly acquired a great respect for Mr. Yeats.... it began to occur to me that his Celticism might be genuine, or might be a pose, but that in any case it did not matter very much beside the importance of the personality.'

[2] See II. 142–3. This encounter had taken place, as AG recorded in her diary (Pethica, 163), on 19 Dec 1897, when she and WBY had 'set out for Chiswick — where he had heard of "an old lady with folk lore & a weakness for bullseyes" — We found & interviewed her, & got some stories — a reward for what had seemed rather a wild goose chase.' The stories were used by AG in *Visions and Beliefs* (146–7) and by WBY in 'Away' (*UP* II. 278).

occurred to me I have had a pang of shame that I had never written to thank you. I procrastinated for some time, and then thought I would postpone writing till my book was out, but when that may be I do not know, my hands are so full of other things.[3]

Yr ever
W B Yeats

TLS Berg.

## To W. A. Henderson, [c. 24 July 1907]

Mention in letter from Henderson, 25 July 1907.
Enquiring about Abbey Theatre expenditure and asking for box-office returns.[1]

NLI.

## To Katharine Tynan Hinkson, 28 July [1907]

C/o Lady Gregory | Coole Park | Gort | Co Galway.
July 28.

My dear M[rs] Hinkson: I am sorry to have to return to you your husbands play.[1] I dont think any body can write well in dialect unless he has been brought up talking it like Boyle, or has made a most exaustive & even scientific study of it like Synge & Lady Gregory. Every body else (so far as I can judge of the plays sent to the Abbey) copies the purely literary dialect of the Irish Novelists. Then too we always advise our dramatists to have nothing to do with love as a theme. The moment they begin to write of

---

[3] The book became *Visions and Beliefs in the West of Ireland*, not published until 1920, and then under AG's name, although with contributions from WBY.

[1] On 25 July Henderson sent an account of box-office returns at the Abbey from 20 Oct 1906 to 27 Apr 1907 which amounted to £758 19*s*. 5*d*. He added a note 'hurriedly prepared not checked', and another hand, probably that of Swayne the auditor, recorded that Henderson 'can't trace plays produced on Apl. 13. Payne hasn't given returns yet for £31.18.1 & £7.15.4. . . . Down to Feb 29 H says the figures are accurate. After that, he thinks correct but may be a few pence out.' A later and more detailed version of these accounts made the total receipts £763 19*s*. 9*d*.

[1] Henry Albert Hinkson (1865–1919) had married Katharine Tynan in May 1893. After reading classics at Trinity College, Dublin, he had become a barrister, and turned his hand to writing novels and plays without great success. His play was *Love in a Mask*, a copy of which he had sent to William Archer in December 1906, although it was never published nor produced. It may have been a dramatization of Honoré de Balzac's story *L'Amour masqué*, rendered into Irish dialect.

it, they forget life & write out of a memory of the Colleens & young Countrymen of the Anglo Irish tradition. Very few people I find can see life with their own eyes, if they choose some thing in life that many others have described. Your husband should ask himself at every moment while he writes have I seen this, just as I describe it, or have I felt this just as I express it. All sincere literature lies between, or at one or other extreme.

I wish I saw you sometimes when I am in London but you are always so many miles away.[2]

Y ever<br>W B Yeats

ALS Harvard, with unstamped envelope marked '*Immediate*', and addressed 'M<sup>rs</sup> Hinkson'.

## To A. H. Bullen, 28 July [1907]

Coole Park | Gort, Co Galway<br>July 28

My dear Bullen,

I return the proof sheets.[1] I have modified a word in one poem in obedience to a suggestion of your own, and have changed one little poem, but as this practically I think brings you very near the end of the lyrics without any other change, you will not be greatly alarmed.[2] I enclose the correct version of the poem which I call 'The Hollow Wood' and I want you to substitute it for 'I heard under the ragged Hollow Wood'. I think you will admit the improvement. The old poem was always spoiled by the poverty of rhyme. This is practically only a change of four lines.[3]

Yr ever<br>W B Yeats

[2] The Hinksons had lived in the west London suburb of Ealing since 1893 but were just about to move to Chipperfield, Kings Langley, Hertfordshire.

[1] These proofs were evidently for the section of *CW* I which included 'In the Seven Woods'.

[2] The modification was probably the inclusion of a hyphen in 'well beloved' in the second line of 'The Folly of Being Comforted' (VP, 199).

[3] 'The Hollow Wood' (see p. 694), a poem of three quatrains, was an addition to 'In the Seven Woods' in *CW* I. It had first appeared, without title, in the story 'The Twisting of the Rope' in *Stories of Red Hanrahan* (1904), when its first line read 'I heard under a ragged hollow wood', and it was later retitled 'The Ragged Wood'. The main change that WBY made to the poem for *CW* was to reverse the order of the first and second stanzas, but he also revised the language and, as he suggests here, the rhyme scheme from 'wood/cry/hood /I! // trees/cry/images/I!' to 'trees/sigh/images/I! // silver-shoed / sky/ hood /I!' (see *VP*, 210–11).

[*In WBY's hand*]
I have not yet had the section called 'The Rose'. I suppose that comes next.[4]

TLS Buffalo. Wade, 489–90.


## To A. H. Bullen, [*? 29 July 1907*]

COOLE PARK, | GORT, | CO. GALWAY.

My dear Bullen

I wrote yesterday & sent proofs but owing to accident this was not posted until this morning. The lad who takes the post went looking for cows that had gone swimming across the lake & did not get back in time.

In calculating whether you can get two volumes out of the verse plays remember that we shall give the three versions of Shadowy Waters[1] & that there is a new play (which can if necessary go in the book of prose plays) about as long as Hour Glass.[2]

Yr ev
W B Yeats


Prose book will contain the new 'Where there is nothing', 'Hour Glass' 'Kathleen ni Hoolihan' & I dare say 'Pot of Broth'.[3]

APS Kansas.


## To Florence Farr, [*early August 1907*]

Coole Park, | Gort, | Co. Galway.

My dear Florence Emery: Here is the music—your old *Shadowy Waters* among the rest. I don't know if you have a version of the Stage Version (but you might leave that over for a little as I am hoping for copies of the American edition which contains it.)[1] Keep the music safe for me. I don't

---

[4] 'The Rose' poems comprised the final section of *CW* I.

[1] Bullen did get two volumes out of the verse plays and there were three volumes of plays in all. Vol. II contained two, not three versions of *The Shadowy Waters*.

[2] i.e. *The Golden Helmet* (see p. 693, n. 4), which appeared in vol. IV.

[3] *The Pot of Broth* was omitted, and the new version of *Where There Is Nothing* (i.e. *The Unicorn from the Stars*) appeared in vol. III with *The Countess Cathleen* and *The Land of Heart's Desire*.

[1] Vol. II of *The Poetical Works*, published by Macmillan, New York, on 8 July 1907, contains the acting version of *The Shadowy Waters* in appendix III.

find here that music you did for the womans song in *On Bailes Strand* and I must write again for it.[2]

Miss Horniman is starting in Manchester on I think September 25 with that play of cockney life by MacEvoy the Stage Society brought out a while back.[3] I don't know what else she has but she claims to have lots of plays— they must be pretty bad if she has.[4] I hear that Shaw advised Payne to have nothing to do with her as she fights with everybody but Payne thinks he can manage.[5] Lady Gregory says that Miss Horniman is like a shilling in a tub of electrified water—everybody tries to get the shilling out. Lady Gregory is now quite definitely added to Miss Hornimans list of truly wicked people.[6] I am looking forward to the moment when Manchester will

[2] The music for the plays appears at the end of *CW* III, prefaced by WBY's note, 'The Music for Use in the Performance of these Plays' (222–33). It includes FF's setting of the Fool's song and the chanting of the Three Women in *On Baile's Strand* (see pp. 221, n. 2, 342, 377, 380–1), but the setting for *The Shadowy Waters* is by Arthur Darley.

[3] AEFH apparently settled on Manchester as the base of her new theatre company because it was the city that had bought the most books when the Irish players visited it, and because Payne, her first manager, had grown up there and knew it well. The venture opened on 23 Sept 1907 with Charles McEvoy's *David Ballard*, which WBY and Payne had seen together when it was produced by the Stage Society on 9 June 1907. The play involves the attempt by David Ballard, a poet manqué, to escape from his vulgar, materialist, and snobbish lower-middle-class London family. Destitution forces him to return home, but he finally wins a £100 prize for the 'best poem on Sunlight Soap', and elopes with a sympathetic young woman called Mercy. Charles McEvoy (1879–1929) had originally trained as an ordnance engineer, but became a journalist in 1902 and from 1907 wrote a number of plays and novels. AEFH was also to present his *Gentlemen of the Road* and *Lucifer* in her first season, and his *When the Devil was Ill* at the opening of the renovated Gaiety Theatre, Manchester, in September 1908.

[4] Despite Shaw's reservations about AEFH's temper, the main productions of her first Manchester season were his *Candida* and *Widowers' Houses*. William Poel of the Elizabethan Stage Society directed a widely discussed production of Shakespeare's *Measure for Measure*, and there were translations of plays by Rostand and Maeterlinck. Otherwise, the plays were relatively unremarkable pieces by Nigel Playfair, George Paston, Basil Hood, J. Sackville Martin, St John Hankin, and A. R. Williams, although *The Subjection of Kezia* by Mrs Edith Havelock Ellis received wide press coverage. Over time the Gaiety's main discoveries were to be the playwrights Stanley Houghton and Harold Brighouse.

[5] The day after resigning from the Abbey Theatre, Ben Iden Payne was astonished to receive a note from AEFH, asking him to call. When he arrived, she 'wasted no time in explaining why she had asked to see me. "I want," she declared, "to teach those impossible people in Dublin that I have other fish to fry." She said that she had decided to use £25,000 of the money she had reserved for public purposes for further theatrical activities. She would like me to undertake this project for her.' Payne was 'far from being elated' at this 'extraordinary opportunity' because he wanted to be an actor rather than a manager and director. Nevertheless, he accepted because he 'saw this stroke of fortune as a step toward creating the kind of theatre that I had longed for but never found . . . a chance to experience, and to help advance, the New Drama.' After toying with the idea of a base in London, or a Scottish National Theatre (Payne warned her that, after her Dublin experience, 'she should be leery of any enterprise that bore a nationalistic tag'), they decided upon Manchester, and he wrote to several newspapers there announcing the project. WBY had warned Payne against AEFH, telling him that she was 'a vulgarian', and advising him to make sure that he had a watertight contract, advice for which Payne 'learned to be grateful' (*Life in a Wooden O*, 80).

[6] AEFH's simmering jealousy of AG had taken a more strident tone earlier this year. On 27 Feb she had scolded WBY (NLI) for bringing her 'that impudent *message from Lady Gregory* that I might

begin to add our names. The strange thing is that any old hatred years after you think it dead will suddenly awake. They are like the stops of an organ.

I am reading Norths Plutarch and I find a beautiful thing. Alcebiades refused to learn the flute because he thought it ill became a gentleman either to put his cheeks out of shape or to make music he could not speak to. He had so much influence that ever after the flute was despised. This might help you with your lectures—you will find it in the account of Alcebiades. Alcebiades said the flute should be left to Thebans that did not know how to speak. He also claimed that the patrons [of] Athens, Pallas and Apollo, objected to the flute and that Apollo skinned a man for playing on it.[7]

Yours ever
W B Yeats

Printed copy; Bax 60–1, Wade 490–1.

---

mortgage the Abbey', and in an undated letter of late July 1907 (NLI) had warned him that he was 'ceaselessly victimized by Lady Gregory on the score of your gratitude for her kindness. You are being made a slave, your genius is put under a net in that precious "garden" and you are only let out when you are wanted to get something out of *me*.' When Payne first met AEFH in Oxford earlier this year, he discovered that his encounters with her 'consisted mainly in listening to her complaints about the cavalier way in which she was treated by everyone in the Abbey Theatre including the directors, especially Lady Gregory' (*Life in a Wooden O*, 76). WBY's name was added to AEFH's list of enemies after a dispute over the Abbey subsidy in 1911.

[7] Plutarch, in North's translation, recounts that when Alcibiades 'was put to schoole to learne, he was very obedient to all his masters that taught him any thing, saving that he disdained to learne to playe of the flute or recorder: saying, that it was no gentlemanly qualitie. For, sayed he, to playe on the vyoll with a sticke, doth not alter mans favour, nor disgraceth any gentleman: but otherwise, to playe on the flute, his countenaunce altereth and chaungeth so ofte, that his familliar friends can scant knowe him. Moreover, the harpe or vyoll doth not let him that playeth on them, from speaking, or singing as he playeth: where he that playeth on the flute, holdeth his mouth so harde to it, that it taketh not only his wordes from him, but his voyce. Therefore, sayed he, let the children of the Thebans playe on the flute, that cannot tell howe to speake: as for us Athenians, we have (as our forefathers tell us) for protectours and patrones of our countrie, the goddesse Pallas, and the god Apollo: of the which the one in olde time (as it is sayed) brake the flute, and the other pulled his skinne over his eares, that played upon the flute. Thus Alcibiades alledging these reasons, partly in sporte, and partly in good earnest: dyd not only him selfe leave to learne to play on the flute, but he turned his companions mindes also quite from it. For these wordes of Alcibiades, ranne from boye to boye incontinently: that Alcibiades had reason to despise playing of the flute, and that he mocked all those that learned to play of it. So afterwards, it fell out at Athens, that teaching to playe of the flute, was put out of the number of honest and liberall exercises, and the flute it selfe was thought a vile instrument, and of no reputation' (*Plutarch's Lives of the Noble Grecians and Romans, Englished by Sir Thomas North* [1579], ed. W. E. Henley [1895], II. 93–4).

## To A. H. Bullen, [? 4 August 1907]

COOLE PARK, | GORT, | CO. GALWAY.

Sunday

My dear Bullen: I return proofs 'waving' is right the other a misprint.[1] Please let me know if Dierdre is out.[2] I have just finished a new play except for verbal revision—it is one of the Cuchulain cycle for the collected edition[3] but am still stuck in 'Where there is Nothing'.[4]

Yrs ever

W B Yeats

ALS UCLA.

## To A. W. Henderson, [c. 7 August 1907]

Mentioned in following letter.
Asking for the MS of John Eglinton's version of *Oedipus Rex*.

## To W. K. Magee ('John Eglinton'), 9 August [1907]

Coole Park | Gort,

August 9

My dear Magee,
    Henderson tells me (I had written to him for the M.S. of Edipus) "Magee told me Payne had it, and that he had given him permission to produce it in Manchester being under the impression that only peasant plays would be produced in the Abbey in future". He says also that you will get the play back if we wish for it.[1]

---

[1] Probably '*Our arms are waving, our lips are apart*' from 'The Hosting of the Sidhe' (*VP*, 140). *The Celtic Twilight* (1893) had printed 'a-waving'.
[2] *Deirdre* was published later this month.
[3] i.e. *The Golden Helmet*, which appeared in *CW* IV.
[4] AG was taking an increasingly large part in the writing of the play, and in a programme note for the first performance of *The Unicorn from the Stars* (21–3 Nov 1907), WBY explained that while rewriting *Where There Is Nothing* for *CW* this summer he had 'decided that I could not include it in its old form, which was written too much from the point of view of the chief character for sanity, and had too much heterogeneous life for artistic unity. I felt that the central idea of the play would seem vague and shadowy unless it were imbedded in the circumstances of real life. I therefore asked Lady Gregory, the greater portion of whose work has been a study of the actual life of Ireland, to collaborate with me.'

[1] See pp. 22, n. 2, 390. Magee's translation of *Oedipus* was produced neither by the Abbey nor the Gaiety. WBY finally wrote versions of both *Sophocles' King Oedipus* (1928) and *Sophocles' Oedipus at Colonus* (1934) himself.

We certainly do wish it, we are publicly pledged to produce it, and mean to do so as soon as possible. If you wish to give it to Manchester also please do not let them do it till after our performance. We would be very much obliged if you would give us a good start with it, as we want the honour of being very obviously the first to play Edipus the King in English. Payne wanted to play Edipus himself, but we refused, as the part was intended for Frank Fay.[2] It will be one of our earliest plays in all probability. The sooner we have the text the better as we are now arranging our winter programme. It is your own text we want, not Payne's paraphrase of it. It is quite possible we shall begin the winter with it. I dont know what put it into Payne's head that we are only a peasant theatre, though of course we acknowledge that our main capacity is peasant.

Yrs sny
W B Yeats

TLS Southern Illinois.

## *To J. B. Yeats,* c. *9 August 1907*

Mention in letter from JBY, 11 August 1907.
Complimenting JBY on his article on George Frederick Watts.[1]

[2] See p. 643.

[1] JBY's article on George Frederick Watts (see p. 335, n. 5), a version of a controversial lecture he had delivered in January 1906, appeared in the summer 1907 number of the *Shanachie* (113–26), under the title 'The Rationale of Art'. For JBY Art had no Rationale, at least none that the moralist would understand: the artist, he insisted, 'works only to please himself...he admires wrong as often as right...he inculcates no lessons, and preaches no dogma'. Art's advice was 'Seek temptation; run to meet it; we are here to be tempted.' He wove these observations into his discussion of Watts, and, musing on the 'polite indifference' of the English public towards Watts's imaginative painting, suggested that 'had he lived in Dublin his fate would have been worse. Indifference, however polite and respectful, is bad; but destructive criticism kills.' The Dublin critics, he maintained, admitted only one thing more than themselves, 'the *fait accompli*, a mundane success. Had Watts been born in Dublin, he would have read for the "Indian Civil," and perhaps—passed.' In her review of the magazine in the *Peasant* of 27 July 1907, 'E.K.' dismissed the article (3) as 'a rather silly article on Watts', a reproof that had evidently stung JBY since in his reply he confided that he 'was very glad to get yr letter & to hear that you approved of my article on Watts—your compliments came very opportunely, because I had just settled down to the belief that I ought not to have published it at all. Altho' I did not quite accept the criticism of the Peasant that it was "silly", the author of that criticism a Miss Knox, an ominous name for the poor fine arts—'

## To John Millington Synge, 15 August [1907]

COOLE PARK, | GORT, CO. GALWAY.
August 15

My dear Synge,

I agree with you about the cheques, we had been intending to write to you on the subject. When you are at the Abbey next will you see if you can arrange some system of working. There is no reason why we should not draw out two or three weeks expenses at a time and so save trouble. Or one of us might sign a number of cheques, and you when in Dublin might fill them in to the amount and sign your name. Vaughan is probably all right but we don't know anything about him.[1]

Our suggestion was (but nothing was settled) that instead of having week shows every month we should play three nights every week. There would be drawbacks, but then we should avoid those drops at the beginning of every week. The last weeks show was an agreeable surprise we did not think we should take so much, and were regretting having assented to it.[2] We thought it best to let Fay have a free hand in the tours as none of us could go running after him. You know of old that I dont believe that Fay is a very competent man to run a theatre, that in fact I think him particularly unfitted for it, but Miss Horniman has definitely announced that she will do nothing more for us at the end of the two years. In all probability Fay may survive us (theatrically), and at the end of that time may carry on some sort of touring company with our good will and what he wants of our plays.

---

[1] WBY had obviously read Synge's letter to AG of 14 Aug, and on 19 Aug a startled Synge told Maire O'Neill (*JMSCL* II. 36), 'I wrote to Lady G. the other day about various matters, and got an answer from *Yeats*—and I fancied rather a stiff one.' His letter to AG (*JMSCL* II. 29–30), had taken up the question of Vaughan signing cheques now that he had replaced Henderson: 'I think of course as he is managing everything that he will have to sign as Secretary. But I think, now that the business is not quite so much a matter between personal friends as it used to be, that the Directors i.e. two of the Directors should not in future sign blank cheques. Obviously the rule that the Directors must sign is to ensure that they should control and be responsible for all the money that goes out—and I think the method we fell into with Ryan of signing blank cheques "en bloc" is not a business like one. If you are of the same opinion it would be well to begin the other method now when we are making a change of hands. I do not mean for a moment that I have any doubts about any one in the place but I think it is not well to be too lax.'

[2] For the annual Horse Show week the Abbey had revived WBY's *Cathleen ni Houlihan* and *The Hour-Glass* and AG's *The Rising of the Moon* and *Hyacinth Halvey*. WBY evidently feared that the production of old work would deter audiences, but in fact the theatre broke even, as Synge explained in his letter of 14 Aug: 'The expenses—cut down to their lowest—were about £30 and the takings up to and including Sat. Matinée were about the same. I do not know what was taken on the last night.' He went on to say that W. G. Fay had told him 'of your decision about playing the three nights weekly instead of the Saturday only. I hope it will work well, but I dont feel greatly taken with the scheme.' Despite Synge's misgivings, the new arrangement was introduced from the beginning of the autumn season on 3 Oct.

I wanted somebody in control over Fay but now that plan has failed and that we have lost Miss Horniman I think we must give Fay every opportunity to acquire experience and amend his faults. So far as practical things are concerned he is bound to be captain of the ship, and our interference would only prevent him from picking up a little knowledge without improving the navigation. Of course if you take a different view you should tell us, and we had hoped you would have been down here to settle these things, we may arrange some other plan. Please write to us exactly what you think. I need hardly say that if anybody gave us some thousands of pounds I should for one insist upon Fay giving up everything but acting and such parts of stage management as he is competent for. I am very doubtful of his being able to hold the company together, considering his queer temper, but I dont see what else we can do. We want him to work for us as enthusiastically as possible with a view to his ultimately making his living out of the thing and helping others to make theirs. The Theatre is now a desperate enterprise and we must take desperate measures.[3] We did not expect to make at present by the country tours, but we determined to spend £50 of Miss Horniman's £150[4] on Irish tours, to make ourselves a part of the National life. There is always the remote chance of money coming to us from some other quarter at the end of the Patent period, and that chance would be much better if we have made ourselves a representative Irish institution. A Theatre with an uncertain hold on Dublin and a much stronger hold on London and the English provinces would have less chance of being capitalised than if it were a part of the public life of Ireland. Some Frenchman has said 'to be representative is to be famous'.[5]

Yrs sny
W B Yeats

[*In AG's hand*]
I am so sorry you are ill again, & hope you will get all right & away[6]—AG

TLS TCD. Saddlemyer, 235–6.

---

[3] Despite WBY's challenging tone, Synge, in his letter of 14 Aug, had declared himself happy with this scheme: 'Fay gave me to understand that he was to have a free hand more or less with these tours etc. to see what he could do with them. I think it is the best plan.'

[4] Evidently a mistyping for £250, the sum which AEFH had sent in July (see p. 674).

[5] This was said by the French writer and politician, Honoré Gabriel Riquetti, Comte de Mirabeau (1749–91), who argued in the National Assembly in July 1789 that those who represented the people were a 'virtual aristocracy'.

[6] Synge was at this time confined to his house with 'one of my regular influenza-ish turns with my usual cough as bad as ever' (*JMSCL* II. 27). He had hoped to join his friend Henri Lebeau in Brittany in quest of better health.

## *To A. H. Bullen, 18 August [1907]*

COOLE PARK, | GORT, | CO. GALWAY.
August 18

My dear Bullen: Many thanks for 'Dierdre' which looks very well.[1] You might send press copies to Masefield & Arthur Symons on the chance.[2] But please remember to send no press copies to Irish papers.[3] Have you seen A. P. Watt.[4]

Yr ev
W B Yeats

APS Kansas, with envelope addressed to Shakespeare Head Press, Stratford-on-Avon, postmark 'ORANMORE AU ?19 07'.

## *To Florence Farr, [c. 18 August 1907]*

COOLE PARK, | GORT, | CO. GALWAY.

My dear Florence Emery: I send you 'Dierdre' at last. I think it looks well & I have just read it through with some content.[1] I can judge it now for the first time for the actors voices have begun to fade. I send you (or rather I

[1] *Deirdre* was the fifth volume in the series 'Plays for an Irish Theatre', and was uniform in appearance with volumes ii and iv: issued in grey paper boards with green cloth spine, white label printed in black inside green rule border on spine, white end-papers, and all edges untrimmed.

[2] i.e. the chance of a review. Masefield, who had worked for the paper until 1905, may have been the author of the anonymous notice of *Deirdre* in the *Manchester Guardian* of 3 Sept 1907 (5), which concentrated on the quality of the verse and expression, rather than the dramatic force: 'The verse . . . is easier and more various than ever before, without the conscious-seeming heave of departure from the strict iambic form with which Mr. Phillips, for example, takes the liberty of allowing himself an occasional anapaest.' The notice went on to say that 'the play is rich in beautiful and close expression of fugitive drifts of feeling nowhere expressed before, in fine combinations of modern ease and idiom in speech with dignity and mystery of theme, and in cadences which have something of the quality of curious and beautiful sounds in nature rather than of deliberate constructions'. *Deirdre* was also reviewed very favourably twice by the poet Edward Thomas, first in the *Daily Chronicle* of 28 Sept (3) and in the October number of the London *Bookman* (47), and by F. G. Bettany in the *Athenaeum* on 5 Oct (415–16). A further anonymous review appeared in the *Guardian* of 1 Jan 1908 (18–19). Arthur Symons was now living mainly at Island Walk, a cottage in Wittersham, Kent, and repairs to this had landed him in debt. He was trying to get a number of his plays produced and was currently seeing his *William Blake* through the press. Although he wrote nearly forty reviews and articles in 1907, he does not appear to have noticed *Deirdre*.

[3] This was now firm policy with WBY (see III. 341–2), and no review of *Deirdre* in any Irish periodical or newspaper has been traced.

[4] He had not, and was not to do so until mid-September.

[1] WBY inscribed this copy of *Deirdre* (Halladay): 'Mrs Emery from her friend WB Yeats.' It also contains the bookplate of Patrick Cairns Hughes and a note by him: 'Mrs. Emery (Florence Farr) was

will send both books to morrow) American collected edition of my plays for the sake of the dedication of a section to yourself & the Appendix IV (an old essay) & preface both of which mention you—they may be of use to you in America.[2] I shall follow up the American book with a volume of prose plays 'Hour Glass' 'Pot of Broth' Kathleen ni Houlihan & the new version [of] Where there is nothing by Lady Gregory & myself & called 'The Unicorn from the Stars'. It is now almost finished—three acts & thrown back in time a little over a hundred years & tamed enough to be possible in Dublin.[3]

There is double 'war of sex' going on here now which delights me. A young man is staying here with his bride. A month ago they eloped & they are here I think in hopes of softening the parental hearts who are in the next county.[4] Then there is Robert Gregory & his betrothed.[5] The young husband is the most depressed man I have ever seen & as his depression

indeed more than "my friend" to W.B. Yeats. She was his mistress—or so my parents told me. And they should know: she introduced them to each other.'

[2] As well as *Deirdre*, WBY was sending the second volume of *The Poetical Works of William B. Yeats*, published by Macmillan in New York on 8 July. This included *The Land of Heart's Desire*, with a dedication to FF, and the preface, dated December 1906, concluded: 'The labour of two players, Miss Florence Farr and Mr Frank Fay, have done enough to show that all is possible, if the summer be lucky and the corn ripen.' Appendix IV, 'The Work of the National Theatre Society at the Abbey Theatre, Dublin: A statement of principles', was extracted from his essay 'Literature and the Living Voice', first published in the *Contemporary Review*, October 1906. At the end of his plea for the rediscovery of the old art of 'regulated declamations', he described and praised FF's experiments with speaking to the psaltery. On 6 Sept FF wrote to Quinn (NYPL) 'I have just received Macmillans American edition of Yeats with allusions to me at the end of the Preface & end of Appendix 4. He says he hopes it will help me in America.' WBY inscribed the flyleaf of this volume: 'Mrs Emery from her friend W. B. Yeats'.

[3] The volume, published as *The Unicorn from the Stars and Other Plays*, was issued by Macmillan in New York on 13 May 1908. As well as the title play, it contained *Cathleen ni Houlihan* and *The Hour-Glass*, but not *A Pot of Broth*. On 17 Aug AG explained to Quinn (NYPL) that WBY was very anxious to rewrite *Where There Is Nothing* (which Quinn had copyrighted in America) for Bullen's *CW*, 'and wanted my help, and we spent a good deal of time over it, rather unprofitably. Now I am working at it alone, and he will come back to it when it is in a new setting, but it is a hundred times harder redoing an old play than starting a new one. He doesn't like the magistrate and I don't like the tinkers, and we neither of us like the Sermon on the Mount, or think of the monastery scene possible for Irish playing. So, you see, there is a great upset.'

[4] The young husband and his bride were Francis Macnamara (1885–1945), minor poet, man of letters, and later father-in-law of Dylan Thomas, and his first wife Yvonne Majolier. Although neither side approved of the match, the main opposition, according to their daughter Nicolette Devas, came from the Majoliers, their objection being that Macnamara 'had no money': 'In my mother's words, "Mother did not like Francis's manners"' (*Two Flamboyant Fathers* [1966], 22). The two had eloped earlier that summer and married secretly at Paddington Registry Office. Macnamara's father Henry Valentine Macnamara, High Sheriff of Co. Clare and an extensive landlord in the west of that county, temporarily cut off his allowance, but soon became reconciled to the marriage.

[5] Robert Gregory was to marry the artist Lilly Margaret Graham Parry (1884–1979) on 26 Sept 1907. In her letter of 17 Aug to Quinn (see above) AG described her as 'a very charming girl . . . clever, pretty and very bright and good. She is Welsh, with a Spanish grandmother and French great grandmother and has no English blood, and that I am just as glad of. She is artistic and will keep Robert's painting before her, as he does before himself, and they will spend the winter in Paris, that he may work there.

grows his bride grows more & more cheerful. She grows pinker & whiter & her hair seems yellower every day & she eats enormously. He watches with a look that seems to say 'I never thought you would be like this—I wonder how much longer I shall last—O my God'.[6] They have no conversation & no ideas & can have nothing to do or think of but—being kind to one another.[7] Robert & his betrothed are fighting for mastery on the other hand in the most amusing way. The depressed husband brought a dangerous little yact here which upset twice in the first three days.[8] Robert forbid his young woman to go out in it unless in calm weather. Two days ago she walked into the library holding the cheerful bride by the hand & said to the depressed husband 'take us out for a sail' (Robert was present). 'No' he said 'it is too stormy'. 'Then we are going by our selves' she said. They set off for the lake but the bride got afraid & came back. Then Robert set out for the lake & found his betrothed up to her middle in the water trying to clime

I shall for the present stay here to look after things for them but will fade away by degrees so they can be here more, for young people should have their own chance.'

[6] According to Nicolette Devas (see n. 4), her father was very tall and her mother very small. The daughter of a French father and an Irish mother, she had grown up in London and was 'a very pretty woman in an essentially feminine way; light on her feet, size three shoes, masses of soft fair hair, milk and roses skin. It was her charm, her flirtatious manner and spontaneous gaiety that enhanced her prettiness. Next to Francis with his violent man's gestures (he flung his arms and legs about) my mother was reduced to Dresden china delicacy. She was a curious blend of high intelligence and frivolity' (21). However, Macnamara's depression may have been caused as much by the atmosphere at Coole, and by WBY's criticism of his poetry, as by his bride's appetite and demeanour. Nicolette Devas, evidently recording first-hand her mother's recollections of this visit, reports that 'Yeats was treated as the Sacred Great Man and when he spoke everyone hushed. If a visitor did not know this rule of the house, Lady Gregory held up a small imperious hand for silence, and in her indignation looked more than ever like Queen Victoria. For she was a small cottage-loaf shape and like the Queen always dressed in widow's weeds.' The new Mrs Macnamara 'found this sacred atmosphere particularly galling', but 'sat in a deceptively meek adoration', and found that when AG was called away to Dublin 'the Sacred Poet got down from his throne and prattled away like anybody else and my mother enjoyed giggles all round until Lady Gregory's return' (127). At this time Macnamara, who was about to abandon his law studies for poetry, was 'full of awe' for WBY, but 'after the honeymoon visit the relationship deteriorated. For Yeats thought that Francis as a young aspiring poet needed a few hints on his craft and these he obligingly gave him: Francis was not grateful' (127). When Arland Ussher suggested in September 1935 that WBY should include some of Macnamara's poems in *OBMV*, WBY replied (Kansas): 'No, no, no. Francis Macnamara had a strain of talent once, but he has lost it through never mastering the technique of verse.' Macnamara was, however, pleased by WBY's description of him as 'that frustrated Dionysius' (*Two Flamboyant Fathers*, 127).

[7] It was not only the dauntingly reverential atmosphere of Coole that inhibited conversation: Macnamara fancied himself a philosopher, and in pursuit of this vocation would often strike the pose of Rodin's statue *The Thinker*, and banned all small talk from his house. WBY was prescient about the fragility of the relationship, for although the marriage produced four children it lasted only seven years, after which Macnamara deserted his family for the wife of the artist Henry Lamb. According to Nicolette Devas (36–7), this came as a complete surprise to Yvonne, and was a terrible blow: 'In many ways immature, my mother had never taken Francis's ideas very seriously, believing romantically that love was on her side.'

[8] Macnamara was a keen and sometimes foolhardy sailor. Nicolette Devas recalls (24) that he nearly drowned three of his children when he capsized a yacht he kept on the Thames.

into the yact which was anchored. Then he gave in. That night to his great joy she had a cold & she has it still but insists that it is hay fever. Like struggles are going on every day & yet they are the best of friends.

I am writing for 'the New Age'.[9]

I have Saturn in my first house □ Sun & Jupiter & it will be there for months. The result is that I feal like my uncle.[10]

Yr ev<br>W B Yeats

[*At top of first page*]
PS. I may want to hire your rooms from you when you go so let me know if you have let them. I cannot say [*for* stay] on in Woburn Buildings.[11]

ALS NYPL.

## To A. E. F. Horniman, [c. 25 August 1907]

Mention in letter from AEFH, 27 August 1907.
Telling her of the difficulty in getting books he wants from Woburn Buildings,[1] discussing her astrological predictions on his behalf,[2] complaining of the work involved in advising the Dun Emer Press,[3] telling her that he has

---

[9] WBY does not mean that he was writing articles for the *New Age* (and nothing by him was published there at this time), but writing for a copy of the magazine to read FF's contributions. She had evidently told him that her 'Marie Corelli and the Modern Girl' had appeared there on 1 Aug and that another article, 'The Rites of Astaroth', contrasting the degraded positions of prostitutes in Western cultures with their sacred status in certain Eastern civilizations, was to be published on 5 Sept.

[10] The 'square' is a 90-degree angle, always regarded as more stressful than the other astrological angles. Saturn transits slowly, so that WBY's natal opposition of Jupiter and sun would have been under the prolonged sobering and saddening influence of Saturn, and poor health, melancholy, or a period of heavy responsibility might be predicted—cf. his poem 'Conjunctions' (*VP*, 562): 'If Jupiter and Saturn meet, | What a crop of mummy wheat!' In WBY's horoscope, the sun is in the 5th house and Jupiter in the 11th, so he could expect trouble in the Theatre (a 5th house matter) or from friends or groups (11th house matters). WBY's uncle George Pollexfen was a chronic hypochondriac and melancholic (see p. 96, n. 9).

[11] FF had rooms at 107½ Holland Road, Kensington. WBY was evidently thinking of leaving Woburn Buildings permanently, but in fact he remained there until June 1919. Since FF did not return to America, he could not have borrowed her apartment in any case.

[1] AEFH, who was on holiday in Annecy, France, replied that she 'would gladly have fetched you any books or sent you my own astrology. I only sent back the keys when there was no more time to hear from you.'

[2] AEFH was worried by WBY's stars and replied: 'That transit of ♄ in your first won't be as bad as it would be if he were ill-dignified there but the □ ♃ & ☉ look bad for your prosperity & fame. You must be very determined not to take any fresh serious course of action under those aspects. I cannot help being anxious about you, you ought to be doing your greatest work now.'

[3] WBY had evidently told AEFH of the trouble he was taking over the Dun Emer books. In her reply she warned him that he could not 'possibly find & write enough books for your sisters, they must get hold of material themselves sooner or later. I don't blame you for starting them, but they must run

been sailing in a boat on the Coole Lake,[4] mentioning that he and AG are giving the rewritten *Where There Is Nothing* the title *The Unicorn from the Stars*.[5]

NLI.

## To A. H. Bullen, 26 August [1907]

COOLE PARK, | GORT, CO. GALWAY.
August 26

My dear Bullen,
    Would you mind looking through the Samhains that you have, and noting as you suggested what seems to you most suitable for the book of essays, and sending them to me. I will be glad if you will do this as soon as possible.[1] Please also send me the John Sherman and Dhoya if you can get one.[2] I am anxious to get all the scrappy work done that I may go on to original work. I intend that you shall have four volumes to go on with before I leave this. That will give me time to try a couple of plays which are to go in the final volume before you come to it.[3] But go to A. P. Watt. I have no agreement yet about POEMS '99 nor about Deirdre.[4] There is a good deal of music ready to go to print for the plays, but it wants to be written out legibly. You had somebody in the office I understand who did that for Mrs Emery when you brought out Cathleen ni Houlihan.[5] Have you got that man with you still? Some of the music is Irish folk music, some is by

their own business in time. You are not valued enough by your own people, either your relations or your fellow countrymen.'

    [4] WBY had evidently been tempted out for a sail in Francis Macnamara's boat.
    [5] See p. 696, n. 2. AEFH was delighted with the new name, which she would have recognized as deriving from the Practicus (3°=8°) Ritual of the GD (see p. 342, n. 6), writing that it was 'a splendid title, it gives one a feeling of the marvellous & the unexpected'.
    [1] The latter part of *CW* IV was entitled 'The Irish Dramatic Movement', comprising largely of WBY's contributions to the annual theatrical magazine *Samhain* 1901–6.
    [2] 'John Sherman' and 'Dhoya', two of WBY's short stories first published in the same volume in 1891, were the final items in *CW* VII.
    [3] These were not written in time for *CW*. The most recent of WBY's plays published there were *The Unicorn from the Stars* and *The Golden Helmet*.
    [4] Bullen did not see Watt until at least the middle of September, but on 10 Sept wrote to him (Watt) to say that the 'agreements for *Poems 1899–1905* and for *Deirdre* are to be precisely the same as for *Ideas of Good & Evil*'. He went on to remind Watt that '*Poems* were published at 6/net and *Deirdre* at 3/6 net. You have the agreement for *Ideas of Good & Evil*. So if you will kindly draw [up] the agreements for *Poems 1899–1905* and *Deirdre* I will sign them.' The agreement for *Deirdre* was initially drawn up on the same day, but caused unforeseen problems because of the size of the advance demanded (see below, pp. 744–5), and Bullen did not sign a revised contract until 27 Dec.
    [5] The music printed at the end of *CW* III (see p. 702, n. 2) is very legibly copied, and, apart from the traditional airs, is by FF and Arthur Darley. FF's music for *Cathleen ni Houlihan* had been published in the English edition of vol. II of 'Plays for an Irish Theatre', issued by Bullen in March 1904, and a copy of this, in her hand, is now at Northwestern University.

Arthur Darley, but a good deal is by Mrs Emery.[6] This music is essential to the completeness of my record, even apart from its own merits it is necessary to show how I want the things set. I mean the degree of attention to the speaking voice.[7] I dont want therefore to leave them to the last moment especially as Mrs Emery goes to America in November.[8]

Yrs sny
W B Yeats

TLS Harvard. Wade, 491.

## To W. A. Henderson, 26 August [1907]

COOLE PARK, | GORT, CO. GALWAY.
August 26

Dear Henderson,

As I believe you are still in our employment for a few days I send you the £4 to pay into the Bank in payment of that debt of mine.[1]

I hope this weeks show will go as well in Dublin as it has done in Cork.[2]

I hope we shall very often see you at our performances. Of course you understand that you can always come into the Theatre free.

With kind regards from Lady Gregory

Yrs ever
W B Yeats

TLS Kansas.

---

[6] See p. 702, n. 2.

[7] The music published at the end of *CW* III has a section on the music used in WBY's plays and another on the music for his lyrics, which contains a note by FF and notation for some of WBY's poems recited to the psaltery.

[8] Having recently returned from America (see p. 651, n. 7), FF was now contemplating a second trip there and told Quinn in a postcard on 12 Sept (NYPL): 'I have just arranged to sail with Mrs. Patrick Campbell in the "Lusitania" on 2nd November.' At this time she had an engagement in Buffalo on 21 Nov, but others may not have materialized, and she wrote to Quinn on 17 Sept that she had decided to postpone the trip until the end of January. That plan, too, collapsed, and she never returned to America.

[1] The debt is unidentified but was probably for private typewriting among that relating to the Abbey, and may have come to light in the thorough auditing of the accounts undertaken by Swayne (see pp. 678, 679).

[2] The Company had undertaken a two-week tour of Waterford, Cork, Kilkenny, and Cork again, from 12 to 24 Aug. During the first visit to the Opera House, Cork, 15–17 Aug, they made £26, and D. J. O'Donoghue told Holloway on 21 Aug (NLI) that W. G. Fay had written that 'the manager of the Cork Theatre was delighted with the Company & wanted them to stay on. They had to fill their engagement at Kilkenny, but return to Cork for the weekend.' These 'Special Re-engagement' performances took place from 21 to 24 Aug. When Holloway called at the Abbey on 27 Aug the Company 'all spoke of their reception at Cork in terms of delight. About Waterford & Kilkenny they were silent. Frank Fay said Kilkenny was scarcely a one night show. The people were alright but very poor!' Synge told AG on 14 Aug (*JMSCL* II. 29) that he had 'had rather bad accounts from

## To Maud Gonne, [*late August 1907*]

Mention in an undated letter from MG, [late August 1907].
Sending her *Deirdre*[1] and telling her of Robert Gregory's engagement.[2]

*G–YL*, 245.

## To Agnes Tobin, [*? late August 1907*]

Abbey Theatre | Dublin

My dear Friend,
    Everything is packed & I have nothing but this soiled sheet of paper. Dear Friend the more I run over things in my mind the more do I know that I belong to this ship of mine, & that the crew & I are bound together for life. Have we not sworn something of a pirates oath—a sacred thing ever—& I am nothing but a pirate. You are kind & good, & I thank you, but do not put your treasure where there is nothing but a crazy ship & a troubled sea.[1] Send me the printed pages of this beautiful book, & I shall be very grateful for so fine a gift—the best America has today—this treasure takes nothing from the giver.[2] I am going back to my ship & must welcome all with a clear eye. "Comrades" it must say "my oath also is unbroken. I belong to you, to that old flag & to the [?]sword. Therefore you can trust

Waterford. . . . the programme had to be rearranged the first night. The audience was thin and jeered at Vaughan in the Wise man, and hissed the Rising of the Moon, and Spreading the News—I suppose on the score of the Playboy.' On 27 Aug AEFH wrote to WBY (*LWBY* I. 191) that she had 'had some long cuttings from the agency about Cork & Waterford. There will be always a difficulty in first visits at a bad time of the year. If you cover expenses it is something.' In *Ireland's Abbey Theatre* Seaghan Barlow recalled (75) the difficulty of getting the scenery into the Town Hall, Waterford, and that part of a stage cottage had been forgotten (*JMSCL* II. 29).

[1] WBY sent MG's letter about his *Deirdre* on to AG (see below) and it is now lost. It was evidently enthusiastic and cheered him up 'very much'. In a letter written the following day MG explained (*G–YL*, 245) that the 'post man came while I was writing & . . . I had to send your letter unfinished yesterday as I couldn't wait longer to tell you what I thought of your Deirdre'. She had long been interested in the play's progress, and on 29 Apr 1906 (*G–YL*, 229) had congratulated him on having the 'courage you have to begin a great work like Deirdre all over again—I don't think I could do that'. In May of the same year she told him that she had 'just begun a picture of Deirdre as a child' (*G–YL*, 230).

[2] See p. 709. In her reply MG asked him to give her 'congratulations & good wishes' to Robert Gregory on his marriage, and she added that she hoped 'he & his wife will come to see me if they are in Paris this winter'.

[1] Agnes Tobin had evidently developed a romantic interest in WBY, and had apparently telegraphed him, offering to subsidize his plays and enter into a partnership with him.

[2] Presumably Agnes Tobin's translation of Racine's *Phèdre*, which was published posthumously in 1958. WBY had given her help in the preparation of her earlier translations, including Petrarch's *On the Death of Madonna Laura*, published in November 1906 (see pp. 144, 569).

me." (How could they trust were I to murmur even under my breath "there is some little I keep from you".)

When you send me your proofs I will go through them very carefully—it will be a great pleasure to do this for you.

Yours affectionately

W B Yeats

ALS Private.

## To Hugh Lane, [late August 1907]

My dear Lane:

I am only passing through on my way to London so cannot see you this time. I have to go over for a few days. I wanted to tell you how indignant I feal over Count Plunkett affair.[1]

Yrs ev

W B Yeats

ALS Private.

---

[1] Earlier this year Lane had been asked to apply for the directorship of the Irish National Museum of Science and Art, and to AG's delight agreed to do so. He had already begun to collect items for the Museum when he heard rumours that another candidate was to be appointed. AG went to Dublin to find out what was happening and was told that the position had been given to George Plunkett. As she recalls in her *Hugh Lane* (75) she 'sent a telegram home, as well as one to Hugh in London, telling the dreary news. Yeats was staying with us, and had raged when it was received. It was, in his mind, one of the worst of crimes, that neglect to use the best man, the man of genius, in place of the timid obedient official. That use of the best had been practised in the great days of the Renaissance. He had grown calmer before my arrival, because when walking in the woods, the sight of a squirrel had given him a thought for some verses, the first he had ever written on any public event.' This poem was 'An Appointment' (*VP*, 317–18), written on a blank leaf in one of the books he had given to AG, and in this form it was entitled 'On the appointment of Count Plunkett to the Curatorship of Dublin Museum, by Mr T. W. Russell and Mr Birrell, Hugh Lane being a candidate.'

George Noble Plunkett (1851–1948) was a barrister who contributed poetry, often under the name of 'Killeen', to a number of periodicals and anthologies, and he had been created a papal count in 1884. He had edited the short-lived but enterprising magazine *Hibernia* in 1882, and, besides several books of verse, published works on Botticelli (1900), Pinelli (1904), and *The Architecture of Dublin* (1908), as well as editing and revising Margaret Stokes's *Early Christian Art in Ireland* (Dublin, 1911). He was inducted into the directorship of the National Museum on 16 Oct 1907, and remained in office until 1916, while also acting as vice-president of the Royal Irish Academy from 1908 to 1909, and 1911 to 1914. His son Joseph Mary Plunkett was executed as one of the leaders of the 1916 Easter Rising, after which Count Plunkett became involved in politics. He was elected Sinn Fein member for North Roscommon in 1917 and served as Minister of External Affairs in the first Dail Eireann and as Minister for Fine Arts in 1921–2. AG believed that Plunkett had been appointed because he was 'in the opinion of the Castle officials "a safe man"', and because he was a Catholic. Augustine Birrell later told her that, although Chief Secretary of Ireland, he had not been told of the appointment until it had been made and that he was enraged when he heard of it (*Hugh Lane*, 75–6).

## *To Lady Gregory,* [*1 September 1907*]

18 Woburn Buildings

My dear Lady Gregory: I had a fine passage but boat more crowded than I ever saw it.[1] Best of friends with Miss Tobin & likely to remain so & at that only. There was a simple enough explanation of telegram etc.[2] I shall stay for Binyon play on 4 Sept or for 5 Sept if I cannot get in on first night probably not longer.[3] I have however to see Barker for Fay[4] & dentist for myself. I enclose a letter I have had from Maud Gonne about Deirdre.[5] It has cheered me up very much. Bullen has gone to Ireland where I rather think he expected to see me.[6]

Yrs ever
W B Yeats

ALS Berg, with envelope addressed to Coole, postmark 'LONDON SP 1 07'. No enclosure.

[1] After an unsettled and unusually wet summer, the weather had improved, and the *Irish Times* of 31 Aug issued a special three-day forecast of moderate south-westerly winds and increased sunshine. WBY probably crossed on Sunday, 1 Sept, after attending the Saturday night performances at the conclusion of the Abbey's Horse Show week. The good weather for the Horse Show, the Phoenix Park Races, and the Irish International Exhibition at Ballsbridge had brought a more than ordinarily large attendance for these events.

[2] Agnes Tobin's telegram to WBY does not apparently survive. She evidently nursed her romantic interest in WBY, and on hearing in May 1909 that she had formed a friendship with MG, AG tartly observed (Berg) that it would be 'cemented by the offer of you by one to the other'.

[3] Binyon's *Attila*, produced on 4 Sept at His Majesty's Theatre by Oscar Asche, who also took the title role (see p. 545, n. 2), is a four-act poetic play which dramatizes the tragic love affair of the Hun chieftain and a Burgundian princess, who kills him in the erroneous belief that he has betrayed her to the Romans. Charles Ricketts designed the costumes and scenery, and the production, which had a run of thirty-two performances, was financed by Lord Howard de Walden. The critics were respectful rather than enthusiastic; *The Times*, commenting that Binyon could 'write good verse' and indulged 'in no preciosities, no glittering digressions, no descriptions for descriptions sake', reflected that it was 'agreeable to think that we still have a poet or two left capable of writing for the stage', and concluded that on the whole 'this *Atilla* must be counted an honourable achievement for all concerned'.

[4] This was about the possibility of the Abbey using the Savoy Theatre on their next visit to London.

[5] See p. 714. AG evidently did not send back this letter, since it is not among those which GY returned to MG after WBY's death.

[6] This was indeed the case: on 10 Sept Bullen wrote to Watt (Private) that he had 'been in Ireland, where I expected to see Mr. W. B. Yeats; but he had crossed to England'.

## To Lady Gregory, 3 September 1907

18, Woburn Buildings, | London, N.W.

Sept. 3, 1907.

My dear Lady Gregory

I am hoping to be able to stay here long enough to see Binyon's play which begins to-morrow night. I don't particularly want to go to-morrow night however as if I don't like the play which is probable I shall have to say so, and I don't want to have to do that. Everybody one knows will be there. I want to go Thursday night when I shall see a better performance as well as probably finding it easier to get a seat. I should probably have to get Binyon to help me to get in tomorrow night.[1]

I have just had a long letter from John Quin[n] all about Playboy. He seems to be a little out with Hyde, indeed Mrs. Emery tells me the same, but I will show you the letter, so there is no use writing about it.[2] I haven't seen much of anybody. Bullen is in Ireland, rather expecting to see me there I imagine, for his niece, Miss Lister, who has charge of the printing press in a letter to-day rather suggests my seeing him on my passing through Dublin. I don't think I will however, as I don't see what there is to do that cannot be done by letter.[3]

I am trying to see Granville Barker at Fay's suggestion to find out if we could go to the Savoy or send a single play there (your Hyacinth by

---

[1] In fact, WBY did get a ticket for the first night, and on 6 Sept FF wrote to tell Quinn (NYPL) that WBY had 'been on tour for a few days this week but has, I think, returned to Ireland now to go on staging there. . . . We were all at Binyon's *Attila* on Wednesday. The scenery by Ricketts & dresses very delightful designed by him & made by people I know, who have helped in our Literary theatre production.' In a letter to Cockerell of 16 Sept (*The Best of Friends* [1956], 15) Binyon confessed himself 'decidedly pleased with the performance of Attila. Asche is very good, and Ricketts has made wonderful pictures out of the play. I fear it won't run long, but that was not to be expected.'

[2] Quinn's letter of 23 Aug extended over more than twelve typewritten pages and was, by his own admission, 'a long rambling letter . . . my, how one goes on when one is dictating. This is a long letter. Please tear it up and so be merciful to my biographer.' It was mostly taken up with attacks — on those who opposed *The Playboy of the Western World*, on Sinn Fein, on the Irish in general, on Seumas MacManus's article in the *North American Review*, and on the Catholic Church. In commenting towards the end of his letter on 'the narrowness of Irish leaders', he criticized Horace Plunkett for implicitly taking all the credit for the Irish Revival: 'Then Hyde came and the glory was to the Gaelic League — increase and revival of industry, stopping or reducing of emigration, anti-treating and anti-drinking Gaelic League Crusade, and so on, but nothing about Plunkett or the IAOS. You are the only Irishman who gave just praise to all.'

[3] In the event, WBY probably did see Bullen in Dublin. Edith Georgina Lister (see p. 30, n. 10) was secretary of the Shakespeare Head Press in Stratford, which also published some of her writings under the name 'E. M. Martin' and other pseudonyms. Her sister Alys Oswald Lister (see p. 30, n 10), was Bullen's mistress (a position that both may have occupied). Edith Lister was to be actively engaged in the preparation of *CW* over the coming months, and even published an enthusiastic and informed review of the project in the *Fortnightly Review* of February 1909 over the initials 'E.M.D.' (253–70).

preference) from last year's bill.[4] I should think that the revival with our own people in the parts of a past play would help rather than otherwise our next visit with new work.

When I saw Fay in Dublin, he was very full of his meeting with Judge Keogh, who said he could raise enough money for us to run through the States for three months, and asked to have particulars sent to him. Fay wants either you or me to write to Judge Keogh and find out whether he was in earnest.[5] I should think that about the best thing would be to write assuming that he was in earnest and that we would send particulars as soon as possible. I confess I don't know how we are to get the particulars of expenses. We know something about expenses of touring in England, but I don't know how we are to find out about America. The matter, however, is of great importance. I wonder who knows Keogh's address which Fay doesn't seem to have asked him for. Perhaps you might write him a note care of Dun Emer and mark it Immediate.[6] When I see Barker I will ask him if he can give me any advice about expenses for three months in America as I know he has contemplated tours, but I should think his expenses would be incomparably heavier than ours.

Yrs ever
W B Yeats

[*in WBY's hand*]
no change about Miss Tobin & there will not be.

TLS Berg.

---

[4] Granville-Barker and J. E. Vedrenne had moved from the Court (see p. 23, n. 4) to the Savoy Theatre in the Strand, hitherto the home of the works of Gilbert and Sullivan. The move, to a theatre which was more central than the Court and twice its size, was largely Vedrenne's idea and was intended to increase audiences and revenues, but the venture failed: the new patrons did not materialize, and the old ones disliked the new venue. On 1 Aug Shaw was to describe Vedrenne as 'an incorrigible spendthrift', and, in sending him a further £500 on 19 Dec of this year, wrote (*BSCL* II. 742): 'I am stony. The enclosed is all I can scrape up.... Will it take you over the new production? If not—the brokers!' Although Shaw advised Granville-Barker that the 'thing to aim at now is a season without a single Shaw evening bill', the Savoy depended upon Shaw revivals and had just mounted the first West End production of his *Caesar and Cleopatra* by arrangement with Forbes-Robertson, but the plan to revive Abbey plays there came to nothing, and the whole venture lurched to a financially disastrous close on 14 Mar 1908.

[5] Judge Martin Jerome Keogh had been in Dublin in August 1906 with his wife, son, and Agnes Tobin, and the Abbey players had mounted a special show for them (see p. 503, n. 5). Keogh had been so impressed with this performance that he had suggested getting up a fund to underwrite a visit by the Abbey Company to the USA, and discussions about this continued throughout the autumn.

[6] The Keoghs had visited the Dun Emer Press the previous year, and SMY was a particular favourite with Martin Keogh.

## *To W. A. Henderson, 3 September 1907*

18, Woburn Buildings, | London, N.W.
Sept. 3, 1907.

Dear Henderson,

I shall write to Bullen asking him to give your book his careful attention.[1]
I could do nothing with Murray whom I know slightly.[2]

Yrs sny
W B Yeats

TLS NLI.

## *To A. E. F. Horniman, [c. 6 September 1907]*

Mention in two letters from AEFH, 8 September 1907.[1]
Telling her that he is out of the hands of the dentist[2] and has left London,
discussing a proposed American visit by the Abbey Theatre and a possible
series of lectures by him while they were there,[3] asking her if she has the

---

[1] With more time on his hands after his dismissal from the Abbey, Henderson evidently intended to
buckle down to finishing a book. He was, according to Payne (see p. 477, n. 1), writing on Shakespeare at
this time, but he was also extremely interested in the Arthurian legends and the various treatments of
the Tristan and Iseult story. Although he wrote a great number of articles on these and other topics, he
never published a book.

[2] The firm of John Murray were AG's publishers, with offices in Albermarle Street, London, and
WBY had occasionally negotiated with them about AG's books (see pp. 213, 218, and III. 134–7).

[1] AEFH was still in Annecy, and sent two replies to this letter, one marked '*Personal*' and the other a
'formal letter to you so that you may have something to shew to Judge Keogh if he wishes to know my
attitude'.

[2] WBY had chronic trouble with his teeth (see II. 514), and had arranged to see his dentist, Charles
Baly of 140 Harley Street, on his brief return to London. In her reply AEFH said that it was 'a pity that
you have gone away from London although release from the dentist's hands must be a relief'.

[3] WBY had told AEFH of Keogh's proposals. She had no objection to an American tour, and even
thought it might keep the Company 'up to the mark', but suspected that it would lead to the politiciza-
tion of the Abbey. Even in her '*Personal*' letter she warned 'as a matter of justice to the guarantors as
well as the Society, that if the Company is run in America on political lines that that will stop the
subsidy. They ought to know this clearly. I daresay that if Irish-American sympathies were raised and
the Abbey run on those lines, a large sum might be raised & I could be bought out.' She also advised him
to be 'very careful not to get left in the lurch, the way Mr Quinn stopped his £50 subscription without a
word of warning should make you cautious about American help'. Her 'formal' letter was even more
emphatic on the matter of politics: 'I hope that it is quite understood by everyone that I shall not
interfere either for or against any performances anywhere. That this visit to America will be practically
under political auspices alone would have always prevented me from having anything to do with it. As a
matter of policy I hope that I shall not have the political side impressed on me, as you all know perfectly
well that if the company be used in any way as a political instrument, it would be a matter of conscience

accounts for the last British tour,[4] and discussing the continuation of her subsidy for further tours.[5]

NLI.

## *To Letitia Darragh*, c. *10 September* [*1907*]

Mention in letter to Quinn, 4 October 1907.
Refusing her permission to perform *Cathleen ni Houlihan* in America, since the Abbey[1] Company would need it there if they toured, and telling her that he would need to write to a friend in New York about the contractual arrangements with Margaret Wycherly in respect of *Deirdre* and *The Shadowy Waters*.[2]

## *To Alexander Strahan Watt*, c. *11 September* [*1907*]

Mention in letter to Bullen, 4–5 October 1907.
Asking Watt to remind him of the terms of his contract with Bullen for *Ideas of Good and Evil*.

with me to stop the subsidy & to close the Abbey Theatre.' She thought it worth putting this formally as she supposed that Judge Keogh might 'not know my horror of politics which has been much intensified by my connection with Ireland'. She was 'very glad for you to go & lecture again'.

[4] WBY wanted to get some estimation of what an American tour might cost (see p. 718), and had asked for the accounts of the recent British tour as some sort of guide. Although AEFH pointed out that she would hardly have brought them to France with her, she revealed that she had 'kept them back on purpose as I had had the experience of sending previous accounts to Coole & their being lost without a word of apology from anyone. I will send them to you as soon as I get home though I fear that they cannot be posted until Tuesday.'

[5] AEFH warned that the American expenses would 'be very large if the poetical plays be taken too. Of course I shall continue the subsidy during the tour but if you go away for several months I think that I should be told when you will be absent so that I may make an effort to let the Abbey then.'

[1] Letitia Darragh had written to WBY to ask for rights to produce *Cathleen ni Houlihan*, *Deirdre*, and *The Shadowy Waters* during her forthcoming season in New York.

[2] The friend in New York was John Quinn. Margaret Wycherly (see pp. 50, 59–61) had produced *Cathleen ni Houlihan* in the USA, but not *Deirdre* or *The Shadowy Waters*, although WBY had evidently given her permission to stage the former (see p. 61, n. 6). Since the agreement was vague and she was unlikely to take up the option, there was no real need to consult Quinn, and WBY was using this as an excuse 'partly to get time to think' (see below, p. 735).

## To Edith Lister, 14 September [1907]

COOLE PARK, | GORT, CO. GALWAY.
Sept 14

Dear Miss Lister,

I heard from a friend in London that Bullen is very much against the inclusion of the three versions of Shadowy Waters. If this is so I dont want to press the point as the acting version is in my American edition appendix.[1] I can merely put a note mentioning the edition published at sixpence for sale in the theatre. It is in no way a vital matter with me, though I would sooner have it in. If the plays are to go into two volumes I think there is a better order than you have chosen. But first let me say that there will be one new play not two, about Cuchulain. This play is in prose and about as long as Cathleen ny Houlihan.[2] The new Where there is Nothing is not at all so long as the old being three acts instead of five.[3] If it does not matter having one volume bigger than its companion volumes it might be well to put Baile's Strand and Deirdre into the volume you have marked Vol II. and the prose plays into volume three (but I am at the present moment rather inclined to drop Pot of Broth).[4] If this arrangement is adopted we will begin the volume of verse plays with Deirdre and King's Threshold, in fact with my most mature work, and begin the prose plays with the new Where there is nothing.

If on the other hand the two volumes have to be of equal size, and not to include verse work, I think it will be best to print the plays in chronological order, Deirdre, and the new Where there is Nothing coming last, Hourglass and Cathleen ny Houlihan after Land of Hearts Desire.

Only I should like to know fairly soon as it will make a difference as to what I put into the appendix. In either case the second volume of the two will have to be delayed a considerable time, the prose stories &c coming first. I have to put the new wor[k] into rehearsal to test it.

I have written to Mrs Emery about the music. You will probably find yourself out of sympathy with this music but it gets its meaning from the method of speaking and is a necessary record of that method.

---

[1] WBY was corresponding with Edith Lister because Bullen was in London, partly to meet with Watt on WBY's behalf. WBY's 'friend in London' was probably AEFH, who had left Annecy on 8 Sept and who was taking a proprietorial interest in *CW*. In the end only two versions of *The Shadowy Waters* were published in *CW* II.

[2] The new play about Cuchulain was *The Golden Helmet* (see p. 693).

[3] i.e. *The Unicorn from the Stars*.

[4] Finally, there were three volumes of plays (see p. 695), and *A Pot of Broth* was dropped.

It is important to me that people whom I cannot personally teach and who may produce my work shall know my intentions. I will write a short appendix to go with the music.[5]

Yrs sny

W B Yeats

TLS Harvard. Wade, 491–2.

## To Sir Edward Grey,[1] [mid-September 1907]

RIGHT HON: SIR EDWARD GREY, M.P., &c., &c., SECRETARY OF STATE FOR FOREIGN AFFAIRS.[2]

SIR,

We, the undersigned, respectfully invite you to consider the advisability of an immediate release of the persons concerned in an assault on certain British officers near the village of Denshawai, on Wednesday, 13th June, 1906.[3]

---

[5] Both WBY and FF wrote notes on the method of speaking to the music for his plays and poems (see p. 702, n. 2), and music by FF, Sara Allgood, Arthur Darley, WBY, and A. H. Bullen was published in *CW* III.

[1] Sir Edward Grey, later 1st Viscount Grey of Fallodon, (1862–1933), Liberal politician and statesman, had been Under-Secretary for Foreign Affairs from 1892 to 1895, and Secretary of State for Foreign Affairs 1905–16. He acted as temporary British ambassador to the USA in 1919, and served as chancellor of Oxford University from 1928 to his death. He recalls the Denshawai incident in chapter VIII of his autobiography *Twenty-Five Years* (1925), defending the action of the court and his response to it. Reading the book in November 1925, AG commented (*Journals* II. 52) that 'Grey seems to have himself been shocked at the Egyptian pigeon shooting business, though he had officially to support it'.

[2] This petition was drafted by Shaw and published in the *New Age* on 24 Oct 1907. Apart from its main purpose of gaining the release of the Egyptian prisoners, it was also part of a longer-term campaign, as Shaw confessed to Holbrook Jackson on 12 Nov, to force the Prime Minister, Sir Henry Campbell-Bannerman, to reshuffle his cabinet: 'I believe that by a steady singling out of Morley ... and Grey (for Denshawai), and some grumbling about Gladstone's reactionary free-contract attitude at the Home Office, we might make black sheep of them among the Liberals, and even compel C.B. to reconstitute his Cabinet on more popular lines' (*BSCL* II. 712–13).

[3] On 13 June 1906 a party of five uniformed British officers (two of whom were Irish), led by Major J. E. Pine-Coffin (1866–1919) went to shoot pigeons near the village of Denshawai (or Denshawi) in the Nile delta. They failed to get permission for this from the Omdeh, or headman, of the village, who was away. Some, and probably all, of the pigeons they were shooting were not wild, but had been bred by the local fellahin, many by Hassan Mahfouz, a pigeon-farmer, who was incensed at this depredation of his stock. Shortly after the shoot began a threshing floor nearby caught fire, and, although the flames were rapidly doused, this incited a group of villagers to attack the soldiers. In the fracas a Lieutenant Porter's gun was discharged, wounding four protesters, including a woman, the wife of Abd-el-Nebi, who was erroneously reported dead. The attack on the soldiers with sticks and stones intensified and they attempted to escape on foot to their camp, a distance of six miles. One succeeded in this, and raised the alarm; another, Captain Bull, collapsed on the way with sunstroke and was later found dead; the others were captured by their pursuers and brought back to Denshawai, where they were shown the wounded woman and threatened with death. At this point a party of Sheikhs and Gaffirs intervened to

The impression under which public opinion was reconciled to the Denshawai sentences (always excepting the resort to flogging, which many Englishmen consider inadmissible under any circumstances) has been completely changed by the publication of the official papers, (White Papers, Egypt, 1906 Nos 3 & 4).[4] That impression was that a party of British officers had been attacked without provocation in an Egyptian village, and one of them put to death in an outburst of anti-English prejudice and Moslem fanaticism. The White Papers prove that the affair had no political or religious significance; that the officers thoughtlessly gave very serious provocation; that those officers who did not escape were rescued from the mob by the sheikhs and gaffirs of the village, and sent on to the English camp;[5] that the deceased officer, who took to flight, died of sunstroke at a considerable distance from Denshawai; that one of the prisoners, now undergoing sentence of penal servitude for life, assaulted

protect the captives from their attackers, gave them water, and assisted them to return to camp. An army patrol subsequently arrested fifty-two villagers and they were tried on 24–7 June by a special tribunal. On 27 June four of the accused were sentenced to death, two to penal servitude for life, another to fifteen years, six others to seven years, three to one year and fifty lashes, and five to fifty lashes. The sentences were carried out in public the following day on a gallows which had been erected in view of the village, in a protracted alternation of hangings and floggings which apparently lasted from 1 to 4.40 p.m. (although the official account claimed they only went on until 2.30).

[4] The reports in the English press at the time of the incident and trial echoed official communiqués in suggesting that this was a premeditated insurrection, inspired by extremist political and religious motives, and signalled by the fire at the threshing floor. On 18 June 1906 *The Times* reported (5) that the 'district bears a bad name, and the fact that cries of "Death to the Christians" were raised is of some significance'. The following day it commented (5) that official accounts gave the impression that 'the Denshawi fellaheen are quite capable of attacking strangers at any time, but that the unrest of this year made their attack more ferocious than it would otherwise have been'. The paper gave accounts of the case for the prosecution at the trial, but not for the defence, and in reporting the sentences on 18 June maintained that opinion 'among Europeans and many respectable natives supports the verdict, the evidence having proved that the attacks had been premeditated for months, and that the wounded officers had been treated with cowardly brutality by the mob, who attacked only when Major Pine-Coffin had ordered the party to surrender their arms in the vain hope of quieting the threatening crowd.' Sir Edward Grey repeated this view when challenged by the Irish MP John Dillon in the House of Commons on 28 June 1906, asserting that the evidence clearly established premeditation and concerted action, and insisting that the British officers had behaved with extreme forbearance and self-restraint.

[5] Despite Grey's reassurances, there was widespread concern in Britain at the unsound legal processes involved in the trial, and about the severity of the sentences. This led to a demand that the transcript of the trial and ancillary papers should be published and this was done in two White Papers (*Accounts and Papers* 1906, cxxxvii, Egypt 3 and 4), issued in July and September 1906. The full transcript called the hitherto official account into doubt on a series of crucial points, and this, together with protests against the conduct of the trial in the Egyptian press, provoked an agitation for a full inquiry and the quashing of the sentences. Wilfrid Blunt's pamphlet *Atrocities of British Rule in Egypt*, dated August 1906, presented a powerful indictment of the soldiers' behaviour and the irregularities in the judicial process, while Shaw devoted the final section of his preface to *John Bull's Other Island* (1907) to a withering exposé of the contradictions and hypocrisies in the official account of 'The Denshawai Horror'. At the same time, Irish and Radical MPs, particularly John Dillon and Hugh Law, continued to raise the topic in Parliament, Law insisting on 31 Aug 1907 that the White Papers proved the attack had not been premeditated and that the executions were judicial murders.

the officers under a reasonable (though mistaken) impression that the wound his wife had received in consequence of the discharge of Lieut. Porter's gun was fatal;[6] and that, in short, nothing had happened that might not have been expected in any English village if a shooting party of foreigners, ignorant of our language and customs, had begun to shoot the domestic animals and farm stock under the impression that they were ferae naturae.

When we add that the tribunal which awarded the sentences of hanging (4), flogging (8), penal servitude for life (2), and a number of shorter sentences, including one for 15 years, was constituted in a manner altogether repugnant to English practice, in that there was no Jury, we have said enough to show how strong and justifiable the feeling in Egypt (and in England) is against the sentences,[7] and how many of our own countrymen are deeply discouraged, as long as the sentences are maintained, in their faith in the impartiality, equity and humanity of the English administration in Egypt.

We deeply regret that the severest sentences are beyond recall; the hangings and floggings are irrevocable; but we would urge you to remember that every day's delay creates an impression unfavourable to the Foreign Office and to English justice in Egypt.

Under these circumstances, without asking you to retract your personal support of what we may call the official view of the calamitous incident at Denshawai, we do venture most strongly to press upon you, Sir, the necessity of relieving the present strain and anxiety by the speedy release of the prisoners from an imprisonment which has already lasted fifteen months.[8]

---

[6] The evidence as to whether Lieutenant Porter had fired the shots which wounded the wife of Abd-el-Nebi and three others, or whether his gun had gone off after it had been seized from him, was contradictory. He claimed that he had tried to unload his gun and put on the safety-catch before it was snatched form him, but (before being ordered to quit the witness-box) an Egyptian policeman, Ahmed Hassan Zakzouk, who had accompanied the shooting party, claimed that the officers had deliberately fired on the mob twice.

[7] The trial was conducted under a khedival decree of 25 Feb 1895 which instituted a special tribunal to deal with crimes of violence against the officers and men of the British army of occupation. There was no jury and the tribunal was under the jurisdiction of Boutros Ghali, a Copt and the Egyptian acting Minister of Justice; William Hayter (1869–1924), Assistant Legal Adviser in Egypt; Colonel Ludlow, Officiating Judge Advocate of the Army of Occupation; Ahmed Bey Fathi Zaghul, President of the Native Tribunal of Cairo; and the Vice-President of the Native Court of Appeal. Technically neither the Egyptian government nor the British Agency in Egypt had any legal power to intervene in the execution of the decrees of the court, but a telegram from Grey as Minister for Foreign Affairs would have suspended the executions had he chosen (as urged by John Dillon) to send such a directive. British opinion was disconcerted not only by the executions and the floggings, but also because they were carried out in public.

[8] This petition was presented to Sir Edward Grey on 9 Oct 1907. *The Times* reported on 19 Oct (3) that a 'memorial, signed by Lord Coleridge, Lord Courtney of Penwith, Lord Eversley, Lord Weardale,

We have the honour to be,

Sir,
Your most obedient, humble servants,
W B Yeats
Augusta Gregory

TLS Emory. Marked at top in another hand '*Confidential.* Please sign & return to C H Norman. 4N. Hyde Park Mansions, London, N. W.'⁹

## To Elizabeth Sharp, [c. *17 September 1907*]

Mention in letter from Elizabeth Sharp, 19 September 1907.
Asking for details of William Sharp's birth so that he can cast his horoscope.¹

*LWBY* I. 192.

## To Elizabeth Sharp, [c. *21 September 1907*]

Mention in letter from Elizabeth Sharp, late September 1907.
Asking for more precise details of William Sharp's birth in order to cast his horoscope,¹ and evidently sending her an account of his lecture to the Franco-Scottish Society in Aberdeen on 25 Jan this year.²

*LWBY* I. 192–3.

Lady Gregory, Mr. Wilfrid Blunt, Mr. H. R. Fox Bourne, Professor Caird, General Sir William Butler, Mr. George Meredith, Mr. Bernard Shaw, and Sir William Wedderburn, and a number of prominent Radical politicians, writers, and others, has been addressed to Sir Edward Grey urging the immediate release of the Denshawi prisoners should be considered.' The report went on to quote Grey's reply to the petition, issued through his assistant under-secretary Walter Langley on 16 Oct, that 'the subject has been very recently discussed in Parliament, and that Sir E. Grey cannot at present add to the statements which he then made concerning it'. In spite of this apparently dusty answer, Grey and the Liberal government were acutely embarrassed by the whole affair, and the letter was not without effect: by the end of the year all the Denshawi prisoners had been released on a full pardon, and the khedival tribunal was never used again.

⁹ Clarence H. Norman was a journalist and legal shorthand writer. Shaw also employed him to take down verbatim reports of his public lectures, and had persuaded him to act as secretary and co-ordinator of the Denshawi petition, for which he collected 53 signatures.

¹ In her reply, Elizabeth Sharp told him that 'The Year of Will's birth was 1855' and added that she was 'so interested in this matter of his horoscope'.

¹ WBY had evidently written to tell Mrs Sharp that he would need more than the year of birth to cast her husband's horoscope accurately, and she replied from London sometime after 26 Sept with 'valuable' information on the matter from 'an old friend': 'that he was born about *two o'clock*, on Friday the 12ᵗʰ. September.'

² Mrs Sharp was 'interested' to see the account of the meeting (see p. 610, n. 2), and wished she 'had been there to hear your address'. The newspaper account, which he was presumably sending her,

## To A. H. Bullen, [*23 September 1907*]

COOLE PARK, | GORT, | CO. GALWAY.
Monday

My dear Bullen: There will be no difficulty about the five volumes.[1] You can have the volume of stories any time. I am not quite sure if I shall put the stage version of 'Shadowy Waters' or the second version of the other but there will be only two. Augustus John has just left with sketches to do his etching from—if it is satisfactory there need be no delay.[2] I doubt if I shall be able to get the coloured designs of stage scenes as Robert Gregory is getting married & has his hands full. I had discussed the process with my brother & his experience of hand-colouring went to show that they could be done without too great expense.[3]

Your letters do not irritate me. It was your use of that text without consulting me & not your letters that put me out.[4] I should think the best order for the plays will be

---

informed her that he had read a poem of Fiona Macleod's, and in the concluding chapter of her biography, *William Sharp*, she quoted (424) WBY's speech at length: 'He considered that "Sharp had in many ways an extraordinarily primitive mind. He was fond of speaking of himself as the representative of the old bards," and the Irish poet thought there was really something in the claim. . . . He continued that W.S. was the most extraordinary psychic he had ever encountered. He really believed that "Fiona Macleod was a secondary personality—as distinct a secondary personality as those one reads about in books of psychical research. At times he (W.S.) was really to all intents and purposes a different being." He would "come and sit down by my fireside and talk, and I believe that when 'Fiona Macleod' left the house he would have no recollection of what he had been saying to me".'

[1] Bullen was hoping to print off five volumes of CW as a group, before going on to the remaining three.

[2] The flamboyantly bohemian artist Augustus John (1878–1961) had been invited to Coole Park by Robert Gregory, for whom he was to act as best man on 26 Sept. Since Charles Shannon was too busy to do a portrait of WBY in London, Robert Gregory suggested that John, who would be in Coole anyway, should do one instead. AG sent John a fee of £18 in advance and on 21 Sept wrote a cheque for a further 25 guineas (Emory). John wrote to Alexandra Schepeler from Coole on 17 Sept 1907: 'Painting Yeats is becoming quite a habit. He has a natural and sentimental prejudice in favour of the W. B. Yeats he and other people have been accustomed to see and imagine for so many years. He is now 44 and a robust virile and humorous personality (while still the poet of course). I cannot see in him any definite resemblance to the youthful Shelley in a lace collar. To my mind he is far more interesting as he is, as maturity is more interesting than immaturity. But my unprejudiced vision must seem brutal and unsympathetic to those in whom direct vision is supplanted by a vague and sentimental memory' (Huntington). Perhaps for this reason, none of WBY's friends, including Bullen, thought the etching 'satisfactory' and it was not used in *CW*. John did a number of studies for the etching, but the final version now hangs in the Manchester City Art Gallery (although in *Expl* [308] WBY erroneously describes this as 'a Birmingham gallery'). John also painted WBY again in the summer of 1930.

[3] This had been a matter of controversy between Bullen and WBY earlier in the summer (see p. 691). In the end, there were no coloured designs of stage scenes in *CW*.

[4] See pp. 690–1, 692.

The Kings Threshold (or 'Dierdre')
Dierdre (or the Kings Threshold)
Bailes Strand.
Countess Cathleen.
The Shadow[y] Waters
Land of Hearts Desire.⁵
What do you think.

Yr ever
W B Yeats

ALS Kansas.

## *To A. E. F. Horniman,* [c. *23 September 1907*]

Mention in letter to AEFH, 27 September 1907.
Wishing her success with the opening week of the Playgoers' Theatre,¹
discussing the writing of *The Unicorn from the Stars*,² and telling her that
FF is seeing a lot of Robert Farquharson.³

NLI.

---

⁵ The final arrangement of *CW* II was *The King's Threshold, On Baile's Strand, Deirdre,* and *The Shadowy Waters. The Land of Heart's Desire* was published as the second play in *CW* III.

¹ Having announced on 11 July that she was setting up a repertory company in Manchester, AEFH took the Midland Hotel Theatre there for four weeks from 23 Sept (see p. 702), and WBY had evidently written to wish her well. She was to hire the venue for a further week from 5 Nov, while she was negotiating for the Gaiety Theatre as a permanent home. In her reply on 27 Sept, she told him that the 'fine weather is bad for all the theatres but we are going along all right & the interest is growing.... The great thing is to make people believe that this is a serious undertaking, not a philanthropic passing idea. Of course wild tales of my wealth are being circulated in Manchester, so I'm asking my friends to say that I live in a flat with one servant.'

² In her reply AEFH said that she was 'very curious as to how you will turn Paul into a Unicorn from the Stars. Will it be put into rehearsal at once? Will it be a play to tour?'

³ WBY had evidently told AEFH that FF was seeing a good deal of Farquharson, whom he despised (see pp. 134, 145, 150–1), but AEFH rallied to the defence of her sex and age: 'Mʳˢ Emery & I are at the age to like young admirers & when elderly men give them *rude* nicknames & call them "loathly" etc. we accept that as their natural arrogance. Why should she not have Farquarson in tow? Its a queer taste though!'

## *To Florence Farr, [23 September 1907]*

Coole Park, | Gort, | Co. Galway.

My dear Florence Emery: Augustus John has just left and I have time for letters. He has done numberless portraits of me to work up into an etching—all powerful ugly gypsey things.[1] He behaved very well here, did the most wonderful acrobatic things on the floor and climbed to the top of the highest tree in the garden and did not talk much about his two wives and his seven children. Lady Gregory was always afraid some caller would say 'How many children' 'Seven' 'You must have married very young' 'About four years' 'Twins I suppose' 'Oh no but—' and then all out.[2] He wears hair down to his shoulders and an early victorian coat with a green velvet collar. Robert watches him with ever visible admiration and dicipleship. To day Miss Horniman opens her Manchester theatre[3] and for the next few months lives under the following secondary directions (nearly all from fifth house—house of theatres)

| | | |
|---|---|---|
| ☽ sep for ☍ ♃ R | | Sept and Oct |
| ☽ | □ ☽ R | about Oct and Nov |
| ☽ | ☍ ♀ R | about Jan |
| ☽ | □ ☉ P | about March |
| ☽ | ☌ ♂ P | abt July |
| ☽ | ☍ ♄ R | Nov and Dec |

If this (and the transits are nearly as spirited) does not make hay with her Manchester theatre, Ananias was an astrologer and a planet and a star.[4]

---

[1] In *Pages from a Diary written in Nineteen Hundred and Thirty* WBY recalled (*Expl*, 308): 'When I was painted by John years ago, and saw for the first time the portrait (or rather the etching taken from it)...I shuddered....He had found Anglo-Irish solitude, a solitude I have made for myself, an outlawed solitude.'

[2] John's first wife Ida Nettleship had died on 14 Mar of this year of puerperal fever and peritonitis, following the birth of her fifth son. John's 'two wives' legend grew up after Dorothy (Dorelia) McNeill (d. 1969) was admitted to the ménage in 1903, but, though she bore him four children, and lived with him until her death, John never married her. By 1907 John had seven children, the five by Ida and two by Dorelia.

[3] The venture had opened on 23 Sept (see previous letter) with two plays by Charles McEvoy: a curtain-raiser, *His Helpmate*, and *David Ballard*. The latter, and the venture as a whole, received a good press.

[4] Secondary directions depend on progressing the movement of the planets in the zodiac at the rate of a day for a year. It is much easier to calculate 'secondaries' than primary directions, since the astrologer counts off the days in the ephemeris following birth to find the new positions. The moon is most commonly studied because it moves quickly. AEFH was born on 3 Oct 1860, and WBY's astrological notebook for 1906–10 (NLI) shows a very thorough analysis of her horoscope and its progressions for 1907–8. He notes the moon's secondary progression (taking a day for every year of her life, roughly a degree of lunar progression for a month of 'real time') from October 1907 to April 1908. He also dated his analysis 'Oct 3, 1907', i.e. from AEFH's forty-seventh birthday. In this list WBY has noted the

Many thanks about the music.[5] The first five volumes are to come out almost at once. I think Miss Lyster wrote as she did about Sidgewick because he and Bullen are I think in slightly strained relations.[6] I have just glanced at your horoscope (but will work it out carefully). I note that ☽ is going to ☌♅, Δ♀R, Δ♃P, which should give you success in America (♃ ♂ ♀).[7]

Yours ever<br>W B Yeats

Printed copy; Bax 61–2, Wade 492–3.

## To Maud Gonne, [late September 1907]

Mention in letter from MG, 28 September [1907].
Complaining that he feels depressed about politics,[1] telling her of plans for the publication of his *Collected Works* and his book of essays, *Discover-*

---

stressful squares and oppositions to her natal (Radix) planets, and also to the progressed positions of the other natal planets:

    Moon opposite Jupiter Radix
    Moon square Moon Radix
    Moon opposite Venus Radix
    Moon square Sun Progressed
    Moon conjunct Mars Progressed
    Moon opposite Saturn Radix

The transiting planets were activating many of the same planets, and planetary stresses were likely to cause dangerous energies. In Ben Jonson's *The Alchemist* (1610) the zealous Puritan deacon Ananias returns to London from Amsterdam to purchase the philosopher's stone, with which he hopes to free his exiled brethren, but he is duped and fleeced by Subtle, a fake alchemist and astrologer who plays on his ignorance and gullibility with a flood of alchemical processes and assurances. In Act II scene V Subtle asks him rhetorically whether he is an alchemist: 'A Lullianist? A Ripley? Filius artis?' WBY's interest in astrology had deepened recently and from 24 June 1906 he kept an MS book of horoscopes. On 17 Sept 1907 he had even contemplated a lyric on the topic. See also Acts 5.

[5] WBY had written to FF for copies of her musical settings of his plays and poems (see p. 721), and she had evidently obliged.

[6] Edith Lister's letter to FF is untraced. Presumably she had asked FF to communicate with her or Bullen at Stratford-upon-Avon rather than with Frank Sidgwick, who was in dispute with Bullen over their financial relationship and who was to dissolve their partnership on 14 Feb 1908.

[7] The moon going to opposition Uranus, and is also trine (120 degrees) her Venus Radix and trine her Jupiter Progressed. Jupiter conjunct Venus is an extremely fortunate combination. Nevertheless, FF did not return to the USA (see p. 713, n. 8).

[1] MG could not understand WBY's depression (intensified no doubt by the backwash of the *Playboy* disputes and the hostile attitude of the Dublin Council and Arthur Griffith over the Lane picture gallery) and replied (*G–YL*, 246) that although she was 'away from it all I feel hopeful & see many signs of progress'. She was particularly gratified by the success of Sinn Fein: 'I started the Sinn Fein Movement, but I never thought it would progress as rapidly as it has. Griffith really has worked well at it which must make one lenient to many aggravating traits in his character, he has great tenacity of purpose.'

*ies*,[2] stating that he does not attack directly those in Irish life who annoy him,[3] and apparently asking if her direct work for Ireland is over.[4]

*G–YL*, 246–7.

## To Edith Lister, 28 September [*1907*]

COOLE PARK, | GORT, CO. GALWAY.
Sept 28

Dear Miss Lister,

Would you mind telling me exactly how much of my collected edition has been printed? I have had a letter from Mr Bullen which I cannot understand. He writes among other things 'I have not got an unlimited quantity of type . . . I have a whole volume in type. . . . which I cant release'. This can only mean that there is some volume which he cannot print off, owing to having received incomplete copy. I am puzzled. He has had complete copy for four volumes. (a) Celtic Twilight and Red Hanrahan. (b) Ideas of Good and evil. (c) Poems. (d) Verse Plays. The copy for the remaining three volumes is all in my hands. There has evidently been some mistake, it is very important to have this cleared up, as I am most anxious not to keep the Press waiting.[1] Since I arranged with Mr Bullen some time ago that I should get a reasonable time for my revisions, there has been no reason whatever for any hitch. Mr Bullen also speaks of beginning the Verse Play volume with Baile's Strand. I had written asking him whether he thought it better to begin with Deirdre or Kings Threshold and then saying that I thought it had better be Deirdre. I have an impression that I wrote to you from London, suggesting an order with Kings Threshold first. If you

---

[2] MG replied that she was 'looking forward to your collected edition & to reading the essays'.

[3] MG was pleased to hear this, replying that she was 'glad you don't attack directly those who annoy you in Irish life. I too am beginning to think that direct personal attack is GENERALLY a mistake.'

[4] MG answered that she did 'not know if my direct work for Ireland is over or not—now as ever, in this matter I am in the hands of the gods'. But she added that 'for the moment I am forming a wonderful instrument. I will tell you all about this when we meet. I am not good at writing of things that interest me very deeply.' At a personal level, she was 'quite content with my life as it is & find so much that interests me. You know for years I wore blinkers so as to never cease working for the cause & only see the one end & object. Now I have taken them off & find so much to look at—'

[1] Since the Bullen archives are incomplete and dispersed, it is difficult to trace with any exactitude the printing history of *CW*. Bullen had placed an initial order for fifty reams of paper from R. Tanner & Co. on 30 May of this year. In the early autumn of 1907 he was occupied with the publication of *Deirdre* and the third edition of *Ideas of Good and Evil*, as well as with *CW*, and it was not until 5 Feb 1908 that he instructed James Burn & Co. to bind what was presumably the first run of 150 copies of vols. I, II, V, and VI.

have my letter would you please look it up.[2] When I wrote these letters I did not know that the Press was at work on anything but Countess Cathleen. I had received two lots of proofs of Countess Cathleen and as the proofs left off at I think the second act I concluded that the Press had been put to something else. If I know what the Press is doing, and when things are wanted I shall be able to let you know exactly what I want done and send copy punctually. But I must always know. It is also necessary that I should know when the next volume is wanted. I have done all my own work but it is necessary that I get the text of my revisions typed. Mr Bullen asked me some time ago for five volumes which he could put upon the market without waiting for the last two.

However I think it very unwise going on as we are without definite agreements. I am sorry that A. P. Watt wasnt there to meet him the other day, but I imagine that he has all but retired, in which case the sooner his sons get the grip of my affairs the better. I shall write to A. P. Watt on hearing from you.[3]

I havent sent you the music I spoke of, as Bullen seems anxious to have the appendix which will contain it at the end of the Prose Plays and this will enable me to look through a drawer I have of various musical odds and ends in London. The only thing absolutely necessary as a record is Miss Farr's music, and some fragments of folk music for the prose plays, as I dont want to burden the book with too much I may as well wait till I look through the mass.[4]

Yrs sny
W B Yeats

TLS Harvard. Wade, 493–5.

[2] No letter from London has been traced, but WBY discussed the order of his plays in his letters of 14 and 23 Sept from Coole (see pp. 721–2, 726–7), in both of which he had suggested that either of these plays could be placed first.

[3] In his letter to Watt of 10 Sept (see p. 712, n. 4) Bullen said that he had 'been intending to call upon you in connection with the collected edition of Yeats' writings; and I will try to see you in the early part of next week, if you are in town'. When he called he found not A. P. Watt but his son and partner Alexander Strahan Watt (see p. 141), who had been handling most of the correspondence for some time. Bullen apparently refused to negotiate with him and returned to Stratford in high dudgeon. No correspondence or agreement relating to *CW* survives in the Watt archives, and there may have been no formal contract for the project, since any contract would have been complicated by AEFH's subsidy.

[4] See pp. 712–13.

## *To A. H. Bullen, 30 September* [*1907*]

COOLE PARK, | GORT, CO. GALWAY.

Sept 30

My dear Bullen,

You can begin with King's Threshold. Deirdre would be rather better as it has more popular qualities being a love story, and I have noticed that reviewers have a way of judging one by whatever comes first. For years every review said it was such a pity Mr Yeats had fallen off so after writing the Wanderings of Oisin. So next edition, I put the Wanderings of Oisin at the end of the book instead of the beginning, and nobody has ever mentioned it since.[1] However let the order be: Kings Threshold, Baile's Strand, Deirdre, Land of Hearts Desire, Shadowy Waters, Countess Cathleen.[2] What I would have objected to altogether would have been Baile's Strand first as you said in your last letter but one. You need not keep Deirdre back for the music for I want the music to go in an appendix, not in the text. If you will look up my letters you will find that I stated this some little time ago. You suggested that the Appendix would have come better in the Volume of prose plays, and I asked if it would be anomolous having the music to the verse plays as well as that to the prose plays in that appendix. You had better look up my letter. If you think it necessary to have the music at the end of the verse volume, then all the appendix to the verse plays had better go in at the same time. But I must know, as I shall have to write something about the music. I gave certain arguments in my letter besides for preferring to have all the music together in an appendix at the end of the prose volume.[3]

The reason why I dont want the music in the text this time is that it is not folk music as it was in the case of the Pot of Broth. There is

[*The rest of this letter is missing*]

TL Kansas.

---

[1] 'The Wanderings of Oisin' had appeared at the beginning of the first edition of *Poems* in October 1895 (after the short prefatory poem 'To some I have talked with by the fire'), but in the second, revised, edition of 1899 it was placed at the end of the volume, a position it continued to occupy in all subsequent printings.

[2] *The Land of Heart's Desire* and *The Countess Cathleen* were finally placed in *CW* III. With these omissions, the order of the plays in *CW* II was as WBY suggests here.

[3] WBY is probably thinking of his letters to Edith Lister of 14 and 28 Sept (see pp. 721–2, 730–1), but may be referring to a more specific letter to Bullen which is now lost.

## To John Quinn, 4–6 October 1907

Nassau Hotel, | D U B L I N,
4th Octr., 1907.

My dear Quinn

Very many thanks for your long letter, which I was very glad indeed to get.[1] I have just come up from Coole for the production of a new play called "The Country Dressmaker". It is by a new writer called Fitzmaurice. A harsh, strong ugly comedy. It really gives [a] much worse view of the people than the "Playboy". Even I rather dislike it, though I admire its sincerity, and yet it was received with enthusiasm.[2] The truth is that the objection to Synge is not mainly that he makes the country people unpleasant or immoral, but that he has got a standard of morals and an intellect. They never minded Boyle, whose people are a sordid lot, because they knew what he was at. They understood his obvious moral, and they don't mind Fitzmaurice because they don't think he is at anything, but they shrink from Synges harsh, independent, heroical, clean, wind-swept view of things. They want their clerical conservatory where the air is warm and

---

[1] i.e. of 23 Aug 1907; see p. 628, n. 8.

[2] In George Fitzmaurice's three-act peasant comedy *The Country Dressmaker*, the heroine, Julia Shea, keeps her memories of her emigrant sweetheart alive through the influence of cheap romantic fiction and the machination of her unscrupulous neighbours the Clohesys, who forge letters from him in order to exploit her. The emigrant returns, and the Clohesys try to marry him off to one of their daughters, but he meets Julia again, and, after a series of complications, marries her. Fitzmaurice (1877–1963) was born in Kerry, the son of a Church of Ireland clergyman, and, after working in a bank in Cork, moved to Dublin where, except for army service in the Great War, he remained a clerk in the civil service for the rest of his life. *The Country Dressmaker* was so well received that its run was extended, and in his diary for 3 Oct (NLI) Holloway explicitly compared its reception with that of *The Playboy*: 'No troops required, not even a policeman, at the Abbey tonight. . . . Irish people can stand any amount of hard things being said of them if there is truth at the back of them, but what they wont stand for a moment is libellous falsehoods such as those contained in *The Playboy* & such-like foreign tainted stuff, that makes them out sensual blackguards, cruel monsters, & irreligious brutes. Now the new dramatist, George Fitzmaurice . . . hits hard enough at times, & his Clohesy family are anything but a lovable lot; nevertheless, their faults are human & Irish.' However, the play's success was not so unquestioning as this and WBY suggest. The *Evening Mail* (Dublin) noted that 'it displays the Irish peasant of Kerry in a light scarcely less loveable than Mr Synge's "Parricide". Yet, no murmur of dissent impedes its easy flow.' The *Evening Telegraph* of 4 Oct thought (2) that the author 'might, without straining beyond the borders of accuracy, have introduced a few more lofty and more Irish types than appear in his conception. . . . There is no breath of the Gaelic League in the whole play, and no suggestion of the new National Spirit which is sweeping over the country.' The play continued to attract adverse comment, and the most hostile review appeared in the *Peasant* on 4 Jan 1908, after its revival. Fred Ryan told Holloway on 4 Oct (NLI) that he thought the play 'promising', but that it showed the Irish people in as sordid a light as Synge, except that 'Synge with all his faults gripped you in his plays just like Ibsen—you wanted to know what was coming on. They were strange & they interested you!' As early as 22 Mar 1907 Holloway had heard of WBY's warning to Fitzmaurice 'that they would require 200 police when they produced his play, seeing that 150 were required during the run of Synge's *Playboy*'.

damp. Of course, we may not get through to-morrow night, but the row won't be very bad. Nothing is ever persecuted but the intellect, though it is never persecuted under its own name. I don't think it would be wise for me to write a reply to that absurd article by M'Manus. As I never now write about politics people would think I was paying him off or his Party off for the "Playboy".[3] I argued that question at the meeting not because I thought I should convince anybody but because the one thing that seemed possible to do was that we should all, players and playwrights, show that we weren't afraid. The result has been that we have doubled the enthusiasm of our own following. The principal actors are now applauded at their entrances with a heartiness unknown before, and both Lady Gregory & myself received several times last Spring what newspapers writers call "an ovation". We have lost a great many but the minority know that we are in earnest, and if only our finances hold out we will get the rest. You were quite right about my father being the proper person to introduce Synge. I have seen so little of him lately having been in the country, that I don't know what he is doing in the matter.[4] Just one thing more and I am done with theatrical things for the moment. Miss Darragh, who played Deirdre here has gone to America touring in somebody or others Company. She left in the middle of last month, and just before doing so asked me if I would give her permission

---

[3] A not inconsiderable portion of Quinn's long letter (see above, n. 1) had been taken up with an attack on Seumas MacManus's article 'Sinn Fein: Its Genesis and Purposes', which had appeared in the *North American Review* on 16 Aug 1907, and which, Quinn claimed, fraudulently ascribed all the recent advances in Irish industrial, social, and cultural life to Sinn Fein: 'the whole article is disgusting. Why can't you write a letter to the editor of the *North American Review* protesting against its down right deliberate dishonesty?' Quinn had sent a copy of the offending article, complete with his markings and comments, to WBY and had also sent copies to Hyde, AE, Rolleston, and Gill. Quinn had been nominated president of Sinn Fein in New York in August 1907, but, according to the *Gaelic American* of 17 Aug (1), declined for business reasons.

Seumas MacManus (*c.* 1868–1960), a prolific author of popular stories, verse, and plays, had emigrated to America shortly after the death of his wife, the Irish poet Anna Johnston ('Ethna Carbery'), in 1902. His one-act comedy *The Townland of Tamney* had, to WBY's disgust, been produced by the INTS in January 1904 (see III. 540–1), but his attacks on the Abbey Company during their first USA tour in 1911 were so virulent that AG was to dub him 'Shame-Us MacManus'. His autobiography, *The Rocky Road to Dublin*, appeared in New York in 1938.

[4] Although Quinn felt that the debate over *The Playboy* (see p. 617, n. 4) 'was a mistake' (a view with which Synge agreed), he was tickled by JBY's observation that Ireland was a country of plaster saints and an island of sinners. He added that he was trying to arrange for Baker & Taylor to become Synge's American publishers, and that he needed an introduction to the plays: 'I have written to Synge and to Roberts that the man of all others in Ireland to do this would be — can you guess — your father. He has an extraordinary gift of expression.... Your father would write a winning introduction — one that would help and tend to disarm criticism.' In an undated letter, written at this time (NLI), JBY told WBY that he had received 'a long letter from Quinn ... he writes to make two requests: — that I write the general introduction to Synge's plays, which I am quite ready to do provided it is done on approval (by which I chiefly mean my own approval), and the other request is *that I do a portrait of you for £30*. I need not say it would be an immense kindness and help to me if you could manage to come up sometime reasonably soon, and give me a few sittings.'

to play "Deirdre", "Shadowy Waters", and "Kathleen Ni Houlihan" in the States. I cannot let her play "Kathleen" as our own people may be going out, but the other two plays are possible as our own people could not do them adequately. When she wrote to me I replied, partly to get time to think, that I had a friend in New York who had arranged about previous performances and that I knew he had some arrangement with Miss Witcherly about her having the rights upon my work for a certain time, and that I should have to write to you. Miss Darragh wanted your address but I don't see why I should trouble you with her. If you think it well that she should do "Deirdre", or the other, please send her the affirmative letter which I enclose, and if you don't think it, please send her the negative one. I imagine that Miss Witcherly's rights have lapsed, but I really want to ask you to advise.[5] The point is this "Deirdre" is the one play I am likely to write for sometime which has a good woman's part in it. I am going to write lyrics for a year.[6] Should I keep it back on the chance of some considerable actress taking it up, or should I let Miss Darragh do it on the principle of a bird in the hand? I liked her performance (though I must say Lady Gregory and many others did not) and everybody liked her performance in the "Shadowy Waters". She is an extremely well taught actress, indeed most learned in her business, but has not a sufficiently sympathetic personality on the stage to make a success of herself probably in this age. She is also rather artificial, in fact rather too obviously knows her business; she has power but no charm. I don't know what to say about business arrangements with her, but I think the simplest thing will be to leave them in abeyance, until she gets an opportunity to perform it which she may never do. If that opportunity comes perhaps you might be so kind as to write her a letter stating terms. I hate putting work on you.

Saturday.

We have had another performance of "The Country Dressmaker" since I wrote, and the success was greater than before. The dear "Freeman", or rather its evening issue which is called by another name, has congratulated us on having got a play at last "to which nobody can take the slightest

[5] Letitia Darragh was performing with the James K. Hackett company at the Hackett Theatre, New York. For Miss Wycherly see pp. 59–60.

[6] Quinn already knew this since AG, enumerating in her letter of 17 Aug (see p. 629, n. 11) the difficulties caused to the Abbey by AEFH's decision to withdraw her financial support, concluded that it had 'had one good effect, that Yeats no longer feels himself bound to write plays and is inclined to go back to lyrics, which I shall be very glad of, for lyric work will always be his highest expression, and he had been away from it for too long'.

exception" or some such words,[7] and yet Fitzmaurice that wrote it, wrote it with the special object of showing up the sordid side of country life. He thinks himself a follower of Synge, which he is not.[8] I have now no doubt that there will be enthusiasm to-night, and that the author who has been thirsting for the crown of martyrdom will be called before the curtain for the third night running.[9] We are putting the play on again next week owing to its success. Synge has just had an operation on his throat, and has come through it all right. I am to see him to-day for the first time.[10] When he woke out of the ether sleep, his first words to the great delight of the doctor who knows his plays were: "May God damn the English they can't even swear without vulgarity." This tale delights the Company, who shudder at the bad language they have to speak in his plays. I don't think he has done much this summer owing to bad health, but will probably set to work now.

Mrs. Robert Gregory is charming. She is 23, pretty, very clever, and with beautiful manners. While she was at Coole she was quite the great lady. I sometimes think that the combination of joyous youthfulness with the simplicity and conscious dignity that makes up what we call the great lady is the most beautiful thing in the world. Many a high born woman has it not, though most have something of it. The form at any rate without the substance. Maud Gonne had it, especially in her young days before she grew tired out with many fools, and the little Countess of Cromartie has it more than anyone I have ever known.[11]

[7] A review in the *Evening Telegraph*, the *Freeman*'s evening sister-paper (see above, n. 2), praised Fitzmaurice for presenting 'some remarkably true types of Irish character', and congratulated him 'on the success of his first essay in drama, and it is refreshing to think that one can get a realistic representation of ordinary Irish country life which cannot in the slightest degree offend even the most captious'.

[8] This was a cause of dispute when Holloway first met Fitzmaurice on 11 Oct 1907 (cf. *Abbey Theatre*, 95): 'I was introduced to young Fitzmaurice . . . & found him a nice, unassuming, fellow, with I am sorry to say, a hankering after Synge & his methods of presenting the Irish character on the boards. We had a long argument over the matter but he was of the same opinion at the end, I fear. . . . I like Fitzmaurice & hope he won't be spoiled by the cult.'

[9] On 3 Oct (see n. 2) Holloway recorded the delight of the audience on the first night of the play: 'Applause followed each act, & repeated calls for author at the end had to be acceded to before the audience would be satisfied. Quite a young man modestly bowed his thanks in acknowledgement of the applause. The large audience dispersed delighted with the comedy.'

[10] Synge underwent an operation in the Elphis Nursing Home on 14 Sept to ease the swelling of his neck glands caused by as yet unacknowledged Hodgkin's disease, and was now convalescing at his mother's house in Glenageary. On 20 Sept he had written to AG from the Elphis that the operation had been 'a rather severe one', but that he was 'able to see people now if WB.Y should be in town again' (*JMSCL* II. 59).

[11] Robert Gregory had married Margaret Parry in London on 26 Sept (see p. 709). WBY also celebrates simplicity and dignity in women in 'Michael Robartes and the Dancer' (*VP*, 385–7), 'A Prayer for my Daughter' (*VP*, 403–6), and 'In Memory of Eva Gore-Booth and Con Markiewicz' (*VP*, 475–6). In 'Beautiful Lofty Things' (*VP*, 577–8) he recalled a youthful MG: 'Maud Gonne at Howth station waiting a train, | Pallas Athene in that straight back and arrogant head', and he was to use the

Manchini, the Italian painter, you will know his work. He is the man who splashes on great masses of colour, so that his painting looks at times as if it were modelled in relief, is here in Dublin now. He has come to paint Lady Gregory for Hugh Lane's new Gallery. He is a dear creature with no English. I met him last night. I am naturally delighted with him as he presented me with a large chrysanthemum and with a vehement gesture of his lifted hand, and standing on tip toes cried out in French, "The master is very tall—very beautiful."[12] Which reminds me that I have done nothing about Shannon. After you left I heard that he got always 300 for a portrait, and I did not think that he would make an exception in my case. However, Robert Gregory now says that he is sure Shannon would do me for £100.[13]

Countess of Cromartie as the model for 'A Guitar Player' (see p. 312, n. 5), first published as 'The Banjo Player' in the *Gentleman's Magazine* in September 1906: 'Her voice, the movements of her body, the expression of her face, all said the same thing. . . . A movement not of music only but of life came to its perfection. . . . The little instrument is quite light, and the player can move freely and express a joy that is not of the fingers and the mind only but of the whole being; and all the while her movements call up into the mind, so erect and natural she is, whatever is most beautiful in her daily life' (*E & I*, 268–9).

[12] Antonio Mancini (1852–1931), an Italian painter whom Hugh Lane admired, was in Dublin, to execute portraits of Lane's sister Ruth Shine, AG, and, on 6 Oct, WBY. These were Lane's commissions, who was also providing all the materials and, as AG recalled in *Hugh Lane* (81), 'Mancini made at times an over-liberal use of paint, white especially, slapping it on as a mason slaps mortar on the stone. So rumour was, perhaps, well informed in saying that Hugh, returning after dusk to the Gallery, would scrape some of the most extravagant lumps and masses from the canvas, putting them back upon the palette for the unsuspecting artist's use next day.' WBY was to quote Synge's remark that his portrait of AG was the 'Greatest since Rembrandt' in his poem 'The Municipal Gallery Revisited' (*VP*, 602), and in *Hugh Lane* AG remembered that she 'sat in a high chair in an old black dress, in front of a brown curtain', while Mancini set up a frame in front of her, crossed by many threads which corresponded to threads on his canvas. His picture of WBY was reproduced as the frontispiece of *CW* V, and WBY wrote in Quinn's copy: 'if I only looked like the Manchini portrait I should have defeated all my enemies here in Dublin. Manchini did it in an hour or so working at the last with great vehemence and constant cries, "Cristo, O", and so on' (*Bibl*, 87). In *Hugh Lane* (79–80), AG quotes WBY's more circumstantial account of the sitting: 'The pastel . . . was an evening's work. Mancini put his usual grill of threads where the picture was to be and another grill of threads corresponding exactly with it in front of me. He did not know anything about me, we had no language in common, and he worked for an hour without interest or inspiration. Then I remembered a story of Lane's. Mancini, Italian peasant as he was, believed that he would catch any illness or deformity of those whom he met. He was not thinking of microbes but of some mysterious process like that of the Evil Eye. He had just been painting someone who had lost a leg, and whose cork leg he believed was having a numbing effect on his own. He worried Lane with his terror—"My leg is losing all power of sensation," he would say at intervals. The thought of this story made me burst into laughter, and Mancini began to draw with great excitement and rapidity.' In *Samhain* (1908) WBY was to make Mancini a symbol of the art of personality and individuality as practised in the Abbey Theatre against the mechanical realism of the photographer: 'Every trouble of our Theatre in its earlier years, every attack on us in any year, has come directly or indirectly either from those who prefer Mr. Lafayette to Signor Mancini, or from those who believe, from a defective education, that the writer who does not help some cause, who does not support some opinion, is but an idler, or if his air be too serious for that, the supporter of some hidden wickedness' (*Expl*, 238–9).

[13] The question of Charles Shannon painting a portrait of WBY for Quinn had first been raised in November 1904 (see III. 671), but WBY thought Quinn's fee too low. Shannon finally executed the commission in January 1908, at the fee Quinn had offered, and the portrait now hangs in the Houghton Library, Harvard.

Augustus John has been staying at Coole, he came there to do an etching of me for the collected edition. Shannon was busy when I was in London, and the collected edition was being pushed on so quickly that I found I couldn't wait for him. I don't know what John will make of me. He made a lot of sketches with the brush and the pencil to work the etching from when he went home. I feel rather a martyr going to him. The students consider him the greatest living draftsman, the only modern who draws like an old master. But he makes everybody perfectly hideous, beautiful according to his own standard. He exaggerates every little hill and hollow of the face till one looks a gipsy, grown old in wickedness and hardship. If one looked like any of his pictures the country women would take the clean clothes off the hedges when one passed as they do at the sight of a tinker. He is himself a delight, the most innocent, wicked man I have ever met. He wears earrings, his hair down over his shoulders, a green velvet collar and had two wives who lived together in perfect harmony and nursed each others children on their knees till about six months ago when one of them bolted and the other died.[14] Since then he has followed the lady who bolted and he and she are gathering the scattered families. Of course, nobody round Coole knew anything of these facts. I lived in daily terror of some benevolent gossip carrying on conversation with him like this,

"Married, Mr. John? Children?"

"Yes." "How many". "Seven." "You married young."

"Five years ago." "Twins doubtless?"—after that frank horrifying discourse on the part of Augustus John, who considers himself a particularly good well-behaved man. The only difference is in the code.[15] He told me how he tried to reform an old reprobate professor, who is an authority on gipsy lore. The old professor had a series of flirtations unknown to his wife, but one day when he was in a half intoxicated state in a Welsh tavern

---

[14] John's wife Ida Nettleship had died in a Paris hospital of puerperal fever following the birth of a child in March of this year (see p. 728, n.2). After her death, John returned to Dorelia, from whom he had been temporarily estranged, although he continued his affair with Alick Schepeler (who was later to become WBY's mistress) at the same time.

[15] The question of acceptance of a passive 'code', which WBY contrasted with the conscious cultivation of a mask (*Mem*, 151), was to occupy him a great deal in August 1910, in a three-way dispute with AG and Edmund Gosse: 'Since I was fifteen and began to think, I have mocked at that way of looking at the world, as if it was a court of law where all wrong actions were judged according to their legal penalties. All my life I have, like every artist, been proud of belonging to a nobler world, of having chosen the slow, dangerous, laborious path of moral judgment.... Nothing in which strong passions are involved should, if one can help, be dealt with on general principles as if it were a question of manners.... So, far from the moral nature having anything to do with the code, it begins with the rejection of it, and attains to power by listening to minute, almost secret, ungeneralized thought. But of all forms of courage this is the most difficult, for this ungeneralized thought has never any support but in itself' (*Mem*, 256–7).

where he had been studying gipsies he was plunged into deep depression because a gipsey told him that he was getting very bald at the top of his head, "What shall I do?" he said to John. John replied sternly "Return to your innocence," by which he meant sin openly and scandalise the world.[16] He is the strangest creature I have ever met, a kind of faun. He climbed to the top of the highest tree in Coole garden and carved a symbol there, nobody else has been able to get up there to know what it is, even Robert stuck half way. He is a magnificent looking person, and looks the wild creature he is. His best work is etching, he is certainly a great etcher with a savage imagination.

Yr ev<br>W B Yeats

[*In WBY's hand*]
Miss Darraghs address is
             C/o J K Hackett
                  Hackett Theatre
                  New York

PS. The guarrantee I speak of in my letter to Miss Darragh came this way. Judge Keogh said to Fay if Fay could find out the cost he would get up a guarrantee.[17] Fay is now writing in all directions to find out cost but not as yet with success.

[*with enclosures*]

Nassau Hotel, | D U B L I N,<br>4th Octr., 1907.

Dear Miss Darragh,
    I find there is no objection to your performing "Deirdre" or "Shadowy Waters". If you get an opportunity you might perhaps be so good as to write to my friend John Quinn, 31, Nassau Street, New York, about

---

[16] The old reprobate professor was John Sampson, the bohemian librarian of Liverpool University, whom John had met in the spring of 1901. Sampson, a gifted linguist, had taught himself both Romany and Shelta, the jargon of the tinkers, and was to compile *The Dialect of the Gypsies of Wales*. John's advice evidently worked, for on 16 July 1908 Walter Raleigh, Professor of English at Liverpool, wrote to Sampson: 'You are a learned man, and a rogue, one of the sort of fellows who think they can conduct the business of life on inspirationist principles, and who run an office pretty much the same way as they make love to a woman' (*Letters of Sir Walter Raleigh* [1926], II. 333).
[17] Judge Keogh had made this promise during his visit in the summer (see p. 718).

terms.[18] Miss Witcherly's period has lapsed so there is no trouble there. I wish I could be in America to see you play. I don't recommend you to play "Shadowy Waters". Beautiful as your performance is, for the play requires [a] very special audience, and if its day ever come it will not come till we have an audience as learned and as humble for poetical Drama as there is for difficult music.[19] You will do far better with "Deirdre", but I leave you free to do either play. I cannot give you leave to play "Kathleen Ni Houlihan" I am sorry to say for a likelihood has arisen of our own people taking it to America. They have been offered a guarantee and are this moment trying to find out how much it would have to be.

Yr sny
W B Yeats

Nassau Hotel, | DUBLIN;
4th Octr., 1907.

Dear Miss Darragh,

I find after consulting my friend Mr. Quinn that it is impossible to do anything about the plays at present. I hope you will have a great success in America. You have great power, but alas you will probably not get what you want a series of tragic parts to turn knowledge into instinct, and both alike into personality. I am feeling the same difficulty in my own work. I have got to the point now of having knowledge but if I cannot find an audience and players it must remain knowledge, and perhaps help others, by criticism, to more popular forms of creation. We can make something of ourselves always, but it is our age that decides whether it is to be our best or not.[20]

Yrs sny
W B Yeats

TLS NYPL,with envelope addressed to 31 Nassau St, New York, postmark'DUBLIN OC ?o7'. Partly in Wade, 495–7.

[18] Quinn did not send either of these letters to Letitia Darragh, but wrote to her himself on 28 Oct (NYPL), suggesting that they should meet 'in regard to some suggestion or proposition as to your giving some of his plays in America'. She replied that she would be in touch after Christmas about the possibility of producing WBY's plays.
[19] *The Shadowy Waters* had never been popular, but Letitia Darragh's performance received a good press (see p. 540).
[20] An early example of WBY's theory of historical phases, which he was to develop in *A Vision*.

## To T. Sturge Moore, 4 October 1907

Nassau Hotel, | D U B L I N,
4th Octr., 1907.

My dear Sturge Moore,

It was a great pleasure to get your so appreciative letter. I often get rather discouraged about my playwriting at least so far as the verse is concerned. The little plays I have written in prose are ever popular here, but it [is] so difficult to get good performances of verse work, and good audiences for it, that one rather loses heart. There are a little group of enthusiasts here who care for it, but there are only a small number in comparison to those who like prose comedy, and then the critics generally tell one that one should go back to the lyric.[1] A man has just sent me from Australia, with an evident belief that I would like it an article which he has written commending that damned "Inisfree", and repeating phrases out of every article telling me I know nothing about drama, written by a person called Shore, I think, in the "Academy".[2] I find that people have no sense of dramatic Art as an Art, but

---

[1] On 14 Sept Sturge Moore had written (Bridge, 11–12): 'I must write to tell you how much I have enjoyed your *Deirdre*. It is very beautiful and very original; the verse in its very texture is quite an invention of your own, and the construction admirable, although I think the mood one of the most difficult to present dramatically.' In his reply to this letter (Bridge, 14–15) Moore said he was 'sorry you are so discouraged and hope you may get a real chance before long. Think of Shaw's position before the Court started and Shaw's position now. Most people would have said that the more part of his plays were even more hopelessly unfit for the public than verse plays. That may give us hope.'

[2] The article, 'William Butler Yeats', by 'B.S.', appeared in the *Native Companion: An Australian Monthly Magazine of Literature and Life* on 29 June 1907 (4–11). Identifying WBY as 'a poet of rare quality, the successor to Swinburne and Rossetti in the direct line from Shelley, Coleridge and Blake', the author surveyed WBY's early work and quoted 'the well-known lyric, "The Lake Isle of Innisfree"', in its entirety, noting 'the fine effect of the open vowels and also the expression of the desire to get away from the present place to somewhere where there is peace'. 'B.S.' preferred the early work to the later and concluded that 'the latest form of the poetical drama "The Shadowy Waters" may be better for acting purposes (it seems absurd to put it on the stage at all) but it is not so good a poem as the first version. The most disturbing portent is that the last volume "*Poems 1899–1905*"—is not merely not an improvement upon the first volume of collected *Poems*, but falls far short of it in quality and charm. This, however, maybe due to the temporary aberration which led him to write dramas for an Irish National Theatre. His gift is essentially lyrical; he is too little in touch with life and is not endowed with that dramatic instinct the want of which has caused many great poets to fail as dramatists.' The article does not quote Shore, but his comments may have been included in the covering letter, which is now lost. However, the syntax of this sentence is confused and suggests a mistranscription by the typist, so WBY may have been referring to Shore's article separately.

W. Teignmouth Shore (1866–1932), journalist and advertising consultant, was the editor of the *Academy* from October 1903 to February 1905. In a review of *Where There Is Nothing* in the magazine on 2 July 1904 (20) he said that WBY had 'aimed at mysticism and not at reality, but he has so hopelessly muddled up the two and his knowledge of stage-craft is so immature that the result is chaos and dreariness'. In further articles in the same magazine on 3 and 17 Sept 1904 he praised the work of the INTS.

only of the nature of one's subject. You are dramatic if your subject is easily understood and sympathised with by the average man, and you are undramatic no matter how carefully you construct if you look for a special audience. We shall do nothing till we have created a criticism which will insist upon the dramatic poet's right to educate his audience as a musical composer does his. I hope you are not giving up dramatic writing. Miss Horniman who you know has a theatre now at Manchester which is producing verse work, and her manager Payne is quite an intelligent man.[3] I really like "Atilla" though I could see that Binyon was not easy because of having to construct for the first time.[4] The first result of construction when one works at it deliberately is to make one rhetorical. There are such a lot of things that have to be said not because one wants to say them, but because the plot insists on them. I think it is only when one has so mastered construction that one is conscious of nothing but the subject that one is able to think of so arranging the story that one need never go beyond oneself. Please remember me to Mrs. Sturge Moore.

[*Remainder of letter in WBY's hand*]

We produced a crude comedy by a new man three days ago & it is it seems going to be a great success though it represents the people in a worse light than Synge ever did.[5] They object to Synge because he is profound, distinguished, individual. They hate the presence of a mind that is superior to their own & so invent & even beleive the cry of immorality & slander. But it is much the same everywhere—nothing is ever persecuted but the intellect & the one thing Plutarch thought one should never complain of is the people. They are what they are & it is our work to live our lives in their despite.[6] Where they are crude as here they are perhaps less mischiev-

---

[3] Moore had been discouraged after the hostile reception of his play *Aphrodite against Artemis* in April 1906 (see p. 371), but this experience had evidently not blunted his desire to stage his plays and in his reply he asked whether WBY meant 'to suggest that I should do well to send a play to Miss Horniman? And, if so, ought I to address it to her or to Payne? And what address for either of them?'

[4] WBY had been at the first night of Laurence Binyon's *Attila*, which had been produced at His Majesty's Theatre on 4 Sept 1907 (see pp. 716, 717).

[5] i.e. *The Country Dressmaker*, actually produced on 3 Oct, suggesting that this letter, like those to Quinn and Bullen of the same date, was in fact finished some days after it was begun.

[6] WBY had been reading North's *Plutarch* over the summer (see p. 703), and is probably thinking of Plutarch's praise for Metellus, Aristides, and Epaminondas for refusing 'to seeke the good will of the common people by flatterie and dissimulation: which was in deede, bicause they despised that which the people coulde geve or take awaye. Yet would they not be offended with their citizens, when they were amerced, and set at any fines, or that they banished them, or gave them any other repulse: but they loved them as wel as they did before, so soone as they shewed any token of repentaunce, and that they were sorie for the wrong they had done them, and were easely made frendes againe with them, after they were restored from their banishment. For he that disdaineth to make much of the people, and to have their favour, shoulde much more scorne to seeke to be revenged, when he is repulsed' (*Plutarch's Lives of the Noble Grecians and Romans, Englished by Sir Thomas North*, II. 195). A similar idea provides the theme of WBY's poem 'The People' (*VP*, 351–3).

ous than where they beleive themselves educated & read the Spectator, or write it. I have done a tragic farce—I know not what else to call it with Lady Gregory—three acts & will produce it this winter.[7]

Yrs ever

W B Yeats

TLS Texas. Bridge, 12–14.

## To A. H. Bullen, 4–5 October 1907

Nassau Hotel, | DUBLIN,

4th Octr., 1907.

My dear Bullen,

Sidgwick has written apologetically, and has sent me £10.[1] I have just arrived here in Dublin, where we produced a new play last night. By the by don't forget that you have all my Samhains; you offered to look through them and make suggestions as to what extracts I should put into the book of essays. I wish you would do so as there is no reason why you should not, if there is enough material, which I am pretty confident there is, print the volume of criticism immediately after the volume of stories.[2] I have a certain amount of difficulty in giving you a date for its publication as a part of it "discoveries" is coming out with my sister at Christmas. You will remember that I arranged this when I thought that you would be thirteen months getting through the edition.[3] This however need not prevent you from going to press. It is possible that by the time the critical volume and the stories are printed I shall have the volume of prose plays ready, but I cannot promise this. It all depends on how soon I get the "Unicorn from

---

[7] i. e. *The Unicorn from the Stars*, first produced on 21 Nov 1907.

[1] Sidgwick's letter is untraced but the £10 may have been for royalties now earned by *Ideas of Good and Evil*. Bullen had advanced WBY a total of £56 5s. 6d. for the subsequently unfinished novel *The Speckled Bird*. Rather than demanding the money back, he agreed in 1903 that it should be counted as an advance on *IGE* chargeable against royalties, together with an exorbitant 10 guineas paid to E. J. Oldmeadow for the right to reprint WBY's introduction to *A Book of Images* (see III. 781). Since a third edition of *IGE* had just been published, it may have been that the royalties now exceeded this advance, but that Sidgwick had not realized this.

[2] This selection appeared as 'The Irish Dramatic Movement', a section made up of extended extracts from *Samhain*, the *Arrow*, and two articles from the *United Irishman* (see pp. 642, n. 4, 712). It was not published in vol. VIII, the 'volume of criticism', but in vol. IV of *CW*, together with three plays: *The Hour-Glass*, *Cathleen ni Houlihan*, and *The Golden Helmet*.

[3] *Discoveries* was published by the Dun Emer Press on 15 Dec of this year, and the essays were included not with 'The Irish Dramatic Movement' in vol. IV of *CW*, but with other critical essays in vol. VIII.

the Stars" on to the stage, and whether it wants much working on afterwards. I hope to get it on next month, and that a couple of weeks at latest after
that date it would be ready to print. It may happen however that I cannot get
it on until early January. I think you may however calculate upon the end of
January being the latest possible date for its reaching you.[4] You will have two
books to get through before that. But the sooner you send me these "Samhains" again with your suggestions the better. I suppose you will be seeing
Watt in a few days. In your negotiations with him keep in mind that we
mustn't do anything in facilitating that collected edition which will prevent
my having all my ordinary editions in one publisher's hands within a
reasonable time.[5] This edition ought to prepare the way for an ordinary
edition at a moderate price, though not necessarily at once.[6] I intend my next
book after the collected edition to be a volume of lyrics and narrative poems.
I don't see why it should not have a very tolerable success.[7] Why I have been
so insistent upon my revisions etc. in this expensive edition is that I know I
must get my general personality and the total weight of my work into
people's minds. As a preliminary to new work. I know that I have just
reached a time when I can give up constant revisions but not till the old is
right. I used to revise my lyrics as I now do the plays.[8]

                                                                    Saturday.
    I have just got your last letter sent on from Coole. I am very much
amused at that exorbitant demand. I particularly admire the additional
sixpence. When Watt jun wrote to me saying that it was to be the same
terms as "Ideas of Good and Evil", I asked him what those terms were.

---

[4] *The Unicorn from the Stars* was first produced on 21 Nov of this year, and was published in *CW* III
in October 1908 with *The Countess Cathleen* and *The Land of Heart's Desire*, having already appeared in
another edition in New York on 13 May 1908.

[5] To get all his works into the hands of one publisher had long been an ambition of WBY's. He
nearly achieved this in June 1916 when Macmillan & Co. became his main publishers, but *Poems* and the
early plays, originally published by Unwin and from 1927 by Ernest Benn Ltd., did not revert to
Macmillan until May 1933.

[6] Because Unwin and later Benn continued to hold the rights in a considerable portion of WBY's
early work, this did not happen until 1933 when the agreement with Benn lapsed and WBY transferred
the rights to Macmillan & Co., who were subsequently able to issue *Collected Poems* in November 1933
and *Collected Plays* in November 1934. These were to have been the first volumes in an 'ordinary'
edition, but the sequence was interrupted by the Second World War, as were a 'de luxe' edition planned
by Scribner in America, and a 'definitive' edition to be published by Macmillan & Co. in Britain.

[7] This appeared in March 1910, published by Bullen as *Poems: Second Series*. It included thirty-seven
poems from *The Wind Among the Reeds*, 'The Old Age of Queen Maeve', 'Baile and Aillinn', fourteen poems
from *In the Seven Woods*, 'The Musicians' Songs from *Deirdre*', and *The Shadowy Waters*. The success
of the book was 'tolerable' enough for it to be reissued in 1913.

[8] WBY never altered his habit of revision, a practice which has sometimes caused irritation to his
readers and frequently anguish to his editors. He defended his conduct in a short poem of this time, which
he published in *CW* II: 'The friends that have it I do wrong | When ever I remake a song, | Should know
what issue is at stake: | It is myself that I remake.' As late as 27 Dec 1930, when about to revise his work for
an Edition de Luxe, he wrote joyously to OS: 'Months of re-writing. What happiness!' (Wade, 780).

I noticed in his reply that the sum you named was paid in advance, but it did not occur to me that he would consider that fact an integral part of the agreement. I have of course, written to put the matter right. It was a sum paid by you that I might live while writing a novel that was never finished. You very generously considered it as advanced upon the later book. Of course, A. P. Watts son has no recollection of the facts and merely looked up a pigeon hole when you proposed the same terms as on "Ideas of Good and Evil".⁹ Let the agreement be for the usual six years. I say that partly because if my books are going well you will be able to give me at the end of that period the same terms that Unwin gives me for "Poems", which are slightly more, I think, than you are giving. "Poems" however is a very well selling book.¹⁰

I am a little anxious about your arrangements with Matthews and with Unwin, and about the ordinary editions as distinguished from this expensive collected edition. I have written about this to Watt. And I hope that he and you will be able to come to some definite arrangement covering the whole ground.¹¹

Yrs ev
W B Yeats

TLS Harvard. Wade, 497–8.

## To Alexander Strahan Watt, 5 October 1907

Mention in previous letter.
Explaining that Bullen is not liable for an advance of £66 15s. 6d. on publication of *Deirdre*.

---

⁹ Bullen's desire to negotiate with A. P. Watt himself (see p. 731) was clearly sound, as his son Alexander Strahan Watt had demanded an excessive advance for *Deirdre* by not knowing the tortuous history of the agreement over *Ideas of Good and Evil* (see n. 1). That contract had combined the £56 5s. 6d. Bullen had already advanced to WBY in lieu of *The Speckled Bird* with the 10 guineas paid to Oldmeadow, so that the contract stipulated an advance of £66 15s 6d. Not realizing that this had been paid over a period of seven years in special circumstances, the young Watt had demanded a like advance when drawing up the contract for *Deirdre* on 10 Sept, and Bullen had written to complain to WBY on receiving the new agreement. In fact, Bullen was as much to blame as Alexander Watt, since in his letter of 10 Sept he had insisted that the new contract was 'to be precisely the same as for *Ideas of Good & Evil*' (see p. 712, n. 4).
¹⁰ Unwin was notoriously parsimonious in his business dealing, but WBY had managed to extract better terms from him with successive editions of *Poems*, and in November 1900 had negotiated a royalty of 17½%, with £25 on account for the third edition, published in 1901 (see III. 17). The agreement for *Deirdre* was that Bullen should pay royalties of 15% on the first 1,000 copies and 17½% thereafter.
¹¹ Mathews had the rights to 'The Tables of the Law' and 'The Adoration of the Magi', and residual rights in *The Wind Among the Reeds*, while Unwin had the rights to *Poems*, *John Sherman and Dhoya*, *The Countess Cathleen*, and *The Land of Heart's Desire*.

## *To A. P. Watt, 5 October 1907*

Mention in letter to Bullen, 4–5 October 1907.
Asking Watt about Bullen's arrangements with Elkin Mathews and Fisher
Unwin, and the implications of these for the ordinary editions of his work.

## *To Judge Martin J. Keogh, [early October 1907]*

Mention in a letter from Quinn to WBY, 8 December 1907, and from
Quinn to Keogh, 10 December 1907.
Discussing the possibility of an Abbey tour of the USA.[1]

## *To Lady Gregory, [early October 1907]*

For Lady Gregory

Arts Club is upstairs in house opposite old Turkish bath in Lincoln place.
Go in at first door to left opposite bath.[1]

W B Yeats

ALS Berg.

[1] See p. 718. WBY and W. G. Fay had finally estimated the expenses of an American tour by the Abbey
Company (see p. 739), and had written to Keogh about finding the money to underwrite or subsidize this.
On 10 Dec of this year, Quinn told Keogh (NYPL): 'I read Yeats's letter to you, received by you in
October with great interest. I suggest you write to him . . . stating that for the present owing to the
panic . . . it will be impossible to do anything about the company. I am very much interested in the theatre
company and I think that if they came out here under proper business management they would make a
success, but personally I am not enthusiastic about subsidizing them or getting up a fund.'

[1] See p. 630. The first location of the United Arts Club was a suite of rented rooms at 22 Lincoln
Place, a building which also housed the Irish Agricultural Organization Society, near the back gate of
Trinity College and convenient for Westland Row (now Pearse) railway station. On 7 Dec 1910 the club
moved to 44 St Stephen's Green.

### To Johnston Forbes-Robertson, [6 October 1907]

Mention in letter from Johnston Forbes-Robertson, 'Monday' [7 October 1907].
Inviting him and his wife to a special matinee performance at the Abbey on 11 October.[1]

### To Florence Farr, 7 October 1907

Nassau Hotel, | Dublin.
Oct. 7th. 1907.

My dear Florence Farr, I think Bullen is going to put all the music with all my other appendixes at the end of the volume of prose plays as he wants to enlarge that volume. I came up to Dublin last Thursday. We produced a play called the *Country Dressmaker*, a rough but amusing piece of work which is showing signs of being popular. I have got to a typewriter as you see and feel I can tell the news at last. I have got so out of the habit of writing letters with my fingers that even apart from my sight I make them very short. I cannot recollect whether I told you or not about Allen Bennett. The day I left London I was at the dentist's and he began telling me about a friend of his, a man of science, who was interested in Buddhism. He had gone out to Burma and there he met an Englishman who was a Buddhist monk. This Englishman had converted him and now he and the monk were members of a Buddhist missionary Society. The Englishman was Allen Bennett. He showed me a photographic group of the Committee of the Society with Bennett in the middle, evidently the most important person. He also told me that Bennett was now working on experimental science.[1] The friend and a native Burmese widow and a third person paying the expenses. If any

---

[1] WBY was asking Forbes-Robertson to the first of a series of special 'professional' matinées for visiting London companies and although Forbes-Robertson (see p. 283, n. 3) did not attend, members of his company did. As he explained to WBY (Berg) he and his wife would 'have been delighted to come at your kind invitation on Friday, were it not that I have to play "Hamlet" in the evening. I am obliged to remain very quiet all the after-noon before attempting "the Dane". I have lately been on the sick list, so have to take extra care. I am very sorry not to be present, as I need hardly say I am most interested in the movement.'

[1] Allan Bennett (1872–1923) was a member of the Esoteric Section of the Theosophical Society; he had joined the GD in February 1894, proceeded to the second order with the motto 'Iehi Aour' in May 1895, and conducted rituals and experiments with FF. Before leaving for Burma he had worked for an analytical and consulting chemist in London and Aleister Crowley (1875–1947) thought his 'knowledge of science, especially electricity...was vast accurate and profound'. In 1899 Bennett had instructed Crowley in magic, and in 1900 Crowley arranged for Bennett to emigrate to Ceylon (Sri Lanka) as a self-converted Buddhist in the hope that the warm climate would cure his asthma. When the founder of a

profit resulted from Bennett's researches the bulk of the profit is to go to the Missionary Society, but a certain percentage to those who have supplied the capital. The researches are concerned with N Rays.[2] Bennett goes out every morning with his begging bowl as a monk, but always gives the contents of his bowl to some less well-provided-for brother. His own meals are sent in every day to the workshop. I think I told you something of all this but not the details. I don't know when I shall be able to get over. I am desperately hard up owing to the difficulty of getting A. P. Watt and my publisher to meet. They have been playing some sort of a fantastic game for months. I got them together with much urgency last week with the only result that Bullen took offence because it was Watt junior who received him,[3] and so went back to Stratford. In any case a man with Saturn entering his second house by transit has to look out for bad times.[4] Astrology grows more and more wonderful every day. I have some astonishing irrefutable things to show you. I imagine that the stars are beginning to tell on Miss Horniman as since her first elated letter written the day after the start at Manchester I have not heard a word of how they are doing, though she has written about something else.[5] I put the date of some great disturbance concerning her to April, May or June. I am trying to work at primary directions, but my head reels with all the queer, mathematical terms.[6] I am hoping to find in the aspects a basis of evocation, which is really what interests me.

college for girls in Rangoon sought a teacher of physical science, Bennett accepted and took the name 'Ananda Metteyya'. After entering the Burmese branch of the Buddhist Sangha in 1907, he returned to London for six months in 1908 as a 'missionary' and established the English branch of the International Buddhist Society. FF was to follow Bennett's example by emigrating to Ceylon in 1912. WBY's dentist was Charles Baly (see p. 719).

[2] N-rays were a supposed form of radiation discovered in 1903 by René Blondlot (1849–1930), a Professor of Physics at the University of Nancy (from the initial letter of which the name derives). Blondlot thought he had stumbled across the existence of N-rays while attempting to polarize X-rays, and set up experiments using prisms and aluminium lenses to test their properties. Several other scientists apparently replicated his findings, but the American spectroscopist Robert Wood remained sceptical and, after witnessing unconvincing demonstrations in Blondlot's laboratory, exposed the whole theory as spurious in *Nature* on 29 Sept 1904. This effectively ended serious interest in N-rays, although a number of scientists, like Bennett, continued inconsequential experiments over the next few years.

[3] i.e. Alexander Strahan Watt (see pp. 141, 731).

[4] For the influence of Saturn on WBY's horoscope see p. 711.

[5] AEFH had sent copies of the *Manchester Guardian* with accounts of the opening of the Playgoers' Theatre, but the note she probably included with these has not survived. She had subsequently written on 27 Sept (see p. 727, n. 1) to pass on the views of Fr. Maine, a Catholic priest in Ancoats with a large congregation, who thought that it would be all right to produce *The Playboy of the Western World* in Manchester, as long as his parishioners did not hear about it.

[6] Primary directions are extremely difficult to calculate because the dependence on the zodiacal degrees of the planets and the angles of the horizons and meridian require transposition into degrees of Right Ascension (the nautical measure). The obliquity of the planets' positions in relation to the equator also enters into the calculations. Once these figures are determined, the position of each planet directed to another has to be calculated.

Did you see Bernard Shaw's letter in the "Times" a couple of days ago—logical, audacious and convincing, a really wonderful letter, at once violent and persuasive. He knew his opponent's case as well as his own, and that is just what men of his kind usually do not know.[7] I saw *Caesar and Cleopatra* with Forbes-Robertson in it twice this week and have been really delighted and what I never thought [to] be with work of his, moved. There is vulgarity, plenty of it, but such gay heroic delight in the serviceable man. Ah if he had but style, and distinction and was not such a barbarian of the barricades.[8] I am quite convinced by the by that the whole play is chaff of you in your Egyptian period, and that you were the Cleopatra who offered that libation of wine to the table rapping sphinx.[9]

Yours ever<br>W B Yeats

Printed copy; Bax, 59–60, Wade, 498–500.

---

[7] On 5 Oct Shaw had made a trenchant and lengthy intervention (12) into an ongoing controversy in *The Times* on the subject of Kulin polygamy in India. The discussion, which, as Shaw saw, centred on the opposition between cultural relativism and imperialistic uniformity, had been provoked by the insistence of the former Indian civil servant Sir Henry Cotton (1845–1915) that polygamy did not exist among the Kulins of Bengal. In a spirited attack on British parochialism, prejudice, and hypocrisy, Shaw pointed out that if 'the Empire is to be held together by anything better than armed force . . . we shall have to make up our minds to bring the institutions and social experiments of our fellow-subjects to a very much higher test than their conformity to the customs of Clapham'. Noting that the British were more than tolerant of their own 'abominations and superstitions', he insisted that they should be more alert in distinguishing between 'the shock of unfamiliarity and genuine ethical shock'. With this in mind he found 'that the institution of Kulin polygamy . . . does not seem to me on the face of it an unreasonable one', and, comparing Bengali marriage customs with those in Britain, concluded that 'the only difference between India and England is that England holds her beliefs more loosely, less religiously, less thoughtfully, and is less disposed to let them stand in the way of pecuniary gain and social position'. He went on to suggest that the Kulin practice might, in fact, be eugenically more effective than monogamy, since a 'system which limits the fertility of its men of fine physique to the child-bearing capacity of one woman, and wastes the lives of thousands of first-rate maiden ladies in barrenness . . . must not take its own merits for granted'. WBY was to make his own intervention into the debate about eugenics in *On the Boiler* (1938).

[8] Forbes-Robertson was at the Gaiety Theatre 7–12 Oct, presenting *Caesar and Cleopatra* as part of a programme that also included *Mice and Men*, *Hamlet*, and *The Light that Failed*. An ironic treatment of the affair between Caesar and Cleopatra, Shaw had finished the play in 1898, but it was not staged in Britain until Johnston Forbes-Robertson produced it at the Grand Theatre, Leeds, on 16 Sept 1907 for three performances. It transferred to the Savoy Theatre in London on 25 Nov 1907 and ran there for forty performances.

[9] As a former mistress of Shaw, FF would have been interested in the production of the play, and it would also have appealed to her fascination with Egyptian symbolism. Her 'Egyptian period' had been at its most intense after she took charge of the London Temple of the GD in April 1897, and set up her 'Sphere' group, devoted to the study of Egyptian symbolism and rituals. She also collaborated with OS in writing two plays set in ancient Egypt: *The Beloved of Hathor*, first produced at the Victoria Hall, London, on 16 Nov 1901 in celebration of the inaugural meeting of the Egypt Society, with WBY and Shaw in the audience, and *The Shrine of the Golden Hawk*, staged with *The Beloved of Hathor* on 20–1 Jan 1902 in the same venue. WBY reviewed this latter production in the *Star* on 23 Jan (*UP* II. 265–7). In Act IV of Shaw's *Caesar and Cleopatra*, Caesar offers to make Cleopatra a new kingdom and build her a

## To A. E. F. Horniman, [c. 7 October 1907]

Mention in letter from AEFH, 10 October 1907.

A 'long & welcome letter' asking for details of her theatre in Manchester,[1] reporting the production of *The Country Dressmaker*,[2] discussing the Abbey accounts,[3] revealing that the Abbey Company is over-rehearsing and that Beerbohm Tree has offered to come to a rehearsal,[4] speaking of his proposed American lecture tour,[5] asking for her natal details for a horoscope and giving his reading of her astrological aspects,[6] suggesting that he may come less to London and give up Woburn Buildings,[7] and complaining of the delay over the building of the new Abbey annexe.[8]

NLI.

holy city there. She resolves that the spirit of the Nile shall name the new city, and a priest brings in a miniature sphinx, with a tripod and incense, to which she offers wine, declaring she 'will have my city named by nobody but my dear little sphinx, because it was in its arms that Caesar found me asleep.... Now let us call on the Nile all together. Perhaps he will rap on the table.'

[1] See pp. 702, 727, 728. AEFH replied that she was reluctant 'to bore you with long accounts of the doings here.... Shaw is a growing draw—but nothing can undo the unpopularity of the building itself.'

[2] Presumably WBY's account of the play was similar to the one he had given to FF (see previous letter). In her reply AEFH said she would like a copy of the play if it were published.

[3] Given her new expenditure on the Manchester theatre company and her decision to stop subsidizing the Abbey after 1910, AEFH was trying to sort out the less than transparent Dublin accounts. In her reply she complained that it was 'over two years since it was arranged to float a Limited Company & I have never had a definite list of shareholders even. If the current expenses with a rent-free theatre & the subsidy for salaries cannot be covered, the plant must be in a bad way.'

[4] See p. 283, n. 3. Beerbohm Tree, who had set up an 'Academy of Dramatic Art' in 1904 (see III. 640), had evidently invited himself to monitor an Abbey rehearsal, but there is no evidence that he attended one. AEFH was 'surprised to hear of *over* rehearsal, I never saw any signs of it. I daresay that the actors have got tired of some of the plays, but that is not the same thing.'

[5] AEFH had commented on Martin Keogh's suggestions for an American tour by the Abbey (see p. 719), and in taking up her points WBY evidently revealed that he would undertake lectures there at the same time. She replied that she did not 'agree with you about the American lecturing matter.... But I have written & said all I can on that matter.' The first American visit by the Abbey did not take place until 1911.

[6] WBY was concerned by AEFH's ominous astrological aspects (see pp. 728, 748), and had evidently told her of this and offered to cast her horoscope. In her reply AEFH informed him that she 'was born in London at 7–35 p.m. on Oct. 3rd 1860. I see clearly that I have had bad aspects but I cannot sit with folded hands waiting for good ones. Of course I am trying to be cautious & not to over-step the legacy money in any way & to take precautions as to the future.' WBY's horoscope of AEFH is in NLI.

[7] In her reply AEFH commented that it 'would be a great loss to you to give up coming to London— I'm not only thinking of how I should miss you, but the want of society would be so bad for you & your work. You have been away too long & too much already from the circles in which you can live & talk naturally. You know perfectly well what I mean, in Dublin you are too much with your social inferiors.' In fact, WBY gave up this idea and retained his rooms in Woburn Buildings until the lease ended in 1919.

[8] Work on building a new annexe for the Abbey had been long delayed by problems in getting planning permission, but AEFH was able to tell WBY that Tim Harrington had informed her he had seen 'the plans for the Annex through the Passing Committee & Mr. Holloway has explained that there will be some extra items. I have accepted these & now the work should begin. I am very sorry that there should have been so much delay.'

# To Sir Antony MacDonnell, [11 October 1907]

Nassau Hotel | South Fredrick St | Dublin.

Dear Sir Anthony Macdonold:[1] at Lady Macdonolds suggestion I tried to get you on the telephone just now, but I am little familiar with telephones & I put the thing one puts to ones ear down & got rung off. Lady Gregory asked me [to] invite you & Lady Macdonold to the Abbey Theatre this afternoon at three O clock to meet M$^r$ Tree. We are giving a private performance of some of our little plays for him & for various members of his company & of M$^r$ Forbes Robertsons company.[2] I think M$^r$ Birrell is coming.[3] The whole thing has been got up in such a hurry that I hope you will excuse such short notice.

Yr ev

W B Yeats

this hotel is 1205

yr sny

W B Yeats

ALS MBY.

[1] Presumably an error for Sir Antony Patrick MacDonnell (see p. 67, n. 3), the Irish-born Liberal statesman and Catholic. He had married Henrietta, née MacDonnell (see p. 69, n. 3), in 1878.

[2] The visiting London companies and certain distinguished locals were invited as guests to the special 'professional' matinées now being arranged at the Abbey (see p. 747), while the remaining seats were made available to a paying audience. This first such matinée was mounted for the Beerbohm Tree as well as the Forbes-Robertson companies, both of which were performing in Dublin during the week (Tree appeared at the Theatre Royal 1–12 Oct with a repertory of *Julius Caesar*, *The Red Lamp*, *The Van Dyck*, *Colonel Newcombe*, and *Richard II*). For the matinée, the Directors presented three of their own one-act plays, *Riders to the Sea*, *Cathleen ni Houlihan*, and *The Rising of the Moon*, and Holloway recorded (NLI) that the 'performance was well patronised & everything passed off quite nicely': 'Each piece was loudly applauded at the end & you could hear the proverbial pin drop during their enactment. Besides the professional element present, art & letters were well represented. Lady Gregory played the role of hostess perfectly & greeted all new comers in the Vestibule in [a] quite homely way. To mention the notables present would be to almost give a list of all within the theatre. Mr Tree & Miss Violet Tree, Mrs Gunn & Miss Haidee Gunn, Mr Mouillot, Mr W. J. Locke etc. just to mention a few. . . . The Abbey's first professional matinee must be voted a success.' In speaking at a Corinthian Club dinner on the previous day, Tree, as the *Stage* recorded on 17 Oct 1907, had congratulated his audience (15) in having 'in their midst an institution in which they had native dramatists, native actors and actresses. He referred to the Playhouse of the Western World, which some people would persist in calling the Abbey Theatre (Laughter). Well, they were to have the good fortune to listen to one of these Irish plays the following day, and they looked forward with great interest to that. He thought it was a splendid sign that in this City there should be a National—he would not say a Nationalist, but a National—Irish drama. That was a fine thing.' On 12 Oct he wrote to AG (Berg) that he had enjoyed *The Rising of the Moon* 'hugely, but indeed the whole afternoon was an enjoyment'. He also admired WBY's 'imaginative little play. I think the last line showed the true touch of the dramatist. Should he not write a play on the larger world? Poetry expressed in prose instead of prose expressed in poetry as we too often get.'

[3] The Rt. Hon. Augustine Birrell (1850–1933), lawyer, Liberal politician and man of letters, had been appointed Chief Secretary for Ireland earlier this year, and had been working with Sir Antony MacDonnell on the Irish Council Bill, which would have granted Ireland a measure of devolution, but which was rejected by most nationalists. The son of a Nonconformist clergyman, Birrell was educated at Cambridge,

## To Mrs Patrick Campbell, [c. 17 October 1907]

Mention in next letter.

## To Lady Gregory, [17 October 1907]

ADARE MANOR, | ADARE, | IRELAND.
Thursday

My dear Lady Gregory: I enclose M^rs Campbells telegram. I have written to thank her & said that 3 o clock would be the probable hour.[1] I wonder if you know Phillip Carrs address or if it is in my address book & if that is on the table at the Nassau. I think there will be no harm in having information as to rehersal hours at Repetoire theatres. I will write to Miss Horniman for her hours. I am not sure if I shall ask Barker as he puts plays on for longer periods & I am not sure if he has always the same company & his answer would have to cover a more complex situation & I hardly like asking him to take so much trouble as to write it all. Carr & Miss Horniman have on the other hand I think produced a new play every week. It is possible that we may have to re-organize the whole system of rehersals & make them harder & longer—now that our present one has broken down—or we may find we are getting the normal amount of work—in any case knowledge is no harm.[2] This is a

called to the Bar in 1875, and appointed Quain Professor of Law at London University in 1896. In 1899 he was elected Liberal MP for West Fifeshire, subsequently serving as MP for North Bristol from 1906 to 1918, and as President of the Board of Education, 1905–7. As Irish Secretary he steered the Irish Universities Act (1908) and the Land Purchase Act (1909) through Parliament, but his easygoing attitude to Irish nationalism left him wholly unprepared for the Easter Rising in 1916 and he resigned immediately after it. Among his many books were three volumes of *Obiter Dicta* (1884, 1887, 1924), a biography of Charlotte Brontë (1885), editions of Boswell's *Life of Johnson* (1897), *Collected Essays* (1900), and studies of William Hazlitt (1902) and Andrew Marvell (1905). His autobiography, *Things Past Redress*, appeared posthumously in 1937. After meeting Birrell at a dinner party in January 1909 and finding him grown too self-sufficient in middle age, WBY tried to compose an epigram on him: '*Augustine Birrell dreams he has found a trick | To juggle out of sight the natural laws | And grow a self-sufficient man because | He that was once a flea is now a tick*' (see *Mem*, 145–6, 230–1). Nevertheless, Birrell used his political influence to assist AG's successful petition for a Civil List pension for WBY in July 1910.

[1] Following the success of the special matinée for the Tree and Robertson companies on 11 Oct (see above, n. 2), the Abbey Company staged a further matinée on 25 Oct for Mrs Patrick Campbell's company which was booked to perform at the Gaiety Theatre, Dublin, in the week beginning 20 Oct with a repertory including Pinero's *The Second Mrs Tanqueray* and *The Notorious Mrs Ebbsmith*, Sudermann's *Magda*, and Ibsen's *Hedda Gabler*. In the event, the matinée began at 2.30, not 3.00 p.m.

[2] The laxity in the conduct of rehearsals noted by Payne (see p. 667, n. 3) had grown worse under W. G. Fay's management of the Abbey Theatre and AG and WBY had decided to close the Theatre until an adequate programme could be rehearsed. Beerbohm Tree had offered to attend a rehearsal (see p. 750), and WBY now wanted to consult Philip Carr (see p. 3, n. 3) for advice on rehearsal practice at the Royalty and Great Queen Street theatres, where he had produced several plays in 1904–5. In fact, company discipline at rehearsals was to continue to cause problems and in September 1910 WBY was to insist that the players signed a formal undertaking pledging punctuality and good behaviour.

beautiful house & there is a pleasant party of about a dozen. An Austrian and Lord Northland are about the cleverest though not particularly so.[3] They are all playing golf. There is a young man called Chrighton, who was at school & college with Robert. He is Lord Dunravens private secretary.[4] I brought nothing to work at on the chance that I might start a poem but I may not get started as the start is difficult after so long a time at other things.

Lord Dunraven is it seems [?]entirely occupied with growing tobacco. For the moment he seems to have lost interest in politics.[5]

Yrs ev

W B Yeats

ALS Berg, with envelope addressed to the Nassau Hotel, Dublin, postmark 'ADARE OC 17 07'.

## To A. E. F. Horniman, [*17 October 1907*]

Mention in previous letter and in letter from AEFH, 18 October 1907. Informing her that he is staying with Lord Dunraven, who is thinking of establishing a new Irish paper,[1] telling her that both the Mancini

---

[3] Thomas Uchter Caulfeild Knox, Viscount Northland (1882–1915), had served in the Coldstream Guards 1900–6. The Austrian is unidentified. Either before setting out, or in a letter now lost, WBY had evidently asked AG for advice about tipping the servants and in her reply to this letter, dated 'Friday' (18 Oct 1907; Berg), she instructed him: '2/6 to housemaid, 2/6 to footman not butler who attend you will do yr tips.'

[4] Andrew Gavin Maitland-Makgill-Crichton (b. 1881) was private secretary to the Earl of Dunraven for seven years. After distinguished service in the Cameron Highlanders in the First World War, he dedicated himself to the cause of peace and worked for the League of Nations. He had attended Elstree preparatory school, where Robert Gregory had been a fellow pupil 1893–5.

[5] Windham Thomas Wyndham-Quin, 4th Earl of Dunraven and Mount-Earl (1841–1926), had been a soldier and then foreign correspondent for the *Daily Telegraph* before succeeding to the title in 1871. He served as Under-Secretary to the Colonies, 1885–6, 1886–7, and later concerned himself with the condition of the working classes, both as chairman of a House of Lords committee on sweated labour and as a member of London County Council. He published numerous articles on politics and economics as well as on sport (he was a keen steeplechase rider and yachtsman), and was appointed Lieutenant of Co. Limerick in 1894. He was chairman of the Irish Land Conference 1902–3, and president of the Irish Reform Association. Although his forebears had used Dunraven Castle in Glamorgan, Wales, as their main residence, he based himself in his Irish seat, Adare Manor, Adare, Co. Limerick. The cultivation of tobacco in Ireland had been given a boost by William Redmond's recent Tobacco Act, which repealed the Tobacco Cultivation Act of 1831 and statutes of Charles II prohibiting Irish tobacco-growing in order to protect the American colonists. A number of improving landlords were now experimenting with different varieties of seed, and, despite an exceptionally wet summer, good results had been obtained. At this time Dunraven had 7 acres under cultivation in Co. Limerick. He imported a 'Proctor' machine from America and eventually gave 30 acres over to growing tobacco, but abandoned the scheme when all his barns and farm machinery were accidentally destroyed in a fire on New Year's Day 1916.

[1] In her reply AEFH said she was 'was so glad' that he was with Lord Dunraven: 'I hope that he will not waste his money over a paper unless he has the strength of will to make it a *decent* one. I've not forgotten the much heralded "Nationist" & its a vulgar philistinism from the very first. But perhaps he would not be as fastidious as a middle-class spinster.'

portraits of him were good,[2] discussing the method of rehearsing at the Abbey Theatre,[3] asking her if she has met Mouillot,[4] saying he fears that the Abbey will not be ready to produce *The Unicorn from the Stars*,[5] speaking of the Abbey accounts,[6] and evidently discussing her occult and astrological life.[7]

NLI.

[2] AEFH thought that if the pictures were 'both good why should not both go into the Library Edition? I congratulate him if he has put the "irate Demon" on paper!' WBY had evidently spelled the name 'Manchini' and she could not resist treating him to a lecture in elementary Italian: 'M A N C I N I is pronounced Manchini. If spelled in Italian with an "h" it would be pronounced Manheenee.'

[3] AEFH asked Payne 'three questions' on this topic, and enclosed his answers (now lost) as he was 'too busy to write them himself'. She also volunteered her own 'general impression' based upon her observations of Payne and Charles McEvoy: 'Mr. Payne uses technical experience in regard to moving & grouping & gesture & tone of voice etc. to carry out the ideas given him by the reading of the play. The actors do their best with their minds and bodies to carry out these ideas. Mr. Mc'Evoy has of course no such technical experience but he flings himself into each character & shews what he wants done. He discusses with the players (& with me too) as to what the real people would do.' She thought that the Abbey's 'continual rehearsals which let the playing get *flatter* must have something wrong with them', and cited the example of Sara Allgood and W. G. Fay as showing 'the sort of growing monotony in the performances'.

[4] i.e. Frederick Mouillot (see p. 432, n. 7), the theatre manager and impresario. He had presumably told WBY of meeting AEFH, perhaps at her Manchester opening, but she denied any knowledge of him: 'I don't remember anyone of the name of "Moulleot", but I meet such crowds of civil people that my memory gets weak.'

[5] *The Unicorn from the Stars* was produced 21–3 Nov, but AG was still making revisions to it on 18 Oct, as she told WBY in a letter of that day (Berg). Its planned production was, moreover, in danger of interfering with the preparations for the Abbey's Advent tour to Britain (see p. 681). In her reply AEFH robustly reassured WBY that they had 'ample time to put on Unicorn by Nov. 23rd if the players work properly & you don't maul the play about constantly'.

[6] AEFH had long complained that the Abbey accounts never reached her, although she was footing most of the bills, and WBY had evidently enquired about these derelictions. She was more than happy to chronicle her complaints: 'The copy of the auditor's accounts was never sent to me by Henderson, Mr. Payne told him to do so, in vain. The only accounts I have had came about a year (or rather less) ago & I explained them to you as best I could. I have never received a list of shareholders nor a complete salary list of your present arrangements nor even any statement as to how the subsidy is apportioned out. The experience I have gained has taught me well that you are only one director amongst three & that the majority does not direct effectually that I should receive information.' WBY evidently acted upon this complaint at once, and instructed Ernest Vaughan to sent AEFH the information she required. She, in turn, thanked Vaughan on 22 Nov (NLI).

[7] WBY had asked for AEFH's natal details and in casting her horoscope (NLI) supposed that her stars presaged misfortune for her from 1907 onward. She would have none of this, and in her reply was even sceptical about such sources of prognostication: 'I feel now that I am in a vital and intellectual current in which I am right to work with vigour but there is nothing mystic connected with it. I feel no astral strain nor opposition; it is as if what I am doing belongs to the *mental* and *visible* world. If the occult life is to be mine again in this incarnation I shall be ready for it, but the summons will have to prove itself clearly, as coming from a High Source. I will never accept anything which carries a doubt to my mind by the impurity of the channel; I've had enough of that.'

## To Maud Gonne, [*late October 1907*]

Mention in an undated letter from MG, [October 1907].
Telling her that he is trying to get her horoscope cast, asking about significant dates in her life,[1] in particular the birth of Iseult,[2] the beginnings of the trouble with her husband,[3] and whether anything fortunate happened to her in January 1906, suggesting that the problems with MacBride were fated by Saturn's position in mid-heaven in late 1904,[4] asking if she is still evoking Aengus and Lugh,[5] revealing that he wrote her a dull letter on the

---

[1] WBY was trying to cast MG's horoscope, in the hope of discovering whether she would win her appeal against the verdict in her divorce case (see p. 637). It was the latest of many such attempts to interpret her stars, and he had been working on a horary for her as early as December 1898 (Visions Notebook). In her reply she thanked him 'for the trouble you are taking to get my horoscope. The dates you ask I will only be able to give you with any sort of exactitude when I get the papers back from the lawyers after the appeal is heard. I have NO memory for dates—Time as one counts by days & years, it has never meant very much to me & I never can remember the dates, even of the most important things in my life. At the time of the divorce proceeding I was obliged however to get exact dates of some of the principal events of my life both before & after my marriage—but they are *on paper* not *in my head.* When I get my papers back I will note them for you exactly.'

[2] In her letter MG told him that 'Iseult's birth date is 6th August 1894. Her arrival that year in my house may be the event you see marked in my 27th year, it is the only marked change I can remember in my life that year—I think it must have been about 3 or 4 years before that that a terrible tragic event occurred which shook & has certainly altered the whole of my life, but as usual I have no date for it.' This 'terrible tragic event' was the death of her infant son, Georges, which took place in Paris on 31 Aug 1891.

[3] In her reply, MG told him: 'It was as far as I can remember end of October 1904 I learnt the extent of MacBride's infamy or insanity, that date I can get accurately when my papers are returned to me. In Dec. 1904 I was in London trying to settle for a quiet separation without scandal & in February 1905 I think the divorce proceedings began in the French Courts. I was very unhappy all that time but in a dazed dull sort of way as my nerves had been so worn by the strain of the previous year that I was incapable of feeling anything *very* keenly.'

[4] MG could not recollect 'any very fortunate thing happening in Jany, 1906', but thought that what WBY said 'about *fate* (Saturn in mid Heaven) at the time of the discovery about MacBride should be correct, for months before it happened I was like one in a dream waiting for some event I knew not *what,* that would end my marriage. I waited quite calmly knowing only one thing that I must wait & be *quite still* & let fate work—It was one of the reasons I think that made me so reluctant to start divorce proceedings. I felt I ought to remain quite still & trust to fate,—even now I don't feel quite sure that I was passive enough at that time. MacBride had to disappear from my life because fate had ordered it—I need not have troubled about helping fate by going to law—' She apologized for her 'very long & very egotistical letter', but said that 'there are so many horoscope questions in your letter, I can only answer at some length—'.

[5] MG revealed that she did not have 'the same impossibility I used to have of seeing Aengus. I see Lugh less frequently & less clearly than formerly, but I think I am still under his protection.' She and WBY had conducted psychic experiments over a number of years which involved calling up visions of Celtic gods, particularly those of Aengus, the god of love, and Lugh, god of light. On 21 Dec 1898, for instance, WBY recorded in his Visions Notebook that

> Last Saturday evening [i.e. 17 Dec] I was with PIAL [i.e. MG]. We evoked Aengus. He appeared lying down, dressed in green, with an overset cup & a long spear. Asked for his five talismans corresponding to the five of the great initiation he showed a cup, an egg[.] PIAL saw this with a gold ring round it & a cross above—birds & a wand & a stone. He was laughing & mocking. He said we

situation in Ireland which he decided not to send,[6] and telling her that he is publishing a series of essays.[7]

*G–YL*, 247–8.


## To John Quinn, 26 October 1907

Mention in letter to Quinn, 29 October 1907.
Telegram instructing him 'dont give Darragh Deirdre'.[1]


## To Clement Shorter, 28 October 1907

Nassau Hotel, | Dublin.
28th Oct. 1907.

My dear Shorter,
The above address will find me for the present. I know nothing of the memorial but I will sign with pleasure any testimony or the like for

were one in the pre natal life & that this prenatal life was now bringing us togeather. When asked to show us in that life he showed PIAL a stone & me a most beautiful golden flame like form. Presently PIAL saw Lug who said we could now take the initiation of the spear. We saw a tree with a serpent & then a great fountain of fire. The spear was held over us & we were told to hold to this. We rose up through the fire. I saw a kind of feathery flames like the branches of some kind of trees or bush & heard sounds as if made by falling & crashing metal. Presently I saw the spear put upright we holding it no more. I was then drawn up as it seemed into the form of a great goddess who seemed like PIAL & like a stone Artemis[.] I looked out of her eyes. We were told that we would get to real initiation in sleep that night & would remember enough to teach others. We talked hours of certain troubles & this partly unfitted us, PIAL was after wards told. Her vision at night was finer & is in [notebook] A. I saw patterns first of little diamond shaped pieces of dull gold & then patterns made of many colours[.] I saw PIAL three times in ordinary dreams once in a black dress I know but with an embroidered sunflower a [sun symbol] symbol on the skirt a little below the waist.

On the preceding page, opposite this passage, WBY has added 'AE also associated Lug with the fire fountain & speaks of the clashing sounds. Lug said we were given the initiation of the spear before that of the sword that we might have inspiration & master the knowledge.'

  [6] WBY's long but unposted letter evidently explained and justified his views on the political state of Ireland to which she had objected in late September (see p. 729). MG answered that she was 'sorry you didn't send me your letter on the situation in Ireland, I would certainly not have found it dull though perhaps I wouldn't have agreed'. She added that the 'apathy you speak of is every where at present, at least in our part of the world, it is appalling in France—'.

  [7] WBY had told MG that *Discoveries* was going through the Dun Emer Press, and she asked when it would appear.

  [1] Mrs Pat Campbell had unexpectedly announced in Dublin that afternoon that she would play in *Deirdre* the following year and WBY was eager to make sure he retained sole rights in the play for this prestigious production.

Meredith's greatness. Is that what you want?[1] <As a rule> I hate seeing my name in irrevelant crowds of public names and exasperated a good lady of this town by refusing to sign some petition for the release of Gorki from prison. It was nothing to her that I did not know what he was in prison for and had never read a word of his writings.[2] I am sorry to say I have not read very much Meredith and nothing of him these fifteen years, but if one does not join in his praise in whose praise can one join,[3] [*remainder of letter in WBY's hand*] he is the formost of us all to day Swinburne being in his long eclipse and four fifth rhetorician, even when his moon was clear.[4]

Yrs ever<br>W B Yeats

TLS Berg.

## To John Quinn, 29 October 1907

Nassau Hotel, | Dublin.<br>29th October 1907.

My dear Quinn,
    I wired to you on Saturday night "dont give Darragh Deirdre", and this is my letter of explanation. On Friday Mrs. Patrick Campbell came to the

---

[1] Shorter had asked WBY to sign a memorial to be presented to the novelist George Meredith on his eightieth birthday on 12 Feb 1908. The memorial, mounted on vellum, and signed by 250 representatives of art, science, literature, and public life, was delivered in person to Meredith at his home by Shorter, his wife, and the folklorist Edward Clodd. The text of the memorial and its signatories, which included WBY, was published in *The Times* on 12 Feb 1908 (17).

[2] Maxim Gorki, pseudonym of Alexey Maximovich Peshkov (1868–1936), the celebrated social-realist novelist and short-story writer, had played a leading part in the march on the Winter Palace on 22 Jan 1905. He was arrested shortly after this demonstration and incarcerated in the Peter-and-Paul Fortress of St Petersburg. The Russian government wanted a secret trial, but mass support from the West forced the issue into the public eye, and saved him. He was released on bail of 10,000 roubles, and fled Russia shortly afterwards to settle in Capri. From April to November 1906 he made a disastrous trip to the USA, where he was denounced by the press for travelling with his mistress Maria Feodorovna Andreeva. WBY was unsympathetic to Gorki's cause and had angered Ricketts on 30 June 1905 (*SP*, 53) on this account: 'Yeats in evening obviously discouraged by Ireland & things Irish, he got on my nerves once or twice in using the editorial "we" over Ireland, when he started posturing over the Gorki manifesto, I flashed up and said it was of course a matter of common human & artistic interest, one which affected Europe & not to be confused with any local political point of view. The Irish are odious with their barndoor politics & Hen-run ethics.' WBY later had Gorki's *Reminiscences of Tolstoi* (1920) in his library (*YA4*, 283). The 'good lady in Dublin' was probably Con Markiewicz.

[3] WBY seems to have been most interested in Meredith in 1888. In September of that year he read the poem 'Love in the Valley', finding it 'full of a curious intricate richness', and in November the novel *Diana of the Crossways*, which he thought made 'the mistake of making the reader think to[o] much. One is continually laying the book down to think. He is so suggestive ones mind wanders. The really great writers of fiction make their readers minds like sponges' (see I. 97, 108).

[4] WBY's dislike of Swinburne had been intensified by the dispute over Blake (see pp. 434–5). Swinburne's best poetry is generally supposed to have been written before 1880, and for the last

Abbey to a special Matinee given in her honour, was in great enthusiasm about the Plays and the acting, and told me that I might annouce from the stage that she would come to us next year and play with the Company for a week. On Saturday night she made a speech from the stage of the Gaiety calling me "my dear friend and your great poet".[1] This means that if she has any sort of success she will probably put the play on elsewhere. Miss Darragh will understand how important it is to us here. I am very much afraid that if Mrs. Campbell were to find Miss Darragh playing the play while she was in America where she goes next week that she would be put off it. She is very touchy about things of that kind. When I engaged Miss Darragh for Dublin the play was actually promised to Mrs. Campbell and I withdrew it from her because of the overwhelming importance to me of making the Dublin Theatre a success. I mean that I withdrew it so far as Dublin was concerned giving it a first performance there, instead of leaving it to Mrs. Campbell to produce it when she liked somewhere else. Mrs. Campbell likes to produce plays for the first time, and Moore and myself lost her for Dairmuid & Grania by insisting on a first Dublin performance.[2] On Friday afternoon when somebody reminded her of Miss Darragh

thirty years of his life he lived, protected from his own eccentricity and almost total deafness, with the critic and novelist Theodore Watts-Dunton. Nevertheless, WBY stopped his sister in the street the day after Swinburne's death in April 1909 to tell her that he was now 'the King of the Cats' (Hone, 230). Swinburne and Watts-Dunton also signed the Meredith memorial.

[1] The Abbey Company performed *The Gaol Gate*, *In the Shadow of the Glen*, *Spreading the News*, and *Cathleen ni Houlihan* at the special matinée for Mrs Campbell, her company, and a paying audience (see p. 751, n. 2). Holloway recorded (NLI) that the 'professional matinee with the additional attraction of Mrs. Patrick Campbell was a big Success in every way, & the almost "sensational" announcement made by W B Yeats as the audience were dispersing that Mrs. Campbell had promised to appear as Deirdre in his one act play of that name for a week at the Abbey next November twelve month was a stroke of luck to the poet'. The following day, 26 Oct, 'Jacques' in the *Irish Independent* announced (4) the 'great bit of news' that was 'given out yesterday just as we were leaving the Abbey Theatre', and reported that as WBY made the announcement 'he was so plainly overjoyed that one expression of gratitude to Mrs. Pat tumbled over the other. W.B. looked really pleased and honoured. He has good reason to be. A great honour has been done him and those associated with him in the fostering care of the National Theatre Society.' Jacques went on to say that at the tea party in the green room after the matinée Mrs Campbell 'was fairly surprised at all she had seen and heard. The plays she said, were Irish all through, and most truly national, and the soft accents of the players—well, there; that was beyond her.' On Saturday, 26 Oct, Mrs Campbell said in the course of a farewell speech that she and her company had been invited back to the Gaiety 'next year, in the last week of November. The following week I am going to have the happiness of appearing at the Abbey Theatre (hear, hear, and applause), in my friend's and your poet's delightful play, "Deirdre" (applause). This has been my wish for months, and the knowledge that that wish is going to be realised will keep me happy until I see you again' (*Freeman's Journal*, 28 Oct 1907, p. 5). The *Irish Times* of 28 Oct reported her words (6) as 'my dear friend's and your poet's beautiful play, "Deirdre" '. Mrs Campbell was true to her word; she took the leading role in WBY's *Deirdre* at the Abbey Theatre in early November 1908, and presented the play in London later in the same month.

[2] Mrs Campbell had intended to produce *Diarmuid and Grania* in London in 1901 but withdrew when George Moore and WBY insisted on including it in the final ILT productions in Dublin (see II. 615–16, 622–3; III. 20–1).

having produced the play here she seemed inclined for the moment to give up the project. Apart altogether from any question of relative merits of the two actresses Mrs. Campbell means success and that means the future of our players & our Theatre secure. We did not put "Deirdre" on in London as Lady Gregory and Synge, and indeed the whole Company consider that Miss Darragh was not a success in the part. I thought she had very good moments, and that some of her faults were the faults of my own writing in the experimental version of the play she went on in. In any case we should have hesitated about London, as we never gave up the idea of Mrs. Campbell outside Ireland. When I wrote to you sending those two letters,[3] I thought, (though I must say Lady Gregory did not) that Mrs. Campbell had given up the play for good. The play was actually written for her and read to her in Scenario, so I think Miss Darragh will not feel quite the same as if I took it from her to give it to some one else. What makes me particularly anxious not to lose Mrs. Cam[p]bell is that owing to Miss Horniman having said that she will not continue our subsidy after the winter 1909–10, I cannot lose any chance of enlarging our audiences here, and Mrs. Campbell's promise, and her fulfilment of it still more is bound to do more than anything else to break down the feeling on the Unionist side here that our plays cannot be good because they are "Irish", and the feeling among a considerable number of Nationalists that they cannot be good because they are cultivated and intellectual. Our difficulty in keeping up the standard has been increased by Miss Hornaman's decision which makes Fay anxious to put on as little dangerous work as possible, and to press for as many performances as possible of the cruder and more popular plays. Mrs Campbell's promise which is really a beautiful thing from a great Actress has come just in time to help Lady Gregory and myself in the carrying out of our resolution of keeping the Theatre precisely as it has always been. We believe that is our one chance of success apart from every other reason. I hope my wire has not put you to any trouble. Let me know if you have really been in negotiation with Miss Darragh, and have had to withdraw a consent or anything of that kind as I must write her my apologies in that case. I have not really felt for a long time the personal enthusiasm that I feel at this moment for Mrs. Campbell's generosity. She is coming to us without salary, and not only that but will be giving up salary to come. I had got to look upon her as given up to Society and caring little for her art, and now all I have thought has been proved wrong by this generosity of hers. It has put new life into my imagination, and I am already thinking out a new plot not this time a legend but my own invention.[4]

---

[3] See pp. 739–40.
[4] WBY's 'new plot' was to become *The Player Queen.*

When I saw her in the Modern Plays she was doing here I told her that she was a volcano cooking eggs. I am now going myself to see if I cannot make some very passionate thing, and last night the stars gave me a fantastic thought. Lady Gregory and I had a suspicious young man in here to cut a lot of nonsense out of his play and I thought it would be tactful to leave him to Lady Gregory,[5] and so I went out for a walk, and then the stars gave me their gift. I have not forgotten by-the-bye that I have promised you the manuscript of "Deirdre".[6] It needs some little re-arrangement to make it intelligible. There were such a lot of different versions in every part that I cannot get at it just yet.[7] I forgot when writing to you last to answer a question you asked me about the death of Naisi. I am afraid a stage direction has dropped out, he is gagged by the executioner before he is led off which makes quite a little effect.[8]

Yr sny<br>W B Yeats

[*In WBY's hand*]
My type writer woman spells vilely & is very bad at her work in every way—

TLS NYPL, with envelope addressed to 20 [corrected in another hand to 31] Nassau St., New York, postmark 'Dublin OC 30 07'.

[5] The 'suspicious young man' was probably Thomas MacDonagh who had submitted his unwieldy three-act tragedy *When the Dawn is Come* to the Abbey. It was finally produced on 15 Oct 1908.

[6] WBY had sent Quinn a copy of the published *Deirdre*, inscribed 'John Quinn from his friend W. B. Yeats August 17 1907', but it is unclear whether he ever presented the MS of the play to him. Presumably he would have wanted to keep the original text by him until Mrs Pat's production in November 1908, and he was to fall out with Quinn a few months after that. No MS version of *Deirdre* was included in the comprehensive sale of Quinn's library at the Anderson Galleries in 1923 and 1924.

[7] These changes were made in time for Mrs Patrick Campbell's production of *Deirdre* in November 1908, when they were printed in *Samhain* (28–33) as 'Alterations in "Deirdre"', and prefaced by WBY's explanation that there were 'two passages in this play as published which I always knew to be mere logic, mere bones, and yet after many attempts I thought it impossible to alter them. When, however, Mrs. Campbell offered to play the part my imagination began to work again. I think they are now as they should be.' Later in November 1908 Bullen published this as a four-page leaflet under the same title, for insertion in the published copies of the play; see *VPl*, 393–6.

[8] The stage direction '*Unseen by Deirdre, Naoise is gagged*' was inadvertently omitted in the printing of *Deirdre* in vol. II of *The Poetical Works of William B. Yeats*.

## *To the Editor of* The Times, *29 October 1907*

Sir,—The Prime Minister has consented to receive during next month a deputation from the following dramatic authors on the subject of the censorship of plays.[1] In the meantime, may these authors, through your columns, enter a formal protest against this office, which was instituted for political, and not for the so-called moral ends to which it is perverted—an office autocratic in procedure, opposed to the spirit of the Constitution, contrary to common justice and to common sense?[2]

They protest against the power lodged in the hands of a single official— who judges without a public hearing, and against whose dictum there is no appeal—to cast a slur on the good name and destroy the means of livelihood of any member of an honourable calling.[3]

They assert that the censorship has not been exercised in the interests of morality, but has tended to lower the dramatic tone by appearing to relieve the public of the duty of moral judgment.[4]

---

[1] The Rt. Hon. Sir Henry Campbell-Bannerman (1836–1908) had been Leader of the Liberal Party since 1899 and Prime Minister since 1905. He had served as Chief Secretary for Ireland 1884–5. Owing to terminal ill-health, he was unable to receive the deputation of playwrights, which, led by J. M. Barrie, was finally seen by the Home Secretary Herbert Gladstone (1854–1930) on 25 Feb 1908. The deputation had no effect, nor did a Joint Select Committee of the Houses of Lords and Commons set up to enquire into the working of stage censorship in 1909, and censorship in the theatre was not abolished in Britain until 1968.

[2] Stage censorship had been officially established in Britain by the Licensing Act of 1737, a measure designed primarily to curb political satire. New and revised plays had to be submitted to the Lord Chamberlain's office, which would decide whether they should be licensed for performance. Although the Act had been designed to end political satire, it soon became used as a method of moral control, and in the 19th century the majority of banned plays were suppressed because of their sexual content. The arbitrary exercise of this power had long been a matter of contention; WBY had signed a public protest in June 1902 against the banning of Maurice Maeterlinck's *Monna Vanna* (see III. 207), and the danger that *The Playboy of the Western World* might be denied a British licence had caused him to cut short his trip to Italy in May of this year (see pp. 662–3, 664). This new protest had been occasioned by the banning of Harley Granville-Barker's play *Waste*, in which the career and life of an up-and-coming Radical politician are destroyed by a casual sexual relationship and subsequent abortion. The play was not publicly performed until December 1936.

[3] The Lord Chamberlain did not himself read the plays submitted for licensing; this was done by the Examiner of Plays, an office of obscure origin and held since 1895 by the dismally conventional ex-bank manager George Alexander Redford (see p. 24, n. 8). There was no appeal against his decisions, which were absolute, and nor was he legally required to give his reasons for granting or withholding a licence (although, in practice, he usually indicated the changes he considered necessary for an unlicensed play to be performed).

[4] Besides banning *Monna Vanna*, Redford had also refused licences to such serious plays as Shaw's *Mrs Warren's Profession*, Laurence Housman's *Bethlehem* (see III. 280, 285), Shelley's *The Cenci*, Sophocles' *Oedipus Tyrannus*, Edward Garnett's *The Breaking Point*, and D'Annunzio's *La Città morta*. But his attempt to ban Shaw's *The Shewing-Up of Blanco Posnet* was circumvented in Ireland when the Abbey Theatre insisted on producing it in 1909 under the terms of their Dublin Patent. In 1902 *The Times* had observed of Redford that 'any tinge of literary merit seems at once to excite his worst suspicions' (see III. 208). In a more recent onslaught in the *Academy* on 29 June 1907 (628–31), Shaw had shown up the contradictions in the censor's position and concluded that dramatists wanted

They ask to be freed from the menace hanging over every dramatist of having his work and the proceeds of his work destroyed at a pen's stroke by the arbitrary action of a single official neither responsible to Parliament nor amenable to law.

They ask that their art be placed on the same footing as every other art.

They ask that they themselves be placed in the position enjoyed under the law by every other citizen.

To these ends they claim that the licensing of plays shall be abolished. The public is already sufficiently assured against managerial misconduct by the present yearly licensing of theatres, which remains untouched by the measure of justice here demanded.[5]

[*signed by seventy-one men and women of letters including W. B. Yeats*]

Printed letter, *The Times*, 29 Oct 1907, p. 15. Also published in *The Green Room Book* (1908), 603–4.

## To Florence Farr, 29 October 1907

Nassau Hotel, | DUBLIN.
29th October 1907.

My dear Florence Emery

I have no doubt Mrs. Campbell has told you the news and so I feel that you are the less entitled to hear it from me, but why dont you write. I have nobody to tell me your news, and God knows how much longer I shall have to stop here. Another month possibly, certainly three weeks. I see nothing for it in spite of all good resolutions but keeping hard at work here in Dublin, except when I can hand the Theatre over to Lady Gregory. If Fay is not constantly watched he is away idling with his paint box, or what is still worse down at the Theatre painting out our decorative scenery and

'not anarchy and the police, but reasonable liberties in return for reasonable guarantees...let Mr. Redford's doom be a handsome pension, and leisure to write the perfectly moral plays he has failed to extract from the rest of us'. Shaw co-signed this letter, as did Granville-Barker, Housman, and Garnett. Masefield, Sturge Moore, Symons, and Synge were also signatories

[5] In Britain plays could only be publicly performed in venues licensed for the purpose. Before 1843 the Lord Chamberlain was responsible for granting such licences, but in that year the Theatres Act transferred these powers in most towns to the local authorities (although the Lord Chamberlain retained his right of censorship). But the prospect of allowing censorship through licence to depend on the uncertain taste of provincial aldermen did not appeal to the theatre industry as a whole, and the managers preferred a clear-cut and binding ruling by a central authority such as the Lord Chamberlain to the unpredictable vagaries of different local watch committees, which would make the production of any given play legally and financially hazardous. The *Green Room* observed in a paragraph following this letter that it was 'interesting to note that, while practically all the leading dramatists protest against the Censorship, nearly all the responsible managers uphold the retention of the office'.

putting his own damnable landscapes in its stead. M^rs Campbell came in for one of these.[1] Mrs. Campbell has won my heart for ever. I am fifty times more grateful to her than I would have been if she had put the Play on in a London Theatre. It is a really beautiful thing of her to come into our little Theatre and play there bringing us her great name and her great fame— A beautiful romantic thing. You do not often see me in this mood but I am really touched. I have been thinking of her as giving up too much to Society and to the people who are not Artists, but now I see her once more as the great Artist. You who love London will not understand me, but it is this narrow, imbittered, in many ways stupid town that touches my imagination. Elsewhere we become like other people, here perhaps because other people are rather disagreeable we remain ourselves. I believe that this promise of hers, the mere promise, will help me more than anything I have said or written these five years back, and that the performance will win the battle. She made a beautiful speech from the stage of the Gaiety promising to return in November next year to play at the Abbey "in Deirdre by my dear friend and your great Poet." The day before I had caught an old journalist who probably hates the Abbey, because he thinks it the centre of advanced ideas trying to stir up, though naturally in vain, Miss Allgood's feelings, trying to rouse her jealousy <of all things>.[2] On Saturday he began questioning me, with a queer bitter tone in his voice looking I could see for some fact that might help him to prove that this was a mere act of friendship on Mrs. Campbell's part and not a compliment to the Abbey. In reporting Mrs. Campbell's speech which he, for I have little doubt it was he, did for every Dublin paper he left out the word "great".[3] On the other hand those who do care for my work are delighted. This is a litany not a letter, a list of beatitudes what you will, but I will write you a letter before the week ends.

I send you the songs if I can call them songs out of the "golden helmet". There is no hurry but could you manage at your leisure to put some musical notes to them. You will remember the play is noisy and violent.[4]

Yrs ever<br>W B Yeats

TLS Texas.

[1] Fay's scenic designs in these productions attracted no adverse press comment, although Holloway noted (NLI) that 'the lighting of the scene was vile' during AG's *The Gaol Gate*.

[2] This was possibly 'Jacques', the drama critic of the *Irish Independent*.

[3] See p. 758, n. 1. The word 'great' was omitted in all accounts of Mrs Campbell's Gaiety speech in the Dublin press.

[4] WBY had written *The Golden Helmet* at Coole during the summer of this year, and in her letter of 17 Aug (see p. 629, n. 11) AG described it to Quinn as 'a merry little heroic farce about Cuchulain and

## *To Frank Sidgwick, 29 October 1907*

Mention in auction catalogue.

Typed letter, addressed to both Sidgwick[1] and Bullen from the Nassau Hotel, asking that a copy of *Ideas of Good and Evil*[2] be sent to Mrs Pat Campbell: 'Please send this at once as she is leaving for America in a few days.[3] She is going to play *Dierdre* at the Abbey Theatre on her return, and has asked for "Ideas".' Also requesting that a copy of *Deirdre* be sent to B. Iden Payne.

Sold at Sothebys, 21 February 1978, catalogue 'Cadmus', item 468.

## *To A. H. Bullen, [1 November 1907]*

Nassau Hotel | Dublin.
Friday.

My dear Bullen

:No 'John Sherman & Dhoya' comes last in the book & are to be labelled early work—that is essential. The book begins with the following stories & in the following order.

Crusifixion of the outcast
Out of the Rose
Wisdom of the King
Heart of the Spring
Curse of the Fires & the Shadows
Old men of the Twilight

the Championship he had long had in his mind'. In fact, the play, written as an introduction to *On Baile's Strand*, was based on her own version of 'The Feast of Bricriu' in *Cuchulain of Muirthemne*. FF evidently delayed writing music for the four songs (by Leagerie, his wife, Conal's wife, and Emer) until shortly before the first production at the Abbey on 19 Mar 1908, just as WBY was writing "The Music for Use in the Performance of these Plays" for *CW* III, where he placed the musical settings for his plays. Though no settings of songs from the play were finally included there, WBY clearly supposed that they would be when he wrote his introductory essay: 'The degree of approach to ordinary singing depends on the context, for one desires a greater or lesser amount of contrast between the lyrics and the dialogue itself. . . . the little song of Leagerie when he seizes the "Golden Helmet" should in its opening words be indistinguishable from the dialogue itself' (*CW* III. 222).

[1] Sidgwick was still working with Bullen, but their partnership was showing signs of strain (see p. 729).

[2] Bullen had issued the third edition of *Ideas of Good and Evil* (see p. 730, n. 1) in September of this year.

[3] After completing her season at the Gaiety in Dublin, Mrs Campbell returned to London to prepare for an extensive American tour. She sailed on the *Philadelphia* and arrived in New York on 7 Nov before opening at the Lyric Theatre on 11 Nov.

Proud Costello
Rosa Alchemica
Then will come 'Tables of the Law' & John Sherman & Dhoya.[1]

W B Yeats


ALS Kansas.


## *To Maud Gonne,* [c. *1 November 1907*]

Mention in letter from MG, 'Monday' [? 4 November 1907].
Telling her he has found good lodgings,[1] and asking when she is to arrive in Dublin.[2]


*G–YL*, 248.


## *To A. E. F. Horniman,* [c. *1 November 1907*]

Mention in letter from AEFH, 3 November 1907.
A 'long letter' asking about her acquisition of the Gaiety Theatre, Manchester,[1] telling her that he is trying to make himself into a technically good

---

[1]  This is a reply to a letter of Bullen's of 29 Oct (*YL*, 337): 'In regard to the John Sherman volume: I take it that the order is to be John Sherman, Dhoya | Secret Rose (dedicated to A.E.), The Binding of the Hair, Wisdom of the Kings, Where there is Nothing, Crucifixion of the Outcast | Out of the Rose, Curse of the Fires and of the Shadows, Heart of the Spring, Costello the Proud etc. | (The Book of the Great Dhoul not to be included, though it's far better than some of the others), The Old Men of the Twilight, Rosa Alchemica, Tables of the Law, The Three Magi. Is this right? And will you kindly let me have the corrected copy as quickly as you possibly can?' The stories were printed in vol. VII of *CW* in the order WBY gives, except that 'Where there is Nothing, there is God' was included after 'The Curse of the Fires and of the Shadows', and this order was retained in *Mythologies* (1932). 'John Sherman and Dhoya' were printed at the end of the volume as 'Two Early Stories', with a preface dated 14 Nov 1907. 'The Binding of the Hair' and 'The Rose of Shadow' were omitted from *CW*.

[1]  WBY was in fact staying as usual at the Nassau Hotel.

[2]  In her reply MG wrote that she was crossing to Dublin immediately and staying with Ella and Elizabeth Young at 57 Grosvenor Square, Rathmines. She invited him to visit her there at 5.00 p.m. on 5 Nov, or on 6 Nov, and told him she would remain in Dublin until 12 Nov.

[1]  AEFH had now found a permanent home for her new company in the rather run-down Gaiety Theatre, which she was in process of purchasing from United Theatres Ltd. Obtaining a theatrical licence and moving into the Theatre took a good deal longer, and the company (now renamed 'Miss Horniman's Company') was not to open there until March 1908, when it played for six weeks, after which there was a tour while the theatre was being refurbished. In her reply AEFH told WBY that she had 'not told you much about the Manchester affair because I don't see why your time should be taken up with details about what you consider to be "an error of judgement". The Gaiety is one of the well-known theatres, in a splendid position & it holds over 1000 people. Everyone is glad to hear that I am buying it & that I intend if possible to arrange for all the seats to be booked. The date on which I shall take possession is not yet settled, it could be in six weeks or not until the end of July next.'

stage manager,[2] and of Mrs Pat Campbell's offer to play in *Deirdre* the following autumn,[3] hinting that he may establish a second company at the Abbey,[4] asking after her plans and whether he can see her in London,[5] and describing Mancini's portrait of him.[6]

*LWBY* I. 194.

## To Gwen John (Gladys Jones),[1] 2 November [1907]

Nassau Hotel | Dublin
Nov 2nd

Dear Madam: Yes you may play 'The Land of Hearts' desire at Chesterfield for the purpose you speak of.[2] M^r Synge's address is Glendalough House, Glen-na Geary, Kingstown. Co Dublin.[3]

Yr ev
W B Yeats

ALS Private.

[2] AEFH thought this idea 'a sad waste of time', especially since he would 'have to work with unwilling material & neglect the literary tasks which you can carry out as no one else living can do. But what are my words against the wooing of the vampire Kathleen ni Houlihan!'

[3] See pp. 757–8, 763. Although AEFH had constantly urged WBY to let Mrs Campbell have *Deirdre* (see pp. 486, n. 2, 498, n. 4), she replied with waspish jealousy: 'I believe that she admires your poetical powers & very likely she has taken a fancy to you too although you are much too old for a woman of forty who might well go in for someone young. The root matter is whether Willie Fay will let the Directors & the Company consent to allow an Englishwoman to play at the Abbey & whether his permission (if he grant it) be genuine or not. This is the whole gist of it all, but you will only be angry with me for putting it so clearly. But I will not see the rest of your life wasted without raising my voice even if it be useless.'

[4] This idea was shelved with the departure of the Fays from the Abbey in 1908, but was revived with some success during the First Company's extended tour to America in 1911–12. AEFH, however, poured scorn on the idea at once: 'You *must* know that Fay would not permit a second company of actors at the Abbey, they would need to be paid & some would not be Irish & they could not be kept together to do proper work amongst the present company. You have not the discipline amongst the present people which is absolutely necessary—as long as things are going on at the Abbey like this your time is being wasted.'

[5] AEFH replied that she was going to Manchester and Glasgow, but that she would 'indeed be glad to see you in London, *my* dear old friend; but you must bear in mind that your wish that I should trouble you less will be fulfilled. You will have no less kindness from me, but I will not waste the rest of my life on a Lost Cause.'

[6] See pp. 737, 753–4. In her reply AEFH asked him to send her a photograph of the Mancini portrait.

[1] 'Gwen John' was the pseudonym of Gladys Jones, actress, playwright, and biographer. She was born in Chesterfield, and was later a member of PEN. She published a number of plays from 1916 to 1930, as well as a biography of Queen Elizabeth I (1924) and a volume of poems, *Syringa*, in 1922.

[2] Miss John was seeking permission to stage *The Land of Heart's Desire* as part of an amateur production in aid of the Victoria Home for Nurses, Chesterfield, which, as she told Synge on 8 Nov (TCD), was 'in reduced circumstances'.

[3] In her letter of 8 Nov to Synge (see n. 1) Miss John described her theatrical venture and explained that she had experienced 'great difficulty in finding plays worth acting for which there are not heavy fees

## *To A. E. F. Horniman, 5 November 1907*

Nassau St. Dublin 2.12 PM

Reply paid Miss Horniman Manchester
Wire Norreys Connells address your mistake about Piper first production after tour never any question of dropping it.[1]

Yeates

Telegram Southern Illinois.

## *To Ella Young, 6 November [?1907]*

Nassau Hotel | Dublin
Nov 6

Dear Miss Young: could you come on Sunday instead as I find I shall have to take some body to the exhibition on Thursday or Friday I dont know

---

to pay'. She had been entranced by *Riders to the Sea* and *The Shadow of the Glen*, but had only just discovered that they were still in copyright and now 'the only course open to me is to give up the hope of playing them, unless of your charity you will give permission: for being poverty-stricken we can't pay a fee. Of course before giving permission you would like to think that they would be well played. I hope they would be—we should try our best. I am a professional actress. But in any case we could not do such good work harm, it should become classical: and we might muster enough Irish blood to give it the proper colour. And the Celtic movement being almost unheard of here, it would be the thin end of a wedge which should enter. I am afraid it is a great deal to ask you, but one has to ask to get anything. It will be <u>very</u> kind if you will allow us to play them. With apologies for troubling you.' This mixture of disingenuousness and flattery worked, and the performances took place on 17 Dec at 3.30 and 18 Dec at 7.30 at St James's Room, Vicar Lane, Chesterfield, in aid of the Victoria Home for Nurses. They did not use WBY's play but produced Synge's *In the Shadow of the Glen* and *Riders to the Sea*, with Miss Jones taking the leading parts in both.

[1] Despite her repeated protestations that she would never again intervene in the running of the Abbey, AEFH had once more been making mischief by her meddling. After assuring WBY in her letter of 3 Nov (see p. 765) that it would 'be a great relief to your mind, to know that you need never fear any more interference from me', she continued immediately: 'I saw Norris Connell last night, he wrote & asked for an interview. I told him the bare fact you told me, that "Fay did not like his play" & how that your passing it & my liking it were of no avail. The man lives by his pen so it was only just that I should tell him the truth. Naturally I told him that I have no more connection with the Abbey beyond the subsidy & the building itself.' WBY, who was arranging for *The Piper* (see p. 635, n. 3) to be performed in February 1908, was horrified and wired AEFH the moment he received her letter. She in her turn wrote to Connell immediately after receiving this telegram on 5 Nov (Southern Illinois), confessing that she 'was wrong to interfere even so slightly with the Abbey Theatre affairs. I should have been wiser if I had referred you to the Directors. But well-meaning words seem to bring much trouble sometimes. I have wired your address to Mr Yeats. What he said to me most certainly gave me the clear impression that he was troubled because Fay did not like the play & he had a certain dislike to explaining the matter to you. These misunderstandings have arisen very often & they are very trying to all concerned.'

which & Saturday I shall have to be at theatre.[1] MG horoscope is very interesting. The difficulty about ascendant is increased by ☽☍☉ almost exact. Even if end of ♋ rose she would still be very solar. She has ♂ 27 ♋☍♃ (seven apart). I think ♂ must be fairly close to asc & have for various reasons pitched on 3 ♌ but on the other hand there is a primary direction which agrees with either 3 ♌ or 13 ♌. It is a curious figure but her fighting character seems to me to require ♂ near Asc.

The keys of her character are ♃☍♂ & ☽☍☉. This last is of supreme importance & means a climactric period about every 14 years—this period is due at opening of next year.[2]

If Sunday will not suit come on Monday.[3]

Yr sny
W B Yeats

ALS Congress.

[1] WBY would have attended the Irish International Exhibition (see p. 674) before the closing ceremony on Saturday, 9 Nov. The Exhibition Grounds in Herbert Park, Ballsbridge, featured Irish Home Industries, Art and Historical Sections, Village Entertainment Competitions, Canadian and French Pavilions, Indian Theatre, Somali Village, Switchback Railway, Shooting Range, Baby Incubators, Tuberculosis Exhibition, marching bands, dancing, and various musical entertainments.

[2] WBY had asked James Richard Wallace to cast MG's horoscope during this autumn, although her vagueness about exact dates in her life (see p. 755) obliged WBY to call upon his insight into her character, as well as his knowledge of her natal horoscope, to determine her exact time of birth. The ascendant is the point of the zodiac rising on the eastern horizon for the time and place of the event in question. In the present letter, WBY points out that MG's moon opposite sun complicates the matter of the ascendant. She was born on 21 Dec 1866, just before the full moon, and seems to have given him an approximate time of 5 p.m. Her full moon is in fact in conjunct with his sun, and her sun is opposite his, a complementary which, with her problematic ascendant, bedevilled their relationship. WBY writes that even if 'end of Cancer' rose, it would still be nearly Leo, so the leonine qualities would already be apparent. MG's Mars at 27 degrees Cancer opposite Jupiter by a difference of only 7 degrees strengthens both planets even in opposition, and WBY saw this, together with the opposition of sun and moon, as defining the 'keys' of her character. The opposition of sun and moon, together with the return of the moon in twenty-eight days (or, symbolically, years) to its original position, means that fourteen years puts the symbolic moon in opposition to the birth moon, again a strengthening or stressful position. In MG's case, this lunar opposition is at the same time a symbolic conjunction with her natal sun, emphasizing male–female connections. Primary directions (see p. 748) take a degree of the earth's rotation eastward as equivalent to a year of life, so that a mistake of as little as four minutes in the birth time can put calculations of primary directions among the planets and angles out by a year. Birth times were often rectified for exactness by calculating back from accurately detailed events of the subsequent life; in 1908 WBY was to commission Wallace to rectify MG's horoscope in this way, and, like WBY here, Wallace concluded that 3 degrees Leo (3 ♌) was her most likely natal sign. Since MG was born in 1866, a series of fourteen-year cycles would make 1908—the 'opening of next year'—a climacteric period.

[3] MG had arrived in Dublin on 4 Nov and was staying with the Youngs (see pp. 43–4, 94).

## To Norreys Connell, [*7 November 1907*]

Nassau Hotel | Dublin.
Thursday

Dear Norris Connell:

We hope to put your play on immediately on our return from tour. Could you come over in January any time to attend rehersals & would you prefer any other time? Of course it is not necessary that you should come, but you said you thought you would do so & it would be a help.[1] Synge Lady Gregory & I all admire your play extremely and are proud to have the production of it.[2] We shall if it is the great success we are confident it will be tour it afterwards taking it to towns like London, Manchester & Edinburgh.[3]

Yr sny
W B Yeats

ALS Southern Illinois, with envelope addressed to 103 Leith Mansions, Elgin Avenue, London, postmark 'DUBLIN NOV 7 07'.

## To Edward Evans,[1] [*8 November 1907*]

UNITED ARTS CLUB, | LINCOLN PLACE, | DUBLIN.
Friday

My dear Evans: could you come on Sunday week instead of Sunday next. Martin Harvey has asked me to supper & I think it well to

---

[1] WBY was quickly trying to repair the damage caused by AEFH's indiscretion (see p. 767). Connell did come to Dublin in 1908 and *The Piper* was produced at the Abbey 13–15 Feb 1908 and revived for 1–3 Oct in the same year. There were further revivals in 1909 and 1913.
[2] W. G. Fay's name is conspicuous by its absence from this list.
[3] The Abbey Company performed the play in Manchester in February 1909.

[1] Edward Evans, known in Dublin as 'The Bishop', had trained as a stockbroker but emigrated to South Africa where he worked at various manual jobs. On his return from Africa he became, as Page Dickinson explains in *The Dublin of Yesterday* (68), 'exceedingly religious in a fairly conventional way, on the general lines of Anglican Doctrine, but with many strange spiritual ideas of his own added, as the result of his real or imaginary experiences. He took a small and isolated cottage at the foot of the Dublin hills, where he lived the life of a recluse, surrounded by books dealing with every religion under the sun. He used to see spooks and tell one of his conversations with them.' He subsequently became a lay brother in the Anglican Franciscan order and devoted his life to the sick and needy. WBY attended his Bible classes and also went for walks with him in the Dublin mountains, during one of which, as he recalls in *Mem*, Evans, all 'muscular force and ardour', reminded him of Ben Jonson's line ' "So rammed with life he can but grow in life with being". The irregular line of his thought which makes him obscure is itself a sign of this. He is as full of twists and turns as a tree' (163–5).

go on various more or less practical grounds.[2] I am sorry to put you off.

Yrs sny

W B Yeats

ALS Southern Illinois, with two envelopes, one addressed to Doddervale Cottage, Orwell Road, Rathgar, postmark 'DUBLIN NOV 9 07', the other to Mr Evans, Hon Sec of discussion committee, United Arts Club, Lincoln Place.

## To Laurence Binyon, [*11 November 1907*]

Nassau Hotel | Dublin
Monday

My dear Binyon: I hear you are with Judge Madden.[1] I wanted to go & hear you to day but some theatrical correspondence kept me at home.[2] Are you free on Wednesday? If so can you dine with me here — dinner rather bad —

---

[2] Martin Harvey's company had opened at the Theatre Royal in Dublin on 4 Nov for a three-week season, and WBY had arranged a special matinée at the Abbey for both his and F. R. Benson's company (which was to open at the Gaiety on 11 Nov). At the matinée of four plays held on 15 Nov, Holloway observed (NLI) that 'Hugh Lane & J. M. Synge sat together during *Riders to the Sea* & Lady Gregory & W. B. Yeats busied themselves about their principal guests & introduced Jack Magrath to Harvey & Benson to extract copy from them for the *Freeman's Journal*. These professional matinees are a great stroke of business!' In his article in the *Freeman's Journal* of 16 Nov (5), John McGrath reported that 'both were very warm in their praises of the plays; indeed, one might say, remarkably so. . . . The "atmosphere" of the theatre impressed both — something very different from what the actor is used to. Mr. Harvey dwelt especially, not only on the remarkable character of the plays, but also on the exceptional ability of the players. In this respect he referred to the exquisite voice and beautiful intonation of Miss Allgood in "Kathleen ni Houlihan" and the performance of Mr. William Fay in "Hyacinth Halvey" — tragedy and comedy, he said of an extremely high and successful type. Mr. Harvey thinks that the Abbey plays are expressing the thought, the mind, and the genius of Ireland as in another field Wales is expressing herself; and that, he holds, is a great thing gained, for he holds that great art like the Elizabethan, comes from such sources.' Though Benson did not speak so freely as Harvey at first, he finally said, 'very deliberately, that he was impressed more than he could say with the plays he had seen — with the idea of them, and with the acting of them. "These plays," he said, "are beautiful, are art, and are true, and I feel humiliated in listening to them when I think of the ordinary drama of the day".'

[1] Dodgson Hamilton Madden (1840–1928) had been the Unionist MP for Dublin University 1887–92, Attorney-General of Ireland 1889–92, and sat as a High Court judge from 1892 until his retirement in 1919. He also served as Vice-Chancellor of Dublin University from 1895 to 1919. As well as publishing a number of legal works, he also wrote on medieval history and Shakespeare, and is best known for *The Diary of Master William Silence; A Study of Shakespear and Elizabethan Sport* (1897), a new edition of which had appeared this year. JBY had painted portraits of both him and his first wife in the 1880s.

[2] Binyon (see p. 545), visiting from the Department of Prints and Drawings in the British Museum, was in Dublin to give the annual Hermione Lectures at Alexandra College. His four lectures on 'Japanese Art' were announced to begin on 4 Nov, but on that day the *Irish Times* printed an announcement that they had been postponed until 11–13 Nov. On 12 Nov the paper reported that at the opening lecture Justice Madden introduced Binyon and presided over 'a large and fashionable audience', which included the Countess of Aberdeen.

no at 'United Arts Club' at seven on Wednesday. At 8.30 there will be discussion on 'Modernism' opened by William Gibson & no body knows whether the club will survive it in the present state of fealing.[3] 'Arts Club' is at Lincoln Chambers, Lincoln Place but perhaps we could meet here which is quite close to Club. If you are in Town Thursday night I hope you will come to the Abbey Theatre & see 'Dervagilla' a new one act tragedy by Lady Gregory a beautiful thing.[4] You are with nice people but so far as the women kind are concerned politics are all as they are with most people in this country.[5]

Yr ever
W B Yeats

ALS Private.

---

[3] The long simmering controversy over Modernism in the Catholic Church, a movement which sought to reinterpret traditional Catholic teaching in the light of 19th-century philosophical, historical, and psychological theories and which called for greater freedom of conscience and a decentralization of papal authority, had recently come to the boil with Pope Pius X's condemnation of such teaching as heretical in his encyclical *Pascendi Dominici Gregis* of 8 Sept 1907, and his excommunication in late October of the anonymous authors of *The Programme of the Modernists*, a pamphlet written in reply to the encyclical. The Hon. William Gibson (1868–1942; see III. 150), a Catholic convert, Gaelic enthusiast, and the son and heir of Lord Ashbourne, Lord Chancellor of Ireland, was closely involved in the dispute through his friendship with the Irish-born Jesuit priest Fr. George Tyrrell (1861–1909), who had also just been excommunicated for reaffirming modernist principles in his own separate statement. Gibson had established his credentials as a liberal Catholic with *The Abbé de Lamennais and the Liberal Catholic Movement in France* (1896), and as a modernist with a radical article, 'An Outburst of Activity in the Roman Congregations', in the *Nineteenth Century* of May 1899. Tyrrell had stayed with Gibson in January 1907 while under suspension of his priestly faculties, describing him to a friend (St Andrews) as 'above all things kind, and undoubtedly a good religious-minded man, though a wild Irishman in theology — like myself'. Tyrrell had just asked Gibson to write an article for *The Times* arguing that Cardinal Newman would in effect have been condemned by *Pascendi Dominici Gregis* but this he refused to do because, as Tyrrell reported (St Andrews), 'it was against his Sinn Fein principles to acknowledge the existence of the Times'. Gibson did, however, publish an article, 'The Recent Syllabus and Cardinal Newman', in the *Irish Peasant* on 23 Nov (2), stating that Newman's views on faith and probability ran counter to the encyclical. No press reports of the Gibson-led discussion of the controversy at the United Arts Club (see pp. 630, 746) have been traced, but the encyclical and the decree *Lamentabili Sane Exitu* of the Curia's Holy Office effectively broke the Modernist movement, and in a letter of 27 Nov 1910 to *Droits de l'homme* Gibson described himself as an 'ancien "moderniste"' (je dis ancien, car le mouvement n'existe plus)'. In the introduction to his play *The Resurrection* (*Expl*, 394–5) WBY speaks with approval of Pius X's rejection of Modernism. Upon the death of his father in 1913, Gibson became the 2nd Lord Ashbourne.

[4] Sara Allgood took the title role in AG's one-act historical tragedy *Dervorgilla*, which was first produced, with a revised version of her three-act comedy *The Canavans*, at the Abbey Theatre on 31 Oct. This bill was revived on Thursday, 14 Nov, although WBY did not attend that performance as he had been asked to dinner at the Corinthian Club. In the play the aged Dervorgilla reflects upon her life and her adulterous love affair which resulted in the Anglo-Norman invasion of Ireland.

[5] Madden had married Jessie Isabelle Warburton as his second wife in 1896 and the family was strongly unionist.

## *To Laurence Binyon,* [*12 November 1907*]

Nassau Hotel | South Fredrick St | Dublin

My dear Binyon: I know that Lane is anxious that you should see some of the work he has got to geather for the modern Gallery—he has some magnificent Manchinis & a fine old house to put the pictures in.[1] Could you come with me either to morrow (Wednesday) or Thursday. If you come to morrow, come here at 11.30 & you can go to the Arts Club after, or if you come Thursday come at the same time & lunch with me afterward. This house is nearer the pictures & I think nearer you than the Arts Club would be.

Yrs sny
W B Yeats

ALS Private. In Binyon's hand on the final side of the letter: 'The Lecture Agency Ltd | The Outer Temple | Strand. W. C. | Freer. | F.D.B. | Cripps. | Raper[2]

## *To Edith Lister, 14 November* [*1907*]

Nassau Hotel | Dublin
Nov 14

Dear Miss Lister,

I send you John Sherman corrected for the Press, and a little preface.[1] There should be a half title, or whatever you call it, with the words 'John

---

[1] Apart from the portrait of AG (see p. 737), and a very fine portrait of himself, Lane's collection also contained four other works by Mancini: *La Douane*, an early picture of a young woman seated on a trunk and surrounded by other pieces of luggage, executed with a more fastidious eye to detail than characterized his later work; *The Marquis del Grillo*, a portrait of the bearded Chamberlain to the Queen Dowager of Italy dated 1899, although painted some years before that; *En voyage*, a sympathetic study of the artist's father in a railway carriage, which had been presented to the gallery by the artist John Sargent (who described Mancini as 'the greatest living painter'); and *Aurelia*, a half-length portrait of a young woman against a background of flowers. Clonmell House in Harcourt Street, Dublin, had been the home of the Municipal Gallery of Modern Art since 1902. It was built by John Scott, 1st Earl of Clonmell and Lord Chief Justice of the King's Bench in Ireland, in the last quarter of the 18th century, but sold by the 2nd Earl. With a frontage of 120 feet it was the biggest house in the street, and since 1830 had been divided, the larger area serving as an art gallery, and the smaller part annexed into the house next door.

[2] Binyon used a blank page of this letter to jot down some notes of his own: 'The Lecture Agency Ltd | The Outer Temple | Strand. W. C.', had presumably organized the present lecture tour; 'Freer' is probably Charles Freer, a self-made American millionaire and collector of Oriental art, who was corresponding with Binyon at this time and became a good friend; 'F.D.B.' is a member of Binyon's family; 'Cripps' is Arthur Shearly Cripps (1869–1952), a university friend, a poet, and now a missionary in Mashonaland; 'Raper' is perhaps Robert William Raper (1842–1915), Binyon's supportive tutor at Trinity College, Oxford, where Binyon had read classics 1888–92.

[1] *John Sherman*, with a new preface dated 14 Nov 1907, and *Dhoya* were published in vol. VII of *CW*. The preface showed WBY's renewed interest in astrology during this period, and read in part: 'Having

Sherman and Dhoya. Two early Stories', and then on the back of the half title, with no heading to it, the enclosed preface. At least that is what I suggest.[2] I didnt send John Sherman before for the good reason that I had mislaid the book. I did not think the delay mattered as I knew you had plenty of material to go on printing.

Yrs sny<br>W B Yeats

TLS Kansas.

## To Edith Lister, [*17 November 1907*]

Nassau Hotel | Dublin<br>Sunday

Dear Miss Lyster: I return proofs. I am very sorry. Until I got your letter I simply did not know I had received them.[1] They must have come in the rush & excitement of M<sup>rs</sup> Patrick Campbells visit—she came to my little theatre, was so enthusiastic about plays & players that she has announced her intention to play with our people in our theatre next year. This is a great event for us all. If in future I do not send a proof by return please wire. Send proofs & wire always to this address which is much safer than the Abbey.

The contents of John Sherman volume were sent two or three days ago.

Yr sny<br>W B Yeats

ALS Kansas.

been persuaded somewhat against my judgment to include these early stories, I have read them for the first time these many years. They have come to interest me very deeply; for I am something of an astrologer, and can see in them a young man—was I twenty-three? And we Irish ripen slowly—born when the Water-Carrier was on the horizon, at pains to over come Saturn in Saturn's hour, just as I can see in much that follows his struggle with the all-too-unconquered Moon, and at last, as I think, the summons of the prouder Sun.' Among the Bullen papers at Stratford-upon-Avon are sheets of the second edition of *John Sherman and Dhoya*, signed 'W B Yeats, November 1891' and marked in Bullen's hand 'Republished by courteous permission of Mr. T. Fisher Unwin', an acknowledgement which also appears in *CW* VII.

  [2] The half-title was set out as WBY suggests here, except that the preface was printed on a separate page, rather than on the back of the title.

  [1] These were probably the proofs of the plays for *CW* II.

## *To Nancy Maude,*[1] *20 [November 1907]*

Nassau Hotel | Dublin.
Oct 20

Dear M^rs Maude: the vision is most interesting & I have handed it over to Lady Gregory who is now working at faery beleif. The Sidhe move in dust storms & in all whirling winds. There is some connection between them & whirling movement hard to fathom. When the country people see bits of straw or dust whirling on the road they say it is 'the Sidhe'. In the middle ages it was said to be the dance of the daughters of Herodias—an attempt to Christianize something which was pre-christian.[2] The Sidhe are also associated with mist & a dust storm is a kind of mist. The vision is like so many visions seen by the country people and I have no doubt a glimpse of the reality of things. It is easier to see such things when we are young but these hidden people seem to prefer to remain hidden & so we turn away or in some other way lose the sight. The country people fear sometimes their displeasure at being seen. Please thank your cousin for writing it out for me.[3]

Yrs sny
W B Yeats

ALS Southern Illinois, with envelope addressed to 50 Seymour St, London W, postmark 'DUBLIN NO 20 07'.

[1] Nancy Maude (1886–1974), whom WBY has confused with her mother, was the only daughter of Colonel Aubrey Maurice Maude. She had been at St James's School in London with Dorothy Shakespear from 1899 to 1902 and they remained good friends (WBY's future wife George Hyde-Lees attended the same school in 1907–8). She was now living at home and chafing at the conventionality of her parents, but in March this year had made her first trip to Ireland, to stay with cousins in Hillsborough, Co. Down, and with other relatives at Enniskillen. She immediately fell in love with the country, describing her time there (TCD) as 'enchanting days', and she heard many folk stories, as well as going on a hunt for pookas. On 11 and 12 June she had attended the Abbey productions at the Great Queen Street Theatre with the Shakespears, and had seen WBY and Shaw talking together in the stalls (see pp. 677–8, n. 2). In 1909 she was to meet the Irish poet Joseph Campbell, whom, much against her parents' wishes, she married in 1911, living thereafter in Ireland (see p. 357, n. 2). She published a slim volume of verse, *The Little People*, in 1910, and wrote the prologue to *I Was There* (Worcester, 1956), a book of recollections of St James's School. In her diary (TCD) she records 'Nov 22^nd Letter from W. B. Yeats' as among her 'Particularly Happy Days in 1907'.

[2] See 'Nineteen Hundred and Nineteen', ll. 117–21 (*VP*, 433): 'All break and vanish, and evil gathers head: | Herodias' daughters have returned again, | A sudden blast of dusty wind and after | Thunder of feet, tumult of images, | Their purpose in the labyrinth of the wind.' In a note to his poem 'The Hosting of the Sidhe' in *The Wind Among the Reeds* (1899), WBY had written: 'Sidhe is also Gaelic for wind, and certainly the Sidhe have much to do with the wind. They journey in whirling winds, the winds that were called the dance of the daughters of Herodias in the Middle Ages, Herodias doubtless taking the place of some old goddess. When the country people see the leaves whirling on the road they bless themselves, because they believe the Sidhe to be passing by' (*VP*, 800).

[3] Probably Nancy Maude's cousin Antony Maude, who had persuaded her parents to allow her to go to Ireland in March. He was now working in London, but returned to Co. Down frequently.

## *To Mabel Beardsley,*[1] *20 November* [*1907*]

Nassau Hotel | Dublin
Nov 20

Dear M^{rs} Wright: I am in Ireland as you see & have been for months—our little theatre takes up so much time—& shall only get to London for about six weeks this winter. Perhaps I may be so lucky as to see you then—I hope you will excuse me for leaving your note so long unanswered.[2]

Yrs sny
W B Yeats

We produce a new play to morrow night by Lady Gregory & myself 'The Unicorn from the Stars' 3 acts.[3]

ALS Texas.

---

[1] Although WBY knew the artist Aubrey Beardsley (1872–1898) well in the 1890s, he had not apparently meet his sister Mabel Beardsley (1871–1916) at that time. She became an actress, toured extensively, and married the actor George Bealby Wright in 1903. She and WBY, who had a number of acquaintances and interests in common, were to become friends over the coming years and he celebrates her courage during a long battle with terminal cancer in his sequence of poems 'Upon a Dying Lady' (*VP*, 362–7).

[2] The note is untraced, but was presumably an invitation to call.

[3] *The Unicorn from the Stars*, a rewriting of WBY's *Where There Is Nothing* (see p. 686, n. 4), was produced on 21 Nov with *Spreading the News* and turned out to be William Fay's last new production at the Abbey. On 11 Dec AG told Quinn (NYPL) that it had attracted 'very small audiences' because 'Shaw's "John Bull" was going on at the same time. But we are very well satisfied with the production. Lord Monteagle said, "It is a beautiful thing, and few have courage to produce a beautiful thing." And Poel, founder of the Elizabethan Society, said much the same and others also. Griffith broke silence to attack it, and George Moore brought a party of chilly scoffers to run it down.' Although the *Evening Herald* on 22 Nov (4) called it 'one of the most striking plays yet produced by the I.N.T.S.', the Dublin press was generally dismissive. *Sinn Fein*, dubbing it *Where There Is Less*, 'broke silence' only to be reduced to silence, describing it on 30 Nov (3) as 'no more dramatic in its construction and development than any of Mr. Yeats's stage failures.... Before such a hopeless conglomeration of unmeaning phrases and wild speech and "folk" inanities the critic is silent.' An equally damning review in the *Evening Mail* of 22 Nov (6) saw the co-authorship as the problem: 'the work of the two writers is hopelessly incongruous and never fits together, you can separate one from the other with a clean cleavage, there is no organic unity, nor even dramatic cement to keep them together.... No wonder the audience was bewildered and frozen. They tried occasionally to be interested, once or twice they laughed feebly at nothing, for it was all dreariness set forth in the dreariest way.' Holloway, noting (*Abbey Theatre*, 96) the 'thin house (mostly friends of the dramatists)', also blamed collaboration for the play's failure: 'Yeats and Lady Gregory are too violent when taken in one draught, however palatable either may be when taken neat.' The Dublin *Daily Express* of 22 Nov (6) considered 'the central idea...unworthy of the serious treatment accorded to the play. The actors did all they could for it.... But it is unlikely that the efforts of the players will save a play which has for its action nothing more...than the ravings of a maniac. This is a re-cast of another writing; if Mr. Yeats wishes to try again let him go in honestly for "screaming farces."'

## *To the Editor of* The Leader, *21 November* [*1907*]

"Abbey Theatre,
"Nov. 21.

"Dear Sir—I see in your issue of to-day a series of paragraphs beginning 'The author of Cathleen Ni Houlihan, we see, was at a God save the King dinner one night last week'.[1] The dinner you refer to was given in honour of Lady Aberdeen by the Corinthian Club, and my presence there was accident.[2]

"I met Sir Charles Cameron for the first time at a theatrical supper party; he asked me to dine with him at the Corinthian Club a few days later, and to reply to the toast of the guests, but did not mention who they were.[3] I knew nothing of the Corinthian Club, except from a report in the papers of a luncheon party which it had given for Mr. Tree. I expected to find a Bohemian gathering of perhaps twenty of thirty people. I found two or three hundred, and was already sitting in my place when I heard that Lord and Lady Aberdeen were expected.[4] That I have met Viceroyalty at a public

---

[1] Although officially published on Saturdays, the *Leader* usually appeared on Thursdays, and in its issue of 23 Nov had devoted two paragraphs to WBY's presence at a Corinthian Club dinner in the Gresham Hotel on Thursday, 14 Nov: 'The author of "Cathleen ni Houlihan" we see, was at a "God Save the King" dinner one night last week! "Cathleen," we suppose, is alright in theory; but then a dinner is a dinner even to a poet.... "Oh Caithleen [*sic*] ni Houlihan your way's a thorny way"! The toast of "The King," which in this country means for the most part "To hell with the Irish Nation," was drunk with musical honours. Mr. Yeats was among the speakers at this feed, for the British Lord-Lieutenant proposed the toast of "Our Guests," coupled with the names Lord Chancellor, Tony Traill, and the author of "Cathleen ni Houlihan." Poor "Cathleen"!' The second paragraph coupled WBY's hypocrisy in attending a loyalist dinner with his duplicity in denouncing the 'commercial' theatre, while inviting English 'commercial' managers such as Tree, Mrs Patrick Campbell, and Martin Harvey to performances at the Abbey Theatre (see pp. 747, 751). The Corinthian Club had been founded in October 1899 in imitation of the Savage Club in London. It was avowedly non-political, and held Saturday-night dinners in winter to honour the achievements of members and distinguished visitors to Dublin, particularly musicians and actors.

[2] Isabel Maria Marjoribanks, Lady Aberdeen (1857–1939), a Liberal, humanitarian, and leader of the International Council of Women, was the wife of John Campbell Gordon, Lord Aberdeen (1847–1934), Lord-Lieutenant of Ireland in 1886 and again 1905–15. As WBY says, it was she, not her husband, who was being honoured by the Club, and that not on political grounds, but because of her philanthropic work in Ireland, particularly her campaign to eradicate tuberculosis. She replied to the toast, and the Lord Chancellor, Sir Samuel Walker, the provost of Trinity College, Dr Anthony Traill, and WBY all replied on behalf of the guests. In his speech, as reported in the Dublin *Daily Express* of 15 Nov (7), WBY tried to rally educated Ireland to patriotic causes, pointing out that 'they in Ireland were working under many difficulties and required the support of the educated people of Ireland. He was sorry, however, to say they were getting no support from educated Ireland. They were trying to build up in the imagination of this country the noble images of its past and the noble images of its present. He did not think that any of them could realise how quickly the past of Ireland was fading from the life of the people. They required the help of the cultured and educated people of Ireland or their sacrifice was in vain (applause).'

[3] Sir Charles Alexander Cameron (1830–1921) was president and Professor of Hygiene and Chemistry at the Royal College of Surgeons, Ireland. He was co-founder and president of the Corinthian Club.

[4] In fact, the Club had a membership of over 350, drawn from the Irish political, professional, religious, and social establishment, and included members of the Protestant and Catholic hierarchies.

dinner is the fault, doubtless unintentional, of Sir Charles Cameron. If it should happen again it will be my fault.

"I have long ceased to be an active politician, but that makes me the more anxious to follow with all loyalty the general principles defined by Mr. Parnell and never renounced by any Nationalist party. He directed Ireland on the occasion of a Royal visit in 1885 or 1886 to pay no official honour to any representative of English rule until a sufficient National independence had made possible a new treaty.[5] I could have slipped away and so avoided attack, or won a little vain glory by making some protest, but I chose rather to follow those old rules of courtesy in which, as Balzac has said, we are all Conservatives.[6]

Yours sincerely
"W B Yeats"

Printed letter, *The Leader*, 30 November 1907, p. 226.[7]

## *To Count Casimir Markiewicz,*[1] *21 November* [*1907*]

Nassau Hotel
Nov 21

My dear Markiewics,
   I was told last night that you said at the Arts Club to several people that you had met me upon the morning of the Corinthian Club dinner and that I

The Protestant Bishop of Meath had been present at the dinner of 14 Nov and the Catholic Bishop of Waterford, in apologizing for his unavoidable absence, wrote that the 'entire country will unite with the club in wishing every happiness to the noble lady who has done so much for Ireland, and in particular for its industries and its national health'.

[5] The Irish political leader Charles Stewart Parnell (1846–91) had laid down this principle during the visit of the Prince of Wales to Ireland in April 1885. According to the *Leader*, WBY sat at the dinner next to the businessman and politician William Martin Murphy (1844–1919), the 'old foul mouth' (*VP*, 292) who had supported Parnell's enemies and who was to oppose Hugh Lane's proposals for a Dublin municipal gallery.

[6] WBY also used this comment by Balzac (whom he had been rereading extensively at this time) in *Discoveries* (*E & I*, 284).

[7] Moran devoted three paragraphs to replying to this letter which, he said, cleared WBY 'of the charge of having knowingly and with malice intent assisted at a God save the King dinner', and which suggested two lines of reflection. The first was the attitude which Ireland ought to adopt towards the crown; the second was on the reasons for the Corinthian Club being so called, and WBY's simplicity in supposing it to be 'a Bohemian gathering': 'a more conventional, common-place, phlegmatic, greasy crowd it would be hard to find than these beef-eaters who book an actor or someone like that and hang an evening sing-song and a heavy dinner on to him.'

[1] Count Casimir Dunin-Markiewicz (1874–1932) had been born in the Ukraine, the second son of a Polish landowner. In 1895 he went to study art in Paris, where, shortly after the death of his estranged

was "greatly delighted at being invited to meet Vice-Royalty". Your
memory deceived you, for I have several times refused to meet Viceroyalty,
and only met them that night by accident. I did not know they were
expected until I was in the room and at the table, and so unable to withdraw
without discourtesy. I hope you will take any opportunity that may arise to
put yourself right with any of those you may have said this to. It was a
natural error to fall into, for knowing Dublin so much better than I do you
probably knew that Viceroyalty was going to be present, and thought that I
knew it also.

Yours sinly
W B Yeats

TLS Harvard.

## *To A. H. Bullen, 22 November* [*1907*]

Nassau Hotel | Dublin
Nov 22.

My dear Bullen: I thought you were leaving all the notes for Vol 3 of the
plays & so did not send you any.[1] I have now however done what is
necessary but cannot at this moment get a type-writer. You are the sinner
of the acting version of 'Shadowy Waters' & as I warned you the American
edition was the final one, but the change is not very great.[2] We should have
written it down when you were here had I remembered.[3] The long note

first wife in 1899, he met the artist, suffragette, and nationalist Constance Gore-Booth, daughter of Sir
Henry Gore-Booth of Lissadell, Sligo. They married in 1900, and settled in Dublin in 1903, where they
were to play a vigorous part in artistic and theatrical circles. Markiewicz, described by Padraic Colum as
'the only stage Irishman I ever met', was a bon viveur and an active member of the Arts Club. He also
wrote plays, and formed his own dramatic society. In December 1913 he left Dublin to become a war
correspondent in the Balkans, and in 1914 joined the Russian army. The family estate was burned down
in the Bolshevik revolution and he spent the rest of his life in Warsaw.

[1] See pp. 731, 732. In the event, both *CW* II and *CW* III contain notes (in appendices) appropriate to
the plays included in them. The four appendices in *CW* II comprise the acting version of *The Shadowy
Waters*, a variant scene from *Deirdre*, a note on 'The Legendary and Mythological Foundation of the
Plays', and three short notes on the dates and performance of the plays. The appendix to *CW* III
contains a preface relating to *The Countess Cathleen*, notes on the plays, and on the music for use in them
(see p. 702, n. 2).

[2] Two versions of *The Shadowy Waters* appeared in *CW* II (see pp. 701, 721, 726), and Bullen had
evidently set the acting version from the text he had published earlier this year and not from the later,
revised version which appeared in appendix III of vol. II of *The Poetical Works of William B. Yeats*.
Apart from slight verbal and punctuation emendations, the major changes between the two texts were
the omission of eighteen lines from a speech by Aibric, as well as other, shorter cuts elsewhere (see *VPl*,
322, 324–5, 330, 337).

[3] WBY had evidently seen Bullen in Dublin in early September (see p. 717).

from the English edition is no use, as it refers to a rejected version of the play.[4]

Yr sny<br>W B Yeats

ALS Kansas.

## To Count Casimir Markiewicz, 23 November [1907]

Nassau Hotel | Dublin.<br>Nov 23

My dear Marcovi-evicz: many thanks for your letter which is quite satisfactory.[1] I have to be careful about such things for I am the shepherd of a flock which is accused of having been tempted from ancestral fields by the rich pastures of Merrion Square.[2]

Yr ever<br>W B Yeats

ALS Harvard.

## To John Quinn, [c. 24 November 1907]

Mention in letter from Quinn, 8 December 1907.
Telegram replying to a wire from Quinn asking for instructions about the proprosed production of *Cathleen ni Houlihan* and *The Hour-Glass* by Margaret Wycherly in New York.[1]

---

[4] This note appeared in *Poems, 1899–1905*, which had been published by Bullen in October 1906. It described Robert Gregory's design for the play and the changes to the text necessitated by using a psaltery instead of a harp (see *VP*, 815–17).

[1] Markiewicz's letter is untraced, but obviously explained his alleged comments on WBY's delight at dining with the Viceroy (see above). WBY's difficulties in spelling the name were persistent (see III. 680).

[2] Merrion Square is an expensive and fashionable part of Dublin, and at this time its inhabitants were overwhelmingly unionist. The Abbey Company was sometime accused of seeking audiences there rather than among the people.

[1] This was a reply to a telegram from Quinn of 23 Nov, which read (Himber, 92): 'Lieblers reputable extensive theatrical managers have small theatre (stop) Arnold Daly star one act plays (stop) Have announced Cathleen Houlihan and Hour Glass series matinees alternating one act performances Japanese actress and Daly plays, in ignorance your plays copyrighted (stop) Announcement made

## To *J. B. Yeats,* [*25 November 1907*]

Monday

My dear Father:
I cannot get to you to morrow as I shall be busy all day. Please dont come round as very little puts me off my work. I will either look in at studio before you go or write & make apointment. I am very sorry but cannot do other wise.[1]

Yrs ever
W B Yeats

ALCS Boston, addressed to Gurteen Dhas, Churchtown, Dundrum, Co Dublin, postmark 'DUBLIN NO 25 07'.

## To *A. E. F. Horniman,* [c. *25 November 1907*]

Mention in letter from AEFH, 26 November 1907.
Telling her that he is getting on with the *Collected Works* for Bullen,[1] denying that the Abbey actors have been involved in a demonstration at

advertised (stop) Want permission customary royalties (stop) Miss Wycherly leading (stop) Whatever course adopted regarding your Company's tour here do not feel consent not exceeding three weeks pending formal arrangements if trial succeeds would damage (stop) Cable instructions (stop)'. Decoded, this meant that Liebler & Company, a firm of theatrical managers and impresarios, in ignorance of the copyright position, had arranged for WBY's plays to be performed in a series of matinées at Arnold Daly's Berkeley Theatre, with Margaret Wycherly in the leading roles. Since Quinn knew of Judge Keogh's proposal to bring the Abbey Company to America (see p. 739), he did not want to authorize any agreement that might impair its potential success.

[1] JBY was trying to arrange a sitting for an oil portrait of WBY, commissioned by Quinn for £30 (see p. 734, n. 4). JBY had begun it in early October of this year and was to take the finished picture with him when he and SMY sailed for New York on 21 Dec.

[1] AEFH took a proprietorial interest in *The Collected Works* (or 'Library Edition' as she called it) since she was subsidizing the project. In her reply she said that she was 'glad that you are getting on with the work for Bullen'.

the Theatre Royal, Dublin,[2] and explaining why her name was left out of the publicity for the forthcoming tour of Britain.[3]

NLI.

## *To Gwen John (Gladys Jones)*, [c. 25] November 1907

Nov | 1907

Of course with pleasure.[1] W B Yeats

APS Private, addressed to Spital Lodge, Chesterfield, England, postmark 'DUBLIN NO 2[?] 07'.

[2] AEFH was raking up old news, since the two 'demonstrations' at the Theatre Royal had taken place over a year before. On 3 Oct 1906 Beerbohm Tree had produced *The Man Who Was*, a dramatization of Rudyard Kipling's story by F. Kinsey Peile, which begins with the drinking of the Queen's health. At this, as Holloway reported (NLI), 'the untimely applause of a few nearly caused an unpleasant diversity of opinion, but luckily was checked in time to prevent a disturbance'. Six weeks later Martin Harvey's production of Rosamund Langbridge's *The Spell* received a mixed reception, which Holloway put down to bad acting (see p. 521, n. 5). An unnamed informant had recently told AEFH that the manager of the Theatre Royal had refused Abbey players the usual theatrical free passes because they had joined in these disturbances, and she had written to WBY for an explanation. He saw the manager on 20 Nov 1907, but AEFH, apparently suspecting WBY of partiality on the matter, wrote to the manager herself on 23 Nov: 'I think it necessary to write to you direct about the matter on which M$^r$ Yeats spoke to you last Wednesday. At Manchester, about Oct 25$^{th}$ I was told distinctly that you would not give any passes to the actors of the National Theatre Society because they had made a demonstration at your theatre. As this was said in the presence of a man connected with the press, I carefully abstained from asking any questions although I was extremely annoyed. During the next few days I wrote and asked M$^r$ Yeats to make enquiries and he sent me what was practically an alibi for the "Spell" demonstrations. But as I had heard of a smaller & more political fuss during the performance of "The Man Who Was", I asked for further enquiries without mentioning the name of the play. . . . I am not asking you to tell me any names only I beg you to believe that I want to clear up a matter concerned with people with whom I am publicly connected. To have spread such a rumour would be damaging myself as well as the others implicated.' Once again AEFH had jumped the gun in an attempt to implicate the Abbey Company in unseemly behaviour, a fact she was reluctantly forced to admit on 2 Dec: 'I have heard from my original informant that he unwittingly confused matters—that he did not intend to imply that the company were refused tickets because they had made a demonstration at the Theatre Royal. . . . I wish that I had written to him immediately, before asking you to investigate the matter. But this does not cast any light upon the things you wrote to *me* that *I* was said to have brought the accusation against them, does it? . . . It shows a very horrid spirit & is a warning to me to let Dublin affairs severely alone in future.'

[3] As well as the supposed row over the Theatre Royal, AEFH had found another occasion of grievance. The publicity pamphlet for the Abbey tour of Manchester, Glasgow, and Edinburgh from 24 Nov to 15 Dec did not mention her, an omission which she regarded as a studied slight. WBY had evidently assured her that no discourtesy was intended, but she was not to be 'mollified': 'Please do not trouble to write "to explain" matters.—The little pamphlet . . . was not sent to me at all but given to me by Vaughan. . . . Long ago when you spoke of people being "mollified" I asked why I was left out & you said that that task was left to you. Your time is of value, don't waste it uselessly. I know that you are helpless when you want to treat me fairly & I am most intensely anxious to put an end to the wrangling between us. It will destroy our friendship.' The reason her name had been left out was because this was the first Abbey tour that she had not subsidized.

[1] See p. 766. On 21 Dec Miss Jones gave Synge a very fulsome account of the performances (TCD) and thanked him 'for the great pleasure those two parts of Maurya and Nora Burke have given me. I

## *To Thomas MacDonagh,*[1] *3–7 December 1907*

<Nassau Hotel, | DUBLIN.
3rd. December, 1907.>
18 Woburn Buildings | Euston Road | London.

Dear Mr. MacDonough,

I could not write to you before about your play, as we had not heard from the reader it had been submitted to. He now writes "it is hard to know what to do with it. It has real dramatic gifts of characterization, and arrangement, and general power of building up something that can stand by itself; but the treatment of the hero at the end is so sentimental, I hardly see how we can stage it." I have myself read your play, and considered it very carefully, and I find myself on the whole at one with the reader's decision, which goes on to say that if we decide to play it "I suggest that he should carefully revise the part of his principal character, as he would be likely in his present form to appear ridiculous on the stage."[2] Your play puzzled me more than I can

have had many congratulations for which I am grateful, for I should not like to think I had played them quite unworthily—and though not myself appreciably Irish I have been told that my accent & intonation were successful!...I have received letters of thanks for an artistic treat, both in acting and choice of plays. On the other hand I have heard vague rumours of ladies who have not been able to sleep since for thinking of bodies in sheets, who nearly went into hysterics at what someone called my "passionate acting" of Maurya—and of persons who dispose of the matter by saying that such gruesome plays have no business to be acted at all!...I hope when we have got things settled up that we may realise £8 or so for the object—but the actors are repaid by their labours.' She concluded by asking Synge to remember her if any of the Abbey actresses fell ill as she would love the opportunity of playing the parts again.

[1] Thomas MacDonagh (1878–1916), poet, playwright, and a leader of the Easter Rising, was at this time teaching at the Diocesan Seminary in Fermoy. In November 1902 WBY had advised him about his first book of poems, *Through the Ivory Gate* (see III. 246–7), and a second book, *April and May*, had appeared later in the same year. On 26 Jan 1904 he had submitted 'a little play which I think may suit your Irish theatre' to the INTS, informing Fred Ryan in a covering letter (Harvard) that 'it is the nearest approach I have made to the folk spirit....I trust that whether you accept this or not you will let me have the opinion of Mr Yeats.' MacDonagh had been teaching in Fermoy since 1903, but in 1908 took up an appointment in St Enda's College, Padraic Pearse's Gaelic school in Dublin. D. J. O'Donoghue had published his most recent book of poems, *The Golden Joy*, in December 1906, but MacDonagh had been disappointed by its reception. Soon after taking an MA at University College, Dublin, in 1911 he joined the staff of the English Department there. Further volumes of poems appeared in 1910, and 1913, and his study *Thomas Campion and the Art of English Poetry*, which draws upon WBY's theories of 'speech-verse', in 1913. He co-founded the *Irish Review* (1911–15), and became a friend of WBY, whom he nevertheless satirized as Earl Winton-Winton de Winton in his play *Metempsychosis*, published in the *Irish Review* in February 1912. In 'Easter 1916' WBY celebrated him (*VP*, 392–3) as one who 'might have won fame in the end, | So sensitive his nature seemed, | So daring and sweet his thought'. His study of Gaelic and Anglo-Irish poetry, *Literature in Ireland*, appeared shortly after his execution in 1916.

[2] MacDonagh had submitted his then two-act tragedy, *A Fragment*, to the Abbey. The unidentified reader was Synge, who made his report in a letter to AG of 29 Nov (*JMSCL* II. 91). The play was not produced until 15 Oct 1908, and then in a revised form under the title *When the Dawn is Come*. The

say. If we had a larger company, and so could produce work more rapidly, I would be inclined to get it up that you yourself might gain necessary experience. And if you care to make drastic revisions it is possible, though I cannot say more than that, that we should be able to fit it in at some time.[3] I would, however, rather suggest that you make a scenario of a new play, and submit the scenario to us, as this would save you a good deal of time. I am going to London in a couple of days, but if you are ever in town I would like to see you a month or so hence on my return. I am sorry about the delay in sending back your manuscript, but the puzzling nature of it is responsible for that delay. It was read by several of us, and left us so uncertain that we decided to submit it for a final judgement to the reader I have quoted. When his opinion came it was practically the same as that which we had arrived at unknown to him. I can see, by the by that you are considerably influenced by Brownings plays, a salutary and interesting influence, but one that leads, I think to somewhat over much dialectical dialogue for dramatic force.[4] That however, you would attain by the work of composition, should you go on.

Yrs sy
W B Yeats

[*In WBY's hand*]
PS. I wrote above in Dublin. Since writing it we have been considering the possability of certain avowedly experimental matinees of new writers work. We [*for* When] we do this I will write to you for your play in all likelihood.

action of the play takes place fifty years in the future, when an Irish insurgent force is negotiating with the British army. Thurlough MacKieran, elected commander of the Irish army, conducts secret negotiations with the British, which lead to his conviction for treachery. As he is about to be sentenced the British attack, and he leads the Irish to a decisive victory, but is mortally wounded. A philosopher and poet rather than a man of action, Thurlough associates himself with Savonarola, and sees all sides of every question. He thus has affinities with a number of Robert Browning's heroes, and the play, as most Dublin reviewers pointed out, is wordy and undramatic. At the end of the version of the play WBY is discussing here Thurlough is sentenced to death for treason by the Irish military tribunal and thus dies a disgraced failure. Heeding WBY's advice, MacDonagh added a short third act in which Thurlough dies victorious (but hardly less sentimentally), and in this form the play was accepted by the Abbey in March 1908.

[3] This would have been a great disappointment to MacDonagh, who had been working on the play since 1904, and who told D. J. O'Donoghue on 30 Oct 1907 (*Irish Book Lover*, 13, Feb–Mar 1922) that those who had seen the play 'think it wonderfully good; it breaks new ground, being a play of Ireland fifty years hence in time of insurrection, in the main, a study of a subtle Hamlet-like character. I have used a kind of noble, rhythmic prose, the best version, I think, of what may be a noble Gaelic idiom of that time. One friend of mine, who is a fine dramatic critic, in one way, too, an Abbey critic, says it will be an [*sic*] unique success' (134).

[4] In his youth WBY had admired Browning as one of the few 19th-century English poets to write plays that were theatrically viable and, while at the Dublin Art School, had been moved by Browning's 'air of wisdom' (see p.143, n. 5). His *The Land of Heart's Desire* was toured in America in 1901 with Browning's *Two in a Balcony*, but in 1929 he was to describe Browning as 'a dangerous influence'.

Please excuse the dirt of this paper—the letter has been in the bottom of my bad [*for* bag].

TLS Texas.

## Minutes of Abbey Theatre Directors' Meeting, 4 December 1907

December 1907

At a Directors meeting held December 4 1907, to consider W.G. Fay's letter of Dec 1 about re-organization of the company[1] it was decided:—

1.   That we could not agree to his proposal about dismissal of the Company and re-engagement by him personally.

2.   That we cannot enlarge the powers already given under contract.

3.   We cannot abrogate the right of appeal to the Directors already possessed by the Company.

4.   That an improvement in discipline is necessary, and that rules with this object be drawn up in consultation with the Company. That the Company be asked to elect, say, three members to consult with the Stage Manager and Directors as to the rules of discipline. That the rules so drawn up be put to the company as a whole for their decision.

5.   That it be explained to the Company that this Theatre must go on as a theatre for intellectual drama, whatever unpopularity that may involve. That no compromise can be accepted on this subject, but that if any

---

[1] The simmering trouble between W. G. Fay and the rest of the Company which had nearly boiled over a year previously (see pp. 553, 571–2) was now once more approaching crisis point. Vaughan confided to Holloway on 23 Nov (NLI) that he and the Fays were 'quite sick of the Yeats–Gregory management. Willie Fay thinks them both off their heads.' Fay thought that AG and WBY were pushing their own unpopular plays, while they and the Company found his behaviour ever more authoritarian and capricious. On 1 Dec he had confronted the Directors with five peremptory demands that would have given him absolute power over the other members of the Company. He stipulated that they should terminate the contracts of all the members of the Company and instruct those 'wishing to re-engage [to] write in to W. G. Fay'; that all future contracts should be for one season only and terminable by a fortnight's notice on either side; that if the Directors required special actors for specific performances, Fay should be responsible for engaging them on terms decided between him and the Directors; that he should have the power to dismiss members of the Company; and that there should 'be no appeal to any other authority than mine by the people engaged by me on all matters dealt with in their contracts'. Although Fay later defended these demands as 'the usual power of a manager and producer' (*Fays of the Abbey*, 230), they were wholly unrealistic in the present context, and the Directors met on 4 Dec to frame their answer to him. In a letter of 6 Dec (Berg) AG wrote: 'Poor Fay has completely delivered himself into our hands by that proposal of his. We might dismiss him tomorrow on it, and I doubt that even his brother would blame us. I think he is either crazed or has been worked up by Vaughan and Mrs Fay for their own ends. Now, we want re-organization and a new start, and we can do it, and have the company with us on this question.'

member find himself unable to go on with us under the circumstances, we will not look upon it as unfriendly on his part if he go elsewhere, on the contrary we will help him all we can.[2]

6. That henceforth a Director must always go with the Company upon the more important tours.[3]

TD NLI.

## *To A. E. F. Horniman,* [c. *4 December 1907*]

Mention in letter from AEFH, 5 December 1907.
Defending his right not to inform her of all that goes on at the Abbey Theatre,[1] discussing repairs to the Theatre,[2] and asking her about the inclusion of the Mancini portrait in the *Collected Works.*[3]

NLI.

---

[2] Discontent at the uncommercial nature of the Abbey plays was general throughout the Company and had been aggravated by the recent production of AG's revised *The Canavans*, which had embarrassed a number of the actors, and the disappointing audiences for *The Unicorn from the Stars.* Meanwhile Shaw's *John Bull's Other Island*, which WBY had rejected for the Abbey, was playing to packed houses on its Dublin tour.

[3] Fay's dictatorial behaviour was more pronounced on tours. As Henderson told Holloway on 26 Oct (NLI): 'When in Oxford, A Power was late to fill his role as policeman in *Spreading the News*, Fay would not let him on in the peasant plays.' The current British tour was full of tensions and difficulties, culminating in Mrs Fay (Brigit O'Dempsey) taking over the roles of the indisposed Sara Allgood without any announcement of the change, and in Kerrigan's resignation after being sworn at by Fay.

[1] WBY had evidently taken AEFH to task for meddling in the Abbey generally, and with the arrangements with Norreys Connell over the production of *The Piper* in particular (see pp. 767, 769), but she refused to accept his criticism: 'I do not consider that anyone has any right to conceal from me anything bearing even remotely on the affairs of the Abbey Theatre & the National Theatre Society, so I shall decline to listen to any carefully selected pieces of information which may be given to me. . . . I treated Mr Connell honourably & answered his questions truthfully & I do not regret it.'

[2] WBY had apparently told her that the Abbey needed a certain amount of refurbishment, and she replied that she was 'writing to tell Mr Holloway to get an estimate for the necessary repairs and doing up at the Abbey'. A long-running attempt to get planning permission for the conversion of an annexe for the Abbey Theatre from the Dublin Corporation had recently been successful (see p. 750).

[3] WBY had sent a photograph of the Mancini portrait to AEFH at her request (see p. 766, n. 6), and had evidently asked her what she thought of it. She, as he was soon to discover, did not like it, and she replied tersely that when he returned to London 'I will talk over the Mancini portrait with you & such other affairs as we can discuss fairly & honestly'.

## *To Lady Gregory, 5 December* [*1907*]

Nassau Hotel | Dublin
Dec 5

My dear Lady Gregory:
   I have just found programes—one of which I have sent on. These programes must have been printed before the Allgood trouble, & Hour glass put on.[1] I feal very much inclined to give Vaughan notice. I enclose a note for him which post if you agree with it. Does your memory bear mine out about 'Hour Glass' not to be in programe. My beleif is that we told him & Fay repeatedly.

Yr sny
W B Yeats

PS. If your memory bears out mine I cannot see how we can pass the matter over.[2] On hearing from Vaughan I would write that I will lay his explenation what ever it is before a meeting of the directors. In no circumstances would I let him go on without a written apology, & I think even that concession unwise. This shows that we cannot trust him.

[*With enclosure*]

18 Woburn Buildings | Euston Road
Dec 5

Dear M$^r$ Vaughan: I see that 'The Hour glass' was included in the programme for Manchester and not as I first thought put on in an emergency caused by Miss Allgoods illness. I told you it was not to be played & await your explenation.

Yr sny
W B Yeats

ALS Berg, with envelope addressed to Coole, postmark 'DUBLIN DEC 5 07'. Enclosure NLI.

[1] Vaughan had put WBY's *The Hour-Glass* on the programme of the Abbey's Manchester tour. In her reply of 6 Dec (Berg) AG wrote: 'I know you didn't mean Hour-Glass to go to Manchester, but it is just possible Vaughan may have made a mistake. I got, with great difficulty, the Manchester programme from him, while we were playing Unicorn but had not quite decided. It was written in pencil and was on the chimney-piece at the Nassau—and it seems to me Hour-Glass was on it—and if so, he will say we should have remonstrated then. He probably put it on, as I am inclined to believe his way is, chancing our not looking into things or making a row.' Sara Allgood had been taken ill in Manchester and could not fulfil her roles.
[2] AG's main reason for not wishing WBY to dismiss Vaughan was that it might give W. G. Fay 'something else to ground his dissatisfaction on. If Vaughan left in consequence of your letter he might complain of such a useful man being driven from the Co. Indeed I am not for noticing anything that may go wrong until our crisis with him.'

## *To Lady Gregory,* [*5 December 1907*]

Nassau Hotel | Dublin

My dear Lady Gregory: I have decided to stay till to morrow for my fathers sake—he wants another sitting.[1]

If you think the letter unwise, burn it, or suggest some other form of letter.[2] One dislikes passing over a serious matter like this without some prompt action, on the other hand one may precipitate a crisis. My fealing is that a letter is necessary and a prompt one but that it is possible a letter asking simply for explenation might cover the ground—but still one wants to make them beleive we are in earnest.

A civil letter about Corinthian in Leader to day.[3]

My father tells me that Isaac did not show us the best of the family treasures—a silver cup presented to a member of the family in 1515 and beleived to be very valuable. It should have been my fathers but they were afraid he might pawn it.[4]

Lane was round to day about Mancini readiness to do you for £50. I suppose he has written & that you will go to London. I think Lane thought you should go before Mancini started on a round of visits he has planned.[5]

Yrs ever<br>W B Yeats

I enclose an alternative letter to Vaughan.

---

[1] i.e. for the portrait of WBY commissioned by John Quinn (see pp. 734, n. 4, 780, n. 1).

[2] i.e. the letter to Vaughan, printed below

[3] The *Leader* of 7 Dec (which had appeared, as usual, two days before its official date of publication) printed an extract from a letter (244) by a correspondent signing himself 'Idolator', praising WBY's speech at the Corinthian Club dinner (see pp. 776–7): 'Mr. Yeats does not do himself justice about the Lady Aberdeen dinner. Of course we all accept at once his assurance that when he was invited to a dinner, he had no idea Her Excellency would be present, or that the British Anthem would be sung. For my part, I do not think that an exhibition of boorishness is required from a Nationalist who happens to find himself at a public dinner where the usual toasts are given. . . . But what Mr. Yeats did—and what was most creditable, though he does not say so—was to introduce a claim for the crying necessity of a Catholic University in his after-dinner speech, replying to the toast of "The Guests." This, we must admit, was a nervy proceeding. As a kind of apology Mr. Yeats claimed the irresponsibility of the true Bohemian and Artist, but poor Sir Charles Cameron spent the most agonizing eight minutes of his life listening to Mr. Yeats' speech—wondering whether he ought to pull him up, as out of order, or let him go on—though many of the guests were annoyed and a few delighted.'

[4] Isaac Butt Yeats (1848–1930) was WBY's paternal uncle. After graduating from TCD he became secretary to the Artisan Drilling Company, and lived unmarried with his sisters Jenny and Grace in Morehampton Road, Dublin.

[5] Mancini had already painted AG in early October of this year, and that portrait now hangs in the Municipal Gallery, Dublin (see p. 737) but, as AG explained in her *Hugh Lane* (79), the artist was 'not quite satisfied' with it and 'begged me to come to London and sit for another portrait that would immeasurably excel this one'. In a letter of this time, dated 'Thursday' (Berg), AG told Lane that she was feeling exhausted and reluctant to face a journey, but enquired about arrangements with Mancini:

[*With enclosure*]

<Nass>
18 Woburn Buildings | London.
Dec 5

Dear M^r Vaughan: I have just seen Midland Theatre programe & I notice that 'Hour glass' was included. I thought from what I saw in the papers that it was put on in an emergency. But these programes must have been printed before Miss Allgoods illness. I gave specific & repeated directions that 'Hour glass' was not to be played in Manchester. This is the second time my directions have been disobeyed & I await your explenation.

Yrs siny
W B Yeats
Managing director

ALS Berg.

## To Sarah Martha Old,[1] [*early December 1907*]

Mention in letter to AG, 14 December 1907.
Complaining of the infestation of 'insect life' at 18 Woburn Buildings.[2]

---

'If he is not ready for my sittings, perhaps you cd let me have a *wire early* tomorrow—I told Yeats to ask you this if he shd see you tonight.' In *Hugh Lane* (79) she reveals that she never made the journey, and that it was 'one of my lasting regrets that I allowed opportunity . . . to escape me then'. On 11 Dec AG sent Quinn a photograph of the original picture (NYPL), explaining that 'Hugh Lane had it done for his Modern Art Gallery. . . . It is a wonderful picture, luminous and radiant and triumphant.'

[1] Mrs Sarah Martha Old (1855–1939) was WBY's cook and housekeeper, inherited from Arthur Symons. In *Some Memories*, Masefield described her (14) as 'a tall, strong country-woman', who at their last meeting, in 1928, told him, 'I shall never forget the blessed days with Mr. Yeats at Woburn Buildings, for, oh, they were blessed days.' A. E. Waite described her as a 'vast female' in his diary for 20 Jan 1903; but St John Ervine recalled that WBY 'could not have been more gracious to a duchess . . . than he was to the middle-aged woman who cooked his meals and kept his rooms clean' (*I & R1*. 102–3). Mrs Old died in the same month as WBY.

[2] WBY's rooms were liable to infestation, especially when he was away for any length of time. Bullen had apparently used his apartment during the autumn and may have alerted him to the problem. In June 1902 Sturge Moore's younger sister had rented the rooms with a friend, who was bitten by a bedbug, and although, according to Sylvia Legge (*Affectionate Cousins* [1980], 204), Mrs Old insisted that they must have brought it with them, 'she thoroughly searched the room and parafinned the bed and used Keatings with a lavish hand'. WBY told Sturge Moore that he had caught a bedbug in his room and kept it under a wineglass for Mrs Old to see before she could be persuaded to take action (see III. 201).

## *To Lady Gregory, [8 December 1907]*

18 Woburn Buildings | Euston Road
Sunday

My dear Lady Gregory

Miss Horniman was worse than usual last night. Her conversation was one long song of joy that she had neither wit, beauty, genius, good birth or manners but was 'a spinster of London'. She is very indignant at not being mentioned in our pamphlet for the tour, & delights in Vaughan[1] who however applied to be taken into her theatre but was refused by Payne.

I am going out to see M[rs] Emery to get rid of the impression of Miss Hornimans loud timbril. The Mancini she will not have but has taken Augustus John into her family & is herself through M[rs] MacEvoy trying to get the drawing out of him.[2]

I have no doubt you are right about Vaughan though I have no doubt he put that play down out of rascality.[3]

Yrs ever
W B Yeats

You could come over later for Mancini—Lane thought you could come after Robert got back.

ALS Berg, with envelope addressed to Coole Park, Gort, Co Galway, London,[4] postmark 'LONDON 9 DE 07'.

---

[1] i.e. the publicity pamphlet for the Abbey tour of Manchester, Glasgow, and Edinburgh, about which AEFH had already complained in writing (see p. 781). Vaughan had given her a copy of the offending document in Manchester, but even before this she had welcomed him as an ally. Writing on 22 Oct (NLI) to thank him for sending financial and production details about the Abbey, she speculated that 'the Directors as a body do not wish me to receive full information on that subject. . . . I write all this because I do not want you to get into trouble with the Directors for giving me information which they do not wish to reach me; yet of a nature of which it seems *to you* quite obviously right for me to hear.' In her reply of 11 Dec (Berg), AG commented: 'Miss Horniman is a joy—I sometimes think it will be a real blessing when we *know* she will do no more for us, & you will be free of all except the gratitude which we can show by doing our best with the theatre.'

[2] Mary Spencer McEvoy, née Edwards, was the sister-in-law of the realist playwright Charles McEvoy (see p. 702), a number of whose plays AEFH staged at the Gaiety Theatre (see p. 702, n. 3). She had been introduced to Charles's brother, the painter Ambrose McEvoy (1878–1927), by Augustus John, who had befriended him at the Slade School in 1894 and shared studios with him in 1898, and the two had married in 1902. John did an etching of Charles McEvoy in 1908, and visited the McEvoys with his children at their home in Berkshire that year.

[3] See p. 786, n. 1.

[4] This piece of absent-mindedness meant that AG did not receive this letter until the evening of 10 Dec.

## To Lady Gregory, 10 December 1907

18, Woburn Buildings, | Euston Rd., N.W.
Dec. 10, 1907.

My dear Lady Gregory

I dictate a few words in the middle of a lot of correspondence and will write more in a few days. I kept away from Miss Horniman on Sunday but she came round last night and was so subdued that, I think, she understood that I was a little out with her. There was nobody else except Mrs. Emery who came after Miss Horniman at sight of whom Miss Horniman went away.[1] Later on Orage came in. I think he will do something about Lane's exhibition, or get something done. He offered me £5 to do a column and a half in the New Age on the subject, but I said I didn't think I would.[2] I haven't seen Masefield or anybody else. Orage told me a very curious story of a half fulfilled astrological prophecy. He was lecturing in Sheffield and a man spoke to him after the lecture. I recognised from his description my uncle's old correspondent,[3] who made that prophecy about Miss Mitchell's friend.[4] He got into talk with Orage and sat up half the night working his horoscope. He told him the most minute details of his past life and then said: "Next September (that is to say last September) you will go out riding, you will catch a violent cold and if you recover from that cold it will be with some disease that will make you an invalid."

He told him the exact day that he would go that ride. Orage is quite well but last September on the very day spoken of he got a letter, asking him to bicycle down to spend the night with some friends or friend who had taken a lodging in a wood. No sooner had he started than it came on to pour with rain and it rained until he got to the town where he had a rendezvous with a friend. He wanted to change his clothes but the friend persuaded him that it would not matter if he kept moving, so they set out together for the lodging in the wood. It was late at night when they got there but the landlady told

---

[1] AEFH had fallen out with FF over the Golden Dawn in 1900 (see p. 193, n. 5), and the breach had never been made up.
[2] A. R. Orage was now editor of the weekly *New Age* (see p. 663, n. 1), and consequently in a position to publicize Lane's latest enterprise, an exhibition of Irish artists as part of the Franco-British Exhibition, to be held in the spring of 1908.
[3] Perhaps James Richard Wallace who lived in Manchester, and whom WBY also knew (see p. 768, n. 2). None of the biographies of Orage contains this story, but he had immersed himself in occult studies and was an avid theosophist. His essay *Consciousness, Animal, Human and Superhuman* had been issued by the Theosophical Publishing Society earlier this year, and was to become in later life a devoted disciple of the Greek-Armenian spiritual teacher George Ivanovitch Gurdjieff (*c.* 1866–1949).
[4] This may refer to Norma Borthwick (1862–1934), who had become an ardent Gaelic Leaguer after settling in Dublin in the 1890s, but who was wrongly accused in 1900 of forgery and embezzlement, and temporarily imprisoned (see II. 595). She was a close friend of Susan Mitchell (see p. 488).

them that she could not let them have the rooms as her husband had just been brought in with a broken leg. They slept in a barn and Orage awoke in the morning, wet through & now for the first time, remembering the prophecy—but perfectly well. It was evidently more clairvoyance than astrology, with something of the misunderstanding of a dream. I have no doubt you have had the same report I have from Glasgow. A small profit.[5] I don't know whether I wish for a small profit or a small loss. My feeling at the moment is that a loss would be better, as it would make it more easy to get drastic change and make it more certain that whoever stayed with us understood the facts and meant to stay for intellectual work. That £15 may be enough to set Fay and Vaughan dreaming of melodrama and independence. Orage and Mrs. Emery admired the photograph of your portrait immensely. Orage gave an exclamation of surprise and delight before I had said a word. They agree with Miss Horniman, I am sorry to say, in disliking mine.[6]

Yrs sny
W B Yeats

TLS Berg.

## To Norreys Connell, *10 December 1907*

18, Woburn Buildings, | London N.W.
Dec. 10, 1907.

Dear Norreys-Connell,

I am not sure that I posted a letter which I wrote to you in Dublin and so must repeat what I then said.[1]

I am sorry to say that Miss Horniman had a quarrel with Fay some years ago and has never seen him as he really is from that moment. He is really an excitable, hot-tempered, grown-up child, whose moods change with the weather, with the receipts of the last performance, with whatever other trivial accident moves him at the moment. He has very little influence with the Company and certainly none over the Directors and his own dislike of a

---

[5] WBY had heard that the Abbey Company had made a profit of £15 in Glasgow, although, as she revealed in her letter of 11 Dec (see p. 789, n. 1), AG knew nothing of this, since she had 'not had reports from tour since I left Dublin, though you wired Vaughan to send them'.

[6] i.e. the portraits of WBY and AG done by Mancini. WBY had sent a photo of his to AEFH in November (see p. 766).

[1] WBY had in fact posted the earlier letter; see p. 769.

play certainly does not mean that he will play it badly.[2] There is a little play by Lady Gregory called "The Rising of the Moon" which he hated, heaven knows why, with the greatest intensity, and now it is his favourite of all our plays and he still hates a play of hers called The Canavans and yet gives in it, what is probably his finest performance. In fact I think it is rather necessary for him to dislike a play for then he makes a great effort, believing that it requires all his effort to prevent disaster. After The Cavanans I have heard him say: "The sweat is pouring down me, as you see because it is such hard work to make that go."[3] And the hard work was precisely what made it a fine performance. On the other hand I have seen him give a miserable performance in a play which he thought was doing all the work itself. He is the only member of the Company who has seen your play, so it is too soon, in any case, to say whether they will like it or dislike it. Can you dine with me some day next week, towards the end of it?

Yr sny

W B Yeats

TLS Southern Illinois.

## To Wilfrid Meynell,[1] 10 December 1907

18, Woburn Buildings, | London, N. W.

Dec. 10, 1907

Dear Mr. Meynell,

It was kind of you to send me the Memorial Card for Francis Thompson.[2] I have always thought him at moments a very great poet, and now I

---

[2] AEFH had told Connell in late October that WBY was hesitant about his play, and on 5 Nov, in writing to apologize for interfering in the matter, repeated that WBY had seemed troubled because Fay did not like the play and he felt uncomfortable in explaining this to Connell (see pp. 767, n. 1, 769).

[3] W. G. Fay's portrayal of the Ballad Singer in AG's *The Rising of the Moon* and of Peter Canavan in her *The Canavans* had been widely praised in the Dublin press. He had disliked *The Rising of the Moon* at first, but on 7 Mar 1907 AG told WBY (Berg) that he was 'now enthusiastic' about the play, '& wishes it had another act'. He did not, however, change his view of the later play, and on 23 Nov complained to Holloway (NLI) that at the final curtain of *The Canavans* he was sometimes 'in a fever-heat . . . trying to keep the piece going'.

[1] Wilfrid Meynell (1852–1948), poet, biographer, and editor, had married Alice Christiana Gertrude Thompson (1847–1922), essayist, poetess, and journalist, in 1877 and both were Catholic converts. For many years they co-edited the Catholic *Weekly Register*, and the more popular *Merry England*.

[2] The Meynells had befriended the highly strung Catholic poet Francis Thompson (1859–1907) after he had contributed verses to *Merry England* in 1888, and rescued him from the abject poverty in which he was then living. After a period of rehabilitation in a monastery in Sussex, where he wrote 'The Hound of Heaven', his most famous poem, Thompson lodged with the Meynells for the rest of his life. His *Poems* appeared in 1893, *Sister Songs*, written for the Meynells' daughters, in 1895, and *New Poems*

regret that I never met him, except once for a few minutes.[3] There seems to be some strange power in the forms of excess that dissolve, as it were, the external will, to make the character malleable to the internal will. An extreme idealism of the imagination seems to be incompatible in almost all with a perfectly <harmless> harmonious relation to the mechanics of life.[4]

Yrs ever<br>W B Yeats

TLS Private, with envelope addressed to 4 Granville Place Mansions, Portman Square, W., postmark 'LONDON W.C. DE 10 07'.

in 1897. He also wrote essays, some of which were published posthumously, and, as a frequent reviewer, had noticed WBY's *Wind Among the Reeds, Poems* (1900), *Literary Ideals in Ireland*, and *The Shadowy Waters*. He had died of tuberculosis on 13 Nov of this year.

[3] This was on Thompson's only visit to the Rhymers' Club in the early 1890s, reported in *Aut* (165). WBY had previously alerted the Rhymers to Thompson's existence: in *OBMV* (p. x) he recalls that he read out a letter to them 'describing Meynell's discovery of Francis Thompson, at that time still bedded under his railway arch, then his still unpublished *Ode to the Setting Sun*', and in *Aut*, discussing the reasons why Thompson never joined the Rhymers, suggests that it 'was perhaps our delight in poetry that was, before all else, speech or song, and could hold the attention of a fitting audience like a good play or good conversation, that made Francis Thompson, whom we admired so much—before the publication of his first poem I had brought to the Cheshire Cheese the proof-sheets of his *Ode to the Setting Sun*, his first published poem—come but once and refuse to contribute to our book. Preoccupied with his elaborate verse, he may have seen only that which we renounced, and thought what seemed to us simplicity, mere emptiness' (301–2). WBY included 'The Hound of Heaven' in *OBMV* (54–9). Wilfrid Blunt had invited Thompson to tea with WBY in May 1902, but he was unable to come because of a previous engagement, writing (Private): 'I should very much have liked to meet Yeats, whom I have long wished to see. You know I heartily admire his work, which in its consistent contempt for popularity and research of what is fine and delicate appeals to my own soul. . . . He has followed English—or Celtic—literary tradition, in which I think is the truest inspiration for a poet of the English tongue.'

[4] Thompson remained an example of spiritual ecstasy to WBY, and as late as 1937, in his introduction to *The Ten Principal Upanishads*, he recalled that when young he and his companions 'talked much of tradition, and those emotional young men, Francis Thompson, Lionel Johnson, John Gray, found it in Christianity'. In a review of Arthur Symons's *Amoris Victima* in April 1897 he praised Thompson's 'distinguished catholic ecstasy and his preoccupation with personal experience' (*UP* II. 40), and the following year identified him as the only contemporary English poet who was 'preoccupied with a spiritual life' (*UP* II. 116). In *Aut* (228) WBY suggests that his own quarrel with the morally orthodox Charles Gavan Duffy over the New Library of Ireland (see I. 343–6, 349–52) may have arisen in part because he preferred Francis Thompson, 'but half rescued from his gutter', over 'the humanitarian Stephen Phillips', and elsewhere in *Aut* places Thompson among those who seek 'unities not of the mind, but unities of Nature, unities of God . . . whose preoccupation is to seem nothing': 'The wholeness of the supernatural world can only express itself in personal form, because it has no epitome but man, nor can the Hound of Heaven fling itself into any but an empty heart. We may know the fugitives from other poets because, like George Herbert, like Francis Thompson, like George Russell, their imaginations grow more vivid in the expression of something which they have not themselves created, some historical religion or cause' (246–7).

## *To Lady Gregory*, [*12 December 1907*]

18 Woburn Building

My dear Lady Gregory: I have just had a letter from Miss Horniman in which she says "after mature consideration I have come to the conclusion that it is just to tell you that Sarah Allgood has 'written in' to M^r Payne. I have told him that I did not wish to take any one from the National Theatre Society as long as it holds to geather. Miss Allgood must know that I should hear of this & probably tell you."[1]

Fay told me that Miss Allgood had been trying for jobs. It is nothing new. It makes it all the more desirable to take the company into our confidence.

Yr ev

W B Yeats

Excuse paper. I began it without seeing I had been working astrology on the back.

```
8. 50. 25      7.  2. 41
               1. 17. 35
               5. 45.  6
10.  8. 0
 5. 45. 6
 4. 22. 54²
```

[*On back flap of envelope*]
John writes that he has just finished etching[3]
WBY

Letter just arrived.[4] Company made £15 in Glasgow.

ALS Berg, with envelope addressed to Coole, postmark 'LONDON W.C. DEC 12 07'.

[1] AEFH's letter appears not to have survived. In her reply of 13 Dec (Berg) AG thought the 'news about Miss Allgood rather discouraging—not much use in fighting her battle with Fay if she wants to be off'. Synge had also heard that Sara Allgood was looking out for a new job, and that she had approached Vedrenne of the Court Theatre as well as Payne, adding (*JMSCL* 11. 107) that he did 'not blame her. They are in want of money and people tell her she could get wonderful salaries on the English stage, and Fay and Vaughan tell her that we are no use, and cannot last.' He prophesied, however, that nothing would come of this and said he would write to her 'to ask her not to do anything in a hurry'.

[2] WBY was continuing with his astrological studies and casting horoscopes of most of the people he knew. He had recently read Synge's stars, and had asked for Maire O'Neill's hour of birth (*JMSCL* 11. 94–5).

[3] Augustus John's letter is untraced.

[4] i.e. AG's letter of 11 Dec telling him that she did not know how much the Abbey had made in Glasgow (see p. 791, n. 5).

# To Lady Gregory, [*14 December 1907*]

18 Woburn Buildings | Euston Road | London
Saturday

My dear Lady Gregory: I am working at the British Museum which looks very clean in its new paint[1] that M[rs] Old may scrub the floor at home—this the result of my letter about 'insect life'.[2] It is to be scrubbed once a week. Last night I had Ralph Shirley a very good astrologer to dinner[3] & showed him your horoscope he looked at [it] with delight as if it were the photograph of a young beauty & presently he said (I had said nothing) 'what firmness of character, what a horoscope'.[4] I am going to him to morrow for a lesson. I went yesterday to the new gallery & heard Rothenstein praise the Manchini picture of Lane—a man who was with him disliked it but Rothenstein said "If I were wearing seven hats I would take them all off before it".[5] He then said "it is horrible, it is like a bad Italian building something Boroco[6] but all the same it is magnificent inimatable—It kills everything else." Miss Horniman tells me that Miss Allgood has twice written to Lane [*for* Payne] but would in any case be no good to them as she

---

[1] The British Museum Reading Room had been closed in April for six months for extensive refurbishment and redecoration. The October number of the *Bookman* explained (7) that the 'new scheme of colouring is not an ambitious one . . . but it is applied so much more skilfully in the new dome than in the old that it seems to increase its height by thirty feet, and almost entirely does away with that squat appearance which was generally considered deforming . . . A different scheme of decoration in which lightness is made the chief aim, is applied to the cap of the dome above the lights, and produces a very airy and agreeable effect.'

[2] See p. 788, n. 2

[3] The Hon Ralph Shirley (1865–1946) was the brother of the 11th Earl Ferrers and a direct descendent of Robert Devereux, Earl of Essex. He had a keen interest in all forms of occultism, mysticism, psychical research, and particularly astrology. From 1892 to 1925 he was director of William Rider & Son, the foremost British publishers of occult material, edited the *Horoscope* under the pseudonym 'Rollo Ireton' 1902–4, and from 1905 to 1926 was editor of the *Occult Review*. He also became vice-president of the International Institute for Psychic Investigation, and published a number of books on mysticism and the occult.

[4] WBY cast AG's horoscope so often and so thoroughly that she became very familiar with her planetary fortune, describing her natal positions in the opening of *70 Years* (1): 'At the midnight hour between the fourteenth and fifteenth of March 1852, the planet Jupiter, so astrologers say, being in mid heaven, a little girl was born at Roxborough that is in Connacht.' Her horoscope appears in WBY's book of horoscopes (NLI), dated 1907, and in 1908 Wallace also cast horoscopes for her and for Robert and Margaret Gregory.

[5] An exhibition of portrait painters was being held at the New Gallery, 121 Regent Street, and included Mancini's portrait of Hugh Lane, which had been executed in Rome, probably in 1905. In his *Hugh Lane and his Pictures* (Dublin, 1932) Thomas Bodkin describes the painting (plate III) as 'probably the best of all the portraits of Lane. The pose is singularly characteristic of his alert highly-strung disposition.' In her *Hugh Lane*, AG thought it had 'rather too much confusion of background, yet friends notice that his custom of sitting on the edge of his chair shows something of his character, as if he was but poised for a moment'.

[6] Apparently a portmanteau word made up by Rothenstein—or WBY—from Baroque and Rococo.

only suits our sort of plays. The first time she 'wrote in' was at their first start. I enclose Glasgow account the last two Edinburgh nights have been £31 & then £19 if I remember rightly.[7]

Yr ev
W B Yeats

ALS Berg, with envelope addressed to Coole, postmark 'LONDON N.W. DEC 16 07'.


## To the Manager of the National Bank, Dublin, *16 December 1907*

Mention in letter from J. S. Birmingham, 17 December 1907.
Enclosing a cheque for £17 10*s.*, drawn on the National Bank Ltd., Dublin, signed by WBY in favour of the National Theatre Society's deposit account.[1]


## To Lady Gregory, [*? 16 December 1907*]

... I had a long lesson in the mathematical part of astrology from Ralph Shirley yesterday, I think I must ask you to meet him, he was struck with your horoscope.[1] 'Those Jupiter and Scorpio people,' he said, 'have such a grand way with them.' I showed him the Mancini photograph to prove it.[2]

Printed extract, *Hugh Lane*, 93.


[7] The Glasgow account has not been traced but evidently showed a profit of £15 (see p. 794). On 12 Dec AG had written (Berg) that she was glad there had been a profit on the tour, but that she was 'sorry it was Glasgow, for they will say it was the "Dressmaker"'.

[1] On behalf of the manager of the National Bank Ltd., Dublin, J. S. Birmingham returned WBY's cheque on 17 Dec, explaining that, since WBY wanted to move the money from the deposit to the current account, no cheque was required, but that he must send 'the Deposit Receipt before we can place the money to credit of the Current Account of the National Theatre Society'. He also pointed out that the 'signatures of two Directors and the Secretary' would be required for this.

[1] Ralph Shirley was teaching WBY how to calculate the mathematically difficult primary directions (see p. 748), and his illustrative horoscope using this method, heavily scrawled with figures, survives among WBY's astrological papers in NLI, together with Shirley's notes on semiarcs and directions for the calculation of primaries.

[2] For Mancini's portrait of AG see p. 737.

## To Ernest Vaughan, [c. 16 December 1907]

Mention in letter to AG, 18 December, and from Fay, 17 December 1907.[1] Asking about the script of *The Hour-Glass*,[2] passing on his sister's complaint about the lack of heating in the Theatre,[3] and evidently asking about the receipts for the Edinburgh performances.[4]

## To Maud Gonne, [c. 17 December 1907]

Mention in an undated letter from MG, [December 1907].
Sending her a photograph of Augustus John's etching of him[1] and a copy of *Discoveries*,[2] complaining that theatre worries are again absorbing him, telling her that he has postponed an intended trip to Paris until her legal affairs are settled,[3] and discussing her horoscope.[4]

*G–YL*, 249.

[1] Although WBY had written to Vaughan, his letter was answered by W. G. Fay.

[2] The Company had played *The Hour-Glass* at Manchester against WBY's wishes, as he wanted to rewrite it, but this unauthorized production had evidently spurred him on to consider a more radical revision. On 7 Jan 1908 he informed Quinn (NYPL) that he had been working on *The Hour-Glass*, 'which I have been gradually ridding of its conventional religiousness', but it was not until 1913 that he finally published a fundamentally rewritten edition of the play.

[3] SMY had complained about the lack of heating at the Abbey during the Theatre of Ireland productions there on 13 Dec.

[4] Given the foreseeable withdrawal of AEFH's subsidy, the success of the Abbey in cities with large educated audiences like Edinburgh was of increasing importance, a point that Synge made on 22 Nov in thanking James Paterson (see p. 406) for helping with publicity there: 'the *financial* future of our movement . . . is giving us a good deal of anxiety and it is important for us to be able to make a little money in towns like Edinburgh where our work gets the sort of audiences that it needs' (*JMSCL* 11. 83). Fay replied to WBY's query on 17 Dec that their share of the Edinburgh receipts was £66 4s. 3d., with expenditure of £69 12s. 3d., and a deficit £3 8s. He promised to send full particulars of the whole tour in a few days, but thought that they had made roughly £30 (see below, p. 806). On 20 Dec Henderson told Holloway (NLI) 'that a friend had written from Edinburgh stating that it was pitable to see the thin audiences that attended the Irish plays in that city'.

[1] MG agreed with the rest of WBY's friends in deploring 'your portrait which I think is horrid. I shouldn't like you if you were like that & if you had not sent it I should never have recognised it at all.'

[2] *Discoveries* had been published on 15 Dec by the Dun Emer Press in an edition of 200 copies. A copy (Private) is inscribed on the title page: 'Maud Gonne from her friend W B Yeats.' In thanking him for the book, MG said she liked it 'very much', although she did not 'always agree with your philosophy, but it is very living'.

[3] WBY had evidently discussed a trip to Paris with MG when he saw her on her recent visit to Dublin (see p. 765), but had now written to say that this would be impossible, given the problems over the Theatre. This did not disappoint MG, who replied that she was 'not sorry you have postponed your visit to Paris as until my proces is over I am so worried by absurd legal difficulties & complications that my mind is not free for intelligent thought.'

[4] See pp. 755, 768. MG thanked him for having taken so much trouble about her horoscope, and apologized that the 'dates are so vague'. He had evidently told her of a letter so full of ominous predictions that he had not posted it, but she regretted this, since 'even if wrong about events it would

## *To Lady Gregory, 18 December [1907]*

18 Woburn Buildings | Euston Road
18 Dec

My dear Lady Gregory: I send one of the John etchings. I admire it very much as an etching & shall hang it on my wall with joy but it is of course a translation of me into tinker language. I showed it to Miss Horniman with the remark 'It is a very fine drawing' & she flew into a rage over it. If she could afford it she would buy up the plate & destroy it. I am sending one to Bullen but Miss Hornimans word is final I conclude.[1] I went thereon to look for Robert but was told that he called at Delamere Terrace on Monday but had not been seen since.[2] I then went to see Shannon myself, to ask him to draw me but both he & Ricketts were out.[3] If you know Roberts real address you might wire it. There is so little time that I must sit to somebody at once. I dont know what to write to John—whatever I say he will think I want to be flattered.

I am very glad about the good sail [*for* sale] of 'Saints & Wonders'.[4]

Yr ev
W B Yeats

PS.
Miss Horniman consents to our plan for painting the auditorium a different colour if it does not cost more than the old colour but if it is not to it must

have been very interesting & you know my nerves are very good & bad prophecies wouldn't have worried me overmuch'.

[1] The etching did not reach Coole until 21 Dec, and AG, like most of WBY's friends, hated it, reporting to Synge on 21 Dec: 'John has done such a horrible etching of Yeats!' Since AEFH was subsidizing the publication of *CW*, she had the final say in the portraits to be included. WBY had probably shown it to her on 16 Dec when he presented her with a copy of *Discoveries* inscribed 'Miss Horniman from her friend the writer' (Private). She thought John should do a fresh drawing and wrote to WBY on 7 Jan 1908 that she was getting Charles McEvoy (see p. 702) to 'stir up Augustus John about the fresh drawing if an opportunity should arise. I gather that Augustus John's work varies so from his habits, it is a great pity.'

[2] Robert and Margaret Gregory had returned to London from Paris, and in a letter of 18 Dec (Berg) AG informed WBY that they would be staying at 28 Delamere Terrace until 24 Dec. Before his marriage Robert had shared the house, overlooking the canal at Little Venice in the Royal Oak district of London, with his fellow artist Wilfred Cave.

[3] The original plan of commissioning a portrait of WBY by Charles Shannon (see pp. 651, 726, n. 2, 737) was now resuscitated in light of the controversy over the drawing by Augustus John. Robert Gregory was a friend of Shannon, who had, somewhat leisurely, painted a large portrait of him from 1904 to 1906.

[4] AG's *A Book of Saints and Wonders* had first been published in an edition of 200 copies by the Dun Emer Press on 20 Oct 1906, and had soon sold out (see p. 557, n. 1). In October 1907 a new and enlarged edition was published by John Murray in London and Charles Scribner's Sons in New York. In her letter of 18 Dec AG reported that 940 copies of this edition had been sold and that it was being reprinted.

not it seems require the scraping off of the old colour. Our colour must be darkish.[5]

ALS Berg, with envelope addressed to Coole, postmark 'LONDON.W 19 DE 1907'.

## *To Henry Meade Bland, 18 December 1907*

18, Woburn Buildings, | Euston Road, N.W.

Dec. 18, 1907.

Dear Sirs,

I thank you for making me an Honorary Member of your Club, which I imagine to myself somewhere under the shadow of the palm trees.[1] I remember how the moon light fell amongst them one night in San Jose, I wish I could attend your meetings. But alas! Marconi has not yet discovered how to transport so weighty a thing.[2]

Yrs sny

W B Yeats

TLS Bancroft. Printed in the *Overland Monthly* (San Francisco), July 1908 (55).

[5] In her reply on 19 Dec (Berg) AG wondered 'how long the theatre will be in the painters hands— That is Holloway's fault, it might have been done while they were on tour.'

[1] Henry Meade Bland, who had met WBY at San Jose State College in January 1904 (see p. 452), had now made him an honorary member of the 'Pacific Short Story Club', which he had founded in San Jose in 1905 'to foster a soul in Western literature'. Bland, the president of the Club, had declared in its first circular that it was intended for those who 'want to be the very best possible teachers of school English.... Those who want to keep in touch with the literature of the West.... Those who want to train their talents at literary work.... Those who love poetry and prose.' Other honorary members included Joaquin Miller and Jack London.

[2] Guglielmo Marchese Marconi (1874–1937), the pioneer of the radio, was born in Bologna of an Italian father and Irish mother. After experiments with wireless telegraphy in Bologna and La Spezia, he set up the Marconi Telegraph Co. in London. In 1898 he transmitted signals across the English Channel and in 1901 broadcast Morse code across the Atlantic. He had been much in the Irish newspapers since 17 Oct of this year, when his new wireless transmitter station opened in Ballyconneely, Clifden, Co. Galway, and sent the first transatlantic wireless message to his station in Nova Scotia. A report of this event in the *Irish Times* of 18 Oct also contained (5) a personal message from Marconi: 'On inauguration Transatlantic wireless service, I send "Irish Times" cordial greetings. Happy that corresponding European station situated in Ireland.' The paper celebrated the event as marking 'a new era in telegraphic communication', and noted that Marconi's 'mother was a native of Ireland, and his wife is also a native of this country, so that Irish people naturally feel more than a mere professional interest in the epoch-making system which has now been successfully launched on its career.' Marconi continued to improve and refine his electronic inventions and was to win the Nobel Prize for physics in 1909.

## *To John Millington Synge, 18 December 1907*

18, Woburn Buildings, | Euston Road, N.W.
Dec. 18, 1907.

My dear Synge,

I am very sorry to give you a job that will send you into town for a few hours, few things are so necessary at this moment as that you should get on with your play, but I don't quite know what else I can do. I have been trying to pay to the National Theatre Society the extra expenses of Deirdre.[1] I sent the enclosed cheque to the bank to receive back a letter asking for the Deposit Receipt and for two other signatures, The Secretary and one director.[2] I enclose the cheque to you and I want you to go to the theatre and ask for the Directors' box. I conclude you have a key. At the same time there is another matter you must attend to—the salary cheques are required, I enclose the cheque book and I have signed four or five cheques. You will please put your signature and fill in, say a couple of weeks. I don't think it is a good principle to give a number of blank cheques to Vaughan. Apart from the obvious reason I don't think it wise to do anything which makes the management feel independent of us just now.

I have had a letter from Fay which I have sent on to Lady Gregory.[3] The important thing about it is two statements:

1st. he says: "I wish to bring to your notice that out of seven rehearsals on tour, Miss M. Allgood was only in time for one, and on one occasion was an hour late. A rehearsal is called for this evening, and her sister told me (Miss Sarah Allgood) that she, Miss Sarah Allgood, could not come to rehearsal as she had an appointment. I asked her what the appointment was and she said it didn't matter. Owing to the fact that I have no direct control over these people and, consequently, have no power to make them obey my orders, I must refuse to accept any responsibility as to the date of production arranged."[4]

---

[1] WBY had used professional actresses (Letitia Darragh and Mona Limerick) for both the November 1906 and April 1907 productions of *Deirdre* and this had meant extra salaries. Furthermore, because of Mona Limerick's illness (see pp. 639–40, 646) the preparations for the April performances were unusually drawn out.

[2] See p. 796.

[3] In fact, this letter probably precedes that to AG, since WBY tells her, 'I have written to Synge' (see p. 802). Moreover, he quotes verbatim from Fay's letter, which he evidently still had before him.

[4] Since Synge was secretly engaged to Maire O'Neill, this point would have been particularly important to him, but he already knew that there was trouble between Fay and both the Allgoods, confiding to AG in a letter written on this day (*JMSCL* II. 107–8) that Fay was 'very bitter against Miss O'Neill. She is, I dare say, hard to manage, all artists with highly excitable tempers are, but I know a whole series of little things by which Fay has broken down his authority with her.' And he revealed that Fay was deeply hurt by Sara Allgood's admission to the press that Brigit O'Dempsey had appeared in her name on the recent tour.

2nd. That they made on the whole tour "roughly speaking if we include Miss Horniman's guarantee about £30."

The letter winds up with various complaints about our allowing people to appeal directly to us, a right that we certainly cannot give up. The whole situation is perilous, and all the more so, because it is quite obvious that Fay hasn't the least intention of resigning.[5] I mean that we must have a change somehow, or we shall all be worn out, and that change must be something more than good resolutions on everybody's part.[6]

Yrs sry

W B Yeats

TLS TCD. Saddlemyer, 253–4

## To George Brett, *18 December 1907*

Mention in following letter.

Sending an MS of *The Unicorn from the Stars*, and asking them to publish it as soon as possible, or, if it is rejected, to send it to John Quinn.[1]

## To Lady Gregory, *18 December 1907*

18, Woburn Buildings, | Euston Road, N.W.

December 18, 1907.

My dear Lady Gregory

I enclose a letter from Fay. I had heard from my sister that the theatre, though entirely full for the Theatre of Ireland, was icy cold. I wrote to Vaughan and received the enclosed reply from Fay.[1] Last winter my recollection is that I was told by Holloway that the stoves could not possibly warm the place unless they were lighted between 8 and 11 in the morning. I gave directions upon the subject and was very indignant one day, to find the fires still unlighted between 1 and 2 in the afternoon. All that winter Fay

---

[5] Synge was not so sure about this and in his letter told AG that Fay 'seemed depressed and nervous, and, I think, quite decided to go if he does not get what he wants'.

[6] Synge agreed with this, and in his letter to AG (which he asked her to send on to WBY) urged that 'the matter is so very important, that we *three* MUST MEET and talk it over with Fay, and then with the company'.

[1] WBY was trying to secure the American copyright to his new play, and, had the Macmillan Company chosen not to publish it, he wanted them to send it on to Quinn who would issue it in one of his small copyright editions (see pp. 17, 28, 178). In fact, Macmillan did issue a very small edition of the play, which was entered for copyright in America on 15 Jan 1908, and followed this up with a full edition on 13 May 1908 under the title *The Unicorn from the Stars and Other Plays*. This volume also included *Cathleen ni Houlihan* and *The Hour-Glass*.

[1] See below.

insisted that he was having the fires lighted at the time I said. He now writes to me that the fires were lit from 4 o'clock each evening and that this is the usual time. His whole letter is most unsatisfactory. I have replied about the fires, but merely stated that my recollection is that they were to be lit much earlier. Meanwhile I have written to Holloway and asked him to inspect the stoves. When I get his letter I shall have to deal with Fay. We are responsible now for the comfort of Miss Horniman's tenants. I have written to Synge and sent the cheque book and also the £17 odd cheque returned by the bank for extra signatures and for the deposit receipt, which must be in the directors' box. I don't know what to do about Fay. It is evident that he never meant his threats and that he does mean to drift on in the usual way, and I don't think any of our nerves will stand that.[2] I think, however, it will be better for me to postpone my meeting with the company for a little bit. For one thing, it will let everybody's temper cool down. It will enable Synge to get the Allgoods into some permanent frame of mind. At the moment I am inclined to think, but I have said nothing about this to Synge, that Miss Molly Allgood had better continue her demand for a directors' meeting to hear her complaint. The investigation of that complaint would probably result in getting Fay to realise that there is another side to all he says, and that we know it. I don't see that new good resolutions on everybody's part will do us much good, unless we have some new form of organization to give them effect. I feel at this moment more inclined to get into closer relations with the members of the company than to allow Fay to go on in the present way. I think it might do him good if it were put to him quite clearly that he must go or fall in with a new arrangement lessening his power. I think it is pretty clear now that he doesn't want to go. I think also from what I hear of Miss Horniman that none of them are very likely to get berths elsewhere, as they would find their special training with us of little use to them anywhere else. She certainly apart from her special reasons doesn't seem to want them, whereas I can see, she does, for instance, want Synge's plays, though how she expects to play them, God only knows![3] I think she is quite honest in saying

---

[2] In fact, W. G. Fay was in a depressed and vacillating state, as Holloway discovered during a long conversation with him on 20 Dec (NLI), during which he spoke of 'the impossibility of working the Abbey into a success with Yeats, Gregory & Synge at the helm. He was for chucking the whole thing & I advised him not to until he saw his way clearly ahead. . . . He was most despondent—he had trained several companies & had arrived at the age of 35—& had made nothing. Had he worked 14 hours for over five years in America he would be a rich man today & not a poor fellow without a copper. Even the Company are getting out of his control & come & go when they like.'

[3] Presumably AEFH had given WBY this impression in conversation, as there is no suggestion of it in her letters, and she had a low opinion of Synge's character (see pp. 491, n. 2, 550–1, n. 1, 562, n. 5). For his part, Synge was unimpressed with the opening repertoire of AEFH's company (*JMSCL* II. 39). In a letter of 14 Dec AG had commented (Berg) that 'Kerrigan may settle down when he finds Miss H won't take him, I am sure he counted on Payne.'

that Miss Allgood who, alone out of the company, has always had her praise would be quite useless to her.[4] The only importance of this opinion is that it is probably Payne's. The prospect for us is a discontented company which stays with us, not because it wants to, but because it can't go anywhere else. I really cannot at the moment see any way out and that is another reason for delaying our meeting with them for a little while. Of course if you think it better for me to go over at once, I will. The chief burden of managing Fay falls upon you now and I don't want to do anything you do not approve of. I must say this small detail of the theatre fires comes to me as a reminder of many intolerable things. A far less competent man who told the truth would in the end, have been better for us, and, at any rate, I think so at this moment. I am sure, at any rate, we should all have written better plays and more of them.

Remember that I am dictating this and so it is like talk, not quite so deliberate as writing.

I enclose a long letter from Quinn, which will amuse you. Please return it to me that I may answer it. I wonder what I should do about the Charles Shannon portrait. It is a matter for a third person to arrange as it would be embarrassing both for myself and for Shannon if he thought the price offered inadequate. I might ask Sturge Moore to negotiate, but if Robert were passing through London and inclined to speak to Shannon, that would be much better, as he has the precedent of his own portrait.[5] There is no knowing that Shannon may not like keeping up appearances before so near a neighbour as Sturge Moore, who is also, I think, rather afraid of Ricketts and Shannon. Of course I should very much like to be painted by Shannon. If I had that I should feel that with the Mancini and the Augustus John I had done all I need do. Shannon will be as emphatic in one way as Mancini is in another. I send to you two papers which I have had sent me from Japan. Please keep them for the theatre book. If our own company breaks up we shall be all the better pleased to have these foreign tributes, besides they will help me to a Samahain.[6] I also send various paragraphs which have been sent by Quinn about my New York performances. I haven't read

---

[4] AEFH did in fact employ Sara Allgood, with great success, in a production of Shakespeare's *Measure for Measure* produced by William Poel at the Gaiety Theatre in April 1908.

[5] For Quinn's letter of 8 Dec see below. Shannon had started a portrait of Robert Gregory in May 1905 but then put it aside until late November of that year. He continued to work at it intermittently until early March 1906, when it was finally finished. In her reply on 19 Dec AG told WBY that if 'Robert will speak to Shannon about the picture it wd be best. But if he doesn't, you might just write to Shannon, quoting the bit from Quinn's letter. He will probably do it.'

[6] AG did not apparently paste the Japanese articles into her 'Theatre Book', and they are untraced, although WBY made use of them in a short article, 'The Abbey Theatre', which he included in the programme for the British Association's visit to the Abbey in September 1908: 'In Japan there are some who believe very erroneously that we are a great success, and even making money, and one of their distinguished critics uses our example to urge upon his countrymen the support of their native drama.' In her reply of 20 Dec AG thought the 'Japan paper is nice'.

them, but so far as I can see by a hasty glance they are favourable.[7]
Leighton[8] once said to somebody I know, or knew, that he never read
articles about his pictures, because the bad ones annoyed him, and the good
ones gave him no pleasure. He has also sent me a rather absurd interview
with Mrs. Campbell in which [s]he abuses Shaw and praises me, though
whether as a man or a writer, I don't know. I will send it to you when I have
shown it to Mrs. Emery. It looks to me like a private conversation,
published as an interview.[9]

[7] Quinn had sent WBY 'all the notices' of the Wycherly production of *Cathleen ni Houlihan* and *The Hour-Glass* at the Berkeley Theatre. The acting was generally praised, although there were differences over the importance of the plays themselves. The two best notices appeared in the *Sun* and the *World*. The former observed on 3 Dec (7) that in both plays 'Margaret Wycherly was put forward prominently': 'Miss Wycherly is a stranger neither to New York nor to dramatic symbolism, having been seen previously in plays by this same Irish poet-dramatist. She then appeared to be an elocutionist of some ability and to some extent possessed of the power to suggest the wistfulness and the transcendental yearnings of the Celt. Both of these qualities she again exhibited last evening. . . . Holbrook Blinn was the Wise Man and exhibited sincerity and power, though not much poetry.' It added that in *Cathleen ni Houlihan* 'Miss Wycherly had the assistance of Mrs. Annie Yeamans and William Harrigan and they and their associates furnished the requisite background against which was displayed the symbolic picture of Ireland, for whom her sons must sacrifice all and count it well lost. The audience, though not overflowing in numbers, was enthusiastic and there were several recalls after each curtain.' On the same day the *World*, under the byline 'Two Little Plays with Real "Ideas" | Margaret Wycherly in Yeats's Dramas Puts First Gilt Edge On Daly's Scheme', asserted (6) that if 'at the outset of his experiments with his "theatre of ideas", Arnold Daly had hit upon as intelligent and competent an actress as Miss Margaret Wycherly and presented her in one-act plays of such deep import, poetic inspiration and literary excellence as the symbolic dramas of William Butler Yeats his project at the Berkeley Lyceum would not have resulted in failure'. It added that Margaret Wycherly had 'greatly pleased a small audience', and wondered whether perhaps it was 'not too late for her to put the Daly scheme on its feet. At any rate her performances are gems, and they appeal directly to the special audiences which the little theatre is attempting to attract. . . . The little plays were as well produced as they were acted.' The *New York Herald* of 3 Dec (10) was less certain of the importance of the pieces, describing them as two 'Irish poetic fantasies—they can hardly be called plays', and went on to assert that while 'Mr. Yeats's little sketches have a certain poetic, elusive charm of their own, it may be doubted whether the every day theatrical audience find in them more than an interesting puzzle'. It reported, however, that 'Miss Wycherly acted with skill and much sympathy with the poetic sentiment of the parts she undertook', and praised the performance of Holbrook Blinn as the Wise Man in *The Hour-Glass*. The *Gaelic American* of 7 Dec (4) also agreed that Miss Wycherly had 'made a decided hit' in the two plays and that her parts, and the quality of the supporting actors, gave her 'ample opportunity to display her undoubted dramatic talent'. The *Evening Post* of 3 Dec (9) thought that *The Hour-Glass* owed a great deal to *Everyman* but judged that both plays 'were impressively and simply acted'.

[8] For Frederick Leighton, the Victorian artist, see p. 188, n. 3.

[9] The interview with Mrs Patrick Campbell by Charles Darnton appeared in the New York *Evening World* of 16 Nov (9), and versions of it were published in other New York papers. She assured Darnton that Shaw was ' "quite out of it in London. Shaw offends good taste. When one meets an Irishman like Yeats—an Irishman of truly cultured taste—one sees that Shaw has no taste. The Irish won't have him because, as they say, he is not a true Irishman, and the English won't have him for various reasons, and so, I suppose, he'll have to be called an American, if he is to be called anything." ' Darnton then asked her if she would be 'one of a committee of two to go down to the dock and meet poor George Bernard Shaw when he swims ashore?' ' "Shaw's 'Major Barbara,' " ' pursued Mrs. Campbell, javelin in hand, "was a particular offence to good taste. No, it wasn't much of a play—are any of Shaw's plays for that matter? His characters are not characters—they are merely mouthpieces for Shaw's views. And one

I have sent the Unicorn to Macmillan, New York, and asked them to get out an edition, if they will, as soon as possible, and if they will not, to send it to John Quinn.[10]

On consideration I have sent rather different letters both to Fay and Holloway. I realised as I thought over it that my first letters were merely postponing the difficult moment, as my recollection was perfectly distinct. The only thing I can think of now is to have a notice printed, stating the hour when the fires are to be lit and have this pasted up in the theatre. It won't be obeyed, but it will be a way out of the difficult situation, which it is better to deal with on the main issue.[11] The trouble is, that they are all probably anxious to drift on, merely because it is more convenient than going anywhere else and not anxious, while the discipline remains as at present, to do efficient work.

Yr sny

W B Yeats

[*In WBY's hand*]
I enclose copies of letters to Fay & Holloway.

[*With enclosures*]

Abbey Theatre

17 December 1907

Dear Mr. Yeats

Your letter to hand this morning. We have no script of The Hour Glass. We use the printed book. I enclose typewritten alterations you left here a short time before we went away.[12]

About the fires in the theatre during performance of theatre of Ireland, the fire was lit from four o'clock each evening, the usual time. The night your sister was present, people here say was a particularly cold night and

---

grows tired of mouthpieces, doesn't one? Tell me, is there any interest here in serious plays?" ' At this time Mrs Pat thought Shaw superficial and she had told D. D. Lyttleton the previous year, 'It's that journalistic cleverness of his that I detest', although it is conceivable that her animosity towards him on this occasion may have been further fuelled by a recent letter in which he addressed her as 'Princess with the Sixteen Chins', and by his description of her beloved pet dog Pinkie as 'a cheese maggot under a microscope' (Peters, *Mrs Pat*, 270).

[10]  See p. 801, n. 1

[11]  AG told WBY (Berg) that she was 'sorry you wrote about the fires, just as I am sorry that I wrote mentioning not being sent reports (I did it as an excuse to mention Xmas holidays) for we ought to keep to the one definite question of discipline & not stray into any other.'

[12]  See p. 797. Although eager to rewrite *The Hour-Glass* extensively, WBY did not find time to do so until 1912. The Company were presumably using the slightly revised text issued as a 'theatre edition' by Bullen earlier this year, to which WBY made a number of subsequent corrections.

that may account for it.[13] No one made any complaint at the theatre about it.

Have you the National Bank cheque book for subsidy salaries, if so, you might send it to us with some signed cheques, as we will want it this week.

The Edinburgh receipts (our share) £66.4.3. The expenditure was £69.12.3. deficit £3.8s.

We shall send you full particulars re the whole tour in a few days. Roughly speaking if we include Miss Horniman's guarantee we made about £30.

I wish to bring to your notice that out of seven rehearsals on tour, Miss M. Allgood was only in time for one and on one occasion was an hour late. A rehearsal is called for this evening and her sister Miss Sara Allgood told me that she Miss Sara Allgood could not come to rehearsal as she had an appointment. I asked her what the appointment was and she said it didn't matter. Owing to the fact that I have no direct control over these people, and consequently have no power to make them obey my orders, I must refuse to accept any responsibility as to the date of productions arranged. My agreement with the Directors on taking over the management of this theatre again, at a reduced salary, was that there was to be no communication between any of the employees of the theatre and the Directors, except through me as Manager. This agreement has been repeatedly broken through during the last season, the inevitable result being that the members of the company think that if they don't like to obey my orders, they can appeal to the Directors. If you and Mr. Synge have a plan for getting into better working order here, the sooner it is put in operation, the better.

Yours faithfully
William G. Fay

Dec. 8, 1907

My dear Yeats: I received your two letters and the cable about *Deirdre*.[14] I had written to Miss Darragh asking when I could see her and got a letter from her which I enclose you with this.[15] If she writes after Christmas I shall say that Mrs. Campbell has the play now and that is all there will be to it. Mrs. Campbell by the way said some good things about you and took a rap at Shaw. I didn't see the papers, but I was told about them. Mr. White of my office got one of the papers for me and I send you a cutting with this. Mrs. Campbell was in New York only one week; she could not get a theatre

---

[13] See pp. 801–2. Holloway described the evening of the first night, 13 Dec, as 'one of the most disagreeable days of the season' (NLI).

[14] This is an answer to WBY's letters to Quinn of 4 and 29 Oct, and his telegram of 26 Oct (see pp. 733–40, 756, 757–60).

[15] This letter has not been traced.

for a longer time. It is splendid of her to be willing to act in your company for a week next spring. It ought to do a great deal of good.

I am delighted to get your new *Poems* and I am delighted with *Deirdre*. I think *The Shadowy Waters* has been greatly improved, but two new lines of it struck me as a little too homely for a dream play, which is what it seems to me to be:

> 'I've nothing to complain but heartburn,
> And that's cured by a boiled liquorice root.'

I can't make any rhythm out of these lines and they break the mood that the rest of the play brings on one. But you know and I don't.[16]

I was much amused by your account of John, the artist. Can I buy the drawing he has made of you for the collected edition? To whom should I write about it? To him or to Bullen or to whom?[17]

If Shannon will make a portrait of you for a hundred pounds, as you think he will, and if you will give him the time I shall be delighted. Shall I write to him? Perhaps you could manage it better. You can tell him that I'm not a millionaire or a Tom Kelly.[18]

I think *Deirdre* is your best acting play yet. I can feel the proud scorn with which Naisi treats the King, but it seems to me that Naisi should let himself go a bit more after he rebukes Deirdre for her suggestion to free him on the King's terms. Treachery of the foulest kind, betrayal of the cruellest sort, of a man who trusted to the hospitality of a King ought, it seems to me, to call for a blast from the victim upon the King—a prophecy of the extinction of his house and so on. I believe it was Fergus or some other one who either cursed him or made a prophecy, but Naisi could do it quite as well in the play. It's the best woman's part you have ever written, but it seems to me you have not let yourself go towards the end. However and again I am no

---

[16] Quinn had been reading the second volume of *The Poetical Works of William B. Yeats*, which contained the new version of *The Shadowy Waters*, including the lines to which he here objects (*VP*, 227v, ll. 116a, b). He had evidently forgotten that WBY had 'very joyfully' cited 'liquorice-root' in his letter of 16 Sept 1905 as an example that 'the element of strength in poetic language is common idiom' (see p. 179). Although WBY was currently proud of the lines, he seemingly came round to Quinn's judgement, and cut them in *Later Poems* (1922) and in all subsequent printings of the play.

[17] See pp. 738–9. Quinn did in fact purchase John's portrait of WBY, and later became one of John's most loyal patrons.

[18] Thomas Hughes Kelly (1865–1933), son of the wealthy Irish-American banker Eugene Kelly (1804–1884), was a millionaire, treasurer of the Irish Industrial League of America, and an enthusiastic member of the Irish Literary Society of New York. He was patron of Irish artists and writers (although, much to James Joyce's indignation, he declined to underwrite the *Goblin*, a projected Dublin paper to be edited by Joyce and Francis Skeffington); in 1903 he had endowed Padraic Colum with an annual subsidy so that he could devote himself to literature, and Colum dedicated *The Land* to him in 1905. He had a house at Celbridge, Co. Kildare.

judge.[19] I'm glad you have written it and if Mrs. Campbell does it here it will add to your reputation immensely.

We have had a bad panic. It originated in two or three bank failures caused by bad banking methods and then spread to the trust companies. They had been doing a banking business on an investment basis and when a run was started on one it spread to others and the panic was on. I was in the very midst of it. My bank, the National Bank of Commerce in New York, was the clearing agent for the Knickerbocker Trust Co. and it was the latter's failure that caused the flurry. All the big banks helped out the smaller ones and saved the day. But it was terrible. As my uncle wrote to me—"I see that money is tight in New York but Hell is loose."

In the middle of it came the failure of a big mill and print works in Massachusetts and the bank I am attorney for was involved $2,200,000; supposed to be secured. But now its whole position as a secured creditor is assailed and we have a fight on that will be carried up to the United States Supreme Court. So you see I have a load to carry.[20] Fortunately I took things easy in the late summer and was in good shape to stand the shocks. But I am a little tired now. For some days I had only four to five hours' sleep—conferences late into the night and so on.

[19] Quinn had taken a lively interest in the progress of *Deirdre*, with AG keeping him abreast of its writing. WBY's treatment of the legend is more economical than many others, most of which culminate in a prolonged battle between Conchubar's men and the sons of Usnach, who are only overcome when Conchubar tricks Cathbad the Druid into putting a spell on them. At the end of WBY's play Naoise pursues Conchubar off-stage to kill him but is caught in a net and, when brought into Conchubar's presence, is more occupied with refusing Deirdre's offer to save him by becoming Conchubar's wife than in denouncing Conchubar's treachery. And whereas in most other renditions Deirdre ends with her famous elegy, 'The Lament for the Sons of Usnach', in WBY's version she devotes her last words to persuading Conchubar to allow her to take a final farewell of Naoise. The original versions of the tale present the whole episode as triggering the collapse of the Red Branch order, when Fergus, enraged at Conchubar's treachery, destroys his seat of power, Emain Macha, and joins the enemy forces of Maeve and Ailell, while the now undeceived Cathbad puts a curse on Conchubar and his descendants.

[20] Quinn was retained by the National Bank of Commerce, a clearing agent for the Knickerbocker Trust Company, which had recently gone into liquidation. Its collapse had contributed to a financial panic which, Quinn assured AG (NYPL), was caused by 'yellow journalism and yellow magazines and yellow statesmen'. The banks tightened their terms for credit and the number of American business failures reached a ten-year high with over 8,000 companies going under, leaving liabilities of $116,000,000. One of the victims of the general turmoil was the Arnold Print Works of North Adams, Massachusetts, of which the National Bank of Commerce was the secured creditor. Quinn's acumen in dealing with these financial upheavals greatly enhanced his reputation as a company lawyer, although he was disappointed not to be appointed a receiver of the Knickerbocker Trust.

I should be delighted to have the MS. of *Deirdre* when you have it ready.[21] I have three fine MSS. of William Morris now[22] and the complete MS. of John Davidson's *Ballads and Songs* and several MSS. of Ernest Dowson;[23] and the MS. of William Carleton's autobiography[24] and the page-proofs of Lady Gregory's *Gods and Fighting Men*.[25] So you see your MS. of *Deirdre* will be in good company.

Liebler & Co. had announced the plays—*Cathleen ni Houlihan* and *The Hour-Glass*—before they knew they had been copyrighted here. When they found out that they were copyrighted they came to me and that's why I cabled.[26] I saw only the end of *The Hour-Glass*. Miss Wycherly is, in my opinion, a much conceited person. The rest of the company was good. Your friend Miss Quinn played the angel.[27] The press notices were quite

---

[21] See pp. 632, 636. AG had promised Quinn the MS of *Deirdre* on WBY's behalf as early as 6 May 1905, writing (NYPL) that she was 'sure he wd. like you to have it'.

[22] Quinn had admired the writings of the William Morris (see p. 152) since his youth. He owned the MSS of Morris's *The Glittering Plain* and his translation of the *Aeneid*, and in 1911 he was to acquire the MS of the first draft of Morris's translation of the *Odyssey*. In 1915 he sold these and other manuscripts to Henry E. Huntington to raise money to purchase pictures by Puvis de Chavannes, but retained the MS of *The House of the Wolfings* until 1923.

[23] The Scottish poet John Davidson (1857–1909) was a fellow member with WBY of the Rhymers' Club in the 1890s, although the two men did not get on (see *Aut*, 316–18). Quinn built up a magnificent collection of Davidson's works, including an autograph MS of his *Ballads and Songs* (1894), which he acquired for $260, as well as the autograph MSS of two of his most celebrated poems, 'A Ballad of a Nun' and 'A Ballad in Blank Verse of the Making of a Poet'. The poet Ernest Christopher Dowson (1867–1900) was also a member of the Rhymers' Club and an acquaintance of WBY, who thought his 'best verse immortal' but found him 'too vague and gentle for my affections' (*Aut*, 312). Quinn owned twenty-eight items by Dowson, among which were the autograph MSS of his 'The Eyes of Pride' (published in the *Savoy*, January 1896), 'Countess Marie of the Angels' (published in the *Savoy*, April 1896), 'The Dying of Francis Donne' (published in the *Savoy*, August 1896), and *The Pierrot of the Minute* (1897), as well as the corrected proof sheets of *Decorations* (1899).

[24] The Irish novelist William Carleton (1794–1869) was best known for his *Traits and Stories of the Irish Peasantry* (Dublin, 1830; 2nd series, 1833), and also published eighteen full-length novels as well as further collections of short stories. WBY had edited *Stories from Carleton* in 1889, describing him in the introduction (pp. xvi–xvii) as 'the great novelist of Ireland, by right of the most Celtic eyes that ever gazed from under the brows of storyteller', and as recently as October 1906 had, as the *Freeman's Journal* of 15 Oct 1906 reported, claimed (6) that the Abbey Theatre owed 'its inspiration to the immortal Tyrone schoolmaster and stone-mason who, with many faults, is a great honour to Irish literature. If we have in Ireland to-day a Jane Barlow and an Emily Lawless we owe it to the genius of Carleton.' Carleton's unfinished autobiography, written in the last year of his life and published posthumously in 1896, gives a vigorous account of his childhood and youth, and offers a rare insight into rural life in the north of Ireland in the first twenty-five years of the 19th century. Quinn had acquired the 178-page autograph MS, headed 'My Life—September 21st 1868', from D. J. O'Donoghue, who had purchased it from Carleton's daughter.

[25] WBY had himself given these to Quinn in March 1904, at the close of his first American tour.

[26] See p. 779.

[27] The 'friend' is ironical, since Maire Quinn (see pp. 78, n. 2, 271) had caused a great many difficulties when an actress with the INTS and secretary of Inghinidhe na hEireann ('The Daughters of Ireland'). She had left the INTS with her husband-to-be Dudley Digges in 1903, following a dispute over Synge's *In the Shadow of the Glen*, and the two further angered WBY by performing as the 'Irish National Theatre' at the St Louis Exhibition of 1904 (see III. 590–4). In 1905 she had partly redeemed

good, but the pieces will be taken off on Tuesday of this week. I send you enclosed all the notices. Mrs. Thursby got her brother Arthur Brisbane, who edits the *Journal* to say a good word yesterday,[28] but the ordinary actor can't talk well much less speak beautiful words beautifully. Miss Wycherly's idea of speaking beautiful words seems to be "to baby them"—to half articulate them—I could hardly make out half of what she said and I know the words very well. So what could an audience that did not know the words make out of it?

Berkeley Theatre is a small theatre which accommodates about five or six hundred people. I should say it was a little larger than the Abbey Theatre. Arnold Daly played there last year in a series of Shaw plays, which were successful. Later he put on *Mrs. Warren's Profession* but it was stopped by the police on the complaint of a stupid Police Commissioner. Later on the Court held that the play was not criminally indecent but was only vulgar and tiresome, so the Judges said.[29]

Liebler & Co. are good people and some time I hope to have the time to take up with them seriously the suggestion that they bring out your company on a business basis. Judge Keogh sent me your letter to him. If a *business* venture with the company is impossible, then it will be time enough to talk of a guaranty fund. But a regular business management is better.[30] Liebler & Co. said they would pay a royalty of five dollars (one pound) for each performance. If that means one pound for *each* play, then there would be due you for the six evenings and two matinees last week, sixteen pounds; if not, eight pounds. I will send you a draft for whatever amount I receive and

herself by helping Quinn with depositions on behalf of MG (see p. 76), and WBY had recommended Digges to Arnold Daly in 1905 (see p. 177). Of her current performance in *The Hour-Glass* Charles Darnton commented in the New York *World* of 3 Dec: 'Any one who could have any faith in angels after seeing and hearing Miss Maire Roden Quinn, in a red robe and a gilt halo, deserves to go to heaven.'

[28]   Mrs Alice Brisbane Thursby (1861–1953) was the sister of Arthur Brisbane (1864–1936), editor of the New York *Evening Journal*. Apparently no file of the paper for this date has survived.

[29]   Arnold Daly had put on *Mrs Warren's Profession* (against Shaw's advice) at the Garrick (not Berkeley) Theatre on 30 Oct 1905 (not 'last year'). The play, which was banned in England, gives a rational account of the 'profession' of prostitution through Mrs Warren, a prosperous and matter-of-fact brothel-keeper, and was denounced before its opening by the obsessive Anthony Comstock (1844–1915), secretary of the New York Society for the Suppression of Vice. At Comstock's instigation the New York Police Commissioner William McAdoo arrested Daly together with other members of the cast and management for 'disorderly conduct', although in the event only the house manager, Samuel Gumpertz, was charged, and then with the lesser offence of causing a public nuisance. Meanwhile Daly surrendered to the public and press outcry, and withdrew the play after only one night.

[30]   Liebler & Co., a company of theatrical and tour managers, based in New York and headed by Theodore A. Liebler (1852–1941), had been in negotiation with Martin Keogh over a proposed Abbey tour (see pp. 718, 739). In her letter of 19 Dec AG had suggested that WBY 'shd copy the bit re theatre for Fay when you write—I felt that Judge K not answering you went against us—& Fay wd know in making up his mind that America was still a possibility'. Liebler's in fact organized the first American tour by the Abbey 1911–12.

also for the two nights of this week.[31] They are the people who are managing Mrs. Campbell and I fancy that it was due perhaps to her enthusiasm that they thought of doing your plays with Daly's company and Miss Wycherly. That's the chief reason why I did not want to shut them off from giving the plays a trial.

Mr. Bullen has written me a letter asking me to see Brett in regard to his taking a small edition of your collected edition in eight volumes. I will see him in a few days and will at once write to Bullen. Brett ought to take three hundred sets at least.[32] Their sale would not interfere at all with the sale of the collected edition in two volumes. Of course, you have seen the two volume edition. They look very grand and you must be pleased with them. I am sending Lady Gregory a set, each of your sisters a set, and a set to Mrs. Emery.[33]

I hope all is going well at the Abbey Theatre this winter. I am not surprised at Miss H's action.[34] Women are unreliable as a rule in business matters and whimsical and changeable. That's why I never have a woman as a client, if I can help it.

You ought to feel proud of that collected edition in eight volumes; so my friend there are some compensations. But editions and successes of that sort don't make all of life. One wants affection and friendship and sometimes love too. If one doesn't care for a legal wife he should be entitled to a "visiting wife"—that's the phrase a clever lady used at a dinner that I attended today. Her husband seemed to enjoy the joke.

I was shocked to hear a day or two ago of Hyde's illness. I hope he is out of danger by this. His loss would be irreparable for Ireland. Any man is influenced by those who are close to him, and Mrs. H. hasn't had an altogether good influence over him.[35]

---

[31] On 13 Dec Quinn forwarded a draft for £16 8s. 7d. in payment of these royalties.

[32] Bullen had contacted Quinn on 20 Nov, asking him to persuade George Brett of the Macmillan Company to issue some sets of *CW* in America, and Quinn was quick to oblige, sending Brett a prospectus of the edition on 10 Dec, and urging him 'to make some arrangement with Bullen by which you could offer two or three hundred sets of this edition to the American public'. He assured Brett that such a scheme 'would not only not interfere with the sale of the regular works, but would help them a great deal', reminded him 'that you have your market practically all ready', and offered to give him any help he needed. On the same day Quinn informed Bullen that he had urged Brett to take up 'the American end' of the *Collected Works*, and hoped for a favourable answer: 'I think it would help Yeats's reputation if your edition was put before the American public, and I entirely agree with you that it wouldn't do a dollar's worth of damage to Brett's own books'. Brett replied on 13 Dec that he 'certainly' wished that 'it might be possible to handle this charming edition in this country', but that American copyright law made this impossible.

[33] AG's copies arrived in late December and she thanked him on 22 Dec (NYPL): 'How very good of you to send me those two books of Yeats. They do indeed look imposing.'

[34] i.e. AEFH's action in abandoning the Abbey for her new company in Manchester.

[35] Douglas Hyde had suffered a prolonged and dangerous attack of pneumonia shortly after his return from his American tour. He was bedridden for several months in the autumn of 1907, and for a time

I've written to no one for months. Hardly had time to sleep and dress. But that doesn't mean that I am any the less keen on hearing from and about my friends, and you and Lady Gregory come first on the list. So don't wait to have letters from me before writing.

I am sending you also a copy of my letter to Liebler & Co. But that is all off now—because Daly wants to be the whole thing and he is going back to Shaw's plays on Wednesday, reviving *Candida*, which draws the women.[36]

[*The remainder of this letter is missing.*]

TLS Berg; enclosures NLI and NYPL.

## *To W. G. Fay, 18 December 1907*

18, Woburn Buildings, | Euston Rd., N.W.

Dec. 18, 1907.

My dear Fay,

Last winter Holloway told me that there was no likelihood of the theatre being warm on cold days unless the fire was lighted from 8 to 11 in the morning. I told you this at the time and you undertook to have the fire lighted at 11. One day I came in at 2 o'clock and was indignant not to find any fires, and you then lighted them. I now hear that the usual hour is 4 o'clock.[1] <I am in communication with Holloway> I have sent a cheque to Synge.

[*unsigned*]

TS copy NLI.

there were fears that he was dying. He did not fully recover until the following spring. Many of Hyde's other friends shared Quinn's reservations about his wife Lucy, whom he had married in 1893, and who had little affection for his friends or interest in his work for the Irish language. On 12 July 1906, in the course of a lengthy diatribe against her, Quinn had complained to AG (NYPL) that 'Mrs Hyde is not friendly to Yeats.... I am sorry to say that I found her jealous and most unkind in her remarks.'

[36] Quinn's letter to Leibler, discussing terms for the production of WBY's plays in America, is untraced. Daly had made a moderate success with Shaw's *Candida* in December 1903 and gave 132 performances of the play between then and late April 1904. He had just revived it with *The Man of Destiny* and *How He Lied to Her Husband* at the Berkeley Theatre from 15 Oct to 10 Dec 1907.

[1] See pp. 801–2.

## To Joseph Holloway, 18 December 1907

18, Woburn Buildings, | Euston Road, N.W.
Dec. 18, 1907.

Dear Mr. Holloway,

You told me last winter that the fires at the theatre should be lighted in cold weather between 8 and 11. I have had complaints of the theatre being icy cold the other day when every seat was taken. I am convinced, therefore, that the fires were not lighted early enough and I want a written statement from you that we may base upon it more stringent regulations.[1]

Y sny
W B Yeats

TLS NLI.

## To Lady Gregory, 20 December [1907]

18 Woburn Buildings | Euston Road | London
Dec 20

My dear Lady Gregory: I enclose Synges letter.[1] I can go to Dublin at any time you & he decide.[2] I have been expecting this revolt against Fay for a considerable time. If he goes we shall have to get rid of Vaughan too. It is a lamentable situation. It is a question whether it might not be better for Kerrigan[3] & the Allgoods to formally set out in writing or other wise their

---

[1] See p. 802.

[1] i.e. Synge's reply to WBY's letter of 18 Dec; see below.

[2] AG replied on 'Saturday' (21 Dec 1907; Berg): 'I will write to Synge that I can go up any day after Xmas—though I dont know that it will do much good. We shall have to snub Synge and Molly in the end—her being late in assignations with him is no excuse for her upsetting rehearsals—and we all have "artistic temperaments"—if we choose to flaunt them. I believe America and a break up would be best of all.'

[3] J. M. Kerrigan (see p. 576) had resigned from the Abbey Company in early December, during the British tour, although Synge had urged Maire O'Neill to do all she could to dissuade him. According to Synge, who interviewed him on 18 Dec (*JMSCL* II. 107–8), the cause of his resignation was that Fay had falsely accused him of being late on a cue and 'swore and cursed at him and spoke badly to him personally—as he puts it—but there was nothing out of the way. Kerrigan, however, lost his head and temper and gave notice. He says Fay is unfortunate in his manner with them; at one time too confidential, and then the next lowering himself by undignified personal abuse so that none of them can feel any respect for him.' Earlier Synge told AG that Kerrigan reportedly 'wrote a letter to the Directors giving his reasons for resigning, and gave it to Fay to forward to them. Fay it seems has suppressed it' (*JMSCL* II. 106). On 14 Jan 1908 Ambrose Power told Holloway (NLI) that Kerrigan was likely to act with the Theatre of Ireland and that the 'National Theatre Society threatened to leave him at Glasgow

complaints of Fay as this would leave us in the position of arbitrators between two parties, & not ourselves a party.[4] It would also make it impossible for Fay to make a public cry against us—in case of our deciding against him. <I am writing this to> I agree with what Synge says about working more in future in consultation with the company. I think it is only fair to them—of course artistic policy must be in our hands. About the Allgoods & Kerrigan. I have it in my mind that it will be better to so arrange the matter that if Fay goes no one will have the chance to say that we are impossible to work with & have driven him out, as they may say we did Colum & the rest.[5] If the company revolts Fay will be held responsible for all—other wise we will. If we are arbitrators & not negociators we can keep out of the dispute. If you agree with me about this you might ask Synge to suggest that Fays opponents meet & draw up their complaints in definite form & invite us to interfear.[6]

Yours always
W B Yeats

If you think it well to get the matter over now & are well enough to get up[7] that will please me best. A free mind is impossible with all this still to come, but if Shannon is to draw me I should have to return here.
PS.2
Of course I see the humour of Synges letter—he no longer needs Fay & does need Kerrigan but could any of us stand a continuance of the present state of things.

---

last tour until he appealed to Yeats and Lady Gregory and got a ticket back to Dublin.' AG warned Synge on 14 Dec that Kerrigan's 'going could throw us into Fays hands even more than we are', and on 16 Dec told WBY (Berg) that Kerrigan's loss 'would be a greater loss than Miss A—he is so good in Unicorn, besides Synge's Deirdre—and men seem scarcer than women. Besides, we cant put Fay in the wrong so clearly as about Miss A.—and any weakening of the company will put us more and more in Fay's hands. . . . I dont think we have ever been at such a boggy place, no enemy to fight in the open, but the ground sinking under us.' But she reflected that Kerrigan might become more amenable when he discovered that AEFH would not take him on at the Gaiety Theatre, Manchester.

[4] In her reply (see above, n. 1) AG wrote: 'I think it is a very good idea getting the company to make their statement. I am very much afraid we shall lose the Fays, and that puts an end to America, But we must keep our position clear. I think we ought to have met this week.'

[5] i.e. over the reorganization of the Irish National Theatre Society into a limited liability company; see pp. 270, n. 1, 292–8.

[6] AG did write to Synge on receipt of this letter (Saddlemyer, 258–9), saying that she quite agreed with WBY 'that the members of the Company who have complaints against Fay ought to put them in writing & send them to us. I thought we ought all or anyhow you & Yeats to have met this week & settled the matter, but as it has been missed, I dont think next week wld. be a good one with the "show" on as well as Xmas. However I will go up whenever you say it is necessary.' She also told him that Quinn was trying to arrange an Abbey tour to the USA (see p. 746, n. 1), and that it would be better to hold the Company together for that, especially since 'Fay, & most of the Company, would stay out there—so we cld. anyhow make a fresh start'.

[7] AG had been suffering from influenza.

[*With enclosure*]

Glendalough House | Kingstown
Dec 19th/07

Dear Yeats

I have received cheque-book etc, and your letter.[8] I will see to the deposit business the first day I am in town—tomorrow or next day. I understood the money for salaries was in a separate account now, that could be drawn on by Vaughan and Fay, however I will find out if they need money. Vaughan I suppose is our Secretary now so that it is his signature that will be needed for the deposit money. Do you know if there is any minute recording his appointment?

As to the other troubles, I wrote hurried notes to you and Lady Gregory last night, and I have thought over matters a good deal since. Yesterday in his depressed mood Fay—I think—really meant to leave if he does not get autocratic power. One does not know what he may think in a fortnight. Further in going over our talk again I can see a carefully hidden, but bitter animosity against the Allgoods—both of them. It is the same feeling that he had against the Walkers and Roberts two years ago, and that he has had since against Miss Horniman, and the Directors in varying degrees. I do not see any hope of *peace* while he is at the head of the company. I like him in many ways, in spite of all draw-backs, but I do not think he is now suitable for his position, especially as his wife is using his irratability for her own ends.[9] His perfectly definite refusal to remain stage-manager if Kerrigan is brought back, is a plain issue on which to work, but it seems not a sufficiently broad one. The difficulty of our position is that Fay's claims are logical and reasonable if he was the right man for the position, but are impossible when we take into consideration all the details of his personality which we have learnt by long cooperation with him.

If it was possible for Lady Gregory to come up now—her presence is essential if anything is to be done—I half think it would be better for you to come over and clear things up at once, as it is a matter where we want to work on clear issues, and not on compromises that will only lead to worse confusion. The danger of delay is the danger of compromise, and none of us want an arrangement that will lead to a fresh crisis in two or three months.

I was pleased with Kerrigan yesterday he seemed really intelligent and in sympathy with what we are trying to do. I told him, vaguely, of what we

[8] See pp. 800–1.
[9] The Directors suspected that Brigit Fay was trying to usurp the Allgood sisters in the Company and to insinuate herself into their parts, a suspicion deepened by her behaviour over Sara Allgood's parts in Glasgow (see p. 800, n. 4).

propose to put before the company, and he seemed to think the plan would work. He admits the need of discipline to the fullest.

One other matter. I think Miss M. Allgood's unpunctuality is very serious, but it is not, as Fay thinks, merely agressive insubordination. She is just as unpunctual in everything she does. Further, on this tour when she had her sister seriously ill in rough theatrical lodgings, and was playing and learning new heavy parts, a reasonable stage-manager would have treated her with a little extra consideration, instead of singling her out as Fay has done.[10]

Yours

J. M. Synge

P.S. My Deirdre is impossible without Kerrigan.[11]

I think in future—I suggest at least—that there should be a permanent committee—the Directors—Stage-manager—and two or three of the company elected by themselves, who will keep up a link between us and the rank and file and aid discipline. I am all for more democracy *in details*.

ALS Berg, with envelope addressed to Coole, postmark 'LONDON DEC 20 07'. Enclosure Berg.

## *To John Millington Synge, 20 December* [*1907*]

18 Woburn Buildings | Euston Road

Dec 20

My dear Synge: I will go to Dublin when ever you & Lady Gregory decide. I agree about our consulting the company more in future & was myself coming to the same opinion as that you have come to about a consultative committee at the same time all artistic matters should be outside its control. In any case we had better meet & consider the question before making any announcement on the subject. <My only hesitation> The chief difficulty & danger is that we do not want ourselves to create the organization for strikes against unpopular plays, I was thinking out some such title as 'di[s]ciplinary committee' or the like—a wider referance may be necessary. I have written to Lady Gregory that it may be better for the Allgoods, Kerrigan etc to meet & formulate their complaints in writing—better for us as I mean as

[10] See p. 800.
[11] In November of this year Synge had begun work on what turned out to be his final play, *Deirdre of the Sorrows*, a three-act treatment of the same legend as WBY's *Deirdre*. Presumably he had earmarked Kerrigan for the leading part of Naisi, but when the play was produced, posthumously, in January 1910, Kerrigan took the part of Ainnle, Naisi's brother.

this would put us out side the dispute, & make us arbitrators, & make it impossible for Fay, if we decide against him, to raise a popular cry against us. It is important that we should not seem to be the agressers. But wait till you hear from Lady Gregory. It is possible for us to put the company as Fay wishes into the power of one we know to be unjust & untruthful <& I doubt if now it has come to the present state>. I too think that compromise is out of the question or drifting on—but I wont act without Lady Gregory as the loss of Fay affects her work chiefly. She knows what I think. If he is to stay it should be as a defeated man. I beleive him to be unfit to manage the company.

Yrs ever<br>W B Yeats

PS—I should think the old secretaries signature would do if the new ones name is not upon the minutes.[1] The current saleries is the really pressing matter. I drew a certain number of checques before I left but these are I conclude exausted. We must not give blanck checques as Vaughan wanted.

I have <written> on the matters contained in this letter to Lady Gregory so you need not send it on.

[*On back of envelope*]

instead of the phrase 'formulate demands' or the like I should have written 'formulate greivances'.

ALS TCD, with envelope addressed to Glendalough House, Glen-na-geary, Kingstown, Co Dublin, Ireland, postmark 'LONDON. W.C. DEC 20 07'. Saddlemyer, 256-7.


## *To Augustus John, 20 December 1907*

Mention in following letter.

Praising John's etching of him as an etching but telling him that he expected a violent letter about it from Bullen.[1]

---

[1] i.e. W. A. Henderson, who, although no longer business manager at the Abbey, was still legally able to countersign the necessary cheques for the Theatre's expenses (see pp. 678, 713).

[1] See p. 798. In his reference to Bullen's violent reaction WBY was preparing John for the fact that the portrait might not after all be used in *CW*.

## *To Lady Gregory, 20 December 1907*

18, Woburn Buildings, | Euston Rd., N.W.
Dec. 20, 1907.

My dear Lady Gregory

I have written to you to-day, but I feel so cramped and irritated sometimes when writing, instead of dictating, especially when I have bad eyes, as I have to-day, that finding myself with a few moments I go over the same ground in this, or partly the same ground, for I have had your letter since I wrote.[1] I made no reply to Fay about Miss Allgood, because that matter is sub judice. It is necessary to hear her statement. I am rather anxious to know whether you agree with me that the Miss Allgoods, Kerrigan and Mac should put their complaints in a definite form.[2] I feel this, for the reasons I wrote to-day and because, so long as there is no formal complaint of him we are in the position of refusing to Fay something which must seem quite reasonable to all who do not know his character. The existence of a formal complaint at once changes the situation and complicates the thing for him very greatly should he desire to appe[a]l to the public against us. So far as I can see it is better also for our chances of keeping Fay. At the present moment he has a sense of grievance probably against us. He would probably feel that we, alone, for the sake of unpopular plays or some such thing are withholding him from his legitimate authority. If there is a formal complaint upon the other hand we are in a better position with him, as well as in a better position with the company for we interfere to protect one party from the other, and we are the antagonist of neither party. They may be unreasonable towards each other, but they will be reasonable to us, and we win the gratitude of the party whose side we take in case of there being a split. We ought to hear everybody's suggestions and choose amongst them. A hint from Synge would I have no doubt result in grievances taking a definite form. At the present moment I have Fay's complaint against Sally Allgood and Molly Allgood, and I know that complaint, however true in itself, to be complicated by misrepresentation, and yet if we refuse Fay redress we are distinct[l]y failing to uphold our stage manager in what is, on the face of it, a legitimate complaint. We have no official knowledge of the other side and can hardly act on gossip. The sooner we get that official knowledge the better. We can then proceed to invite, according to the resolution of the last Directors Meeting, the general body to appoint three members to confer with us, or with us and

---

[1] AG had written on 'Thursday' (19 Dec 1907) wondering what reply WBY had made to Fay's letter of 17 Dec (see pp. 805–6).

[2] AG did agree, and wrote to Synge on 21 Dec recommending this course of action (see p. 814, n. 6).

Fay on the situation.[3] Fay will be on the defensive and by so much in the weaker position. I want to qualify what I wrote in the postscript about Synge's motives.[4] He is an unintelligible creature, but I think he has some feeling of my wasted time and still more of yours. I said to him in Dublin, that I did not think either of us could endure the undisciplined state of the company without losing more than we would gain. I remember he agreed to this. I told him that you would be the main sufferer and I think he honestly feels that. We have so much to blame Vaughan for that I don't want to blame him unjustly. He may have thought that he had done all that was necessary in sending accounts to me, which he did pretty regularly, though he missed a time or two at the end. I have been keeping them to take round to Miss Horniman who has had weekly accounts but not daily. I rather thought that you had written and expostulated and were getting your duplicate set. I have been hoping, though vainly, to get some suggestion from her or new offer. I have been rather working towards her financing an American tour for us, but she has made no hint and so I have remained silent.

I have written to Augustus John praising the etching as an etching but telling him that I expect a violent letter about it from Bullen. I am going out to-night to see Ricketts and Shannon. As I can't find Robert I shall have to try if I can do anything myself. There is no particular hurry about the portrait, but it is better to propose both that and the sketch together.

I dined last night with Norreys-Connell, who will come over when we want him, but seems anxious for rather a large caste. I described Power to him and he seemed to think he would be the right man for Black Mike, but he wouldn't hear of Fay in the part. However if we lose both Fay and Vaughan we may find it difficult to caste it.[5] <and I am not quite sure>

I feel that the sooner we get rid of Vaughan the better.

I am told that Augustus John, under the pressure of his friends has decided to marry number 2, but says that he must first mourn a year for number 1. As he has never parted from number 2 all the time, it shows a charming sense of appearances which one did not expect.[6]

Yrs ever
W B Yeats

---

[3] See pp. 784-5.     [4] See p. 814.

[5] Ambrose Power moved in and out of the Company. He had not accompanied them on their recent tour to Manchester, Glasgow, and Edinburgh, and had in fact acted for the rival Theatre of Ireland, taking the part of Naisi in AE's *Deirdre* on 13 and 14 Dec. He did, however, play the part of Black Mike (see p. 638, 640, n. 1) in the first production of *The Piper* on 13 Feb 1908. Including extras, the play had a cast of fourteen. Connell did not want Fay in the part because he knew that he did not like the play (see pp. 767, n. 1, 769, n. 2).

[6] After the death of his wife Ida following childbirth on 14 March of this year (see p. 728, n. 2) John had oscillated between Dorelia McNeill and Alick Schepeler, a London secretary, later WBY's mistress, with whom he had been infatuated for over a year. He had planned to escape Ida and Dorelia by setting up with Alick and Frieda Block in Paris, but the affair came to an end in January 1908.

[*In WBY's hand*]
If you aggree with what I say about a formal complaint please write to
Synge.[7]

TLS Berg.

## To Lady Gregory, [*23 December 1907*]

18 Woburn Buildings | Euston Road | London.
Monday

My dear Lady Gregory: I enclose a letter from Quinn which I think puts
America somewhat into the distance again.[1] I dont feal I can write to Fay
about Kerrigan. First of all I have just found Fay out in a big fable & do not
want to ask favours.[2] Then it is really our business & not Fays. Kerrigan has
resigned & we can do nothing unless he formally write in to one of us & ask
to be re-instated.[3] Then what if Fay say[s] he will go at once if we re-instate
Kerrigan even in this temporary way? If you like to ask Fay to do it well &
good but I cannot—not only for that lies sake but because I think he is
more likely to make impossible demands & therefore to go if we all start
humouring him. He will feal indespensable especially with America in the
wind. I see no objection to your writing if you like. I spent three full hours
yesterday trying to write to Fay about Kerrigan & America & then in trying
to explain to you why I could not—finally I destroyed the letters. If we lose
Fay it will be a great loss but it will be a rest to our nerves & that will be
much. I would not consent to that Galway programe but insist on Canavans. <I am writting to Synge on subject> If you agree [I] will write Fay &

---

[7]  AG did write to Synge on receiving this letter (see p. 814, n. 6).

[1]  Judge Keogh's proposal to bring the Abbey Company to the USA had roused Quinn's interest in
the ways and means of doing this, and AG had been sending WBY extracts from his letters on this topic.
On 20 Dec she told WBY (Berg) that Quinn had spoken 'about the company going out, and says "I will
go through the matter with Tyler soon after Xmas." So we had better not hurry a crisis—for we
couldn't go there without the Fays.' And in a letter of 22 Dec (Berg) she quoted at length from the same
letter.

[2]  Synge's letter of 19 Dec had asserted that Fay absolutely refused to have Kerrigan back (see p. 815),
but AG had written to WBY the previous day that she was 'of opinion you ought to write to Fay saying
we intend to hold a meeting in January to decide on best means of keeping discipline. That it is your
wish & the wish of directors, he should arrange with Kerrigan to stay on until after that date.' Despite
Synge's misgivings, she held to this view and on 20 Dec told WBY, 'I still think you had better write
about the January meeting and about keeping Kerrigan on for it.' Fay's 'big fable' was his assertion that
the fires in the Abbey had been lit at the proper times (see pp. 801–2, 805–6).

[3]  In her reply to this letter on 26 Dec (Berg), AG wrote: 'I did not mean you to *ask* Fay to keep
Kerrigan, but merely to say, as a business matter, he had better arrange for him to stop until we have
made our proposals. However Synge will do all he can to keep him, so I daresay we needn't interfere.'

Synge. It should be tried in the country while we have Fay.[4] I will write to John as you suggest.[5] Ricketts told me that John tried to bring a No 3 into the house but No 2 said it was not fair to M^rs John & became a perfect fury on the subject, & so kept No 3 out.[6] Bullen of course refuses the John picture with violent language.[7]

Yr ever
W B Yeats

[*With enclosure*]

Dec 13 1907

Dec. 13 1907

My dear Yeats: Your plays weren't put on this week. I thought they would be put on Monday and Tuesday, but the theatre was closed Monday and Tuesday and it opened Wednesday for the revival of *Candida*.[8] Liebler & Company have sent me a check for $80, which is at the rate of $5 a performance for each of the two plays. There were six evening performances and two matinees, and at the rate of $10 a performance the total eight performances amounted to $80. I have accordingly obtained a Dublin draft to your order for the full amount thereof, which is £16 8s. 7d. and which I enclose you herewith. I hope that you will receive this in time to use it for Christmas presents.[9]

---

[4] Fay and Vaughan had set their own agenda for the Abbey's tour to Galway, in defiance of WBY and AG who wanted a country production of her play *The Canavans* (see pp. 785, n. 2, 792). The final programme, presented at the Court Theatre from 6 to 10 Jan, was *Riders to the Sea*, *The Rising of the Moon*, *The Hour-Glass*, and *Hyacinth Halvey*.

[5] On 'Saturday' (21 Dec 1907; Berg) a distinctly underwhelmed AG had written in consternation about the Augustus John etching: 'The etching has only now arrived — it is a horror — the features don't seem to belong to each other, and there is something of the same pained look he has got into mine. . . . If it is a tinker it is one in the dock, and not enjoying his chicken stealing. What do you think of telling John that I had reminded you he had promised to do 2 or 3 to choose from? It is not very likely there will be one fit for the book, but it is possible, and anyhow there might be one that we could see people buy with resignation. I hope Shannon's may turn out all right.' On 'Monday' (23 Dec 1907; Berg) she reported that Robert, who had just arrived to spend Christmas at Coole, 'thinks the etching *bad*, says just as I do there is no composition, He saw John who told him "Yeats is delighted with it". I really think you had better ask him for the others he promised to choose from.' AG eventually sold the portrait, but not until 26 June 1928, when she recorded that 'Oliver Brown of the Leicester Galleries writes that he has at last sold John's portrait of Yeats "to a public Gallery". Doesn't say for how much but I am glad it is to a Gallery. I don't really like it and there is no regret in parting with it (*Journals* II. 283).

[6] See p. 738, n. 14.

[7] WBY carried on an unsuccessful campaign through the first half of 1908 to persuade Bullen to use a John sketch in *CW*. On 8 Aug 1908 (Kansas) he told him that 'I am myself not a Johnite. His work is an expression, as are Ibsens plays, of the school opposed to everything I care for or try to accomplish myself but that hardly comes into the matter, especially as I have enough portraits to balance this particular impression. I look on John as a painter who has a profound instinct for selecting the decaying elements to represent, but his picture exists, cannot be got rid of, and will I believe strengthen the edition.'

[8] See p. 812.

[9] These were the royalties for Margaret Wycherly's New York productions of *Cathleen ni Houlihan* and *The Hour-Glass*.

Miss Wycherly was a distinct disappointment to me. I had never seen her before.[10] However, no harm has been done by the giving of the plays, and sometime in the course of the next two or three months I hope to be able to have a talk with George Tyler of Liebler & Company, a man of some ideas,[11] in regard to the company generally. I should like sometime to have the Fays send me or to have you send me a list of all the plays that you are doing. I cannot do anything with this for the next two or three months. It is almost impossible for me to get time to write a letter to my sister and I don't want to enter now into any correspondence with the Fays about it. In my judgment the thing cannot be done unless some theatrical manager is interested. As I think I wrote you, or as I wrote Judge Keogh, the key to the situation is the securing of a chain of theatres in several of the large cities.[12] Unless this is done you would find the company here ready to act, but with no stage. The time of all the different theatres is booked up solidly for every week and every day of every week and in many cases every Sunday of every week, from the beginning of the theatrical season until the end. You must therefore start with the fact that you must interest someone of the big managers (the Jews say "producers") of dramatic companies who have a chain of theatres or who can get time at different theatres. If you can interest them at all, you can interest them sufficiently to put it on a business basis, which means paying the expenses of the actors over here and their salaries while here. Novelli, the Italian actor,[13] is here now, and came under a guaranty. The same was true of Duse and her company[14] and the same is true of a dozen French and German companies that have been here in the last two or three years. In no case was there any fund raised; they all were brought out on their merits or lack of merits. Some made brilliant successes; others did not. Mrs. Campbell could only get a week's time here this autumn and then she had to go out on the road. I believe she will be able to get a little more time in the spring,[15] but the

---

[10] The New York reviewers did not share Quinn's poor opinion of Margaret Wycherly (see p. 804, n. 7). Describing the productions to Jack Yeats on 10 Dec (NYPL), Quinn told him that Miss Wycherly had 'a very good opinion of herself. Her idea of acting seems to be to talk in a baby way and to half-articulate the words. She played the part of the Fool in "The *Hour-Glass*" and no woman ever yet could take the part of a man or boy and carry it off well.'

[11] George Crouse Tyler (1867–1946), executive head and founder of the New York firm of theatrical managers Liebler & Co.

[12] Quinn had written to Judge Keogh on 10 Dec, advising him to shelve plans for the proposed Abbey tour, and to ensure that when it did take place it was financed by 'proper business management' and not by a subsidy (see p. 746, n. 1).

[13] Ermete Novelli (1852–1919), Italian actor and manager. He had just enjoyed a successful autumn season at the Lyric Theatre, New York, with a repertoire which changed every night and which included Italian versions of *Othello*, *Papa Lebonnard*, *The Merchant of Venice*, *The Outlaw*, *The Taming of the Shrew*, *Louis XI*, and *The Benevolent Bear*.

[14] Eleonora Duse (see p. 604), the most famous Italian actress of her generation.

[15] Mrs Pat Campbell's current American tour had begun with a week at the Lyric Theatre, New York, from 11 Nov (see p. 764, n. 3), followed by a long and gruelling series of mainly one-night stands,

getting of the theatres in a consecutive chain is the real key to the situation, and that means getting one of the large managers interested.

A fund or subsidy or anything of that sort would be in my opinion money thrown away. The management of a theatrical company is a business by itself and quite a different thing from lectures or Gaelic League work or anything of that sort. So much for that.[16]

I enclose you a clipping from the New York Sun of Sunday, November 17th, which gives some of the story about the Knickerbocker Trust Company, the receivership of which I thought was in my hands.[17] It was taken from me by my "dear friend" Bourke Cockran. You might care to take a glimpse through the eyes of the New York Sun at this phase of New York politics and finance.[18] After you have read the clipping I should be glad if you would send it to Mrs. Emery.

which took in New England, Canada, the Mid-West, and Chicago. She returned to New York in February 1908 for a brief and very disappointing run at the Garden Theatre, before going out to California and making her way back to the Mid-West by way of Seattle. The tour came to a close on 7 May.

[16] In her reply of 26 Dec (see above), AG was of the opinion that Quinn had written 'in a bad humour, caused by the demands of the Gaelic League. It seems doubtful if we can ever go out. But one wd like to know definitely. Of course if we break up it means neither America or London.' Quinn had complained to her on 2 Aug (NYPL) about the Irish in general, and particularly that the 'American Irish hurl abuse at the drop of a hat, and such abuse! I came in for all sorts of criticism over the Hyde tour, and I haven't darkened the door of an Irish "society" since Hyde left the country.'

[17] On Sunday, 17 Nov, the New York *Sun* (13) discussed the financial and political shenanigans that were continuing to dog the Knickerbocker Trust after its collapse (see p. 808). The scandal had been revived by the recent suicide of Charles E. Barnes, the former president of the Company. A. Foster Higgins, the current president, had told the New York press that Barnes had killed himself over illegal transactions with another financier Charles W. Morse, who might face criminal prosecution before a Grand Jury. These charges had been countered by William A. Tucker, a director, who, in a desperate attempt to restore confidence in the Company, insisted that Barnes's death was caused by the humiliation of failure not fraudulence, that Morse owed the Trust far less than Higgins had suggested, and that the underlying financial position of the firm was so secure that it would soon become a going concern again. Both Tucker and Morse hinted that Higgins was an old man who would not long remain in post as president. Meanwhile, opposing petitions as to whether the list of depositors in the Trust should be made public was being heard by the Supreme Court of Staten Island.

[18] William Bourke Cockran (1854–1923), Co. Sligo-born lawyer, political orator, and US Congressman from New York, had introduced WBY at his big public lecture at Carnegie Hall on 3 Jan 1904 (see III. 467–9, 513). Quinn described his recent machinations at more length in a letter to AG of 10 Dec (NYPL): 'I was the choice of all the Directors to be one of the three Receivers of the Knickerbocker Trust Company, which failed, and when the appointment was within my grasp Burke Cockran put in his oar and did me up and got the place for his father-in-law, an old man named Ide, long a place-holder under the Government. . . . It would have meant a great reputation for me as well as a good fee. If I had got it I could have afforded to subsidize the Abbey Theatre for a year myself. But my friend Cockran spoiled it all. I am not sore about it. . . . He is nearly sixty and has a young wife on his hands and evidently feels so anxious to please her that he betrays his friends to get his father-in-law a job. No man lives who can truthfully say that I ever deceived him; but Cockran is disliked by all who know his real character.' In 1906 Cockran had married as his third wife Anne, the daughter of Hon. Henry C. Ide, formerly Governor-General of the Philippine Islands and Chief Justice of Samoa.

When Hyde left here I told him that I wanted him to make it plain to the Gaelic League in Dublin that my work had been done and that thereafter I would contribute or give my money, but not myself. Yesterday there came a fat letter from the Secretary of the Gaelic League[19] (with the signature in Irish and so indecipherable to me) containing a lot of stuff about organizing a Gaelic League Alliance, and so forth. This originated with Dr. Dunn, the nominal professor of Irish at the Catholic University in Washington, an innocent young man who has been a student of philology.[20] Dunn saw me in the spring and I told him distinctly that I could have nothing to do with it, that I considered that I had done my share, and that somebody else must do the rest. Dunn wrote over to Dublin and the result is that the Council of Dublin has "consented" to the establishment of the Gaelic League Alliance here with four Treasurers; and now comes to me a copy of Dunn's letter, a copy of a lot of resolutions and a long three or four page letter from the Secretary asking my advice and cooperation, and so on. I don't blame Hyde for this, because the letter from the Secretary starts off by alluding to his illness and rejoicing over his recovery and by saying that the letter is written in his absence and without being overlooked by him. There will be no ambiguity about the letter which I shall write to the Secretary of the Gaelic League. If I think of it I will send a copy to you. I certainly shall send one to Hyde.[21]

Well, my dear Yeats, I hope that this will reach you before Christmas and that it will find you well and full of fight and vigor and that you will have a very pleasant Christmas and a good new year. Sincerely, your friend,

[John Quinn]

ALS Berg, with envelope addressed to Coole, and postmark 'LONDON W.C. DEC 23 07'. Enclosure NYPL.

## *To Lady Gregory, [23 December 1907]*

Mention in letter from AG, 24 December 1907.
Telegram insisting that, against W. G. Fay's wishes, *The Canavans* should be performed on the coming tour to Galway and not *The Country Dressmaker*.[1]

---

[19] Pádraig Ó'Dálaigh had been appointed the first paid secretary of the Gaelic League in late 1901 and retained the post until 1915, when he resigned with Hyde over the decision to rescind the 'no politics' rule.

[20] Dr Joseph Dunn (1872–1951), was Assistant Professor of Celtic Languages and Literature at the Catholic University of America.

[21] Quinn wrote to Hyde on 11 Dec (NYPL) and to the Gaelic League, telling them that organizing Hyde's visit to the USA had exhausted him, and that he had resolved to be 'done with such things'. Without his support the proposed Gaelic League Alliance foundered.

[1] In a PS to a letter of 22 Dec (Berg) AG wrote that she had just received 'enclosed telegram & answered "Best consult Yeats—Am against Dressmaker"—It is awkward—for we cant have Cana-

## *To Lady Gregory,* [25] *December* [1907]

18 Woburn Building | Euston Rd
Dec 24
Wed.

My dear Lady Gregory: I sent two letters.[1] I have answered to Synges that if really necessary (though I would much sooner not) I am prepared to reinstate Kerrigan & tell Vaughan to pay him his money pending enquiery. Fays letter has a tone I have not seen before in his letters—his refusal to play in Canavans outside Dublin is insolent. I think we may look on his connection with us as at an end & that it is not worth losing the rest of this season from the training & arrangin[g] of the new company on the hope of America. Even if America were immediate who would go out with them to represent us. Quinn would never take up the work nor could he if he would. They would quarrel again & perhaps involve us in a heavy penalty with the theatres out there. I dont think we could endure Fay in his present mood at home either. I have made no answer to his letter for though I suggested lime-light for Canavans sake it is at least as much wanted for Rising of the Moon. I wish we could get out of Galway for heaven knows how the work will be done in their present mood.

Vaughan did his work in Glasgow pretty scandalously I hear. It was his duty to count the tickets in the boxes. He did not do so on the Saturday at any rate for Payne's man (they followed us) was made furious by finding his tickets & ours all mixed togeather, Vaughan had never it seems opened the boxes. I hear that Payne as a result will not re-commend Vaughan—that he has quite turned against him.[2]

Yr ever
W B Yeats

vans without Kerrigan—or even Spreading the News—tho' that they might get someone for—That is just what I was afraid of about the delay, some side issue turning up.' The telegram had been from W. G. Fay and evidently suggested that they should take Fitzmaurice's *The Country Dressmaker* to Galway in early January 1908, in preference to her *The Canavans*. On receiving this letter on 23 Dec, WBY had wired that she should insist upon them playing *The Canavans*, and the following day AG told him that she 'had your wire last night. I am writing to Fay, saying I think Canavans wd be best, & that it is time to try it on a new audience. But I had heard nothing from him about it.' The Company generally had a very low opinion of *The Canavans* (see pp. 785, n. 2, 792).

[1] For Synge's letter see below. Fay's letter is untraced, but, as AG reported to Synge on 26 Dec (Saddlemyer, 261), it asserted that he had 'put on Gaol Gate for Galway . . . & says he was given leave to choose the Galway programme. . . . He also refuses to play in Canavans anywhere out of Dublin.' Fay had evidently also claimed that they could not take *The Canavans* to Galway because they lacked limelight there.

[2] The practice in receiving theatres at this time was that collectors, stationed at various entrances, would take in the tickets purchased at the box office and place them in locked boxes. The boxes would subsequently be unlocked by the local theatre manager together with the touring company's manager, the tickets counted independently by both, and the count checked against the numbers provided by the ticket office. The touring manager would then sign the night's 'return' in duplicate, and keep his

I have not answered Fay & will, if I can help it, not write to him at all as I can write nothing but what would make things worse & I want the company & not the directors to shove him out if he is to go. I am afraid that his whole generation in Dublin was flawed—It took to the arts too late to get any kind of habit of work or dicipline. Our new people are better di[s]ciplined because the generation is better. At the same time I have no doubt that Vaughan has ripened the seed. It [is] a pity but we must not waste time now. If Fay stays it can only be as utterly conquered.

[*Sent on*]

Glendalough House | Kingstown
Dec. 23rd 07

Dear Yeats,

In order to draw the money from the Deposit, the receipt, itself, must be endorsed by two Directors and Secretary, then the whole can be drawn out, what we want deducted, and the rest put back, on a new Deposit Receipt. According to Vaughan the £17, is to go into the 'running expenses account' in the Munster and Leinster Bank, and not into the ordinary account of the National Bank, where Miss Horniman's guarantee fund is kept only.[3] I found the receipt all right, but I think, as we have waited so long, it will be easier to settle the matter when you come over. The Deposit receipt is rather a valuable document to set adrift on the Xmas post. You do not give me any direction as to what I am to say to Kerrigan, and he is anxious to know what we are going to do. If Fay is allowed to keep him out, he will try and get rid of any other members of the company that he does not like, by the same simple means, I am afraid. If Kerrigan will wait, it will, I suppose, be easier to deal with his case when you are over.

On Saturday—<I was at the Abbey copyrighting the Tinkers> after the rehearsals—I found that the Galway contract was fully signed on both sides, it had just come in, but Fay was going to break it on the pretext that the Galway man had delayed some days, a week I think, in sending back

---

copy as the only proof of what was owed. Payne would have been particularly angry at Vaughan's neglect of this vital chore, as he himself 'disliked the job at best' (*Life in a Wooden O*, 21). Hitherto he had been well disposed towards Vaughan, finding him more efficient than the bookish Henderson, and in the spring of this year it was arranged that the two should work in tandem, Vaughan looking after the backstage when Payne had to attend to the front of house. In fact, Vaughan was not generally admired. On 24 Dec (see pp. 824–5, n. 1) AG told WBY that 'Robert, before I had told him anything, said he had taken a gr dislike to Vaughan, & hoped we wd get rid of him; & Hugh Lane said much the same. So I feel it is not only our susceptibilities that suffer.' On 3 Nov Lawrence had described him to Holloway (NLI) as a 'commonplace style of fellow'.

[3] The cheque for £17 was WBY's contribution for the extra expenses involved in the production of his *Deirdre* (see p. 800).

his—the Galway man's half of the contract. I did not think that that was a desirable thing to do, especially as Lady Gregory is a Galway person, so I told them they had better go, and got them to wire a proposed bill to Lady Gregory for her approval.[4] Not having Kerrigan the plays will suffer a good deal. Still it is not possible to force him back for the moment.

I suppose Lady Gregory will go to Galway, the date is the 6th of January. Vaughan says we are likely to lose thirty pounds on the trip—that should have been said when the matter was proposed not after the contract had been signed on both sides.

It seems bad management, somewhere, that the theatre should be painted now,[5] when we have important work coming on, and not during the three weeks when the company was away.

Things are now, apparently, as usual.

Are the company to have a holiday, if theatre is being painted and there is nothing special to do?[6]

Yours sincerely
J. M. Synge

ALS Berg, with envelope addressed to Coole, postmark 'LONDON W.C. DEC 25 07'.

## To John Millington Synge, [25 December 1907]

18 Woburn Building
Wed

My dear Synge: If you find it necessary get Kerrigan to write to me asking to be re-instated, (or if you like to you yourself) & I will at once direct Vaughan to pay him his screw as usual, pending investigation. I mean that

---

[4] The Galway tour took place from 6 to 10 January 1908, but did poor business. AG only went there for the final two days, partly because she did not want to precipitate a crisis with Fay and partly because she felt that the programme he had arranged was too nationalistic and too gloomy for her to be able to persuade her upper-class friends to attend. On receiving this letter on 26 Dec she told WBY (Berg): 'I wish Synge had let them give up Galway. I particularly didn't wish to have Gaol Gate there in the present state of agrarian excitement, it would be looked on as a direct incentive to crime. Fay was never told he was to choose programme for anywhere—we allowed him to suggest it for most places—but about Galway you always said "Lady Gregory must choose for there" and I especially remember the last time we spoke of it at the Nassau and he said something against Canavans, and I said "Well we will talk of that later." I think he is looking for a good pretext to leave upon, and we must be most careful not to give it, but to choose our own ground. For this reason I am not, as I first intended, wiring you to stop Galway. I wouldn't like his going to be based on that. But of course it is insubordination.'

[5] See pp. 798–9.

[6] The question of the Company's Christmas holiday had been complicated by the 'dismissal' of Kerrigan, which meant that Fay had to call extra rehearsals for the performances arranged for 26 and 27 Dec.

we can only re-instate him until the whole question between Fay & company has been gone into—we owe this to Fay. If Fay <is found in the wrong> makes no case against Kerrigan then of course all is well. I would sooner however that Kerrigan remain out for a little longer, as his coming back now may send Fay out—& on a side issue. I am very certain that Fay is going out but I am anxious not to seem to push him out. I want the pushing to come from the company. The Allgoods etc should at once ask for a directors meeting or put their case in writing.

Yr ever<br>W B Yeats

As soon as we have the application for a meeting from the Anti Fay party Lady Gregory & I can go to Dublin & we will have our enquiery.
[*On back of envelope*]
Yes—the company are to have a holiday at once.[1]

ALS TCD, with envelope addressed to Glendalough House, Gen-na-Geary, Kingstown, Dublin, postmark 'LONDON W.C. DEC 25 07'. Saddlemyer, 260–1.


## *Agreement with A. H. Bullen,*[1] *27 December 1907*

MEMORANDUM OF AGREEMENT made this <10th> 27th day of <September> December 1907 on this and the following two folios of paper between WILLIAM BUTLER YEATS ESQ: of 18 Woburn Buildings, Euston Road, London, W.C. of the one part and A. H. BULLEN ESQ. of The Shakespeare Head Press, Stratford-on-Avon of the other part WHEREBY it is mutually agreed as follows:—

   1. That the said W. B. Yeats shall grant to the said A. H. Bullen the right of printing and publishing in book form in the United Kingdom of Great Britain and Ireland its Colonies and Dependencies a new book entitled "DEIRDRE" of which the said W. B. Yeats is the author and the nominal selling price of which shall be 3/6d. (three shillings and

---

[1] See above. Synge reported to AG on 16 Dec (*JMSCL* II. 106) that Fay had said nothing to the Company about holidays, and he urged her to 'please write to Fay at once and tell him to let them off for a few days. I think it would do good to let them have a few days rest—to quiet down.' On 18 Dec he explained the reason for Fay's behaviour: 'Fay, as it is, flatly refuses to have Kerrigan back, he is putting Vaughan into the Yankee part! in the Dress-maker that is why he cannot give holidays' (*JMSCL* II. 108). AG, as she told WBY on 19 Dec (Berg), wrote to Fay that she supposed the company 'will get the usual Xmas holidays', but received an unsatisfactory reply from him.

[1] This was a standard agreement and was based on that drawn up for *Ideas of Good and Evil* (see pp. 712, n. 4, 744–5, 1012–14). As often in WBY's dealing with Bullen, it was signed some time after the book concerned had been published. Bullen initialled the corrections and deletions.

sixpence) nett and in consideration thereof the said A. H. Bullen shall pay
to the said W. B. Yeats the following royalties:—a royalty of fifteen per cent
(15%) of the nominal selling price (3/6d) on all copies of the said book
which he may sell up to the number of one thousand (1,000) copies and a
royalty of seventeen and a half per cent (17½ %) of the nominal selling price
(3/6d) on all copies of the said book which he may sell over and above the
first one thousand (1,000) copies.

    <2. That the said A. H. Bullen shall pay to the said W. B. Yeats on the
signing of this agreement the sum of £66.15.6 (sixty six pounds fifteen
shillings and sixpence) in advance and on account of the above mentioned
royalties.>[2]

    3. That the said A. H. Bullen shall bear all the expense of the produc-
tion, publication and advertisement of the said new book.

    4. That the copyright of the said new book is to remain the property of
the said W. B. Yeats and at the expiration of five years from the first day
of July 1908 or at the expiration of any subsequent period of five years
thereafter this agreement may be terminated by either party on giving
three months notice of intention so to do. Provided that if it shall be
terminated by the said W. B. Yeats before royalties amounting to the sum
of £66.15.6 (sixty six pounds fifteen shillings and sixpence) shall have
become payable under this agreement he shall refund to the said A. H.
Bullen the difference between the amount of the royalties which shall have
become payable and the sum of £66.15.6 (sixty six pounds fifteen shillings
and sixpence) which will have been paid to him by the said A. H. Bullen in
advance and on account of such royalties. Further, that in the event of this
agreement being terminated by the said W. B. Yeats he shall purchase
the plates and stock in hand at the cost of manufacture—such plates and
stock to be in good order—and if there is any wear or damage at such less
price than the cost of manufacture as is fair having regard to the wear or
damage. But if this agreement be terminated by the said A. H. Bullen no
liability whatever shall attach to the said W. B. Yeats but he shall have the
option of purchasing the stock and plates on the before mentioned terms
should he think it to be in his interest to do so but should the said W. B. Yeats
not purchase such stock and plates the said A. H. Bullen shall be at liberty to
sell the stock accounting for the royalties thereon as provided above.

    5. That if after three years from the date of publication the sales of the
said new book shall in the opinion of the said A. H. Bullen cease to be
remunerative he shall be at liberty to dispose of the unsold stock by auction

---

[2] Bullen deleted this clause because the large advance which had been appropriate for the unusual
arrangements under which *Ideas of Good and Evil* had been published was not applicable to *Deirdre*,
although subsequent references to the £66 15s. 6d. have been left uncancelled through an oversight.

or otherwise and any profit so realised shall after deducting the original cost of production be equally divided between the said W. B. Yeats and the said A. H. Bullen.

6. That in the event of the said A. H. Bullen declining or neglecting within six months after the said new book shall have become out of print to publish a new edition of the same all rights granted or assigned under this agreement shall then revert to the said W. B. Yeats and the said W. B. Yeats shall then have the option of purchasing the moulds or plates of the said new book on the terms detailed in Clause 4 of this agreement but he shall not be bound to do so.

7. That the said W. B. Yeats shall be entitled to receive on publication the usual six presentation copies of the said new book.

8. That an exact account of the sales of the said new book shall be made up every six months to the thirtieth day of June and the thirty-first day of December, delivered on or before the following October the first and April the first and settled by cash on November the first and May the first.

9. That the rights of dramatization and all rights in the said new book other than those herein granted are reserved by the said W. B. Yeats.

The said W. B. Yeats hereby authorises and empowers his Agents Messrs. A. P. Watt & Son, of Hasting House, Norfolk Street, Strand, London, W.C. to collect and receive all sums of money payable to the said W. B. Yeats under the terms of this agreement and declares that Messrs. A. P. Watt & Son's receipt shall be a good and valid discharge to all persons paying such monies to them. The said W. B. Yeats also hereby authorises and empowers the said A. H. Bullen to treat with Messrs. A. P. Watt & Son on his behalf in all matters concerning this agreement in any way whatsoever.

Witness to the signature of                                          A. H. Bullen
John Joseph Seeney
11 Warwick R$^d$
Stratford on Avon


TS Doc Watt.

## To Lady Gregory, [28 December 1907]

18 Woburn Buildings | Euston Road
Saturday

My dear Lady Gregory

I agree but I too doubt their spirit.[1] I think failing resignation they should demand an enquiery. I am afraid you must come to Dublin too as we must all obviously act togeather. Even if two members of the company should make this demand it would strengthen us.

I dont know whether they are printing for Galway but if they are it cannot be help[ed] & the thing must be changed at the last moment.[2] I think you are probably right abt Fay wanting an excuse. If the company wont complain then I think I must at once re-appoint Kerrigan pending enquiery & see if Fay takes up that challenge. It is of the first importance that we make plain that the trouble is between Fay & the company—
John is doing another etching or is to.[3]

Yrs ev
W B Yeats

ALS Berg, with envelope addressed to Coole, postmark 'LONDON W.C. DE 28 07'.

## To Lady Gregory, [29 December 1907]

Mention in the following letter.
A telegram, telling her that he agreed with her proposals about the crisis at the Abbey,[1] but doubting if the Company has the spirit to resign.[2]

---

[1] On 26 Dec AG wrote (Berg) that 'it might be well for the Allgoods and Mac to send in their notices to us. We could call our meeting to enquire into this, and not leave Fay the only one making complaints. We could then investigate, and do what we thought just—and if Fay resigned, it would be because of the action of the company, not ours. But I doubt their having grit to do this, and go openly against Fay.' She added that she would 'suggest it to Synge, and you can write to him'.

[2] AG was enraged by the programme Fay had arranged for Galway (see pp. 820–1) and had concluded her letter of 26 Dec by speculating whether 'we should be able to put Galway off or change programme as now with the contract signed. I have never heard (till I saw it in Synge's letter to you) that 6th was the date. They had not told me if it was 6th or 20th.'

[3] This was at AG's instigation. In a letter written on 'Xmas Eve' (Berg) she revealed that she had asked Robert Gregory what WBY should do 'about the etching, & he says take it to Rothenstein & consult him. John says he is the only man with a great mind, & would, R. thinks, possibly take his opinion. He will only be ruffled by amateur opinions. It looks very bad, as an etching, beside his other etchings. So Rothenstein wd probably make him try to do better for his own sake.' AEFH was also using Charles McEvoy's influence to persuade John to do more drawings (see p. 789).

[1] WBY was spurred into sending this telegram by the reproach in a letter from AG of 28 Dec (Berg) that she 'thought I might have heard from you by second post, but have had nothing'.

[2] On 27 Dec AG had written and wired WBY about the situation at the Abbey. In her letter (Berg) she suggested that 'the resignation of the Allgoods & Mac would be simplest', since the Directors 'could refuse to accept them without a meeting—then propose our plan of discipline—They would accept it, Fay in his present mood is unlikely to, & we have a clear issue for the public.'

## *To John Millington Synge,* [*29 December 1907*]

18 Woburn Buildings | Euston Road

My dear Synge:

I have wired that I aggree with Lady Gregory but I doubt the company having spirit for that policy—resignation.[1] I think however that they should as an alternative demand an enquiery—if two even would do so that would be a great help. I think Fay is looking for an excuse & we must try & keep him from getting one. Like us he wants to be right with public opinion. Please wire or write the moment the company has made a move.

Yrs ever
W B Yeats

PS.

If the company wont move please wire.[2] I can then take up Kerrigans case & let that be the ground of action—though not so good a one as the other. I dont like time passing & nothing done—as we shall have new people to get Etc. I wish Galway was over. It will be a real pleasure giving Vaughan notice.

ALS TCD. Saddlemyer, 263.


## *To John Millington Synge, 30 December 1907*

18, Woburn Buildings, | London, N.W.
Dec. 30, 1907.

My dear Synge,

The more I hear and the more I think about what I hear the more do I think that we need a signed demand for an investigation from members of the company, especially from Sally Allgood. I don't think a threat of resignation is essential, but a signed statement is.[1] You mention a letter of

---

[1] AG had written to Synge on 26 Dec (Saddlemyer, 261–2) that a break with W. G. Fay was inevitable, and that the Company, 'the Allgoods & Mac, should send in their resignations, basing it on dissatisfaction with Fays management—& then he would be on the defensive'. She had written in similar terms to WBY on 26 and 27 Dec.

[2] There is no evidence that Synge did write or wire.

[1] This letter was prompted by one from AG of 28 Dec (see p. 831, n. 1), which complained of Synge's prevarications, and enclosed a 'not very spirited letter' of *c.* 27 Dec from him (Saddlemyer, 263–4, where it is dated '[30 December 1907]'). In the letter Synge had suggested that the Company were now 'in a less bitter frame of mind', that their objections to Fay were 'not easy to formulate', and that 'nothing can really be done till after Galway'. This was all the more provoking as WBY was convinced that it only needed a 'hint from Synge' for the Company's grievances to take 'a definite form' (see p. 818).

Sally Allgood's saying that she wants an investigation or implying so. Why should not you put down in writing what she has said to you, of what you know to be her grievances, and get this signed by herself and the others. It needn't be particularly definite, the point is that we get a signed statement which will prevent the members going back upon us. It is also necessary on other grounds.[2] What I would propose is, that you enumerate, let us say, the following complaints:

    1.　　Violent language.[3]

    2nd.　　Irregularity at rehearsals, sometimes no importance being put on punctuality and at other times unexpected indignation[4] (possibly this may be difficult to formulate)[5]

    3rd.　　Mrs. Fay being put into Sally Allgood's place in Glasgow and no attention drawn to the fact on the programme. The company are not concerned with Fay's explanation which concerns us, he has done, so far as Sally Allgood is concerned, something upon which she could base an action.[6] What we want is, first of all violent language complained of and

---

[2] Sara Allgood had emerged as the leading lady at the Abbey and had a wide popular following in Dublin, so her help against Fay would be of great propaganda value. Moreover, she had very strong professional grounds for an investigation, in that Fay had allowed his wife to act under her name in Glasgow. Synge had informed the other Directors of the mutual antipathy between Sara Allgood and W. G. Fay, and on 16 Dec said he was writing to her 'to tell her that there is going to be a meeting in January' (*JMSCL* II. 107). He was particularly close to her views, since he was engaged to her sister, but had said nothing of her writing a letter. On 7 Jan 1908 he told Yeats that 'Sara Allgood has still sent me no statement' (*JMSCL* II. 123).

[3] This had been a long-standing criticism of Fay, and had come to the fore again as a result of his outburst against Kerrigan. On 16 Dec Synge had told AG (see p. 828, n. 1) that 'Fay appears to have used violently bad language to Kerrigan and he bases his resignation on that. I have heard Fay on one occasion using impossible and unmentionable language to the scene-shifters.'

[4] The proper conduct of rehearsals was a perennial problem (see p. 667, n. 3), and remained so long after the Fays had left the Abbey. In the course of a 'long talk' at the Abbey Theatre on 20 Dec a 'despondent' W. G. Fay told Holloway (see p. 802, n. 2) that the Company were 'getting out of control & come & go when they like'.

[5] In his letter to AG of *c.* 27 Dec (see above, n. 1), Synge complained that the Company's disagreements with Fay, although 'quite real', would be difficult to formulate 'as they are based on a general and growing dissatisfaction with Fay's bad temper, untruthfulness, and his whole attitude towards them.' Synge evidently brooded over WBY's remarks in this letter, and did not reply until 6 Jan 1908, when he told WBY (*JMSCL* II. 123): 'I have been thinking over the matters you raise. Apart from my personal <fell> feelings I do not think your scheme—that I should draw up a statement and get it signed by company—is workable. They have all different grievances which would not go into any general statement. (2) the violent language was used in heated scenes that are now more or less forgotten or blurred. (3) I do not know how many of the company would be on our side in such a move—. it would soon be known that I (or we) were moving definitely in the matter—O'Rourke, is on the Fays' side, Kerrigan is a very peacable [*sic*] creature, and Sara Allgood, as I said, is quite uncertain.' Synge himself 'entirely' agreed 'as to the usefulness of the statement you propose, but there is no good trying to get it, if there is no likelihood of <any> getting what we need'.

[6] See p. 800, n. 4. During Sara Allgood's illness in Manchester *Dervorgilla* was withdrawn, and her roles in the other plays taken by her sister Maire O'Neill, and by W. G. Fay's wife Brigit O'Dempsey. In Glasgow her part in *The Country Dressmaker* was again taken by Brigit O'Dempsey, but no announcement was made of this change. *Dervorgilla*, billed for 2 Dec, was withdrawn at the last moment, but it

then some definite thing, which prevents the whole thing from seeming too vague. I don't want to put words into their mouths, but merely to get their own thoughts recorded. I don't want to prejudge the thing, but we can't very well investigate their complaint unless it is before us. The meeting to consider the matter will have to be extremely formal, minutes very carefully kept and signed. There is the possibility of an appeal to the public against us and of our justification being the publication of the Minutes. We cannot state the case of the members, they must do that. If they would threaten to resign so much the better, but we have no right to demand that of them. When the moment comes we will restore Kerrigan to his membership that he may sign the statement and have his case investigated too. At least we can consider this. Lady Gregory is afraid and I think rightly so, that Fay and Vaughan are looking for a cause of quarrel[7] and that the cause they will try for is that we are suppressing, or trying to suppress, a popular work like The Dressmaker in the interests of our own unpopular work. This is an issue very difficult to fight, for we will never make the ordinary man of the pit with the Leader and Sinn Fein taking up the case against us, believe that we are not suppressing young talent.[8] How can we make them understand

was played on 4 Dec, with a recovered Sara Allgood in the title role. This caused a good deal of confusion and drew a sharp rebuke from the drama critic of the *Glasgow Herald*, who had had reservations about the acting in Fitzmaurice's play, and whose notice on 5 Dec (4) concluded: 'Those of last night's audience who attended Monday's and Tuesday's performances also must be considerably puzzled as to the identity of Miss Sara Allgood, whose name has appeared in almost every cast. The truth is that Miss Allgood, who took Dervorgilla's part last night, appeared then for the first time this week. Owing to illness, her parts have been taken in "The Country Dressmaker"—both tonight and on Monday—by Mrs Fay, and in the three other plays where her name was printed by the talented Miss Maire O'Neill.' The critic continued: 'Nationalism is all right, but a player, even an Irish national player, has a reputation to make or mar, and we cannot but feel that a manager is to blame for giving the public no sign when there is a change of cast. From now onwards Miss Allgood, we hope, is to be seen in her own roles, and from her performance of to-night much is to be expected.' On 6 Dec, Synge told AG (*JMSCL* II. 98) that 'Fay did not slip programmes or announce in any way that Miss Sarah Allgood was not playing. . . . Miss S. Allgood is not unnaturally very much annoyed at having Mrs Fay masquerading in her name.' He went on to tell her in a postscript that 'a lady reporter got hold of Sally Allgood *after* Dervorgilla in the stalls and asked her if she was Miss Sarah Allgood and if so who were the ladies they had been seeing, and Miss Sarah told her that she had just come, and appeared for the first time that week. The press, they say, is very angry.' It transpired that Fay was not trying to push his wife's interests illicitly, but, as Synge reported (*JMSCL* II. 108), 'thought there would be a penalty if he changed the cast and he was trying to trick the Management. As no penalty was claimed he was evidently wrong!'

[7] In her letter of 26 Dec (see p. 820, n. 3) AG wrote that 'Fays mind must be giving way—he must know we won't give him choice of plays or allow him to refuse to act where we wish—His stand about Canavans puzzles me, for I think Mrs Fay likes it—but as Vaughan was hostile to it his influence is probably supreme—But Fay giving me that rebuff shows I think that he knows he cannot stay.'

[8] This was a recurrent complaint in Dublin, and had been aired again recently in the course of a debate over *John Bull's Other Island* at the Contemporary Club on 30 Nov. AG was thought to be the main culprit, and the success of *The Country Dressmaker*, which had been put on instead of *The Canavans* at the post-Christmas shows on 26 and 27 Dec, gave credence to the charge. As she told WBY on 29 Dec (Berg), Vaughan had sent her Dublin papers with good notices of the *Dressmaker*:

that The Playboy which they hate is fine art and that The Dressmaker which they like is nothing? When the meeting comes, Fay, I have very little doubt will have enough sense to try and forestall our action by delivering some sort of an ultimatum. Vaughan has possibly persuaded him that he is indispensable. Or he may be merely in a temper, but whichever it is, I have no doubt whatever that he will make a case against us. I shall be in the chair. If I have a written statement before me of the company's grievance I can give it priority and force Fay to fight on that issue. If I haven't I must hear the first speaker, or the first amendment. This will be equally the case whether we three Directors hold the meeting with nobody there except Fay and a few representatives of the company, or with the whole company or with any possible arrangement of <membership> attendance. I mean everything must be in the most perfect order.[9] If we met alone by ourselves and Fay were to send in a written complaint it would have to be considered, and any counter action upon our part would seem a reply to it and not the cause of it. Of course I hope the Minutes won't have to be published, but we must prepare for their publication. Fay is a man of genius and often a very pleasant fellow, but he is just the kind of man who will make a very unfair opponent.

We have our own complaints against them, but these should not arise until the company have been heard. I have just detected him in a particularly fine lie[10] and he has refused to play Canavans in Galway or anywhere

'They are trying you see to force the quarrel on the merits of it against Canavans—which is just the worst ground for us, the public wd be ready to believe we were pressing our own work & keeping back young authors. Fay meanwhile is sitting down comfortably till "after Galway"—& seems to have consented to sending the Dressmaker there, so that all the indignation fell on me.' William Boyle was aggrieved to the point of paranoia by what he saw as the neglect of his more popular work and on 17 Jan 1908 wrote to Holloway (NLI) endorsing a recent newspaper comment 'that the directorate of the Abbey "shelved plays that drew audiences and insisted upon the performance of others towards which the public evince no great liking."' Yeats can't deny that *The Eloquent Dempsy* was a play which drew audiences. Yet, on the British tour next after its production, he would not allow it to be played though Fay wanted it (he told me). Then in the visit which they paid to London two years ago they kept back *The Land* and *The Building Fund* till the day of a first performance of a Shaw play at the Stage Society knowing well the critics would be at Shaw's play and the newspaper space occupied with it.... Of course only the directors' own stuff was played at such high critical places as Oxford and Cambridge.' On 15 May 1907 Synge had told Frank Fay that AG had 'protested very strongly' against the Company 'ever going to important towns without some of Yeats' verse plays, the production of which she considers the most important part of our work' (*JMSCL* I. 347). On 17 Jan 1908 Holloway amused himself (cf. *Abbey Theatre*, 99) by listing all the dramatists who had had plays rejected by the Abbey: 'Rosamund Langbridge, James H. Cousins, Stephen Gwynn, Arnold Graves, T. O'Neill Russell, John Guinan, Edward McNulty, George Bernard Shaw, W. P. French, Edward Martyn, Kingsley Tarpey, Colum, Seumas MacManus, Anthony P. Wharton, Fitzmaurice, etc., etc.' D. P. Moran's *Leader* and Arthur Griffith's weekly paper *Sinn Fein* were particularly vociferous on this topic.
  [9] There was no formal meeting with the Fays, as they pre-empted it by resigning before it could take place. On 11 Jan WBY, AG, and Synge held a meeting about Abbey Theatre affairs that went on all afternoon.
  [10] i.e. the question of the Abbey heating (see pp. 801–2, 805–6, 812–13).

out of Dublin[11] and has chosen his own programme for Galway. This makes me suspect that he and Vaughan may have some scheme founded on the basis of Fay's indispensability. This may be all moonshine, but we must prepare for everything. On the other hand the success of the Dressmaker and the cooling down of his temper may make him come to the meeting with the desire of going on with us. If he does we must see to it that he goes on manifestly beaten. So far as I can see we shall have to insist for one thing upon a return visit to Galway with Canavans and upon the dismissal of Vaughan, who is probably at the bottom of the whole mischief, and is in any case a bad actor. I have had a letter of complaint about him from a professor's wife in Edinburgh and my sister writes that he was the one blot on the performance of the Dressmaker.[12]

I am not corresponding at all with Fay now though there are several things I should write about as I don't want to give him any opportunity for raising side issues. I am doing the same about Vaughan, though there is a financial matter which wants attention. For when Miss Horniman's last subsidy money was paid into the bank there was a deficit there of about £14. A sum to meet this should be paid out of the Current Expenses Fund into the bank and if it is found on investigation that the cause of the deficit is a permanent one, a further sum of £14 should be paid in to meet the next deficit. If you see Vaughan you might speak of this matter.[13] If you prefer I will write to him, but last time I wrote I got letters of complaint from Fay to whom I had not written.[14] I am writing to Kerrigan.

---

[11] AG had already told Synge (Berg) that Fay refused 'to play in Canavans anywhere out of Dublin', and had reminded WBY of this in her letter of 26 Dec (see n. 7). W. G. Fay told Holloway that he had to strain every nerve to make the play work (see p. 792, n. 3), and his dislike of the piece was shared by the Company—on Christmas Day 1907 Henderson told Holloway (NLI) that when AG asked him what he thought of *The Canavans* 'he answered "He thought it a poor play". Frank Fay who stood near chimed in with—"A damned bad play".' In fact, Synge sympathized with this opinion, and warned WBY on 7 Jan 1908 (*JMSCL* 11. 124) that they 'should keep Fay from getting the quarrel fixed on the Canavans . . . as in that case he would have the company and the public with him—I do not like the Canavans myself and I have not met anyone who does, except you.'

[12] Since both letters are untraced it is impossible to identify the professor's wife, but the Abbey visits generally attracted an intelligent audience at Edinburgh (see p. 429, n. 8). When Holloway attended the same performance as ECY on 28 Dec he noted 'with regret the absence of Mr Kerrigan from the cast; his original role of Pats Connor being filled by Ernest Vaughan in rather colourless style. . . . His accent was distinctly affected under the nasal twang.'

[13] It is unlikely that Synge did speak to Vaughan, although, like the other Directors, he was sure that he should be dismissed.

[14] See pp. 786, 788, 797.

I enclose my letter to Kerrigan[15] which please send on if you think it suitable as you know his state of mind. I have come to the conclusion that you had better see it.

Yrs ev
W B Yeats

TLS TCD. Saddlemyer, 264–7.

## To J. M. Kerrigan, 30 December 1907

Mention in previous letter.

Evidently assuring Kerrigan that he would be reinstated in due course, and urging him to write out a statement of his complaints against W. G. Fay.

[15] This is untraced.

# BIOGRAPHICAL AND HISTORICAL
# APPENDIX

THE CHRONOLOGY OF THE PERFORMANCES BY THE ABBEY THEATRE COMPANY, 1905–1907, gives an account of the week-by-week programmes offered at the Abbey Theatre and on tour, and not merely the first productions. The list bears witness to the effort and organization that went into the theatre project, and shows a steady increase in activity over the three years concerned as the Company became more professional and more ambitious. It also reveals the frequency with which plays were, or were not, revived. It was a perennial complaint in Dublin that the Abbey Directors favoured their own work, and some critics even claimed that they actively suppressed the work of others that might prove more popular. In theory it should have been impossible for them to exercise undue influence since the Reading Committee had been devised expressly to prevent such bias, but in practice it was dominated by the Directors and after the end of 1905 this domination was absolute. Nevertheless, while WBY certainly did have a higher opinion of the plays of AG and Synge than his fellow Dubliners, time has by and large vindicated his judgement. Moreover, he (and to a lesser degree Synge) spent a great deal of time and effort in helping aspiring dramatists such as Padraic Colum and William Boyle put their ideas into better dramatic shape. They also took risks on promising work by young playwrights such as Winifred Letts and Thomas MacDonagh that they knew would be unpopular. Thus, although Joseph Holloway and the Dublin press frequently reproached the Directors by listing dramatists who had had plays rejected by the Abbey, and although the list contained important names — including Padraic Colum, James H. Cousins, Percy French, Arnold Graves, John Guinan, Stephen Gwynn, Rosamund Langbridge, Seumas MacManus, Edward McNulty, Edward Martyn, T. O'Neill Russell, George Bernard Shaw, Kingsley Tarpey, and Anthony P. Wharton — on closer inspection most of the plays so declined turn out to be either pedestrian or worse, or (as in the case of Colum, Martyn, and Guinan) inferior work by dramatists whose better efforts were welcomed and performed. The one exception is the rejection of Shaw's *John Bull's Other Island*, although there were plausible technical reasons for thinking this play beyond the resources of the Abbey, and the Directors were otherwise eager to produce Shaw's work.

The Abbey Theatre opened on 27 Dec 1904 with the production of *On Baile's Strand* (WBY), *Cathleen ni Houlihan* (WBY), and *Spreading the News* (AG), and this programme (with Synge's *In the Shadow of the Glen* alternating with *Cathleen ni Houlihan*) continued for the rest of the week and on the Monday and Tuesday following. At this period the Company was still amateur and could only afford to mount productions for one week in every month. The first season continued until 16 June and there were five separate weekly programmes, but they were scheduled irregularly, with no productions at all in May. Nevertheless, what was lacking in the quantity of performances was made up for by their variety, and the season saw four completely new productions as well as WBY's *The King's Threshold* in a substantially revised form. Synge's *The Well of the Saints* was produced in February, but audiences shied away from the harshness of a plot in which two beggars, cured of blindness by a holy man, find the visible world so inferior to the world of their imaginations that they ask him to restore them to sightlessness, and an imperceptive press dismissed the dialogue as 'wearisome'. AG's *Kincora*, based on the life of the tenth-century Irish king Brian Boru, was better received, and it was now that reviewers began to appreciate that an Abbey style of acting was emerging, in which the actors 'move but little, subordinating gesture to fine speaking, recognising that in any play which gets part of its effect out of literature speech is of paramount importance'. The first of William Boyle's plays to be produced at the Abbey, *The Building Fund*, in which a son and niece compete for the money of a dying miserly woman, was a palpable success, despite some grumbling about its satirical view of Irish character, and Padraic Colum's *The Land*, with another contemporary theme, the causes and effects of emigration in rural Ireland, was also greeted with enthusiasm.

By late spring it was clear that if the Theatre had pretensions to professionalism the leading players would have to be paid, and this initiative triggered a set of negotiations which transformed the Society from a loose-knit co-operative venture into a far more centralized limited liability company in which the power was concentrated in the hands of the new three Directors, WBY, AG, and Synge. Owing to the meetings connected with this profound upheaval, and because the Company needed time to rehearse for an ambitious tour to Oxford, Cambridge, and London in November, there was only one week of performances in Dublin during the autumn, consisting of a double revival of *The Building Fund* and *The Land*. The English tour was an artistic and financial success, but caused resentment in Dublin, where it was claimed that the Company was neglecting their faithful home audience to chase foreign esteem, and that the new Directors had manipulated the London programme so as to showcase their own work. Back in Dublin, the Company produced AG's historical comedy *The White Cockade*, a broad account of James II's cowardly betrayal of Ireland in 1690, to appreciative notices, but Boyle's new comedy, *The Eloquent Dempsy*, scheduled for Boxing Night, was delayed until 20 January 1906.

By that time the old Company had fallen apart when simmering discontent with the new reforms led to the secession of a majority of the members, at least one of whom, the actress Maire Walker, was a considerable loss. WBY's ill-advised threat to sue her for breach of contract was widely condemned in Dublin where the seceders set about organizing a rival company and were given the rights to Colum's *The Land*. This was counterbalanced by William Boyle's *The Eloquent Dempsy*, a comedy of political trimming in a country town, radically rewritten by the Directors, which scored a lasting popular success at the Abbey, as did another comedy, AG's *Hyacinth Halvey*, in which a newcomer to the little town of Cloon finds it impossible to throw off an inhibiting reputation for virtuousness. AG's adaptation of Molière's *Le Médecin malgré lui*, produced in April, was so successful that some of the audience archly called for the long-dead author at the end of the performance, although WBY's rewritten *On Baile's Strand* on the same bill received a more restrained reception. The Abbey had returned to its practice of putting on productions for one week a month, and also initiated a policy of Irish country tours with visits to Wexford and later to Dundalk. As part of the new arrangements, Frank Fay was appointed instructor in voice production and verse-speaking, which augmented his salary as a leading actor.

Despite this creative vitality audiences remained obstinately small. Holloway remarked WBY wandering 'about amongst the empty seats like a lost soul', and on 17 April the *Leader* counted only sixty-two patrons in a theatre built to hold 562, commenting that 'sixty two persons do not make a nation'. The recent schism and the defection of Colum no doubt thinned the hitherto regular audience, as did the expense. On AEFH's orders the cheapest seat at the Abbey cost one shilling, a sum well in excess of comparable charges at the commercial theatres, which could also offer the best London companies on tour.

The Company also did its share of touring, visiting Manchester, Liverpool, and Leeds in late April with a repertory comprising *In the Shadow of the Glen, Cathleen ni Houlihan, Spreading the News, A Pot of Broth, Riders to the Sea*, and *The Building Fund*. The critical response to both the plays and the acting was extremely enthusiastic, but although the audiences were warm they were not large. One of the reasons for this appeared to be the unsuitability of the theatres and halls in which the Company was obliged to appear, and W. G. Fay complained to Alfred Wareing, a new theatrical acquaintance, of his many but unsuccessful attempts to get the managers of regular English theatres to give the Abbey an engagement. Wareing, who had managed some of the leading English companies, and knew the proprietors of most of the principal provincial theatres, volunteered his help. The Abbey's performances had impressed him when he was on tour in Dublin and he believed that the Company 'had an audience waiting for them in England'. In collaboration with Fay, the Directors, and AEFH he began to plan an ambitious tour of Britain for the early summer.

Even with his expertise and AEFH's financial guarantees, this was a risky undertaking. It was taking place in the summer, a time when, as many of the reviewers pointed out, potential audiences were either on holiday or disinclined to spend long sunny evenings cooped up in a theatre. Moreover, not only was the Company still recovering from a major upheaval in its membership and management, it was also very young and inexperienced in the ways of the professional theatre. This had been one of its charms for Wareing, who on his first visit to the Abbey had found Sara Allgood sewing canvas and Willie Fay and other actors lending a hand with painting and set-building, but a gruelling six-week run (something it had never yet attempted even in Dublin) was to test its artistic stamina severely. That the tour was so gruelling was apparently the whim of AEFH who, as Wareing recalled, 'expressed a preference for certain towns and disregarded the increased travelling expenses and the fatigue of long journeys'. The Company had won golden opinions on its previous English tours, and she as its known benefactor evidently wanted to bathe in its reflected glory as well as to realize her dream of recreating something like the German municipal theatre in Britain.

The tour began in Cardiff on 28 May 1906 and then took in Glasgow, Aberdeen, Newcastle, and Edinburgh, before finishing in Hull on 7 July. Of the seven plays in the repertory two were by WBY, two by AG, two by Synge, and one by Boyle. Again, it may appear that the Directors were favouring their own work, but with Colum's *The Land* denied them and given the parochial nature of *The Eloquent Dempsy*, the selection was sensible and perhaps even inevitable.

Things began to go wrong fairly quickly. The Company was not at its best at Cardiff, where the audiences were thin but respectful, and their high spirits got out of hand on the long journey from there to Glasgow. The musician Arthur Darley had been injudicious enough to present Brigit O'Dempsey with a toy trumpet which she 'tootled most of the time in the corridor of the carriage', an irritation which did nothing to dampen the ardour of Arthur Sinclair, who 'was drunk at Cardiff station & wanted to travel with Miss O'Dempsey. Mr Wareing objected, & put him in a compartment at one end & the girls at the other & took a central one himself.' Such boisterousness, which continued intermittently throughout the six weeks, shocked the Victorian sensibilities of AEFH and her rather priggish friends, as did Synge's tolerant view of such misdemeanours and his open carrying-on with Maire O'Neill. This unconstrained behaviour would not perhaps in itself have alienated AEFH from the Company; it was the lack of consistent production values and professional standards in such matters as make-up and costume that really exasperated her. She had advertised the performances among her friends, particularly in Edinburgh, but now, instead of being feted as the benefactress of a great artistic movement, she was in danger of becoming an object of ridicule for puffing a troupe of embarrassingly inadequate amateurs. There was, in fact, no real possibility of this since the reviews, while noting that some of the Company might lack technique in the ordinary sense, thought that their freshness more than compensated for any shortcomings. But the fear of looking foolish was of all things unendurable to AEFH and in Glasgow it led her to nag Fay with disastrous short- and long-term consequences. As Synge explained, 'a Mr Bell' had been brought in to help with the tour, a 'profoundly self-satisfied and vulgar commercial man, that none of us can abide. He got Miss H[orniman] more or less into his hands, and at last she sailed round to Fay one evening just before the show to suggest that Bell should "make up" the company. Fay broke out forthwith, and she describes her exit as that of "a strange cat driven out of a kitchen with a broom-stick"! She complains pathetically to me that everyone knows in Glasgow that she is paying for our show, and that she feels in rather a foolish position when she has to confess that she had no authority over it!!' W. G. Fay's flash of anger cost him dear; AEFH never forgave him, and her complaints about his behaviour henceforth became the recurring theme of her letters to WBY. The tour ended with a detailed list of AEFH's accusations, and her determination to have as little as possible to do with the Company in future. It was also decided that Fay did not have the capacity to combine the roles of player, director, and administrator and that a business manager should be appointed.

This, after somewhat prolonged negotiations, turned out to be W. A. Henderson, a clerk in an accountants' office, who was also secretary of the National Literary Society and an enthusiastic student of the theatre. Henderson's immediate remit was to increase the size of the audiences at the Abbey, and he set about this as soon as he took up office. His task was made easier by the fact that in her new aloofness AEFH no longer insisted that the minimum entrance cost should be a shilling and it was accordingly reduced to half that sum for the new season. For his part, Henderson inaugurated an imaginative scheme of subscription tickets and produced a brochure detailing forthcoming plays into the new year. The consequence of these two initiatives surpassed expectations and a delighted Holloway noted on 10 October that despite heavy rain 'the stalls were better attended than any night save the opening ones of the theatre. The new sixpenny seats were crowded to overflowing, and some who sought shilling seats had to be accommodated in the balcony. This was all very refreshing to those who have followed the fortunes of the little company through thick and thin, and Mr. Henderson, the new secretary, must feel very proud that his untiring exertions met with such instant success.'

Henderson's brochure had announced an ambitious bill of translations for the new season, including Sophocles's *Antigone* and *Oedipus* and Racine's *Phèdre*, but none of these were in fact staged. The autumn did, however, see four new plays, and two of them, AG's *The Gaol Gate* and Boyle's *The Mineral Workers*, opened the season on 20 October. AG's short curtain-raiser, in which his mother and wife discover that a young moonlighter, so far from being a shameful informer as alleged, has sacrificed his life to save his friends, split the reviewers down political lines but deeply affected the audience which gave it a rousing ovation. Although very different in theme and style, *The Mineral Workers*, which dramatizes the attempts of a returned emigrant to establish a mining industry in a conservative Irish rural community, was also a tremendous success. Not only were the receipts for this evening greater than for any other night in the Theatre's history apart from the first night, they remained well up on previous seasons, the Saturday performances being particularly popular.

The next new production was WBY's long-awaited *Deirdre*. Much against the wishes of the Company and other Directors he imported Letitia Darragh, a London actress of Irish descent, to take the title role. As Henderson confided to Holloway, she did nothing to endear herself to her fellow players: 'At first she sort of sneered & looked down on them as mere amateurs, & they naturally resented the slight & gave her the cold shoulder in return! . . . Her engagement was not popular with the patrons of the theatre either, & did much to lessen the audience.' Her unpopularity with the audience was caused by the sensuousness of her performance, her low-cut costume, and the perceived voluptuousness of WBY's treatment of the legend. A number of critics even purported to prefer AE's limp version of the legend as more wholesome.

Miss Darragh also starred as the heroine in the revival of WBY's extensively rewritten *The Shadowy Waters*. Her performance in this role was deemed to be much more stately, although the play, notwithstanding the time and trouble WBY had lavished on revising it during the summer of 1905, was once more dismissed as undramatic. AG's *The Canavans*, an extravaganza set in Elizabethan Ireland, was saved by W. G. Fay's inspired comic acting but was considered too wordy and even childish by many reviewers. However, the season ended with a popular revival of *The Hour-Glass* and *The Mineral Workers*, Holloway describing the latter as 'the play of the theatre up to the present'. This ensured that things went on very tolerably and WBY was able to assure Clement Shorter that they had 'trebled our audience here and are paying our way—even without our subsidy'.

Nevertheless, the controversy over Letitia Darragh brought to a head WBY's concerns about the treatment of his own plays at the Abbey. Egged on by AEFH, he argued that his intense poetic tragedies required a different kind of acting (particularly by the women) from that of the comic 'dialect' plays of AG, Synge, and Boyle. It was also evident to him that the expanding theatre needed managerial and administrative skills superior to those possessed by W. G. Fay and Henderson. AEFH was now automatically opposed to everything that Fay did or said, but her reservations were echoed to varying degrees by the Directors and the Company. WBY found both the Fays inadequate for his purposes: W. G. Fay had no ear for verse and although Frank Fay was training exact verse speakers, they came from his classes devoid of passion. During the winter of 1906–7 there was a sometimes incensed four-way debate on the future shape of the Theatre between the three Directors and AEFH, whose prolonged absence in north Africa over the New Year made negotiations even more difficult. The battle lines were far from absolute, but in general terms AG and Synge, who were both more sympathetic to W. G. Fay, opposed WBY's and AEFH's attempts to force a new manager on the Company. Their views seemed to have prevailed when Fay turned down a package whereby he would accept a new manager in return for a financially advantageous redefinition of his own duties. But WBY, with AEFH's purse at his command, would not allow his interests to be thwarted; he fought back and on 14 January was able to tell MG that he was 'putting a professional theatrical manager at a fair salary in charge of the Abbey Theatre and it has been & huge fight. . . . Fay struggled hard to keep his authority threatened even to go on the music hall stage but it is done now, I mean it is agreed to, and everybody seems quite content, even I think a little relieved.' The new manager was to be appointed at the very impressive sum of £500 per annum, far more than the combined salaries of the two Fays and Henderson, and after taking advice in London and canvassing several possibilities, the Directors offered the job to the 25-year-old Ben Iden Payne. He was to direct all the plays other than those in Irish dialect, and was to take ultimate responsibility for the management of the Theatre and for organizing tours.

But, even as Payne was taking up his position, the Abbey was racked by the greatest crisis of its existence—the riots over *The Playboy of the Western World* (see pp. 862–85). The protesters and many less extreme patrons thought that by calling in police protection WBY had effectively destroyed the Abbey, and great numbers announced that they would never again darken its doors. WBY cannily responded by including his ever-popular nationalist play *Cathleen ni Houlihan* in the two programmes following *The Playboy* disturbances and was, as he informed Quinn, rewarded with 'an extraordinary reception from the audience, which was certainly meant to imply approval of our action'. He had no doubt that the fight over *The Playboy* was unavoidable and that it had been 'for some time inevitable that the intellectual element here in Dublin should fall out with the more brainless patriotic element, and come into existence as a conscious force by doing so'. Ironically, the massive challenge from without helped to bind the Directors, the Fays, and the Company together, and fissures that might otherwise have burst open irrevocably in the late spring of 1907 were held precariously together until the following year. Not that it took much to detect the lava seething beneath the thin crust of unity. The volatile and resentful AEFH was always ready to discharge hysterical accusations on her acid-yellow notepaper and the Fays were working quietly but assiduously to undermine Payne's authority. Although everyone agreed that Payne was a pleasant and efficient man, as a better-paid English interloper he faced hidden and open opposition in the Company and only lukewarm support from AG and Synge. A recurrent cause of friction was the demarcation between 'Irish' plays and 'poetic' plays. On 5 March 1907 Frank Fay announced his resignation from the Company on the grounds that Payne was to take over the direction of *On Baile's Strand*, but was reminded that he had already agreed to this and finally made to see sense. *The King's Threshold*, although technically part of Payne's remit, was left in the Fays' hands to avoid unnecessary trouble, although when AEFH heard of this compromise she made trouble enough for all of them. She was even more strident when, owing to an obvious oversight, W.G. Fay was mistakenly designated as manager on new Abbey stationery and she accused the Directors of a conspiracy to deceive her.

Against this background of incipient strife the show went on. Productions were now more regular and more frequent than in the previous two years, and new plays continued to come. In the spring season of 1907 the majority of these were from the pen of AG, with *The Jackdaw*, a one-act comedy, in late February and the short patriotic play *The Rising of the Moon* in early March. These were followed in April by *The Poorhouse*, another one-act comedy that she had written in collaboration with Douglas Hyde. Meanwhile Payne made his debut as a director with a production of Maurice Maeterlinck's *Interior*, the first foreign work at the Abbey to be translated into standard English rather than Irish dialect. A play of pathos and tragic irony, it received excellent reviews in Dublin and delighted AEFH, who would have much preferred the Abbey to dedicate itself to modern European plays than peasant drama, and she urged WBY to include it in the next British tour. Winifred Letts's *The Eyes of the Blind*, which was staged in Easter Week, is a slight, mildly melodramatic piece in which a blind beggar perceives the ghost of a victim behind the chair of his murderer, but has an historical interest in that it is an early example of an Abbey play inspired by the Abbey itself. Miss Letts and her family normally patronized the Dublin commercial theatres with their London touring companies, but earlier this year she had found herself almost by accident at the Abbey where she was overwhelmed by a performance of *Riders to the Sea*. She went home and wrote *The Eyes of the Blind*, which to her astonished delight was immediately accepted for production.

It was on the first night of her play, which was on a bill with *Deirdre*, *The Rising of the Moon*, and *Spreading the News*, that the influential transatlantic impresario Charles Frohman made his only recorded visit to the Abbey. Much was hoped of this: an American tour certainly, and there were even rumours in the London press that he might take over the Theatre altogether. In the event, the evening did not go well. Because Mrs Payne, who acted as Mona Limerick, had been unwell, *Deirdre* was under-rehearsed and the general nervousness at Frohman's impending arrival was intensified when a fist fight between the two Fays broke out behind the scenes and one of them had to be locked away in the dressing room. Holloway noted that Frohman, who 'went unrecognised by Yeats & Co', came in 'when Deirdre was half-over, & a person behind [him] heard him express delight at *The Rising of the Moon*'. If WBY did not recognize Frohman, the compliment was returned, for

Frohman later enquired if Yeats was 'the long, black fellow who was passing continually between the audience and the footlights?' Apart from a few polite words about the Abbey by Frohman, nothing came of this visit, although the following year he was to give an American contract to the Fays after their departure from Dublin.

The last new play to be staged in the spring season of 1907 was Wilfrid Blunt's *Fand*, a three-act tragedy in alexandrines based on the Irish legend that also inspired WBY's *The Only Jealousy of Emer*. It was directed by Payne, who decided to shorten it by omitting the second act, an economy which resulted in a good deal of puzzlement among the audience. Holloway noted that it 'was followed with interest if not always with understanding', while an admirably restrained Blunt plaintively enquired whether it could be revived in its uncut form. WBY did not see *Fand*; by the time of its production he was in Italy with AG and Robert Gregory, taking a well-earned rest after the stresses and strains of *The Playboy* dispute and theatre politics generally. Before leaving Dublin he had given a pep talk to the members of the Company, who were about to leave on a British tour and apprehensive about the reception they would get when they staged *The Playboy* there.

The tour began in Glasgow on 11 May and the Company went on to Cambridge, Birmingham, Oxford, and London. William Boyle had already denounced the planned London production of *The Playboy* in the *Catholic Herald* and the same paper had broadly hinted at violent disturbances unless the performance was banned. This so alarmed the English censor George Redford that he contemplated withholding a licence for the play, news that AEFH passed on to AG in Italy on 17 May. AEFH also wrote to Redford, making a powerful defence of the production, and, while this correspondence was still in progress, WBY and AG hurried back to England. Redford finally permitted the play, apparently after the intervention of the Irish Secretary Augustine Birrell, subject to the omission of Pegeen's reference in Act I to 'loosèd kharki cut-throats' and 'any other allusion derogatory to the army', although the Directors voluntarily withdrew it from the Birmingham programme. Its first English performance took place in Oxford where it received an appreciative welcome. In London it had mixed fortunes; the first production on 10 June was received with great applause and Synge called for and cheered to the echo, but at its second performance on 14 June the opposition was present in more force and barracking continued throughout the evening. After this, the Company refused to give any further performances of the play in London, much to the wrath of AEFH, who considered it a political act.

Payne's position in the Company had never been easy—apart from the sniping from the Fays he had also irritated the actors by trying to insist on punctuality and discipline at rehearsals, and while in London further infuriated them by revealing personal details about them in a newspaper interview. In London he necessarily saw a good deal of AEFH and almost certainly voiced to her the qualms about his managerial position that he was shortly to express to WBY—notably that he considered the Company unsuited to WBY's verse work, and the regret that his own attempts to direct WBY's plays had been thwarted by animosity towards him, so that he had been reduced to concentrating on his business rather than artistic duties. AEFH's impatience with the Company was in any case becoming more embittered. Having wilfully misinterpreted the mistake over the stationery headings, she now went so far as to insinuate that the Directors had colluded in cheating her financially. At AG's behest, WBY at once wrote her an angry refutation, in which he also tendered his resignation from the Company, although it is uncertain whether this letter was ever actually sent. Whether it was or not, there followed three days of extraordinary discussions which finally obliged WBY to define his position, and that of his work, in the Irish dramatic movement.

On 16 June WBY and Payne called on AEFH to suggest that she should set up 'another theatrical scheme', using the Abbey 'as a "pied a terre"'. She considered the proposal but rapidly reached the conclusion that she wanted nothing more to do with Dublin, nor with AG and Synge. Various other towns were proposed for the new initiative, Manchester amongst them, and WBY was tempted to throw in his lot with her; he was not writing fluently in either dramatic or lyrical mode, the experiment of bringing Payne in to facilitate the production of his plays in Dublin had manifestly failed, and AEFH was losing no opportunity to insinuate that Synge and AG were exploiting him to further their own work. He evidently thought the matter over carefully and discussed it with AG, who on 20 June informed Synge that AEFH would have no more to do with the Abbey Theatre, but would 'just continue the subsidy she was bound to, & open a Theatre elsewhere—in Manchester probably...will make Payne Manager, & asked Yeats to be a sort of Head Manager, & to assign his plays to her for a term of years'. But WBY had already come to his decision. He backed out of the scheme, explaining to AEFH on 18 June that he could not change his nationality and that he only fully understood his 'own race': 'in all my work, lyric or dramatic I have thought of it. If the theatre fails I may or may not write plays,—there is always lyric poetry to return to—but I shall write for my own people—whether in love or hate of them matters little—probably I shall not know which it is.'

WBY jumped one way, Payne jumped the other. He formally resigned as manager at the Abbey on 22 June and was immediately offered the same position in AEFH's new theatrical venture in Manchester. WBY was sorry to see him go, and warned him to watch AEFH, telling him that she was 'a vulgarian', and advising him to make sure that he had a watertight contract, advice for which Payne 'learned to be grateful'. For his part, WBY embarked upon yet another reorganization of the Abbey administration, and began by going through the accounts with AEFH. He also put Fay back in sole command of the Company, confessing to Synge: 'I wanted somebody in control over Fay but now that plan has failed and that we have lost Miss Horniman I think we must give Fay every opportunity to acquire experience and amend his faults.' Then Henderson had to be dismissed and Ernest Vaughan, an old chum of W. G. Fay's, put in his place, although with the Directors' profound misgivings. WBY also proposed a new system of programming for the autumn. Instead of one week of productions a month, with additional Saturday night performances, he now wanted the Company to play for three nights every week. Despite Synge's misgivings, the new arrangement began on 3 October and worked well.

Before that the Company reintroduced themselves to Dublin during the fashionable Horse Show Week, for which they revived *Cathleen ni Houlihan*, *The Hour-Glass*, *The Rising of the Moon*, and *Hyacinth Halvey*. Although WBY feared that the production of old work would deter audiences, they managed to break even, if only because expenses were cut to the bone. It was also decided, for strategic purposes, to mount an Irish tour. As WBY informed Synge, the Theatre was 'now a desperate enterprise and we must take desperate measures'; although he did not expect such tours to be profitable, they were necessary 'to make ourselves a part of the National life. There is always the remote chance of money coming to us from some other quarter at the end of the Patent period, and that chance would be much better if we have made ourselves a representative Irish institution.' In fact, the tour of Waterford, Cork, and Kilkenny from 12 to 24 August surpassed expectations — at least in Cork. In Waterford the audiences were small and hostile, and in Kilkenny small and compliant, but the manager of the Cork Opera House was so delighted with the performances there from 15 to 17 August that he asked the Company back for a 'Special Re-engagement' for four days from 21 August. They rounded off the month with a week at the Abbey, where the audiences were disappointing, and Holloway found the acting lacklustre.

An attempt to coax Boyle's plays back to the Abbey by offering him a retainer of £1 a week failed, but Colum agreed to restore *The Land* to the repertory. Meanwhile the Directors went on exploring the possibility of improving the Theatre's international prestige and perhaps financial standing with an American tour. Since Frohman had neglected to make an offer after his trip to the Abbey at Easter, WBY began to follow up suggestions by Judge Martin Keogh, a prominent Irish-American and friend of John Quinn's, who had been cultivated by the Directors on his visit to Ireland the previous year. Keogh now proposed raising a fund to underwrite a tour to the USA, or finding some sort of subsidy, and discussions and calculations as to the sums required continued for several months. In December the more practical Quinn pointed out that the current panic in the New York money markets made such a venture too risky that at that time, but that a trip might be arranged in the new year under proper business management.

The autumn season began in Dublin on 3 October with the production of a new play by a new author, *The Country Dressmaker* by the self-effacing Kerry playwright George Fitzmaurice. Fitzmaurice, who saw himself as a disciple of Synge, had expected the play to cause as much trouble as *The Playboy*, a view which WBY evidently shared as he warned him that 'they would require 200 police when they produced his play'. In fact, rather to WBY's chagrin, the audience were so enchanted with this three-act peasant comedy, in which true love triumphs over double-dealing and forgery, that it had to be retained for further performances, and Holloway bore witness to the applause which 'followed each act, & repeated calls for author at the end had to be acceded to before the audience would be satisfied'. The return of Colum's popular play *The Land*, slightly revised in the second act, was also greeted with loud and continuous calls for the author at the closing curtain, and helped to retain the audience attracted by Fitzmaurice.

Shortly before the production of *The Land*, the Directors had adopted the shrewd practice of the 'Professional Matinée' to which visiting London companies and certain distinguished locals were invited as guests, while the remaining seats were made available to a paying audience which wanted to gawk at the visiting celebrities. This not only raised the profile of the Company among famous actors with an international following, but also introduced or reintroduced the leading lights in Dublin life to the habit of attending the Abbey, besides attracting any amount of free publicity in the Dublin press. The first such matinée was mounted for the Beerbohm Tree and Forbes-Robertson companies on 11 October, while the second, on 25 October, caused even more excitement when Mrs Patrick Campbell, the guest of honour, sensationally announced as the audience was dispersing that she would take the title role in WBY's *Deirdre* the following year. The *Irish Independent* reported that WBY was so plainly overjoyed that 'one expression of gratitude to Mrs. Pat tumbled over the other', and he repeated these feelings of profound appreciation in a private letter to Florence Farr: 'It is a really beautiful thing of her to come into our little Theatre and play there bringing us her great name and her great fame—A beautiful romantic thing. You do not often see me in this mood but I am really touched.'

There were two new productions before Christmas. On 31 October Sara Allgood took the title role in AG's one-act historical tragedy *Dervorgilla*, which was presented with a revised version of her three-act comedy *The Canavans*. The plot of *Dervorgilla*, in which the now aged Queen of Breffney reflects upon her life and her adulterous love affair with Diarmuid MacMurrough, which resulted in the Anglo–Norman invasion of Ireland, was generally thought to be moving but essentially undramatic, while the rewritten *Canavans* was pronounced no improvement on the widely derided first version. *The Unicorn from the Stars*, a rewriting of *Where There Is Nothing* by WBY and AG so radical that it constituted a new work, was staged for the first time three weeks later. It attracted very small audiences, partly because it was competing with Shaw's *John Bull's Other Island* at the Theatre Royal, but also because of overwhelmingly hostile reviews. Although the *Evening Herald* thought it 'one of the most striking plays yet produced by the I.N.T.S.', other commentators dismissed it variously as 'the ravings of a maniac', 'a hopeless conglomeration of unmeaning phrases and wild speech', and as being 'all dreariness set forth in the dreariest way'.

The unpopularity of *The Canavans* and *The Unicorn from the Stars*, as well as the muted reception of *Dervorgilla*, further lowered the morale of an already depressed and fractious Company. Through the autumn the laxity in the conduct of rehearsals noted by Payne had grown worse under W. G. Fay's erratic management and the Directors had to close the Theatre in September until an adequate programme could be prepared. Later in the autumn Beerbohm Tree offered to attend a rehearsal and give his advice, and WBY also consulted the English director Philip Carr for guidance growing out of his rehearsal practice at the Royalty and Great Queen Street theatres. This aggravated the already simmering trouble between W. G. Fay and the Directors, and Ernest Vaughan confided to Holloway that he and the Fays were 'quite sick of the Yeats–Gregory management.

Willie Fay thinks them both off their heads.' But for their part the Company were growing quite sick of Fay's stage management, and especially of his violent temper and dictatorial manner.

These problems came to a crisis during the Advent tour to Manchester, Glasgow, and Edinburgh, which began on 26 November. On 1 December, at the end of the week in Manchester, Fay confronted the Directors with five peremptory demands that would have given him absolute power over the Company: he stipulated that all contracts should be cancelled forthwith and those wishing to re-engage be required to apply to him; that all future contracts should be for one season only and be terminable at a fortnight's notice on either side; that any special actors requested by the Directors for specific performances should be hired by him; that he should have the power to dismiss members of the Company; and that there should 'be no appeal to any other authority than mine by the people engaged by me on all matters dealt with in their contracts'. Although Fay later defended these terms as 'the usual power of a manager and producer', they were wholly unrealistic in the present context, and when the Directors met on 4 Dec to frame their answer they turned down all his requests for increased powers, although they quite agreed that 'an improvement in discipline is necessary'. They advocated that this should be brought about democratically rather than autocratically, and suggested that the Company should elect a committee of three to discuss the question in consultation with the Stage Manager and Directors, and that any rules subsequently drawn up should be put to the Company as a whole for their decision. They also insisted that the Company (and here they were aiming at Fay more than the other actors) should accept that the Abbey was 'a theatre for intellectual drama, whatever unpopularity that may involve', and that anyone who had difficulty accepting this should resign. They also specified that in future a Director must always accompany the Company on major tours.

It might have been supposed that this brisk exchange would settle the dispute one way or another. Certainly AG believed that Fay had 'completely delivered himself into our hands by that proposal of his': 'We might dismiss him tomorrow on it, and I doubt that even his brother would blame us. I think he is either crazed or has been worked up by Vaughan and Mrs Fay for their own ends. Now, we want re-organization and a new start, and we can do it, and have the company with us on this question.' But it was not that easy. Although the Company returned from the Advent tour with a long charge-sheet against Fay, they were reluctant to press the charges home or bring things to a head. AG was also reluctant to act too precipitately against Fay, as he would be crucial if they were to mount, as Quinn was now urging, an American tour in the near future. She also hoped that in any case an American tour would solve the problem, since Fay and most of the Company would stay there, thus clearing the way for a fresh start in Dublin. Meanwhile, Kerrigan had resigned from the Company because Fay had sworn at him, Sara Allgood was applying for jobs with AEFH in Manchester and Vedrenne at the Court Theatre, and Fay was altering the Abbey's programme against the express wishes of the Directors. WBY was at his wits end with frustration: 'I don't know what to do about Fay.

It is evident that he never meant his threats and that he does mean to drift on in the usual way, and I don't think any of our nerves will stand that.' For his part, Fay was caught in a depressing cycle of resentment, vacillation, and self-pity, and complained to Holloway on 10 December of 'the impossibility of working the Abbey into a success with Yeats, Gregory & Synge at the helm. He was for chucking the whole thing & I advised him not to until he saw his way clearly ahead. . . . He was most despondent—he had trained several companies & had arrived at the age of 35—& had made nothing. Had he worked 14 hours for over five years in America he would be a rich man today & not a poor fellow without a copper. Even the Company are getting out of his control & come & go when they like.'

The Directors felt that they needed the unambiguous support of the Company if they were to act against Fay, otherwise Dublin would accuse them of high-handed arrogance, and AG lamented that they had never before been 'at such a boggy place, no enemy to fight in the open, but the ground sinking under us'. In the end it was decided that the Company should prepare a statement of complaints to be presented to the Directors, but even this presented problems. As Synge pointed out, although the Company's disagreements with Fay were 'quite real', they would be difficult to formulate 'as they are based on a general and growing dissatisfaction with Fay's bad temper, untruthfulness, and his whole attitude towards them'. He also explained that the actors all had different grievances which would not go into any general statement, that they were far from united, and that if pushed too hard it would become obvious that the agitation originated with the Directors not them.

And so things might have drifted in indefinitely, as WBY feared they would, had not the Fays decided to cut the Gordian knot by giving a month's notice on 13 January 1908, and leaving Ireland to seek their fortunes at first in America and then Britain. It was yet another upheaval in the short history of the still young Company, and, as during the other upheavals, the Dublin Cassandras jostled to prophesy that it marked the end of the Abbey Theatre.

## 1904–1905

### Abbey Theatre, 27 December 1904–7 October 1905

| | |
|---|---|
| 27–31 Dec 1904, 2–3 Jan 1905 | *On Baile's Strand* (WBY); *Cathleen ni Houlihan* (WBY), alternating with *In the Shadow of the Glen* (Synge); *Spreading the News* (AG) |
| 4, 6–11 Feb 1905 | *The Well of the Saints* (Synge); *A Pot of Broth* (WBY) |
| 25–30 Mar, 1 Apr 1905 | *Kincora* (AG) |
| 15 Apr 1905 | Lady MacDonnell organized a special INTS performance of *The Hour-Glass* (WBY), *A Pot of Broth*, and *Spreading the News*, all proceeds going to the New Gallery of Modern Art. |
| 24, 26, 28 Apr 1905 | *Kincora* (revised version) |

| | |
|---|---|
| 25, 27, 29 Apr 1905 | *The King's Threshold* (WBY: revised version); *The Building Fund* (Boyle) |
| 9–10, 12–16 June 1905 | *The Hour-Glass*; *The Land* (Colum) |
| 2–7 Oct 1905 | *The Building Fund*; *The Land* |

**The Corn Exchange, Oxford, 23 November 1905**

| | |
|---|---|
| 23 Nov 1905 | 2.30 p.m.: *On Baile's Strand*; *In the Shadow of the Glen*; *Spreading the News*<br>8.30 p.m.: *The Well of the Saints*; *Cathleen ni Houlihan*; *Spreading the News* (repeated by request) |

**Victoria Assembly Rooms, Cambridge, 24 November 1905**

| | |
|---|---|
| 24 Nov 1905 | 8.30 p.m.: *On Baile's Strand*; *In the Shadow of the Glen*; *Spreading the News* |

**Small Guildhall, Cambridge, 25 November 1905**

| | |
|---|---|
| 25 Nov 1905 | 2.30 p.m.: *The Well of the Saints*; *Cathleen ni Houlihan* |

**St George's Hall, London, 27–8 November 1905**

| | |
|---|---|
| 27 Nov 1905 | 2.30 p.m.: *The Well of the Saints*; *Spreading the News*<br>8.30 p.m.: *On Baile's Strand*; *Cathleen ni Houlihan*; *Spreading the News* |
| 28 Nov 1905 | 2.30 p.m.: *The Land*; *In the Shadow of the Glen*<br>8.30 p.m.: *On Baile's Strand*; *The Building Fund*; *Cathleen ni Houlihan* |

**Abbey Theatre, 9–16 December 1905**

| | |
|---|---|
| 9, 11–16 Dec 1905 | *The White Cockade* (AG) |

## 1906

**Abbey Theatre, 20 January–22 February 1906**

| | |
|---|---|
| 20, 22–7 Jan 1906 | *Riders to the Sea* (Synge); *The Eloquent Dempsy* (Boyle) |
| 19–20 Feb 1906 | *The Hour-Glass*; *Hyacinth Halvey* (AG); *Cathleen ni Houlihan* |
| 21–2 Feb 1906 | *Riders to the Sea*; *The Eloquent Dempsy* |
| 23–4 Feb 1906 | *The Hour-Glass*; *Hyacinth Halvey*; *Cathleen ni Houlihan* |

**Theatre Royal, Wexford, 26–7 February 1906**

| | |
|---|---|
| 26 Feb 1906 | *Riders to the Sea*; *The Eloquent Dempsy* |
| 27 Feb 1906 | *Cathleen ni Houlihan*; *The Eloquent Dempsy* |

**Town Hall, Dundalk, 17 March 1906**

| | |
|---|---|
| 17 Mar 1906 | *A Pot of Broth*; *The Eloquent Dempsy*; *Cathleen ni Houlihan* |

**Abbey Theatre, 16–21 April 1906**

16, 18, 20–1 Apr 1906 (Easter Week)

*On Baile's Strand*; *The Doctor in Spite of Himself* (Molière adapted by AG)

17, 19 Apr 1906      *In the Shadow of the Glen*; *The Building Fund*; *Spreading the News*

**Midland Hall, Manchester, 23–4 April 1906**

| | |
|---|---|
| 23 Apr 1906 | *In the Shadow of the Glen*; *Cathleen ni Houilihan*; *Spreading the News* |
| 24 Apr 1906 | *A Pot of Broth*; *Riders to the Sea*; *The Building Fund* |

**St George's Hall, Liverpool, 25–6 April 1906**

| | |
|---|---|
| 25 Apr 1906 | *In the Shadow of the Glen*; *Cathleen ni Houilihan*; *Spreading the News* |
| 26 Apr 1906 | *A Pot of Broth*; *Riders to the Sea*; *The Building Fund* |

**Albert Hall, Leeds, 27–8 April 1906**

| | |
|---|---|
| 27 Apr 1906 | *In the Shadow of the Glen*; *Cathleen ni Houilihan*; *Spreading the News* |
| 28 Apr 1906 | *A Pot of Broth*; *Riders to the Sea*; *The BuildingFund* |

**Town Hall, Dundalk, 15 May 1906**

| | |
|---|---|
| 15 May 1906 | *Cathleen ni Houlihan*; *The Building Fund*; *Spreading the News* |

**Theatre Royal, Cardiff, 28 May–2 June 1906**

| | |
|---|---|
| 28, 30, 31, May 1906 | *In the Shadow of the Glen*; *Hyacinth Halvey*, *Cathleen ni Houlihan*, *Spreading the News* |

29 May, 1 June 1906      *A Pot of Broth*; *Riders to the Sea*; *The Building Fund*; *Spreading the News*

2 June 1906      2.00 and 7.30 p.m.: *A Pot of Broth*; *Riders to the Sea*; *The Building Fund*; *Spreading the News*

## King's Theatre, Glasgow, 4–9 June 1906

4, 6, 7 June 1906      *In the Shadow of the Glen*; *Hyacinth Halvey*; *Cathleen ni Houlihan*; *Spreading the News*

5, 8 June 1906      *A Pot of Broth*; *Riders to the Sea*; *The Building Fund*; *Spreading the News*

9 June 1906      2.00 p.m.: *In the Shadow of the Glen*; *Hyacinth Halvey*; *Cathleen ni Houlihan*; *Spreading the News*

     7.30 p.m.: *A Pot of Broth*; *Riders to the Sea*; *The Building Fund*; *Spreading the News*

## Her Majesty's Theatre, Aberdeen, 11–16 June 1906

11–12 June 1906      *A Pot of Broth*; *Riders to the Sea*; *The Building Fund*; *Spreading the News*

13–15 June 1906      *In the Shadow of the Glen*; *Hyacinth Halvey*; *Cathleen ni Houlihan*; *Spreading the News*

16 June 1906      2.15 and 7.30 p.m.: *A Pot of Broth*; *Riders to the Sea*; *The Building Fund*; *Spreading the News*

## Tyne Theatre, Newcastle, 18–23 June 1906

18–19 June 1906      *A Pot of Broth*; *Riders to the Sea*; *The Building Fund*; *Spreading the News*

20–2 June 1906      *In the Shadow of the Glen*; *Hyacinth Halvey*; *Cathleen ni Houlihan*; *Spreading the News*

23 June 1906      2.00 p.m. and 7.30 p.m.: *A Pot of Broth*; *Riders to the Sea*; *The Building Fund*; *Spreading the News*

## Royal Lyceum Theatre, Edinburgh, 25–30 June 1906

25–6 June 1906      *A Pot of Broth*; *Riders to the Sea*; *The Building Fund*; *Spreading the News*

27–9 June 1906      *In the Shadow of the Glen*; *Hyacinth Halvey*; *Cathleen ni Houlihan*; *Spreading the News*

30 June 1906      2.00 and 7.30 p.m.: *A Pot of Broth*; *Riders to the Sea*; *The Building Fund*; *Spreading the News*

### Theatre Royal, Hull, 2–7 July 1906

| | |
|---|---|
| 2–3 July 1906 | *A Pot of Broth*; *Riders to the Sea*; *The Building Fund*; *Spreading the News* |
| 4–6 July 1906 | *In the Shadow of the Glen*; *Hyacinth Halvey*; *Cathleen ni Houlihan*; *Spreading the News* |
| 7 July 1906 | 2.00 and 7.30 p.m.: *A Pot of Broth*; *Riders to the Sea*; *The Building Fund*; *Spreading the News* |

### Temperance Hall, Longford, 12–13 July 1906

| | |
|---|---|
| 12 July 1906 | *Hyacinth Halvey*; *Riders to the Sea*; *The Building Fund* |
| 13 July 1906 | *A Pot of Broth*; *The Hour-Glass*; *Spreading the News* |

### Abbey Theatre, 13 October–31 December 1906

| | |
|---|---|
| 13 Oct 1906 | Conversazione and Concert to mark opening of new season; the *conversazione* started at 8 p.m. in the new Annex; the concert in the Theatre at 8.45 |
| 20, 22–7 Oct 1906 | *The Gaol Gate* (AG); *The Mineral Workers* (Boyle); *Spreading the News* |
| 10 Nov 1906 | *Riders to the Sea*; *The Doctor in Spite of Himself*; *Hyacinth Halvey* |
| 17 Nov 1906 | *The Eloquent Dempsy*; *Cathleen ni Houlihan* |
| 24, 26–30 Nov 1906 | *Deirdre* (WBY); *The Building Fund* (substituted for *The Canavans*) |
| 1 Dec 1906 | 2.30 p.m.: *Deirdre*; *The Building Fund* (substituted for *The Canavans*) |
| | 8.15 p.m.: *Deirdre*; *The Building Fund* (substituted for *The Canavans*) |
| 8, 10–14 Dec 1906 | *The Shadowy Waters* (WBY: revised); *The Canavans* (AG) |
| 15 Dec 1906 | 2.30 p.m.: *The Shadowy Waters* (revised); *The Canavans* |
| | 8.15 p.m.: *The Shadowy Waters* (revised); *The Canavans* |
| 29, 31 Dec 1906 | *The Hour-Glass*; *The Mineral Workers* |

## 1907

**Abbey Theatre, 1 January–27 April 1907**

| | |
|---|---|
| 1–4 Jan 1907 | *The Hour-Glass*; *The Mineral Workers* |
| 5 Jan 1907 | 2.30 p.m.: *The Hour-Glass*; *The Mineral Workers* |
| | 8.15 p.m.: *The Hour-Glass*; *The Mineral Workers* |
| 12 Jan 1907 | 2.30 p.m.: *Riders to the Sea*; *The Eloquent Dempsy* |
| | 8.15 p.m.: *Riders to the Sea*; *The Eloquent Dempsy* |
| 19 Jan 1907 | 2.30 p.m.: *Hyacinth Halvey*; *In the Shadow of the Glen*; *Spreading the News*; *Cathleen ni Houlihan* |
| | 8.15 p.m.: *Hyacinth Halvey*; *In the Shadow of the Glen*; *Spreading the News*; *Cathleen ni Houlihan* |
| 26, 28 Jan–1 Feb 1907 | *Riders to the Sea*; *The Playboy of the Western World* (Synge) |
| 2 Feb 1907 | 2.30 p.m.: *Riders to the Sea*; *The Playboy of the Western World* |
| | 8.15 p.m.: *Riders to the Sea*; *The Playboy of the Western World* |
| 4 Feb 1907 | Public discussion on the production of *The Playboy of the Western World* ('The Freedom of the Theatre') |
| 9 Feb 1907 | 2.30 p.m.: *A Pot of Broth*; *The Doctor in Spite of Himself*; *Cathleen ni Houlihan* |
| | 8.15 p.m.: *A Pot of Broth*; *The Doctor in Spite of Himself*; *Cathleen ni Houlihan* |
| 23, 25 Feb–1 Mar 1907 | *The White Cockade*; *Cathleen ni Houlihan*; *The Jackdaw* (AG) |
| 2 Mar 1907 | 2.30 p.m.: *The White Cockade*; *Cathleen ni Houlihan*; *The Jackdaw* |
| | 8.15 p.m.: *The White Cockade*; *Cathleen ni Houlihan*; *The Jackdaw* |
| 9 Mar 1907 | 2.30 p.m.: *The Hour-Glass*; *The Gaol Gate*; *Hyacinth Halvey*; *The Rising of the Moon* (AG) |
| | 8.15 p.m.: *The Hour-Glass*; *The Gaol Gate*; *Hyacinth Halvey*; *The Rising of the Moon* |
| 16 Mar 1907 | 2.30 p.m.: *On Baile's Strand*; *Interior* (Maeterlinck); *Cathleen ni Houlihan*; *The Rising of the Moon* (by special request) |
| | 8.15 p.m.: *On Baile's Strand*; *Interior*; *Cathleen ni Houlihan* |

| | |
|---|---|
| 23 Mar 1907 | 2.30 p.m.: *The Doctor in Spite of Himself*; *Interior*; *The Rising of the Moon*; *Spreading the News* |
| | 8.15 p.m.: *The Doctor in Spite of Himself*; *Interior*; *The Rising of the Moon*; *Spreading the News* |
| 1 Apr 1907 | (Easter Week) |
| | *The Eyes of the Blind* (Letts); *Deirdre*; *The Rising of the Moon*; *Spreading the News* |
| 2 Apr 1907 | *Hyacinth Halvey*; *Riders to the Sea*; *Spreading the News*; *Cathleen ni Houlihan* |
| 3, 5 Apr 1907 | *Deirdre*; *The Poorhouse* (AG and Hyde); *The Gaol Gate*; *The Jackdaw* |
| 4 Apr 1907 | *The Rising of the Moon* (substituted for *Hyacinth Halvey*); *Riders to the Sea*; *Spreading the News*; *Cathleen ni Houlihan* |
| 6 Apr 1907 | 2.30 p.m.: *Deirdre*; *The Poorhouse*; *The Rising of the Moon*; *The Jackdaw* |
| | 8.15 p.m.: *Interior* (substituted for *Deirdre*); *The Poorhouse*; *The Rising of the Moon*; *The Jackdaw* |
| 13 Apr 1907 | 2.30 p.m.: *The Hour-Glass*; *On Baile's Strand*; *The Jackdaw* |
| | 8.15 p.m.: *The Hour-Glass*; *On Baile's Strand*; *The Jackdaw* |
| 20 Apr 1907 | 2.30 p.m.: *The Eyes of the Blind*; *Fand* (Blunt); *A Pot of Broth* |
| | 8.30 p.m.: *The Eyes of the Blind*; *Fand*; *A Pot of Broth* |
| 27 Apr 1907 | 2.30 p.m.: *The Eyes of the Blind*; *Fand*; *A Pot of Broth* |
| | 8.30 p.m.: *The Eyes of the Blind*; *Fand*; *A Pot of Broth* |

### Royalty Theatre, Glasgow, 13–18 May 1907

| | |
|---|---|
| 13, 15–16 May 1907 | *Riders to the Sea*; *On Baile's Strand*; *The Rising of the Moon*; *Hyacinth Halvey* |
| 14, 17 May 1907 | *The Gaol Gate*; *The Hour-Glass*; *Cathleen ni Houlihan*; *The Jackdaw* |
| 18 May 1907 | 2.00 p.m.: *Riders to the Sea*; *On Baile's Strand*; *The Rising of the Moon*; *Hyacinth Halvey* |
| | 7.15 p.m.: *Spreading the News*; *The Rising of the Moon*; *Cathleen ni Houlihan*; *The Jackdaw* |

## Victoria Assembly Rooms, Cambridge, 20–4 May 1907

| | |
|---|---|
| 20, 24 May 1907 | *The Rising of the Moon*; *The Hour-Glass*; *Riders to the Sea*; *The Jackdaw* |
| 21, 23 May 1907 | *On Baile's Strand*; *Cathleen ni Houlihan*; *Spreading the News* |
| 22 May 1907 | *The Gaol Gate*; *A Pot of Broth*; *In the Shadow of the Glen*; *Hyacinth Halvey* |

## Birmingham and Midland Institute, Birmingham, 27 May–1 June 1907

| | |
|---|---|
| 27 May, 1 June 1907 | *The Rising of the Moon*; *The Hour-Glass*; *Riders to the Sea*; *Spreading the News* |
| 28, 29 May 1907 | *A Pot of Broth*; *The Rising of the Moon*; *On Baile's Strand*; *Hyacinth Halvey* (substituted for *The Playboy of the Western World* and *Spreading the News*) |
| 30 May 1907 | 2.30 p.m.: *A Pot of Broth*; *The Rising of the Moon*; *On Baile's Strand*; *Hyacinth Halvey* (substituted for *The Playboy of the Western World* and *Spreading the News*) |
| | 8.00 p.m. *The Gaol Gate*; *In the Shadow of the Glen*; *Cathleen ni Houlihan*; *The Jackdaw* |
| 31 May 1907 | *The Gaol Gate*; *In the Shadow of the Glen*; *Cathleen ni Houlihan*; *The Jackdaw* |

## New Theatre, Oxford, 3–5 June 1907

| | |
|---|---|
| 3 June 1907 | *The Gaol Gate*; *Hyacinth Halvey*; *The Shadowy Waters*; *The Rising of the Moon* |
| 4 June 1907 | *Riders to the Sea*; *On Baile's Strand*; *Cathleen ni Houlihan*; *The Jackdaw* |
| 5 June 1907 | *The Playboy of the Western World*; *Spreading the News* |

## Great Queen Street Theatre, London, 10–15 June 1907

| | |
|---|---|
| 10 June 1907 | *The Playboy of the Western World*; *Spreading the News* |
| 11 June 1907 | *Riders to the Sea*; *The Jackdaw*; *The Shadowy Waters*; *Spreading the News* |
| 12 June 1907 | 2.30 p.m.: *The Playboy of the Western World*; *The Jackdaw* |
| | 8.30 p.m.: *The Gaol Gate*; *The Rising of the Moon*; *On Baile's Strand*; *Hyacinth Halvey* |
| 13 June 1907 | *The Jackdaw*; *Cathleen ni Houlihan*; *The Shadowy Waters*; *Hyacinth Halvey* |
| 14 June 1907 | *The Playboy of the Western World*; *The Jackdaw* |

| | |
|---|---|
| 15 June 1907 | 2.00 p.m.: *The Gaol Gate*; *The Rising of the Moon*; *On Baile's Strand*; *Hyacinth Halvey* |
| | 8.30 p.m.: *Spreading the News*; *The Shadowy Waters*; *The Rising of the Moon*; *Cathleen ni Houlihan* |

**Abbey Theatre, 5–10 August 1907 (August Bank Holiday Week)**

| | |
|---|---|
| 5–9 Aug 1907 | *The Rising of the Moon*; *The Hour-Glass*; *Cathleen ni Houlihan*; *Hyacinth Halvey* |
| 10 Aug 1907 | 2.30 and 8.15 p.m.: *The Rising of the Moon*; *The Hour-Glass*; *Cathleen ni Houlihan*; *Hyacinth Halvey* |

**Theatre Royal, Waterford, 12–14 August 1907**

| | |
|---|---|
| 12, 14 Aug 1907 | *Hyacinth Halvey*; *Riders to the Sea*; *The Rising of the Moon*; *Spreading the News* |
| 13 Aug 1907 | *The Rising of the Moon*; *The Hour-Glass*; *Cathleen ni Houlihan*; *The Jackdaw* |

**Opera House, Cork, 15–17 August 1907**

| | |
|---|---|
| 15 Aug 1907 | *Hyacinth Halvey*; *Riders to the Sea*; *The Rising of the Moon*; *Spreading the News* |
| 16 Aug 1907 | *The Rising of the Moon*; *The Hour-Glass*; *Cathleen ni Houlihan*; *The Jackdaw* |
| 17 Aug 1907 | 2.00 p.m.: *The Rising of the Moon*; *The Hour-Glass*; *Cathleen ni Houlihan*; *The Jackdaw* |
| | 8.00 p.m.: *Hyacinth Halvey*; *Riders to the Sea*; *The Rising of the Moon*; *Spreading the News* |

**The Theatre, Kilkenny, 19–20 August 1907**

| | |
|---|---|
| 19 Aug 1907 | *Hyacinth Halvey*; *Riders to the Sea*; *The Rising of the Moon*; *Spreading the News* |
| 20 Aug 1907 | *The Rising of the Moon*; *The Hour-Glass*; *Cathleen ni Houlihan*; *The Jackdaw* |

**Opera House Cork (special re-engagement), 21–4 August 1907**

| | |
|---|---|
| 21, 23 Aug 1907 | *Hyacinth Halvey*; *Riders to the Sea*; *The Rising of the Moon*; *Spreading the News* |
| 22 Aug 1907 | *The Jackdaw*; *The Hour-Glass*; *The Rising of the Moon*; *Cathleen ni Houlihan* |
| 24 Aug 1907 | 2.00 p.m.: *Hyacinth Halvey*; *Riders to the Sea*; *The Rising of the Moon*; *Spreading the News* |
| | 8.00 p.m.: *The Jackdaw*; *The Hour-Glass*; *The Rising of the Moon*; *Cathleen ni Houlihan* |

## Abbey Theatre, 26 August–23 November 1907

| | |
|---|---|
| 26–31 Aug 1907 | *The Jackdaw*; *Riders to the Sea*; *Spreading the News*; *Cathleen ni Houlihan* |
| 3–4 Oct 1907 | *The Country Dressmaker* (Fitzmaurice) |
| 5 Oct 1907 | 2.30 and 8.15 p.m.: *The Country Dressmaker* |
| 10–11 Oct 1907 | *The Country Dressmaker* |
| 11 Oct 1907 | 3.00 p.m.: Special professional matinée for the Beerbohm Tree and the Forbes-Robertson companies: *Riders to the Sea*; *Cathleen ni Houlihan*; *The Rising of the Moon* |
| 12 Oct 1907 | 2.30 and 8.15 p.m.: *The Country Dressmaker* |
| 17–18 Oct 1907 | *In the Shadow of the Glen*; *The Land*; *The Rising of the Moon* |
| 19 Oct 1907 | 2.30 and 8.15 p.m.: *In the Shadow of the Glen*; *The Land*; *The Rising of the Moon* |
| 25 Oct 1907 | 2.30 p.m.: Special professional matinée for Mrs Patrick Campbell's company: *The Gaol Gate*; *In the Shadow of the Glen*; *Spreading the News;* *Cathleen ni Houlihan* |
| 31 Oct, 1 Nov 1907 | *Dervorgilla* (AG); *The Canavans* (new version) |
| 2 Nov 1907 | 2.30 and 8.15 p.m.: *Dervorgilla*; *The Canavans* (new version) |
| 7–8 Nov 1907 | *Hyacinth Halvey*; *The Hour-Glass*; *The Land* |
| 9 Nov 1907 | 2.30 p.m.: *Hyacinth Halvey*; *The Hour-Glass*; *The Land* |
| | 8.15 p.m.: *Hyacinth Halvey*; *The Hour-Glass*; *The Land* |
| 14–15 Nov 1907 | *Dervorgilla*; *The Canavans* (new version) |
| 15 Nov 1907 | 2.30 p.m.: Special professional matinée for the Martin Harvey and Frank Benson companies: *Riders to the Sea*; *Hyacinth Halvey*; *Cathleen ni Houlihan*; *The Rising of the Moon* |
| 16 Nov 1907 | 2.30 and 8.15 : *Dervorgilla*; *The Canavans* (new version) |
| 21–2 Nov 1907 | *The Unicorn from the Stars* (AG and WBY); *Spreading the News* |
| 23 Nov 1907 | 2.30.: *The Unicorn from the Stars*; *Spreading the News* |
| | 8.15.: *The Unicorn from the Stars*; *Spreading the News* |

## Midland Theatre, Manchester, 26–30 November 1907

| | |
|---|---|
| 26 Nov 1907 | *The Rising of the Moon* (substituted for *The Gaol Gate*); *In the Shadow of the Glen*; *Hyacinth Halvey*; *Cathleen ni Houlihan* |
| 27, 29 Nov 1907 | *Riders to the Sea*; *The Rising of the Moon*; *The Hour-Glass*; *Spreading the News* |
| 28 Nov 1907 | *The Goal Gate*; *In the Shadow of the Glen*; *Hyacinth Halvey*; *Cathleen ni Houlihan* |
| 30 Nov 1907 | 2.00 p.m.: *The Goal Gate*; *In the Shadow of the Glen*; *Hyacinth Halvey*; *Cathleen ni Houlihan* |
| | 7.30 p.m.: *Riders to the Sea*; *The Rising of the Moon*; *The Hour-Glass*; *Spreading the News* |

## King's Theatre, Glasgow, 2–7 December 1907

| | |
|---|---|
| 2 Dec 1907 | *The Rising of the Moon* (substituted for *Dervorgilla*); *The Country Dressmaker* |
| 3, 5, 7 Dec 1907 | *The Rising of the Moon*; *The Hour-Glass*; *Hyacinth Halvey*; *Cathleen ni Houlihan* |
| 4, 6 Dec 1907 | *Dervorgilla*; *The Country Dressmaker* |

## Lyceum Theatre, Edinburgh, 9–15 December 1907

| | |
|---|---|
| 9, 11, 13 Dec 1907 | *The Rising of the Moon*; *The Hour-Glass*; *Hyacinth Halvey*; *Cathleen ni Houlihan* |
| 10, 12, 14 Dec 1907 | *Dervorgilla*; *In the Shadow of the Glen*; *The Gaol Gate*; *Spreading the News* |

## Abbey Theatre, 26–8 December 1907

| | |
|---|---|
| 26–8 Dec 1907 | *The Rising of the Moon*; *The Country Dressmaker* |

THE PLAYBOY OF THE WESTERN WORLD CONTROVERSY was of long gestation, but actually began shortly before 11 p.m. on Saturday, 26 January 1907, the night of the first performance. In 'J. M. Synge and the Ireland of his Time', WBY recalls that just after delivering a lecture in Aberdeen he was handed a telegram which read 'Play great success': 'It had been sent', he explains, 'from Dublin after the second act of *The Playboy of the Western World*, then being performed for the first time. After one in the morning, my host brought to my bedroom this second telegram, "Audience broke up in disorder at the word shift." I knew no more until I got the Dublin papers on my way from Belfast to Dublin on Tuesday morning. On the Monday night no word of the play had been heard.' From a modern vantage point, when Synge is part of the syllabus in Irish schools and universities, the reaction of the Dublin audience in 1907 seems bizarre and almost inconceivable; in the context of the times it was a reaction waiting to happen and almost inevitable. It was a flashpoint fuelled by a combustible mix of social, cultural, religious, linguistic, and even generic factors.

The plot of the play, while not obviously inflammatory, contained much that ran counter to contemporary myths about the Irish countryside. A young, downtrodden peasant Christy Mahon strikes his father in an argument over his refusal to marry an aged widow with an evil reputation. Believing that he has committed murder, he takes to the roads, and seeks shelter in a small Mayo village, where the curious inhabitants extract his story from him. Isolated and thirsting for excitement, they are impressed with the tale Mahon has to tell, a story that becomes more theatrical at every retelling. Pegeen Mike, the feisty daughter of the local publican, on the point of marrying her milk-sop cousin, is particularly taken with Mahon, and resists the attempts of a local widow called Quin to carry him off to her house. He falls in love with her, but, just as he gains her father's permission to marry her, his own father reappears, heavily bandaged but far from dead. Mahon at once falls from hero to despised impostor, but seeks to restore himself to his former glory in Pegeen's eyes by attempting to kill his father a second time. Far from impressing the villagers, the actual rather than the narrated deed horrifies them; as Pegeen remarks 'a strange man is a marvel, with his mighty talk, but what's a squabble in your backyard, and the blow of a loy, have taught me that there's a great gap between a gallous story and a dirty deed'. They bind Mahon prior to handing him over to the police, and Pegeen burns his leg with a hot turf to keep him quiet, when his father crawls though the door, still alive. Both old and young Mahon pour scorn on the Mayo people and, to Pegeen's anguish, leave together to 'go romancing through a romping lifetime'.

In portraying Irish country people as sexual beings, as energetic and outspoken in their daily communication, and by showing that this energy arises out of a frustration with the harsh and limited life of the countryside, the play challenges the sentimental stereotypes of the peasant propagated by the Celtic Twilight and Gaelic League. Synge had attended the Sorbonne, where Celtic studies were associated with a vigorous ethnological primitivism rather than the feminine sensitivity postulated by Matthew Arnold and adopted by many English and Irish commentators. The myth of the pure Celtic peasant was also underpinned by powerful Irish orthodoxies. Changing demographic patterns after the Great Famine meant that marriages now took place later in life and an already puritan Catholic clergy policed a strict code of sexual morality to try to ensure chastity through this prolonged pre-marital period. They saw their task becoming harder as rural Ireland was increasingly open to imported periodicals and literature, and vocal campaigns were mounted against the potentially corrupting influence of such an influx. There were regular and widely reported missions led by leading clergymen against such literature, and one had taken place only a few weeks before the production of *The Playboy*. The idea of Irish purity under attack from alien filth clearly had a political dimension, and it was one exploited by Arthur Griffith's newspapers and D. P. Moran's weekly *Leader*, which had mounted a successful campaign to close down a number of Dublin music halls as places of iniquity. Even WBY was not immune from such propaganda and in the late 1890s had claimed that England was now fighting Ireland with the filth off her streets. The Gaelic and Irish-Ireland movements had embraced such ideas enthusiastically, alleging not only that it was impossible to be coarse in the Irish language, but that the language itself was a linguistic barrier which kept Irish purity immune from the encroaching sensuous tides of modernity.

Synge presented a particular problem in this respect. Many of the treatments of the Irish people that ran counter to the national myths were by British or foreign writers and could be set down as politically or racially motivated lies, peddled by those whose real aim was to demonstrate that the Irish were incapable of Home Rule. But Synge manifestly did know both the Irish people and the Irish language, and had spent long periods on the Aran Islands, a kind of Mecca for Irish-Ireland. That he knew the people better than his Dublin critics was readily conceded in regard to plays such as *Riders to the Sea*, but led to a major generic misunderstanding in the reception of his work. Holloway (who compares him to Gorki), Griffith, and almost all of the Dublin reviewers believed that he was a realist pure (or, as they saw it, impure) and simple, and that he intended everything relating to the life of the Irish peasantry in his plays to have documentary force. Such commentators also supposed that he believed that what was true of any one of his characters was applicable to Irish country people as a whole. *In the Shadow of the Glen* had been denounced both at its first production and again at its first printing not merely for daring to suggest that not all Irish married women were chaste but for implying that none of them were. Given Synge's familiarity with Ireland, his deviation from received wisdom could be explained either by the fact that he was using tainted and alien sources or that his exposure by long residence to the decadence of Paris had warped his mind in unhealthy ways. Griffith had insisted that the plot of *In the Shadow of a Glen* was based on Petronius, and Holloway explained *The Playboy* in terms of a creative schizophrenia whereby Synge knew the people were pure but when he wrote of them they turned out sensual.

Undisguised sexual attraction, and particularly female sexuality, was the focus of critical unease, and involved with this was his frankness of language which shocked the false gentility of post-Victorian Dublin to a degree that is hard to comprehend today. Thus it was that Holloway, like many of his fellow citizens, was relieved in February 1905 that 'the curtains have closed in on *The Well of the Saints*, Mr. Synge's harsh, irreverent, sensual representation of Irish peasant life, with its strange mixture of lyric and dirt, for the last time as far as Dublin is concerned', and noted that ever since seeing *In the Shadow of the Glen* he had 'always thought that Synge would be the rock on which the Society would come to grief, and that time has arrived I am sorry to say'.

Although none too soon for Holloway, the curtain had at least fallen on *The Well of the Saints* after the appointed number of performances had been staged. This did not always happen in Dublin, where there was a tradition of audiences hooting unpopular productions off the stage. As early as 1903 it had been hinted that this should also happen in the case of Synge: a correspondent to the *Irish Independent*, on hearing that the controversial *In the Shadow of the Glen* was to be repeated, hoped that that the audience might 'not be rewarded for their forbearance during last week by having this production... again put upon the stage'. The implication that forbearance was not inexhaustible hints that more physical means may be needed to suppress the play. In the year before the production of *The Playboy of the Western World* demonstrations at the Theatre Royal forced the withdrawal of Rosamund Langbridge's one-act play *The Spell* and there was serious unrest during a dramatization of a Rudyard Kipling short story, *The Man Who Was*, staged by Beerbohm Tree. A more serious riot occurred at the Theatre Royal in April 1902 when a production of *The Dandy Fifth* led to eleven arrests, and the theatre being patrolled by the police. These were productions by English companies, who excited a traditional mistrust, but even WBY and his friends were not immune from suspicion. There had been demonstrations at the first production of *The Countess Cathleen*, and members of the INTS thought *The Land of Heart's Desire* too dangerously unorthodox for production in Ireland, and the priests of Kilkenny even tried to suppress *The Nativity* by Douglas Hyde. In 1907 the Abbey was more liable to such disturbances since it had recently halved the price of its cheapest seats, so encouraging those used to the more robust atmosphere of the commercial Dublin theatres to become patrons. On 19 January 1907, a few days before the production of *The Playboy*, the amateur actor Harry Young, who was taking small parts at the Abbey, told Holloway that he had heard 'there was an organised opposition present to hiss Synge's play'. Holloway 'pooh-poohed the idea', and the play, *In the Shadow of the Glen*, being produced that night was in fact received 'with great applause... & not the slightest note of dissention. So much for the bogey—organised opposition!'

It seems that the rumour was right, but Young had attached it to the wrong play. Not that the audience on the first night of *The Playboy of the Western World* appeared to be troublemakers. The Abbey on 26 January was, as Holloway reported, 'thronged' with everyone 'who is anyone in artistic & literary Dublin'. A distinguished audience, then, but given Synge's reputation not an entirely neutral one. According to Holloway many men left their wives at home for fear that the play might be offensive, and these included D. P. Moran of the *Leader*, who also stayed away himself because he 'feared something nasty would be in it' and 'sent Arthur Cleary to do the notice instead'. Despite these apprehensions, the evening got off to a good start with the respectful and enthusiastic reception of *Riders to the Sea*. Most of *The Playboy of the Western World* was also well received and, as Holloway noted, the 'audience bore with it for two & a half acts & even laughed with the dramatist at times, but an unusually brutally coarse remark put into the mouth of Christopher Mahon, the "playboy" of the title, set the House off into hooting & hissing amid counter applause, & the din was kept up till the curtain closed in.' The precise flashpoint on the first night was at once linguistic, social, and sexual: when in the third act the Widow Quin urges Christy to make his escape from the village he retorts that 'It's Pegeen I'm seeking only, and what'd I care if you brought me a drift of chosen females, standing in their shifts itself maybe'. The image is erotic but hardly 'brutally coarse' since 'shift', although at that time giving way to the more genteel 'chemise', was a perfectly acceptable and widely used term for a female flannel undergarment. Holloway confirmed that it was 'this phrase that settled it!' and added that it 'was made more crudely brutal on the first night by W. G. Fay. "*Mayo girls*" was substituted for "chosen females".' In fact, Fay may have weakened the line by putting 'shift' in place of the more direct 'stripped itself' which Synge had written in the final typescript.

From the beginning the audience was divided over the play, and divided by and large on social lines. Even Holloway acknowledged that the 'stalls for the most part backed up the Author's freedom of speech by their applause'. On the first night, as on the next three nights, the objectors came from the new half-price pit and the gallery, while the supporters occupied the stalls and the balcony. Holloway and his friends, particularly W. J. Lawrence, were incensed by the play. When he heard a voice from the pit exclaim 'This is not Irish life!', he agreed immediately: 'I maintain that . . . *The Playboy* is not a truthful or just picture of the Irish peasants, but simply the outpouring of a morbid, unhealthy mind ever seeking on the dunghill of life for the nastiness that lies concealed there. . . . Synge is the evil genius of the Abbey and Yeats his able lieutenant.' These are not words of unexpected revelation but the confirmation of views long held, and so it was with most of the other protesters. Holloway was also typical of others in his sweeping and absolute condemnation of every aspect of the play ('All the characters were the scum of the earth. Not one of them expressed a decent thought'), in his praise of the curtain-raiser *Riders to the Sea* (unaffected apparently by the unhealthiness of Synge's mind), and in his praise for the players: 'I only pitied the actors & actresses for having to give utterance to such gross sentiments & only wonder they did not refuse to speak some of the lines.'

Yet, angry though he was, Holloway was a good deal cooler on Saturday and Sunday than he was later to become. The following morning he met the Fays out for a Sunday walk '& we chatted about last night's fiasco, & the feeling of the actors'. W. G. Fay revealed that the 'players had expected the piece's downfall sooner' and supposed that that 'had he not cut out a lot of the matter the audience would not have stood an act of it', while Frank Fay defended Synge's language on the score that he 'was influenced by the Elizabethan dramatists and loved vigorous speech'. Both Fays not unnaturally 'wondered what would be the result of last night's scene', and Holloway was almost benignly reassuring: 'I said, bad houses next week, but a return when the right stuff would be forthcoming again.' He, although strongly opposed to the play, evidently did not foresee the continuation let alone the intensification of the disturbances, and anticipated a boycott rather than a riot.

And this is the way things might have turned out had it not been for an inflammatory anonymous review by William O'Hara, the drama critic the *Freeman's Journal*, in that paper on Monday morning, although it is probable that this article merely further worked up an already organizing opposition. As outraged by the play as Holloway, O'Hara also contemplated the solution that Holloway had proposed to the Fays—'least said soonest mended'—but rejected it at once on the grounds that the growing prestige and pretensions of the Abbey Theatre demanded a more antagonistic response. A 'strong protest', he insisted, must be 'entered against this unmitigated, protracted libel upon Irish peasant men and, worse still, upon Irish peasant girlhood'. His protest took the form of a bludgeoning emotive assault on the raw sensitivities of his nationalist readers. 'The blood boils with indignation', he exclaimed, 'as one recalls the incidents, expressions, ideas of this squalid, offensive production, incongruously styled a comedy.' He was particularly incensed that Pegeen was left alone for the night with the 'murderer' and, after presenting a truncated parody of the plot, bereft of motivation or explanation, turned to attack the 'barbarous jargon, the elaborate and incessant cursings of these repulsive creatures. Everything is a b———y this or a b———y that, and into this picturesque dialogue names that should only be used with respect and reverence are frequently introduced. Enough! the hideous caricature would be slanderous of a Kaffir kraal.' The references to the libel on the Irish people and the allusion to the kraal reveal that the underlying motivation of the article is less moral indignation than political mortification. For O'Hara, Synge's play takes its place in a genre of covertly pro-unionist literature which justifies continuing British rule by presenting a picture of the Irish as a people racially and culturally unfitted for self-government. The only remedy is immediate suppression ('The piece is announced to run for the week; it is to be hoped it will be instantly withdrawn'), and, tacitly recalling the violent treatment meted out to certain offending British companies in recent years, O'Hara hints how this might be achieved, remarking that if 'a company of English artistes attempted such an outrage the public indignation would be rightly bitter'. 'Indeed', he continues, 'no denunciation could be sufficiently strong. . . . It is not necessary to inquire whether, even if such things were true, they should be brought upon the stage. It is quite plain that there is need for a censor at the Abbey Theatre.' Who or what that censor should be is left to the reader.

O'Hara's article was supported by a letter, ostensibly written by 'A Western Girl' but, given its anonymity and suspicious speed off the mark, probably composed in the *Freeman's* office. It repeated and supplemented O'Hara's charges with the assumed authority of a native: 'I am well acquainted with the conditions of life in the West, and not only does this play not truly represent these conditions, but it portrays the people of that part of Ireland as a coarse, besotted race, without one gleam of genuine humour or one sparkle of virtue.' As a 'girl' herself, the writer is especially horrified by the portrayal of the women and particularly distressed that Sara Allgood is forced, 'before the most fashionable audience in Dublin, to use a word indicating an essential item of female attire, which the lady would probably never utter in ordinary circumstances, even to herself' (a delicacy which must have made for interesting mime-shows in contemporary dress-shops). But the letter also reinforces O'Hara's nationalist agenda ('Fancy such a play being produced in England!') and, like him (although with a calculated attempt to drive a wedge between the Abbey actors and the management), advocates instant suppression: 'It is a pity that the Messrs. Fay, Miss Allgood, Miss O'Neill, Mr. Power, and the other capable members of this excellent company should for once, through no fault of their own, find themselves unable to please their audience. I understand that the play was produced for the first time on Saturday night—let us hope it will be for the last.'

The other major nationalist paper, the *Irish Independent*, was more balanced in its criticism, even going so far as to acknowledge that the play was 'at least the work of a writer with ideas, although he still lacks the skill to put them into acceptable shape'. It found, too, that 'the story is told with such a light touch through crisp and sparkling, sometimes rather coarse, dialogue as tends to amuse the audience, and by inciting their laughter at its pungent witticism prevents them from thinking of the social incongruities masked behind the play of words.' But, finally, 'the whole thing' is declared 'impossible' in its plot and motivation, and, like the *Freeman's Journal*, the reviewer hints at violent suppression by drawing a similar parallel with the reception of offending English companies: 'How would it be, say, if such a type of stage Irishman appeared in a play brought across-Channel and presented in Dublin? Wouldn't there be an uproar, and wouldn't the uproar be all the greater if the author seriously affirmed that his delineations of characters and incidents were true to Irish life?'

If the first and subsequent audiences divided between the pit and the stalls in their reception of the play, then a similar division can be discerned in the Dublin press. The unionist papers, although finding fault with aspects of the plot and as old-maidish about the language as their nationalist rivals, were more appreciative of the play as a work of dramatic art. Much hinged on the interpretation of Synge's 'realism' and the political consequences of that interpretation. The *Irish Times* thought that he had tried to give his audience 'a realistic picture of peasant life in the far west of Ireland', and that 'he succeeded in accomplishing his purpose with a remarkable degree of success'. And although it criticized his occasional broadness of language, it did so not because that language was inauthentic, as the nationalist papers alleged, but because it was inappropriate: 'While there is not a word or a turn of expression in the play that is not in common use amongst peasants, it is quite another matter to reproduce some of the expressions on a public stage in a large city.' Another unionist paper, the Dublin *Daily Express*, found the dialogue 'in many parts sparkling and witty', although, like the *Irish Times*, it thought it would be 'the better for some slight revision here and there', and considered the notion that Mayo girls would become besotted with a parricide preposterous, especially with 'this Christy, a curious-looking little scamp. . . . It can scarcely be true that Irish girls contend for murderers as husbands.' The reference to the 'curious-looking little scamp' reminds us that reaction to the play depended not merely on its text but also upon its presentation on the stage. Although W. G. Fay was almost universally praised for his performance, many commentators drew attention to his unkempt and furtive appearance and George Moore maintained that the 1909 Dublin revival of the play passed without incident because the part was then taken by the more wholesome Fred O'Donovan.

The notices in the *Freeman's Journal* and to a lesser extent in the *Irish Independent* had their impact on the Monday evening performance, a consequence perhaps anticipated by the former, which sent a reporter to record every incident on this and the following nights. Although the Monday audience was generally thin, the pit was ominously full, even 'congested'. As on Saturday night, *Riders to the Sea* was 'most favourably received', and again as before, the first minutes of *The Playboy* were applauded. But on this evening the protests began at a far earlier point in the play. As the *Freeman's Journal* reported, an 'extraordinary change' occurred 'when it was decided that Mahon was to remain during the night in Flaherty's public house, the only other inmate of which would be the publican's daughter'. This incident, which had aroused no antagonism at the first perform-ance, had been specifically condemned in O'Hara's article and now sparked an 'uproar' of 'gigantic dimensions': 'stamping, boohing, vociferations in Gaelic, and the striking of seats with sticks were universal in the gallery and pit.' W. G. Fay stopped the play and came down to the footlights. Although receiving 'anything but a cordial reception', he managed to call for the play to be heard and offered their money back to those who did not like it. But money was not the issue: as they made plain, what the protesters wanted was to suppress the play altogether ('We protest against the play going on. We won't have it'). When Fay insisted that there were people present who wanted to see the play and that if they were not permitted to do so he would 'pull the curtain down, and have the disturbers removed', a voice retorted 'If you don't pull the curtain down we will pull it down for you (deafening cheers)'.

Cries were then raised of 'Where is the author? Bring him out, and we will deal with him.'

Mr. Fay—What do you want the author for? You can have your money back.

Hundreds of Voices—We don't want the money. It is a libel on the National Theatre. We never expected this of the Abbey.

This last cry also betrays the influence of the press: both O'Hara and the *Irish Independent* had been indignant that this play was not the usual English libel but was being produced at an institution that claimed to be an Irish National Theatre.

At this point the Abbey management called the police, but it was some time before they arrived, and not until a quarter of an hour later 'close on a dozen policemen entered the theatre and took up a position commanding the left side of the pit, whilst another body of constables were stationed outside the building. Their advent was hailed with a torrent of boos.' The performance resumed, but in dumb-show, since not a word could be heard, and 'cries of "Sinn Fein for ever" were strenuously uttered'. The management lost its nerve and when the curtain was lowered at the end of the first act in obedience to 'some apparently mystic sign or command, the constables turned right about and marched in stately style out of the building'. The pit and gallery, supposing that they had won, 'signalised their success by triumphant yells, shouts, tramping of feet, and the belabouring of seats and walls with sturdy sticks, mingled with the singing of "The West's Awake", "A Nation Once Again" and such like well-known patriotic compositions, in which nearly all the audience joined.' The second and third acts received similar treat-ment, and no word was heard 'owing to the din created by the audience, many of whom cried—"Sinn Fein"; "Sinn Fein Amhain"—and "Kill the Author". Still the author was adamant, and despite many personal calls to him, he refused to make a speech, and the final curtain fell amid a scene of great disorder in the house.'

The audience remained on after the play, excitedly gloating and expressing 'their elation in energetic outbursts in both Irish and English on the success they had achieved, and energetically declared that they would adopt a similar attitude on every occasion the play would be produced'. Synge and AG also registered their resolve not to surrender and informed a reporter from the *Irish Independent* of their intention to produce the play for its full run. Synge unwisely added to these views in a rushed and over-excited interview given to a persistent representative of the *Evening Mail* at the end of the evening. Even the journalist confessed that he 'was scarcely in a mood for being interviewed. He looked excited and restless, the perspiration standing out in great beads over his forehead and cheeks.' Synge denied that he had a realist intention in writing the play, or indeed any intentions at all; nor, he claimed, had he ever considered how it might be received by an Irish audience: 'I wrote the play because it pleased me, and it just happens that I know Irish life best, so I made my methods Irish.' To this extent, the play's Irish setting was 'a mere accident', and nor did he think its action probable, although that did not matter: 'Was Don Quixote probable? and still it is art.' While the play was not realism but 'a comedy, an extravaganza, made to amuse', he revealed that it had been inspired by a real incident in the Aran Islands where the people befriended a young man who had killed his father, and he further insisted that the speech used by his characters was the actual speech of the people, and that 'in art a spade must be called a spade'. ' "But the complaint is, Mr. Synge, that you call it a bloody shovel." "We shall go on with the play to the very end, in spite of all", he answered, snapping his fingers, more excited than ever. "I don't care a rap." '

On Tuesday the press reaction to the previous evening's events again divided along nationalist and unionist lines. The *Irish Times* and *Evening Mail* deplored the attempted suppression of free speech, while Matthias Bodkin in an editorial in the *Freeman's Journal* fulminated against the decision to continue with the play in the face of public opposition. In developing this position, he laid bare the political animus of the criticism:

Grossness of language is, of course, an offence to be condemned. But the calumny on the Irish people, of which the whole play is an embodiment, deserves still more scathing condemnation. Let us remember this calumny runs on old and familiar lines. It has ever been the custom of traducers of the Irish people to charge them with sympathy with all forms of crime. Over and over again this same lie has been made the justification for Coercion. To those who think that the calumny in Mr. Synge's play be safely condoned as too grotesque to be offensive may be commended the views of the 'Irish Times', which commends the squalid and repulsive travesty as 'remorseless truth', even to the profane and foul-mouthed dialogue.

Central to the question of freedom of speech in the theatre was the extent to which the demonstration had been pre-planned or a spontaneous reaction to a perceived affront. The repeated cries of 'Sinn Fein' and the suspicious congestion in the pit suggests that a certain amount of organization had been involved and the Tuesday edition of the *Evening Mail* had no doubt of the fact, and deplored it. Though 'far from attempting to limit the right of an audience to express its disapproval of any performance', the paper declared its opposition 'to organised demonstrations of the kind that took place last night', and alleged that many 'of those who listened quietly to the piece at its first production on Saturday' had 'returned last night for no other purpose than that of creating a disturbance'. But the protesters would not admit to conspiracy: they preferred the demonstration to appear as a spontaneous overflow of indignant, righteous feeling. Indeed, they could not admit preplanning since to confess to a prearranged demonstration would leave them open to prosecution under theatrical law.

On Tuesday morning Holloway called at the Abbey on business and 'found the players all agog about the events of last night, & defending the play & pitching in to the audience for their behaviour'. The imminent arrival of WBY from Scotland made continued resistance a certainty, especially since, as Henderson was to recall in October, he returned pumped up for action: 'He rushed into the theatre exclaiming "We must have columns & columns in the newspapers & 30 or forty sandwidge [sic] men to advertise the play" & then dictated what he wanted inserted about "the freedom of the theatre" etc.' Ben Iden Payne also retained a 'vivid recollection' of a meeting with the Abbey Directors, probably held on this afternoon: 'Yeats had been absent at the opening of *Playboy*, but at this meeting he was the dominant figure. . . . Synge very tentatively suggested that they throw in the sponge by stopping the run of the play, though it had been advertised to last for a week. Yeats would not hear of it. His manner was high-spirited, even elated. The fire of combat lighted up his eyes as he said they must at all hazards give the play its full allotted time. If they gave way to clamor, he said, they would ever afterward be at the mercy of the whims and prejudices of their audiences. The play must go on, he said, even if they had policemen stationed by every row of seats to throw out the disturbers.'

The police were not the only allies at that evening's performance. Hugh Lane recruited a posse of beefy students from the loyalist Trinity College to act as pro-Synge claque. As shock-troops their value was limited, but they may have been more valuable in inadvertently converting the potentially violent passions of the occasion into high farce. Woods, the assiduous reporter from the *Freeman's Journal*, described the battle lines with military precision: at 7.30 he noticed about forty young men seeking admission at the entrance leading to the pit. At the same time a file of policemen, led by a sergeant, took up position in the dressing rooms ready for action. At 8.00 p.m. a 'gentleman, stated to be from Galway' (presumably Hugh Lane) led about twenty young men into the stalls 'without the formality of purchasing tickets'. As they entered the hall, one of them ('a gentleman wearing a smart-fitting overcoat', identified by Holloway as Moorhead, and probably a member of the Dublin medical family of that name) challenged any man in the pit to fight him:

'Come on, any of you,' he shouted; and immediately came the response, 'We would wipe the streets with you,' followed by a good deal of uproar, and some good-humoured banter at the expense of the overcoated gentleman, whom the audience refused to take seriously. Some of his friends tried to restrain the gentleman's loquacity, but he was apparently determined to make himself heard.

His antics continued to be 'more provocative of mirth than of resentment'; he sat down for a time, and then stood up, to proclaim that he was 'a little bit drunk and don't know what I am saying'. He then made his way to the piano in front of the stage, 'stood up on a chair and bowed in mock courtesy to all parts of the house, after which he sat down and attacked the piano, from which he succeeded in torturing some stray notes of a waltz before he was suppressed by one of the stewards. There were cries of "Put him out," whereupon the gallant gentleman, facing the audience, and presenting what he evidently regarded as a heroic figure, shouted defiantly, "Put me out if you are fit", a challenge which provoked more merriment.'

The actual performances began punctually at 8.15. and after the end of *Riders to the Sea* WBY spoke from the stage. He offered an open debate on the merits of *The Playboy* and its production on the following Monday evening; in the meantime he hoped that the play would be given a fair hearing: 'We have put this play before you to be heard and judged. Every man has a right to hear and condemn it if he pleases, but no man has a right to interfere with another man who wants to hear the play. We shall play on and on, and I assure you our patience will last longer than their patience (applause and groans).'

*The Playboy* was heard in silence for a few minutes but uproar soon broke out in the pit; the lights were raised, Moorhead again offered to fight anyone who dared, the actors gave up the attempt to continue against the incessant noise, and WBY once more mounted the stage and

asked the audience to remain seated and to listen to the play of a man who, at any rate, was a most distinguished fellow-countryman of theirs (applause, groans, and hisses). Mr. Synge deserved to be heard. If his play was bad, it would die without their help; and if it was good, their hindrances could not impair it either (applause and hisses); but they could impair very greatly the reputation of this country for courtesy and intelligence.

Moorhead was finally persuaded by his friends to leave the hall, and after WBY failed to quell the noise by another appeal to the pit (someone was even blowing a bugle), the Directors reluctantly decided to call in the police. Since they were already waiting on the premises, they arrived far more quickly than on the previous evening, and this time they remained. WBY and Hugh Lane pointed out those most causing disruption and they were ejected amid much confusion. After this the police took up strategic positions throughout the hall, and although the noise continued it was not so loud as before. Sporadic attempts were made to restart the play, all of them interrupted by fresh disturbances, cat calls, boos, and hisses. More protesters were put out, and now actual arrests were made. This state of affairs continued throughout the second and third acts, and Holloway recorded that from 'start to finish not half a dozen consecutive sentences had been heard by the audience. When the performance came to a close the gentlemen in the stalls who had supported the play sang "God save the King".' The College boys had ultimately to be forcibly ejected by the police '& they marched off in a body singing, police-protected to the College'. One of them, Lady Gregory's nephew John Persse, was arrested for striking a policeman and fined £5.

Reports of these events appeared in the Dublin press on Wednesday morning, as did an interview with WBY in the *Freeman's Journal*. In this he claimed that *The Playboy* was Synge's masterpiece and discussed the Freedom of the Theatre 'with a good deal of vehemence'. He argued that 'All great literature . . . dealt with exaggerated types, and all tragedy and tragicomedy with types of sin and folly. A dramatist is not an historian.' He traced the disturbances to new and sinister forces in Irish life: in the old days Irishmen followed a few leaders

but during the last ten years a change has taken place. For leaders we have now societies, clubs, and leagues. Organised opinion of sections and coteries has been put in place of these leaders, one or two of whom were men of genius. Instead of a Parnell, a Stephens, or a Butt, we must obey the demands of commonplace and ignorant people, who try to take on an appearance of strength by imposing some crude shibboleth on their own and others' necks. They do not persuade, for that is difficult; they do not expound, for that needs knowledge.

He argued that the forty young men 'who came down last night, not to judge the play, but to prevent other people from doing so, merely carried out a method which is becoming general in our national affairs', and that this struck at the freedom of Ireland. For this reason those at the Abbey were determined not to surrender: 'We will go on until the play has been heard, and heard sufficiently to be judged on its merits. We had only announced its production for one week. We have now decided to play all next week as well, if the opposition continue.' He offered to send free tickets to anyone who had been unable to hear the play—even if they were opposed to it—and also renewed his promise to debate the freedom of the theatre with the opposition.

Once again, attitudes to the disturbances divided along sectarian and political lines. The fact that the *Freeman's Journal* had published an interview with WBY did not prevent it criticizing his position in a different part of the paper, but the *Irish Times* continued to be more even-handed. While disliking the play and agreeing that its central incident would be 'uncommon in any civilised country', it nevertheless maintained that 'no well-balanced mind can defend for a single moment the *Sinn Fein* party's crude and violent methods of dramatic criticism'. The 'Sinn Fein shouters', it alleged, had altogether ignored those aspects of the play that might 'be justly and severely criticised', and had 'founded their objections on a theory of Celtic impeccability which is absurd in principle, and intolerable, when it is sought to be rigidly imposed as a canon of art'. It 'heartily endorsed' Yeats's position on the freedom of the theatre and recommended that it was 'high time for thoughtful Irishmen of all parties to make a stand for freedom of thought and speech against bodies which seek to introduce into the world of the mind the methods which the Western branches of the United Irish League have introduced into politics. For this reason we sympathise with the plucky stand which the National Theatre Company is making against the organised tyranny of the clap-trap patriots.' It however deplored Synge's remarks in the *Evening Mail* that he had written the play merely to please himself: 'The idle aim of a mere extravaganza does not justify the grimly realistic treatment of a distinctly unpleasant theme. A serious purpose, clearly brought home, would have vindicated the play.'

Some of the play's more serious themes were by now being discussed by more informed commentators, notably by Patrick Kenny, who had tried to address the pit on Tuesday evening, and now contributed a thoughtful article to the *Irish Times*, arguing that the play was highly moral and commending Synge's courage for shooting 'his dreadful searchlight into our cherished accumulation of social skeletons. He has led our vision through the Abbey street stage into the heart of Connaught, and revealed to us there truly terrible truths, of our own making, which we dare not face for the present'.

The following day Synge himself wrote to the *Irish Times* to counter their criticism of his rushed interview in the *Evening Mail* and to acknowledge Kenny's insights:

SIR,—As a rule the less a writer says about his own work the better, but as my views have been rather misunderstood in an interview which appeared in one of the evening papers, and was alluded to in your leader today, I would like to say a word or two to put myself right. The interview took place in conditions that made it nearly impossible for me—in spite of the patience and courtesy of the interviewer—to give a clear account of my views about the play, and the lines I followed in writing it. 'The Playboy of the Western World' is not a play with 'a purpose' in the modern sense of the word, but although parts of it are, or are meant to be, extravagant comedy, still a great deal that is in it, and a great deal more that is behind it, is perfectly serious, when looked at in a certain light. That is often the case, I think, with comedy, and no one is quite sure to-day whether 'Shylock' and 'Alceste' should be played seriously or not. There are, it may be hinted, several sides to 'The Playboy'.

'Pat', I am glad to notice, has seen some of them in his own way. There may be still others if anyone cares to look for them.

Despite Kenny's attempt to justify the play in the morning paper, the Wednesday night performance apparently followed the rowdy pattern of the previous two nights, although there were slight hints of the change that was to take place over the rest of the week. The theatre was even more crowded than ever, and the internal division between pit and stalls as before, but it seemed evident to Holloway that many of those attending had come to watch the row itself rather than the play. He also noted that for the first time since Saturday *The Playboy* was at least listened to 'in patches'. The *Freeman's Journal* revealed that the comic turn on this evening was provided by an opponent of the play, who made a protest from the gallery and then said he would leave, 'although he had paid for his seat', but immediately afterwards 'stated that he had changed his mind and would remain. He, however, did not do so, as he was soon afterwards ejected. But he was evidently irrepressible. He quickly reappeared in the stalls, and was proceeding to thank the audience for the cordial reception they had accorded him, when once more he was what is termed "shown the door".' Once again Synge was hissed and booed on entering the theatre, once again *Riders to the Sea* and part of the first act of *The Playboy* were listened to with respect, once again the police were used, once again WBY helped point out troublemakers for arrest. An actual brawl broke out and was settled with fisticuffs in the vestibule, although no one could tell in the melee how it all ended. As usual the third act caused the most trouble but on this occasion the protests went on long after the performances had ended: 'Matters appeared rather critical. A number of gentlemen began to address knots of admirers. Mr. Monahan, a prominent Sinn Feiner, mounted a seat and denounced the piece, saying he had never seen or heard anything like it.' He was cut short by the police, who cleared the auditorium, but the protests continued outside, where the 'rival sections marched through Abbey street,

O'Connell street, and other thoroughfares giving vent to the faith that was in them. They were followed by strong detachments of police, whilst other bodies of the force were stationed at points of 'vantage. So far as could be ascertained, no serious disturbance occurred.' As Holloway exclaimed on this evening: 'All eyes are on the Abbey this week. The audience & not the play is the thing since Monday's disturbances!'

The consequences of the disturbances now began to filter through the Northern Police Court and WBY spent most of his Wednesday and Thursday mornings there helping to prosecute the protesters. In the main these were young men such as Piaras Béaslaí, Patrick Hughes, and John Duane, who were associated with Sinn Fein and the Gaelic League, and whose affiliations suggest an organized claque. More unexpectedly was the arrest of Padraic Colum's father, who, apparently carried away by the occasion, was charged with using obscene language (a charge not without its irony, given the protesters' denunciation of the swearing in Synge's play). An important point of law was at issue in these prosecutions. Hostile comment on plays in Dublin theatres was of long tradition and, up to a point, protected as a legitimate freedom of speech, which had been established by a ruling of Lord Chief Justice Bushe in 1822. The magistrate Thomas Wall spelt out this point on Thursday morning when he reminded his court that members of a theatre audience

might cry down a play which they disliked, or hiss and booh the actors who depended for their positions on the good-will of audiences, but they must not act in such a manner as had a tendency to excite uproar or disturbance. Their censure or approbation, though they might be noisy in expressing it, must not be riotous, and must be the expression of the feeling of the moment. If premeditated by a number of persons combined beforehand to cry down a performance or an actor it became criminal.

Unlike Mahony, the magistrate who had presided on the previous morning, Wall did not think that the cases before him constituted a riot, nor a conspiracy, and, although obliged to fine the defendants, he did so with great reluctance (and then only ten shillings), strongly hinting that he thought that it was the Abbey Directors, not the protesters, who should be appearing before him. These observations made Wall a hero to the protesters and his name was cheered in the Theatre and at a demonstration against the play in nearby Marlborough Street on the following night. Quizzed by a representative of the *Freeman's Journal* on this development, WBY acknowledged that Wall clearly supposed that the Abbey was 'behaving in a high-handed way in face of popular opposition, or rather of the opposition of portion of our audience', but went on to point out that a 'very large number of the great plays of the world have been produced in the face of intense popular opposition. . . . Fine drama, by its very nature, rouses the most fiery passions.' He also offered Wall a complimentary ticket for the play.

Given the state of the law, all those on trial insisted that there had been no conspiracy, and it is clear that some of the protesters, no doubt with drink taken, had been caught up in the excitement of the moment. Nevertheless, Padraic Colum certainly took it for granted that there had been an organized opposition and in a letter to the *Freeman's Journal* defended his father as not being part of the 'gang'. There is also strong circumstantial evidence—the phalanx in the pit, its association with Sinn Fein, its premeditated possession of bugles and sticks—to suggest that WBY was right in alleging that this was a prearranged attempt to force the play off the stage.

If so, it did not succeed. By Thursday, the steam was going out of the protests and although the *Freeman's Journal* called once more for the play's withdrawal, it did so with a weary lack of conviction and devoted most of the article to attacking the commercial motives of the Directors. There were a number of reasons for the change in attitude, among the most important of which was the Directors' determination—reiterated by AG in Thursday morning's papers and by each of them individually in Friday's press—that the play would go on, even if this required an extended run. By Thursday, with half the performances completed, it was evident that the play would now go the full distance. In this situation, the expense of a nightly visit to the theatre, let alone the risk of a substantial fine, must have seemed hardly worth it. Moreover there was evidence that the audience was becoming part of the attraction, which was not at all the purpose of the exercise, and was actually providing the play with valuable free publicity. There was also in some more thoughtful quarters a growing sense that the whole thing had got out of hand, that the protests were out of proportion to their occasion. Kenny's intelligent article on the play had been followed by further eloquent defences of it by Ellen Duncan and others. Colum's letter to the *Freeman* defending his father had also ended sensibly: 'The opposition to "The Playboy of the Western World" has only prevented a sane estimate of the play. Many people interested in Irish drama have been unable to hear this latest contribution to a National Theatre. Let us hear the play, and judge it as a play. After all, human nature is fairly uniform, and if "The Playboy of the Western World" is false to Irish nature, it is probably false to human nature.'

The protesters, including Holloway, now cheered themselves up with the conviction that the play was irredeemably dull as well as dirty-minded, and that by putting it on and then defending it with police protection WBY and Synge had effectively destroyed the National Theatre Society as a credible Irish institution. As one of the ejected demonstrators put it in the *Freeman*: 'There is no pleasure in kicking a dead dog, especially if when alive we thought well of it; and the Abbey Theatre is now dead and rotten as a National Theatre.' On Thursday night Holloway admitted that the 'police-protected drama by the dramatist of the dung-heap . . . got a fair hearing tonight, & was voted by those around me very poor, dull, dramatic stuff indeed. After the first act all interest of any kind ceases, & were it not for the claque imported into the stalls very little applause would be forthcoming. . . . The theatre is for ever damned in the eyes of all right thinking Irishmen.' The theatre was still heavily guarded inside and out by the police and there were still boos and counter cheers, but the *Evening Mail* noted that 'no disorder of a serious nature took place' even during the second and third acts. Although 'for no particular reason apparently about a dozen young men in the pit rose and left the building, booing and hissing as they went', and 'one man in the pit became so disorderly that he had to be forcibly removed by the police', on the whole 'the piece received . . . a fair hearing, and the audience left the building in good order'.

The Directors sensed victory. The *Irish Independent* reported that Synge 'was beaming at the reception' of the play and, interviewed after the performance, WBY 'expressed himself pleased with the progress of events. "Gradually", he said, "the audience are beginning to see what the play means. We always had the stalls with us, but to-night for the first time we had the majority of the pit on our side, and any protests that there were were perfectly fair. If members of the audience object to certain parts of the play, of course they have a perfect right to express their dissent in a reasonable way".'

Further referring to the hostile demonstrations that had taken place, Mr. Yeats said that events were taking the normal course of the work of a man who had a curious, a very new and harsh kind of imagination. There had been a great deal of unreal sentimentalising and idealising of the Irish peasant, and possibly there was now taking place a reaction in the other direction in Irish types of character. That was the way of literature.

By Friday night the protesters had all but disappeared, although worrying news from London reached the Directors in the form of a letter from the dramatist William Boyle, withdrawing his very popular plays from the Abbey. He announced this publicly on 1 February 1907 in a letter to the *Freeman's Journal*:

As the writer of plays recently produced at the Abbey Theatre, I beg to say that I have written to Mr. Yeats to-day withdrawing from his company my sanction to the perform-ances of any play of mine in future. This is my protest against the present attempt to set up a standard of National Drama based on the vilification of any section of the Irish people, in a theatre ostensibly founded for the production of plays to represent real Irish life and character.

In a private letter to WBY he regretted that he was 'obliged to write to withdraw my three plays—The Building Fund, The Eloquent Dempsy and The Mineral Workers from the repertoire of the National Theatre Company, as a protest against your action in attempting to force, at the risk of a riot, a play upon the Dublin public against their protests of its being a gross misrepresentation of the character of our western peasantry.' Questioned about this on 2 February in an interview in the *Evening Telegraph*, WBY suggested that 'Mr. Boyle evidently did not know the facts about the new play', and further added that Boyle was 'the last man who should take up such an attitude; for his own admirable plays have by no means been approved of by the class of critics who are so antagonistic to Mr. Synge'. WBY was to reinforce this point later this spring by republishing Irish press attacks on Boyle's plays in the next number of the *Arrow*.

Holloway, chagrined that the play continued to attract a large audience, began to disparage the members of that audience: 'It pained me to see the class of people who eagerly paid 2/- or 3/- shillings to hear the play in the hope of getting their value out in nastiness. It was the sort of an audience one would expect to see at the Empire on a Saturday night. As all the very crudely coarse & indecent passages are now omitted these seekers for foulness were disappointed & I heard several say it was a fraud when the piece had concluded. Poor human nature! . . . Great numbers of all sorts & conditions of people are going to the Abbey to see what is all the fuss about for themselves.'

Predictably the weekly press—particularly *Sinn Fein* and the *Leader*—slated the play, but they were too late to add much to the damage already done. The account of the play in *Sinn Fein* reiterated much that had already been said more effectively by O'Hara and Bodkin almost a week before, and the too deliberately worked-up outrage issued in ludicrously sweeping generalizations ('Mr. Synge's play . . . is one of the worst constructed we have witnessed . . . it is a vile and inhuman story told in the foulest language we have ever listened to from a public platform'). Inevitably there were also glaring inaccuracies: Old Mahon, for instance, was said to utter a word 'so obscene that no man of ordinary decency would use it'. Ambrose Power, the actor who played the part, wrote to point out that the word concerned was in fact 'stuttering'.

The *Leader* printed two articles on the play. The first, curiously limp but presumably by D. P. Moran, implied that both protesters and supporters had succeeded in their aims, and while thinking the staging of the play 'a great blunder', found it 'impossible not to admire the pluck of the actors and actresses in a situation that called for all their reserve of nerve'. Indeed, he even praised the Directors for the same quality: 'the Abbey Theatre people, we see, have decided to fight the matter out. The manifesto they have issued may indicate pluck, but we do not think it is wise.' The other *Leader* piece, evidently written by Cleary, was a more direct onslaught on the Abbey and its latest work, and in customary pietistic *Leader* style condemned 'the extraordinary decadence of tone which pervades it from start to finish. . . . Throughout the play there runs an undercurrent of animalism and irreligion. . . . One looks in vain for a glimmer of Christianity in the acts or utterances of the characters.'

And so the tumultuous week drew to a close. On Saturday the indefatigable Holloway attended both the matinée and the evening performances of the play he so hated. The police were still present on both occasions, but 'had no work to do & idly stood by'. At the matinée 'W. B. Yeats came & had a few words with me re arrest last night & I told him what I thought of it & others, & also of the drunken Trinity students of Tuesday night. He replied, "There were plenty of drunken men in the pit, & he preferred drunken men who applauded in the right than drunken men who hissed, etc., in the wrong."—A beautiful sentiment quite worthy of his pal Synge, I thought. When I pressed him further about the freedom of every man to judge for himself, & yet if a man hissed or left the theatre before the play was over he was likely to be taken, he fled. He would not work in the art-for-art's-sake theory into an answer to that question, and so his flowers of speech did not blossom on the subject. "Humbug," thy name is Yeats.' Holloway noticed that at the matinée the 'audience was not very large & mostly ladies'; by the evening it had apparently transmogrified into a freak show: 'one would imagine that the Empire & the Tivoli emptied themselves out into the pit & balcony to judge by the cut of the customers with patches over the eye, week-old unshorn beards, smelly pipes. . . . The police were as thick as blackberries in September. . . . I noticed as I stood in the Vestibule the same set of young fellows as I has seen the previous evenings, were to act as a claque'. He reported a certain amount of hissing and deliberate coughing, but nothing on the scale of the noise earlier in the week, and by the end of the play 'the claques hadn't the heart to applaud vigorously nor the opponents to hiss with a will. Faint applause & hisses marked the fall of the welcome curtain.' And so it all apparently ended—not with a bang but with a (not altogether unpleasing) whimper.

Not that this was by any means the end of the affair. WBY attempted to turn the dispute into a moral and artistic crusade, placing an advertisement in the papers urging in capital letters support of the Abbey Theatre against 'organized opposition', with the reminder that 'he who strikes at freedom of judgment strikes at the soul of the nation'. In support of these precepts he also arranged the promised debate on 'The Freedom of the Theatre', which he held in a packed Abbey Theatre on Monday, 4 February. Synge was too ill to attend and AG, who disapproved of the whole 'dreadful' exercise, congratulated him on his absence. She sent him and Robert Gregory identical letters which gave an account of the occasion from the Directors' point of view. The chairman, P. D. Kenny, she thought good: he 'didn't lose his temper and made himself heard but no chairman could have done much', and the meeting turned out to be as rambunctious as the early performances of the play itself. WBY's first speech was reasonably well received, and in any case he had taken a precaution he was wont to adopt on such occasions of writing it out in advance and giving the reporters a copy. AG was particularly aggrieved by the cowardice and desertion of Abbey supporters: 'Russell [AE] was in the gallery we heard afterwards but did not come forward or speak. Colum "had a rehearsal" and didn't speak or come. T. W. Russell didn't turn up. We had hardly anyone to speak on our side at all, but it didn't much matter for the disturbances were so great they wouldn't even let their own speakers be well heard.' She thought that Piaras Béaslaí, who had been arrested and fined for his part in the protests, was 'the only one with a policy for he announced his intention of never entering the place again, and called on others to do so, but the cheering grew very feeble at that point.' She added that 'Dr. Ryan supported us fairly well' and revealed that in 'the thick of the riot Mrs. Duncan sent up her name to the platform offering to give an address! But Pat sent back word he would not like to see her insulted!' She also told how 'a young man forced his way up and argued with Dossy [Wright] till a whisky bottle fell from his pocket and broke on the stage, at which Dossy flung him down the steps, and there was great cheering and laughing, and Dossy flushed with honest pride'. The meeting descended into chaos in which the last speakers could hardly be heard at all: 'There was a tipsy man in the pit crying "I'm from Belfast! Ulster aboo!"'. Many of our opponents called for order and fair play and I think must have been disgusted with their allies. The scene certainly justified us in having in the police. The interruptions were very stupid and monotonous. Yeats when he rose for the last speech was booed but got a hearing at last and got out all he wanted to say. He spoke very well, but his voice rather cracked once or twice from screaming and from his sore throat. I was sorry while there that we had ever let such a set inside the theatre, but I am glad today, and I think it was spirited and showed we were not repenting or apologizing.'

The Dublin press gave a more objective account of the proceedings, the fullest of which appeared in the *Freeman's Journal* of 5 February:

Last night the promised discussion at the Abbey Theatre took place on the Freedom of the Theatre and 'The Playboy of the Western World'. The proceedings were noisy, farcical, and at one period disgusting. The Theatre was crowded. Precisely to time the curtain was raised amid cheers and hisses, and Mr. W. B. Yeats, accompanied by Mr. P. D. Kenny ('Pat') appeared on the stage. 'Pat' took the chair.

Mr. W. B. Yeats, who met with a very mixed reception, said he saw it again and again said that they tried to prevent the audience from the reasonable expression of dislike. He certainly would never like to set plays before a theatrical audience that was not free to approve or disapprove ('Oh,' groans, and cries of 'What about the Police?') even very loudly, for there was no dramatist that did not desire a live audience (laughter, cheers and hisses). They had to face something quite different from reasonable expression of dissent ('Oh'). On Tuesday and on Monday nights it was not possible to hear six consecutive lines of the play. ('Quite right', and cheers), and this deafening outcry was not raised by the whole theatre, but almost entirely by a section of the pit ('Oh'), who acted together ('No, no')—and even sat together ('No'). It was an attempt to prevent the play from being heard and judged (cheers and cries of 'Quite right!'). Mr. O'Donoghue said in that day's Freeman that the forty dissentients were doing their duty (cheers), because there is no Government Censor in Ireland. The public, he said, was the Censor (cheers) where there is no other. But were these forty alone the public (groans) and the Censor? (groans). What right had they to prevent the far greater number who wished to hear from hearing and judging? (hisses and cheers). They called to their aid (cries of 'The police', and hisses) the means which every community possessed to limit the activities of small minorities who set their interests against those of the community—the police (great groaning). When the 'Countess Kathleen' was denounced with an equal violence they called in the police—that was in 1899, when he was still President of the Wolfe Tone Commemoration of Great Britain (cheers and groans). The struggle of last week had been a long necessity (cheers). Various paragraphs in newspapers, describing Irish attacks on theatres, had made many, mostly young men, come to think that the silencing of a stage at their own pleasure might win them a little fame (hisses), and, perhaps, serve their country. The last he heard of was in Liverpool (cheers), and there a stage was rushed, and a priest who set a play upon it came before that audience and apologised (cheers, and cries of 'You should have done the same'). They had not such pliant bones, and did not learn in the house that bred them a so suppliant knee ('Oh,' groans and hisses). It needed eloquence to persuade and knowledge to expound ('Oh!') but the coarser means came to every man's hand as ready as a stone or a stick (A Voice—'Or a spade', and laughter). It was not approval of Mr. Synge's play that sent the Abbey Theatre receipts up nearly £100. The generation of young men and girls who were now leaving schools and colleges were weary of the tyranny of clubs and Leagues (uproar).

The Chairman appealed to them to give a fair hearing as they expected a fair hearing for their spokesmen.

Mr. Yeats concluded by saying that manhood was all (laughter, cheers, groans, and noise).

Mr. W. J. Lawrence, who was loudly cheered, said he spoke as an Irishman and an Irish play boy (laughter and applause). He was not a member of any League or Society in Ireland. In some of his recent writings Mr. Yeats had said that praise, except it came from an equal, was an insult. He was not going to praise Mr. Yeats that night—'I come to bury Caesar, not to praise him' (laughter and cheers). He was present four nights last week, and he was present on the first occasion. Mr. Yeats was not. He was therefore in a position to speak in regard to the reception it got on the first night. He had twenty-five years' experience as a playgoer, and he had never seen a more thoroughly intellectual, representative audience. There was no predisposition to damn the play. It got a fair and honest hearing (A Voice—'It didn't on Monday', and another voice, 'Throw him out'). At the end the protest was made on the indecent verbiage, blasphemy, and Billingsgate that was indulged in (cheers, and a Voice—'Nonsense'). There was not one single call for author. That was the registration of the condemnation of the play (hear, hear). He said that viewing the reception the play got on Saturday night and the verdict of the Press that the National Theatre Society would have been well advised if they had at once, in deference to public opinion, taken the play off the boards (loud cheers). Mr. Yeats had won a Pyrrhic victory. This was not the first time in their history that a wrongly administered English law had violated Irish freedom (cheers). Mr. Yeats had struck one of the strongest blows in modern times against the freedom of the theatre (cheers). There was a movement in other countries for the abolition of censorship. If the censorship was abolished the English manager had only to adopt the method of Mr. Yeats to obtrude any indecent, vulgar play on the public. Mr. Yeats's action was an argument in favour of the creation of a censorship in Ireland (applause and dissent).

The Chairman thought they should keep within relevant limits.

Mr. Sheehy Skeffington said he was both for and against (laughter). The play was bad (hear, hear), the organised disturbance was worse (hear, hear), the methods employed to quell that disturbance were worst of all (cheers and dissent). Mr. Yeats's view would entitle him to put anything he liked on the stage and force it on his audience. As to the methods referred to when a play was rushed off the boards, such methods were, under certain circumstances, not only necessary, but the only possible methods (cheers). Mr. Yeats would have enlisted the support of the public if he had acted as he had said he would—if he had endeavoured to wear out the patience of his opponents (hear, hear). It would have been better to have enlisted the support of the public than the support of the garrison (hear, hear).

Mr. Cruise O'Brien said they protested against what they considered coercion (hear, hear). If Mr. Yeats objected to bullying so did he (cheers), and so did the audience (cheers).

Mr. O'Hoey, who first spoke in Irish, said he had never seen a play which placed the Irish people in such a disgusting light (loud cheers).

Mr. T. Cuffe, rising in the pit, said there were a number of G men in the background.

Mr. Yeats, who was hissed, rose and said so far as he knew, there were no police whatever in the house (cries of 'Put them out').

Mr. O'Hoey said he was quite sure Mr. Yeats was not responsible for the presence of the G men there that night any more than for the excitement and disturbance they caused trying to create a riot amongst a handful of people outside, when they had a force sufficient to wipe them out (hisses and cheers). He thought if this play had been produced on the other side it would have been either openly or tacitly put down on the bills as a sketch of Irish peasant life (cheers). He was glad that most of those who sympathised with his view had seen fit to absent themselves that night, as a protest against the introduction of the police (cheers). There was no organised disturbance on Monday night. They objected to the attribution to the Irish people of characteristics which had not been, were not, and never would be theirs (cheers). He hoped all right-minded Irish people would teach Mr. Yeats and the management the lesson they richly deserved without further letter-writing or speeching (cheers).

Mr. R. Sheehy said their audiences when the satire was well directed and just, reproved their faults and approved the satire. Mr. Yeats claimed freedom without limits. What was to be said if, instead of slandering an individual, he slandered a nation (cheers). Mr. Yeats's position was that so long as a man paid his money and had not heard this slander, the slander must be continued until he heard it. The play was rightly condemned as a slander on Irishmen and Irishwomen. An audience of self-respecting Irishmen had a perfect right to proceed to any extremity (cheers).

Mr. C. P. Gavan said that he had been accused of giving information to the police last week (groans, hisses, and boos). He was referring to the moral objectors (hisses). We have a worse murderer (the speaker's conclusion could not be heard in the storm of groans and hissing).

Mr. Beasley said he found it very hard to understand Mr. Yeats's view that night; but he found it easy last week when he (Mr. Yeats) charged him in the Police Courts (groans and cries of 'Police'). They had as chairman a gentleman who had already expressed his views in the congenial atmosphere of the 'Irish Times' (A voice—'He ought to be very impartial', and laughter.) Mr. Yeats said he came as an artist (laughter). Well, he (Mr. Beasley) hoped Irishmen would never forget his pose in the Police Court (cheers). Nature breaks out through the eyes of the cat (cheers and laughter). They had called in the claque of the garrison and police, and had rendered that place a place to which no Irishman could give the slightest support (cheers).

Mr. Molloy (Cork) said the play was not true (cheers). They protested against the squalid language poured on the stage during the last week (cheers).

Mr. J. B. Yeats said he had not read the play; he had seen it twice, but had not heard it. He knew Mr. Synge. He knew he had an affection for these people (loud laughter and cat-calls) he had described in 'Riders to the Sea'. His affection for them ('Oh,' and laughter) was based on a real knowledge ('No, no', and groans). He lived amongst them, and was their friend (disorder), and intimate with their households (cries and groans). He knew this was the Island of Saints—plaster saints (disorder and groaning). He (Mr. Yeats) was no great believer in saints, but he engaged to think that this was a land of sinners (cries of 'Police, police', and laughter). The speaker went on to compare Mr. Synge's peasants and Carleton's peasants, amid much interruption. Carleton's peasants, he said, were a real insult and degradation (noise), and Mr. Synge's peasant was a real, vigorous, vital man, though a sinner (loud laughter and hisses). The speaker could not proceed with the noise.

Mr. D. Sheehan said he came to defend the play. He did so as a peasant who knew peasants, and also as a medical student (loud laughter and groans).

The Chairman—Listen to a peasant on peasants (loud laughter).

Mr. Sheehan claimed that a man who came up and lived in Dublin for four or six years had as much right to speak of peasants as a man who lived down in the country (A Voice—'Wonderful', groans and laughter). He claimed his right to speak as a medical student (laughter). Mr. Synge had drawn a type of character that ever since he studied any science he had paid strong attention to (laughter), and that was the sexual melancholic (hisses and disorder). He said that in any country town in Ireland they would get types of men like Christy Mahon. He would refer them to the lunacy reports of Ireland (disorder), and to Dr. Connolly Norman's lectures at the Richmond Lunatic Asylum (some laughter and great disturbance). He came that night to object to the pulpit Irishman just as they objected to the stage-Irishman (renewed noise). A type of life had been brought on and held up to their praise lately in Ireland utterly unproductive altogether (cries of 'Order'). Further references to this point were received with cries of 'Shame'. Mr. Sheehan continued, when some quiet was restored. He had never seen the doctrine of the survival of the fittest treated with such living force as by Mr. Synge in his play (noise). It was they who ought to defend the women of Ireland from being unnatural pathological—(the rest of the sentence was lost in the noise). Mr. Synge had drawn attention to a particular form of marriage law which, though not confined to Ireland, was very common in Ireland (disorder). It was with a fine woman like Pegeen Mike (hisses) and a tubercule Koch's disease man like Shaun Keogh (some laughter, groans, hisses, and noise)—and the point of view was not the murder at all (hisses), but when the artist appears in Ireland who was not afraid of life (laughter) and his nature (boos), the women of Ireland would receive him (cries of 'Shame' and great disorder).

(At this stage in the speech many ladies, whose countenances plainly indicated intense feelings of astonishment and pain, rose and left the place. Many men also retired).

Mr. Sheehan continued, but his sentences could not be followed owing to the din.

A young fellow from the stalls, under the influence of drink, here ascended the stage and tried to speak, but was removed.

Dr. Ryan said one point they were anxious to know was whether the management put forward a play as representative of the life of the West of Ireland or only a burlesque (laughter). Mr. Yeats, in the Police Court, said it was an exaggeration (a Voice—'Apropos').

A young fellow, who gave a name in Irish, said suppression was not criticism (hisses). Was the author of the play incapable of appreciating the good qualities of his country men and women? (cries of 'Yes', and cheers). The answer would be found in 'The Riders to the Sea' (hisses and noise). If the thing was a slander the scoundrel (cheers) should be kicked out of Ireland (cheers). But they could not accept that verdict ('Yes, Yes') against a man who wrote 'The Riders to the Sea' ('Oh', and hisses). He had laid bare the strength and weakness of the Irish character (noise). There was undoubtedly a want of moral courage in our people ('Oh', and groans). They undoubtedly said one thing and think another sometimes (laughter and 'Oh').

Mr. P. Carroll said Mr. Synge's play was the result of brutal ignorance, born almost of idiocy (great noise and cheers).

Mr. W. B. Yeats asked, as to the introduction of the police, did they realise the effect upon actors of the kind of thing, of the disgraceful behaviour of Monday and Tuesday evening last ('Oh') the wear and tear of nerve, and the physical exhaustion? His business was to secure a hearing for author and actors, and to do that as quietly as possible. He had been asked why he charged Mr. Beasley. Having called in the police he thought it right and manly to go the full length (hisses). He deliberately walked down and charged a man—he did not want to charge a rowdy like some of those who were then making a noise (groans and boos). He chose a man he could respect ('Oh, oh,' and hisses). Knowing that the dispute that lay between them was one of principle (A Voice—'That won't wash'). There was one thing no one there would say he flinched from his fight (cheers). He was not a public entertainer (laughter), he was an artist (renewed laughter), setting before them what he believed to be fine works (hisses and laughter), to see and insist that they shall receive a quiet and respectful attention (laughter, hisses, and cheers).

After some disorder he arose again.

Mr. Yeats said—The author of 'Kathleen Ni Houlihan' appeals to you (cheers). They were offered support from the 'garrison' if they took 'Kathleen Ni Houlihan' from the list of their plays, and they refused (cheers), and now the author of that play, holding what he believed to be right, refused to give up the work of one whom he believed to be a man of genius (cries and laughter), because the mob cried at him (cheers and noise). The groups of men and women formed a spirited section, extravagant he admitted ('Oh!'). There were two peasants in that play—one dutiful man, just such a man as Irish novelists had represented, that was the young man who would be afraid to be jealous of a man who had killed his father (groans). The other was not, he admitted, an admirable ideal, but where they had a group of girls appealed to to choose between the man who was so docile to Father Reilly, and the man who killed his father, he did not think there was one woman in that room who would have hesitated (cheers and hisses). He could tell them where Mr. Synge got the central idea of the play; he would leave them to explain the facts themselves. Some ten years ago, before Mr. Synge went to the Middle Island of Arran to live there, he (Mr. Yeats) went there out of a fishing boat with Mr. Edward Martyn, Mr. Arthur Symons, and Lord Killanin. Mr. Arthur Symons had just put on record the incident. They came out of the fishing boat—a somewhat unusual thing. A crowd of people gathered around, and looking upon them as, he imagined, people flying from justice (A Voice, 'No wonder', and laughter), they brought up to them a very old man, one they said who was the oldest man on the island, and they all gathered round him in reverent admiration while he made this speech. He said if any gentleman had done a crime, we will hide him. There was a gentleman that killed his father, and I had him in my house six months till he went away to Amerikay (cries of 'Oh', laughter and cheers).

Mr. Yeats and 'Pat' then retired, and the meeting broke up with cheers and hisses and the singing of 'A Nation Once Again'.

The immediate effect of the disturbances over *The Playboy of the Western World* was the boycotting of those associated with the Abbey. On the very night of the debate Sara Allgood was to have appeared at a Boys' Brigade Concert, but had been told that her services were not required, while at roughly the same time the Gort District Council unanimously passed a resolution denouncing the production of the play and punishing AG for her part in it by banning the local workhouse children going to Coole to attend her parties and treats. Another immediate effect was the felting of the floor of the Abbey pit, so that stamping and the pounding of sticks would not in future be so disruptive.

It is harder to judge the long-term effects of the dispute on audience numbers. Holloway, who was biased, went on insisting that it took years for the Theatre to recover, but, although there was a dip in attendance in the immediate aftermath, recuperation seems to have been reasonably swift. The more intelligent patrons remained faithful, including even those like Holloway, Lawrence, and O'Donoghue who had condemned the play, and the permanent absentees were soon replaced by new faces. In truth, there was no alternative. Although there was brave talk of founding a new and more authentic National Theatre, sponsored by the Gaelic League and the Theatre of Ireland, nothing came of this and the Abbey remained the only show of its kind in town.

Boyle's absence from the Abbey, which had been prompted by AEFH's triumphalism as well as his objections to *The Playboy*, was to be longer and more expensive in lost takings than WBY anticipated or wanted. When asked about it by the *Freeman's Journal* a few days after Boyle's announcement, he was fairly sanguine, refusing to believe that this was a final rupture, and expressing confidence that he had 'acted precipitately, and on mere rumour; and I hope he will reconsider his position'. He began to make overtures to Boyle almost immediately through Holloway and D. J. O'Donoghue, to get him to 'reconsider his position', but it was not until nearly three years later, in November 1909, that his plays returned to the repertory.

In essence the riots over *The Playboy* represented a clash between two definitions of freedom: the freedom of an artist to express himself as he wished versus the freedom of audiences to protest against a work that for good or bad reasons they deemed offensive. And here the question of conspiracy was crucial. Some, perhaps most, of the protests were spontaneous expressions of individual outrage, but there was also more sinister evidence of an organized group which, inflamed by inaccurate and tendentious newspaper accounts, was determined to suppress the play altogether. Defeating this core group was a battle that WBY and the other Directors knew had to be won, not merely for the sake of the Abbey but for the future freedom of Irish literary expression. Their victory made it easier to outface hostility to Norrys Connell's *The Piper* in the following year, to counter repressive opposition to *The Playboy* in Liverpool and London, and later New York and Philadelphia, and to win similar battles over the production of Sean O'Casey's plays in the 1920s.

The determination and courage of the Abbey Company, both Directors and players, were crucial in this, but so, in a paradoxical way, was the curious if partial self-discipline of the dissenters and their propensity to humour. The opposition was focused entirely on *The Playboy*, and *Riders to the Sea*, although also by Synge, was heard with respect and admiration throughout the disturbances. And although Synge was roundly hissed and sometimes threatened verbally, there was no actual attempt to harm him physically, and nor, apparently, did he have any fear on this score since he circulated nightly in the theatre. Even the civil war between the stalls and the pit rarely went further than alcohol-fuelled posturing and bravura — at least in the auditorium — and the divided house could always be united in laughter at a wisecrack or tipsy absurdity. As Holloway reflected after the last performance: 'If all the comic things that took place at the Abbey during the week were put in a book they would make the world laugh.'

But a different outcome would have made the world weep, and Synge was prophetic when he wrote to Maire O'Neill on the morning after the first night that it was 'better any day to have the row we had last night, than to have your play fizzling out in half-hearted applause. Now we'll be talked about. We're an event in the history of the Irish stage.'

THE PSALTERY PROSPECTUS was a four-sided publicity leaflet put together by WBY and FF to advertise their experiments with the psaltery. They had presented their 'new art' before a paying audience for the first time on 16 February 1901 when, with the aid of a harp and a piano to sound the notes and indicate the changes of pitch, FF and Anna Mather chanted poems while WBY explained the method in a lecture entitled 'New Methods of Speaking Verse'. By October 1901 the musician Arnold Dolmetsch had constructed a psaltery to accompany their chanting, and over the next few years they undertook a number of recitals in London and elsewhere to publicize and spread the art. In 1906 they took their lecture-demonstration, now entitled 'Literature and the Living Voice', on a provincial tour to Liverpool and Leeds, while WBY also spoke on the same topic in Aberdeen and Dundee. Given this level of demand, it was felt necessary to print the circular which follows. The circular could be used to advertise combined lectures or demonstrations given by FF alone, and she distributed it to encourage bookings on her American tour of 1907. WBY and FF gave their final lecture-demonstration on 16 February 1911, the tenth anniversary of their first recital, at the Little Theatre, London, and shortly before she emigrated to Ceylon FF performed her final solo performance on the psaltery to a crowded audience at the Clavier Hall on 18 July 1912.

## LECTURES by Mr. W. B. YEATS
## on POETRY & the LIVING VOICE.
*Illustrated by Miss FLORENCE FARR.*

---

*Professor Herford, in the 'Manchester Guardian,' 9th May.*—For some months past various London audiences, public and private, have been making acquaintance with what its professors claimed to be 'a new art.' A certain mystery hung, and probably for most minds still hangs, about the invention, for neither performers nor auditors seemed able to find exact and definite terms for the effects they produced or the impressions they received. If you tried to catechise them you were met by evasions or negatives, and probably given to understand that 'it' was wonderfully impressive but beyond description. Songs and poems were rendered to the accompaniment of a psaltery; so much was clear. But the 'rendering' was declared to be neither speech, nor music, nor recitative, but something combining the virtues and the charm of all three. The point of real interest and importance in this 'new art' which at once disengaged it from the crowd of fashionable pastimes and elegant excitements, was that it claimed to be the one ideally satisfying mode of rendering poetry to the ear—the kind of utterance most consonant, in its delicate poise between the ways of song and of speech, to the poetic temper itself.

Such claims might well have provoked scepticism. But they happened to be advanced, with the ardour of conviction, by two persons peculiarly qualified to put them to the test—a distinguished actress, Miss Florence Farr, and a yet more distinguished poet, Mr. W. B. Yeats. In a striking article in the 'Monthly Review' for May, 1902, Mr. Yeats described his first impressions with engaging frankness:—

'I have always known that there was something I disliked about singing, and I naturally dislike print and paper, but now at last I understand why, for I have found something better. I have just heard a poem spoken with so delicate a sense of its rhythm, with so perfect a respect for its meaning, that if I were a wise man and could persuade a few people to learn the art I would never open a book of verses again. A friend who was here a few minutes ago has sat with a beautiful stringed instrument upon her knee, her fingers passing over the strings, and has spoken to me some of my own poems and some verses from Shelley's "Skylark." . . . Wherever the rhythm was most delicate, wherever the emotion was most ecstatic, her art was most beautiful, and yet, though she sometimes spoke to a little tune, it was never singing, never anything but speech. A singing note, a word chanted as they chant in churches, would have spoiled everything; nor was it reciting, for she spoke to a notation as definite as that of song, using the instrument, which murmured sweetly and faintly under the spoken sounds, to give her the changing notes. Another speaker could have repeated all her effects except those which came from her own beautiful voice, that would have given her fame if the only art that gives the speaking voice its perfect opportunity were as well known among us as it was known in the ancient world.'

Mr. Yeats goes on to describe his earlier gropings after a perfectly expressive vocal medium for his verse, such as he now believed that he had found. Musical friends advised him to have his songs set to music; but that meant, as he well knew, an absolute surrender of the poet to the musician, the 'natural music' of his words being altered or 'drowned in another music which I did not understand.' 'What was the good of writing a love-song if the singer pronounced love "lo-o-o-o-ove," or even if he said "love" but did not give it its exact place and weight in the rhythm?' Of technical music he was wholly ignorant. But he heard the 'natural music' of his own and others' poetic speech with all the greater delicacy and distinctness. 'Like every other poet, I spoke verses in a kind of chant when I was making them.' When he repeated them he could not always 'chant' them in the same way, but he 'always felt that certain ways were right, and that I would know one of them if I remembered the way I first spoke the poem.' His object was, then, to find a means, available for others, of fixing these 'right ways.' After various experiments with musicians, who mostly declared that his 'chant' could not be written down in musical notation since it contained quarter-tones, he finally had the good fortune to encounter Mr. Arnold Dolmetsch, who contrived an instrument, 'half psaltery, half lyre,' containing all the chromatic intervals within the range of the speaking voice, and taught Mr. Yeats and his associate to 'regulate their speech by the ordinary musical notes.'

The result might be described as a subtly modulated monotone—the monotone which in the hands of a great artist can often thrill us with a more potent magic than all the bright play of contrasts—the monotone of Rembrandt's shadows, of twilight, of the tolling bell. The faint undertone of the psaltery does for the poetry which it accompanies something of what is done for a landscape by far-off notes of music exquisitely fitted to sustain the mood it excites. Ordinary recitation of verse tends to vary between the sing-song manner, which sacrifices it to an idle tune, and the prose manner, which sacrifices it to the formless jumble of common speech. These are gross and garish effects, encouraged and diffused by modern acting. Mr. Yeats, himself a master of subtly modulated monotone, of glimmering twilights and lustrous glooms, has unusual title to be heard when he claims as the true principle of vocal expression in poetry 'a monotony in external things for the sake of internal variety, a sacrifice of gross effects to subtle effects, an asceticism of the imagination.'

Many readers may be inclined to dismiss this as another vagary of the 'Celtic Renascence,' of which they think, excusably, that they have had enough. But impartial witnesses of other schools have testified to the singular heightening of effect which is attained by this simple and subtle blending of psaltery and voice practised by Miss Farr and Mr. Yeats. In particular, Mr. William Archer, whose trained judgment is not lightly imposed upon, has publicly admitted the impressiveness of their performance.

'THE TIMES,' 7th May, 1903.—The natural intonation of words, in fact, is the important thing, and the tune is no more than the embodiment of the spirit of unity which runs through a poem, and holds together the subtle varieties of separate lines or phrases. The office of music, as Gluck said, is to enforce the expression of the sentiment without weakening it by superfluous ornament; and the art of chanting is the invention of the revival of a conscious attempt to systematise in poetry the natural music which should exist in every sentence of ordinary conversation, and does, as Hazlitt noted, in moments of exaltation and excitement. . . . After all, what is the essential difference between the chanting of the Mass, always the same words to the same notes, and the more liberal course of Miss Farr's sympathetic and perfectly managed voice? . . . Many people would be interested if Mr. Yeats dilated further on this revived art, and those who were not would forgive him for the sake of Miss Farr's chanting to the Psaltery.

*Mr. E. K. Chambers, in 'The Academy,' 9th May.*—Mr. Yeats' 'new art' of spoken poetry. . . . It was a very charming performance, and if the dramatic recitation were to give way to the musical recitation, one would have reason to be grateful.

*Mr. G. K. Chesterton, in the 'Daily News,' 16th May.*—I have within the last two or three days twice had the pleasure of hearing Mr. W. B. Yeats give some of his admirable expositions of the right vocal treatment of poetry and of the primary nature of the poet, once at the recitals which Miss Florence Farr has been giving at Clifford's Inn, and once at the Westminster Lectures. No one assuredly has done so much for the right appreciation of primitive literature in the modern, intellectual world as Mr. Yeats. In his view, as is well known, verse should be neither sung nor said; it should be intoned, as it were, to a simple notation, whereby every word is pronounced so as to reach the ear like a conversational utterance, but also to reach a certain tone, like a definite note in a song. This, he maintains, is the original art of the minstrels and the troubadours, the original art in which all love, religion, and history were once expressed. It is clear, of course, that the very use of the words 'sing' and 'song' and 'lyre,' as connected with poetry, still refers back to this age before pen and ink; it is as absurd to talk of the modern Poet Laureate singing his poems as to talk of him playing them on the trombone. Miss Florence Farr has developed a beautiful manner of so intoning some selections on a weird-looking instrument as to illustrate Mr. Yeats's meaning almost to perfection. And it is Mr. Yeats's theory that the remedy—at least the only feasible remedy at present, for this reign of vulgarity and cynical inattention which now, as he said in a fine phrase, 'has made all the arts outlawed'—is to draw yet closer the circle of culture, and to go on performing as specialities the things which were once universal habits of men, singing, telling stories, and celebrating festivals.

*The Musical Critic of the 'Manchester Guardian,' 19th May, 1903.*—An obvious comment on the art of speaking to the psaltry—as contrived by Mr. Yeats, Mr. Dolmetsch and Miss Florence Farr—and practised by Miss Farr—is that it consists in mixing ordinary speech and a rudimentary kind of song. Mr. Yeats's idea is an important one—I believe a sound one. Like other poets, he hates the musical apparatus which, in an ordinary way, simply distracts attention from the words, or, if it does at all interpret the words, catches them up into an alien sphere and interprets them not in the manner desired by the poet. Mr. Yeats feels sure that in the Hellenic world this was not so, and that it ought not to be so now. He has here laid hold upon a most important fact—the modern impoverishment both of music and of poetry by the divorce between those arts. This is part of the broader fact that we have not any such harmony among the arts as the Greeks of the great age possessed, but are harassed by 'the sick hurry, the divided aims,' of which Matthew Arnold complained. If we are ever to find a way back to a true harmony between music and poetry it will almost certainly be by some such way as Mr. Yeats's—that is to say, by consulting the poet, who has hitherto not been allowed to exercise the slightest influence over the musician, except in the very rare cases where poet and musician have been identical, as with Wagner and Cornelius. Such cases are too exceptional to be of much interest for Mr. Yeats, who desires to alter the entire attitude of the public towards poetry, and make them regard it essentially as something to be heard rather than something to be read in silence. For such a purpose nothing depending on the extremely elaborate and difficult *technique* of modern music will serve, and it is, therefore, possible that Mr. Yeats may be on the track of an important discovery.

## THE CHORUS of CLASSICAL PLAYS TO THE MUSIC OF A PSALTERY BY FLORENCE FARR

Miss JANE ELLEN HARRISON, LL.D., Aberdeen, D.Ltt. Durham, Lecturer and sometime Fellow of Newnham College, Cambridge, writes:—
'I have twice, at the recent reproductions in London of the *Hippolytus* of Euripides, had the great pleasure of hearing Miss Florence Farr lead the chorus. Miss Farr is an artist with a wonderful mesmeric voice, that to hear is a joy; and her method of recitation is all her own. Something of this method she was good enough to explain to me. It is neither spoken recitation, nor singing, nor, in the ordinary sense, intoning. It is really more natural than any of these yet, so accustomed are we to artificial methods, that it strikes the ear at first as strange. After a long experience in listening to Greek choruses, I felt, when I heard Miss Farr, that at last a method had been found which, while it kept much of the emotional poignancy of music, yet left the words articulate and their natural rhythm unclouded and unhampered by an alien tune.'

The translator of Euripides into English verse, Professor GILBERT MURRAY, M.A., LL.D., Emeritus Professor of Greek in the University of Glasgow, sometime Fellow of New College, Oxford, writes:—
'Miss Farr's method of speaking or chanting lyrical verse to the accompaniment of a psaltery, seems to me to possess not only unusual charm but also very great scientific and historical interest. The methods of ancient bards, Greek or Celtic, are very little known to us, and it is difficult to see how any exact knowledge of them could now be recovered. But Miss Farr has developed a treatment of poetry, which must be very like theirs in spirit. It was after hearing her for the first time that it first seemed to me possible to produce Greek choruses on the English stage.

To my feeling her method provides lyrical poetry with just the means of expression that it needs.'

Mr. W. B. YEATS in 'Samhain,' December, 1904:—
'When I heard the Æschulean Trilogy at Stratford-on-Avon last spring I could not hear a word of the chorus, except in a few lines here and there which were spoken without musical setting. The chorus was not without dramatic, or rather operatic effect; but why should those singers have taken so much trouble to learn by heart so much of the greatest lyric poetry of Greece. "Twinkle, twinkle, little star," or any other memory of their childhood would have served their turn. If it had been comic verse, the singing-master and the musician would have respected it, and the audience would have been able to hear.

Mr. Dolmetsch and Miss Florence Farr have been working for some time to find out some way of setting serious poetry, which will enable us to hear it, and the singer to sing sweetly and yet never to give a word, a cadence, or an accent, that would not be given it in ordinary passionate speech. They are trying to re-discover an art that is only remembered or half-remembered in ships and in hovels and among wandering tribes of uncivilised men, and they have to make their experiment with singers who have been trained by a method of teaching that professes to change a human being into a musical instrument, a creation of science, "something other than human life." In old days the singer began to sing over the rocking cradle or among the wine cups, and it was as though life itself caught fire of a sudden; but to-day the poet, fanatic that he is, watches the singer go up on the platform, wondering and expecting every moment that he will punch himself as if he were a bag. It is certainly impossible to speak with perfect expression after you have been a bagpipes for many years, even though you have been making the most beautiful music all the time.

The success of the chorus in the performance of *Hippolytus* last Spring—I did not see the more recent performance, but hear upon all hands that the chorus was too large—the expressiveness of the greater portion as mere speech, has, I believe, re-created the chorus as a dramatic method. The greater portion of the singing, as arranged by Miss Farr, even when four or five voices sang together, though never when ten sang together, was altogether admirable speech, and some of it was speech of extraordinary beauty. When one lost the meaning, even perhaps where the whole chorus sang together, it was not because of a defective method, but because it is the misfortune of every new artistic method that we can only judge of it through performers who must be for a long time unpractised. This new art has a double difficulty, for the training of a modern singer makes articulate speech, as a poet understands it, nearly impossible, and those who are masters of speech very often, perhaps usually, are poor musicians. Fortunately Miss Farr, who has some knowledge of music, has, it may be, the most beautiful voice on the English stage, and is in her management of it an exquisite artist.'

Miss DOROTHEA BEAL, Principal of Cheltenham Ladies' College, writes:—
'Miss Farr gave an exposition of speaking to the music of a psaltery here in the summer of 1903. The kind of chant would be most suitable for a chorus of

Euripides, and would be heard at a great distance, so I dare say the Greeks adopted this stately recitative, which would be in harmony with the whole spirit of the performance.'

THE RULES AND ADMINISTRATION OF THE IRISH NATIONAL THEATRE SOCIETY went through a number of transformations in its formative years. Beginning as an amalgam of several smaller organizations—the Irish Literary Theatre, the Fays' amateur Ormond Dramatic Society, the Inghinidhe na hEireann (Daughters of Ireland), and AE's Hermeticists—each with a different aesthetic and political agenda, it formally constituted itself on 9 August 1902 with W. G. Fay, Frank Fay, Dudley Digges, P. J. Kelly, Maire Walker, Maire T. Quinn, Helen Laird, Fred Ryan, James Starkey, and George Roberts as founding members. At this first General Meeting they appointed WBY as president (after AE had declined); AE, MG, and Hyde as vice-presidents (Edward Martyn, also proposed as vice-president, declined the office); and Frederick Ryan as secretary. The same meeting elected James Cousins, Frank Walker, Thomas Keohler, H. Norman, Synge, Colum, and Sara Allgood as members, and AG, Stephen Gwynn, Maire Garvey, Udolphus Wright, and Vera Esposito were admitted at a subsequent meeting.

A series of disputes over the selection of plays, political bias, and the conditions of membership showed the need for clear rules. Early in 1903 the Society, prompted by a letter from MG, and under the guidance of AE and Fred Ryan, set about drafting these. It is significant that the Society was registered under the Friendly Societies Act of 1896 as a co-operative venture, and not under the Companies Act as a commercial undertaking. A copy of the draft was sent to WBY whose amendments were incorporated into the final version, which was approved at a General Meeting on 15 February 1903.

The acquisition of the Abbey Theatre as a permanent home in 1904 depended upon the granting of a Patent, and this not only set out conditions for the running of the new Theatre, but also laid legal restrictions on the kinds of play that the Society was permitted to produce. The desirability of now paying the more important actors made it necessary to rewrite the rules in August 1905. At first, this was envisaged as no more than a revision of the existing constitution, but as AE and Ryan worked at drafting, and with the enthusiastic support of WBY, it became clear that a more radical rewriting was required. At the end of September AE suggested the step of reconstituting the Society as a limited liability company rather than as a Friendly Society. This was probably the most far-reaching step taken in the history of the Abbey Theatre, and entirely altered its power structures and policies. The new rules were drawn up under the Industrial and Provident Societies Act of 1893, and later amended to comply with the Companies Consolidated Act of 1908. Despite unease in the Company at these changes (unease that was shared by AE and Ryan who had drafted them) the new constitution was adopted at a meeting of the Society on 24 Oct 1905. What follows are the various rules and constitutions arranged chronologically, including AE's transitional document of September 1905.

## 1. ORIGINAL RULES OF THE IRISH NATIONAL THEATRE SOCIETY, AUGUST 1902

### I.

The name of the society shall be 'The Irish National Theatre Society'

### II.

Its objects shall be to create an Irish National Theatre, to act and produce plays, in Irish or English, written by Irish writers, or on Irish subjects, and such dramatic works of foreign authors as will tend to educate and interest the public of this country in the higher aspects of dramatic art.

### III.

The Society shall consist firstly of President, Vice Presidents, Stage Manager, Secretary, Assistant Secretary, and Actors and Members: and secondly of associates who may hereafter be admitted by a three quarters majority of the votes of the members of the Society at a meeting called for the purpose and who shall pay an annual subscription of [*space left blank*] yearly, but who shall have no vote in the selection of plays or in the management of the Society.

### IV.

A Reading Committee of five members shall be elected who shall first consider all plays proposed for performance by the Society. No play shall be performed until it has been recommended by this Committee. Final acceptance or rejection of any play thus recommended shall rest with the members of the Society, to whom such plays shall be read at meetings summoned for the purpose when a three quarters majority of those present shall decide. The author shall not be allowed to be present when the vote is taken.

### V.

No official of the Society shall have power to accept a play or to reject one which shall have been accepted and passed in accordance with the foregoing rules. The Stage Manager and Author shall have the sole right to decide on questions as to how a scene shall be acted and the choice of actors shall be left to the decision of the Stage Manager upon consultation with the Author.

These rudimentary rules, almost certainly drawn up by AE and Fred Ryan, gave the Society an official existence and addressed themselves to defining correct practice in those areas—the mechanism for choosing plays and the remit of the stage manager—that had already proved contentious in the Company's short life. But any organization that had ambitions to be a National Theatre needed a legal status, and thus it was that AE and Ryan carried on with the labour of drafting a more elaborate constitution that would conform to the requirements of the Friendly Societies Act.

## 2. 1903 CONSTITUTION UNDER THE FRIENDLY SOCIETIES ACT
### RULES
of the
### Irish National Theatre Society.

### I.—NAME AND PLACE OF OFFICE OF THE SOCIETY

(*a.*) The Society shall be called the 'IRISH NATIONAL THEATRE SOCIETY.' Its registered office shall be at 34 Lower Camden Street, Dublin, in the County of Dublin.

(*b.*) In the event of any change in the situation of the registered office, notice of such change shall be sent to the Registrar within fourteen days.

### II.—OBJECTS OF THE SOCIETY

(*a.*) The objects of the Society shall be to create an Irish National Theatre, to act and produce plays in Irish or English, written by Irish writers, or on Irish subjects; and such dramatic works of foreign authors as would tend to educate and interest the public of this country in the higher aspects of dramatic art.

(*b.*) The funds of the Society shall be applicable only to further the objects mentioned in Section (*a*).

### III.—MEMBERSHIP

(*a.*) The Society shall consist, in the first instance, of the seven signatories to these rules, and hereafter of those whom they may admit at the first General Meeting of the Society.

(*b.*) After the first General Meeting of the Society, no one shall become a member who shall not have been admitted by a three-quarters' majority of the votes of the members of the Society who are present at a meeting called for the purpose.

(*c.*) The President, Vice-Presidents, and Secretary shall *ex officio* be members of the Society.

(*d.*) The Society may admit associate-members, persons who shall pay an annual subscription of not less than ten shillings. They shall be admitted as Associates by the Committee on application and payment of the subscription, but shall have no vote in the selection of plays, or in the management of the Society. They shall be entitled to free admission to such performances as may be specified by the Committee.

(*e.*) Members may withdraw from the Society by giving written notice to the Secretary.

(*f.*) A member may be expelled by the vote of two-thirds of the members present at a Special General Meeting of the Society upon a charge, in writing, of conduct detrimental to the Society, communicated to the Secretary one fortnight before the meeting is summoned.

(*g*.) Associates who have not paid their annual subscription when due lapse from membership.

(*h*.) The Committee shall have power to give a retaining fee to any member or actor if it seems desirable. If a retaining fee is given to a member he or she shall engage on his or her part not to act in any play not produced by the Society during the period for which the retaining fee is given, without the permission of the Committee.

## IV.—GENERAL MEETINGS

(*a*.) The first meeting of members shall have the same powers as are herein given to the Annual General Meeting.

(*b*.) An Annual General Meeting of members shall be held during the months of April or May in each year.

(*c*.) The functions of the Annual General Meeting shall be:—

(1.) To receive from the Committee, Auditors, or other officers of the Society a report and full statement of accounts for the preceding year, and the audited balance sheet, and, if satisfactory, to adopt them.

(2.) To decide any appeal referred to, if from a decision of the Committee, provided that not less than seven days' notice of any such matter being brought before the meeting has been given to the Secretary.

(3.) To elect the President, Vice-Presidents, Committee of Management, Reading Committee, Auditor and Treasurer as required by the rules.

(4.) To transact any other general business of the Society.

(*d*.) A Special General Meeting of members may be called at any time by the Committee, and on receipt of a demand signed by no less than one-fifth of the members, it shall be the duty of the Secretary to call such a meeting.

(*e*.) No member shall be entitled to more than one vote upon any matter submitted for consideration at any general meeting.

(*f*.) Ten members shall constitute a quorum of an Annual or Special General Meeting.

(*g*.) Any resolution which commands a three-quarter's majority of the votes of those present shall be considered carried.

## V.—THE DUTIES AND POWERS OF THE COMMITTEE

(*a*.) The Committee of Management shall be elected at the Annual General Meeting of the Society. They shall be eligible for re-election on the expiry of their term of office.

(*b*.) Members of Committee must also be members of the Society. They shall not receive salary or other remuneration.

(*c*.) The Committee shall be seven in number, and three shall form a quorum. In case of parity of voting the Chairman shall have a casting vote. They shall have control of the business arrangements. All questions relating to the payment of money and the terms on which engagements may be entered upon shall be decided by them. No engagement shall be made without their sanction. The stage manager shall, *ex-officio*, be a member of the Committee, who shall nominate their own chairman. The Committee may from time to time, as may be found necessary, appoint an acting manager, whose duty it shall be to see that all arrangements decided upon by them shall be carried out. The Committee shall meet as often as the business of the Society requires.

(*d*.) The Committee shall have power, if they deem it necessary, to remunerate any official of the Society or actor for his work.

(*e*.) The Committee shall have the rules of the Society printed, and shall provide the Secretary with a sufficient number of copies of the rules to enable him to deliver to any person on demand a copy of such rules on payment of a sum not exceeding one shilling for non-members.

(*f*.) The Committee shall provide the Secretary with a sufficient number of copies of the last annual return or balance sheet, or other document duly audited, containing the same particulars as in the Annual Return, as to receipts and expenditure for supplying gratuitously every member or person interested in the funds of the Society, and it shall be the duty of the Secretary to supply such gratuitous copies on application. The Committee shall always keep a copy of the last annual balance sheet of the Society for the time being, together with the Auditor's report, hung up in a conspicuous place at the registered office of the Society.

(*g*.) The Committee shall every year before the 1st of June, cause the Secretary to send to the Registrar, in the form prescribed by the Chief Registrar of Friendly Societies, a General Statement, to be called the Annual Return of the receipts, expenditure, funds, and effects of the Society as audited, which shall show separately the expenditure in respect of the several objects of the Society, and shall be made out on the 31st [*sic*] April then last inclusively. A copy of the Auditor's Report shall also be sent to the Registrar with the Annual Return, and such annual return shall state whether the audit has been conducted by a public auditor, appointed under the Friendly Societies' Act, and by whom; and if such audit has been conducted by any persons other than a public auditor, shall state the name, address, and calling of each of such persons, and the manner in which they were appointed.

(*h*.) The Committee shall have power to open a banking account if they consider it desirable, and any payments by cheque shall be signed by two members of the Committee, and be countersigned by the Secretary.

(*i*.) All properties, scenery, and dresses which are acquired by the Society shall belong to the Society, and their disposal or use, or the lending of any such properties, shall be decided by the Committee.

(*j*.) Any decision of the Committee affecting the Society shall be communicated to the members, and if any objection be made by one-fifth of the members, the vote of the Society shall be taken in the matter, when three-quarter's majority shall decide.

(*k*.) Any acting member taking part in any performance other than those given by the Society, shall give notice of such engagement to the Secretary, who shall submit same to the Committee, who shall decide whether or not such performance is prejudicial to the interests of the Society. If, against the decision of the

Committee, any such acting member should take part in performances other than those given by the society, the Committee shall have power to suspend any such person from membership until the matter has been brought before a Special General Meeting of Members, whose decision shall be final.

(*l.*) The Committee shall have the appointment of the Stage Manager and Secretary of the Society.

## VI.—THE READING COMMITTEE AND THE SELECTION OF PLAYS FOR PERFORMANCE

(*a.*) The Reading Committee shall be elected at the Annual General Meeting of the Society. The Members shall be eligible for re-election on the expiry of their term of office.

(*b.*) The Reading Committee shall be six in number; and they shall first consider all plays proposed for performance by the Society. No play shall be performed until it has been recommended by the Reading Committee. The final acceptance or rejection of any play thus recommended shall rest with the Members of the Society, to whom such plays shall be read at meetings summoned for the purpose, when a three-quarters' majority of those present shall decide. The author shall not be allowed to be present when a vote is taken.

(*c.*) No official of the Society shall have power to accept a play on behalf of the Society, or to reject one which shall have been accepted and passed in accordance with the foregoing rules.

(*d.*) No play shall be accepted or rejected on political grounds solely, and the literary, dramatic, and acting merits of the play shall primarily be considered, and no objection raised to a play on the ground that its performance would antagonize any political party shall be valid unless it should be considered that there is any degradation of National ideals in the work submitted.

## VII.—THE STAGE MANAGER

The Stage Manager and Author shall have the sole right to decide on questions as to how a scene shall be acted, and the choice of actors shall be left to the decision of the Stage Manager in consultation with the author.

## VIII.—THE TRUSTEES

(*a.*) The General Meeting shall elect one or more Trustees to hold the property of the Society. These Trustees shall be entitled to invest any money belonging to the Society, which is not required as working capital, in such of the following manners as the Committee shall sanction:—

In the Post Office Savings' Bank; Public Funds; Government Securities in Great Britain or India or the Colonies; Debentures or other Securities of any Company incorporated by Charter or Act of Parliament, and paying dividend; or in the Securities of any County, Borough, Parish, Council, or Rates authorised to be levied and Mortgaged by Act of Parliament.

(*b*.) A copy of every resolution appointing a Trustee shall be sent within fourteen days to the Registrar in the form prescribed by the Treasury regulation.

## IX.—THE TREASURER

(*a*.) The Annual general Meeting shall appoint a Treasurer, who shall be a member of the Committee. Security may be given by him in the form prescribed by the Act, and for such amount as the Annual General Meetings may determine. He shall receive from the Secretary all moneys paid to him on behalf of the Society.

(*b*.) The Treasurer may also hold the position of Secretary if the latter office is an honorary one.

(*c*.) All moneys paid to the Treasurer, if the Committee so decide, shall be placed by him to the account of the Society in such bank as the Committee select.

(*d*.) In the temporary absence of the Treasurer, the Committee shall appoint two of their number to perform his duties. Should he resign his position, a Special General Meeting shall be called to elect another member to take the office.

## X.—THE SECRETARY

(*a*.) The Committee shall appoint and shall have power to remove a Secretary, and shall also have power to fix some remuneration for his services. The duties of the Secretary shall be:—

(1.) To summon and attend all meetings of the Society and the Committee.

(2.) To record the whole of the transactions of the Society in books provided for the purpose; to conduct correspondence on behalf of the Society; to prepare the Annual Return and the Balance Sheet, and to have charge of the documents, books, and vouchers for payment made on behalf of the Society, and to pay all accounts passed by the Committee.

(*b*.) The Committee may sanction the appointment of an Assistant Secretary, if they deem it necessary, who shall act in the absence of the Secretary.

(*c*.) The Books and Accounts of the Society shall be open to the inspection of any members at the registered office, or at any place where the same are kept, and it shall be the duty of the Secretary to produce them for inspection if called upon at any reasonable time.

(*d*.) The Accounts shall show the Expenditure and Receipts and the expenses of Management.

## XI.—AUDIT OF ACCOUNTS

The Committee of Management shall, once at least in every year, submit the accounts, together with a general statement of the same, and all necessary vouchers up to the 31st December then last for audit, either to one of the public auditors appointed under the Friendly Societies' Act, or two or more persons appointed as auditors by the members of the Annual General Meeting each year, and shall lay before every such meeting a balance sheet showing the receipts and expenditure, funds and effects of the Society, together with a statement of the affairs of the Society since the last ordinary meeting, and of their then condition. Such auditors shall have access to all the books and accounts of the Society, and shall examine every balance sheet and annual return of the receipts and expenditure, funds and effects of the Society, and shall verify the same, with the accounts and vouchers relating thereto, and shall either sign the same as found by them to be correct, duly vouched, and in accordance with law, or shall specially report to the meeting of the Society before which the same is laid, in what respects they find it incorrect or not in accordance with law.

## XII.—ALTERATION OF RULES

The Rules of the Society can only be altered or rescinded by vote of a Special General Meeting, a statement of the suggested amendments being given in the notice convening the meeting, which shall be issued not less than fourteen days prior to the meeting.

## XIII.—SETTLEMENT OF DISPUTE

Any dispute arising between the members or officials of the Society shall first of all be referred to the Committee, and, if their decision be not accepted, it shall be brought before a Special General Meeting of members, whose decision shall be final.

## XIV.—DISSOLUTION OF THE SOCIETY

The Society at any time may be dissolved by the consent of five-sixths of the members, testified by their signature to an instrument of dissolution in the form provided by the Treasury regulations in that behalf.

The foregoing are the Rules of the Irish National Theatre Society.

> WILLIAM G. FAY.
> PATRICK J. KELLY.
> FREDERICK RYAN.
> HELEN S. LAIRD.
> MAIRE WALKER.
> JAMES STARKEY.
> F. J. FAY.
> GEORGE ROBERTS, *Secretary*

These rules guided the conduct of the Society through its first two years, and, with their provision for Special General Meetings as well as an Annual Meeting, indicate the co-operative and democratic spirit in which the Society was first conceived. Although it was found necessary to amend the rules governing the Reading Committee, there was no reason to suppose in 1903 that this constitution would not serve the Society for the rest of its existence. It was issued from 34 Lower Camden Street, but this was less a 'registered office' than a small and inadequate hall which was the Company's first permanent home and which was so inconvenient that it could only be used for rehearsals. Although both WBY and the Fays had hopes of finding some more satisfactory base, they could not have anticipated the effect of AEFH's extraordinary generosity in providing them with a fully equipped theatre on a site in the heart of Dublin. But before moving into the Abbey Theatre in late December 1904 certain essential legal steps were necessary, in particular the application for a theatrical patent, and this, like the 1903 constitution, further defined, and in some aspects, circumscribed the emerging Theatre.

In 1786, during the reign of George III, the Irish Parliament passed 'An Act for Regulating the Stage in the City and County of Dublin', requiring theatres to secure a patent, valid for twenty-one years but usually renewable, from the Crown. The Hall of the Mechanics Institute, which AEFH and Joseph Holloway converted into the Abbey Theatre, had in fact been granted a patent in the mid-nineteenth century when it opened as the Princess Theatre on the site of the old Theatre Royal. It was rebuilt following a severe fire, and reopened in 1874 as the New Princess Theatre of Varieties, but neglected to renew the patent and so it was necessary for AEFH to apply for a new one. Her application was opposed by the existing Dublin theatres on commercial grounds, and she had to argue her case before J. H. Campbell, the Irish Solicitor-General, on 4 August 1904. She mustered a strong supporting team, including WBY, W. G. Fay, T. P. Gill, T. W. Rolleston, T. C. Harrington, Horace Plunkett, and the Rt. Hon. William Frederick Bailey, and their testimony won the day. However, although favourably disposed towards the granting of a patent, Campbell was sympathetic to some of the objections raised by the other Dublin managers and on 5 August 1904, in the presence of AEFH's legal representatives, asked the lawyers on both sides to see if they could not draft a series of conditions which would limit the patent 'for the special purpose for which Miss Horniman required it and safeguard the rights of the existing theatres'. This they did and on 20 August placed certain 'restrictive clauses' before him in the library of Dublin Castle. These included the stipulation that the Abbey should confine itself to 'plays in the Irish or English language written by Irish writers or on Irish subjects, and such dramatic works of foreign authors as would tend to educate and interest the public of this country in the higher works of dramatic art, all the foregoing to be selected by the Irish National Theatre Society under the provisions of part 6 of its rules now existing and subject to the restrictions therein contained'. There were also clauses against assigning the rights in the patent to any person other than a trustee for Miss Horniman, and insisting that the patent would cease if the Irish National Theatre Society were to be dissolved. No physical enlargement of the Theatre was to be permitted and no licence for the sale of alcoholic drinks was to be granted. These alterations satisfied Campbell and were incorporated into the final version of the deed. Although drawn up in consultation with AEFH's lawyers and acceptable to her and to WBY, two of these late additions—the stipulations about choosing plays according to rule six and the cessation of the patent in case of dissolution—were to cause difficulties after the schism in the Company early in 1906.

Another complication was that only those domiciled in Ireland could be granted an Irish theatre patent, and to comply with this requirement AEFH nominated AG as her trustee, legally indemnifying her against any liability that this might incur. Although ostensibly granted for twenty-one years, the patent had to be renewed after only six, meaning that there would have to be serious renegotiations before December 1910. If AEFH decided to carry on supporting the Abbey these negotiations would be straightforward, but if, as turned out, she declined to continue with the arrangements, the Directors would have to find the resources to buy her out.

Thus, for all its quaint formulaic phraseology, the patent was an important legal and indeed practical document, which not only set out the justification for the new Theatre but also described the conditions under which the patentee was to retain her rights, spelt out the mechanism for the selection of plays, gave detailed instructions on the safety measures to be employed in the Theatre, and stipulated the conditions under which the patent would lapse. AEFH later complained that the process of applying for a patent cost her in all £405-2s.-10d. (the price of an equivalent licence in London would have been less than £10). The final portion of the fee – £48 – went to the Crown and Hanaper Office for copying the document onto five richly decorated sheets of vellum about four feet long by three feet wide, with an attached seal, six inches in diameter. This elaborate, costly, and unwieldy artefact apparently perished in the Abbey fire of 1951 and is reconstructed here from typescript copies.

## 3. THE ABBEY PATENT, DECEMBER 1904.

WARRANT FOR LETTERS PATENT for a new Theatre in the City of Dublin
(Signed) Edward R & I.

Right Trusty and Well-Beloved Cousin and Councillor we greet you well!
Our Will and Pleasure is that you forthwith cause effectual Letters to be passed under the Great Seal of that part of Our United Kingdom of Great Britain and Ireland in the form and to the effect following.
EDWARD THE SEVENTH, by the Grace of God, of the United Kingdom of Great Britain and Ireland and of the British Dominions beyond the Seas KING, Defender of the Faith, to all to whom these Presents shall come
GREETING!

WHEREAS by a certain Act of Parliament of Ireland passed in the Twenty-sixth year of the reign of His late Majesty King George III entitled: "An Act for regulating the stage in the City and County of Dublin" it is amongst other things enacted that it should and might be lawful to and for His Majesty His Heirs and Successors to grant under the Great Seal of Ireland for such term not exceeding Twenty-one years and under such restrictions, conditions and limitations as to him or them should seem meet from time to time and when and so often as he or they should think fit one or more Letters Patent to one or more persons for establishing or keeping one or more well-regulated Theatre or Theatres, Play-house or Play-houses in the City of Dublin and in the liberties, suburbs and County thereof and in the County of Dublin.

AND WHEREAS Annie Elizabeth Fredericka Horniman of H-1, Montague Mansions, Portman Square, in the County of London, Spinster, by her Memorial represented unto you Our Lieutenant General and General Governor of that part of Our United Kingdom of Great Britain and Ireland called Ireland.

That by the Act of Parliament passed in the Twenty-sixth year of the reign of His late Majesty King George III, Chapter 57, entitled "An Act for regulating the stage in the City and County of Dublin" it was amongst other things enacted that it should be lawful for His said Majesty and His Successors to grant under the Great Seal of that part of the United Kingdom called Ireland for any term not exceeding Twenty-one years as therein mentioned from time to time Letters Patent for establishing one or more Theatre or Theatres, Play-house or Play-houses in the City of Dublin and in the suburbs and County thereof and in the County of Dublin.

That Memorialist was an English woman residing in London but being a patron of good dramatic art was very anxious to assist the Society known as the Irish National Theatre Society registered under the Friendly Societies Act, 1896. That the Society was formed to continue on a more permanent basis the work begun by the Irish Literary Theatre. Its objects were to endeavour to create an Irish National Theatre by producing plays written in Irish or English by Irish writers or on Irish subjects or such dramatic works of foreign authors as would tend to educate and interest the Irish public in the higher aspects of dramatic art. That it was not a Society having profit as its basis but the encouragement of dramatic art in Ireland. That the Society had already produced several plays both in Dublin and in London and had from all quarters met with great praise and encouragement. Memorialist referred to certain extracts from newspapers showing the opinions of some of the leading critics in England. That many of these critics had pointed out that Ireland had evidenced by the plays the beginnings of a distinctive dramatic school growing out of the life of the Country and inspired by a high intellectual idea. That however successful this school of writers might become it was not likely that the performances would ever attain so great a degree of popularity as to become a serious rival to the existing theatres. That such movements no matter how deeply they might affect the more thinking people could never under modern conditions reach a popularity which would make them of commercial importance:

That Memorialist recognised the fact that the Irish National Theatre laboured under the great disadvantage of not having any suitable premises in which to produce its plays:

That Memorialist being possessed of some means and very anxious to encourage the Irish National Theatre had agreed to take a lease for ninety-nine years from the First day of May one thousand nine hundred and four of the Theatre belonging to the Dublin Mechanics Institute, Lower Abbey Street, in the City of Dublin, and a lease for a similar term of adjoining premises in Marlborough Street now known as the old Morgue so as to afford better access to the Theatre and the necessary accommodation for dressing rooms, etc.:

That the Theatre of the Dublin Mechanics Institute was firstly known as the Theatre Royal (there being in Dublin another theatre of the same name) and subsequently as the Princess Theatre and had attached to it a Patent for theatrical representations:

That this Patent appeared to have expired about the year 1850 and never to have been renewed:

That the object of Memorialist in taking the premises was solely to benefit the Irish National Theatre. That her intention was to allow this Theatre to have the use of the premises free of charge whenever required: at other times that Memorialist would desire to let the premises for concerts, lectures, amateur performances and such dramatic performances as those of the Elizabethan Stage Society. That she would, however, seek a general Patent:

That Memorialist did not contemplate lettings to ordinary travelling companies. For this reason and as the premises would only seat some six hundred people Memorialist submitted that the premises of which she had agreed to take a lease could never rival those of the existing Theatres:

And Memorialist prayed that a Patent under the Great Seal of Ireland under the provisions of the said Act of the 26th. George III, Chapter 57, entitled "An Act for regulating the stage in the City and County of Dublin" might be granted to Memorialist for a term of twenty-one years to enable Memorialist to establish and keep a well-regulated Theatre within the said City of Dublin and County of Dublin and therein at all lawful times publicly to act represent or perform or cause to be acted represented or performed all Interludes, Tragedies, Comedies, Preludes, Operas, Burlettas, Plays, Farces, Pantomimes or any part or parts thereof and of what kind or nature whatsoever:

AND WHEREAS Our Lord Justices General and General Governors of that part of Our said United Kingdom of Great Britain and Ireland called Ireland aforesaid in the absence of Our said Lieutenant General and General Governor of Ireland did on the eleventh day of July One thousand nine hundred and four, refer the said Memorial to Our Attorney-General and Solicitor-General for Ireland to consider thereof and to report unto Us what might be proper to be done thereon:

AND WHEREAS Our said Attorney-General and Solicitor-General duly considered the said Memorial and heard the statements of Counsel on the part of the said Memorialist and Counsel on behalf of patentees of the Theatre Royal, Dublin, the Gaiety Theatre, Dublin and the Queen's Theatre, Dublin, and what was offered on behalf of the said theatres and having received the consent of the said Annie Elizabeth Fredericka Horniman that any Patent that might be granted should be granted to Dame Isabella Augusta Gregory, of Coole Park, Gort, in the County of Galway, widow of the late Right Honourable Sir William Henry Gregory, K.C.M.G., as trustee for the said Annie Elizabeth Fredericka Horniman her executors, or administrators were of the opinion that We might if We should be pleased so to do, grant Letters Patent under the Great Seal of Ireland unto the said Dame Isabella Augusta Gregory for establishing and keeping a well-regulated Theatre or Play-house at the premises in Lower Abbey Street and Marlborough Street in the City of Dublin which were formerly known as the Dublin Mechanics Institute and the Morgue respectively for the term of six years under such conditions, restrictions and limitations as are herein set forth and We are graciously pleased to condescend thereto:

KNOW YE THEREFORE that We of Our special grace, certain knowledge and mere motion by and with the advice and consent of Our Right Trusty and Well-beloved Cousin and Councillor, William Humble, Earl of Dudley, Knight Grand Cross of Our Royal Victorian Order, Our Lieutenant General and General Governor of that part of Our said United Kingdom of Great Britain and Ireland called

Ireland, DO HEREBY grant unto the said Dame Isabella Augusta Gregory, her executors, administrators and such assigns as are hereinafter mentioned in trust for the said Annie Elizabeth Fredericka Horniman her executors or administrators, under the restrictions, conditions and limitations hereinafter mentioned, full power and authority to establish and keep in the building formerly known as the Dublin Mechanics Institute and the Morgue in the City of Dublin and indicated in the plans deposited in Our Privy Seal Office in Our Castle of Dublin a well-regulated Theatre or Play-house and therein at all lawful times (except when We or Our Chief Governor or Governors of that part of Our said United Kingdom of Great Britain and Ireland for the time being shall see cause to forbid the acting or performance of any species of plays, shows or theatrical amusements) publicly to act represent or perform or cause to be acted represented or performed all Interludes, Tragedies, Comedies, Plays in the Irish or English language written by Irish writers or on Irish subjects and such dramatic works of foreign authors as would tend to educate and interest the Irish public in the higher works of dramatic art and as may be selected by the Irish National Theatre Society under the provisions contained in part six of the Rules of the Irish National Theatre Society that is to say:

(a)  The Reading Committee shall be elected at the Annual General Meeting of the Society. The members shall be eligible for re-election on the expiry of their term of Office.

(b)  The Reading Committee shall be six in number and they shall first consider all plays proposed for performance by the Society. No play shall be performed until it has been recommended by the Reading Committee. The final acceptance or rejection of any play thus recommended shall rest with the members of the Society to whom such plays shall be read at meetings summoned for the purpose when a three-quarters majority of those present shall decide. The author shall not be allowed to be present when a vote is taken.

(c)  No official of the Society shall have power to accept a play on behalf of the Society or to reject one which shall have been accepted and passed in accordance with the foregoing rules.

(d)  No play shall be accepted or rejected on political grounds solely and the literary dramatic and acting merits of the play shall primarily be considered and no objections raised to a play on the grounds that its performance would antagonize any political party shall be valid unless that it should be considered that there is any degradation of National ideals in the work submitted PROVIDED that all such Interludes, Tragedies, Comedies and Plays shall be decent and becoming and not profane or obnoxious: TO HAVE AND TO HOLD the premises unto the said Dame Isabella Augusta Gregory her executors administrators and such assigns as are hereinafter mentioned in trust for the said Annie Elizabeth Fredericka Horniman her executors or administrators and for them to act represent and perform all such hereinbefore mentioned Interludes, Tragedies, Comedies, Plays or any part or parts thereof of the said nature or kind decent and becoming and not profane or obnoxious for and during the term time and space of six years from the first day of December one thousand nine hundred and four fully to be completed and ended:

AND WE DO HEREBY for Us Our Heirs and Successors strictly prohibit and forbid all persons whatsoever for and during the term time and space hereinbefore limited from presuming to erect build or keep open in any manner whatsoever or howsoever any theatre or theatres, stage or stages whatsoever within Our said City of Dublin or County of Dublin or therein to act represent or perform any Interlude, Tragedy or Comedy, Prelude, Opera, Burletta, Play, Farce, Pantomime or any other exhibition such as shall be authorised by these Our Letters Patent or any part or parts thereof unless they have been or shall be thereunto duly authorised and appointed by Us Our Heirs and Successors. AND WE DO HEREBY for Us Our Heirs and Successors grant unto the said Dame Isabella Augusta Gregory her executors administrators and such assigns as are hereinafter mentioned full power and license and authority from time to time to gather, entertain, govern, privilege and keep such and so many players and persons to exercise and act represent and perform all such Interludes, Tragedies, Comedies and Plays as aforesaid or any part or parts thereof as the said Dame Isabella Augusta Gregory her executors administrators or such assigns as are hereinafter mentioned shall think fit and requisite for that purpose which said Company shall be servants of Us Our Heirs and Successors and shall consist of such number of players and persons as the said Dame Isabella Augusta Gregory her executors administrators and such assigns as are hereinafter mentioned shall from time to time think fit and such persons to continue during the pleasure of the said Dame Isabella Augusta Gregory her executors administrators and such assigns as are hereinafter mentioned for the performance of the entertainments stated therein peaceably and quietly without any impediment or interruption of any person or persons whomsoever for the honest recreation of all such as shall desire to see the same. AND it shall and may be lawful to and for the said Dame Isabella Augusta Gregory her executors administrators and such assigns as are hereinafter mentioned to take and receive of such persons as shall resort to hear or see any such plays and entertainments of the stage as aforesaid such sum or sums of money as have customarily been taken in the like kind or shall be thought reasonable by the said Dame Isabella Augusta Gregory her executors administrators and such assigns as are hereinafter mentioned in regard to the great expense incurred in the erection of the said Theatre and for scenes, music, decorations and other requisites:

AND FURTHER for Us Our Heirs and Successors we do give and grant unto the said Dame Isabella Augusta Gregory her executors administrators and such assigns as are hereinafter mentioned full power from time to time and at all times for and during the term time and space hereinbefore mentioned to make such allowances out of the monies which they shall so receive by such performances and entertainments as aforesaid to the performers and other persons employed in acting or representing or in any quality whatsoever about the said Theatre or so as they shall think fit.

AND WE ALSO empower and appoint the said Dame Isabella Augusta Gregory that she her executors administrators and such assigns as are hereinafter mentioned do and shall from time to time and at all times eject out of the said Company all scandalous disorderly or other persons as they shall think meet and that all and every person and persons so by them ejected and discharged shall be disabled from playing or acting with the said Company in the said Theatre and shall from the time of such their ejectment or discharge stop and altogether cease from receiving any part proportion or salary out of the profits of the representations in the said Theatre or from the said Dame Isabella Augusta Gregory her executors administrators and such assigns as are hereinafter mentioned and for the better obtaining Our Royal purpose in this behalf We have thought fit hereby to declare that henceforth no representations shall be admitted on the stage by virtue or under cover of these Presents whereby the Christian Religion may in any manner suffer reproach. AND WE HEREBY strictly prohibit all and any degree of abuse or misrepresentation of Sacred characters which may in any degree tend to expose Religion or bring it into contempt and that no such characters be introduced or played in any other light than such as may increase the just esteem of those who answer the end of those sacred functions. AND WE FURTHER enjoin the strictest regard to such representations as anywise concern the civil policy or the Constitution of Our Government that these may contribute to support Our Sacred Authority and to the preservation of order and good Government. AND it being Our Royal Will and pleasure that for the future the said Theatre may be instrumental in the promotion of virtue and instruction of human life WE DO HEREBY enjoin and command that no entertainment or exhibition whatsoever be acted or produced under the authority hereby granted which does or may contain any expression or passage or gesture offensive to piety or good manners until the same shall be corrected or purged by the Manager or Managers for the time being by expunging all such offensive expressions, passages and gestures. AND if the said Dame Isabella Augusta Gregory her executors administrators and such assigns as are hereinafter mentioned shall permit to be brought forward any representations at such theatre hereby authorized which shall be deemed or construed to be immoral and shall not forthwith discontinue and cease representing playing or acting the same on receiving notice from or in the name and by the authority of Our Lieutenant General and General Governor or other Chief Governor or Governors of that part of Our United Kingdom of Great Britain and Ireland called Ireland for the time being by any person or persons lawfully authorised by him or them in such cases these Presents and every grant privilege and immunity hereby given or granted shall become null and void to all intents and purposes whatsoever:

PROVIDED ALWAYS that the said Dame Isabella Augusta Gregory her executors or administrators shall not assign or transfer her rights under these Presents to any person other than the person or persons residing in Ireland who shall be nominated in writing by the said Annie Elizabeth Fredericka Horniman her executors or administrators as Trustee or Trustees for her or them, and in the event of any breach or attempted breach of this provision or in the event of the said Irish National Theatre Society being dissolved during the term of these Presents then on the happening of either of these events these Presents and every grant privilege and immunity hereby given or granted shall become null and void to all intents and purposes whatsoever:

PROVIDED ALWAYS and We do hereby declare and command that these Presents shall be and remain upon the conditions that if at any time during the said term hereby granted it shall be made to appear to Our Lieutenant General and General Governor of that part of Our said United Kingdom of Great Britain and Ireland called Ireland or other Our Chief Governor or Governors thereof that the said Theatre is not duly ventilated or kept in due or proper repair and in accordance with the said plans or that fit and proper commodious means of ingress and egress are not maintained and provided for those who frequent the same or that owing to the character of the performance carried on therein or the class or conduct of the audience or persons frequenting the said Theatre or from any other cause whatsoever the said Theatre shall not be or shall cease to be an orderly well conducted and respectable place of public entertainment then and in such case upon signification in that behalf made by Us under the hand of one of Our Principal Secretaries of State or made by Our Lieutenant General and General Governor of that part of Our said United Kingdom of Great Britain and Ireland called Ireland or Our Chief Governor or Governors thereof for the time being under his or their hand or hands or hand of the Chief Secretary for Ireland and which signification shall be published in the Dublin Gazette these Presents shall forthwith cease and determine and be utterly void to all intents and purposes anything herein contained to the contrary whereof in anywise notwithstanding.

AND WE DO FURTHER HEREBY declare and command that these Our Letters Patent are upon the further condition that the said Theatre shall be constructed, maintained and conducted subject to and in accordance with the rules and regulations following that is to say:—

(1) The said Theatre shall not be enlarged so as to be capable of accommodating more persons than the number which the said Theatre can accommodate at the date of these Presents and which amounts to five hundred and sixty two persons.

(2) All doors and barriers to open outwards or to be fixed back during the time when the public are within the Theatre.

(3) All gangways passages and staircases intended to be used for the exit of the audience to be kept entirely free from chairs or any other obstruction whether permanent or temporary.

(4) All chairs or seats intended for the use of persons listening to the representations or performances in the said Theatre to be fixed and immovable.

(5) An ample water supply with hose and pipes to be available to all parts of the house where possible on the high pressure main.

(6) All fixed and ordinary gas burners to be furnished with efficient guards moveable and occasional lights to be where possible protected in the same manner or put under charge of persons responsible for lighting watching and extinguishing them, a separate and independent supply of light for the stage and auditorium no white metal gas pipes to be used in the building.

(7) The foot-lights or floats to be protected by a wire guard, the first ground line to be always without and unconnected with gas whether at the wings or elsewhere sufficient space to be left between each ground line so as to lessen risk from accident to all persons standing or moving amongst such lines.

(8) The rows or lines of gas burners at wings to commence four feet at least from level of the stage wet blankets or rugs with filled buckets or water pots to be always kept in the wings and attention directed to them by placards legibly printed or painted and fixed near them, some person to be responsible for keeping the blankets buckets and so forth ready for immediate use.

(9) A fire proof curtain to be always in use in the said Theatre and to be lowered at least once during every performance to test its efficiency and condition.

(10) Hatchets hacks or other means to cut down hanging scenery in case of fire to be always in readiness. The regulations as to fire to be always posted in some conspicuous place so that all persons belonging to the Theatre may be acquainted with their contents.

(11) Counter weights where possible to be carried to the walls of the building and cased in and the ropes attached to them to be constantly tested. No structural alterations to be made in the Theatre without the sanction of the Commissioner of Public Works in Ireland or such person as Our Lieutenant General and General Governor of that part of Our United Kingdom of Great Britain and Ireland called Ireland or other Chief Governor or Governors thereof for the time being may afterwards appoint for that purpose, plans for such alterations to be sent to the Privy Seal Office Dublin Castle.

(12) Admission to be given at all times to authorized Officers of the Police.

(13) Permission to the Gallery in the interior of the Theatre to be given to so many persons as there shall be seating accommodation for.

(14) No profanity or impropriety of language to be permitted on the stage.

(15) No indecency of dress, dance or gesture to be permitted on the stage.

(16) No offensive personalities or representation of living persons to be permitted on the stage nor anything calculated to produce riot or breach of the peace.

(17) No exhibitions of wild beasts or dangerous performances to be permitted on the stage, no women or children to be hung from the flies nor fixed in positions from which they cannot release themselves.

(18) No public masquerade to be permitted in the Theatre.

(19) No encouragement to be given to improper characters to assemble or to ply their calling in the Theatre.

(20) No wines, spirits or beer or any other intoxicating or spirituous liquor to be sold in the Theatre or in any part of the Theatre premises.

(21) All refreshments to be sold in the Theatre to be sold only in such positions as do not interfere with the convenience and safety of the audience.

(22) All suitable and proper dressing rooms and accommodation to be provided for male and female performers in the said theatre premises.

(23) No smoking to be permitted in the Auditorium and if at any time there shall be a breach or breaches of any of the said rules and regulations or of any rules and regulations to be substituted therefor as hereinafter provided then and in such case upon signification on that behalf made by Us under the hand of one of Our Principal Secretaries of State or made by Our Lieutenant General and General Governor of that part of Our United Kingdom of Great Britain and Ireland called Ireland or other Chief Governor or Governors thereof for the time being under his

or their hand or hands or hand of the Chief Secretary for Ireland and which signification shall be published in the Dublin Gazette these Presents shall forthwith cease determine and be utterly void to all intents and purposes anything hereinbefore contained to the contrary thereof in anything notwithstanding.

PROVIDED ALWAYS that if the said Dame Isabella Augusta Gregory her executors administrators or such assigns as are hereinbefore mentioned shall at any time apply to Our Lord Lieutenant or other Chief Governor or Governors of Ireland to alter or modify any of the rules or regulations numbered 1 to 23 above and such alteration or modification shall be permitted then and in such case the said rules and regulations shall be deemed to be altered and modified accordingly: And further Our Will and Pleasure is AND WE DO HEREBY DECLARE that these Our Letters Patent or the enrollment or exemplification thereof shall be in all things good sufficient valid and effectual in the law according to the true intent and meaning of the same unto them the said Dame Isabella Augusta Gregory her executors administrators or such assigns as are hereinbefore mentioned and shall be taken and construed and adjudged in the most favourable and beneficial sense for the best advantage of the said Dame Isabella Augusta Gregory her executors administrators or such assigns as aforesaid as well within all Our Courts of Record within that part of Our said United Kingdom of Great Britain and Ireland called Ireland or elsewhere as amongst all and singular the subjects of Us Our Heirs and Successors whatsoever and wheresoever:

PROVIDED ALWAYS that these Our Letters Patent be enrolled in the Record and Writ Office of Our High Court of Justice, Chancery Division, in that part of Our said United Kingdom of Great Britain and Ireland called Ireland within the space of six months next ensuing the date of these Presents:

AND We do hereby direct and require that you cause to be inserted in the said Letters Patent all such other powers and clauses as are usual in like cases or necessary or proper for rendering the same firm valid and effectual as Patents or Grants of the like nature:
And for so doing this shall be as well unto you as to all other Our Officers and Ministers a sufficient Warrant.

And so We bid you heartily farewell!

Given at Our Court at Saint James's the twenty-second day<br>of December 1904; in the Fourth year of Our Reign.<br>By His Majesty's Command<br>[Signed] Lansdowne.

The patent established the INTS's legal right to take residence and perform in the Abbey Theatre, an occasion that was, quite properly, the cause of much rejoicing and congratulation. But the strains of running what was now in effect a professional company on a rule book designed for a society of amateurs soon began to tell.

As the new Theatre began to exact increasingly arduous demands on the time and energy of the Company it became clear that certain members would need to be paid and given professional contracts. Although there was provision under rule V (*d*) for the management committee 'to remunerate any official of the Society or actor for his work', this was evidently intended to apply to ad hoc payments for specific extra duties, and indeed 'or actor' did not appear in the text as originally printed but was added by hand as an afterthought. WBY saw that substantial redrafting would be required to make regular payment possible and once again called upon the expertise of AE, who quickly came to the conclusion 'that if the actors are to be paid the whole society must be put on an entirely different basis'. He was appalled at the slovenly way in which the Society had been administered and saw the need to separate its business and artistic sides. As he worked on, later with the help of Fred Ryan, he altered the rules of the Society so radically that it ceased to be a co-operative venture and turned into a limited liability company with a small executive board of directors. This was a process of evolution that cost AE a great deal of labour, especially since he found WBY's interventions and contributions less than helpful. An interim draft of the new rules, in AE's hand, shows how his mind was working in late August 1905. He is still thinking in terms of the Friendly Societies Act and the draft is still based on the earlier constitution. But already the new division between general members and actor members has been established and the powers of the General Meeting, and therefore of all the ordinary members, are being curtailed as power is transferred to the management committee. AE also severely limits the ordinary members' say in the selection of plays, while the grounds for suspending and expelling actors are widened from the precise crime of taking part in rival shows without permission to any conduct 'calculated to injure the usefulness of the society and to obstruct it in its work'. The management committee is also given much greater financial authority than hitherto, and is now empowered to raise loans, overdrafts, and mortgages, while control over the petty cash is strengthened by the insistence that only cheques are to be used in transactions costing more than one pound.

This is an early but serious attempt to reform the Society. AE is still guided in his thinking by the 1903 model and his more significant emendations of those rules are marked in bold. But, as he soon realized, the implications of the ideas he was formulating here pointed to a far more radical solution to the Company's maladministration and finally to the abandoning of the co-operative model altogether.

## 4. AE'S AUGUST 1905 INTERIM EMENDATIONS TO THE 1903 RULES

### Rules of the
### Irish National Theatre Society

I    Name & Place of Office of the Society

The Society shall be called 'The Irish National Theatre Society' its registered office shall be at **the Abbey Theatre. Abbey St Dublin**. In the event of any change in the situation of the registered office notice of such change shall be sent to the Registrar within fourteen days.

## II     Objects of the Society

The objects of the Society shall be to create an Irish National Theatre, to act and produce plays in Irish or English written by Irish writers or on Irish subjects; and such dramatic works of foreign authors as would tend to educate and interest the public in the higher aspects of dramatic art. The funds of the Society shall be applicable only to further these objects.

## III     Membership

(a)  The Society shall consist in the first instance of the **eight** signatories to these rules and hereafter of those who may be admitted at the <first> general **or special** Meetings of the Society.

(b)  **There shall be three classes of members:**

    (1)  **General members in whom shall be vested the control of the society, the election of President, Vice Presidents, Reading and Business Committee and the direction of the general policy of the society. General members shall be only admitted by a three quarters majority of the votes of their own class who are present at meetings called for the purpose. The number of general members shall not exceed twenty.**

    (2)  **Actor members to be admitted only by a three quarters vote of members of the same class who are present at a meeting called for the purpose**

    (3)  **Honorary members who shall consist of such persons as may be admitted by the general members in recognition of services to literature, drama, music or art in Ireland. They shall have no power to take part in the management of the society but shall be entitled to free admission to any of its performances**

(c)  The President and Vice President shall *ex officio* be members of the Society

(d)  Members may withdraw from the society by giving written notice to the Secretary.

(e)  Members may be expelled by the vote of two-thirds of the members present at a special general meeting of the society upon a charge in writing of conduct detrimental to the Society communicated to the secretary one fortnight before the meeting is summoned.

(f)  **Actor members who have not attended rehearsals or taken part in any performances for one year shall lapse from membership.**

## IV     General Meetings

(a)  An Annual General Meeting of Members shall be held during the months of April or May in each year.

(b)  The functions of the Annual General Meeting shall be:

    (1)  To receive from the **Business** Committee, auditors or other officers of the Society a report and full statement of the Accounts for the preceeding year together with the audited balance sheet, and if satisfactory to adopt them.

(2) To elect the President, Vice Presidents, Committee of Management, Reading Committee, Auditor and Treasurer as required by the rules.

(3) To transact any other general business of the Society.

(c) **The Committee of Management, the Reading Committee, Auditor and Treasurer shall be elected from and by the general members with the exception of the Auditor who may be a non-member.**

<(d) **The stage manager shall be elected by a vote of the actors members but his election shall be subject to the approval of the business committee.**>

(d) A special general meeting of members may be called at any time by the Committee, and on receipt of a demand signed by no less than one fifth of the members, it shall be the duty of the Secretary to call such a meeting.

(e) No member shall be entitled to more than one vote upon any matter submitted for consideration at any general meeting.

(f) **Proxy voting shall be allowed only when the notice and full information about the question to be decided has been sent by post to the absent members. No general delegation of voting power shall be allowed at a general meeting.**

(g) **One** <fourth third> **half** of the general members shall constitute a quorum of an Annual or Special general meeting.

(h) Any resolution which commands a three quarters majority of the votes given shall be considered carried.

V   The Duties and Powers of the Committee.

(a) The committee of management shall be elected at the annual general meeting of the society. They shall **retire at the expiry of their year of office** but shall be eligible for re-election. <The committee must be chosen from the general members.>

(b) Members of Committee shall be chosen from the **general** members of the Society. They shall receive no salary or other remuneration.

(c) The Committee shall be **five in number of whom the President shall be one**. Three members shall form a quorum. **Matters discussed shall be decided by the majority of votes.** In case of parity of voting the Chairman shall have a casting vote. The committee of management shall have control of the business arrangements. All questions relating to the payment of money and the terms on which engagements may be entered upon shall be decided by them. No engagement shall be made without their sanction. **The stage manager shall be required to attend meetings** of the committee which shall be called as often as the business of the society requires. The committee may appoint a **business manager** whose duty it shall be to see that all arrangements decided upon by them shall be carried out. <**The stage manager may if thought advisable also hold the office of business manager.**> **Or this office may if thought advisable be combined with that of secretary, stage manager or actor.**

(d) The Committee shall have power if they deem it necessary to remunerate any official of the society for their work.

(e) The Committee shall have power to give a retaining fee to any actor or member [*three words indecipherable*]. If a retaining fee is given to a member or actor he or she shall engage on his or her part not to act in any plays other than those produced by the Society during the period for which the retaining fee is given without the consent of the Committee. Any actor or official who is paid for his services shall enter into an agreement with the Society for the use [and] performance of his duties.

(f) The Committee shall have power to open a banking account if they deem it desirable, **or to obtain advances from their bankers by way of loan or overdraft or mortgage on the property of the Society. All payments of money over one pound shall be made by cheque.** Every cheque shall be signed by two members of the **business** committee and be countersigned by the secretary.

(g) The Committee shall have power to suspend any actor from membership if they deem that his conduct is calculated to injure the usefulness of the society and to obstruct it in its work. The question of the expulsion of such a member shall rest with the general members at annual or special general meetings.

(h) All properties, scenery and dresses which are acquired by the Society shall be **under the care of the stage manager**, and their disposal or the lending of any such properties shall be decided by the business committee.

   (i)  Present rule V section (e)

   (j)  Present rule V section (f)

   (k)  Present rule V section (g)

### VI   The Reading Committee

(a) The reading committee shall be elected at the annual general meeting of the society **by and from the general members**. The members of the committee shall be eligible for reelection on the expiry of their term of office.

(b) The Reading Committee shall be **five** in number and they shall consider all plays proposed for performance by the society **and their decision as to the acception or rejection of a play shall be final.** No play shall be performed until it has been recommended by the Reading Committee. A member of the reading committee shall not be entitled to vote if a play of his own should be submitted for its consideration. The stage manager shall attend any meeting of the Reading Committee <if required>.

### VII   The Stage Manager

**The stage manager shall be nominated by the business committee.** The stage manager and author shall have the sole right to decide on questions as to how a scene shall be acted or what actors shall be selected for the performance. **In case of dispute on the latter point the business committee shall appoint** <a third>

one of <its own> the members of the society to arbitrate. His decision shall be final.

## VIII    The Trustees

Same as before.

## IX    The Treasurer

Remains same as before.

## X    The Secretary

(a) As at present except in clause 1 add
'To summon and attend all meetings of the Society, **the Reading Committee and business committee.**'

## XI    Audit of Accounts

As at present

## XII    Alteration of Rules

Insert after 'by vote' the words '**of the general members** at a special general meeting' etc.

## XIII    Settlement of disputes

As at present

## XIV    Dissolution

As at present

The final version of the rules, which was published in early 1906, would have perplexed the original and largely working-class members of the Society as having little to do with its central purpose as they conceived it, beginning as it does with legalistic accounts of share-dealing, nominations, legacy duty, intestacy, illegitimacy, and probate. Apart from a brief mention of overall aims and the qualification for membership, the only reference to the artistic aspect of the Society's mission in the opening pages is an ominous paragraph on 'Expulsion', after which the text returns to directives on loans, investments, and share options. Sections V, VI and VII, which deal with management and administration, reveal the extent to which the new arrangements had effected a constitutional putsch: the Society is now to be run 'by a Board of Directors, not less than three or more than five', which can fix its own time and place to meet. The general and special meetings, previously democratic if cumbersome forums for discussion, are reduced to little more than rubber stamps since rule 44 stipulates that all questions are to 'be decided by a majority of votes, and each individual member shall have one vote for every fully paid up share held by him'. As the Directors each held 63 shares, far more than the rest of the Company (allotted one share each) put together, this, as WBY told AG, gave the Directors absolute power, and rules 46 and 47 confirmed their right to appoint and remove any of the Society's employees at will, including the secretary and stage manager. Even on those few issues—the expulsion of members, appointment of new Directors, and amendment of the rules—for which a policy of one-man-one-vote operated, the percentages needed to effect any change of the status quo still assured the Directors of dominance. The first constitution of the National Theatre Society had lasted barely two years; the new constitution, with minor amendments, was, with the Letters Patent, to remain the enabling charter for its continuing existence.

## 5. 1906 CONSTITUTION UNDER THE INDUSTRIAL AND PROVIDENT SOCIETIES ACT

THE
**National Theatre Society, Ltd.**
RULES.

### I.—*INTERPRETATION.*
*Construction of Rules.*

1. In construing these rules, the following words and expressions shall have respectively the meanings herein stated, provided that such meaning does not conflict with the subject matter of the rule or the context:—

(*a*) Words importing the singular or plural number include the plural and singular numbers

(*b*) Words importing the masculine gender shall include the feminine gender.

(*c*) "Member" shall mean an individual of Society holding the shares required by the rules and duly admitted to membership.

(*d*) "The Society" shall mean the Society to which these rules refer.

(*e*) "The Committee" shall mean the Committee of Management of the Society.

(*f*) "The Act" shall mean the Industrial and Provident Societies Act, 1893.

(*g*) "A Society" shall mean a Society registered under the Act.

(*h*) "He," "him," "they," and "person" include a Society.

(*i*) "The special members" mean those persons who sign the application for registration of the Society.

(*j*) "Registrar" shall mean the Assistant Registrar of Friendly Societies for Ireland.

### II.—*NAME, REGISTERED OFFICE, AND OBJECTS.*
*Name.*

2. The Name of the Society shall be the "NATIONAL THEATRE SOCIETY, LIMITED."

*Registered Office.*

3. The registered office of the Society shall be in The Abbey Theatre, Dublin, but may be changed by the Committee. Notice of any change of the office shall be sent to the Registrar within fourteen days after such change in accordance with the Treasury regulations.

*Objects.*

4. The objects of the Society shall be to create an Irish National Theatre, to act and produce plays in Irish or English, written by Irish authors, or on Irish subjects, and such dramatic works of foreign authors as would tend to educate and interest the public of this country in the higher aspects of dramatic art. It shall be lawful for the Society to do all things necessary and expedient to accomplish its objects.

## III.—*MEMBERSHIP.*
### *Members.*

5. The Society shall consist in the first instance of the special Members and of all such persons as the special members, and, subsequently, the Directors may admit to membership.

*Nominations: How Made.*

6. Any member being of the age of sixteen years and upwards may nominate in writing under his hand and send to the Registered Office during his lifetime the names of any person or persons other than a member of the Society to whom his shares shall be transferred at his decease in such proportion as he shall declare and specify in such nomination.

*Nominations: How Revoked.*

7. A nomination so made may be similarly revoked, but shall not be affected by any will or codicil thereto made by the nominator.

*Nominations: How Recorded.*

8. Nominations shall be carefully preserved and duly recorded in a book kept by the Society for the purpose.

*Proceedings on Death of Nominator.*

9. On receiving satisfactory proof of the death of a nominator, the Directors shall either transfer the property comprised in the nomination in manner directed by it, or pay to every person entitled thereunder the full value of the property given to him, unless the shares comprised therein, if transferred as directed by the nominator, would raise the share capital of any nominee to a sum exceeding two hundred pounds, in which case they shall pay him the value of such shares.

*Succession or Legacy Duty.*

10. If the total property of the nominator in the Society at his death exceeds eighty pounds the Directors shall, before making any payment, require production of a duly stamped receipt for the succession or legacy duty payable thereon, or a letter or certificate stating that no such duty is payable, from the Commissioners of Inland Revenue, who shall give such receipt, letter, or certificate, on payment of the duty, or satisfactory proof of no duty being payable, as the case may be.

*Intestacy.*

11. If any member of a registered Society entitled to property therein in respect of shares, not exceeding in the whole, at his death, one hundred pounds, dies intestate, without having made any nomination thereof then subsisting, the Directors may, without letters of administration, distribute the same among such persons as appear to them, on such evidence as they deem satisfactory, to be entitled by law to receive the same, subject, if such property exceeds eighty pounds, to the obtaining from the Commissioners of Inland Revenue a receipt for the succession or legacy duty payable thereon, or a letter or certificate stating that no such duty is payable.

*Illegitimacy.*

12. If any such member is illegitimate and leaves no widow, widower, or issue, the Directors shall deal with his property in the Society as the Treasury shall direct.

*Probate.*

13. For the purpose of probate the Directors may require, before making a payment to any claimant, that a statutory declaration shall be made by the claimant that the total personal or movable estate of the deceased, including the sum in question, does not exceed, after the deduction of debts and funeral expenses, the value of £100.

*Transfer to Claimants.*

14. Upon the death of any member who has an interest in the Society exceeding £100, or transmitted by his will, and a notice in writing given by his executor or administrator to the Secretary of the Society, stating the death of such member, and the Christian name, surname, profession or business of such legal representative, and specifying the nature and amount of his interest or claim; and the production, if the case requires, of the probate of the will of, or letters of administration to, such member, and of such evidence (if any) of his death as may be required by the Directors, the Directors shall either transfer the shares or other interest of the member specified in such notice, in the books of the Society to his legal representative, or shall pay to him the sum which represents the full value

thereof, and may make such transfer or payment at their discretion, unless the transfer would increase the interest of the transferee in the Society to more than £200, in which case they shall make the payment in money.

### Insane or Lunatic Member.

15. If a member becomes insane, and no committee of his estate or trustee of his property has been duly appointed, the Directors may, when it is proved to their satisfaction that it is just and expedient so to do, pay the amount of his property in the Society, not exceeding £100, to any person whom they shall judge proper to receive the same on his behalf.

### Bankruptcy.

16. If any member becomes bankrupt, his interest in the Society shall be transferable or payable to the assignee of his property.

### Cessation of Membership.

17. Any member whose shares have been transferred or repaid or who shall have been expelled shall cease to be a member of the Society.

### Expulsion.

18. A member may be expelled if found guilty of conduct detrimental to the Society, provided:—

(a) That he shall have received, in writing, one month previously, complete particulars of the charge alleged against him; and
(b) That two-thirds of the members present at a Special General Meeting vote for his expulsion, each member to have one vote only irrespective of his share holding.

The full amount paid or credited upon the shares held by an expelled member shall be paid to him on expulsion and an entry of the cancellation of his shares shall be made thereupon in the share Register.

### Re-Admission.

19. An expelled member shall only be re-admitted by the vote of two-thirds of the members present at an Ordinary General Meeting and on a motion of which notice has been given at the preceding Ordinary General Meeting.

### IV.—CAPITAL.
### Ordinary Shares.

20. The capital of the Society shall consist of shares of £1 each, which shall be transferable only. They shall be held only by individuals. Five shillings per share

shall be paid on application and the balance in such calls as the Directors may from time to time direct, provided, that a fortnight's notice of each such call shall be sent to the registered address of each member. Members may elect to pay up their shares in full at any time.

### Interest and Liability.

21. Interest at the rate of not more than 4 per cent. per annum may be paid on shares but shall not be calculated on fractions of £1 or of a calendar month. The liability of members shall be limited to their shares. No member may have an interest in the funds of the Society exceeding £200 sterling.

### Loans.

22. The Directors may obtain loans for the purposes of the Society, from members or other persons, on the security of bonds, agreements, promissory notes or mortgages to the extent of £10,000, for such periods as they deem expedient and at a rate of interest not exceeding 5 per cent. per annum. Should any member of the Board become personally liable for any debt incurred on behalf of the Society he shall not be removed from office without his consent until such liability has ceased.

### Investments.

23. The Directors may invest any portion of the Society's capital as follows:—
(*a*) In any security in which Trustees are for the time being by law authorised to invest; and
(*b*) In the shares of any other registered Society or Company provided such Society or Company shall be one with limited liability.

### Voting re Investments.

24. The Directors may appoint one of their number to vote on its behalf at meetings of any Society or Company in which any portion of the Society's funds are invested.

### Application for Shares: How Made.

25. Application for shares shall be made in the forms prescribed in Appendix I. Applications shall be considered by the Directors at the next ensuing meeting, and notice of admission or otherwise shall be sent to the applicant within one week after the meeting of Directors at which the application is considered.

### Share Register.

26. The Shares shall be numbered consecutively and in the order of their allotment, and shall be registered in the name of the holder in a share register in which shall be recorded the dates of allotment and transfer (if any), particulars of

any shares transferred and of the name of the person to whom the transfer was made together with the date thereof.

### *Transfers.*

27. Transfers of shares may only be made with the consent of the Directors and in the form prescribed by Appendix IV. This form shall bear a sixpenny stamp which shall be affixed by the transferrer.

### *Lien on Shares.*

28. The Society shall have a first lien on the shares held by any member and may set off any sum credited thereon towards the payment of any debt due by the member to the Society.

### *Sale of Shares to Pay Debts.*

29. The Directors may sell and transfer any shares standing in the name of a member who is indebted to the Society, provided a fortnight's notice in writing has been given to the defaulting member, and apply so much of the proceeds as may be necessary to the discharge of the debt due together with the necessary expenses in its recovery.

### *Recovery of Debts.*

30. All moneys payable by a member to the Society, whether in respect of shares or otherwise, shall be debts due from such member to the Society and shall be recoverable as such either in the County Court of the District in which the registered office of the Society is situate or in that of the district in which such member resides, at the option of the Society, and the Directors may take legal proceedings for the recovery thereof.

## V.—MANAGEMENT.
### *The Board of Directors*

31. The Society shall be managed by a Board of Directors, not less than three or more than five in number, who shall be appointed by the members, and who shall be shareholders in the Society. Any addition made to first three Directors must be nominated by the Directors, but elected by vote of the members at a general meeting called for the purpose, each member having one vote only irrespective of his share holding. Two members shall retire by rotation at each yearly general meeting, but shall be eligible for re-election.

### *Removal of Directors.*

32. A member of the Board of Directors may, subject to the provisions of Rule 22, be removed from office by the vote of two-thirds of the members present and

voting in accordance with Rule 44 at a General meeting specially convened, and such meeting may thereupon fill the vacancy so caused.

### Vacancies.

33. Casual vacancies in the Board may be filled by co-option, subject to confirmation by the next ensuing General Meeting.

### Quorum.

34. The quorum of a meeting of Directors shall be two.

### Meetings.

35. The Board of Directors shall fix their own time and place to meet. Special meetings may be held at any time on giving twenty-four hours' notice.

### Chairman.

36. The Directors shall appoint one of their body as Chairman of the Society. He shall hold office for one year and shall be eligible for re-election. He shall preside at all Board and General Meetings and shall have a vote and a casting vote at the former and a casting vote only at the latter.

## VI.—GENERAL MEETINGS.
### Nature of Meetings.

37. General meetings shall be ordinary and special. Ordinary meetings shall be held yearly.

### Notice of Ordinary Meetings.

38. Notice of the First Ordinary General Meeting shall be given by the Special members as soon as practicable after these rules are registered and thereafter fourteen days notice shall be given of every ordinary General Meeting.

### Notice of Special Meetings.

39. Special General Meetings may be convened by the Directors, or by a requisition to the Secretary signed by ten members. The notice for a special General meeting shall not be less than six clear days except in cases of urgency, when the Directors unanimously may decide on giving notice of not less than forty-eight hours.

### Quorum.

40. The quorum of General meetings shall be one-half the members of the Society, if the number be less than twenty, and ten if the membership be over

twenty. If there be no quorum present one hour after that fixed for the holding of the meeting, the proceedings shall be adjourned to the same day, hour and place the following week, when the business shall be disposed of whatever number of members may be present, provided, however that if the meeting be convened on the requisition of members it shall in the absence of a quorum be dissolved.

### Adjournments.

41. Duly constituted meetings may be adjourned from day to day or to any specified date, as the members present may direct, provided that absent members shall receive notice of such adjournment and that no business other than that on the original agenda be brought forward at such adjournments.

### Business of Ordinary Meetings.

42. The functions of Ordinary General meetings shall be:—

(a) To consider the yearly statement of accounts and the report of the Directors.

(b) To elect Directors, Reading Committee, save where the power of appointment is hereinafter stated to be in the Directors.

(c) To transact other business incidental to such meetings.

### Business of Special Meetings.

43. Special General meetings shall transact no business other than that appearing on the Agenda paper which shall accompany the notice convening the meeting. An ordinary General meeting may, at the conclusion of its ordinary business, be made special for any purpose of which notice has been duly given.

### Voting.

44. All questions shall be decided by a majority of votes, and each individual member shall have one vote for every fully paid up share held by him, except in votes on Rule 18, 62, and 31, when the votes shall be subject to the provision in those rules.

## VII.—THE MANAGER, SECRETARY, AND OFFICERS.
### Manager.

45. The Chairman of the Board shall be managing director and shall have such functions and powers as the Directors shall from time to time decide.

### Secretary.

46. The Directors may appoint and remove a Secretary, or may make such other provision as they deem expedient for the discharge of secretarial work and arrange the terms of remuneration therefor.

*Employees.*

47. The Directors shall appoint and may remove the stage manager, business manager and all other employees of the Society, fix their salaries and arrange their duties.

*Security.*

48. All officials and employees of the Society having charge of money or property belonging to the Society shall, before entering into employment, provide such security as the Directors deem adequate, and in such form as they may approve.

*Bank Account.*

49. The Directors shall open a bank account which shall be operated as they determine.

## VIII.—*ALLOCATION OF PROFITS.*

*Profits.*

50. The net profits of the Society, after payment of interest on loan capital, shall be applied firstly in:—

(*a*) Depreciation on property and fixtures at 5 per cent. on their original cost.

And afterwards in such proportion as the Directors may decide in any of the following manners:—

(*a*) Interest on shares at 4 per cent.
(*b*) Bonus to actors and employees.
(*c*) Fund for old age pensions.
(*d*) General Reserve Fund.

Ordinary General meetings may further apply a sum not exceeding 10 per cent. of the total net profit to any lawful purpose connected with the work of the Society.

## IX.—*STATUTORY OBLIGATIONS AND MISCELLANEOUS.*

*Seal.*

51. The Society shall have its name engraven in legible characters upon a seal which shall be in the custody of the chairman. It shall only be used under the authority of a resolution of the Directors, and shall be attested by the signatures of two members of the Board and the Secretary.

*Name.*

52. The name of the Society shall be legibly painted or affixed on the outside of its registered Office and other places of business; it shall also be legibly set forth in all documents, notices, advertisements, etc., as required by section 12 of the Act.

*Change of Name, &c.*

53. The Society may by Special resolution: —

(*a*) Change its name.

(*b*) Amalgamate with or transfer its engagements to another Society, or Company, or accept a similar transfer.

(*c*) Convert itself into a Company.

(*d*) Voluntarily dissolve by resolution to wind up under the Companies Acts, or

(*e*) Wind up by an instrument of dissolution signed by three-fourths of the members for the time being.

*Auditor.*

54. The accounts of the Society shall be audited by a Public Auditor, who shall be appointed by the first Ordinary General meeting of the Society and subsequently by the First Ordinary General meeting in each year, which shall also fix his remuneration. No employé of the Society shall act as its Auditor. Casual vacancies in the position of Auditor may be filled up by the Directors. The Auditor shall present statements of accounts in such form for such periods as the Directors may decide; he shall also prepare the Society's Annual Return and shall duly fulfil the obligations imposed and enjoy the rights conferred on Public Auditors by the Act and the Treasury Regulations.

*Annual Return.*

55. The Directors shall before the 31st day of March in each year furnish to the Registrar the form of Annual Return in the manner prescribed by the Treasury Regulations, accompanied by a copy of every Auditor's report relating to the preceding year.

*Members and Return.*

56. A copy of each Annual Return shall be delivered gratuitously on application to every member or person interested in the funds of the Society.

*Balance Sheet.*

57. A copy of the last annual balance sheet for the time being, together with the Auditor's report, shall be always kept hung up in a conspicuous place in the Society's Registered Office.

*Rules.*

58. Each member shall receive a copy of the Society's rules free; other persons shall on demand be furnished with a copy on payment of one shilling.

### Inspection of Accounts by Members.

59. Any member or person interested in the funds of the Society may inspect his own account and the register of members during business hours at the Society's registered Office.

### Inspection by Registrar.

60. Any ten members may apply to the Registrar to appoint an accountant to inspect the books of the Society and to report thereon.

### Application to Registrar.

61. One-tenth of the members may make application to the Registrar:—

(*a*) To appoint one or more inspectors to examine into and report upon the affairs of the Society; or
(*b*) To call a Special meeting of the Society in accordance with Section 50 of the Act.

62. Rules may be altered, rescinded or amended, on the proposal by the Directors by a majority of two-thirds of the votes of the members present at a Special General Meeting, each member shall have one vote only irrespective of his share holding, and such alterations shall be duly registered and on registration embodied in or issued with the rules of the Society for the time being.

### Disputes and Arbitrations.

63. Any dispute arising between the Society and its members shall be submitted to arbitration. The costs of the arbitration shall be borne as the arbitration body directs and such sums as the arbitrating body decides shall be deposited prior to the hearing of the case. The award of the arbitrating body shall be final.

### Contentious Subjects.

64. No sectarian discussion shall be raised, nor shall any resolution which deals with irrelevant and contentious subjects be proposed at a General meeting of the Society.

*APPENDICES.*

...........................................

## I.—APPLICATION FOR ORDINARY SHARES.

.........................................................................*Limited*

I, the undersigned, hereby apply for ................................................................ ordinary transferable £1 shares in the above-named Society, in respect of which I agree to make the payments required by the rules of the Society and otherwise to be bound thereby.

*Signature of Applicant* ............................

*Address* ............................

*Occupation* ............................

*Witness* ............................

Date ............................

## II.—FORM OF TRANSFER BETWEEN INDIVIDUALS.

.........................................................................*Limited*

This instrument, made the   day of 19 , between   , of   , and   , of   , witnesses, that in consideration of the sum of £  , paid by said          to me, I, the said   , hereby transfer to the said   , his executors, administrators, and assigns, the        shares, numbered   , now standing in my name in the books of the above-named Society, to hold the said shares upon the same conditions on which I now hold the same; and that I, the said   , hereby accept the said shares, subject to the said conditions. In witness whereof we have hereto set our hands.

................................ *Name of Transferer.*

................................ *Name of Transferee.*

The foregoing are the rules of the NATIONAL THEATRE SOCIETY, LIMITED.

F. J. FAY,
*Secretary.*
AUGUSTA GREGORY,
W. B. YEATS,
W. G. FAY,
VERA ESPOSITO,
J. M. SYNGE,
SARA ALLGOOD,
U. WRIGHT.

# ADDENDA TO VOLUMES I–III

The following letters should have appeared in volumes I, II, or III of this edition, but came to light after their publication. In a few cases, a version of the letter concerned, taken from an imperfect copy, did appear, and is now reprinted in its more authentic form.

## To Thomas Edwin Yeats,[1] [22 December 1887]

My dear Edwin

Come by all means. Come about 1$^{oc}$ if you can. I see by your letter you are still at Palmerston Park if I had realized that you were so near, and not at Clontarf still,[2] I would have gone to see you long ago. I hope all your people are well.[3]

W B Yeats

APS Private, addressed to 10 Windsor Road, Palmerston Park, Dublin, postmark 'DUBLIN DE 22 87'. This letter would have appeared in 1. 44.

[1] Thomas Edwin Yeats (1867–1949) had been born in Coregg, Sligo, the son of Matthew Yeats (1816–85), JBY's uncle and land agent. He settled in Canada in the late 1890s, where he worked for the Bank of Montreal. In a letter to his daughter Grace on 12 Feb 1949 (Private), Jack Yeats, who had been a particular friend of his, recalled him 'as a jovial young man'.

[2] Edwin Yeats and his family had moved from 4 Belview Terrace, Dollymount, Clontarf to 10 Windsor Road, Palmerston Park, Dublin, in 1886. Their new residence was on the same side of Dublin as KT's house, Whitehall, Clondalkin, where WBY stayed from December 1887 to January 1888.

[3] Edwin Yeats was living with his mother Ann Grace Yeats.

# To D. J. O'Donoghue,[1] 23 May [1888]

3 Blenheim Road | Bedford Park
May 23rd

Dear M[r] O Donaghue,

The first Wednesday in June will suit me quite well. About the matter of chairman. Dr Todhunter will come with me.[2] I would <be glad> like to make him chairman.[3] I am sure Mr Fahy,[4] or who ever your usual chairman is, will not mind giving way to so <disk> distinguished a writer & student as Dr Todhunter.

Yours sincerely
W B Yeats

ALS Private. This letter would have appeared in 1. 70.

[1] David James O'Donoghue (1866–1917), born in London of Cork parents, was at this time a leading light in the Southwark Irish Literary Club, an organization which in 1883 had grown out of the Southwark Junior Irish Literary Club, founded two years earlier to foster a sense of Irish identity among the children of Irish immigrants in London. In 1892 he was to help WBY establish the Irish Literary Society, London, and in the same year produced the first edition of his compendious *Poets of Ireland*. In 1896 O'Donoghue moved to Dublin, where he set up as a bookseller. He published biographies of William Carleton (1896) and Robert Emmet (Dublin, 1902), and a *Life and Writings of J. C. Mangan* (1897). O'Donoghue had evidently asked WBY to lecture in mid-May, and he replied that he would 'be very glad to lecture. I have a never delivered lecture on the "Folk lore of the West of Ireland" already written; so I am ready for any date you name.' The lecture took place on Wednesday, 13 June 1888.
[2] John Todhunter (1839–1916; see 1. 515–16), a friend and later neighbour of the Yeatses who had abandoned medicine for literature. WBY had long been an admirer of Todhunter's work, and on 4 Apr 1885 JBY wrote to thank him (Reading) for his interest in WBY, adding that 'Willie on his side watches with an almost breathless interest your course as dramatic poet & has been doing so for a long time—he has read ... everything you have written most carefully—he finished when at Howth your Rienzi at a single sitting—the sitting ending at 2 oclock in the morning. Your book on Shelley he has also read.' Todhunter, who was at this time collaborating with WBY, Katharine Tynan, and John O'Leary on the anthology *Poems and Ballads of Young Ireland*, was eager to further Irish cultural projects and on 27 Nov 1887 told Herbert Horne (Reading) that hitherto Irishmen had 'suffered from invincible ignorance about both the literature & history of their country. I am happy to say, however, that the national spirit seems now roused as it never was before in my memory.'
[3] A few days after the talk WBY reported to Katharine Tynan (1. 71) that his 'lecture on Sligo fairies at the Southwick Irish Literary Club went off merrily. Todhunter took the chair.' W. P. Ryan described the occasion in *The Irish Literary Revival* (1894): 'Some of us thought till then that we had a very tolerable acquaintance with the ways and doings of the Irish fairies, but Yeats's lecture (of course it was on the good people) was something of a revelation to us—in fact he spoke as one who took his information firsthand. His only error was to speak unduly of the *soulths* and *sheogues* of his own county, but the South had a sturdy champion in John Augustus O'Shea, who gave it as his experience that there were more fairies on a square foot of Knockshegowna [in Tipperary] than in all the County Sligo' (29–30). Todhunter Ryan remembered as 'a gifted Irishman ... destined to be a comrade later on'.
[4] Francis Arthur Fahy (1854–1935), poet, songwriter, and humorist, was born in Galway. After joining the civil service he moved to London where in 1883 he helped found the Southwark Irish Literary Club. Later he became a member of the Irish Literary Society, London, and president of the London Gaelic League. He contributed poems and sketches to a number of Irish periodicals, sometimes under the pseudonym of 'Dreoilin', and is best known for his poem 'The Ould Plaid Shawl'. His *Irish Songs and Poems* had been published in Dublin in 1887 by M. H. Gill & Son. He had met WBY on 23 Feb of this year, when he was introduced to him at the British Museum.

## To John Lane,[1] 27 September 1889

3 Blenheim Road | Bedford Park | Chiswick
Sept 27. 89.

Dear M{r} Lane
I shall turn up on Monday at 8–30 with great pleasure.
Yours very Sincerely
W B Yeats

ALS Huntington. This letter would have appeared in 1. 189.

## To John O'Leary,[1] [after 19 June 1891]

3 Blenheim Road, | Bedford Park, | Chiswick W.

Dear M{r} O'Leary
I did not answer before because I knew I should have to write almost at once again if I took your hint about the post card, as I want you to address the enclosed to Rolleston whose Irish address I have mislaid.[2] I could not however write before to day as I have been very busy. Todhunter has had a play on & I have had to review it twice & write only on chance of reviews being printed too, to see it twice, & loose time helping to hunt up people to fill empty places[3] as well as writing hard at Blake.[4] This last because I want

---

[1] This may have been WBY's first meeting with John Lane (see p. 138, n. 2), who had set up the Bodley Head publishing house with Elkin Mathews in 1887, and was an active partner in the firm, although still employed at this time as a clerk in the Railway Clearing House. He gave frequent parties for young writers, and on this occasion evidently discussed the possibility of the Bodley Head taking some copies of WBY's *The Wanderings of Oisin*, published in January of this year, on a sale-or-return basis (see 1. 190–1). In 1891 and 1892 Lane was to be a prime mover in the publication of *The Book of the Rhymers' Club*, to which WBY contributed.

[1] John O'Leary (see p. 530, n. 6) was at this time WBY's chief Irish mentor, and was trying to establish with him a network of Irish literary societies.

[2] Thomas William Hazen Rolleston (1857– 1920; see 1. 508–9), was a disciple of John O'Leary and at this time regarded as a potential successor to Thomas Davis, leader of the Young Irelanders. He founded and edited the *Dublin University Review* (published 1885–7), where WBY's early work appeared, had translated Epictetus into English and Walt Whitman into German, and wrote a life of Lessing. Rolleston had recently taken a house in London, at Spencer Hill, Wimbledon, but was probably spending the summer holidays in Ireland, at Glasshouse, Shinroane, near Roscrea, Co. Tipperary. WBY may have been sending him a copy of *Representative Irish Tales*, which Rolleston reviewed in the *Academy* on 10 Oct 1891 (300–7).

[3] Todhunter's *The Poison Flower*, a poetic drama based on Hawthorne's *Rappaccini's Daughter*, was produced, with his *Sicilian Idyll*, in matinée performances at the Vaudeville Theatre, 15–19 June 1891. WBY reviewed the play in the *Providence Sunday Journal*, 26 July 1891, and in the *Boston Pilot*, 1 Aug 1891 (*LNI*, 111–15, 50–1). He further noticed it, with *A Sicilian Idyll*, in *United Ireland*, 11 July 1891 (*UP* 1. 190–4).

[4] WBY and Edwin Ellis were working on an ambitious edition of the *Works of William Blake*, which did not in fact appear until February 1893.

to be in Ireland by the middle of July & must see a lot for the printers done before then. I am going to stay with Charles Johnston who will have Ballykilbeg to himself for a couple of weeks[5] & shall then endeavour to spend a week in Dublin if the Tynans will take me in.[6] I can only get away for a very short time pending the completion of Blake & am afraid of facing Dublin distractions before I give a little while to country placidity. I see by your note that you hope to be in London. I hope your visit here will not coincide by any ill chance with mine to Dublin.

I am rather in a difficulty about Miss O'Leary poems. I find it almost impossible to review it for so Ultra-Tory a paper as the National Observer but when I do an article I intend for Providence Journal (there article of mine finally came off though late) I shall try again. In any case I shall again remind Todhunter about Academy (I did so remind him once but he has been busy with his plays). If he is not going to do it I can try & get it from Cotton & can write review either before leaving this three weeks hence or when in Ballykilbeg. When I consented to Henley's suggestion that I should review it for him I had no idea how difficult it would be. If I were a Tory it would be easy enough or if I could descend to writing as a Tory who did not let his politics quite kill his literary sympathies. A few saving clauses would make all well but they are just what I cannot put in.[7]

The article on Blake you sent me has proved most useful. When did it appear?[8]

I saw Miss Leonard the other day. She has got a new and larger house & seems flourishing.[9] I know nothing of Miles. I made a number of attempts to see him about Xmas but found him always either out or away from home

[5] The Johnston family home was at Ballykilbeg, Co. Down; WBY stayed there in late July 1891.

[6] WBY stayed with the Tynans and her family for a few days in mid-July on his way to Ballykilbeg, at their farmhouse, Whitehall, in Clondalkin, Co. Dublin, described by Katharine Tynan in her reminiscences *Twenty-Five Years* (1913) as 'a small cottage building with little windows under immense overhanging eaves of thatch and a hall door within a porch of green trellis' (31). The village of Clondalkin is $4\frac{1}{2}$ miles south-west of Dublin, on the Grand Canal.

[7] Although WBY had already noticed Ellen O'Leary's volume of poems *Lays of Country, Home and Friends* in the *Boston Pilot* (*LNI*, 45–6), the O'Learys were eager that he should also review it in W. E. Henley's weekly *National Observer*, for which he was writing regularly. The journal was, as WBY observes here, imperialist and conservative in its outlook and opposed to the Irish nationalism with which the O'Learys were associated, and, in the event, he did not notice the book there, nor in the *Providence Sunday Journal*. J. S. Cotton was editor of the *Academy*, where Todhunter reviewed the book on 25 July 1891 (70), finding that the 'unpretending little volume' charmed 'by its absolute simplicity and absence of literary artifice'. It was 'racy of the soil' and demonstrated a 'stern reticence of feeling', though he occasionally wished that Miss O'Leary had 'studied the art of versification a little more closely'.

[8] This may have been the notice of an exhibition of Blake's books, watercolours and engravings held at the Boston Museum of Fine Art which appeared in the *Academy* on 7 Mar 1891 (240). While praising the 'scholarly' exhibition catalogue, the reviewer pointed out some omissions, notably Blake's illustrations for J. G. Stedman's *Narrative of a five years' expedition against the revolted Negroes of Surinam* (1796). The description of Blake's portrayals of the punishments meted out to the Surinam slaves would have been of interest to WBY as they inform parts of Blake's *Jerusalem* (45:19) and *Visions of the Daughters of Albion* (1:21). O'Leary took, and occasionally contributed to, the *Academy*.

[9] This was probably the daughter of John P. Leonard, a Young Ireland sympathizer who taught English in Paris and had been O'Leary's closest friend in Paris, during his exile there. Together they had

altogether.[10] I cannot find where I put P B notice but will ransack my pockets & table for it, in a day or two. I *promise*.[11]

My novel has gone to press but does not come out until September. I have sent in with it to be put in the same volume a short tale of ancient Irish legendary days & called this book "John Sherman & The Midnight Rider". The second part of the title refers to second story. My pseudonym is Ganconagh the name of an Irish spirit.[12] I am very glad to hear both about the progress of your book & the course of events in Tipperary.[13]

Yours very sincerely

W B Yeats

ALS Private. Partly in Wade, 168–9. A version of this letter appeared in 1. 249–51.

## To John McGrath,[1] [late June 1891]

3 Blenheim Road | Bedford Park | Chiswick | W

Dear Sir

I <enclose> send an article on D^r Todhunters plays at the Vaudeville the other day on chance that you may think it suitable for your paper. If it

formed the St Patrick's Society, made up of descendants of the Wild Geese and Irish expatriates living in France, and in an article in the *Boston Pilot* on 30 July 1892 WBY recalled that the 'late Mr. Leonard tried all his life to make the people of Paris listen to the true story of England and Ireland' (*LNI*, 61).

[10] Alfred Henry Miles (1848–1929), author, composer, and journalist, was currently editing the ten-volume *The Poets and Poetry of the Century* (1891–7), and WBY wanted to see him about contributing the introductory note to Ellen O'Leary's poems, which subsequently appeared in vol. VII (1892) of the anthology.

[11] This was probably WBY's *Boston Pilot* review of *Lays of Country, Home and Friends*, which had appeared on 18 Apr 1891.

[12] WBY's two stories *John Sherman and Dhoya* appeared as No. 10 in Fisher Unwin's Pseudonym Library in November 1891 over the pseudonym 'Ganconagh'. At this time *Dhoya* had the title 'The Midnight Ride' (or 'Rider').

[13] As part of the agrarian agitation connected with the 'Plan of Campaign', the tenants of A. H. Smith-Barry, part of whose estate included the town of Tipperary, had been withholding their rents since the autumn of 1889. Smith-Barry responded with wholesale evictions and the tenants established a substitute town, 'New Tipperary', outside his property. Since much of John O'Leary's income was derived from rents on property in old Tipperary, this agitation. which he vehemently opposed, had a disastrous effect upon his finances. By 1891 the Tenants' Defence Association was finding New Tipperary to be financially disastrous and the whole project showed signs of collapsing; 'there has never been', wrote O'Leary in a letter to the *Freeman's Journal*, 26 June 1891 (2), 'in the whole history of Irish agitation, anything so reckless, ruthless and utterly ruinous as this Tipperary affair from beginning to end.' O'Leary was working on a book of memoirs, *Fenians and Fenianism*.

[1] John McGrath (1861–1956) was at this time sub-editor of *United Ireland*, and had done much to shape the literary policy of the paper. Born in Portaferry, he contributed poems to *Young Ireland* in his youth and later served on the staff of the *Freeman's Journal* but, after its defection to the anti-Parnellites, moved to *United Ireland*. In 1891 he published 'the famous article that accused the anti-Parnellites of the

does not suit you please return it as soon as possible as I think I can use it elsewhere.[2]

Yours truly

W B Yeats

to

The Editor of United Ireland.

ALS Private. With a draft of a political article in McGrath's hand on the blank pages.[3] This letter would have appeared in I. 255.

## *To Lionel Johnson,*[1] [c. 4 September 1891]

3 Upper Ely Place | Dublin.

My dear Johnson,

My brother Jack has done illustrations to Rhy's Cockney Tragedy and Unwin has published them. Could you say a good word for them in the

---

murder of Parnell' (*Mem*, 57) and the following spring helped WBY to set up the National Literary Society. Recalling this period in his article 'W. B. Yeats and Ireland', *Westminster Review*, July 1911 (3–4), McGrath wrote that he and Leamy had 'decided that "United Ireland" must be, not only the propagandist paper of Parnellism, but also a literary national organ after the style of the old *Nation* of Davis and Duffy', and that of all the writers they attracted to its pages the 'most interesting one to me . . . was Mr. Yeats, and not so much because of his contributions, as because, personally, he was something in the nature of an enigma. He looked the character — in a long yellow coat and sombrero hat — far more than he spoke it. But he did undoubtedly speak it also. He talked in the most amazing way about poetry.'

[2] WBY's review appeared in *United Ireland* on 11 July 1891 (see p. 928, n. 3).

[3] McGrath used the blank sheets of this letter to draft the beginning of his article 'Holy Ireland', denouncing the smear tactics used against Parnell in the recent Carlow bye-election, which appeared in *United Ireland* on 11 July 1891: 'There is one feature of contest in Carlow to wh we feel ourselves bound in conscience as public journalists solemnly to call attent. of our countrymen & countrywomen who h. not allowed heat & bitterness of a political struggle to obliterate those characteristics wh for many hundreds of years h. been the distinguishing features of Catholic people of Ireland, & who h won for this green island of ours the noble name wh stands at the head of this article, the grandest & proudest & most beautiful name of all nations. We mean to speak plainly: & we say deliberately that the methods by wh Mr Healy & his disciples are conducting their campaign agst Mr Parnell is demoralising, utterly demoralising numbers of young men & young girls of this country. The evidence of this fact during the fight in Carlow was emphatic startling, conclusive. It was given in the light of day, within stone-throw of Catholic Churches, in the presence of Catholic priests. The exhibitions are shocking. Young girls, tender maidens in their teens under instigation of ?others we might hope for the honor of Irish . . .'

[1] Lionel Johnson (1867–1902; see I. 496–7), poet and critic, had recently come down from New College, Oxford, and was living at 20 Fitzroy Street, London, with the aesthetes Herbert Horne, Selwyn Image, and Arthur Mackmurdo. He had greatly admired *The Wanderings of Oisin* before knowing WBY, and the two were now fellow-members of the Rhymers' Club. During the early 1890s Johnson became WBY's closest friend in London, and under his influence discovered a supposed Irish ancestry. In June of this year he had been received into the Catholic Church, and this letter was perhaps partly written to tease his new orthodoxy. He visited Ireland in the autumn of 1893, and again in April 1894, March 1896,

Anti Jacobin. They seem to me to have a genuine tragic intensity a much rarer thing than mere humourous sketching.[2] In anything being done with the Rhymers book?[3] I am drifting about with no very clear purpose except to get to London sometime this month but shall return here again for a time in October if all goes well.[4] I was in Co Down for a bit[5] and am now studying folklore and black magicians—have discovered a whole colony of them of the most interesting and iniquitous kind. They are great mesmerists and thorough blackguards but picturesque in their hideous costume of black cloth which covers all but their eyes.[6] They have the inverted pentagon upon their foreheads and are followers of the goddess Isis.[7]

and the spring of 1898, by which time his heavy drinking and irregular hours circumscribed his friendship with WBY and others. He died in September 1902 after a fall in a public house, and in 1904–5 WBY selected and edited a collection of his poems for the Dun Emer Press (see p. 49).

[2] Jack Yeats had provided seven illustrations for Ernest Rhys's *The Great Cockney Tragedy*, a sequence of sonnets narrating the birth, ill-fortune, and suicide of a Jewish tailor in London. It had been published in late August 1891, and WBY also wrote to W. E. Henley on 4 Sept, suggesting that he might put in a good word for the illustrations in the *National Observer* (see I. 263–4). Johnson, like Henley, obliged with a short but enthusiastic review in the *Anti-Jacobin* of 12 Sept 1891, praising (791) both Rhys's 'curious sonnets', which 'by their humour and simplicity . . . manage to touch our sympathies', and, even more fulsomely, Jack Yeats's sketches, which 'notwithstanding an obvious exaggeration of manner, are exceedingly remarkable. . . . In their tragic energy and life, their fearless and true realism, they are admirable. Experience will supply the rest; and meanwhile, Mr. Yeats' work shows an experienced mind, which is better than the dextrous hand of a mindless man.' The originals of the drawings, together with an eighth which was not used, are now in the Berg Collection and are reproduced in Hilary Pyle's *The Different Worlds of Jack B. Yeats* (Dublin, 1994), pp. 177–8.

[3] The first *Book of the Rhymers' Club*, an anthology of fifty-seven poems, had been suggested by WBY earlier in the summer, largely because, as he wrote in a copy of the book inscribed to AG (Emory), he wanted to have copies of Ernest Dowson's as yet unpublished poems. Johnson was the 'Receiver of Verse' and one of a committee of four charged with the initial selection, which was then submitted to the whole Club for final approval. The book did not appear until February 1892.

[4] In fact, WBY remained in Dublin until late October and did not subsequently return until May 1892.

[5] WBY had stayed at Ballykilbeg, Co. Down, the home of his former schoolfriend Charles Johnston, in late July; see p. 929.

[6] WBY was associating with a group of Dublin black magicians, led by the English-born Captain Roberts (fl. 1893–1951), who indulged in animal sacrifice, and who is identified by Lionel Johnson in a letter to Edmund Gosse of 29 Dec 1893 (BL) as the model for the magician in WBY's essay 'The Sorcerers' (*Myth*, 37–40; see also *Aut*, 249–50 and II. 524). Austin Clarke records that at about this time AE had met WBY staggering out of a session with Roberts, 'hurrying along Pembroke Road, his olive complexion turned to a bilious green. He had just been present in a nearby house where an Englishman, adept in the Black Art, had sacrificed a cock. The sensitive poet rushed out into the street, horror-stricken by the bloody rite, and never again had anything to do with this ancient cult' (*A Penny in the Clouds* [1968], 56). It is possible that Captain Roberts also served as the model for a black magician who practises animal sacrifice in Althea Gyles's unpublished novel of the early 1890s, 'The Woman without a Soul' (NLI).

[7] The pentagram, a five-sided figure derived from the Temple of Solomon, was supposed to gain satanic power if it was reversed. The Egyptian goddess Aset, or Eset, Isis in the Greek form, was one of the most important of Egyptian deities. As the wife of the murdered god Osiris, she reunited the fragments of his dismembered body and restored him to life through her magical powers, and she also protected their child Horus from attack and danger. The paramount magical powers attributed to her attracted a wide devotion: she was revered as a guardian of the sick, and, with the goddesses Nephthys, Neith, and Selket, as protector of the dead, while as the mother of Horus she was associated with life-

Certain good Theosophists aver to seeing them in visions of the night, and do in truth shake in their shoes at the mention of their name.[8] They and a woman who saw a vision of St Joseph with "a lovely shiny hat on him and a shirt buzzum that was never starched in this world" are the best supernaturalism that I have found this expedition.[9] The black magicians have invited me to drop in at an incantation now and then as a sort of compliment to my knowledge of the black art. They have not got enough in the way of souls left to cover a sixpence but that does not matter much—for the present.[10]

My blessing on the Rhymers and may they prosper & get their book out & on before Le Gallienne or some one else print his and so rob them of his poem.[11]

Yours

W B Yeats

TS copy NLA. This letter would have appeared in 1. 264.

giving. Her cult spread from Egypt throughout the Mediterranean, and flourished particularly in Greece and Rome. Knowledge of these mysteries was transmitted by Apuleius' *Metamorphoses*, which contains a detailed account of an initiation rite, and Plutarch's treatise 'About Isis and Osiris', which gives an interpretation of the Isis Mysteries. Recent archaeological discoveries in Egypt had revived occult interest in Isis, and WBY's sometime friend MacGregor Mathers, one of the chiefs of the GD, was to revive Isis mysteries in Paris in the late 1890s, while two other friends, OS and FF, collaborated on a play, *The Beloved of Hathor*, Hathor being a goddess associated with Isis (see p. 749, n. 9).

[8] Madame Blavatsky had warned her followers against magic and spiritualism, and the leader of the Dublin theosophists, Charles Johnston (1867–1931), had dissuaded his fellow-theosophists from accompanying WBY to meetings where such arts were practised, as AE reported to his friend Carrie Rea in an unpublished and undated letter of *c*. 17 Jan 1888 (Armagh): 'There have been private spiritualistic seances in Dublin lately. I would like to have gone to one, but Johnston thinks it would be bad for me. Willy Yeats has not recovered from the effects of one which he attended.' This was probably the seance to which WBY accompanied KT in January 1888, and at which, alarmed by a violent nervous impulse, he tried to pray. Unable to recall any prayers, he recited the opening lines of *Paradise Lost*: 'For years afterwards I would not go to a séance or turn a table . . .' (*Aut*, 103–5; see also Tynan, *Twenty-five Years*, 208–9).

[9] This vision was experienced by a Clondalkin laundress, who recounted it to Katharine Tynan, who in turn passed it onto WBY while he was staying with her in mid-July (see 1. 260). WBY included it in his introduction to *Irish Fairy Tales* (5).

[10] In his essay 'The Sorcerers', WBY describes one of the magicians cutting the throat of a black cock, and then beginning 'an invocation, which was neither English nor Irish, and had a deep guttural sound. . . . I saw nothing with any definite shape, but thought that black clouds were forming about me. I felt I must fall into a trance if I did not struggle against it, and that the influence which was causing this trance was out of harmony with itself, in other words, evil' (*Myth*, 38–9).

[11] Richard Le Gallienne (1866–1947), poet, novelist, and literary journalist, had moved to London from Liverpool in the April of this year, and had already established a reputation as a poet and influential man of letters (he reviewed regularly as 'Logroller' for the *Star* and was a reader for Elkin Mathews and John Lane). WBY had met him at John Todhunter's house in 1890, saw him frequently at the Rhymers' Club, and cultivated his friendship (see 1. 249), for which he was rewarded with a number of friendly reviews, two of which Le Gallienne reprinted in his *Retrospective Reviews* (1896). He was just about to publish a book of belle-lettriste prose sketches, *The Book-Bills of Narcissus*, but his next book of verse, *English Poems*, did not appear until late September 1892, and he contributed four poems to *The Book of the Rhymers' Club*.

# To John McGrath, [early January 1892]

3 Blenheim Road | Bedford Park | Chiswick. W

Dear M$^r$ M$^c$Grath

I have written so few stories that a new one needing as it does a plot is a very considerable labour—much more than an article of the same length[1]— & as I am busy with Blake up till the end of February or the beginning of March when it has to be finished[2] & with my new book of poems which go to press in about three weeks,[3] I am afraid that the Shamrock story is impossible. Many thanks however—when this bulk of work is off my hands I shall be much more able to do things of this kind.

If Leamy[4] would write an article on Todhunter's book it would be a very good thing & would help the book much more than any article of mine. Get him to do so if you can for I think it is a shame that Irish people dont buy a book like the "Banshee" when they can get it for 1/-. So far the 1/- edition has done very badly unless some recent good reviews may have helped it. If Leamy writes on this subject, please return my article to me & I will send it to the Boston Pilot.[5]

The Truth about the article you refer to is that Miss Gonne & I are very old friends <& that she sent me the papers I used—she sends & was pleased> & that the article was written because she is anxious to help us

---

[1] McGrath had evidently asked WBY to contribute a story to the *Shamrock*, a weekly magazine aimed at an adolescent audience and also published by *United Ireland*. In 1892 the magazine printed a great number of stories, including some by WBY's friends, such as Richard Ashe King, Katharine Tynan, and McGrath himself.

[2] Progress on WBY's and Edwin Ellis's *Works of William Blake* (see p. 928) was slower than anticipated and the edition did not appear until almost a year after this letter was written.

[3] i.e. WBY's second major collection of poems, *The Countess Kathleen and Various Legends and Lyrics*. In fact, WBY did not send Unwin copy for the book until mid-March, and it did not appear until late August.

[4] Edmund Leamy (1848–1901) had helped Parnell to seize the *United Ireland* offices by force on 10 Dec 1890, after the split in the Irish Party, and was now the paper's editor. Born in Waterford, he qualified as a solicitor but abandoned the law for politics and literature, becoming Nationalist MP for Waterford in 1880, for N E Cork in 1885, for South Sligo in 1887, and for Kildare in 1900. He published verse in a number of Irish journals; his *Irish Fairy Tales* appeared in 1890 and *The Fairy Minstrel of Glenmalure* in 1899; and his play, *Cupid in Kerry*, was produced posthumously in Dublin in 1906. Under his editorship *United Ireland* became the leading Parnellite organ until the setting up of the *Irish Independent*. WBY recalled him (*Mem*, 57) as 'a pleasant, indolent man', and he was evidently too indolent to review the new edition of Todhunter's book, as WBY did it himself.

[5] WBY had reviewed the first edition of *The Banshee and Other Poems*, published in the spring of 1888 by Kegan Paul, Trench & Co., in the *Providence Sunday Journal* on 10 Feb 1889 (LNI, 78–90). The book had been reissued in late 1891 in a cheaper 1*s.* edition by the Dublin firm of Sealy, Bryers & Walker, and WBY was eager to get it as widely noticed as possible. He persuaded Katharine Tynan to review it in the *Irish Daily Independent* on 14 Jan 1892 (6), and noticed it himself in *United Ireland*, 23 Jan 1892 (*UP* 1. 215–18). In the course of his review, WBY pointed out how inexpensive the new edition was and urged that it 'should be incumbent on all good Irishmen to know something of their old legends'. Todhunter himself had consulted John O'Leary about possible American reviewers for the book (Reading).

with the Young Ireland League & with the Irish Literary Society of London which we have now on foot over here & it seemed to me that she could help the better if people knew that she was doing a quite practical & useful work in Paris, & that her faculty as a speaker was recognized there.[6] By the by she often asked me to bring you to see her when I was in Dublin but either I left too soon or you were away or for some other reason which I forget I was unable to find you at the right moment.[7]

Yours very truly
W B Yeats

ALS Private. This letter would have appeared in I. 280.

## To William Praeger,[1] [1 April 1892]

My dear Praeger: We are "at Home" on Monday evening next as usual & hope to see you—The day before yesterday I came on your letter by chance & found there you had asked for Horniman address[2]—I am sorry to say I do not know their number—It was horribly forgetful of me not to have written to you about it. It was completely out of my mind.

W B Yeats

APS Kentucky, addressed to 23 Brackenbury Road, Goldhawk Road, W, postmark 'CHIS-WICK AP 1 92'. This letter would have appeared in I. 293.

---

[6] WBY had published an article on MG under the title 'The New "Speranza" ', in *United Ireland* on 16 Jan 1892 (*UP* I. 212–15). This described the influence in Paris of her Association Irlandaise in bringing 'the Irish of Paris into touch with one another, and to keep France informed of the true state of the Irish Question'. He went on to quote enthusiastic reports of a speech she had recently delivered in Paris which had appeared in a number of French newspapers, including *Figaro*, *L'Étendard national*, and *Le Bien publique*. McGrath was evidently intrigued to know how the monolingual WBY had access to this material. WBY was to publish further articles in praise of MG in *United Ireland* (*UP* I. 218–21) and in the *Boston Pilot* (*LNI*, 61–3).

[7] MG and McGrath did meet, and he stood by her during the controversy over her separation from MacBride.

[1] William Praeger, a friend of WBY, was seeking admission to the Golden Dawn, which he joined on 28 May of this year, taking the motto 'Perficit qui mavult'. He attained the grade of 4°= 7°on 3 Mar 1893 but resigned in November 1894. He was possibly a relative of Robert Lloyd Praeger, librarian of the Royal Irish Academy.

[2] Praeger wanted to contact AEFH, who was Sub-Praemonstratrix of the Isis-Urania Temple and living at The Mount, Lordship Lane, Dulwich, London, for a pledge form to join the Golden Dawn. He evidently succeeded in contacting her and on 21 May she forwarded his pledge to Percy William Bullock (1867–1940), who was Sub-Cancellarius in the order.

## To Lionel Johnson, [mid-September 1892]

53 Mountjoy Square | Dublin

My dear Johnson,
I found that Todhunter cannot do me for Academy as he does not want to follow up a review he has done of Ellis by a notice of a brother [? another] rhymer.[1] Could you do it?[2]

Yours
W B Yeats

TS copy NLA. This letter would have appeared in 1. 316.


## To Richard Le Gallienne,[1] [mid-October 1892]

C/o George Pollexfen | Thorn Hill | Sligo

My dear Le Gallienne
We are getting up in connection with the country branches of our National Literary Society small lending libraries & are asking every body to give us books.[2] Do you ever have any review copies that you have finished with & need no more? If so we would be glad of them & they would lighten up some dull minds & make less loutish some country lads. Miss Gonne who is working at the scheme asks me also to get her names of people who review

---

[1] John Todhunter reviewed Edwin Ellis's book of poems *Fate in Arcadia* in the *Academy* on 24 Sept 1892 (256–7), praising its 'easy grace' and noting Ellis's 'sympathy with the mystical method'. This latter attribute made Ellis a 'happy choice' as one of the editors of Blake: 'His imagination superficially resembles Blake's . . . but, unlike Blake's, it is held in leash by a singularly subtle and self-conscious intellect.' This 'stuff of thought' Todhunter found impressive, 'though it is too often expressed in a form which is puzzling rather than illuminating'.

[2] Johnson stepped into the breach, and his enthusiastic review of *The Countess Kathleen and Various Legends and Lyrics* appeared in the *Academy* on 1 Oct 1892, and is reprinted in *W. B. Yeats: The Critical Heritage*, ed. A. Norman Jeffares (1977), 78–82. Johnson argued that, while Irish of the Irish and possessed of all the Celtic qualities of style and feeling, WBY's poetry also displayed classical virtues of intelligence and organization (virtues which Matthew Arnold had famously found wanting in the Celtic genius). Thus 'he produces poems, rational and thoughtful, yet beautiful with the beauty that comes of thought about imagination'.

[1] For Le Gallienne see p. 933.

[2] At a meeting on 15 Sept 1892, the Committee of the National Literary Society had set up a Libraries Subcommittee 'for the establishment of Libraries through the country'. There were seven members: MG, Mary Hayden, John O'Leary, WBY, W. P. Coyne, J. P. Quinn, and J. F. Taylor, with WBY subsequently appointed honorary secretary. The project was inspired by the Repeal Reading Rooms of the 1840s.

and she will herself write to them & ask for books. Do you know any likely folk? She is going to London next week & meens to try round for books there & wants me to get her names before that week is over if I can.[3]

I hope I am not giving you a great lot of trouble—Thank you again very much for your splendid notices of my "Countess".[4]

I am yours truly
W B Yeats

ALS Brandeis (black-bordered paper). This letter would have appeared in 1. 324.

## To Lionel Johnson, [mid–October 1892]

Mention in letter from Johnson, 26 October 1892.
Asking for Johnson for review and spare copies of books for Irish country libraries,[1] thanking him for his review of *The Countess Kathleen* in the *Academy*,[2] evidently asking about the Rhymers' Club,[3] and whether he has seen Edwin Ellis about Blake.[4]

NLI. This letter would have appeared in 1. 324.

[3] In a note to John O'Leary on 4 Oct 1892 (NLI) MG had told him that she was 'writing to all my friends for books for the libraries'. Libraries were eventually founded at Loughrea, New Ross, and Listowel, and the effort to gather books for these and other reading rooms in Arklow, Ballygarret, and Westport went on throughout 1893.

[4] Le Gallienne, writing as 'Logroller' in his regular review column in the *Star*, had given two very favourable notices of WBY's play *The Countess Cathleen*. The first, which appeared on 28 Apr 1892, before *The Countess Kathleen and Various Legends and Lyrics* was published, anticipated (2) that the play would demonstrate that WBY had 'solved that Crux of the poetic drama—the necessary union of a lyrical intensity with vivid dramatic action'. Le Gallienne also devoted his second and longer review on 1 Sept 1892 to the play, which he claimed showed an increase of control and economy over WBY's earlier poetry (see 1. 320–1).

[1] WBY had evidently written to Johnson in similar vein to the preceding letter to Le Gallienne. In his reply Johnson regretted that he had 'no books just at present to part with: I have done little reviewing of late, and have already got rid of my last batch of unnecessary books. And I fear that I know of no reviewer sufficiently patriotic, and not too poverty-stricken, to be of any use. But I will put the wants of Ireland in mind, both as regards myself and others. Would a paragraph in some of the literary papers be of any service?'

[2] See p. 936. In his reply to this letter he told MBY he was 'delighted to know that you are pleased with my review: though those abominable misprints still grieve me'.

[3] Johnson replied that the Rhymers' had 'been meeting, with some good results in the way of rhyme: but do come back, and put some new life into us. Sligo must have inspired you sufficiently by this time.'

[4] Johnson told WBY that Edwin Ellis had 'talked to me about my Blake notes, to my perfect satisfaction'. Johnson was to review WBY's and Ellis's edition of *The Works of William Blake* in the *Westminster Review* on 16 Feb 1893 and in the *Academy* on 26 Aug 1893.

## To John McGrath, [7 November 1892]

C/o George Pollexfen | Thorn Hill | Sligo.

My dear Mcgrath
    I enclose an article on an important Gaelic book—if you cannot use it keep it for me as I will send it to Independent.[1] You thought you might perhaps manage an article after a couple of weeks. I accordingly send it on chance.
    I return on Monday.

Yours sincerely
W B Yeats

ALS Private (black-bordered paper).[2] This letter would have appeared in 1. 329.

## To John McGrath, [19 January 1893]

3 Blenheim Road | Bedford Park | Chiswick
| London. | W

My dear Mcgrath.
    Please attend next Council meeting early as O'Leary or Plunkett will propose the formation of the literary committee origonally suggested by you.[1]

[1] In a letter to John O'Leary written at this time, WBY told him that he had written an article for *United Ireland* (1. 327), but no further reviews by WBY appeared there, and there was no review in the *Irish Independent*. It is possible that WBY had sent McGrath his notice of the recently published *Vision of MacConglinne*, edited and translated by Kuno Meyer, which eventually appeared in the *Bookman* for February 1893, and which he described there as 'one of the most singular and suggestive Irish books I have ever come across' (*UP* 1. 261).

[2] WBY's maternal grandmother had died in Sligo on 2 Oct. His grandfather William Pollexfen was taken ill shortly after he wrote this letter, so that he had to postpone his return to Dublin until 20 Nov. Pollexfen died on 12 Nov 1892.

[1] A dispute had broken out in the National Literary Society in Dublin over control of the New Irish Library, a scheme for a series of inexpensive Irish books (see 1. 500–1). WBY had been in negotiation about the project with his publisher, Fisher Unwin, since early 1892, but in the early summer of that year, Sir Charles Gavan Duffy (1816–1903; see 1. 483–4), the Young Irelander who had been general editor of the original 'Library of Ireland' in the 1840s, returned to Dublin with a rival plan. When Duffy's initial intention of working with the Irish-born publisher Edmund Downey fell through, he opened negotiations with Unwin through T. W. Rolleston, so usurping WBY's initiative. WBY and his allies were now trying to regain some control of the scheme, not merely out of pique, but because they suspected that the books Duffy chose for the series would be didactic rather than imaginative. WBY had returned to London to persuade the Irish Literary Society to insist upon their right to advise on the selection of books, through a specially appointed three-man committee, while O'Leary, Count George Plunkett (1851–1948), and McGrath were working in the National Literary Society in Dublin to the same end.

I[t] must be done at once if we are to get our books.[2] Unwin will not go on without our support.[3]

The proposed series will be printed in Ireland & have an Irish publishers name on together with Unwins. Please tell this to council.

Yrs ever

W B Yeats

[on back of envelope]

The picture you speak of was done from me & is probably like though it was not intended as a portrait. Be sure I would never have had myself painted as the mad "King Goll" of my own poem had I thought it was going to turn out the portrait it has. I was merely the cheapest & handiest modle to be found.[4]

ALS Private, with envelope addressed to "United Ireland", Abbey St., Dublin, postmark 'Chiswick JA 19 93'. This letter would have appeared in 1. 346.

## To Lionel Johnson, [late October 1893]

56 North Circular Road | Dublin.

My dear Johnson,

I enclose Langbridge's[1] prospectus which he has asked me to send you. He is anxious for anything possible in the way of paragraphs or leaders or

[2] So strong were suspicions on both pro-and anti-Duffy sides of the National Literary Society that McGrath and O'Leary failed to get agreement on the three-man subcommittee WBY had recommended (see 1. 343–6). Discussions of the proposal became extremely acrimonious, and a meeting, not on the following Thursday but on Friday, 27 Jan 1893, at which WBY was present, broke up after a violent row. At a subsequent meeting on 2 Feb O'Leary moved that a committee of six should be appointed to advise on the projected series of books and that the six should be Sigerson, Ashe King, Count Plunkett, WBY, McGrath, and himself. Such a committee would have had a majority in favour of WBY's views, but the proposal was overturned when an amendment 'That the committee appointed consist of the entire council' was carried by 7 votes to 4. This substantial enlargement would have rendered the committee all but ineffectual, and on 27 Feb a proposal by Sigerson was carried with only O'Leary dissenting, 'That the Council of the Irish National Literary Society approves of the arrangement by which Sir Charles Gavan Duffy is editor and Mr Rolleston and Dr Hyde sub-editors of a series of Irish books:—That so long as this arrangement is maintained this council will loyally and cordially promote the circulation of the series.' WBY evidently supported his motion, since he was present at the meeting.

[3] In fact, the above resolution of the Council of the National Literary Society, and support from the Irish Literary Society, London, persuaded Unwin to go ahead with Duffy's scheme, despite last-ditch attempts by WBY and O'Leary to retain some control of the project (see 1. 349–52). The first of the twelve volumes issued by the New Irish Library, Duffy's edition of Thomas Davis's *The Patriot Parliament of 1689*, appeared later this year, with Unwin as the main publisher, and Sealy, Bryers & Walker in Dublin and P. J. Kennedy in New York as co-publishers.

[4] JBY's portrait of WBY as King Goll had been published opposite the first printing of the poem in the *Leisure Hour* in September 1887. The poem was republished in *The Wanderings of Oisin* as 'King Goll' and later retitled 'The Madness of King Goll' (*VP*, 81–6).

[1] The Revd Frederick Langbridge (1849–1922), poet, novelist, and playwright, was born in Birmingham, educated at Oxford, and ordained in 1877. In 1883 he became rector of St John's and Canon

leaderettes thereon.[2] I suppose you will be at the meeting of the Literary Committee tomorrow and might show them prospectus.[3] They talk of a quarterly magazine. I shall be in London on December 2 for the dinner.[4] Let me hear what and how you are doing.

Yours ever

W B Yeats

[*With enclosure*]

*The Old Country* , the new Christmas Annual which we have the honour to introduce to the public represents—not a creed, or a party, or a province; not an interest, an -ism, or a hobby—but the Literature of Ireland.

While fully assured that Irishmen will regard with kindly good will a genuine Irish Magazine, we feel that it is expecting too much of patriotism to ask it to give a penny for a halfpenny bun, because it is home-manufactured.

We offer, therefore, a large bun, with plenty of currants.

*The Old Country* consists of 200 royal octavo pages, well printed, on good paper, and profusely illustrated by the best and newest processes.

Eschewing politics and theology, and all controversial matters, we have tried to make its pages light and bright, pure and wholesome. We hope that our readers will enjoy many hearty laughs—laughs of which it may be said: 'There is not a heart-ache in a hogshead of them.' Not that serious interest

---

of St Munchin's, St Mary's Cathedral, Limerick, a living he retained until his death. At this time he had already published four books of verse, as well as children's stories, and was contributing prose and verse to a large number of periodicals. His ambition to found an Irish literary magazine was to result, in December 1893, in the publication of the *Old Country*, which although advertised as a Christmas annual, was intended to be the first of a monthly series.

[2] WBY had also sent a copy to McGrath, who printed the complete prospectus on the front page of *United Ireland* on 4 Nov 1893 and described it as 'very businesslike and smart'. He also gave a list of contributors (which included WBY and Katharine Tynan, along with Langbridge himself, Edwin Hamilton, Edmund Downey, Samuel K. Cowan, W. G. Wills, Mary H. Tennyson, Mrs Henniker, Edward Dowden, and 'Dick Donovan') and, while questioning whether all of these were really Irish, added that there would also be unpublished poems by Lord Byron and Thomas Moore, and 'illustrations by Walter Osborne, W. C. Mills, J. B. Yeats, and others'. He anticipated that the 'Christmas number promises well, and should have a large circulation. Of its merits, apart from the writers, of course it is impossible to speak till we see the publication itself.'

[3] i.e. the Literary Committee of the ILS, sponsor of the Irish literary magazine which WBY had been planning since January of this year (see I. 344, 355). He and Johnson had negotiated with printers about production costs during the latter's recent visit to Dublin (see I. 362–3), and the *Irish Home Reading Magazine* finally appeared in May 1894 under the co-editorship of Johnson and Eleanor Hull. Although intended as a quarterly, it folded after the second number in October 1894.

[4] This was a dinner at the Criterion restaurant to mark the resignation of T. W. Rolleston as secretary of the Irish Literary Society, but WBY was unable to attend because of a cold (see I. 521).

will be lacking. There is the story with a grip; the song that reaches the heart. The harmless necessary ghost unobtrusively keeps his tryst, and other seasonable 'creeps' are not lacking.

Our pages will be found distinctively, but aggressively, Irish. They *smack*, but not *thump*, of the soil. For we look for a welcome in Great Britain, and in Greater Britain, as well as in the old country.

The Bill of Fare will, we venture to believe, tempt the very coyest shilling out of its owner's pocket.

TS copy NLA. Text of the Proposal from *United Ireland*, 4 Nov 1893, p. 1. This letter would have appeared in 1. 367.


# To John McGrath, 27 August [1894]

3 Blenheim Road | Bedford Park | Chiswick. W
August | 27th

My dear M<sup>c</sup>grath

I want you to send me a copy of the paper with my letter in it should you publish it this week as I am very busy & find it hard to get into town to see it at the 'Irish Lit' or to buy it in the Strand. I may want to write again should you comment.[1] I saw last weeks paper but suppose the letter arrived later. The last sentence of the letter as I wrote it was I think 'I accept your phrases' Etc. I wish you would put 'I accept your amendation' Etc instead.[2]

I have been much interested in Sigersons letter about 'The Irishman' & find Davitt very feable & full of all manner of purposeless spite. It is always amazing to me the way Irish politicians destroy their dignity by personal-

[1] WBY's letter did appear in the following number of *United Ireland*, that of 1 Sept (see 1. 397–8). It was a response to comments of McGrath's arising out of his criticism of the New Irish Library, and particularly of Thomas Davis's *The Patriot Parliament of 1689*, which had been published in 1893 as the first volume in the series. In the *Bookman* of August 1894, WBY had described the book as 'an historical tractate which, if modified a little, had done well among the transactions of a learned society, but it bored beyond measure the unfortunate persons who bought some thousands of copies in a few days'. Commenting on these views in *United Ireland* on 18 Aug, McGrath agreed with WBY's general condemnation of the New Irish Library but defended *The Patriot Parliament* as good history and noted that it had 'a bigger sale than any Irish book of our time'. Although he prefaced WBY's letter with the explanation that it was written 'with reference to some paragraphs which appeared in this column a fortnight ago on the New Irish Library', he did not comment further on it.

[2] WBY's letter arrived in time for this alteration to be made and his final paragraph read: 'If you re-read my remarks in the *Bookman* upon "The Patriot Parliament" you will find that instead of criticising its historical merits I assumed them and called it a good book for the proceedings of a learned society. I made no other criticism than that it was "dull," whereas, you prefer the words "not brilliant" or "particularly readable." I accept your amendations with pleasure, and we are at one again.'

ities & Irish journalists not less.[3] Your paper is the only Irish one it is possible to read with pleasure & just because you keep to greater matters than persons.[4] M^rs Hinkson tells me that you think of going to Australia & I hope you will only think of going.[5] I am convinced that the next few years will see an immense shifting of all the centres of political influence in Ireland & that those who have kept their dignity intact through present squabbles shall prosper the best.

---

[3] The *Irishman*, a radical Irish nationalist newspaper, and the direct forerunner of *United Ireland*, had appeared in the 1860s and 1870s under the proprietorship of Richard Pigott (1828–89), who was later to forge letters implicating the Irish leader Charles Stewart Parnell in agrarian crime. A controversy about the paper raged in *United Ireland* from July to the end of September 1894, after Michael Davitt condemned it as anti-national during an attack on Timothy Healy's *Irish Catholic*: 'there has not been in Ireland since the death of Richard Pigott's *Irishman* a paper more malignant in its systematic lying about Nationalist leaders, more venomous in its attacks upon the characters of men who have devoted their lives to the National cause, or a greater reproach to, and outrage upon, true Catholic journalism than this paper' (*United Ireland*, 21 July 1894 [5]). A lengthy correspondence followed which included six letters from George Sigerson, four from Davitt himself, two from John O'Leary, two from Count George Noble Plunkett and one from T. O'Neill Russell. Sigerson argued consistently throughout that by simply labelling the paper 'Pigott's *Irishman*' Davitt was slandering everyone else who wrote for the paper, including those 'who recognised sincerity, and understood the true spirit of patriotism. . . . The Irishman did not die on Mr. R. Pigott ceasing to be proprietor' (28 July 1894, p. 1). In his four letters Davitt insisted that he meant no disrespect to the writers who contributed to the *Irishman*, but maintained that Pigott had had full editorial control of the paper and refused to withdraw his contentious description of it. While Davitt's exchanges with Sigerson retained a tone of mutual respect, his correspondence with the other contributors to the debate became much more personal, and on 1 Sept he launched a sustained attack (5–6) on the papal count, George Plunkett, for his aristocratic condescension. Responding the following week (1–2) O'Leary commented that 'the sneers of Mr. Davitt upon the title of Count Plunkett . . . are in such horrible bad taste that they more than answer themselves. . . . I know him [Plunkett] to be a gentleman and a scholar, and I don't think Mr. Davitt's deadliest enemy could ever accuse him of being either.' In a counterblast on 15 Sept (5), Davitt claimed that the 'posturing and posing, the pretensions and the patronising airs of Mr O'Leary in National politics, during the past twenty years, have been fruitful subjects of mirthful comment to those who have had most opportunities of witnessing his peacock-like self admiration. Without a single act of real service to any National, social, literary, or educational interest to his credit . . . except a comparatively short term of imprisonment; without ever having written a line that lifted any Irish theme, National or literary, above the level of the most commonplace mediocrity, or that has lived in individual or popular memory for five minutes after being read in "Pigott's Irishman"—this gentleman has for years assumed the role of censor-in-chief upon every man and movement associated with Irish National or literary affairs! Truly, a most amusing personality in Irish contemporary life and politics is the unequalled "scholar" and "gentleman," the "Blade" O'Leary.' Old-style Fenians like O'Leary and Charles Kickham had vehemently opposed Davitt's Land League, and *United Ireland* was hostile to him because he had sided with the anti-Parnellites after the fall of Parnell in 1891. At this time, WBY was still a staunch disciple of O'Leary, but he was soon to alter his opinion of Davitt (see II. 163, 464–6).

[4] WBY had a high opinion of *United Ireland*, the Parnellite Dublin weekly, which since late 1891 had devoted a great deal of space to literary and cultural matters. His 'The Prose and Poetry of Wilfrid Blunt' (*UP* I. 122–30) had appeared there on 28 Jan 1888, the first of many articles he was to contribute regularly, particularly in the early 1890s. On 15 Jan 1892 he thanked O'Leary 'very much for United Ireland I am always very glad to get it' (I. 281), and on 23 Dec 1893 congratulated the paper on keeping 'up the good fight bravely' (I. 370)

[5] McGrath did not emigrate to Australia but remained in Dublin, working as a journalist, for the rest of his life.

Will be in Dublin in a month. I waited here for my brothers marriage & as that has taken place[6] should return but for an uncle who wants to find me here in September,[7] Shall probably go to the west with him after a short time in Dublin.

I have had a very kind letter from Robert Louis Stephenson praising my poetry which he avers has taken him 'captive' [as] he was taken captive by [Swi]nburne when a boy & by Merediths verse ten years ago. Such praise is worth numberless reviews so far as ones own pleasure is concerned.[8]

I shall publish a new Irish poem 'The Shadowy Waters' before Xmas.[9]

Yours sincerely<br>W B Yeats

ALS Private. This letter would have appeared in 1. 397.

[6] Jack Yeats had married Mary Cottenham ('Cottie') White (1868–1947) at Emmanuel Church, Gunnersbury, on 23 Aug 1894.

[7] i.e. George Pollexfen (see p. 96, n. 9). WBY went to stay with him in Sligo on 23 Oct of this year.

[8] Robert Louis Stevenson (1850–1894), novelist, poet, essayist, and author of *Treasure Island, Kidnapped, The Master of Ballantrae*, and numerous other stories; for health reasons, he had settled at Apia in Samoa in 1890. He had written to WBY on 14 Apr 1894 to tell him that he had been deeply moved as a boy by Swinburne's poems and later by Meredith's *Love in the Valley* and that it might 'interest you to hear that I have a third time fallen in slavery: this is to your poem called the *Lake Isle of Innisfree*. It is so quaint and airy, simple, artful, and eloquent to the heart—but I seek words in vain. Enough that "always night and day I hear lake water lapping with low sounds on the shore," and am, yours gratefully, Robert Louis Stevenson' (*The Letters of Robert Louis Stevenson*, ed. S. Colvin [1911], IV. 254–5). McGrath used this piece of literary intelligence at once, and announced in a note in *United Ireland* on 1 Sept 1894 (1): 'One of Mr. Yeats's latest admirers is Mr. Robert Louis Stevenson, the celebrated novelist, who has just written him from his far-away home in Samoa to say that his poetry has taken him "captive." This is a remarkable tribute from such a critic. Mr. Stevenson was taken captive by Swinburne when a boy, and ten years ago by the verses of George Meredith. Our Irish bard, you see, is climbing up into high company.'

[9] McGrath also used this piece of information in his *United Ireland* note: 'By-the-way, I hear Mr. Yeats is working on a new Irish poem, which he expects to publish before Christmas.' WBY had been writing his heavily symbolic play *The Shadowy Waters* for many years, and had recently returned to it with renewed enthusiasm after seeing a performance of the poetic drama *Axël*, by the Symbolist writer Philippe-Auguste Villiers de l'Isle Adam (1838–89), at the Théâtre de la Gaîté in Paris on 26 Feb 1894 (see 1. 382). Although he continued to work at *The Shadowy Waters* throughout the 1890s, and although it was regularly announced as forthcoming, it was not published until May 1900, and not produced until 4 Jan 1904, when the Irish National Theatre Society staged it in Dublin. He radically revised the play during the summer of 1905, after seeing a production mounted under the auspices of the Theosophical Society (see pp. 134, 139, 145).

## To John McGrath, [c. 11 February 1895]

Thorn Hill | Sligo[1]

My dear M^{ac}Grath

I enclose a letter which I hope you will kindly find room for.[2]

Yrs sinly

W B Yeats

ALS NLI. This letter would have appeared in 1. 439.

## To the Editor of United Ireland, 16 February 1895

SIR—I see by your issue of last Saturday that the National Musical Festival[1] is to be held, if possible, on the anniversary of the birth of Moore;[2] and is intended, I gather from the general tone of the article, to be a kind of annual proclamation of his greatness. I urge the committee, if this be so, to consider the change that has taken place in the attitude of the best critics towards the greater portion of his works. As the fame of Keats, Shelley, and Wordsworth has risen, the fame of Southey, Campbell, and

---

[1] WBY had been staying with his uncle George Pollexfen at his house Thornhill since 23 Oct 1894, working on *Poems* (1895) and *The Shadowy Waters*.

[2] i.e. the following letter.

[1] *United Ireland* first mentioned the plan for a national Irish musical festival on 9 Feb (2), suggesting that it would be 'something like the Eisteddfod', and that it was 'intended to embrace all music of a National character, and will be called by the appropriate Irish name—of, the Feis'. A further article in the same issue (5) suggested that the festival should be associated with the anniversary of Thomas Moore's birth on 28 May. This article claimed that Moore was 'almost as forgotten by the English and their Irish Shoneen followers as is the most obscure rhymer of the seventeenth century', and that this was 'just the reason why the Irish people ought to honour Moore and love Celtic music'. Insisting that the 'Irish should love Moore for the enemies he has made', the writer pointed out that the 'achievement of Burns is observed in every part of the world', and insisted that the 'Irish have as great a right to honour Moore'. And it reported that a meeting in favour of associating the proposed Feis with the anniversary of Moore's birth had been attended by George Sigerson and other members of the National Literary Society of Dublin.

[2] The Irish poet Thomas Moore (1779–1852) was the son of a Catholic Dublin grocer, but studied at Trinity College, Dublin, after which he moved to London to study law at the Middle Temple. He achieved enormous popularity in his time for the songs and lyrics in his ten-volume *Irish Melodies* (1808–34), as well as for *Lalla Rookh*, a series of four Eastern tales which he published in 1817, but later Irish writers and critics tended to find his work sentimental and shallow, and despised his social climbing. In the preface to *A Book of Irish Verse* (1900) WBY complained that 'all but all of his Irish melodies are artificial and mechanical when separated from the music that gave them wings' (pp. xviii–xix), and Joyce's Stephen Dedalus jibes that Moore 'was a Firbolg in the borrowed cloak of a Milesian' (*A Portrait of the Artist as a Young Man* [1968], 183).

Moore has declined,[3] and if this change of opinion be justified, a "Musical Festival" permanently connected with his name will repel more strongly every year many educated people whom it might otherwise attract; for it is not possible to celebrate his unquestionable service to Irish music without also celebrating his more questionable service to literature. The writer of the article I refer to seems to consider that only English opinion, and the opinion of those Irishmen who despise Irish literature—at least so I understand him—refuse to Moore the title of a great poet. You, sir, can settle the matter in a way which will be interesting, and at the same time help to draw attention to the projected Festival, by asking the Irishmen who have most excelled in the making as in the criticism of imaginative literature—Mr O'Grady, Mr Stopford Brooke, Mr King, Mr Johnson, Mr Graves, and their fellow-workers[4]—to send you for publication in UNITED IRELAND a short expression of their opinion.[5] It is, of course, possible, though always unlikely, that the cultivated people of a particular age may be wrong, but the only court of appeal from their judgement

[3] This was a feature of 19th-century literary history. The poetry of John Keats (1795–1821) and Percy Bysshe Shelley (1792–1822), both of whom influenced WBY, grew in critical esteem, as did that of William Wordsworth (1770–1850), although WBY was less enthusiastic about his work. Meanwhile, the poetic reputation of Robert Southey (1774–1843), author of a series of long narrative poems, including *Thalaba* (1801), *Madoc* (1805), and *A Vision of Judgement* (1821), was already in steep decline before his death, notwithstanding his appointment as Poet Laureate in 1813. Thomas Campbell (1777–1844) was born in Scotland, but moved to London from 1803. He never lived up to the promise and popularity of his first poem, *The Pleasures of Hope*, which he wrote at the age of 21. In *Samhain* (1904) WBY wrote (21) that there 'never have been men more unlike an Englishman's idea of himself than Keats and Shelley, while Campbell, whose emotion came out of a shallow well, was very like that idea'.

[4] For A. P. Graves and Lionel Johnson, see pp. 419–20, 49, n. 1. Standish James O'Grady (1846–1928; see I. 501–3), historian, novelist, barrister, and journalist, whose versions of heroic tales had helped inspire the Irish Literary Revival, had been leader writer on the Conservative *Daily Express* since 1873. The Revd Stopford Augustus Brooke (1832–1916), clergyman, author, and scholar, was born near Letterkenny, Co. Donegal, and educated at Trinity College, Dublin. Ordained in 1857, he held various fashionable London incumbencies, and in 1863 went to Berlin as chaplain to Prince Frederick of Prussia. In 1867 he was appointed chaplain to Queen Victoria, but in 1880 he left the English Church and became a Unitarian. His *Primer of English Literature* (1876) sold half a million copies during his lifetime, and among his other publications were a *History of Early English Literature* (1892), studies of Tennyson (1894) and Browning (1902), and an anthology, *A Treasury of Irish Poetry* (1900). He was a vice-president of the Irish Literary Society, London. Richard Ashe King (1839–1932) took holy orders after graduating from Trinity College, Dublin, but left the Anglican Church in disillusion. He became a literary journalist in London, but subsequently moved to Blackrock, Co. Dublin, where he became an active member of the National Literary Society, and where WBY saw a good deal of him in the late 1880s and early 1890s (see *Mem*, 54). King returned to London early in 1897, and married in April 1898. He served as literary editor of *Truth* for many years, and was later elected president of the Irish Literary Society.

[5] None of the writers WBY mentions took up his invitation and the only response to his letter was a hostile retort from T. O'Neill Russell the following week (2): 'I was never more pained by reading anything in an Irish National journal than by reading the letter on Moore. . . . I only know what harm to the Festival may be done even by the apparently wholly un-Irish and somewhat demented person who wrote the letter, I would not take any notice of it whatsoever. . . . Take away the name of Moore from Irish National literature and what is left?' Thomas O'Neill Russell (1828–1908) was a strong supporter of the revival of the Irish language, and a controversialist, who had associations with the IRB and

is time. Should their verdict be against Moore, it would be easy to find some other date, such as the anniversary of Carolan's death, if it be known,[6] or of the death of one of the old Gaelic musicians, which would be full of national suggestion, and perpetuate no uncritical enthusiasm. I only press this matter because I believe that Irish literature, if it disentangle itself from artificiality and insincerity, will in the next few years penetrate all classes in Ireland, and bring something of patriotic fire into even the dim corners of West Britonism. Every one of the small nationalities of Europe has gone through the struggles we are now passing through; and in almost all it has been national literature and history which have filled the educated classes with patriotism, but in none were they able to do so until they learned to set truth above the national glory.—Yours truly.

A STUDENT OF IRISH LITERATURE.

Printed letter, *United Ireland*, 16 February 1895 (1). This letter would have appeared in 1. 439.

## To Jane Cobden Unwin,[1] 8 June [1895]

3 Blenheim Road | Bedford Park | Chiswick. W
June 8th

Dear Mrs Unwin
Thank you very much for your kind invitation for Tuesday the 11th. I accept with great pleasure.

Yours sincly
W B Yeats

AS West Sussex. Dated '1895' in another hand. This letter would have appeared in 1. 466.

emigrated to America for thirty years after the Fenian rising of 1867. WBY describes him anonymously in *Aut* (207–8) as 'an old commercial traveller, a Gaelic scholar who kept an erect head and the animal vigour of youth, frequented the houses of our leading men, and would say in a loud voice, "Thomas Moore, sir, is the greatest heroic poet of ancient or modern times". I think it was the Fire-Worshippers in *Lalla Rookh* that he preferred to Homer; or, jealous for the music of the *Melodies*, he would denounce Wagner, then at the top of his vogue; "I would run ten miles through a bog to escape him", he would cry.'

[6] Turlough Carolan (Toirdhealbhach Ó Cearbhalláin; 1670–1738), one of the most celebrated Gaelic harpers, composers, and poets, was born in Meath but grew up in Ballyfarnan, Co. Roscommon. Mrs MacDermott Roe, the wife of a wealthy local man, had him trained as a harper after he was blinded by smallpox at the age of 18, and he became an itinerant bard, mainly in Meath, Connaught, and north Munster, travelling around the big houses, where he would play and compose songs in praise of the resident family. He settled in Mohill, Co. Leitrim, after his marriage to Mary Maguire, but, following her death, resumed his wandering life, and died on 25 Mar 1738 at Alderford, the house of the MacDermott Roes, his first and most loyal patrons.

[1] Jane Cobden Unwin, née Cobden (1851–1946), the daughter of the radical politician and economist Richard Cobden (1804–65), had married WBY's publisher Thomas Fisher Unwin (see p. 106) in February 1892. In *The Truth about a Publisher* (1960) Sir Stanley Unwin describes her as 'a power behind the throne . . . a forceful personality, but highly emotional and unreliable in her judgements. Her enthusi-

# To Miss Allport, 24 September [? 1895][1]

3 Blenheim Road | Bedford Park | Chiswick W.

Sept | 24 | th

My dear Miss Allport,
   please type write the enclosed for me; & if possible sometime this week.[2]

Yours sincerely

W B Yeats

ALS Private. This letter would have appeared in 1. 475

# To John McGrath, [c. 5 April 1896]

IRISH LITERARY SOCIETY LONDON | 8, ADELPHI TERRACE,
| ADAM STREET, | STRAND.[1]

Dear Sir,
   You have kindly reprinted a couple of poems of mine from 'The Senate' but perhaps you will permit me to send you a correct version, as that in 'The Senate' owing to the miscarriage of my proof sheets is so inaccurate as to get a good deal on my nerves.[2]

Yours sinly

W B Yeats

PS.
Please let me know if you like getting books for review or are they only an embarrassment. If you like getting them I may be able to get some

asm for such causes as Women's Suffrage, the Protection of Aborigines, anti-vivisection, was unbounded. Invitations to lunch at No 3 were "royal commands" that had to be obeyed, but they were disconcerting occasions if for any reason (usually political) the feeling of "The Jane" had been aroused. One was apt to be greeted with a tirade as if one was personally responsible for what she disapproved. But it was unwise to assume that she would hold the same views two days running' (97–8). Although the Unwins had a country house, Oatscroft, in Heyshott, near Midhurst, Sussex, this invitation (probably for lunch) would have been for 3 Adelphi Terrace, where the Unwins had, according to Sir Stanley Unwin, 'a beautiful top-floor flat'. Mrs Unwin edited *The Hungry Forties: Country Life under Protection* (1900), and in the same year published a pamphlet denouncing the Boer War, *The Recent Development of Violence in our Midst*.

[1] Miss Allport lived close to the Yeatses at 4 Marlborough Road, Bedford Park, and did typing on a part-time basis; WBY frequently called on her services in the early 1890s.

[2] WBY may have wanted his story 'St. Patrick and the Pedants' typed prior to sending it to the *Weekly Sun Literary Supplement*, where it appeared on 1 Dec 1895. It was reprinted in the *Chap Book* (Chicago) and, under the title 'The Old Men of the Twilight', in *The Secret Rose* (1897).

[1] The Irish Literary Society, London, had moved to Adelphi Terrace from Bloomsbury Mansion on 24 Oct 1894, to provide its members with easier access to the railway stations.

[2] The poems, 'Two Poems by O'Sullivan the Red concerning Mary Lavell', had first appeared in the *Senate* of March 1896, and were republished in *United Ireland* on 4 Apr 1896 (see II. 21–2). After revision, both were published in *The Wind Among the Reeds*, and subsequently became part of the canon as 'He tells of the Perfect Beauty' (*VP*, 164) and 'A Poet to his Beloved' (*VP*, 157).

publishers here to send to you more continually than they have done. By living in the midst of London as I do now[3] I am more able than before to influence publishers in a matter of the kind.

I have two books – one prose & one verse – coming out this autumn.[4] In the summer I go to Ireland – probably to Tory Island where I want to lay some chapters of a novel.[5]

Yrs ever<br>WBY

ALS NLI. Marked in another hand 'Addressed to McGrath'. This letter would have appeared in II. 19.

## *To Miss Allport, 11 August [1896]*

C/o Edward Martyn Esq., | Tillyra Castle, | Co Galway, | Ireland.
August | 11th

My dear Miss Alport: would you please type write the enclosed & pay your self for doing so; & also the 6d—was it not 6d?—I owe you for work since you last type-wrote.[1] Take it out of the enclosed postal order—I think it is sufficient.

Yours sincerely<br>W B Yeats

Please send the MS & copy to me here.

T. copy Private. This letter would have appeared in II. 43–4.

[3] WBY had moved into Woburn Buildings in February of this year.
[4] i.e. *The Secret Rose*, not published until April 1897, and *The Wind Among the Reeds*, which did not appear until 1899.
[5] In a letter to SMY, probably written in April 1896 (*LBP*, 29), JBY had reported that WBY was 'very shortly to set about writing a long novel for Lawrence and Bullen. He is to write it in Ireland beginning with a few days in *Tory Island*!!' In the event, WBY visited the Aran Islands instead (see II. 36, 47), and his attempts to write the novel *The Speckled Bird* (which was never completed or published in his lifetime) were to continue for more than a decade. Tory (Tòrach, the 'Towery') Island lies off the northwest coast of Donegal; WBY used to pass it on the Liverpool-Sligo boat as a boy, and recollects it in *Aut* (50).

[1] WBY was again calling upon Miss Allport's typing skills, this time probably for a fair copy of his review of Lucy M. Garnett's *Greek Folk Poesy*, published in the *Bookman* in October 1986, and his story 'Where there is Nothing there is God', which appeared in the *Sketch* on 21 Oct.

## To John McGrath, [? 16 September 1896]

Rosses Point | Sligo.
Wednesday

My dear MacGrath: I return to Dublin to morrow & cross to London probably on Saturday.[1] Can you meet me at 11.30 on Friday morning at the resteraunt in Westminster Street which used to be called 'Thompsons'?[2] We can talk there at that hour without interruption.

Yours very sincerely W B Yeats

my Dublin address will be C/o Standish O'Grady 4 Earlsfort Place.[3]

ALS NLI. This letter would have appeared in II. 55.

## To John McGrath, 4 December [1896]

Hotel Corneille, | 5 Rue Corneille, | Paris.[1]
Dec 4th

My dear Mac Grath: You have not told me anything about the newspaper project.[2] I did my part of the bargain. I saw both Mark Ryan & Barry O Brien & found the first open to conviction & the second most cordial about it[3] &

[1] WBY had been in Ireland since mid-August with Arthur Symons, staying with Edward Martyn at Tillyra Castle, visiting the Aran Islands, and, lately, Sligo (see II. 46–55).
[2] 'Westminster' is evidently an error for 'Westmorland' Street. Harrison & Co. had recently taken over the restaurant and business of Thompson & Co. at 29 Westmorland Street.
[3] WBY was to stay with the O'Gradys at the same address in May 1897.

[1] The Hôtel Corneille, rue Corneille, was popular with expatriate Irishmen. John O'Leary had lived there in 1859, and used it on trips to Paris. WBY found it 'expensive' (Aut, 343), and usually stayed at 203 boulevard Raspail or with the Matherses, but they had lately expelled AEFH from the GD, and relations may have been temporarily sensitive.
[2] At their meeting the previous September McGrath had broached the prospect of setting up a new Dublin newspaper, which would take an advanced nationalist line but avoid the factionalism of the rest of the Irish press. It was also to continue and amplify the policy of publicizing Irish cultural developments that McGrath had initiated in the United Ireland in 1891.
[3] Dr Mark Ryan (1844–1940), Galway-born, Irish-speaking medical doctor and Fenian. Ryan had been initiated into the IRB in 1865 by Michael Davitt, and engaged in successful gun-running in the north of England, making enough money to fund medical degrees from Dublin and Edinburgh. A member of every significant Irish political or cultural organization in London, he was elected to the Supreme Council of the IRB, and travelled to both America and Paris on its behalf. In 1894 he withdrew from the IRB to become one of the heads of the INA in Britain and Ireland, a more radical Fenian organization founded by members of the American Clan-na-Gael, which was strenuously opposed by the IRB. With his brothers Drs Patrick and Michael Ryan (also Fenians), he ran two medical practices in London, and used the one in Chancery Lane for political meetings. It was Ryan who initiated MG into the IRB, and he was the dedicatee of Lionel Johnson's poem 'Right and Might' (1896). His Fenian Memories, published by M. H. Gill, appeared in 1945. WBY's attitude to Ryan was ambivalent; he

ready to agree to everything you suggested about neutrality between parnellites & anti parnellites.[4]

I do not write about this but because the chairman of the Committee of
the Irish Literary society asked me in the name of the committee to ask you
if you would be likely to be in London soon. Stopford Brook has asked to
have a special meeting to hear a project of his for a magazine.[5] He beleives
he has got a publisher. The committee are on the look out for an editor &
want if possible to get both you & Rolleston to meet Brooke[6] <?again
nothing is urgent ?without a ?combination ?>

If you were to come over, & if the magazine can be managed (it is not to
be exclusively literary but also industrial) & if you would agree on hearing
Brooke to take the post I think you would probably be chosen editor. You
would be paid of course.

If you still think of the newspaper you could see about that the same visit.
Write to me here. I shall be here for a month or so

Yrs ever
W B Yeats

[*At top of first page*]
PS. please excuse these half sheets I have no paper & am too busy to go out
just now.

ALS NLI. This letter would have appeared in II. 64.

## To John McGrath, 3 March 1897

Whitehall Terrace | P.O. Clontarf | March 3, 1897

---

Handed in at Nassau St. Dublin Office at 11.27     Received here at 11.52

---

TO McGrath Arduladh Clontarf

---

described him (*Mem*, 83) as 'naturally indulgent. . . . naïve', but at this time he was working closely with
him on the London '98 Centenary Committee. Although a confirmed Parnellite, Richard Barry O'Brien
(see p. 8) was now eager for a united Irish national party.
    [4] The nationalist press in Dublin at this period was divided between the *Freeman's Journal*, which
was anti-Parnellite and inclined to John Dillon's faction; the *Irish Daily Independent*, also anti-Parnellite
and sympathetic towards Tim Healy; and *United Ireland*, a Parnellite weekly.
    [5] The Revd Stopford Augustus Brooke (see p. 945) was a vice-president of the Irish Literary Society,
London, and also Rolleston's father-in-law.
    [6] Parallel discussions about establishing a new Irish periodical continued over the coming months,
and as late as March 1898 Rolleston was negotiating 'with C. Graves who is now literary adviser of
S[mith] E[lder] & Co. about an Irish magazine—as to which he asked me to submit a detailed scheme'
(diary, Private). Nothing came of this plan, and, with the early demise of McGrath's *New Sunday World*

Come if possible to Morrisons Hotel one today Meet Macbride O'Donnell and Self possibly important.[1]

Yeates

Telegram NLI. This telegram would have appeared in II. 78.

## To John McGrath, [14 July 1897]

At | Tillyra Castle, | Ardrahan, | Galway.<br>Wednesday

My dear MacGrath: please send me the 'New Sunday World' from the start (you have had three numbers I think) & at once if possible as I shall be leaving this for Sligo, on Sunday next & would like to show them to Martyn.[1] We are

the initiative passed to a revamped Dublin *Daily Express*, which for a few months in 1898–9, under the control of Horace Plunkett and T. P. Gill, became the mouthpiece of the Irish Co-operative and Industrial Movement and the Celtic revival.

[1]  Morrison's Hotel, 1 Dawson Street, Dublin, was known as 'Parnell's hotel'. WBY was staying there with Frank Hugh O'Donnell (1848–1916; see II. 707–12) as London delegates to a large Dublin meeting of those interested in organizing the centenary celebrations of the 1798 uprising, to be held on 4 Mar. One of its most important duties was to set up an official Central Centenary Committee, but it was already clear that this would be contentious, since the agenda (see II. 78–80) proposed that the Committee should be formed largely from those present, which meant in effect that it would be controlled by the Dublin IRB party, plus whoever they might care to co-opt, and so be unrepresentative and factional. This telegram was to summon McGrath to a council of war to try to confound these machinations, and at the meeting the provincial delegates, supported by O'Donnell, moved an amendment which called for a national convention as the first step towards appropriate provincial representation. This was defeated; the original resolution was passed, and an Executive Committee dominated by the IRB was immediately appointed. WBY tried to put matters right, but was 'suppressed by O'Leary, who was in the chair and did not understand my intentions' (*Mem*, 110), and thereafter took no further part in the voting or business of the meeting. On 6 Mar WBY gave 'a lurid picture of the hatreds & jealousies' prevailing among the delegates to T. W. Rolleston, who recorded in his diary (Private) that there were 'roughly' Mark Ryan's party and the Dublin party of P. N. Fitzgerald and Allan: 'The latter being on the spot in Dublin want to have things all their own way & make the thing a mere Fenian manifestation while Y[eats] & F. H. O'Donnell . . . want to put it on a larger basis.' On 9 Apr 1897 the *Freeman's Journal* published a hurt letter from Alice Milligan, complaining (5) of her shock on receiving the agenda and of her fruitless attempts to obtain concessions regarding representation from the Dubliners. Dr Anthony MacBride of Westport, brother of John MacBride, was Dr Mark Ryan's locum in several London medical practices. He was INA treasurer, although, according to a police report (PRO), so 'timid and nervous' that he left the collecting of monies to others. He had evidently accompanied WBY, and O'Donnell to the Dublin meeting, as he, with WBY, endorsed O'Donnell's contentious report of the proceedings to the London Committee (see II. 91–2).

[1]  Planning for John McGrath's new newspaper (see p. 949) had continued through the spring of this year and T. W. Rolleston reported in his diary (Private) on 7 Mar that WBY had brought McGrath to see him in Dublin to talk over a 'new weekly newspaper' which 'Magrath is to edit, in connection with Ryan's movement'. Finally McGrath purchased the *Sunday World*, a weekly which ceased publication in April 1897, and relaunched it as the *New Sunday World* on 20 June 1897. The short-lived paper supported Home Rule, but was palpably less factional in its nationalism than the Parnellite *United Ireland*, for which McGrath had previously worked. McGrath also increased the literary content, with particular emphasis on Irish books and writers, including WBY.

about to try & found a Celtic dramatic school in Ireland[2] & will give a performance next May (do not make this public yet).[3] I would like, when the plan has taken fuller shape to do an article on it for you.[4]

Yr ever
W B Yeats

ALS NLI. This letter would have appeared in II. 123.

## To Lord Castletown,[1] 26 August [1897]

Coole Park, | Gort, | Co. Galway.
August 26th

Dear Lord Castletown; Lady Gregory has given me a kind message from you. I would endeed very much like to have a talk with you about Irish matters, particularly Irish folk lore.[2] I am writing a book about Irish fairy

[2] The decision to attempt to found an Irish theatre was taken by AG, WBY, and Martyn, at Duras, the house of Comte de Basterot, probably in late June (see *Mem*, 117; *Aut*, 398–9; II. 121, 123–6). AG recorded later (Pethica, 152–3) that 'E. Martyn & Yeats drove to Duras one drenching day', where she discussed with WBY the possibility of staging their plays in Dublin, hoping that this 'would be a development of the literary movement, & help to restore dignity to Ireland, so long vulgarised on the stage as well as in romance—& we talked until we saw Dublin as the Mecca of the Celt—This was the beginning of our movement.' AG also alleged (*OIT*, 20–1) that 'the word "Celtic" was put in for the sake of Fiona Macleod whose plays we never acted'.

[3] Legal problems, as well as the difficulty in securing a suitable venue, led to the postponement of the Irish Literary Theatre (as the project soon became known) for a year and the first season was mounted in the Antient Concert Rooms, Dublin, in early May 1899. This initiative led to the formation of the Irish National Theatre Society and to the purchase of the Abbey Theatre in 1904 (see III. 713–18).

[4] There is no evidence that WBY contributed an article on the Irish Literary Theatre to the *New Sunday World*, which folded before plans had 'taken fuller shape'. Nevertheless, McGrath continued to support the Irish dramatic movement and he frequently attended performances at the Abbey Theatre.

[1] Bernard Edward Barnaby Fitz-Patrick, 2nd Baron Castletown of Upper Ossory (1849–1937). Lord Castletown, educated at Eton and Oxford, was leader of the New Unionist Party 'which wished to secure a fairer fiscal arrangement with England' (*Mem*, 110), and at this time was thought of as a possible successor to Parnell. Castletown was later to take a prominent part in the Pan Celtic Movement (see II. 132, 300, 304).

[2] AG records that when she met Castletown at a luncheon party in London on 7 Apr of this year (Pethica, 142–3) she discovered that he 'also has been collecting folk lore—& believes as firmly as Yeats in the "dim nation"'. His 'The Piper', an unpublished version of a folk tale recorded from an oral source, is preserved in NLI, and he appears to have shared WBY's belief in the supernatural. See also his *Ego* (1923), 86–7, 123–5, for an account of his own folklore researches.

belief³ from quite [a] new point of view⁴ and as I hear you are interested in the subject & have been working at it I feal sure I have much to learn from you.⁵ I would gladly spend a day with you as you suggest & could go any time that would suit you early next month.⁶

Yrs sinly

W B Yeats

ALS NLI. This letter would have appeared in II. 131–2.

## To Lord Castletown, 1 September [1897]

at | COOLE PARK, | GORT, | CO. GALWAY.

Sept 1

Dear Lord Castletown: the sixth will suit me admirably. I shall bring some of my folk lore with me¹—A great many thanks.

Yr sinly

W B Yeats

What is your station? I am quite ignorant of the railways.²

ALS NLI. This letter would have appeared in II. 132.

³ WBY was in process of publishing a series of six articles on Irish fairy belief, and intended these to be the core of an ambitious book on Irish folklore. The articles were based on materials in the main collected and transcribed by AG, but published with a mystical frame of reference entirely WBY's. By the time the plan finally came to fruition, as *Visions and Beliefs in the West of Ireland* in 1920, AG was to be named as the sole author, although the book included notes by WBY and two essays by him, 'Witches and Wizards in Irish Folklore' and 'Swedenborg, Mediums, and the Desolate Places', both dated 1914.

⁴ WBY had always entertained a contempt for what he called 'scientific' folklorists, and his intention in collecting such material was to get down to what he considered the primitive religion on which it was based. In 'The Message of the Folklorist' (*UP* 1. 284) he claimed that folklore 'is at once the Bible, the Thirty-nine Articles and the Book of Common Prayer. . . . Homer, Aeschylus, Sophocles, Shakespeare, and even Dante, Goethe, and Keats, were little more than folk-lorists with musical tongues', and he returned to this theme in 'The Evangel of Folk-Lore' (*UP* 1. 326–8).

⁵ 'I have heard the words "tetragrammaton agla" in Doneraile—the floating debris of mediaeval thought', WBY recalled in 'A General Introduction to my Work' (*E & I*, 514–15), and in *Aut* (401) remembered spending 'a few days' at Doneraile, where he talked to 'an old shepherd' about fairy games. He cites folklore from Doneraile in 'The Broken Gates of Death' (*UP* II. 97), 'Ireland Bewitched' (*UP* II. 182), and 'Swedenborg, Mediums, and the Desolate Places' (*Expl*, 69), and he also took down accounts of 'The Children of Lir' from fishermen and of the 'Good People' and fairy raths from local peasants.

⁶ Castletown had invited WBY to Doneraile Court, Doneraile, Co. Cork, one of his two seats.

¹ As well as discussing folklore, WBY also told Castletown about plans for the Irish Literary Theatre. Castletown became a guarantor of the Theatre (for £1), and explained to AG in a letter of 10 Oct 1897 (Berg) that he was 'strongly in favour of doing all that can be done to give a sound national basis to any movement of this kind and to give our people pure food for their minds. . . . Whatever tends to keeping before a people its national poetry, thought, literature and scenic art is good . . . for all within the country.'

² The nearest railway station to Doneraile was Buttevant, then served by the Great Southern and Western Railway.

## To Lord Castletown, 20 November [1897]

27 South Fredrick St, | Dublin
(After Monday next | 18 Woburn Buildings, | Upper Woburn Place, |
London.)
Saturday. Nov <19> 20th

Dear Lord Castletown: I send you an article on 'The Tribes of Danu'.[1] I
should have sent it before but I was waiting in the hope of getting a second
article out, as the second article is much better. My second has been delayed
& so I must put my worst foot foremost.[2] The article I send you is not
exaustive or scientific enough but the article to follow will be both I think.[3] I
have articles on the following subjects planned out or on the stocks (1) one
on the shape shifting & general habits of the fairies, their music, their
dancing, their houses etc[4] (2) one on the dead who are taken by them at
death (all who die young go to them for a time according to most peasants
that I have met)[5] (3) one on the dead who are brought back by various
means[6] (4) one on changlings[7] (5) one on 'people away'[8] (6) one or perhaps

[1] WBY's folklore article 'The Tribes of Danu', published in the November issue of the *New Review*,
gave accounts from a number of informants of the Irish country belief that the tribes of goddess Danu,
perfect in their beauty, live on to the present day in forts or 'forths' ('little fields surrounded by clay
ditches') and in certain trees and bushes. His informants also told of the friends of the tribes of Danu, a
few favoured people who are permitted to see them.

[2] This second article, 'The Prisoners of the Gods', was also to have appeared in the *New Review*, but
WBY had just learned that W. E. Henley had been dismissed as editor and therefore could not publish
it. The article, which appeared in the January 1898 number of the *Nineteenth Century* (*UP* II. 74–87),
records folklore about the desire of 'the others' to capture the dead or dying, and WBY pursued this
theme in 'The Broken Gates of Death' (*UP* II. 95 ff.).

[3] Castletown told AG on 3 Mar 1898 (Berg) that WBY was not 'practical enough' in his folklore
researches, and WBY had evidently already sensed this objection and was stressing the 'scientific' nature
of his investigations.

[4] In 'The Prisoners of the Gods' WBY describes the fairies' love of hurling and dancing, and their ability
to transform themselves into birds and beasts. He also gives an account of their dwellings in forts and caves.

[5] Some stories of this kind appear in 'The Prisoners of the Gods', and yet more are given in 'The
Broken Gates of Death', which was published in the *Fortnightly Review* for April 1898.

[6] The latter part of 'The Broken Gates of Death' recounts numerous stories of this kind.

[7] Stories of changelings (fairy children who are substituted for kidnapped humans) appear in 'The
Prisoners of the Gods', and in 'The Broken Gates of Death'. The greater part of 'Irish Witch Doctors'
concerns those who have been spirited 'away' without any changeling being substituted in their stead. In
his article, 'Away', WBY writes that the 'Irish country people always insist that something, a heap of
shavings or a broomstick or a wooden image, or some dead person ... is put in your place, though
sometimes they will forget their belief until you remind them, and talk of "the others" having put such
and such a person "into a faint," or of such and such a person being "away" and being ill in bed' (*UP* II.
275). A wooden changeling is substituted for Mary Bruin at the end of WBY's *The Land of Heart's
Desire*, and for Cuchulain in his *The Only Jealousy of Emer* (*VPl*, 209, 537, 542).

[8] The article 'Away', published in the *Fortnightly Review* of April 1902, is entirely taken up with
accounts of people who are thought to be in the power of the fairies for varying periods. Such 'men and
women and children are said to be "away," and for the most part go about their work in a dream, or lie
all day in bed, awakening after the fall of night to a strange and hurried life' (*UP* II. 267).

two on witch doctors & witches & wizards generally[9] (7) one on priest cures[10] (8) a miscellaney article or two.[11] I do not expect to have any difficulty in placing these articles. I have already made some arrangements.[12] In any case <with add> they will be the neucleus of a rather considerable book which I think of calling 'The Land of the Living Heart', an old Irish name for faery land. I intend to get the book illustrated with drawings of the old castles, & bushes & forts & of the hills & woods Etc that come into the stories.[13] I shall deposit the names & address of the story teller with either the Royal Irish Academy or with some well known Celtic scholour, that folklorists may if they like verify my information but will not print the real names.[14] One must protect the story teller from the priests at any rate.[15] The folklore I have gives importance to every new scrap I get, & if you could send me some <? subjects I and folk on that subject> it would <will make a great difference in> help me very much.[16] I will of course make the most ample acknowledgements. I hope to make a big authoritative & beautiful book, which will influence Irish poets & scholours for years to

[9] Accounts of witch doctors and fairy doctors appear in 'Ireland Bewitched', published in the *Contemporary Review* of September 1899, and in 'Irish Witch Doctors', which was published in the *Fortnightly Review* of September 1900. The first gives numerous examples of the powers of Biddy Early, the celebrated 19th-century wise woman and healer from Co. Clare, and the second contains an extended account of a fairy cure prepared for WBY's own eye complaint.

[10] WBY did not devote an article to this topic: he mentions briefly in 'Away' that 'sometimes a priest works the cure' (*UP* II. 279), but gives no examples. However, the last section of *Visions and Beliefs* deals with 'Friars and Priest Cures'.

[11] Besides the six main articles, WBY published 'Notes on Traditions and Superstitions' in *Folk-Lore*, March 1899, as well as contributing a number of essays on folkloric themes to the *Speaker* in 1902, which were republished in the 'Revised and Enlarged' edition of *The Celtic Twilight* later that year.

[12] In fact, WBY appears to have had more difficulties than he anticipated in placing the six articles and they appeared over a five-year period in four different periodicals: the *New Review*, the *Nineteenth Century*, the *Contemporary Review*, and the *Fortnightly Review* (which published three of them).

[13] *Visions and Beliefs* did not contain any illustrations.

[14] In all six folklore articles WBY and AG identify their informants pseudonymously but with correct locations; the actual names are given in *Visions and Beliefs*. In a note to 'The Prisoners of the Gods', WBY wrote: 'These names are not, of course, the real names. It seems better to use a name of some kind for every one who has told me more than one story, that the reader may recognize the great number of strange things many a countryman and woman sees and hears. I keep the real names carefully, but I cannot print them' (*UP* II. 74).

[15] Parish priests almost universally disapproved of stories about elemental creatures, and of their parishioners frequenting fairy doctors, an attitude which is mentioned by a number of WBY's and AG's informants. In 'The Prisoners of the Gods', WBY records a woman at Spiddal telling him that the 'priests know all about them, more than we do, but they don't like to be talking of them, because they might be too big in our minds' (*UP* II. 74), and in 'Ireland Bewitched' reports that 'a woman near Coole' confided to him that she 'never let on to Father Curran' about her visit to Biddy Early (*UP* II. 176). See also *Myth* (44–6).

[16] Castletown told AG on 10 Oct 1897 (Berg) that he had found WBY 'a most earnest and pleasant companion', and promised to send him 'a funny old rhyme' which he had collected on his estate.

come & help perhaps with a further impulse the growing idealism of our movement. I want to make people understand how a beautiful invisible world pervades all Irish peasant life—even in the slums of Dublin as I have heard lately.

Yr sny

W B Yeats

Standish O'Grady is about to publish a book on the Finance movement. It will be out almost at once he tells me.[17] I have a book of verse coming out shortly & will send you a copy. There is a lot of folk lore in the notes, which are much better than the article I send you. I will probably get it out by Xmas.[18]

ALS NLI. This letter would have appeared in II. 149.

---

[17] Standish James O'Grady's *All Ireland*, published in December 1898, was a response to the agitation in Ireland which followed the majority finding by a Royal Commission that Ireland had been overtaxed by the British government since the Act of Union. Castletown had himself played a focal role in beginning this agitation, when at a meeting in Cork on 13 Dec 1896, as reported in *The Times* of the following day (10), he warned English ministers who might be 'inclined to stand in the way of peace with honour . . . to pause and think solemnly and seriously of what a nation such as a United Ireland could do when her very life depended upon the result of the contest. He did not wish to use words that might be misinterpreted, but he felt so deeply upon that great question that he would like to draw attention to the fact that sometimes history repeated itself, and an obstinate statesman and cruel taxation lost to England her greatest colony—the United States. He hoped that Cork would never have to follow the example of Boston, but if it was necessary they would be right, because they had justice on their side. (Loud cheers.)' This speech made Castletown an immediate national hero, but he subsequently toned down his language and his keenly anticipated speech in the House of Lords on 5 Mar 1897 was a disappointing anticlimax. O'Grady, who saw this controversy as the last chance for the Irish landlords to reassume the political and moral leadership of Ireland, had written his book (which makes numerous references to Castletown) to urge them to seize their opportunity.

[18] *The Wind Among the Reeds*, a collection of thirty-seven lyrics, was not in fact published until April 1899. The very extensive notes, incorporating much folkloric material, occupied pp. 65-108 of the book, and WBY later confessed (*VP*, 800) that being 'troubled at what was thought a reckless obscurity, I tried to explain myself in lengthy notes, into which I put all the little learning I had, and more wilful phantasy than I now think admirable, though what is most mystical still seems to me the most true'.

# To Thomas Ekenhead Mayne,[1] [21] December 1897

18 Woburn Buildings | Euston Road. | London—
Wednesday. Dec 97.[2]

Dear Sir: I have been a long time about sending you the price of 'Black-thorn Blossoms'. I have been very busy, as well as travelling about, & this & many other things went out of my head. I believe the price is 1/- & 3[d] for postage—If [I] have made a mistake let me know & I will set it right.[3]

I like a great deal about the little book very much you really observe & set down what you observe carefully & musically. I think I like *Tir-In-nan-Oge* a good deal the best a line like 'asleep on the flowers the white hours lie' is not observation, but creation a much better thing. If you work on in that direction you will some day do really memorable work. The poem is good deal spoilt for me by the last line, which turns what should be a vision of ideal beauty into a piece of moralizing. Much better close with the question 'How shall I reach? Etc', 'through the way of the wind' etc. I think I see some new influence in this poem.[4] Elsewhere you are in too close a bondage to Tennysons rythms.[5] One should I think, if one wishes to write celtic poetry, read <our Irish ballads> Allingham, perhaps <above> Allingham

---

[1] Thomas Ekenhead Mayne (1867–1899) was the son of a Belfast bookseller and wrote short stories and poetry for several Irish newspapers, including the *Limerick Leader*. After joining the nationalist Henry Joy McCracken Society in 1895 he began to publish in its journal the *Northern Patriot*, but when Alice Milligan and Anna Johnston left the Society in 1896 to establish the *Shan Van Vocht*, Mayne gave them his full support by contributing articles, poems, and stories to this new Belfast-based magazine, which henceforth became his most important publishing forum. While the relationship between Mayne and his editors was generally harmonious, Milligan dissociated herself from a bloodthirsty article 'The Development of Ireland', which she nevertheless printed in October 1896 on the grounds that while 'the opinions expressed in this paper on the French Revolution are not those of the editor, nor would we say, of the majority of our readers . . . the tone of the writer is so thoughtful and patriotic, that we gladly afford him the opportunity of expressing his views'. *Blackthorn Blossoms* was his first, and, as it unhappily turned out, his only book of verse since he died suddenly at the age of thirty. A volume of short stories and sketches *The Heart o 'the Peat*, funded by Alice Milligan and Anna Johnston, appeared posthumously in 1900.

[2] This date is not in WBY's usual form and was probably written by the recipient. The letter was posted on Tuesday, 21 Dec.

[3] *Blackthorn Blossoms* had been published in Belfast earlier this year, priced 1s. A slim volume of ninety-one pages, it nevertheless contains a number of ambitious and technically uneven long poems. Although Mayne proclaimed his cultural allegiances by printing the title of the book in Irish as well as English, and while he took his inspiration mainly from Irish legend, folklore, landscape or character, the poems show the influence of a number of English writers, particularly Wordsworth and Tennyson.

[4] The line WBY quotes occurs in the fourth stanza of the poem 'An Tir-nan-Og': 'The seasons change not, the birds do not die, | Asleep on the flowers the white Hours lie; | It is Beauty's own land, whose sway is so strong | Time's hand is not lifted against her for wrong.' The closing lines read: 'How shall I reach this land that I love? | Through the way of the wind the high hills above? | Down through the blue wide ways of the sea? | Ah, no! the soul's way mine must be.'

[5] WBY's estimation of the former Poet Laureate Alfred Lord Tennyson (1809–92) had sunk over the 1890s. Earlier in the decade he had described him as a 'supreme artist' (I. 325), and praised his 'marvellous picturesque power' (*UP* I. 251–6), but had now come to regard him as too prone to preaching and too indulgent in his poetic diction, quoting with approbation Verlaine's remark that 'Tennyson was

a great deal for he is very careful, & Hydes 'Love Songs of Connaught' & Fergusson at his best & try & catch, as I think, what is essential in the tune or substance of such things.[6] And with them one should read the great English poets of the past, the Elizabethans constantly. If one reads the English poets of the present one picks up what is merely temporary in them because one is too near them. If one reads the poets of the past one picks up only their eternal part, because the rest has become a bore—it was the illusion of a past age & is gone.[7]

I have myself always found that one is helped to perfect a manner fit to write celtic thought, if one reads the great primitive writers of any country[8]—the folk songs of Roumania,[9] the Kalawala which is the Finnish

too noble, too *Anglais*, and when he should have been broken-hearted had many reminiscences' (*UP* I. 399; see also *UP* II. 413 and *Aut*, 342). In the introduction to *The Oxford Book of Modern Verse* WBY identified the 'revolt against Victorianism' with a revolt against the 'irrelevant descriptions of nature, the scientific and moral discursiveness of *In Memoriam*' (p. ix), but in these judgements forgot the influence on 'The Wanderings of Oisin' of Tennyson's Irish poem 'The Voyage of Maeldune', and the fact that Tennyson's melancholy and attitude to Nature conform more closely to Arnold's definition of 'Celticism' than the work of many Irish poets. In March 1898 WBY turned down a commission to write a book on Tennyson because he was 'a very essentially English writer' (see II. 197).

[6] WBY's admiration for the Donegal poet William Allingham (1824–89) had increased throughout the 1890s (see I. 394). He made a selection of his poems for Miles's *The Poets and Poetry of the Century* (1892), and in the introduction to *A Book of Irish Verse* (p. xx) placed him 'among those minor immortals who have put their souls into little songs to humble the proud'. On 7 Dec 1904, he told Allingham's widow Helen (Illinois), 'I have the greatest possible admiration for Mr Allingham's poetry. I am sometimes inclined to believe that he was my own master in Irish verse, starting me in the way I have gone whether for good or evil.' His edition, *Sixteen Poems* by William Allingham, was published by the Dun Emer Press on 27 Nov 1905 (see p. 459). WBY thought Douglas Hyde's *Love Songs of Connacht*, published in 1893, an exemplary collection of Irish folklore, 'one of those rare books in which art and life are so completely blended that praise or blame become well nigh impossible', and that it grew out of a world where everything was 'so old that it was steeped in the heart, and every powerful emotion found at once noble types and symbols for its expression' (*UP* I. 292, 295). The poetry of Sir Samuel Ferguson (1810–86), like Mayne a native of Belfast, had been an early enthusiasm of WBY, who in 1886 had described him as 'the greatest poet Ireland has produced because the most central and most Celtic' and praised his work over that of Tennyson (*UP* I. 103, 95). Lately WBY had become more critical and in the introduction to *A Book of Irish Verse* (xviii–xix), written in August 1894, he complained that Ferguson was 'frequently dull, for he often lacked the "minutely appropriate words" necessary to embody those fine changes of feeling which enthral the attention', although he described his 'Vengeance of the Welshmen of Tirawley' as 'the best Irish ballad', and his 'Conary' as 'the best Irish poem of any kind'. In the same essay he claimed that 'Allingham was the best artist, but Ferguson had the more ample imagination'.

[7] The recommendation to read the Elizabethans was to become WBY's standard advice to aspiring poets (see p. 355).

[8] WBY's mind was preoccupied with primitive literature at this time as he was writing his lecture 'The Celtic Movement', which he delivered to the ILS on 4 Dec. Later recast in essay form as 'The Celtic Element in Literature' (*E & I*, 173–88), WBY argued that what had been taken has peculiarly Celtic in literature was in fact 'but the ancient religion of the world, the ancient worship of Nature', and he cited Slavonic lore, the Finnish *Kalevala*, the Welsh *Mabinogion*, and the Icelandic Sagas in support of this, commenting that the 'old Irish and the old Welsh, though they had less of the old way than the makers of the *Kalevala*, had more of it than the makers of the Sagas' (*E & I*, 175).

[9] WBY had been much impressed with *The Bard of the Dimbovitza: Roumanian Folk-Songs*, collected from Romanian peasants by Carmen Silva and translated by Alma Strettell and Hélène Vacaresco. A first series had appeared in 1892, with a second in 1894, and in a review of October 1896 WBY had praised the poems for their 'superhuman preoccupations and extravagant beauty' (*UP* I. 411).

epic,[10] the <Norw> Icelandic Sagas[11] & the Welsh stories & poems.[12] We have to combine a music which we can only learn from English writers, for we write in English, with a substance much wilder, much more primitive, than any substance they have moulded. Miss Hopper in verse & Miss Macleod in prose are doing this very <power> beautifully & both have I know read enormously in all primitive literatures <& Irish ?myth> as well as in the legends of their own countries.[13]

The deliberate self possessed spirit of Tennyson is I think very alian to our spirit.

I think some of your poems are dangerously long. One should accustom one self to work within narrow limits that one may be as <perfect> careful as possible. A single perfect stanza should & must take a great deal of time & if one writes many stanzas one grows careless & says the same thing to[o] many ways instead of the one way.

Yours sinly<br>W B Yeats

ALS Private, with envelope addressed c/o R Aickin & Co, Donegall St Place, Belfast,[14] postmark 'LONDON W.C. DE 21 97'. Marked in WBY's hand *Please Forward*. This letter would have appeared at 11. 161.

---

[10] The first edition of the *Kalevala*, based on Finnish and Karelian epic folk poems collected and edited by Elias Lönnrot, had appeared in 1835, followed by an expanded and definitive version in 1849. The poem not only articulated but helped to define Finnish national identity, long submerged under Swedish and Russian influences, and an English translation by John Crawford in 1888 had attracted wide attention in Britain. WBY would have come across references to it in Andrew Lang's article, 'The Celtic Renascence', which had appeared in *Blackwood's Magazine* in February 1897, and also in *Finnish Legends* (1893) by R. Eivind. He was to continue to study the poem during the first two months of 1898 (see 11. 169, 185).

[11] WBY had read the Icelandic sagas in William Morris's versions and in 'The Celtic Element in Literature' commented (*E & I*, 186) that the 'Scandinavian tradition, because of the imagination of Richard Wagner and of William Morris and of the earlier and, as I think, greater Henrik Ibsen, has created a new romance, and, through the imagination of Richard Wagner, become all but the most passionate element in the arts of the modern world.'

[12] WBY's knowledge of traditional Welsh poetry was derived at this time from the work of his friend Ernest Rhys (see p. 229) and from Sir John Rhys's and Matthew Arnold's redactions of Lady Charlotte Guests's translation, *The Mabinogion from the Welsh of the Llyfr Coh O Hergest*. In February 1898 Enid Layard, Lady Charlotte Guests's daughter, was to present WBY with a copy of *The Mabinogion* (*YL*, 1166), a group of Welsh tales surviving in MSS of the 14th and 15th centuries, and he found it 'a perfect example of the right way to tell old tales' (see 11. 186, 250).

[13] According to the *Pall Mall Gazette* of 7 Dec 1897 (12), WBY cited the work of Fiona Macleod and Nora Hopper (see pp. 526–7) in his lecture to illustrate the 'belief in the presence everywhere of something which the eye cannot always see, and the ear can only hear when it is opened . . . [which] the Celts alone among civilized people retain; and out of it arises that "curious troubled ecstasy" in the contemplation of nature which is the distinguishing mark of the Celt'. He cut both these allusions when rewriting the lecture as 'The Celtic Element in Literature'. In a review of her *From the Hills of Dream* in December 1896 (*UP* 1. 423) WBY had criticised her poetry in terms close to those he applies to Mayne's work in this letter, detecting 'two influences — a Gaelic influence, which Miss Macleod has mastered and remoulded, and an influence from modern literature which she has not yet been able to master and mould'.

[14] R. Aickin & Co. were booksellers

## To Lord Castletown, 12 January 1898

18 Woburn Buildings | Euston Road.
Jan 12th — 98 —

My dear Lord Castletown: I put off answering you until I got my second article to send you; & then, when it came out, <in the Nineteenth Century> being busy over a third article, & having besides a talent for procrastination, I put off writing again. However I send you the article now.[1] You will find it more thorough & scientific than the first. It is to be followed by one on the people who are taken 'prisoner' but manage to return after having apparently died.[2] I have written this article & expect to follow it with a fourth on people, who do not die, but go away with the fairies from time to time—people 'away' in fact.[3]

Thank you very much for your kind idea about getting people who would collect for me, & for your good suggestions generally. I shall hardly need subscribers, I think, but will certainly follow some part of your suggestion about collectors. I am thinking of asking the Irish Lit Society & Nat Lit Society & perhaps the Gaelic League to circularize their members on the matter.[4]

I should very much like to have a talk with you about these things. I shall hardly be in Ireland just yet, but may I have a talk with you when you come over for your lecture?[5]

Yrs sinly
W B Yeats

The one or two corrections at the opening of the article are merely getting rid of changes made by Knowles whose ideas of style are elementary.[6]

ALS NLI. This letter would have appeared in II. 171.

[1] This was 'The Prisoners of the Gods', which could not appear in the *New Review* (see p. 954, n. 2). In November 1897, shortly after Henley's dismissal, AG met James Knowles, editor of the *Nineteenth Century*, at lunch and he urged her to send him an article on folklore. She sent WBY's 'The Prisoners of the Gods' (which also contained some of her material), and WBY was delighted with Knowles's acceptance, believing that only titled people or those introduced by 'someone with a title' were published in the *Nineteenth Century* (Pethica, 156).

[2] i.e. 'The Broken Gates of Death' (see p. 954, n. 5), which gives many accounts of changelings returning from the dead, and which includes a story from Doneraile.

[3] WBY's article 'Away' was in fact the last of the six to be published (see p. 954, n. 8). The next article to appear was 'Ireland Bewitched', published in the *Contemporary Review* in September 1899 (see p. 953, n. 5).

[4] WBY did not do this, and almost all the lore in his articles and in *Visions and Beliefs* was collected by him or AG.

[5] This was 'Our Celtic Inheritance', published in the *Irish Literary Society Gazette* in June 1899.

[6] James Knowles (1831–1908) had given up his career as an architect in 1870 to become editor of the *Contemporary Review*. He founded the *Nineteenth Century* in 1877, and under his editorship it developed

## To Dora Sigerson Shorter, [? 26 March 1898]

18 Woburn Buildings
Saturday

My dear M^rs Shorter: I did not let you know about Sunday before, because I had given Sunday as one of two alternate days to Lady Gregory[1] who wanted me to bring a friend to see her.[2] She has unfortunately chosen Sunday & so please excuse my long delay & ask me some other Sunday instead. Yours

W B Yeats

ALS Private. This letter would have appeared in II. 204–5.

## Agreement with Dodd, Mead & Co., 4 January 1901

MEMORANDUM OF AGREEMENT made this fourth day of January 1901 between W. B. Yeats Esq., of 18 Woburn Buildings, Upper Woburn Place, London, W.C., hereinafter called the Author of the one part, and Messrs. Dodd, Mead & Co., of 372 Fifth Avenue, New York, in the United States of America, hereinafter called the Publishers of the other part. WHEREBY it is mutually agreed as follows:—

(1). That the said Author shall assign to the said Publishers the exclusive right of printing and publishing in book form in the United States of America a new book at present entitled "THE SHADOWY WATERS" written by the said Author the nominal selling price of which shall be hereafter fixed at the discretion of the said Publishers and in consideration thereof the said Publishers shall pay to the said Author a royalty of ten per

into an immensely successful and influential journal, whose contributors included Gladstone, Ruskin, and Tennyson. However, he declined to publish any more of WBY's folklore articles. Since WBY's corrected copy has not apparently survived, it is impossible to know which changes he made. As printed in the *Nineteenth Century*, the article begins rather stiffly: 'None among people visiting Ireland, and few among the people living in Ireland, except peasants, understand that the peasants believe in their ancient gods, and that to them, as to their forbears, everything is inhabited and mysterious.'

[1] WBY often dined with the Irish poet and writer Dora Sigerson and her husband, the London journalist Clement King Shorter (see p. 537, n. 2). On 24 Mar he had written to AG (II. 203) that he 'could dine with you on Sunday evening. I had intended to go to Shorters' but I can go there any Sunday quite as well' and asked her to confirm the new arrangement the following day.

[2] The friend was Lionel Johnson, whom AG had recently met for the first time at WBY's Monday Evening on 7 Mar 1898. Johnson had already started drinking heavily but in a letter of 25 Mar (II. 204) WBY assured her that he was 'quite safe at dinner. He does his drinking mostly in his own rooms. I conclude we are not to dress but if I am wrong send me word tomorrow.' In fact, this dinner did not take place because the death of AG's favourite brother, Gerald Dillon Persse, on 26 Mar changed all her plans.

cent (10%) of the nominal selling price on all copies of the said new book which they may sell up to the number of one thousand (1000) copies and a royalty of fifteen per cent (15%) of the nominal selling price on all copies of the said new book which they may sell over and above the first one thousand (1000) copies.[1]

(2).   That all details as to the manner of production, publication and advertisement and the number and destination of free copies shall be left to the sole discretion of the said Publishers who shall bear all the expenses of the production publication and advertising of the said new book.

(3).   That the said Author guarantees to the said Publishers that the said new book is in no way whatever a violation of any copyright belonging to any other party and that it contains nothing of a libellous character and that he and his legal representatives shall and will hold harmless the said Publishers from all suits and all manner of claims and proceedings which may be taken on the ground that the said new book is such violation or contains anything libellous.

(4).   That the rights of translation and all rights other than the right of publication in book form in the United States of America are hereby reserved by the said Author.

(5).   That the said Author shall be entitled to receive on publication six presentation copies of the first edition of the said new book.[2]

(6).   That no royalty shall be paid to the said Author by the said Publishers on copies of the said new book given away for review—for the purpose of advertising the book—on author's copies, on travellers' samples or on copies of the said new book sold at or below cost.

(7).   That the said Publishers shall after 'copy' of the said new book has been placed in their hands take all precautions and steps which may be necessary under the United States Copyright Acts to secure their own rights and those of the said Author in the said new book.[3]

(8).   That the copyright of the said new book is to remain the property of the said Author and that at the expiration of five years from the day on which the book is first published by the said Publishers or at the

---

[1] This agreement is broadly similar to the contract for the British and colonial rights to *The Shadowy Waters*, signed with Hodder & Stoughton on 16 Oct 1900 (see II. 577–80). The main differences were that the royalties on the English edition were a flat 15% and there was a clause stipulating the date of publication, and specifying an advance of £20. This was probably the first time that WBY had managed to retain his American rights rather than allowing an English publisher to negotiate them, and he thought Watt had got 'good terms' (see III. 11).

[2] Dodd, Mead & Co. published the American edition of *The Shadowy Waters* in April 1901, and two copies were received at the Library of Congress on 25 Apr 1901. WBY thought that this version was 'much nicer than the English edition' (III. 64).

[3] Paragraphs 6 and 7 had not been included in the Hodder & Stoughton agreement.

expiration of any subsequent period of five years thereafter this agreement may be terminated by either party on giving three months notice of intention so to do. Provided that if this agreement be terminated by the said Author he shall purchase the plates and stock in hand at the cost of manufacture. But if this agreement be terminated by the said Publishers no liability whatever shall attach to the said Author but he shall have the option of purchasing the stock and plates on the before mentioned terms should he think it to be in his interest to do so, but should the said Author not purchase such stock and plates the said Publishers shall be at liberty to sell the stock accounting for the royalties thereon as provided above.

(9). That an exact account of the sales of the said new book shall be made up every six months to the first day of February and the first day of August, delivered and settled in cash on or before the following February 28th and August 31st.

The said Author hereby authorizes and empowers his Agents Messrs. A. P. Watt & Son, of Hastings House, Norfolk Street, Strand, London, W.C., to collect and receive all sums of money payable to the said Author under the terms of this agreement and declares that Messrs. A. P. Watt & Son's receipt shall be a good and valid discharge to all persons paying such monies to them. The said Author also hereby authorizes and empowers the said Publishers to treat with Messrs. A. P. Watt & Son on his behalf in all matters concerning this agreement in any way what-soever.

Witness to the
signature of Dodd Mead & Co

L.K. Esselstyn

TS Doc Watt. This document would have appeared in III. 6.

# To A. P. Watt,[1] [8 January 1901]

18 Woburn Buildings | Euston Road.
Tuesday

Dear M^r Watt: I send you a copy of my Unwin agreement, and also a letter about it.[2]

Yr sny
W B Yeats

ALS Watt. This letter would have appeared in III. 13.


# Agreement with T. Fisher Unwin, [3 February 1901]

MEMORANDUM OF AGREEMENT made this day of [*blank space*] 1901 BETWEEN W. B. YEATS of 18 Woburn Buildings, Euston Road, N.W. of the one part and THOMAS FISHER UNWIN of 11 Paternoster Buildings E.C. of the other part.[1]

---

[1] The literary agent Alexander Pollock Watt (see p. 65) had just begun to act for WBY, who reported to AG on this very day (III. 11) that 'Watt has got good terms for the American rights of "The Shadowy Waters"'. This had presumably persuaded him to send Watt the correspondence with Unwin for advice, as it related mainly to American rights, although, since the agreement with Unwin was of long standing, he did not ask Watt to act professionally in this matter. In May of this year he was to tell AG that he had 'handed all my books to Watt except the book Unwin has. I think I should hand that over too although he can do nothing for me there at present, & will of course take ten percent' (III. 72).

[2] Thomas Fisher Unwin, WBY's main publisher since 1891, had issued the second revised edition of *Poems* in May 1899, and WBY was now renegotiating the contract for a third edition. The letter mentioned here as an enclosure was probably the one WBY wrote to Unwin on this same day (see III. 12–13), challenging the arrangements over translation and American rights, which Unwin had proposed to split half and half with him. WBY pointed out that as Unwin was acting as an agent in this matter, he should receive only the usual agent's fee of 10%. He also insisted that the new agreement should run for only six years, not the seven years that Unwin had wanted. Since Macmillan (New York) were shortly to take over WBY's American publications, there was in fact no American issue of this or subsequent editions of *Poems*.

[1] See previous letter. The precise date of publication has been left open in this contract, but the new (third) edition of *Poems* appeared in April 1901; the fourth and fifth editions were published in June 1904 and 1908 respectively. WBY had opened negotiations with Unwin for a collection of his poems, provisionally entitled *Under the Moon: Poems Mainly Legendary*, on 11 Oct 1894, and on 19 Oct of the same year stated as his terms that the rights should revert to him after four years, that he should be paid a royalty of 12½ % (rather than the 10% suggested by Unwin), and that he should receive six free copies. After some haggling, contracts were exchanged on 5 Nov 1894 and the book finally appeared in October 1895 (see I. 401–4, 407, 439). A second edition appeared in May 1899 with a new cover designed by Althea Gyles, and when the initial agreement, which had been for four years, expired in November 1899, WBY consulted Clement Shorter as well as Watt about renegotiating it on better terms (see II. 418, 420–1). WBY contributed a critical preface for this new edition, and made major revisions to *The Countess Cathleen* and *The Land of Heart's Desire*, as well as making a number of slight revisions in other parts of the book. He sent Unwin the MSS of the revised book on 2 Feb 1901, and this corrected agreement the following day.

WHEREBY it is mutually agreed as follows:—

1.   That the said W. B. Yeats hereby concedes to said T. Fisher Unwin the exclusive right of printing and publishing in Great Britain, its Colonies and Dependencies, and in English on the Continent of Europe a work to be entitled "Poems by W. B. Yeats", and in consideration thereof said T. Fisher Unwin shall pay to said W. B. Yeats on publication of the said work the sum of Twenty Five Pounds (£25.) on account of a Royalty of $17\frac{1}{2}$ per cent on the published price of all copies sold at above half the published price and a Royalty of $17\frac{1}{2}$ per cent on the net receipts of all copies sold at below one half the published price. <In reckoning the above Royalties 13 copies shall be counted as 12.>[2]

2.   That the said T. Fisher Unwin shall bear all expenses of production, publication and advertisement, except the amount if any by which the cost of corrections of proofs other than printers' errors exceeds an average of 5/- per sheet of 16 pages of printed matter, which amount shall be borne by said W. B. Yeats.

3.   That the said W. B. Yeats guarantees to the said T. Fisher Unwin that the said work is in no way whatever a violation of any existing copyright, and that it contains nothing of a libellous or scandalous character, and that he will indemnify the Publisher from all suits, claims, proceedings, damages and costs which may be made, taken or incurred by or against him on the ground that the work is an infringement of copyright, or contains anything libellous or scandalous.

4.   That the rights of dramatisation are reserved by the said W. B. Yeats.[3]

5.   That the said W. B. Yeats shall be entitled to receive on publication six presentation copies of the first edition of the work and three copies of every subsequent edition and shall be entitled to purchase further copies for personal use at half the published price net.

6.   That the said W. B. Yeats shall not transfer the rights of translation in the above work without the consent of the said T. Fisher Unwin.

7.   That the copyright of the said work shall remain the property of the said W. B. Yeats and at the expiration of six years from the date of publication or at the expiration of any subsequent period of six years

---

[2] The 1894 agreement had given WBY a royalty of $12\frac{1}{2}$% on the published price, but he was determined to improve this, and on 20 Dec 1900 accepted Unwin's offer of $17\frac{1}{2}$%. Unwin, however, had tried diminishing this percentage by treating the book as a non-net volume, and counting thirteen copies as twelve. WBY had protested against this on 14 Jan 1901 (III. 17), on receiving a copy of the agreement, telling Unwin that had he offered '16 per cent I should have refused as I could get 20 per cent else where. You offered me $17\frac{1}{2}$ and I accepted as I wished to go on publishing with you, but the 13 as 12 would reduce the $17\frac{1}{2}$ to practically 16 per cent. On these grounds I must continue to object to 13 counting as 12.' Unwin initialled the deletion of this sentence.

[3] Since *Poems* included two plays (see above, n. 2), this clause was of importance.

thereafter this agreement may be terminated by either party on giving three months' notice of intention so to do.[4]

8.   That accounts of sales of the said work shall be made up to the 30th of March in each year and rendered on September 30th following when payment shall be made in cash.

9.   That this agreement cancels the agreement dated the 5th day of November 1894 between the said W. B Yeats and the said T. Fisher Unwin for a one volume edition of Works.[5]

AS WITNESS the hands of the parties

SIGNED                                                                    T. Fisher Unwin

SIGNED                                                                    W B Yeats

TS Doc signed; Watt. This document would have appeared in III. 31.


## *To John McGrath, [16 May 1901]*

4 ELY PLACE, UPPER, | DUBLIN.
Thursday,

My dear MacGrath: I wish you could come in here tomorrow evening (Friday). This is as you know I dare say Moores house.[1] He has asked me to

---

[4] Unwin had insisted on extending his rights in the book in return for the improved financial terms. The original agreement in 1894 had vested the rights in Unwin for four years, and on 18 Nov 1900, WBY had asserted that the 'longest period of years for which I would arrange, would be three or four' (II. 591). Unwin countered with the suggestion that he should hold the rights for seven years, but on 8 Jan 1901 WBY complained that this was 'a longer period than we agreed for last time. . . . 5 is I think long enough, but you can have it for 6' (III. 13).

[5] Apart from the improved royalties and extended rights, the major difference between this contract and that of November 1894 related to the question of American rights. The draft agreement, probably echoing that of 1894, had stated that 'the proceeds of the sale of rights of translation & of advance rights to the United States of America shall be received by the said T Fisher Unwin & divided in the proportion of one half to the said T Fisher Unwin & one half to the said W B Yeats'. Since this, in WBY's eyes, made Unwin 'practically a literary agent' in the matter, he argued that he should be entitled to no more than the 10% fee that A. P. Watt would have taken for his services (see III. 12–13). Although WBY offered him 10%, Unwin evidently capitulated and withdrew his claim to American rights altogether, and there was no American issue of this or subsequent editions of *Poems*. Copeland & Day had purchased copies of the 1895 edition in bulk for the US market, and may still have had copies on their hands.

[1] George Moore had moved permanently to Dublin at the beginning of April (see III. 55), and WBY was eager to introduce him to leading figures in Irish cultural life; see III. 68–9, 72. The present meeting was to discuss the possibility of organizing a travelling stock company under William Fay's management to tour with plays in Irish and English.

ask you. Russell,[2] Magee,[3] Griffith,[4] & I hope Dixon[5] are coming. We will talk over the theatre & other things.[6]

Yrs sinly

W B Yeats

Come any time after 8.30.


ALS Private, with envelope addressed to Ard-Uladh, Clontarf Crescent, Dublin, postmark 'DUBLIN MY 17 01'. This letter would have appeared in III. 68.


## *To William Sharp,* [c. *21 May 1901*]

&lt;18 Woburn Buildings | Euston R&gt;

C/o George Pollexfen | Sligo.

My dear Sharp: I send a typed copy of the Rite.[1] I wish you would try & get a vision of the coming of the seven races, which I have done in a very perfunctory way.[2] Please let me have the Rite back with your notes as soon

[2] i.e. George Russell (AE). See pp. 5–6, n. 7.

[3] i.e. the Dublin-born William Kirkpatrick Magee, who wrote under the pseudonym John Eglinton (see p. 296).

[4] Arthur Griffith (see p. 25, n. 1), radical nationalist and founder of the Sinn Fein movement, had started the weekly *United Irishman* with his friend William Rooney on his return from South Africa in 1899, and it soon established itself as one of the most radical mouthpieces of Irish nationalism. Griffith, a close friend of MG and of John MacBride, had supported WBY in the controversy over *The Countess Cathleen* and at this time still regarded him as an ally; later he was to attack both WBY and the Abbey Theatre because he thought they sacrificed nationalist sentiment to aesthetic ideals (*Mem*, 211; *VP*, 601).

[5] For Henry Dixon, Fenian and the initiator of the 1892 scheme to establish libraries throughout Ireland, see p. 33.

[6] The Irish Literary Theatre was coming to the end of the three-year cycle that WBY and its other founders had envisaged for it, and he was now airing various possibilities for continuing the dramatic movement.

[1] WBY was sending Sharp (see p. 177) a version of the first, Neophyte, ritual for the Celtic Mystical Order (see II. 663–9), 'a ritual system of evocation and meditation—to reunite the perception of the spirit, of the divine, with natural beauty' which he intended to be 'mysteries like those of Eleusis and Samothrace'. He had been working on the rites since 1895, and received help from fellow-members of the Golden Dawn, from AE, MG, and her sister, as well as from Sharp. Sharp's assistance became of growing importance and on 12 Feb 1900 WBY had recorded in his 'Visions Notebook' (Private):

> Some months ago I gave S[harp] my rough draft for an initiation of Celtic wisdom and asked him to use it as a foundation or symbolic rapport to get the truth forms by.... We evoked Semias, who appeared with a mauve-heather coloured stripe down long white robe and with pointed grey beard. He told us that we must question the water. We must look in the water under the dew drenched hazel bough. We asked if he would henceforth protect in the labour of this rite. He said yes if we gave him the signs. We asked what signs. He said we must hurry because there were four hounds coming. After some doubt as to what to do we waved a dew drenched hazel bough over some water. Radiant face came in water and said it was the face of the three sons of Aengus and that the first sign was to bow to the star of the west and that the second was to uplift the cresent to the south with left hand and that we must ourselves know the third.

[2] In the Neophyte ritual the seven races who invaded Ireland in prehistoric times are invoked in chronological order: the race of Queen Cesar, the Fomor, the Children of Nemedh, the Children of

as possible. Try to get Miss Macleod to try her hand at any part that may seem weak. I am bent on starting definitely next autumn on my return from Ireland & on then going on Rite by Rite till the whole fabric is finished.

Yrs always
W B Yeats

AS Private. This letter would have appeared in III. 73.

## To Fiona Macleod, [*? 26 May 1901*]

C/o George Pollexfen | Rosses Point, | Sligo.
Sunday.

My dear Miss Macleod: M$^r$ Sharp has I beleive sent you my draft for an initiation into celtic 'Mysteries'.[1] It needs to be better written but I feal that the structure is right. The seven lamps are each of a different colour— seven symbolic colours of which I have a note. The next initiation is that of the Cauldron or of elemental water, the next of the stone or of earth, the next of the sword or of air, the next of the spear or of fire. The last of the mountain cave, or of the spirit.[2] I have worked out the symbolism pretty minutely for all these. The great problem is structure, just as the great problem in a play is structure. Once that has been got the actual writing comes readily enough.

The teaching in the grades or degrees should be I think as follows—

1st degree,   study of ordinary sources of Celtic knowledge.
2nd  "   study of symbolism, symbolical, astrological, Etc.
3rd  "   study of methods of devination making of talismans etc.

Parthalon, the race of Firbolg, the Tuatha de Danaan, and the Children of Mil. WBY had probably first come across the idea of the seven consecutive races of mankind in H. P. Blavatsky's *The Secret Doctrine*, although her application of the notion is very different from his.

[1] The major symbols of Celtic Mystical Order rituals were the talismans of the Tuatha de Danaan— the cauldron, stone, sword, and spear. WBY's source for these was Geoffrey Keating's *The History of Ireland*, which describes the four magical cities of the Danaans, Falias, Gorias, Finias, and Murias, and their respective talismans, the Lia-Fail or stone of destiny, the sword of Lugh, the spear of Lugh, and the cauldron of the Dagda.

[2] WBY completed a Neophyte ritual and four Outer Order rituals (in two versions): Cauldron, Stone, Sword, and Spear. He also drafted a Portal ritual for an Inner Order. In the Neophyte ritual, the Wayfarer (Neophyte) is told the mythological history of Ireland by the office-bearers (the Herdsman, the Incense-Bearer, and the Messenger), while six out of seven mystic, coloured lamps are extinguished. The ceremony concludes with a symbolic closing of gates against the four coloured winds of Ireland. Following this, the candidate was to read Irish mythological texts (after their publication, 'Lady Gregory's books' were specified). Each of the four initiation rituals has two parts, and involves figurative rites of passage. In one version of the Neophyte ritual, the colours of the seven lamps are said to be indigo, dark blue, purple, red, orange, yellow, and green.

4   ″      study of mystical philosophy
5   ″      study of clairvoyance
6   ″      Thaumaturgies.
7   ″      White Magic[3]

This brings the different subjects under their proper elements—symbols under water, practical magic under earth, philosophy under air Etc.[4]

Can you tell me when the "Queen of the Fort", the queen of the sidhe, gives her "touch"? I am particularly anxious to know. The "fool" gives his in June.[5] My own work will be more & more, so far as my prose is concerned, with this kind of thing. I have hesitated for a long time about throwing myself into it as I knew it would raise fealing against me. But the growing Catholic party in this country is already so suspicious of me, that I will lose nothing by saying all I have to say. I will indeed rather gain.[6] I hope to bring out a rather revolutionary book of essays this autumn & then my big book of folklore.[7]

Yrs sny
W B Yeats

ALS Private. This letter would have appeared in III. 75.

[3] 'White Magic' appears to have been added in another hand.

[4] As in the Outer Order of the Golden Dawn, members of the Celtic Mystical Order advanced through a hierarchy of five grades after undertaking the ritual associated with the appropriate grade, and there is a considerable overlap between the procedures of the two societies. The members of the Golden Dawn were also required to study astrological symbols and practice, learn to make talismans, and study mystical philosophy and clairvoyance.

[5] WBY was working on an article to be published as 'The Fool of Faery' in the *Kensington: A Magazine of Art, Literature and the Drama* of June 1901, and as 'The Queen and the Fool' in the revised edition of *The Celtic Twilight* in 1902. In this essay WBY recalls (*Myth*, 112) an Irish witch doctor telling him 'that in "every household" of Faery "there is a queen and a fool," and that if you are "touched" by either you never recover, though you may from the touch of any other in Faery.' Although WBY cites the belief of several of his informants that the fool, 'the *Amadán-na-Breena*', gives his stroke in June, he says nothing about November in relation to the queen. In a letter of 26 July 1901 (*LWBY* 1. 84), Fiona Macleod requested that should WBY 'know or come across anything about "the Queen's touch," or "the Fool's laughter" in *November*, please tell me. By the way, be very careful this November. It is always a month of suffering and mischance for some of us and especially about the 21st. (the seven days before or after)—'

[6] WBY had found himself increasingly attacked by Irish Catholic writers and journalists, and particularly in the *Leader*, recently founded by D. P. Moran (see p. 295). In late May of this year he told AE that he thought conflict with the Catholic clerical party in Ireland was inevitable (see III. 76).

[7] i.e. *Ideas of Good and Evil*, not published until May 1903. On 13 Apr 1901 WBY told AG that the essay on Shakespeare he planned to write would 'go into the book of essays rather well'. For the 'big book of folklore' see p. 953, n. 3.

## *To William Gibson,*[1] *3 June* [*1901*]

C/o George Pollexfen Esq | Rosses Point, | Sligo
June 3

Dear Mr Gibson: I cannot accept co-option in the general committee of the Irish Literary Society under the present circumstances. To do so would be to make altogether too little of the grave circumstance that made me resign from it last session. At the same time I thank the committee for their kindness in appointing me.[2]

Yours sinly
W B Yeats

ALS India Office. This letter would have appeared in III. 78–9.

[1] The Hon. William Gibson (see p. 771, n. 3), had recently become honorary secretary of the Irish Literary Society, London. Gibson, whose father Lord Ashbourne had been Lord Chancellor of Ireland since 1895, was also an enthusiastic member of the Gaelic League and was described by W. P. Ryan in *The Pope's Green Island* (213) as 'easily the most picturesque, the most social, and yet in some respects the most elusive individuality. In his Gaelic garb he goes everywhere. He is the Happy Traveller and philosophic enthusiast of Gaeldom.' The Gibsons visited Coole later this summer and WBY was to stay with them at their house in Surrey in 1902.

[2] WBY had resigned from the General Committee of the Irish Literary Society in March of this year, after a dispute over the membership of George Moore (see III. 49–51). Moore's attempts to join the ILS had been thwarted by the threat of resignation by R. Barry O'Brien, a founding member and current Chairman of the Society. Moore had inadvertently been invited to apply for membership by Charles Russell, the Society's Treasurer, who, not realizing what he had done, subsequently insisted that the Committee should blackball him. Much of the opposition to Moore stemmed from his treatment of sexual themes, and from the contemptuous attacks he had made on Ireland and Catholicism in a number of his early works. WBY recalled the incident in *Aut* (433): 'I got rid of Charles Russell by producing his letter of invitation, but Barry O'Brien remained, and after a long fight I withdrew Moore's name and resigned rather than force his resignation'. WBY's letter of resignation, of 16 Mar 1901 stated the issue as one of personal gratitude to Barry O'Brien versus an institutional commitment to artistic freedom: 'as I believe that my duty to my own Order as a man of letters makes it impossible for me to share the most indirect responsibility for what I consider an act of intolerance I resign my position on the Committee and ask that this letter be placed upon the Minutes. I shall not seek re-election so long as the principle of tolerance I have defended is unable to govern the actions of the Society.'

## *A. P. Watt to Henry Newbolt,*[1] *24 June 1901*

HASTING HOUSE | NORFOLK STREET, STRAND
| LONDON, W.C.

24th, June 1901.

(Copy)
Henry Newbolt Esq.,
      "The Monthly Review",[2]
            50, Albemarle Street,
                  W.

Dear Mr. Newbolt,
   I take pleasure in handing you herewith complete typewritten 'copy' of an article by Mr. W. B. Yeats, entitled, as you will note, "MAGIC".
   I shall be glad to hear that you have read this article and that you think so well of it as to be willing to purchase the British serial rights for use in some forthcoming number of "The Monthly Review" (after which all rights would, of course, revert to Mr. Yeats).[3]
   Awaiting your early decision and trusting that it may be a favourable one,
                  I am,

Yours sincerely,
(signed) A. P. Watt.

'Copy' enc:.

TS copy Watt. This letter would have appeared in III. 84.

[1] Henry John Newbolt (1862–1938), poet and editor of the *Monthly Review*, had published two volumes of poetry, *Admirals All* (1897) and *The Island Race* (1898), containing the patriotic naval poems and ballads that led Walter de la Mare to dub him the 'nautical Kipling'. He had evidently elicited this essay on 29 Apr of this year, when WBY had invited him to dinner followed by a 'Monday Evening'; as he records in *The Later Life and Letters of Sir Henry Newbolt* (1942), he 'went accordingly, asked for a contribution, and got it'. Newbolt adds that he 'enjoyed every moment' he spent in WBY's company: 'As a host he was unconventional and amusing: as a talker he was miraculous—almost too miraculous, for he would recount experiences of his own which, though told with convincing sincerity, left the hearers in a desperate plight—faced with the impossible necessity of reconciling the world of science with a strongly contrasted world of magic' (5–6).
[2] Newbolt had been editor of the *Monthly Review* since its inception in 1900. Issued by the publisher John Murray, the journal printed poems and articles of literary, cultural, and political matters, and other contributors included T. Sturge Moore, Arthur Symons, AG, and William Archer.
[3] Despite his 'desperate plight' over WBY's beliefs, Newbolt replied on 26 June (Watt) that he was 'happy to accept' WBY's essay, which subsequently appeared in the September number of the *Monthly Review*.

# *A. P. Watt to Henry Newbolt, 28 June 1901*

HASTING HOUSE | NORFOLK STREET, STRAND
| LONDON, W.C.

28th, June 1901.

(Copy)
Henry Newbolt Esq.,
    "The Monthly Review",
    50, Albemarle Street, W.

Dear Mr. Newbolt,
    Many thanks for yours of the 26th informing me that you have decided to accept my offer of Mr. Yeats "MAGIC".[1] You do not mention, however, at what rate of payment you propose to remunerate Mr. Yeats for the rights which you have purchased in his article and perhaps you can kindly let me have a line from you on this point before I write to Mr. Yeats informing him that his work is to appear in "The Monthly Review".[2]
    Please also let me have proofs and as long notice as possible of the date upon which you are going to publish the article in "The Monthly Review" so that I may have ample opportunity of dealing with the American serial rights.

                  I am,

                          Yours sincerely,
                       (signed) A. P. Watt.

TS copy Watt. This letter would have appeared in III. 85–6.

# *To Oliver Sheppard,[1] 20 July [1901]*

c/o Lady Gregory | COOLE PARK, | GORT, | CO. GALWAY.
July 20

My dear Shepherd: I heard when in Dublin that Hughes having got enough work to take all his time for the next year and a half had resigned his post in

---

    [1] See above.
    [2] Newbolt replied on 4 July, enclosing proofs of 'Magic', and informing Watt that he proposed 'to pay you £20 for it and to publish it on Aug 28 for Sept 1'. He also asked Watt to tell WBY that he was 'very glad to have his paper, and that I don't care a Daily Mail how unpopular his opinions are'.

    [1] Oliver Sheppard (1865–1941), the Irish sculptor, was born in Co. Tyrone, but moved as a child to Dublin, where he lived in the same neighbourhood as John Hughes. He attended the Metropolitan

the art school Dublin.[2] I ventured without consulting you to write to the sec of the tecnical board suggesting you for the vacant post. I <did this because you> explained in my letter that I had had no communication with you. I enclose his reply, which please return to me. I hope you will see your way to send him what he asks.[3] I do not know in any way how you are circumstanced but I feal that it is our duty to get as much talent into Ireland as we can in the present crisis. I dare say you know that Edward Martyn has been given a free hand in the decorating of the new cathedral at Loughrea—[4] Hughes & Sarah Pursur are already at work[5] & there is a great liklehood that

School of Art from 1884, and was for a time a fellow-student of WBY, John Hughes, and AE. In 1889 he won a scholarship to the National Art Training School in South Kensington, where he remained until 1891. After leaving South Kensington, he was appointed to teach modelling at the Science and Art School in Leicester, and subsequently moved to a similar post at the Nottingham Art School. In 1905 he helped found the Royal Society of British Sculptors. Sheppard executed busts of John O'Leary, AE, and Sir Horace Plunkett, among others, and in September 1898 WBY had written of his 'charming sculpture with old Celtic subjects' (II. 269–70). His most celebrated work, the bronze statue of the dying Cuchulain, probably executed in 1911, which now stands in the Post Office, O'Connell Street, Dublin, helped inspire WBY's poem 'The Statues' (VP, 610–11), and, after an invocation to the 1916 Easter Rising, The Death of Cuchulain concludes: 'A statue's there to mark the place, | By Oliver Sheppard done' (VPl, 1063).

[2] John Hughes (1865–1941), sculptor and friend of WBY, had been a student at the Metropolitan School of Art from 1879, and was appointed instructor in modelling there in 1894. An able sculptor in a classicizing mode, he had executed the monument of the novelist and Fenian Charles Kickham, unveiled in Tipperary in November 1898. On 14 Sept 1898 WBY had praised Hughes's 'beautiful and vivid' sculpture (see II. 269), and in E & I (209) picks out his 'beautiful, piteous Orpheus and Eurydice' for particular commendation. Hughes, who is the model for Rodney, the sculptor in the opening story of George Moore's The Untilled Field, had given up his teaching post to work on his Man of Sorrows and Madonna and Child for Loughrea Cathedral, although completion of the latter was delayed until 1908–9 because in 1903 he won a commission for a memorial statue of Queen Victoria. In that year he left Ireland, and spent the rest of his life working abroad.

[3] Thomas Patrick Gill (1858–1931), journalist and politician, born in Tipperary, had edited the New York Catholic World before becoming Irish Party member for South Louth, 1885–92. A man of moderation, he retired from politics following the Parnellite split, and in the late 1890s edited the Dublin Daily Express with flair. From 1900 to 1923 he served as Secretary of the Department of Agriculture and Technical Instruction for Ireland, which, on 1 Apr 1900, had taken the Metropolitan School of Art under its management. Gill's reply to WBY's letter has not been traced, but presumably suggested that Sheppard should make a formal application for the job, and submit a curriculum vitae.

[4] Edward Martyn, long a critic of Irish ecclesiastical art, had persuaded the Bishop of Clonfert to use Irish artists to decorate the new cathedral at Loughrea, and he retained a strong influence on the project. Aided by Sarah Purser (see p. 72), he had also lobbied T. P. Gill to establish classes in stained glass at the Metropolitan School of Art. Together they consulted the English designer Christopher Whall, who promised them his best pupil, A. E. Child, as instructor, and Purser set about founding a stained-glass co-operative, An Túr Gloine (Tower of Glass), which opened at 24 Upper Pembroke Street in January 1903. The commission for St Brendan's Cathedral, Loughrea, occupied the early years of the firm, but it also executed windows for the Abbey Theatre.

[5] Sarah Purser designed a panel depicting St Brendan in the porch of the cathedral, and Hughes sculpted two statues for it (see n. 2 above) as well as executing much of the carving. But she did not approve of WBY's present initiative. As he recalled in a letter to AG of 24 June 1915 (Berg) she was thrown into 'the most manaical state of fury' with him for writing to Gill in support of Sheppard: 'She wished to suggest him herself or to get Hughes, she said, to do so.'

many other catholic churches will follow.⁶ There may be a great market here. One cannot of course feal certain; and certainly I would not have you give up your substance for a shadow; but if you can get a post under the tecnical board the substance will be assured.⁷ You would find Dublin very different from what it was when we were fellow students at Kildare St.⁸ The artistic, & literary movement, in which I include the gaelic movement, has changed the face of the town. There is quite a stirring little group of writers & artists too—George Russell, George Moore, Hughes & others. Thus in Dublin you would be among the living forces of Ireland, shaped & shaping.

I wrote to Duffy for your address & was glad to find from his letter that they have made you a full Academician.⁹

Yr ev<br>W B Yeats

I think you should write at once to Gill if you care to move in the matter.¹⁰

ALS NCAD. This letter would have appeared in III. 92.

## To Fiona Macleod, 4 August [1901]

COOLE PARK, | GORT, | CO. GALWAY.<br>August 4

My dear Miss Macleod: It occurs to me that instead of starting afresh on that first initiation you might prefer to work on the second.¹ The order of the initiations or 'Mysteries' as I plan them will be as follows

⁶ The other impressive church to have been inspired by the revival of Irish art was the Honan Hostel Chapel in Cork, completed in 1916. It has stained glass by Harry Clarke (1889–1921) and a carving of St Finn Barr over the west door by Sheppard.

⁷ Details of Sheppard's contract at the Metropolitan Art School have not survived, but the terms were probably similar to those offered to John Hughes: a salary of £150 a year, rising by annual increments of £10 to £250 for a 21-hour working week.

⁸ WBY, like AE and Hughes, was critical of the teaching he had received at the Metropolitan School of Art, and on 13 Oct 1905 told a committee appointed to inquire into the work of the School (see p. 216) that 'the whole system of teaching' there was 'boring, and destructive of enthusiasm, and of all kinds of individuality'.

⁹ Sheppard had been elected an associate of the Royal Hibernian Academy in July 1898, and on 18 July 1901 became a full member. Patrick Vincent Duffy (1836–1909), painter and art administrator, was auditor, resident keeper, and librarian of the Academy.

¹⁰ Sheppard, who was still teaching in Nottingham, did write to Gill and was appointed Hughes's successor from April 1902. He told his cousin H. O. White (later Professor of English at Trinity College, Dublin) that 'it was a letter from Yeats which was instrumental in his coming back to Dublin to teach in the School of Art here' (Alan Denson, John Hughes, [Kendal, 1969], 490).

¹ WBY had sent Sharp a copy of the Neophyte ritual in March (see p. 967), asking him to forward it to Fiona Macleod. She replied in a letter now lost, and on 26 July wrote again (see p. 969, n. 5), asking

1. Taking the obligation (This is the Rite or Mystery that I sent you.)
2. The Mystery of the Cauldron
3. "    "    "   " Stone
4. "    "    "   " Sword
5. "    "    "   " Spear
6. final initiation—that of the mountains heart.[2]

I have had clear directives to complete them one by one—not to skip any but to work in the order of initiation. The plan for the initiation of the Cauldron which has floated before me is to make the officers speak as the prow, stern, rudder etc of a symbolic ship, which is taking the candidate on his way, & then to let the initiation change to a purifying ceremony (the candidate standing symbolically in the stone vessal one sees in New Grange).[3] I got the ship from a ship in 'The Book of the Dead' & from a certain Irish peasant ceremony, said to have been obscene by the priests who put it down, which was called 'The building of the ship' and about which I could discover nothing but that the people who performed it sat round in the shape of the bulwarks of a ship.[4] I know that you are beyond comparison a greater clairvoyant than I & I would

whether he would 'object to a complete reconstruction of the Rite, as for some reason we both still feel either an inveterate hostility or an insuperable difficulty. By a reconstruction I mean a Rite identical in end but wholly distinct in externals. In other words, has your Rite *finality* to you?'

[2] This list corresponds to the initiations that WBY did finally draft. The final initiation, at 'the mountains heart', was part of the Portal ceremony through which a candidate would move from the Outer Order to the Inner Order of the Celtic Mysteries. It is closely modelled on a similar ritual in the Golden Dawn where the mountain (which WBY associated with Abiegnos, the mountain which supported the planes of the Cosmos and under which Father Rosycross lies in his tomb) is described as 'the Eternal Stone of the Wise, which will become the Mountain of Initiation, whereby the whole Earth shall be filled with the Knowledge of God' (Israel Regardie, *The Golden Dawn* [St Paul, Minn., 1971], II. 201). In a draft ritual for the Celtic Mysteries, 'The Mountain of God' (NLI), the initiate is told of the struggle he must undergo for enlightenment, but is also granted additional powers as a new member of the Inner Order. An invocation cancelled in another draft ritual reads: 'May the Light out of the Sacred Mountain descend upon us. May the Fire from the Hollow Stone descend upon us. May the Water from Conla's Well descend upon us.'

[3] The initiation of the Cauldron, subtitled 'The Voyage of Life', remained the second ritual in WBY's planned cycle. In the first part of the ritual, the three initiators stand respectively in the prow, amidships, and in the stern of a symbolic ship. The first announces that the ribs of the ship are made out of the moon and the sails of bird feathers; the second that the ship is made of a dragon, and that the Wayfarer is in the ship of the Seven Stars, that he has always been in it but has not known it, and that it will be beached upon the Island of the Blessed. This part of the ritual concludes with a symbolic voyage to Tir na nOg. The second part of the ritual involves the initiate immersing his hands in a symbolic cauldron as a rite of purification. The Cauldron is described as 'a very shallow basin raised on a low stand about 18 inches from the ground...an oval shallow unpainted wooden bowl, half full of clear water'. On 12 Sept 1898 WBY had invoked 'the stone vessel, apparently in New Grange...and certain little stones were put into it' after MG had sent him earth from there ('Visions Notebook').

[4] The ships of Osiris and Ra feature substantially in the Egyptian *Book of the Dead*, particularly in chapters 98–102 and 134–37. WBY could have come across the Irish peasant ceremony of the 'building of the ship' in the *Transactions of the Kilkenny Archaeology Society for the year 1852* (Dublin, 1853) or in Lady Wilde's *Ancient Legends, Mystic Charms, and Superstitions of Ireland* (1888), but his most likely source was W. G. Wood-Martin's two-volume *Traces of the Elder Faiths of Ireland* (1902), a book he

gladly have your rehandling of 'the Mystery of the Obligation'[5] but if you feal that we may find it hard to get the time to finish this considerable scheme it would I think be better for you & M[r] Sharp to try your hands at the second Rite 'the Mystery of the Cau[l]dron', (Elemental Water). If your impulse is strong the other way follow your impulses. It is possible that you are prevented working at 'the Rite of the Obligation' because [it] is sufficiently right as it is. I am very uncertain.

My s[c]heme of general organization is to give the initiate after the first initiation books of a literary kind about ancient gaelic mythologies to study[6] & to give him after the initiation of the Cauldron a great mass of detailed symbols astrological & mythological (water being the element of all images)[7]

knew well and which gives the most circumstantial account of this rite in the chapter on 'Plays and Games at Wakes' (I. 315):

> The play entitled 'The Building of the Ship' was divided into scenes or acts, severally entitled, 'Laying the Keel,' 'Placing the Stem and Stern Post,' 'Painting the Ship,' 'Erecting the Mast,' and 'Launching,' or 'Drawing the Ship out of the Mud.'
> In the first proceedings the laying down of the keel, several lads were placed on their backs in line, on the floor. The hierophant, or master of the ceremonies, accompanied by his attendants, then walked on the row, tapping them pretty smartly with his wand or stick, to ascertain if the timber was sound.
> The stem and stern posts were then put into position by placing two young men at the end of the line in a sitting posture. The ribs and planking were then arranged. These consisted of a double line of young men, the first row lying, the second sitting. The body of the ship being completed, the master of the ceremonies, followed by one of his attendants, walked down on the line of legs representing the ribs, kicking and striking them to see that the timbers were sound, examining the rivets, and giving an opinion as to whether they were sound or not.
> When the inspection was finished, needless to say, after much severe practical joking, a huge bucket of dirty water and a mop were produced. The water was then poured over the performers, to represent the process of painting.
> In erecting the mast, one of the youngest of the lads was selected, placed in the centre of the ship as a mast, and gestures, expressions, and acts were used, proving that this part of the play was an undoubted relic of the most primitive times.
> In launching or drawing the ship out of the mud, the men engaged in the performance actually presented themselves before the assembled company in a state of nudity. It would be now difficult to obtain further details. Those here given were extracted from old countrymen, a little from one, and a little from the other, the fragments then pieced together. When inquiries were instituted of one informant regarding the ceremony of 'erecting the mast,' he looked surprised, and said, 'Lord, how did you know that? it's nearly sixty years since I saw it, and sure the priests won't let it be acted now.'

Wood-Martin also makes a much briefer reference to this play in the second volume of his *History of Sligo* (Dublin, 1892), where he cites it (348) among ceremonies 'which appear to have been essentially of pagan origin, and most certainly of such character that they were necessarily suppressed by the clergy'.

[5] i.e. the Neophyte ritual.

[6] Instructions at the end of the Neophyte ritual read: 'After the admission give them something for their minds, Lady Gregory's books approved— one Celtic, one Universal. . . . Put together a book of selections such as will lead the reader to study further for himself. Include what is simple with what is profound, so that a simple soul may not be discouraged.'

[7] The rituals instructed that after the Cauldron ceremony initiates were to study 'simple mystical symbolism . . . such as elements of astronomy, merely to erect a figure and note aspects. Plain elemental Tatwas only, not Akasa; use Tatwa colours as published. . . . Give complete Tatwa set, with stringent

& after "the Initiation of the Stone", practical astrology & divination, making of talismans etc (earth being realization)[8] & after "the Initiation of the Sword" theoretic teaching, philosophy etc & after (Air = thought speculation)[9] & after the initiation of the spear, instruction in vision (fire = vision, magical perception)[10] & after the initiation of the mountain heart which is also the initiation of the speaking adept & of his awakening, thaumaturgy & all the central mysteries.[11]

I beleive that there is a great contest going to come on here in a few years between the Church & the mystics. There have been some premonitory mutterings already. It is absolutely necessary to begin our organization at once. I propose to initiate certain people who I have in my mind into the Mystery of the Obligation this autumn, & to give them the second initiation after they have been reading certain books for about two months & then to use them to organize the initiations more perfectly. It is important to get the first two initiations ready, as the preparation of the mass of symbolical teaching for those who have passed the second will take some time. Lady Gregorys book of the heroic tales—(a book of condensed & harmonized new translations) will be out before Xmas in all likelihood & forms an admirable basis for the reading of those who have passed the obligations. It is a very great book, our *Morte D'Arthur* or *Mabinogian* at last.[12] Your book

directions.' Tatwas were different coloured cardboard shapes to aid visionary experiments, while the Akasa were the more advanced Spirit Tatwas. WBY took a good deal of his information about Tatwas from Râma Prasâd's *The Science of Breath and the Philosophy of the Tatwas* (1890; rev. edn. 1894, with a preface by G. R. S. Mead), and Dorothea Hunter told Ellmann on 27 Oct 1946 (Private) that with these symbols WBY had 'experimented in season and out of season. . . . Later he used in the same way forms found in Celtic work & legend; & it was in the deciphering of these that I was helpful to him.'

[8] According to the final draft of the rituals, after undertaking the Stone ceremony initiates were to learn to 'judge an astrological figure. Mixed Tatwas to be given here, no Akasa yet. System of Cromlechs with Celtic colours. Recommend personally chosen reading.'

[9] After the Sword ceremony initiates were to experiment with '[s]eeing with the Zodiac and Planets, using a disc of the colour with the symbol thereon in white. Learn the Celtic Planetary names and forms of the gods.'

[10] The rituals directed that after the Spear ceremony the adepts were to study 'Clairvoyant working of Astrology. Use of all Tatwas now permitted.'

[11] At the end of 'The Mountain of God' Portal ceremony the adept was, for the first time in the rituals, called upon to speak by repeating words of the First Initiator calling for the 'Active Spirit of the Divine Life', 'Informing Genius', 'Life', and 'Joy' to awaken in him or her. The invocation concluded: 'Rejoice, rejoice, a new staff is in the hands Eternal, a new sword is in the hands of the Eternal.' After this the new member of the Inner Order was asked to study 'Invocation of the gods, building up of Talismanic Forms, building up Divine Forms'.

[12] AG's *Cuchulain of Muirthemne* was not in fact published until April 1902. In his introduction to the book, WBY described it as 'the best that has come out of Ireland in my time. Perhaps I should say that it is the best book that has ever come out of Ireland; for the stories which it tells are a chief part of Ireland's gift to the imagination of the world—and it tells them perfectly for the first time' (*Expl*, 3). He went on to compare it to *The Mabinogion*, the collection of Welsh tales translated from *Llyfr Coh O Hergest* in 1877 by Lady Charlotte Guest, the mother of AG's great friend Enid Layard (see p. 959, n. 12). WBY also compared *Cuchulain of Muirthemne* to the *Morte DArthur*, the prose retelling of the Arthurian

will be valuable too—very valuable.[13] However I need not go on to give you details as yet. I have worked out clairvoyantly a great many details of organization &, as you know, Maud Gonne has given me numberless details of symbolism. I have also quantities of material got from Russell.[14]

Yrs sny
W B Yeats

ALS Private. This letter would have appeared in III. 103.

## *To A. P. Watt, 12 September* [*1901*]

COOLE PARK, | GORT, | CO. GALWAY.
Sept 12

Dear M[r] Watt: I got an urgent letter from M[r] George Moore, who is on committee of our theatre, wanting to know why Beltaine was not out. I replied that we could not get a definite offer from Bryers.[1] He went at once it seems to Bryers & I got the enclosed this morning. It should have been written to you but Moore & his hurry are I have no doubt responsible. I have written to accept & sent the MSS as there is no time to lose. Please put enclosed if it is formal enough with my other agreements.[2]

legends which Sir Thomas Malory completed in 1469 and which was published by Caxton in 1485. WBY owned an 1893 edition (*YL*, 1214).

[13] *The Winged Destiny*, which was not published until 1904.

[14] MG had sent WBY notes on Celtic colour symbolism the previous August (see *G–YL*, 133, 483), but AE had forbidden him to show Sharp any of his material and on 13 Aug 1900 repeated the prohibition through a letter to AG (Berg): 'Please tell Yeats on no account to show Sharp or Fiona the Celtic symbols I gave him nor any of the auras. If he does they will be desecrated and I will never speak on Celtic things to him again.'

[1] Three issues of *Beltaine*, an occasional review given over to theatre matters, appeared in May 1899 and February and April 1900. The magazine was published for the ILT by E. J. Oldmeadow, proprietor of the Unicorn Press (see p. 117), and the name was derived from *La Bealtaine*, the Irish for the first day of May, the Irish fire festival that marked the beginning of summer. There were in fact no further numbers of *Beltaine*; it was superseded in October 1901 by *Samhain* which had a similar format. As he explained in the first issue, WBY changed the magazine's name to *Samhain*, 'the old name for the beginning of winter, because our plays this year are in October, and because our Theatre is coming to an end in its present shape'. *Samhain* was published in Dublin by Sealy, Bryers & Walker and in London by T. Fisher Unwin. George Bryers (1854–1908) was chairman of Sealy, Bryers & Walker, which had published WBY's first book, *Mosada*, in 1886. Earlier he had been a director of the Dublin Steam Printing Works and was associated with both the Irish Protestant Home Rule Association and the Imperial Home Rule Association. The firm was less a regular publisher than a printing firm which occasionally issued small books and pamphlets.

[2] Moore was eager for the appearance of the magazine as it was to contain his article on 'The Irish Literary Theatre'. In a letter of 18 Aug (MBY) he had asked WBY 'What about Beltaine. When will it be out? The sooner the better', and on 3 Sept had again demanded to know 'What about Beltaine?' Part of

I am writing to Unicorn Press, the old publisher, to put him in communication with Bryers. They are both highly unbusiness like & will waste a
great deal of each others time.[3]

Yrs sinly
W B Yeats

[*With enclosure*]
SEALY, BRYERS & WALKER | 94, 95 & 96 MID ABBEY STREET & SOUTH
BROWN STREET | DUBLIN.
10 Sept 1901

We propose to print & publish "Beltaine" at our own risk & expense,
allowing for fifteen per cent on the published price that is to be fixed at
sixpence on all copies sold by us.[4]

The copies supplied to the London publisher, will be supplied at
Threepence & the Royalty he will pay you will be in proportion.

The price is not to be reduced without the consent of the holders of the
Copyright.

Sealy, Bryers & Walker
W. B. Yeats Esq,

[*In WBY's hand*]
I agree to the terms in this letter.
W B Yeats

APS Watt. This letter would have appeared in III. 115.

the delay was caused by finding a London publisher. As early as 28 May WBY had told AG (III. 75–6)
that they would 'have to get an English publisher also for Beltaine I expect, as there are a good many
English readers. If (say) Sealy Bryers took it in Ireland & Hodder & Staughton in England this might
result in Hodder & Staughton advertizing in it. A P Watt might draw up both agreements. I am rather
anxious to let some publisher who has books of mine have some share in it as I have a vague idea of turning
it some day into a kind of Irish *Fors Clavigera* in which I could comment on what ever Irish matter I liked.
In any case I think A P Watt should do the busines[s] part. This will keep the Irish publisher up to the
mark. We could of course go to the publisher & say will you bring out this magazine? If you will A P Watt
will write to you. As I may have to go to Dublin before I go to you I may be able to see Bryers.'

[3] Suspicious of Oldmeadow's business methods and efficiency (see p. 117, n. 1), WBY and AG had
already decided to find a new English publisher for *Samhain*, and had enlisted Moore's help. He
obliged, and on 10 Sept wrote to T. Fisher Unwin urging him 'to publish this interesting "brochure" in
London. The Dublin firm will supply you with copies at 3d each, half price. Will these terms satisfy
you? I hope so for there is no time for bargaining; the matter must be settled at once' (*George Moore in
Transition*, ed. Helmut Gerbler [Detroit, 1968], 218–19).

[4] Although Sealy, Bryers & Walker printed all seven numbers of *Samhain* (1901–8), they ceased to
publish it from 1906, when Maunsel & Co. became the Irish publishers. Unwin remained the British
publisher for the first four and the last (1908) numbers, while Bullen co-published the 1905 number
with Maunsel, who were the sole publisher in 1906. All seven numbers were priced 6*d*., with the
exception of the 1904 issue, which, enlarged to mark the opening of the Abbey Theatre, sold for 1*s*.

# To William Sharp, [? early October 1901]

COOLE PARK, | GORT, | CO, GALWAY.

My dear Sharp: I enclose another letter for Miss Macleod which please read
& send on. I am looking forward to the new 'Hills of Dream' very much.[1]

Do what you can about the Rite. I do not feal we can safely delay much
longer. On[c]e we have got the first ceremonies you will find that you are
much less attacked. They will be a protection—that is endeed a part of
their purpose. A Rite woven into other Rites is a ceaseless invocation of
strong protectors.[2]

Make a circle of light about the room before you begin & if you think
well—this I got once through Maud Gonne—set the 4 hosts of the Feanna
to guard the cardinal points.[3]

Yrs snly
W B Yeats

Dict AEFH, signed WBY; Private. This letter would have appeared in III. 117.

[1] A revised American edition of *From the Hills of Dream* had just been published by Thomas B.
Mosher of Portland, Maine. The book had originally appeared in 1896, and WBY possessed both
editions (YL, 1193, 1193A).

[2] Sharp had evidently told WBY that he and Fiona Macleod had been unable to work on the
Neophyte rite because of psychic attacks, and she described these at length in apologizing on 31 Oct
of this year (*LWBY* I. 91–2) for her lack of progress on 'magical matters': 'I have never known such
continuity of hostile will, of the which I am persuaded: and though, owing to the visionary power of our
common friend, much has been seen and overcome, and much seen and avoided, there is still something
to avoid, something to overcome, and something to see. But very soon now, possibly in this very month
of November where the dark powers prevail (and if so, a double victory indeed!) that which has been
impossible may become possible. Even yet, however, there is much to work against: and not only here:
for you, too, move often into the Red and the Black, or so at least it seems.' Sharp frequently warned
WBY about such phenomena; on 12 Feb 1900, for instance, WBY's 'Visions Notebook' records
(Private) that Sharp had sent an earlier version of the rite to Fiona Macleod, 'but she had replied that
great powers of evil were against them she could find out nothing. He himself had had his foot injured in
a railing and when at last he had tried the rite he had gone off into a dead trance and awoke to remember
vaguely some dream about Murias and to find the copy of the Rite burned to ashes in his hands (? had he
burned it while in trance). I gave him a lunar talisman and made him promise to come to me Tuesday to
work at it. He came though seriously ill from shock.'

[3] The Fianna were an elite band of warriors and huntsmen, who are traditionally supposed to have
flourished in the 3rd century AD, and who inspired numerous tales and lore over subsequent centuries.
They took upon themselves the defence of Ireland, insisted on stringent tests in arms and physical
fitness for those wishing to join them, and observed a rigorous code of chivalry and personal discipline.
They were divided into seven battalions, three in service and four in reserve.

# A. P. Watt to the Editor of the Cornhill Magazine,[1]
## 14 October 1901

HASTING HOUSE | NORFOLK STREET, STRAND
| LONDON, W.C.
14th, Octr., 1901.

(Copy)
The Editor,
    "The Cornhill Magazine",
        15, Waterloo Place, S.W.
Dear Sir,
    I take pleasure in handing you herewith complete typewritten 'copy' of a new article entitled, as you will note "THE HUT, THE CASTLE AND COUNTING HOUSE", the author being Mr. W. B. Yeats.
    I shall be glad to hear that you have read the above and that you think so well of it as to be willing to purchase the British serial rights for use in "The Cornhill Magazine" only (after which all rights will revert to the author) and on terms likely to be satisfactory to Mr. Yeats.
    Awaiting your early decision and trusting that it may be a favourable one,
        I am,

Yours sincerely,
(signed) A. P. Watt.

P.S.
    Mr. Yeats writes with regard to the above, "Popular Poetry" or "What is Popular Poetry" are alternatives to the "present fanciful title."[2]
'Copy' enclosed.

TS copy Watt. This letter would have appeared in III. 118.

---

[1] The editor of the *Cornhill Magazine* since 1897 had been Reginald John Smith (1857–1916), a barrister, who was also a director of Smith, Elder, & Co., the firm which published it. The *Cornhill*, a literary monthly, had been founded by his father-in-law George Smith (1824–1901) in 1860, and its first editor, until March 1862, was the novelist William Makepeace Thackeray (1811–63). The magazine survived until 1975.

[2] The article was retitled 'What is "Popular Poetry"?'. It appeared in the *Cornhill Magazine* in March 1902, and was reprinted as the first essay in *Ideas of Good and Evil*.

# To Fiona Macleod, [? 23 November 1901]

18 Woburn Buildings | Euston Road | London.
Saturday

My dear Miss Macleod: I have been a long while about thanking you for
your book of poems but I have been shifting from Dublin to London & very
busy about various things—too busy for any quiet reading.[1] I have been
running hither & thither seeing people about one thing & another. But now
I am back in my rooms & have got things straight enough to settle down at
last to my usual routine. Yesterday I began arranging under their various
heads some hitherto unsorted folk stories on which I am about to work[2] &
today I have been busy over your book. I never like your poetry as well as
your prose, but here & always you are a wonderful maker of myths. They
seem your natural method of expression. They are to you what mere words
are to others. I think this is partly why I like you better in your prose,
though now & then a bit of verse comes well, rising up out of the prose. In
prose, in your simplest prose the most, the myths stand out clearly, as
something objective, as something well born & independent. In your verse
as in your more elaborate prose they seem subjective, a mere way of looking
at things assumed by a single mind. They have little independent life &
seem vague. Your words bind them to you. If Balzac had written with a very
personal, very highly coloured style, he would have always drowned his
inventions with himself. You seem to feal this, for when you use elaborate
words you invent with less conviction with less precission, with less
delicasy than when you forget every thing but the myth. I will take as
example, a prose example. That beautiful story in which the child finds the
Twelve apostle[s] eating porridge in a cottage is quite perfect in all the first
part for then you think of nothing but the myth but it seems to me to fade to
nothing in the latter part.[3] For in the latter part the words rise up between
you & the myth. You yourself begin to speak & we forget the apostles & the
child & the plate of porridge. Or rather the mere mortal part of you begins

---

[1] On 31 Oct 1901 Fiona Macleod had sent WBY a copy of what she described in an accompanying
letter (*LWBY* 1. 92) as 'the much changed, cancelled, augmented, and revised American edition' of
*From the Hills of Dream* (see p. 980). The section entitled 'Foam of the Past', containing poems written
between 1896 and 1900, opens with a lengthy dedication to WBY.

[2] WBY, in preparing the new edition of *The Celtic Twilight* (see p. 969, n. 5), was rereading
Macleod's collection of Celtic folktales, *The Washer of the Ford* (1896).

[3] 'The Last Supper', a story from *The Washer of the Ford* (1896), describes the dream of a lost child
who is carried by 'the Fisher of Men', Iosa, into the Shadowy Glen where he meets the Twelve Weavers
gathered for porridge at the last supper. All weave immortal shapes on the shuttles of Beauty, Wonder,
and Mystery, except Judas, who weaves Fear on the shuttles of Mystery, Despair, and the Grave.
Restored to his mother by Iosa, the child looks back but sees only the Weaver of Hope singing a song
learned from the Weaver of Joy.

to speak, the mere person, not the god. You, as I think, should seek the delight of style in utter simplicity, in a self effacing rhythm & language; in an expression that is like a tumbler of water rather than like a cup of wine. I think that the power of your work in the future will depend on your choosing this destiny. Certainly I am looking forward to 'The Laughter of the Queen'.[4] I thought your last prose that pilgrimage of the soul & mind & body to the Hills of Dream promised this simple style. It had it endeed more than anything you have done.[5]

To some extent I have an advantage over you in having a very fierce nation to write for. I have to make everything very hard & clear, as it were. It is like riding a wild horse. If ones hand fumble or ones knees loosen one is thrown. You have in the proper sense far more imagination than I have & that makes your work correspondingly more difficult. It is fairly easy for me who do so much of my work by the critical, rather than the imaginative faculty to be precise & simple but it is hard for you in whose mind images form themselves without ceasing & are gone as quickly perhaps.

But I am sure that I am right. When you speak with the obviously personal voice of your verse, or of your essays you are not that Fiona who has invented a new thing, a new literary method. You are that Fiona when the great myths speak through you.

In a few minutes I must begin work on the Celtic Rite which is unfolding very fully. But if you have any notes do send them to me for there are places where I need the qualities of a different mind from mine.

Yr ev<br>W B Yeats

I like your verses on Murias & like them the better perhaps because of the curious coincidence that I did in summer verses about lovers wandering 'in long forgotten Murias'.[6]

---

[4] 'The Laughter of the Queen' appeared in *Barbaric Tales* (1897), reviewed by WBY in the *Sketch* on 28 Apr 1897 (*UP* II. 42–5). It tells how Scathach, the Amazonian Queen of Skye, runs mad through unrequited love for Cuchulain and has twenty Vikings strung up by their hair in oak trees 'like drooping fruit. . . . Then Scathach the Queen laughed loud and long . . . for then the madness was upon her' (59–60). WBY had evidently seen the dedicatory poem in Mosher's edition and had forgotten that he had already reviewed the tale from which it came.

[5] *The Divine Adventure: Iona: By Sundown Shores* (1900) is a collection of symbolic and legendary tales in which the narrator explores the spiritual history of the self, the island of Iona, and the Highlands. In 'The Divine Adventure' the Body, the Will, and the Soul discover their relation to each other on their pilgrimage to 'the dim blue hills in the west, the Hills of Dream, as we called them'.

[6] 'Murias', one of the five poems that make up her sequence 'The Dirge of the Four Cities', had been published in the October *Fortnightly Review* under the title 'Requiem'. Macleod had directed WBY to the poem in her letter of 31 Oct (see above, n. 1). It was not included in the new Mosher edition, and first appeared in book form in the English edition of *From the Hills of Dream* (1907). In WBY's 'Baile

I think 'The Silver Flutes' is the best of the titles you have & very pretty.[7]

ALS Private. Partly in Sharp, 334–6. Partly in Wade, 357–8. A version of this letter appeared in III. 123–5.

## *A. P. Watt to the Editor of the* Cornhill Magazine, *25 November 1901*

HASTING HOUSE | NORFOLK STREET, STRAND
| LONDON, W.C.
25th. November 1901.

The Editor,
  "The Cornhill, Magazine,"
    15, Waterloo Place, S.W.
Dear Sir,
  Referring to your letter of the 28th. ult: I now have the pleasure of informing you that I am authorised by Mr. W. B. Yeats to accept the offer which you are good enough to make therein for the British serial rights of his article entitled, "THE HUT, THE CASTLE AND THE COUNTING HOUSE."[1]

---

and Aillinn' (*VP*, 196) two swans are said to 'know all the wonders, for they pass | The towery gates of Gorias, | And Findrias and Falias, | And long-forgotten Murias'. When this poem was published in the *Monthly Review* in July 1902 WBY added a note (*VP*, 188), explaining that 'Findrias and Falias and Gorias and Murias were the four mysterious cities whence the Tuatha De Danaan, the divine race, came to Ireland, cities of learning out of sight of the world, where they found their four talismans, the spear, the stone, the cauldron, and the sword'. In *From the Hills of Dream* (105) Murias is described as 'the sunken city', one of the four cities 'that no mortal eye has seen but that the soul knows'. The cities were cited in the drafts for the rites of the Celtic Mystical Order.

  [7] In a postscript to her letter of 31 Oct, Fiona Macleod had asked WBY for his 'opinion as to the title' of a new book of poetry she intended to publish the following year, and offered three suggestions: 'For a Little Clan', 'The Immortal Hour' and 'The Silver Flutes'. The last title was evidently suggested by the account (later recorded in her essay 'The Magic Kingdom' [see p. 999, n. 2]) of a man who, after his return from being 'away' with the fairies, asked constantly, 'who will now be playing the silver flute'. In the event, she ignored WBY's advice and her next book, called *The Winged Destiny*, was not published until 1904.

  [1] See p. 981. On 28 Oct Smith wrote (as 'The Editor') to tell Watt that he had 'now read' WBY's article, 'The Hut, the Castle, and the Counting House', and had 'pleasure in accepting it . . . at our usual rate of payment, viz: one guinea per page'.

I shall be glad if you will kindly let me have a proof of the article at your convenience and also a note of the exact date on which you will publish it in the "Cornhill Magazine". I require this proof and this information in order that I may make the necessary arrangements for the simultaneous publication of the article in America.[2]

I am,

Yours sincerely,

TS copy Watt. This letter would have appeared in III. 125–6.

## A. P. Watt to W. L. Courtney,[1] 28 November 1901

HASTING HOUSE | NORFOLK STREET, STRAND
| LONDON, W.C.
28th. November 1901.

W. L. Courtney Esq:
"The Fortnightly Review,"[2]
11, Henrietta Street, W.C.

Dear Mr. Courtney,

I am in receipt of your letter of yesterday's date and note with pleasure that you have decided to accept my offer of the British serial rights of Mr. Yeats' essay "THE HAPPIEST OF THE POETS" and that for these rights you will pay us a sum to be calculated at the rate of Three guineas (£3.3.0.) a thousand words.[3] I presume that you will publish the essay in the "Fortnightly Review" within a reasonable time, say six or seven months from date and that you will give us not less than two months'

---

[2] In his letter Smith said that he was 'at present unable to fix a date for the appearance of the article, which I should prefer to publish under the alternative title of "What is Popular Poetry?"' There is no evidence that the article was published in America before its appearance in the New York edition of *Ideas of Good and Evil* in 1903.

[1] William Leonard Courtney (1850–1928) had been editor of the *Fortnightly Review* since 1894. A scholar and man of letters, he published books on a number of literary topics, as well as on ethics, and a biography of John Stuart Mill.

[2] The *Fortnightly Review* was founded as a bi-monthly journal in 1865, but, despite its name, had appeared monthly since November 1866. It was issued by the publishers Chapman & Hall, and WBY had published three of his folklore articles there (see p. 955, n. 12).

[3] Watt's initial letter, making the offer of 'The Happiest of the Poets', has apparently not survived. In his reply to it, on 27 Nov (Watt), Courtney suggested a rate of 'three guineas per thousand words', but said that the date of publication 'is for the present to remain indefinite'. In fact the essay, a study of William Morris, did not appear until March 1903. It was republished in *Ideas of Good and Evil* the following month.

notice of the exact date of publication in order that we may make the necessary arrangements for the simultaneous publication of the essay in America.

I am, dear Mr. Courtney,<br>Yours sincerely,

TS copy Watt. This letter would have appeared in III. 130.

## To A. P. Watt, [*13 January 1902*]

18 Woburn Buildings | Euston Road. | London.<br>Monday night.

Dear M<sup>r</sup> Watt: I return Bullens letter, which seems to me perfectly right in its general features. He can have the copy for the enlarged 'Celtic Twilight' any time he likes—it is practically ready. I am putting the last touches to it now.[1] Many thanks for the trouble you are taking in my affairs.

Yrs sny<br>W B Yeats

ALS Watt. Stamped 'A. P. WATT & SON | 14 JAN 1902 | LONDON'. This letter would have appeared in III. 147.

[1] Bullen's letter has not been traced, but evidently referred to the 'Revised and Enlarged' edition of *The Celtic Twilight*, which he published in July 1902, and probably to the more complicated contractual arrangements over *Ideas of Good and Evil* (see pp. 1012–14).

## To Helen Laird,[1] 2 April 1902

*April 2nd 1902.*

Dear Friend,

Both plays went splendidly, magnificent reception.[2] Deirdre sends love[3] & a thousand thanks for your thoughtful wire[4]—The only regret is that you were nor with us to share our pleasure.

Kindest regards from all.

> Maud Gonne, Mary T. Quinn, W. B. Yeats, Maire nic Siúblaig, Dudley Digges, F. J. Fay, Bill Fay, Charles Caulfield,[5] P. J. Kelly, Frederick Ryan, P. J. Columb

Pencilled note in the hand of Maire Quinn, signed WBY; UCD. This letter would have appeared in III. 166.

## Agreement with A. H. Bullen, 14 April 1902

MEMORANDUM OF AGREEMENT made this <fourth> fourteenth day of April 1902 on this and the following one folio of paper between W. B. Yeats Esq., of 18 Woburn Buildings, Euston Road, London, N.W., of the one part and A. H. Bullen Esq., of 18 Cecil Court, Charing Cross Road,

[1] Helen S. Laird (see p. 153, n. 2) was a founding member of the Fays' Irish National Theatre Society, acting under the name of 'Honor Lavelle', and was to appear as Mrs MacFadden in Frederick Ryan's *The Laying of the Foundations* in October of this year. She acted with the Company until her secession from the NTS in December 1905, although in a letter to WBY of 9 Feb 1903 Frank Fay numbered her among those in the Company 'not strong at acting', and on 18 March 1903 described her as 'not primarily interested in acting at all'.

[2] AE's *Deirdre* and WBY's *Cathleen ni Houlihan*, with Maire Quinn and MG respectively in the title roles, were produced by the Fays' Irish National Dramatic Company at St Teresa's Hall, Dublin, 2–5 Apr 1902. The success of these productions persuaded WBY to combine with the Fays in making an Irish National Theatre a continuing reality. On 3 Apr 1902 WBY reported to AG (III. 166–7) that both plays were 'really very great successes. They took to Dierdre from the first. The hall was crowded & great numbers could not get in.... Kathleen Ny Hoolihan was also most enthusiastly received.' Summing up the productions on 5 Apr, after the last night, he reported (III. 167–8) that 'Crowds have been turned away from the doors every night & last night was the most successful of all the performances.... It was realy a wonderful sight to see crowds of people standing up at the back of the hall where they could hardly ever see because of the people in front—I heard this from one of them—& yet patient & enthusiastic.'

[3] i.e. Maire Quinn.

[4] Helen Laird's wire has not been traced but evidently wished the Society well for this, its most important production to date.

[5] Charles Caulfield played Illaun, one of the sons of Fergus, in *Deirdre* and Patrick Gillan in *Cathleen ni Houlihan*. He left the INTS in late 1902, alarmed by the theological discussions arising out of WBY's *The Hour-Glass*. He did not become a permanent member of the INTS, and took small parts in various amateur productions in Dublin over the next few years. In 1904 he was part of the company that Dudley Digges and Maire Quinn took to the World Fair in St Louis (see III. 566–71).

London, W.C., of the other part WHEREBY it is mutually agreed as follows:—

(1)    That the said W. B. Yeats shall grant to the said A. H. Bullen the exclusive right of printing and publishing in book form in Great Britain its Colonies and Dependencies a book entitled "THE CELTIC TWILIGHT" of which the said W. B. Yeats is the author and the nominal selling price of which shall be six shillings (6/-) and in consideration thereof the said A. H. Bullen shall pay to the said W. B. Yeats a royalty of seventeen per cent (17%) of the nominal selling price on all copies of the said book which he may sell.[1]

(2)    That the said A. H. Bullen shall publish the said book on a date hereafter to be fixed by him in consultation with the said W. B. Yeats, but which shall not in any case unless mutually arranged be later than the first day of June 1902[2] and it is further provided that the said A. H. Bullen shall pay the said W. B. Yeats the sum of thirty guineas ($£31.10.0$) in advance and on account of the above mentioned royalties the said thirty guineas ($£31.10.0$) being paid as follows:-viz., fifteen guineas ($£15.15.0$) on the receipt by the said A. H. Bullen of the complete 'copy' or manuscript of the said book and fifteen guineas ($£15.15.0$) on the day on which the said A. H. Bullen first publishes the said book.

(3)    That the said A. H. Bullen shall bear all the expense of the production publication and advertisement of the said book.

(4)    That the United States rights the rights of translation and dramatization together with the right to publish the said book in English on the Continent of Europe are reserved by the said W. B. Yeats.[3]

(5)    That the said W. B. Yeats shall be entitled to receive on publication the usual six presentation copies of the said book.

(6)    That the copyright of the said book is to remain the property of the said W. B. Yeats and that at the expiration of five years from the day on which the said A. H. Bullen shall first publish the said book or at the expiration of any subsequent period of five years thereafter this agreement may be terminated by either party on giving three months notice of intention so to do.[4] Provided that if it shall be terminated by the said

---

[1] See pp. 982, 986. This was a standard contract, drawn up by A. P. Watt & Sons.

[2] The book was actually published in July 1902.

[3] An American edition, comprising the imported sheets of the English edition and bound in the USA, was published by the Macmillan Company of New York later in 1902. There was an Irish edition, published by Maunsel & Co., in 1905.

[4] Bullen retained the rights to the book, and issued a further edition in December 1911. WBY corrected a copy of this edition in 1914 with a view to a revised version, but this never appeared, and the book was transferred to Macmillan & Co. when they became WBY's main publishers in June 1916.

W. B. Yeats before royalties amounting to the sum of thirty guineas
(£31.10.0) shall have become payable under this agreement he shall refund
to the said A. H. Bullen the difference between the amount of the royalties
which shall have become payable and the sum of thirty guineas (£31.10.0)
which will have been paid to him by the said A. H. Bullen in advance and
on account of such royalties. Further, that in the event of this agreement
being terminated by the said W. B. Yeats he shall purchase the plates and
stock in hand at the cost of manufacture—such plates and stock to be
in good order—and if there is any wear or damage at such less price than
the cost of manufacture as is fair having regard to the wear or damage. But
if this agreement be terminated by the said A. H. Bullen no liability
whatever shall attach to the said W. B. Yeats but he shall have the option
of purchasing the stock and plates on the before mentioned terms
should he think it to be in his interest to do so but should the said
W. B. Yeats not purchase such stock and plates the said A. H. Bullen
shall be at liberty to sell the stock accounting for the royalties thereon as
provided above.

(7)   That if after three years from the date of publication the sales of the
said book shall in the opinion of the said A. H. Bullen cease to be remunerative he shall be at liberty to dispose of the unsold stock by auction or
otherwise and any profit so realised shall after deducting the original cost of
production be equally divided between the said W. B. Yeats and the said A.
H. Bullen.

(8)   That in the event of the said A. H. Bullen declining or neglecting
within six months after the said book shall have become out of print to
publish a new edition of the same all rights granted or assigned under this
agreement shall then revert to the said W. B. Yeats and the said W. B. Yeats
shall then have the option of purchasing the moulds or plates of the said
book on the terms detailed in Clause 6 of this agreement, but he shall not be
bound to do so.

(9)   That an exact account of the sales of the said book shall be
made up every six months to the thirtieth day of June and the thirty-
first day of December, delivered on or before the following October the first
and April the first and settled by cash on November the first and May the
first.

The said W. B. Yeats hereby authorises and empowers his Agents
Messrs. A. P. Watt & Son of Hastings House, Norfolk Street, Strand,
London, W.C., to collect and receive all sums of money payable to the said
W. B. Yeats under the terms of this agreement and declares that Messrs.
A. P. Watt & Son's receipt shall be a good and valid discharge to all persons
paying such monies to them. The said W. B. Yeats also hereby authorises
and empowers the said A. H. Bullen to treat with Messrs. A. P. Watt & Son

on his behalf in all matters concerning this agreement in any way whatsoever.

Witness to the
  signature of    A. H. Bullen
                  J. M^cCall

TS Doc Watt. This document would have appeared in III. 173.

## To John McGrath, [? 20 April 1902]

18 Woburn Buildings | Euston Road.
Sunday

Dear Mcgrath: Lady Gregory has asked Murray to send you her book[1] &
both she & I hope that you will do an article on it in Freeman, if possible &
keep it out of the hands of some ignorant Gaelic Leaguer, who will know
nothing but the dead words of Irish & will think that he knows all about
Cuchullain because he knows that he has never read any English literature.[2]

I send you also a very important French article on the Irish Literary
Movement which should I think be translated somewhere—with its little
Foreign ignorances unchanged. The *Revue de Deux Monds* carries such
great weight this article should not be wasted.[3]

Yrs ever
W B Yeats

---

[1] i.e. *Cuchulain of Muirthemne*, published this month.

[2] McGrath had moved back to the *Freeman's Journal*, upon which he had begun his career. He did not
review AG's book, and failed to keep it out of the hands of just such a virulent critic as WBY had feared.
This was Robert Donovan (1862–1934), a journalist and critic, who wrote leaders and literary articles for
the *Freeman's Journal* from 1891 to 1923. His notice was largely taken up with an attack on WBY's
observation in his preface to *Cuchulain of Muirthemne* that if 'we but tell these stories to our children the
Land will begin again to be a Holy Land, as it was before men gave their hearts to Greece and Rome and
Judea'. In reviewing the book on 2 May, Donovan accused WBY (5) of 'literary blaspheming' and an
'affectation of neo-Paganism. The blend is anything but Irish. It is a corruption of the French decadent
school, from which the virility of France has already succeeded in rescuing French literature. . . . Mr.
Yeats, who sees all things through a pair of esoteric spectacles, borrowed from the Englishman Blake, has
rather seriously injured the Irish revival by these attempts at a foreign grafture.' This was not the first
time Donovan had attacked WBY: in a *Nation* review of 25 May 1889 (3), he had found little 'promise of
better things' in *The Wanderings of Oisin* and asserted that WBY's 'imagination will never be brighter or
more active in the future'; while later in the same year he criticized WBY for printing an anti-Catholic tale
in his *Stories from Carleton* (see I. 205–7). WBY was to describe him as 'a bigoted Voteen' in the *Irish
Packet* of 27 Apr 1908, but the following year Donovan got the Chair of English literature at University
College, Dublin, instead of WBY.

[3] This was Louis Paul-Dubois's long, seven-part article 'Le Recueillement de l'Irlande', which
appeared in the *Revue des deux mondes* of 15 Apr 1902 (765–802). It gave an informed account of

PS.

If by any chance Lady Gregory's book (which comes out on Tuesday) does not reach you. Please write to her at

Coole Park,

Gort

Co Galway.

If you translate that French article it will certainly annoy TCD & that is always a pleasure. When you are writing on Lady Gregorys book you should look up the Gaelic League pamphlets with Mahaffey & Atkinson evidence. They put their heads so nicely in a bag by saying there is no "idealism" or "imagination" in Old Irish Literature.[4] Blunt has an enthusiastic essay on the Book in the Nineteenth Century.[5]

ALS Private. This letter would have appeared in III. 170.

the Irish Literary Revival from a Gaelic League viewpoint, and not only traced the 'renaissance intellectuelle de l'Irlande' from the fall of Parnell to 1902 but fitted this into an overview of the political and cultural position of Ireland in the nineteenth century. Identifying the revival of the Irish language as 'le facteur d'une transformation profonde de l'Irlande moderne', resulting in an 'émancipation psychologique', Paul-Dubois turned in the fifth section of his essay to Irish literature in English and the recent 'magnifique floraison poétique', discovering that 'tous ces divers courans poétiques se rencontrent enfin, à leur suprême puissance, dans la personne d'un maître, d'un artiste incomparable, W. B. Yeats' (791). Although extremely impressive in its reach and grasp, the article contains a few minor errors of emphasis and fact, exaggerating, for instance, the influence of the Young Irelanders on Mangan, citing William Blake as an Irish poet, and alleging that Sir Charles Gavan Duffy founded the *Dublin Magazine* in 1887. No translation of the article has been traced in the *Freeman's Journal* or in the *Weekly Freeman*.

⁴ WBY's irritation with Trinity College, Dublin, for neglecting or belittling Irish literature in both English and Irish went back as far as his public attacks on Edward Dowden in early 1895 for disparaging the Irish literary movement (see I. 427, 430–1, 433, 437–8, 448–50). A later article, 'The Academic Class and the Agrarian Revolution', published in the Dublin *Daily Express* on 11 Mar 1899 (*UP* II. 148–52), was a response to the hostile and ill-informed evidence about the Irish language given to the Intermediate Education (Ireland) Commission by two TCD dons, Robert Atkinson (1839–1908) and John Pentland Mahaffy (1839–1919). Mahaffy, a classicist and ignorant of Irish, had relied very heavily on Atkinson's authority when giving his evidence on 12 Feb 1899, and had asserted that Old and Middle Irish literature was 'either silly or...indecent' (Dublin *Daily Express*, 13 Feb, p. 2). In a letter responding to Mahaffy's evidence, Hyde referred to 'that Stygian flood of black ignorance about everything Irish which, Lethe-like, rolls through the portals of my beloved Alma Mater' (*Daily Express*, 17 Feb, p. 5). Atkinson had also asserted that it would be difficult to find an Irish text which was not 'silly or indecent' (*Minutes of Evidence*, 642). The Atkinson controversy continued for several weeks in the Dublin *Daily Express* and other Dublin papers (see II. 371, 373–5), and in 1900–1 the entire controversy was collected in a series of Gaelic League pamphlets (nos. 12–21, n.d.), and WBY's article was reprinted in pamphlet no. 20 (23–6). In *Aut* (455–6) WBY reveals that it was Atkinson's denigration of ancient Irish literature that motivated AG to compile *Cuchulain of Muirthemne* and *Gods and Fighting Men*. Paul-Dubois had gone into the dispute at some length in his article in the *Revue des deux mondes* and criticized the anti-Irish stance of Trinity College.

⁵ The review of *Cuchulain of Muirthemne*, 'The Great Irish Epic', by Wilfrid Blunt, a close friend and former lover of AG (see p. 80, n. 1), appeared in the *Nineteenth Century and After* of May 1902 (811–16). Blunt, quoting with approval WBY's judgement that this was 'the best book that has ever come out of Ireland', praised AG's 'monumental translation into noble and rhythmic Anglo-Irish prose', which he

# To Dr Robert W. Felkin,[1] [8] May 1902

18 Woburn Buildings, | Euston Road.
May 10th/02
Thursday.[2]

My dear F. R.

My eyes are bad so I am dictating this letter, the Theorici have got to make themselves useful as you may see.[3] I shall have to go out to-morrow at about half past twelve as I am lunching with a friend at 1–15.[4] I was not quite sure from your note in which you said you would see me early upon Friday, whether you would see me early upon Friday evening or whether you would see me in the morning. It is my evening as you may know. I shall be delighted to see you even before mid-day or any time in the evening, from say 7–15. Or I could see you at any time you cared to name on Sunday.[5]

found not only original but absolutely fitted to 'the text translated', and he went on to applaud her synthesizing powers which 'succeeded in giving to a series of discontinuous episodes a single romantic form, building them into a single tragic story'. Unlike WBY (see III. 163–6, 166–8), he also approved of the skill with which AG had 'steered her course between the rocks and shoals of taste in sexual matters', and doubted whether 'for general reading' there would ever be a version 'more acceptable, more brilliant and more popular than Lady Gregory's'.

[1] Dr Robert William Felkin (d. 1922) had begun medical studies in the late 1870s, but interrupted them to go as a missionary to Uganda in 1878. He returned to Edinburgh University, where he qualified in 1884, taking a further medical degree at Marburg the following year. He joined the Amen-Ra Temple of the GD in Edinburgh in March 1894, taking the motto Finem Respice (F. R.), but subsequently transferred to the Isis-Urania in London. He joined WBY, AEFH, and FF in the Second Order in November 1896, when he and his wife were living in north London, and they both became members of FF's heterodox 'Sphere Group' (see II. 32–3). Felkin began to take a more central part in the order after the convulsions following the expulsion of MacGregor Mathers in April 1900, and early in 1902 claimed that he had established a link with the Secret Chiefs of the Third Order. With the kudos this brought, he helped to thwart a radical reform of the order in May 1902, and it reverted instead to its original constitution under the governance of three chiefs. This initiative did not last long: in 1903 differences with A. E. Waite led Felkin to secede with a majority of members, including WBY, to form the Amoun Temple of the Stella Matutina. Felkin continued to be troubled by doubts about the authenticity of the GD and made several trips to Germany to try, unsuccessfully, to seek out information about its origin. In 1916 Felkin emigrated with his family to New Zealand and the Stella Matutina fell into decline, finally disintegrating in 1923, the year after Felkin's death.

[2] AEFH had apparently added 'Thursday' because she was uncertain of the date. Thursday fell in fact on 8 May, and an '8th' has been written in another hand next to 'Thursday'.

[3] An occult in-joke; AEFH, to whom WBY was dictating this letter, was a Theoricus Adeptus Minor (5°= 6°) in the Golden Dawn.

[4] Unidentified, but perhaps the journalist and classical scholar Stephen MacKenna (1872–1934), who was in London and wanted to introduce WBY to his fiancée (see III. 182).

[5] This letter was in reply not to a note, but to a telegram from Felkin, asking to see WBY. In his reply (Private) Felkin explained that his telegram meant that he 'would try to be in time to have a chat with you before your meeting tomorrow night, and I will endeavour to be with you about 7.30'.

I have several things to talk over. May I congratulate you on your election.[6] The Chiefs may feel perfectly confident that everybody will support them in their authority to the utmost.[7]

Vale,
DEDI[8]

Dict AEFH, signed WBY; Private. This letter would have appeared in III. 182.

## To William Sharp, 12 June [1902]

18, Woburn Buildings,
June 12th

My dear Sharp,

I enclose that P.O. I am sorry to say I had forgotten about it.[1] I was very sorry not to get to your At Home yesterday but I was dictating a play to a friend and did not like to lose my day's work.[2] I got the names of the twelve

[6] It had recently been decided that the Golden Dawn would revert to the authority of 'Three Chiefs' following serious disagreements in the order in February and March 1901 (see III. 25–7, 29–35, 36–40, 42–7), and the public scandal provoked by the trial of Mr and Mrs Horos, two bogus members, in December (see III. 14–16). Felkin had been elected one of the chiefs, with Percy W. Bullock ('Levavi Oculos'; 1868–1940) and Brodie-Innes (1848–1923; 'Sub Spe') as his fellows. In his reply he thanked WBY 'very sincerely for your congratulations upon my election and for your assurance that the chiefs may feel perfectly confident that everyone will support them to the utmost. Indeed I earnestly hope & trust that this may be the case and that for . . . the future all personal ideas and preferences may be entirely sunk in a whole-hearted striving for the good of all the members of the Order and with the great object always in view of reestablishing the link with the Third Order upon the material plane, which I am personally so confident may be done if we will work harmoniously together and agree to bury the various tomahawks which have been too prominently exhibited in the past and which I am sure have almost disintegrated and abolished the material manifestation of our Order.' He added that although the powers of evil worked against the order, 'their strength is in our weakness', and that 'perfect confidence in each other' and the 'earnest fulfilling' of all obligations would put the enemy to flight.

[7] This optimism proved unfounded: AEFH fell out with the new chiefs when they suspended the Ritual Sub-Committee, and she resigned from the order in February 1903. Later that year Percy Bullock resigned his office of chief and was not replaced, while in the autumn there was a complete schism when A. E. Waite and his followers formed the mystical Independent and Rectified Rite, while Felkin established a rival magical group, the Stella Matutina. WBY tried to reconcile the two camps, suggesting that they should use a common Temple for the Outer Order and share private rooms for the Second Order, but his attempts came to nothing.

[8] WBY's Golden Dawn motto, 'Demon Est Deus Inversus' (the Devil is God Inverted), an occult expression of his enduring belief that polarity and opposition are constitutive of a final Unity. He had probably taken it from the chapter-title of section IX, Part II, book I, of Madame Blavatsky's *The Secret Doctrine* (1888).

[1] The 'P.O.', a postal order whereby money could be sent through the mail more securely than cash, was perhaps to cover Sharp's postage costs in returning revised CMO rites to WBY.

[2] WBY had been dictating an early draft of *The Hour-Glass*, which at this time he called 'The Fool and the Wise Man', to AEFH. On 13 June, his 37th birthday, he wrote to AG that he had 'almost finished a first draft of that little play' (III. 201).

winds from something of Whitley Stokes'. I cannot now recollect exactly where I got them but I know they are quite accurate. The system is manifestly the order of colours in the rainbow though all the mixed colours do not come into the scheme. The rainbow goes from east to west but from west to north & NE are muddy colours. I cannot find what system these muddy colours are arranged in. What is your authority for the Nine Winds? and for their colours? The book I got my colours from was a book I read in the National Library in Dublin, but I forget its name. It gave the colours of the winds, not only in Ireland but in various parts of Asia. One of the most curious things about it was that all the colour schemes were different. One Asiatic tribe made the north wind yellow for instance, while another if I recollect rightly made the west wind yellow.[3] I wish that you would give me an opinion as to the arrangement of the seven notes. There are two mediaeval systems. One makes the note Do correspond to the moon, and the highest note correspond to the planet Saturn (This is the system I adopted—) while there is another system that exactly reverses the process making the note of the most rapid vibration correspond to the moon, the nearest and (so far as its apparent motions are concerned) the swiftest of the planets. According to general symbolism both systems would be correct, one signifying the intensity of mortal life which dies out before the immortal life, whilst the other would signify the intensity of immortal life growing faint and sluggish as it approaches mortality. What I want to find out is which of these two methods enters most into the Gaelic habit of mind and into Gaelic symbolism.[4] Lilly the astrologer when he spoke of the Angels as speaking much in the throat like the Irish probably intended to attribute the

---

[3] The ancient Irish believed that there were twelve winds, each of a different colour. These winds are described in the *Seanchas Mór*, or Ancient Laws, and WBY would have found references to them in would have an edition of Middle Irish poems, *Saltair na Rann* Oxford, 1883), by the noted philologist and Celtic scholar Whitley Stokes (1830–1909). In a précis of the first poem in this collection, Stokes speaks (iii) of 'the four chief winds, the eight sub-winds' mentioned in ll. 45–52, and 'the colours of the winds cited in ll. 53–80. Although unable to decipher the poem itself, WBY may have sought a translation from Hyde or some other Gaelic authority. He would also have come across coloured winds in vol. III of Eugene O'Curry's *On the Manners and Customs of the Ancient Irish* (1873; *YL*, 1478): 'He (the Lord) then created the colours of the winds, so that the colour of each differs from the other; namely, the white and the crimson; the blue and the green; the yellow and the red; the black and the gray; the speckled and the dark; the dull black (*ciar*) and the grisly. From the east . . . comes the crimson wind; from the south, the white; from the north, the black; from the west, the dun. The red and the yellow are produced between the white wind and the crimson; the green and the gray are produced between the grisly and the white; the gray and the dull black are produced between the grisly and the jet black; the dark and the mottled are produced between the black and the crimson; and those are all the sub-winds contained in each and all of the cardinal winds' (133–4). In early versions of 'The Adoration of the Magi', WBY refers slightly inaccurately to the colours of the Irish winds (*VSR*, 170ᵛ), and in his 'Visions Notebook' records that on 10 July 1898 he tried to invoke the spirits 'that inhabit the green or grey colours associated with the West Wind in old Irish symbolism'. Fiona Macleod subsequently published an 'Invocation of Peace' in which the 'grey wind of the west' and other coloured winds are summoned (*From the Hills of Dream* [1907]).

[4] Medieval theories of music were predicated on Pythagorean and Platonic notions of the harmony of the spheres as representative of cosmic truth and proportion. Such harmonies were thought to be

higher being to the deep notes.[5] On the other hand the Highland seer who said that the fairies had voices that were like whistling may have meant that they were inferior powers falling under the influence of the moon and mercury and therefore of notes of rapid vibration.[6] However the Easterns I understand, speak their mantrums in such a way as to invoke the higher spirits by intoning upon notes of rapid vibration. My lecture on Tuesday evening was a great success, many were standing up and many others could not get in at all.[7] Come round on Monday evening as Mrs. Emery is going to speak to the psaltery. I go away on the Thursday following.

Yrs sny
W B Yeats

TLS Private. This letter would have appeared in III. 200.

# A. P. Watt to Henry Newbolt, 10 October 1902

HASTING HOUSE | NORFOLK STREET, STRAND
| LONDON, W.C.
10th. October 1902.

Copy.
Henry Newbolt Esq:
   "The Monthly Review",
      50a. Albemarle Street, W.

Dear Newbolt,
   I take pleasure in sending you herewith typewritten 'copy' of two new poems written by Mr. W. B. Yeats entitled, as you will

governed, as WBY suggests here, by numerical proportion based on the planets' speed of revolution and distance from the earth. The relationship between the heavenly spheres and musical notes is stated differently by various medieval commentators, and Ptolemy and Boethius correlated celestial and human psychic harmonies.

   [5] 'It is very rare, yea, even in our Days, for any Operator or Master to have the Angels speak articulately; when they do speak, it's like the *Irish*, much in the Throat' (*Mr Lilly's History of his Life and Times* [1715], 88). William Lilly (1602–81), the English astrologer, was born in Leicestershire but moved to London, where he gained financial independence by marrying a rich widow. He took up astrology, through which he gained fame and wealth and on which he published nearly twenty books, including an annual book of prophecies, *Merlinus Anglicus, Junior*, from 1644 until his death. His support for the Cromwellians in the English Civil War led to his temporary imprisonment after the Restoration, and he was also suspected for a time of having had a hand in the Great Fire of London.

   [6] WBY also cites this in his essay 'Kidnappers' (*Myth*, 70) where he describes the faery hosts trooping by night and filling the air 'full of shrill voices—a sound like whistling, as an ancient Scottish seer has recorded'. WBY took this belief from *Popular Tales of the West Highlands* (1860–2) by the scholar and folklorist John Francis Campbell of Islay (1822–85).

   [7] On Tuesday, 10 June, WBY gave a well-attended lecture on 'Speaking to Musical Notes' at Clifford's Inn, illustrated by Florence Farr's first public performance with the Dolmetsch psaltery.

note, "THE OLD AGE OF QUEEN MAEVE" and "ADAM'S CURSE".[1]

I shall be glad to hear that you have read these poems and that you think so well of them as to be willing to purchase the British serial rights for use in "The Monthly Review" between now and the end of January next, after which date Mr. Yeats will publish them in volume form.[2]

Awaiting your early decision and trusting that it may be a favourable one,

I am, dear Newbolt,

Yours sincerely,

A. S. Watt.

TS copy Watt. This letter would have appeared in III. 234–5.

## *A. P. Watt to the Editor of the* Pall Mall Magazine,[1] *18 November 1902*

HASTING HOUSE | NORFOLK STREET, STRAND | LONDON, W.C.

COPY.                                                18th Nov. 1902.

G. R. Halkett Esq:
    "The Pall Mall Magazine,"
        18, Charing Cross Road, W.C.

Dear Mr. Halkett,

I now have the pleasure of informing you that I am authorised by Mr. W. B. Yeats to accept the offer which you were good enough to make in

The circular announced that the 'lecture will be given in order to start a fund for the making of Psalteries for these purposes'. Arnold Dolmetsch was in the chair and provided musical explanations.

[1] Newbolt accepted 'Adam's Curse', but declined 'The Old Age of Queen Maeve', perhaps because of its length.

[2] On 24 Nov Newbolt, in acknowledging the corrected proof of 'Adam's Curse', told Watt that he had put the poem 'into my Dec. no. . . . and I will pay you £4.4.0 for the two pages' (Watt). Watt wrote to WBY in some consternation the following day, telling him that he had asked Newbolt to postpone publication 'until his January number' since if the poem appeared 'in the December number issued at the end of this month, there is neither time to offer them for simultaneous publication in America nor even to copyright them'. But it was far too late to postpone publication; the poem did appear in the December 1902 number of the *Monthly Review*, and was subsequently reprinted in the *Gael* (New York) in February 1903 and in *In the Seven Woods* in August of the same year.

[1] George Roland Halkett (1855–1918), artist, writer, and editor, was born in Edinburgh and became a strong supporter of Gladstone, writing and illustrating *The Irish Green Book* in 1887, during the

your letter of the 22nd. ult: for the British serial rights of his poem entitled
"THE OLD MEN ADMIRING THEMSELVES IN THE WATER".[2]

I presume that as the amount is small you will be willing to pay it now
and that you will publish the poem within a reasonable time, say six months
from date.

I am,

Yours sincerely,
A. P. Watt.

P.S. Please let me have ample notice, say not less than two months, of the
exact date on which you will publish the poem in the "Pall Mall Magazine". I shall be glad if you will at the same time furnish me with proofs in
order that I may take the necessary steps for the disposal of the American
serial rights.[3]

TS copy Watt. This letter would have appeared in III. 254.

## To Henry G. O'Brien, 22 November 1902

18 Woburn Buildings, | Euston Road. | London.
Nov 22nd,/02.

Dear M[r] O'Brien,

I hope that you will excuse me for dictating this letter, but I can hardly
help myself, I have had a trouble of the eyes for some little while & dictate
everything. I need hardly say that your letter has interested me very much.
Yes, our movement in Ireland is becoming good & stirring & it is very
natural that with your desires and tastes you should wish to be in the midst
of it. But after all nobody is the worse for having to struggle for a while
against adverse circumstance. Besides it will take you some little time to
really know whether you will ever take to the sea-faring life. You should not
think of leaving it unless you have some other work ready to your hand. I
should be sorry to recommend any young man in whom I had not reason to
see, at least, a knack for literary journalism to try to make his living by

controversy over the First Home Rule Bill. He became political cartoonist of the *Pall Mall Gazette* in
1892 and also contributed drawings to *Punch*. In 1897 he became art editor of the *Pall Mall Magazine*,
and served as its editor from 1900 to 1905. He was a close friend of William Sharp, who dedicated his
*Literary Geography* (1904) to him.

[2] On 22 Oct Halkett had written to Watt to say that if WBY would 'accept Two Guineas for his verse
"The Old Men admiring themselves in the Water" we shall be glad to take it for this Mag.'

[3] The poem was published in the *Pall Mall Magazine* in January 1903, and in the *Gael* (New York) in
September of the same year. It appeared in *In the Seven Woods* in August 1903.

literature.[1] That literary journalistic knack is not as common amongst us Irish as it is amongst the English. We can write about our own subjects, but we make a poor hand of it when they set us to general reviewing, We are ready enough for political journalism, but that kills the literary faculty. There is no reason why you should not write away out there in China & send your work to the magazines here; then if you began to do pretty well, you could take to literature altogether if you liked. Even if you want to write about Ireland, you may have some store of boyish recollections and if you get into the habit of writing down descriptions of the scenes about you, & your own thoughts about them and other things, you will be training yourself for whatever you may write later on. Of course I don't know what kind of work you are gifted for, but one can write stories anywhere & one can dramatize one's self anywhere. Pierre Loti a sailor like yourself on a war-ship has written of his daily thoughts and the scenes about him & has made a great reputation.[2] Of course I can well imagine that it is about Ireland that you want to write, but after all you are yourself Irish earth & if you dramatise yourself in any form, verses, stories, sketches, in a way you write of Ireland. Some day you will come back & become a part of our movement I have no doubt. After all if you take a dull task of your daily work on ship-board as a sort of a discipline, I daresay that you would not find it so bad. If you wish to write to me at any time, do so by all means. I shall always try to answer, though sometimes you must find a little delay. I am just back from Ireland where we have started a little theatre with Irish actors. It is doing wonderfully well. The acting is excellent and we are producing plays of the most serious kind and getting good audiences.

Yours sincerely<br>
W B Yeats

Dict AEFH, signed WBY; Pierpont Morgan. This letter would have appeared in III. 259.

---

[1] Henry G. O'Brien, an Irish midshipman serving in Hong Kong, who had written to WBY on 6 Oct to explain that he was incompetent and unhappy as a sailor and wanted to become an Irish farmer and write books like WBY's (see p. 40). He concluded his letter 'by asking your advice in my own case, as I should dearly like to know your ideas on the subject and if it will not trouble you to reply to this appealing letter. What I should like to have done myself of course would have been, to be a farmer in some part of Ireland and my idea of happiness would be to write verses or prose, compliments apart, such as you do in the Celtic Twilight and John Sherman and Dhoya which I believe are also yours, and which have given me more pleasure than anything else I have read so far. To conclude once more, I have to thank you sincerely if you have troubled to read so far, and hoping that you will consider this letter as a purely private question to you from Your Sincere Admirer Henry G. O'Brien Midn.' O'Brien left the navy in 1903, but became a priest rather than a farmer.

[2] Pierre Loti, pseudonym of Louis Marie Julien Viaud (1850–1923), was a French writer who was also a naval officer. He used his experiences of the world in a series of descriptive and melancholic exotic novels such as *Rarahu* (1880), *Madame Chrysanthème* (1887), and *Fantôme d'Orient* (1891).

## To William Sharp, 12 January 1903

18 Woburn Buildings, | Euston Road, | London
Jan. 12ᵗʰ,/03.

My dear Sharp,

I have never heard the phrase "The Kingdom of Laughter" but you will find in my "Fairy & Folk Tales" (Scott Library) under the heading "*Tirn'anoge*" this phrase quoted from a letter of Hyde's "The country where you buy joy for a penny."[1] I wish you would tell me, when Miss Macleod is going to publish the book to which the "Monthly Review" article is a prelude? I particularly want to know.[2]

I send you "Samhain",[3] I would have sent it to you before but I was not certain of your address. Your letter came from one place & your picture post-card from another.[4]

---

[1] WBY's anthology *Fairy and Folk Tales of the Irish Peasantry* was published in late September 1888 by Walter Scott as part of the Camelot Series. In a note to the section of tales about 'T'yeer-na-n-Oge' (323) WBY quotes Douglas Hyde that Tir na nOg 'is the place where the Irish peasant will tell you *geabhaedh tu an sonas aer pighin*, "you will get happiness for a penny," so cheap and common it will be'. There are various names for the Irish Other World, the happy paradise of old Irish belief, supposedly situated to the west of Ireland, where there is freedom from death and decay. The most common is 'Tir na nOg' (Land of the Young), but it was also known as 'Tir innambeo' (Land of the Living Ones), and 'Tir tairngeri' (Land of Promise); in his essay on 'Magic' (*E & I*, 52), WBY also calls it 'The Land of the Living Heart' (see p. 955).

[2] Fiona Macleod's article 'The Magic Kingdom', largely an account of Celtic other worlds such as Tir na nOg, had appeared in the current, January, number of the *Monthly Review* (99–112). A footnote in the article (104) states that the essay was 'the prologue to a volume to appear later, under the same title (formerly announced as "The Chronicles of the Sidhe")'. In fact, Sharp changed the book's title several times, and it finally appeared as *The Winged Destiny*, a collection of essays on Celtic lore, culture, and philosophy, which was delayed until 1904 because of illness, and which did not contain 'The Magic Kingdom'. WBY was eager to know about both publications, not primarily because he thought they might help him with the Celtic Mystical Order (see pp. 967–9), but because AG feared they might rival her books, a matter upon which he reassured her the following day (III. 302): 'I have written to William Sharpe asking your question about Fiona Macleod's book. At the same time I doubt if any book of hers will interfere with either you or me. She is quite certain to turn it all into her own sort of wild romance while both you and I give the foundations themselves. Neither does it follow that her book is really on the edge of publication for she has been announcing books for years which have never come out. I should not wonder at all if her plans were to completely change before my question reaches her.'

[3] The latest issue of *Samhain*, published jointly by Bryers and Unwin (see p. 978, n. 1), had appeared in October 1902. Besides the customary 'Notes' on the preceding year, it also contained AE's essay 'The Dramatic Treatment of Heroic Literature', and the texts of WBY's *Cathleen ni Houlihan*, Hyde's *An Naomh ar Iarraid* in Irish, and AG's translation of it into English as *The Lost Saint*.

[4] Neither letter nor postcard have been traced. Because of chronic illness, Sharp was spending most of his winters in the Mediterranean, particularly Sicily. Since the end of October he had been in Taormina, but had visited his friend Alexander Nelson Hood at his estate at Maniace in the Sicilian highlands in early November, and at the end of the month was to pay an extended visit to Greece.

I agree with you about the rite but you will find it all re-done by the time you arrive. I should be very glad for any detailed suggestions you can send me or get F. M. to send me.[5]

Our theatre is doing very well in Dublin, they revived my little farce "A Pot of Broth" last month & will revive it again in a few days.[6] We have got a real dramatist in a man called Ryan[7] & a very promising beginner called Collumb.[8] Russell is writing a play on the death of Cuchullian. It is sure to be full of eloquence but like his Deirdre will be lacking in invention.[9] Wilfrid Blunt is also doing us a play on the Cuchullian & Fand episode. He is English, but his three months in prison for the cause should, but probably will not, make our people feel friendly to him.[10]

Yrs sny
W B Yeats

Dict AEFH, signed WBY; Private. This letter would have appeared in III. 301.

[5] There had evidently been no let up in the 'continuity of hostile will' which was preventing Sharp revising the Neophyte and Cauldron rites (see pp. 967–9, 974–8, 980, n. 2).

[6] *The Pot of Broth* had first been produced by the INTS on 30 Oct 1902. It was revived from 4 to 6 Dec in the Camden Street Hall, and at the Town Hall, Rathmines, on 10 Jan 1903 under the auspices of the Gaelic League.

[7] Frederick Ryan (see p. 153) was at this time secretary of the INTS. His Ibsenite play *The Laying of the Foundations*, on the theme of municipal corruption in building contracts, had been produced by the INTS at the Antient Concert Rooms on 29 Oct, and revived at the Camden Street Hall on 4–6 Dec.

[8] As yet none of the plays of Padraic Colum (see p. 28) had been produced, but he had published three short dramatic pieces in the *United Irishman* over the previous year. His one-act play *The Saxon Shilling* was staged by the Daughters of Erin on 15 May of this year and the three-act *Broken Soil* by the INTS on 3 Dec 1903. Colum had read one of his plays to WBY in early April 1902, and WBY had recently sent him a volume of Ibsen's plays as a Christmas present so that he could study dramatic technique.

[9] AE had achieved a theatrical success with the production of his *Deirdre* (see p. 987, n. 2), and on 24 May 1902 wrote to tell WBY (MBY): 'I am trying to think out a play on Cuchulain's death but cannot get the last scene clear in my mind as drama.' In fact he soon abandoned playwriting altogether, and never finished the Cuchulain play.

[10] Wilfrid Scawen Blunt (see p. 80) had served two months in Galway Gaol in 1888 for resisting the police during the suppression of a Land League meeting at Woodford, Co. Galway, an exploit which WBY celebrated in an article in *United Ireland* on 28 Jan 1888 (see p. 942, n. 4). The reception of his play *Fand*, when it was finally produced at the Abbey on 20 and 27 Apr 1907, was perplexed rather than unfriendly, since the second act had been axed, and the third act was difficult to understand without it (see p. 661, n. 6).

# *A. P. Watt to W. L. Courtney, 15 January 1903*

HASTING HOUSE | NORFOLK STREET, STRAND
| LONDON, W.C.
15th. Jan. 1903.

W. L. Courtney Esq:
"The Fortnightly Review,"
11, Henrietta Street, W.C.
Dear Mr. Courtney,

I now have the pleasure of informing you that I am authorised by Mr. W. B. Yeats to accept the offer of £12. (twelve pounds) which you were recently good enough to make for the British serial use of his poem entitled "THE OLD AGE OF QUEEN MAEVE".[1] As, however, the poem is to be included in a volume to be published, probably in the month of March, I shall be glad to hear that you can publish it in "The Fortnightly" either in your February or March number.[2]

Please let me hear from you on this point at your convenience and
Believe me,
Yours sincerely,

TS copy Watt. This letter would have appeared in III. 304–5.

[1] Since Newbolt had declined 'The Old Age of Queen Maeve' for the *Monthly Review* (see pp. 995–6), Watt had sent it to Courtney to see if it would do for the *Fortnightly*, and on 10 Jan he replied that, 'after consultation with our Managing Director', he was able to 'offer twelve pounds (£12) for the serial use of Mr Yeats's poem: that is at the rate of three guineas a page – our extreme price for contributions. I am aware that publications enjoying a large and varied sale probably find it profitable to offer a large price; but of course conditions are altered in the case of a half-crown Review:—a smaller circulation, but a much more select audience.'

[2] 'The Old Age of Queen Maeve' (*VP*, 180–7) was published in the *Fortnightly Review* in April this year, reprinted in the *Gael* (New York) in June, and subsequently appeared in *In the Seven Woods*, which was published in late August not March 1903.

## *To Louise Imogen Guiney,*[1] *17 January* [*1903*]

18 Woburn Buildings | Euston Road.
Jan 17

Dear Miss Guiney: I want M^r Days address.[2] I want to introduce to him a young Irish priest, Father O'Donovan, who is very cultivated & intelligent, the best priest I know & deeply connected with our Irish Intellectual movement.[3] Father O'Donovan is going to America to collect for some church or other but of that I know nothing.[4] I want him to meet one or two imaginative & well read people.

Yr ever
W B Yeats

ALS Pierpont Morgan. This letter would have appeared in III. 305.

[1] Louise Imogen Guiney (1861–1920), daughter of a Boston lawyer from Tipperary, published poems in a number of American papers during the 1880s and 1890s. She had first met WBY during a prolonged visit to England from May 1889 to February 1891, and she settled permanently there in 1901, living in or near Oxford for the rest of her life. She published a number of books of verse as well as critical studies of Henry Vaughan and Lionel Johnson, and an edition of Mangan.

[2] The American Fred Holland Day (1864–1933), aesthete, bibliophile, spiritualist, publisher, and photographer, was a distant relative of Louise Guiney. He had met WBY on his second trip to England, in the summer of 1890, when WBY had taken him to meetings of the Rhymers' Club and discussed theosophy and spiritualism with him. In later years Day became increasingly involved with art photography, and in the late 1890s gained notoriety for his depictions of the Crucifixion with himself posing as Christ. But his attempts to found a new school of American photography failed, and in 1917, after a series of disappointments and disasters, he took to his bed at his home in Norwood, Massachusetts, and remained there until his death.

[3] Father Jeremiah O'Donovan (see p. 219), administrator of Loughrea parish, a member of the Gaelic League and the Irish Agriculture Organization Society, was committed to the revival of Irish crafts. He had lectured on 'Native or Foreign Art' to the National Literary Society on 25 Mar 1901, and put his ideas into practice by commissioning Irish artists, including Sarah Purser and Jack Yeats, in the construction and decoration of St Brendan's Cathedral, Loughrea (see p. 973). Under these auspices and those of the IAOS, he had been invited by the 'Irish Industrial Society of America' to lecture in the USA in the autumn of 1903, and, by chance, travelled over on the same boat as WBY, who was also beginning a lecture tour then (see III. 459, 461, 463). In 1904, shortly after his return to Ireland, O'Donovan left both Loughrea and the priesthood, moving to London, where he married, took up a literary career, and later became the lover of Rose Macaulay. He was a friend of George Moore, who based the priests in his short story 'Fugitives' and novel *The Lake* on him.

[4] This is disingenuous: Loughrea Cathedral was a major architectural and cultural project, and one with which WBY, his sisters, and Jack Yeats had all been actively engaged (see III. 410–11, 419–20). But presumably WBY wanted Guiney and Day to understand that he was introducing O'Donovan for his intellectual and cultural interest, and not touting for a subscription to his cause.

# *A. P. Watt to A. H. Bullen, 11 February 1903*

HASTING HOUSE | NORFOLK STREET, STRAND
| LONDON, W.C.
11th. Feb. 1903.

A. H. Bullen Esq:
  47, Great Russell Street, W.C.
Dear Mr. Bullen,
 I have the pleasure of informing you that I am just in receipt of a letter from Mr. W. B. Yeats authorising me to accept the offer detailed in your letter of the 29th. January, which you have been good enough to make for the British and Colonial book rights of his Volume of Plays entitled "WHERE THERE IS NOTHING". I shall at once draft the usual formal agreement and send you a copy of it for your approval and signature.[1]
       I am,
               Yours sincerely,

TS copy Watt. This letter would have appeared in III. 317–18.

# *Agreement with A. H. Bullen, 11 February 1903*

MEMORANDUM OF AGREEMENT made this eleventh day of February 1903 on this and the following 2 folios of paper between W. B. Yeats Esq., of 18, Woburn Buildings, Euston Road, London, N.W. of the one part and A. H. Bullen Esq., of 47, Great Russell Street, London, W.C., of the other part WHEREBY it is mutually agreed as follows:-[1]
 (1) That the said W. B. Yeats shall grant to the said A. H. Bullen the exclusive right of printing and publishing in book form in Great Britain its Colonies and Dependencies a new Play entitled "WHERE THERE IS

[1] Bullen had written to Watt on 29 Jan (Watt), telling him that WBY had handed him *Where There Is Nothing* 'and I have had a specimen page, which he approves, set up at the Chiswick Press. He seems to think that these plays are likely to find a large public, and I need hardly say that I should be very glad if he were to prove a true prophet.' He proposed to print a thousand copies in the first instance, and to pay a royalty of 15% on the published price of 3s. 6d., rising to 20% after the first thousand, and to 25% after 2,500. He added that he had already given WBY a five-guinea advance, but confessed that he was 'very doubtful whether this prose play will have any success.... the first thing is that I should get a proper text of the play. I understand that he wishes to make large alterations (and certainly there is room for plenty of revision). Naturally I do not want a big bill for printing corrections.' Watt evidently conveyed these proposals to WBY in an untraced letter on 6 Feb, WBY accepted them on 9 Feb (see III. 779–80), and they were incorporated in the following agreement.

[1] See above. This was a standard contract, drawn up by A. P. Watt & Sons.

NOTHING" of which the said W. B. Yeats is the author and the nominal selling price of which shall be three shillings and sixpence (3/6.) and in consideration thereof the said A. H. Bullen shall pay to the said W. B. Yeats the following royalties:— a royalty of fifteen per cent (15%) of the nominal selling price (3/6.) on all copies of the said new Play which he may sell up to the number of one thousand (1,000) copies, a royalty of twenty per cent (20%) of the nominal selling price (3/6.) on all copies of the said new Play which he may sell over and above the first one thousand (1,000) copies and up to two thousand five hundred (2,500) copies, and a royalty of twenty five per cent (25%) of the nominal selling price (3/6.) on all copies of the said new Play which he may sell over and above the first two thousand five hundred (2,500) copies.[2]

(2)    That the said A. H. Bullen shall publish the said new Play on a date hereafter to be fixed by him in consultation with the said W. B. Yeats, but which shall not in any case unless mutually arranged be later than the thirtieth day of April 1903[3] and it is further provided that the said A. H. Bullen shall pay the said W. B. Yeats the sum of ten guineas (£10.10.0) in advance and on account of the above mentioned royalties, such ten guineas (£10.10.0) to be paid not later than the day on which he first publishes the said new Play.

(3)    That the said A. H. Bullen shall bear all the expenses of the production, publication and advertisement of the said new Play.

(4)    That the United States rights, the rights of translation and dramatic representation together with the right to publish the said new Play in English on the Continent of Europe are reserved by the said W. B. Yeats.[4]

(5)    That the said W. B. Yeats shall be entitled to receive on publication the usual six presentation copies of the said new Play.

---

[2]  The publication history of *Where There Is Nothing* was tortuous. On 3 July 1901 George Moore had sent WBY a five-part scenario (MBY) which sketched the bohemian career of a university student after his meeting with a tinker, culminating in his death at the hands of a mob in a ruined monastery. When WBY subsequently withdrew from the proposed collaborative play on this topic, Moore announced that he was writing a novel based on the plot, and would get an injunction if WBY used it. Hearing from AE that Moore had actually begun not a novel but a play, WBY went to Coole and dictated his own version to AG and Hyde in a fortnight. He secretly arranged for the publication of this, now entitled *Where There Is Nothing*, as a supplement to the *United Irishman* of 1 Nov 1902 (see III. 228, 232–3, 238–9). Before this publication, John Quinn had the play printed at his own expense by John Lane in New York to secure the American copyright. This edition, based on WBY's unrevised first draft, was entered for copyright at the Library of Congress on 24 Oct 1902, and filed there on 30 Oct. WBY continued to revise the play, which was performed by the Stage Society in June 1904, but it was never produced by the Irish National Theatre Society. It was omitted from *Collected Plays*, and replaced by *The Unicorn from the Stars*, a radical rewriting largely undertaken by AG (see pp. 686, 693, n. 6, 704, n. 3).

[3]  Bullen's heavily revised edition of *Where There Is Nothing* appeared in May 1903. This was the first of a three-volume series entitled 'Plays for an Irish Theatre'.

[4]  An identical American edition was issued by the Macmillan Company of New York shortly after Bullen published his edition.

(6)   That the copyright of the said new Play is to remain the property of the said W. B. Yeats and that at the expiration of five years from the day on which the said A. H. Bullen shall first publish the said new Play or at the expiration of any subsequent period of five years thereafter this agreement may be terminated by either party on giving three months notice of intention so to do. Provided that if it shall be terminated by the said W. B. Yeats before royalties amounting to the sum of ten guineas (£10.10.0) shall have become payable under this agreement he shall refund to the said A. H. Bullen the difference between the amount of the royalties which shall have become payable and the sum of ten guineas (£10.10.0) which will have been paid to him by the said A. H. Bullen in advance and on account of such royalties. Further, that in the event of this agreement being terminated by the said W. B. Yeats he shall purchase the plates and stock in hand at the cost of manufacture—such plates and stock to be in good order—and if there is any wear or damage at such less price than the cost of manufacture as is fair having regard to the wear or damage. But if this agreement be terminated by the said A. H. Bullen no liability whatever shall attach to the said W. B. Yeats but he shall have the option of purchasing the stock and plates on the before mentioned terms should he think it to be in his interest to do so but should the said W. B. Yeats not purchase such stock and plates the said A. H. Bullen shall be at liberty to sell the stock accounting for the royalties thereon as provided above.

(7)   That if after three years from the date of publication the sales of the said new Play shall in the opinion of the said A. H. Bullen cease to be remunerative he shall be at liberty to dispose of the unsold stock by auction or otherwise and any profit so realised shall after deducting the original cost of production be equally divided between the said W. B. Yeats and the said A. H. Bullen.

(8)   That in the event of the said A. H. Bullen declining or neglecting within six months after the said new Play shall have become out of print to publish a new edition of the same all rights granted or assigned under this agreement shall then revert to the said W. B. Yeats and the said W. B. Yeats shall then have the option of purchasing the moulds or plates of the said new Play on the terms detailed in Clause 6 of this agreement but he shall not be bound to do so.

(9)   That an exact account of the sales of the said new Play shall be made up every six months to the thirtieth day of June and the thirty-first day of December, delivered on or before the following October the first and April the first and settled by cash on November the first and May the first.

The said W. B. Yeats hereby authorises and empowers his Agents Messrs. A. P. Watt & Son of Hastings House, Norfolk Street, Strand, London, W.C., to collect and receive all sums of money payable to the said

W. B. Yeats under the terms of this agreement and declares that Messrs.
A. P. Watt & Son's receipt shall be a good and valid discharge to all persons
paying such monies to them. The said W. B. Yeats also hereby authorises and
empowers the said A. H. Bullen to treat with Messrs. A. P. Watt & Son on his
behalf in all matters concerning this agreement in any way whatsoever.
Witness to the
signature of      A. H. Bullen
                 J. McCall

TS Doc Watt. This document would have appeared in III. 318.


## To William Sharp, [early April 1903]

at | COOLE PARK, | GORT, | CO. GALWAY.

My dear Sharp: I never got Miss Macleods letter nor yours. I wonder what
can have happened [to] them. I am sorry too that I missed you. I shall be
back in London about May 1 or at end of this month rather. Our Theatre
performs three plays of mine for Irish Lit Society on May 2 & I have to be
over to look after some arrangements.[1]

I am very anxious to see you. I have now quite finished the Rites that
old one (which I have remade in a very simple folklike spirit) & the twofold
Rite of the Water which follows.[2] I am quite certain that they are finished
now. If you have seen anything concerning me or our plans lately I would
gladly know it for much has changed—I hardly care to write of these things.[3]

I have worked very hard lately but almost wholly at plays. I have finished
'Cuchullain' which is in the press[4] & am deep in a new one about 'Senchan
Torperst'.[5] 'Where there is Nothing' should be out this Spring & in a few
days my book of essays 'Ideas of Good & Evil' which you might ask for
somewhere. It is quite a big book.[6]

---

[1] Neither Sharp's nor Fiona Macleod's letter has been traced, but Sharp's presumably announced
that he was back in London, having spent the first part of the year in Athens. The Irish National Theatre
Society made its historic first visit to London on 2 May 1903, when it included in its repertory WBY's
*The Hour-Glass, Cathleen ni Houlihan*, and *The Pot of Broth*.

[2] i.e. the Neophyte and the Cauldron rites (see pp. 967–9, 974–8).

[3] The greatest change was the marriage of MG to Major John MacBride in Paris on 21 Feb of this
year. MG had been a crucial influence on, and inspiration for, the Celtic Mysteries, and after her
removal from active participation in them WBY gradually lost interest in the project.

[4] i.e. *On Baile's Strand*, which was being published in *In the Seven Woods*.

[5] Seanchan 'Torpest' was the name given to the chief poet at the court of King Guaire of Gort, who is
the hero of WBY's play *The King's Threshold*.

[6] *Ideas of Good and Evil*, published in May 1903, comprised viii+344 pages. WBY is suggesting that
Sharp should ask to review the book in some periodical or paper.

I got your letter to day & so I have replied promptly.[7]

I go to Loughrea on Easter Monday for the day to see a play of Russells & a play of mine.[8]

Yrs ev<br>
W B Yeats

Dict AEFH, signed WBY; Private. This letter would have appeared in III. 342.

## To Henry G. O'Brien, 6 April [1903]

COOLE PARK, | GORT, | CO. GALWAY.<br>
April 6

Dear M[r] O'Brien—

I will not write at any length, as I see by your last letter that you will be home so soon—[1]

I hope to be in London about May 1. And if you are there at any time, I shall be very glad to see you any Monday evening—between 9 & 11[oc] at 18 Woburn Buildings—[2]

Our little theatrical society is going over to give some plays on May 2 for the Irish Literary Society, 20 Hanover Square (I dont know where place of acting[3] [*part of letter cut away*][4] interested me—I hope you may receive this letter, I send it to c/o Admiralty—

[*signature cut away*]

Dict AG; Pierpont Morgan. This letter would have appeared in III. 344.

---

[7] This has not been traced, but was evidently a follow-up to Sharp's earlier letter, which never reached WBY (see above, n. 1).

[8] The INTS made its first tour to the West of Ireland during the Easter holidays this year, playing at the Court Theatre, Galway, and the Town Hall, Loughrea. The repertoire included WBY's *Cathleen ni Houlihan* and *The Pot of Broth*, AE's *Deirdre*, and *Eilis agus an Bhean Déirce*, a play in Gaelic by P. T. MacGinley. During this trip, on 13 Apr, WBY dined with the Revd Jeremiah O'Donovan (see p. 1002).

[1] O'Brien's letter has not been traced. He had just been dismissed from the Royal Navy for failing his seamanship examinations for the third time, and was being sent home from China.

[2] O'Brien did not manage to see WBY in London, and in fact the two never met.

[3] The first London productions of the INTS took place in the afternoon and evening of 2 May at the Queen's Gate Hall, South Kensington.

[4] In cutting off WBY's signature for an autograph, O'Brien also excised part of the text on the other side of the sheet.

## To F. J. Fay, [mid-April 1903]

New passages for Shadowy Waters.[1]
Page 30. line 1.[2] Instead of 'The oar can hardly' &c insert the following
Because the wind is light
And this great Lochlann galley lashed against us
She will not answer to the helm, and I
(He leaves Helm)
That would be at the streams where the world ends
Must idle among the streams of the world because
These fools believe that women taken in war
Are better than the woods—(&c as before.)[3]

Page 36, after the words 'until you die' at the end of page insert the following passage:—

FORGAEL
Cry to them, cry them on that you may know
In what a dreamy net the stars have taken
your heart, and mine.

A SAILOR
She bids us follow her.
FORGAEL.
You <are wasting> have wasted words for they have but their swords
And I am guarded by a dream.

---

[1] On 30 Jan 1903 Frank Fay told WBY (NLI) that he and his brother were eager to have practice 'in the sort of acting which you like', and that 'those of us who took an interest in verse should get up some play and do it as a "Costume Recital", that is to say largely in a decorative way'. The Fays thought that *The Shadowy Waters* would be 'the very thing for such treatment', and by 23 Mar it had been decided to give the play a full production in the third week of May, and it was put into rehearsal. Although WBY told Quinn (III. 334) that this was 'rather against' his wish as he could not think it would be popular, he did not like to refuse, and was now busy 'arranging the scene'. He enlisted the help of Sturge Moore with the setting (III. 336–9), and, since he was in Ireland during March and April, would have attended some of the rehearsals. Frank Fay bombarded him with questions about the staging, music, and meaning of the play during these months, and had evidently asked him for the changes registered here. In the end the production of the play was put off until 14 Jan 1904, when WBY was in America.

[2] The page references are to the first edition of *The Shadowy Waters* (1900). Since the play was radically revised in the summer of 1905, none of the following emended passages was ever published, but they appear in two typescript prompt copies, now in the Berg Collection.

[3] These emendations and additions emphasize Forgael's impatience at being forced to remain against his will until the captured Dectora is brought aboard his galley. They replace the lines (*VP*, 754): 'The oar can hardly move her, | And I must lose more time because these fools | Believe that gold and women taken in war | Are better than the woods where no love fades . . .'

## A SAILOR

I am weary
Of following Forgael's dream from wind to wind. (And so on as before)[4]

Page 37. after last line 'I give you all as much' read
FORGAEL (taking up his harp and
beginning to tune it)

I will find out if you have all your sweetness
For I'll have need of it, strings of the seven stars.
The high string of the moon has all its sweetness.

### A SAILOR

What sounded there.

### ANOTHER SAILOR

<And> you will not be avenged
For those among your people that are dead. (So on as before.)[5]
Sunday.

Dear Fay,
    Here are the passages for the Shadowy Waters. You will notice that I
have marked strongly the uselessness of the helm. Nobody should touch it
until Dectora cuts the rope. Forgael can then go to it if he likes.[6] You will
see that Forgael is now made to busy himself with the tuning of his harp,
whilst part of that long scene of the mutiny is passing. I dont think he
should make much noise about the tuning of it, and I think when he strikes
one clear note from "the high string of the moon", the sailor who says
'What sounded there?' should have turned towards him with a tremor.
Perhaps you would find it effective to make the other sailors too, turn
towards him for a moment as if in half fear before they take up the
conspiracy again with the words '<And> you will not be avenged'. My
recollection of the rehearsal is that the play will have a curious dreamy
effect and that it will be remembered for the beautiful speaking of the
actors.

---

[4] In this insertion, only Forgael's lines are new, and emphasize the obsessiveness of his dream. In the
previous speech (*VP*, 757) Dectora has urged his already disaffected sailors to follow her in return for
worldly riches, an offer that precipitates a mutiny against him.

[5] These new lines of Forgael demonstrate both his lack of concern about the mutiny and his
(justified) faith in the power of his harp to quell the turbulence (see *VP*, 758–9).

[6] At the end of this version of the play, Dectora, having vowed to follow Forgael, cuts the rope
lashing his galley to the one in which she was captured, so that she and he can sail together in quest of his
dream (*VP*, 768–9).

Please let me know if there are any other passages or words you want altered. I think you mentioned some, but I forget what.[7]

Yrs sny
W B Yeats


TLS Kansas. This letter would have appeared in III. 347.


## To F. J. Fay, [? late April 1903]

My dear Fay

I want to see you. I go 9.30[1]—if you are in time come & dine at 7. If not I will go to Hall[2] at 8. I go at 9.20.

Yrs ever
W B Yeats


ALS NLS. This letter would have appeared in III. 350.


[7] In a letter of 23 Mar 1903 (*LWBY* I. 120–2), Frank Fay had bombarded WBY with questions about the play: 'Are the battle axes to be ordinary shape. What shape are the swords to be or do you wish any but Forgail to have a sword. . . . and if Forgail wears a helmet or hat, do you wish him to remove it at the lines commencing "The harvest's in, the granary doors are shut", which I take to be the entrance of Love. Am *I right* as to the interpretation of that speech. Forgail says "give her to Aibric if he will, I wait for an immortal woman, as I think"; and then he goes to Dectora and gazes on her, eventually giving utterance to the speech "The Harvest's in", which I interpret – I don't know if rightly – as above.' A further letter of 30 Mar (Private) enquired whether he had 'rightly interpreted the speech commencing "all comes to an end". I shall from time to time want to be guided as to the meaning of speeches etc. in Forgail. . . . What is the meaning of the "*loud*" streams. I have a vague notion of it; but would like to hear your explanation. Then there is a line of Forgail's on the last page but one, at the end of his speech – "pity these weeping eyes". Does that refer to *himself* or to Dectora? Another part that troubles me is "The stars would hurl their crowns amid the foam were *they* but lifted up." Does "they" refer to Dectora's eyelids. Let me know about these matters soon.'

[1] WBY was in Dublin on his way back to London after an extended stay at Coole, and evidently wanted to discuss last-minute arrangements for the INTS's imminent London productions (see p. 1007) before leaving on the Holyhead boat from the North Wall station at 9.20 p.m. There was much to discuss, since, as WBY explained to AG on 1 May (III. 351), the Company were 'all tired & excitable & flying at each other every moment'.

[2] The INTS had rented the Camden Street Hall from 8 Aug 1902 (see III. 219, 220) and continued to use it as their headquarters until they moved into the Abbey in late 1904. Although it proved inadequate for public performances, it provided a valuable rehearsal space, scene dock, and workshop, as well as serving as an administrative and social centre.

# To Mary MacMahon,[1] 12 June [1903]

RATRA | FRENCHPARK | CO. ROSCOMMON.[2]
June 12

Dear Miss MacMahon: I have only just noticed your note on the back of an old note of M[r] Gwynns asking for receipt for expenses over plays.[3] I now forget the amount but it was quite correct.

Yr siny
W B Yeats

ALS India Office. This letter would have appeared in III. 385.

# To Henry G. O'Brien, [late June 1903]

C/o Lady Gregory, | Coole Park, | Gort, | CO. GALWAY.

Dear Mr. O'Brien,
   I am so sorry to have missed you in London. When I got your letter I had just left.[1] I think it is probable however, that I will be back in London for a week or so, at the end of the month, or early in July. I shall be passing through Dublin on the way to and fro, but otherwise I shall be in the West of Ireland. If you write to the above address it will reach me sooner or later, though I am more likely to be in Sligo or Roscommon for some little time. I wrote to you a while ago but the letter must have just missed you. The verse "The Golden Age" is much better than any of the others you have sent me.[2] It has really a good deal of charm. Whether you do or do not develop a literary faculty, you will only gain in happiness by trying to write such things. It is hardly ever possible to say who has or has not, literary faculty till it is actually there as an accomplished power. I myself, have made

---

[1] Mary Catherine MacMahon (1866–1938) was born in Tralee, Co. Kerry. She had become assistant secretary of the Irish Texts Society, of which WBY was a member, in 1898, after some years as a governess to a French family, and in 1900 was appointed the first paid secretary to the Irish Literary Society, London, a post she held until 1906 when some injudicious remarks about members of the Society made to a journalist, but not intended for publication, appeared in the *Daily News* and she was obliged to resign. In 1908 she went to Canada, where she taught the piano in Toronto, but returned to London in 1916 to help bring up the family of her widowed brother.
[2] WBY stayed with Douglas Hyde at his home in Frenchpark, Co. Roscommon, 8–13 June.
[3] As honorary secretary of the Irish Literary Society, London, Stephen Gwynn (see p. 87) had arranged for the INTS's visit to London on 2 May (see p. 1007), and guaranteed £50 for expenses.

[1] WBY had arrived in Dublin from London in early June, and then went off to stay with Hyde (see above), before going on to visit his uncle George Pollexfen at Rosses Point, Sligo, 14–21 June. From Sligo he went to Coole, but returned to London, by way of Dublin, on 3 July to attend a meeting of the Masquers Society on 6 July, before returning to Ireland on 9 July.
[2] No poems by O'Brien have been traced, and he never published a book of verse.

mistake after mistake. I have thought that people had not got it who came to something in the end, and that others who came to nothing had got it. When literary power is actually there, there is no mistake possible, but one can be infinitely mistaken about what seems the promise of it.

Yrs sny<br>W B Yeats

TLS Pierpont Morgan. This letter would have appeared in III. 388.

## *Agreement with A. H. Bullen, 14 September 1903*

MEMORANDUM OF AGREEMENT made this 14th day of September 1903 on this and the following 2 folios of paper between WILLIAM BUTLER YEATS ESQ: of 18 Woburn Buildings, Euston Road, London, W.C., of the one part and A. H. BULLEN ESQ: of 47 Great Russell Street, London, W. C., of the other part. WHEREBY it is mutually agreed as follows:-

(1).   That the said W. B. Yeats shall grant to the said A. H. Bullen the right of printing and publishing in book form in Great Britain its Colonies and Dependencies and in the United States of America a volume of Essays entitled "IDEAS OF GOOD AND EVIL"[1] of which the said W. B. Yeats is the author and the nominal selling price of which shall be 6/- (six shillings) and in consideration thereof the said A. H. Bullen shall pay to the said W. B. Yeats the following royalties:—a royalty of fifteen per cent (15%) of the nominal selling price (6/-) on all copies of the said volume which he may sell up to the number of one thousand (1,000) copies and a royalty of seventeen and a half per cent ($17\frac{1}{2}$%) of the nominal selling price (6/-) on all copies of the said volume which he may sell over and above the first one thousand (1,000) copies.

(2).   That the said A. H. Bullen shall do his best to dispose of copies or an edition of the said volumes for sale in the United States of America and should be successful in doing so he shall pay to the said W. B. Yeats a royalty of twenty per cent (20%) of the actual price he receives for all copies of the book sold in the United States of America.

(3).   That the said A. H. Bullen shall pay to the said W. B. Yeats on or before the day on which he first publishes the said volume the sum of £66.15.6 (sixty six pounds fifteen shillings and sixpence)—the receipt of which is hereby acknowledged—in advance and on account of the above mentioned royalties.[2]

---

[1] *Ideas of Good and Evil* had actually been issued in early May 1903 (see pp. 969, n. 7, 1006, n. 6).

[2] This was an exceptionally large advance since Bullen had taken the book in lieu of the unfinished *The Speckled Bird*, for which he had already given WBY £56 5s. 6d. Rather than demanding the money

(4). That the said A. H. Bullen shall bear all the expense of the production, publication and advertisement of the said volume.

(5). That the copyright of the said volume is to remain the property of the said W. B. Yeats and that at the expiration of five years from the first day of July 1903 or at the expiration of any subsequent period of five years thereafter this agreement may be terminated by either party on giving three months notice of intention so to do. Provided that if it shall be terminated by the said W. B. Yeats before royalties amounting to the sum of £66.15.6. (sixty six pounds fifteen shillings and sixpence) shall have become payable under this agreement he shall refund to the said A. H. Bullen the difference between the amount of the royalties which shall have become payable and the sum of £66.15.6 (sixty six pounds fifteen shillings and sixpence) which will have been paid to him by the said A. H. Bullen in advance and on account of such royalties. Further, that in the event of this agreement being terminated by the said W. B. Yeats he shall purchase the plates and stock in hand at the cost of manufacture—such plates and stock to be in good order—and if there is any wear or damage at such less price than the cost of manufacture as is fair having regard to the wear or damage. But if this agreement be terminated by the said A. H. Bullen no liability whatever shall attach to the said W. B. Yeats but he shall have the option of purchasing the stock and plates on the before mentioned terms should he think it to be in his interest to do so but should the said W. B. Yeats not purchase such stock and plates the said A. H. Bullen shall be at liberty to sell the stock accounting for the royalties thereon as provided above.

(6). That if after three years from the date of publication the sales of the said volume shall in the opinion of the said A. H. Bullen cease to be remunerative he shall be at liberty to dispose of the unsold stock by auction or otherwise and any profit so realised shall after deducting the original cost of production be equally divided between the said W. B. Yeats and the said A. H. Bullen.

(7). That in the event of the said A. H. Bullen declining or neglecting within six months after the said volume shall have become out of print to publish a new edition of the same all rights granted or assigned under this agreement shall then revert to the said W. B. Yeats and the said W. B. Yeats shall then have the option of purchasing the moulds or plates of the said volume on the terms detailed in Clause 5 of this agreement but he shall not be bound to do so.

(8). That the said W. B. Yeats shall be entitled to receive on publication the usual six presentation copies of the said volume.

back, he agreed in 1903 that it should be counted as an advance on *Ideas of Good and Evil* chargeable against royalties, together with an exorbitant ten guineas paid to E. J. Oldmeadow for the right to reprint WBY's introduction to *A Book of Images*. This unusual agreement was to cause trouble over the contract for *Deirdre* (see p. 745).

(9).   That an exact account of the sales of the said volume shall be made up every six months to the thirtieth day of June and the thirty-first day of December, delivered on or before the following October the first and April the first and settled by cash on November the first and May the first.

The said W. B. Yeats hereby authorizes and empowers his Agents Messrs A. P. Watt & Son, of Hastings House, Norfolk Street, Strand, London, W.C., to collect and receive all sums of money payable to the said W. B. Yeats under the terms of this agreement and declares that Messrs A. P. Watt & Son's receipt shall be a good and valid discharge to all persons paying such monies to them. The said W. B. Yeats also hereby authorizes and empowers the said A. H. Bullen to treat with Messrs A.P. Watt & Son on his behalf in all matters concerning this agreement in any way whatsoever.

Witness to the
    signature of    A. H. Bullen
                    J M<sup>c</sup>Call

TS Doc Watt. This document would have appeared in III. 423.


## To A. P. Watt, 20 September [1903]

At | COOLE PARK, | GORT, | CO. GALWAY.
Sept 20


Dear M<sup>r</sup> Watt: I return agreement with my sister about 'seven woods'.[1] The book is, as you will see by enclosed circular not published in the ordinary way.[2] Some of the clauses of your draft agreement are therefore irrelevant. My arrangement with my sister was for a single edition & the book will be published shortly by Bullen in the ordinary way. The edition is already sold out so the clauses about 'remainders' Etc are not wanted. My corrections are to show you what the circumstances are & must [? not] be taken as binding you to any particular form of words. I have signed this

[1]  This was the original draft of the agreement for *In the Seven Woods*, the first of WBY's books to be published by ECY at the Dun Emer Press. Although dated 7 Jan the contract was not in fact signed by ECY until 2 Oct 1903, after the book's publication, and WBY heavily emended Watt's standard agreement form to register both this, and the fact that it was a one-off limited edition (see below). The version of the contract that ECY signed reflected these changes, and did not include any of the clauses WBY had deleted. The book comprised viii+68 pages, and contained twelve poems and the play *On Baile's Strand*.

[2]  The prospectus for the Dun Emer Press had been drafted by WBY and issued earlier in the summer. It announced that an attempt to revive the art of book-printing was being made at the Press, using good, uncluttered type and Irish rag paper, and that the 'first book printed has been "In the Seven Woods", a new volume of poems by W. B. Yeats. The Edition has been limited to 325 copies and the book will not be reprinted in this form. Price 10/6 per copy'. It made clear that the books would only be available through subscription and gave intending subscribers ECY's name and address.

draft as it is possible that may save further trouble, should you think the corrected agreement fair to all concerned & care to send a copy to my sister. I am sorry to give you so much trouble.

Yrs sinly
W B Yeats

ALS Watt. Stamped 'A.P. WATT & SON | 22 SEP 1903 | LONDON'. This letter would have appeared in III. 427–8.

## *Agreement with E. C. Yeats, [20 September 1903]*

**MEMORANDUM OF AGREEMENT** made this 7th day of January 1903 on this and the following 1 folio of paper between William Butler Yeats Esq., of 18 Woburn Buildings, Euston Road, London, W.C. hereinafter called the said Author, of the one part, and Miss Elizabeth C. Yeats, of Gurteen Dhas, Churchtown, Dundrum, Co. Dublin, hereinafter called the said Publisher, of the other part. WHEREBY it is mutually agreed as follows:-

(1)   That the said author shall assign to the said publisher the rights to print and publish in Great Britain its colonies & dependencies an edition of 325 copies of a new volume of poems[1] entitled "IN THE SEVEN WOODS" written by the said Author and the nominal selling price of which shall be fixed at the discretion of the said Publisher[2] and in consideration thereof the said Publisher shall pay to the said Author a royalty of twenty per cent (20%) of the nominal selling price on all copies of the said new volume which she may sell. Corrected by WBY.[3]

<(2).   That the said Publisher shall pay to the said Author ten per cent (10%) of the nett receipts from all copies of the said new volume sold as a remainder, all copies of the said new volume sold at or below one quarter of the nominal selling price being considered to be sold as a remainder. It is further provided that such ten per cent (10%) shall be in lieu of other royalty.> Crossed out by WBY.[4]

---

[1] WBY wrote out the emendation to clause 1 to this point in his own hand and pasted the slip of paper over the typed agreement, so obliterating the standard reference to 'exclusive rights', and spelling out the exact size of the edition. In the fair copy of the agreement signed by ECY this is further emphasized, since the figure '325' is followed by the written form '(three hundred and twenty five)'. At this time WBY planned that Bullen should bring out a cheaper edition immediately after the publication of the Dun Emer version (see III. 300), but finally waited to include the collection in *Poems, 1899–1905*.

[2] The book was sold at the price of 10s. 6d.

[3] This and all following annotations 'Crossed out by WBY' have been added in WBY's own hand.

[4] Since the book was now sold out, WBY deleted clauses 2 and 3 as irrelevant.

<(3). That the said Publisher shall publish the said new volume on a date hereafter to be fixed by her in consultation with the said Author but which shall not in any case unless mutually arranged be later than the thirtieth day of April 1903.>[5] Crossed out by WBY.

(4). That all details as to the manner of production, publication and advertisement and the number and destination of free copies shall be left to the sole discretion of the said Publisher who shall bear all expenses of production, publication and advertisement of the said new volume.[6]

(5). That the said Author guarantees to the said Publisher that the said new volume is in no way whatever a violation of any copyright belonging to any other party and that it contains nothing of a libellous character and that he and his legal representatives shall and will hold harmless the said Publisher from all suits and all manner of claims and proceedings which may be taken on the ground that the said new volume is such violation or contains anything libellous.

(6). That the American book rights, the right of translation together with the right to publish the said new volume in English on the Continent of Europe are reserved by the said Author.[7]

(7). That the said Author shall be entitled to receive on publication six presentation copies of the <first edition of the> said new volume. Crossed out by WBY.

<(8). That the copyright of the said new volume is to remain the property of the said Author and that at the expiration of five years from the day on which the said Publisher shall first publish the said new volume or at the expiration of any subsequent period of five years thereafter this agreement may be terminated by either party on giving three months notice of intention so to do. Provided that in the event of this agreement being terminated by the said Author he shall purchase the plates and stock in hand at the cost of manufacture—such plates and stock to be in good order—and if there is any wear or damage at such less price than the cost of

---

[5] In fact, the book was not finished until 16 July and published on 25 Aug 1903, partly because WBY went on rewriting *On Baile's Strand* until late spring.

[6] In March 1904 WBY wrote in Quinn's copy that this was 'the first book of mine that it is a pleasure to look at—a pleasure whether open or shut' (*Bibl*, 65).

[7] Although John Lane was eager to issue *In the Seven Woods* in America, WBY arranged for it to be published there by Macmillan & Co. of New York simultaneously with the Dun Emer edition, to secure the American copyright of *On Baile's Strand*.

In Quinn's copy of the Macmillan edition WBY wrote (*Bibl*, 68): 'The printer followed my sister's edition in this book without consulting me, & spoilt in copying.' On 13 July 1903 WBY sent George Brett (see p. 64) the copy for the Macmillan edition made up of spoiled pages from the Dun Emer edition (III. 397), and added, 'I think you were to give me 15 per cent. As my sister's book is ready for the binder, I hope you will let me know the date of publication as soon as possible, in order that I may publish on the same day here.'

manufacture as is fair having regard to the wear or damage. But if this agreement be terminated by the said Publisher no liability whatever shall attach to the said Author but he shall have the option of purchasing the stock and plates on the before mentioned terms should he think it to be in his interest to do so, but should the said Author not purchase such stock and plates the said Publisher shall be at liberty to sell the stock accounting for the royalties thereon as provided above.> Crossed out by WBY.

<(9). That should the said Publisher allow the said new volume to become out of print and should she decline or neglect—within a period of three months after being requested by the said Author to do so—to print and publish a new edition of the said new volume then and in that event all rights of printing and publishing the said new volume in book form in Great Britain its Colonies & Dependencies shall thereupon revert to the said Author.> Crossed out by WBY.

<(10).  That an exact account of the sales of the said new volume shall be made up every six months to the thirtieth day of June and the thirty first day of December, delivered on or before the following October the first and April the first and settled by cash on November the first and May the first.>[8] [*In WBY's hand*] The edition is already sold out so this is not wanted. WBY.

The said Author hereby authorizes and empowers his Agents Messrs A. P. Watt & Son, of Hastings House, Norfolk Street, Strand, London, W.C. to collect and receive all sums of money payable to the said Author under the terms of this agreement and declares that Messrs A. P. Watt & Son's receipt shall be a good and valid discharge to all persons paying such monies to them. The said Author also hereby authorizes and empowers the said Publisher to treat with Messrs A. P. Watt & Son on his behalf in all matters concerning this agreement in any way whatsoever.

Witness to the
    signature of    W B Yeats
                    W R Gregory


TS Doc signed; Watt. This document would have appeared in III. 428.


[8] Since, as WBY told AG on 6 Jan 1903 (III. 298), the book was 'merely a specially beautiful and expensive first edition of certain of my best things', there was no question of further editions in this form and so these clauses were irrelevant. Watt however added a further clause in the amended agreement: '(7). That when the said 325 (three hundred and twenty five) copies of the said new volume have been sold all rights of printing and publishing the said new volume in Great Britain its Colonies and Dependencies shall thereupon revert to the said Author.'

# To Will David Howe,[1] 2[5] October [1903]

18 Woburn Buildings | Euston Road, London.
Oct 2[5],

Dear Sir,

I am leaving for New York next week, but all my lectures are being arranged by my friend Mr John Quin, 120 Broadway New York.[2] If you still wish to have a lecture from me will you please write to him as I do not know what arrangements he may have made.

I should have written sooner, but my plans have been uncertain.

Yrs snly
W B Yeats

TLS Butler College, with envelope addressed to Butler College, Indianapolis, USA, postmark 'LONDON W. Oct 26 1903'. This letter would have appeared in III. 457.

[1] Will David Howe (1873–1946) was educated at Butler University, whence he returned on completion of his Harvard doctorate in 1899, teaching English there until 1906, when he took up an appointment at Indiana University. In 1919 he joined the publishing house of Harcourt, Brace & Howe and in 1921 moved to Charles Scribner's Sons as editor and director, retiring in 1942. He published books on Rhetoric, Charles Lamb and his circle, and on English and American literature, as well as editing Longfellow's and Byron's poems, Lowell's essays, and Sheridan's plays.

[2] WBY was just about to leave on his first American lecturing tour, which was being organized by John Quinn (who had suggested it) and which lasted from November 1903 to March 1904. Howe had also written to Quinn on 15 Oct, commissioning a lecture from WBY, and Quinn replied on 17 Oct (Butler) that it was not yet possible 'to fix any definite schedule'. The lecture was not for Butler College, but the Athenaeum Club of Irvington, and the date was not finally fixed until 2 Jan 1904, when Quinn asked Howe to confirm the hour and subject by writing direct to WBY, care of Miss J. M. A. Jones, 4500 Cook Avenue, St Louis.

## To Will David Howe, [7 January 1904]

TERMINAL HOTEL, | EUROPEAN. | UNION STATION. | ST. LOUIS

Dear Prof Howe:

I shall leave this tomorrow (Friday) by the noon train which gets to Indianapolis[1] at 6.50. I get [?*for* think] the theatre a good choice as I always fight that battle which is my own with some fervour.[2]

Yours snly<br>W B Yeats

ALS Butler College, with envelope addressed to 377 S. Audubon Road, Indianapolis, postmark 'ST. LOUIS MO TERMINAL STA' date indecipherable. This letter would have appeared in III. 514.

## To Lady Gregory, [? 10 January 1904]

... You would have been pleased if you had heard the compliments that have been paid to-day,[1] for they commended me for doing just what you have wanted me to do. The Irish in this land often explain to me that I have done what no other Irishman has done for the dignity of Ireland here....[2]

Printed fragment, *Hugh Lane*, 52. This letter would have appeared in III. 517–18.

[1] WBY had arrived in St Louis from New York on 5 Jan, lecturing to the Society of Pedagogy on the same day, and to the Wednesday Club of St Louis on 6 Jan.

[2] On the evening of 9 Jan WBY lectured on 'The Theatre' to the Athenaeum Club at Butler University, Indianapolis. James Whitcomb Riley (1853–1916), an American poet of Irish descent familiarly known as 'the Hoosier Poet', presided, and at the end of the lecture WBY was presented with a four-foot harp of moss and roses (see III. 517 n.).

[1] On 10 Jan the Emmet Club of Indianapolis gave a banquet luncheon for WBY, when he spoke on 'The Intellectual Revival'. In an interview with the *St. Louis Post-Dispatch* on 10 Jan 1904 (11) he had told Willis Clanahan that the 'ultimate effect' of the Irish Literary Revival would be 'the uplifting of the Irish people through their literature'.

[2] AG had first been attracted to the Irish dramatic movement because it would 'help to restore dignity to Ireland' (Pethica, 153), and raising the dignity of Ireland became her watchword. On 25 May 1902 she admonished WBY that 'anything we write must show kindly dignity, not vexation'.

## To William Sharp, 17 April 1904

18 Woburn Buildings, | Euston Road.
April 17<sup>th</sup>,/04.

My dear Sharp,

I hope that this will catch you before you go on to Paris.[1] I have been overwhelmingly busy for months now as you can imagine. In America I was continually moving from place to place & when I came back here, I had the theatre on my hands. It has just given certain very successful London performances.[2] I am indeed glad to hear that you are in good health again. I had no idea that you had been so ill.[3] Yes, I think that I shall be in London in May & shall have plenty to tell you when we meet. I was several times on the edge of writing to you when I was in America, but the whirl I was in, put it out of my head again. All is going well with the theatre in Dublin, we will start in the Autumn with a better place to perform in & with better plays. Synge, whose work had a great success here, has done us quite a long play & Shaw is writing us one.[4] I met quite a number of friends & readers of yours in America and found many admirers of Fiona M<sup>c</sup>Cleod everywhere.

Yrs snly,
W B Yeats

Dict AEFH, signed WBY; Private. This letter would have appeared in III. 583.

---

[1] Sharp had spent the winter in Athens, where he suffered a severe feverish attack. He had begun to recover at the end of February and was now recuperating in the south of France, at Hyères, Nîmes, and Le Puy. He subsequently went to Paris, and returned to London in July.

[2] The INTS's second visit to London took place under the auspices of the Irish Literary Society at the Royalty Theatre in the West End on 26 Mar 1904. They produced five plays: WBY's *The King's Threshold* and *The Pot of Broth*, Synge's *In the Shadow of the Glen* and *Riders to the Sea*, and Colum's *Broken Soil*. As in the case of the first visit, the London press was extremely enthusiastic.

[3] Apart from his fever in Athens (see above, n. 1), Sharp had been taken dangerously ill in Perthshire the previous autumn, and had to seek special treatment at Llandrindod Wells.

[4] Synge's three-act play *The Well of the Saints* was put into rehearsal in September 1904, but not produced until 4 Feb 1905. George Bernard Shaw was completing his long-promised play *John Bull's Other Island* for the Abbey, but when it was finished in the autumn of this year WBY thought it beyond the Abbey's resources, and the first production was at the Royal Court Theatre, London, from 1 to 11 Nov 1904. It was not finally staged at the Abbey Theatre until 25 Sept 1916 (see p. 79).

# To Charles Welsh, 1 June [1904]

18 Woburn Buildings | Euston Road | London
June 1.

Dear M{r} Welsh—

I send you my preface,[1] & am sending photograph to O'Donoghue as you said[2]—I am sorry for the long delay but when I got back here I found myself in a whirl of many things to do, chiefly the production of plays— Please send me a proof sheet of enclosed which I will send back to you by return of post—

Yrs sny
W B Yeats

I shall be very glad indeed to be represented in your book by any selection 'AE' has made from my writings.[3]

WBY.

Dict AG, signed WBY; Providence College. Marked in another hand: 'ans{d} June 10/04'. This letter would have appeared in III. 602.

# To Lady Gregory, [early July 1904]

...Hugh Lane tells me that Watts has left a number of his pictures to British galleries, not, it seems, specifying what galleries.[1] He is very anxious

---

[1] WBY was contributing an article, 'Modern Irish Poetry', a revised version of the introduction to his *A Book of Irish Verse* (1900), to vol. III of *Irish Literature*, a ten-volume anthology edited by the Irish politician and man of letters Justin McCarthy (1830–1912). The project had been seen through the press by George James Bryan and Charles Welsh (see p. 3), managing editor of J. D. Morris & Co., Philadelphia. WBY was not a member of the editorial and advisory board (which included Douglas Hyde and AG), but he was listed as one of the authors of 'Biographies and Literary Appreciations', which are identified in the index.

[2] For D. J. O'Donoghue see p. 927. In the end there were no photographs in *Irish Literature*.

[3] In addition to his essay on 'Modern Irish Poetry', fifty-four pages of WBY's poetry, drama, and prose were printed in vol. IX. This material had been selected by AE, who also contributed a biographical and critical introduction.

[1] George Frederick Watts (see p. 335, n. 5), the English artist, had died on 1 July 1904. Long an advocate of a National Gallery devoted entirely to British art, he left the greater part of his own works to the nation, the largest sections of this making up the Watts Collection at the National Gallery, a substantial collection in the National Portrait Gallery, and the Watts Gallery at his house, Limnerslease, near Guildford.

that you should take the first opportunity of putting in a claim for Ireland.[2]
I promised to tell you, but write for fear of being delayed . . .

Printed fragment, *Hugh Lane*, 72. This letter would have appeared in III. 614.

## Agreement with A. H. Bullen, 21 July 1904

MEMORANDUM OF AGREEMENT made this twenty-first day of
July 1904 on this and the following two folios of paper between W. B.
Yeats, Esq., of 18, Woburn Buildings, Euston Road, London, N.W. of the
one part and A. H. Bullen, Esq., of 47, Great Russell Street, London,
W.C., of the other part WHEREBY it is mutually agreed as follows:—

(1).    That the said W. B. Yeats shall grant to the said A. H. Bullen the
exclusive right of printing and publishing in book form in Great Britain its
Colonies and Dependencies a new book entitled "THE HOUR GLASS"
being the second volume of "PLAYS FOR AN IRISH THEATRE" of
which the said W. B. Yeats is the author[1] and the nominal selling price of
which shall be three shillings and sixpence (3/6) and in consideration
thereof the said A. H. Bullen shall pay to the said W. B. Yeats the following
royalties:—a royalty of fifteen per cent (15%) of the nominal selling price
(3/6) on all copies of the said new book which he may sell up to the number
of one thousand (1,000) copies, a royalty of twenty per cent (20%) of the
nominal selling price (3/6) on all copies of the said new book which he may
sell over and above the first one thousand (1,000) copies and up to two
thousand five hundred (2,500) copies, and a royalty of twenty five per cent
(25%) of the nominal selling price (3/6) on all copies of the said new book
which he may sell over and above the first two thousand five hundred
(2,500) copies.

(2).    That the said A. H. Bullen shall bear all expense of the production,
publication and advertisement of the said new book.

---

[2] Lane probably knew that AG and Robert Gregory had visited Watts at Limnerslease shortly before
his death, and that, as AG recalled in *Hugh Lane* (72), inspired by her Cuchulain tales, he promised 'to
give one of his pictures to Ireland'. Although this had not been recorded in his will, his wife sent his
picture *Faith, Hope and Charity* to the Irish Gallery.

[1] On 7 June 1904 Watt told Bullen that WBY had recently mentioned that 'he had never received any
formal agreements' covering the publication of *The Hour-Glass* and *The King's Threshold* in the 'Plays
for an Irish Theatre' series: 'Assuming this is so, I shall be glad if you will kindly draft and send me
formal agreements at your early convenience, which I can submit to Mr. Yeats for his approval and
signature' (Watt). Bullen had already published both plays in March 1904. The agreements for both
plays are identical, apart from the names and the volume numbers.

(3).   That the United States rights, the rights of translation and dramatic representation together with the right to publish the said new book in English on the Continent of Europe are reserved by the said W. B. Yeats.

(4).   That the said W. B. Yeats shall be entitled to receive on publication the usual six presentation copies of the said new book.

(5).   That the copyright of the said new book is to remain the property of the said W. B. Yeats and that at the expiration of five years from the day on which the said A. H. Bullen shall first publish the said new book or at the expiration of any subsequent period of five years thereafter this agreement may be terminated by either party on giving three months notice of intention so to do. Further, that in the event of this agreement being terminated by the said W. B. Yeats he shall purchase the plates and stock in hand at the cost of manufacture—such plates and stock to be in good order—and if there is any wear or damage at such less price than the cost of manufacture as is fair having regard to the wear or damage. But if this agreement be terminated by the said A. H. Bullen no liability whatever shall attach to the said W. B. Yeats but he shall have the option of purchasing the stock and plates on the before mentioned terms should he think it to be in his interest to do so but should the said W. B. Yeats not purchase such stock and plates the said A. H. Bullen shall be at liberty to sell the stock accounting for the royalties thereon as provided above.

(6).   That if after three years from the date of publication the sales of the said new book shall in the opinion of the said A. H. Bullen cease to be remunerative he shall be at liberty to dispose of the unsold stock by auction or otherwise and any profit so realised shall after deducting the original cost of production be equally divided between the said W. B. Yeats and the said A. H. Bullen.

(7).   That in the event of the said A. H. Bullen declining or neglecting within six months after the said new book shall have become out of print to publish a new edition of the same all rights granted or assigned under this agreement shall then revert to the said W. B. Yeats and the said W. B. Yeats shall then have the option of purchasing the moulds or plates of the said new book on the terms detailed in Clause 5 of this agreement but he shall not be bound to do so.

(8).   That an exact account of the sales of the said new book shall be made up every six months to the thirtieth day of June and the thirty-first day of December, delivered on or before the following October the first and April the first and settled by cash on November the first and May the first.

The said W. B. Yeats hereby authorises and empowers his Agents Messrs. A. P. Watt & Son of Hastings House, Norfolk Street, Strand, London, W.C., to collect and receive all sums of money payable to the said W. B. Yeats under the terms of this agreement and declares that Messrs. A. P. Watt & Son's receipt shall be a good and valid discharge to all persons paying such monies to them. The said W. B. Yeats also hereby authorises and empowers the said A. H. Bullen to treat with Messrs. A. P. Watt & Son on his behalf in all matters concerning this agreement in any way whatsoever.

Witness to the
   Signature of     A. H. Bullen T. Kearns,
                      Shanklin,
                      Benhill Rd,
                      Sutton.

TS Doc Watt. This document would have appeared in III. 626–7.

## To the Incorporated Stage Society, 7 August 1904

THE INCORPORATED STAGE SOCIETY
   To the Council of the Management of
     The Incorporated Stage Society
       9 Arundel Street, Strand, W.C.

I desire to become a Member of THE INCORPORATED STAGE SOCIETY,[1] in accordance with the Memorandum and Articles of Association, which contain the Clauses quoted on the back hereof; and I undertake, so long as I remain a Member to comply with the Regulations and By-laws for the time being of the Society, and to make due payment of all Subscriptions or other sums payable by me as a Member under said Regulations and Bye-laws.

           Name in full           \<W B Yeats> William Butler Yeats
           *State whether*
           *Mrs. or Miss*

           Address               18 Woburn Buildings
                                Euston Road

           Description          Writer

[1] See p. 354. The Incorporated Stage Society had been founded on 19 July 1899 'to promote and encourage Dramatic Art', to 'serve as an Experimental Theatre', and 'to provide for the establishment of a Repertory Theatre in London'. Its first production, on 26 Nov 1899, was Shaw's *You Never Can Tell*, and by late 1902 it had 480 subscribers, of whom about thirty were actors, but no permanent theatre. It made its reputation in performances of Ibsen, but had produced plays by thirteen different dramatists, including Maeterlinck, Hauptmann, and Hardy. The Society had produced WBY's *Where There Is Nothing* from 26 to 28 June of this year.

| Date | August 7 |
|------|----------|
| Signature | W B Yeats |
| Proposed by *Signature of Member* | A E F Horniman |

It is important that the Candidate's profession (if any) should be stated. Married women should be described "Wife of

Printed form signed; Private. This document would have appeared in III. 632–3.

## A. P. Watt to W. L. Courtney, 8 August 1904

HASTING HOUSE | NORFOLK STREET, STRAND
| LONDON, W.C.
August 8th, 1904.

(Copy)
The Editor,
    "The Fortnightly Review",
        11, Henrietta Street, W.C.
Dear Sir,
    I take pleasure in sending you herewith typewritten 'copy' of a new article by Mr. W. B. Yeats entitled "AMERICA AND THE ARTS".
    I shall be glad to hear that you have read this article and that you like it so well as to be willing to purchase the British serial rights for use in "The Fortnightly Review" only and on terms likely to be satisfactory to Mr. Yeats.
    Awaiting your early decision and trusting that it may be a favourable one,[1]
                I am,
                                    Yours sincerely,
                                    (Sgd) A. P. WATT.
'copy' encl.

TS copy Watt. This letter would have appeared in III. 634.

[1] WBY told Quinn as early as 6 July 1904 that he had sent Watt this article (see III. 614), and Courtney compounded the delay in placing it by not getting back to Watt until 5 Oct, when he informed him that, while he hoped to be able to use the article, he could not yet fix a date for its publication (Watt). On 31 Oct he again wrote to Watt to point out that since the article was only 1,800 words it would make no more than four pages of the *Fortnightly Review*, and that he did not think 'Messrs. Chapman & Hall would give more than 30/-per page, that is to say six guineas for the article'. Watt wrote to WBY on 2 Nov to enquire whether this was 'a proposal which you care to accept' (Watt); apparently it was not, for the article did not

# To W. K. Magee [John Eglinton],[1] [early October 1904]

at | COOLE PARK, | GORT, | CO. GALWAY.

My dear Magee: I want two copies of your two books at once[2] that I may cut them up into selections for my sister.[3] Could I have them by return? I pretty well know what I will give—the essay on 'Patriotism' is your best essay I think.[4] If you have any recent essay I would like to see them.[5]

'Dana' has improved greatly & I think doing good work—even in the eyes of a beleiver like myself[6]—but I wish you had kept Russell & Moran

appear in the *Fortnightly Review*, although on 7 Nov WBY told Quinn that he had 'just heard that the "Fortnightly Review" has taken it on this side' (III. 669). It was eventually published by the New York *Metropolitan Magazine* in April 1905 (see pp. 15–16).

[1] For Eglinton see p. 296.

[2] John Eglinton had published two books of essays, *Two Essays on the Remnant* (Dublin, 1894) and *Pebbles from a Brook* (Kilkenny, 1901). WBY had reviewed the former in the *Bookman* of May 1895 (*UP* 1. 356–8), describing Eglinton as 'none the less a theorist and a thinker because he wraps his theories and his thoughts in sentences which are rich and elaborate as old embroidery'. Eglinton's 'remnant' was a 'Chosen People', or spiritual elite, of 'liberated individuals' who withdrew themselves from popular life and culture, but WBY argued that such people should be leaders, not exiles. In his review of *Pebbles from a Brook* for the *United Irishman* on 9 Nov 1901 (*UP* II. 255–62), he found Eglinton's criticism of modern life 'formidable', but confessed that 'that which has made John Eglinton turn from all National ideas and see the hope of the world in individual freedom . . . has made me see the hope of the world in re-arrangments of life and thought which make men feel that they are part of a social order, of a tradition, of a movement wiser than themselves.' James Joyce celebrated his essays more frivolously in a limerick: 'There once was a Celtic librarian | Whose essays were voted Spencerian, | His name is Magee | But it seems that to me | He's a flavour that's more Presbyterian' (Richard Ellmann, *James Joyce* [Oxford, 1982], 118).

[3] WBY was making a selection from Eglinton's books for *Some Essays and Passages by John Eglinton*, published by ECY at the Dun Emer Press in 1905. Eglinton was not happy about the inclusion of extracts from *Two Essays on the Remnant*, especially the entire text of the second essay, 'The Chosen People at Work', and published a note of disavowal at the foot of the list of contents: 'The writer of the following pages would like to say that he has had no hand in the selection, which Mr. Yeats has done him the honour to make for the Dun Emer Press Series, and in particular, that if consulted he would hardly have approved of the inclusion of the last essay, written over twelve years ago, in which a metaphor [i.e. of the 'Chosen People'] is pressed to the point of being recommended as a gospel.' In a copy of *Some Essays and Passages* inscribed for James Healy in July 1938 (Stanford), WBY wrote that 'Eglinton was the sceptic of our movement, always for the individual against the race. We lived in our better moments.'

[4] i.e. Eglinton's essay 'Regenerate Patriotism', published in *Pebbles from a Brook* (65–81), and republished in its entirety under the title 'Dying Nations and Regenerate Patriotism' as the first of WBY's selections. The essay argues that traditional patriotism, like traditional religion, is dying as new discoveries modify the significance of the facts on which it has rested, facts which have led to an increase of self-conscious individualism. Englinton thought that this would result in what he calls the 'higher or regenerate patriotism', which 'has its ground in the relation of man to his fellow men and to nature, rather than in his political relation to the state'.

[5] As well as contributing essays with WBY and AE to *Literary Ideals in Ireland* in 1898 (see II. 289–90, 293–8), Eglinton was currently publishing essays and reviews in the magazine *Dana*, and was to publish *Anglo-Irish Essays* in 1917. In fact, all WBY's extracts were taken from *Two Essays on the Remnant* and *Pebbles from a Brook*.

[6] From 1904–5 Eglinton co-edited the rationalist monthly *Dana*. His accounts of WBY appeared in *Irish Literary Portraits* (1935), and in the *Dublin Magazine* (July-September 1953, pp. 22–6). In an inscription in a copy of *Dana* he presented to AG (Emory), Eglinton lamented that WBY did not approve of the magazine.

out of the ring. Russell should have replied in Dana. He could have dared Moran to come on there if he had a mind to. If Moran was to be faught in his own paper it should have been on purely public impersonal grounds.[7]

Yrs ever

W B Yeats

ALS Pierpont Morgan. This letter would have appeared in III. 659–60.

## To Charles Elkin Mathews, 30 October [1904]

18 Woburn Buildings | Euston Road

Oct 30

My dear Mathews,

The Income Tax people have assessed my income at a preposterous sum & I have to appear before them next Thursday morning. I shall be greatly obliged if you will write me a letter stating roughly what you have paid me during the three years up to April 1904.[1]

Yours ever

W B Yeats

Dict AG, signed WBY; Connecticut College. A version of this letter appeared in III. 665.

## To Lady Gregory, [early December 1904]

... The wretched Academicians never go near him and are openly obstructive. They have lent the Academy to a Paper-Hangers' Exhibition for one week in January, so Lane will have to close after a month. The

[7] Following journalistic attacks on Horace Plunkett's *Ireland in the New Century* for its allegedly anti-Catholic bias (see III. 463, 658–9) AE published an article, 'Physical Force in Literature', in the September number of *Dana* (129–33), denouncing the 'thoughtless savagery' and blind bigotry of the Irish press, and calling for humanity, tolerance, and independent thought. Although not mentioned by name, the *Leader* was clearly one of his main targets and in a coat-trailing rejoinder there on 10 Sept (37–9) its editor, D. P. Moran (see p. 295, n. 11), describing AE as an 'eminently business-like and skilfully advertised minor poet', challenged him to 'join issue with us on the Bigotry ... question and we will give him space'. AE took up the gauntlet on 17 Sept (52), and asked permission to reprint Moran's article with his own in a pamphlet, *Controversy in Ireland*, published *c.* 23 Sept 1904. The *Leader* returned to the attack on 24 Sept, and AE replied in a 'long letter' of 1 Oct (88–90) which WBY did not like, and which oscillated unhappily between hauteur and apology. Printing the letter under the heading 'A Minor Poet in Eruption', Moran gibed at the 'pretty exhibition he makes of himself. ... Biddy Moriarty has her arms akimbo and is giving forth.' The controversy continued in the paper until 15 Oct.

[1] The Income Tax inspectors refused to believe that a man so well–known as WBY could earn so little, and had estimated the tax they thought payable on his supposed income. He also wrote an identical letter to Bullen on this day (see III. 665), and presumably sent to Unwin the same request. He visited the tax office in person accompanied by Quinn, who on 26 Feb 1916 recalled (Himber, 168) 'smoking in the outer room of the income tax office, when ... the little cockney Englishman, greater in

paper-hangers being Nationalists with some public zeal are very sorry, and
are ready to do anything, but they have sent out all the announcements, etc.
The Academicians are stony. . . .[1]

Printed fragment, *Hugh Lane* 62. This letter would have appeared in III. 680.

## To Lady Gregory, [c. 12 December 1904]

. . . The last event is that Sir Thomas Drew[1] has written to Lord Drogheda,
who had, as you remember, promised £100, remonstrating with him for
belonging to a committee which included such rebellious persons as Edward
Martyn and myself. Lord Drogheda is very valuable, as he is nearly the only
entirely 'safe' person Lane has.[2] Even Mayo seems to be suspected of red
republicanism.[3] Lord Drogheda won't let his wife go on the committee as a
result,[4] but whether he has himself resigned I don't know. Edward Martyn is
to be asked to resign and to state his reason in a letter to the *Freeman*, offering
a subscription.[5] I have offered to resign at any time Lane likes. . . .

Printed fragment, *Hugh Lane*, 61. This letter would have appeared in III. 683.

circumference than in height, came out and said: "See ere, don't yu know ware yu arr? Yu arr in er
Majesty's tax orrfice. Yu mite as well smauke in Sommerset aause."' WBY evidently managed to
convince the Inquiry that his figures were correct.

[1] Hugh Lane's Loan Exhibition of Modern Art (see III. 680–2) had opened at the Royal Hibernian
Academy on 21 Nov, but the Academicians had a long-standing contract to let the galleries to the
Decorators' Guild of Great Britain for their Triennial Exhibition in January 1905. George Moore
made a public protest about this in a letter to the *Daily Express* on 5 Dec, and the following day Stephen
Catterson Smith (1849–1912), portrait painter and secretary of the Royal Hibernian Academy, wrote to
the paper (5) to point out that the Decorators' Guild had booked the rooms many months before Lane,
that it had been made perfectly clear to Lane that he must vacate the premises by 7 Jan 1905, that the
Academy was legally bound to its agreement with the Decorators' Guild, that it had abandoned its own
Winter Exhibition to accommodate Lane, and that it had received no formal request from Lane for an
extension of time. WBY replied to this letter (see III. 681–2), arguing that 'possibly even as late as last
week, the paper-hangers could have been persuaded to forego their contract if the Academy had
approached them. The attempt should, at any rate, have been made.' In fact, Lane managed to have the
Exhibition moved to the Round Gallery of the National Museum of Ireland in Kildare Street after 7 Jan.

[1] Sir Thomas Drew (1838–1910), the Irish architect, was president of the Royal Hibernian Academy
from 1900 until his death. On 23 Oct 1907 JBY recalled (NLI) that 'Sir Thos. Drew wrote a venomous
letter against the Lane Collection—he is also moved by a special spite against H. Lane and *you*, he is
singularly ignorant of art, and his only idea of doing his duty as President of the Academy is to make
himself on all occasions as obnoxious as possible, he thinks that making himself prominent he pushes the
R.H.A. fortunes; in reality he ought to keep his disagreeable appearance as much out of sight as
possible.'

[2] William M. Ponsonby, 9th Earl of Drogheda (see p. 324), chaired a committee of thirty-three,
including WBY, Edward Martyn, the Earl of Mayo, Sir Thomas Drew, Colonel Sir W. Hutcheson Poe,
C. B. and T. Harrington, the artist Dermod O'Brien (treasurer), and Hugh Lane (secretary). He ignored
Sir Thomas Drew's letter, and remained on the committee.

[3] Dermot Robert Wyndham Bourke, 7th Earl of Mayo (see p. 324), took an active interest in the
agricultural and industrial welfare of Ireland, as well as in the development of Irish art.

[4] Lord Drogheda had married Anne Tower (d. 1924) in 1879.

[5] Martyn did not in the end resign from the committee.

## To Lady Gregory, [c. 18 December 1904]

...I went to see Hugh Lane to-day and asked him if I should reply to a stupid little paragraph about him.[1] I am not to do so, however, as he finds association with us Nationalists too injurious with the monied people. Many of his rich friends are saying that they will not help him now, that he is a part of the Movement. It's only the Gaelic League over again, etc., etc., and they had thought it something quite different. I am not even to speak of my father's lecture.[2] All this amuses me very much. My father says that the Unionist classes are secretly angry with themselves, and that this is the one sort of anger a man never gets out of....[3]

Printed fragment, *Hugh Lane*, 60–1. This letter would have appeared in III. 688.

## To Lady Gregory, [c. 19 December 1904]

...At first the editor denied that there was any insinuation that Lane is making money out of the Forbes collection,[1] but finally he owned up and said he wrote it because three Academicians had told him that Lane had made large sums out of the Guildhall, and would make large sums out of the present collection if it was bought.[2] You can imagine the scene that

---

[1] In a paragraph on the 'squalid...if not unamusing' dispute between Lane and the Academicians, the *United Irishman* of 17 Dec three times drew attention to the fact that Lane was a professional picture-dealer. The implication was that Lane expected to take a percentage out of the exhibition and sale of the pictures. On 7 Feb 1908 WBY told Quinn (NYPL) that his 'first serious quarrel with Arthur Griffith was when I went down to the Office and told him what I thought of his conduct in hinting at a preposterous scandal against Hugh Lane in his paper'.

[2] JBY lectured at the Royal Hibernian Academy on 'The Art Instinct' on 29 Dec (see III. 691). The *Freeman's Journal* reported on 30 Dec (7) that the chairman, Robert Elliott, spoke afterwards 'strongly in favour of establishing a modern art gallery in Dublin', and WBY also spoke.

[3] In her reply of 20 Dec (Berg) AG agreed that it was 'a great worry about the pictures, & I have not been able to write a line to anyone yet — it is maddening to think of the stupidity of those "classes" — '.

[1] See above.

[2] AG wrote in *Hugh Lane* that she did 'not know who these three Academicians were, or if many gave credence to their statement that Hugh was making money out of his public work'. The three were probably Sir Thomas Drew, Stephen Catterson Smith, and Lieutenant-Colonel George Tindall Plunkett (1942–1922), who was not an Academician but director of the Science and Arts Institutions in Dublin since 1895, and a bitter enemy of Lane. Lane had organized 'An Exhibition of a Selection of Works by Irish Painters' at the Guildhall Art Gallery, London, after negotiations about an exhibition of Irish paintings for the St Louis World Fair of 1904 broke down (see III. 564). The Exhibition opened on 30 May 1904 in the presence of a large gathering which included WBY, AG, John O'Leary, and Wilfrid Blunt, and proved a success, running until 23 July 1904 and attracting 80,000 paying visitors. Its 465 exhibits included works by C. H. Shannon, J. J. Shannon, Lavery, Orpen, Mark Fisher, Furse, Brabazon, Hone, JBY, and others. Lane immediately began to make plans for a Dublin show, and AG wrote in *Hugh Lane* (54) that he 'looked on the success of the Guildhall Exhibition as another step toward the fulfilment of his purpose, now very definite, of creating a modern picture gallery in Ireland'.

followed. I said, 'My dear [Griffith], you have published just enough of a slander to give wings to it, while keeping yourself out of the Law Courts.' He promised some sort of retraction next week, but I can imagine the grudging spirit it will be made in.[3] As I was coming away, I said, 'It is a custom of gentlemanly life to presume that a man's motives are good until they are proved the contrary.' He answered without a smile, and in obvious earnestness, 'I don't agree with that principle at all. If any Irish newspaper were at this moment to act on the assumption, or to say that Lord Dunraven's motives were good, the country would be wrecked in six months.'[4]

Printed fragment, *Hugh Lane*, 60. This letter would have appeared in III. 688.


## To Lady Gregory, [*20 December 1904*]

... I hear from Robert that you may get up for a little to-day.[1] I hope you will take a long rest. I shall see about the awning for the old woman's stall to-night.[2] Synge has a photograph, which will give us a picturesque form. We changed all the lighting on Saturday, and the costumes look much better now. In any case everything looks so much better on the new stage. G[ogarty] came in last night with a Boer, who went to Trinity, because, so far as I could make out, he thought he would find himself among sympathetic surroundings. He and some other young Boers, including one who is said to have killed more Englishmen at Spion Kop than anybody else, had to go to a university in Europe and chose Ireland. Finding the sort of place

---

[3] In fact, Griffith made an honourable apology the following week (24 Dec), explaining (1) that he had been 'assured the inference which might be drawn from a fact we referred to last week—that Mr. Hugh Lane is a professional picture-dealer, would do Mr. Lane injustice...Mr. Lane, we are assured, has gathered the present collection solely with the object of advancing art in Ireland, and his efforts in that direction, instead of benefiting, have involved him in heavy pecuniary loss. We have been invited to verify the assurance by examining his accounts. It is quite unnecessary. The word of a gentleman is sufficient in such a matter.'

[4] Windham Thomas Wyndham-Quin, 4th Earl of Dunraven and Mount-Earl (see p. 753), was a progressive landlord, who published numerous articles on politics and economics. He was chairman of the Irish Land Conference 1902–3, and president of the Irish Reform Association. As a sympathetic and ameliorating landlord, he posed a greater threat to uncompromising nationalism than more clear-cut political and class enemies.

[1] AG had been struck down with influenza, and WBY was keeping her abreast of preparations for the opening of the Abbey Theatre on 27 Dec.

[2] i.e. the awning for Mrs Tarpey's apple-stall in AG's *Spreading the News*, one of the plays performed at the opening of the Abbey Theatre.

it is, they look at the situation with amusement and are trying to get out more men of their own sort to form a rebellious coterie.³...I mention G[ogarty], in order to say that he wants to try his hand at translating *Oedipus the King* for us.⁴ To-night we go on experimenting in lighting and after that will come the great problem of keeping the bottom of the trews from standing out like frilled paper at the end of a ham bone.⁵

Printed fragment, Gregory, *Our Irish Theatre*, 35–6. This letter would have appeared in III. 688.

## *To Lady Gregory, [24 December 1904]*

....I have a project for Lane to get a private Art Committee together the Committee to include one member of each of the seven or eight Art Classes in Dublin. This Committee to arrange that each of the classes will write to the papers giving a subscription list, 2/6 from one 1/- from another a letter from an art class or industry should appear every day or two for some weeks....¹ The Company are very disappointed that you will not be up for the first night. Fay says they would all act better if you were here.²

TL fragment Berg and printed fragment, Gregory, *Our Irish Theatre*, 35. This letter would have appeared in III. 689–90.

---

³ A number of Boers had enrolled in Trinity College, Dublin, including Jacobus Van Staden, Wilhelm Van Zijii, James Van Zyl, Johannes de Villiers, and Cornelius Dijkman, not realizing that, although an Irish university, it had a long Anglophile and unionist tradition. Nevertheless, it began a tradition that continued well into the century. Spion Kop was the scene of one of the greatest British defeats during the Boer War.

⁴ i.e. Oliver St John Gogarty, who did not, in the end, finish his translation (see pp. 22, n. 2, 42, n. 3).

⁵ The trews, i.e. trousers, were worn by the warriors and kings in WBY's *On Baile's Strand* and had been the topic of discussion between F. J. Fay, WBY, and AEFH (who was designing the costumes) in January 1904 (see III. 528). In his *A Social History of Ancient Ireland* (1903) P. W. Joyce confirmed (II. 207) that the 'ancient Irish wore a trousers.... The usual Irish name was *triubhas*...which is often correctly anglicised *trews*, and from which the modern word "trousers" is derived.'

¹ Nothing appears to have come of this rather cumbersome suggestion.

² AG was still suffering from influenza but she managed to write on 20 Dec (see p. 1029, n. 3) for the first time in many days: 'I dont know what to say—fever & headache have gone, but I am dreadfully weak & cough a gt deal & food will not always stay down & neuralgia comes & settles in the eyes—But no doubt I am on the mend, & only want patience—I was sure you cd not come & it is best for I dont know when I can leave my room—Many thanks for yr letters.... We have the house full for shooting Monday to Friday—next week—I cling to the hope of a glimpse of the plays after tho.'

## To Lady Gregory, [c. 26 December 1904]

. . . . My father has just come in and read me his lecture, he lectures at the Hibernian Academy on Thursday. Alas, he thought he had an hour's lecture written, and when he read it to me it took about a quarter of an hour.[1]

Printed fragment, Gregory, *Hugh Lane*, 71. This letter would have appeared in III. 690.

[1] JBY lectured on 'The Art Instinct' at the Royal Hibernian Academy on Thursday, 29 Dec 1904. According to a report in the *Freeman's Journal* of 30 Dec (7), he was 'imperfectly heard', but argued that the modern painter was a magician who unlocked the secrets of ancient art 'and there was no peace like that breathed out by the galleries of old masters'. He maintained that the 'art instinct established within them was like a divine voice which summoned out of the void innumerable worlds', and he defended Millet, whom he thought not 'sentimental' but 'sympathetic'. He confessed that he found the Protestant mind too literal and, although a Protestant himself, preferred the Catholic mind where religion was like the pages of Dante. WBY spoke after the lecture (see III. 691, n. 3).

# INDEX OF RECIPIENTS

# GENERAL INDEX

Abbey Theatre and Irish National Theatre Society, 6, Pixie Smith designs scenery for, 10; 13n, asks Quinn to copyright *The Well of the Saints* in USA, 17, 28; Company 'excited' at prospect of Murray translating *Oedipus* for, 22–3; no censorship in Ireland and Abbey 'a beautiful little theatre', 23; Abbey to be 'a great dramatic school', 24; revival of *The Shadow of the Glen* attacked, 25–7, 24n, 29n, 31–3, 34, 35; designs for *The Well of the Saints* 'quite a new thing', 27; plays 'beginning to come in to us', 28; 29n, 30; George Moore praises Abbey acting, 37; audiences 'rather thin' but theatre making a small profit, 37; audiences friendly but general atmosphere 'one of intense hostility', 38; possible designs for Abbey productions, 44; 52, 57; 58n, Abbey will make 'no sudden leaps', 61; regular audience of 'about a thousand people', 61; 'severely decorative' scenery 'has conquered everybody', 62; audience diminishes in Lent, 67; profit on *Kincora*, 69–70; 78; 75n, need to pay Company, 81; 86n, 88n, 90, 95–6, 102, 104; WBY reflects on first Abbey season, 112; 114; AEFH to guarantee actors' wages, 119, 120, 279; 126n, 143, 287; WBY anticipates a 'fine' second season, 145; AE begins to rewrite the Company's constitution, 148–9; 151; discussions about the Company's new constitution, 153–9, 163, 164, 167–8, 169–71, 172, 173; 176, abolishing 'democracy in the Theatre' 178; new plays to be produced, 178–9; discussions about the Company's new constitution, 180–5; proposal that INTS should become limited liability company, 186, 187, 188, 189–90; Directors to have 'absolute majority' in reorganized INTS, 192–3; 194–8; plans for autumn 1905 programmes and English tour, 194; AE tries to persuade reluctant INTS members to accept new constitution, 197; 200–1, 203, 206, 236–7; players think WBY's plays draw best audiences 204; 207, 208–9, 212; plans for theatre orchestra, 214, 215, 221–2; WBY does advance publicity for English visit, 218–19, 230, 232; proposal for establishment of Gaelic company 222–6; plans for 1906 tour to Leeds,

Manchester, and Liverpool, 228–9 235–6, 240, 243, 249 266, 288, 323, 333, 367, 370, 374, 386, 390, 392, 398; 1905 English tour, 233–5, 236, 237, 239–40, 241, 243; proposed tour in Ireland, 240, 275; 245; Directors offer Company shares in new Company, 248, 251–2; complaints that Directors pushed their own work in London, 249–51; difficulties with Maire Walker over her contract, 255–8, 260–1, 263–4, 270–80, 283; seeking new actors to replace those who have seceded from, 258, 261, 263, 265, 266, 269, 273, 274, 280, 282–4, 291, 301, 376–7; dramatists asked to assign their work to Company, 259, 284–5; plans for a re-united Society would be five wild cats struggling in a bag, 280; WBY drops idea of legal action against Maire Walker, 280–82, 285–7, 290, 291, 292, 300; audience 'almost entirely general public', 290; AEFH gives extra £200 per annum, 291; Colum secedes from, 292, 299; WBY welcomes rival company, 299; legal disputes with rival Theatre of Ireland, 304–21, 323, 329–33, 344, 346–7, 348–9, 351–2, 396, 409, 427; problem of heating Abbey, 325; Frank Fay appointed to teach voice production and verse speaking, 345; attack on in *United Irishman*, 348–9; 361, 362, 365; 'going on with decorative scenery and with nothing else', 368; 370, AEFH provides funds for duplicate touring scenery, 371; raising Abbey salaries, 371, 376; 374; design for *On Baile's Strand*, 377, 379–80, 382–3, 384–5; plans for Irish tour, 378, 381–2, 401, 403–4, 417; think of producing Shaw's plays, 378–9; production of *On Baile's Strand* 'the first thoroughly efficient performance' of a WBY verse play, 387; 388; Company improving, 392; Wareing arranges British tour in summer of 1906, 392, 399; holding their audiences, 393–4, will defeat the cavilling of their detractors, 394; disappointing reception in Dundalk, 403; AEFH suggests further tour to Manchester, 404–5; mistake to tour 'indefinitely with a practically comedy programme', 405; academic people 'most suspicious' of the Abbey, 406; ill-discipline during British 1906 summer tour, 413, 414–16, 426, 427–34, 437–9, 441–2, 443, 447; W. G. Fay

**Yeats, William Butler:** (*cont.*)

the terms she has offered MacBride are too generous, 6; offers to go to Paris to help MG, 6; tells AG of MG's marital difficulties, 7–9; MG's situation 'has awakened nothing of the old fealing – a little to my surprize – no feeling but pity & anger', 9; feels 'that strength shapes the world about itself, & that weakness is shaped about the world – & that the compromise is weekness', 9; sees Pixie Smith about design for scenery for *The Well of the Saints*, 9; now 'utterly certain' that MG must get 'divorce or legal seperation, with entire control of her child' and will 'urge this on her ceaselessly', 10; learns that MacBride has made false counter charges about him, 10; Barry O'Brien informs him that MacBride has not signed MG's deed of settlement and a suit for divorce or separation seems inevitable 11; hears that, besides him, MacBride has cited Millevoye, Cipriani and probably W. T. Stead as having been MG's lovers, 11–12; WBY suggests that MG show her evidence to leading Republicans 'to make it obvious that Mac Bride must dissappear', 12; is 'in a whirl of varying occupations', 13; places 'America and the Arts' with the *Metropolitan Magazine* through Watt, 15–16; asks Bullen for the MS of Synge's *The Well of the Saints*, to send to Quinn for copyrighting in the USA, 16, 17; asks AG to join him in London as he cannot bear the burden of MG's 'terrible case', knows 'nothing about lawyers & so on', and sees that he will 'have to do a great deal', 18; learns that MacBride has threatened to shoot him, 'the only cheerful peice of news I have had for days – it gives one a sense of hightened life', 18–19, 50; sends MG a letter from AG's lawyer about divorce proceedings, 20; takes interest in establishing a publishing house in Ireland, 20; arranges to meet art critic D. S. MacColl in London to enlist his aid in dispute over value of Lane pictures, 21; invites Gilbert Murray to translate Sophocles' *Oedipus* for Abbey, 22–4; assures Murray that Ireland 'is in its first plastic state, and takes the mark of every strong finger', 23; WBY 'trying to persuade Ireland . . . that she is very liberal, abhors censors delights in the freedom of the arts, is prepared for anything', 23; quotes English censor's objections to *On Baile's Strand*, 24; believes they are 'going to make a great dramatic school' in Ireland, and that *The Well of the Saints* is 'a great play', 24; defends Synge's *The Shadow of the Glen* against attacks in *United Irishman*, 25–7, 31–3, 34; thinks it 'no

bad thing that our two so different points of view should find full and logical expression' but that 'differences that arise out of mistakes of fact are useless', 27; meets AG in Dublin for rehearsals of *The Well of the Saints*, 27; occupied with design – 'our first attempt to do decorative open air scenes' – of *The Well of the Saints* with W. G. Fay, AG and Pixie Smith, feeling that 'the remoteness, the abstractedness of the scenic arrangements, will make the play safer', 27; has written preface for the play, 28; plays beginning to come in to Abbey and believes 'we will have a whole dramatic literature before long', 28; Colum reads him simplified scenario of *The Land*, with dialogue 'full of country idiom and character', 28; starting an Abbey Theatre series of plays, 28; delighted with ten-volume anthology *Irish Literature*, which is 'is the evidence of the scholarship and criticism of a generation', 29, 36; re-writing *On Baile's Strand* and intends to re-write *The King's Threshold*, 30; shames *United Irishman* into publishing Synge's letter on sources of *The Well of the Saints*, 34; production of *The Well of the Saints* a success despite thin audiences and reduced returns, as it was 'the finest piece of acting as a whole the company has done', 37; Ireland 'has never produced an artistic personality in the modern sense of the word', 38; foresees 'a hard fight in Ireland before we get the right for everyman to see the world in his own way admitted', 38; Synge invaluable for his 'intense narrow personality', which raises issue of personality and freedom, 40; contrasts Colum's 'unbeautiful' dialect with that of AG and Synge, 40; detects a 'great intellectual stir and awakening now coming up on Ireland', 41; health 'much better', 42; making fair copy of revised *On Baile's Strand*, which has 'delighted' Frank Fay, 43; anxious about MG's divorce case, 43; AE regularly exhausts up to two hours of his day, 43; making 'one or two very slight changes' to *On Baile's Strand* at W. G. Fay's suggestion, 44; AE wrongly accuses him of slander, 45; busy on Abbey affairs, 46–7; sees performances of Shakespeare by Edmund Tearle, 47; discusses MG's divorce with Henry Dixon, 47; writing poem 'O Do Not Love Too Long', 48; returns to London, 49; asks Quinn's help in getting affidavits testifying to MacBride's insobriety while in New York, 49–50; MacBride continuing to make 'wild counter charges', including an allegation against WBY, 50; WBY sees a London production of *The Pot of Broth* which he thinks 'bad & vulgar beyond words' and for which he receives £5, 50–1, 52–3; sees Bullen, and goes to Whistler Memorial Exhibition, 52; tells Archibald Henderson that he would not write about Shaw 'unless at considerable length & after weighing my words', because Shaw 'is a very brilliant man & my friend', 54; has had 'a multitude of things to do', including dictating 'scores of letters' and listening to Masefield's plays, 56; meets Irish folk musician Herbert Hughes, 56; 'greatly bored' by Stage Society production of Brieux's *The Three Daughters of M. Dupont*, 66; sees Eric Maclagan, 57; sends Dunsany a circular about the new Municipal Gallery and asks him for a subscription, 58; thanks Quinn for looking after his interests in Bayard Veiller's and Margaret Wycherly's productions of his plays in New York, 59–60; hardly knows 'what sort of a play' *The Countess Cathleen* is, because of circumstances of its first production and because he 'had no stage experience' so that it 'rambles all over the place', 59–60; intends 'to put more logic into the construction', 60; suggests cuts and revisions to *The Countess Cathleen*, 60–1; has been 'thinking of very little but construction for a couple of years now', 61; Abbey production of *Kincora* 'a magnificent success' but WBY has warned Company that a 'theatre like ours makes no sudden leaps', 61; Abbey now has core audience of 'about a thousand people who come to everything we do', 61; has finished new version of *The King's Threshold*, 61; scenery for *Kincora* 'the most beautiful in effect' he has ever seen, 62; invites J. P. Quinn to the post-production party for *Kincora*, where WBY also talks to Martin Ross, 63, 64n; negotiates with Macmillan (NY) about *The Poetical Works of William B. Yeats*, 64–6; suggests Macmillan (NY) should publish his projected multi-volume *Collected Works* in USA, 66; discusses with Quinn the financial arrangements for the production of his plays in New York by Margaret Wycherly, 67; 'One learns something from every performance of a play of one's own', 67; Lent is reducing size of Abbey audiences, 67; a 'rather exhausting' cold is better but has left his eyes 'very bad', 68; gives G. K. A. Bell permission to anthologize some of his poems, 71; sends AEFH to Mayo to spy on the MacBrides, 72; urges Bullen to see Watt or Brett about American publication of *Collected Works*, 73; Macmillan (NY) agree to Quinn's suggestion that *The Poetical Works of William B. Yeats* should be in two volumes, 73; Macmillan (NY) decline to publish *Collected*

*Works* in USA on legal grounds, 73–4; Quinn send him New York reviews of Margaret Wycherly's production of *The Countess Cathleen*, 74, 75n; asks Quinn to give him an account of the production with a view to a future rewriting of the play, 74–5; Colum at Coole with WBY and AG, 'working very hard' on *The Land*, 75; WBY working on his 'rather elaborate' article 'Literature and the Living Voice', 76; hears that *The Hour-Glass* has been successfully staged in Chicago by Anna Morgan, 76, 101; receives an enthusiastic reception at the Royal University, where he speaks to paper on 'The New School of Literature and Drama in Ireland' and defends Synge, 77; complains of rheumatism, 78; tells MG that AEFH failed to find any witnesses to MacBride drunkenness in Mayo, 78; sends MG a copy of *Stories of Red Hanrahan*, 78; declines MG's request to re-employ Dudley Digges at the Abbey, 78–9; resigns the Abbey's production rights in Shaw's *John Bull's Other Island*, 79; writes to Blunt about his play *Fand*, 80–2; Abbey has 'only two women who can be relied upon in the speaking of blank verse', 81; believes that Company will 'very shortly' have to be regularly paid, which will give more time for rehearsal, 81; trying to arrange an Abbey tour to London 'for a couple of days in June, but nothing is settled yet', 81; believes that MacBride is making his first move towards 'surrender', 82, 83–6, 94, 104; sees Henry Irving in Tennyson's *Beckett*, and thinks the play largely 'sentimental melodrama', 82; asks Bullen for help in advising George Roberts and Joseph Hone to set up a publishing firm (later Maunsel & Co.) in Dublin, and opposes AE's possible appointment as literary adviser over Stephen Gwynn, 86–9, 92, 94; encourages AG in her dispute with her tenant grass farmers, 89; advises her that 'Life in its last analysis is a war of forces & it is right that it should be, for it makes us strong & I think that is the root of happiness – certainly not to fear is', and that 'a day comes in everything almost when one has to fight, & wisdom is not in avoiding it but in keeping no bitterness when the day is over', 89; delighted with Carr's 'extravagant joyous' production of Jonson's comedy *The Silent Woman*, 90; writes 'a new passage of some length' for *On Baile's Strand*, and revises long opening speech in *The King's Threshold*, 90; takes Julia Worthington to a production of Wilde's *Salome* but dislikes the play, 90, 103–4; sends Hone to Bullen for tips on setting up Maunsel & Co., 91, 94; advises Roberts not to

**Yeats, William Butler**: (*cont.*)

hold out for a partnership, 91–3, 94; reminds him that 'Every bad Irish book published injures the whole trade in Irish books'. 92; generally a mistake to try and tie a man 'down too closely for it makes him suspicious' and 'all life is a gamble, we bet on "black or white"', 93; congratulates AG on the way she has resolved the dispute with her tenants, 93; dissuades Philip Carr from producing AE's *Deirdre*, 94; defeats FF in a dispute over the design of her forthcoming production of *The Shadowy Waters*, 94–5; contemplating technical innovations in the staging of the play, 95, 102–3; finishing revision of opening speech in *The King's Threshold*, which has 'lost nothing & gained much', 95; Abbey's London tour postponed until November, 96, 102; feels rather lost without AG, 96; annoyed at AE's continuing interference in Maunsel & Co. and his support for Roberts's demands to be a partner, 97–100; sees Shaw's *Man and Superman* and thinks 'the construction bad' but likes the last act, 99; wants to get his three recent verse plays as perfect as revision after performance can make them, 103; has re-written every word of early part of *On Baile's Strand*, 103; has made *The King's Threshold* 'much more animated', 103; stays with Bullen in Stratford where they plan *Poems, 1899–1905* and decide to postpone the *Collected Works*, 103; has a lot of work to revise, 103; Quinn sends him a copy of Wilde's *The Rise of Historical Criticism*, 103; thinks Wilde's 'wonderful sense of the stage' deserted him in tragedy and that *Salome* 'has every sort of fault, the speeches don't work to any climax, and there are moments when the principle people have nothing to do but look like fools', 103; has 'just completed the revision of "Shadowy Waters" but . . . a few lines more to do on "The King's Threshold"', 106; *Poems, 1899–1905* 'should sell very well' as it is 'the first big mass of verse that I have published for years', 106; Marie Corelli presses her gondola on WBY, 107; reading the forty volumes of Balzac which he has bought from Bullen, 107; sees W. S. Gilbert's *The Palace of Truth* and thinks it bad, 107–8; advises Synge on translation rights, 108, 130–1; Eric Maclagan gives him the 'beautiful' Vale Press edition of Sir Thomas Browne, 110; sees 'wonderful' production of Molière's *Les Précieuses ridicules*, 111; Colum's *The Land* at Abbey 'wonderfully simple & natural & wonderfully played', 112, 126; Abbey has 'done 12 plays since Xmas – six of them being new &

all I think good & all staged in a more or less new way', 112; plans Abbey tours to small Irish towns, 112; sits up talking to W. G. Fay, who wants FF to play Emer in Blunt's *Fand*, 112; attends General Meeting of INTS which agrees to pay some of the actors, 112, 114; has begun a sexual relationship with FF, 112, 114; pleased with production of *The Hour-Glass* in which Maire Walker is 'a delight' and Frank Fay 'very varied and powerful', 114–15; consults Bullen about retrieving rights to *The Wind Among the Reeds* from Elkin Mathews, 115–16; FF dines with him and he makes corrections to *The Shadowy Waters*, which is in rehearsal, 117–18; disgusted with Robert Farquharson's playing of Forgael, 118, 124, 126, 131, 145, 150–1, 400, 425; speaks at a dinner of the women's Lyceum Club, and congratulates it on 'the destruction of the Home which I described as the source of all bad art', 118; AEFH guarantees £400 for Abbey actors' salaries, 119, 120, 277, 285; signs Agreement with Macmillan (NY) for *The Poetical Works of William B. Yeats*, 121–3; negotiates with Patrick D. Kenny about joining a syndicate to back a new Irish weekly, 124, 125, 128; sees Pinero's *The Cabinet Minister* with FF, 124; thanks Quinn for contributing to his birthday present, the Kelmscott Press's edition of *The Works of Geoffrey Chaucer*, 'the most beautiful of all printed books', just as he is 'setting out to read Chaucer', 125, 129; an illustration to the Kelmscott *Chaucer* has suggested an important change in the setting of his *Deirdre*, 125–6; performance of *The Shadowy Waters* will allow WBY the 'chance of making a lot of changes and testing them', 126; criticizes the characterization of the heroine in *The Land*, which Colum is trying to improve, 126; Irish 'not yet sufficiently deep in their new artistic education to understand what temperament is', 127; criticizes AG's *Kincora* as 'a wonderful achievement of dramatic logic' but not the product of an individual mind, 127; hopes that after her divorce MG will organize a women's 'radical movement for personal freedom', 127; thinks the 'woman's question is in a worse state in Dublin than in any place I know', 127–8; prophesies that 'we are going to have a very active time in the next year or two in Dublin', 128; believes that 'all most powerful convictions have their roots in personal suffering', 128; turning a lecture by JBY into an article, 128; some years ago WBY 'had the need of Spenser and read him right through', but now 'it is Chaucer, a much wiser and saner man', 130; negotiates with Frank Washburn-Freund about German translations of his and other Abbey plays, 130; sees FF's production of *The Shadowy Waters*, 131; negotiates through Watt to retrieve the rights to *The Shadowy Waters* from Hodder & Stoughton, 132, 137, 138, 139, 141, 146, 148; at Coole working on *The Shadowy Waters*, 'changing it greatly, getting rid of needless symbols, making the people answer each other, and making the ground work simple and intelligible', 133; *To-Day* compares him to Ibsen and Maeterlinck as a great dramatist, 133; 'changing *The Shadowy Waters* on almost every page', 134–5, 139; describes his daily routine at Coole, including angling and 'sandow exercises', 135; dines with Edward Martyn at Tillyra Castle, 136; discusses poems suitable for the psaltery with FF, 136, 151–2; refuses to write an essay on Shakespeare for Bullen because he will be 'reading nothing but Chaucer for some time', 139–40, 161–2; turns down a play on Robert Emmet submitted to the Abbey by Stephen Gwynn, 141–3; asks Symons for his essay 'The Ideas of Richard Wagner', and send him Agnes Tobin's translations from Petrarch, 144; feels 'a sort of pathetic interest in books of good poetry, as if they were waifs in the street with tragic stories', and 'wishes to send them to some benevolent home where they will get a little encouragement', 144; believes he is 'making a really strong play out of the Shadowy Waters and am certainly losing no poetry', 145, 148; consults Watt, Bullen, Brett, and the Society of Authors about retrieving the rights to *The Wind Among the Reeds* from John Lane and Elkin Mathews, 146, 147, 167, 174, 185, 207–8, 216, 227, 338–9, 353, 369, 374, 410–11, 413, 439, 462; 'my imagination is getting so deep in Chaucer that I cannot get it down into any other well for the present', 147; encourages AE to consult W. G. Fay about altering the INTS rules to enable certain actors to be paid, 148–9, 153–9; catches fish for Catholic guests' Friday dinner at Coole, 149–50; attempts to get Henry Paget's design for *The Shadowy Waters*, 151, 160, 191; planning a 'large scene dock' for the Abbey, 151; suggests FF and he should trace the route of Chaucer's Canterbury pilgrims on bicycles, 151; thinks the 'danger of the Psaltery is monotony', 152; reading Chaucer has convinced him of need for 'vivid irresistible phrase in all verse to be spoken aloud – it rests the imagination as upon the green ground', 152, 166; necessary to put the INTS on a business footing if they are to

mount country tours, 155; agrees with AE's general plan for reform of the INTS, 157–8; takes an unsympathetic attitude to his sisters' financial and personal difficulties in Dun Emer Industries, 159–60; dreams of FF, 160; Lady Cromartie's and Lady Margaret Sackville's visit to Coole leads to a busier social life, 160–1; like AG, thinks Boyle's *The Eloquent Dempsy* 'impossibly vulgar in its present form' and suggests that Colum help revise it, 162–3, 164–5; urges AE to complete his revision of the INTS rules as soon as possible, 167; writes in praise of a play by W. P. Ryan, 168; agrees with AE's latest revisions to the INTS rules, apart from size of the reading committee and the status of Norman and Helen Laird, 169–71, 181–2, 184, 185; wants 'a strong solid centre' to the Society, 170; calls a General Meeting of the INTS, 171; asks W. G. Fay to help AE with new INTS rules, 172; informs MG that Martyn is now troubled by the religious aspect of her divorce petition, 172; urges Synge to attend forthcoming INTS General Meeting as the 'whole future of the Society in all probability' depends upon its decisions, and suggests a prior meeting at Coole, 173; asks Synge for the MS of *The Tinker's Wedding* for possible production and publication in *Samhain*, 173; Symons's essay 'The Ideas of Richard Wagner' touches his 'own theories at several points, and enlarges them at one or two', 175; 'not more than about thirty lines' of old version of *The Shadowy Waters* remain, 175, 179; revisions indicate 'how much I have learned by watching rehearsals in Dublin', 175; *The Shadowy Waters, On Baile's Strand*, and *The King's Threshold* have 'all been rewritten after rehearsal or actual performance, and the King's Threshold has been changed and rehearsed and then changed again and so on, till I have got it as I believe a perfectly articulate stage play', 175–6; has 'learned a great deal about poetry generally' in revising his plays and is now convinced 'that all the finest poetry comes logically out of the fundamental action', 176; the modern error 'is to believe that some things are inherently poetical, and to try and pull them on to the scene at every moment', 176; recommends Dudley Digges to Arnold Daly for his New York production of *John Bull's Other Island*, 176; finds Fiona Macleod's articles on 'The Irish Muse' 'curiously bad', 177; delighted by the success of Synge's plays in Germany and Bohemia, 178, 203; although 'not out of the wood yet', thinks 'we have seen the end of the democracy' in the Abbey

in Baile's Strand', 221; WBY gives his reasons
for and against establishing a Gaelic Company
at the Abbey, 222–6; 'if we are ever to establish
a Gaelic Company we must do it during the
next year possibly during the next few months',
222; 'In England the Philistines attack the
morals of a writer in Ireland he attacks his
nationality', 223; asks Rhys for tickets for his
musical play *Gwenevere*, 229; a revised *Where
There Is Nothing* 'is beginning to shape itself in
my mind', 231; alerts Gosse to the 1905 Abbey
performances in London, 232; travels to
Oxford with AG and Synge for Abbey
performances there, 233; advises A. B. Walkley
to attend afternoon performance of the INTS
in order to see *The Well of the Saints*, 233; sends
Mrs Pat Campbell two tickets for the 1905
Abbey performances in London, 234; writes to
the Pond Bureau via Quinn suggesting a joint
US lecture tour with FF, 237–9, 395; gives
Quinn an account of Abbey's recent British
tour, 239–40; thinks AG's *The White Cockade*
'a fine play', but not yet in its final shape
because it 'takes a long time making out a new
dramatic form', 240; 'for some reason or other,
every current dramatic form looks curiously
foreign when you try to put Irish material into
it', 240; describes corrections to *On Baile's
Strand* and believes he is 'getting it right this
time', 240; 'a couple more years' before the
Abbey playwrights 'get a mastery of our
different forms, or at any rate get a mastery of
them for any kind of ambitious purpose', 241;
discusses the removal of Tom Kettle from the
editorship of the *Nationist* and Kenny's
removal from the editorship of the *Irish Peasant*
through clerical influence, 241–2, 258; reminds
seceding INTS actors that they can claim a
share in the new Society, 248, 251–2; lectures
in Cork on 'What is a National Theatre?', 249,
253–4, 295, 299; asks Colum how far he has got
with *The Fiddler's House*, 249; explains how the
Abbey's London programme was arranged,
249–51; describes to AG the way shares are to
be apportioned in the NTS in return for
costumes, 255; sees Maire Walker who is
equivocating about joining the NTS, 255–6;
thanks Maire Walker for signing her NTS
contract and explains her duties as wardrobe
mistress, 257; attacked by Sarah Purser for
disparaging some of the stain-glass designs of
her firm, *An Túr Gloine*, 259–60, 262–3;
threatens to prosecute Maire Walker, who has
reneged on her NTS contract, 260, 261, 263–5,
270–80; invites the actress Vera Esposito to join
the NTS, 261; wires W. G. Fay to engage

Arthur Sinclair at once, 261; confident that
prosecution of Maire Walker will 'stop the
vagueness & drifting', 264; sends 'Never Give
All the Heart' to *McClure's Magazine*, 265;
declines to sign letter deploring war-mongering
between Britain and Germany, 268; sends a
'blood curdling letter' to his sisters about Maire
Walker, 271; 'good friends with Sarah Pursur
again. . . . It has been a drawn battle, I think',
272; considers Masefield's *The Campden
Wonder* 'a magnificent play', 275; had 'a kind of
illumination' on receiving Maire Walker's
letter breaking her contract, 276; 'one has at
times to act on something which is the reverse
of scient[if]ic reasoning or scholourly reasoning
& this is why sedentary reasoning is
dangerous', 276; instead 'of merely deducing
ones actions from existing circumstances, one
has to act so as to create new circumstances by
which one is to be judged. It is all faith', 276;
'pretty confident' that Maire and Frank Walker
will return to Abbey 'in the course of a few
months', 277; has 'written the lyrical bit' for *On
Baile's Strand*, 278, 282; wants to sue Maire
Walker to show Dublin people that the
'fundamental fact of all business is – *contract*',
278; assures Colum that the NTS 'is
flourishing' and 'is now a business, run on the
ordinary lines of a business', 279; 'No
compromise is possible' with those who have
seceded from the INTS and a 're-united
society would be "five wild-cats struggling in a
bag"', 280; decides not to proceed against
Maire Walker, 280–2, 285–6; threatened to sue
Maire Walker because after 'a long period of
wasted time & worry I thought I could change
things by a sudden action', 282; he and the
other Abbey dramatists 'have all signed a paper
granting the Irish rights of our plays to the
National Theatre Company', 284; believes that
'a rival theatre would only show the power of
ours . . . all we have to do is to hold firm', 285;
confesses that he has 'no doubt I was wrong' in
the controversy over Maire Walker and that
'this theatre row has been a good deal of a
strain', 286; advises Masefield on the
construction of *The Campden Wonder*, 288–9;
candid exchange of views with AE, 290–8;
WBY desires 'the love of very few people, my
equals or my superiors', and the 'love of the
rest would be a bond & an intrusion', 290; feels
he is 'a fairly strong & capable man & that I
have gathered the strong & capable about me, &
all who love work better than idle talk will
support me', 290; knows he 'will never have the
support of the clubs, but I will beat the clubs',

**Yeats, William Butler:** (*cont.*)
290; wishes he 'could keep from calling people
"poultry" but I cant', 291; with AEFH's extra
£200 a year Abbey can go on 'whether we have
audiences or not', 291; finds it 'often very hard
to know why one does a thing. . . . I sometimes
find that one acts because one sees clearly a
number of detached pieces, which one never
sees again. Looking back afterwards one either
doubts or affirms the act, but not from reason
in either case', 292; AE informs him that he has
'few or no friends in Dublin', 293; that
*Samhain* (1905) did him 'endless harm', 295;
AE has 'felt for some years' that their 'old
friendship . . . was worn very thin', 297; WBY
prophesies that the Theatre of Ireland 'will
either collapse after a performance or two or
they will become more and more crudely
propagandist', 300; sympathizes with Mrs
Sharp on the death of William Sharp, 302–3; in
facing legal challenge from the seceders, 'better
a clean stroke & have done with it', 305–6;
lectures successfully in Edinburgh and
Aberdeen, 308, 316; discovery that the terms of
the patent greatly strengthen the seceders'
hand forces Abbey Directors to reconsider
their legal and negotiating position, 308–10,
311–14, 315–16, 319–21, 329–33, 344, 348,
351–2; stays with Lady Cromartie, 310; not
being able to fight the seceders as he would like,
WBY now proposes 'a scheme so generous that
it will . . . help us with the public as well
as . . . bring back everybody we want', 311–12;
'there is in the long run no worthy way to be
popular except good plays', 314; ready to
consider anything the seceders suggest
'provided it does not weaken discipline or delay
the work in any way', 314; 'in long run popular
support is not got by concession to it, but by
strength – by the quiet doing of ones work. Of
the demigogue Ireland has enough', 314–15;
has 'done well' at *On Baile's Strand* and has 'at
last got a grip on the thing', 320; has 'always
felt that Byron was one of the great problems,
the great mysteries – a first-rate man, who was
somehow not first-rate when he wrote', 322;
signs appeal for presentation to Hugh Lane,
323–4; delighted with *Astarte*, Lord Lovelace's
'very vivid powerful book' about Byron and
Augusta Leigh, 327, 362; tells FF what 'a
pleasure it is to be fond of somebody to whom I
can talk – as a rule any sort of affection
annihilates conversation, strikes one with a
silence', 328; negotiates through AG with the
seceders, offering hire of the Abbey and a fair
proportion of the old INTS funds in return for

their formal resignation, 329–32; sends Mrs Pat
Campbell copy of the new *Shadowy Waters*,
334; his and FF's reputations are 'too esoteric
for the general public', 334; in lecturing finds
he can 'move people by power not merely . . . by
"charm" or "speaking beautifully"', and feels
'this change in all my work and that it has
brought a change into the personal relations of
life – even things seemingly beyond control
answer strangely to what is within', 334–5; he
'once cared only for images about whose necks
I could cast various "chains of office" as it
were . . . so many aldermen of the ideal, whom I
wished to master the city of the soul', but now
does 'not want images at all, or chains of office
being contented with the unruly soul', 335; has
'begun eastern meditations . . . with the object
of trying to lay hands upon some dynamic and
substantialising force as distinguished from the
eastern quiescent and supersentualizing state of
the soul – a movement downwards upon life
not upwards out of life', 336; believes that if
Lane gets a Dublin gallery, he 'will make it one
of the great galleries', 337; in Coole finishing
*On Baile's Strand*, which has given him 'the
devil of a time', 338; *Poems* (1904) 'now
bringing me about thirty-five pounds a year',
339; does 'magnificent work' at Coole: 'a sketch
of a strange little play about the capture of a
blind Unicorn', and a choral ode for *On Baile's
Strand*, 341–2; asks FF to teach him how to
meditate since he gets 'partly hypnotized at
once', and that 'makes it very difficult to get the
mood of fiery understanding which must
represent the spirit which is . . . "that which
moves itself"',' 342–3; appoints Frank Fay
teacher of voice-production and verse-speaking
for an extra 10/- a week, 345; the possibility
that AEFH may impose a too rigorous embargo
on 'propagandst' plays is 'the most serious
matter we have yet had to deal with', 347; stays
with Lord Howard de Walden, 347; has 'been
dining out a great deal', 347; lectures with FF
in Leeds and Liverpool, 349, 351; stays with
Emily Ladenburg, 351, 375–6; sees production
of Murray's version of *Electra*, 352–3; resigns
his membership of the Stage Society, 354;
recommends a would-be poet 'to read as much
good poetry as possible, and the older the
better', particularly Elizabethan and Jacobean
lyrics, 355; comments on Joseph Campbell's
*Rushlight*, 356–8; young Irish poets 'seldom get
deeper than rhetoric', 357; thinks an Irish
writer of thirty 'is at the most where an
Englishman gets to at 20', because 'all the
traditions in Ireland are undeveloped, and we

have to find out everything for ourselves', 357; commissions Sargent to make a drawing of Lane on behalf of the Dublin Picture Committee, 358–9, 363; AG sends him money during a financial crisis, 360; is 'really working hard just now' and has 'rewritten a lot of my Spenser & sent off a lot of proofs', 360; 'Science has robbed us of our courage', 362; the false morality of Pinero's *His House in Order* puts him into an extended state of depression, 364–5; doing a round of theatres: sees Murray's version of *Hippolytus*, Phillips's *Nero*, and Sturge Moore's *Aphrodite against Artemis*, 365; lunches at T. P. O'Connor's and meets Prince Christian, 366; thinks that 'the habit of construction is too deep' in him to adopt AG's suggestion that he should redraft *The Speckled Bird* as series of philosophical reflections, but may turn it into 'a kind of spiritual autobiography', 366; 'very anxious to get to Dierdre' as he wants 'to put into practice the technical knowledge I have got lately', 367; a little disappointed with FF's performance as the nurse in *Hippolytus*, 367; suspects that the ILS 'is going to collapse or join with the Gaelic League', 367; has dictated the new version of the introduction to his selection from Spenser, 368; winding up *On Baile's Strand*, 370; discusses theatre business with AG, 370–1; detects in the failure of Sturge Moore's *Aphrodite against Artemis* 'all the mistakes I had ever committed myself', 371–2; writes 'eulogistic letter' about Masefield's *The Tragedy of Nan* to Granville-Barker, 372; sees Anstey's *The Man from Blankley's* with AEFH, 372; visits Cockerel and hears him abuse Tonks and the Slade School of Art, 372–3; describes forthcoming Abbey productions to Quinn, 373–4; *The Poetical Works of William B. Yeats* delayed by dispute with John Lane, 374; Hyde praises WBY in an interview in the *San Francisco Bulletin*, 375; hears that W. G. Fay is going to marry Brigit O'Dempsey, 376; discusses theatre business with AG, 376–9; his opposition to a revival of *The Well of the Saints* upsets Synge, 378; reading Shaw's plays with a view to staging them at the Abbey, 378–9; sends Bullen the final proofs for *Poems, 1899–1905*, but substitutes a part of *On Baile's Strand*, 380–1; Watt sends 'Literature and the Living Voice' to the *Contemporary Review*, 384, 401; discusses German productions of his and Synge's plays with Freund, 385; thinks current Abbey productions 'have shown our people at their very best', and that of *On Baile's Strand* 'is the first thoroughly efficient performance of a

verse play of mine that there has been', 387; Abbey audiences disappointing, 388; Tree's business manager asks if he can offer Sara Allgood an engagement, 388; WBY rewriting *Deirdre*, 389; makes up copy for *The Poetical Works of William B. Yeats* from proofs of *Poems, 1899–1905*, 390–1; thinks Hyde 'in a certain sense the race tradition embodied', 391; WBY 'becoming more and more certain that new form, new technical mastery, comes more from the shock of new subject matter than deliberate effort', 392; believes that with sufficient audiences 'to keep our players and our playrights busy with the expression of Irish life, we shall make a great movement in the end', 392; both Fays 'have developed a power they never had before of building up a part ... of making a character change with events, and we have a really fine actress in Miss Allgood', 392; Alfred Wareing has arranged a British tour for the NTS in the summer of 1906, 392; fine works of art 'all come home to roost in the end' so that Synge may have to 'find his way home through England and America', 393; thanks to AG's encouragement *Deirdre* 'has at last come right' but he has had to alter a great deal, 393; 'pretty confident' that some Abbey plays would succeed in USA, 394; considers AG's *The White Cockade* 'too loosely constructed for a normal audience', 395; 'have at last got things into our own hands here with the theatre' by making a bargain with the seceders whereby they all resigned 'in return for fifty pounds ... and costumes, to start a theatre of their own', 396; cannot send a poem to *McClure's Magazine* because he has 'been buried in plays this last year', 397; the existence of the Abbey provides him with 'an opportunity that no dramatic poet has had for generations of mastering the technique of dramatic verse' and he will 'have time for lyrics later on', 397; deep in *Deirdre* 'which I think my best poem as well as my best play', 398; has 'done apparently very little work for some two or three years, but really a great deal, for I have been rewriting old work stuff to make it fitting for the stage. It is just the kind of work one gets no credit from but learns most from', 398; Abbey Company 'are setting out on the first regular professional engagement at the ordinary theatres' but will 'take nothing but peasant work', 399; criticizes the 'empty, sluggish & pretentious' dialogue of Wilde's *Salome*, and claims it 'has nothing of drama of any kind', 399; describes the structure of a good play, 399; 'No good actor will ever succeed in

**Yeats, William Butler**: (*cont.*)
inorganic work', 399; thinks the third act of
*Man and Superman* 'has no real dramatic life',
400; WBY's 'Irish work gets every day more
exacting', 400; a great deal depends on Abbey
tours to Irish country places, 401; tells Synge
that the 'country towns in Ireland are mainly
animal, but can sometimes be intoxicated into a
state of humanity by some religious or political
propagandist body, the only kind of intellectual
excitement they have got used to', 403;
discusses Irish tours with Synge, 403–4; writes
to AEFH about a proposed Abbey tour to
Manchester and Edinburgh, 404–6; a mistake
to tour a comedy programme indefinitely:
'Comedy must make the ship sail, but the ship
must have other things in the cargo', 405;
discusses the Countess of Cromartie's
horoscope with George Pollexfen and describes
her recollections of a previous life, 406–8;
reminds his sisters not to miss the Annual
General Meeting of the INTS, and provides
addresses of wealthy acquaintances to invite to
the London exhibition of Dun Emer work, 409;
instructs the printers to add dedications to
Frank Fay and FF to *Poems, 1899–1905*,
411–12; busy time in Edinburgh overseeing the
now strained Abbey tour, and dispatched by
AEHF to Glasgow, where W.G. Fay has been
rude to her, and where there has been a row
between Fay and the business manager,
414–17; spends nearly all his time in
Edinburgh absorbed in Phoebe Traquair's art
work, 417–18; has given one good and one bad
lecture in Edinburgh, 418, 418; criticizes the
concept and editing of the Irish periodical
*Shanachie*, 419–20; 'what Dublin wants is some
man who knows his own mind and has an
intolerable tongue and a delight in enemies',
420; helps to plan the Abbey's visit to
Longford, 421, 422, 423; finds that the notes
that are to become *Discoveries* have 'more
coherence than I had hoped for', 421; begins
each day 'with a few pages of Sir Thomas
Brown to keep me in key', 421; Bullen asks to
publish *Discoveries* in the *Gentleman's
Magazine* but only offers £2 per thousand
words, 423; WBY realizes that AEFH more
upset by her quarrel with Fay in Glasgow than
he supposed, and now refuses to do theatre
business through him, 423–4; she proposes to
hand over entire control of the Abbey to the
Directors, 424; AEFH urges the Directors to
hire a business manager, 425; having finished
his proof-corrections, he is now 'able to begin
work the moment I come down in the morning

and to work for three or four hours without
difficulty.... I am even paying calls and taking
exercise', 425; sends Fred Ryan £50 for the
Theatre of Ireland, 427; AEFH renews her
attack on W. G. Fay, 427–30; post mortem on
the long British tour suggests that 'the
discipline of the company has got dangerously
loose' and is on its way to scandal, 431; WBY
'perfectly convinced that we must take
advantage of the present upset to get the
discipline permanently right', 431; eager to
restore AEFH's relationship with the Abbey
for fear she may abandon them altogether, and
the first step is the appointment of a business
manager, 431–2; 'rather disappointed about
Synge', who 'is afraid of Fay and does not take
trouble', 433; Swinburne makes 'a wild attack'
on WBY's Blake scholarship in the *Athenaeum*,
434–5, 449–50; spends 'a most delightful time'
at Katharine Horner's with Cockerell, Lady
Cromartie, Lady Margaret Sackville and
Raymond Asquith, to whom he reads Agnes
Tobin's translations of Petrarch, 435; makes
'little corrections' to Tobin's sonnets, and
informs her that she is 'the greatest poet of
America since Whitman', 436; draws up a
catalogue of the Company's bad behaviour
during the recent British tour and suggests that
the time is now 'ripe for a further
strengthening of our hold on the company' by
taking entire administrative responsibility for
the Abbey, 437–8; going to Longford with the
Company, 440, 446; worried about Synge's
relationship with Maire O'Neill, 441; sees W.
G. Fay, who 'is very humble & himself asked
for a business man, who will take over all
accounts & wants to have nothing but his
artistic work to do', 442; thinks Synge's
intention to marry Maire O'Neill 'lunacy' but it
would avoid scandal, 442; agrees to condense
his selections from Spenser, 444; discusses
changes in the management structure at the
Abbey, believing 'that the existence of the
theatre is at stake', 445; is 'quite aware of the
danger to the theatre from the tension between
myself & Fay', and will not let this affect the
theatre even if he has to 'fade out of the
practical side of the work & leave it to Synge',
445; defends W. G. Fay to AEFH, 446–7;
praises Letitia Darragh's acting over that of the
Abbey actresses, 448, 450, 457–8, 468–73, 612;
settled in Coole for the summer and questions
Bullen about the sequence of copy for a
possible *Collected Edition*, 448; eager to make
new versions of *Where There Is Nothing* and
*The Countess Cathleen*, 448; Mrs Pat Campbell

**Yeats, William Butler:** (*cont.*)
threatens to resign as Abbey Director over
quarrel with AEFH about the duties
apportioned to Fay and Payne, 668–9; declines
AEFH's suggestion that he leave the Abbey
and join her in an English theatrical venture,
671; although he seeks 'a universal audience',
for his plays, 'there is always an immediate
audience also', 671; would fail to find an
immediate theatrical audience in England
'through lack of understanding on my part
perhaps through lack of sympathy', 671;
understands his 'own race & in all my work,
lyric or dramatic I have thought of it', 671; will
'write for my own people – whether in love or
hate of them matters little – probably I shall not
know which it is', 671; 'a slight breakdown
from overwork', 673; Abbey receipts less than
thought, 673–6; declines to join in protest
against unfair criticism of Shaw, 677–8; WBY
attacked by Alfred Noyes, 678; dismisses
Henderson as business manager of the Abbey,
and reallocates his work between Ernest
Vaughan and W. G. Fay, 678–9, 681; asks for
complete statement of Abbey accounts, 679,
687–8, 699; reluctantly agrees to putting W. G.
Fay back into Abbey management, 680, 681;
Fay's temper and evasions 'exasperate' WBY,
680; at FF's instigation WBY reluctantly asks
AEFH to finance Mrs Pat Campbell's
production of his *Deirdre*, 680–11, 690; meets
Fay and Payne to sort out Abbey accounts and
plan a British tour in Advent, 681; will play a
less active part in the practical running of the
Abbey, 681; feels that he has 'lost myself – my
centre as it were, has shifted from its natural
interests, and that it will take me a long time
finding myself again', 681; will not resign from
the Abbey altogether as his presence is a
protection against AEFH's capriciousness, 681;
dines with Eveleen Myers and meets Revd
Campbell, 682; at Grierson's suggestion has
read Edmund Gardner's books on Italian
culture, 683; fails to meet Henry O'Brien again,
684; there will never be a 'serious literature in
Ireland' if people do not give respect to talented
writers, 684–5; wants nothing to do with
translation rights, 685; intends to leave up
open for popular editions of his books after *CW*
finished, 686; agrees to a two-year extension in
Elkin Mathews' rights in *The Wind Among the
Reeds* in return for his taking 50 sets of *CW*,
685–6; insists that Watt should be consulted in
any negotiations with Elkin Mathews, 686; has
started to rewrite *Where There Is Nothing* with
AG's help, 686; discusses Henderson's terms of

employment, 687; unwell and close to nervous
breakdown, 688; begins to get proofs of *CW*,
689–90; not arranging contents of *CW* on a
chronological system, nor on the system
adopted in the American *Poetical Works of
William B. Yeats*, 689; quarrels with Bullen
over arrangements for printing *CW*, 690–11;
sends Bullen a list of poems in the order in
which they are to be printed, 691; demands
colour illustrations in the *CW* volume of
dramatic criticism, 691; discovers he and
Bullen have been at cross-purposes, Bullen was
'too hasty' and WBY 'too vague', 692;
discovers he has far less time to prepare text for
*CW* as Bullen will take three weeks to print
each volume, not six to eight weeks, 692–3; asks
Bullen for as much extra time as possible, 693;
is making 'a powerful play' of *Where There Is
Nothing*, 693; Bullen agrees to find more time
for WBY's preparation of the *CW* texts, 694;
has rewritten poem 'Maid Quiet', 694; working
on revised notes for *The Wind Among the Reeds*,
694, 696; sends Bullen a draft proposal for four
volumes of *CW*, 695; disagrees with Bullen's
arrangement for a volume of plays, 695; is
'working very hard, and mean to work hard',
696; sends AEFH good wishes for her
theatrical venture in Manchester, 696–7; asks
Connell to revise *The Piper*, 697; declines to
contribute to an anthology because too busy
with *CW*, 698; rejects a play by H. A. Hinkson,
699; nobody 'can write well in dialect unless he
has been brought up talking it . . . or has made a
most exaustive & even scientific study of it like
Synge & Lady Gregory', 699; most plays sent
to the Abbey copy 'the purely literary dialect of
the Irish Novelists', 699; Directors advise
would-be Abbey dramatists to avoid using love
as a theme, 699–10; very few people 'can see
life with their own eyes, if they choose some
thing in life that many others have described',
700; sends corrected proof sheets for *CW* 1,
700; corrects poem 'The Hollow Wood', 700;
suggests that *CW* should include two volumes
of verse plays, 701; sends FF her music for the
plays to keep for him, 701–702; discusses
AEFH's Manchester theatre with FF, 702–3;
reading North's *Plutarch*, 703; finishes *The
Golden Helmet*, but 'still stuck' in *Where There
Is Nothing*, 704; asks Eglinton to reserve his
translation of *Oedipus* for the Abbey and not
give it to AEFH, 704–5; counters Payne's
allegation that the Abbey is 'only a peasant
theatre', 704–5; congratulates JBY on article
about the artist Watts, 705; discusses with
Synge mechanisms for dealing with Abbey

**Yeats, William Butler:** (*cont.*)
criticizes the poems of T. E. Mayne, 957–9;
Irish poets must combine an English music
with a wilder, more primitive substance, 959;
agreement for *The Shadowy Waters*, 961–3;
agreement with Unwin for *Poems* (1901),
964–6; arranges meeting to discuss future of
Irish dramatic movement, 966–7; discusses
rites for the Celtic Mystical Order with
William Sharp, 967–9, 974–8, 980, 993–5,
1000, 1006; declines co-option onto the
committee of the ILS, 970; Watt arranges
publication of essay 'Magic' in the *Monthly
Review*, 971–2; urges Oliver Sheppard to apply
for post at the Metropolitan School of Art,
972–4; cultural revival has 'changed the face' of
Dublin, 974; believes 'there is a great contest
going to come on here in a few years between
the Church & the mystics', 977; arranges
publication of *Beltaine*, 978–9; Watt arranges
publication of essay 'What is "Popular
Poetry"?' in the *Cornhill Magazine*, 981, 984–5;
comments on Fiona Macleod's work, 982–4;
WBY has an advantage 'in having a very fierce
nation to write for', so has 'to make everything
very hard & clear', 983; Watt arranges
publication of essay 'The Happiest of the
Poets' in the *Fortnightly Review*, 985–6;
arranges for publication of the revised *Celtic
Twilight*, 986; agreement with Bullen for the
revised *Celtic Twilight*, 987–90; tries to place
AG's *Cuchulain of Muirthemne* for review,
990–1; sees Felkin to discuss GD matters,
992–3; Watt tries to arrange publication of
poems 'The Old Age of Queen Maeve' and
'Adam's Curse' in the *Monthly Review*, 995–6,
1001; Watt arranges publication of poem 'The
Old Men Admiring Themselves in the Water'
in the *Pall Mall Magazine*, 996–7; WBY
advises a midshipman on his career, 997–8,
1011–12; INTS doing well, 1000; arrangement
with Bullen for publication of *Where There Is
Nothing*, 1003–6; 'almost wholly at plays',
1006; goes with INTS to Loughrea, 1007;
sends F. J. Fay a new passage for *The Shadowy
Waters*, 1008–10; agreement with Bullen for
publication of *Ideas of Good and Evil*, 1012–14;
sends Watt the agreement with Dun Emer
Press for *In the Seven Woods*, 1014–17; arranges
American lectures, 1018–19; all going well with
plays in Dublin, 1020; sends contribution to
*Irish Literature*, 1021; agreements with Bullen
for publication of *The Hour-Glass* and *The
King's Threshold*, 1022–4; joins the Stage
Society, 1024–5; Watt tries to arrange
publication of essay 'America and the Arts' in

the *Fortnightly Review*, 1025–6; WBY working
on his edition of selections from Eglinton,
1026; praises the magazine *Dana*, 1027; over-
assessed by income tax commissioners, 1027;
attacks Royal Irish Academy for its obstructive
attitude towards Hugh Lane's Loan
Exhibition, 1028–9; remonstrates with Griffith
over insinuations against Lane in *United
Irishman*, 1029–30; experimenting with
lighting at the Abbey, 1031; Gogarty asks to
translate *Oedipus* for Abbey, 1031; suggests an
Art Committee to support Lane, 1031

*Drama and Dramatists*: delights in a performance
of Francis Beaumont's *The Knight of the
Burning Pestle*, 3; asks Pixie Smith to design for
scenery for *The Well of the Saints*, 9; procures
MS of *The Well of the Saints* for Quinn to
copyright in USA, 16, 17; invites Gilbert
Murray to translate Sophocles' *Oedipus* for
Abbey, 22–3; 'trying to persuade
Ireland . . . that she is very liberal, abhors
censors delights in the freedom of the arts, is
prepared for anything', 22–3; quotes English
censor's criticism of *On Baile's Strand*, 24;
believes they are 'going to make a great
dramatic school' in Ireland, and that *The Well
of the Saints* is 'a great play', 24; defends
Synge's *The Shadow of the Glen* against attacks
in *United Irishman*, 25–7, 31–3, 34; in Dublin
for rehearsals of *The Well of the Saints*, 27;
occupied with Abbey's 'first attempt to do
decorative open air scenes' of *The Well of the
Saints* with W. G. Fay, AG and Pixie Smith,
feeling that 'the remoteness, the abstractedness
of the scenic arrangements, will make the play
safer', 27; has written preface for the play, 28;
plays beginning to come in to Abbey and 'we
will have a whole dramatic literature before
long', 28; Colum reads him simplified scenario
of *The Land*, with dialogue 'full of country
idiom and character', 28; starting an Abbey
Theatre series of plays, 28; re-writing *On
Baile's Strand* and intends to re-write *The
King's Threshold*, 30; shames *United Irishman*
into publishing Synge's letter on sources of *The
Well of the Saints*, 34; production of *The Well of
the Saints* a success despite thin audiences and
reduced returns, as it was 'the finest piece of
acting as a whole the company has done', 37;
contrasts Colum's 'unbeautiful' use of dialect
with that of AG and Synge, 40; Frank Fay
'delighted' with revised *On Baile's Strand*, 43;
making 'one or two very slight changes' to *On
Baile's Strand* at W. G. Fay's suggestion, 44;

**Yeats, William Butler:** (*cont.*)

'a wonderful achievement of dramatic logic'
but not the product of an individual mind,
127; negotiating with Frank Washburn-
Freund about German translations of his
and other Abbey dramatists' plays, 130; sees
FF's production of *The Shadowy Waters*,
131; negotiates through Watt to retrieve the
rights to *The Shadowy Waters* from Hodder
& Stoughton, 132, 137, 138, 139, 141, 146,
148; working on *The Shadowy Waters*,
'changing it greatly, getting rid of needless
symbols, making the people answer each
other, and making the ground work simple
and intelligible', 133; *To-Day* compares him
to Ibsen and Maeterlinck as a great
dramatist, 133; 'changing *The Shadowy
Waters* on almost every page', 134–5, 139;
asks Symons for proofs of his essay 'The
Ideas of Richard Wagner', 144; WBY
believes he is 'making a really strong play out
of the Shadowy Waters and am certainly
losing no poetry', 145, 148; encourages AE
to consult W. G. Fay about altering INTS
rules to enable actors to be paid, 148–9,
153–9; attempts to get Henry Paget's design
for *The Shadowy Waters*, 151, 160, 191;
planning a 'large scene dock' next door to the
Abbey, 151; realizes 'danger of the Psaltery
is monotony', 152; necessary to put INTS on
business footing if they are to mount country
tours, 155; agrees with AE's general plan for
reform of INTS, 157–8; WBY and AG think
Boyle's *The Eloquent Dempsy* 'impossibly
vulgar in its present form' and suggest that
Colum help Boyle to revise it, 162–3, 164–5;
urges AE to complete his revision of the
INTS rules as soon as possible, 167; writes
in praise of a play by W. P. Ryan, 168; agrees
with AE's latest revisions to the INTS rules,
apart from size of the reading committee and
status of Norman and Helen Laird, 169–71,
181–2, 184, 185; wants 'a strong solid centre'
to the Society, 170; calls a General Meeting
of the INTS, 171; asks W. G. Fay to help AE
with new INTS rules, 172; urges Synge to
attend coming INTS General Meeting as
'whole future of the Society in all
probability' depends upon its decisions, 173;
suggests a prior meeting at Coole, 173; asks
Synge for the MS of *The Tinker's Wedding*
for possible production and publication in
*Samhain*, 173; Symons's essay 'The Ideas of
Richard Wagner' 'touches my own theories
at several points, and enlarges them at one or
two', 175; 'not more than about thirty lines'

of old version of *The Shadowy Waters*
remain, 175, 179; revisions indicate 'how
much I have learned by watching rehearsals
in Dublin', 175; *The Shadowy Waters*, *On
Baile's Strand*, and *The King's Threshold* have
'all been rewritten after rehearsal or actual
performance, and the King's Threshold has
been changed and rehearsed and then
changed again and so on, till I have got it as I
believe a perfectly articulate stage play',
175–6; delighted with success of Synge's
plays in Germany and Bohemia, 178, 203;
although 'not out of the wood yet', thinks
'we have seen the end of the democracy' in
the Abbey Theatre owing to AE's new rules,
178; pleased with his revisions to *The
Shadowy Waters*, which is now 'full of
homely phrases and of the idiom of daily
speech', and 'has become a simple passionate
play', 179; suggests that under new rules
INTS stage manager should be appointed by
the reading and business committees in
consultation, 180; Synge, WBY and AG
insist that under the new INTS rules those
working full-time for the Abbey 'must have a
working majority among the general
members', 181; WBY tells AE that the new
INTS constitution is 'a compromise arising
out of the local circumstances', 182;
confesses he has 'no tact', and bullies
people, 185; negotiations over the INTS
'going better than well', 186; AE 'has himself
proposed a limited liability company' with
WBY, AG and Synge as directors, 186;
AEFH announces she will not be a member
of the new limited company, 186; acceptance
of INTS limited company complicated by
Fred Ryan's fear that distribution of shares
'may give the directors an over mastering
influence', 187, 189, 192; WBY writes to FF
for information about 'the articles of
association' of commercial theatres, 188;
orders 'a delightful model theatre' from Fay
to experiment with new scenes, 188, 191,
194; AEFH influences shape of INTS as
limited liability company by insisting on the
security of her capital, 190, 236–7; WBY
decides with Fay and Synge that publication
and production of *The Tinker's Wedding*
'would be dangerous at present', 190;
difficulties in getting theatre delays 1905
Abbey tour to London until late November,
190; Synge plans to bring a Gaelic Company
from the Blasket islands, 190; WBY still
revising *The Shadowy Waters*, 191, 193, 198;
discusses INTS rules with AE, Ryan and

cultural revival has 'changed the face' of Dublin, 974; believes 'a great contest [is] going to come on here in a few years between the Church & the mystics', 977; WBY has an advantage 'in having a very fierce nation to write for', so has 'to make everything very hard & clear', 983; remonstrates with Griffith over insinuations against Lane in *United Irishman*, 1029–30

*Occult Interests*: 128; asks William Sharp if he has sent anyone to him 'on a veiled mission', 212; begins 'eastern meditations... with the object of trying to lay hands upon some dynamic and substantialising force as distinguished from the eastern quiescent and supersentualizing state of the soul – a movement downwards upon life not upwards out of life', 336; asks FF to teach him to meditate as he finds it difficult 'to get the mood of fiery understanding which must represent the spirit which is, according to the old definition, "that which moves itself"', 342–3; discusses Countess of Cromartie's horoscope with George Pollexfen and describes her recollections of a previous life, 406–8; sends FF adverse astrological predictions about AEFH's Playgoers' Theatre, 728; 'Astrology grows more and more wonderful every day' and has produced 'some astonishing irrefutable things', 748, 750, 754, 755; discusses MG's horoscope with Ella Young, 767–8; discusses a vision of the sidhe with Nancy Maude, 774; hears a clairvoyant story from A. R. Orage, 790–1; dines with astrologer Ralph Shirley, who is teaching him to calculate primaries for horoscopes, 795, 796; has discovered 'a whole colony' of black magicians, 932–3; discusses rites for the Celtic Mystical Order with William Sharp, 967–9, 974–8, 980, 993–5, 1000, 1006; sees Felkin to discuss GD matters, 992–3

*Poetry and Poets*: writing 'O Do Not Love Too Long', 48; negotiates with Macmillan (NY) about *The Poetical Works of William B. Yeats*, 64–6; suggests Macmillan (NY) should publish his projected multi-volume *Collected Works* in USA, 39; gives G. K. A. Bell permission to anthologize some of his poems, 71; urges Bullen to arrange American publication of *Collected Works*, 73; Macmillan (NY) agree to Quinn's suggestion that *The Poetical Works of William B. Yeats* be issued in two volumes, 73; Macmillan (NY) decline to publish *Collected Works* in USA on legal grounds, 73–4; plans *Poems,*

*1899–1905* with Bullen and they decide to postpone *Collected Works*, 103; a lot of work to revise, 103; *Poems, 1899–1905* 'should sell very well' as it is 'the first big mass of verse that I have published for years', 106; consults Bullen about retrieving rights to *The Wind Among the Reeds* from Elkin Mathews, 115–16; signs Agreement with Macmillan (NY) for *The Poetical Works of William B. Yeats*, 121–3; given Kelmscott Press's edition of *The Works of Geoffrey Chaucer*, just as he is 'setting out to read Chaucer', 125, 129; some years ago 'had the need of Spenser and read him right through', but now 'it is Chaucer, a much wiser and saner man', 130; reading Chaucer every morning, 135; discusses suitable poems for the psaltery with FF, 136, 151–2; refuses to write essay on Shakespeare for Bullen because he will be 'reading nothing but Chaucer for some time', 139–40, 161–2; sends Symons Agnes Tobin's translations from Petrarch, 144; feels 'a sort of pathetic interest in books of good poetry, as if they were waifs in the street with tragic stories' and 'wishes to send them to some benevolent home where they will get a little encouragement', 144; consults Watt, Bullen, Brett, and the Society of Authors about retrieving rights to *The Wind Among the Reeds* from John Lane and Elkin Mathews, 146, 147, 167, 174, 185, 207–8, 216, 227, 338–9, 353, 369, 374, 410–11, 413, 439, 462; 'my imagination is getting so deep in Chaucer that I cannot get it down into any other well for the present', 147; Chaucer convinces him that one wants 'vivid irresistible phrase in all verse to be spoken aloud – it rests the imagination as upon the green ground', 152, 166; has 'learned a great deal about poetry generally' in revising his plays and is now sure 'that all the finest poetry comes logically out of the fundamental action, and that the error of late periods like this is to believe that some things are inherently poetical, and to try and pull them on to the scene at every moment', 176; believes 'that the element of strength in poetic language is common idiom, just as the element of strength in poetic construction is common passion', 179; sends copy for *Poems, 1899–1905* to Sidgwick, 187; advises Bullen to publish *Poems, 1899–1905* at a lower price, even if this means not using poems from *The Wind Among the Reeds*, 207–8, 209, 216; sends 'Never Give All the

to Spenser, 360; 'the habit of construction is too deep' in him to adopt AG's suggestion that he redraft *The Speckled Bird* as series of philosophical reflections, but may turn it into 'a kind of spiritual autobiography', 366; dictates new version of introduction to selection from Spenser, 368; Watt sends 'Literature and the Living Voice' to *Contemporary Review*, 384, 401; finding that notes for *Discoveries* have 'more coherence than I had hoped for', 421; begins each day 'with a few pages of Sir Thomas Brown to keep me in key', 421; Bullen asks to publish 'My Thoughts and my Second Thoughts' (*Discoveries*) in *Gentleman's Magazine* at modest fee of £2 per thousand words', 423; Swinburne makes 'a wild attack' on WBY's Blake scholarship in the *Athenaeum*, 434–5, 449–50; agrees to condense his selections from Spenser, 444; is 'nothing of a novel reader' and Huysmans' *En Route* is last modern novel he has read, 446–7; *Discoveries* 'almost a spiritual diary', 486; receives £15, the remaining payment, for his selection from Spenser, 491; 'groaning over task of copying next instalment of *Discoveries*, 495; contemplates an essay on 'the ideal of life' suggested to the Jacobeans 'when they thought of the Court', 496; delivers copy for *Arrow*, 511; sends Bullen third instalment of 'Discoveries', 513; reading dull novel by D'Annunzio, 652; writing further instalments of *Discoveries*, 656; sends copy for forthcoming *Arrow*, 658–60; plans new stories for *The Secret Rose*, 693; reading North's *Plutarch*, 703; asks Bullen's help in selecting drama criticism from the run of *Samhains*, 712; discusses the order of the stories in *CW* VII, 764–5; sends 'John Sherman' to Bullen for *CW* VII, 772–3; made an honorary member of the Pacific Short Story Club, 799; working hard on the *Works of William Blake*, 928–9; *John Sherman and Dhoya* in press, 930; writing stories requires 'a very considerable labour', 934; MG sends him material for articles on her, 934–5; Watt arranges publication of essay 'Magic' in the *Monthly Review*, 971–2; arranges publication of *Beltaine*, 978–9; Watt arranges publication of essay 'What is "Popular Poetry"' in *Cornhill Magazine*, 981, 984–5; WBY comments on Fiona Macleod's stories, 982–4; Watt arranges publication of essay 'The Happiest of the Poets' in *Fortnightly Review*, 985–6; arranges for publication of the revised *Celtic Twilight*,

986; agreement with Bullen for the revised *Celtic Twilight*, 987–90; agreement with Bullen for publication of *Ideas of Good and Evil*, 1012–14; sends contribution to *Irish Literature*, 1021; Watt tries to arrange publication of essay 'America and the Arts' in the *Fortnightly Review*, 1025–6; working on his edition of selections from Eglinton, 1026; praises the magazine *Dana*, 1026

*Publishing*: places 'America and the Arts' with the *Metropolitan Magazine* through Watt, 15–16; helping Starkey to revive the Dublin publishing firm of Whaley, 20; advises Roberts on design of the Abbey Theatre series, 24; Quinn copyrights plays in USA, 28; starting an Abbey Theatre series of plays, 28; a 'real Irish publishing house' a possibility, 28; WBY delighted with ten-volume US anthology, 29, 36; negotiates with Macmillan (NY) about *The Poetical Works of William B. Yeats*, 64–6; trouble with John Lane and Mathews over rights to *The Wind Among the Reeds*, 65–6; suggests Macmillan (NY) should publish his projected multi-volume *Collected Works* in USA, 66; gives G. K. A. Bell permission to anthologize some of his poems, 71; urges Bullen to see Watt or Brett about American publication of *Collected Works*, 73; Macmillan (NY) agree to Quinn's suggestion that *The Poetical Works of William B. Yeats* should be in two volumes, 73; Macmillan (NY) decline to publish *Collected Works* in USA on legal grounds, 73–4; asks Bullen for help in advising George Roberts and Joseph Hone, who are setting up a publishing firm (later Maunsel & Co.) in Dublin, and firmly opposes AE's proposed role as literary adviser over Stephen Gwynn, 86–9, 92, 94; sends Hone to Bullen for guidance on setting up Maunsel & Co., 91, 94; advises Roberts not to hold out for a partnership in new firm, 91–3, 94; reminds Roberts that 'Every bad Irish book published injures the whole trade in Irish books', 92; annoyed at AE's continuing interference in Maunsel & Co. and his support for Roberts's demands to be a partner, 97–100; stays with Bullen in Stratford where they plan *Poems, 1899–1905* and decided to postpone the *Collected Works*, 103; has a lot work to revise, 103; thinks *Poems, 1899–1905* 'should sell very well', 196; Eric Maclagan gives him the 'beautiful' Vale Press edition of Sir Thomas Browne, 110; consults Bullen about retrieving rights to *The Wind Among the Reeds* from Elkin

**Yeats, William Butler:** (*cont.*)
Mathews, 115–16; signs Agreement with
Macmillan (NY) for *The Poetical Works of
William B. Yeats*, 121–3; thinks the
Kelmscott Press's edition of *The Works of
Geoffrey Chaucer*, 'the most beautiful of all
printed books', 125, 129; negotiates through
Watt to retrieve the rights to *The Shadowy
Waters* from Hodder & Stoughton, 132, 137,
138, 139, 141, 146, 148; consults Watt,
Bullen, Brett, and the Society of Authors
about retrieving the rights to *The Wind
Among the Reeds* from John Lane and Elkin
Mathews, 146, 147, 167, 174, 185, 207–8,
216, 227, 338–9, 353, 369, 374, 410–11, 413,
439, 462; takes an unsympathetic attitude to
his sisters' financial and personal difficulties
with Dun Emer Industries, 159–60; sends
copy to Sidgwick for *Poems, 1899–1905*, 187;
advises Bullen to publish *Poems, 1899–1905*
at a lower price, even if this means not using
the poems from *The Wind Among the Reeds*,
207–8, 209, 216; sees John Murray about
new editions of AG's books, 213; *The
Poetical Works of William B. Yeats* delayed
by dispute with John Lane, 374; makes up
copy for *The Poetical Works of William
B. Yeats* from proofs of *Poems, 1899–1905*,
390–1; questions Bullen about delivering
copy for a possible *Collected Edition*, 448;
seeks Katharine Tynan Hinkson's
permission to make a selection from her
lyrics for the Dun Emer Press, 459–60; falls
out with ECY over her commissioning of a
selection of AE's poetry for Dun Emer
without reference to him as literary adviser,
460, 463–5, 466, 467; discusses with Brett
the contents and copy for *The Poetical Works
of William B. Yeats*, 460–61; explains to JBY
that the only chance of making the Dun
Emer Press a permanent success is 'to get the
books a reputation for fine literary taste
and … what was finest in our movement',
463–4; insists that there 'are only two things
possible' in his dispute with Dun Emer: 'one
that I should have the usual control of an
editor, and the other is that Lollie shall do
the work herself or get some person she can
trust to do it', 465; informs Katharine Tynan
Hinkson he cannot edit her poems because
he has resigned as literary editor to the Dun
Emer Press, 482; asks Katharine Tynan
Hinkson to help him in his dispute with the
Dun Emer Press, 484; trying to keep
'imitative poetry' from publication, 484;
dealing 'with three very emotional people,

my sisters and my father', 485; 'vital' to
prevent Dun Emer 'drifting into the
amateurish Dublin way', 485; receives £15,
the remaining payment for his selection from
Spenser, 491; dictates terms to ECY for
continuing as literary adviser to the Dun
Emer Press, 504–7; sends Bullen the third
instalment of *Discoveries*, 513; tells Unwin
that he wishes to transfer all his books to
Bullen, 520; settles his dispute with ECY
over the Dun Emer Press, 525; begins his
selection of Katharine Tynan Hinkson's
poems for the Dun Emer Press, 526;
finishing copy, revisions, and proofs for vol
II of *The Poetical Works of William B. Yeats*,
544, 545; quarrels with ECY over her
business methods and her erratic payment of
Dun Emer authors, 557; 584, 594, 605, 606,
611–12; financial difficulties about proposed
*CW*, 603, 608; arranges with Watt to have all
his books transferred to Bullen, 636; sends
revised *Deirdre* to Macmillan in New York,
639; AEFH arranges terms for *CW* with
Bullen, 641–3, 651; wants nothing to do with
translation rights, 685; intends to leave way
open for popular editions of his books after
*CW* finished, 686; agrees to a two-year
extension of Elkin Mathews' rights in *The
Wind Among the Reeds* in return for his
taking 50 sets of *CW*, 685–6; insists that
Watt should be consulted in any negotiations
with Elkin Mathews, 686; begins to get
proofs of *CW*, 689–90; not arranging
contents of *CW* on a chronological system,
nor on the system adopted in the American
*Poetical Works of William B. Yeats*, 689;
quarrels with Bullen over arrangements for
printing *CW*, 691–2; sends Bullen a list of
poems in the order in which they are to be
printed, 691; demands colour illustrations in
the *CW* volume of dramatic criticism, 691;
discovers he and Bullen have been at cross-
purposes, Bullen was 'too hasty' and WBY
'too vague', 692; discovers he has far less
time to prepare text for *CW* as Bullen will
take three weeks to print each volume, not
six to eight weeks, 692–3; asks Bullen for as
much extra time as possible, 693; Bullen
agrees to find more time for WBY's
preparation of the *CW* texts, 694; sends
Bullen a draft proposal for four volumes of
*CW*, 695; disagrees with Bullen's
arrangement for a volume of plays, 695;
declines to contribute to an anthology
because too busy with *CW*, 698; sends
corrected proof sheets for *CW* I, 700;